Routledge Handbook of Sustainable and Resilient Infrastructure

To best serve current and future generations, infrastructure needs to be resilient to the changing world while using limited resources in a sustainable manner. Research on and funding towards sustainability and resilience are growing rapidly, and significant research is being carried out at a number of institutions and centers worldwide.

This handbook brings together current research on sustainable and resilient infrastructure and, in particular, stresses the fundamental nexus between sustainability and resilience. It aims to coalesce work from a large and diverse group of contributors across a wide range of disciplines including engineering, technology and informatics, urban planning, public policy, economics, and finance. Not only does it present a theoretical formulation of sustainability and resilience but it also demonstrates how these ideals can be realized in practice. This work will provide a reference text to students and scholars of a number of disciplines.

Paolo Gardoni is a Professor and Excellence Faculty Scholar in the Department of Civil and Environmental Engineering at the University of Illinois at Urbana-Champaign. He is the founder and Editor-in-Chief of the international journal *Sustainable and Resilient Infrastructure*.

Routledge Handbook of Sustainable and Resilient Infrastructure

Edited by Paolo Gardoni

LONDON AND NEW YORK

First published 2019
by Routledge
2 Park Square, Milton Park, Abingdon, Oxon OX14 4RN

and by Routledge
52 Vanderbilt Avenue, New York, NY 10017

First issued in paperback 2020

Routledge is an imprint of the Taylor & Francis Group, an informa business

British Library Cataloguing-in-Publication Data
A catalogue record for this book is available from the British Library

Library of Congress Cataloging-in-Publication Data
Names: Gardoni, Paolo, editor.
Title: Routledge handbook of sustainable and resilient
infrastructure / edited by Paolo Gardoni.
Description: Abingdon, Oxon ; New York, NY : Routledge, 2019. |
Series: Routledge international handbooks | Includes bibliographical references and index.
Identifiers: LCCN 2018034617 (print) | LCCN 2018047896 (ebook) |
ISBN 9781315142074 (eBook) | ISBN 9781138306875 (hbk) | ISBN 9781315142074 (ebk)
Subjects: LCSH: Infrastructure (Economics)–Environmental aspects.
Classification: LCC HC79.C3 (ebook) |
LCC HC79.C3 R68 2019 (print) | DDC 338.9/27–dc23
LC record available at https://lccn.loc.gov/2018034617

ISBN 13: 978–0–367–65962–2 (pbk)
ISBN 13: 978–1–138–30687–5 (hbk)

Typeset in Baskerville
by Out of House Publishing

This book is dedicated to Engineer, Artist and Entrepreneur Giuseppe Sala

Contents

Contents

Contents

Contents

Figures

Tables

Contributors

Ahmed U. Abdelhady is a research assistant and a PhD student in the Department of Civil and Environmental Engineering at University of Michigan. Ahmed earned his Bachelor of Science in Civil Engineering in May 2014, and his Master of Science in Structural Engineering in July 2016 from Cairo University. His Master's research focused on the structural analysis of tall buildings using the boundary element method. His current research focuses on evaluating resilience of communities subject to natural hazards.

Umberto Alibrandi obtained his BS, MS, and PhD from the University of Messina, Italy, in Civil and Environmental Engineering. He was postdoctoral researcher at the University of California at Berkeley (2008–2009), National University of Singapore (2013–2015), Nanyang Technological University under the programme 'Singapore Berkeley Building Energy Efficiency and Sustainability in the Tropics' (2015–2017), while he is currently Senior Research Fellow at Berkeley Education Alliance for Research in Singapore (BEARS). From 2010 to 2012 he worked as a structural engineer, where he also contributed to the structural analysis of a bio-technology centre in Sicily. His research interests are in the broad area of Structural Reliability, Risk Analysis and Random Vibrations, Structural Optimization, and Decision Making under uncertainty, using Machine Learning and Artificial Intelligence. Currently he is applying these methods of Computational Intelligence for the development of an integrated Socio-Technical Platform under uncertainty for sustainability and resilience of the urban communities and smart cities.

Yasser Almoghathawi is an Assistant Professor in the Department of Systems Engineering at King Fahd University of Petroleum and Minerals (KFUPM) in Dhahran, Saudi Arabia. He received BS and MS degrees from KFUPM and a PhD from the University of Oklahoma (OU), all in Industrial and Systems Engineering. His research interests broadly deal with applications of operations research, including optimization, mathematical modelling, facility location, and sequencing and scheduling. His graduate work within OU's Risk-Based Systems Analytics Laboratory developed optimization models and approaches for the restoration problem of interdependent networks to enhance their resilience. He is a member of INFORMS and IAENG.

Dilanthi Amaratunga is a Professor of Disaster Risk Management at the University of Huddersfield, UK. She is a world leading expert in disaster resilience with an international reputation. She leads the Global Disaster Resilience Centre, a global leader in interdisciplinary research, education, and advocacy to improve the resilience of nations and communities at the

University of Huddersfield, UK. Her research interests include socio-economic measures for disaster risks; preparedness for response, recovery and reconstruction; built environment dimensions of climate change and sustainability; gender and protection; and public policy, governance and procurement. Her research leadership in disaster management has been recognized in the international research community by her appointment as the Editor-in-chief of the *International Journal of Disaster Resilience in the Built Environment*. She has project managed to successful completion several international research projects generating significant research outputs. To date, she has produced over 200 publications, refereed papers, and reports, and has made over 50 key note speeches in around 30 countries, over 80 invited speeches and keynotes for international audiences. She is regularly invited to provide expert advice on disaster resilience by national and local governments and international agencies. Dilanthi has lead and chaired a large number of international conferences. These events demonstrate her role, as a leader in the disaster mitigation and reconstruction field and as a conduit for international collaboration and engagement. Many of these conferences have brought together major international networks to address global challenges and advance research agendas. She led the international peer review panel of the UN Global Assessment Report input papers in 2015. Dilanthi has also lead and chaired a large number of international conferences, demonstrating her role as a leader and as a conduit for international collaboration and engagement. She is also a member of the Steering Committee of the UNISDR 'Making Cities Resilient' Campaign. She has also been appointed by the UNISDR as the Working Group Leader of the Words into Action on Accountability and Governance. Full details of Dilanthi's publications, projects, and national and international activities can be found at www.dilanthiamaratunga.net. Dilanthi can be contacted via d.amaratunga@hud.ac.uk.

Navid Attary is a research scientist at the Center of Excellence for Risk-Based Community Resilience Planning in the Department of Civil and Environmental Engineering at Colorado State University. He received his PhD in Civil/Structural Engineering in 2013 from Rensselaer Polytechnic Institute (RPI). His research has mainly been focused on multi-hazard mitigation techniques to enhance community resilience, using performance-based engineering, often addressing different types of natural hazards at multiple scales. Dr Attary's research evolved from experimental and numerical studies of seismic response mitigation devices to modelling of physical infrastructure sectors and their coupled response to earthquakes, tsunamis, and tornados.

Emilio Bastidas-Arteaga is Associated Professor at the University of Nantes since 2010 where he is affiliated to the Research Institute in Civil and Mechanical Engineering. His research works aim at providing robust stochastic frameworks to optimize design, inspection, and maintenance of aging coastal and offshore infrastructure and buildings. Since 2009, he has been working in the assessment of effects and adaptation of reinforced concrete structures and buildings subjected to climate change and deterioration. His research activities allowed him to benefit from a Doctoral Training and Research Award since 2015 and have resulted in the publication of more than 100 scientific and technical documents including more than 28 peer-reviewed journal papers in recognized scientific journals and one international patent. He is also participating in several technical committees related to climate change and civil engineering: AFNOR (France), American Concrete Institute (USA), and IABSE (International). He has been involved in 14 research projects on reliability and maintenance of deteriorated reinforced concrete structures granted by regional (7 projects), national (3 projects), European (3 projects), and international (1 project) funds. He has lead two of these projects (Chlordetect 2016–17 and eADAPT 2013) and participated as work-package leader for two other projects (RI-ADAPTCLIM 2014–17, and ANR JCJC CLIMBOIS 2013–17).

Kash Barker is an Associate Professor and Anadarko Petroleum Corporation Presidential Professor in the School of Industrial and Systems Engineering at the University of Oklahoma. His work broadly dealing with reliability, resilience, and economic impacts of infrastructure networks has been funded by the National Science Foundation, Department of Transportation, Department of the Navy and Army Research Office, among others, and has resulted in over 55 refereed journal publications. He received BS and MS degrees in Industrial Engineering from the University of Oklahoma and a PhD in Systems Engineering from the University of Virginia. He is an Associate Editor of IISE Transactions and is on the editorial board of Risk Analysis.

Emanuele Bellini gained a PhD in Telematics and Information Society from the University of Florence, Italy in 2012 and MSc cum laude in Communication Science from the University of Siena, Italy in 2006. He is researcher and senior project manager at UNIFI and an expert in Complex Socio-eco-technical Systems, Resilience Engineering, and Quantification, Human Factors, and Communication Science. He was lecturer in Database and Programming Languages at the University of Florence and he is Lecturer in Risk Perception and Complex Systems at Steinbeins Universität. He is coordinator of H2020 DRS7 RESOLUTE and is involved as Work Package leader in several EU funded programmes as H2020, FP7, CIP, Eurostar, Leonardo, etc. with projects like CyberTrust, SCC1-REPLICATE, CloudSocket, ECLAP, APARSEN, SHARES, JamTODAY, etc. He is president of LOGOS, a not-for-profit research association on Occupational Health and Safety assessment for disabled people and biometric-based quantification of human reliability. He is also a member of PIN-MOSIS laboratory on Statistical Information System and Knowledge Management for knowledge-driven risk management and government data quality. Dr Bellini is member of IEEE, IEEE System Council, Integrated Mission Group for Security (IMG-S) TC4-Resilience, CEN TC 88 Resilience Information Portal, EU-VRI, European Technology Platform for Industrial Safety ETPIS, ESRA TC Human Reliability and TC Risk Assessment.

Jessica Boakye is a research assistant and a PhD candidate in the Department of Civil and Environmental Engineering at the University of Illinois at Urbana-Champaign. Jessica earned her Bachelor of Science in Civil and Environmental Engineering in May 2014 from University of Massachusetts at Amherst, and her Master of Science in Civil and Environmental Engineering from University of Illinois at Urbana-Champaign in May 2016. Her current research focuses on the definition of metrics to evaluate the societal impact of natural hazards on communities.

Emily Bondank is a PhD candidate in the department of Civil, Environmental, and Sustainable Engineering at Arizona State University. Her research interest lies in informing and facilitating decision making for infrastructure adaptation. In her dissertation work funded by National Science Foundation grants, she evaluates future reliability and resilience of coupled water and power infrastructure under climate change stress by developing statistical fault tree, network, and agent-based models. To explore mitigation and adaptation pathways, she hosts workshops with decision-makers wherein she gamifies the use of the models by developing simulation scenarios and board games.

Michel Bruneau, Professor in the Department of Civil, Structural and Environmental Engineering at the University at Buffalo, is recognized nationally and internationally for the impact of his research contributions to the design and behaviour of steel structures subjected to earthquakes and blasts. His work has been instrumental in the inclusion in national and international standards of specifications for ductile steel plate shear walls, tubular eccentrically braced frames, ductile bridge diaphragms, and ductile composite sandwich walls, leading to implementation in countless structures worldwide. For example, his development and validation of the tubular eccentrically braced frames concept for bridges was implemented in the $1B temporary supports of the new San-Francisco Oakland Bay Bridge. He has authored over 500 technical publications, including over 150 articles in the leading peer-reviewed journals in his field. He is one of the most cited researchers in structural engineering and earthquake engineering. Notably, he is the lead author of the 900-pages textbook *Ductile Design of Steel Structures*, used worldwide by structural engineers and considered by many to be the reference for the seismic design of steel structures, and the lead author of the 2003 pioneering paper 'A framework to quantitatively assess and enhance the seismic resilience of communities', which has formulated the concept and expression of disaster resilience in a manner that has since driven research in this field. He also published four fiction books. Bruneau has received several national awards and recognitions for his work and has been inducted as fellow of the Canadian Academy of Engineering. He is also an ASCE Fellow, a member of various AISC and CSA committees developing design specifications for bridges and buildings. He has conducted numerous reconnaissance visits to disaster stricken areas and has served as Director of MCEER. He has also participated in various expert peer review panels, project advisory committees, and special project design teams. A detailed outline of his qualifications is available at www.eng.buffalo.edu/~bruneau.

Daniel Burillo is a PhD Candidate in the Department of Civil, Environmental and Sustainable Engineering at Arizona State University. He is a cross-functional researcher with transdisciplinary expertise in engineering, business, and law. He is lead author on several studies with innovative statistical and geographical methods for quantifying uncertainty in heat waves due to climate change, modelling electricity demand, and estimating impacts on energy infrastructure. Daniel's contributions to the field have been recognized with membership appointments to the editorial boards of Energies and Insight – Energy Science.

Mikhail Chester is an Associate Professor in Civil, Environmental, and Sustainable Engineering at Arizona State University, where he runs a research laboratory focused on studying the resilience to climate change and sustainability of infrastructure systems. His work spans a number of infrastructure systems (including power, water, and transportation) and hazards (including heat, precipitation, and wildfires). The research focuses on characterizing how infrastructure fail with climate hazards and the strategies that can be used to mitigate against failures. He and his team have developed several approaches for understanding and mitigating failure including stochastic models, long-term network interdependency simulations for vulnerability propagation, hydrologic analyses, and coupled travel-hazard simulations.

Gian Paolo Cimellaro's primary field of investigation is Earthquake Engineering with emphasis on defining Quantification of Resilience of systems. Cimellaro's interdisciplinary research investigates representations of health system properties and processes, creating quantitative modelling solutions for a better understanding systems resilience. This often challenges collaborating teams consisting of scientists, social scientists, engineers, lawyers, and extension specialists across a wide spectrum of disciplines. His major contribution has been the quantification of the concept of disaster resilience. More information is available at: http://staff.polito.it/gianpaolo.cimellaro/faculty_bio.html

Maxwell Coar is a PhD candidate at Princeton University in the Department of Civil and Environmental Engineering, in Dr Maria Garlock's Creative and Resilient Urban Environment research group. He received his Bachelor of Science degree in Mechanical Engineering and Materials Science from Duke University, where he was a National Science Foundation Grand Challenge Scholar and a Pratt School of Engineering Research Fellow. His research interests include urban resiliency, computational hazard simulation, structural art, and pedagogy in engineering.

Alessandro Contento is a research assistant and a PhD candidate in the Department of Civil and Environmental Engineering at the University of Illinois at Urbana-Champaign. Alessandro earned his Master of Science in Civil Engineering in October 2005, and his 'Dottorato di Ricerca' in Civil and Environmental Engineering in April 2009 at the University of L'Aquila. The research started during his Master and 'Dottorato di Ricerca' focuses on the study of the dynamics of rigid blocks and in particular on the use of passive control systems to prevent their overturning. His current research interests are in the development of a framework for hurricane risk analysis, with a particular focus in developing probabilistic models for storm surge.

Jennifer E. Cross, PhD, is the Director of Research for the Institute for the Built Environment, Co-Director of the Center for Energy and Behavior, and Associate Professor of Sociology at Colorado State University. Dr Cross is a community sociologist who works with community agencies and local governments to develop effective programmes and create transformational change. Her areas of expertise include behaviour change, community development, inter-agency collaboration, place attachment and community connection, professional social networks, and urban sustainability. Current research projects include applied projects assessing the health impacts of green schools, developing innovative programmes to help cities and campuses meet their climate action goals, designing for urban regeneration, and enhancing social connectedness. She teaches courses on social research methods, community development, and applied social change. Dr Cross has developed two upper division courses that engage students in Community Based Research, where the students work with community partners to conduct sociological research that solves community problems, enhances organizational capacity, or develops programmes for social change.

Nuwan Dias has over eight years of research experience as an academic in the Higher Education sector both in the UK and Sri Lanka. He is a Post-Doctoral Researcher at the University of Huddersfield. Currently, Nuwan is working on a Horizon 2020 project called ESPREssO (Enhancing Synergies for disaster Prevention in the European Union) which aims at contributing to a new strategic vision to approach natural risk reduction and climate change adaptation, thereby opening new frontiers for research and policy making. He actively engaged in several EU funded research projects which addressed disaster resilience and management issues in post disaster reconstruction and disaster resilience education. In addition, Nuwan has engaged in several urban development and urban networking projects in Sri Lanka. His research publications include refereed journal and refereed conference papers and various high impact reports. Nuwan has been actively engaged in organising varies international events and conferences. Nuwan currently conducts PhD assessments and willing to undertake PhD supervision. He completed PhD from the University of Huddersfield in January 2016 and he has a MSc in Urban Design from the University of Salford and BSc (Hons) in Town and Country Planning from the University of Moratuwa, Sri Lanka.

Max Didier is a PhD Candidate at the Chair of Structural Dynamics and Earthquake Engineering at the Institute of Structural Engineering (IBK) of the Swiss Federal Institute of Technology (ETH) Zurich. His research interests are in design and evaluation of earthquake-resilient communities and elements of the built infrastructure.

Negar Elhami Khorasani is an assistant professor in the Department of Civil, Structural and Environmental Engineering at the University at Buffalo. Negar obtained her PhD degree in 2015 from the Department of Civil and Environmental Engineering at Princeton University. Negar's main area of research is investigating performance of the built environment under extreme loading and multi-hazard scenarios, specially fire and fire following earthquake within probabilistic frameworks. She was a Gordon Wu Fellow at Princeton, and has received several scholarships including NSERC-Canada. Negar is a member of several ASCE committees, including the ASCE/SEI Fire Protection Committee.

Bruce R. Ellingwood, PhD, PE, NAE, is College of Engineering Eminent Scholar and Co-Director of the Center for Excellence in Risk-Based Community Resilience Planning in the Department of Civil and Environmental Engineering at Colorado State University. His main research and professional interests involve the application of probability and statistics to structural engineering, particularly to performance of structures under service, environmental, and abnormal load conditions, structural reliability theory and probabilistic risk assessment of engineered facilities. He is internationally recognized as an authority on the technical development and implementation of probability-based codified structural design standards.

Simona Esposito is an Earthquake Specialist at Swiss Re Management Ltd. She worked as postdoctoral researcher at University of Canterbury, New Zealand, and at the Swiss Federal Institute of Technology (ETH) Zurich. She is an expert in probabilistic seismic risk and resilience analysis of complex infrastructure systems, seismic regional hazard, and spatial correlation of ground motion.

Kasey M. Faust is an Assistant Professor in Construction Engineering and Project Management in the Department of Civil, Architectural, and Environmental Engineering at the University of Texas at Austin. Her research on sociotechnical systems aims to improve service to communities. Dr Faust's work spans the life cycle of infrastructure systems between the project phase during construction through the operations phase, exploring human-infrastructure interactions, infrastructure interdependencies, and the institutional environment. Studies within her research group include: human-infrastructure interdependencies in cities experiencing urban decline; disaster migration and the resilience of the built environment; sociotechnical modelling of infrastructure systems including gentrification and water/energy poverty; the impact of policies and regulations on the built environment; understanding the impact of institutional elements on projects; and modelling of public perceptions.

Dan M. Frangopol is the inaugural holder of the Fazlur R. Khan Endowed Chair of Structural Engineering and Architecture at Lehigh University. He is recognised as a leader in the field of life-cycle engineering of civil and marine structures. His main research interests are in the development and application of probabilistic concepts and methods to civil and marine engineering. He is the Founding President of the International Associations for Bridge Maintenance and Safety (IABMAS) and Life-Cycle Civil Engineering (IALCCE). Dr Frangopol has authored/co-authored over 370 articles in archival journals including nine award-winning papers. He is the Founding Editor of Structure and Infrastructure Engineering. Dr Frangopol is the recipient of several medals, awards, and prizes, from ASCE, IABSE, IASSAR, and other professional organizations. He holds four honorary doctorates and 12 honorary professorships from major universities. He is a foreign member of the Academia Europaea (Academy of Europe, London) and of the Royal Academy of Belgium, an Honorary Member of the Romanian Academy, and a Distinguished Member of ASCE. Additional information can be found at www.lehigh.edu/~dmf206.

Andrew Fraser, PhD, is a Research Associate Professor in Civil Engineering at Arizona State University (ASU). His research addresses questions surrounding sustainability and climate change adaptation and resilience as each relates to transportation systems. He has specialised in the effects of extreme heat and inherent and emergent risks to transportation infrastructure, intra-regional mobility, and public health. In addition, his recent work has focused on the combined hazards of wildfires and precipitation and the vulnerability of rural transportation systems.

Paolo Gardoni is a Professor and Excellence Faculty Scholar in the Department of Civil and Environmental Engineering at the University of Illinois at Urbana-Champaign. He is the Director of the MAE Center that focuses on creating a Multi-hazard Approach to Engineering, and the Associate Director of the Center of Excellence for Risk-based Community Resilience Planning funded by the National Institute of Standards and Technology (NIST). He is the founder and Editor-in-Chief of the international journal *Sustainable and Resilient Infrastructure* published by Taylor and Francis Group. He is internationally recognised for his work on sustainable and resilient infrastructure; reliability, risk and life cycle analysis; decision making under uncertainty; earthquake engineering; performance assessment of deteriorating systems; ethical, social, and legal dimensions of risk; policies for natural hazard mitigation and disaster recovery; and engineering ethics.

Maria Garlock is Professor at Princeton University in the Department of Civil and Environmental Engineering, and also the co-Director of the Architecture and Engineering Program. She is a Fellow of the American Society for Civil Engineers (ASCE) Structural Engineering Institute (SEI), and the recipient of awards such as AISC's 2016 T.R. Higgins Lectureship Award and the President's Award for Distinguished Teaching (the highest teaching award at Princeton University). Dr Garlock received her Bachelors of Science degree from Lehigh University, a Masters of Science degree from Cornell University, and a PhD degree from Lehigh University. Dr Garlock is also a licensed Professional Engineer, having earned her license while working for Leslie E. Robertson Associates of New York City as a structural engineer prior to obtaining her PhD.

Katsuichiro Goda is a Reader in Earthquake Hazards and Risks at the University of Bristol, United Kingdom. He is an expert on earthquake and tsunami risk analysis and conducts multi-disciplinary research on catastrophic multi-hazard risk management from economic and societal viewpoints.

Roberto Guidotti is a Research Assistant in the Department of Civil and Environmental Engineering at University of Illinois at Urbana-Champaign and in the Center of Excellence for Risk-based Community Resilience Planning funded by the National Institute of Standards and Technology (NIST), with expertise in analytical and quantitative modelling towards informed decision making in the catastrophe modelling area. He earned a PhD in Structural Engineering from the University of Illinois at Urbana-Champaign and a PhD in Structural, Seismic, and Geotechnical Engineering from the Milan Technical University (Politecnico di Milano). His research interests encompass risk, reliability, and resilience of interdependent urban infrastructure subject to extreme-loading events, and earthquake engineering and seismology, with focus on the modelling of soil–structure interaction, site–city interaction, and seismic hazard characterization via 3D physics-based approaches.

Richard Haigh is Professor of Disaster Resilience and Co-Director of the Global Disaster Resilience Centre at the University of Huddersfield, UK. His research interests are in the field of disaster resilience in the built environment, with a focus on disaster risk governance and accountability, multi-hazard early warning and the last mile, convergence of disaster risk reduction and climate change adaption, and post-conflict reconstruction. He is the Co-Founding Editor-In-Chief of the Scopus indexed *International Journal of Disaster Resilience in the Built Environment*, Founder and Co-Chair of the Co-Chair of the International Conference on Building Resilience series, and Working Group Leader and Editor for two United Nations Words into Action Guides on 'Governance and Accountability' and 'Construction Policy and Practice', to be distributed to all 187 member states who are signatories to the Sendai Framework for Disaster Risk Reduction 2015–30. Richard has secured 21 research grants since 2005, delivered over 60 invited speeches and keynote presentations for audiences in over 20 countries across the world. He has published an edited book with Wiley Blackwell, seven book chapters in three edited books, and over 40 peer reviewed journal articles, the majority in ISI or SCOPUS indexed journals.

James Robert Harris, PhD, PE, SE, NAE, is Principal of J.R. Harris & Co., a leading structural engineering firm in Denver, CO. He is internationally recognized for his numerous contributions to the profession of structural engineering and the advancement of structural codes and standards over a career of more than four decades. His technical and professional leadership in the development and implementation of improved provisions for earthquake-resistant structural design into ASCE Standard 7 through the voluntary consensus standard approval process is among the most noteworthy of his contributions. He also is recognised as a leader in the advancement of performance-based engineering in structural engineering practice.

Michael Havbro Faber is Professor in the area of Risk Informed Decision Support for Structures at the Department of Civil Engineering at Aalborg University, Denmark. Prior to this position he was head of the Department of Civil Engineering from 2011 to 2015. In the period from 2000 to 2011 he was tenured professor and head of the group on Risk and Safety at ETH, Zurich, Switzerland. His research interests are directed on decision theory, risk assessment, resilience, sustainability, global catastrophic risks, uncertainty modeling, life safety management, Bayesian probability theory, and applied statistics. Application areas include offshore installations, ship structures, bridges, tunnels, buildings, roadway traffic systems and space structures as well as management of natural hazards. His industrial experience mostly originates from COWI, Denmark, Det Norske Veritas, Norway and on-going consultancy work through the specialist consulting company Matrisk GmbH of which he is a founding partner since 2001. He has taken leadership in several international committees, including: The Joint Committee on Structural Safety (JCSS); President, the International Forum on Engineering Decision Making (IFED); founding President, the ISO 2394 Principles of Reliability of Structures; Convener, the international Civil Engineering Reliability and Risk Association (CERRA); past President, The World Economic Forum, member of Global Expert Network on Risk and Resilience, the OECD High Level Risk Forum, Research Fellow of the Global Risk Forum in Davos,

Honorable Professor at the Harbin Institute of Technology, and is elected member of the Danish Academy of Technical Sciences (ATV) since 2012.

Christopher Hoehne is PhD candidate in Civil, Environmental, and Sustainable Engineering at Arizona State University, and a 2017 recipient of the Dwight David Eisenhower Transportation Fellowship. His research interests concentrate on identifying sustainable, resilient, and safe solutions to emerging problems in the transportation sector. His dissertation research focuses on examining how the transportation sector influences extreme heat exposure in urban populations. He received his Bachelors of Science in Civil and Environmental Engineering from the University of Missouri, and he received his Masters of Science in Civil, Environmental, and Sustainable Engineering from Arizona State University.

Lorenzo Hofer is a Postdoctoral Researcher in the Department of Civil, Environmental and Architectural Engineering at the University of Padova, Italy. He earned his MSc in Civil Engineering from the University of Padova in 2014, and PhD from the Doctoral School in Civil and Environmental Engineering Sciences, at the University of Padova, Italy, in 2018. During the spring and summer 2017 terms, he spent a period as visiting PhD student in the Department of Civil and Environmental Engineering at the University of Illinois at Urbana-Champaign. His main research interests are in the area of earthquake engineering, reliability, risk and resilience analysis. His research covers seismic risk assessment for enterprises and productive processes, extreme events modelling and loss analysis for insurance purposes and catastrophe bond pricing.

Gaofeng Jia is an Assistant Professor in the Department of Civil and Environmental Engineering at Colorado State University. His expertise lies in the areas of uncertainty quantification and propagation, robust analysis/design optimization of complex engineering systems, risk-informed decision making, modeling of infrastructure aging and deterioration, and life-cycle cost analysis. His research leverages the versatility of generalized simulation-based approaches and the efficiency of soft computing and high performance computing to address the challenges associated with solving complex engineering problems.

Maria C. G. Juenger is a Professor and holder of the John A. Focht Centennial Teaching Fellowship in the Department of Civil, Architectural, and Environmental Engineering at the University of Texas at Austin, where she has been since 2002. She is a fellow of the American Concrete Institute (ACI) and the American Ceramic Society (ACerS). Dr Juenger received her BS degree in Chemistry from Duke University and PhD in Materials Science and Engineering from Northwestern University. After completing her PhD, she was a postdoctoral researcher in Civil Engineering at the University at California, Berkeley. Dr Juenger's teaching and research focus on materials used in civil engineering applications. She primarily examines chemical issues in cement-based materials; these include phase formation in cement clinkering, hydration chemistry of portland cement, calcium sulfoaluminate cement, and supplementary cementitious materials, and chemical deterioration processes in concrete. In 2005 she received a Faculty Early CAREER Award from the National Science Foundation. She has received several awards from ACI for her research, teaching, and service, including the Walter P. Moore, Jr. Faculty Achievement Award in 2009, the Young Member Award for Professional Achievement in 2010, the Wason Medal for Materials Research in 2011, and the Delmar L. Bloem Distinguished Service Award in 2018. She is an associate editor of *Cement and Concrete Composites* and is on the editorial boards of both *Cement and Concrete Research* and *ACI Materials Journal*.

Golam Kabir is currently an Assistant Professor in the Department of Mechanical, Automotive, Materials Engineering at the University of Windsor, ON, Canada. He received his PhD in Civil Engineering from the School of Engineering at UBC-Okanagan Campus, Canada on 2016. He received his MSc and BSc in Industrial and Production Engineering from Bangladesh University of Engineering and Technology (BUET) in 2011 and 2009, respectively. His research interests include infrastructure asset management, system risk, reliability, resilience assessment, multi-criteria decision analysis under risk and uncertainty, Bayesian inference, and data driven decision making.

Vineet R. Kamat is a Professor at the University of Michigan. He received a PhD in Civil Engineering at Virginia Tech. His primary research interests include automation and robotics, and their applications in various civil engineering and building system domains. His email address is vkamat@umich.edu and his web page is located at http://live.engin.umich.edu.

Sabarethinam Kameshwar is a post-doctoral research scholar at Oregon State University. He is also affiliated with the NIST-sponsored Center of Excellence for Risk-based Community Resilience Planning. Sabarethinam received his doctoral degree in Civil Engineering from Rice University. His research interests are in the area of multi-hazard fragility, risk, and resilience assessment of infrastructure systems and the use of surrogate models and machine learning for civil engineering problems.

Jessica A. Kaminsky is an Assistant Professor in the Construction, Energy, and Sustainable Infrastructure group in the Department of Civil and Environmental Engineering at the University of Washington. Dr Kaminsky is a scholar of engineering projects and organizations. She conducts research on infrastructure in developing communities, with a particular interest in topics of social sustainability. While her work is usually in the context of the global south, Dr Kaminsky is interested in any context that is experiencing significant change in civil infrastructure (or, is developing). The practical goal of her research is to enable increased human capabilities through better civil infrastructure for all the world's people.

Omar Kammouh has received his BSc (Honour, 2013) from Beirut Arab University and his MSc (Honour, 2015) from University of Bologna. He is currently assigned a PhD position at the Politecnico di Torino with a full scholarship. His undergraduate study was in the field of civil engineering and structural control. Kammouh's current research focuses on the evaluation of critical infrastructure resilience during natural and manmade disasters. He is one of the team members working on the Ideal Rescue project sponsored by the European Research Council, 2015–2019. More information regarding Kammouh's research can be found at: www.researchgate.net/profile/Omar_Kammouh.

Kaushal Keraminiyage has over 15 years of experience as an academic in the Higher Education sector both in the UK and Sri Lanka. He is a Senior Lecturer at the University of Huddersfield. Dr Keraminiyage is an experienced researcher with a good publication profile and funded research projects. His research publications include book chapters, refereed journal and refereed conference papers, and various high impact reports. During the last few years he has actively been engaged in organising high profile research conferences at various international locations creating strong links with various Built Environment and Disaster Management experts and stakeholders. Dr Keraminiyage is currently supervising a number of PhD students, and engaged in conducting PhD assessments. He is keen to utilise his knowledge to create better virtual collaborative environments to address teaching, learning and research needs in the field. His research interests are: disaster induced relocations and resettlements; use of ICT for improved disaster resilience; complexity in project management, financing, and estimating; collaborative virtual environments for construction education and research; and disaster resilient urban infrastructure.

Yeowon Kim is a PhD candidate in Sustainability at Arizona State University (ASU), where she studies advancing safe-to-fail and resilient infrastructure to increase the adaptive capacity of cities under non-stationary climate. Her work spans quantitative analyses that measure flood resilience of infrastructure, identification of susceptible regions/populations to risks, and demonstration of trade-offs of solutions using decision support tools, alongside qualitative analysis of conducting stakeholder workshops to foster resilience-based climate risk management policies. Prior to joining ASU, Yeowon received her BS and MS in Civil and Environmental Engineering from Korea University in South Korea, where she studied desalination and water purification by forward osmosis membranes.

Ryan Levitt is a PhD Candidate in the Economics Department at Colorado State University. His concentrations are in Environmental Economics and Political Economy. Ryan's dissertation work is on the economic impacts of natural disasters and community resilience.

Da Li is a PhD candidate in Civil and Environmental Engineering department at the University of Michigan. He received his Masters in Construction Engineering and Management from the University of Michigan. His major research focus is modeling occupants' energy use behaviours in buildings, and predicting thermal comfort using heterogeneous data sources. His email address is dliseren@umich.edu.

Fangjin Li is a PhD student in the Department of Civil and Environmental Engineering at the Hong Kong Polytechnic University. She obtained both her bachelor and master degrees in civil engineering. Her research interest mainly includes pavement materials, especially the asphalt pavement recycling, material characterisation, and material rejuvenation.

Abbie B. Liel, PhD, PE is an Associate Professor of Civil, Environmental and Architectural Engineering at the University of Colorado, Boulder. She earned undergraduate degrees in Civil Engineering, and the Woodrow Wilson School of Public Policy, at Princeton University. She started her graduate studies in the United Kingdom on a Marshall Scholarship, where she received a MSc in Civil Engineering and a MSc in Building and Urban Design and Development. Dr Liel did her PhD at Stanford University, focusing on collapse risk of older non-ductile concrete frame structures. At CU, Liel has worked on problems related to performance of concrete buildings, snow loads on structures, and flood damage in the 2013 Boulder, CO floods. She recently received the Shah Family Innovation Prize from the Earthquake Engineering Research Institute.

Peihui Lin is a postdoctoral research fellow in the School of Civil Engineering and Environmental Science at the University of Oklahoma (OU). She obtained her MS degree from Tongji University, China, in 2014 and her PhD degree from OU in 2018. Dr Lin's research at OU has been focused on stochastic resilience modelling of interdependent physical systems at community or city scales. Dr Lin is affiliated with the NIST-sponsored Center of Excellence for Risk-based Community Resilience Planning, taking an active role in recovery analysis and decision modeling of community's building portfolio as an integrated system.

John W. van de Lindt is George T. Abell professor in Infrastructure and co-director of the Center of Excellence in Risk-Based Community Resilience Planning in the Department of Civil and Environmental Engineering at Colorado State University. Over the past two decades, his research has sought to improve the built environment by focusing on the performance-based engineering of building systems exposed to earthquakes, hurricanes, tornados, and floods.

Samuel Markolf is a postdoctoral research associate within the Urban Resilience to Extremes Sustainability Research Network (UREx SRN) at Arizona State University. His research focuses on understanding the relationship between vulnerability, resilience, and inter-dependent infrastructure systems. He also explores the impact of integrated Social-Ecological-Technological Systems (SETS) on urban resilience. Prior to joining ASU, Sam received his BS in Chemical Engineering from the University of Texas at Austin and his PhD in Civil & Environmental Engineering and Engineering & Public Policy from Carnegie Mellon University. Outside the office, Sam can be found hiking, travelling, and spending time with friends and family.

Hassan Masoomi is a research assistant and a PhD candidate in the Department of Civil and Environmental Engineering at Colorado State University. His research interests are in the area of risk, reliability, and resilience assessment of interdependent infrastructure systems; performance-based engineering; optimization; and decision analysis.

Therese P. McAllister, PhD, PE, is the Community Resilience Group Leader and Program Manager in the Materials and Structural Systems Research Division of the Engineering Laboratory (EL) at the National Institute of Standards and Technology (NIST). She is the federal program officer for the NIST-funded Center of Excellence, Center for Risk-Based Community Resilience Planning led by Colorado State University. Her current research emphasises the integrated performance of physical infrastructure systems and interdependencies with social and economic systems. She has expertise in structural reliability, risk assessment, and failure analysis of buildings and infrastructure systems.

Jason McCormick is an Associate Professor in the Department of Civil and Environmental Engineering at the University of Michigan and a registered professional engineer in the state of Michigan. His research focuses on the performance of steel systems under extreme loads and innovative methods for damage mitigation.

Carol C. Menassa is an Associate Professor at the University of Michigan. She received her PhD in Civil Engineering from the University of Illinois at Urbana-Champaign. Her main research area is building energy modelling and simulation including developing occupancy energy use behavioural models. Her email is menassa@umich.edu and her web page is https://sites.google.com/a/umich.edu/sicislab/.

Steven Moddemeyer is Principal for Planning, Sustainability and Resilience at Seattle-based CollinsWoerman. He advises and guides large-scale master plans that implement affordable, resilient, and sustainable buildings and infrastructure. He applies socio-ecological resilience strategies to urban policy, capital spending, and decision-making. He serves on the National Academies of Sciences Roundtable on Risk, Resilience, and Extreme Events; is a member of the International Union for the Conservation of Nature Resilient Theme group; and advises the University of Washington Masters in Infrastructure Planning and Management as well as the

Evergreen Center for Sustainable Infrastructure. Steve helped to launch the International Water Association's Cities of the Future programme and Singapore International Water Week.

Khalid M. Mosalam obtained his BS and MS from Cairo University and his PhD from Cornell University in Structural Engineering. In 1997, he joined the Department of CEE, UC-Berkeley where he is currently the Taisei Professor of Civil Engineering and the Director of the Pacific Earthquake Engineering Research (PEER) Center. He conducts research on the performance and health monitoring of structures. He is active in areas of assessment and rehabilitation of essential facilities, and in research related to building energy efficiency and sustainability. His research covers large-scale computation and experimentation including hybrid simulation. He is the recipient of 2006 ASCE Huber civil engineering research prize, 2013 UC-Berkeley chancellor award for public services, and 2015 EERI outstanding paper award in Earthquake Spectra. He was a visiting professor at Kyoto University, Japan, METU, Turkey, and NTU, Singapore. He was a High-end Expert in Tongji University and is a core-PI for 'Internet of Things & Societal Cyber Physical System Lab' of Tsinghua-Berkeley Shenzhen Institute.

Ario Muhammad is a Research Associate at School of Earth Science, University of Bristol, United Kingdom. His research interest is on tsunami and earthquake hazard and risk analysis, and tsunami evacuation modelling.

Colleen Murphy is a Professor of Law, Philosophy, and Political Science, as well as Director of the Women and Gender in Global Perspectives Program at the University of Illinois at Urbana-Champaign. She is the author of *A Moral Theory of Political Reconciliation* (Cambridge University Press, 2010) and The Conceptual Foundations of Transitional Justice (Cambridge University Press, 2017), as well as co-editor of Engineering Ethics for a Globalized World (Springer, 2015) and Risk Analysis of Natural Hazards (Springer, 2016). Dr Murphy is an Associate Editor of the *Journal of Moral Philosophy*, and a member of the Editorial Board of the journal *Sustainable and Resilient Infrastructure*.

Zoltan Nagy is an assistant professor in the Department of Civil, Architectural, and Environmental Engineering at The University of Texas at Austin, directing the Intelligent Environments Laboratory. He holds a diploma (MSc) in Mechanical Engineering and a PhD in Robotics from ETH Zurich, Switzerland. He was an academic guest at DTU Copenhagen, Denmark, and a visiting researcher at MIT, Cambridge, USA. Prior to his appointment at UT Austin, he was a senior researcher at the Department of Architecture at ETH Zurich working on kinetic façade systems. As a roboticist turned building scientist, his research interests are in smart buildings and cities, renewable energy systems, control systems for zero emission building operation, machine learning and artificial intelligence for the built environment, and the influence of building occupants on energy performance. He co-leads an IEA EBC Annex subtask on occupant centric control systems. He is a member of ASHRAE.

Paolo Nesi is full professor since 2001. He obtained his PhD in the University of Padova and conducted a period in the IBM research labs in Almaden (California). He has been coordinator of the Ad-Hoc Group for ISO MPEG-SMR standard and co-author of the ISO MPEG-SMR defined in the MPEG-4 format, and on MPEG21 on DRM. For two years he has been included among the first 15 researchers at international level in the Software Engineering area, the only Italian. His research skills include distributed systems technologies, intelligent content, digital rights management and licensing, formal methods, artificial intelligence, grid and cloud systems, middleware, realtime systems, digital content distribution, smart systems, smart city, e-learning, crawling, LOD, data mining. He has been member of many international conference committees and editor of international publications and journals. Paolo Nesi has published more than 250 articles in international journals and congresses and has been chair and/or programme chair of: IEEE SC2, IEEE ICSM, IEEE ICECCS, DMS, AXMEDIS, WEDELMUSIC, CSMR, and programme committee member of IEEE ICSE, IEEE ICECCS, IEEE ICSM, IEEE METRICS, DMS, ICSOFT, DATA, SPIE, SEKE, WEDELMUSIC, IIMS, SEW, Virtual Content, IFIP, and others. Prof. Paolo Nesi is full professor of Distributed Systems in Software Engineering, University of Florence, where he teaches distributed architectures, cloud, virtualization systems, middleware, collaborative systems, mobiles, semantic grid, semantic computing, etc. in bachelor degrees and PhD courses. He has been project manager of many large European research and innovation projects, including: RESOLUTE, ECLAP, AXMEDIS, MOODS, I-MAESTRO, WEDELMUSIC, MUSICNETWORK and for the Department in many other European Projects, including REPLICATE, ICCOC, MUPAAC, VISICON, OPTAMS, IMUTUS, and IMEASY; and of many industrial large projects such as ICARO CLOUD, TRACE-IT, RAISSS, SACVAR, Coll@bora, and Sii-Mobility. Prof. Paolo Nesi is coordinator and responsible of the DISIT Lab of the University of Florence (www.disit.dinfo.unifi.it); he is scientific member of CSAVRI (Centre for the Technology Transfer and University Incubator management); and coordinator and scientific officer of APRE Toscana & Regional Committee of APRE Toscana.

Fabrizio Nocera is a research assistant and PhD Candidate in the Department of Civil and Environmental Engineering at the University of Illinois at Urbana-Champaign. He received his Bachelor of Science from Politecnico di Bari in 2014 and his Master of Science from Politecnico di Torino in 2016. Nocera's research focuses on risk, reliability, and resilience of infrastructure systems with particular emphasis on the resilience of transportation networks, business interruption, and socioeconomic impact following natural hazards.

Maria Nogal, PhD, MSc, MRes is an Assistant Professor in Trinity College Dublin (Ireland). Her expertise includes resilience of interconnected systems, involving land transport networks and their critical infrastructure, and transport modelling. She is also the Principal Investigator of TrinityHaus-School of Engineering. She has published over 60 peer-reviewed scientific papers, and has been awarded the International Abertis Prize, and the XIV Talgo Award.

Alan O'Connor is a Professor in the Dept. of Civil Engineering at Trinity College Dublin, Ireland. He is a Chartered Engineer and Fellow of the Institution of Engineers of Ireland. He has extensive national/international experience in infrastructural risk analysis and probabilistic safety assessment. He has advised clients such as: Irish Rail, The Irish National Roads Authority, The Danish Roads Directorate, Danish Railways, Swedish Railways, The Norwegian Roads Authority, and The Dutch Ministry of Transport, Public Works and Water Management. At Trinity College Dublin, the research group which he leads are focused on investigating: infrastructural asset management and optimised whole life management, cross asset maintenance optimisation, structural health monitoring, wind engineering infrastructure, stochastic modelling of engineering systems, risk analysis of critical infrastructure for extreme weather events, and structural reliability analysis. He has authored over 150 peer-reviewed academic papers in these areas. He has delivered keynote addresses at international conferences in Europe, the United States, and Australia.

Jamie E. Padgett is an Associate Professor in the Department of Civil and Environmental Engineering at Rice University in Houston, Texas. Padgett's research focuses on the application of probabilistic methods for risk assessment of structures and infrastructure, including the subsequent quantification of resilience and sustainability. Her work emphasises transportation and energy related infrastructure exposed to multiple hazards, including earthquakes, hurricanes, or aging and deterioration. Dr Padgett was the founding Chair of the ASCE / SEI technical committee on Multiple Hazard Mitigation. She currently serves on editorial boards for the *ASCE Journal of Structural Engineering* and *Sustainable and Resilient Infrastructure*.

June Young Park is a PhD student at the University of Texas at Austin in the Department of Civil, Architectural, and Environmental engineering, in the Intelligent Environment Laboratory. He received Master of Science in Building Performance & Diagnostics from Carnegie Mellon University, Pittsburgh PA (thesis title: 'Data-driven building metadata inference framework'). In his doctoral work, research interests are in smart building and cities: occupant centred building control using reinforcement learning, occupancy detection and travel estimation using smart technologies, and data-driven building performance benchmarking.

Dorothy A. Reed is Professor of Civil and Environmental Engineering and Adjunct Professor of Industrial and Systems Engineering at the University of Washington. A native of Savannah, Georgia, Reed received a PhD in Civil Engineering from Princeton University. She joined the University of Washington faculty in 1983, following two years as a research associate at the National Institute of Standards and Technology (NIST). Her research interests include the investigation of the resiliency and sustainability of civil infrastructure systems with particular emphasis on post-hurricane performance of power delivery systems. Her research has been featured in the NSF Science Nation series. She serves as vice-chair of the ASCE Wind Engineering Division. She is a registered professional engineer in Washington state.

Andrei M. Reinhorn is a retired (2013) and former chaired professor (Clifford C. Furnas Eminent Professor) in the Department of Civil Structural and Environmental Engineering at University at Buffalo (SUNY), where he taught courses in structural engineering and mechanics with emphasis on experimentation and simulations in structural dynamics and earthquake engineering. His research activity focused on structural control and on inelastic seismic behaviour of buildings and bridge systems. He holds four patents and authored several computer platforms for nonlinear analysis of structures under dynamic excitations. All computational tools were based on experimental evidence from shake table simulations. He is a former member (1996–2006) of the executive committee of MCEER (Multidisciplinary Center for Earthquake Engineering Research), a national centre of excellence dedicated to the development of new technologies that equip communities to become more disaster resilient in the face of earthquakes and other extreme events. He is a co-author of the 2003 pioneering paper 'A framework to quantitatively assess and enhance the seismic resilience of communities', which has formulated the concept and expression of disaster resilience. Moreover, he developed more recently in collaboration with other colleagues the P.E.O.P.L.E.S computational concept for quantification of temporal-geospatial dimensions of resilience of communities. He is the author/co-author of over 750 technical articles and reports in archival journals, conference proceedings, and institutional publications. His articles were cited more than 15,000 times according to Google Scholar. Reinhorn is the founding Director (2000–2007) of the University at Buffalo's Structural Engineering and Earthquake Simulation Laboratory, which hosted the most versatile equipment site of the George E. Brown Network for Earthquake Engineering Simulation (NEES). He is the recipient of the 2015 ASCE Moisseiff Award, 2011 ASCE Nathan M. Newmark Medal, the 2007 SUNY Chancellor Award for Excellence in Scholarship and Creative Activity, the

2005 ASCE-CREF Charles Pankow Award for Innovation, among numerous others. Additional information can be found at http://civil.eng.buffalo.edu/~reinhorn.

Javier Riascos-Ochao is currently Assistant Professor at the Department of Basic Sciences at Universidad Jorge Tadeo Lozano (Bogotá Colombia). Dr Riascos is physicist with a MSc in applied mathematics and he has a PhD in Engineering. His current research areas include stochastic modelling of deteriorating systems and time-dependent evolution of biological and physical systems. He has also worked actively in optimisation and computational modelling in engineering.

Mark Reiner. Prior to co-founding WISRD, Mark was a founding Principal and CEO of Symbiotic Engineering in Boulder, Colorado, a utility data tracking and life-cycle assessment-based company which was acquired by ICF International in September 2012. Mark received his PhD in Civil Engineering at the Urban Sustainable Infrastructure Engineering Program (USIEP) at the University of Colorado Denver in 2007. There he focused on the life-cycle energy/emissions and sustainable solutions for the primary infrastructure sectors in the urban environment. Mark's publications in the past year include: *The Weight of Cities* (UNEP), 'Resource requirements of inclusive urban development in India: Insights from 10 cities' (IOPScience), 'Dependency model: reliable infrastructure and the resilient, sustainable, and livable city' (*Jour. Sus and Resil Infra*), and 'Foundational infrastructure framework for city resilience' (*Jour. Sus and Resil Infra*).

Raffaele De Risi is an experienced structural engineer, specializing in performance-based earthquake engineering. He is also an expert in advanced probabilistic and statistical analyses for modelling natural hazard impact. His research interests cover a wide range of environmental risks (e.g. seismic, tsunami, flooding, and climate change).

David V. Rosowsky is the Provost and Senior Vice President at the University of Vermont in Burlington, Vermont (USA). Dr Rosowsky served previously as Dean of Engineering at Rensselaer Polytechnic Institute, and as Head of the Zachry Department of Civil Engineering at Texas A&M University, where he also held the A.P. and Florence Wiley Chair in Civil Engineering. Dr Rosowsky earned BS and MS degrees in civil engineering from Tufts University, and a PhD in civil engineering from Johns Hopkins University. Dr Rosowsky maintains an active research programme in wind and earthquake engineering and continues to supervise graduate students and post-doctoral researchers. He was a registered Professional Engineer in Texas and holds the rank of Fellow of the American Society of Civil Engineers and Fellow of the Structural Engineering Institute. A recognised expert in structural reliability, design for natural hazards, stochastic modelling of structural and environmental loads, and probability-based codified design, Dr Rosowsky has authored or co-authored more than 250 papers in peer-reviewed journals and conference proceedings. He is the recipient of the American Society of Civil Engineers (ASCE) Walter L. Huber Research Prize, the T.K. Hseih Award from the Institution of Civil Engineers (UK), and the ASCE Norman Medal.

Rehan Sadiq is a Professor and an Associate Dean at School of Engineering UBC-Okanagan Campus. For the past 20 years he has been involved in research related to environmental risk analysis, water supply systems, lifecycle assessment, and infrastructure reliability. He is author of more than 450 peer-reviewed journal and conference articles, book chapters, and technical reports in the related areas. Citations of his research work has now reached ~7000 in the Google Scholar and other scientific databases with a current H-index of 45.

Mauricio Sánchez-Silva's area of expertise is risk analysis and stochastic modelling to support the decision making process in engineering under uncertain conditions. He works extensively on Probabilistic Risk Analysis (PRA) and approximate measures to estimate potential risks for infrastructure, network systems, and industrial facilities. Furthermore, he has experience on estimating risk in complex problems under conditions where information is partial, incomplete, and difficult to quantify. Finally, he has been involved in projects where the socioeconomic and environmental contexts play a significant role and, therefore, traditional risk modelling and engineering methods can only be applied partially. Some of his current areas of research include planning and development of infrastructure systems (structures and lifelines); design for changeability, stochastic modelling of deteriorating systems and structures, decision-making for resource allocation and cost effectiveness of investments in the design and operation of various types of facilities.

Amir Sarreshtehdari is a PhD candidate in the Department of Civil, Structural and Environmental Engineering at the University at Buffalo. Amir obtained his MS degree in 2017 from the Department of Civil, Structural and Environmental Engineering at the University at Buffalo. His research focuses on the probability-based assessment of infrastructure performance under natural hazard scenarios, mainly fire and earthquake.

Neetesh Sharma is a PhD Candidate in the Department of Civil and Environmental Engineering at the University of Illinois at Urbana–Champaign. He received his BTech in Civil Engineering from NIT Trichy, India in 2010. He thereafter worked for four years in construction and maintenance of power plants at NTPC Ltd. He received his MS in Civil Engineering from University of Illinois at Urbana-Champaign in 2016. His current research focuses on mathematical modeling of risk, reliability, and resilience of critical infrastructure systems.

Seymour M.J. Spence is an Assistant Professor in the Department of Civil and Environmental Engineering. He earned his MS in Civil Engineering in 2005 from the University of Perugia and PhD from the Universities of Florence and Braunschweig in 2009. His research interest is focused on harnessing the computational and technological revolution of the last decades with the aim of developing models that better predict and optimise the performance of the built environment to natural hazards.

Christine D. Standohar-Alfano is an Associate Engineer at Haag Engineering. She holds degrees in both meteorology and civil engineering. Her research interests include risk analysis for meteorological hazards and methods for improved performance of the built environment to natural hazards including tornadoes, straight-line winds, and hail.

Mark G. Stewart is Professor of Civil Engineering and Director of the Centre for Infrastructure Performance and Reliability at The University of Newcastle in Australia. He is the author of *Probabilistic Risk Assessment of Engineering Systems* (Chapman & Hall, 1997), *Terror, Security, and Money: Balancing the Risks, Benefits, and Costs of Homeland Security* (Oxford University Press, 2011), *Chasing Ghosts: The Policing of Terrorism* (Oxford University Press, 2016), and *Are We Safe Enough? Measuring and Assessing Aviation Security* (Elsevier, 2018) as well as more than 400 technical papers and reports. He has 30 years of experience in probabilistic risk and vulnerability assessment of infrastructure and security systems that are subject to man-made and natural hazards. Mark has received over $4.5 million in Australian Research Council (ARC) support in the past 15 years. Mark recently led a consortium of five universities in Australia for the $3.5 million CSIRO

Flagship Cluster Fund project Climate Adaptation Engineering for Extreme Events (CAEx). The CAEx Cluster is assessing the impact of climate change on damage and safety risks to infrastructure, and assessing the cost-effectiveness of engineering adaptation strategies. The three year project ended in 2016. A new book co-authored with Emilio Bastidas-Arteaga, *Climate Adaptation Engineering: Risks and Economics* will be published by Elsevier in late 2018. Mark also has significant expertise in time and spatial dependent reliability analysis of new and existing deteriorating structures such as bridges and buildings. This has utility for Structural Health Monitoring (SHM) and assessing the safety and service-life prediction of new and existing structures. He is also a leading investigator with the reliability-based calibration of the Australian Masonry and Concrete Structures Codes. Since 2004, Mark has received continuous ARC support to develop probabilistic risk-modelling techniques for infrastructure subject to military and terrorist explosive blasts and cost-benefit assessments of counter-terrorism protective measures for critical infrastructure. In 2011, he received a five-year Australian Professorial Fellowship from the ARC to continue and to extend that work. This work was further extended to 2019 by the ARC.

Božidar Stojadinović is the Chair of Structural Dynamics and Earthquake Engineering at the Swiss Federal Institute of Technology (ETH) Zürich. His main research is in the probabilistic performance-based seismic resilience evaluation and design of civil structures and infrastructure systems. He is also working on response modification techniques, such as rocking and seismic isolation, and on the development of new hybrid simulation methods to evaluate the response of structures to dynamic excitation. Dr Stojadinović teaches courses in Seismic Design, Structural Dynamics, and Theory of Structures. He is a graduate of the University of Belgrade (1988), Carnegie Mellon University (1990), and the University of California Berkeley (1995).

Armin Tabandeh is a PhD candidate in the Department of Civil and Environmental Engineering at the University of Illinois at Urbana-Champaign. He has done research on a range of topics related to the development of probabilistic and stochastic models for the performance analysis of dynamical systems. His current research centres on risk, reliability, and resilience analysis of civil infrastructure-social systems.

Solomon Tesfamariam is a professor at the School of Engineering UBC Okanagan Campus. His research group is developing multi hazard risk-based decision support tools for civil infrastructure systems management. His buried infrastructure research group is working on integrated asset management by developing analytical- and numerical-based pipe failure models. He has published over 100 peer reviewed journal papers with H-index of 25 and over 2000 citations.

Iris Tien's research work focuses on probabilistic methods for modelling and reliability assessment of structures and infrastructure systems. She explores subjects that encompass traditional topics of civil engineering as well as sensing and data analytics, stochastic processes, probabilistic risk assessment, and decision-making under uncertainty. Her recent major contributions have been in the areas of complex interdependent infrastructure systems modelling, structural risk and reliability, and big data analytics for real-time infrastructure assessment. Tien received her PhD in Civil Systems Engineering from the University of California, Berkeley.

David Trejo is Professor and Hal Pritchett Endowed Chair in the School of Civil and Construction Engineering at Oregon State University. His interests and expertise are in durability and performance of reinforced concrete systems, corrosion of steel in cementitious materials, service-life analyses, innovative concrete materials for improved construction and service life, and modelling deterioration mechanisms in cementitious and metallic systems. His research focuses on the design, development, and assessment of materials and systems for efficient construction processes and durable constructed products. His research in these areas has resulted in over 150 publications, and he has been recognised as a NASA research fellow and a fellow of the American Concrete Institute.

José Ramón Vázquez-Canteli is a PhD Candidate in Civil Engineering at the University of Texas at Austin, in the Intelligent Environment Laboratory. He obtained his BS in Electromechanical Engineering, and his MS in Industrial Engineering at the Comillas Pontifical University, Spain. He did his Master thesis on building energy simulation at the urban scale at École Polytechnique Fédérale de Lausanne (EPFL). His doctoral research is on the use of multi-agent reinforcement learning for demand response in the built environment at the urban scale. His objective is to integrate occupants into the control loop of urban energy management systems. He has also been a visiting researcher at NREL.

Navya Vishnu is a graduate research assistant and PhD student in the Department of Civil and Environmental Engineering at Rice University. Her research interests are in the area of infra-structure sustainability and resilience under multiple threats, with a focus on bridges and bridge networks.

Naiyu Wang, PhD, is an Assistant Professor in the School of Civil Engineering and Environmental Science at the University of Oklahoma. Her work focuses on structural safety and reliability assessment, natural hazard modelling, and risk-informed sustainable decisions for civil infra-structure. She is especially interested in modelling and analysis of resilience of civil infrastructure systems using stochastic process models of recovery and the impact of climate change on risk to civil infrastructure exposed to natural hazards.

Shuoqi Wang is a postdoctoral research associate at the University of Washington. He received his MS and PhD in Industrial and Systems Engineering from University of Washington. His research interest includes system reliability and resilience in civil infrastructure, as well as healthy buildings and indoor environment quality assessment. He is experienced in post-hurricane elec-tric power network recovery modelling, data management, and geospatial fragility analysis. He has also been involved in several indoor environment quality and indoor air quality assessment investigations for buildings owned by the university and by a city government. He is a certified Fitwel Ambassador.

Yuhong Wang is an Associate Professor in the Department of Civil and Environmental Engineering at the Hong Kong Polytechnic University. Dr Wang's main research areas include the structural design of pavements, asphalt/concrete pavement materials, pavement construc-tion and management, management of infrastructures in their life cycles. Dr Wang has led and participated in many research projects in his research areas with extensive publication records.

Sarah J. Welsh-Huggins, PhD, EIT, LEED Associate is an Urban Resilience and Sustainable Development Consultant based in Washington DC. She earned undergraduate degrees in Civil Engineering and International Studies at Lafayette College. She earned her MS in Structural Engineering and a graduate certificate in Engineering for Developing Communities at the University of Colorado, Boulder, before completing her PhD in Civil Systems (Civil Engineering), also at CU Boulder. Dr Welsh-Huggins's dissertation focused on life-cycle analysis of economic cost and environmental impact tradeoffs for buildings designed to jointly meet goals for sustainable and resilient performance. Welsh-Huggins has worked for the US Federal Emergency Management Agency supporting Hurricane Irma recovery initiatives in Florida and was recently selected as a finalist for a Science & Technology Policy post-doctorate fellowship by the American Association for the Advancement of Science.

Hao Xu is a PhD student and graduate research assistant in the Department of Civil and Environmental Engineering at the University of Illinois at Urbana-Champaign. Hao earned his Bachelor of Science degree in Civil Engineering from Harbin Institute of Technology in 2012, and his Master of Science degree in Structural Engineering from the University of Illinois in 2014. His research focuses on non-stationary space-time random field formulations, and multi-scale multi-variate modelling of engineering systems.

David Y. Yang is a postdoctoral research associate at Lehigh University. He obtained his BEng in Civil Engineering in 2012 from Zhejiang University, China, and his PhD in Structural Engineering in 2017 from the Hong Kong Polytechnic University, Hong Kong. His research interest includes structural strengthening, structural reliability, multi-hazard risk and resilience assessment, robust decision-making under uncertainty, and life-cycle management of civil infrastructure. His current work is focused on the risk management of civil infrastructure under climate change and risk-informed decision-making for deteriorating civil and marine structures.

Sammy Zahran is an Associate Professor in the Department of Economics at Colorado State University. Sammy is also an Associate Professor in the Department of Epidemiology in the Colorado School of Public Health. From 2012 to 2014, he was Robert Wood Johnson Health and Society Fellow at Columbia University. His published research appears in *Proceedings of the National Academy of Sciences, Risk Analysis, Journal of Risk and Uncertainty, Ecological Economics, Environmental Science and Technology, Climatic Change, Science of the Total Environment, Environmental Research, Journal of the Association of Environmental and Resource Economists (JAERE), American Journal of Public Health, Environment International*, and the *International Journal of Epidemiology*.

Mariano Angelo Zanini received his MSc in Civil Engineering from the University of Padova, Italy in 2011, and PhD from the Doctoral School in Engineering of Civil and Mechanical Structural Systems, at the University of Trento, Italy in 2015. From 2015 to 2017 he held the position of Professor of Structural Design for the Civil and Environmental MSc degrees, and is currently Professor of Seismic Risk Assessment for the Civil and Industrial Safety Engineering MSc degree at the University of Padova. His main areas of research interest are reliability, safety, durability, and resilience of bridges and reinforced concrete structures, Bridge Management Systems, seismic risk assessment and emergency management, enterprise risk management, loss and business continuity analysis, development of risk mitigation strategies, seismic risk rating for insurance coverage and CAT bond pricing purposes.

Kecheng Zhao is a PhD candidate in the Department of Civil and Environmental Engineering at the Hong Kong Polytechnic University. He obtained his bachelor degree in chemical engineering and his MS degree in environmental engineering. His research focuses asphalt binder characterization, asphalt long-term aging behaviours, new rejuvenation methods for aged asphalt binder, and new anti-aging methods for long-life pavement.

Part I
Introduction

1

Toward sustainable and resilient physical systems
Current state and future directions

Paolo Gardoni[1]

[1] DEPARTMENT OF CIVIL AND ENVIRONMENTAL ENGINEERING,
MAE CENTER: CREATING A MULTI-HAZARD APPROACH TO ENGINEERING,
UNIVERSITY OF ILLINOIS AT URBANA-CHAMPAIGN, URBANA, IL, USA; GARDONI@ILLINOIS.EDU

1.1 Introduction

Structures and infrastructure (i.e., physical systems) play a fundamental role in promoting and enhancing the sustainability and resilience of communities. Specifically, physical systems enable individuals to have genuine opportunities to achieve different dimensions of well-being, such as being mobile, nourished and educated. The resilience of physical systems promotes the availability of such opportunities with minimal disruptions. The sustainability of physical systems promotes the availability of such opportunities to both current and future generations and addresses considerations of environmental and social justice.

Significant research has been conducted to assess the performance and reliability of individual structures, such as bridges, buildings and electrical substations (e.g., Gardoni et al. 2002, 2003; Choe et al. 2007, 2009; Ramamoorthy et al. 2006, 2008; Mardfekri & Gardoni 2013, 2015; Mardfekri et al. 2015; Tabandeh & Gardoni 2014, 2015) and individual infrastructure systems, such as transportation, water and power networks (e.g., Kang et al. 2008; Guikema & Gardoni 2009; Lee et al. 2011; Frangopol & Bocchini 2012; Guidotti et al. 2017a) when subject to natural hazards. However, the functionality of individual physical systems often also depends on the functionality of other supporting physical systems as well as the response of the supported socio-economic systems. As a result, assessing the functionality of physical systems, modeling the impact of hazards, and developing effective mitigation and recovery strategies require capturing the dependencies/interdependencies among physical systems and socio-economic systems. In addition, predicting the functionality of physical systems requires considering the effects of aging and deterioration, as well as the impact of climate change and multiple hazards.

Promoting the resilience of physical systems demands a comprehensive framework and new multidisciplinary models to predict the impact of hazards on physical systems over time. The time period of interest needs to be extended from immediately after the occurrence of a hazard up to the entire service life of physical systems, including the possible recovery process following

3

a hazard. The time of recovery is critical information for the evaluation of risk (Murphy & Gardoni 2008; Gardoni & Murphy 2018). As a result, resilience (defined in the next section) is both one of the most pressing characteristics of physical systems and communities as well as a source of necessary information for risk evaluation and decision-making. The needed framework has to be probabilistic so that it can properly account for the uncertainties inherent in the phenomena of interest as well as in the prediction process. Such uncertainties include, for example, aleatory uncertainties in the characteristics of natural hazards and physical phenomena and epistemic uncertainties due to the limited availability of data and simplification in the mathematical models of complex systems (Gardoni et al. 2002; Murphy et al. 2011).

The impact of hazard on physical systems and communities over time needs to be quantified in terms of informative decision variables or metrics. Common metrics measure the direct physical damage and consequences such as deaths, dollar loss and duration of downtime (May 2001, Gardoni & LaFave 2016). However, Murphy and Gardoni (2006) noted that such traditional metrics are incomplete. In addition, hazards often have larger impacts on the more vulnerable households and populations (e.g., An et al. 2004, van Willingen et al. 2005; Kajitani et al. 2005; Dash & Gladwin 2007; Dash et al. 2007). Traditional metrics typically do not capture such heterogeneity in the distribution of the impact. As a result, new metrics have to be introduced to properly describe the broader socio-economic impact along with its spatio-temporal variability (Murphy & Gardoni 2006).

In addition, sustainability brings in a set of normative considerations that need to be included in the design of physical systems and planning of communities, as well as in the evaluation of the impact of hazards on communities and the recovery processes. There are three components of sustainability (Gardoni & Murphy 2008, 2018): (a) environmental justice, (b) global justice and (c) intergenerational justice. Environmental justice is about promoting a flourishing natural ecosystem, which may be good in itself or for instrumental reasons, insofar as a flourishing natural ecosystem is an important element for the well-being of individuals. Both global justice and intergenerational justice are linked with social justice, which is about the distributional fairness in economic, political and social domains. Since certain population groups may be more impacted by a hazard than others or recover more slowly, global justice focuses on the spatial distribution within as well as across communities. Intergenerational justice focuses on distributions over time, considering the availability of goods and services as they are distributed across generations.

Finally, a holistic framework that optimally addresses societal needs and successfully promotes individuals' well-being has to take advantage of the continuous advances in information and communication technology, and in big data analytics (Boakye et al. 2018). The framework has to include the fundamental role played in achieving resilience and sustainability by urban planning and public policies, as well as critical economic and financial considerations that shape both the immediate impact as well as the recovery process.

The remaining sections of this chapter first discuss in more details the concepts of resilience and sustainability and then define the overarching goal and contributions of the book. Finally, the chapter describes the organization of the book.

1.2 Resilience

The concept of resilience has received increasing attention in the last few decades in multiple disciplines and it is now seen as a desirable characteristic of physical systems and communities (Bruneau et al. 2003; McAllister 2013; Caverzan & Solomos 2014; Ellingwood et al. 2016; Gardoni 2017; Guidotti et al. 2016; Sharma et al. 2017). There are a number of discipline-specific definitions of resilience in the literature (e.g., Bruneau et al. 2003; Cimellaro et al. 2010; Bocchini et al. 2012; United States National Research Council 2012; United Nations International Strategy for Disaster Reduction 2015; Koliou et al. 2018). A common characteristic to all definitions is that resilience is "the ability of a system to withstand external perturbation(s), adapt, and rapidly recover to the original or a new level of functionality" (Gardoni & Murphy 2018). Doorn et al. (2018) also gives a multidisciplinary definition of resilience going beyond the engineering domain, incorporating philosophical and social science considerations, and accounting for social justice.

1.2.1 Resilience and recovery of physical systems

Considering physical systems, resilience can be described as the ability of a structure or infrastructure to reach and maintain a desired level of reliability or provide a desired level of service or functionality, Q, promptly after the occurrence of a hazard. The recovery of a system is influenced by several factors including the type and level of damage, availability of resources required for the repair, environmental conditions and the possible occurrence of disrupting events that could occur during the recovery process. As a result, the recovery curve $Q(t)$ can have different shapes as a function of time t (Figure 1.1). To increase the resilience of a system, we need to increase its robustness (the residual functionality in the immediate aftermath of a hazard) (moving along Arrow 1), and reduce the recovery time (moving along Arrow 2).

Resilience analysis requires the development of a mathematical formulation to model the recovery process, as well as the definition of metrics for the quantification of the resilience associated with a given recovery process. To replicate the actual work progress occurring during the recovery process, Sharma et al. (2017) proposed a stochastic formulation that captures the effects on $Q(t)$ of the completion of recovery activities as well as possible disrupting events that might occur during the recovery process. The stochastic formulation captures the completion time of different groups of recovery activities that improve the system state (i.e., reliability or functionality of the system), models the occurrence of possible disrupting events that might reduce the reliability or functionality of the system, and predicts the system state after the completion of each recovery step or the occurrence of disrupting events. The formulation accounts for the type and level of damage, availability of resources, and the environmental conditions.

The recovery of physical and socio-economic systems depends also on the recovery of the supporting systems. For example, the recovery of the functionality of buildings depends on

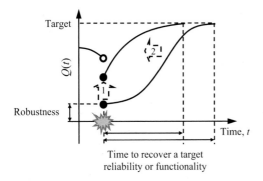

Figure 1.1 Illustration of the change in functionality Q as a function of time t.

the recovery of the supporting infrastructure like potable water and electric power networks. Similarly, the recovery of the potable water network depends on the recovery of the electric power network since power is needed at the pumping stations and control systems. Guidotti et al. (2016, 2018) modeled the role on the resilience of dependencies and interdependencies of physical and socio-economic systems.

The recovery curve $Q(t)$ of a system completely describes the resilience of a system. Resilience metrics can be used as partial descriptors of the recovery curve, and are particularly valuable in decision-making. The integral of the recovery curve over time can be used as a possible resilience metric (Bruneau et al. 2003). An alternative metric is the probability of a system's recovery (Chang & Shinozuka 2004). Different variations of these initial metrics can be found in the more recent literature (e.g., Decò et al. 2013; Ayyub 2014). However, a single metric is generally incomplete. Sharma et al. (2017) proposed resilience metrics defined by analogy to the moments of random variables in probably theory. Such resilience metrics are simple and intuitive, have clear interpretations that facilitate the understanding and communication of the level of resilience to the public, and any (sub-)set of metrics can be expanded with additional ones of higher order to capture additional information about the system resilience up to describing the entire information in the recovery curve.

1.2.2 Resilience and recovery of society

Going beyond the impact of hazards on physical systems and the modeling of their recovery over time, the concept of resilience needs to be extended to include the societal impact of hazards and the recovery of the well-being of individuals. In this broader context, the United Nations International Strategy for Disaster Reduction (UNISDR) (2015) defines resilience as "[t]he ability of a system, community or society exposed to hazards to resist, absorb, accommodate to and recover from the effects of a hazard in a timely and efficient manner, including through the preservation and restoration of its essential basic structures and functions." Similarly, the United States National Research Council (2012) defines resilience as "[t]he ability to prepare and plan for, absorb, recover from, or more successfully adapt to actual or potential adverse events." Such "ability" introduced in both definitions depends on the resilience of the physical systems as well as on the contextual characteristics of social, economic and political institutions (Murphy & Gardoni 2011a; Gardoni & Murphy 2018). The ability of societies to recover is linked to the ability of the impacted society to repair and rebuild the physical systems (possibly with the help of external support – federal or international), and the ability of individuals and communities to adapt and recover in a more creative and self-reliant way independently from the recovery of the built infrastructure (Olshansky 2018).

A capability approach can be used to quantify the societal recovery and convert the predicted recovery of the physical systems into societal recovery (Gardoni & Murphy 2018, Tabandeh et al. 2018). Specifically, the estimates of the functionality of different physical systems obtained from the modeling of the recovery of physical systems can be used as time-dependent input values in predictive models that give the genuine opportunities that individual have (e.g., avoiding escapable morbidity and mortality, being adequately nourished, being sheltered, and having mobility). In a capability approach, such opportunities (or capabilities) are used as measures of well-being of individuals in the aftermath of a hazard (Murphy & Gardoni 2006, 2007, 2008, 2010, 2011a, b, 2012; Gardoni & Murphy 2008, 2009, 2010, 2013, 2014). Using such time-dependent values, we can obtain time-dependent estimates of the well-being of individuals as the physical systems recover over time. The prediction over time of the well-being of individuals can then be used in risk evaluation to judge a risk from a hazard as acceptable, tolerable or not tolerable (Murphy & Gardoni 2008; Tabandeh et al. 2018).

1.3 Sustainability and social justice

Three normative considerations need to be included in the design of physical systems, and in the evaluation of the impact of hazards on communities and the recovery processes (Murphy & Gardoni 2008; Gardoni & Murphy 2018). These normative considerations are: (a) environmental justice, (b) global justice and (c) intergenerational justice.

Environmental justice is about the state of the environment. A flourishing natural ecosystem may be desirable in itself and worth protecting and promoting for its own sake. At the same time, a flourishing natural ecosystem may matter instrumentally as it contributes to the well-being of individuals. Environmental justice calls for mitigation strategies and recovery processes that protect and ideally promote the ability of ecosystems to flourish. If negatively impacted by a hazard, mitigation strategies or recovery processes of the physical systems, ecosystems should also be restored and rehabilitated (Anderson & Woodrow 1989). There is a need for a general formulation that is able to account for environmental concerns in the definition and quantification of the impact of a hazard. A capability approach allows us to account for environmental justice by explicitly considering the ecosystem per se (Martins 2011; Ballet et al. 2011, 2013) as well as how ecosystems serve individuals (Gardoni & Murphy 2018).

Certain population groups may be more impacted than other ones or recover more slowly (Guidotti et al. 2018). Global justice calls for considering and addressing the differential impact and recovery rates across communities as well as sub-groups within a community. Global justice also requires fairness in the distribution of mitigation and recovery resources and that opportunities for a prompt recovery are available to all individuals (World Commission on Environment and Development 1987; Alexander 2002). Assessing the recovery of communities and sub-groups within a community requires having a formulation of the kind outlined in the previous section that can predict, measure and track resilience with a sufficient level of granularity to capture the spatial heterogeneities (Guidotti et al. 2018). Evaluating the fairness in the resource allocation for mitigation strategies and recovery processes requires looking at the genuine opportunities to access resources as well as the opportunities generated by such resources.

Finally, sustainability also requires consideration of intergenerational justice (Gardoni & Murphy 2008; Gardoni et al. 2016). Intergenerational justice refers to the idea of fairness or justice between generations. Mitigation strategies and recovery processes must respect and ideally promote intergenerational equity (Mileti 1999; World Commission on Environment and Development 1987). Issues that need to be considered when discussing future scenarios include the effects of climate change (in particular on the likelihood and magnitude of some natural hazards), population growth (in particular in coastal regions) and migration (for example from rural to urban areas), as well as the likely advent of new technologies. There are a number of uncertainties when dealing with the assessment of intergenerational justice because by nature of the problem we are considering future scenarios that are not perfectly known (Goodin 1999; Murphy et al. 2018). For example, there are uncertainties surrounding the advent of future technologies, unknown harms associated to current technologies may be discovered, and new solutions might become available. Evaluating intergenerational justice requires using our best current knowledge while accounting for the relevant uncertainties (Murphy et al. 2011).

Addressing the three normative considerations associated to sustainability is challenging also because they often bring to bear competing needs. For example, in discussing the moral dimensions of climate change, MacLean (2016) argues that global justice and intergenerational justice may pull in competing directions.

1.4 Overall goal and contributions of the book

This book provides a targeted perspective on sustainability and resilience aiming to outline a comprehensive underlying narrative across topics typically presented in isolation and to define the directions of future developments. The book includes a unique collection of contributions from some of the foremost scholars in the field covering a broad spectrum of topics across multiple disciplines that play a fundamental role in achieving sustainability and resilience. The book brings conceptual clarity and mathematical rigor to the fast growing fields of sustainability and resilience. It discusses some of the modeling tools for sustainability and resilience analysis, and introduces a broader discussion of interdisciplinary considerations that should be accounted for to achieve resilient systems that address societal needs and are sensitive to sustainability considerations. The book discusses the role of dependencies/interdependencies among networks, the impact of aging and deterioration of infrastructure, the role played by climate change, the role of information and communication technologies, the role of urban planning and public policies, and the need to involve economic and financial considerations in developing optimal mitigation strategies and recovery processes.

1.5 Structure of the book

The 44 chapters within this book are organized into 12 parts. Part I gives a general introduction of the book, including a discussion of its goal and contributions, and presents an overview of the field of sustainable and resilient infrastructure. Part II focuses on situating and motivating sustainability and resilience, and discusses metrics and quantification of sustainability and resilience, as well as how they affect societal well-being. Part III discusses methods for resilience analysis of different systems (including buildings, and transportation, electric and power, water and cyber infrastructure). Part IV focuses on sustainable materials, design and construction. Part V discusses how sustainability and resilience should come together so that physical systems can best serve current and future generations. Part VI talks about the role of dependencies and interdependencies of physical systems in achieving sustainability and resilience. Part VII discusses the role and impact of aging and deterioration of physical systems. Part VIII focuses on the role and impact of climate change. Part IX talks about smart cities and the role of information and communication technologies in achieving sustainability and resilience. Part X focuses on multi-objective optimization of physical systems. Part XI is about the role of urban planning and public policies. Finally, Part XII covers economic and financial considerations, and discusses the role of insurance, re-insurance and catastrophe bonds.

References

Alexander, D. (2002). *Principles of Emergency Planning and Management.* Oxford University Press: New York.
An, D., Gordon, P., Moore II, J.E., and Richardson, H.W. (2004). Regional economic models for performance based earthquake engineering, *Natural Hazards Review,* 5(4), 188–95.
Ayyub, B.M. (2014). Systems resilience for multihazard environments: Definition, metrics, and valuation for decision making, *Risk Analysis,* 34, 340–55.
Ballet, J., Bazin, D., Dubois, J.-L., and Mahieu, F.R. (2011). A note on sustainability economics and the capability approach, *Ecological Economics,* 70(11), 1831–4.

Ballet, J., Koffi, J.M., and Pelenc, J. (2013). Environment, justice and the capability approach, *Ecological Economics*, 85, 28–34.

Boakye, J., Gardoni, P., and Murphy, C. (2018). Using opportunities in big data analytics to more accurately predict societal consequences of natural disasters, *Civil Engineering and Environmental Systems*, (under review).

Bocchini, P., Decò, A., and Frangopol, D.M. (2012). Probabilistic functionality recovery model for resilience analysis. In Biondini, F. and Frangopol, D.M. (eds.), *Bridge Maintenance, Safety, Management, Resilience and Sustainability*, London: CRC Press, 1920–27.

Bruneau, M., Chang, S.E., Eguchi, R.T., Lee, G.C., O'Rourke, T.D., Reinhorn, A.M., Shinozuka M., Tierney K., Wallace W.A., and von Winterfeldt, D. (2003). A framework to quantitatively assess and enhance the seismic resilience of communities, *Earthquake Spectra*, 19(4), 733–52.

Caverzan, A. and Solomos, G. (2014). Review on resilience in literature and standards codes for critical built-infrastructures, *JRC Science and Policy Report*. http://publications.jrc.ec.europa.eu/repository/bitstream/JRC90900/resilience_report.pdf (last accessed September 10, 2018).

Chang, S.E. and Shinozuka, M. (2004). Measuring improvements in the disaster resilience of communities, *Earthquake Spectra*, 20, 739–55.

Choe, D., Gardoni, P., and Rosowsky, D. (2007). Closed-form fragility estimates, parameter sensitivity and Bayesian updating for RC columns, *ASCE Journal of Engineering Mechanics*, 133(7), 833–43.

Choe, D., Gardoni, P., Rosowsky, D., and Haukaas, T. (2009). Seismic fragility estimates for reinforced concrete bridges subject to corrosion, *Structural Safety*, 31, 275–83.

Cimellaro, P.G., Reinhorn, A.M., and Bruneau, M. (2010). Framework for analytical quantification of disaster resilience, *Engineering Structures*, 32(11), 3639–49.

Dash, N. and Gladwin, H. (2007). Evacuation decision making and behavioral responses: Individual and household. *Natural Hazards Review*, 8(3), 69–77.

Dash, N., Morrow, B.H., Mainster, J., and Cunningham, L. (2007). Lasting effects of hurricane Andrew on a working-class community, *Natural Hazards Review*, 8(1), 13–21.

Decò, A., Bocchini, P., and Frangopol, D.M. (2013). A probabilistic approach for the prediction of seismic resilience of bridges, *Earthquake Engineering & Structural Dynamics*, 42, 1469–87.

Doorn, N., Gardoni, P., and Murphy, C. (2018). A multidisciplinary definition and evaluation of resilience: The role of social justice in defining resilience. *Sustainable and Resilient Infrastructure*, DOI: 10.1080/23789689.2018.1428162.

Ellingwood, B.R., Cutler, H., Gardoni, P., Peacock, W.G., van de Lindt, J.W., and Wang, N. (2016). The Centerville virtual community: A fully integrated decision model of interacting physical and social infrastructure systems, *Sustainable and Resilient Infrastructure*, 1(3–4), 95–107.

Frangopol, D.M. and Bocchini, P. (2012). Bridge network performance, maintenance and optimization under uncertainty: Accomplishments and challenges, *Structure and Infrastructure Engineering*, 8(4), 341–56.

Gardoni, P. (ed.) (2017). *Risk and Reliability Analysis: Theory and Applications*. New York: Springer.

Gardoni, P. and LaFave, J., (eds.) (2016). *Multi-hazard Approaches to Civil Infrastructure Engineering*. New York: Springer.

Gardoni, P. and Murphy, C. (2008). Recovery from natural and man-made disasters as capabilities restoration and enhancement, *International Journal of Sustainable Development and Planning*, 3(4), 1–17.

Gardoni, P. and Murphy, C. (2009). Capabilities-based approach to measuring the societal impacts of natural and man-made hazards in risk analysis, *ASCE Natural Hazards Review*, 10(2), 29–37.

Gardoni, P. and Murphy, C. (2010). Gauging the societal impacts of natural disasters using a capabilities-based approach, *Disasters*, 34(3), 619–36.

Gardoni, P. and Murphy, C. (2013). A capability approach for seismic risk analysis and management, in Solomon Tesfamariam and Katsu Goda (eds.) *Handbook of Seismic Risk Analysis and Management of Civil Infrastructure Systems*. Cambridge, UK: Woodhead Publishing Ltd.

Gardoni, P. and Murphy, C. (2014). A scale of risk, *Risk Analysis*, 34(7), 1208–27.

Gardoni, P. and Murphy, C. (2018). Society-based design: Developing sustainable and resilient communities, *Sustainable and Resilient Infrastructure*, DOI: 10.1080/23789689.2018.1448667.

Gardoni, P., Der Kiureghian A., and Mosalam K.M. (2002). Probabilistic capacity models and fragility estimates for RC columns based on experimental observations, *ASCE Journal of Engineering Mechanics*, 128(10), 1024–38.

Gardoni, P., Mosalam K.M., and Der Kiureghian A. (2003). Probabilistic seismic demand models and fragility estimates for RC bridges, *Journal of Earthquake Engineering*, 7(Special Issue 1), 79–106.

Gardoni, P., Murphy, C., and Rowell, A., (eds.) (2016). *Societal Risk Management of Natural Hazards*. New York: Springer.

Goodin, R. (1999). The sustainability ethic: Political, not just moral, *Journal of Applied Philosophy*, 16(3), 247–54.

Guidotti, R., Chmielewski, H., Unnikrishnan, V., Gardoni, P., McAllister, T., and van de Lindt, J. (2016). Modeling the resilience of critical infrastructure: The role of network dependencies, *Sustainable and Resilient Infrastructure*, 1(3–4), 153–68.

Guidotti, R., Gardoni, P., and Chen, Y. (2017a). Network reliability analysis with link and nodal weights and auxiliary nodes, *Structural Safety*, 65, 12–26.

Guidotti, R., Gardoni, P., and Chen, Y. (2017b). Multi-layer heterogeneous network model for inter-dependent infrastructure systems. In *Proceedings of the 12th International Conference on Structural Safety & Reliability (ICOSSAR 2017)*, TU Wien, Vienna (Austria).

Guidotti, R., Gardoni, P., and Rosenheim, N. (2018). Integration of physical infrastructure and social systems in communities' reliability and resilience analysis, *Reliability Engineering & System Safety* (under review).

Guikema, S. and Gardoni, P. (2009). Reliability estimation for networks of reinforced concrete bridges, *ASCE Journal of Infrastructure Systems*, 15, 61–9.

Kajitani, Y., Okada, N., and Tatano, H. (2005). Measuring quality of human community life by spatial-temporal age group distributions-case study of recovery process in a disaster-affected region, *Natural Hazards Review*, 6(1), 41–7.

Kang, W.H., Song, J., and Gardoni, P. (2008). Matrix-based system reliability method and applications to bridge networks, *Reliability Engineering and System Safety*, 93, 1584–93.

Koliou, M., van de Lindt, J.W., McAllister, T.P., Ellingwood, B.R., Dillard, M., and Cutler, H. (2018). State of the research in community resilience: Progress and challenges, *Sustainable and Resilient Infrastructure*, DOI: 10.1080/23789689.2017.1418547.

Lee, Y.-J., Song, J., Gardoni, P., and Lim, H.-W. (2011). Post-hazard flow capacity of bridge transportation networks considering structural deterioration of bridges, *Structure and Infrastructure Engineering*, 7(7), 509–21.

MacLean, D. (2016). Climate change and natural hazards. In Gardoni, P., Murphy, C. and Rowell, A. (eds.), *Societal Risk Management of Natural Hazards*. New York: Springer.

Mardfekri, M. and Gardoni, P. (2013). Probabilistic demand models and fragility estimates for offshore wind turbine support structures, *Engineering Structures*, 52(2013), 478–87.

Mardfekri, M. and Gardoni, P. (2015). Multi-hazard reliability assessment of offshore wind turbines, *Wind Energy*, 18(8), 1433–50.

Mardfekri, M., Gardoni, P., and Bisadi, V. (2015). Service reliability of offshore wind turbines, *International Journal of Sustainable Energy*, 34(7), 468–84.

Martins, N. (2011). Sustainability economics, ontology and the capability approach, *Ecological Economics*, 72, 1–4.

May, P. (2001). *Organizational and Societal Consequences for Performance-Based Earthquake Engineering*. PEER 2001/04. Berkeley, CA: Pacific Earthquake Engineering Research Center, College of Engineering, University of California, Berkeley.

McAllister, T. (2013). *Developing guidelines and standards for disaster resilience of the built environment: A research needs assessment*. NIST Technical Note 1795, Gaithersburg, MD.

Mileti, D.S. (1999). *Disasters by Design: A Reassessment of Natural Hazards in the United States*. Washington, DC: Joseph Henry Press.

Murphy, C. and Gardoni, P. (2006). The role of society in engineering risk analysis: A capabilities-based approach, *Risk Analysis*, 26(4), 1073–83.

Murphy, C. and Gardoni, P. (2007). Determining public policy and resource allocation priorities for mitigating natural hazards: a capabilities-based approach, *Science and Engineering Ethics*, 13(4), 489–504.

Murphy, C. and Gardoni, P. (2008). The acceptability and the tolerability of societal risks: A capabilities-based approach, *Science and Engineering Ethics*, 14(1), 77–92.

Murphy, C. and Gardoni, P. (2010). Assessing capability instead of achieved functionings in risk analysis, *Journal of Risk Research*, 13(2), 137–47.

Murphy, C. and Gardoni, P. (2011a). Design, risk and capabilities. In Jeroen van den Hoven and Ilse Oosterlaken (eds.), *Human Capabilities, Technology, and Design*. Heidelberg: Springer.

Murphy, C. and Gardoni, P. (2011b). Evaluating the source of the risks associated with natural events, *Res Publica*, 17(2), 125–40.

Murphy, C. and Gardoni, P. (2012). The capability approach in risk analysis. In Sabine Roeser (ed.), *Handbook of Risk Theory*. Heidelberg: Springer.

Murphy, C., Gardoni, P., and Harris, C.E. (2011). Classification and moral evaluation of uncertainties in engineering modeling, *Science and Engineering Ethics*, 17(3), 553–70.

Murphy, C., Gardoni, P., McKim, R., (eds.) (2018). *Climate Change and Its Impact: Risks and Inequalities*. Cham: Springer.

Olshansky, R.B. (2018). Recovery after disasters: How adaptation to climate change will occur. In C. Murphy, P. Gardoni and R. McKim (eds.), *Climate Change and Its Impact: Risks and Inequalities*. New York: Springer.

Ramamoorthy, K.S., Gardoni, P., and Bracci, M.J. (2006). Probabilistic demand models and fragility curves for reinforced concrete frames, *ASCE Journal of Structural Engineering*, 132(10), 1563–72.

Ramamoorthy, K.S., Gardoni, P., and Bracci, M.J. (2008). Seismic fragility and confidence bounds for gravity load designed reinforced concrete frames of varying height, *ASCE Journal of Structural Engineering*, 134(4), 639–50.

Sharma, N., Tabandeh, A., and Gardoni, P. (2017). Resilience analysis: A mathematical formulation to model resilience of engineering systems, *Sustainable and Resilient Infrastructure*, 3(2), 49–67.

Tabandeh, A. and Gardoni, P. (2014). Probabilistic capacity models and fragility estimates for RC columns retrofitted with FRP composites, *Engineering Structures*, 74, 13–22.

Tabandeh, A. and Gardoni, P. (2015). Empirical Bayes approach for developing hierarchical probabilistic predictive models and its application to the seismic reliability analysis of FRP-retrofitted RC bridges, *ASCE-ASME Journal of Risk and Uncertainty in Engineering Systems Part A: Civ. Eng.*, 1(2), 04015002.

Tabandeh, A., Gardoni, P., Murphy, C., and Myers, N. (2018). Societal risk and resilience analysis: dynamic Bayesian network formulation of a Capability Approach, *ASCE Journal of Risk and Uncertainty Analysis*, DOI: 10.1061/AJRUA6.0000996.

United Nations International Strategy for Disaster Reduction, Terminology (2015). www.unisdr.org/we/inform/terminology (last accessed October 21, 2015).

United States National Research Council (2012). *Disaster Resilience: A National Imperative*. Washington, DC: The National Academies Press.

van Willingen, M., Edwards, E., Lormand, S., and Wilson, K. (2005). Comparative assessment of impacts and recovery from Hurricane Floyd among student and community households, *Natural Hazards Review*, 6(4), 180–90.

World Commission on Environment and Development (1987). *Our Common Future*. Oxford University Press: New York.

Part II

Situating and motivating sustainability and resilience

2

Aligning community resilience and sustainability

Therese P. McAllister[1] and Steven Moddemeyer[2]

[1] NATIONAL INSTITUTE OF STANDARDS AND TECHNOLOGY, GAITHERSBURG, MD, 20899, USA

[2] COLLINSWOERMAN, SEATTLE, WA, 98104, USA

2.1 Introduction

Many communities want to be sustainable and resilient. If goals and strategies for improving resilience and sustainability are developed independently, chances are high that the goals will differ, and may even be in conflict. This chapter explores the concepts of resilient and sustainable communities, how changing conditions in the natural and built environment and sustained stressors may require new approaches, and suggests methods and tools to advance community resilience and sustainability.

The best outcome for communities occurs when their resilience and sustainability strategies are aligned. Yet, resilient and sustainable development has significant issues to overcome before delivering on promises to future generations. Challenges include reduction in impacts to ecological systems, governance, the time it takes to replace the existing infrastructure through normal rates of renewal, and changing current practices. Yet even where governance capacity may be present and investments in sustainability and resilience follow, intergenerational equity is challenged by assumptions that natural systems (our environment, ecosystems, and climate) are stable and unchanging. Initial concepts of sustainability and resilience for the built environment failed to fully appreciate the dynamic nature of natural systems, with their complex interactions across space and time and their predilection for tipping points and thresholds. Many professionals are faced with the dilemma of designing infrastructure based on hazard models that do not include future changes in hazard intensity or frequency, as scientific consensus on this issue has yet to be established. Additionally, current design practice does not address consideration of damage levels and associated impacts on recovery of building functions – an essential element of resilience.

Comprehensive community planning that includes resilience specifies performance levels and time frames for recovery of building and infrastructure functionality, so that existing infrastructure can be evaluated and prioritized for targeted modifications to improve building and infrastructure performance. Prioritization of actions to improve the built environment are based on meeting the community's social and economic goals. Alignment of and compatibility between community resilience and sustainability goals with economic development goals is the best approach for addressing local needs, based on the role of each facility or infrastructure

15

system in the community. Resilience and sustainability goals sometimes have different time frames (decades vs. generations) and different goals (rapid recovery of function vs. prioritized use of renewable resources).

When strategies and solutions for both of these important goals are aligned, there will be benefits at the community and individual levels, and a reduction in unintended consequences from competing goals. The *Community Resilience Planning Guide for Buildings and Infrastructure Systems* (NIST 2016) helps communities address these challenges through a practical approach that helps develop plans to improve resilience of the community. While the Guide process is intended to focus on the built environment, it can be expanded to include natural and nature-based systems, as well as sustainability goals.

Resilience and sustainability challenges are examined in the following sections: Section 2.2 considers paradigms and associated challenges in resilience and sustainability practices, Section 2.3 addresses considerations related to traditional approaches and changing conditions, Section 2.4 highlights the impacts of nonstationary processes on current practices, Section 2.5 examines the local community perspective for developing unified resilience and sustainability goals and the NIST Guide, and Section 2.6 looks at next steps toward advancing community resilience and sustainability.

2.2 Resilience and sustainability paradigms and challenges

Sustainable development is a simple and powerful concept to ensure that humanity, "meets the need of the present without compromising the ability of future generations to meet their own needs" (United Nations 1987). This idea was first articulated by the visionary Bruntland Commission's report on sustainable development. With the adoption of the Sustainable Development Goals in 2015, sustainability continues to be an international consensus that has inspired and guided governments and individuals around the world to moderate some of humanity's more extreme impacts to global ecosystem function.

At the same time, the concept of resilient communities has evolved. The term resilience is applied and uniquely defined for a range of topics and scales that include psychology, sociology, public health, security, continuity in business operations, emergency planning and response, hazard mitigation, and the capacity of the built environment (e.g., buildings, transportation systems, utilities, and other infrastructure) to physically resist and rapidly recover from disruptive events. With regards to communities and hazard events it has been defined as "the ability to adapt to changing conditions and withstand and rapidly recovery from disruptions" (PPD-21 2013). The resilience premise for buildings and infrastructure systems is that they can resist hazard impacts up to a specified threshold and recover or be restored within a specified period of time to minimize disruption to the community, expenditures for repair and rebuilding, and economic impacts. Given the range of infrastructure age and conditions across a community, in practice there will often be situations where the built environment may not be able resist even a threshold level hazard event. In those cases, the resilience planning process can be used to identify performance gaps and temporary measures that allow the community to continue to provide services, even though the affected building(s) or infrastructure system(s) cannot. These performance gaps also offer opportunities to initiate an adaptive process to improve the performance of the built environment.

Resilient and sustainable development can potentially be in conflict. For example, strategies used to protect communities, such as levees that limit flooding but disconnect riverine habitats, can undermine ecological systems. Or, when older sites and buildings are re-purposed as part of community sustainability, which conserves land and saves energy and resources (GEF

2017), the buildings may not meet resilience performance goals. Some sustainable materials may be less resilient in terms of their performance and capacity. Conversely, strategies that reduce waste or damage to physical systems may also reduce impacts on social and natural systems. When buildings and infrastructure systems continue to operate with minor repairs, they produce less debris and waste (Brown et al. 2011) and require significantly less resources for recovery, operation, and maintenance.

Without intending it, the presumption that sustainability can be addressed through efficiency, optimization, and economic growth can reduce a community's capacity to be resilient. When systems are optimized for a particular scale, unintended consequences can emerge at other scales. "Green" strategies applied to buildings sometimes fail to account for a larger context and ironically lead to "sustainable buildings" in unsustainable locations that ultimately negatively impact community resilience. Similarly, buildings "well engineered within their defined parameters" may miss larger impacts to the surrounding natural and infrastructure systems (Mehaffy & Salingaros 2015). For example, extensive damage occurs to buildings and infrastructure from coastal and inland flooding each year that takes years of recovery, such as the coastal flooding during Hurricane Sandy in 2012. Some of the buildings and infrastructure were constructed prior to the establishment of flood plains in the 1970s, but many others were more recent developments. The rebuilding in New York that is still underway requires elevation of buildings in flood plains and other mitigation measures (NYC 2018). In some cases, sustainability strategies that improve efficient use of resources may reduce adaptive capacity of natural and infrastructure systems by pushing them closer to their tipping points where there is less ability to absorb stresses and shocks. For example, local supply chains for food efficiently deliver a range of foods and products to communities. When transportation systems are damaged and disrupted in a disaster, residents may find reduced local supplies. The adaptive capacity of local suppliers to respond to these circumstances may be minimal or brittle, and insufficient to interact with ongoing competition from distant suppliers who capitalize on pre-disaster efficiencies of scale, vertical integration, and certification schemes (Smith 2016). Such systems may be more brittle, less flexible, less adaptable, and less resilient to changes in other systems.

Despite ongoing efforts in codes, standards, and best practices to improve the performance of the built environment, hazard events often result in significant losses and damage, as evidenced by an average of 40 Presidential Disaster Declarations each year between 1964 and 2013 (FEMA 2013). This is primarily because older, existing infrastructure often contributes more to losses than new construction. For example, given that buildings are designed assuming an average 50-year service life (ASCE 2017), then the building stock is renewed at an average of a 2 percent annual rate. Yet even current codes and design standards for buildings do not preclude structural damage, damage to the contents, or the loss of function when a building is subject to a design level hazard event or worse. Significant damage and losses to both old and new building stock in a community result in large financial and functional impacts that can extend the recovery period. Yet functional disruption and time to recovery is often treated as an externality to the original design or performance expectations of a facility.

In addition to integrated planning, tools are needed that can better characterize and anticipate the dynamics of future change due to climate impacts, technological developments, and coastal population growth. The population in coastal counties increased from 47 million people in 1960 to 87 million people in 2008 (Wilson & Fischetti 2010). Many coastal areas are being impacted by sea level rise, which is projected to increase between 0.3 m and 2.5 m by 2100 (Sweet et al. 2017). This means that the increase in population has more people living in areas with increased risk due to sea level rise, as well as the corresponding greater investment in

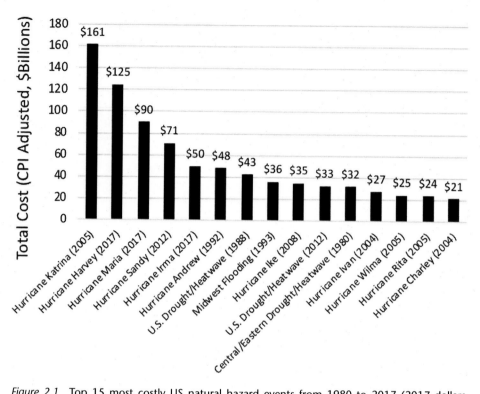

Figure 2.1 Top 15 most costly US natural hazard events from 1980 to 2017 (2017 dollars adjusted for inflation but not population or wealth, developed from NOAA 2018a).

buildings and infrastructure. Future climate changes in the next century at both the coastal and continental scale also includes changes in precipitation patterns, drought and heat waves, and stronger and more intense hurricanes (Melillo et al. 2014).

Natural disasters can affect communities through loss of life, displacement of residents and businesses, injuries, property damage, and economic impacts. Chronic stressors, such as high unemployment, inefficient infrastructure, or food shortages, can amplify these effects and further slow community recovery. The National Centers for Environmental Information (NOAA 2018a) estimates that there have been 218 natural weather disaster events, each resulting in at least $1 billion in damage and economic losses in the US between 1980 and 2017. Figure 2.1 demonstrates the level of damage and loss of functionality to communities from natural hazards. Improving the resilient and sustainable performance of buildings and infrastructure can help communities avoid these significant economic costs and long-term impacts.

In 2002, Carl Folke wrote an important perspective on change that can inform approaches to both sustainability and resilience, "The world view of nature and society as systems near equilibrium is being replaced by a dynamic view, which emphasizes complex non-linear relations between entities under continuous change and facing discontinuities and uncertainty from suites of synergist stresses and shocks" (Folke 2002). First Folke states that our worldview is changing: that nature and society are not in equilibrium but are instead dynamic and constantly changing. Second, they are constantly changing in ways that are not linear, but non-linear. In non-linear systems, the relationships are complex where there might be varying outcomes from similar inputs. Third, change can become abrupt or "discontinuous." Finally, relationships between nature and society are uncertain because of chronic stresses and sudden shocks to either system that may be "synergistic," where the combined effects can be greater than the sum of their separate effects.

However, in the absence of training, guidance, and tools about future changes that affect design practice, many designers continue to address their systems with a stationary worldview. In failing to recognize the dynamism of natural and human systems interaction, the likelihood of failure may increase, as the performance is based on standards with a stationary reliability basis that are used to justify the investments. When the frequency of damage or failure of a building or infrastructure system is higher than expected, then the cost effectiveness of the investments is questionable. Additionally, the impacts of failure are often disproportionately born by the occupants rather than the developers and builders. For example, the population of New Orleans fell from approximately 485,000 before Katrina in 2000 to an estimated 230,000 in 2006, a loss of over half of the city's population. Much of the lost population did not return to city, which led to significant changes to demographic and other aspects of the city's social and economic makeup. By 2015, the population had reached 80 percent of what it was in 2000 (Plyer 2016).

Sustainability and resilience remain important consensus goals for communities and regions when informed with knowledge of dynamic processes. If intergenerational equity is still a good idea – and we argue that it is – then resilience and sustainability goals need to be integrated into community planning. Communities need to realize that the most important element to the sustainability and resilience of people, culture, economies, infrastructure, and nature is a systems-based perspective that helps navigate and manage the dynamic reality of their changing conditions, dependencies, and interactions.

Resilience is a powerful framework for understanding and managing change. Early resilience thinking was based on the study of natural species, ecosystems, and social systems that persist, adapt, or are transformed by change over time. "Resilience thinking provides a basis for understanding and developing strategies for sustainable transformation in turbulent times. Resilience – the ability to deal with change, often sudden and surprising, to move on and continue to develop – can help turn crises into opportunities" (Folke et al. 2009).

Communities can improve their resilience and sustainability as sudden or gradual changes in the built environment and natural environment offer opportunities. Both sustainability and resilience seek to develop thriving social, environmental, and economic conditions that allow the community to adapt to changing conditions. Sustainability also focuses on minimizing social, environmental, and economic impacts and resilience focuses on minimizing disruption and accelerating recovery of community functions when shocks or stressors occur. With a focus on long term planning, resilient and sustainable development can extend beyond disaster risk reduction to an essential increase in the capacity of the community to manage systems and maintain social functions in the face of hazard events and dynamic processes. Resilience thinking will help develop approaches to becoming "adaptive managers" (Fabricius et al. 2007) with skills to manage and the will to adapt to change as future generations experience natural, technological, and social changes at multiple scales.

2.3 When traditional methods are appropriate and when they will come up short

In 1996, ecologist C.S. Fritz Holling clarified the difference between "ecological resilience" and "engineering resilience" (Holling 1996). He describes engineering resilience as concentrating on "efficiency, constancy, and predictability – all attributes at the core of engineers' desires for fail-safe design." Holling writes that on the other hand ecological resilience, "focuses on persistence, change, and unpredictability" (Holling 1996). Holling acknowledged that the two types of resilience can become "alternative paradigms." Two significant distinctions between Holling's definitions of ecological and engineering resilience are their time horizon and addressing environmental impacts. Ecological resilience refers to how life forms continuously adapt to changing environmental conditions over decades to centuries whereas engineering resilience refers to how built systems resist the forces of nature for a specified service life that typically spans 50–75 years.

Moving forward, both types of resilience provide tools and perspectives that are essential for adaptive managers. Since Holling's observations 20 years ago, leaders, planners, and designers of built and natural systems are beginning to consider when traditional resistance methods are appropriate and when these methods need to be augmented with adaptive design approaches that address future environmental changes and uncertainties, as well as new designs for rapid recovery following a disruptive hazard event.

The traditional resistance approach to engineering resilience is intended to benefit human activities and support continuity and growth. It is when the design parameters no longer reflect the future that it becomes problematic, especially when accepted probabilistic models of future hazard events are missing. Despite the desire for stability, the combined effects of infrastructure development and changes in natural systems and climate are affecting the intended performance of built systems. Bridges may become inundated if undeveloped areas upstream of the bridge lose their absorbency following new development and paving. Roadway drainage designed for weather patterns of the past may fail as storm rainfall and temperature intensities increase with atmospheric temperatures. Seawalls may begin to be overtopped more frequently as sea level rises. Nuisance flooding is occurring more frequently in coastal communities subject to sea level rise, and is expected to increase in frequency and intensity (NOAA 2018b).

When to resist? When to adapt? When to transform? Alternative approaches that consider adaptation and recovery are under development by a number of planners and designers. For example, community development and renovation projects are considering how to incorporate adaptability and recovery into engineered designs for uncertain future events, such as sea level rise, increased precipitation, or elevated temperatures. Such designs may include a mix of civil engineering, land-use planning, landscape architecture, and natural shoreline systems that can be adjusted or modified in 10–20 years as needed (Russell 2017). All communities need to develop approaches to adaptation, not only to natural and environmental conditions but also for social and economic conditions that can affect their ability to manage and recover from shocks and stressors.

Leaders and decision-makers need the ability to discern when different strategies should be considered, depending on the situation. The Cynefin framework, described below, helps leaders determine the prevailing context for decision making by determining whether they are dealing with a simple, complicated, complex, or chaotic situation. Simple and complicated contexts assume an ordered universe, where cause-and-effect relationships are perceptible, and right answers can be determined based on the facts. Complex and chaotic contexts are unordered – there is no immediately apparent relationship between cause and effect, and the way forward is determined based on emerging patterns (Snowden & Boone 2007). For example, if a situation is complicated, then experts can analyze a way forward using existing tools and data. However, if a situation is complex, then experts need to extrapolate their knowledge to some degree and sense the way forward, looking for emerging patterns where adaptation is likely appropriate. A third suite of strategies around transformation may be appropriate in a chaotic context, where relationships between cause and effect are no longer apparent, and some level of order needs to be re-established. In such cases, actions may bring enough order to identify patterns and new opportunities for moving forward.

Built systems are expected to provide continuous, reliable services; natural systems are expected to continue functioning in a predictable manner. However, the complexity of changing future conditions affecting built and social systems, as well as the environment, the uncertainty, and risk that influences performance of these systems need to be explicitly accounted for in design and decision making.

2.4 Stationarity, uncertainty, and risk issues

Stationarity is a property of a stochastic (random) process. A stationary process varies at any point in time but can be measured through probability distributions with a mean value and variance that are constant. In other words, while there is natural variability in processes and events, this variability is aligned around a mean that is stable over time. Probability distributions are based on past events for use in predicting future events, such as the frequency of occurrence of hazard events. Many hazard events are characterized in this fashion, and are the basis of system design in the built world. Virtually every road, bridge, culvert, energy distribution system, water supply line, water reservoir, flood control dam, levee, dike, stormwater system, wastewater line, and wastewater treatment system has been designed with a stationary hazard assumption.

Milly et al. (2008, 2015) assert that some hazard events, such as those associated with water management, are no longer stationary due to anthropogenic (human caused) impacts. The stationarity assumption for water management has always been challenged by human disturbances in river basins, such as channel modifications, drainage works, and changes in land-cover and land-use. However, rising average temperatures of the atmosphere and ocean can lead to increasing the intensity of wind storms and precipitation in future decades, due to the increased amount of water vapor held in the atmosphere (Chung et al. 2014). These "complex non-linear" changes introduce uncertainty into future climate forecasts.

Designers of built systems are faced with a dilemma: How to design a reliable system that meets current design requirements, minimizes risks, and can be adapted for future hazard events that are nonstationary? The consequences of failing to address loss of stationarity appropriately can be profound. Infrastructure might be undersized or oversized, depending on the intensity of future hazard events. If it is undersized, it will fail more frequently and not provide the intended performance that was used to calculate benefits and costs of the investment. Or if it is oversized, its capacity may never be needed, thus wasting funds and resources.

One approach to addressing uncertain conditions is to use scenarios to simulate a range of potential hazard event conditions, based on the best information available, for community planning. These scenarios can be based in available science, but as currently developed they are not probabilistically defensible. Scenarios may address a single building, or they may be developed for events that affect buildings and infrastructure across a region, such as earthquakes (USGS 2018), floods (FEMA 2015), or windstorms (FEMA 2015). Scenarios are a set of possible event conditions based on a selected hazard intensity; while the selected hazard intensity may be based on a probabilistically determined design-level hazard (e.g., design wind speed), the extension of the scenario to a geospatial region is based in physics or expert judgement. Additionally, there is often a variation in design levels for a given hazard between buildings and infrastructure systems – they are not all designed to the same hazard design level, hence a variation in performance is expected. However, even with these qualifications, scenarios are useful for understanding the broad range of possible impacts, including dependencies and cascading events.

So, is it possible to rationally design infrastructure if it there is significant uncertainty in setting a threshold performance target for the next 50–100 years? In the absence of consensus, decisions must be made, and one approach is to increase design criteria in the interim. Highway departments may add an additional 0.6 m (2 ft) to new culverts to address current knowledge about future conditions or sea wall designers may add an additional 0.6 m (2 ft) to perhaps buy a few more decades of protection (FEMA 2014). However, these interim approaches may not meet long-term resilience or sustainability goals because they may not be sufficient, be adaptable, or support rapid recovery. Some designers are beginning to develop "adaptive designs" that allow for future modifications or improved solutions in the next 10–15 years, as a series of short term solutions, rather than designing for 50 or more years (Russell 2017). Adaptive designs also include approaches that work with the hazard (e.g., dual purpose parks that act as flood basins when needed).

As communities and regions invest in infrastructure, social systems, and natural systems, it is becoming increasingly important to ask about resilience and sustainability goals, the associated design assumptions, the levels of uncertainty and risk that are being accepted, and the integrated capacity to adapt to future conditions.

2.5 Local community perspectives

In the United States, there are a number of communities recovering from a hazard event each year. Over the last 50 years an average of 40 Presidential Disaster Declarations have been made each year for hazard events (FEMA 2013). Communities are where hazard impacts are first felt and can be best managed. Although communities cannot stop natural hazards, they can minimize the consequences with long term planning and prioritized set of actions that are implemented over time. The extent of recovery and the ultimate outcome depend upon the nature and severity of the event and community actions to mitigate risk, protect assets, respond in a timely and coordinated way, and recover community functions within a specified time period. Together, these measures determine a community's resilience.

Resilience offers a comprehensive approach to address risks associated with hazard events as well as sustainability challenges with social, economic, environmental, and built systems that give future generations the same opportunities to thrive as this one. Communities can work toward designing a more socially and economically just and sustainable world by managing performance gaps and significant risks in a comprehensive, integrated approach. Possible approaches include: incorporating adaptability, flexibility, and recovery into community planning and designs for infrastructure, using a system of systems approach that addresses multi-scale relationships and dependencies, and finding methods to address the uncertainty of future hazard event intensity.

The NIST Guide (2016) helps communities address these challenges through a six-step planning process (see Table 2.1) that promotes comprehensive and integrated planning between the physical, social, and economic systems in a community to meet long-term resilience goals. It is a flexible approach that can incorporate other systems or goals (such as sustainability goals) that may be of interest. Sustainability goals for social, economic, environmental, and built systems can easily be integrated into the community planning process. It is important that all community plans and their goals be aligned and coordinated, even if they have differing time or geospatial scales, or they may unintentionally undermine progress through competing goals.

Table 2.1 NIST guide six-step planning process and key activities for community resilience

Planning Steps	*Key Activities*
1. Form a collaborative planning team	• Identify resilience leader for the community • Identify team members, and their roles and responsibilities • Identify key public and private stakeholders for all phases of planning and implementation

2. Understand the situation	• Social Dimensions –
	  • Identify and characterize functions and dependencies of social institutions, including business, industry, and financial systems, based on individual/social needs met by these institutions and social vulnerabilities
	  • Identify how social functions are supported by the built environment
	  • Identify key contacts and representatives for evaluation, coordination, and decision making activities
	• Built Environment –
	  • Identify and characterize buildings and infrastructure systems, including condition, location, and dependencies between and among systems
	  • Identify key contacts/representatives for evaluation, coordination, and decision making activities
	  • Identify existing plans to be coordinated with the resilience plan
	• Link social functions to the supporting built environment
	• Define building clusters and supporting infrastructure

3. Determine goals and objectives	• Establish long-term community goals • Establish desired recovery performance goals for the built environment at the community level based on social needs, and dependencies and cascading effects between systems • Define community hazards and levels • Determine anticipated performance during and after a hazard event to support social functions • Summarize the results
4. Plan development	• Evaluate gaps between the desired and anticipated performance of the built environment to improve community resilience and summarize results • Identify solutions to address gaps including both administrative and construction options • Prioritize solutions and develop an implementation strategy
5. Plan preparation, review, and approval	• Document the community plan and implementation strategy • Obtain feedback and approval from stakeholders and community • Finalize and approve the plan
6. Plan implementation and maintenance	• Execute approved administrative and construction solutions • Evaluate and update on a periodic basis • Modify short or long-term implementation strategy to achieve performance goals as needed

Source: NIST 2016.

The NIST process is intended to help communities:

• Set resilience performance goals to prioritize and rapidly restore vital social functions, like healthcare, education, and public safety, and supporting buildings and infrastructure systems – transportation, energy, communications, and water and wastewater following a disruptive event, accounting for dependency relationships and cascading consequences.

23

- Recognize that the community's social and economic needs and functions should drive goal-setting for how the built environment performs when subjected to a disruptive event.
- Provide a comprehensive method to align community priorities and resources with resilience goals.

The six steps may look obvious at first glance, but frequently a number of individual plans are developed for a community without any common goals or awareness of other plans, which can lead to unintended conflicts or vulnerabilities. The first three steps are essential for integrated community goals setting, prioritization, and plan development. Having all the key stakeholders at the table, either as community participants or industry collaborators, builds community resilience by increasing community connectivity and access to diverse points of view, experiences, and cultures. Inclusiveness of perspectives improves the quality of the planning and the buy-in and acceptance of the final plans. A challenging but necessary step is termed "understand the situation," where the social dimensions and built environment need to be characterized as to their role in the community before and after a disruptive hazard event, and their interactions and dependencies. The NIST *Community Resilience Economic Decision Guide for Buildings and Infrastructure Systems* (Gilbert et al. 2015) helps communities evaluate economic investments for alternative solutions identified in step 4. With the stakeholders and a community assessment of existing systems, recovery goals to minimize disruption to community functions can be set. These goals can then inform and align other community plans.

Fort Collins, Colorado used the NIST Guide to conduct comprehensive resilience planning (Konz 2016). The community experienced a series of weather events that highlighted their vulnerability. In 2012, the High Park Fire on the edge of the community was recorded as the third worst fire in the state. One year later, the community experienced flooding due to 0.3 m (12 in) of rain in two days. The city normally receives about 0.5 m (17 in) a year. The wildfire scarring from the 2012 fire exacerbated the impact of the flooding in 2013. After a 1997 flood, Fort Collins had upgraded culverts, built pre-sedimentation basins to separate particulates from raw water before it entered the water treatment plant, and integrated the Flood Management Plan with strong local regulations. The community sustained only minor property damage after the 2013 event, despite the magnitude. In addition, a 2014 study showed that the number of extremely hot days has increased over 20 years. It revealed that Fort Collins had experienced twice as many 90-degree days in the past 14 years as it had in the previous 39 years – signaling a need to adapt to a changing climate.

Fort Collins used Guide steps 1–4 to set performance goals for recovery of vital social functions and the supporting buildings and infrastructure systems, and as a comprehensive method to align community priorities and resources with its goals. The process allowed Fort Collins to include its commitment to sustainability, expressed through the triple bottom line, through policies and regulations on the economic, environmental, and social health of the community. The community characterized its built environment, dependencies among social services, and identified prevailing hazards. This information was used to develop long-term resilience goals and an action plan with identified strategies and periodic progress evaluation. Importantly, this plan will be integrated with other community plans.

Integrating all community plans ensures a unified approach across the community that benefits from inclusion of multiple disciplines and stakeholder perspectives. Integrated planning around time to recover functions is a powerful metric for changing the way communities plan for, design, and implement policy, programs, and capital expenditures.

2.6 Next steps

In communities around the globe, natural and built systems will continue to be developed and adapted in the face of hazard events, changing environmental conditions, and sustained stressors. Infrastructure systems built under stationary assumptions may have reduced performance and reliability. The corresponding reduction in infrastructure services will place stress on built systems, food systems, economic systems, and cultural and human systems and threaten human life. Repeated damage and rebuilding by communities result in losses and are inefficient and disruptive; in other words, are non-sustainable and non-resilient. How our communities resist, and adapt, and are transformed by changes in climate as well as natural and built systems is still an open question.

The development and adoption of the following methods and tools will continue the advancement of community resilience and sustainability:

- Recognition of the complexity of non-linear interdependencies between social, economic, environmental, and built systems that suggest more adaptable and flexible solutions designed to speed recovery.
- A comprehensive, integrated community planning methodology that identifies and aligns resilience and sustainability goals and long-term plans for physical, natural, social, and economic system. The NIST Guide (2016) provides such a comprehensive, flexible approach.
- Models that consider system of systems dynamics to simulate dependencies, functions, performance, and recovery for physical, natural, social, and economic systems. Research by the NIST Community Resilience Program (NIST 2016) and the Center for Risk-Based Community Resilience Planning (CSU 2018) are both conducting research to develop analytical models that can address these issues at the community scale.
- Methods to estimate future nonstationary hazards, based on the best available science, and their magnitudes, frequencies, and associated uncertainties for planning and design purposes. Examples include global climate models (IRI 2018) and hurricane forecast models (Hurricane Science 2018).
- Guidance for developing hazard scenarios for community resilience and sustainability planning with a scientific basis to link design-level hazards for individual buildings and infrastructure systems to community-level hazard intensities with geospatial distributions.
- Guidance on when it is appropriate to use traditional design criteria based on stationary processes, when adaptation planning approaches are required, and which design criteria and methods should be used to address uncertain future conditions.
- Science-based community metrics that are used to monitor progress on resilience and sustainability goals over time and to inform decision support tools.
- Sensors that monitor building and infrastructure performance and can identify when degradation of function is underway prior to failure to avoid failure and improve recovery.
- Enhanced training and design solutions for design teams to create infrastructure that is readily adaptable to changing conditions throughout its service life to aid rapid recovery of critical social and economic functions supported by infrastructure.

2.7 Conclusions

As leaders, planners, and designers continue to develop metrics, methods and tools to support the resilience and sustainability of our communities, there are three key issues that need to be addressed. First, any community approach needs a system of systems perspective that includes dependencies and consequences. Second, infrastructure needs to be designed to minimize damage and rapidly recover from a hazard event that may reach or exceed design levels. Third, fundamental inequities need to be addressed for those who are impacted by failed infrastructure and have the least capacity to recover. Incorporating these issues into tools and practice will improve the resilience and sustainability of communities as they strive to align their long-term goals and address sustained stressors and changing conditions in the natural and built environment.

References

ASCE (2017) Minimum Design Loads and Associated Criteria for Buildings and Other Structures. ASCE/SEI 7–16, American Society of Civil Engineers, Reston, VA.

Brown, C., Milke, M., and Seville, E. (2011) Disaster waste management: A review article, *Waste Management*, 31(6), June, 1085–98.

Chung, E.S., Soden, B., Sohn, B.J., and Shi, L. (2014) Upper-tropospheric moistening in response to anthropogenic warming, *PNAS*, 111(32), 11636–11641.

CSU (2018) Center for Risk-Based Community Resilience Planning, A NIST-Funded Center of Excellence. http://resilience.colostate.edu/ (last accessed August 29, 2018).

Fabricius, C., Folke, C., Cundill, G., and Schultz, L. (2007) Powerless spectators, coping actors, and adaptive co-managers: a synthesis of the role of communities in ecosystem management, *Ecology and Society*, 12(1), 29.

FEMA (2013) Presidential Disaster Declarations, December 24, 1964 to December 31, 2013. Federal Emergency Management Agency, Washington, DC. https://gis.fema.gov/maps/FEMA_Presidential_Disaster_Declarations_1964_2013.pdf (last accessed August 9, 2018).

FEMA (2014) Building Higher in Flood Zones: Freeboard – Reduce Your Risk, Reduce Your Premium. Federal Emergency Management Agency, Washington, DC. www.fema.gov/media-library-data/1438356606317-d1d037d75640588f45e2168eb9a190ce/FPM_1-pager_Freeboard_Final_06-19-14.pdf (last accessed August 9, 2018).

FEMA (2015) Organizational Tabletop Exercise – Customizable Hazard-Specific Scenarios. Federal Emergency Management Agency, Washington, DC. www.fema.gov/media-library-data/1426103634437-a1928f190773b74ca029bf2f5793e958/ap_organizational_ttx_ppt_all_6_hazards_form_031015_final_508.pdf (last accessed August 9, 2018).

Folke, C., Carpenter, S., Elmqvist, T., Gunderson, L., Holling, C.S., and Walker, B. (2002) Resilience and Sustainable Development: Building Adaptive Capacity in a World of Transformations, *Ambio*, 31(5), 437–40.

Folke, C., Chapin III, F. S., and Olsson, P. (2009) Transformations in Ecosystem Stewardship. In F.S. Chapin III, G.P. Kofinas, and C. Folke (eds.), *Principles of Ecosystem Stewardship: Resilience-based Natural Resource Management in a Changing World* (pp. 103–25). New York: Springer Verlag.

GEF (2017) Adaptive Reuse, Creating a Sustainable Future Through Education, Green Education Foundation. www.greeneducationfoundation.org/green-building-program-sub/learn-about-green-building/1223-adaptive-reuse.html (last accessed August 9, 2018).

Gilbert, S.W, Butry, D.T., Helgeson, J.F., and Chapman R.E. (2015) Community Resilience Economic Decision Guide for Buildings and Infrastructure Systems. NIST Special Publication 1197, National Institute of Standards and Technology, Gaithersburg, MD.

Holling, C.S. (1996) Engineering Resilience versus Ecological Resilience, Engineering Within Ecological Constraints. The National Academies Press. www.nap.edu/read/4919/chapter/4#41 (last accessed August 9, 2018).

Hurricane Science (2018) Hurricane Forecast Models, Hurricanes: Science and Society, Graduate School of Oceanography. The University of Rhode Island. www.hurricanescience.org/science/forecast/models/ (last accessed August 9, 2018).

IRI (2018) Climate, International Research Institute for Climate and Society. Earth Institute, Columbia University, New York. https://iri.columbia.edu/our-expertise/climate/ (last accessed August 9, 2018).

Konz, P. (2016) How the City of Fort Collins is Making Community Resiliency a Reality, CitiesSpeak. National League of Cities, July 18, 2016. https://citiesspeak.org/2016/07/18/how-the-city-of-fort-collins-is-making-community-resiliency-a-reality/ (last accessed August 9, 2018).

Mehaffy, M.W. and Salingaros, N.A. (2015) *Design for a Living Planet*. Sustasis Foundation.

Melillo, J.M., Richmond, T.C., and Yohe, G.W. (eds.) (2014) Climate Change Impacts in the United States: The Third National Climate Assessment. U.S. Global Change Research Program, pp. 841 http://s3.amazonaws.com/nca2014/low/NCA3_Full_Report_0a_Front_Matter_LowRes.pdf?download=1 (last accessed August 9, 2018).

Milly, P.C.D., Betancourt, J., Falkenmark, M., Hirsch, R.M., Kundzewicz, Z.W., Lettenmaier, D.P., and Stouffer, R.J. (2008) Stationarity is dead: Whither water management, *Science Magazine*, 319 (5863), 573–4. American Academy for the Advancement of Science. http://en.vedur.is/media/loftslag/Milly_etal-2008-Stationarity-dead-Science.pdf.

Milly, P.C.D. Betancourt, J., Falkenmark, M., Hirsch, R.M., Kundzewicz, Z.W., Lettenmaier, D.P., and Stouffer, R.J. (2015) On Critiques of "Stationarity is Dead: Whither Water Management", Water Resources Research, American Geophysical Union. https://agupubs.onlinelibrary.wiley.com/doi/full/10.1002/2015WR017408 (last accessed August 9, 2018).

NIST (2016) Community Resilience Planning Guide for Buildings and Infrastructure Systems, NIST Special Publication 1190, National Institute of Standards and Technology, Gaithersburg, MD.

NOAA (2018a) Billion-Dollar Weather and Climate Disasters: Overview 2018, National Oceanographic and Atmospheric Administration, Washington, DC. www.ncdc.noaa.gov/billions/ (last accessed August 9, 2018).

NOAA (2018b) What Is High Tide Flooding? National Oceanographic and Atmospheric Administration, Washington, DC. https://oceanservice.noaa.gov/facts/nuisance-flooding.html (last accessed August 9, 2018).

NYC (2018) NYC Build It Back, NYC Housing Recovery, New York City, New York. www.nyc.gov/html/recovery/html/home/home.shtml (last accessed August 9, 2018).

Plyer, Allison (2016) Facts for Features: Katrina Impact. The Data Center, New Orleans, LA. www.datacenterresearch.org/data-resources/katrina/facts-for-impact/ (last accessed August 9, 2018).

PPD-21 (2013) Presidential Policy Directive PPD-21, The White House, February 12, 2013. https://obamawhitehouse.archives.gov/the-press-office/2013/02/12/presidential-policy-directive-critical-infrastructure-security-and-resil (last accessed August 31, 2018).

Russell, P.R. (2017) Special Report: How Engineers Are Preparing for Sea-Level Rise, *Engineering News Record*, August 10, 2017.

Smith, K., Lawrence, G., MacMahon, A., Muller, J., and Brady, M. (2016) The resilience of long and short food chains: a case study of flooding in Queensland, Australia, *Agric Hum Values*, 33, 45–60.

Snowden, D.J. and Boone, M.E. (2007) A leader's framework for decision making, *Harvard Business Review*, November. https://hbr.org/2007/11/a-leaders-framework-for-decision-making (last accessed August 31, 2018).

Sweet, W.V., Kopp. R.E., Weaver, C.P., Obeysekera, J., Horton, R.M., Thieler, E.R., and Zervas, C. (2017) Global and Regional Sea Level Rise Scenarios for the United States, NOAA Technical Report NOS CO-OPS 083, National Oceanic and Atmospheric Administration, Silver Spring, MD.

United Nations (1987) Report of the World Commission on Environment and Development: Our Common Future. www.un-documents.net/our-common-future.pdf (last accessed August 9, 2018).

United Nations (2015) Transforming Our World: The 2030 Agenda for Sustainable Development. https://sustainabledevelopment.un.org/post2015/transformingourworld (last accessed August 9, 2018).

USGS (2018) Earthquake Scenarios, Earthquake Hazards Program, US Geological Survey, Golden, CO. https://earthquake.usgs.gov/scenarios/ (last accessed August 9, 2018).

Wilson, S.G. and Fischetti, T.R. (2010) Coastline Population Trends in the United States: 1960 to 2008, Population Estimates and Projections, U.S. Census Bureau, Economics and Statistics Administration, U.S. Department of Commerce, Washington, DC. www.census.gov/prod/2010pubs/p25-1139.pdf (last accessed August 9, 2018).

3

On sustainability and resilience of engineered systems

Michael Havbro Faber

DEPARTMENT OF CIVIL ENGINEERING, AALBORG UNIVERSITY, DENMARK

3.1 Introduction

Scientists increasingly apply the term "anthroposphere" to highlight that the present geological era is significantly shaped by human activities. Exponential population growth, technological developments and industrialization have reached a state where the interactions between human enterprise, the Earth system at global scale and the environment at local scales harmfully affect the conditions for future societal developments. Scarcity of natural resources, arable and inhabitable land, drinking water and threats to livelihoods in general, are progressively affecting societal developments – with social unrest and migration as a consequence. Emissions from human activities to the environment are broadly recognized to adversely affect the geology and biosphere of the Earth system itself and thereby in several ways, including global climate change, affect the very same living conditions facilitating human civilization as we know it today. At the scales of regions and cities, pollution of air, drinking water and soil, substantially impairing welfare, health and livelihoods for present and future generations is not only a threat but already a reality for millions of people. Failure to achieve and maintain sustainable societal developments, a global catastrophic risk (Faber 2011), must be taken seriously at all levels of societal decision making.

At the same time as society is directing focus on sustainable societal developments there is an increasing demand for improved public welfare, calling for enhanced efficiency and reliability in all activities of the free market as well as in public and private governance. Globalization and technological developments associated with an ever increasing volume and complexity of critical infrastructure, financial, industrial and market systems, on one hand enable meeting such demands; on the other hand they comprise a new challenge, namely the management of risks due to systems failures and possible cascading failures across systems. Such failures are associated with substantial consequences in terms of service provision losses. Over the last 1–2 decades significant research and development efforts have addressed this challenge through the concept of resilience, aiming to minimize risks associated with service disturbances and disruptions by means of an integral consideration of governance and technological measures.

Whereas sustainability addresses decision making for the management of adverse effects of human activities on the Earth system with derived consequences to welfare, resilience may be seen to address decision making for the management of adverse effects originating from the

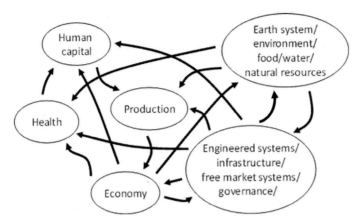

Figure 3.1 Illustration of principal societal mechanisms governing welfare, sustainability and resilience.

Earth system and human activities on the functionalities of social institutions which facilitate welfare. It is thus evident that there is a strong coupling between sustainability and resilience, and that the two terms ultimately express the same mechanisms from two different perspectives, see also Figure 3.1.

However, the more precise character of the coupling between sustainability and resilience is as yet not fully understood in either theoretical or practical terms. Consequently, improved knowledge facilitating decision support for sustainable and resilient societal developments is a highly ranked topic on both the political and the academic agendas.

The present chapter addresses resilience and sustainability of interlinked human and natural systems in the context of providing decision support for societal developments. Based on earlier works of the author (Faber et al. 2017, 2018; Faber & Qin 2016), concepts of resilience and sustainability, and especially their interrelations, are addressed and explored in the context of providing decision support for societal developments.

Section 3.2 starts out with an abridged overview of central insights and ideas from the vast literature on resilience, sustainability and decision analysis, achieved over the past 3–4 decades in the fields of mathematics, economy, ecology and engineering. The purpose of this overview is to provide a basis for the development of a framework facilitating decision making with respect to resilient and sustainable societal developments. Section 3.3 provides a proposition for such a framework. To this end the recent concept of Planetary Boundaries forwarded in Rockström et al. (2009) and Steffen et al. (2015), together with the framework for systems risk modeling from Faber et al. (2007) and JCSS (2008) and the novel formulations of resilience and sustainability failure introduced in Faber et al. (2017) play important roles. The constituents of this framework are addressed in Section 3.4 with focus on the probabilistic representation of system characteristics, modeling of disturbances[1] (or hazards/exposures) and modeling of consequences in different metrics in the particular context of sustainability and resilience. To this end the systems risk modeling framework proposed in JCSS (2008) is utilized and extended to represent the joint functionalities of interlinked systems, the characteristics of their performances with respect to disturbances and the multidimensional attributes and criteria associated with their performances. To accommodate for the utilization of the proposed framework for ranking of decision alternatives, a generic probabilistic representation of possible system states associated with benefits and losses is provided. This modeling basis also facilitates for the representation and analysis of cascading system failures. To account for the impacts to the environment and health and safety originating from human activities such as land use, applied technology and the built environment, life cycle analysis (LCA) is introduced. Societal preferences for investments into health and life safety are accounted for through the marginal life saving principle and the Life Quality Index (Nathwani et al. 1997). Absolute limits for impacts to the environment are included in terms of limited budget constraints, derived using the concept of Planetary Boundaries (Rockström et al. 2009).

Finally, in Section 3.5 a short discussion and outlook is provided on practical challenges associated with resilient and sustainable societal developments and suggestions for future research and educational activities are summarized.

3.2 Abridged appraisal of knowledge developments in resilience, sustainability and decision analysis

During the last 3–4 decades substantial research efforts have been devoted to improving the understanding of resilience and sustainability of human and natural systems and decision analysis in support of societal developments. The following sections provide an abridged overview and discussion of these topics with the objective of providing a conceptual basis for supporting decisions on resilient and sustainable developments and management of interlinked human and natural systems.[2]

3.2.1 Developments in the area of resilience

Fundamental work on resilience is presented in Pimm (1984) and Holling (1996) in which resilience of ecological systems is associated with the ability of systems to sustain disturbances and the time it takes until systems recover to their original states of functionality after disturbances. It is highlighted that not only the strength characteristics of the systems with respect to disturbances are important but the capacity building; facilitating recovery from disturbances are of key significance. As underlined in Derissen et al. (2011), however, the actual state of operation of a resilient system is not necessarily desired; the Earth system as an example has in several prehistoric eras taken resilient states which did not accommodate for the existence of humans. In fact one system may possess several states of equilibrium which on an individual basis could be considered resilient, however, which may exhibit functional characteristics differing significantly with respect to associated benefits – for humans and societal developments.

In Holling (1996) it is argued that engineered or designed systems are fundamentally different from natural systems. Whereas natural systems, such as in the case of organisms relying on endothermy, tend to seek optima in the vicinity of instability points where the potential gain is the highest, engineered systems are generally optimized such that their normal mode of operation is far away from regions of instability. Natural systems as Holling (1996) explains, ensure safe operation through functional diversity, i.e. by means of a number of highly reliable and redundant mechanisms. Moreover, different strategists may be recognized in natural systems. Holling (1996) elaborates on the r- and K-strategists; r-strategists being simple, fast in replication, less efficient and short lived and K-strategists being more complex, slower in replication, more efficient and long lived. In the event of disturbances of ecological systems comprised by K-strategists it is not unusual to see the less specialized r-strategists multiplying and dominating the system after the disturbance. This domination lasts until a certain time has passed and the K-strategists, due to their higher efficiency, have had time to outcompete the r-strategists. Considering engineered systems similar mechanisms may be recognized. When for instance infrastructure systems developed and optimized over time have been subject to major disturbances, it is normal to re-establish the most fundamental functionalities of the disturbed system by means of less expensive and short lived – interim – infrastructures. These then provide sufficient functionality at typically lower levels and less efficiently until efficient long term renewals may be put in place. Moreover, as described in Nishijima and Faber (2009) the choice between quality and quantity (less expensive and less durable infrastructure versus more expensive and long lived; r- vs. K-strategist) engineered solutions for the development of infrastructure can be optimized in balance with the economic capacity of a society. In Nishijima and Faber (2009) the term quality covers the aggregate susceptibility to degradation and damage caused by, e.g. natural hazards, corrosion and fatigue.

Anderies et al. (2004) address resilience characteristics of interlinked ecological societal systems in general and in Anderies (2014) in particular the role of the built societal infrastructure is discussed from the perspective of optimal allocation of available resources for enhancing resilience. It is suggested that different strategies for enhancing resilience may be devised optimally in dependency of the magnitude and frequency of disturbances (e.g. earthquakes, floods and wind storms). It is interesting to note that such strategies indeed have been in place for many years in the area of civil engineering where design criteria have been developed and broadly applied for design of structures with respect to earthquake excitation not only as a function of frequency and intensity but also as a function of consequences. In Janssen and Anderies (2007) resilience characteristics of systems are related to their robustness characteristics and it is highlighted that these are strongly dependent, to an extent that the terms resilience and robustness might indeed be synonymous. This dependency is illustrated and discussed further in Section 3.3.

Cutter et al. (2010), address community resilience in the context of natural hazards, terrorism risk management and protection of infrastructure. It is underlined that resilience is understood as the capacity of a community to recover from disturbances by their own means in the sense of Mileti (1999) and that community characteristics and governance are of key importance for resilience. This perspective is opposed to the engineering perspective of Bruneau et al. (2009) in which resilience is considered an inherent quality of the infrastructure and built environment; by means of inbuilt redundancy, robustness, resourcefulness and rapidity. Cutter et al. (2010) propose a framework for base-line assessments for the resilience of communities in terms of the Disaster Resilience Of Place (DROP) model, see also Cutter et al. (2003). Based on this model, data analysis is undertaken for different communities and the baseline resilience performances of local communities are assessed and mapped.

The developments in research on resilience of systems in the different areas of research have led to a range of definitions, see also Doorn et al. (2018), including:

Ecological systems
Pimm (1984) – *Resilience…the time it takes till a system which has been subjected to a disturbance returns to its original mode and level of functionality.* Holling (1996) – *Resilience…the measure of disturbance which can be sustained by a system before it shifts from one equilibrium to another.*

Social systems
Cutter et al. (2010) – *Resilience…capacity of a community to recover from disturbances by their own means.*

Engineered systems
Bruneau (2009) – *Resilience…a quality inherent in the infrastructure and built environment; by means of redundancy, robustness, resourcefulness and rapidity.*

In the following, however, the definition formulated by The National Academy of Science (NAS) will be pursued as basis for design and management of engineered systems:

NAS (2012) – *Resilience…a systems ability to plan for, recover from and adapt to adverse events over time.*

3.2.2 Developments in the area of sustainability

In 1987 the Gro Harlin Bruntland report "Our Common Future" (Bruntland 1987) put sustainability on the global political agenda for the first time. Since then the emphasis on the need for sustainable societal developments fueled by global warming has been intensified and remains one – if not the main – topic on the global political agenda. Sustainability has attained a prominent focus point for very substantial collaborative research and development projects of supra-national organizations such as the United Nations, the World Economic Forum, OECD etc.

Sustainability is also not new on the academic agenda. In the fundamental contributions by Solow (1974) sustainability is introduced from the perspective of economics. The economics of equity in markets of exhaustible resources are addressed and analyzed through ideal cases of scalable markets with different assumptions with respect to technological developments, population growth and exchangeability. In Solow (1991) a wider account of the concept of sustainability is provided highlighting the controversial aspects associated with intra- and inter-generational equity and posing the idea that economic gains from exploitation of exhaustible natural resources are fully reinvested into human capital and thereby transferred to the future. The assumption of exchangeability between human capital and exhaustible natural resources is associated with the concept of weak sustainability. Hard sustainability, conversely, assumes that exhaustible natural resources and human capital are strictly complementary.

Kates et al. (2001) introduce sustainability as a science and highlight a number of central and pressing challenges for the research community including: (i) the need for better representations of the dynamic interactions (including time lags and inertia effects) in integral systems models of society and nature; (ii) improved understanding of how trends in society and environment affect sustainability; (iii) identification of what determines vulnerability and resilience of interlinked human and natural system for particular ecosystems and livelihoods; (iv) assessment of possible criteria for early warning of developments or conditions which seriously change interlinked human and natural systems; (v) identification of incentive structures, markets and regulatory frameworks which lead society on more sustainable tracks: (vi) utilization and improvement of present operational tools for monitoring and reporting for enhanced sustainable developments; (vii) better coordination, integration and dissemination of research and developments on decision support systems, systems modeling, etc. to enhance sustainable developments.

Preferences for investments into health and life safety at societal level is considered in Nathwani et al. (1997) who propose the Life Quality Index (LQI) as a demographical indicator expressing the societal preference for trade-offs between leisure time and time spent in productive activities. Based on the LQI, a criterion is derived that allows the assessment and prioritization of investments into health and life safety improvements at societal level in the same manner as applying the marginal lifesaving cost principle from health economics, see also Blomquist (1979). The concept of the LQI is further utilized in support of socio-economic sustainable decisions on design and maintenance of the built environment in Rackwitz et al. (2005), using renewal theoretical principles first proposed by Rosenblueth and Mendoza (1971). Optimal socio-economic sustainable decisions are derived on the design and maintenance of the built environment which accounts for discounting in consistency with societal preferences and economic growth.

With the objective to better understand the impact of human activities on the environment, Hauschild (2015) suggests to couple quantitative sustainability assessment (from product oriented Life Cycle Analysis) with the concept of Planetary Boundaries (Steffen et al. 2015; Rockström et al. 2009). This in turn facilitates assessing the aggregate impacts of human activities at global level with respect to the main parameters controlling safe operating conditions for the planetary system. Moreover, such an approach may be utilized to account for environmental emissions in decision analysis for sustainable and resilient societal developments – as a consequence associated with decision alternatives which not only might have impacts at local spatial and short term temporal scales, but also at global spatial and long term temporal scales.

Based on the definition of resilience by the National Academy of Science (NAS 2012) and the concept of Planetary Boundaries proposed by Rockström et al. (2009) and Steffen et al. (2015), a novel decision analytical framework is proposed in Faber et al. (2017, 2018) for the representation and quantification of resilience and sustainability of interlinked systems. The novelty in the formulation is twofold, namely (i) the events of resilience and sustainability failure of systems are formulated in absolute and quantifiable terms and (ii) accounting for lack of knowledge and inherent natural uncertainty, they are assessed probabilistically so as to facilitate assessment of the annual probability of resilience and sustainability failure, respectively. Furthermore, through this modeling framework decisions relating to the design and operation of engineered systems as well as to the social capacity to react, deal with and learn from disturbance events can be optimized and ranked in accordance with their associated expected value of (service life) benefits. Possible acceptance criteria with respect to the probability of system resilience failure, welfare and risks to individuals and safeguarding qualities of the environment may moreover be accounted for. In this manner Faber et al. (2017) demonstrate how systems efficiency, robustness and resilience may be related and assessed. In Faber and Qin (2016) the framework and the results presented in Faber et al. (2017) are extended to consider one dimension of sustainability through the representation of resource consumption and thereby also indirectly CO_2 emissions associated with construction, operation and failure of infrastructure systems. First insights are achieved on how resilience, efficiency and sustainability relate to each other, which in turn facilitates the assessment of how resilient is resilient enough.

3.2.3 Developments in the area of decision analysis

Since the formulation of the Bayesian decision analysis by Raiffa (1961), Raiffa and Schlaifer (1961) and axioms of expected utility theory first postulated by Bernoulli (Cramer 1728) and later formally proven by von Neumann and Morgenstern (1943), the theoretical and methodical basis for decision support in the face of uncertainty may be stated to be available. A full account of the utilization of decision analyses in different fields of science and application is beyond the scope of the present text as focus is directed on developments with a particular relevance for the present problem setting.

In a normative decision analysis context, Fischoff (2015) provides a discussion of some of the main challenges in the utilization of decision analysis and concludes that decision analysis provides a very strong basis for supporting societal processes on communication and development of informed preferences. Miettinen and Hämäläinen (1997) highlight the merits of utilization of decision analysis in the context of life cycle analysis. Lawrence (2015), besides providing a very full account of the development of decision analysis, proposes decision analysis as a strong means of informed decision support in pursuit of sustainable societal developments

33

and set focus on the potential of decision analysis in providing transparency regarding value settings and their impacts on the decision process.

In the context of descriptive decision analysis, a main scientific interest has been directed on the understanding of which factors and circumstances affect the preferences of decision makers and their decisions, and how this might be reflected in the formulation of utility functions. Empirical evidence from a substantial experimental basis has formed background for a general questioning of whether decision makers in reality can be assumed to be rational in the sense of following the axioms of expected utility theory (von Neumann and Morgenstern (VNM) rationality); see e.g. Kahnemann and Tversky (1979) and Slovic and Tversky (1974). Whereas it has been found that the concept of relative utility as proposed in the prospect theory (Kahnemann & Tversky 1979) may resolve this problem, the identified psychological effects affecting our ability to model and predict the behavior of decision makers also have bearings on normative decision making. Not least, the framing of the decision problems as highlighted in Tversky and Kahnemann (1981) is recognized to play a significant role and constitutes an important ethical dilemma. This of course also relates to the development of decision support for resilient and sustainable societal developments. How should such decision problems be formulated, which are the objectives and values to be pursued?

With respect to the practical application of decision analysis the vast number of publications on risk informed decision making across the engineering disciplines underline a general tendency to focus on the adverse consequences associated with a decision alternative, i.e. risks, see e.g. Aven and Zio (2011) and Fischoff (2015). Risk assessments have undergone significant regulation and unification over the last 2–3 decades (e.g. ISO31000:2009), however the emphasis of regulations on risk management also for the different specific application areas is mostly directed on procedural aspects and only rarely addresses systems modeling aspects (see e.g. ISO2394:2015; JCSS 2008). As a result the best practices on risk management have, over the different application areas, evolved somewhat uncoordinated and subject to rather different industrial needs and regulatory requirements which is why, in the context of decision analysis, they may at best be termed informal. Generally it is the case that both the bases, methods and the results of risk informed decision analysis conducted in different application areas are not consistent and compatible; see e.g. Faber and Stewart (2003).

It is interesting to note that Linkov et al. (2014) identify risk assessment as an inadequate means for assessing and ensuring resilience in the context of societal decision making. The perspective is taken that systems are too complex, that risk based strategies for ensuring appropriate system performances focus on hardening of the system against the effect of disturbances and do not capture the essentials of resilience. It is proposed in Linkov et al. (2014) that more research must be undertaken to understand resilience of systems and to facilitate implementation of strategies ensuring resilience already at early stages in their design.

In conclusion, following the framework proposed by the Joint Committee on Structural Safety (JCSS 2008), normative Bayesian decision analysis, provides an adequate methodical framework for the development of informed societal decisions on resilient and sustainable developments. Insights and results from descriptive decision analysis may and should however be accounted for in the representation of consequences.

3.3 Framework for decision making for resilience and sustainable developments

To facilitate the development of decision support for resilient and sustainable societal developments it is necessary to establish a representation of the considered system which facilitates a ranking of decision alternatives that is consistent with available knowledge, coherent with preferences and objectives and conforming with possibly given requirements. Such a systems representation framework is presented in the following, closely following Faber et al. (2018).

3.3.1 Hierarchical decision analytical system representation

When providing decision support for the management of systems it is essential to establish representations of the systems which consistently map possible different decision alternatives into achievement of preferences of decision makers and involved stakeholders. This implies that the context of the systems are identified in terms of decision makers, stakeholders and their preferences, temporal and spatial boundaries, the physical characteristics of the systems, the performances of the system and possible and relevant decision alternatives together with their effect on the systems performances, see also Faber et al. (2007) and JCSS (2008).

A modeling issue which is often overlooked in decision analysis for systems concerns the organizational aspects of management; the governance structure. The governance of societal systems is typically organized hierarchically into subsystems each under their own management and decision makers, and with defined interfaces to both over- and underlying management levels and decision makers. Such hierarchies can and should be established prior to their detailed modelling and management optimization supported by decision analysis.

An example of a hierarchical representation considering management of infrastructure systems is illustrated in Figure 3.1. The lowest hierarchical level in the representation provided in Figure 3.1 is infrastructure management at municipality or community level. The idea being that the services provided by infrastructure at community level provide benefits to the same level but also that a part of this benefit is transferred to higher organizational levels e.g. in the form of a tax. This tax may then be used in order to establish and manage infrastructure systems which facilitate sharing and utilization of resources as well as service provision capacities across communities. To the extent that higher level management apply taxes from underlying levels also as a means for building financial reserves, these may also be utilized for the purpose of risk financing. Figure 3.1 also illustrates that service provision at community level takes basis in local conditions with respect to environment and natural resources, and of course are subject to the local conditions regarding disturbances, in the form of geo- and anthropological hazards.

At each individual level in the governance hierarchy, decision makers and stakeholders in principle are concerned mainly about ensuring the efficient management of their infrastructure on the basis of their available resources. Their objectives being to ensure adequate resilience and sustainability performance from their perspective. In pursuing these objectives any boundary conditions imposed on them – e.g. through environment, natural resources and hazards, but also in terms of regulations, codes and standards defined at higher levels in the governance hierarchy – must be accounted for and adhered to.

The general idea underlying the hierarchical governance structure illustrated in Figure 3.2 can be applied to other contexts of governance, e.g. for private organizations or industrial activities.

From a theoretical perspective it is fundamental that decision alternatives which are considered for the purpose of optimizing the design and/or management of engineered systems subject to uncertainty and incomplete knowledge in a normative decision context shall be ranked in accordance with their expected value of utility (or benefit) in accordance with Bayesian decision analysis and the axioms of expected utility theory, see e.g. Raiffa and Schlaifer (1961) and von Neumann and Morgenstern (1943).

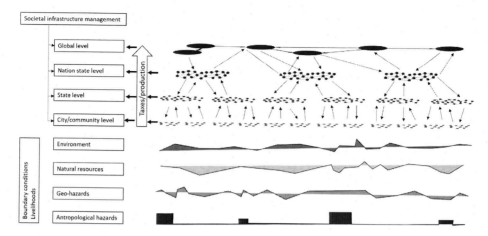

Figure 3.2 Illustration of the hierarchy of governance of interlinked infrastructure systems.
Source: Modified from Faber et al. 2018.

To benefit fully from this theoretical and methodical basis for decision optimization it is necessary to formulate probabilistic models for the performances of the systems as well as to identify and represent the preferences of the decision maker with respect to the possible outcomes of the decisions. Crucial issues concern the probabilistic modelling of the considered systems and also the identification of strategies and options for their design, operation and management.

An illustration considering design and management of infrastructure systems is provided in Figure 3.3. The considered system is comprised of the infrastructure system, the social system (governance), the geo-hazards and anthropological hazard systems (disturbances), the ecological/life support system (environment) and the regulatory system. The temporal performance of the interlinked system must be accounted for, e.g. through time-slicing, whereby the condition of the system is modeled, e.g. on an annual basis, and the condition of the system at one particular time (e.g. one year) depends on the system performance history in the past.

The performances of the interlinked system at any given point in time (in the time slice model from Figure 3.3) may be assessed from the principal framework illustrated in Figure 3.3. As opposed to most common approaches for risk informed decision support the framework illustrated in Figure 3.4 includes not only risks in the sense of expected value of losses of different relevant metrics (e.g. loss of lives, damages to the qualities of the environment and financial losses) but also the benefits associated with decision alternatives – the main objective of engineered systems. This extension facilitates as will be addressed in Section 3.4 that resilience and sustainability may be modeled and quantified and thereby adequately addresses the shortcomings of traditional risk modeling as a basis for resilience assessments highlighted by Linkov et al. (2014).

Based on the systems modeling framework illustrated in Figure 3.4 it is possible to assess and rank different decision alternatives for the design and management of engineered systems in accordance with expected value of utility or any particular metric of preference.

As indicated in the figure the space of acceptable decision alternatives might be limited by e.g. maximum acceptable risks to life, loss of qualities of the environment and financial losses. The concept of the Life Quality Index proposed by Nathwani et al. (1997) readily provides a framework for assessing the acceptability of life risks to individuals.

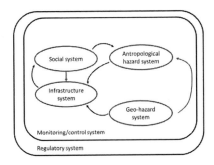 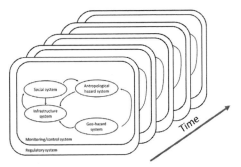

Figure 3.3   Illustration of interlinked system with time slicing.
Source: Modified from Faber et al. 2018.

The scenario based modeling also facilitates assessments of e.g. intensity and duration of loss of critical services, which are typically of particular interest in the context of resilience optimization, and additional requirements in this respect may straightforwardly be added. At smaller geographical and temporal scales, which are normally assumed when considering resilience performance of engineered systems, requirements with respect to impacts on the qualities of the environment are most often specified in regulations, standards and codes. Requirements relating to the performance of interlinked governance and technical systems on the other hand are as of yet not available but can, as shown in Section 3.4.4, be formulated in probabilistic terms.

At global geographical scale and considering long time horizons, acceptance criteria with respect to environmental impacts are not yet available. One possible approach to the identification and formulation of such requirements is however available through the concept of Planetary Boundaries introduced by Rockström et al. (2009) and Steffen et al. (2015). The general idea behind the concept of Planetary Boundaries is that the Earth system has limited capacities to sustain the stresses imposed by human activities. These capacities may be expressed in terms of Planetary Boundaries, quantified in accordance with best available knowledge. At the present time 11 such Planetary Boundaries have been identified. Much research is still necessary on the quantification of associated capacities but already now so-called domains of safe operation of the Earth system are suggested in terms of value ranges for several of these, see Steffen et al. (2015). As described in Section 3.4.5 the concept of the Planetary Boundaries facilitates a quantitative probabilistic assessment of impacts together with associated acceptance criteria.

3.4 System representation and characteristics

To proceed in the presentation of the proposed framework the following sections closely following Faber et al. (2018), provide additional details on the representation of systems as well as on the individual systems characteristic indicated in Figure 3.4.

3.4.1 Exposures and disturbance events

As illustrated in Figure 3.4 a system is assumed subjected to exposure events (disturbances) representing, in principle, all possible events with the potential to generate consequences. In the context of resilience and sustainability modeling and assessments, exposures may be

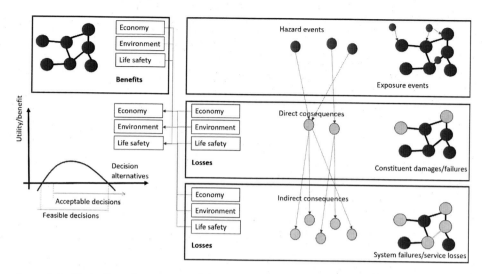

Figure 3.4 Illustration of systems modeling framework accounting for both the generation of capacities as well as losses.

Source: Modified from Faber et al. 2018.

understood in the sense of disturbances. However, it should be underlined that disturbance events as addressed in the vast majority of research on resilience are associated with relatively rare, sudden and high intensity damaging events. Here the perspective is taken that not only such events should be accounted for but rather any type of exposure event. These may be categorized as (see also Faber 2011):

- Type 1 hazards: Large scale averaging rare and high consequence events: Rare in place and time, potentially associated with catastrophic consequences. Over sufficient large scales in time and space the associated risks are predictable, which greatly facilitates their management. Typical examples of this type of hazards include geo-hazards, e.g. earthquakes, floods, strong wind storms, etc.
- Type 2 hazards: Frequent in time and space with relatively small consequences, which is why they are commonly overseen or collectively ignored. Cognition biases such as tunneling and framing (see Kahnemann & Tverski 1984) play important roles in this. Over sufficient scales in time and space they might be associated with devastating cumulative consequences. Moreover, their cumulative effects may trigger more disastrous consequences of the same characteristics as those of Type 3 hazards. Typical examples are emissions to the environment, exploitation of resources, extinction of species, inefficient or inadequate regulations, inadequate budgeting, human errors etc.
- Type 3 hazards: Extremely rare and potentially disastrous events which are unpredictable even over large extents in time and space and for which basically no knowledge is available. May be triggered by the cumulative effects of Type 2 hazards. Examples include super volcano eruptions, impacts by asteroids, high intensity solar storms, global climate change as well as major malevolent actions. The management of risks due to this type of hazard cannot be planned for in the same manner as Type 1 hazards since little is understood with respect to probability of occurrence and evolution of consequences. Conditional risk assessments might

be utilized to quantify speculation on the robustness and resilience of society at different scales – by basing risk assessments on certain extents of damages of the systems providing societal functionality – conditional, or "what if" assessments.

- Type 4 hazards: Events triggered by incorrect information and knowledge. Examples include consciously and unconsciously omitted or manipulated information, "fake news" as well as censored and erroneous observations. Consequences associated with this type of hazard may resemble the consequences associated with Type 1–Type 3 hazards. The management of this type of hazard may be supported by means of sensitivity analysis (see e.g. Faber et al. 1997) and by means of inclusion of options for validation of information and knowledge playing a significant role for the ranking of decision alternatives.

3.4.2 Modeling of cascading failures

The system modeling approach suggested by the JCSS (2008) subdivides the scenarios of events leading to consequences into three parts, namely the hazard (or disturbance) events, direct consequences and indirect consequences, see also Figure 3.5. The direct consequences comprise either (i) all losses caused directly by the disturbance event or (ii) all losses caused by failure states of the constituents of the system except functionality related losses. The indirect consequences are assumed to be caused by (a) all losses caused in the process of internal redistribution after the disturbance event or b) the functionality losses alone. Besides the differentiated consequence modeling, two phases are introduced in the modeling of the progression of failure of the system: the initiation phase and the propagation phase, see also Faber et al. (2017). In the initiation phase m_{H_i} constituent failures are assumed generated by the hazard event H_i. In the propagation phase furtherl_{H_i} constituent failures are generated by the joint effect of internal redistribution of system demands and hazard events, see also Figure 3.5.

It is assumed that all possible $i = 1, 2, ... n_S$ different scenarios of hazard events with their occurrence probabilities $p(i)$, direct consequences associated with constituent failure events during the initiation phase $C_{D,I}(i)$ and propagation phase, respectively $C_{D,P}(i)$ and the indirect consequences $C_{ID}(i)$ have been identified and assessed. The probabilistic system representation **S** can then be written as:

$$\mathbf{S} = (i, p(i), C_{D,I}(i), C_{D,P}(i), C_{ID}(i)), \quad i = 1, 2, .., n_S. \tag{3.1}$$

3.4.3 Quantification of robustness

The robustness of systems may be understood as the degree to which a system is able to contain or limit the immediate consequences of disturbance events. Risk based formulations for the quantification of systems robustness are first provided in Baker et al. (2008) and JCSS (2008) and later enhanced in Faber (2015) where the robustness index of a system with respect to a given scenario i, i.e. $I_R(i)$ is:

$$I_R(i) = \frac{c_D(i)}{c_T(i)}. \tag{3.2}$$

The direct and total consequences $c_D(i)$ and $c_T(i)$ entering Equation (3.2) may be interpreted in dependence on the focus of the system assessment (or rather the definition of the system

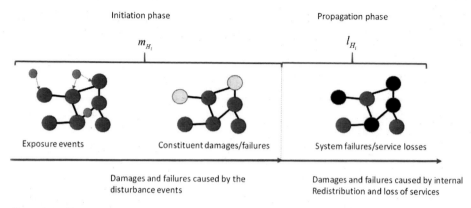

Figure 3.5   Illustration of the representation of cascading failure events.
Source: Modified from Faber et al. 2018.

boundaries). If the focus of the system assessment is directed on the representation and analysis of cascading failures Equation (3.2) may be rewritten as:

$$I_R(i) = \frac{c_{D,I}(i)}{c_{D,I}(i) + c_{D,P}(i)}, \tag{3.3}$$

where $c_{D,I}(i)$, $c_{D,P}(i)$, represent the direct consequences associated with the initiation phase and the propagation phase of the ith failure scenario of the system, respectively.

If the emphasis is directed on the ability of the system to contain the development of consequences Equation (3.2) may be rewritten as:

$$I_R(i) = \frac{c_{D,I}(i) + c_{D,P}(i)}{c_{D,I}(i) + c_{D,P}(i) + c_{ID}(i)}. \tag{3.4}$$

As the scenarios i are random in nature, as reflected by their occurrence probabilities $p(i)$, it is realized that the robustness index $I_R(i)$ itself is a random variable which may be analyzed further by categorization and ordering of the different scenarios in accordance with the hazard, damage, failure and consequence events they are composed of. In this manner robustness indexes for a given system can be assessed probabilistically conditional on e.g. the type and/or intensity of the hazard event as well as the magnitude of direct, indirect or total consequences. Moreover, the scenario based approach allows for keeping account of which constituent damages and failures contribute the most to, e.g. poor robustness performance as well as to the total consequences.

3.4.4 Quantification of resilience

A relatively large variety of propositions for the modeling and quantification of systems resilience are available in the literature, see e.g. Tamvakis and Xenedis (2013), Cimellaro et al. (2009), Linkov et al. (2014) and Sharma et al. (2017). Most often the suggested models are directed on the short term representation of the ability of the system to sustain and recover from disturbances, without substantial loss of functionality and without the support from the outside. Typically the attention in resilience modeling is directed on the representation of the

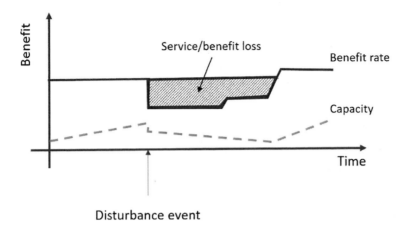

Figure 3.6 Illustration of principal resilience model.
Source: Modified from Faber et al. (2018).

effect of specified disturbances on service provision and the characteristics of the recovery in terms of degree of recovered service versus time and total loss of service, see Figure 3.6.

Until recently, only implicit consideration has been devoted to the modeling of the capacity of systems to recover from disturbances. However, following the life-cycle benefit considerations in the resilience model presented in Faber et al. (2016), systems resilience should account for not only the loss of functionality, but also for the generation of the capacity which is critically important for the successful – and fast – reorganization, adaptation and rehabilitation, following disturbances and hazard events, see Figure 3.6.

Therefore a life-cycle model of systems resilience is proposed here in which scenarios of both benefit generation and losses are modeled and analyzed and where insufficient resilience or systems resilience failure is defined as exhaustion of system capacity (social, economic and/or environmental). Resilience, in the same manner as robustness is thereby a system characteristic of a random nature and requirements to resilience may only be specified meaningfully in probabilistic terms, e.g. through an acceptable annual probability of resilience failure.

In Figure 3.7 this idea is illustrated for the simple case of a system for which the only explicitly considered capacity is a financial reserve established as a fixed percentage of the annual benefit generated by the system over time. The general shape of the benefit loss curves in the aftermath of disturbances reflects that a period of time will pass before the service can be reestablished. In the first instance only up to a certain level, reflecting that interim solutions are foreseen, implemented and operated, while waiting for the preparation and implementation of complete and possibly even improved system rehabilitation.

Resilience failure occurs if at some point in time one or more of the available capacities are exhausted. It should be underlined that resilience failure in principle can also occur as a consequence of disturbances of a "slow burner" character, such as the effect of inefficient governance and cognitive errors (Type 2 Hazard from Section 3.4.1).

In Figure 3.7 two time histories of benefit generation and accumulated economic reserves are illustrated. It is seen how disturbance events both reduce the capacity generation as well as the accumulated capacity reserves. In the time history illustrated with a green line it is seen that a disturbance event exhausts the accumulated reserves and causes a resilience failure.

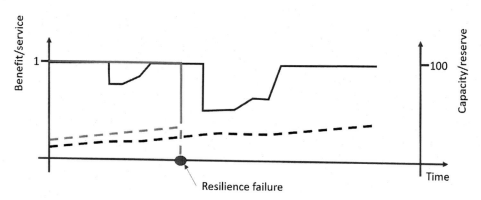

Figure 3.7 The proposed resilience model in terms of time histories of benefit generation and corresponding time histories of accumulated economic reserves.
Source: Modified from Faber et al. 2018.

The probability of resilience failure $P_{RF}(t,\mathbf{a})$ may in this manner be represented and assessed probabilistically as:

$$P_{RF}(t,\mathbf{a}) = 1 - P\left[\left\{r_r(\mathbf{X}(\tau),\mathbf{a}) - s_r(\mathbf{X}(\tau),\mathbf{a}) > 0, \forall \tau \in [0,t[\right\}\right], \tag{3.5}$$

where $r_r(\mathbf{X}(\tau),\mathbf{a})$ is a function representing a given capacity of the system at time τ and $s_r(\mathbf{X}(\tau),\mathbf{a})$ is a function representing the demand or stress on the system caused by a disturbance event at time τ. $\mathbf{X}(\tau)$ is a vector of random variables which may depend on time and $\mathbf{a}$ is a vector containing all decision alternative which may affect the resilience performance of the system. It may be realized that Equation (3.5) indeed represents a first excursion problem.

As for the case of robustness, conditional resilience failure may be modeled and assessed utilizing the scenario based life-cycle oriented approach. Conditioning on disturbance events of given characteristics, the conditional event of a system being resilient can be defined as the event of successful recovery within a given time horizon without exceeding available resources.

Examination of Figure 3.7 reveals that the first immediate drop in the benefit rate (service provision or functionality) after a disturbance event relates directly to the systems robustness as described by Equation (3.3). However, the index of robustness defined by Equation (3.4) can be seen to also represent the resilience characteristics of a system. If this index for a given scenario is equal to 1 it implies that the system suffers no functionality related losses. This in turn is only possible if the services provided by the system are successfully reestablished immediately after the disturbance event – implying perfect resilience performance. Even with moderate assumptions concerning the contribution of indirect consequences to total consequences it is apparent that cascading failures and loss of functionality play a significant role for the resilience of the system.

3.4.5 Quantification of sustainability

Addressing sustainability necessitates a joint consideration of impacts to the environment, health and welfare of people, economy and exhaustion of natural resources from the perspective of intergenerational and intra-generational equity. In addition to the impacts already considered in the modeling of resilience, the focus is directed on how to account for impacts to the environment.

The general idea followed is to apply the concept of Planetary Boundaries as a means to represent the capacities of the Earth system which are central for the continued development of society as we know it today. In the following these characteristics of the Earth system are referred to as the Earth Life Support System (ELSS). It is further assumed that to any decision alternative relating to the design and management of an engineered system it is possible to assign system states and corresponding consequences relating to impacts on the qualities of the environment imposing stresses on the ELSS. Following Hauschild (2015) this relationship might be established through Life Cycle Analysis as applied in support of Quantitative Sustainability Assessments (QSA) in the context of product development. The principle is illustrated in Figure 3.8.

According to Steffen et al. (2015), the ELSS may become unstable if its capacities to cope with emissions and other disturbances caused or influenced by human activities are exhausted. Research is still ongoing to understand and assess the capacities of the ELSS with respect to CO_2 emissions, acidification of the oceans, extinction of species, fresh water use etc. However, it may be assumed that for each of the presently identified 11 critical boundary variables it is (or will soon be) possible to formulate criteria of the form:

$$r_i(\mathbf{x}, \tau, \mathbf{a}) - s_i(\mathbf{x}, \tau, \mathbf{a}) \leq 0, \ i = 1, 2, ..n_B, \tag{3.6}$$

where $r_i(\mathbf{x}, \tau, \mathbf{a})$ and $s_i(\mathbf{x}, \tau, \mathbf{a})$ are complex functions describing the capacities and the stresses or demands acting on the ELSS with respect to its n_B Planetary Boundary variables at a given point in time τ. $\mathbf{x}$ is a vector of variables entering the functions and $\mathbf{a}$ is a vector of decision alternatives which may influence both the capacities and the stresses.

Assuming that the variables $\mathbf{x}$ are associated with uncertainty we may assess system sustainability probabilistically along the same lines as system resilience failure, i.e.:

$$P_{SF,ELSSi}(t, \mathbf{a}) = 1 - P\left[\left\{r_i(\mathbf{X}(\tau), \mathbf{a}) - s_i(\mathbf{X}(\tau), \mathbf{a}) > 0 \forall \tau \in [0, t[\right\}\right]. \tag{3.7}$$

The probability of sustainability failure $P_{SF,ELSSi}(t, \mathbf{a})$ may, as for the case of resilience failure, be assessed as a first excursion problem. In the general case where all n_B planetary boundary variables are considered this becomes a vector valued first excursion problem.

The dimension of sustainability relating to health and welfare may be represented through the indirect relation between economy and life expectancy as provided by the Life Quality Index (LQI) see e.g. Kübler (2005):

$$LQI = g^w l^{1-w}(1-w)^{1-w}. \tag{3.8}$$

The parameter in Equation (3.8) represent three demographic social indicators, namely the gross domestic product per capita (g), the life expectancy (l) and the fraction of life spent to earn a living (w). By introducing an elasticity labor factor β, a factor indicating, the trade-off between wealth and longevity can be expressed as $q = w / (\beta(1-w))$.

The GDP may be modeled through the monetary benefits generated from the services provided by the engineered systems, less the expenditures associated with construction, maintenance, reconstruction and renewals. The relationship between the development of the economy and life expectancy at birth at nation state level is studied in Kuebler (2005) and Faber and Virguez-Rodriguez (2011):

$$\frac{dg}{g} = \frac{1-w}{w}\frac{dl}{l}. \tag{3.9}$$

43

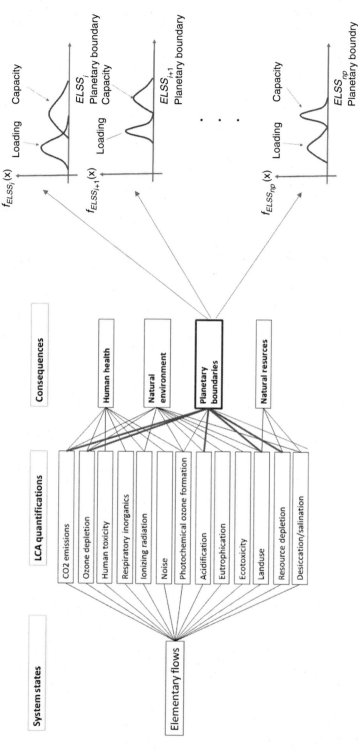

Figure 3.8 Illustration of the mapping of system changes imposed by a given decision alternative to elementary flows, LCA quantifications and consequences in metrics of relevance for resilience and sustainability assessments.

As a function of different decision alternatives **a** it is thus possible to model trajectories over time of the development of the LQI and thereby to assess the development of societal welfare for given policies affecting the decision alternatives contained in **a**, see Equation (3.10):

$$\text{LQI}(\mathbf{x}, \tau, \mathbf{a}) = g(\mathbf{x}, \tau, \mathbf{a})^{w} l(\mathbf{x}, \tau, \mathbf{a})^{1-w} (1-w)^{1-w}. \tag{3.10}$$

Moreover by relating the social capacity to deal with disturbances in terms of reorganization, restructuring and adaptive learning in and after the event of a disturbance, to the LQI as a function of time, the dynamic effect between general societal welfare and resilience can be represented. Using this model a societal sustainability failure criterion may be formulated through the event that the LQI decreases below a critical level LQI_{LIM} and the probability of societal sustainability failure $P_{SF,Soc}(t, \mathbf{a})$ can be assessed along the same lines as resilience failure and sustainability failure, i.e.:

$$P_{SF,Soc}(t, \mathbf{a}) = 1 - P\big[\{\text{LQI}(\mathbf{X}(\tau), \mathbf{a}) - LQI_{LIM} > 0, \forall \tau \in [0, t[\}\big]. \tag{3.11}$$

Figure 3.9 provides an overview of the various metrics, system characteristics and assessments entering the decision analysis of systems in the context of supporting decisions for resilient and sustainable societal developments.

3.5 Conclusions

Research in resilience and sustainability has attracted tremendous resources and efforts over the past 3–4 decades. The fundamental principles and concepts mostly originate from the fields of economy, ecology and social sciences but applications of these for the design and management of engineered systems may be found in a relatively wide range of engineering disciplines. For engineered systems, however, research in resilience and sustainability has developed largely in parallel, the two fields to a large extent considered and approached as individual topics. It is nevertheless evident that at a fundamental level the two concepts are strongly related or even equivalent depending on the boundaries assumed when defining the considered system. Traditionally resilience of engineered systems is addressed at scales in time and geography which are much smaller than those assumed when addressing sustainability, with a strong focus on safeguarding the services provided by the systems – in part from the environment. Sustainability on the other hand puts emphasis on the safeguarding of the qualities of the environment from adverse effects originating from these services in the long run and at the scale of Earth. In the formulations of resilience and sustainability provided in the foregoing sections it is shown that resilience and sustainability of engineered systems may be approached in the exact same manner by introducing resilience and sustainability failure as the event that one or more capacities of considered systems are exhausted. If resilience of the global Earth systems is considered it is thus clear that resilience failure is equivalent to sustainability failure if resilience is addressed in a long term perspective. Moreover, resilience of engineered systems at smaller scales necessitate resilience (or sustainability) at global scale.

Another important point from the foregoing sections is that resilience and sustainability of engineered systems in the same manner as the system characteristic robustness, due to lack of knowledge and inherent natural variability, only meaningfully can be approaches and modeled probabilistically. Requirements to resilience and sustainability as a consequence must defined, e.g. in terms of acceptable annual probabilities of resilience failure and sustainability failure, respectively. From this perspective it immediately becomes clear that tradeoffs exist and

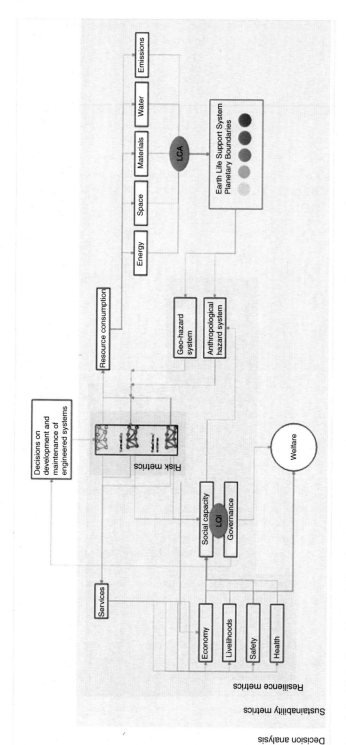

Figure 3.9 Illustration of interrelations between risk, resilience and sustainability as well as associated metrics and techniques for their assessments.

must be accounted for when deciding how resilient engineered systems and sustainable societal developments should be. The more short term welfare in society will depend on what is considered to be acceptable risks associated with resilience failures at local geographical scales (e.g. at community level) as well as society's risk appetite for the risk of sustainability failures at global scale. More research on these tradeoffs must be achieved in the nearer future to facilitate timely and informed societal decision making.

Notes

1　Various alternative terms are used in the literature: in ecology the term is typically "disturbance," in disaster risk and environmental risk management the terms "hazards" is frequently applied and in engineering and insurance a typical term is "exposures."
2　In the following the term "engineered systems" refers to in principle all societal systems originating from human decisions, including systems sometimes referred to as "self-organized systems." This inclusion is made since self-organized systems only exist in the context of decision making if they are known and if they are allowed to be self-organized.

References

Anderies, J.M (2014). Embedding built environments in social-ecological systems: Resilience-based design principles, *Building Re-search and Information (BRI)* 42(2): 130–42.

Anderies, J.M., Janssen, M.A., and Ostrom, E. (2004). A framework to analyze the robustness of social ecological systems from an institutional perspective, *Ecology and Society* 9: 18.

Aven, T. and Zio, E. (2011). Some considerations on the treatment of uncertainties in risk assessment for practical decision making, *Reliability Engineering and System Safety* 96: 64–74.

Blomquist, G. (1979). Value of life saving: implications of consumption activity. Journal of Political Economy, 87(3): 540–58.

Bruneau, M., Chang, S.E., Eguchi, R.T., Lee, G.C., O'Rourke, T.D., Reinhorn, A.M., Shinozuka, M., Tierney, K.T., Wallace, W.A., and von Winterfeldt, D. (2003). A framework to quantitatively assess and enhance the seismic resilience of communities, *Earthquake Spectra* 19(4): 733–52.

Bruntland, G.H. (1987). *World Commission on Environment and Development (1987). Our Common Future.* Oxford: Oxford University Press.

Cimellaro G.P., Reinhorn, A.M., and Bruneau, M. (2009). Framework for analytical quantification of disaster resilience. *Engineering Structures* 32: 3639–49.

Cramer, G. (1728). Letter from Cramer to Nicholas Bernoulli. Translated into English by Louise Sommer in Bernoulli, Daniel (1954), *Exposition of a New Theory on the Measurement of Risk, Econometrica* 22: 23–36.

Cutter, S.L., Boruff, B.J., and Shirley, W.L. (2003). Social vulnerability to environmental hazards. *Social Science Quarterly* 84(1): 242–61.

Cutter, S.L., Burton, C.G., and Emrich, C.T. (2010). Disaster resilience indicators for benchmarking baseline conditions, *Journal of Homeland Security and Emergency Management* 7 (2010): 1271–83.

Derissen, S., Quaas, M., and Baumgärtner, S. (2011). The relationship between resilience and sustainability of ecological-economic systems, *Ecological Economics* 70: 1121–8.

Doorn, N., Gardoni, P., and Murphy, C. (2018). Multidisciplinary definition and evaluation of resilience: the role of social justice in defining resilience, *Journal of Sustainable and Resilient Infrastructure*, DOI: 10.1080/23789689.2018.1428162.

Faber, M.H. (2011). On the governance of global and catastrophic risks. *International Journal of Risk Assessment and Management* 15(5): 400.

Faber, M.H. (2015). Codified risk informed decision making for structures. *Symposium on Reliability of Engineering System*, SRES2015, Hangzou, China. October 15–17, 2015.

Faber, M.H. and Qin, J. (2016). On the relationship between resilience and sustainability for infra-structure systems. In *International Symposium on Sustainability and Resiliency of Infrastructure (ISSRI2016)*, S.-S. Chen and A.H.-S. Ang (eds.), Taiwan Tech, Taipei, Taiwan, 2016.

Faber, M.H. and Stewart, M.G. (2003). Risk assessment for civil engineering facilities: Critical overview and discussion. *Reliability Engineering and System Safety* 80: 173–84.

Faber, M.H. and Virguez-Rodriguez, E.A. (2011). Supporting decisions on global health and life safety investments. *Proceedings of 11th International Conference on Applications of Statistics and Probability in Civil Engineering – ICASP11*, August 8–10, 2011. Zurich, Switzerland.

Faber, M.H., Maes, M.A., Baker, J.W., Vrouwenvelder, T., and Takada, T. (2007). Principles of risk assessment of engineered systems. *Proceedings of 10th International Conference on Application of Statistic and Probability in Civil Engineering*, 31 July–3 August 2007. Tokyo, Japan.

Faber, M.H., Qin, J., Miraglia, S., and Thöns, S. (2017). On the probabilistic characterization of robustness and resilience, *Procedia Engineering* 198: 1070–83.

Faber, M.H., Miraglia, S., Qin, J., and Stewart, M.G. (2018). Bridging resilience and sustainability – decision analysis for design and management of infrastructure systems, *Journal for Sustainable and Resilient Infrastructure*, Taylor and Francis.

Fischhoff, B. (2015). The realities of risk-cost-benefit analysis. *Science* 350(6260): 527.

Hauschild, M.Z. (2015). Better – but is it good enough? On the need to consider both eco-efficiency and eco-effectiveness to gauge industrial sustainability. In *The 22nd CIRP conference on Life Cycle Engineering – Procedia CIRP* 29: 1–7.

Holling, C.S. (1996). Engineering resilience versus ecological resilience. In Engineering Within Ecological Constraints, ed. Peter Schulze, Washington: National Academy of Engineering, p. 224.

ISO 2394:2015 (2015). General Principles on Reliability for Structures, International Standards Organization.

ISO 31000:2009 (2015). Risk Management – Principles and Guidelines, International Standards Organization.

Janssen, M.A. and Anderies, J.M. (2007). Robustness trade-offs in social-ecological systems, *International Journal of the Commons* 1: 43–65.

JCSS (2008). Risk Assessment in Engineering – Principles, System Representation & Risk Criteria, June 2008.

Kahneman, D. and Tversky, A. (1984). Choices, values and frames, *American Psychologist* 39: 341–50.

Kates, R.W. et al. (2001). Sustainability science, *Science, New Series* 292(5517): 641–2.

Kübler, O. (2005). Applied Decision-Making in Civil Engineering. Dissertation ETH No. 16394.

Linkov, I., Bridges, T., Creutzig, F., Decker, J., Fox-Lent, C., Kröger, W., Lambert, J. H., Levermann, A., Montreuil, B., Nathwani, J., Nyer, R., Renn, O., Scharte, B., Scheffler, A., Schreurs, M., and Thiel-Clemen, T. (2014). Changing the resilience paradigm, *Nature Climate Change* 4, June.

Miettinen, P. and Hämäläinen, R.P. (1997). How to benefit from decision analysis in environmental life cycle assessments (LCA), *European Journal of Operational Research* 102: 279–94.

Mileti, D.S. (1999). *Disasters by Design: A Reassessment of Natural Hazards in the United States, Natural Hazards and Disasters*. Washington, DC: Joseph Henry Press.

NAS (2012). *National Research Council Disaster Resilience: A National Imperative*. The National Academies Press, 2012.

Nathwani J.S., Lind N.C., and Pandey M.D. (1997). Affordable safety by choice: the life quality method. Institute for Risk Research, University of Waterloo, Canada.

National Research Council. (2012). *Disaster Resilience: A National Imperative*. Washington, DC: The National Academies Press.

Nishijima, K. and Faber, M.H. (2009). Societal performance of infrastructure subject to natural hazards, *Australian Journal of Structural Engineering* 9(1), March 2009, Special issue on Disaster & Hazard Mitigation (IFED 2007), pp. 9–16.

Pimm S.L. (1984). The complexity and stability of ecosystems, *Nature* 307: 321–6.

Rackwitz, R., Lentz, A., and Faber, M.H. (2005). Socio-economically sustainable civil engineering infrastructures by optimization, *Structural Safety* 27(3): 187–229.

Raiffa, H. (1961). Risk, ambiguity, and the savage axioms: comment, *Quarterly Journal of Economics* 75: 690–4.

Raiffa, H. and Schlaifer, R. (1961). *Applied Statistical Decision Theory*. Cambridge, MA: Harvard University Press.

Rockström, J. et al. (2009). Planetary boundaries: exploring the safe operating space for humanity, *Ecology and Society* 14(2).

Rosenblueth, E. and Mendoza, E. (1971). Reliability optimization in isostatic structures, *Journal of the Engineering Mechanics Division* 97(6): 1625–42.

Sharma, N., Tabandeh, A., and Gardoni, P. (2017). Resilience analysis: a mathematical formulation to model resilience of engineering systems, *Sustainable and Resilient Infrastructure* 3(2): 49–67.

Slovic, P. and Tversky, A. (1974). Who accepts Savage's axiom?, *Behavioral Science* 19: 368–73.

Solow, R.M. (1974). Intergenerational equity and exhaustible resources, *The Review of Economic Studies*, Vol. 41, Symposium on the Economics of Exhaustible Resources, pp. 29–45.

Solow, R.M. (1991). Sustainability: An economist's perspective. Paper presented at the Eighteenths J. Seeward Johnson Lecture to the Marine Policy Center, Woods Hole Oceanographic Institution, at Woods Hole, Massachusetts, on June 14, 1991.

Steffen, W. et al. (2015). Planetary boundaries: Guiding human development on a changing planet, *Science* 347: 1259855.

Tamvakis, P. and Xenidis, Y. (2013). Comparative evaluation of resilience quantification methods for infrastructure systems, 26th **IPMA** World Congress, Crete, Greece, 2012, Elsevier, *Procedia – Social and Behavioral Sciences* 74: 339–48.

Tversky, A. and Kahneman, D. (1981). The framing of decisions and the psychology of choice, *Science* 211(4481): 453–8.

von Neumann and Morgenstern (1943). *Theory of Games and Economical Behavior*. Princeton, NJ: Princeton University Press.

4

Resilience and sustainability goals for communities and quantification metrics

Jessica Boakye,[1] Colleen Murphy[2] and Paolo Gardoni[3]

[1] DEPARTMENT OF CIVIL AND ENVIRONMENTAL ENGINEERING, MAE CENTER: CREATING A MULTI-HAZARD APPROACH TO ENGINEERING, UNIVERSITY OF ILLINOIS AT URBANA-CHAMPAIGN, URBANA, IL, USA; BOAKYE3@ILLINOIS.EDU

[2] COLLEGE OF LAW, UNIVERSITY OF ILLINOIS AT URBANA-CHAMPAIGN, CHAMPAIGN, IL, USA; COLLEENM@ILLINOIS.EDU

[3] DEPARTMENT OF CIVIL AND ENVIRONMENTAL ENGINEERING, MAE CENTER: CREATING A MULTI-HAZARD APPROACH TO ENGINEERING, UNIVERSITY OF ILLINOIS AT URBANA-CHAMPAIGN, URBANA, IL, USA; GARDONI@ILLINOIS.EDU

4.1 Introduction

Communities can experience significant impact from natural (and anthropogenic) hazards. Goals need to be defined in terms of the acceptable impact in the aftermath of a hazardous event. Resilience and sustainability goals can be defined to explicitly consider recovery time, environmental justice, and social justice (i.e., global and intergenerational justice) when evaluating the impact on well-being (Gardoni & Murphy 2018). To measure the impact of a hazardous event on well-being, we need to define quantification metrics. Such quantification metrics need to be defined at different times to be able to express the changes in well-being from before the occurrence of a hazard to immediately after and throughout the recovery process. The well-being of individuals is complex and depends on many factors including the service provided to a community by infrastructure, societal norms, and societal status. Societal norms and status are often described as social vulnerability factors (e.g., Bates & Peacock 1992). To accurately predict and evaluate the effect a natural disaster has on well-being, goals and quantification metrics have to account for these factors.

One of the relevant factors that influence well-being is infrastructure. Critical infrastructure such as transportation or water/wastewater networks are vulnerable to natural hazards such as earthquakes or floods (Gardoni & LaFave 2016). Direct damage caused by natural disasters must be translated into a reduction in functionality to infrastructure networks (Gardoni & Murphy 2018; Guidotti & Gardoni 2018). For example, an earthquake may cause a bridge to fail which in turn reduces the functionality of the transportation network that supports the community by transporting goods and people to locations of interest (Nocera et al. 2018; Nocera & Gardoni 2018). Much research has been devoted to measuring the performance of individual infrastructure networks (Kang et al. 2008; Guikema & Gardoni 2009; Lee et al. 2011; Frangopol & Bocchini 2012; Guidotti et al. 2017a) and their components (e.g., bridges, buildings) (Gardoni et al. 2002, 2003; Choe et al. 2007, 2009; Ramamoorthy et al. 2006, 2008; Mardfekri & Gardoni 2013, 2014; Mardfekri et al. 2015; Tabandeh & Gardoni 2014, 2015) in the aftermath of a natural hazard. The focus of such research is on creating quantitative models that predict the state of infrastructure and their components as a function of the characteristics of the physical systems and the hazard intensity. Although the failure of critical infrastructure can be devastating to community well-being, it also presents an opportunity for improvement (Murphy & Gardoni 2006). Infrastructure recovers over time following a natural disaster and the options of rebuilding to better standards may improve the well-being of individuals, as well as potentially address inequalities among individuals that existed before the occurrence of a disaster and that were likely exacerbated by the disaster. Therefore, quantification metrics should be able to account for both the positive and negative impacts of natural disasters.

Natural hazards tend to exacerbate societal inequalities across communities (Gardoni et al. 2016; Doorn et al. 2018). Many studies identify vulnerability factors for individuals (Fothergill et al. 1999; Peacock et al. 1987; Masozera et al. 2007), which can be social, political, and/or economic, and include: socio-economic status, local development, race/ethnicity, political ideology, gender, sexual orientation, employment/occupation, and disability. These factors influence the impact of a hazard as well as the process of recovery post-disaster and should be accounted for in any study of the impact of a hazard on well-being (Bates et al. 1992; Kajitani et al. 2005; Peacock et al. 1987, 1997). The focus of many of these studies is to enhance risk mitigation and community resilience by alerting decision makers and planners to these vulnerability factors. (A multidisciplinary definition of resilience that can account for the role of social justice can be found in Doorn et al. 2018.) Once these factors are identified, vulnerable groups can be given additional resources to help mitigate the effects of the natural hazard. However, many studies on risk factors and social vulnerability are case-specific and qualitative. Therefore, it is difficult to combine social vulnerability factors with the quantitative modeling of physical infrastructure.

This chapter defines quantification metrics as proxies for well-being that can account for social vulnerability and be used throughout the recovery of physical infrastructure and communities as time-varying measures that describe both positive and negative impacts. The Capability Approach (CA) provides a rational and normative framework for selecting metrics to quantify societal well-being in the context of risk analysis. According to the CA, the well-being of individuals should be measured and evaluated based on the opportunities (or capabilities) people have (Robeyns 2006). Such opportunities are a function of what individuals have and what they can do with what they have, and thus are impacted by the built infrastructure and factors shaping vulnerability. This chapter also defines resilience and sustainability goals based on acceptability and tolerability limits on capabilities as well as the distribution of the capabilities across individuals.

There are eight sections in this chapter. The next section presents a literature review on the CA in the context of risk analysis, the third section reviews the implementation of the CA, the fourth section defines quantification metrics, the fifth section defines the resilience and sustainability goals, the sixth section outlines the advantages of the CA, the seventh section shows an illustrative example, and the eighth section concludes the chapter.

4.2 Background of the capability approach

The CA was first developed by Sen (1989, 1992, 1993, 1999a, 1999b) and Nussbaum (2000a, b, 2001) in the context of development economics and policy. Since then it has been adopted by the United Nations Development Program for multiple uses including the annual global Human Development Report and studies of food security (Burchi & Muro 2012, UNDP 2016). The CA offers a conception of some of the constitutive components of well-being. According to the CA, the well-being of individuals should be measured and evaluated based on the opportunities people have to live valuable lives (Robeyns 2006). This differs from a utilitarian approach which puts emphasis on the satisfaction of individuals' personal preferences. There are two key definitions in the CA: *functionings* and *capabilities*. Functionings refer to what an individual does or becomes in his or her life that is of value, such as being educated, being mobile, being employed and being adequately nourished. Capabilities refer to the functionings that are feasible for an individual to choose to achieve given what he/she has and what he/she can do with that given, for example, the built infrastructure, legal norms, and economic institutions (Sen 1993). Functionings can be seen as dimensions of well-being. As a result, defining goals in terms of capabilities can drive policy decisions that focus on promoting opportunities for individuals to achieve well-being. Capabilities depend on many societal factors. To illustrate, consider the opportunity for an individual to live in a permanent and safe residence. To have such an opportunity, a person may need to have money to purchase or rent a residence, as well as the legal right to obtain property.

The CA was introduced in risk analysis by Murphy and Gardoni (2006, 2007, 2008, 2010, 2011a, 2011b, 2012) and Gardoni and Murphy (2008, 2009, 2010, 2013, 2014) to conceptualize and quantify the societal impact of natural hazards. Their key claim is that the impact of a natural hazard should be measured in terms of how much it affects individuals' capabilities. Risk analysis involves estimating the consequences and associated probabilities of a hazard. It also involves evaluating the risks in order to guide decision makers in issues of risk management and mitigation. Using a CA, we can formulate risk assessment focused on changes to the well-being of individuals within a society (Murphy & Gardoni 2006), frame risk evaluation based on goals for societal well-being (Murphy & Gardoni 2008), define recovery strategies that restore and enhance well-being (Gardoni & Murphy 2008; Tabandeh et al. 2018), and promote environmental and social justice (Gardoni & Murphy 2018).

4.3 Implementation of a capability approach in the assessment of societal well-being

The steps needed to implement a CA are: (1) selection of capabilities and indicators, (2) development of predictive models, and (3) development of an aggregate measure of achievement. This section discusses these steps in detail. The section also reviews the implementation of a CA using a Dynamics Bayesian Network (DBN) following Tabandeh et al. (2018) and how to deal with the relevant uncertainties and infrastructure (inter)dependencies following Guidotti et al. (2016).

4.3.1 Selection of capabilities and indicators

Gardoni and Murphy (2009, 2010) proposed three criteria for selecting relevant capabilities. First, capabilities should be relevant. In the context of risk analysis, this means that the selected capabilities should be potentially affected by the natural hazard(s) of interest. Such vulnerability

Table 4.1 Example capabilities and indicators

Capability (opportunity to …)	Indicator	Indicator type
Maintaining health	Access to a hospital	Categorical
Being sheltered	Access to a permanent residence	Categorical
Being mobile	Travel time	Real-valued

should be identified by either theoretical justification or empirical evidence. Second, capabilities should be parsimonious to avoid problems with data collection and storage. Third, capabilities should be orthogonal. Each capability chosen should provide information that cannot be ascertained from another capability to avoid weighting one capability group higher than another. Based on the third criterion, capabilities can be assumed to be incommensurable and to be all necessary to the well-being of an individual (Sen 1993; Gardoni & Murphy 2009, 2010).

When modeling the capabilities, we identify some key characteristics. First, capabilities are often interdependent (Robeyns 2006; Murphy & Gardoni 2010). For example, having access to energy may affect the capability of being sheltered. Without having energy for three days, a family may choose to leave their permanent residence regardless of the structural condition of the residence (Guidotti et al. 2018). Moreover, one capability may be a necessary condition for another. For example, being alive is a necessary condition for all of the other capabilities considered. To properly model this interaction between capabilities, it is important that the modeling technique used is dynamic and can accurately account for any interdependencies.

Next, indicators are chosen that are easily quantifiable since capabilities are not easily measured (Raworth & Stewart 2003). Indicators should be metrics that can be easily measured before, during, and after a natural disaster. They can be either real-valued or categorical (Tabandeh et al. 2018). We present possible capabilities and the corresponding indicators in Table 4.1. We propose to use indicators as quantification metrics of the impact of a hazard (as discussed in further detail in Section 4.4).

4.3.2 Development of predictive models for indicators

Predictive models for the indicators are needed to estimate the values of the indicators as a function of the influencing factors (regressors) that describe the state of functionality of the infrastructure and various socio-economic factors contributing to community vulnerability. Tabandeh et al. (2018) proposed the following form for probabilistic predictive models for real-valued indicators:

$$\mathrm{T}\left[I_l\left(\mathbf{x}_l;\Theta_l\right)\right]=\mathrm{T}\left[\hat{I}_l\left(\mathbf{x}_l\right)\right]+\sum_{j=1}^{n_l}\theta_{l,j}x_{l,j}+\sigma_l\varepsilon_l, \tag{4.1}$$

where: $\mathrm{T}(\cdot)$ is a variance stabilizing transformation; $I_l(\mathbf{x}_l;\Theta_l)$ is the predicted value of the lth indicator; $\mathbf{x}_l := (x_{l,1},...,x_{l,n_l})$ is the set of regressors; $\Theta_l := (\theta_l,\sigma_l)$ is the set of unknown model parameters that need to be estimated, in which $\theta_l := (\theta_{l,1},...,\theta_{l,n_l})$; $\hat{I}_l(\mathbf{x}_l)$ is an existing (if any) deterministic model for predicting the value of the lth indicator (e.g., the mean of the measured values of the indicator for all individuals); $\sigma_l\varepsilon_l$ is the model error term, in which σ_l is the standard deviation of the model error and is assumed to be independent of $\mathbf{x}_l$ (homoskedasticity assumption) and ε_l is a standard normal random variable (normality assumption). Different statistical techniques can be used to estimate the model parameters. A Bayesian approach might be best suited so that the model parameters can be updated as new data become available (Gardoni et al. 2002; Choe et al. 2007). To create parsimonious models, a model selection can be used to eliminate unimportant regressors (Gardoni et al. 2002; Tabandeh et al. 2017).

For the categorical indicators, Tabandeh et al. (2018) proposed a multinomial logit model form

$$P\left[I_l\left(\mathbf{x}_l,\Theta_l\right)=k\right]=\begin{cases}\dfrac{\exp\left(\sum_{j=1}^{n_l}\theta_{l,k,j}x_{l,j}\right)}{1+\sum_{k=1}^{K_l-1}\exp\left(\sum_{j=1}^{n_l}\theta_{l,k,j}x_{l,j}\right)}, & k=1,\ldots,K_l-1,\\[3ex]\dfrac{1}{1+\sum_{k=1}^{K_l-1}\exp\left(\sum_{j=1}^{n_l}\theta_{l,k,j}x_{l,j}\right)}, & k=K_l,\end{cases}\tag{4.2}$$

where $k=1,\ldots,K_l$ are the possible categories for the indicator and $P\left[I_l(\mathbf{x}_l,\Theta_l)=k\right]$ is the probability that $I_l = k$.

The indicators are time-varying since $\mathbf{x}_l$ generally changes with time. The measured values of the regressors can be used in the probabilistic models to assess the values of the indicators before a natural hazard occurs. The occurrence of a hazard changes the values of some or all of the regressors due to the damage to the built environment and the corresponding loss of functionality. Using the predictions of the values of the regressors after the hazard occurence gives new values of the indicators. The impact of the natural hazard can then be defined as the difference between the indicators before and after the hazard occurrence. As infrastructure recover their functionality, the values of the regressors changes again with time thus changing the values of the indicators during the duration of the recovery process.

An indicator could be in three possible states: acceptable, tolerable, or intolerable (Murphy & Gardoni 2008; Gardoni et al. 2018; Tabandeh et al. 2018). The acceptable threshold specifies the minimum level of capabilities that communities should allow over any period of time. It is a "necessary condition of justice for a public political arrangement is that it deliver to citizens a certain basic level of capability" (Nussbaum 2000). Murphy and Gardoni (2008) argued that a lower attainment should be allowed under special conditions such as in the immediate aftermath of a natural hazard. An indicator is in the tolerable state when it falls below the acceptable threshold but (a) is above the even lower tolerable threshold and (b) recovers in a sufficiently short time (Murphy & Gardoni 2008; Gardoni & Murphy 2018; Tabandeh et al. 2018). To know if an indicator has reached the acceptable threshold in a sufficiently short time, the recovery must be modeled. For example, it may be tolerable to live without access to clean water piped into a permanent residence for a few days following an earthquake (Guidotti et al. 2018) but not if the lack of potable water is prolonged, where water is critical for meeting physiological needs. To determine if the situation is tolerable or not, it is necessary to model the recovery of the water network. Defining the time threshold for tolerability can be left up to decision makers and the general public that is affected. Practically, these definitions may change across different communities and governments as a function of environment, social norms, and political systems. Section 4.5 discusses the definition of "sufficiently short time" as a community resilience goal.

4.3.3 Development of an aggregate measure of achievement

To define the state of well-being, the indicators need to be combined to create an aggregate measure of achievement. Because the capabilities are incommensurable (as discussed in

Section 4.3.1), the well-being for each individual can be seen as a series system where each capability (and the corresponding indicator) is a component of the system (Tabandeh et al. 2017). Following a system reliability approach (Gardoni 2017), the system fails if any component fails to reach a desired level.

4.3.4 Use of a dynamic Bayesian network for risk evaluation

Tabandeh et al. (2018) integrated the probabilistic models for the indicators (i.e., Equations (4.1)–(4.2)) into a Dynamic Bayesian Network. A Bayesian Network (BN) is a probabilistic graphical model that represents the statistical relation among a set of (random) variables by means of a directed acyclic graph. The graphical structure is defined by nodes and directed links where the nodes are the random variables and links represent the statistical relationship between them. In the BN terminology, a node u is a parent of the node v if (u,v) is a directed link from u to v. The probabilistic relationships between the notes are quantified by attaching Conditional Probability Table (CPT) to each node of a function as its parents. If a node has no parents (i.e. regressor nodes), a marginal probability table is used instead. Following Tabandeh et al. (2018), the CPTs are constructed using Equations (4.1) and (4.2). The BN is then generalized to a Dynamic BN (DBN) that accounts for the joint distribution of the random variables over time and models the recovery of well-being over the recovery time. The DBN graphically represents the statistical relation of well-being with indicators and their regressors over the recovery time. Figure 4.1 (adapted from Tabandeh et al. 2018) shows a generic BN for the well-being analysis at a given time t.

4.3.5 Dealing with relevant uncertainties and infrastructure (inter)dependencies

Components of critical infrastructure such as bridges, buildings, and power lines are vulnerable to physical damage from natural disasters and are part of larger complex infrastructure systems that are both interdependent and necessary for community well-being. Damage to a component in Network A could lead to loss in functionality of Network B. For example, if a substation in a power network is damaged, it may affect the functionality of water network that needs

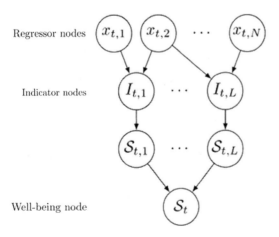

Figure 4.1 A generic BN for the well-being analysis.
Source: Adapted from Tabandeh et al. 2018.

power for its pumps. To have informative regressors that describe the functionality of salient infrastructure systems, it is necessary to have a methodology that translates the physical impact of a natural event onto particular components into a loss in functionality of the corresponding infrastructure system (and other dependent infrastructure systems). Since natural disasters have large degrees of uncertainty, the methodology should also be probabilistic.

An example of a probabilistic methodology to translate the physical damage into loss or reduction in functionality accounting for the dependencies and the relevant uncertainties can be found in Guidotti et al. (2016). The methodology provides an estimate of the functionality of infrastructure in the immediate aftermath of a natural hazard as well as during the recovery process. Specifically, recovery functions (Sharma et al. 2018) for the infrastructure components are incorporated in the methodology to model the recovery process and the change with time of the functionality of the infrastructure.

4.4 Definition of quantification metrics

As previously noted, indicators are chosen because capabilities are not easily quantifiable. These indicators can serve as quantification metrics for the different capabilities and the corresponding functionings that can be measured through the disaster impact and recovery. Issues with data availability make it difficult to create ideal indicators and regressors. For example, it is generally desirable to have the regressors at the household level. However, it is often not possible to obtain socio-economic information such as income, race, or age at the household level. Additionally, the complexity of capabilities makes it difficult to find an indicator that is always representative given differences among communities in the functionality of infrastructure and the socio-economic conditions before the occurrence of a hazardous event. For instance, a desirable indicator for having access to clean water in a developed country may be access to potable water piped into a dwelling whereas for a developing country it may be more beneficial to examine different sources of potable water such as water tanks or wells. Therefore, indicators need to be selected based on data availability and relevance to the region of interest. Selecting data sources for indicators/regressors is crucial for creating accurate predictive models. The data source should be reliable and updated frequently so that the models can be used in the future. An example data source may be the US Census which is updated regularly and available to the public. If real-time data becomes available, Bayesian updating could be used to update the models.

Factors such as seasonality and scale of population should also be taken into consideration. Some regions have varying populations at different times of year (e.g., touristic cities, college towns) so it may be necessary to have multiple data sources or models to represent the location of interest at the time of interest. Different geographic scales should also be treated differently. When looking at a location of interest which spans a large region such as a state or statistical area, data sources that span over counties or cities can be used directly. If the location of interest is smaller, statistical techniques can be used to incorporate data from a larger scale into a region at a smaller scale. For example, count data at the census block aggregation can be assigned to individual houses using statistical methods accounting for the relevant uncertainties in the de-aggregation process (Rosenheim et al. 2018).

4.5 Definition of resilience and sustainability goals

In this section, we introduce normative principles to define community resilience and sustainability goals. We also discuss some common challenges decision makers may face when defining these goals and provide some recommendations/solution strategies.

4.5.1 Defining resilience goals based on acceptability and tolerability limits

After quantification metrics for well-being have been defined, they can be evaluated before, immediately after, and throughout the recovery. The values of these quantification metrics can then be used to define an impact as acceptable, tolerable, or intolerable as defined in Section 4.3.2.

The United States National Research Council (2012) defines resilience as "[t]he ability to prepare and plan for, absorb, recover from, or more successfully adapt to actual or potential adverse events." In terms of the CA, resilience is concerned with how quickly the indicators can return to their pre-hazard condition or better. Resilience goals can be expressed in terms of what constitutes a sufficiently fast recovery of the capabilities/indicators. For example, a possible resilience goal is to have the entire community in an acceptable state in 1.5 years following an earthquake of a given magnitude. To meet this goal, the aggregate measure (discussed in Section 4.3.3) should be in the acceptable state for all households in the region of interest.

The spatial distribution of the quantification metrics can be useful for decision makers to see which areas of a community are likely to recover more quickly and which ones are more likely to recovery more slowly. Decision makers can then decide if the current predictions of recovery time matches the resilience goals.

4.5.2 Defining sustainability goals based on acceptability, tolerability and distribution limits

Gardoni and Murphy (2008, 2018) highlight three generally recognized normative considerations related to sustainability: (a) environmental justice; (b) global (or distributive) justice; and (c) intergenerational justice. Sustainability goals can be created to address these considerations (Gardoni & Murphy 2018). As with resilience, modeling recovery is an integral part also of sustainability in the context of risk analysis because of the possible exacerbation of inequalities that can arise during recovery.

Environmental justice is noteworthy not only for the environment itself, but recognizes the fact that a healthy environment is linked to the well-being of individuals. For example, air pollution is not only harmful to the environment per se, but for the individuals living in the polluted region. In a CA, capabilities/indicators can be selected to capture the role of natural ecosystems on the well-being of individuals (Gardoni & Murphy 2018). Sustainability goals concerning environmental justice can then be created by (1) defining acceptability and tolerability limits of these environmental capabilities/indicators, and/or (2) putting time thresholds on the recovery of environmental regressors or the dependent capabilities/indicators.

Global justice and intergenerational justice link sustainability with social justice which deals with inequalities across distributions in the economic, political, and social domains (Gardoni & Murphy 2018). Global justice is concerned with inequality in distributions across groups of individuals or communities, while intergenerational justice is concerned with inequality across different generations of people. For the social justice portion of sustainability, the distribution of capabilities should be examined. Sustainability goals for distributive and intergenerational justice can then be created to prevent unfair distributions of impacts and of recovery opportunities across communities and generations. These goals can be specified in terms of ranges of permissible inequalities (or inequality thresholds) across the distributions of capabilities/indicators in space and time. For example, it is expected that there will be some level of exacerbation of preexisting inequalities in the metrics in the aftermath of a natural hazard (Peacock & Girard 1997). If the exacerbation is significant, such exacerbation might be permissible if it is temporary and reversed in a sufficiently short time (Gardoni & Murphy 2018).

4.6 Advantages of a capability approach

First, the CA focuses directly on the impact of a hazard on individuals' well-being by examining the hazard's effects on individual capabilities. By looking directly at capabilities instead of estimating immediate impacts such as physical damage or fatalities, the CA provides a normative framework that can be used to examine more broadly and holistically the effects of a natural hazard and capture both the negative impact and the positive impact (e.g., opportunities that comes from rebuilding). Additionally, the CA rejects the assumption that dimensions of well-being are substitutable (i.e., the approach rejects the premise that an improvement in opportunity for education can compensate for a lack of an opportunity to find adequate shelter). The capability approach also avoids the moral dilemma and distortions introduced by trying to convert every consequence into a monetary value to create an aggregate measure of achievement (Gardoni & Murphy 2009). Instead, each consequence is analyzed and evaluated separately by examining the effect on each individual capability.

Second, the predictive models account for social vulnerability (through socio-economic regressors) and can be linked naturally to results from a regional risk analysis (through the regressors that define the functionality of the physical infrastructure). Much work has focused on either physical infrastructure modeling or the identification of socio-economic factors that can influence community vulnerability. A CA can integrate the state-of-the-art models and findings from both fields of research to predict the impact over time of natural hazards considering all of the relevant factors. These models can better capture the underlying inequalities that exist before the natural hazard and can show how these inequalities might be exacerbated by a natural hazard and affect the recovery. In many cases, more vulnerable communities not only experience higher impacts but are plagued by slower recoveries (Olshansky & Johnson 2010). By considering the role of the physical systems on the societal impact, a CA provides levers that decision makers can use to foster better mitigation and recovery strategies.

Third, the acceptability and tolerability thresholds allow for easy communication with the public. Since the language of acceptability and tolerability can be easily understood, there is an opportunity for the public to democratically decide on thresholds and/or disagree with thresholds created by decision makers (Murphy & Gardoni 2006; Gardoni & Murphy 2018). Public participation in the creation of acceptability and tolerability thresholds is crucial to ensure that the metrics created are fair and equitable. Additionally, it allows for a public endorsement of the level of acceptable risk (Stallen et al. 1998). Similarly there can be a democratic debate on the permissible levels of inequality (inequality threshold) in the capabilities among individuals.

Finally, the CA is adaptable and scalable. The formulation is general and can be used to predict the well-being of each household if the information has a sufficient level of granularity. The adaptability of the method is evidenced by its use in a variety of fields including development and food security (Burchi & Muro 2012; UNDP 2016). As the interdependency across these fields becomes more apparent, it is important to have frameworks that are consistent. Using a CA in risk and resilience analysis allows for decision and policy makers to make more informed value judgements.

4.7 Example considering a real community

To illustrate some of the concepts discussed in this chapter, we consider the city of Seaside, Oregon subjected to a hypothetical seismic hazard. Seaside is a coastal community with a population that fluctuates between 6,000 and 14,000 people depending on the time of year. Based on counts from the 2010 Decennial Census, 6,440 inhabitants are assigned to various buildings throughout the city (Guidotti et al. 2018). The seismic hazard has magnitude $M_w = 7.0$ and an epicenter located 25 km southwest of the city. Ground Motion Prediction Equations (Boore & Atkinson 2008) are used to generate maps of the ground motion intensity measures over the relevant study region.

In this example, two quantification metrics are selected to illustrate the use of the CA. First, the quantification metric of having access to a permanent residence is used to assess the capability of "Being Sheltered" in the immediate aftermath of the seismic event. This metric is used to illustrate the prediction of the values of a metric. In this case the metric is a function of the predicted structural damage of residential buildings and the predicted probability of people dislocation. Then, the indicator of having access to a hospital is used to assess the capability of "Maintaining Health" through the recovery of the transportation network. This quantification metric is used to show how a resilience goal can be used in risk evaluation.

4.7.1 Being sheltered

For this capability, the selected quantification metric is having access to a permanent residence. For a given intensity measure at the site of a residential building, fragility curves (Gardoni et al. 2002, 2017) are used to find the probability that the building is in one of four different damage states (FEMA 2015). The mean damage is then calculated following Bai et al. (2009). Figure 4.2 shows the mean damage for each residential building in Seaside. The definitions of insignificant, moderate, heavy, and complete used in Figure 4.2 are according to Bai et al. (2009).

After the damage to the buildings is estimated, it is necessary to predict if people can dislocate from their original residence. Dislocation of a household is a function of the probability mass function of the structural damage of the building of residence and socio-economic factors including race. The probability of dislocation of a household is estimated using a logistic model (Guidotti et al. 2018). Figure 4.3 shows the predicted probabilities of population dislocation.

The structural damage and the ability of people to dislocate are then used to define the indicator for the capability of being sheltered. Higher values of the indicator represent the ability of an individual to stay at his/her permanent residence (this corresponds to not having significant structural damage), if there is significant structural damage the indicator assumes a lower value if the individual is able to dislocate to a temporary residence, and an even lower value if the individual is not able to dislocate to a temporary residence (the information on the ability of an individual to dislocate comes from the dislocation model.) Figure 4.4 shows the probability that people have access to a permanent residence.

4.7.2 Maintaining Health

The second capability considered in this example is "Maintaining Health". For this capability, the selected indicator is having access to a hospital. We monitor the access to a hospital of

Figure 4.2 Mean damage to buildings.

individuals over time as well as the inequalities in the access. Seaside has one hospital located inside the city that is assumed to be the primary hospital for residents. An additional hospital located about 15 miles north of Seaside is also considered despite being outside the city boundaries. Within Seaside, all the local roads are modeled, while, outside of Seaside we only consider the major roads. We assume residents would only use major roads to go to the northern hospital. Modeling only the major roads outside of Seaside greatly reduces the computational time, however, modeling all roads would be methodologically the same thing. The bridges along the roads are assumed to be the vulnerable elements in the transportation network to a seismic hazard. Information about the bridges is found from the National Bridge Inventory (NBI), which is maintained and updated by the US Department of Transportation (www.fhwa. dot.gov/bridge/nbi/ascii.cfm). Geographic information for each bridge is available as well as important bridge characteristics including geometry, year built, construction material, and maintenance responsibility. Information on the roads are obtained from the Census Bureau

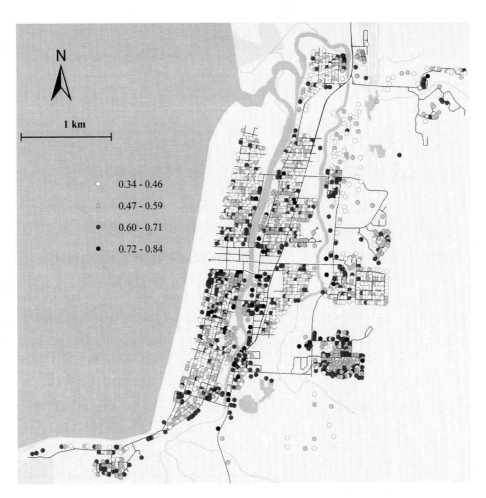

Figure 4.3 Probability of household dislocation.

(www.census.gov/geo/maps-data/data/tiger.html). Figure 4.5 shows the considered transportation network and the location of the two hospitals.

To determine if the residents have access to a hospital, we conduct a connectivity analysis of the transportation network. For this example, we assume that the hospitals are still functional following the example earthquake. A transportation network can be represented using nodes (points of interest, i.e. origins and destinations) and edges based on the basics of graph theory (Liu & Frangopol 2005; Ruohonen 2013; Guidotti et al. 2018). In this example, the residential buildings and the two hospitals are the considered nodes and the roads are considered to be the edges. Bridges are modeled as a potential barriers along the edges. If a bridge is damaged, it can disconnect the corresponding edge and potentially interrupt the connectivity between nodes. When a bridge is repaired (either temporarily or permanently), and the barrier is removed.

We assess the vulnerability of the bridges using fragility functions (Gardoni 2017). Specifically, we use physics-based fragilities from Gardoni et al. (2002, 2003) for the reinforced

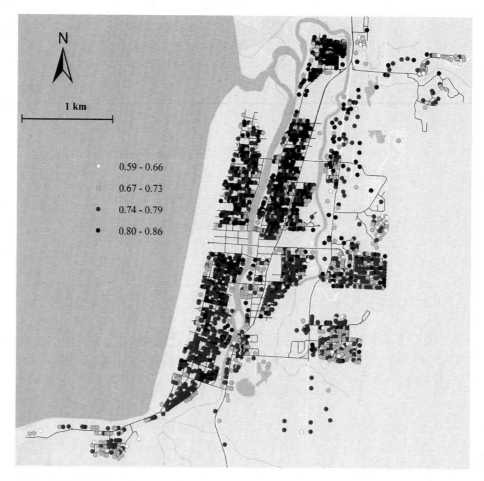

Figure 4.4 Probability that a household has access to a permanent residence.

concrete bridges. Using the NBI data, bridges are separated by year built (pre- and post-1990) to determine if they were seismically designed or not. Within Seaside, the blueprints of each specific bridge are used to find the design variables such as span length, concrete strength and deck width needed in the physics-based fragilities. For missing data such as reinforcement ratio, we use typical bridge design parameters from the Oregon Department of Transportation (ODOT) ((www.oregon.gov/ODOT/Bridge/Pages/Bridge-Design-Manual.aspx) for pre- and post-1990. For bridges outside of Seaside, typical design parameters from ODOT are used. We find the fragility functions for the complete damage state using the probabilistic capacity models in Gardoni et al. (2002). To find the fragility functions for slight, moderate, and heavy damage states, we considered the drift capacity of 1, 2 and 4% respectively following Simon et al. (2010). For the steel, wood, and pre-stressed concrete bridges, we use empirical fragility functions from HAZUS-MH (FEMA 2015).

Immediately following the seismic hazard, the population that needs access to the hospital are those that are injured. To estimate the population at risk of injury, we use the

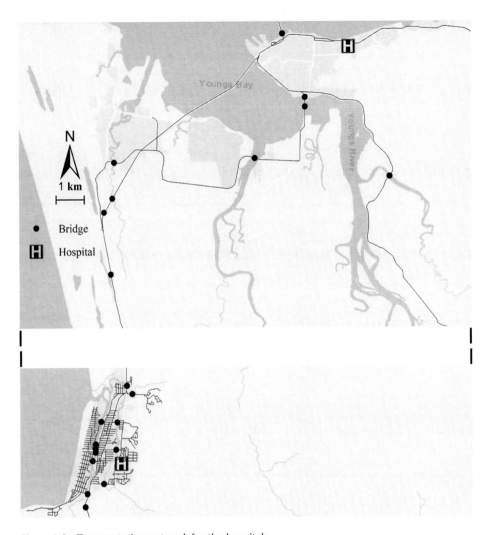

Figure 4.5   Transportation network for the hospitals.

procedure in HAZUS-MH (FEMA 2015). Casualties are grouped into four levels of severity. Severity 1 is for injuries that require basic medical aid such as bandages or observations (no hospitalization necessary); Severity 2 is for injuries that involve medical technology such as x-rays or surgery (but are not life-threatening); Severity 3 includes injuries that are life-threatening; and Severity 4 is for instantaneous mortality. Severities 2 and 3 include the severe injuries that need access to a hospital. We write the probability that at least a casualty in a building is of Severities 2 or 3 given the set of demand variables $\mathbf{s}$ (i.e., hazard intensity measure) $P(S_2 \cup S_3 | \mathbf{s})$ as

$$P\left(S_2 \cup S_3 | \mathbf{s}\right) = P\left(S_2 | \mathbf{s}\right) + P\left(S_3 | \mathbf{s}\right), \tag{4.3}$$

63

where $P(S_2 \,|\, \mathbf{s})$ and $P(S_3 \,|\, \mathbf{s})$ are the probabilities of having at least one individual having an injury of Severity 2 and Severity 3 respectively in a building experiencing $\mathbf{s}$.

The damage states are insignificant, moderate, heavy and complete already discussed in Section 4.7.1. Following the procedure in HAZUS-MH, we further divide the complete damage state into collapse and no collapse, which gives a total of five damage states. We use the total probability rule to obtain the probability that at least one individual in a building experiences an injury of Severity m given $\mathbf{s}$, $P(S_m \,|\, \mathbf{s})$, as follows:

$$P\left(S_m \middle| \mathbf{s}\right) = \sum_{n=1}^{5} P\left(S_m \middle| DS_n\right) \times P\left(DS_n \middle| \mathbf{s}\right), \tag{4.4}$$

where $P(S_m \,|\, DS_n)$ is the probability that at least one individual experiences an injury of Severity m given that the building is in the nth damage state, which is obtained from HAZUS-MH (FEMA 2015); and $P(DS_n \,|\, \mathbf{s})$ is the probability of being in each damage state obtained from the differences between the fragility functions following the procedure in Bai et al. (2009).

Immediately following the earthquake, we conducted a connectivity analysis with the households that are at risk modeled as origins and the two hospitals modeled as destinations. Figure 4.6 shows the accessibility to a hospital for households at risk for injury (Figure 4.6a shows the locations of the closed bridges and Figure 4.6b shows the locations of the households).

After the immediate impact, the analysis moves into the recovery of the transportation network. As the individual bridges recover, the connectivity between nodes also restores. We can use the total probability rule to find the expected recovery time t given $\mathbf{s}$

$$E[t\,|\,\mathbf{s}] = \sum_{i=1}^{5} E\left[t\,|\,DS_i\right] \times P\left(DS_i \,|\, \mathbf{s}\right), \tag{4.5}$$

where $E[t\,|\,\mathbf{s}]$ is the expected recovery time given $\mathbf{s}$; $E[t\,|\,DS_i]$ is the expected recovery time given the damage state obtained from HAZUS-MH (FEMA 2015); and $P(DS_i \,|\, \mathbf{s})$ is the probability of being in each damage state obtained from the fragility functions. For edge, e_k the recovery time is defined as the maximum recovery time for the bridges on it. In this example, we use

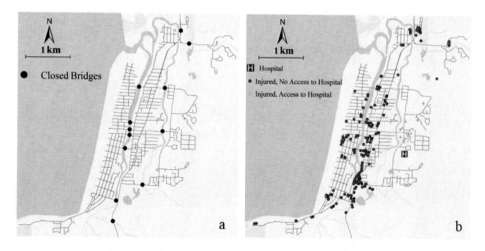

Figure 4.6 Accessibility to a hospital for households at risk for injury.

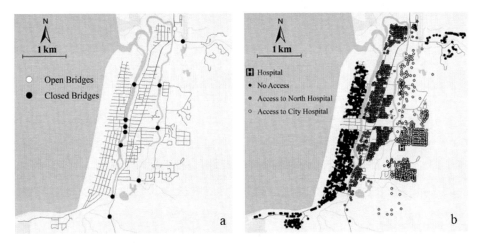

Figure 4.7 Hospital access on day 90.

the ownership of the bridges to determine the allocation of resources (available construction crews). It is assumed that more federal bridges can be fixed simultaneously than city bridges.

According to the assumed recovery plan, the northern route is fixed first (through a combination of temporary and permanent bridge repairs.) By Day 90, this open route gives some residents of Seaside access to the northern hospital. However, the bridges inside Seaside are still damaged at this time so the residents on the west portion of town still do not have access to a hospital (Figure 4.7a shows the locations of the open/closed bridges and Figure 4.7b shows the locations of the buildings). It is assumed that the bridges within Seaside cannot be fixed until after the northern route is open since some resources (construction materials and workers) might come from outside of the city boundaries (the southern route experiences mode damage and so it is expected to recovery after the northern route). By Day 120, we expect that two bridges within Seaside will be repaired giving close to complete access to a hospital to the residents of Seaside (Figure 4.8a shows the locations of the open/closed bridges and Figure 4.8b shows the locations of the buildings). By Day 370, Seaside's southern bridge is expected to re-open giving complete access to the hospital to all residents. Therefore, the complete recovery time for the indicator "Having Access to a Hospital," that represents the capability of "Maintaining Health" is 370 days. Figures 4.7 and 4.8 show that different parts of Seaside regain access at different times. These results can be used to evaluate the consideration of global justice.

4.8 Conclusions

Natural hazards often exacerbate social inequalities that exist in communities before the hazard occurs. To mitigate these effects, decision makers create community resilience goals and use quantification metrics to describe societal well-being. This chapter reviewed a capability approach for well-being assessment after a natural hazard. The approach is general and can be applied to a multitude of locations and hazards. The CA provides a rational framework for quantifying the impact of a natural hazard by examining the natural hazard's impact on the genuine opportunities of individuals. These opportunities are known as capabilities. The indicators chosen (to quantify the capabilities) can be probabilistic and properly account for the inherent uncertainties. Models are presented which can predict the values of the indicators as a

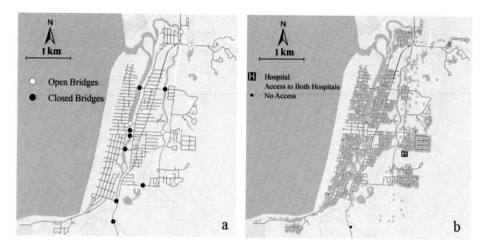

Figure 4.8 Hospital access on day 120.

function of regressors. The indicators can also combine regressors from the built environment with social vulnerability to accurately estimate the unequal consequences that natural hazards inflict on communities. Regressors which come from the built environment should represent the functionality of relevant infrastructure systems while regressors which come from social vulnerability should be theoretically justified or be supported by empirical evidence. Within the CA framework, this chapter presented community resilience and sustainability goals that can be useful for decision makers. Resilience goals are concerned with the rapidity of recovery while sustainability goals are concerned with equity in recovery with respect to the environment and individuals. To illustrate, the chapter presented two quantification metrics for a real community.

Acknowledgement

This work was supported in part by the Graduate College at the University of Illinois at Urbana Champaign, the Civil and Environmental Engineering Department at the University of Illinois at Urbana Champaign and the SURGE program at the University of Illinois at Urbana Champaign. Opinions and findings presented are those of the writers and do not necessarily reflect the views of the sponsor.

References

Bai J-W., Hueste M., and Gardoni P. (2009) "Probabilistic assessment of structural damage due to earthquakes for buildings in mid-America," *Journal of Structural Engineering*, 135(10): 1155–63.

Bates F. and Peacock W.G. (1992) "Measuring disaster impact on household living conditions," *International Journal of Mass Emergencies and Disasters*, 10(1): 133–60.

Boore D.M. and Atkinson G.M. (2008) "Ground-motion prediction equations for the average horizontal component of PGA, PGV, and 5%-damped PSA at spectral periods between 0.01 s and 10.0 s," *Earthquake Spectra*, 24(1): 99–138.

Burchi F. and Muro P. (2012) "A Human Development and Capability Approach to Food Security: Conceptual Framework and Informational Basis." Background Working Paper no. 9 to the Africa Human Development Report, UNDP.

Choe D., Gardoni P., and Rosowsky D. (2007) "Closed-form fragility estimates, parameter sensitivity and Bayesian updating for RC columns," *ASCE Journal of Engineering Mechanics*, 133(7): 833–43.

Choe D., Gardoni P., Rosowsky D., and Haukaas T. (2009) "Seismic fragility estimates for reinforced concrete bridges subject to corrosion," *Structural Safety*, 31: 275–83.

Doorn N., Gardoni P., and Murphy C. (2018) "A multidisciplinary definition and evaluation of resilience: The role of social justice in defining resilience," *Sustainable and Resilient Infrastructure*, DOI: 10.1080/23789689.2018.1428162.

Federal Emergency Management Agency (FEMA) (2015) HAZUS 2.1 technical and user's manuals, available at www.fema.gov/media-library/assets/documents/24609 (last accessed August 11, 2018).

Fothergill A., Maestas E.G.M., and Darlington J.D. (1999) "Race, ethnicity and disasters in the United States: A review of the literature," *Disasters*, 23(2): 156–73.

Frangopol D.M. and Bocchini P. (2012) "Bridge network performance, maintenance and optimization under uncertainty: accomplishments and challenges," *Structure and Infrastructure Engineering*, 8(4): 341–56.

Gardoni P. (ed.) (2017) *Risk and Reliability Analysis: Theory and Applications*. New York: Springer.

Gardoni P. and LaFave J. (eds.) (2016) *Multi-hazard Approaches to Civil Infrastructure Engineering*. New York: Springer.

Gardoni P. and Murphy C. (2008) "Recovery from natural and man-made disasters as capabilities restoration and enhancement," *International Journal of Sustainable Development and Planning*, 3(4): 1–17.

Gardoni P. and Murphy C. (2009) "Capabilities-based approach to measuring the societal impacts of natural and man-made hazards in risk analysis," *ASCE Natural Hazards Review*, 10(2): 29–37.

Gardoni P. and Murphy C. (2010) "Gauging the societal impacts of natural disasters using a capabilities-based approach," *Disasters*, 34(3): 619–36.

Gardoni P. and Murphy C. (2013) "A capability approach for seismic risk analysis and management," in Solomon Tesfamariam and Katsu Goda (eds.), *Handbook of Seismic Risk Analysis and Management of Civil Infrastructure Systems*. Cambridge, UK: Woodhead Publishing Ltd.

Gardoni P. and Murphy C. (2014) "A scale of risk," *Risk Analysis*, 34(7): 1208–27.

Gardoni P. and Murphy C. (2018) "Society-based design: promoting societal well-being by designing sustainable and resilient infrastructure" *Sustainable and Resilient Infrastructure*, DOI: 10.1080/23789689.2018.1448667.

Gardoni P., Der Kiureghian A., and Mosalam K.M. (2002) "Probabilistic capacity models and fragility estimates for reinforced concrete columns based on experimental observations," *Journal of Engineering Mechanics*, 128(10): 1024–38.

Gardoni P., Mosalam K.M., and Der Kiureghian A. (2003) "Probabilistic seismic demand models and fragility estimates for RC bridges," *Journal of Earthquake Engineering*, 7(Special Issue 1): 79–106.

Gardoni P., Murphy C., and Rowell A. (eds.) (2016) *Societal Risk Management of Natural Hazards*. New York: Springer.

Guidotti R. and Gardoni P. (2018) "Modeling of interdependent critical infrastructure for regional risk and resilience analysis," in Gardoni P. (ed.), *Handbook on Sustainable and Resilient Infrastructure*. New York: Routledge.

Guidotti R., Chmielewski H., Unnikrishnan V., Gardoni P., McAllister T., and van de Lindt J.W. (2016) "Modeling the resilience of critical infrastructure: The role of network dependencies," *Sustainable and Resilient Infrastructure*, 1(3–4): 153–68.

Guidotti R., Gardoni P., and Chen Y. (2017) "Network reliability analysis with link and nodal weights and auxiliary nodes," *Structural Safety*, 65: 12–26.

Guidotti R., Gardoni P., and Rosenheim N. (2018) "Integration of physical infrastructure and social systems in communities," *Reliability Engineering and System Safety* (submitted).

Guikema S. and Gardoni P. (2009) "Reliability estimation for networks of reinforced concrete bridges," *ASCE Journal of Infrastructure Systems*, 15: 61–9.

Kajitani Y., Okada N., and Tatano, H. (2005) "Measuring quality of human community life by spatial-temporal age group distributions-case study of recovery process in a disaster-affected region," *Natural Hazards Review*, 6(1): 41–7.

Kang W.H., Song J., and Gardoni P. (2008) "Matrix-based system reliability method and applications to bridge networks," *Reliability Engineering and System Safety*, 93: 1584–93.

Lee Y.-J., Song J., Gardoni P., and Lim H.-W. (2011) "Post-hazard flow capacity of bridge transportation networks considering structural deterioration of bridges," *Structure and Infrastructure Engineering*, 7(7): 509–21.

Liu M. and Frangopol DM (2005) "Balancing connectivity of deteriorating bridge networks and long-term maintenance cost through optimization," *Journal of Bridge Engineering*, 10: 468–81.

Mardfekri M. and Gardoni P. (2013) "Probabilistic demand models and fragility estimates for offshore wind turbine support structures," *Engineering Structures*, 52: 478–87.

Mardfekri M. and Gardoni P. (2014) "Multi-hazard reliability assessment of offshore wind turbines," *Wind Energy.*

Mardfekri M., Gardoni P., and Bisadi V. (2015) "Service reliability of offshore wind turbines" *International Journal of Sustainable Energy*, 34(7): 468–84.

Masozera M., Bailey M., and Kerchner C. (2007) "Distribution of impacts of natural disasters across income groups: A case study of New Orleans," *Ecological Economics*, 63(2–3): 299–306.

Murphy C. and Gardoni P. (2006) "The role of society in engineering risk analysis: a Capabilities-based Approach," *Risk Analysis*, 26(4): 1073–83.

Murphy C. and Gardoni P. (2007) "Determining public policy and resource allocation priorities for mitigating natural hazards: A capabilities-based approach," *Science and Engineering Ethics*, 13(4): 489–504.

Murphy C. and Gardoni P. (2008) "The acceptability and the tolerability of societal risks: A capabilities-based approach," *Science and Engineering Ethics*, 14(1): 77–92.

Murphy C. and Gardoni P. (2010) "Assessing capability instead of achieved functionings in risk analysis," *Journal of Risk Research*, 13(2): 137–47.

Murphy C. and Gardoni P. (2011a) "Design, risk and capabilities," in Jeroen van den Hoven and Ilse Oosterlaken (eds.), *Human Capabilities, Technology, and Design*. Heidelberg: Springer.

Murphy C. and Gardoni P. (2011b) "Evaluating the source of the risks associated with natural events," *Res Publica*, 17(2): 125–40.

Murphy C. and Gardoni P. (2012) "The capability approach in risk analysis," in Sabine Roeser (ed.), *Handbook of Risk Theory*. Heidelberg: Springer.

Nocera F. and Gardoni P. (2018) "Modeling business interruption as a function of the reliability and resilience of physical infrastructure and social systems," in Gardoni P (ed.), *Handbook on Sustainable and Resilient Infrastructure*. New York: Routledge.

Nocera F., Tabandeh A., Guidotti R., Boakye J., and Gardoni P. (2018) "Physics-based fragility and recovery functions: Mathematical formulation and their relevance in reliability and resilience analysis of transportation networks," in Gardoni P (ed.), *Handbook on Sustainable and Resilient Infrastructure*. New York: Routledge.

Nussbaum M. (2000a) "Aristotle, politics, and human capabilites: A response to Antony, Arneson, Charlesworth, and Mulgan," *Ethics*, 111(1): 102–40.

Nussbaum M. (2000b) *Woman and Human Development: The Capabilites Approach*, Cambridge: Cambridge University Press.

Nussbaum M. (2001) "Adaptive preferences and women's options," *Econ Philos*, 17: 67–88.

Olshansky R. and Johnson L. (2010) *Clear as Mud: Planning for the Rebuilding of New Orleans*. American Planning Association, Planners Press.

Peacock W.G. and Girard C. (1997) "Ethnic and racial inequalities in hurricane damage and insurance settlements," in W.G. Peacock, B.H. Morrow, and H. Gladwin (eds.), *Hurricane Andrew: Ethnicity, Gender and the Sociology of Disasters*. London: Routledge.

Peacock W.G., Killian C.D., and Bates F.L. (1987) "The effects of disaster damage and housing aid on household recovery following the 1976 Guatemalan earthquake," *The International Journal of Mass Emergencies and Disasters*, 5(1): 63–88.

Ramamoorthy K.S., Gardoni P., and Bracci M.J. (2006) "Probabilistic demand models and fragility curves for reinforced concrete frames," *ASCE Journal of Structural Engineering*, 132(10): 1563–72.

Ramamoorthy K.S., Gardoni P., and Bracci M.J. (2008) "Seismic fragility and confidence bounds for gravity load designed reinforced concrete frames of varying height," *ASCE Journal of Structural Engineering*, 134(4): 639–50.

Raworth K. and Stewart D. (2003) "Critiques of the human development index: A review," in S. Fukuda-Parr and A.K. Shiva Kumar (eds.), *Readings in Human Development* (pp. 140–52), Oxford, UK: Oxford University Press.

Robeyns I. (2006) "The capability approach in practice," *The Journal of Political Philsophophy*, 14(3): 351–76.

Rosenheim N., Guidotti R., and Gardoni P. (2018) "Integration of detailed household characteristic data with critical infrastructure and its implementation to post-hazard resilience modeling," *Sustainable and Resilient Infrastrcuture* (in preparation).

Ruohonen K. (2013) *Graph theory*. Tampereen teknillinen yliopisto. Originally titled Graafiteoria, lecture notes translated by Tamminen J., Lee K.C., and Piché R, available online at http://math.tut.fi/~ruohonen/GT_English.pdf (last accessed August 11, 2018).

Sen A. (1989) "Development as capabilities expansion," *J Dev Plan*, 19: 41–58.

Sen A. (1992) *Inequality reexxamined*. Cambridge, MA: Harvard University Press.

Sen A. (1993) "Capability and well-being," in Nussbaum M. and Sen A. (eds.), *The Quality of Life* (pp. 30–53), Oxford: Clarendon Press.

Sen A. (1999a) *Commodoties and Capabilities*. Oxford: Oxford University Press.

Sen A. (1999b) *Development as Freedom*. New York: Anchor Books.

Sharma N., Tabandeh A., and Gardoni P. (2018) "Resilience analysis: A mathematical formulation to model resilience of engineering systems," *Sustainable and Resilient Infrastructure*, 3(2), 49–67.

Simon J., Bracci J.M., and Gardoni P. (2010) "Seismic response and fragility of deteriorated reinforced concrete bridges," *ASCE Journal of Structural Engineering*, 136: 1273–81.

Stallen P.J.M., van Hengel W., and Jorissen R. (1998) "Summary of the issues discussed," in R.E. Jorissen and P.J.M. Stallen (eds.), *Quantified Societal Risk and Policy Making: Technology, Risk, and Society* (pp. 212–29), Dordrecht: Kluwer Academic Publishers.

Tabandeh A. and Gardoni P. (2015) "Empirical Bayes approach for developing hierarchical probabilistic predictive models and its application to the seismic reliability analysis of FRP-retrofitted RC bridges," *ASCE-ASME Journal of Risk and Uncertainty in Engineering Systems, Part A: Civil Enginering*, 1(2): 04015002.

Tabandeh A. and Gardoni P. (2014) "Probabilistic capacity models and fragility esimates for RC columns retrofitted with FRP composites," *Engineering Structures*, 74: 13–22.

Tabandeh A., Gardoni P., and Murphy C. (2017) "Reliability-based capability approach: A system reliability formulation for the capability approach," *Risk Analysis*, 38(2): 410–24.

Tabandeh, A., Gardoni, P., Murphy, C., and Myers, N. (2018) "Societal risk and resilience analysis: Dynamic Bayesian network formulation of a capability approach," *ASCE- ASME Journal of Risk and Uncertainty in Engineering Systems, Part A: Civil Engineering*, DOI: 10.1061/AJRUA6.0000996.

UNDP (United Nations Development Program) (2016) *Human Development 2016*. New York: Oxford University Press.

United States National Research Council (2012) *Disaster Resilience: A National Imperitive*. Washington DC: The National Academies Press.

5

Structural engineering dilemmas, resilient EPCOT, and other perspectives on the road to engineering resilience

Michel Bruneau[1] and Andrei M. Reinhorn[2]

[1] 130 KETTER HALL, DEPT. OF CIVIL, STRUCTURAL AND ENVIRONMENTAL ENGINEERING, UNIVERSITY AT BUFFALO, BUFFALO, NY, 14260, USA; TEL: (716) 645–3398; BRUNEAU@BUFFALO.EDU (CORRESPONDING AUTHOR)

[2] 142 KETTER HALL, DEPT. OF CIVIL, STRUCTURAL AND ENVIRONMENTAL ENGINEERING, UNIVERSITY AT BUFFALO, BUFFALO, NY, 14260, USA; REINHORN@BUFFALO.EDU

5.1 Introduction

The first time the authors heard the word resilience used in a professional context was in 2002 when participating as members of a Multidisciplinary Center for Earthquake Engineering Research (MCEER) Task Group that was mandated to identify the most pressing challenge to be addressed by earthquake engineering research for decades forward. As the main outcome of this effort, the need to establish "earthquake resilient communities" was determined to be the most important priority to enhance the state-of-the-art and state-of-practice in this field; the proposed framework that resulted from this process is documented in Bruneau et al. (2003). Little did the authors of this document know that resilience was then to become a buzzword that would drive research and implementation activities to the extent it is today throughout the entire world.

In the 15 years following the pioneering work of that Task Group, major initiatives conducted under the banner of "resilience" of critical (and non-critical) infrastructures have appeared almost everywhere. To cite a few examples, San Francisco celebrated resilience weekend in 2003, Tokyo established an initiative for a "lower carbon and resilient city," New York used "a stronger and more resilient New York" as one of its logos, and the Rockefeller foundation established the "100 resilient cities" initiative. Even within the professional earthquake engineering community, the 2013 Distinguished Lecturer Award was given to Mary Comerio for her lecture on "resilience and engineering challenge," and the byline of the 16th World Conference in Earthquake Engineering was "Resilience, the new challenge in earthquake engineering" (which, interestingly, could be interpreted in more than one way).

The purpose here is to provide some perspectives on what (in the minds of two of the authors that were involved in the pioneering work on resilience) are important dimensions to consider in resilience-research to be relevant to the definition of disaster resilience as originally conceived, and that should be considered in the formulation of resilience frameworks. Furthermore, building on those perspectives, the objective here is to highlight some challenges that exist, from a structural engineering perspective, to achieve disaster resilient communities. Focus here is on seismic resilience, with an understanding that much of the enunciated principles could be adapted to encompass other hazards and disasters.

5.2 Dilution of resilience's essence: The need to focus on functionality

In the span of 15 years, "resilience" has grown from a rarely used word intended to describe the "ability" to recover from a trauma, stress, or deformation, to become an overly used "buzz word," even in the fields of disaster research. Informally assessing the emerging popularity of the term can be done by Google searches (not rigorously a scientific approach, it is nonetheless informative). In July 2016, searches on the word "resilience" alone returned 47,000,000 "hits" on the internet, up from 7,880,000 six years earlier. Most significantly, combining the words "Obama" and "Resilience" returned nearly ¾ million hits, up from roughly 0.4 million hits six years earlier, which is not surprising since President Obama issued a presidential directive requiring all federal agencies to implement policies enhancing resilience (White House 2013). When searching for the combination of "engineering resilience," 17,300 results were found, up from 6,200 six years earlier. The combination "quantifying resilience" was only found 2470 times, up from 953 six years earlier, and the combination "quantification of engineering resilience" was only found three times, up from only one result six years earlier (a Google search returning a single hit is called a "Googlewack," which is a rare event). Interestingly, the numbers of hits obtained from these searches show that results have approximately tripled from 2010 to 2016, except for the case of "resilience" alone, which has increased six-fold.

The above results also indicate that activities focusing on the quantification of resilience may not have been as extensive as one may wish, from an engineering perspective. Furthermore, the immense number of hit returned by the above search on "resilience" suggests an inordinate use of the term, and possibly more definitions than the term warrants; perusal of some of the hits indeed revealed a considerable diversity in what is considered to be "resilience."

In one example that caught the eyes of the authors, as an example of resilience that maybe defies quantification, the US Department of State has a web page devoted to the definition of resilience (US Department of State 2017). There, following a general definition of resilience, a bullet list provided under the heading "Ways to become more resilient" spells out ways to increase individual resilience; the last bullet in that list recommends "laughing." Quoting from the website: "Laugh: Even when things seem to be falling apart around you, try to find time to smile and laugh. It is very healing and it will help you forgive your worries for a few moments. Rent a movie that makes you laugh or spend time with a friend with a good sense of humor." (Note: As indicated in Appendix 5.1, the authors concur that laughing is healthy and has psychological and potential curative benefits.)

Either the term "resilience" has evolved with an incredible elasticity while remaining relevant, or the above suggests that "resilience" may have become the foundation of a new Tower of Babel where all the occupants talk without necessarily understanding each other. Arguably, a concept of resilience that means everything and anything for anybody is not a particularly useful concept as it escapes definition and qualification, therefore making it an intangible concept for practical purposes when the goal is to enhance resilience of the community in a

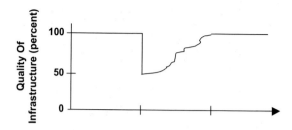

Figure 5.1   Schematic representation of seismic resilience concept.

measurable way. This underscores the urgency to re-establish some principles and rigor on the use of "resilience" within that specific context. This is done below, focusing here on resilience in a way that is relevant for engineers.

Even though dictionary definitions are never similar from one dictionary to the other, all of them agree on a number of common characteristics when it comes to defining resilience. First, resilience in "physical terms" is defined as the ability of something to *"return to its original shape after it has been pulled, stretch, pressed, bent, etc."* (Merriam-Webster 2018). Some definitions used "return to the original form" (Dictionary.com 2017), "resume its original shape" (American Heritage Dictionary 2017), "spring back into shape" (Oxford Living Dictionary 2017), and other variants. Second, dictionaries define it in "life terms" as the ability to *recover* readily from illness, change, depression, adversity, misfortune, or the like. Some definitions use "recover quickly" (American Heritage Dictionary 2017), "become healthy, happy, or strong again" (Merriam-Webster 2018), and other variances. Bottom line, in the perspective of dictionary definitions, resilience is essentially and fundamentally, the quality of being able to return quickly to a previous good condition after problems have occurred. This is the concept embodied (and initially presented by Bruneau et al. (2003)) in the schematic shown in Figure 5.1, which has been widely used in the literature since and needs no detailed explanations here.

This highlights the fact that any functional definition of resilience must refer to a baseline that defines the original condition. In essence, to define and quantify resilience, this baseline must be defined as a functionality of some kind, which could be, for example, the function-ality to maintain operation or intended function of either communities, services, organizations, infrastructures, physical facilities, either individually or considering their combined interactions. Furthermore, quantification of resilience must be able to address both the *loss* of this function-ality (which can be quite sudden in the case of a disastrous event, such as an earthquake), and the path of this *recovery* of functionality both in time and space as presented by Renschler et al. (2010) and Cimellaro et al. (2016b).

In other words, "functionality" is at the core of a workable definition of resilience that can be quantified. In that perspective, functionality can be defined in a number of ways that vary as a function of the services that are provided. For example, functionality can be expressed as residual strength over needed strength when it comes to quantification of physical infrastructures; or it could be defined as available space divided by original space for the phys-ical, the economical, and the environmental dimensions of resilience; or it could be defined as the number of customer served compared to the total number of customers when it comes to infrastructure networks, health of a population, or organizational networks; or even waiting time in emergency conditions compared to waiting time in normal conditions when dealing with public transportation, distribution of goods, and emergency rooms. These are only *some examples* among many.

There could be many definitions of functionality for a given service, depending on the objective sought, constraints in the availability of data, or the resources needed to achieve quantification. For example, residents in seismic areas have expressed their strong expectation that acute care facilities should be available and operational following an earthquake (Alexander 1996; Nigg 1998). To quantify the seismic resilience of acute care facilities, the measure of functionality shown by the vertical axis of the resilience chart of Figure 5.1 must first be defined. This could be done in a number of different ways, depending on the type and range of mitigation actions that are contemplated.

A first option is to quantify *quality of life* as functionality expressed as the percentage of healthy population (Figure 5.2(a)). Using the total healthy population in absence of an earthquake as

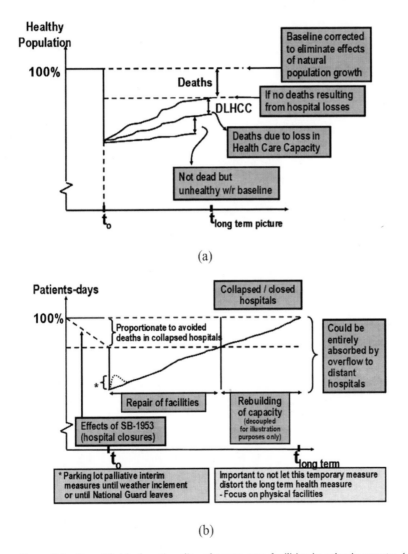

(a)

(b)

Figure 5.2 Quantifiable functionality of acute care facilities in seismic events: (a) in terms of "healthy population"; (b) in terms of "patients-days" treatment capacity.

a reference basis, and normalizing it to eliminate the effect of population growth over time, the horizontal line drawn at 100% on the vertical axis represents the healthy population that resides in an area that could be affected by a scenario earthquake. A first drop in population health would occur when individuals are killed by seismically deficient structures or from other causes during the earthquake (Peek-Asa et al. 1998). At a community scale, this number would not change whether hospitals are seismically retrofitted or not, except for those deaths that would have occurred in seismically deficient hospitals. Injuries suffered during the earthquake would account for the remaining reduction in the healthy population at time t_0. In the best of scenario, in absence of hospital losses, all these injuries would heal, and no more deaths would be added to the toll. Conversely, deaths due to loss in health care capacity (DLHCC) would occur, i.e., deaths that could have been prevented, if the health care system capability had not been reduced by the disaster. Furthermore, a number of individuals, although alive, would likely suffer debilitating injuries or other scars/impairments forever as a result of being unable to receive appropriate treatments immediately following the earthquake, or due to loss of the specialized health care units they need for proper treatment of their chronic disease; these would translate into a marked loss of population health, even though not necessarily deaths (note that while earthquakes are used here for illustration purpose, other types of hazards could yield similar outcomes, as observed for example in the aftermath of Hurricane Maria in Puerto Rico).

This approach has the advantage that it seeks to quantify the impact of an earthquake on the health of a population, a true global societal measure of seismic resilience for a community, which is probably a significant measure for the purpose of policy making. However, it suffers a number of shortcomings. First, the quantification of unhealthy versus healthy may be difficult (although not impossible). Second, establishing how many deaths were directly or indirectly caused by the earthquake could be a challenge. Third, definition of the relevant geographical boundaries can be problematic given that the more wealthy and mobile segment of the population may find its health needs answered in other states (or countries). Fourth, development of accurate data may require substantial resources, requiring at least a coordinated effort between multiple government agencies. Furthermore, if one is interested in providing an engineering contribution to the quantification of resilience, in this broader context, it might not be possible to provide linkages between population health and integrity of the engineered infrastructure in the foreseeable future.

A second option focuses instead on relating the seismic resilience of acute care facilities to the number of patients/day that can be provided as a measure of functionality of the treatment capacity of the health care facilities (Figure 5.3). This could be done for a single institution or for all facilities across a geographical region. The following discussion focuses on the latter. This format allows the illustration of some short term and long term issues whose true impact have often been misinterpreted or exaggerated. For example, prior to an earthquake, the impact of California Senate Bill 1953 requiring the seismic retrofit of hospitals (SB1953) is shown (in Figure 5.2b) as resulting in the loss of some patients/day capacity, as some hospitals are expected to close rather than invest to meet the seismic retrofit goals of that Ordinance. However, since these would likely be facilities identified as suffering from (expensive to correct) severe seismic deficiencies, one could argue that this loss of functionality (i.e. capacity) would have occurred anyhow at time t_0 (the time of an earthquake), but with severe collateral loss of lives. Also illustrated, following the major loss of patients/day capacity directly attributed to the earthquake, is the short burst of recovered patients/day capacity provided in the aftermath of the disaster. This is a consequence of the "parking-lot" MASH-like medicine often provided outside of hospital facilities that have suffered debilitating damage. This burst has typically been observed in warm-climate regions to treat earthquake-related injuries when transportation to a remote facility is difficult, or impossible. This emergency setting usually last but a few days or weeks, and is not a viable solution for an earthquake that would occur in a less accommodating weather or urban setting (such as in New York City, in January). In Figure 5.2(b), for convenience, two distinct and concurrent recovery activities have been illustrated as sequential, namely: repair of capacity and rebuilding of capacity, the first dealing with replacement of capacity lost during the earthquake, the second related to increasing capacity to the level needed to service the needs of the population.

The advantage of this second approach is that it focuses on the physical infrastructures and their ability to provide their intended function, which facilitates engineering quantification (Chang et al. 2002). This is not to imply that engineering issues are more important than the health issues described in the previous option, but only that this framework makes it possible for a coordinated earthquake engineering research effort to contribute in a focused and effective manner to the broader problem. While the engineering effort and resources needed to completely address all issues likely still requires the concerted efforts of multiple government agencies and considerable funding, it is possible for smaller scale engineering efforts to develop some of the tools and methodologies that could be integrated into decision support systems intended to consider multiple complex options related to seismic retrofit, and identify the most effective allocation of limited resources. In this respect, these engineering quantification tools could be used to assess whether the seismic resilience is enhanced or not, i.e. whether a specific intervention (or set of interventions) effectively and significantly reduce the probability of a loss in patient-day capacity, assess if a specific overflow locally (due to loss of capacity) can be absorbed globally, and how long it might take to restore this capacity.

While this approach is more suitable for engineering quantification, it nonetheless remains a complex endeavor. For completeness and reliability of the results provided by a decision support system build upon a strong engineering basis (among many things), this quantification must encompass all equipment and units in a given hospital, as well as capture their interdependencies; whether some equipment would require replacement or repair following an earthquake is a priori difficult to quantify in engineering terms. Modeling of linkages between geographically distributed hospitals adds another layer of complexity, and for simplicity one may have to assume that the performance of a network of hospitals can be established by simple aggregation of the performance of individual facilities. Cimellaro et al. (2010) has also shown that actual relationships can also depend on the post-earthquake condition of the transportation network needed to establish effective linkages, which therefore requires knowledge on the fragilities of that network.

If anything, this illustrates how defining functionality in a manner that can lead to quantification of resilience is a challenge for which extensive research is still needed. Engineers can play an important role in that process and within the broader field of disaster resilience. The obvious one is that engineers can create resilient infrastructure to minimize *loss of functionality*, and to achieve *fast recovery* at minimum cost. Beyond that, however, engineers should participate in the discussions and decision-making activities to formulate multidisciplinary, multidimensional platforms that will be used to quantify resilience, because they can help define the "weight" to give to the resilience of the physical (engineered) infrastructure in an integrated global resilience framework spanning many dimensions (Renschler et al. 2010; Cimellaro et al. 2016b). In particular, one of the engineers' most important roles when part of such discussions (and beyond) is to emphasize that the mitigation of disastrous effect is key to the implementation of any resilience framework if one wishes to manage and prevent disasters. As such, they can help "engineer" the entire decision-making process (Bruneau et al. 2003).

When it comes to structural engineers, though, there are a number of dilemmas that engineers must contend with while trying to serve in the above role. These are not trivial. This chapter provides an overview of three of those dilemmas and highlights some of the challenges that must be overcome in these regards.

5.3 First dilemma

Resilience of the engineered infrastructure is something that most people do not care about, until after a disaster occurs.

Most people in North America are familiar with the Three Little Pigs story (many versions of it can be easily found on YouTube). In this classic nursery rhyme, the first two little pigs expeditiously construct their homes of straw and wood, respectively; the third pig dutiful labors day and night to build a brick home while being ridiculed by the other two who are frivolously spending their free time. Evidently, a "big bad wolf" destroys the first two houses in a single blow, and (depending on who is retelling the story) the first two little pigs either finish in a pulled-pork sandwich or find refuge in the magnanimous third little pig's house that can't be blown away. The moral of the story is obvious and engineers typically identify themselves with the third little pig, agreeing that it is desirable and wise to invest time and resources to achieve a more resilient structure (although, parenthetically, engineers would specify at least *reinforced* masonry to minimize earthquake damage, but that goes beyond the scope of the nursery rhyme).

The Three Little Pigs analogy had been used by a colleague of the authors after a major earthquake to explain to homeowners who had suffered losses that not all houses are created equal when it comes to resisting disasters. However, as pointed out by that same colleague in private philosophical discussions, it remains that, in the Three Little Pigs story, if no wolf ever comes, the first two little pigs have had a more enjoyable life (i.e., more free time and resources) – which is essentially the archetype underscored by the nursery rhyme. Likewise, when it comes to earthquakes, investments in earthquake protection measures, while enhancing resilience, may never actually provide any return on investment in the lifetime of the investor if no damaging earthquake occurs. The same is true for other extreme hazards. Even in full awareness of the risks, probabilistically speaking, betting on the absence of a disaster occurring and hoping to reap an immediate benefit rather than a possible future one is always an option. Tolerance to risk is a complex topic, and a fundamental driver of human behavior. However, in societies that encourage and value immediate rewards, advocating disaster resilience can be an uphill battle.

The problem is partly compounded by the fact that the design philosophy embedded in building codes is one of "life safety," not "damage prevention," which is often not communicated or not completely understood by the consumer. This philosophy is often justified, by analogy, by the rational decision to buy a car with good crash-test ratings that would provide high expectations of survival of passengers in a major collision but where the car itself would be "totaled," against the option of buying a more costly Sherman tank that would allow one to drive oblivious of the risk of collisions (although the analogy is imperfect as the percentage increase in cost from a car to a tank is grossly superior to that from a "life-safety" to a "damage prevention" building design). This philosophy of minimum design for "life-safety" performance often comes as a surprise to the public, generally after an earthquake when structural and non-structural damage has occurred, but also to those contracting a project at the design stage when the structural engineering consultant is offered the opportunity to discuss issues of seismic performance. In those latter cases, faced with the option of buying superior seismic performance at the onset, many owners chose the less expensive "life safety" option. Arguably, it is effectively a decision to bet against the occurrence of an extreme event and use the liquidity for other immediate purposes, which can be a defendable position provided it is a conscientious decision, recognizing consequences, and using insurance instead (or self-insurance) to cover the risk. Fundamentally, this is a pay-now versus pay-later decision, with all the trappings that come with it.

However, a fatal flaw of the car crash analogy lies in the fact that car collisions, most of the time, involve no more than a few vehicles. When the majority of buildings in an urban area are designed following the life-safety perspective, the proper analogy should be that of a massive car pile-up involving hundreds of vehicles (the type that sometimes happen on icy roads in foggy driving conditions), where everybody ends up in the same car crash at the same time. When it comes to buildings, such widespread damage can lead to paralysis of a region or urban center, as happened following New Zealand's Christchurch earthquake where the entire central business district was evacuated, cordoned, and then fenced-off for months to all except professionals involved in authorized response and recovery activities. Owners and residents were prevented access to the area, even if only to recover their belonging, effectively turning the central business district into a ghost town (the first author witnessed restaurants with food rotting on the counters, stores with intact inventory exposed through broken windows – as shown, for example, in Figure 5.3a – and belongings and passports left in hotel rooms. As harshly criticized as this tight control has been, it has nonetheless happened. On the second anniversary of the earthquake, a large percentage of the central business district was still fenced-off, with new types of damage progressively taking roots as a consequence of delayed repairs/reconstruction (Figure 5.3b).

Six years after that earthquake, most of the buildings in the central business district had been demolished and the area was in the midst of a massive rebuilding effort expected to continue until 2020. Incidentally, among the ensemble of new buildings that have arisen as a results of the reconstruction process, a few are base isolated, a couple have viscous dampers, and most new construction is in structural steel (Bruneau & MacRae 2017), with a large number of steel frames having buckling restrained braces, eccentrically braced frames with or without replaceable links, and to a lesser degree moment-frames with or without friction connections, and

(a)	(b)

Figure 5.3 Damage in Christchurch Central Business District: (a) store front a week after the earthquake; (b) fenced-off commercial area two years after the earthquake.

some rocking frames (note that reinforced concrete buildings were the norm for new buildings in Christchurch prior to the earthquake). Interestingly, a major debate is still raging about the desire of parishioners to rebuild the heavily-damaged Christchurch cathedral in the same stone masonry it was originally built from, but possibly strengthened to achieve a "collapse-prevention" level (thus, again prone to damage in a future earthquake).

To some degree, denial of risk when it comes to rare extreme events may be rooted in human nature and urban legends. When living in Berkeley in the 1980s (prior to the Loma Prieta and Northridge earthquakes), the first author heard many Californians state that earthquakes were "not a big deal" and were nothing to worry about (these were obviously not words from engineers, but mindboggling nonetheless considering the history of San Francisco and the 1906 earthquake – particularly to the ears of an earthquake engineering student). Interestingly, the same attitude is found to exist with other hazards; over the years, the first author has met multiple residents of Florida living along the coast from Saint-Augustine to Melbourne who adamantly believed that this particular part of Florida could not be hit by a hurricane, due to either the shape of the ocean floor, the shape of the coast where Cape Canaveral projects into the ocean, or both (in spite of the fact that historical maps showing the path of past hurricanes provide evidence to the contrary). Interestingly, with the 2016 Hurricane Matthew hugging the coastline short of landfall, and producing extensive wind and storm-surge damage along a part of that coast north of Cape Canaveral, this urban legend has been quieted (for now).

Whether such denial of risk is a mechanism to cope with the vagaries of life is a topic best left to psychologists, anthropologists, and other such specialists. However, the above illustrates that promoting disaster resilience is not something that clients will readily embrace, which is a challenge to structural engineers interested in enhancing the resilience of communities.

5.4 Second dilemma

How can a structural engineer contribute to quantifying resilience?

Much research is on-going to quantify or measure resilience. To a large degree, this valuable work focuses on the resilience of distributed networks or of communities. If engineers are to contribute to such quantification/measurement, then a few things are needed for this purpose, namely:

- a resilience framework that both defines resilience and what is to be measured;
- a method to quantify resilience;
- strategies to enhance resilience (i.e., to engineer greater resilience); and
- multidisciplinary collaborations to comprehensively address the problem.

These are considered in the following.

A resilience framework that both defines resilience and what is to be measured

While defining resilience as a measure of changes in functionality in time and space, consistently with the above definitions of resilience (as expressed in Figure 5.1), a *functionality* must be defined and measured – one that will vary depending on the specific application considered. An integrated approach to resilience requires that resilience be considered at many levels, from global (community) resilience, to various dimensions of resilience of dimensions (i.e., sub-systems of a community), or components within such dimensions.

Many approaches can be used for this purpose (see special issue of ASCE, Cimellaro et al. 2016a). For example, the MCEER PEOPLES Framework (Renschler et al. 2010; Cimellaro et al. 2016b) provides seven Resilience Dimensions (i.e., seven realms of a community), that each regroup Resilience Component (i.e., components within a dimension of a community, which incidentally can have interdependencies to resilience components of other dimensions), and corresponding Resilience Indicators (that are quantitative measure of resilience/systems functionality based on quantitative and/or qualitative data sources). The seven dimensions characterizing community functionality (not necessarily in any order of importance as represented by the acronym PEOPLES) are: Population and Demographics, Environmental/ Ecosystem, Organized Governmental Services, Physical Constructed Infrastructure, Lifestyle and Community Competence, Economic Development, and Social-Cultural Capital. The proposed PEOPLES Resilience Framework provides the basis for development of quantitative and qualitative temporal–spatial models that measure continuously the changes of functionality and resilience of communities against extreme events, or disasters, in any or in combination of the above-mentioned dimensions. Over the longer term, this framework will enable the development of geospatial and temporal decision-support software tools (Cimellaro 2016) that help planners and other key decision makers and stakeholders to assess and enhance the resilience of their communities.

The above is used for illustration purpose, and other frameworks are possible. No universally accepted framework exists in this regard, as described below.

Quantification of resilience

Once the resilience framework has been selected, it remains that resilience must be quantified. Here again, no consensus has been reached.

Cutter (2015) has stated that "the landscape of disaster resilience indicators is littered with wide range of tools, scorecards, indices that purport to measure disaster resilience in some manner," and has described the advantages and disadvantages of the major ones developed in the USA. While there indeed exists different expressions of resilience and frameworks that measure it, a large number of those consists of qualitative check lists or score sheets that are filled such as to give either a score or an aggregated index of resilience. Such score sheets are convenient in that they can provide measures that are readily usable by communities that need something immediately and cannot wait for further research developments, but risk becoming enshrined in standard operations of the adopting community and unquestioned over the years in spite of their shortcomings. Arguably, these might also be less compatible with the goal of developing and using engineering tools and approaches to enhance resilience.

The frameworks that may be more appropriate for this purpose are those that have been explicitly created with the goal to quantify using a mathematical framework that treat the resilience data as a continuum rather than from the consideration of discrete or subjective measures. The main drawbacks of quantitative continuum approaches are that they are data intensive and that the tools to achieve the quantification itself are still the subject of on-going research (and the scale of multidisciplinary research needed to fulfill the vision may be orders of magnitude greater above the funding levels currently devoted to the task). The promise is that rigorous mathematical formulations allow integration of resilience across dimensions, but also investigation of sensitivity of various factors to either global (community) resilience, or the resilience of dimensions (sub-systems of a community) or components within such dimensions.

A common quantitative approach to quantify resilience (R) is related to the variations in the functionality curve, generically shown in Figure 5.4, and which could be specified for

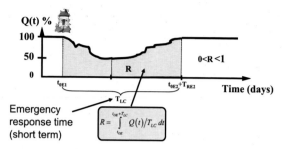

Figure 5.4 Functionality curve and resilience.

a given building, bridge, lifeline network, or community, over a period defined as the control time (T_{LC}). The control time is usually decided by building owners or society at large, for example, and could be taken to correspond to the expected life cycle or life span of the building or other system, or any other fixed time reference. Resilience, R, is defined graphically as the normalized shaded area underneath the function describing the *functionality* of a system, defined as $Q(t)$. $Q(t)$ is a non-stationary stochastic process, and each ensemble is a piecewise continuous function as shown in Figure 5.4, where $Q(t)$ is the functionality of the region considered. The community functionality is an aggregation of all functionalities related to different facilities, lifelines, etc.

The change in functionality due to extreme events is characterized by a drop, representing a loss of functionality, and a recovery. It should be noted that for communities, the loss of functionality can be gradual (see Figure 5.4), or can be sudden (see also Figure 5.1) as well known for earthquakes for example (Bruneau & Reinhorn 2007). In this approach, changes in functionality is evidently at the core of quantification, as it naturally should be.

Again, functionality in quantitative approaches is key to the original definition of resilience, to the extent applicable to the field of disaster mitigation, were the loss and recovery of functionality over time is what matters. Note that in some application, this information can be readily acquired, particularly when functionality is a service and its measure is embedded into a metered distribution network (such as electricity, or water). Not surprisingly, a dominant segment of all resilience studies has focused on such distribution networks. However, one must carefully interpret this data. For instance, the electrical grid can report on the number of households served by the power utility, but the community may be a lot more resilient than indicated by this measure. This is the case in many neighborhoods (such as the authors') where many owners, having suffered through a severely disruptive multi-days power outage have added back-up gas power generation capabilities to their residence or commerce, freeing themselves from the grid's unreliability, thus rendering inaccurate all measures of resilience based solely on data from the utility providers.

The use of single resilience index integrating all resilience dimensions of a region can be valuable, but must also be subject to careful interpretation. For example, Figure 5.5 shows a regional resilience index calculated for every region by combining using weighting coefficients the individual functionality based resilience curves for the power, water, and gas networks obtained following the 2011 Tohoku earthquake (Cimellaro et al. 2014). On that map, different prefectures are shown to have different resilience indices. However, those with higher indices are not necessarily more resilient communities – they only happened to be communities farther from the earthquake epicenter and thus less disturbed by the event. Their resilience might have all been identical had they had been at the same distance from the epicenter. This suggests the

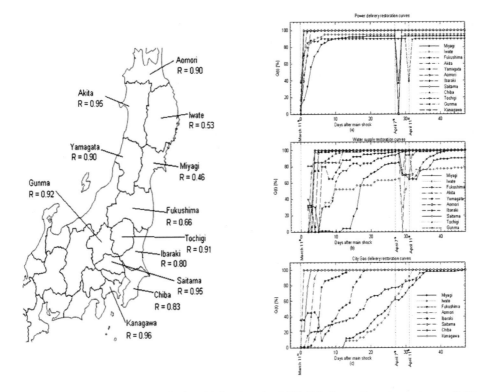

Figure 5.5 Resilience index calculated following the 2011 Tohoku earthquake, in Japan: (left) regional resilience indices; (right) resilience curves for various utilities.

Source: Courtesy of Gian Paolo Cimellaro, Civil Engineering Department, University of Torino, Italy.

need to develop techniques to normalize resiliency measures as a function of the intensity of the hazard (in terms of earthquake magnitude and epicentral distance, for example).

While the resiliency framework is a useful and valuable concept to provide a quantitative measure of resilience (related to the area under the functionality curve, be the units of that area be in kW*days for a power-distribution grids, or patient/days for hospitals), it might be necessary to introduce weighting factors over different regions of this area. Otherwise, when resilience is calculated over a similar reference time period, similar areas could correspond to the same lack of resilience, irrespectively of the shape of that shaded area, which could be misleading. The two graphs in Figure 5.6 illustrate this, whereas a total loss for 2 days is compared to a 10 percent loss for 20 days. Even though the areas are the same, the two events are certainly not perceived to have the same impact. Furthermore, a difficulty arises as the event perceived to be less desirable may vary depending on the audience. For service providers, the preferred scenario might be the one in which most customers are not adversely affected by the disaster, at the cost of loss-of-service to a small base of customers. However, the recipient of services might prefer the "equitably shared hardship" scenario in which all severely suffer but only for a shorter time period, as individuals are apparently most concerned with the possibility of being one of the "lucky" few left without service for a long period of time. This is even more so if the 2 days and 20 days in the above examples are replaced by 10 days and 100 days. This is not to imply that the resiliency framework is invalid, but rather that the single number that

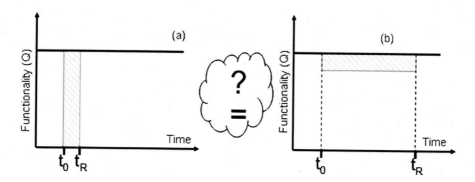

Figure 5.6 Non-linearity of resilience concept: (a) area of 200 days-percent, corresponding to two days of 100% loss of functionality; (b) area of 200 days-percent, corresponding to 20 days of 10% loss of functionality.

defines lack of resilience is non-linear and it might need to be calibrated differently to address the specific needs of different audiences.

However, in some cases, the trade-offs are not so polarized. For example, for hospitals, one could argue that, for a given amount of resources, initial loss of capacity and time to recovery are linked; in other words, it may take longer to restore a system to its original capacity if the initial loss is more significant. As such, it could be argued that investing in limiting initial losses might be, in some instances, the preferred approach to enhance seismic resilience as it automatically translates into a consequent reduction in time to recovery; it is an investment that pays benefits along both axes.

When it comes to individual engineered structures, the achievement of a resilient design is less directly obvious, particularly given that considering resilience from its greater context can effectively void efforts invested in making more resilient a single structure that is part of the total urban landscape (as the New Zealand's Christchurch earthquake demonstrated well). This will be further addressed later, but in spite of this, there may be a need to quantify the resilience of individual buildings.

No consensus has emerged either on how this could be done, but, for illustration purpose, in one approach to quantify seismic resilience, Bruneau and Reinhorn (2007) used a probability distribution surface (i.e. 3-D "bell-curve"), shown in Figure 5.7 as viewed from above to be iso-probability contours (shown as spherical contours for simplicity) in a capacity spectral space defined by floor pseudo-accelerations (PSa floor) and inter-story drifts (Sd floor), and conceptually demonstrated how the intersection of these surfaces with specific structural and non-structural limit states (shown by dotted lines in Figure 5.7) can be used to calculate the probability that response exceeds a specific limit state, and from there the fragility curves and corresponding resilience curves shown in Figure 5.8. Figures 5.8a and 5.8b also illustrate how structural repairs (arbitrarily shown at equal time increments here) progressively shift the curve of probable losses back to the original condition that existed at the instant before t_o (thus equal to the condition at t_1). This requires a financial investment and one could quantify the cost required to shift from one probabilistic curve to another (unlikely to be a linear relationship). The rate of repair also provides a measure of the rapidity dimension of the resilience curve. Note, as shown in Figures 5.8c and 5.8d, repairs to non-structural components may also be required, and that it is possible to increase the value of the investments (on the basis of the same non-structural components and equipment here, not by adding more of them) to above the pre-earthquake condition, enhancing seismic

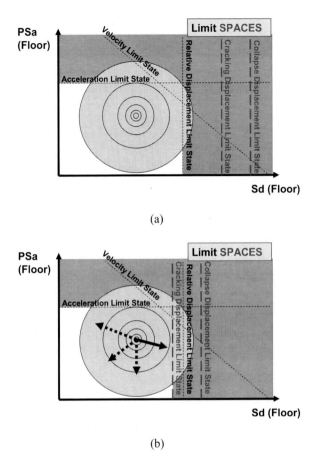

(a)

(b)

Figure 5.7 Probability that response exceeds limit space: (a) non-structural limit states reached prior to structural limit states; (b) different sequence of limit states.

resilience by reducing the probability of losses in a future repeat of the same earthquake. More sophisticated approaches focusing on the structural problem are also possible.

Strategies to enhance resilience

"Mitigation," which involves either retrofitting the existing infrastructure or making new constructions more resilient, is key to achieve the goal of resilient communities, but that is often forgotten or dismissed on the premise that it is "too expensive." Obviously, this begs the question: "Too expensive compared to what?" There seems to exist quite a generous cost tolerance to eliminate all risks in some other regulated areas, for example calling for crews in hazmat suits to remove traces of asbestos, or requiring baby car seats to be discarded after a few years due to aging of the plastic.

It is imperative to recognize that, complementary to improvements in response/recovery, enhancing the Nation's disaster resilience requires mitigating the disaster vulnerability of its facilities and lifelines, i.e. reduce loss of functionality. A perfect response and recovery plan will not eliminate the massive initial losses. Mitigation is needed; otherwise, communities (and the

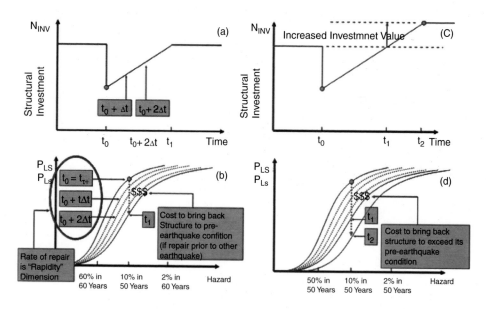

Figure 5.8 Case of non-linear structural seismic response: (a) improvement in structural resilience as structure is repaired over time; (b) corresponding reduction in probability of structural losses; (c) increased resiliency to above pre-earthquake condition; (d) corresponding improvement in probability of structural losses.

nation) will be stuck in an endless cycle of destruction–reconstruction–destruction. Strangely, even though the public expects *critical* facilities and lifelines to be operational following a disaster, this is not necessarily the case – not to forget the rest of the infrastructure.

There are enormous pressures not to upgrade design codes and specifications for new construction beyond minimum requirements, or to a level above "life-safety" protection, even though "life-safety" alone implies eliminating loss of life while most buildings will suffer considerable damage during an earthquake, thus greatly affecting the functionality and consequently the resilience of the affected communities. It is not the purpose here to analyze the economic pressures or mindset that justify this approach. However, continuing to build less resilient (or even to build disaster-vulnerable) facilities and lifelines simply adds to the inventory of such infrastructure, not helping. For example, in 2001, the National Home Builders Association reported building 2,000,000 new homes per year, and a total inventory of 119,117,000 housing units in the United States. Two decade later, at that rate, they will have added 40,000,000 new homes that will become 30 percent of the existing inventory. Any new measure implemented in 2001 would therefore now be found in a progressively growing number of homes. The argument that adding new requirements to enhance the resilience of homes is prohibitively expensive is of dubious merit, given the fact that the cost of residential homes has increased significantly during that same 20-year period without the addition of any disaster resilience features. Except for a lapse of a few years due to the implosion of the housing bubble, homes are still bought and sold (and prices are going up again).

When it comes to mitigation, it is worth re-emphasizing that (generally speaking) enhancing the robustness of the infrastructure simultaneously translates into a greater rapidity to

Figure 5.9   Close-up view of replaceable link in an eccentrically braced frame.

recover. In the context of Figure 5.1, robustness refers to the inherent strength of a system and its ability to reduce the initial loss/degradation in functionality, and rapidity refers to the rate of recovery to an acceptable level of performance either lower, identical, or higher than previously (Bruneau et al. 2003).

In the perspective of mitigation, the Christchurch reconstruction experience is showing that some new structural engineering concepts that prevent/minimize disruption can be implemented without necessary incurring higher initial cost (Bruneau & MacRae 2017). In particular, most of Christchurch is being reconstructed (partly consciously, partly unconsciously) with structural systems that will allow a more rapid return to functionality following future earthquakes. As such, reinforced concrete frames are not used anymore, and as part of the new inventory of steel structures, most structures rely on buckling restrained braces, that have a large low-cycle fatigue life and can sustain multiple earthquakes, and eccentrically braced frames, with either conventional links, which past experience has shown to be expeditiously repairable, or with specially detailed replaceable ductile link intended to further accelerate post-earthquake repairs (Figure 5.9), consistent with the philosophy that hysteretic energy dissipation should instead occur in "disposable" structural fuse elements (a more rigorous definition of "structural fuses" is also presented in Vargas and Bruneau 2009a; 2009b). Note that, as indicated earlier, rocking frames, base isolation, dampers, and other types of advanced structural engineering strategies are also occasionally implemented as part of this reconstruction effort.

Similarly, multi-hazard design also holds a promise of producing more resilient infrastructure, as the development of single structural systems able to provide adequate performance to multiple hazards can be cost-effective. For example, past research has shown that concrete-filled steel tubes fall within this category (Fujikura et al. 2008; Imani et al. 2015; Zaghi et al. 2016). These are only some of the areas within which the structural engineer is poised to make great contributions to resilience.

Multidisciplinary collaborations to comprehensively to address the problem

The quantification of community resilience is a complex temporal and spatial problem (Renschler et al. 2010) that also evidently requires an integrated multidisciplinary effort commensurate with the inherent multidisciplinary nature of the problem. Whatever framework is chosen, engineers must ensure that the weight given to infrastructure as part of this quantification recognizes the predominant impact that infrastructure damage has on a region's resiliency.

For example, taking again the PEOPLES Resilience Framework (Renschler et al. 2010) for illustration purpose, consider that each dimension and/or service and its indicators or terms of functionality can be represented with a GIS layer of the area of interest as suggested in the example portrayed in Figure 5.10. In that figure, Q_{POP} = functionality of population in the community; Q_{ENV} = functionality of environmental fabric; Q_{ORG} = functionality of organizations; Q_{PHY} = functionality of physical infrastructure systems; all terms are function of location ($\mathbf{r}$) and of time ($\mathbf{t}$). The other temporal functionality maps include lifestyles, economics, and social/cultural aspects. For each layer, it is possible to define a *resilience index contour map* after integrating the functionality for the control time (T_{LC}) period.

Each dimensional layer has a specific spatial functionality dictated by the influence area of the grid, jurisdiction, economic environment, social cultural fabric, etc., as shown in Figure 5.10. Moreover, each layer of component functionality in that figure can be represented by a combination of sub-dimensions (or layers), each having spatial-temporal dependent functionalities, each representing a subcomponent.

A global community resilience index can be obtained to assess the entire community by summing (or integrating) over space and time the total functionality $Q_{TOT}(\mathbf{r},t)$, that combines the different dimensions of resilience, such that the final *community resilience index* is given by:

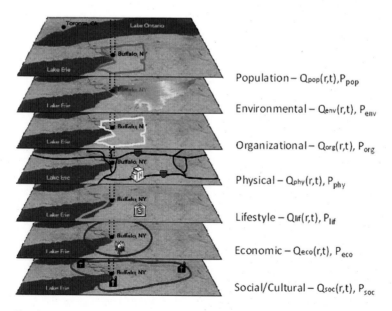

Population – $Q_{pop}(r,t), P_{pop}$

Environmental – $Q_{env}(r,t), P_{env}$

Organizational – $Q_{org}(r,t), P_{org}$

Physical – $Q_{phy}(r,t), P_{phy}$

Lifestyle – $Q_{lif}(r,t), P_{lif}$

Economic – $Q_{eco}(r,t), P_{eco}$

Social/Cultural – $Q_{soc}(r,t), P_{soc}$

Figure 5.10 Schematic representation of time dependent community functionality maps.
Source: Courtesy Chris S. Renschler, Department of Geography, University at Buffalo, Buffalo, NY.

$$R = \int_{\mathbf{r}_{LC}(t)} R(\mathbf{r})dr = \int_{\mathbf{r}_{LC}(t)} \int_{T_{LC}(t)} Q_{TOT}(\mathbf{r},t) / T_{LC}dtdr, \qquad (5.1)$$

where $Q_{TOT}(\mathbf{r},t)$ is the global functionality that combines *all* functionality terms considered; $\mathbf{r}_{LC}$ is the region of interest that can change with time; t is the time parameter; T_{LC}= control time that can itself change through time.

In that expression, the global functionality can be defined by

$$Q_{TOT} = E\{Q(\mathbf{r},t)\} = \sum_{i=1}^{n} p_i(\mathbf{r},t)Q_i(\mathbf{r},t), \qquad (5.2)$$

where n is the number of dimensions considered relevant in the functionality, $p_i(\mathbf{r},t)$ = priority (probability) factors; Q_i = functionality associated to a given dimension of the PEOPLE framework. The priority factor is a weighting factor to determine the relative importance of each dimension to the total resilience index. It is obvious that not all functionalities might have the same weight; it is the responsibility of engineers to ensure that the predominant significance of infrastructure damage (as part of the physical dimension of resilience) is appropriately recognized by a weight factor of proportionate magnitude.

5.5 Third dilemma

Making a disaster resilient community requires multiple owners and stakeholders (with varied priorities, values, and interests) to similarly embrace resilience.

Much of the work on the quantification of resilience has been done on network systems, such as highway networks, power grids, water distribution systems, and other similar networks. These networks are fundamentally different from the ensemble of buildings within a community for a number of reasons.

- First, the assets within a network system are typically owned either by a single owner or by a consortium of a few interdependent large owners. For example, the highways in a state are, with a few exceptions, owned by the state Department of Transportation.
- Second, the design of these networks is often self-regulated, meaning that the design requirements of these facilities are adopted by specification committees on which only these owners have the right to vote.
- As a consequence to the first two points above, these owners have the ability to proceed forward and set priorities regarding the resilience of their infrastructure; for example, state Departments of Transportation have taken the initiative to identify critical routes on which infrastructure shall be functional after an earthquake, typically designated as lifelines roads and bridges.

The situation is quite different for the ensemble of buildings within a community.

First, it is generally the case that there are a large number of owners within a specific community.

Second, the concept of a "lifeline building" does not exist, unless that building is surrounded entirely by lifeline buildings, on a self-sufficient "lifeline island." Even if a single building had been made resilient to earthquakes, it could suffer damage from other surrounding buildings,

Figure 5.11   Damage to low-rise building in Santa Cruz, California, due to collapsed parapet from adjacent building, from 1989 Loma Prieta earthquake.

as shown in Figure 5.11, where the low-rise building might have had, by itself, a satisfactory performance during the earthquake, but was nonetheless destroyed under the shower of bricks created by the out-of-plane failure of the neighboring building's unreinforced masonry wall. Likewise, many buildings that have performed well during the Christchurch earthquake were rendered inaccessible (and therefore had no functionality) when owners were kept out of the Christchurch Business District after the earthquake. For these reasons, truly resilient communities may be decades away for some hazards.

This is further complicated by the fact that achieving resilience requires integrated interaction between stakeholders. This was illustrated by Cimellaro et al. (2008), where resilience of a hospital network was calculated with or without the existence of a coordination agent (Operative Center). Without the benefit of this coordination center, patients typically go to the nearest hospital. In a scenario where functionality is defined as the waiting time in emergency rooms, the nearest hospital is overwhelmed and its resilience is low (long waiting times), all while a hospital away is underutilized and its resilience is high (low waiting time). With the benefit of the coordination center, patients were optimally distributed according to a rule that considers both the waiting time at the respective hospitals and the corresponding transportation time to reach each hospital, and the resulting resilience of the hospital network taken as a whole was found to be higher.

5.6 Possible solutions to the core resilience problem

It has been argued before that the key to making a community resilient was to ensure that its critical infrastructure would be operational in a post-disaster context. However, a community cannot really be considered resilient when all of its lifelines (such as bridges along major evacuation and supply routes, and/or hospitals designed by strict state-enforced guidelines) are made resilient, if no other buildings are resilient. This was demonstrated by the situation in Christchurch, where hospitals were functional following the earthquake, and adequate road access to the Central Business District remained, but where the Central Business District lost its functionality for years – and still has not recovered to its pre-earthquake condition, more than seven years after the event. Although some have said that Christchurch was "highly resilient" during the February 22, 2011 earthquake, on account of the fact that "only two buildings collapsed," in a context where resilience is tied to functionality, one can only disagree. In that perspective, whenever resilience is pursued without ensuring that regular buildings are resilient, it could be said that community efforts at enhancing resilience are counter to the best intentions of structural engineers.

Therefore, if resilience is to be achieved, there needs to be a mechanism to ensure that resilience is part of the discussion in the design of *all* buildings. Given the unlikeliness that building codes and specifications will require resilient design in the foreseeable future, and given that the interest in achieving resilient infrastructure has a tendency to subside as time from past damaging earthquakes increases, it is not clear how such a discussion will proceed. It is commendable that the US Resiliency Council (USRC) has proposed an Earthquake Building Rating System, similar to the LEED rating system for green buildings, where buildings volunteered for such an evaluation will be rated from one to five stars for the respective performance measures of Safety, Damage (in terms of repair cost), and Recovery (in terms of time to return to pre-earthquake functionality). While there is a risk that this initiative may give the wrong impression that all is known about resilience, it remains commendable in that it engages owners in a dialogue on some of the key issues on this topic. In such case, the criticisms must be weighed in light of the benefits, and time will be needed to perform such an assessment as implementation of the rating system is still in its infancy.

In the meantime, it remains that:

(i) Most owners do not want resilience (or don't know why they should want it);
(ii) A resilient building may be pointless unless the entire community is collectively resilient, and;
(iii) Resilient buildings are good, but community resilience requires more than resilient buildings.

Therefore, achieving community resilience "one building at the time" may end-up taking a long time. This creates an overwhelming challenge.

It will be interesting to see how the challenge is met over time, but if one wishes to speed things up, as with all challenges of that magnitude, "unorthodox" ideas might be needed (in the same manner that spanning the Golden Gate with a bridge, or sending a man on the moon, were once deemed to be absolutely unachievable endeavors). In that mindset, the authors herein propose "The Lifeline (Resilient) Building District" concept. Figuratively speaking, such a community would be a self-contained "island" of buildings all having 5-Stars USRC resiliency rating, connected to transportation lifeline (to prevent Christchurch-type "encapsulation" and to link to critical facilities if needed), and having emergency back-up power generation, independent water purification and waste-treatment capabilities, and (possibly if too close to other non-resilient communities) its own security forces. By analogy to the original Experimental Prototype Community of Tomorrow (EPCOT) that was envisioned by Walt Disney (the living community EPCOT, not the amusement park EPCOT, as described by The-original-epcot.com (2002)), the proposed "The Lifeline (Resilient) Building District" would be a "Resilient EPCOT." As originally envisioned, EPCOT was to be a prototype community built from scratch from a virgin plot of land, and systematically created to include a business district, an industrial park, a commercial zone, a residential green belt, and an "airport of the future," among many things, all relying on the latest technologies and advanced designs – in essence, it was Walt Disney's expression of urban planning, with aspects conceived, designed, and engineered from the onset to match his vision. As he stated it himself, EPCOT was to be "like the city of tomorrow ought to be. A city that caters to the people as a service function. It will be a planned, controlled community, a showcase for American industry and research, schools, cultural and educational opportunities." However, Disney died in 1966 and all efforts towards that goal stopped a few years later.

Conceptually, the resilient EPCOT could be modeled in many shapes and forms to the EPCOT model, it that it would be an entirely new community built from scratch, but built to be highly resilient, thus able to most rapidly (or maybe even immediately) return to full functionality of all its systems and parts after an extreme event. It is recognized that, in the globally integrated economical context, an earthquake in Japan can have a ripple effect across the entire world, but a resilient island is still better than no resilient island.

This "unrealistic" idea is subject to receive the same social criticisms that the original EPCOT concept did, and it may be argued to reek of elitism and exclusivity. However, while only Lincolns and Cadillacs offered power windows in the 1950s (i.e., exclusivity), many automakers nowadays offer no models with hand crank windows (it might not necessarily be a cheaper option anymore) and no youth nowadays would understand the rotary hand-gesture that used to mean "lower your car window." Furthermore, given the current trend in many parts of the United States towards gated communities, the step to a full Resilient-EPCOT is much smaller nowadays than it was in Disney's 1960s.

Whether the Resilient-EPCOT idea is desirable and achievable, or not, time will tell. In the meantime, while waiting for bolder practical ideas, it will not hurt to follow the advice from the State Department to be more resilient.

5.7 Conclusions

The concept of resilience is intricately tied to the expression and quantification in time and space of the *functionality* of communities and its components. To achieve resilient communities, one therefore needs a resilience framework, methods to quantify resilience, strategies to enhance resilience, and multidisciplinary collaborations. Most critically, it requires the ability to track how the functionality of all systems and buildings within a specific geographical space evolves over time after a specific event of interest.

Innovative and integrated solutions are key to enhance the resilience of infrastructure against extreme events. The need to expand "single-hazard solutions" to address satisfactorily multiple hazards (without incremental costs) is desirable in that perspective. Multidisciplinary research requires a substantial investment of time and resources, which will be desirable to help acquire a better understanding of how to achieve truly resilient communities.

A community will never be resilient unless it has a resilient infrastructure. However, by the same token, a community peppered by a handful of resilient infrastructures (be they critical infrastructures or not) risks not being as resilient as intended. An integral approach is necessary. In light of the above, it is proposed that developing one (or many) "Resilient EPCOT" might be the best approach forward to provide a possible integrated solution to achieve some resilient communities.

Acknowledgment

This chapter expresses views of the authors resulting from decades of research sponsored by a wide range of sponsors (including the National Science Foundation and the National Institute for Standards and Technology, among many), and this funding has been sincerely appreciated. However, the opinions expressed here are those of the authors alone. In particular, where examples were included in this chapter, this was done solely to facilitate the understanding of the approaches underlined in the chapter, and not intended to be critical of specific individuals, groups, or agencies.

Appendix 5.1

During post-earthquake reconnaissance activities in the Christchurch Business District, which was an urban area closed to all unauthorized personnel, the first author ran into a member of the Clown Doctors organization (www.clowndoctors.org.nz/), whose mission at the time was to relieve the stress of the individuals involved in building safety assessments and emergency repairs/stabilizations (Figure 5.A.1). The organization website states:

Their silly interactions gave people "permission to laugh" at a time and place when they were not able to do so and it has truly made a difference to the community's morale. We aim to relieve tension and create an atmosphere of hope among the grief and sadness of post-earthquake Christchurch.

(a)

(b)

Figure 5.A.1 Clown doctors of New Zealand: (a) Encounter in Christchurch Central Business District following Feb. 22, 2011, earthquake; (b) official badge.

References

Alexander, D. (1996). "The health effects of earthquakes in the mid-1990's," *Disasters* 30(3), 231–47.

American Heritage Dictionary (2017). "Resilience," *The American Heritage® Dictionary of the English Language*, Fifth Edition, Houghton Mifflin Harcourt Publishing Company. www.dictionary.com/browse/resilience?s=t (last accessed September 23, 2017).

Bruneau, M. and MacRae, G. (2017). *Reconstructing Christchurch: A Seismic Shift in Building Structural Systems*. The Quake Centre, University of Canterbury, NZ.

Bruneau, M. and Reinhorn, A. (2007). "Exploring the concept of seismic resilience for acute care facilities," *EERI Spectra Journal*, 23(1): 41–62.

Bruneau, M., Chang, S.E., Eguchi R.T., Lee, G.C., O'Rourke, T.D., Reinhorn, A.M., Shinozuka, M., Tierney, K., Wallace, W.A., and Von Winterfeldt, D. (2003). "A framework to quantitatively assess and enhance the seismic resilience of communities," *Earthquake Spectra*, 19(4): 733–52.

Chang, S.E., Svekla, W.D., and Shinozuka, M. (2002). "Linking infrastructure and urban economy: Simulation of water disruption impacts in Earthquakes, Environ. Plan. B: Plan." *Disasters* 29(2), 281–301.

Cimellaro, G.P. (2016). *Urban Resilience for Emergency Response and Recovery – Fundamental Concepts and Applications*. Netherlands: Springer.

Cimellaro, G.P, Reinhorn, A.M. and Bruneau, M. (2010). "Framework for analytical quantification of disaster resilience," *Engineering Structures*, 32(11), 3639–49Cimellaro, G.P., Solari, D., and Bruneau, M. (2014). "Physical infrastructure interdependency and regional resilience index after 2011 Tohoku earthquake in Japan," *Earthquake Engineering and Structural Dynamics*, 43(12): 1763–84.

Cimellaro, G.P., Duenas-Osorio, L., and Reinhorn, A.M. (2016a). "Special issue on resilience-based analysis and design of structures and infrastructure systems", *ASCE Journal of Structural Engineering*, 142(8). DOI: 10.1061/(ASCE)ST.1943-541X.0001592, C2016001(online).

Cimellaro, G.P., Renschler, C., Reinhorn, A.M., and Arendt, L. (2016b). "PEOPLES: A framework for evaluating resilience." *ASCE Journal of Structural Engineering*, 142(10). DOI: 10.1061/(ASCE)ST.1943-541X.0001514- Editor's Choice (December 2016) (online).

Cutter, S.L. (2016). "The landscape of disaster resilience indicators in the USA", Natural Hazards, 80(2): 741–58.

Dictionary.com (2017). "Resilience", www.dictionary.com/browse/resilience?s=t (last accessed September 23, 2017).

Fujikura, S., Bruneau M., and Lopez-Garcia, D. (2008). "Experimental investigation of multihazard resistant bridge piers having concrete-filled steel tube under blast loading," *ASCE Journal of Bridge Engineering*, 13(6): 586–94.

Imani, R., Mosqueda, G., and Bruneau, M. (2015). "Experimental study on post-earthquake fire resistance of ductile concrete filled double-skin tube columns", *ASCE Journal of Structural Engineering*, 141(8). DOI: 10.1061/(ASCE)ST.1943-541X.0001168 (online).

Merriam-Webster (2018). "Resilience", Merriam-Webster Dictionary, www.merriam-webster.com/dictionary/resilience (last updated August 23, 2018).

Nigg, J.M. (1998). "Empirical findings based on research conducted under NSF Grant No. CMS-9812556, Perceptions of Earthquake Impacts and Loss." Reduction Policy Preferences among Community Residents and Opinion Leaders, J.M. Nigg, principal investigator, MCEER, Buffalo.

Oxford Living Dictionary (2017). "Resilience", Oxford University Press. https://en.oxforddictionaries.com/definition/resilience (last accessed September 23, 2017).

Peek-Asa, C., Kraus, J.F., Bourque, L.B., Vimalachandra, D., Yu, J., and Abrams, J., (1998). "Fatal and hospitalized injuries resulting from the 1994 Northridge earthquake," *Int. J. Epidemiol*, 27(3), 459–65.

Renschler, C.S., Frazier, A.E., Arendt, L.A. Cimellaro, G.P., Reinhorn, A.M., and Bruneau, M. (2010). "Framework for defining and measuring resilience at the community scale: The PEOPLES Resilience Framework", Technical Report to Sponsor – NIST GCR 10–930, US Department of Commerce National Institute of Standards and Technology (NIST), Office of Applied Economics Engineering Laboratory Gaithersburg, Maryland 20899–8603 [cross listed with MCEER Technical Report MCEER-10-0006, University at Buffalo – the State University of New York].

SB1953 (1994). "California Senate Bill 1953 – Chapter 740 - amend the Health and Safety Code, relating to building standards." Legislative Counsel's Digest.

The-original-epcot.com (2002). "Walt Disney's Original E.P.C.O.T." https://sites.google.com/site/theoriginalepcot/the-florida-project (last accessed July 3, 2017).

US Department of State (2017). "What is resilience?" www.state.gov/m/med/dsmp/c44950.htm (last accessed July 3, 2017).

Vargas, R. and Bruneau, M. (2009a). "Analytical response of buildings designed with metallic structural fuses," *ASCE Journal of Structural Engineering*, 135(4): 386–93.

Vargas, R. and Bruneau, M. (2009b). "Experimental response of buildings designed with metallic structural fuses", *ASCE Journal of Structural Engineering*, 135(4): 394–403.

White House (2013). "Critical infrastructure security and resilience." Presidential Policy Directive/PPD-21, The White House, Office of the Press Secretary, https://obamawhitehouse.archives.gov/the-press-office/2013/02/12/presidential-policy-directive-critical-infrastructure-security-and-resil (last accessed February 27, 2017).

Zaghi, A.E., Padgett, J.E., Bruneau, M., Barbato, M., Li, Y., Mitrani-Reiser, J., and McBride, A., (2016). "Forum paper: establishing common nomenclature, characterizing the problem, and identifying future opportunities in multi-hazard design," *ASCE Journal of Structural Engineering*, 142(12).

6

Performance-based engineering to achieve community resilience

Bruce R. Ellingwood,[1] Naiyu Wang,[2] James Robert Harris,[3] and Therese P. McAllister[4]

[1] DEPARTMENT OF CIVIL AND ENVIRONMENTAL ENGINEERING, COLORADO STATE UNIVERSITY, FORT COLLINS, CO 80523, USA; BRUCE.ELLINGWOOD@COLOSTATE.EDU

[2] SCHOOL OF CIVIL ENGINEERING AND ENVIRONMENTAL SCIENCE, UNIVERSITY OF OKLAHOMA NORMAN, OK 73019, USA; NAIYU.WANG@OU.EDU

[3] J.R. HARRIS & COMPANY, 1775 SHERMAN STREET, SUITE 2000, DENVER, CO 80203, USA; JIM.HARRIS@JRHARRISANDCO.COM

[4] ENGINEERING LABORATORY, NATIONAL INSTITUTE OF STANDARDS AND TECHNOLOGY, 100 BUREAU DRIVE, GAITHERSBURG, MD 20899, USA; THERESE.MCALLISTER@NIST.GOV

6.1 Introduction

The resilience of communities under disruptive events depends on the performance of the built environment, as well as on supporting social, economic and public institutions which are essential for immediate community response and long-term recovery (e.g., Bruneau et al. 2003; Miles & Chang 2006; Cutter et al. 2010; Cimellaro et al. 2010; Bocchini & Frangopol 2012; Franchin & Cavalieri 2015; Jia et al. 2017). The built environment is susceptible to damage due to disruptive natural hazards, such as hurricane wind storms and floods, tornadoes, earthquakes, tsunamis, and wildfires, as well as anthropogenic hazards, such as industrial accidents and malevolence. The human and economic losses and social disruptions caused by failures within the built environment are often disproportionate to the physical damage incurred. The potential exists for even larger losses, given the growth of population and economic development to hazard-prone areas in many countries, including the United States, and global climate change.

Investigations conducted in the aftermath of recent natural disasters have revealed the importance of planning, development and mitigation policies that focus on the resilience of the community as a whole, rather than those that simply address safety and functionality of individual civil infrastructure facilities (McAllister 2013). Nevertheless, the performance of buildings, bridges, and other civil infrastructure systems, which are key to community resilience, is largely determined by codes and standards that are developed by different professional groups, (e.g., ASCE Standard 7–16 (ASCE 2016); American Association of State and Highway Transportation Officials (AASHTO) Load and Resistance Factor Design (LRFD) Bridge Design Specifications (AASHTO 2017)), often with different objectives, and the consistency of these governing standards with community goals seldom has been achieved (McAllister 2016). For example, building codes are applicable to individual facilities and generally consider the role of the building within the community indirectly through risk category assignments. Such risk categories aim to provide higher levels of structural performance under extreme events, but may not result in the desired levels of functionality following an event. In the United States, these codes and standards are – and have been – primarily focused on occupant safety goals. The role played by the performance of individual buildings, both existing and newly constructed, in fulfilling community resilience goals is unknown.

The importance of the built environment to community resilience means that a fundamental change must occur in the way that code and standard-writing groups approach the development of guidelines and requirements for design of buildings, bridges, and other civil infrastructure, to ensure that performance of physical infrastructure will support a resilient community. Community resilience planning requires communication across broad disciplines and stakeholder groups, including engineering, socioeconomic sciences, information technology, urban planning, government and the public at large. The National Institute of Standards and Technology (NIST) *Community Resilience Planning Guide* (NIST 2015), hereafter referred to as the Guide, provides a general framework for developing community resilience plans with performance objectives for building clusters and infrastructure that are aligned and based on performance needs of social institutions. However, the Guide does not provide technical approaches to linking component, system and community-level performance goals with the design standards for individual facilities.

This chapter takes a first step at filling this gap, drawing upon the paradigm of performance-based engineering (or PBE), which provides a framework for engineers and planners to respond to evolving public expectations and to achieve desired levels of performance and functionality of civil infrastructure that is essential for community resilience. A structural engineering perspective is presented on some of the major challenges faced in extending PBE concepts for individual facilities to align with and support community resilience goals, including the process of de-aggregating those goals to achieve practical design criteria for buildings and other structures.

6.2 Community resilience goals and metrics

Community resilience goals are *aspirational statements* of how the community should perform given the occurrence of a disruptive event. Some high-level goals are common to virtually all communities, such as continuity of physical and social services, population and economic stability, and availability of critical services (e.g., health, fire, police, schools, etc.). Other goals might be community-specific. Performance metrics measure whether the performance goal is achieved, rely on available data, and should support community decision making. The metrics should be meaningful, both before the disruptive event and during the post-event recovery period to be useful in pre-event planning, design, and mitigation and to support long-term assessment of community resilience. For example, continuity of services might be measured by the percentage of buildings that remain functional by occupancy, or by functionality of the urban transportation network in terms of connectivity or travel time. Population stability might be measured by the percentage of people leaving the community, by those remaining in shelters or in their homes following a disruptive event, or by population count (Burton et al. 2015). Economic stability might be measured by household income, employment or earnings by sector of the economy. Examples of social services stability include the availability of health care and educational facilities. Governance stability may include public safety services, such as police, fire, and emergency operation centers. Such metrics must be quantified in a risk-informed manner because of the large uncertainties in hazard levels and the associated response of the existing built environment (NAE 1996; Bocchini & Frangopol 2010; Lin & Wang 2016).

The performance objectives for individual buildings, building portfolios, and infrastructure can be derived from resilience goals defined at the community level (Mieler et al. 2015), through a process known as de-aggregation (see Figure 5.1) (Wang & Ellingwood 2015; Lin et al. 2016; Wang et al. 2018) which will be illustrated subsequently. While each community might develop a unique set of goals related to its functionality and recovery, it is not readily apparent how these goals can be related to current design practice based on building codes. Thus, general models that communities can follow for deriving performance objectives and metrics for their specific goals are essential.

6.3 PBE objectives and metrics for community infrastructure

For a community to be resilient against natural or anthropogenic hazards, the built environment must be designed to function in a predictable manner as an integrated system of systems. Community infrastructure is interdependent; for example, availability of water depends on electrical power; healthcare depends on building integrity and availability of water, electrical power, and transportation services. Since the design requirements for civil infrastructure systems have been developed by different professional groups with different performance objectives and with limited coordination, it is not surprising that communities seldom perform as integrated systems during or following a disruptive event.

PBE is a process that facilitates the development of engineered buildings that have predictable performance when subjected to a spectrum of external conditions and demands. The International Code Council *Performance Code for Buildings and Facilities* (ICC 2015) is one of the few regulatory documents that has explicitly incorporated the notion of performance requirements. However, PBE as a design concept, to date, has focused on design of individual facilities. In some cases, PBE has been applied to modify specific features that otherwise would be required by prescriptive codes in order to achieve cost savings for equivalent performance. When extended to building inventories and infrastructure, PBE should begin with performance objectives based on social, economic, and infrastructure resilience goals for the entire community. Depending on the role of buildings, bridges, and other civil infrastructure in the community, a differentiated and prioritized approach for design may be needed (Gardoni & Murphy 2009). This includes checks related to public safety, infrastructure damage, and recovery of functionality for key infrastructure. For example, a community may decide to address its resilience, given the occurrence of an earthquake with magnitude $M_w = 6.8$, by setting performance goals that 90 percent of the population can shelter in place, 30 percent of essential services would be recovered within two weeks, and 75 percent of the essential services would be recovered within three months. To meet these community goals using PBE, engineering requirements should be coupled to socioeconomic performance expectations and cost constraints, and provide support for risk-informed decision-making in the public interest. Given the large uncertainties associated with hazard demands and with the response of civil infrastructure, it is important that the performance objectives be articulated probabilistically, and in a manner that can be understood by stakeholders. Furthermore, for many disruptive events, scenario events need to be selected to represent the spatial distribution of the hazard and its impact correctly over a geographic area.

6.4 PBE objectives and metrics for individual buildings

In the traditional practice of structural engineering, design acceptability is measured through conformance to given criteria on materials, configuration, detailing, strength, and stiffness. Such procedures have been deemed to provide buildings and other structures with acceptable performance throughout their service life in terms of public safety, health, and welfare; however, performance goals are not evaluated explicitly in terms of building functionality or recovery characteristics. While PBE guidelines offer more flexibility in meeting desired performance objectives, a means to implement them in structural design practice is needed. At a fundamental level, this may take the form of a set of risk-consistent safety checks (load factors and load combinations and design strengths) similar to those appearing in ASCE Standard 7–16 (ASCE 2016) and other design standards. Many of these safety checks focus on member or component performance; however, to support community resilience, the checks should also address system behavior. At a community or building cluster level, one could envision a set of structural system performance levels, defined by target fragilities, for different functionality goals (e.g., continued occupancy, impaired occupancy, life safety) that would need to be matched by the design to support the resilience objective (Wang et al. 2018); see Sections 5.6 and 5.7. PBE for earthquake provides an example (ASCE Standard 7-2016, Section 21.2.1): the probability of total or partial collapse, given the occurrence of the Maximum Considered Earthquake, must be lower than 10 percent. Note that this example focuses on the life safety performance goal by limiting the likelihood of building collapse; this is an important part of public safety, but not sufficient for the various functionality goals for evaluating buildings in a community resilience assessment, either immediately following an earthquake or during an extended recovery period. Similar design criteria that can be used as reliable metrics of community system performance need to be identified for other hazards. Finally, it should be noted that resilience-based design will not replace traditional safety requirements for the built environment entirely; probability-based limit states design, as currently practiced, will still control the design of most facilities. However, resilience-based functionality requirements may influence traditional design requirements and increase them beyond traditional levels.

6.5 Hazard definitions for buildings and communities

Natural hazard events can be specified for community resilience assessment from either scenario or probabilistic hazard analysis (PHA). PHA has been widely used for the past decades in simulating the intensity of a hazard demand variable (ground motion intensity, three-second gust wind speed, flood elevation, etc.) for purposes of design, insurance underwriting, and other applications directed toward evaluating the performance of a single facility. PHA most often yields a mean return period event for a particular location, and it is often used to design individual facilities (ASCE Standard 7-2016). However, a PHA cannot capture the spatial variation in the demand that is necessary for resilience assessment at community or regional scales. To capture the spatial variation in the community, a hazard scenario is often used in community resilience assessment to represent one possible realization of a future event (e.g., an earthquake with $M_w = 6.8$ and known epicenter and fault rupture geometry; a Category 4 hurricane with postulated track and time of landfall). However, since a mean annual return period generally cannot be associated with a scenario event, a range of scenarios associated with the intensity levels of interest must be considered to assess the vulnerability of the community to a specific hazard. Resolving the dichotomy between PHA-based and scenario-based hazards for structural design purposes presents one of the major challenges to PBE-based design of individual facilities and their role in supporting community resilience performance objectives.

6.6 Development of risk-informed criteria for building design from community performance goals

One of the major challenges to using PBE for community resilience assurance is the development of performance objectives for *individual buildings* and other structures that collectively achieve *community* resilience goals. Accordingly, to achieve an optimal allocation of resources in the community, a de-aggregation process must be followed in which the *performance of individual buildings and building clusters (sets of buildings that support a social function)* is optimized in such a way as to achieve the *community performance goals*. De-aggregation is the process by which the performance goals for a community are transformed into performance objectives that are meaningful for the development of practical performance-based design criteria, as explained in the following paragraph.

The link between community goals and PBE objectives for individual buildings can be developed through the tiered de-aggregation framework (Wang et al. 2018) shown in Figure 6.1. The upper-level de-aggregation (ULD) can be formulated as an inverse multi-objective optimization problem, where a search is performed to identify the minimum performance criteria

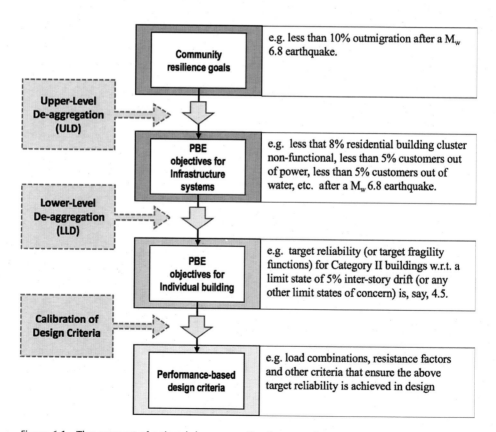

Figure 6.1 The concept of a tiered de-aggregation framework.

for each community system (i.e., community building inventories and infrastructure networks). When satisfied simultaneously they enable the overarching community resilience goals to be achieved. This ULD is performed at the community scale, and it decouples the interdependencies among the community systems for the subsequent analysis. The ULD depends on the unique value system of a specific community and is outside the scope of this chapter. However, once the set of minimum resilience goals are obtained for the community systems, they are de-aggregated further in a lower-level de-aggregation (LLD) to obtain the minimum performance objectives for the individual components (e.g., individual buildings or bridges) in each system (e.g. building cluster or roadway network). The LLD can also be formulated as an inverse multi-objective optimization problem. Finally, once the performance objectives for individual structures are established, performance-based design can be implemented at the individual facility level, in which building (or infrastructure component) attributes can be identified and parameterized to meet the performance objectives resulted from the LLD. In the following section, we will illustrate the feasibility of LLD considering the tornado hazard (Wang et al. 2018).

6.6.1 Lower level de-aggregation under tornado hazard

Building cluster performance metrics

To illustrate the LLD to develop the minimum performance criteria for residential buildings under tornado hazard, we use the Direct Loss Ratio (DLR) and Un-Inhabitable Ratio (UIR) (Lin & Wang 2016) as the metrics that measure the performance of a residential building cluster. The DLR is defined as the ratio of hazard-induced direct loss of residential buildings to the overall replacement cost of the residential cluster, while the UIR is defined as the ratio of the dwelling units that are uninhabitable following a hazard event to the total number of dwelling units in the building cluster under investigation. The DLR is a damage-related metric and contributes directly to the hazard-induced economic impact, while the UIR is a functionality-related metric that is relevant to the social well-being of the community following a disaster. These two metrics are highly correlated because they both depend on the collective performance of individual buildings in the cluster. By considering the two metrics simultaneously, we balance the social and economic considerations in deriving the performance criteria for building design. Detailed formulation of the DLR and UIR is presented in the subsection below on "Relating building cluster metrics to individual buiding permance criteria."

Hazard characterization

The Enhanced Fujita (EF) scale (Texas Tech 2006) is the standard method for describing the intensity of tornadoes. According to the historical data from 1950 to 2015 (NOAA 2015), approximately, 90 percent of tornadoes are categorized as EF2 or below in the US. The current ASCE Standard 7 design wind speed for buildings in the Central US lies between EF1 and EF2 (Standohar-Alfano and van de Lindt 2014). EF5 tornadoes, on the other hand, have had massive economic and social impacts in the US in recent years (e.g. Joplin 2011; Moore 2013). The tornado strike probability at a building site is very low, its impact is localized, and its wind field varies spatially within the tornado footprint. Accordingly, we consider a suite of scenario events in this LLD illustration with intensities EF2 and EF5, which are representative of *design* and *extreme* intensity levels. This approach eliminates the single-event focus often associated with scenario analysis and, at the same time, maintains the spatial variation in hazard demand for each scenario to enable resilience metrics to be assessed on the community scale.

Probabilistic statement of resilience goals

The uncertainties associated with both hazard characterization (H) and metric quantification (M) require community resilience goals to be expressed in probabilistic forms:

$$P(M_{j,i} < G_{j,i} | H_i) = a\% \tag{6.1}$$

where $M_{j,i}$ represents a community resilience metric of interest j (e.g., DLR or UIR) evaluated under hazard intensity H_i (e.g., tornados) with an intensity level of i (e.g., EF2 or EF5). $G_{j,i}$ is the prescribed building cluster resilience goal corresponding to $M_{j,i}$, and $a\%$ is a prescribed probability level. An example of the goal statement expressed in Equation (6.1) is $P(M_{UIR,EF5} < 2\% | EF5) = 95\%$, meaning "less than 2% of the residential buildings are uninhabitable immediately following any EF5 tornado event with 95% probability." The presence of the $a\%$ in the goal statement acknowledges the uncertain nature associated with any community resilience assessment, reflects the risk level that a community is willing to tolerate, and should be related to a community's value systems and preferences. The cluster resilience goal, $G_{j,i}$, may be determined by any one or a combination of the following: (1) de-aggregating socio-economic resilience goals at a higher-level (ULD) using quantitative models (e.g., population outmigration models, computable general equilibrium models) that relate the functionality of building clusters to social-economic consequences of a tornado; (2) selecting goals through the local political process; or (3) calibrating against predicted performance of existing well-constructed building clusters. In this illustration, a calibration method is used, as detailed later in the subsection on "Calibrating the building cluster performance goal."

Relating building cluster metrics to individual building performance criteria

Following the approach developed in earthquake engineering (Cornell & Krawinkler 2000) and recently adopted by Lin and Wang (2016) in community building portfolio resilience assessment, we estimate building cluster resilience metrics probabilistically from:

$$P\left(M \le z | H\right) = \iiiint_{M<z} f_{DV|DS}(u|v) f_{DS|V}(v|y) f_{V|TS}(y|S_T) f_{TS|H}(x|H) du\,dv\,dy\,dx \tag{6.2}$$

where the bold-faced symbols denote vector-valued variables; from right to left, $f_{TS|H}(x|H)$ is the probability density function (PDF) of the parameters defining a tornado scenario (*TS*) conditioned on a tornado intensity (*H*) characterized by EF-scale; $f_{V|TS}(y|S_T)$ is the PDF of the wind field *V* describing the wind gradient given each *TS*; $f_{DS|V}(v|y)$ is the PDF of damage state *DS* of buildings in the cluster conditioned on *V*; $f_{DV|DS}(u|v)$ is the PDF of damage value *DV* conditioned on *DS*; and *DV* is the loss to individual buildings with respect to the resilience metric of interest as a result of its physical damage (Lin & Wang 2016). The community resilience metric, M (i.e. DLR or UIR), is a function of *TS*, *V*, *DS*, and *DV*. Therefore, the cumulative distribution function (CDF) of M conditioned on H can be estimated by integrating the joint PDF of the four random vectors, namely, *TS*, *V*, *DS*, and *DV*, over the multi-dimensional region where $M(TS, V, DS, DV) < z$. The dimensions of *V*, *DS*, and *DV* equal the number of buildings in the cluster. Equation (6.2) relates the performance of individual buildings (represented by building fragility functions, $f_{DS|V}(v|y)$) to the resilience metrics of the cluster as a whole (represented by M, measured in terms of DLR or UIR). Generally, Equation (6.2) cannot be evaluated in a closed-form and a multi-layer Monte Carlo Simulation (MCS) is employed to estimate the probability distributions of UIR and DLR.

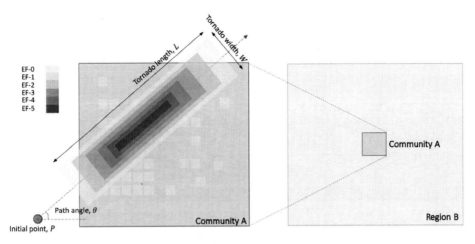

Figure 6.2 Tornado scenario (TS) simulation using MCS: (left) footprint of one TS; (right) the spatial region for tornado path simulation.

We begin by generating the tornado scenarios for events with intensities EF2 and EF5 by MCS. A tornado path can be effectively determined by four parameters (Strader et al 2016): initiation point (P), path angle (θ, east-heading to be 0°), path length (L) and width (W), as shown in Figure 6.2(a) on Community A. In the MCS, we define a Region B, which surrounds Community A and is 36 times large than Community A, as illustrated in the Figure 6.2(b). We assume that the tornado initiation point P is equally likely over Region B, and only tornados initiated in Region B can possibly pass through Community A. A statistical study of historical tornado records for the State of Oklahoma during the period 1950–2015 (NOAA 2015), tabulated in Table 6.1, indicates that tornado path angle θ can be described by a normal distribution, approximately with a mean of 30°~45° and standard deviation (SD) of 30°~50°, while the path length L and width W can be most effectively modeled by Weibull distributions. Using the parameters tabulated in Table 6.1, we generate 4,000 tornado scenarios for Community A, 2,000 each for EF2 and EF5 intensity levels, in order to obtain a probabilistic representation of the UIR and DLR. For each simulated tornado scenario, we generate the spatial variation of wind speed along and across the path, i.e. $f_{V|TS}(y\,|\,S_T)$, using the approach proposed in Standohar-Alfano and van de Lindt (2014), in which wind speed gradients take concentric rectangular shapes and the wind speed in each gradient is expressed in terms of EF-scale, as illustrated in Figure 6.2(a). The classification error associated with subjectively defining the wind intensity in terms of EF-scale can be captured by a normal distribution (Lu 1995). Accordingly, we model uncertainties of the wind speed within the gradients by a normal distribution, as tabulated in Table 6.2, in which the 98th and 2nd percentiles of the normal distribution coincide with the upper and lower bounds of the wind speed range for the corresponding gradient associated with a EF-scale. The simulated tornado path and spatial gradient of wind speed for each path provides a full spatial characterization of the demand field imposed scenario event ($\boldsymbol{TS}$) on a spatially distributed building cluster.

The probability of damage states ($\boldsymbol{DS}$), as defined in Table 6.3 (Masoomi & van de Lindt 2016), can be estimated for each building by fragility functions. Furthermore, the $\boldsymbol{DV}$, conditional on $\boldsymbol{DS}$ (i.e., DV^{DL}- the loss percentage of a building with respect to its replacement cost,

Table 6.1 Statistics of the path parameters for tornadoes in Oklahoma(From the NOAA SPC data, 1950 to 2015, 400 EF2 events and 10 EF5 events)

EF-scale	Length (m) $L \sim Weibull(k,\lambda)$				Width (m) $W \sim Weibull(k,\lambda)$				Angle (°) $\theta \sim N(\mu,\sigma)$	
	Sample		Parameters		Sample		Parameters		Sample	
	Mean	S.D.	Shape, k	Scale, λ	Mean	S.D.	Shape, k	Scale, λ	Mean	S.D.
EF2	11,032	12,993	1.125	12,458	287	327	0.945	280	34.6	31.9
EF5	36,305	23,342	1.691	41,451	1,047	564	2.123	1,195	44.9	36.3

Table 6.2 Statistics of wind speed in each EF-scale

EF-scale	Wind speed (3s gust, mph)	
	Speed range (Texas Tech, 2006)	Normal dist. $N(\mu,\sigma)$
EF0	65–85	$N(75, 5.0)$
EF1	86–110	$N(98, 6.0)$
EF2	111–135	$N(123, 6.0)$
EF3	136–165	$N(151, 7.5)$
EF4	166–200	$N(183, 8.5)$
EF5	Over 200	$N(220, 10.0)$

and DV^{UI}- the uninhabitability of a building) are tabulated in Table 6.4 (FEMA/NIBS 2003). Accordingly, the DLR and UIR can be obtained by aggregating the corresponding $\boldsymbol{DV}$ for each building over the entire building cluster:

$$M_{DLR,i} = \frac{\sum_{k=1}^{N} C_k^{rep} \cdot \sum_{l=1}^{4} DV_i^{DL} \cdot p_{k,l}^i}{\sum_{k=1}^{N} C_k^{rep}}, \qquad i \in (EF2, EF5) \qquad (6.3a)$$

$$M_{UIR,i} = \frac{\sum_{k=1}^{N} U_k^D \cdot \sum_{l=1}^{4} DV_i^{UI} \cdot p_{k,l}^i}{\sum_{k=1}^{N} U_k^D}, \qquad i \in (EF2, EF5) \qquad (6.3b)$$

in which N is the number of buildings in the cluster; $p_{k,l}^i$ is the probability of DS_l of the kth building, obtained from fragility functions with respect to tornado intensity level i; C_k^{rep} is the total replacement cost of the kth building; and U_k^D is the number of dwelling units in the kth building. Estimating M using Equation (6.3) for 2000 EF2 and 2000 EF5 simulated tornado scenarios, a full probabilistic distribution of M is obtained for EF2 and EF5 events, respectively.

6.6.2 Risk de-aggregation to obtain individual building strength criteria

As noted previously, de-aggregating community resilience goals to obtain the strength criteria for individual buildings and engineered facilities is an inverse process of the resilience metric evaluation procedure presented in Section 6.4. The de-aggregation starts with a set of building

Table 6.3 Definition of damage state (Masoomi & van de Lindt 2016)

Damage State (DS)	Roof cover failure	Window/Door failures	Parapet failure	Non-load-bearing wall failure	Roof structural failure	Load-bearing wall failure
0	$\leq 2\%$	No	No	No	No	No
1	$> 2\%$ and $\leq 15\%$	1 or 2	No	No	No	No
2	$> 15\%$ and $\leq 50\%$	> 2 and $\leq 25\%$	No	No	No	No
3	$> 50\%$	$> 25\%$	Yes	Yes	No	No
4	Typically $> 50\%$	Typically $> 25\%$	Yes	Yes	Yes	Yes

Table 6.4 Damage value, **DV** (FEMA 2003)

Damage Value, DV	Damage State, DS_i			
	$i = 1$	$i = 2$	$i = 3$	$i = 4$
DVp for direct loss (DV_i^{DL})	0.05	0.2	0.5	1.0
DV for un-inhabitability (DV_i^{UI})	0	0	1.0	1.0

cluster resilience goals, as expressed in Equation (6.1), and yields the theoretical minimum individual building performance criteria that enable the cluster resilience goals to be achieved. The premise is that the de-aggregation should be independent of the current existing condition of a building cluster. The cluster resilience goal is a long-term target for a community to strive for; and it is this long-term target that governs the de-aggregation, not the existing situation. In other words, de-aggregation answers the question: What are the minimum building performance criteria necessary for a building cluster to achieve the prescribed resilience goals?

Calibrating the building cluster performance goal
In this study, the calibration method is used to illustrate how the building cluster resilience goals with respect to UIR and DLR for residential building clusters might be established. In this illustration, four hypothetical clusters, each consisting of 5000 identical archetype buildings are distributed over a 32 km by 32 km (20-mi by 20-mi) area. The four archetypes, T1 to T4, used to populate the four hypothetical clusters are typical of wood residential buildings (Amini and van de Lindt 2014) that are compliant with the International Residential Building Code. The basic attributes of the four archetypes and the resilience metrics evaluated for the four hypothetical clusters are given in Table 6.5. For these four clusters the 95th percentile of DLR is in the range of 0.23% to 0.42% and 2.64% to 2.99% for EF2 and EF5 tornadoes, respectively, while the 95th percentile of UIR is in the range of 0.22% to 0.44% and 2.64% to 3.08% for EF2 and EF5 tornadoes, respectively. Accordingly, for the subsequent illustration, the resilience goals proposed in the last three columns in Table 6.5 were used for the 32 km by 32 km (20 mi by 20 mi) area. The last three columns each corresponds to a specific design code level: Level 1 – *Baseline code* (focus on life-safety), Level 2 – *Enhanced code* (focus on reparability), and Level 3 – *Continued Use* (focus on continued occupancy and use). When the community area (A_C) varies from 1,035 sq km to 37,400 sq km (400 sq mi to 14,400 sq mi), the DLR and UIR decreases monotonically, as illustrated in Figure 6.3 for DLR_{EF5} because a tornado is a very localized

Table 6.5 UIR and DLR estimated for four 32 km by 32 km (20-mi by 20-mi) hypothetical building clusters consisting of well-performing building archetypes and proposed building cluster goals

Building Cluster Metrics (M)	Hazard Intensity Levels (H)	Building archetype included in each hypothetical cluster (No. of story/No. of dwelling unit) (Amini and van de Lindt, 2014)				Proposed Goals (G)		
		T1 (1/1)	T2 (1/1)	T3 (2/4)	T4 (2/2)	Code Level 1 (Baseline))	Code Level 2 (Enhanced)	Code Level 3 (Cont'd Use)
DLR	EF2	0.23%	0.42%	0.41%	0.37%	**0.18%**	**0.10%**	**0.08%**
	EF5	2.64%	2.99%	2.99%	2.87%	**2.50%**	**1.80%**	**1.50%**
UIR	EF2	0.22%	0.40%	0.44%	0.36%	**0.18%**	**0.10%**	**0.08%**
	EF5	2.64%	2.98%	3.08%	2.84%	**2.50%**	**1.80%**	**1.50%**

T1 – Single family dwelling w/o basement; T2 – Single family dwelling; T3 – Multifamily dwelling; T4 – Multifamily dwelling.
Code Level 1 – Baseline Code; Code Level 2 –Enhanced Code; Code Level 3 –Continued Use.

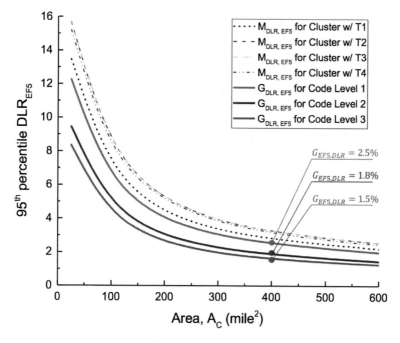

Figure 6.3 95th percentile of DLREF5 as a function of community area (AC).

hazard when compared to other natural events, such as hurricane or earthquake, and its impact on a small-area community can be much more devastating than on a large community. This correlation between DLR (or UIR) and A_C suggests that the cluster goal (G) expressed in term of DLR or UIR should be a function of A_C, as shown in the solid lines.

LLD formulation

The de-aggregation problem is formulated as an inverse optimization problem, where the decision variables are building performance criteria expressed probabilistically in terms of lognormal fragility functions (Rosowsky & Ellingwood 2002):

$$F(x) = \Phi\left[\frac{\ln(x) - \lambda_{Ri}}{\beta_{Ri}}\right], \qquad i = 1, 2, 3, 4 \tag{6.4}$$

where x is the hazard demand; $\lambda_{Ri} \in (\lambda_{R1}, \lambda_{R2}, \lambda_{R3}, \lambda_{R4})$ is the logarithmic median capacity (i.e., the median capacity $= \exp(\lambda_{Ri})$ for each $DS_i \in (DS_1, DS_2, DS_3, DS_4)$) and β_{Ri} is the logarithmic standard deviation of the capacity for damage state DS_i. The analysis of typical, IRC-compliant (IRC 2015) wood residential buildings presented in the literature (Rosowsky & Ellingwood 2002; Amini & van de Lindt 2014) indicate that β_{Ri} is usually in the range of 0.10 to 0.17 under wind load. The source of this uncertainty includes component strength, connection details, modes of failure, construction quality, etc. Accordingly, it assumed (conservatively) that β_{Ri} is 0.17 for all four damage states; this, in turn, focuses the de-aggregation process on determining the target for λ_{Ri}, which is sufficient to define the fragility in Equation (5.4).

De-aggregation is a multi-objective optimization problem (MOOP) in which we seek the minimum building strength parameter, $\lambda_R^T = [\lambda_{R1}^T, \lambda_{R2}^T, \lambda_{R3}^T, \lambda_{R4}^T]$, as illustrated in Figure 6.4, that enables a residential cluster to achieve its resilience goals (see Table 6.5). The MOOP formulation is summarized in Equations (6.5) to (6.8), and Table 6.6. Equation (6.5) defines the decision variable and Equation (6.6) defines the objective of the de-aggregation (i.e., the minimum λ_R) that enables the set of four cluster performance goals expressed in Equation (6.7) to be satisfied simultaneously. The values of $G_{j,i}$ are given in Table 6.5 for the three considered code levels, respectively. Equation (6.8) is a local constraint, which ensures consistency between the relative magnitudes of the four elements in vector λ_R and the characteristics of the four damage states presented in Table 6.3. The optimal λ_R were determined using multi-objective particle swarm optimization (MOPSO), an optimization method for its easy application and fast convergence in solving MOOPs (Kennedy & Eberhart 1995; Reddy & Kumar 2007).

6.7 Minimum performance criteria for residential buildings based on building cluster goals

The optimal minimum performance criteria for residential buildings needed to achieve the building cluster resilience goals presented in Table 6.5 are expressed in terms of optimal decision variables (logarithmic median capacity for each damage state), λ_R, for each goal level. To illustrate, Figure 6.5 presents the Pareto Front for the Code Level 3 – *Continued use*, showing the trade-off between the λ_{R1}, and $\Delta\lambda_R$ (i.e., $(\lambda_{R4}\ \lambda_{R1})$). It is observed that $G_{DLR,EF5}$ governs the lower right portion of the Pareto Front where the optimal λ_R set is relatively narrowly spaced with a comparatively larger λ_{R1} $G_{UIR,EF5}$ dominates the upper left portion of the Pareto Front where there is larger spacing between individual fragility functions of the optimal set starting with a comparatively smaller λ_{R1}; and in between, $G_{DLR,EF2}$ determines the Pareto Front boundaries. This observation can be explained by the fact that, as shown by Table 6.4, all four damage states contribute to DLR while only DS_3 and DS_4 contribute to UIR; thus UIR-related goals require larger values of λ_{R3} and λ_{R4} (corresponding to smaller λ_{R1} and larger $\Delta\lambda_{R1}$) and DLR goals require larger values of λ_{R1}.

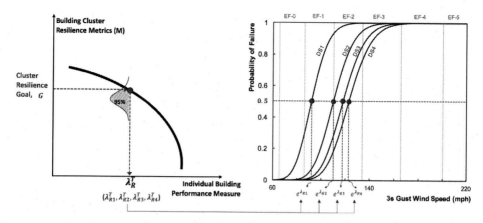

Figure 6.4 Illustration of de-aggregation, demonstrating the relation between (left) the cluster resilience goals and (right) the target building fragility functions.

Table 6.6 Optimal de-aggregation of building cluster goals

Item	Expression	Eq. No.
Decision Variable:	$\lambda_R = [\lambda_{R1}, \lambda_{R2}, \lambda_{R3}, \lambda_{R4}]$	Eq. (5.5)
Objectives	$min \, \lambda_R = \min([\lambda_{R1}, \lambda_{R2}, \lambda_{R3}, \lambda_{R4}])$	Eq. (5.6)
Constraints	$P(M_{j,i} < G_{j,i} \mid H_i) = a\%;$	Eq. (5.7)
	$j \in (UIR, DLR); i \in (EF2, EF5)$	
	$\lambda_R = a + b * \ln(\boldsymbol{DS})$	Eq. (5.8)

To select a target decision variable, λ_R^T, from the Pareto Front, we consider the values of $\Delta\lambda_R$ for typical existing IRC-compliant wood residential building archetypes summarized Table 6.5. The fragility functions for these archetypes can be found in Amini and van de Lindt [2014], where the typical range of $\Delta\lambda_R$ for these archetypes is 0.26 to 0.39, shown as the gray-shaded horizontal band in Figure 6.5. This range reflects the underlying mechanics of four failure modes (see Table 6.3) of typical wood frames. Therefore, the λ_R^T is selected from the Pareto Front within that band and associated with the *smallest* λ_{R1}, as highlighted by the solid red marker on Figure 6.5, as the goal is to identifying the "*minimum*" performance requirement. The value range of λ_{R1} for the same typical wood residential archetypes in Table 6.5 is 4.32 to 4.63, shown as the vertical band in Figure 6.5. The fact that the target λ_{R1}^T falls to the right side of the band suggests that the cluster resilience goals associated with the Code Level 3 objective (*Continued Function*) impose stricter requirements on building performance than those in current building practices aimed at ensuring occupancy safety. The λ_R^T for Code Level 1 (*Baseline*) and Code Level 2 (*Enhanced*) can be derived similarly. The target λ_R^T values for all three code levels are tabulated in Table 6.7, corresponding to the three target fragility functions in Figure 6.6.

The sensitivity of the target λ_R^T to (a) the sample size of MCS of tornado scenarios (N_{MCS}), (b) the number of buildings in a cluster (N_b), and (c) the logarithmic standard deviation of the target fragility functions (β_R) has been examined and is reported elsewhere (Wang et al. 2018), where it was found that the MCS sample size, number of buildings and logarithmic standard deviation, β_R have little impact on the target λ_R^T.

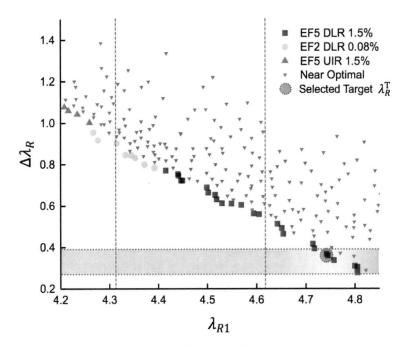

Figure 6.5 The trade-off between λ_{R1} and $\Delta\lambda_R$ for Code level 3 – continued use.

Table 6.7 Minimum performance objectives (Target λ_R^T)for individual residential buildings for the three code levels

Code Levels	Performance Objective	λ_{R1}^T	λ_{R2}^T	λ_{R3}^T	λ_{R4}^T
Baseline Code (BC)	$\lambda_R^{T,BC}$	4.53	4.72	4.82	4.90
Enhanced Code (EC)	$\lambda_R^{T,EC}$	4.67	4.86	4.97	5.05
Continued Use (CU)	$\lambda_R^{T,CU}$	4.74	4.93	5.01	5.11

The fragilities in Figure 5.6 can provide the basis for optimal risk-informed design of individual residential buildings to achieve community resilience goals (see Figure 5.1 and Section 5.4), under the assumptions stated in this chapter. With Figure 5.6, the state of PBE has been advanced beyond a single metric variable to consider two performance metrics – *Direct Loss Ratio* and *Un-Inhabitable Ratio* – the first a damage-related metric and the second a functionality metric. Other target system fragility families could be developed for different functionality goals. From these fragility families, systems of relatively simple equations for practical Load and Resistance Factor Design (LRFD) can be developed. For example, if the probability of unacceptable damage or loss of function is stipulated at 10 percent or less, given the occurrence of a design-basis wind, developing LRFD equations is a straightforward exercise (Ellingwood 2000). Such equations depend on the desired goals of a community which are outside the scope of this chapter.

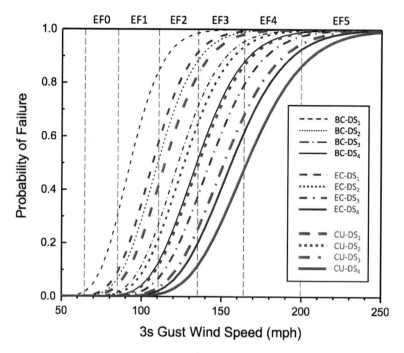

Figure 6.6 Target fragility functions for the three code levels.

6.8 Conclusions

In the coming decades, best practices of architects and engineers and decisions by city planners and regulatory authorities are likely to evolve to support common community resilience goals. At the same time, it seems probable that buildings, bridges, and other civil infrastructure facilities will continue to be designed individually. PBE provides a path forward for addressing and resolving the inherent challenges and constraints that will arise in addressing both facility and community needs. In this chapter, a path forward was proposed to establish the link between community resilience goals and the related performance objectives of individual buildings and civil infrastructure systems through a multi-layered, cascading de-aggregation framework to determine design criteria for PBE. The feasibility of the process was demonstrated with a residential building cluster exposed to tornado hazards and the economic and social aspects of community resilience, represented by two building cluster resilience metrics (UIR and DLR). It was shown that community resilience goals expressed in a probabilistic format yield three sets of target fragilities, each corresponding to a different set of cluster resilience goals (or code levels). Such fragilities can be used as the target building performance for new construction, pre-event retrofitting, or post-event reconstruction and, if desired, the basis for probabilistic design criteria for individual buildings suitable for incorporation in performance standards, such as ASCE Standard 7 (ASCE 2016).

Notwithstanding these advances, the challenges to developing risk-informed procedures for building design to achieve community resilience goals are complex and will likely result in departures from present code development procedures, among them:

- Common resilience goals for communities and building clusters need to be identified by a broadly based stakeholder group.
- Performance objectives for building clusters (e.g., residential, commercial, business, education, health) should be expressed as design requirements that are compatible with engineering practice in the US and are practical to implement from an engineering perspective.
- Hazards for PBE must be stipulated in a risk-consistent manner (PHA vs scenario analysis).
- Reliability targets for individual buildings in current structural design practices (e.g., ASCE Standard 7–16, Section 1.3) set a floor on minimum performance requirements, mostly at the component level; target performance criteria at the system level that support community resilience goals are needed.
- Codes and standards for buildings, bridges, and other civil infrastructure need to be coordinated to support community resilience goals.

Finally, establishing community resilience goals will involve a significant economic analysis component. The questions of how much up-front cost is justified by future risks and the differentiation between who pays the costs and who receives the benefits will drive the debate in most communities. Engineers are presently equipped to address the first question. The second one is inherently political and difficult to predict or model.

6.9 Acknowledgement

The science-based measurement tools to evaluate performance and resilience at community scales, fully integrated supporting databases, and risk-informed decision frameworks to support optimal life-cycle technical and social policies aimed at enhancing community resilience are under development at the Center of Excellence for Risk-Based Community Resilience Planning, established by The National Institute of Standards and Technology at Colorado State University and supported under NIST Financial Assistance Award Number: 70NANB15H044. The views expressed are those of the authors, and may not represent the official position of the National Institute of Standards and Technology or the US Department of Commerce.

References

AASHTO (2017). *AASHTO LRFD Bridge Design Specifications, 8th Edition*. American Association of State Highway and Transportation Officials, Washington, DC.

Amini, M.O. and van de Lindt, J.W. (2014). Quantitative insight into rational tornado design wind speeds for residential wood-frame structures using fragility approach. *J. Struct. Engrg., ASCE* 140(7), 04014033.

ASCE (2016). *Minimum design loads for buildings and other structures (ASCE Standard 7–16)*. American Society of Civil Engineers, Reston, VA.

Bocchini, P. and Frangopol, D.M. (2010). Optimal resilience-and cost-based postdisaster intervention prioritization for bridges along a highway segment. *J. of Bridge Engrg. ASCE*, 17(1): 117–29.

Bocchini, P. and Frangopol, D.M. (2012). Restoration of bridge networks after an earthquake: multicriteria intervention optimization. *Earthquake Spectra*, 28: 426–55.

Bruneau, M., Chang, S., Eguchi, R., Lee, G., O'Rourke, T., Reinhorn, A.M., and Winterfelt, D.V. (2003). A framework to quantitatively assess and enhance the seismic resilience of communities. *Earthquake Spectra*, 19: 733–52.

Burton, H., Deierlein, G., Lallemant, D., and Lin, T. (2015). Framework for incorporating probabilistic building performance in the assessment of community seismic resilience." *J. Struct. Engrg. ASCE*, 142(8) [dx.doi.org/10.1061/(ASCE)ST.1943-541X.0001321].

Cimellaro, G., Reinhorn, A.M., and Bruneau, M. (2010). Framework for analytical quantification of disaster resilience. *Engrg. Struct.*, 32: 3639–49.

Cornell, C.A. and Krawinkler, H. (2000). Progress and challenges in seismic performance assessment. *PEER Center News*, 3(2): 1–3.

Cutter, S.L., Burton, C.G., and Emrich, C.T. (2010). Disaster resilience indictor for benchmarking baseline conditions. *Journal of Homeland Security and Emergency Management*, 7. Article 51: 1–22.

Ellingwood, B.R. (2000). LRFD: implementing structural reliability in professional practice. *Engrg. Struct.* 22(2): 106–15.

Ellingwood, B.R., van de Lindt, J.W., and McAllister, T.P. (2016). Developing measurement science for community resilience assessment. *Sustainable & Resilient Infrastructure*, 1(3–4): 93.

FEMA/NIBS (2003). Multi-hazard Loss Estimation Methodology Earthquake Model (HAZUS-MH MR4): Technical Manual. Federal Emergency Management Agency, Washington, DC.

Franchin, P. and Cavalieri, F. (2015). Probabilistic assessment of civil infrastructure resilience to earthquakes. *Computer-Aided Civil and Infrast. Engrg.*, 30: 583–600.

Gardoni, P. and Murphy, C. (2009). Capabilities-based approach for measuring the societal impacts of natural and man-made hazards in risk analysis. *Natural Hazards Review*, 10: 2.

ICC (2015). *International Code Council Performance Code*. International Code Council, Brea, CA.

IRC (2015). *International Residential Code for One- and Two-family Dwellings*. International Code Council.

Jia, G., Tabandeh, A., and Gardoni, P. (2017). Life-cycle analysis of engineering systems: Modeling deterioration, instantaneous reliability, and resilience, in *Risk and Reliability Analysis: Theory and Applications* (P. Gardoni, ed.), New York: Springer.

Kennedy, J. and Eberhart, R.C. (1995). Particle swarm optimization. In *Proceedings of the 1995 IEEE International Conference on Neural Networks*, pp. 1942–8, Piscataway, New Jersey. IEEE Service Center.

Lin, P. and Wang, N. (2016). Building portfolio fragility functions to support scalable community resilience assessment. *Sustainable & Resilient Infrastructure* 1(3–4):108.

Lin, P., Wang, N., and Ellingwood, B.R. (2016). A risk de-aggregation framework that relates community resilience goals to building performance objectives, *Sustainable & Resilient Infrastructure*, 1(1–2): 1–13.

Lu, D. (1995). A statistically rigorous model for tornado hazard assessment (Doctoral dissertation, Texas Tech University).

Masoomi, H. and van de Lindt, J. W. (2016). Tornado fragility and risk assessment of an archetype masonry school building. *Engrg. Struct.*, 128: 26–43.

McAllister, T. (2013). Developing guidelines and standards for disaster resilience of the built environment: A research needs assessment. *NIST Technical Note 1795*, National Institute of Standards and Technology, Gaithersburg, MD [dx.doi.org/10.6028/NIST.TN.1795].

McAllister, T. (2016). Research needs for developing a risk-informed methodology for community resilience. *J. Struct. Engrg.*, ASCE, 142(8): DOI: 10.1061/(ASCE)ST.1943-541X.0001379.

Mieler, M., Stojadinovic, B., Budnitz, R., and Mahin, S. (2015). A framework for linking community resilience goals to specific performance targets for the built environment. *Earthquake Spectra*, 31: 1267–83.

Miles, S.B. and Chang, S.E. (2006). Modeling community recovery from earthquakes. *Earthquake Spectra*, 22(2): 439–58.

NAE (1996). *Understanding Risk: Informing Decisions in a Democratic Society*. The National Academies, Washington, DC.

NIST (2015). *Community Resilience Planning Guide for Buildings and Infrastructure Systems* (in two volumes). NIST Special Publication 1190 (Vols. 1 and 2), National Institute of Standards and Technology, Gaithersburg, MD.

National Oceanic and Atmospheric Administration. (NOAA). (2015). Severe Weather Database Files (1950–2015): US Tornadoes. www.spc.noaa.gov/wcm/ (last accessed August 13, 2018).

Reddy, M.J. and Nagesh Kumar, D. (2007). Multi-objective particle swarm optimization for generating optimal trade-offs in reservoir operation. *Hydrological processes*, 21(21): 2897–2909.

Rosowsky, D.V and Ellingwood, B.R. (2002). Performance-based engineering of wood frame housing: Fragility analysis methodology. *J. Struct. Engrg.*, ASCE, 128(1): 32–8.

Standohar-Alfano, C.D. and van de Lindt, J.W. (2014). Empirically based probabilistic tornado hazard analysis of the United States using 1973–2011 data. *Natural Hazards Review*, 16(1): 04014013.

Strader, S.M., Pingel, T.J., and Ashley, W.S. (2016). A Monte Carlo model for estimating tornado impacts. *Meteorol. Appl.*, 23(2): 269–81.

Texas Tech (2006). A Recommendation for an Enhanced Fujita Scale. Wind Science and Engineering Center (TTU WiSE), Texas Tech University, Lubbock, Texas.

Wang, N. and Ellingwood, B.R. (2015). Disaggregating community resilience objectives to achieve building performance goals. *Proc., Int. conference on applications of statistics and probability to civil engineering (ICASP12)*, University of British Columbia, Vancouver, BC.

Wang, Y., Wang, N., Lin, P., Ellingwood, B., Mahmoud, H., and Maloney, T. (2018). De-aggregation of community resilience goals to obtain minimum performance objectives for buildings under tornado hazards. *Structural Safety*. DOI: 10.1016/j.strusafe.2017.10.003.

Part III
Resilience of different systems

Buildings

7

Tornado damage modeling

Single buildings, communities, and regions

John W. van de Lindt,[1] Hassan Masoomi,[2] Navid Attary,[3] and Christine D. Standohar-Alfano[4]

[1] CENTER FOR RISK-BASED COMMUNITY RESILIENCE PLANNING, COLORADO STATE UNIVERSITY, DEPARTMENT OF CIVIL AND ENVIRONMENTAL ENGINEERING, FORT COLLINS, CO, 80523, USA; JWV@ENGR.COLOSTATE.EDU

[2] THE B. JOHN GARRICK INSTITUTE FOR THE RISK SCIENCES, UNIVERSITY OF CALIFORNIA, LOS ANGELES, CA, 90095, USA; MASOOMI@UCLA.EDU

[3] CENTER FOR RISK-BASED COMMUNITY RESILIENCE PLANNING, COLORADO STATE UNIVERSITY, DEPARTMENT OF CIVIL AND ENVIRONMENTAL ENGINEERING, FORT COLLINS, CO, 80523, USA; NAVID.ATTARY@COLOSTATE.EDU

[4] HAAG ENGINEERING, CHARLOTTE, NC, 28150, USA; CHRISTINE.STANDOHAR@GMAIL.COM

7.1 Introduction

There are approximately 1200 tornadoes reported annually in the US with the vast majority occurring east of the Rocky Mountains. Tornadoes have not found their way into building codes and standards for two reasons. (i) The probability that any building or structure being impacted by a tornado still remains infinitesimal because of the small geographical area impacted by each tornado. Building codes and standards focus on the design (and retrofit) of individual facilities; thus this low failure (or impact) probability has made it historically difficult to justify the inclusion of tornado loading in codified building design. (ii) Wood-frame building are most severely impacted by tornadoes, many of which are prescriptively and even conventionally constructed meaning a change in a load standard, e.g., ASCE 7 (2016), would not necessarily impact their design. In addition, for buildings constructed of heavier material such as concrete and steel, the majority of the damage occurs to the components and cladding and not the main wind force resisting system.

Interestingly, the study of community resilience (McAllister 2015) ultimately seeks to enable the performance targets of individual facilities and the ability to consider their effect on their community. A recent review of community resilience studies including progress and remaining challenges is available in Koliou et al. (2017b). So, now consider the two reasons that tornadoes have not been duly considered in modern building codes stated above. If one considers that if the ratio of event size to community size is large enough, the recovery responsibility moves from individual facility owners to a collective mentality. In resilience planning, this can be done at planning stages but requires modeling of communities and even regions depending on the level at which decisions are being made.

In this chapter, an overview of tornado damage modeling is provided at different scales, namely the individual building, the community level requiring spatial modeling of the tornado wind speeds, and the regional level for a large outbreak of supercell-spawned tornadoes.

7.2 Building-level analysis

In order to assess the resilience of a community subjected to natural hazards, performance of its components (e.g., residential buildings, industrial buildings, school buildings, water tanks, and electric power towers) under the specified hazard must be studied. Fragility analysis is a common approach to evaluate the performance of structures under extreme loads in which uncertainties in load and resistance estimation can be considered. A methodology to develop tornado damage fragility curves is described herein and more detail is available in Masoomi and van de Lindt (2016).

7.2.1 Fragility modeling

Typically, building-level damage fragility curves are developed for four damage states, namely, Slight, Moderate, Extensive, and Complete. These damage states would be defined based on different limit states for several components of the building according to the approach proposed by Vann and McDonald (1978). Therefore, a fragility curve at component level, can be defined as a conditional probability of exceeding a limit state (LS), based on a specified engineering demand parameter (EDP), for a given hazard intensity (e.g., 3-sec gust wind speed, v), which can be written as:

$$\text{Fr}(V) = P[LS \geq ls_i \,|\, V = v] \tag{7.1}$$

Similarly, at the building level, a fragility curve is defined as the conditional probability of exceeding a damage state (DS) under a given hazard intensity (e.g., 3-sec gust wind speed, v), which can be written as:

$$\text{Fr}(V) = P[DS \geq ds_i \,|\, V = v] \tag{7.2}$$

As shown in Figure 7.1, Monte Carlo simulation can be conducted to develop fragility curves at component and building levels. Usually, fragility curves would be presented by fragility parameters, derived from fitting a lognormal cumulative distribution function to the Monte Carlo simulation results, which can be expressed as:

$$\text{Fr}(V) = \Phi\left(\frac{In(v) - \lambda}{\zeta}\right) \tag{7.3}$$

where $\Phi(.)$ = standard normal cumulative distribution function, v = intensity measure (i.e., 3-s gust wind speed for extreme wind fragility curves), λ = logarithmic median, and ζ = logarithmic standard deviation.

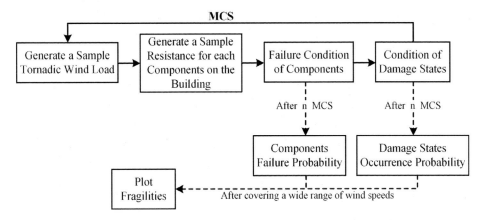

Figure 7.1 Flowchart of developing fragility curves.

7.2.2 Tornado load modeling

To calculate tornado wind loads, van de Lindt et al. (2013), proposed a tornado load coefficient to modify the procedure presented in ASCE 7–10 (2010), based on the study done by Haan et al. (2010). This method has been used in several studies to generate tornado fragility curves (e.g., Amini & van de Lindt 2014; Standohar-Alfano & van de Lindt 2015; Matta et al. 2015; Masoomi & van de Lindt 2016; Koliou et al. 2017a; Memari et al. 2018; Masoomi et al. 2018a). Masoomi and van de Lindt (2016) used this methodology and proposed two approaches to calculate the tornado wind load, namely, Approach A and Approach B. Tornado-induced wind loads for these two approaches can be calculated as follows:

$$q_h = 0.613 K_h K_{zt} V^2 \qquad (\text{N/m}^2); V \text{ in m/s}$$

$$q_h = 0.00256 K_h K_{zt} V^2 \qquad (\text{lb/ft}^2); V \text{ in mph}$$

(7.4)

$$p = q_h \left[T_e \left(GC_p \right) - T_i \left(GC_{pi} \right) \right] \qquad (\text{lb/ft}^2)(\text{N/m}^2),$$

(7.5)

where, K_h = velocity pressure exposure coefficient at mean roof height h, K_{zt} = topographic factor, V = 3-sec gust wind speed, q_h = velocity pressure evaluated at mean roof height h, G = gust-effect factor, C_p = external pressure coefficient, (GC_{pi}) = internal pressure coefficient, T_e = tornado external pressure adjustment, and T_i = tornado internal pressure adjustment.

In Approach A, the ASCE 7–10 (2010) external pressure coefficients, along with tornado pressure adjustments, derived based on the study done by Haan et al. (2010) would be used. In Approach B, the ASCE 7–16 (2016) external pressure coefficients would be used, assuming that both T_e and T_p are equal to unity. Table 7.1 illustrates the differences between the two approaches, for calculating tornado-induced wind load using Equation (7.5).

Wind load parameters statistics can be found from literature. For example, the wind load statistics used to develop fragility curves for the five wood-frame residential building archetypes in Masoomi et al. (2018a) are shown in Table 7.2. Moreover, the statistics for the external

Table 7.1 Difference between approaches A and B for calculating tornado-induced load

Parameters Description					Approach A	Approach B
Tornado Pressure Adjustment	Uplift Pressure	MWFRS	T_e	1.8 – 3.2		1.0
			T_i	0.0		
		C&C	T_e	1.4 – 2.4		
			T_i	0.0		
	Lateral Pressure	MWFRS	T_e	1.0 – 1.5		
			T_i	1.0		
		C&C	T_e	1.2 – 2.0		
			T_i	0.0		
External Pressure Coefficients, GC_p					ASCE 7–10	ASCE 7–16

Table 7.2 Wind load statistics

Parameters	Descriptions	Mean	COV	Distribution	Reference
K_h	Archetype 1	0.85	0.14	Normal	Amini and van de Lindt (2014);
	Archetype 2	0.89			Lee and Rosowsky (2005)
	Archetype 3	0.84			
	Archetype 4	0.82			
	Archetype 5	0.85			
GC_{pi}	Enclosed buildings	0.15	0.33	Normal	Amini and van de Lindt (2014);
	Partially enclosed buildings	0.46			Lee and Rosowsky (2005)
G	Gust-effect factor	0.82	0.10	Normal	Ellingwood and Tekie (1999)
C_p	Roof-to-wall connection	−0.81	0.15	Normal	Ellingwood and Tekie (1999)

pressure coefficients of roof sheathing panels were calculated based on the weighted average method (see Masoomi et al. 2018a, for more details).

7.2.3 Building components resistance modeling

Resistance of the building components subjected to wind loads is the other source of uncertainty in tornado fragility analysis. Statistics for the expected resistance of building components are available in the literature which can be used in fragility development. For example, roof covering, doors, windows, roof sheathing, and roof-to-wall connections, are the building components considered in Masoomi et al. (2018a) to develop damage fragility curves for wood-frame residential buildings. The resistance statistics for these components are summarized in Table 7.3. Since the existence of dead load helps the structure resist uplift loading, the statistics for the dead loads of roof components are also presented in Table 7.3 to be included in the analysis.

7.2.4 Definition of damage states

To develop fragility functions, typically four damage states are defined based on the approach proposed by Vann and McDonald (1978). In this methodology, different limit states are

Table 7.3 Resistance statistics for the components of the wood-frame residential buildings

Component	Mean	COV	Reference
Roof Cover	3.35 (kPa)	0.19	
Doors	4.79 (kPa)	0.20	Unnikrishnan and Barbato (2016)
Windows	3.33 (kPa)	0.20	
Roof Sheathing	6.67 (kPa)	0.21	van de Lindt and Dao (2009)
Roof-to-wall Connection/2H2.5 clips	11.68 (kN)	0.12	Reed et al. (1997)
Roof-to-wall Connection/H2.5 clip	5.84 (kN)	0.12	Reed et al. (1997)
Roof-to-wall Connection/2-16d toe nails	1.83 (kN)	0.16	van de Lindt et al. (2013)
Roof Panel Dead Load	0.168 (kPa)	0.10	Lee and Rosowsky (2005)
Roof-to-wall Connection Dead Load	0.717 (kPa)	0.10	Ellingwood et al. (2004)

Table 7.4 Damage states for the wood-frame building

Damage State	Roof Covering Failure	Window/Door Failures	Roof Sheathing Failure	Roof-to-wall Connection Failure
1	> 2% and ≤ 15%	1	No	No
2	> 15% and ≤ 50%	2 or 3	1–3	No
3	> 50%	> 3	>3 and ≤ 35%	No
4	Typically > 50%	Typically > 3	> 35%	Yes

* Each damage state is defined as occurrence of any of the shaded damage indicators in a given row.

considered for the components of the building envelopes, as well as the structural components, and each limit state participates in the definition of a damage state for the building. As shown in Table 7.4, roof covering, roof sheathing panels, roof-to-wall connections, doors and windows are the building components considered to construct the damage states for the wood-frame residential buildings in Masoomi et al. (2018a). For example, three limit states were considered for the roof covering failure. Limit state c1 (LSc1) was formulated based on the survival of the roof covering failure exceeding 2 percent by area, limit state c2 (LSc2) is when the roof covering failure exceeds 15 percent by area, and LSc3 represents exceeding 50 percent by area of roof covering failure. These three limit states contribute to the definition of damage states DS1, DS2, and DS3 at the building level, respectively. Damage state 1, i.e., minor damage, allows a maximum of one or two failed doors or windows and moderate failure in roof covering such that it can be covered with a tarp to prevent water entering the building. Damage state 2, i.e., moderate damage, allows the building to be occupied safely while there would be major roof covering damage, moderate window breakage, and likely some interior damage due to water intrusion. Damage state 3, i.e., severe damage, prevents the occupation but the building is repairable. Damage state 4, i.e., destruction, is the case of structural failure such that the building is not allowed to be occupied and it is not repairable.

7.2.5 Building-level fragility curves

As mentioned earlier, using the damage states (such as the ones shown in Table 7.4), building-level fragility curves can be achieved. As shown in Table 7.4, each damage state is defined as the occurrence of any of the shaded damage indicators in the corresponding row. However, the occurrence of the damage indicators is not necessarily statistically independent as they may

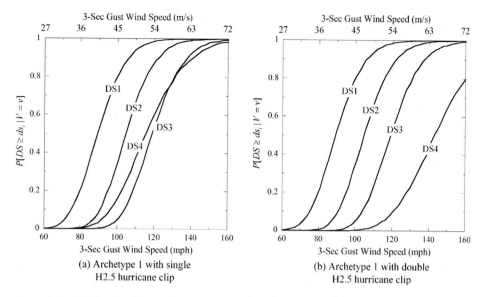

Figure 7.2 Building-level fragility curves for the wood-frame building archetype 1 in Masoomi et al. (2018a): (a) Archetype 1 with single H2.5 hurricane clip as roof-to-wall connections and (b) Archetype 1 with double H2.5 hurricane clip as roof-to-wall connections.

be correlated by wind loads. Therefore, the system fragility curves were developed by Monte Carlo simulation. Regarding damage states presented here for residential buildings (Table 7.4), it should be noted that, since the roof-to-wall connections failures were only considered in the definition of damage state 4, the fragility curve for damage state 4 might cross the curves of the other damage states. This happens if the roof-to-wall connections are more vulnerable than the other damage indicators used in the definition of other damage sates. As an example, the building-level fragility curves are shown in Figure 7.2 for archetype 1 presented in Masoomi et al. (2018a). As shown in this figure, as the resistance of the roof-to-wall connections is reduced from 2H2.5 hurricane clips (Figure 7.2b) to a single H2.5 hurricane clip (Figure 7.2a), the curve for damage state 4 shifts to the left while the other curves remain identical. This results in crossed fragility curves in these cases. The overlap of the fragilities for DS4 with DS3 in Figure 7.2(a) versus Figure 7.2(b) suggests that a load path discrepancy for the roof-to-wall connection. This has been observed in post-tornado field studies where only small portions of the roof covering and sheathing is lost prior to the roof being removed by the tornado. Using this methodology, tornado damage fragilities for different building archetypes may be developed which can be used in damage assessment of communities, subjected to tornadoes.

7.3 Community-level analysis

Tornado fragilities for buildings can be used to estimate the damage caused by tornadoes to individual buildings. Tornado fragilities for different buildings in a community can be developed based on the methodology explained in the previous section. Using tornado fragilities and wind speed at the location of the structure, the probability of reaching different damage states, namely Slight, Moderate, Extensive, and Complete, can be calculated for each building in the community. This process could be performed for all the buildings in a community in order to estimate the total structural damage to a community. However, currently, physics-based tornado fragilities are just becoming more popular and not many of them exists in the literature. Therefore, the building in the community should be categorized to reduce the number of required fragility functions. There is clearly a need for sensitivity analysis to determine how many building types must be modeled for basic community resilience assessment and subsequent risk-informed decisions. As an illustrative example of this process, the damage caused by the EF5 tornado which struck the city of Joplin, MO, USA, on May 22, 2011 is estimated herein. This massive tornado was the costliest tornado ever and the deadliest in the US in the last half a century. For this purpose, geocoded details (GIS data) of all of the buildings in the city of Joplin, at the time of the disaster were gathered. Based on the gathered data, buildings in the city of Joplin were categorized into 19 building types. Table 7.5 shows the details of these 19 building types. As it is clear from the table, since the overarching goal is to assess the resiliency of the community, considering all physical and socio/econ sectors, the selected building archetypes consider the occupancy of each building as well as other characteristics such as building material, area, roof type, etc.

Using the detailed data of the buildings from the city of Joplin, all of the buildings were categorized into the aforementioned 19 archetypes. For example, five typical wood residential buildings (see Amini & van de Lindt 2014, for details) were used to represent all the residential buildings in the city of Joplin. Each of the residential buildings in the city were then assigned to one of these five archetypes based on their characteristics such as foot print area, roof type, number of stories, etc. Figure 7.3 shows the tornado path with red cross hatching closest to the center-line representing the wind speed within the vortex that was estimated to have EF5 wind speeds (>320 km/h (>200 mph)), reducing to yellow for EF4 wind speeds and as the cross hatched areas move laterally outward from the tornado path eventually reaching EF1 rating as light blue. Figure 7.3 also shows different building types (different colors in the figure) assigned to all of the buildings of the city of Joplin.

Table 7.5 Types of buildings assumed to exist in the city of Joplin

Building Type	Building Description
T1	Residential wood-frame building – small rectangular plan – gable roof – 1 story
T2	Residential wood-frame building – small square plan – gable roof – 2 stories
T3	Residential wood-frame building – medium rectangular plan – gable roof – 1 story
T4	Residential wood-frame building – medium rectangular plan – hip roof – 2 stories
T5	Residential wood-frame building – large rectangular plan – gable roof – 2 stories
T6	Business and retail building (strip mall)
T7	Light industrial building
T8	Heavy industrial building
T9	Elementary/middle school (unreinforced masonry)
T10	High school (reinforced masonry)
T11	Fire/Police station
T12	Hospital
T13	Community center/Church
T14	Government building
T15	Large big-box store
T16	Small big-box store
T17	Mobile home
T18	Shopping center
T19	Office building

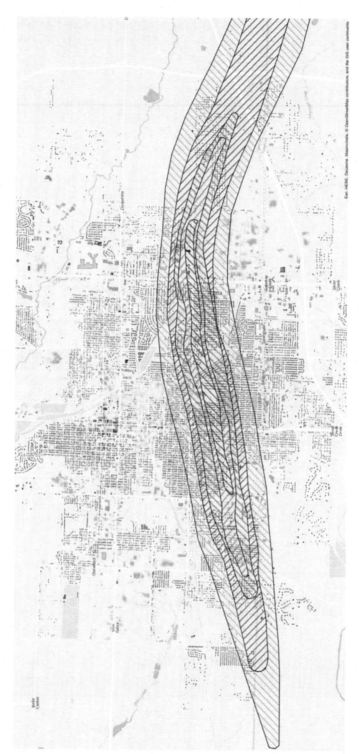

Figure 7.3 Nineteen archetype buildings in the city of Joplin and the actual tornado path and EF zones.

Table 7.6 Fragility parameters of the 19 archetypes buildings used in this chapter (Masoomi et al. 2018a; Koliou et al. 2017a; Masoomi & van de Lindt 2016; and Memari et al. 2018).

Building Type	Damage State (mph)							
	Slight		Moderate		Extensive		Complete	
	λ	ξ	λ	ξ	λ	ξ	λ	ξ
T1	4.52	0.11	4.70	0.11	4.77	0.11	4.81	0.12
T2	4.62	0.17	4.76	0.14	4.80	0.12	4.91	0.12
T3	4.31	0.10	4.44	0.10	4.63	0.10	4.70	0.10
T4	4.42	0.15	4.51	0.13	4.60	0.12	4.69	0.14
T5	4.45	0.13	4.54	0.11	4.67	0.10	4.71	0.10
T6	4.22	0.11	4.43	0.11	4.70	0.11	4.88	0.21
T7	4.29	0.11	4.50	0.10	4.59	0.10	4.67	0.10
T8	4.21	0.12	4.37	0.14	4.77	0.15	4.94	0.19
T9	4.29	0.12	4.56	0.11	4.69	0.11	4.93	0.16
T10	4.33	0.12	4.54	0.11	4.70	0.11	5.07	0.12
T11	4.37	0.25	4.70	0.12	4.85	0.12	4.99	0.19
T12	4.42	0.10	4.59	0.09	4.97	0.09	5.16	0.09
T13	4.06	0.12	4.46	0.11	4.68	0.11	4.95	0.17
T14	4.07	0.12	4.36	0.11	4.62	0.11	4.84	0.13
T15	4.14	0.12	4.37	0.12	4.83	0.12	5.06	0.12
T16	3.99	0.12	4.27	0.12	4.90	0.12	5.05	0.12
T17	4.28	0.12	4.47	0.12	4.60	0.11	4.70	0.12
T18	4.24	0.12	4.44	0.12	4.68	0.10	4.86	0.17
T19	4.23	0.12	4.48	0.12	4.71	0.11	4.97	0.17

Existing fragility functions in the literature were used in this illustrative example for these 19 archetype buildings to estimate the damage caused by the Joplin tornado to buildings. In particular, fragility functions for residential buildings (T1-T5) and big-box stores (T15 and T16) were adopted from Masoomi et al. (2018a) and Koliou et al. (2017a), respectively, while school buildings (T9 and T10), were modified and adopted, from Masoomi and van de Lindt (2016) and the remaining 10 buildings were adopted from Memari et al. (2018). Table 7.6 provides fragility parameters used for the 19 building archetypes.

Figure 7.4 shows the fragility curves for these 19 building types for the four damage states. It is noted that these 19 archetypes might not be sufficient to accurately model individual buildings if one is not within the suite of archetypes, however, since the fragility curves of these 19 building types in the four damage states almost span the entire range of wind speed limits for tornadoes (more than 65 mph), it was felt that this suite of archetypes should be sufficient to reasonably assess a community as a whole. Perhaps as more tornado physics-based fragilities become available, a detailed sensitivity analysis can be performed to assess the number of archetypes needed for this purpose. Using the wind speed and building fragility parameters, the probability of exceeding the four damage states, namely, Slight, Moderate, Extensive, and Complete was calculated for each building in the city of Joplin.

As mentioned earlier, using the estimated EF zones and geocoded details of the buildings, the range of wind speed and fragility parameters for each building are determined. Using Monte Carlo simulation with 10,000 runs, wind speed can be randomly chosen in each run from the associated EF region wind speed range and the probability of each building reaching

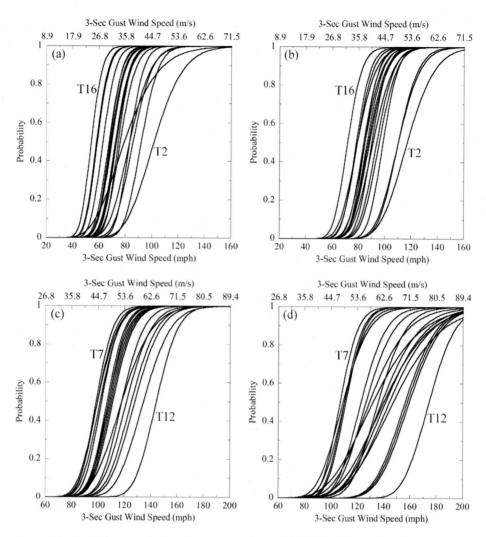

Figure 7.4 Fragility curves for the four damage states of (a) Slight, (b) Moderate, (c) Extensive and (d) Complete for the 19 archetype buildings.

each damage state can then be determined. Figure 7.5 to Figure 7.8 present the probability of damage for the four damage states.

As can be seen from these figures, the number of buildings with higher probabilities is reduced as the damage state goes from Slight (Figure 7.5) to Moderate (Figure 7.6), to Extensive (Figure 7.7), and to Complete (Figure 7.8), which is expected. In order to validate the analysis results both qualitative and quantitative measures were compared with post-disaster data. For example, it was reported by NIST (2014) that a total of 7411 residential buildings had some level of damage with 3181 experiencing severe damage. Simulation results showed that 7156 residential buildings would have more than a 95 percent probability of reaching a Slight (DS1) damage state. In addition, 3633 residential buildings would have more than a 95 percent probability of reaching damage state Extensive, which is consistent with the actual reported results.

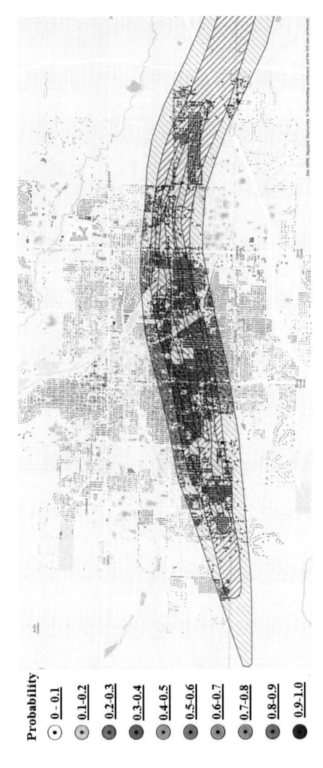

Figure 7.5 Probability of reaching damage state Slight for the buildings of Joplin community.

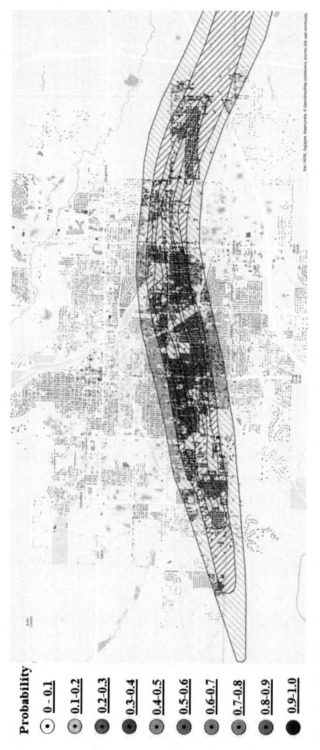

Probability

0 – 0.1
0.1-0.2
0.2-0.3
0.3-0.4
0.4-0.5
0.5-0.6
0.6-0.7
0.7-0.8
0.8-0.9
0.9-1.0

Figure 7.6 Probability of reaching damage state Moderate for the buildings of Joplin community.

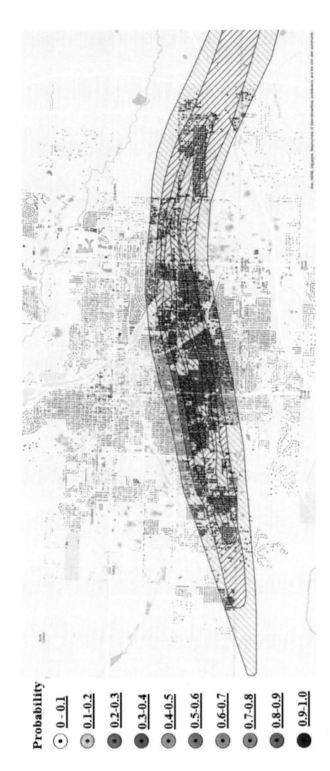

Figure 7.7 Probability of reaching damage state Extensive for the buildings of Joplin community.

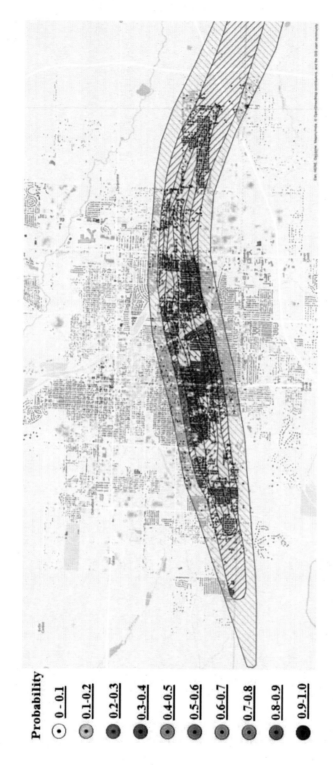

Probability

0 – 0.1
0.1-0.2
0.2-0.3
0.3-0.4
0.4-0.5
0.5-0.6
0.6-0.7
0.7-0.8
0.8-0.9
0.9-1.0

Figure 7.8 Probability of reaching damage state Complete for the buildings of Joplin community.

Alternatively, the results may be compared with aerial images captured after the event (see Attary et al. 2017a).

To fully assess the damage to a community caused by a tornado, in addition to assessing the damage to the buildings, the damage to other physical infrastructure such as the electric power network (Attary et al. 2017b; Masoomi & van de Lindt 2018), water and wastewater networks (Guidotti et al. 2016), telecommunication, etc. as well as socio/economic sectors (Masoomi et al. 2018b) should be considered. Such a complete analysis can be used as a risk-informed decision-making tool, by decision makers and city planners to enhance the resiliency of communities prone to tornadoes.

7.4 Regional-level analysis

While tornadoes can damage individual homes and communities, regional tornado outbreaks also have significant impacts that can cover a large geographic area. In these cases, recovery can be complicated since resources must be shared between multiple communities, counties, and even states. By reducing the degree of damage to wood-frame residential construction in tornadoes, economic losses and societal disruptions can be lessened. For this reason, gaining a better understanding of the impact of improved residential wood-frame construction in tornadoes on a regional level is investigated.

Historically, wood-frame construction has performed poorly when subject to extreme winds (Mehta et al. 1976; Connor et al. 1987; Changnon 2009). However, technological advances in construction methodologies have indicated that improvements in the vertical load path can result in increased performance of this type of construction under high winds (Reed et al. 1997; Lee & Rosowsky 2005; Datin et al. 2011). This was observed in Florida after the active 2004 hurricane season when researchers compared the performance of homes built between 1994 and 2001 to the Standard Building Code and those built after 2001 to the newly adopted Florida Residential Code (FRC) which was created in response to Hurricane Andrew (Gurley & Masters 2011). Results indicated that improved roof sheathing and roof-to-wall connections were effective in limiting structural damage across a broad geographic area associated with land-falling hurricanes. While the wind field in hurricanes and tornadoes do differ considerably, the construction methodologies used in the FRC can be used as the basis for strengthened practices across the interior portion of the US where building codes are substantially weaker under extreme wind loading.

The April 25–28, 2011 tornado outbreak was chosen as a case study to analyze the property loss reduction from tornadoes across a broad region when strengthened construction methodologies were implemented. This was the largest tornado outbreak in the US with a total of 350 tornadoes reported across 21 states (Figure 7.9) resulting in over $5B in property loss (SPC 2011). Due to the extensive nature of the tornado outbreak, the regional analysis performed by Standohar-Alfano et al. (2017) was consolidated to only 60 tornadoes by stipulating a minimum of $1M in property loss per individual tornado. The total property loss for the subset accounts for approximately 99.5 percent of the property loss from the outbreak, thus indicating that the results discussed below are representative of the total tornado outbreak.

It should be noted that the analysis described herein only includes residential construction, both wood-frame and manufactured. Property loss of commercial structures or intangible losses (i.e., fatalities, disruption to economy, damage to interior contents, etc.) was not included, but should be accounted for in future analysis, particularly in the study of resilience.

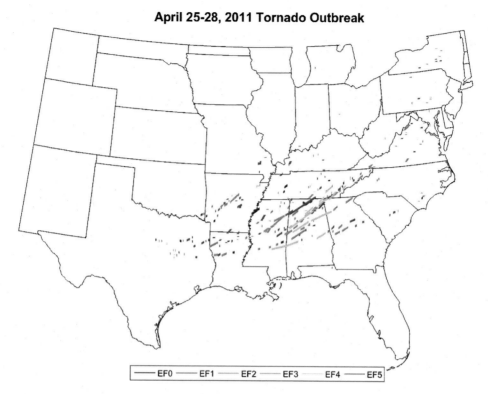

Figure 7.9 Tornado paths of the April 25–28, 2011 outbreak.

The methodology described by Standohar-Alfano et al. (2017) was used to estimate the property loss from a large tornado outbreak. Five wood-frame residential building archetypes described by Amini and van de Lindt (2014) were used in this chapter as representative of typical residential wood-frame buildings in the United States. Using the building code for each state, three different connections along the vertical load path were designed and subjected to tornado wind loading. These connections include the roof sheathing, roof-to-wall, and wall-to-foundation. Using fragility analysis as described earlier, the probability of failure was estimated. Due to uncertainty in the tornado wind field, the fragility analysis included two approaches as discussed before.

For each tornado, a locally-adopted residential building code was assigned to the archetypes based on the state where the tornado occurred. By overlaying the tornado path with census data, the number of homes impacted was determined using Geographic Information System (GIS) software. Similarly, an archetype and real market value (RMV) of each home were assigned based on census data obtained for a given tract impacted by the tornado path. Finally, a tornado wind speed and associated probability of failure were assigned based on the variation of intensity in a tornado path summarized by Standohar-Alfano and van de Lindt (2014).

Once all variables were assigned for a given archetype, property loss was estimated based on two models proposed by Weibe and Cox (2014). Their models provided an estimate for loss at the community level by using fragility curves and a RMV of structures. Method 1 aggregated a percentage of RMV for all buildings with a probability of failure greater than zero. For example, 25 percent of the RMV of a home would be included in the property loss model

Table 7.7 Loss estimation for the April 25–28, 2011 tornado outbreak

Total No. of Tornadoes	No. of Homes Impacted	SPC Record Property Loss ($B)	Property Loss			
			Method 1 – ($B)			
			Approach A		Approach B	
			Local	FRC	Local	FRC
60	22,072	5.1	3.5	2.0	2.3	2.2
			Method 2 – ($B)			
			Approach A		Approach B	
			Local	FRC	Local	FRC
			3.6	2.0	2.3	2.2

Note this only includes tornadoes resulting at least $1M in property loss.

if the associated probability of failure at that location was 25 percent. Similarly, Method 2 aggregated the full RMV of homes with a probability of failure that exceeded a threshold of 50 percent. It should be noted that the threshold can be adjusted based on model use and the discretion of the authors.

Results from the regional property loss estimate for the late April 2011 outbreak are shown in Table 7.7. This table includes the results from using both Approach A and Approach B fragilities, which takes into account the uncertainty in tornado wind loading. The local code varied depending on the state where the tornado was reported, whereas for strengthened construction, all wood-frame residential construction was designed using the FRC (2010). Both Method 1 and Method 2 resulted in similar magnitudes of property loss for Approach A and Approach B for both standard and strengthened construction. For the Approach A estimate of property loss, there was a large difference between local and strengthened construction. The reduction in property loss when using strengthened construction was approximately 43 percent for Method 1 and 45 percent for Method 2. The Approach B estimate of property loss did not result in as large of a reduction in loss with standard versus strengthened construction and was approximately 5 percent for both Method 1 and Method 2. This was anticipated since Approach B treated tornado winds the same as straight-line winds.

The difference in the reduction in property loss between Approach A and Approach B is due to uncertainty in tornado wind loading. Approach B fragility estimation treated tornadic winds as straight line, however, some studies have shown that tornadoes result in higher pressure on buildings as compared to straight line winds (e.g. Haan et al. 2010). This implies that at the same reference wind speed it is likely a tornado would cause more damage than straight line winds.

By investigating a widespread tornado outbreak, the impact of strengthened construction over a broad geographic area can be assessed. Results indicated that by improving construction, the estimated property loss was significantly reduced. It should be noted that the April 25–28, 2011 tornado outbreak did result in 15 violent tornadoes rated EF4 or greater (winds in excess of 74 m/s (165 mph)), which result in catastrophic damage to wood-frame construction and strengthened construction methodologies are of little benefit in areas that receive this magnitude of wind speed. Fortunately, of the 350 tornadoes, 90 percent were rated EF2 or lower on the Enhanced Fujita scale (SPC 2011), implying wind speeds at or below 60 m/s (135 mph). Likewise, in tornadoes rated EF3 or greater, the majority of the damage path experiences wind speeds at or below 60 m/s (135 mph) (Standohar-Alfano & van de Lindt 2014). Thus, utilizing strengthened construction methodologies can mitigate the majority of damage to wood-frame construction subjected to tornadoes. This is extremely beneficial in large-scale outbreaks which can be taxing on local, state, and federal resources used for recovery efforts.

7.5 Conclusions

Tornadoes result in significant losses across the US but are not yet included in building codes and standards. While consideration of tornado risk at the individual building level may still be questionable, consideration at the community and regional level in the context of resilience is more logical. In this chapter, the process of modeling building damage due to tornado wind loads at the building, community, and regional levels are explained. For a tornado outbreak at the regional level, the cost savings of building damage alone is significant if one improves light-frame wood construction practices. In community and regional resilience studies direct losses such as building damage are only one contribution to the information that informs the decision process. Thus, it is imperative that other physical and non-physical sectors within a community or region be added to the modeling process.

Acknowledgements

The work presented in this chapter was supported by the National Science Foundation (NSF) under Grant No. CMMI-1452725, Cooperative Agreement 70NANB15H044 between the National Institute of Standards and Technology (NIST) and Colorado State University, and funds by the Department of Civil and Environmental Engineering at Colorado State University. These sources of support are gratefully acknowledged. All views expressed in this chapter are those of the authors and do not necessarily reflect the views of the funding organizations of government institutes or departments.

References

American Society of Civil Engineers (ASCE). (2010). Minimum design loads for buildings and other structures, Standard ASCE 7–10. Reston, VA.

American Society of Civil Engineers (ASCE). (2016). Minimum design loads for buildings and other structures, Standard ASCE 7–16. Reston, VA.

Amini, M.O. and van de Lindt, J.W. (2014). Quantitative insight into rational tornado design wind speeds for residential wood-frame structures using fragility approach. *Journal of Structural Engineering*, 140(7): 04014033.

Attary, N., van de Lindt, J.W., Mahmoud, H., and Smith, S. (2017a). Hindcasting community level damage for the Joplin MO 2011 EF5 tornado: Buildings-Electric Power Network. *Journal of Natural Hazards Review* (under review).

Attary, N., van de Lindt, J.W., Mahmoud, H., Smith, S. Navarro, C.M., Kim, Y.W., and Lee, J.S. (2017b). Community level building damage assessment for the 2011 Joplin, MO EF5 tornado. *Natural Hazards*, 1–22.

Changnon, S.A. (2009). Tornado losses in the United States. *Natural Hazards Review*, 10(4): 145–50.

Conner, H.W., Gromala, D.S., and Burgess, D.W. (1987). Roof connections in houses: Key to wind resistance. *Journal of Structural Engineering*, 113(12): 2459–74.

Datin, Peter L., Prevatt, David O., and Pang, Weichiang (2011). Wind-uplift capacity of residential wood roof-sheathing panels retrofitted with insulating foam adhesive. *Journal of Architectural Engineering*, 17: 144–54.

Ellingwood, B.R. and Tekie, P.B. (1999). Wind load statistics for probability-based structural design. *Journal of Structural Engineering*, 125(4): 453–63.

Ellingwood, B.R., Rosowsky, D.V., Li, Y., and Kim, J.H. (2004). Fragility assessment of light-frame wood construction subjected to wind and earthquake hazards. *Journal of Structural Engineering*, 130(12): 1921–30.

FRC (2010). Florida Residential Building Code, International Code Council, Country Club Hills, IL.

Guidotti, R., Chmielewski, H., Unnikrishnan, V., Gardoni, P., McAllister, T., and van de Lindt, J. (2016). Modeling the resilience of critical infrastructure: The role of network dependencies. *Sustainable and Resilient Infrastructure*, 1(3–4): 153–68.

Gurley, K.R. and Masters, F.J. (2011). Post-2004 hurricane field survey of residential building performance. *Natural Hazards Review*, 12: 177–83.

Haan, F., Jr., Balaramudu, V., and Sarkar, P. (2010). Tornado-induced wind loads on a low-rise building. *J. Struct. Eng.*, 136(1): 106–16.

Koliou, M., Masoomi, H., & van de Lindt, J.W. (2017a). Performance assessment of tilt-up big-box buildings subjected to extreme hazards: Tornadoes and earthquakes. *Journal of Performance of Constructed Facilities*, 31(5): 04017060.

Koliou, M., van de Lindt, J.W., McAllister, T.P., Ellingwood, B.R., Dillard, M., and Cutler, H. (2017b). State of the research in community resilience: progress and challenges. *Sustainable and Resilient Infrastructure*, 1–21. https://doi.org/10.1080/23789689.2017.1418547

Lee, K.H. and Rosowsky, D.V. (2005). Fragility assessment for roof sheathing failure in high wind regions. *Engineering Structures*, 27(6): 857–68.

McAllister, T. (2015). Research needs for developing a risk-informed methodology for community resilience. *Journal of Structural Engineering*, 142(8): C4015008.

Masoomi, H. and van de Lindt, J.W. (2016). Tornado fragility and risk assessment of an archetype masonry school building. *Engineering Structures*, 128: 26–43.

Masoomi, H. and van de Lindt, J.W. (2018). Restoration and functionality assessment of a community subjected to tornado hazard. *Structure and Infrastructure Engineering*, 14(3): 275–91.

Masoomi, H., Ameri, M.R., and van de Lindt, J.W. (2018a). Wind performance enhancement strategies for residential wood-frame buildings, *Journal of Performance of Constructed Facilities*, 32(3): 04018024.

Masoomi, H., van de Lindt, J.W., and Peek, L. (2018b). Quantifying socioeconomic impact of a tornado by estimating population outmigration as a resilience metric at the community level. *Journal of Structural Engineering*, 144(5): 04018034.

Matta, F., Cuéllar-Azcárate, M.C., and Garbin, E. (2015). Earthen masonry dwelling structures for extreme wind loads. *Engineering Structures*, 83: 163–75.

Mehta, K.C., Minor, J.E., and McDonald, J.R. (1976). Windspeed analyses of April 3–4, 1974 tornadoes. *Journal of the Structural Division*, 102(ST9): 1709–24.

Memari, M., Attary, N., Masoomi, H., Mahmoud, H., van de Lindt, J.W., Pilkington, S., and Ameri, M.R. (2018). Minimal building fragility portfolio for damage assessment of communities subjected to tornadoes. *Journal of Structural Engineering*, 144(7): 04018072.

Reed, T.D., Rosowsky, D.V., and Schiff, S.D. (1997). Uplift capacity of light-frame rafter to top plate connections. *Journal of Architectural Engineering*, 3(4): 156–63.

Standohar-Alfano, C. and van de Lindt, J.W. (2014). An empirically-based probabilistic tornado hazard analysis of the U.S. using 1973–2011 data. *Natural Hazards Review*, 16(1): 04014013.

Standohar-Alfano, C. and van de Lindt, J.W. (2015). Tornado risk analysis for residential wood-frame roof damage across the United States. *Journal of Structural Engineering*, 142(1): 04015099.

Standohar-Alfano, C.D., van de Lindt, J.W., and Holt, E.M. (2017). Comparative residential property loss estimation for the April 25–28, 2011, tornado outbreak. *Journal of Architectural Engineering*, 24(1): 04017026.

Storm Prediction Center (2011). Severe Weather Database Files.

Unnikrishnan, V.U. and Barbato, M. (2016). Performance-based comparison of different storm mitigation techniques for residential buildings. *Journal of Structural Engineering*, 142(6): 04016011.

van de Lindt, J.W. and Dao, T.N. (2009). Performance-based wind engineering for wood-frame buildings. *Journal of Structural Engineering*, 135(2): 169–77.

van de Lindt, J., Pei, S., Dao, T., Graettinger, A., Prevatt, D., Gupta, R., and Coulbourne, W. (2013). Dual-objective-based tornado design philosophy. *Journal of Structural Engineering*, 139(2): 251–63.

Vann, W.P. and McDonald, J.R. (1978). *An Engineering Analysis: Mobile Homes in a Windstorm*. Institute for Disaster Research, College of Engineering, Texas Tech University.

Weibe, Dane M. and Cox, D.T. (2014). Application of fragility curves to estimate building damage and economic loss at a community scale: A case study of Seaside, Oregon. *Natural Hazards*, 71: 2043–61.

Realizing hurricane resilient communities through distributed computing

Ahmed U. Abdelhady, Seymour M.J. Spence, and Jason McCormick

DEPARTMENT OF CIVIL AND ENVIRONMENTAL ENGINEERING,
UNIVERSITY OF MICHIGAN, ANN ARBOR, MI 48109, USA

8.1 Introduction

Hurricanes are one of the costliest natural hazards that can strike the United States. Between 1970 and 2016, the United States suffered seven out of the ten costliest insurance losses in the world, five of which were due to hurricanes (Sigma 2017). In the period 1968–2016, on average 2.4 major hurricanes (Category 3 or greater) occurred each year (Hurricane Research Division 2017). Moreover, risk-prone areas, e.g. coastlines, have experienced population growth, migration, and increased wealth concentration, all of which inevitably lead to increased risk of future losses (Pita et al. 2015). The estimation of resiliency is increasingly recognized as one of the fundamental ways for quantifying this risk as well as providing a rational basis for planning mitigation strategies for its reduction. As such, resiliency is becoming an essential requirement for many coastal communities that seek to ensure long term economic prosperity and quality of life.

By considering different perspectives and fields, various definitions of resiliency were identified in Haimes (2009) while in Righi et al. (2015) a number of new definitions were introduced after having surveyed existing definitions. In particular, in Aven (2011) resiliency was defined as "the ability of the system to withstand a major disruption within acceptable degradation parameters and to recover within an acceptable time and composite costs and risks," while in Cutter et al. (2012) community resiliency was defined as "the ability to prepare and plan for, absorb, recover from, and more successfully adapt to actual or potential adverse events." With the aim of quantifying rather than defining resiliency for communities subject to seismic events, in Bruneau et al. (2003) a conceptual framework was introduced that is based on the following four properties: (1) robustness: defined as the ability to keep a level of functionality after the arrival of a severe hazard event; (2) redundancy: defined as the existence of substitutable components which, in case of disruption, ensure the functionality of the system; (3) resourcefulness: defined through the identification of priorities and mobilization of resources to achieve recovery goals; (4) rapidity: defined as the ability to meet recovery goals in a timely fashion. In Bruneau et al. (2003) these properties are used as a methodology to measure the following four dimensions of community resiliency: (1) technical; (2) organizational; (3) social; (4) economic. In Cimellaro et al. (2010) this conceptual framework was extended through the introduction of analytical functions for describing the technical and organizational dimensions. These functions allowed for the application of the framework to the calculation of resiliency in the case of critical health care facilities subject to severe seismic events.

The quantification of resiliency for communities that are subject to natural hazards (such as hurricanes) is essential for identifying the inevitable interdependencies that exist between the critical infrastructure systems within the community (Ouyang 2014). Critical infrastructure systems are those for which their failure will impact the public and economic security of the community. Examples of such systems are telecommunication systems, transportation systems, water supply systems, etc. It should be mentioned that, even though the interdependencies between critical infrastructure systems can improve operational efficiency, they increase system vulnerability (Dueñas-Osorio & Vemuru 2009). This increase in system vulnerability is due to the phenomena of cascading failure. In other words, the damage in one component can trigger a series of failures in other components. Modeling and simulation of interdependencies across critical infrastructure systems is key to accurately estimating community resiliency (Guidotti et al. 2016). However, due to the often complex nature of the individual systems composing the community, interdependencies will, in general, present a computational problem of non-trivial entity. Figure 8.1 shows an example of the interdependencies that will generally exist, and therefore require modeling, within a computational environment

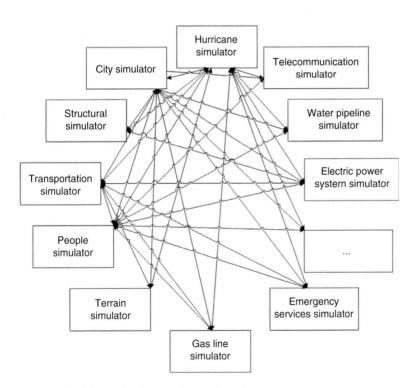

Figure 8.1 Schematic diagram illustrating the computational environment necessary for modeling interdependencies between different simulators of critical systems.

aimed at estimating the resiliency of communities subject to hurricanes, where each critical system is modeled through a numerical simulator. Similar diagrams can be plotted for different types of hazards.

It is clear that modeling those interdependencies is a complex and challenging process. Ouyang (2014) provides a review of modeling and simulation approaches for capturing infrastructure interdependencies and categorized approaches into: (1) empirical approaches: based mainly on historic data about the disaster and expert judgment; (2) agent based approaches: a bottom-up method in which each simulator is an autonomous agent that interacts with other agents in an environment based on a set of rules that simulate their interaction in the real world; (3) system dynamics based approaches: based on modeling the evolution of interdependencies as hazard events occur by capturing the causes and effects (causal-loop), then describing the flow of information through the system (stock-and-flow); (4) economic theory based approaches: based on modeling economic interdependencies by analyzing the intermediate goods that are required by all producers; (5) network based approaches: based on viewing the whole model as a network in which nodes are different infrastructure components while links are used to model interdependency between the different components; (6) other approaches: such as the hierarchical holographic modeling (HHM) method, approaches based on high level architecture (HLA), petri-net (PN) based methods, and Bayesian network (BN) methods. In Ouyang (2014), Ouyang called for "an open modeling framework to capture both short-term and long-term change and evolution of critical infrastructures," but did not provide details on the workings of such a framework.

Within this context, this chapter will give an overview concerning the quantification of resiliency of residential neighborhoods subject to hurricane hazards in which residential neighborhoods are defined as communities consisting of mainly one or two story wooden buildings. First, vulnerability models for the estimation of loss will be discussed (i.e. hurricane damage and loss estimation models). Then, approaches based on distributed computing will be discussed and introduced as a tool to efficiently simulate interdependencies between the models. Finally, the estimation of recovery times and the restoration of functionality curve for estimation of resiliency metrics (recovery model) will be discussed.

8.2 Hurricane damage and loss estimation (vulnerability models)

Estimating the damage that occurs to the envelope of wind excited buildings is one of the key aspects of effectively estimating the damage and losses in typical residential neighborhoods. This damage is caused mainly by two mechanisms: excessive wind pressures and windborne debris. There are two major approaches for estimating damage due to these mechanisms (Yau 2011), the time-stepping method and the point-in-time method, as illustrated in the flowchart of Figure 8.2. In both methods, time histories of wind speeds and directions are required. In the first method, the time history is used to calculate wind pressures, evaluate the performance, and then estimate the cumulative damage for each building at a series of time steps (instants during the passage of the hurricane through the neighborhood). This method is used in HAZUS-MH (Vickery et al. 2006), in the model outlined in Yau et al. (2011), and in the framework outlined in Grayson et al. (2013). The second method uses only one point in time, extracted from the time history, for characterizing the wind speed and direction. This is typically taken as the instant in which the maximum wind speed occurs and is then used to estimate the average damage for each

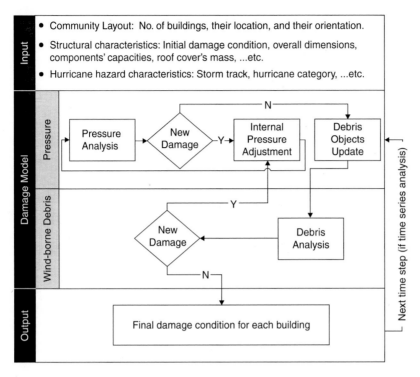

Figure 8.2 Flowchart of vulnerability model.

building in the neighborhood. This approach is used in the Florida Public Hurricane Loss Projection Model (FPHLPM) (Gurley et al. 2005) as well as the model outlined in Yau et al. (2011). The second method is less accurate, but computationally less expensive than the first. In Yau (2011) it is shown that the point-in-time method can lead to underestimates in damage of up to 60 percent. This situation can become even more pronounced when damages caused by debris are included.

As can be deduced from Figure 8.2, the vulnerability model can be divided into four sub-models, namely: building model, hurricane model, pressure damage model, and windborne debris model. The following sub-sections give a brief discussion on each sub-model.

8.2.1 Building model

The main function of this model is to generate a number of residential buildings that form the neighborhood (Grayson et al. 2013). Location (latitude and longitude) and orientation for each building should be specified in this model as damage caused by wind pressure as well as debris is highly dependent on the location and orientation of a building (Yau et al. 2011). After building generation (i.e. location and orientation) the following structural characteristics should be assigned to each building: overall dimensions, initial damage conditions, number of stories (one or two), number of windows, number of doors and garage doors, component resistance to both pressure and impact, dimensions and mass of all wall and roof sheathing as well as wall and roof coverings.

The above-mentioned information and statistics regarding residential buildings should be obtained from the local building stock. Alternatively, previous studies, such as FPHLPM (Gurley et al. 2005) or reports issued by the National Association of Home Builders (NAHB) (National Association of Home Builders 1999), provide a valuable source of information concerning typical building stock.

8.2.2 Hurricane model

A detailed description of the hurricane wind field during its passage through the residential neighborhood is essential for the calculation of the dynamic wind pressures (estimated through a pressure damage model) and the trajectory of windborne debris (estimated through a windborne debris model). Hurricane wind field models that provide a sufficient level of detail can be divided into two main categories: Gradient wind models (i.e. models based on the work of Holland (1980) and frameworks based on the models introduced in Shapiro (1983).

Holland model (gradient wind model)
This model provides the basis for the hurricane model implemented in the framework outlined in (Grayson et al. 2013). In particular, in this model, the equation governing air motion is based on the balance between the force induced by the pressure gradient and the Coriolis and centrifugal forces. Figure 8.3 shows how those forces balance in both the Northern and Southern hemispheres. After solving the equation of motion under these conditions while adding the effect of hurricane translational speed, the following equation provides the mean over-water gradient wind field (Grayson et al. 2013):

$$\overline{V}_g = \frac{1}{2}\left(V_t \sin(\alpha) - fr\right) + \sqrt{\frac{1}{4}\left(V_t \sin(\alpha) - fr\right)^2 + \left(\frac{B\Delta p}{\rho_a}\right)\left(\frac{Rmax}{r}\right)^B e^{-\left(\frac{Rmax}{r}\right)^B}}, \qquad (8.1)$$

where:

V_t = is the hurricane translational speed;
α = is the angle from the hurricane heading to the radius r;
f = is the Coriolis parameter;

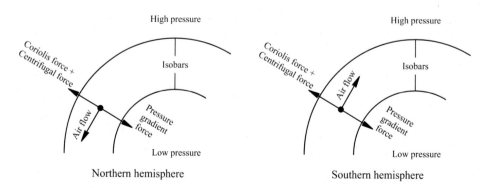

Figure 8.3 Balanced gradient wind in the Northern and Southern hemispheres.

r = is the distance from the hurricane eye to the point at which wind field is calculated;

B = is the Holland pressure parameter (which can be taken between $1 \sim 2.5$ (Holland 1980));

Δp = is the pressure difference between the ambient pressure and the central pressure;

ρ_a = is the air density ($\sim 1.225 \, kg \, / \, m^3$);

$Rmax$ = radius from the eye to the location of maximum wind speed.

For estimating the model parameters B and $Rmax$ for a specific hurricane, the indications provided in Vickery et al. (2000) can be used.

Shapiro model

This model is based on solving the momentum equations for a slab boundary layer of constant depth under an imposed symmetric pressure distribution. In this model, the coordinate system moves with the hurricane vortex, which is in gradient balance with the pressure field above the boundary layer. The radial and tangential momentum equations in cylindrical coordinates (r, λ) are:

$$u\frac{\partial u}{\partial r} - \frac{v^2}{r} - fv + \frac{v}{r}\frac{\partial u}{\partial \lambda} + \frac{\partial \varphi}{\partial r} - K\left(\nabla^2 u - \frac{u}{r^2} - \frac{2}{r^2}\frac{\partial v}{\partial \lambda}\right) + F(c,u) = 0 \tag{8.2a}$$

$$u\left(\frac{\partial v}{\partial r} + \frac{v}{r}\right) + fu + \frac{v}{r}\frac{\partial v}{\partial \lambda} - K\left(\nabla^2 v - \frac{v}{r^2} - \frac{2}{r^2}\frac{\partial u}{\partial \lambda}\right) + F(c,v) = 0, \tag{8.2b}$$

where:

u and v = are the radial and tangential wind speeds;

φ = is the pressure distribution within the storm;

f = is the Coriolis parameter;

c = is the hurricane translational speed;

K = is the constant coefficient of eddy diffusion;

λ = is the azimuth measured counterclockwise from the east;

F = is the frictional drag force.

In Vickery et al. (2000), the above equations are written in Cartesian coordinates and a finite-difference scheme is applied for finding solutions. This formulation of the Shapiro model is implemented in HAZUS-MH (Vickery et al. 2006). Alternatively, in Jakobsen and Madsen (2004) the above equations are solved, and parametric models are provided that can be used directly without invoking the momentum equations. Those parametric models are used in the framework outlined in Yau et al. (2011).

Intensity measures for severe wind events

Both Holland and Shapiro models provide solutions in terms of the mean boundary velocity, V_{mbd}. Many previous studies (Powell 1980; Powell & Black 1990; Thompson & Cardone 1996; Vickery et al. 2000) give empirical relationships to convert this velocity to the mean surface-level (10-m) wind speed over a 1-hour averaging period over open water, $V_{water, 3600s}$. For simplicity, a conversion factor of 0.8 can be used (Yau 2011):

$$V_{water, 3600s} = 0.8 \times V_{mbd}. \tag{8.3}$$

$V_{water, 3600s}$ can then be converted to the 3-second gust wind speed at 10 m in an open-terrain exposure $(V_{land, 3s})$ through the following expression as suggested in Yau (2011) and Simiu et al. (2007):

$$V_{land, 3s} = 1.24 \times V_{water, 3600s}.$$ (8.4)

The 3-second wind speed at 10 m height in open-terrain exposure can be used in wind pressure calculations based on the ASCE 7-16 (American Society of Civil Engineers 2017) as well as wind tunnel driven models and often represents intensity measure for severe wind events. $V_{land, 3s}$ will be referred to as V for the rest of the chapter.

8.2.3 Pressure damage model

In this model, the resistance of each component to external wind pressures is compared to the pressure acting on the component due to the hurricane wind field. If wind pressure acting on any component exceeds this resistance, then the component will fail. Since the resistance of each component is assigned in the building model, the main task of a pressure damage model is to estimate the external wind pressures to apply to the component.

For estimating the pressures acting on a building within the context of resiliency estimation, code-specified wind pressures do not generally provide enough information. Indeed, code-specified pressure represents the envelope of maximum pressures over an envelope of wind directions. This formulation hinders the calculation of wind pressure as a function of wind direction, which is necessary for estimating the progression of pressure induced damage during a hurricane. The most obvious solution is to use wind tunnel data consisting of the directional measurement of external wind pressures. Unfortunately, in many cases, this approach is not viable due to a lack of wind tunnel data and the significant costs associated with gathering such data for an entire community consisting of numerous buildings. To overcome this difficulty, the approach adopted in frameworks such as HAZUS-MH and FPHLPM is to combine available wind tunnel data with code prescriptions, therefore defining a "hybrid code/directional model." The basic idea underpinning this approach is to use the code-specified pressure as a base model and then modify through available wind tunnel data and engineering judgment. This approach enables the consideration of the most important wind directionality effects. A brief discussion of the hybrid code/directional model is presented in the remainder of this section.

The component and cladding wind pressure provided in ASCE 7-16 (American Society of Civil Engineers 2017) is modified according to FPHLPM to represent the actual wind pressure that a residential building will experience during a hurricane event as:

$$q_h = 0.521 \times V^2; V \text{ in } m/s$$ (8.5a)

$$p = 0.8 q_h \left[(GC_p) - (GC_{pi}) \right] (N / m^2),$$ (8.5b)

where:

q_h = is velocity pressure evaluated at mean roof height, h;
0.8 = is to exclude the factor of safety inherent in the code equation;
GC_p = is the external pressure coefficient with built-in gust factor;
GC_{pi} = is the internal pressure coefficient with built-in gust factor.

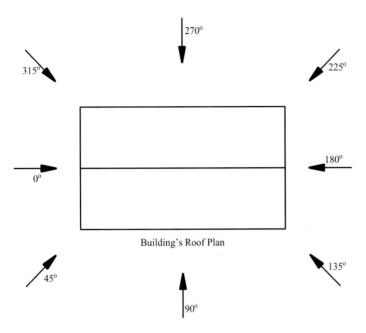

Figure 8.4 The eight nominal wind directions.

The internal pressure coefficient GC_{pi} for an intact building is calculated according to ASCE 7-16 as:

$$GC_{pi} = \pm 0.18.$$ (8.6)

When damage is detected for any of the building components (e.g. windows, doors, garage doors, roof cover), variations in the internal pressure will occur depending on the level of damage. This variation can be estimated as the weighted average of the external pressure acting on the damaged components (Gurley et al. 2005).

The calculation of the external pressure coefficient, GC_p, is key for including effects of wind directionality. To this end, GC_p is estimated for eight nominal wind directions, as shown in Figure 8.4, by combining information gathered from the ASCE 7-16, available wind tunnel test data, and engineering judgment. Following this approach, estimated values for GC_p in the nominal directions of Figure 8.4 are provided in Gurley et al. (2005). For any other wind direction, GC_p can be linearly interpolated.

8.2.4 Windborne debris model

Windborne debris is one of the major causes of damage to buildings subject to severe wind storms such as hurricanes. Indeed, negative wind pressures can cause the failure of components such as roof coverings, roof gravel, roof sheathing, or any other damaged component. Once detached, these objects become windborne debris. In addition to this, any loose object within the neighborhood has the potential to become windborne debris during the passage of the wind storm. Once airborne, this debris can penetrate the envelope of a building and become a threat to human life and property. The damage caused to the building envelope can lead to progressive damage mechanism (American Society of Civil Engineers 2017; Lin & Vanmarcke 2010) due to internal pressure increases that can cause additional damage to the components of the building.

Quantifying damage caused by windborne debris that initiate from the damage caused to the envelope of a given building may be summarized in identifying four quantities: number of debris objects released, landing position, velocity at landing, and impact momentum or energy (Lin & Vanmarcke 2010). The number of debris objects released can be initially determined from the pressure damage model. As shown in Figure 8.5, these debris objects can be geometrically classified as Wills et al. (2002): plate-like, compact-like, and rod-like objects. The other three quantities can be determined through the development of a debris flight trajectory model which involves the aerodynamics and mechanics of the inflight debris object. In the reminder of this section a discussion concerning the available debris flight trajectory models is provided.

Previous studies concerning models for the trajectories of inflight debris can be divided into two-dimensional (2D) and three-dimensional (3D) models. The 2D models are primarily based on the fundamental research of Tachikawa (1983), who reduced the equation of motions of inflight debris objects into a set of simplified dimensionless equations. Tachikawa (1988) then estimated the distribution of missile trajectories through experimental test results and examined the robustness of the proposed 2D models in reproducing the experimental results. Lin et al. (2006) and Holmes et al. (2006) validated the 2D model for plate-type windborne debris using results from wind-tunnel experiments. Lin et al. (2007) used the results from both wind tunnel simulation data and the 2D models associated with compact and rod type debris to improve debris impact criteria currently used in impact testing. Lin and Vanmarcke (2010) introduced a debris risk model that uses empirical data and 2D models to define the debris trajectory. This model (Lin & Vanmarcke 2010) is then incorporated in a structural vulnerability model (Lin et al. 2010) to estimate damage to residential buildings due to debris impact.

While 2D models are easily implemented, they are limited in the debris motions they can reproduce. The 3D models overcome this limitation as they can completely describe the motion of the debris object during the flight time. Radbill and Redmann (1976) introduced one of the first 3D 6-degree-of-freedom (6-DoF) trajectory models, and implemented it to study the flight of a utility pole in a tornado wind field. Richards et al. (2008) presented a 3D deterministic model in which force and moment coefficients were determined experimentally. Grayson et al. (2012) extended this deterministic 3D model to a probabilistic setting and implemented it in their vulnerability framework (Grayson et al. 2013). The process of modeling debris trajectories is of a complex nature. The wind speeds and turbulences that the debris objects experience during their flight are extremely complex to model or measure

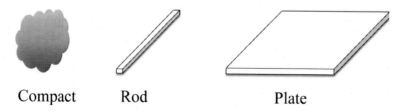

Compact   Rod   Plate

Figure 8.5 Windborne debris types as in Wills, et al. 2002.

experimentally. True progress in the effective modeling of debris flight trajectories would require additional experimental wind tunnel studies to be carried out, the results of which can then be used to better calibrate existing trajectory models and potentially identify new debris flight models.

8.3 Modeling and simulation of interdependencies

The complexity and importance of modeling interdependencies between different infrastructure components was discussed in the introduction. Within this context, Grogan and de Weck (2015) introduced a method to model infrastructure system interoperability using a distributed simulation environment based on a high-level architecture (HLA) approach (IEEE Standards Association 2010) where a distributed simulation environment can be defined as a framework that enables the execution of a model's sub-models across multiple processors (computers) with interoperability enabled through a communication network (Fujimoto 2000). Nouman et al. (2013) developed a distributed hybrid agent-based and discrete event simulation using HLA for modeling interdependencies in emergency medical responses. From a computational standpoint, Gorgan and de Weck (2015) identified that a distributed simulation requires 10–100 times the computational effort of a non-interoperable configuration. They also stated that it requires significantly more code development effort with around 50 percent more software being produced in order to implement federation object models and agreements. However, the physical distribution and interdependent control of constituent models are essential capabilities if community resiliency is to be estimated with high fidelity.

Another aspect of modeling interdependencies between infrastructure components is the realization that the various components are generally specific to a discipline. Therefore, collaboration between researchers from different fields and backgrounds (e.g. structures, meteorology, geography, transportation, economics, social science, etc.) is generally required if results of interest are to be generated. Within this context, Lin et al. (Jan. 2018 submitted; April 19–21, 2018) introduced a framework for modeling the interdependencies between different infrastructure components that fully embraced the multidisciplinary nature of estimating community resiliency. This framework is centered on using the Lightweight Communication and Marshalling (LCM) library for modeling the interoperability between the infrastructure components (Huang et al. 2010; LCM 2018). In particular, each infrastructure component is modeled through a simulator that generally falls within the realm of specific discipline. Each simulator may be viewed as black box that subscribes to data from any other simulator and publishes results for use by other simulators. This LCM platform can be extended to link as many simulators as needed and is the basis of the community resiliency framework used in the applications section of this chapter.

8.4 Community resiliency goals and metrics

The San Francisco Bay Area Planning and Urban Research Association (SPUR 2018) published a set of reports to identify the needs of its seismic mitigation policies in order to ensure San Francisco becomes a "Resilient City". These policies are a set of community resiliency goals that can be applied for any community facing any natural hazard. NIST (The National Institute of Standards and Technology 2015) provided a set of community resiliency goals that were used by Ceskavich and Sasani (2018) to identify quantitative targets for a community's building stock and infrastructure systems. These targets specify the functionality of each component immediately after the hazard and the required recovery time to achieve a certain level of functionality.

Community resiliency goals then require translating into metrics that can be systematically measured and provide a comprehensive assessment of a community's resiliency level. NIST provides four broad categories of community resiliency metrics: (1) time to recovery of function; (2) economic vitality; (3) social well-being; (4) environmental resiliency. For a simple residential neighborhood, restoration of housing within the community is a metric of particular interest (Burton et al. 2016).

Using the guidelines discussed above, the functionality curve for each community resiliency metric can be determined as shown in Figure 8.6. In Cimellaro et al. (2010), simple recovery functions were outlined for average (linear), not well prepared (trigonometric), and well prepared (exponential) communities. These recovery functions take, respectively, the following forms:

$$f_{rec}(t) = a\left(\frac{t - t_{OE}}{T_{RE}}\right) + b \tag{8.7a}$$

$$f_{rec}(t) = \frac{a}{2}\left\{1 + \cos\left[\frac{\pi b (t - t_{OE})}{T_{RE}}\right]\right\} \tag{8.7b}$$

$$f_{rec}(t) = ae^{\frac{-b(t - t_{OE})}{T_{RE}}}, \tag{8.7c}$$

where:

a and b = are fitting constants to fit the model to available data;
t_{OE} = is the time of occurrence of the hazard event (i.e. hurricane);
T_{RE} = is the recovery time required to achieve pre-disaster functionality.

Resiliency can be calculated for each resiliency metric using the following equation (Cimellaro et al. 2010):

$$R_i = \int_{t_{OE}}^{t_{OE} + T_{LC}} Q_i(t) / T_{LC}; i = 1, 2, \ldots, n, \tag{8.8a}$$

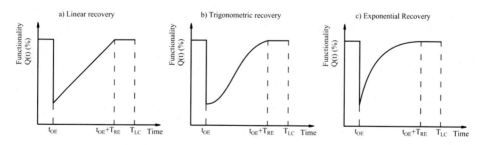

Figure 8.6 Functionality curves: (a) average prepared community; (b) not well prepared community; (c) well prepared community.

Source: Cimellaro et al., 2010.

with

$$Q_i(t) = f_{rec,i}(t)\left[1 - L(I,T_{RE})\right]\left[H(t - t_{OE}) - H(t - (t_{OE} + T_{RE}))\right],$$ (8.8b)

where:

i = is the considered resiliency metric;
n = is the number of considered resiliency metrics;
R_i = is the resiliency measure;
T_{LC} = is the control time (life span of the community);
$Q_i(t)$ = is the functionality function;
$L(I,T_{RE})$ = is the loss function, can be estimated using the vulnerability model;
I = is the intensity of the hazard;
$H(\cdot)$ = is the Heaviside step function.

In Sharma et al. (2017) the limitations of the resiliency metric provided in Equation (8.8a) are discussed, and rigorous mathematical formulations for resiliency metrics that can overcome those limitations are presented.

One of the most challenging aspects in assessing resiliency metrics, such as those outlined above, is the identification of the recovery function $f_{rec}(t)$. Time, geographical region, and interdependencies between different infrastructure components constituting the community significantly influences the recovery process. For example, two identical residential buildings at different locations in the same community may have different recovery paths due to different distances from the repair crews and materials. Also, despite the conceptual recovery framework outlined by Miles and Chang (2006), recovery process models are still limited and require more research. Despite these challenges, the evaluation of resiliency metrics will enable decision and policy makers to gain a deeper understanding into which infrastructure component has the most detrimental effect on the whole system and, consequently, to develop potential mitigation plans.

8.5 Applications

The previous sections have given an overview of possible hurricane damage and loss estimation models (vulnerability models), of solutions for modeling and simulating interdependencies between infrastructure components, and of possible models for quantifying community resiliency. Figure 8.7 shows conceptually how these models can be connected to communicate through a distributed computing platform based on a runtime interface of the type outlined in Lin et al. (Jan. 2018 submitted). In particular, the performance model is divided here into an external pressure estimation model, debris model and damage model. This last is used to estimate damage from both the external wind pressures and windborne debris impact through the comparison between the loads and resistances, where the resistances are provided in the form of fragility functions that model the susceptibility of a given component to multiple damage states. As output, the probability of damage to any of the components defining each building of a given community of interest are estimated.

The output from the damage model can then be used to estimate the community resiliency metrics through an appropriate community resiliency model. In particular, this last should be provided with sufficient data and details about the community under consideration (e.g. available resources, infrastructure, and emergency services) to enable estimation of the time to

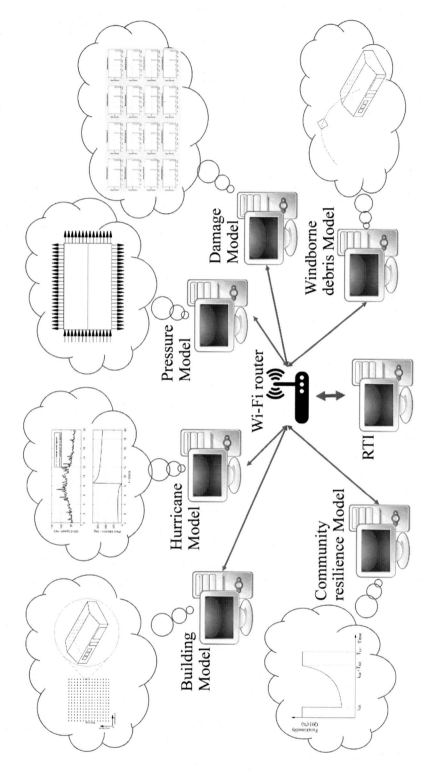

Figure 8.7 Schematic for distributed computing applied to model interdependencies required to quantify community resilience.

restore functionality, for a specified resiliency metric, and the recovery path (i.e. linear, trigono-metric, or exponential).

To illustrate the distributed computing framework discussed above, Figure 8.8 shows a plan view for a virtual residential community that consists of nine residential buildings. In this example, it is assumed that the community is subject to a category 3 hurricane that has the storm track shown in Figure 8.9. To illustrate the type of output that can be obtained from the framework, Figure 8.10 reports the probability of damage due to the external time-varying wind pressure occurring over the duration of the hurricane. In particular, the results have been decomposed for the different components of the buildings. It should be observed that the failure probabilities for all buildings are similar due to the limited size of the virtual community (variation of distance to the storm track between buildings is negligible), which leads to similar external wind pressure, and due to the neglect of windborne debris damage.

From an efficiency and scalability standpoint, it should be observed that the run times for obtaining the results discussed above were in the order of considering a single building subject to a category 3 hurricane. It is this property, coupled with the robustness (i.e. insensitivity to the

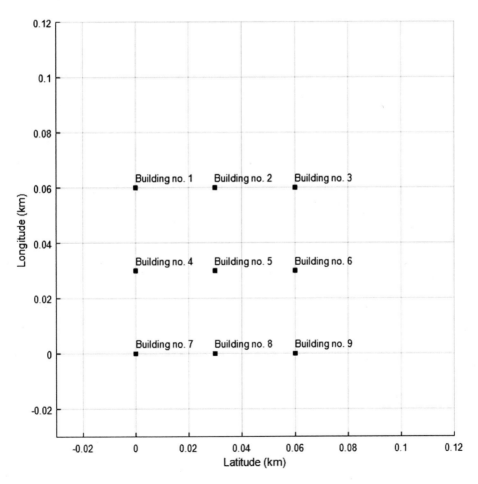

Figure 8.8 Plan view of a virtual residential community.

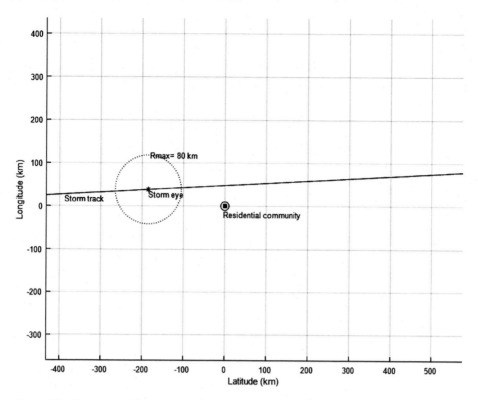

Figure 8.9 Plan view of the storm track passing by the residential community.

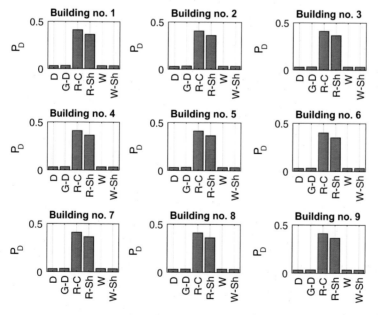

Figure 8.10 Probability of damage (P_D) due to external wind pressure on each component of a residential neighborhood due to a Category 5 hurricane. Nomenclature: door (D); garage door (G-D); roof cover (R-C); roof sheathing (R-Sh); windows (W); and wall sheathing (W-Sh).

individual models characterizing the response of an infrastructure component to a hazard) of the distributed computing framework considered here (and outlined in detail in Lin et al. (Jan. 2018 submitted)), that holds significant promise for future simulations comprising more complex models.

8.6 Conclusions

In this chapter, the evaluation of the resiliency of a residential neighborhood subject to hurricanes through a distributed computing framework has been discussed. In particular, the framework can be decomposed into three main steps: definition of appropriate vulnerability models for the infrastructure components, e.g. buildings defining the community; definition of computational strategies for modeling interdependencies between the infrastructure components; and the translation of damage and loss information into resiliency metrics. For the first step, possible vulnerability models were outlined. For the second step, the development of distributed computing frameworks were identified as an attractive avenue to explore. An approach of this type would allow arrays of detailed computational models (modeling the response of individual infrastructure components) to run on individual computers while allowing full consideration of the complex interdependencies that generally exist between the components of a community. For the third step, the calculation of community resiliency has been discussed and it was concluded that community resiliency should be quantified through resiliency metrics that are specified by society and decision/policy makers. The complexity of estimating the recovery process has been highlighted when in the presence of limited data. Finally, an example was discussed in which the performance of a residential community subject to a category 5 hurricane was estimated through a recently introduced distributed computing platform. It is believed that the use of such platforms in the calculation of community resiliency can lead to significant computational discovery due to their scalability and robustness to the simulators used to model individual infrastructure components.

Acknowledgements

This work was supported by the University of Michigan and the US National Science Foundation (NSF) through grants ACI-1638186 and CMMI-1562388. Any opinions, findings, conclusions, and recommendations expressed in this chapter are those of the authors and do not necessarily reflect the views of the sponsors.

References

American Society of Civil Engineers, 2017. *Minimum Design Loads and Associated Criteria for Buildings and Other Structures, ASCE/SEI 7-16*. Reston, VA: American Society of Civil Engineers.

Aven, T., 2011. On some recent definitions and analysis frameworks for risk, vulnerability, and resilience. *Risk Analysis*, 31(4), 515–22.

Bruneau, M. et al., 2003. A framework to quantitatively assess and enhance the seismic resilience of communities. *Earthquake Spectra*, 19(4), 733–52.

Burton, H.V., Deierlein, G., Lallemant, D., and Lin, T., 2016. Framework for incorporating probabilistic building performance in the assessment of community seismic resilience. *Journal of Structural Engineering*, 142(8).

Ceskavich, R. and Sasani, M., 2018. Methodology for evaluating community resilience. *Natural Hazards Review*, 19(1).

Cimellaro, G., Reinhorn, A., and Bruneau, M., 2010. Framework for analytical quantification of disaster resilience. *Engineering Structures*, 332(11), 3639–49.

Cutter, S. et al., 2012. *Disaster Resilience: A National Imperative.* Washington, DC: The National Academies Press.

Dueñas-Osorio, L. and Vemuru, S.M., 2009. Cascading failures in complex infrastructure systems. *Structural Safety,* 31, 157–67.

Fujimoto, R., 2000. *Parallel and Distributed Simulation Systems.* New York: Wiley.

Grayson, J.M., Pang, W., and Schiff, S., 2013. Building envelope failure assessment framework for residential communities subjected to hurricanes. *Engineering Structures,* 51, 245–58.

Grayson, J.M., Pang, W., and Schiff, S., 2012. Three-dimensional probabilistic wind-borne debris trajectory model for building envelope impact risk assessment. *Journal of Wind Engineering and Industrial Aerodynamics,* 102, 22–35.

Grogan, P.T. and de Weck, O.L., 2015. Infrastructure system simulation interoperability using the high-level architecture. *IEEE Systems Journal,* 12(1), 1–12.

Guidotti, R. et al., 2016. Modeling the resilience of critical infrastructure: The role of network dependencies. *Sustainable and Resilient Infrastructure,* Volume 1, pp. 153–168.

Gurley, K. et al., 2005. *Florida Public Hurricane Loss Projection Model Engineering Team. Final Report,* Miami: International Hurricane Research Center, Florida International University.

Haimes, Y.Y., 2009. On the definition of resilience in systems. *Risk Analysis,* 29(4), 498–501.

Holland, G.J., 1980. An analytic model of the wind and pressure profiles in hurricanes. *Monthly Weather Review,* 108, 1212–18.

Holmes, J., Letchford, C., and Lin, N., 2006. Investigations of plate-type windborne debris – Part II: Computed trajectories. *Journal of Wind Engineering and Industrial Aerodynamics,* 94, 21–39.

Huang, A.S., Olson, E., and Moore, D.C., 2010. *LCM: Lightweight Communications and Marshalling.* IEEE/RSJ International Conference on Intelligent Robots and Systems, Taipei, Taiwan.

Hurricane Research Division, 2017. *National Oceanic and Atmospheric Adminstration.* www.aoml.noaa.gov/hrd/tcfaq/E11.html (last accessed August 13, 2018).

IEEE Standards Association, 2010. *IEEE Standard 1516–2010 - IEEE Standard for Modeling and Simulation (M&S) High Level Architecture (HLA) – Framework and Rules.* IEEE Computer Society.

Jakobsen, F. and Madsen, H., 2004. Comparison and further development of parametric tropical cyclone models for storm surge modelling. *Journal of Wind Engineering and Industrial Aerodynamics,* 92, 375–91.

LCM, 2018. *Lightweight Communications and Marshalling (LCM).* https://lcm-proj.github.io/ (last accessed February 2018).

Lin, N. and Vanmarcke, E., 2010. Windborne debris risk analysis – Part I. Introduction and methodology. *Wind and Structures,* 13(2), 191–206.

Lin, N., Letchforda, C., and Holmes, J., 2006. Investigation of plate-type windborne debris. Part I. Experiments in wind tunnel and full scale. *Journal of Wind Engineering and Industrial Aerodynamics,* 94, 51–76.

Lin, N., Holmes, J.D., and Letchford, C.W., 2007. Trajectories of wind-borne debris in horizontal winds and applications to impact testing. *Journal of Structural Engineering,* 133(2), 274–82.

Lin, N., Vanmarcke, E.,. and Yau, S.-C., 2010. Windborne debris risk analysis – Part II. Application to structural vulnerability modeling. *Wind and Structures,* 13(2), 207–20.

Lin, S.-Y. et al., Jan. 2018 submitted. A distributed simulation framework for modeling interdependencies in community resilience. *Journal of Structural Engineering.*

Lin, S.-Y. et al., April 19–21, 2018. *Modeling Interactions in Community Resilience.* Fort Worth, Texas, USA.

Miles, S.B. and Chang, S.E., 2006. Modeling community recovery from earthquakes. *Earthquake Spectra,* 22(2), 439–58.

National Association of Home Builders, 1999. *An Industry Perspective on Performance Guidelines for Structural Safety and Serviceability of One and Two-Family Dwellings,* MD: Upper Marlboro.

National Institute of Standards and Technology, 2015. *Community Resilience Planning Guide for Buildings and Infrastructure Systems, Volumes I and II,* Gaithersburg, MD: Special Publication 1190, NIST.

Nouman, A., Anagnostou, A., and Taylor, S.J.E., 2013. *Developing a Distributed Agent-Based and DES Simulation Using poRTIco and repas.* Washington, DC, USA.

Ouyang, M., 2014. Review on modeling and simulation of interdependent critical infrastructure systems. *Reliability Engineering and System Safety,* 121, 43–60.

Pita, G., Pinelli, J.-P., Gurley, K., and Mitrani-Reiser, J., 2015. State of the art of hurricane vulnerability estimation methods: A review. *Natural Hazards Review, ASCE,* 16(2), 1–16.

Powell, M.D., 1980. Evaluations of diagnostic marine boundary-layer models applied to hurricanes. *Monthly Weather Review,* 108, 757–66.

Powell, M.D. and Black, P.G., 1990. The relationship of hurricane reconnaissance flight-level wind measurements to winds measured by NOAA's oceanic platforms. *Journal of Wind Engineering and Industrial Aerodynamics*, 36, 381–92.

Radbill, J. and Redmann, G., 1976. *Tornado-Generated Missile Trajectory Calculations with a Six Degree-of Freedom Model.* Texas Tech University, USA.

Richards, P. et al., 2008. Numerical calculation of the three-dimensional motion of wind-borne debris. *Journal of Wind Engineering and Industrial Aerodynamics*, 96, 2188–2202.

Righi, A.W., Saurin, T.A., and Wachs, P., 2015. A systematic literature review of resilience engineering: Research areas and a research agenda proposal. *Reliability Engineering and System Safety*, 141, 142–52.

Shapiro, L.J., 1983. The asymmetric boundary layer flow under a translating hurricane. *Journal of the Atmospheric Sciences*, 40, 1984–8.

Sharma, N., Tabandeh, A., and Gardoni, P., 2017. Resilience analysis: a mathematical formulation to model resilience of engineering systems. *Sustainable and Resilient Infrastructure*, 3(2), 49–67.

Sigma, 2017. *Natural Catastrophes and Man-made Disasters in 2016: A Year of Widespread Damages,* London: sigma 2/2017, Swiss Re.

Simiu, E., Vickery, P., and Kareem, A., 2007. Relation between Saffir-Simpson hurricane scale wind speeds and peak 3-s gust speeds over open terrain. *Journal of Structural Engineering*, 133(7), 1043–5.

SPUR, 2018a. *The Resilient City, SPUR.* www.spur.org/featured-project/resilient-city (last accessed February 2018).

SPUR, 2018b. *SPUR Ideas + Action for a Better City.* www.spur.org/ (last accessed February 2018).

Tachikawa, M., 1983. Trajectories of flat plates in uniform flow with application to wind-generated missiles. *Journal of Wind Engineering and Industrial Aerodynamics*, 14, 443–53.

Tachikawa, M., 1988. A method for estimating the distribution range of trajectories of wind-borne missiles. *Journal of Wind Engineering and Industrial Aerodynamics*, 29, 175–84.

Thompson, E.F. and Cardone, V.J., 1996. Practical modeling of hurricane surface wind fields. *Journal of Waterway Port Coastal and Ocean Engineering*, 122(4), 195–205.

Vickery, P.J., Skerlj, P.F., Steckley, A.C., and Twisdale, L. A., 2000a. Hurricane wind field model for use in hurricane simulations. *Journal of Structural Engineering*, 126(10), 1203–21.

Vickery, P.J., Skerlj, P.F., and Twisdale, L.A., 2000b. Simulation of hurricane risk in the US using empirical track model. *Journal of Structural Engineering*, 126(10), 1222–37.

Vickery, P.J. et al., 2006. HAZUS-MH hurricane model methodology. II: Damage and loss estimation. *Natural Hazards Review, ASCE*, 7(2), 94–103.

Wills, J., Lee, B., and Wyatt, T., 2002. A model of windborne debris damage. *Journal of Wind Engineering and Industrial Aerodynamics*, 90, 555–65.

Yau, S.C., 2011. *Wind Hazard Risk Assessment and Management for Structures.* Available from ProQuest Dissertations & Theses Global.

Yau, S.C., Lin, N., and Vanmarcke, E., 2011. Hurricane damage and loss estimation using an integrated vulnerability model. *Natural Hazards Review, ASCE*, 12(4), 184–9.

Resilience assessment of community building portfolios

Peihui Lin and Naiyu Wang

CIVIL ENGINEERING AND ENVIRONMENTAL SCIENCE; THE UNIVERSITY OF OKLAHOMA, USA

9.1 Introduction

9.1.1 Background

The increasing vulnerability of communities to natural hazards, as manifested in recent disaster events such as Wenchuan Earthquake in 2008, Superstorm Sandy in 2012, the Moore, OK Tornado in 2013, and Hurricane Harvey in 2017, has posed significant research challenges in disaster-related science and technology. While there is a consensus among researchers that effective hazard mitigation requires systematic and holistic community-level planning for disaster resilience, to date there are no science-based tools and measurement frameworks to guide the public and private decision makers to assess and enhance resilience of their communities in a quantitative and integrated manner.

The building portfolio within a community is essential to the day-to-day operation of the community as it provides infrastructure that supports critical community functions such as housing, education, business, health services, and government. Physical damages and functionality losses caused by natural hazard events to a community building portfolio, as a system, can lead to multi-scale social-economic impacts that cascade throughout all sectors of the community during and long after the hazard event. Current research on quantitative resilience assessment of building portfolios is in a rudimentary state of development. Traditionally, the impact of natural hazards on individual buildings has been considered by structural engineers through codes, standards, and regulations in building design, construction, and management (ASCE 2009; ASCE Standard 7 2016). These codes and standards for individual buildings, however, were developed mainly to protect life safety in the events of extreme hazard events, without considering the functional dependences among buildings of different occupancies as well as dependencies between the building portfolio as a whole and the supporting civil infrastructure systems that together contribute to the social-economic stability of a community. This lack of a system-level perspective in building portfolio analysis has led to cascading deficiencies in several critical aspects of resilience assessment for building portfolios, including metric identification, loss evaluation, and recovery modeling.

9.1.2 Research gaps

Building portfolio performance metrics

Existing metrics that have been used in the past as indicators of the performance of building portfolios include direct and indirect economic loss, household dislocation, causality (FEMA/NIBS 2003; Rose & Guha 2004; Peacock et al. 2008), etc. Those metrics are mostly social and economic-centric metrics and are in fact not specifically designed to support resilience assessment of building portfolios. On the other hand, these metrics are often used only as measures of "robustness" (i.e. only being quantified immediately following a hazard event), and are not suitable for "monitoring" or "tracking" the functionality of a building portfolio (or of a community in general) throughout the post-disaster recovery process. Direct and system-level metrics for the functionality of a building portfolio in its entirety are not found in the literature, and must be defined as the first step toward developing a comprehensive and quantitative framework for building portfolio resilience assessment. Such metrics should be firmly rooted in the performance of the building portfolio itself, and at the same time, explicitly reflect the dependence of the building portfolio as a whole on the other infrastructure systems in the same community.

Building portfolio loss estimation

Regarding probabilistic loss estimation of spatially distributed building portfolios, the correlation in building responses caused by a common hazard with a large footprint (i.e. site-to-site correlation) and correlation in structural capacities caused by common structures materials, common structural design code and enforcement, and/or common construction practice (i.e. structure-to-structure correlation) (Lee & Kiremidjian 2007; Goda & Hong 2008; Jayaram & Baker 2009; Vitoontus & Ellingwood 2013) must be considered. The neglect or incomplete consideration of these correlations inevitably leads to underestimation of spatial losses and unconservative errors in portfolio resilience assessment (Vitoontus & Ellingwood 2013, Lin & Wang 2016). However, very limited studies have explicitly modeled the both types of correlation. Common deficiencies in existing correlation models include the lack of data for adequate validation and extrapolation as well as the need of extensive computation efforts to support a fully probabilistic analysis of a large-scale building portfolio. Such deficiencies have confined existing correlation models to be effectively incorporated in even some of the well-accepted loss estimation platforms, e.g. HAZUS–HM (FEMA/NIBS 2003), MAEViz (Steelman et al. 2007). There is a compelling need to develop a systematic and rigorous methodology that is capable of propagating various uncertainties and spatial correlations throughout the entire building portfolio resilience assessment process, including hazard characterization, loss estimation, and recovery modeling.

Building portfolio recovery modeling

Post-disaster recovery is one of the least understood components in disaster research and risk management. A building portfolio traditionally is not perceived as a system of its own; hence, its recovery is rarely investigated from a system perspective. The recovery of a community building portfolio is dependent on the resourcefulness and social-economic characteristics of the community at large and at the same time, is strongly affected by various decisions made by different public and private building owners and stakeholders (Miles & Chang 2003; Burton et al. 2015; Lin & Wang 2017a, b). In contrast to the recovery of lifelines which often resembles a decision-driven process, the recovery of a building portfolio is essentially market-driven (Peacock et al. 2014, Lin & Wang 2017a). Thus, the general-purpose analytical recovery functions assumed in the literature (e.g., uniform cumulative distribution, lognormal distribution or harmonically over-damped functions) are far too simplistic to reflect the intrinsic complexities in the building portfolio recovery process. On the other hand, the empirical recovery models in the literature derived from historical hazard events are often event- and community-specific, making it hard to be generalized to support resilience planning in a quantitative manner (Chang 2010; Xiao & Van Zandt 2012; Peacock et al. 2014). Improvements to recovery outcomes of a building portfolio will be difficult to achieve unless quantitative models revealing the fundamental mechanisms of its recovery processes are developed.

9.1.3 Organization

In this study, a building portfolio resilience assessment framework is presented to address the research gaps identified in Section 9.1.2 by synthesizing studies reported in Lin & Wang (2016, 2017a &b). In Section 9.2, a new functionality definition and metric for building portfolios (i.e. Building Portfolio Functionality Metric, BPFM) is proposed for resilience assessment as an effective indicator of a portfolio's capacity to respond and recover from a hazard event. In Section 9.3, a probabilistic framework for building portfolio functionality loss estimation (BPLE) is developed in which the loss is measured in term of the BPFM. In Section 9.4, a novel simulation-based, two-step stochastic building portfolio functionality recovery model (BPRM) is developed, with the portfolio spatial functionality loss characterized by the BPLE framework as the initial state for recovery. In Section 9.5, the applications of the developed resilience assessment tools for building portfolios – i.e. the BPLE and BPRM – are illustrated through a case study of a testbed community called Centerville. The organization of Sections 9.2–9.5 is illustrated in Figure 9.1.

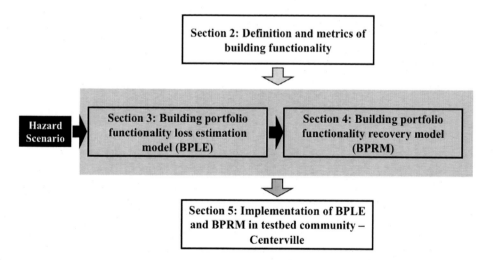

Figure 9.1 The organization of the chapter.

9.2 Building portfolio functionality metric (BPFM): Definition, metrics and notations

Functionality of an individual building can be defined as the availability of the building to be used for its intended purpose, which is a function of its structural integrity and availability of utilities (Almufti & Willford 2013). A main cause of building functionality loss in a hazard event is structural or nonstructural damages, as a building relies on its load-resistant system to provide safety and on its nonstructural components (e.g. lighting, heating, elevators, etc.) to provide serviceability. Another primary cause of building functionality loss is the disruption of basic utilities, i.e., an undamaged building is not functional if critical utilities, such as water and power, are unavailable.

Following an extreme natural hazard, e.g. an earthquake, professional inspections (including structural, nonstructural, or hazardous material damage evaluation) will be initiated for damaged buildings, which are often followed by an ATC-20 placard (Green, Yellow, or Red) to be tagged to each building, ascertaining the state of *building functionality* prior to building restoration (Oaks 1990). Considering the definition of building functionality introduced above, five different functionality states are defined in Figure 9.2, ranging from restricted entry to full functionality, each corresponding to a unique combination of building damage condition and utility availability (Almufti & Willford 2013; Lin & Wang 2017a).

The building functionality state S_j, $j \in (RE, RU, RO, BF, FF)$ introduced above serves as the functionality metric for individual buildings. This metric explicitly expresses the dependence between buildings and other infrastructure systems in the community, which has not been reflected in other typical building-related metrics in the literature, such as deaths, dollar loss, and downtime. Furthermore, this building functionality metric, as presented in Figure 9.2, not only can measure building functionality loss immediately following a hazard event (t_0), but also enables the restoration of a building to be traced throughout its recovery ($t > t_0$). We further

Funtionality States (ATC Placard)		Damage Condition	Utility Availability	Building Repair Classes (RC) & Specific Repair Items	
5	FF	Fully Functionality (Green Placard)	None	All available	N/A	
4	BF	Baseline Functionality (Green Placard)	Minor cosmetic structural and nonstructural damage	Critical ones available	Repair Class 4 (RC4)	• Minor structural damage such as shear wall, link beams, reinforced wall; Minor nonstructural damage such as stairs, partition, tiles
3	RO	Re-Occupancy (Green Placard)	Minor to moderate structural and nonstructural damage	N/A	Repair Class 3 (RC3)	• Minor structural damage; Minor to moderate nonstrutural damage; Mechaical equipment, electrical systems, emergency backup
2	RU	Restricted Use (Yellow Placard)	Moderate structural or nonstructural damage that does not threaten life safety	N/A	Repair Class 2 (RC2)	• Moderate to heavy nonstructural damage such as glazing, exterior partitions, elevator, pipes, fire sprinkler drops
1	RE	Restricted Entry (Red Placard)	Extensive structural or nonstructural damage that threatens life safety	N/A	Repair Class 1 (RC1)	• Heavy structural damage; Heavy nonstructural damage that threatens life safety

Figure 9.2 Functionality states of individual buildings.

Source: Lin & Wang 2017a.

define *building restoration time (BRT)* as the time that a building takes to regain its full function-ality *(FF)* from its pre-restoration functionality state immediately following a hazard event. Note that the building functionality state S_j in Figure 9.2 and the corresponding BRT are defined for risk category II buildings as specified in ASCE 7, which generally includes more than 90% buildings in a typical community in the U.S.

Consistent with the functionality metric for individual buildings, we define the *building port-folio functionality metric* (BPFM) as the percentages of buildings in a portfolio that are in each of the five functionality states, PRI_j, $j \in (RE, RU, RO, BF, FF)$. This BPFM allows the function-ality level of a building portfolio as whole to be quantified both immediately following the hazard event (t_0) and continuously during community recovery as a function of time $(t > t_0)$. Accordingly, we define the *portfolio recovery time (PRT)* as the time required for a target percentage (e.g. 90%) of buildings in a community to regain a prescribed desired functionality state (e.g. *FF*), e.g., $PRT_{FF,90\%}$.

9.3 Building portfolio functionality loss estimation (BPLE)

For an actually-occurred hazard event, the building functionality losses normally are estimated by professional engineers through post-event damage inspections per ATC-20 (Oaks 1990). For pre-event resilience planning, however, the hazard-induced building functionality losses are unknown and need to be estimated probabilistically.

While the BPLE framework developed herein is not limited to a specific hazard type, we use a scenario earthquake hazard to present the BPLE formulation due to its relatively mature development in spatial correlation modeling when compared with other types of hazard. Mathematically, the earthquake-induced functionality losses of building portfolios, in term of the BPFM PRI, exposed to an earthquake scenario event S_{EQ} can be formulated using the total probability theorem as:

$$P\left(PRI \leq z | S_{EQ}\right) = \iiint_{PRI(S) \leq z} f_{S|DS}\left(u|v\right) f_{DS|IM}\left(v|y\right) f_{IM|S_{EQ}}\left(y|S_{EQ}\right) du dv dy, \qquad (9.1)$$

where, reading from right to the left, $f_{IM|S_{EQ}}\left(y|S_{EQ}\right)$ is the PDF of ground motion intensity measure IM^1 at all the building sites conditioned on the scenario event S_{EQ}; $f_{DS|IM}\left(v|y\right)$ is the PDF of damage state DS^2 of all buildings conditioned on IM, which for each building is often given by a fragility function, defined as the probability that the response of a building equals or exceeds a stipulated damage state as a function of hazard intensity; $f_{S|DS}\left(u|v\right)$ is the PDF of functionality state S (i.e. *RE, RU, RO, BF, FF*) conditioned on DS; finally, as introduced in Section 9.2.1, PRI is the percentages of buildings in the portfolio that are in any of the five functionality states of interest; hence $P\left(PRI \leq z | S_{EQ}\right)$, the CDF of $PRI | S_{EQ}$, can be obtained by the convolution of conditional probability distributions associated with the three inter-mediate variables $(IM | S_{EQ}, DS | IM, \text{ and } S | DS)$. The dimension of each of the intermediate variables is consistent with the number of buildings in the portfolio (N).

Accordingly, estimating the CDF of the PRI requires three crucial steps of analysis: (1) char-acterization of the spatially correlated seismic demands, i.e. $f_{IM|S_{EQ}}\left(y|S_{EQ}\right)$; (2) assessment of spatially correlated building damages, i.e. $f_{DS|IM}\left(v|y\right)$; (3) estimation of functionality loss for both individual buildings, i.e. $f_{S|DS}\left(u|v\right)$, and for building portfolio as a whole, i.e. $F(PRI | S_{EQ})$. Each of the three analysis steps is conditional on the previous one. These three analysis steps are illustrated in Figure 9.3.

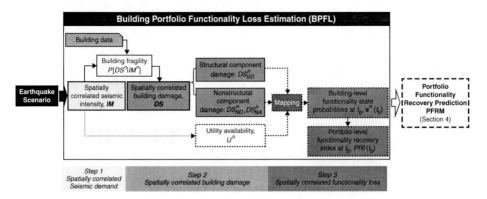

Figure 9.3   Flowchart of community-wide probabilistic pre-recovery damage and functionality loss assessment.

9.3.1 Probabilistic estimation of spatially correlated building damage

For any individual building $n \in \mathcal{N}$ in a portfolio, the mean damage state (μ_{DS^n}) can be estimated as:

$$\mu_{DS_k^n} = \int_{u^n} \sum_{i=1}^{4} ds_i \cdot P[DS_k^n = ds_i | IM^n] f_{IM^n}(u^n) du^n \quad n \in \mathcal{N}; \; i = 0,\ldots,4; \; k \in \{SD, ND, NA\}, \quad (9.2)$$

where $f_{IM^n}(u^n)$ is the probability density function (PDF) of the spectral acceleration IM^n at the site of building n, with median and variance obtained using a ground motion attenuation model and DS_k^n is the seismic-induced damage state to component k of building n, $k \in \{SD, ND, NA\}$ denoting structural (SD), nonstructural drift-sensitive (ND) and nonstructural acceleration-sensitive (NA) components, respectively. Increment $ds_i = i$ represents a specific damage state i, $i = 0,\ldots,4$ denoting *none, slight, moderate, extensive,* and *complete* damage states. The conditional probability, $P[DS_k^n = dsi | IM^n]$, can be obtained from existing fragility functions in the literature (e.g., MAEViz (Steelman et al. 2007) and HAZUS (FEMA/NIBS 2003)).

The covariance between the damage states of any building pair (m,n) resulting from the same scenario earthquake can be expressed as:

$$Covar[DS^m DS^n] = \int_{y^m} \int_{y^n} \rho_{DS^m DS^n | IM^m, IM^n} \cdot \sigma_{DS^m | IM^m} \cdot \sigma_{DS^n | IM^n} \cdot f_{IM^m, IM^n}(y^m, y^n) dy^m dy^n, \quad (9.3)$$

in which $f_{IM^m, IM^n}(y^m, y^n)$ is the joint probability density function (PDF) of IM^m and IM^n; $\sigma_{DS|IM}$ is the standard deviation of the conditional variable $DS | IM$; $\rho_{DS^m DS^n | IM^m, IM^n}$ is the correlation between conditional variables $DS^m | IM^m$; and $DS^n | IM^n$. The formulations Equations. (9.2)–(9.3) for quantifying spatially correlated building damage states can be solved by a multi-layer Monte Carlo Simulation (MCS) as detailed in Lin and Wang (2016).

9.3.2 Probabilistic assessment of portfolio functionality loss

Building-level damage-to-functionality mapping

To link damage of an individual building (as estimated in 9.3.1) to its functionality state (as introduced in Figure 9.1), a damage-to-functionality mapping algorithm must be developed through identifying the mechanism by which building components (both structural and nonstructural) are assembled to collectively support the building functionality as well as the dependencies of the building functionality on the availability of critical utilities.

Accordingly, for the present analysis which is aimed at community-level functionality loss estimation, we introduce a mapping of coarse resolution based on existing studies (FEMA/NIBS 2003; FEMA 2012) to link the damage states of building components to the post-disaster building functionality states as shown in Figure 9.4: (1) buildings with no damage to all of the three buildings components (i.e., structural components, nonstructural drift-sensitive components, and nonstructural acceleration-sensitive components) will achieve *FF*; (2) buildings with no more than slight damage to all of the three components will achieve at least *BF*; (3) buildings with no more than slight damage to the structural components and no more than moderate damage to the two categories of nonstructural components will achieve at least *RO*; (4) buildings no exceeding moderate damage to all of the three building components will achieve at least *RU[3]*.

Further, to express this damage-to-functionality mapping probabilistically to facilitate subsequent analysis, let $S^n(t_0)$ denote the functionality state of building n at t_0 (t_0 is the time when the prescribed hazard event occurs), which takes one of the five predefined functionality states $S_j, j = 1,2,...,5$ (representing *RE, RU, RO, BF, FF*, respectively). Let $e_j^{0,n} = e_j^n(t_0), j = 1,2,...,5$ denote the probability of building n achieving or exceeding functionality state S_j at t_0. The mapping in Figure 9.4 can be expressed as:

$$e_1^{0,n} = P\left[S^n(t_0) \geq RE\right] = 1 \tag{9.4a}$$

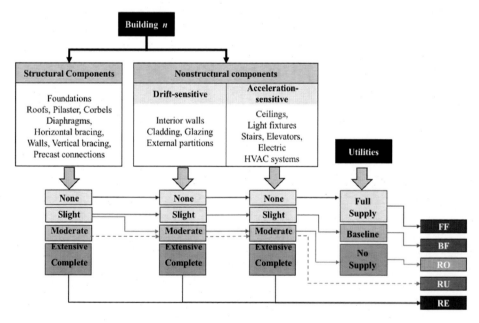

Figure 9.4 Mapping from building damage and utility availability to building functionality states.

Source: Lin & Wang 2017b.

$$e_2^{0,n} = P\left[S^n(t_0) \ge RU\right] = P\left[DS_{SD}^n \le ds_{3,SD}, DS_{ND}^n \le ds_{3,ND}, DS_{NA}^n \le ds_{3,NA}\right] \tag{9.4b}$$

$$e_3^{0,n} = P\left[S^n(t_0) \ge RO\right] = P\left[DS_{SD}^n \le ds_{2,SD}, DS_{ND}^n \le ds_{3,ND}, DS_{NA}^n \le ds_{3,NA}\right] \tag{9.4c}$$

$$e_4^{0,n} = P\left[S^n(t_0) \ge BF\right]$$
$$= \begin{cases} P\left[DS_{SD}^n \le ds_{2,SD}, DS_{ND}^n \le ds_{2,ND}, DS_{NA}^n \le ds_{2,NA}\right], & BU^{0,n} = 1 \\ 0, & BU^{0,n} = 0 \end{cases} \tag{9.4d}$$

$$e_5^{0,n} = P\left[S^n(t_0) = FF\right]$$
$$= \begin{cases} P\left[DS_{SD}^n = ds_{1,SD}, DS_{ND}^n = ds_{1,ND}, DS_{NA}^n = ds_{1,NA}\right], & FU^{0,n} = 1 \\ 0, & FU^{0,n} = 0 \end{cases} \tag{9.4e}$$

where $BU^{0,n}$ and $FU^{0,n}$ are binary variables representing baseline utility and full utility, respectively; the binary states (1– available and 0 – disrupted) of baseline utility ($BU^{0,n}$) or full utility ($FU^{0,n}$) at the site of building n at t_0 can be determined by an integrated interdependent utility network damage and cascading failure analysis which is currently performed by other researchers in the CRCRP (e.g. Zhang et al. 2018a) or found in the literature (e.g. González et al. 2015).

Let $\boldsymbol{\pi}^n(t_0) = [\pi_1^n(t_0), \pi_2^n(t_0), \pi_3^n(t_0), \pi_4^n(t_0), \pi_5^n(t_0)]$ be the functionality state probability vector of building n at t_0, in which the element $\pi_j^n(t_0) = Prob\left[S(t_0) = S_j\right]$ represents the probability of building n being in functionality state S_j. Accordingly, the $\boldsymbol{\pi}^n(t_0)$ is obtained by:

$$\boldsymbol{\pi}^n(t_0) = \left\{1 - e_2^{0,n}, e_2^{0,n} - e_3^{0,n}, e_3^{0,n} - e_4^{0,n}, e_4^{0,n} - e_5^{0,n}, e_5^{0,n}\right\}. \tag{9.5}$$

Portfolio-level functionality loss
While the initial functionality state of any building is determined by $\boldsymbol{\pi}^n(t_0)$, the portfolio functionality losses can be estimated as the following.

Let $I_j^n(t_0), j = 1, 2, 3, 4, 5$ be the functionality state indicator of any building n at t_0:

$$I_j^n(t_0) = \begin{cases} 0 & S^n(t_0) \ne S_j \\ 1 & S^n(t_0) = S_j \end{cases}, \quad n \in 1, 2, \ldots, N. \tag{9.6}$$

The $I_j^n(t_0)$ is a binary variable with probability $Prob\left[I_j^n(t_0) = 1\right] = \pi_j^n(t_0)$.

Accordingly, the PRI_j at initial time t_0, denoting the percentage of buildings in a community that are in functionality state S_j at time t_0, is given by:

$$PRI_j(t_0) = \frac{\sum_{n=1}^{N} I_j^n(t_0)}{N} \quad j \in 1 \ldots 5. \tag{9.7}$$

The overall building portfolio framework formulated in Equation (9.1), unfortunately, cannot be evaluated in closed form when a building portfolio consists of thousands of buildings. To handle the multiple layers of conditional distribution in Equation (9.1), a numerical solution using Monte Carlo simulation (MCS) is employed for obtaining the distribution of PRI, as shown in Figure 9.5. Detailed procedures of the MCS can be found in Lin and Wang (2016).

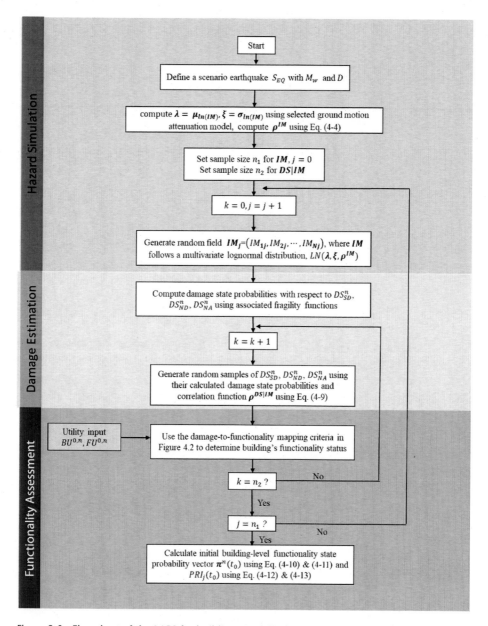

Figure 9.5 Flowchart of the MCS for building portfolio functionality loss estimate.

9.4 Building portfolio recovery model (BPRM)

This section focuses on developing a stochastic building portfolio recovery model (BPRM) to predict the functionality recovery time and recovery trajectory of a community building portfolio following natural scenario hazard events. The BPRM is developed in two steps: building-level restoration is formulated as a discrete-state, continuous-time Markov Chain (CTMC);

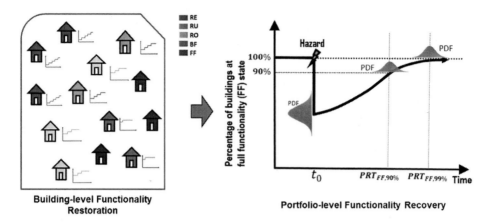

Building-level Functionality
Restoration

Portfolio-level Functionality Recovery

Figure 9.6   Schematic representation of building portfolio recovery.

Source: Lin & Wang 2017a.

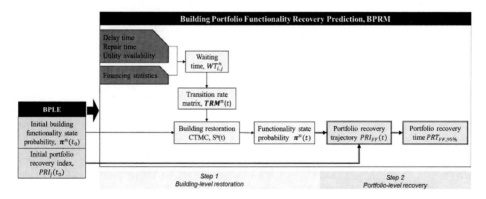

Figure 9.7   Flowchart of the two-step portfolio functionality recovery modeling.

and portfolio-level recovery is formulated as the spatial aggregation of the CTMC restoration processes of individual buildings over the entire recovery time horizon. The BPRM is conceptually illustrated in Figure 9.6, and detailed model components are illustrated in Figure 9.7.

9.4.1 Step 1: Building-level restoration

Discrete-state, continuous-time Markov chain (CTMC)

Let $S(t)$ be the stochastic post-disaster restoration process of an individual building, denoting functionality state at any time t after hazard occurrence at t_0. $S(t)$ is assumed to take one of the five functionality states $S_1, S_2, \ldots S_5$, representing *RE, RU, RO, BF* and *FF*, respectively. A building restoration process $S(t)$ starts at time $t_0 = 0$, from its initial pre-restoration functionality state $S(t_0) = S(0)$, and lasts until $t = BRT$ when the building regains *FF* (i.e. S_5). An illustration of the time-dependent building-level restoration process, $S(t)$, is shown in Figure 9.8 for buildings with $S(t_0) = S_1$.

161

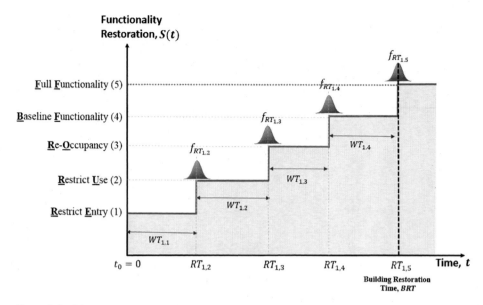

Figure 9.8 Discrete state, continuous time Markov Chain S(t) (for buildings with $S(t_0) = S_1$).
Source: Lin & Wang 2017a.

Due to the uncertainties in $S(t_0)$, introduced by uncertain hazard intensity and structural performance, as well as the uncertainties in the subsequent $S(t)$ for $t > t_0$, introduced by various decisions of building owners with different social and economic status (which ultimately are affected by the resourcefulness of the community as a whole), the building-level functionality $S(t)$ is modeled as a stochastic random process. Moreover, the next functionality state at any time during a building restoration is only dependent on the current functionality state, hence $S(t)$ is modeled as a *discrete-state, continuous-time Markov chain (CTMC)*, characterized by the five-state space (i.e. $S_1, S_2, \ldots S_5$) and a transition probability matrix, **TPM**.

Let $\pi_j(t)$ denote the probability of $S(t) = S_j$ at any time t, i.e. $\pi_j(t) = \text{Prob}\left[S(t) = S_j\right], j = 1, \ldots, 5$, then the state probability vector at any time t is:

$$\pi(t) = \left[\pi_1(t), \ldots, \pi_5(t)\right], \tag{9.8}$$

where $\sum_{j=1}^{5} \pi_j(t) = 1$ for any time t. In particular, the initial $(t = t_0)$ functionality state probability vector $\pi(t_0) = \left[\pi_1(t_0), \pi_2(t_0)\pi_3(t_0), \pi_4(t_0), \pi_5(t_0)\right]$, has been discussed in Section 9.3.

Let **TPM** (t) be the transition probability matrix of the CTMC that represents the building-level restoration process $S(t)$. The non-negative elements of **TPM** (t), $p_{i,j}(t)$, defined as:

$$p_{i,j}(t) = \text{Prob}\left[S(t) = S_j | S(t_0) = S_i\right], \tag{9.9}$$

describe the probability of the restoration process $S(t)$ transiting to state S_j at any time t given that its initial state at t_0 is S_i. Since at a given time a building's functionality either remains at the present state or shifts to any of its higher states, $S(t)$ is a non-decreasing process and the **TPM** (t) takes the form:

Community building portfolios

$$TPM(t) = \begin{pmatrix} p_{1,1}(t) & p_{1,2}(t) & p_{1,3}(t) & p_{1,4}(t) & p_{1,5}(t) \\ 0 & p_{2,2}(t) & p_{2,3}(t) & p_{2,4}(t) & p_{2,5}(t) \\ 0 & 0 & p_{3,3}(t) & p_{3,4}(t) & p_{3,5}(t) \\ 0 & 0 & 0 & p_{4,4}(t) & p_{4,5}(t) \\ 0 & 0 & 0 & 0 & 1 \end{pmatrix}. \tag{9.10}$$

As illustrated in Figure 9.8, let $WT_{i,j}$ represent the waiting time that $S(t)$ stays at state j (or the waiting time takes $S(t)$ to upgrade from the current state S_j to the next state S_{j+1}) given $S(t_0) = S_i$. Further, let $RT_{i,j} = \sum_{k=i}^{j-1} WT_{i,k}$ be the total time to restore the building's functionality to S_j from its initial state S_i. Accordingly, $e_{i,j}(t)$, defined as the probability that $S(t)$ is equal to or exceeds S_j, $j = 1,\ldots,5$, at any time t given the initial functionality state S_i at t_0, can be expressed as:

$$\begin{aligned} e_{i,j}(t) &= \mathrm{Pr}\,ob\left[S(t) \geq S_j \big| S(t_0) = S_i \right] \\ &= \mathrm{Pr}\,ob\left[RT_{i,j} \leq t \right] \\ &= \mathrm{Pr}\,ob\left[\sum_{k=i}^{j-1} WT_{i,k} \leq t \right] \\ &= \int \ldots \int_{\sum_{k=i}^{j-1} wt_{i,k} \leq t} \prod_{k=1}^{j-1} f_{WT_{i,k}} d\left(wt_{i,k} \right), \quad j = 1,\ldots,5, \end{aligned} \tag{9.11}$$

where $f_{WT_{ij}}$ denotes the PDF of $WT_{i,j}$. For a given initial state S_i, $WT_{i,j}$ are treated as independent random variables in Equation (9.11) because each $WT_{i,j}$ is determined only by a set of unique restoration activities that take place during that specific timeframe. The detailed discussion and probabilistic estimation of $WT_{i,j}$ will be presented in the next subsection.

Denote the exceedance probability $e_{i,j}(t)$ as the *conditional building restoration function (CBRF)*, representing the probability of a building achieving or exceeding a predefined functionality state S_j at any post-event time t conditional on its initial (pre-restoration) functionality state S_i immediately following hazard occurrence at t_0. Accordingly, the elements of the $TPM(t)$ become:

$$\begin{aligned} p_{i,j}(t) &= \mathrm{Prob}\left[S(t) = S_j \big| S(t_0) = S_i \right] \\ &= \mathrm{Prob}\left[S(t) \geq S_j \big| S(t_0) = S_i \right] - \mathrm{Prob}\left[S(t) \geq S_{j+1} \big| S(t_0) = S_i \right] \\ &= e_{i,j}(t) - e_{i,j+1}(t), \quad j = 1,\ldots,4, \end{aligned} \tag{9.12a}$$

$$p_{i,j}(t) = e_{i,j}(t), \quad j = 5. \tag{9.12b}$$

Finally, the restoration state probability vector $\pi(t)$ at any time t is:

$$\pi(t) = \left[\pi_1(t),\ldots,\pi_5(t) \right] = \pi(t_0) * TPM(t). \tag{9.13}$$

Define $e_j(t)$ as the *building restoration function (BRF)*, representing the total probability of a building achieving or exceeding a predefined functionality state S_j at any post-event time t regardless of its initial functionality state. The *BRF* can be estimated quantitatively as:

163

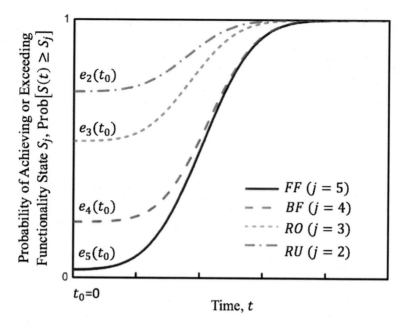

Figure 9.9 Illustration of building restoration function (BRF) of an individual building.
Source: Lin & Wang 2017a.

$$e_j(t) = \mathrm{Prob}\left[S(t) \geq S_j\right] = \sum_{k=j}^{5} \pi_k(t).$$

(9.14)

Figure 9.9 presents an illustration of *BRF* of a building for $j = 2...5$, respectively; when $j = 1$, $e_j(t) \equiv 1$, meaning the probability that a building is in, or exceeds, the worst functionality state S_1 (i.e. *RE*) is always 100%. In particular, $e_j(t_0)$, determined from $\pi(t_0)$, represents the probability of the building at or exceeding functionality state S_j at time t_0 before any restoration activity takes place.

Determination of transition probability matrix (TPM)
The elements of ***TPM***, i.e. $p_{i,j}(t)$, estimated by Equations (11.11)–(11.12), ultimately are functions of waiting time $WT_{i,j}$. The $WT_{i,j}$ vary from building to building, are highly uncertain and are strongly influenced by the social-economic status of building owners as well as the post-disaster construction market within the community. In this study the engineering process of building-level restoration is examined to obtain the probabilistic distributions of $WT_{i,j}$.

Examining the engineering process of building reconstruction, as shown in Figure 9.10, the waiting times are functions of the delay time (T_{Delay}), repair time (T_{Repair}), and the time to regain utility service $(T_{Utility})$, i.e.,

$$WT_{i,j}^n = fcn\left(T_{Delay}^n, T_{Repair}^n, T_{Utility}^n \mid \mathbf{x}^n, \mathbf{X}^c\right),$$

(9.15)

in which the superscript n represents a specific building in a community building portfolio; $\mathbf{x}^n$ represents a vector of building-specific attributes that affect the three components of the

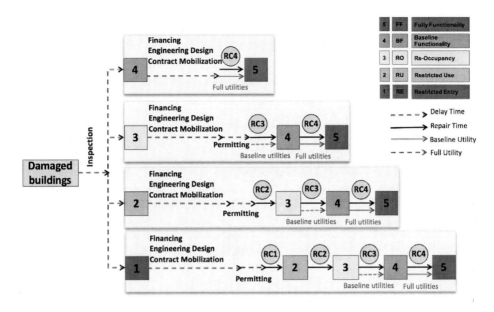

Figure 9.10 An illustration of the general restoration process of individual buildings.
Source: Lin & Wang 2017a.

waiting time, e.g., occupancy type, construction material, post-disaster damage and function-ality loss of the building; and X^c represents community-specific characteristics that have an impact on the three components of the waiting time, such as strength of regional economy, local regulations or policies, financing mechanisms for repair [i.e. private funding or public assistance], human resources and relevant pre- and post-event risk mitigation activities.

The *delay time* (T^n_{Delay}), the time takes to initiate repair for building n, includes three specific phases, as represented by the double-dashed lines in Figure 9.10: (1) time to inspect the building $(T^n_{INSP,i})$; (2) time to secure funding for repair $(T^n_{FINA,i})$, to commission architects and engineers $(T^n_{CONM,i})$, and to design and prepare construction drawings $(T^n_{ENGM,i})$, all of which can occur simultaneously; and finally (3) time to obtain permits, and hire contractors and construction crews $(T^n_{PERM,i})$. The subscript i indicates that these delay time segments are conditional on a building's initial functionality state S_i, $i = 1,2,3,4$. Accordingly, the *delay phase* T^n_{Delay} can be fur-ther expressed as (Almufti & Willford 2013):

$$T^n_{Delay,i} = T^n_{INSP,i} + \max\left\{T^n_{FINA,i}, \ T^n_{CONM,i}, \ T^n_{ENGM,i}\right\} + T^n_{PERM,i}. \tag{9.16}$$

The *repair time* (T^n_{Repair}) is the duration to complete all repair classes (*RCs*) necessary to restore the full functionality of building n, as represented by the solid dark lines in Figure 9.10. The four *RCs* and the mapping between these *RCs* and the five predefined functionality states are presented in Figure 9.2. For example, the repair phase for a red-tagged building, i.e. *RE*, will need to include *RCs* 1–4, while a building with a pre-repair functionality state of *RO* only needs to undergo *RC3* and *RC4* to achieve *FF*. Denote repair class i as *RCi*, representing the repair effort required to upgrade building functionality from S_i to an intermediate state S_{i+1}, and $T^n_{Repair,RCi}$ as the time takes to complete the *RCi*. In general, once a repair construction

165

initiates it will continue until the building regains its full structural and non-structural integrity. Accordingly, it is assumed that there are no arbitrary time breaks between RCs, although the structural and non-structural components being repaired in those RCs are different.

Utilities availability must be considered when a building's restoration process moves beyond the Re-Occupancy (RO) state, as shown in Figure 9.10. Analytically, the time ($T_{Utility}^n$) to bring utility service to building n in a community can be estimated by coupling probabilistic damage assessment and restoration decision optimization regarding resource allocation and repair sequencing within an overarching framework of interdependency modeling of utility networks (e.g. González et al. 2015; Zhang et al. 2018b).

Alternatively, the delay time, repair time, and utility disruption time introduced above can be efficiently represented statistically using data collected from reconnaissance efforts in previous major disasters in the US, supported by opinions from experts in various fields (including engineers, building owners, contractors, cost estimators, and bankers) (FEMA/NIBS 2003; FEMA P58 2012; Almufti & Willford 2013). Moreover, existing database is expected to be further refined and expanded as additional post-disaster field investigations and data collection efforts are completed (e.g. multiple post-event field investigations are included in the work plan of the NIST-funded Center of Excellence (CRCRP)).

Regarding the CTMC, all waiting times conditional on any possible combinations of building damage (ds_p^n) and utility disruption (ua_q^n), denoted as ($WT_{i,j}^n \mid ds_p^n, ua_q^n$), are listed in Table 9.1. Accordingly, the unconditional waiting time variables, $WT_{i,j}^n, j \geq i$, can be obtained using total probability theorem, i.e.,

$$WT_{i,j}^n = \frac{\sum_{(p,q)\in A_i} WT_{i,j}^n \mid ds_p^n, ua_q^n \cdot \mathrm{Prob}\left[DS(t_0) = ds_p^n, UA(t_0) = ua_q^n \right]}{\mathrm{Prob}[S(t_0) = S_i]}, \tag{9.17}$$

where the variables $DS(t_0)$ and $UA(t_0)$ represent the initial damage status of buildings and availability status of utility at the building site, respectively. A_i denotes the collections of the index of building and utility damage scenarios leading to functionality state S_i, as tabulated in Table 9.1. The $\mathrm{Prob}\left[DS(t_0) = ds_p^n, UA(t_0) = ua_q^n \right]$ is calculated from the initial damage evaluation of buildings and performance assessment of the utility networks.

Using Table 9.1 and the statistical or analytical estimation of the time segments involved in these equations, the PDFs of all waiting time $WT_{i,j}^n$ can be obtained. When substituting these PDFs into Equations (9.11)–(9.12), the **TPM** and **BRFs** can be obtained for all different building types in a community building portfolio.

9.4.2 Step 2: Portfolio-level recovery

Portfolio recovery trajectory (PRI)

The portfolio-level recovery can then be obtained by aggregating the CTMC restoration processes of individual buildings across the geographic domain of the community and over the entire recovery time horizon. In order to track the recovery time and trajectory of a building portfolio as a whole, a building *portfolio recovery index*, $PRI_j(t)$ (which is the BPFM introduced in Section 9.2) can be expressed as:

$$PRI_j(t) = \frac{\sum_{n=1}^{N} I_j^n(t)}{N}, \qquad j \in 1\ldots5 \tag{9.18}$$

Table 9.1 Waiting time conditional on initial damage condition and utility availability, $WT_{i,j}^n \mid ds_p, ua_q$

Functionality State $S(t_0)$	Damage State $DS(t_0)$	Utility Availability $UA(t_0)$	Waiting Time $WWT_{i,i}$	Waiting Time $WT_{i,j}, j > i$
RE	ds_1	N/A	$T_{Delay,1} + T_{Repair,RC1}$	$Max(T_{Repair,\,RC_j},\ T_{Utility} - T_{Delay,i} - \sum_{k=i}^{j-1} T_{Repair,\,RCk})$*
RU	ds_2	N/A	$T_{Delay,2} + T_{Repair,RC2}$	$Max(T_{Repair,\,RC_j},\ T_{Utility} - T_{Delay,i} - \sum_{k=i}^{j-1} T_{Repair,\,RCk})$*
RO	ds_3	ua_3	$T_{Delay,3} + T_{Repair,RC3}$	T_{Repair,RC_j}
RO	ds_3	ua_2	$T_{Delay,3} + T_{Repair,RC3}$	$Max(T_{Repair,RC4}, T_{Utility,2} - WT_{3,3})$
RO	ds_3	ua_1	$Max(T_{Delay,3} + T_{Repair,RC3}, T_{Utility,1})$	$Max(T_{Delay,3} + T_{Repair,RC4} + T_{Repair,RC4} - WT_{3,3}, T_{Utility,1} + T_{Utility,2} - WT_{3,3})$
RO	ds_4	ua_1	$T_{Utility,1}$	$Max(T_{Repair,RC4} + T_{Repair,RC4} - T_{Utility,2}, T_{Utility,2})$
RO	ds_5	ua_1	$T_{Utility,1}$	$T_{Utility,2}$
BF	ds_4	ua_3	$T_{Delay,4} + T_{Repair,RC4}$	0
BF	ds_5	ua_2	$T_{Utility,2}$	0
BF	ds_4	ua_2	$Max(T_{Delay,4} + T_{Repair,RC4}, T_{Utility,2})$	0
FF	ds_5	ua_3	0	0

* $T_{Utility} = 0$ if $UA(t_0) = ua_3$; $T_{Utility} = \begin{cases} 0, & j = 3 \\ T_{Utility,2}, & j = 4 \end{cases}$ if $UA(t_0) = ua_2$; $T_{Utility} = \begin{cases} T_{Utility,2}, & j = 3 \\ T_{Utility,1} + T_{Utility,2}, & j = 4 \end{cases}$ if $UA(t_0) = ua_1$

in which $T_{Utility,1}^n$ is the time takes for utility at the site of building n to recover utility status from state ua_1 to state ua_2 and $T_{Utility,2}^n$ is the time to recover from ua_2 to ua_3.

where $I_j^n(t)$ is the functionality state indicator of building n, i.e.:

$$I_j^n(t) = \begin{cases} 0 & S^n(t) \neq S_j \\ 1 & S^n(t) = S_j \end{cases}, \qquad n \in 1,2,\ldots,N \tag{9.19}$$

Accordingly, the Probability Mass Function (PMF) of $I_j^n(t)$ is:

$$P_{I_j^n}(t) = \begin{cases} 1 - \pi_j^n(t) & I_j^n(t) = 0 \\ \pi_j^n(t) & I_j^n(t) = 1, \end{cases} \qquad n \in 1,2,\ldots,N \tag{9.20}$$

where $\pi_j^n(t)$ is the probability of $S^n(t) = S_j$ at any time t for building n, as estimated by Equation (9.13). Moreover, the time-dependent expected value and variance of $PRI_j(t)$ are:

$$E\left[PRI_j(t) \right] = \frac{1}{N} \sum\nolimits_{n=1}^{N} \pi_j^n(t), \qquad n \in 1, 2,\ldots, N \tag{9.21}$$

$$\sigma_{PRI_j}^2(t) = \frac{1}{N^2} \sum\nolimits_{n=1}^{N} \sum\nolimits_{m=1}^{N} \rho_j^{mn}(t) \sigma_j^n(t) \sigma_j^m(t), \qquad n,m \in 1,2,\ldots,N, \tag{9.22}$$

in which, $\sigma_j^n(t) = \sqrt{\pi_j^n(t)\left[1 - \pi_j^n(t)\right]}$ is the standard deviation of $I_j^n(t)$; $\rho_j^{mn}(t)$ is the correlation matrix describing correlations between functionality states of building n, $I_j^n(t)$, and that of building m, $I_j^m(t)$, at any time t. Such correlations are introduced by the correlated initial functionality states between building pairs at t_0 resulting from correlated damage states and are propagated through the building restoration process; temporally, these correlations are strongest at t_0 and decrease monotonically with t as the buildings' restorations progress, and spatially, these correlations depend on the geographical locations of individual buildings and other attributes that affect building's damage state due to the hazard events. A detailed approach to estimate this correlation is presented in Lin & Wang (2017b).

An illustration of the mean values of $PRI_j(t)$ estimated by Equation (9.21) is presented in Figure 9.11, for $j = RE, RU, RO, BF$ and FF, respectively, tracking the temporal evolution of the percentage of buildings falling into each of the five functionality states. Further, define the curve associated with the FF state, i.e. $PRI_{FF}(t)$, as the *portfolio recovery trajectory*, which represents the percentage of the buildings in the FF state at any given elapsed time t from the hazard occurrence and is monotonically increasing with time. The portfolio recovery trajectory $PRI_{FF}(t)$ may not always converge to 100% and the $PRI_{RE}(t)$ may not always diminish to 0, as shown in Figure 9.11, which could be due to the population in- and out-migration following an extreme hazard.

Portfolio recovery time (PRT)
The portfolio recovery time, $PRT_{j,a\%}$, as defined in Section 9.2.1, is the time takes for $a\%$ (e.g. 95%) of community buildings to regain a predetermined functionality state j (e.g. FF). Then, the CDF of $PRT_{j,a\%}$ can be derived as:

$$F_{PRT_{j,a\%}}(t) = Prob\left[PRT_{j,a\%} \leq t \right] = Prob\left[PRI_j(t) \geq a\% \right] = \int_{a\%}^{1} f_{PRI_j}(x,t)dx, \tag{9.23}$$

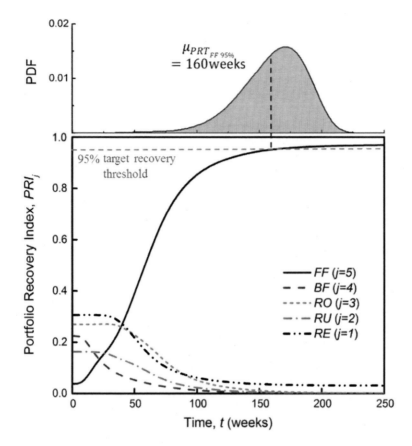

Figure 9.11 Illustration of the mean trajectory of the building portfolio recovery.
Source: Lin & Wang 2017b.

where $f_{PRI_j}(x,t)$ is the PDF of PRI_j at time t. Accordingly, the distribution of portfolio recovery time, $PRT_{FF,95\%}$, estimated using Equation (9.23) is also illustrated in Figure 9.11.

The two-step BPRM developed in this study, when applied to a real community, can provide insights regarding the temporal evolution of the spatial variation in recovery speed in different zones of the community.

9.5 Case study – Centerville community

In this section, the BPLE and BPRM introduced in Sections 9.3 and 9.4 are applied to a testbed community called Centerville. Centerville is a hypothetical community utilized by the NIST-Funded Center for Risk-Based Community Resilience Planning (CRCRP) to embody all typical features of a community and to allow and facilitate research teams to perform various resilience-related analyses of physical, social, and economic infrastructure systems (Ellingwood et al. 2016).

9.5.1 Centerville building portfolio characteristics

Centerville is designed as a typical mid-size community, with a population of approximately 50,000, situated in a Midwestern State in the US, and is approximately 8 km by 13 km (5 miles by 8 miles) in size. As shown in Figure 9.12(a), Centerville includes seven residential zones (Z1–Z7) which are categorized and distributed by the income level of the residents, two commercial zones (Z8–Z9), two industrial zones – one light industry (Z10), and one heavy industry (Z11). More detailed information of Centerville building portfolio can be found in Lin and Wang (2017b).

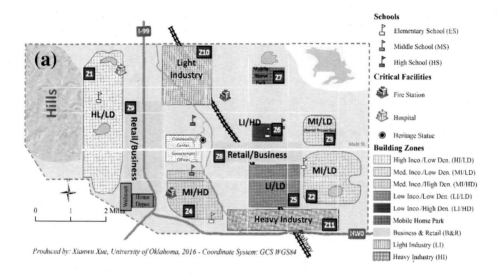

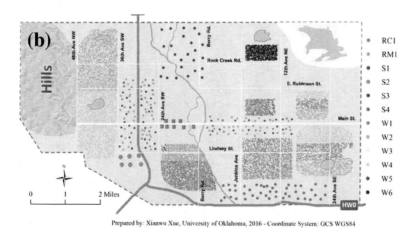

Figure 9.12   Centerville (a) zoning map; (b) building portfolio.
Source: Lin & Wang 2017b.

Table 9.2 Summary of Centerville building types

Type ID	Construction	Occupancy Class	Story	Year Built	Area (ft2)
W1	Wood	Residential, SF*	1	1945–1970	1,400
W2	Wood	Residential, SF	1	1985–2000	2,400
W3	Wood	Residential, SF	2	1985–2000	3,200
W4	Wood	Residential, SF	1	1970–1985	2,400
W5	Wood	Residential, MF*	3	1985	36,000
W6	Wood	Mobile Home	NA	NA	NA
S1	Steel braced frame	Commercial	1	1980	50,000
RC1	RC frame	Commercial	2	1980	50,000
RM1	Reinforced masonry	Commercial	2	1960	25,000
S2	Mix of steel and OWSJ* roof	Commercial	1	NA	125,000
S3	Steel braced frame	Industrial	2	1975	100,000
S4	Steel braced frame	Industrial	1	1995	500,000
RC2	RC frame	Hospital	4	1980	120,000
RM2	Reinforced masonry	Fire Station	2	1985	10,000
RC3	RC frame	School	3	1990	100,000
RM3	Light reinforced masonry	School	1	NA	100,000

*SF – single family
*MF – multiple family
*OWSJ – open web steel joist
Data source: Lin & Wang (2017b).

The Centerville building portfolio of approximately 15,000 buildings consists of 16 building archetypes, including residential, commercial, industrial occupancies, as well as critical facilities such as hospitals, fire stations, schools, and government offices, as tabulated in Table 9.2. The spatial distribution of all buildings within Centerville is shown in Figure 9.12(b). Particularly, the residential building portfolio accounts for nearly 98 percent of the Centerville building portfolio. All residential buildings, located in Z1–Z7, are wood frame structures with different occupancy types, stories, and year built (denoted as W1–W6 in Table 9.2). The number of buildings and the household (HH) income range in each of the residential zones are summarized in Table 9.3.

In Centerville recovery modeling, input data in Table 9.4 and Table 9.5 is synthesized from the information provided in Almufti and Willford (2013) and HAZUS-MH (FEMA/NIBS 2003), for T_{Delay}^n and T_{Repair}^n, respectively. For $T_{Utility}^n$, it is assumed that it takes buildings having no utility service at t_0 (i.e. $BU^{0,n} = 0$; $FU^{0,n} = 0$) 3 weeks on average to regain baseline utility service (i.e. $BU^{t>3weeks,n} = 1$) and 15 weeks to regain full utility service (i.e. $FU^{t>15weeks,n} = 1$); the coefficient of variation (C.O.V) of $T_{Utility}^n$ is assumed 0.7 (Almufti & Willford 2013). It is noteworthy such databases are community-specific, and should be collected and maintained by communities themselves to support their own resilience planning activities. The social-economic characteristics of a community that affect its building portfolio recovery are reflected and categorized in the second column of Table 9.4 as well as in Table 9.6. In particular, the time required to secure finance, $T_{FIN,i}^n$, (Table 9.4) is dependent on the financing resources available to homeowners (Table 9.6).

Table 9.3 Household characteristics of residential zones (Zone 1–Zone 7)

Zone ID	Residential Zones						
	Zone1 (Z1)	Zone2 (Z2)	Zone3 (Z3)	Zone4 (Z4)	Zone5 (Z5)	Zone6 (Z6)	Zone7 (Z7)
Description	High income/ Low density (HI/LD)	Medium income/ Low density (MI/LD)	Medium income/ Low density (MI/LD)	Medium income/ Low density (MI/HD)	Low income/ Low density (LI/LD)	Low income High density (LI/HD)	Mobile Homes
Household ID	HH1	HH2	HH3	HH4	HH5	HH6	HH7
Avg. Household Income	≥$100k	$70k-$100k	$70k-$100k	$40k-$70k	$20k-$40k	≤ $20k	≤ $10k
No. of Household	4,246	2,267	800	4,767	1,856	4,396	1,352
No. of Buildings W1	0	767	300	2,567	1,856	700	0
W2	2,000	700	300	1,000	0	0	0
W3	50	0	0	0	0	0	0
W4	2,196	800	200	0	0	0	0
W5	0	0	0	1,200	0	3,696	0
W6	0	0	0	0	0	0	1,352

Data source: Lin & Wang (2017b).

Table 9.4 Statistics of delay time

Delay Phases, $T_{Delay,i}^n \sim \text{Lognormal}(\theta, \beta)$ (Unit: weeks)

Sequence	Delay Time Components	Building specific conditions	Median (θ)	C.O.V (β)
Delay Phase 1	Inspection ($T_{INSP,i}^n$)	slight	0	0
		above slight	5	0.54
Delay Phase 2	Engineering mobilization & Review/Re-design ($T_{ENGM,i}^n$)	slight	6	0.4
		moderate/extensive	12	0.4
		complete	50	0.32
	Financing ($T_{FINA,i}^n$)	insurance	6	1.11
		private loans	15	0.68
		SBA-backed loans	48	0.57
		Not cover	48	0.65
	Contractor mobilization and Bid process ($T_{CONM,i}^n$)	slight	7	0.6
		above slight	19	0.38
Delay Phase 3	Permitting ($T_{PERM,i}^n$)	slight	1	0.86
		above slight	8	0.32

Source: REDi™ framework (Almufti & Willford, 2013).

Table 9.5 Statistics of building Repair Time with respect to repair classes (RCs)

Repair time $T_{Repair,\,RCi}^n \sim \text{Lognormal}((\theta, \beta))$ (Unit: weeks)

Sequence	Item	Occupancy	Median (θ)	C.O.V (β)
Repair class1 ($T_{Repair,\,RC1}^n$)	Heavily damaged structural and nonstructural components threaten life-safety	Single family	6	0.4
		Multiple family	8	0.4
		Mobile homes	2	0.4
Repair class2 ($T_{Repair,\,RC2}^n$)	Moderately to heavily damaged nonstructural components not threaten life-safety	Single family	6	0.4
		Multiple family	8	0.4
		Mobile homes	2	0.4
Repair class3 ($T_{Repair,\,RC3}^n$)	minor damage to structural components; minor to moderate damage to nonstructural components	Single family	11	0.4
		Multiple family	15	0.4
		Mobile homes	3.5	0.4
Repair class4 $T_{Repair,\,RC4}^n$	Minor cosmetic damage to structural and non-structural component	Single family	0.5	0.4
		Multiple family	0.5	0.4
		Mobile homes	0.5	0.4

Source: Synthesized from HAZUS-MH (FEMA/NIBS, 2003) database.

9.5.2 Building- and portfolio-level functionality loss from BPLE

A hypothetical scenario earthquake with M_w 7.8 and an epicenter located approximately 40 km southwest of Centerville is considered for illustration. The ground motion attenuation model by Campbell (2003) is adopted with mean value of the logarithm of seismic intensity. In this study, Centerville is assumed, for simplicity, to be situated on Site Class A soils.

The spatial variations with respect to the mean damage states of structural components, nonstructural drift-sensitive, and nonstructural acceleration-sensitive components are shown

Table 9.6 Financing resources for Centerville buildings restoration

Zone	Insurance	SBA-backed Loans	Private loan	Savings (personal resources)	Others
Z1(HI)	60%	5%	10%	25%	0%
Z2(MI)	50%	10%	30%	10%	0%
Z3(MI)	10%	10%	10%	5%	65%
Z4(MI)	30%	15%	30%	0	25%
Z5 (LI)	25%	30%	10%	0	35%
Z6 (LI)	25%	30%	10%	0	35%
Z7 (MH)	5%	5%	0	0	90%

Source: Lin & Wang (2017b).

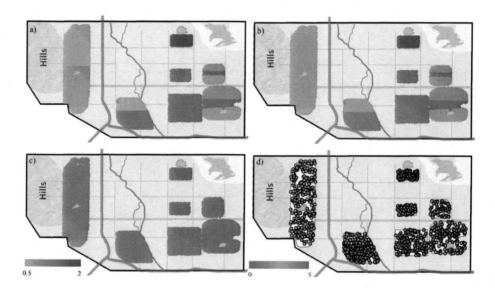

Figure 9.13 Spatial variation in the mean damage state of (a) structural components (SD); (b) non-structural drift-sensitive (ND); (c) acceleration-sensitive components (NA); and (d) the mean initial functionality state at t_0.

Source: Lin & Wang 2017b.

Figure 9.13(a), (b) and (c). It is evident that buildings in the northeast area of the Centerville community (which are mostly medium-income and low-income zones) in average suffer more damage than that of the southwest area (which are high-income zones). The spatial variation in buildings' initial functionality states at t_0 is shown in Figure 9.13(d). The PMF of the initial functionality state for each individual building, obtained by Equations (9.4)–(9.5), is illustrated in Figure 9.14(a), using W2 in Zone 4 as an example. Further, by aggregating the individual buildings' initial functionality states to the portfolio level, the Centerville portfolio recovery index at time t_0, i.e., $PRI_j(t_0)$, $j = RE, RU, RO, BF, FF$, defined as the percentage of buildings in the portfolio that falls in each of the five functionality states prior to restoration in Equation (9.7), are derived and shown in Equation 9.14(b).

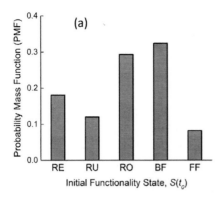
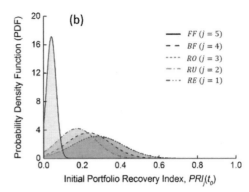

Figure 9.14 Probability assessment of (a) building-level pre-repair functionality state PMF, π^n (t_0), (illustrated using W2 in Zone 4) and (b) portfolio-level pre-recovery functionality index, PRI_j (t_0).

Source: Lin & Wang 2017b.

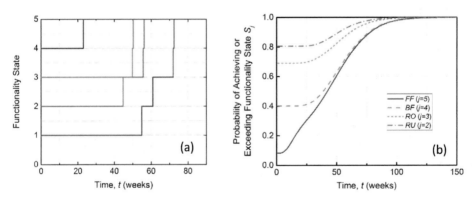

Figure 9.15 Illustration of building-level restoration: (a) conditional mean restoration process; (b) the building restoration function, BRF (both illustrated using W2 building in Zone 4 as an example).

Source: Lin & Wang 2017b.

9.5.3 Building- and portfolio-level functionality recovery from BPRM

Figure 9.15 illustrates (a) the conditional mean restoration process as well as (b) the *BRF* [presenting the probability of a building achieving or exceeding a predefined functionality state S_j at any post-event time t as defined in Equation (9.14)) of any building type in Centerville, using W2 buildings in Zone 4 as an example.

The mean values of $PRI_j(t)$, $j = RE, RU, RO, BF, FF$, are shown in Figure 9.11; the curve associated with *FF*, i.e. $PRI_{FF}(t)$, is the mean portfolio recovery trajectory. The time required for 95 percent of the building portfolio to achieve the *FF* state (i.e. $PRI_{FF}(t) = 95\%$) is defined as the portfolio recovery time and is denoted as $PRT_{FF,95\%}$; the PDF of $PRT_{FF,95\%}$

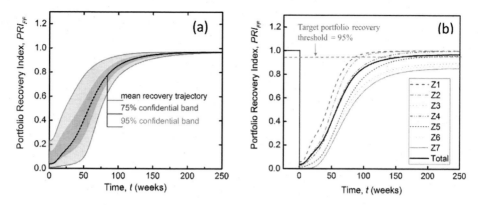

Figure 9.16 An illustration of (a) uncertainty in the portfolio recovery trajectory; and (b) the mean recovery trajectory for each of the seven residential zones (Zone1-Zone7).
Source: Lin & Wang 2017b.

is also illustrated in this figure. Figure 9.11 indicates that the mean portfolio recovery time for Centerville is approximately 160 weeks (approximately three years). The reason that the mean portfolio recovery trajectory PRI_{FF} does not converge to 1.0 is that we assumed 3 percent housing units in Centerville are not restored due to possible population outmigration as discussed previously.

Furthermore, the uncertainty associated with the mean recovery trajectory is shown in Figure 9.16(a), indicating significant variation in portfolio recovery, especially in the early phase, which is due to the uncertainties and spatial correlations in initial functionality states mapped from the community-wide hazard-induced damages and uncertainties in delay time and reconstruction time during building restorations. The mean recovery trajectories for each of the residential zones (Z1–Z7) in Centerville, shown in Figure 9.16 (b), depict the different recovery patterns for different population groups: high income residential zones (Z1 and Z2) recover much faster than low income zones (Z6, and Z7). Houses in Z1 and Z2 are better constructed and experience less damage; moreover, higher-income households in Z1 and Z2 are likely to secure the funding for housing repair more quickly than the households in other zones. Figure 9.17 depicts the spatial variation in mean building functionality states in Centerville at four different points in time during recovery. Notable disparities are observed, reflecting differences in hazard-induced damages and recovery capacities, both underlined by the social and economic disparities among different residential zones.

9.6 Conclusions

The ultimate purpose of developing quantitative, physics-based resilience assessment models, such as the BPLE and BPRM developed in this study, is to guide and support community planning decisions toward achieving community-specific resilience goals. Toward that objective, the community building portfolios resilience modeling framework introduced herein has made several distinct contributions, as compared with approaches that appear in the recent literature:

First, the newly introduced BPFM includes a building-level functionality metric (*RE, RU, RO, BF,* and *FF*) and a portfolio-level functionality metric (*PRI*, defined as the percentage of buildings in a portfolio that are in any of the five pre-defined functionality states). The BPFM explicitly

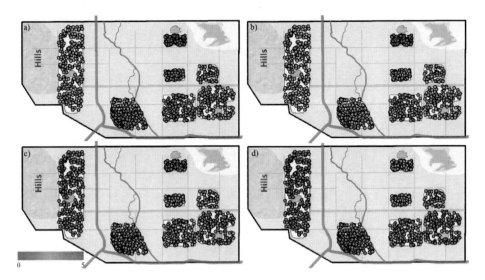

Figure 9.17 Spatial variation of functionality recovery at (a) $t_0=0$; (b) 30 weeks; (c) 60 weeks; (d) 90 weeks following the hazard occurrence.

Source: Lin & Wang 2017b.

reflects the dependency of the building portfolio on other community infrastructure systems in maintaining its desired functionality level, which is not reflected in other typical building-related metrics in the literature. Furthermore, it enables the performance of a building portfolio to be assessed on a consistent measure at various spatial scales (e.g. parcel, block, census, zone, or community) and to be tracked throughout the time domain of resilience assessment (including pre-event planning, immediate post-disaster response, and long-term recovery).

Second, the BPLE framework provides a probabilistic and spatial depiction of functionality losses across a community building portfolio. The BPLE has provided a rigorous and consistent uncertainty modeling scheme enables the uncertainty in the spatial loss of distributed building portfolios to be estimated realistically. Furthermore, a damage-to-functionality mapping is proposed to relate the building functionality states to the joint status of building's physical damage and utility disruption of a building; this mapping, distinguished from some existing building-level functionality assessments supported by detailed building-specific information, effectively facilitates the portfolio functionality loss estimation at regional or community scale. The outcomes of BPLE characterize the initial functionality state for recovery modeling, which is the starting point of the BPRM.

Third, the novel BPRM is constructed in two critical steps: (i) modeling individual building restoration as a discrete state, continuous time Markov Chain (CTMC); and (ii) modeling building portfolio recovery through aggregating the CTMC restoration processes of individual buildings across the domain of the community and over the entire recovery time horizon. The two-step BPRM was calibrated through a review of existing recovery-related databases and variables known to be essential for building portfolio recovery analysis. Uncertainties in these variables were propagated, and the time-variant spatial correlations in buildings' functionality states were quantified throughout the BPRM in the estimation of the portfolio recovery trajectory and recovery time.

The BPLE-BPRM coupled framework is capable of quantifying the impact of different pre- and post-hazard mitigation strategies on the overall resilience – i.e. functionality loss and recovery– of building portfolios. As a result, this framework can facilitate risk-informed community–level decision-making regarding resilience planning and hazard mitigation as discussed in Lin et al. (2016, 2018), Lin and Wang (2018), and Wang et al. (2018).

Acknowledgement

The framework presented herein was supported by the Center for Risk-Based Community Resilience Planning, funded by US National Institute of Science and Technology (NIST) (Award Number: 70NANB15H044).

Notes

1 Ground motion intensity is the ground motion characteristic that can be related to the response of structural systems, nonstructural components, and building contents through engineering analysis, such as peak ground acceleration, peak ground velocity, peak ground displacement, or a spectral response quantity such as spectral displacement, velocity or acceleration.

2 The damage state categorizes the extent of damage to structural and nonstructural components by different damage levels (often related to the structural system deformation or acceleration). In HAZUS-MH (FEMA/NIBS 2003), four damage states (i.e., slight, moderate, extensive, and complete) to structural and nonstructural components of a building and their relationships with building response threshold are identified.

3 There are considerable amounts of nonstructural components suffering from severe damage (such as stairs and suspended ceiling) can threaten life safety and trigger an unsafe placard. However, there are also some nonstructural components that are unlikely to pose threat to life safety (such as elevator, most mechanical equipment and electronical system). In this study we don't distinguish these two types of nonstructural components and assume that the overall nonstructural components with severe damage will threaten life safety and is in restrict entry. This will lead to conservative result in functionality losses.

References

Almufti, I. and Wilford, M. (2013). REDi™ Rating System: Resilience Based Earthquake Design Initiative for the Next Generation of Buildings. Version 1.0. October, Arup.

ASCE (2009). Recommended seismic provisions for new buildings and other structures (FEMA P-750). *Federal Emergency Management Agency*, Washington, DC.

ASCE/SEI (ASCE/Structural Engineering Institute) (2016). Minimum design loads for buildings and other structures. ASCE/SEI 7–16, *Am. Soc. of Civil Engr.*, Reston, VA.

Burton, H.V., Deierlein, G., Lallemant, D., and Lin, T. (2015). Framework for incorporating probabilistic building performance in the assessment of community seismic resilience. *Journal of Structural Engineering*, 142(8), C4015007.

Campbell, K.W. (2003). Prediction of strong ground motion using the hybrid empirical method and its use in the development of ground-motion (attenuation) relations in eastern North America. *Bulletin of the Seismological Society of America*, 93(3), 1012–33.

Chang, S.E. (2010). Urban disaster recovery: a measurement framework and its application to the 1995 Kobe earthquake. *Disasters*, 34(2), 303–27.

Ellingwood B.R., Cutler, H., Gardoni, P., Peacock, W.G., van de Lindt, J.W., and Wang, N. (2016). The Centerville virtual community: A fully integrated decision model of interacting physical and social infrastructure systems. *Sustainable and Resilient Infrastructure*, 1(3–4), 95–107.

FEMA (2012). FEMA P-58-1: Seismic performance assessment of buildings. Volume 1–Methodology.

FEMA/NIBS (2003). Multi-hazard loss estimation methodology earthquake model (HAZUS-MH MR4): Technical Manual. Washington, DC.

Goda, K. and Hong, H.P. (2008). Estimation of seismic loss for spatially distributed buildings. *Earthquake Spectra*, 24(4), 889–910.

González, A.D., Dueñas-Osorio, L., Sánchez-Silva, M., and Medaglia, A.L. (2015). The interdependent network design problem for optimal infrastructure system restoration. *Computer-Aided Civil and Infrastructure Engineering*.

Jayaram, N. and Baker, J.W. (2009). Correlation model for spatially distributed ground-motion intensities. *Earthquake Engineering & Structural Dynamics*, 38(15), 22.

Lee, R. and Kiremidjian, A.S. (2007). Uncertainty and correlation for loss assessment of spatially distributed systems. *Earthquake Spectra*, 23(4): 753–70.

Lin, P. and Wang, N. (2016). Building portfolio fragility functions to support scalable community resilience assessment. *Sustainable and Resilient Infrastructure*, 1(3–4), 108–22.

Lin, P. and Wang, N. (2017a). Stochastic post-disaster functionality recovery of community building portfolios I: Modeling. *Structural Safety*, 69, 96–105.

Lin, P. and Wang, N. (2017b). Stochastic post-disaster functionality recovery of community building portfolios II: Application. *Structural Safety*, 69, 106–117.

Lin, P. and Wang, N. (2018). A resilience-based decision framework to support risk mitigation of community building portfolios. In review.

Lin, P., Wang, N., and Ellingwood, B.R. (2016). A risk de-aggregation framework that relates community resilience goals to building performance objectives. *Sustainable and Resilient Infrastructure*, 1(1–2), 1–13.

Lin, P., Wang, N., Zhang, W., Hu, F., and Nicholson, C. (2018). Post-disaster recovery of community building portfolios: effects of lifeline systems on building functionality. In review.

Miles, S.B. and Chang, S. E. (2003). Urban disaster recovery: A framework and simulation model.

Oaks, D.S. (1990). The damage assessment process: the application of ATC-20. *The Loma Prieta Earthquake, Studies of Short-term Impacts. Program on Environmental and Behavior Monograph*, 50.

Peacock, W., Lin, Y., Lu, J., and Zhang, Y. (2008). Household dislocation algorithm 2: an OLS through the origin approach. Hazard Reduction and Recovery Center. Texas A&M University. HRRC Reports: 08-04R.

Peacock, W.G., Van Zandt, S., Zhang, Y., and Highfield, W.E. (2014). Inequities in long-term housing recovery after disasters. *Journal of the American Planning Association*, 80(4), 356–71.

Rose, A. and Guha, G.S. (2004). Computable general equilibrium modeling of electric utility lifeline losses from earthquakes. In *Modeling Spatial and Economic Impacts of Disasters* (pp. 119–41). Berlin and Heidelberg: Springer.

Steelman, J., Song, J., and Hajjar, J.F. (2007). Integrated data flow and risk aggregation for consequence-based risk management of seismic regional loss. University of Illinois.

Vitoontus, S. and Ellingwood, B.R. (2013). Role of correlation in seismic demand and building damage in estimating losses under scenario earthquakes. *Proc. Int. Conf. on Struct. Safety and Reliability (ICOSSAR 2013)*, New York: Taylor & Francis; The Netherlands: A.A. Balkema.

Wang, Y., Wang, N., Lin, P., Ellingwood, B., Mahmoud, H., and Maloney, T. (2018). De-aggregation of community resilience goals to obtain minimum performance objectives for buildings under tornado hazards. *Structural Safety*, 70, 82–92.

Xiao, Y. and Van Zandt, S. (2012). Building community resiliency: Spatial links between household and business post-disaster return. *Urban Studies*, 49(11), 2523–42.

Zhang, W., Lin, P., Wang, N., Nicholson, C., and Xue, X. (2018a). Probabilistic prediction of postdisaster functionality loss of community building portfolios considering utility disruptions. *Journal of Structural Engineering*, 144(4), 04018015.

Zhang, W., Nicholson, C., Wang, N., Lin, P., and Xue, X. (2018b). Interdependent Networks Recovery Problem. in review.

10

A way forward to resilient infrastructures against earthquake-tsunami multi-hazard

Raffaele De Risi,[1] *Ario Muhammad,*[2] *and Katsuichiro Goda*[3]

[1] DEPARTMENT OF CIVIL ENGINEERING, UNIVERSITY OF BRISTOL; QUEEN'S BUILDING, UNIVERSITY WALK, BS8 1TR, BRISTOL, UK; RAFFAELE.DERISI@BRISTOL.AC.UK

[2] SCHOOL OF EARTH SCIENCES, UNIVERSITY OF BRISTOL; WILLS MEMORIAL BUILDING, QUEENS ROAD, BS8 1RJ, BRISTOL, UK; ARIO.MUHAMMAD@BRISTOL.AC.UK

[3] DEPARTMENT OF EARTH SCIENCES AND STATISTICAL AND ACTUARIAL SCIENCES, WESTERN UNIVERSITY; 1151 RICHMOND STREET NORTH, N6A 5B7, LONDON, CANADA; KGODA2@UWO.CA

10.1 Introduction

Globally, numerous megacities are located along the coast in active seismic regions, and more people migrate to coastal areas for economic reasons. As a result, the population in tsunami-prone regions has been steadily increasing in the last 25 years (Melgar et al. 2016). Figure 10.1 shows the population distribution in the Pacific and Indian Ocean regions according to the NASA's Earth Observing System Data and Information System (http://sedac.ciesin.columbia.edu/). On the map, subduction trenches and plate boundaries are shown with lines, whereas the distribution of historical tsunamis triggered by seismic events in the last 2500 years are indicated by circles, obtained from the National Geophysical Data Center (www.ngdc.noaa.gov/hazard/tsu_db.shtml). The figure highlights the significant exposure of the world population and countries to earthquakes and tsunamis.

As more population migrates to coastal regions, the demand for infrastructures increases rapidly. Infrastructures are a set of physical systems that support day-to-day functions and have major influence on the progress of human society. In coastal areas, there are conventional and strategic infrastructures (Figure 10.2). Conventional infrastructures, such as roads, railways, power and communication networks, water distribution networks, waste water systems, and gas distribution networks, underpin economic and social activities in urban cities. On the other hand, strategic infrastructures in coastal areas typically include harbors that are key points for shipping industry, nuclear power plants that need access to a large amount of water for cooling of boiling water reactors, gas and oil storage containing fossil fuels shipped by tankers, and early warning systems, such as tidal buoys and ocean bottom pressure gauges that detect hazardous

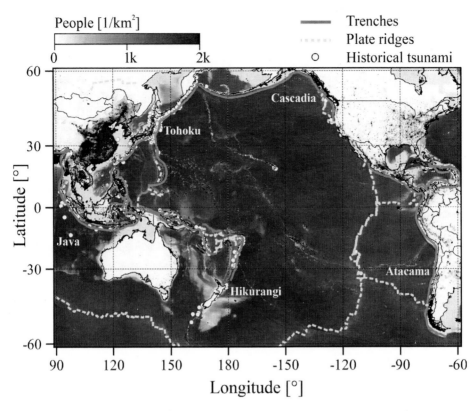

Figure 10.1 Population distribution in Pacific and Indian Ocean regions. Circles represent historical tsunami triggered by seismic events.

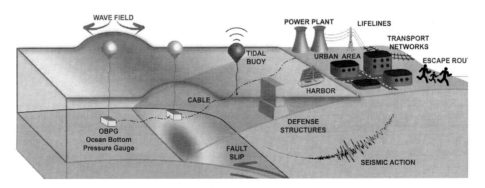

Figure 10.2 Earthquake-tsunami hazard and risk along coasts in a subduction area.

events in open sea. In assessing the infrastructure's response to disasters, it is important to view it as a complex system, composed of several elements; the level of complexity is significantly increased when multiple infrastructures are interconnected and work as interacting systems (Duenas-Osorio & Vemuru 2009).

Resilience and sustainability are the fundamental requirements for modern infrastructures. As highlighted by recent earthquake-triggered disasters, such as the M_w9.1 Sumatra earthquake in 2004, the M_w8.8 Chile earthquake in 2010, and the M_w9.0 Great East Japan earthquake in 2011, during a large-scale seismic event in a subduction zone, coastal communities and infrastructures may be severely affected first by strong shaking and then by tsunami (and other secondary hazards). In such a case, it is essential that infrastructural systems function normally without major disruption; they should facilitate first warning and evacuation, then search and rescue operations, and finally recovery and repairs/reconstruction. For these reasons, it is important that infrastructures are resilient and sustainable. Major progress has been made in the field of disaster risk management (e.g. Bruneau & Reinhorn 2007; Ouyang & Dueñas-Osorio 2012; McCullough et al. 2013; Ayyub 2014; Bozza et al. 2015).

Resilience is the capability to survive, adapt, and grow against unforeseen extreme events, such as earthquakes and tsunamis. There are three main aspects of infrastructure resilience. The first is system resistance and robustness that represent the capacity to withstand and survive to external disturbances. The second is system response and recovery that are the capability of taking actions initially to reduce the adverse impact due to disturbances and eventually to return the community to a normal condition (although it may not be identical to the pre-disaster situation) or even better condition (i.e. the build back better principle). The third is system preparedness that is critical for the subsequent disaster protection-response-recovery cycle.

At the same time, modern infrastructure should be sustainable. Sustainable infrastructures can be defined as functional structural elements that do not diminish the social, economic, and ecological processes by maintaining human equality, diversity, and functionality of natural systems, and therefore do not jeopardize the well-being of future generations (Gardoni 2017). Building infrastructure sustainably increases the resilience, since it improves the overall system performance in terms of satisfaction of citizens' need for basic service. It also strengths various intangible values that are main drivers for long-term social development, such as social vitality, well-being, social and environmental health and safety. Moreover, safeguarding environmental assets reduces the risk and provides resources to facilitate the recovery.

To design new resilient infrastructures or to improve the resilience of existing ones, it is essential to enable a paradigm shift from conventional ones centered around physical protection to more holistic ones that are informed by comprehensive risk management options. The latter will require integration of physical protection strategies (hard measures) with community-awareness/preparedness (soft measures). In fact, hard and soft measures are complementary. It has been demonstrated that they enhance the resilience of stakeholders differently (Kunreuther et al. 2005), and thus they should be integrated into risk management strategies effectively.

This chapter presents an overview of a novel earthquake-tsunami multi-hazard impact assessment methodology that has been developed to evaluate the earthquake-tsunami risk to multiple buildings and infrastructure in coastal areas quantitatively by accounting for uncertainties in earthquake rupture processes. The methodology can be used to improve the resilience of new and existing infrastructures against earthquake-tsunami multi-hazard. Particular attention is paid to studies that approach the problem through the performance-based engineering philosophy (Cornell & Krawinkler 2000) since it offers a nested modular structure that facilitates the quantification of the consequences of future disasters by propagating the uncertainty related to model components (e.g. hazard, exposure, and vulnerability). It helps define the desirable long-term objectives related to disaster risk reduction, quantify the effectiveness of potential mitigation strategies, and implement risk-based management decisions.

The chapter is organized as follows. First, a novel stochastic earthquake-tsunami multi-hazard analysis, developed by De Risi and Goda (2016), is introduced to explain numerical procedures to evaluate the earthquake-tsunami hazard impact to a given coastal location. Subsequently, it is extended to a multi-risk loss estimation framework by incorporating earthquake and tsunami vulnerability components (Goda & De Risi 2018). Possible implementations of the new multi-risk tool in the context of cost-benefit analysis of risk mitigation options are discussed to illustrate their applications in developing more effective disaster risk reduction strategies, including early warning systems and evacuation plans for tsunamis. Finally, a case study of evacuation planning in Padang, Indonesia, is discussed by focusing on tsunami evacuation shelters, which represent a prime example of critical structures and facilities that must withstand against the sequence of earthquake and tsunami.

10.2 Earthquake-tsunami multi-hazard assessment

In the context of multi-hazard assessment of coastal infrastructures in active seismic regions, a hazard module should consider external loadings due to earthquake strong motions and tsunamis as sequential disturbances to a system of complex and interdependent infrastructure and therefore should consider compounding risk due to cascading failure events (Franchin & Cavalieri 2013). In addition, other secondary hazards, such as aftershock, liquefaction, landslide, and fire, can be significant (Daniell et al. 2017). This chapter focuses primarily on a methodology to characterize the sequence of earthquake and tsunami. The term "multi-hazard" is attributed to common source features of strong shaking and tsunami that are captured through physical parameters of earthquake ruptures. Simulations of shaking and tsunami hazard processes are conducted in a joint manner by maintaining the source dependency.

Simultaneous earthquake-tsunami hazard is a serious global issue and may cause grave consequences. Probabilistic hazard analysis is the fundamental step for assessing disaster risk accurately and for deciding upon effective risk mitigation strategies. De Risi and Goda (2016) proposed for the first time a simulation-based probabilistic joint earthquake-tsunami hazard analysis to estimate the likelihood that seismic ground-motion intensity and tsunami inundation at a particular location will exceed given hazard levels within a certain time interval. The methodology is illustrated in Figure 10.3, and a brief overview of the earthquake-tsunami multi-hazard analysis is given below.

Once the geometry of the potential source zone is defined (Figure 10.3a), the first step of the procedure is to define an occurrence model of major tsunamigenic seismic events (e.g. magnitude-recurrence model; Figure 10.3b). This model is used to calculate the annual rate of exceedance of major seismic events that may cause significant ground motions and tsunamis. For example, let **IM** represent the intensity measures, such as peak ground acceleration (PGA) and inundation depth (h). Assuming a Poissonian arrival time process, the probability to observe an earthquake-tsunami sequence having **IM** values equal to or greater than the specific values **im** in t years, is given by:

$$P\left(\mathbf{IM} \geq \mathbf{im} \,|\, t\right) = 1 - \exp\left[-\lambda\left(\mathbf{IM} \geq \mathbf{im}\right) \cdot t\right], \tag{10.1}$$

where $\lambda(\mathbf{IM} \geq \mathbf{im})$ is the mean annual rate at which the intensity measures **IM** will exceed specific values **im** at a given location. The rate $\lambda(\mathbf{IM} \geq \mathbf{im})$ can be expressed as a filtered Poisson process (De Risi & Goda 2017):

$$\lambda\left(\mathbf{IM} \geq \mathbf{im}\right) = \lambda_{M\min} \cdot \int P\left(\mathbf{IM} \geq \mathbf{im} \,|\, \boldsymbol{\theta}\right) \cdot f\left(\boldsymbol{\theta} \,|\, m\right) \cdot f\left(m\right) \cdot \left|\mathrm{d}\boldsymbol{\theta}\right| \left|\mathrm{d}m\right|, \tag{10.2}$$

where λ_{Mmin} is the mean annual rate of occurrence of the seismic events with magnitudes greater than the minimum magnitude considered in the magnitude-frequency distribution. $P(\mathbf{IM} \geq \mathbf{im} | \boldsymbol{\theta})$ is the probability that $\mathbf{IM}$ will exceed $\mathbf{im}$ at a given coastal location for a given set of earthquake source parameters $\boldsymbol{\theta}$. $f(\boldsymbol{\theta} | m)$ represents the scaling relationships of the uncertain earthquake source parameters conditioned on magnitude m, and $f(m)$ is the magnitude–frequency distribution. The integral can be evaluated by Monte Carlo simulations (De Risi & Goda 2017).

For each value of earthquake magnitude, size and geometry of the rupture area as well as other key source parameters (e.g. mean slip and spatial correlation parameters of

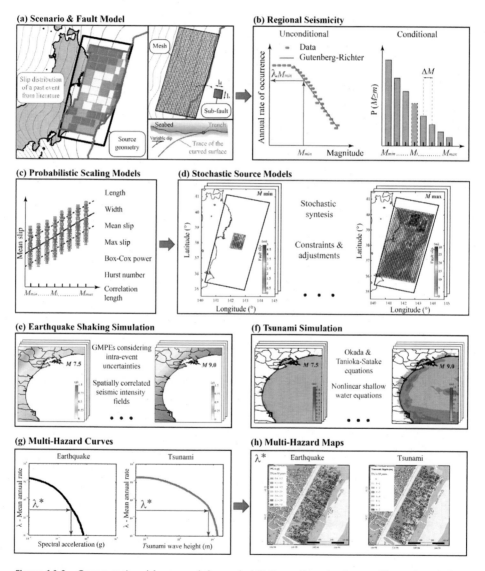

Figure 10.3 Computational framework for probabilistic earthquake–tsunami hazard analysis.

slip distribution) are determined using probabilistic scaling relationships for tsunamigenic earthquakes (Goda et al. 2016; Figure 10.3c). In this step, both aleatory and epistemic uncertainties of model parameters (i.e. position and geometry) are incorporated based on probabilistic information available in the literature. Multiple realizations of possible earthquake slip distributions are generated (Figure 10.3d) according to a spectral synthesis method (Mai & Beroza 2002). In particular, the incorporation of the stochastic slip models in probabilistic earthquake-tsunami hazard analysis is novel with respect to previous studies (e.g. Annaka et al. 2007), where slip distributions within a fault rupture plane are typically considered as uniform or randomly distributed (without realistic spatial correlation of earthquake slip over a fault rupture plane).

Subsequently, estimation of earthquake and tsunami intensity parameters is carried out. For each generated slip distribution, (a) spatially correlated strong motion intensity measures (Goda & Hong 2008) are evaluated through the adoption of suitable ground motion prediction equations (GMPEs) for subduction earthquakes (e.g. Abrahamson et al. 2016) as a function of magnitude and distance from the earthquake rupture (Figure 10.3e), and (b) the seafloor vertical displacement is calculated using analytical formulae (Okada 1985; Tanioka & Satake 1996) and tsunami simulation is performed by solving nonlinear shallow water equations (Goto et al. 1997) using the estimated water surface profile due to the earthquake rupture (Figure 10.3f). It is worth noting that the main difference between simulating earthquake and tsunami hazard processes is that typically, tsunami wave simulation is performed by solving the governing equations of tsunami wave propagation for a given initial wave condition, unlike the use of statistical ground motion prediction models in seismic hazard analysis.

By repeating the above procedure for many stochastic source scenarios, spectral accelerations at multiple locations (i.e. shake maps) can be obtained from the seismic intensity simulation procedure, while the statistics of the maximum wave heights and velocities can be obtained for rigorous tsunami hazard analysis. The site-specific earthquake-tsunami hazard curves (Figure 10.3g) can be derived by integrating the annual occurrence rates of the major earthquakes and the spectral acceleration-tsunami inundation results. De Risi and Goda (2016) showed that a few hundred simulations are sufficient to obtain stable hazard results for a given scenario magnitude, and therefore in total, a few thousands of earthquake scenarios are necessary to cover a range of magnitudes. Moreover, De Risi and Goda (2017) showed that the simulation number can be reduced if the simulated intensity measures are fitted with analytical models adopting a Bayesian procedure.

To obtain earthquake-tsunami uniform hazard maps illustrated in Figure 10.3h, the preceding multi-hazard simulations for a single location can be performed for a set of grid points covering an entire area of interest. Such multi-hazard maps, which are developed by accounting for joint earthquake-tsunami hazards, are particularly valuable for urban planning, since they are effective in identifying risky areas visually, and therefore allow to facilitate more sustainable and resilient development of urban areas. These maps are also useful for increasing the risk awareness of residents and for reducing the gap between real and perceived risks.

10.3 Multi-risk and cost-benefit analysis

Cost-benefit analysis is a systematic approach to identify an optimal choice among alternatives. In the framework of sustainable infrastructures, cost corresponds to investment necessary to realize/upgrade the components of new/old infrastructures and to increase the robustness of dependences/interdependences both within a single infrastructure and between different infrastructures. Cost may account for environmental impact, through a life-cycle assessment procedure (Caruso et al. 2017). It can be extended to the entire life of the infrastructures by considering inspection and maintenance operations, in a life-cycle cost approach (Frangopol & Liu 2007). On the other hand, benefit is generally represented by avoided loss to the exposed assets, in case of extreme natural disasters, associated with available alternatives. A typical exposed asset is a portfolio of buildings in an urban area. Cost–benefit analysis can also be adopted to select the location and the geometry of a breakwater, necessary to protect an urban area, choosing a solution that offers the best trade-off between implementation costs and benefit probabilistically.

To quantify the cost-benefit effectiveness of available options, a methodology that allows the risk quantification in economic terms is needed. Several recent studies have proposed multi-risk approaches (Marzocchi et al. 2012; Selva 2013; Mignan et al. 2014; Ming et al. 2015; Liu et al. 2015) by integrating the performance-based philosophy with new comprehensive methodologies that enable to homogenize multiple risk components in different ways. Three main aspects of the multi-risk framework that have been investigated in literature are: (i) joint probability of relevant hazards, (ii) vulnerability model that accounts for time-variant multi-hazard, and (iii) combination of loss for each hazard in a coherent manner.

In this context, taking advantages of the multi-hazard procedure described in the previous section, Goda and De Risi (2018) have developed a new multi-hazard loss estimation methodology for shaking and tsunami. The formulation of the multi-hazard earthquake impact assessment is based on total probability theorem and it is essentially equivalent to that of performance-based earthquake engineering methodology (e.g. Cornell & Krawinkler 2000). The developed multi-hazard loss estimation method can be regarded as a tool for implementing the performance-based earthquake-tsunami engineering methodology, particularly applicable to multiple buildings in coastal regions. The main equation for the loss assessment of a portfolio of buildings is given by:

$$\nu(L \geq l) = \lambda_{Mmin} \int P(L \geq l|\mathbf{ds}) \, f(\mathbf{ds}|\mathbf{im}) \, f(\mathbf{im}|\boldsymbol{\theta}) \, f(\boldsymbol{\theta}|m) \, f(m) \, |d\mathbf{ds}| \, |d\mathbf{im}| \, |d\boldsymbol{\theta}| \, |dm|, \tag{10.3}$$

where, in addition to the terms presented in Equation (10.2), $f(\mathbf{im}|\boldsymbol{\theta})$ is the joint probability density function of **IM** given $\boldsymbol{\theta}$, $f(\mathbf{ds}|\mathbf{im})$ is the shaking-tsunami fragility function, which predicts the probability of incurring a particular damage state **DS** for given **IM**, $P(L \geq l|\mathbf{ds})$ is the damage-loss function given **DS**, and $\nu(L \geq l)$ is the mean annual occurrence rate that the total loss L for a portfolio of buildings caused by shaking and tsunami exceeds a certain loss threshold l.

As per Equation (10.2), the integral can be evaluated by Monte Carlo simulation. It is important to emphasize that there are not many multi-hazard earthquake-tsunami fragility models that are applicable to a wide range of buildings and infrastructures (Park et al. 2012). Therefore, conventional separate fragility models need to be adopted; the final loss due to shaking and tsunami can be calculated as the dominant contribution from shaking and tsunami damage. Developing seismic-tsunami fragility models that capture damage accumulation due to multi-hazards is an open research area that requires further research.

Similarly to the hazard assessment, the main outcome of the multi-risk procedure is a loss curve that represents the mean annual rate of exceedance of a given loss. Loss curves can be calculated for several alternative configurations of infrastructure and compared with that associated with the current situation. The difference between the curves represents the potential benefit associated with each risk reduction alternative.

10.4 Emergency management

Tools and procedures developed for earthquake-tsunami hazard and risk can be used to improve the disaster preparedness of coastal communities. Specifically, more refined early warning systems are necessary, and more robust horizontal and vertical evacuation plans can be developed and implemented.

Early warning systems

Seismic early warning is a well-established practice around the world. In contrast, tsunami warning systems can still be improved significantly (Monastersky 2012). Tsunami events are characterized by imprecise and/or unreliable real-time forecasting, sometimes underestimating hazards (e.g. 1998 Papua New Guinea and 2011 Tohoku) or overestimating hazards (e.g. 1968 Hawaii). Unsuccessful tsunami warning systems could lead to significant economic losses, potential injuries, and casualties. This is the result of the low-probability high-consequence nature of massive tsunamis with respect to other natural hazards; in fact, tsunami warning systems were not a priority until recently, and in many cases, they did not exist in the majority of countries along subduction zones (Melgar et al. 2016).

In the last two decades, Tsunami Warning Centers (TWCs) around the world, such as the Intergovernmental Coordination Group for the Pacific Tsunami Warning and Mitigation System (ICG/PTWS) and the Indian Ocean Tsunami Information Center (IOTIC), were facing the challenge of issuing tsunami warning reliably based on incomplete or ambiguous information. Many of the existing methods for tsunami warning utilize libraries of potential rupture scenarios and pre-calculated propagating waves; when an event occurs, such libraries are inquired to identify the most likely scenario (Hirshorn et al. 2013; Hoshiba & Ozaki 2014; Tsushima et al. 2014; Inazu et al. 2016). In particular, an initial alarm is generally based on measurements not related to tsunamis (e.g. seismic and GPS data); then fast estimation of the earthquake magnitude and location is performed. The final confirmation from real-time tsunami propagation-inundation analyses or from observations at tsunami buoys, tidal gauges, and ocean-bottom pressure gauges, may be too late for timely evacuation measures. Such situations are further exacerbated when responsible agencies must issue warnings for near-source regions, which may have only several minutes to react. For example, the first waves from a Cascadia tsunami can strike the Pacific Northwest coasts in less than 20 minutes. The situations are even worse in Japan and Aleutian Island, where only a few minutes of lead time may be available (depending on the proximity of tsunami sources). In general, tsunamis triggered by near seismic sources can cause significant tsunami damage, and they should be studied in detail because the slip patterns of earthquake rupture plane have major influence on resulting tsunamis (Geist & Parsons 2006). In comparison to local tsunamis, a simpler parameterization is usually sufficient for far-field tsunamis because seismic moment, source mechanism, and radiation pattern are more influential than slip distribution within a rupture plane.

Only recently, the problem of issuing tsunami warning for local tsunamis has been tackled more rigorously, and new algorithms for tsunami early warning have been developed (e.g. Maeda et al. 2015). The algorithms avoid the estimation of the source. Rather, they calculate the propagating wave field directly in real-time by assimilating real-time data from offshore instruments into tsunami simulation. Related to these new methodological developments, future research is still needed to address the key unresolved issues, including (1) a proper treatment of real-time data coming from offshore instruments (e.g. filtering issues), (2) reducing the effect of bias/uncertainty in estimated earthquake magnitude on hazard forecasting, and

(3) real-time computation and its automation of tsunami wave simulation. In addition, probabilistic treatment of uncertainty (e.g. slip distribution) needs to be improved, and the hazard forecasting should be extended in future to risk forecasting (i.e. estimation of casualties, fatalities, and economic loss) to inform stakeholders and emergency managers and to support them in making critical decisions more effectively.

Along with this new development in tsunami early warning systems, a more extensive real-time observation system of tsunami waves has been implemented in Japan. Figure 10.4 shows a new Japanese early warning system S-net built in the aftermath of the 2011 event (Rabinovich & Eblé 2015); 151 ocean-bottom pressure gauges, mounted on seabed, are connected by optic fiber cables and constantly communicate with five operating stations on land. The new near-source tsunami detecting systems will be particularly useful for advancing the tsunami early warning systems by enhancing the existing algorithms for issuing tsunami early warning.

Tsunami evacuation

The hazard maps generated from the stochastic earthquake-tsunami simulations can be used to develop comprehensive and effective tsunami evacuation plans, consisting of both horizontal evacuation routes to high grounds and vertical evacuation to earthquake and tsunami resistant shelters (Wood et al. 2014; Muhammad et al. 2017). Seismic waves reach buildings in several seconds and usually evacuation from buildings before the shaking is not possible; for this reason, tsunami evacuation shelters should be able to withstand the ground shaking without critical damage (e.g. immediate collapse; FEMA 2012).

With respect to horizontal evacuation, a vital tool for residents is the evacuation time map. The total evacuation time is the sum of initial reaction time and evacuation time. The initial reaction time is composed of the institutional decision time, institutional notification time, and community's reaction time. The first two are strictly related to the warning protocols that responsible authorities implement in issuing the warning. Typical values of initial reaction time vary between a few and 30 minutes depending on technical capability and social preparedness (Post et al. 2009). Finally, evacuation time depends on the physical capacity of transport infrastructures (i.e. roads) and on travel speed that is affected by the traveling method (i.e. pedestrian or vehicular) and evacuees' conditions (age, physical conditions, etc.). Evacuation speed varies between about 1 m/s and 4 m/s (Muhammad et al. 2017). Comparing the total-evacuation-time maps with the arrival time of the first major waves obtained from stochastic simulations, it is possible to evaluate whether transportation infrastructure in place is suitable for evacuation of the exposed population or needs improvements. A potential improvement in evacuation time can be gained by constructing tsunami evacuation buildings in the potential inundation areas (Muhammad et al. 2017). Figure 10.5 shows a schematic representation of a horizontal evacuation map (Figure 10.5a), vertical evacuation map (Figure 10.5b), and combined horizontal-vertical evacuation map (Figure 10.5c). The integrated solution can achieve a significant reduction of the evacuation time, especially for people living close to the coastline.

10.5 A case study of tsunami evacuation planning in Padang, Indonesia

Padang is a highly populated coastal city (more than 850,000 people) in western Sumatra, located in front of the Mentawai segment of the Sunda subduction zone (Figure 10.6a), where major tsunami events occurred in the past (Natawidjaja et al. 2006; McCloskey et al. 2008). Therefore, future tsunami events generated by this subduction zone contribute significantly to

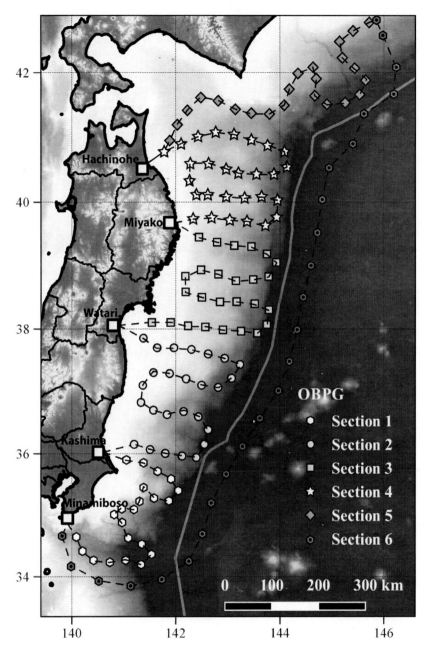

Figure 10.4 Layout of the new Japanese early warning system S-net, consisting of 151 Ocean Bottom Pressure Gauges connected by optic fiber cables.

Source: Data available at www.bosai.go.jp/inline/gallery/index.html).

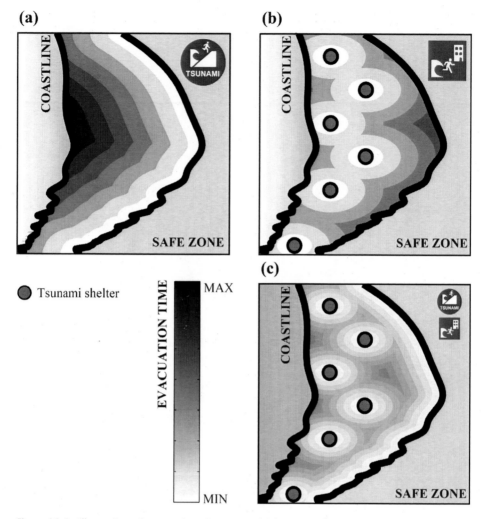

Figure 10.5 Illustration of evacuation time maps: (a) horizontal evacuation, (b) vertical evacuation, and (c) combined horizontal-vertical evacuation.

the risk of this area. Especially, near-source tsunami events, as mentioned above, leave only several tens of minutes to evacuate to the population living in coastal areas; this situation is exacerbated by the low-lying topographic features of Padang. Previous studies estimated a tsunami arrival time of about 20–30 minutes (McCloskey et al. 2008; Schlurmann et al. 2010). It is therefore clear that an integrated tsunami hazard map based on both horizontal and vertical evacuation is necessary.

In Padang, 23 tsunami evacuation shelters have been built and designated in the urban areas, close to the coast, where severe inundations can occur (Figure 10.6b). Muhammad et al. (2017) carried out a comprehensive multi-hazard assessment of the evacuation shelters in Padang by considering the sequence of seismic and tsunami loads to the structures. Such assessment was then incorporated in a city-wide evacuation plan in Padang. Specifically, the

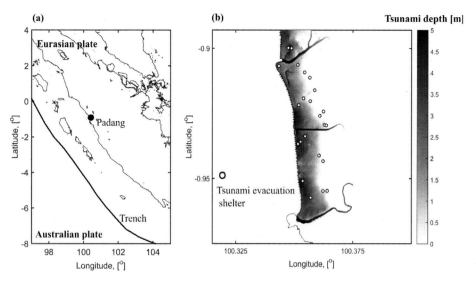

Figure 10.6 (a) Padang geographical location; (b) tsunami inundation map for the M_w9 scenario (circles are the locations of tsunami evacuation shelters in Padang).

horizontal evacuation plan was designed as presented in the previous section. For the vertical evacuation plan, only tsunami evacuation shelters that are considered as safe from the multi-hazard vulnerability assessment were taken into account. The main results from Muhammad et al. (2017) are presented in the following subsection to illustrate how the new multi-hazard earthquake-tsunami impact assessment methodology can be applied to a realistic situation.

Multi-hazard risk analysis of tsunami evacuation shelters

Three different earthquake magnitudes ($M_w8.5$, $M_w8.75$, and $M_w9.0$) are considered. By generating 100 stochastic source scenarios for each magnitude, ground-motion and tsunami simulations are conducted for Padang, as explained in the multi-hazard assessment section of this chapter. The 100 stochastic scenarios capture the uncertainties of earthquake ruptures in the Mentawai-Sunda subduction zone. Subsequently, for each simulation, specific fragility models are adopted and integrated with the simulated hazards to obtain an estimate of the expected damage state.

For the seismic vulnerability assessment, the HAZUS fragility curves (Figure 10.7a) proposed by the Federal Emergency Management (FEMA) are adopted (FEMA 2006). The majority of the 23 vertical evacuation structures in Padang can be classified as mid-rise reinforced concrete moment resistant frames (RC-MRF) designed with high-code seismic standards (category CM1), in terms of HAZUS building classification scheme. Subsequently, for given seismic demand levels (from ground-motion simulations using the 300 stochastic sources), seismic responses of the vertical evacuation structures are first evaluated through the capacity spectrum method (ATC 1996) and then the corresponding fragility curves are used to evaluate the shaking damage probabilities. In the assessment, vertical evacuation shelters that suffer extensive seismic damage with more than 50 percent probability are considered to be unsafe; these unsafe structures are excluded from the further assessment for developing tsunami evacuation maps.

191

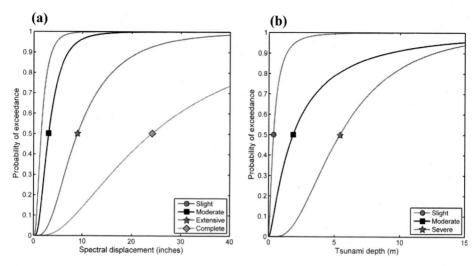

Figure 10.7   (a) Seismic fragility curves and (b) tsunami fragility curves.

For tsunami vulnerability assessment, fragility curves proposed by Suppasri et al. (2011) are adopted to evaluate the damage probability for given levels of inundation depth (from tsunami simulations using the 300 stochastic sources). When the evacuation shelters experience the probability of extensive damage exceeding 50 percent, these structures are considered to be unsafe. The use of the fragility curves by Suppasri et al. (Figure 10.7b) is particularly suitable for the considered case study since they were calibrated on the damage data from the 2004 Indian Ocean tsunami.

Results of the seismic vulnerability assessment of the 23 shelters indicate that for the majority of the 300 cases, the structures are operational in the aftermath of the earthquakes from the Mentawai-Sunda subduction zone. On the contrary, two of the 23 shelters are identified as unsafe for the tsunami actions (M_w9.0 scenario); therefore a structural retrofitting/ improvement is necessary to ensure that they are operational for the evacuation planning.

Figure 10.8 shows the horizontal and vertical evacuation maps obtained for Padang corresponding to a M_w9.0 scenario. Evacuation maps are obtained by adopting an evacuation speed of 0.91 m/s. A long horizontal evacuation time (Figure 10.8a) highlights the necessity of integrating vertical evacuation structures into the overall evacuation strategy. After excluding two shelters recognized as unsafe from the multi-risk analysis, vertical evacuation time as well as combined horizontal-vertical evacuation time (Figure 10.8b–c) are calculated. Resulting evacuation time maps are presented in Figure 10.8b and Figure 10.8c, respectively. The significant reduction of evacuation time due to the integration of vertical shelters emphasizes their importance in saving residents in critical areas.

10.6 Conclusions

Catastrophic events, such as sequences of extreme ground shaking and tsunami, can affect large portions of the whole nation simultaneously; resilient and sustainable infrastructures can help cope with such low-probability high-consequence events. In this chapter, an overview of the earthquake-tsunami multi-hazard and multi-risk assessment framework was provided, and

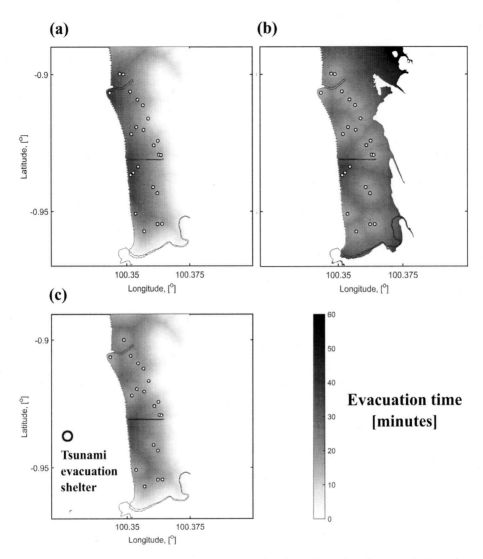

Figure 10.8 Evacuation time maps for Padang under the M_w9 earthquake scenario from the Mentawai fault segment: (a) horizontal evacuation, (b) vertical evacuation, and (c) combined horizontal-vertical evacuation.

subsequently, preparedness measures, such as early warning and evacuation planning, were discussed by highlighting major challenges related to these specific topics.

The performance-based engineering methodology offers the key computational framework for quantifying resilience against major disasters. It constitutes the core for the future resilience-based engineering for urban infrastructures. The modular framework of performance-based engineering facilitates the propagation of uncertainties and the risk quantification associated with different alternatives, and therefore it promotes risk-informed decision-making in managing catastrophic earthquake-tsunami risks. Moreover, performance-based engineering can incorporate maintenance and inspection costs, and environmental impacts from "cradle to grave," to further improve both resilience and sustainability of society and built environments.

Acknowledgements

The authors gratefully acknowledge financial support from the Leverhulme Trust (RPG-2017-006) for the GENESIS (Global Earthquake Resilience for Natural-Engineering-Social Interacting Systems) project.

References

Abrahamson N., Gregor N., and Addo, K. (2016). "BC Hydro ground motion prediction equations for subduction earthquakes," *Earthquake Spectra*, 32(1), 23–44.

Annaka T., Satake K., Sakakiyama T., Yanagisawa K., and Shuto N. (2007). "Logic-tree approach for probabilistic tsunami hazard analysis and its applications to the Japanese coasts," *Pure and Applied Geophysics*, 164(2), 577–92.

ATC (1996). Seismic evaluation and retrofit of concrete buildings, Vol. 1, ATC-40, Applied Technology Council, Redwood City.

Ayyub B.M. (2014). "Systems resilience for multi-hazard environments: Definition, metrics, and valuation for decision making" *Risk Analysis*, 34(2), 340–55.

Bozza A., Asprone D., and Manfredi G. (2015). "Developing an integrated framework to quantify resilience of urban systems against disasters," *Natural Hazards*, 78(3), 1729–48.

Bruneau M. and Reinhorn A. (2007). "Exploring the concept of seismic resilience for acute care facilities," *Earthquake Spectra*, 23(1), 41–62.

Caruso M.C., Menna C., Asprone D., Prota A., and Manfredi G. (2017). "Methodology for life-cycle sustainability assessment of building structures," *ACI Structural Journal*, 114(2), 323.

Cornell C.A. and Krawinkler H. (2000). "Progress and challenges in seismic performance assessment," *PEER Center News*, 3, 4.

Daniell J.E., Schaefer A.M., and Wenzel F. (2017). "Influence of secondary hazards in earthquake loss," *Frontiers in Built Environment*, 3(30) doi: 10.3389/fbuil.2017.00030.

De Risi R. and Goda K. (2016). "Probabilistic earthquake-tsunami multi-hazard analysis: Application to the Tohoku Region, Japan," *Frontiers in Built Environment*, 2(25) doi: 10.3389/fbuil.2016.00025.

De Risi R. and Goda K. (2017). "Simulation-based probabilistic tsunami hazard analysis: Empirical and robust hazard predictions," *Pure and Applied Geophysics*, 174(8), 3083–3106.

Duenas-Osorio L. and Vemuru S.M. (2009). "Cascading failures in complex infrastructure systems," *Structural Safety*, 31(2), 157–67.

FEMA (2006). *Multi-hazard Loss Estimation Methodology, HAZUS-MH MR2 Technical Manual*. Washington DC: Federal Emergency Management Agency.

FEMA (2012). *Guidelines for Design of Structures for Vertical Evacuation from Tsunamis (FEMA P-646, Second ed.)*. Washington DC: Federal Emergency Management Agency.

Franchin P. and Cavalieri F. (2013). "Seismic vulnerability of a complex interconnected infrastructure." In *Seismic Risk Analysis and Management of Civil Infrastructure Systems*, S. Tesfamariam and K. Goda (eds.). Cambridge: Woodhead Publishing Limited.

Frangopol D.M. and Liu M. (2007). "Maintenance and management of civil infrastructure based on condition, safety, optimization, and life-cycle cost," Structure and Infrastructure Engineering, 3(1), 29–41.

Gardoni P. (2017). "Promoting societal well-being by designing sustainable and resilient infrastructure," *Proceedings of the 12th Int. Conf. on Structural Safety and Reliability*, C. Bucher, B.R. Ellingwood, D.M. Frangopol (eds.), Vienna, Austria, 6–10 August 2017.

Geist E.L. and Parsons T. (2006). "Probabilistic analysis of tsunami hazards," *Natural Hazards*, 37(3), 277–314.

Goda K. and De Risi R. (2018). "Multi-hazard loss estimation for shaking and tsunami using stochastic rupture sources," *International Journal of Disaster Risk Reduction*, 28, 539–54.

Goda K. and Hong H.P. (2008). "Spatial correlation of peak ground motions and response spectra," *Bulletin of the Seismological Society of America*, 98(1), 354–65.

Goda K., Yasuda T., Mori N., and Maruyama T. (2016). "New scaling relationships of earthquake source parameters for stochastic tsunami simulation," *Coastal Engineering Journal*, 58(03): 1650010.

Goto C., Ogawa Y., Shuto N., and Imamura F. (1997). "Numerical method of tsunami simulation with the leap-frog scheme," (IUGG/IOC Time project), IOC Manual, UNESCO, No. 35, Paris, France.

Hirshorn B., Weinstein S., and Tsuboi S. (2013). "On the application of Mwp in the near field and the March 11, 2011 Tohoku earthquake," *Pure and Applied Geophysics*, 170(6–8), 975–91.

Hoshiba M. and Ozaki T. (2014). "Earthquake early warning and tsunami warning of the Japan Meteorological Agency, and their performance in the 2011 off the Pacific Coast of Tohoku Earthquake (Mw 9.0)," In *Early Warning for Geological Disasters* (pp. 1–28). Berlin and Heidelberg: Springer.

Inazu D., Pulido N., Fukuyama E., Saito T., Senda J., and Kumagai H. (2016). "Near-field tsunami forecast system based on near real-time seismic moment tensor estimation in the regions of Indonesia, the Philippines, and Chile" *Earth, Planets and Space*, 68(1), 73.

Kunreuther H., Kleindorfer P., and Patricia, G. (2005). "The impact of risk transfer instruments: an analysis of model cities." In *Catastrophe Modeling: A New Approach to Managing Risk* (pp. 189–208). New York: Springer.

Liu Z., Nadim F., Garcia-Aristizabal A., Mignan A., Fleming K., and Luna B.Q. (2015). "A three-level framework for multi-risk assessment," *Georisk: Assessment and Management of Risk for Engineered Systems and Geohazards*, 9(2), 59–74.

Maeda T., Obara K., Shinohara M., Kanazawa T., and Uehira K. (2015). "Successive estimation of a tsunami wavefield without earthquake source data: a data assimilation approach toward real-time tsunami forecasting," *Geophysical Research Letters*, 42(19), 7923–32.

Mai P.M. and Beroza G.C. (2002). "A spatial random field model to characterize complexity in earthquake slip." *Journal of Geophysical Research: Solid Earth*, 107(B11), doi: 10.1029/2001JB000588.

Marzocchi W., Garcia-Aristizabal A., Gasparini P., Mastellone M.L., and Di Ruocco, A. (2012). "Basic principles of multi-risk assessment: a case study in Italy," *Natural Hazards*, 62(2), 551–73.

McCullough M.C., Kareem A., Donahue A.S., and Westerink J.J. (2013). "Structural damage under multiple hazards in coastal environments," *Journal of Disaster Research*, 8(6), 1042–51.

McCloskey J., Antonioli A., Piatanesi A., Sieh K., Steacy S., Nalbant S., Coccob M., Giunchib C., Huanga J.D., and Dunlop P. (2008). "Tsunami threat in the Indian Ocean from a future megathrust earthquake west of Sumatra," *Earth Planetary Science Letters*, 265, 61–81.

Melgar D., Allen R.M., Riquelme S., Geng J., Bravo F., Baez J.C., Parra H., Barrientos S., Fang P., Bock Y., Bevis M., Caccamise II D.J., Vigny C., Moreno M., and Smalley Jr R. (2016). "Local tsunami warnings: Perspectives from recent large events," *Geophysical Research Letters*, 43(3), 1109–17.

Mignan A., Wiemer S., and Giardini D. (2014). "The quantification of low-probability–high-consequences events: part I. a generic multi-risk approach" *Natural Hazards*, 73(3), 1999–2022.

Ming X., Xu W., Li Y., Du J., Liu B., and Shi P. (2015). "Quantitative multi-hazard risk assessment with vulnerability surface and hazard joint return period," *Stochastic Environmental Research and Risk Assessment*, 29(1), 35–44.

Monastersky, R. (2012). "The next wave," *Nature*, 483(7388), 144.

Muhammad A., Goda K., Alexander N.A., Kongko W., and Muhari, A. (2017). "Tsunami evacuation plans for future megathrust earthquakes in Padang, Indonesia, considering stochastic earthquake scenarios," *Natural Hazards and Earth System Sciences*, 17, 2245–70.

Natawidjaja D.H., Sieh K., Chlieh M., Galetzka J., Suwargadi B.W., Cheng H., Edwards R.L., Avouac J.P., and Ward S.N. (2006). "Source parameters of the great Sumatran megathrust earthquakes of 1797 and 1833 inferred from coral microatolls," *Journal of Geophysical Research Solid Earth*, 111, B06403, doi: 10.1029/2005JB004025.

Okada Y. (1985). "Surface deformation due to shear and tensile faults in a half-space," *Bulletin of the Seismological Society of America*, 75(4), 1135–54.

Ouyang, M. and Dueñas-Osorio, L. (2012). "Time-dependent resilience assessment and improvement of urban infrastructure systems," *Chaos: An Interdisciplinary Journal of Nonlinear Science*, 22(3), 033122.

Park, S., van de Lindt, J.W., Cox, D., Gupta, R., and Aguiniga, F. (2012). "Successive earthquake-tsunami analysis to develop collapse fragilities," *Journal of Earthquake Engineering*, 16(6), 851–63.

Post J., Wegscheider S., Mück M., Zosseder K., Kiefl R., Steinmetz T., and Strunz G. (2009). "Assessment of human immediate response capability related to tsunami threats in Indonesia at a sub-national scale," *Natural Hazards and Earth System Sciences*, 9, 1075–86.

Rabinovich A.B. and Eblé, M.C. (2015). "Deep-ocean measurements of tsunami waves," *Pure and Applied Geophysics*, 172(12), 3281–3312.

Schlurmann T., Kongko W., Goseberg N., Natawidjaja D.H., and Sieh K. (2010). "Near-field tsunami hazard map Padang, West Sumatra: utilizing high resolution geospatial data and reasonable source scenarios," *Coastal Engineering Proceedings*, 32, 1–17.

Selva J. (2013). "Long-term multi-risk assessment: statistical treatment of interaction among risks," *Natural Hazards*, 67(2), 701–22.

Suppasri A., Koshimura S., and Imamura, F. (2011). "Developing tsunami fragility curves based on the satellite remote sensing and the numerical modeling of the 2004 Indian Ocean tsunami in Thailand," *Natural Hazards and Earth System Sciences*, 11(1), 173–89.

Tanioka Y. and Satake K. (1996). "Tsunami generation by horizontal displacement of ocean bottom," *Geophysical Research Letters*, 23(8), 861–4.

Tsushima H., Hino R., Ohta Y., Iinuma T., and Miura S. (2014). "tFISH/RAPiD: Rapid improvement of near-field tsunami forecasting based on offshore tsunami data by incorporating onshore GNSS data," *Geophysical Research Letters*, 41(10), 3390–7.

Wood N.J., Jones J., Schelling J., and Schmidtlein M.C. (2014). "Tsunami vertical-evacuation planning in the U.S. Pacific Northwest as a geospatial, multi-criteria decision problem," *International Journal of Disaster Risk Reduction*, 9, 68–83.

Part III
Resilience of different systems

Transportation infrastructure

11

Resilience assessment of transportation networks

Maria Nogal,[1] *and Alan O'Connor*[2]

[1] DEPT. OF CIVIL, STRUCTURAL & ENVIR. ENGINEERING. TRINITY COLLEGE DUBLIN, IRELAND; NOGALM@TCD.IE

[2] DEPT. OF CIVIL, STRUCTURAL & ENVIR. ENGINEERING. TRINITY COLLEGE DUBLIN, IRELAND; OCONNOAJ@TCD.IE

11.1 Introduction

Resilience can be defined as the ability to survive and thrive in the face of a complex, uncertain and ever-changing future. It is a way of thinking about both short-term cycles and long-term trends: minimizing disruptions in the face of shocks and stresses, recovering rapidly when they do occur, and adapting steadily to become better able to thrive as conditions continue to change (RESILENS 2016).

As the previous definition underlies, the term of resilience includes both *regular-basis resilience*, where the intensity of the impact is not severe enough to cause the disruption of the basic functions of the system, but its enhancement results in an improvement of the level of preparedness of the system; and *disaster resilience*, associated with high impact events affecting the critical functions. Most of the literature on resilience of physical systems focuses on the latter, given the potential benefit of improving the disaster resilience of the systems.

The resilience of transportation systems is a topic of growing interest, with increasing number of publications and research works in the previous years. The first papers addressing this topic evidenced a lack of consensus in relation to the operational definition of resilience; moreover, lack of robustness, vulnerability, and resilience were often addressed as equivalent terms. An interesting overview of the existing level of confusion regarding these concepts is given by Reggiani et al. (2015). Similar behaviour has been observed in other fields, such as in Structures, Energy, and even Telecommunications.

Much effort has been also put into the role of the resilience in relation to Risk Science, which is better established and presents a certain overlapping with the first. After great efforts made to define, interpret, and describe resilience in the last years, it seems that we can talk about Resilience Science, where the differences with other sciences become apparent, responding to some necessities that risk analysis does not cover.

In the context of transportation systems, which are especially vulnerable to extreme weather but also to other natural and man-made hazards, and whose disruption is associated with high economic losses and important social and societal consequences, an adequate resilience management may bring enormous benefits. Indeed, extreme weather events resulting in damage to infrastructure assets and delays to users' operations constitute the most frequently reported incidents on transport systems. The total estimated cost in Europe is 2.5 billion of euros per year, of which impacts on road transport represent 80 percent (Doll et al. 2012). Despite being less frequent, man-made event disruptions to transport systems can also have large economic and social consequences. 60 percent of companies surveyed by BCI reported a supply chain disruption as a result of "unplanned IT and telecommunication outages" by comparison with 41 percent for "adverse weather" (BCI 2016). PhishMe (2016) identifies the transportation sector among the top four most susceptible industry groups to cyber-attacks, which has a very strong impact in undermining end-user confidence. Improving the resilience of the transport system will decrease the risk of disruption due to these effects, enhancing operation during such events, and more quickly and safely restoring the system to full operational capacity following an event. Furthermore, it will increase performance during normal operation.

The remainder of this chapter further discusses the main characteristics that make Resilience Science necessary, positioning it as a powerful tool to tackle the emerging problems of the built environment, such as climate change, over-population and cyber-attacks (see Section 11.2). In Section 11.3, an updated overview of the existing approaches to evaluate the resilience of a transport network is presented. Section 11.4 opens the discussion on the future of Resilience Science, discussing potential future research lines, and in Section 11.5 some conclusions are given.

11.2 Why resilience rather than risk?

Resilience analysis has some similarities with risk analysis, but also very important distinguishing features. In this section, the main characteristics defining resilience are discussed in the context of the risk analysis, which seems to be more established in the scientific community. The aspects presented are summarized in Table 11.1 and addressed in detail in the following subsections.

11.2.1 Components of the analysis

Risk analysis requires the inclusion of the two components of the risk, that is, (a) probability of occurrence of the incident *affecting* the system, and (b) magnitude of the consequences, which is linked to system criticality. In addition, some approaches split the first component into system

Table 11.1 Comparison between risk analysis and resilience analysis

	Risk	*Resilience*
Components	Vulnerability (susceptibility to incidents); Prob. of occurrence of the incident; Consequences of a hazardous event	Holistic perspective: system capability at different domains (physical or technical operational, management)
Type of threats	Classical threats (known incidents)	Classical and emerging threats (known and unknown incidents)
System failure	Fixed threshold (acceptable risk)	Threshold as a function of the impact
Temporal dimension	No temporal dimension	Consideration of pre-impact, during impact, post-impact

vulnerability, that is, susceptibility to a given incident, and the probability of occurrence of the incident.

Resilience assessment implies a more holistic perspective, paying attention to system capabilities at different domains. The domains considered varies according to the authors, but basically they encompass the following; (a) physical or technological domain, which in the case of transport systems includes hard infrastructure (network infrastructure and components) and vehicles for freights and passengers. Bruneau et al. (2003) refer to this domain as technical; (b) operational domain, which considers all aspects related to the operation of drivers and travellers, paying specific attention to the interaction, collaboration, and self-synchronization between individuals and entities. This domain is also referred as the social domain (e.g. RESILENS (2016)); and (c) the management or organizational domain, which involves information-related features associated with the system management. Linkov et al. (2013) split this domain into two, namely, the information domain, addressing the creation, manipulation and sharing information, and the cognitive domain, focusing on translating, sharing, and acting upon information to enable system management. Some authors, such as Tierney and Bruneau (2007), propose the inclusion of a last domain related to the economies and business; nevertheless, it can be argued that the economy is generally considered as a social science, being already included in the first domain referred to.

11.2.2 Type of threats

According to ISO31000, risk analysis is a process aimed at comprehending the nature of the risk and determining the level of risk. Therefore, its assessment implies the consideration of those hazardous incidents that can be assessed with a degree of uncertainty, e.g. the extreme weather events, allowing the assessment of the associated probability. It requires dealing with the information of previous events, that is, the known incidents. Those incidents that never happened before cannot be analyzed under a risk perspective; thus the risk-based approaches are clearly unsuitable to deal with the unknown unknowns.

A resilient view implies the consideration of not only those classical threats; but also those emerging threats that cannot be even imagined, such as some terrorist attacks, whose uncertainty in terms of location and intensity invalidates the risk approach. For instance, the September 11th attacks in New York in 2001 showed that the traditional security and risk management was not enough to guarantee the withstanding and recovering from deliberate attacks, accidents, or naturally occurring threats or incidents.

The resilience-based approach pays attention to the potential loss of functionality of the system and its consequences, rather than the probabilities of occurrence of events. This approach is highly recommendable when dealing with unexpected events or long-term trends such as climate change, whose associated uncertainty may lead to misdiagnosing the system behaviour.

In fact, Resilience Science arises as the response to systems that should be prepared to an uncertain future.

11.2.3 System failure

The main difference between risk and resilience lies in the very concept of system failure. A common way to address a risk analysis of a system is by systematically analysing the failure modes of the components, assemblies, and subsystems involved ("what can happen"), and then evaluating their probability of failure or failure rates ("how likely it is"), combined with the corresponding consequences ("what the consequences are"). Within this scheme, popular methods can be listed, such as the cause–consequence analysis; failure modes and effects analysis; failure modes, effects, and criticality analysis; fault tree analysis; and what-if analysis. The approaches can be qualitative, quantitative, and semi-quantitative, and within the qualitative group, boolean, i.e., it fails or not, and probabilistic, rating the results between 0 and 1.

Under the risk perspective, *failure* can be defined as the loss by a system or system element, of functional integrity to perform as intended. The failure will induce a *fault*, that is, an abnormal undesirable state of a system or a system element. Note that not all faults are caused by failures. For instance, a road can be closured by safety reasons. In that case, even when the system does not perform its function, under the risk view, the system did not fail. Finally, the risk evaluation implies the identification of a threshold of acceptable risk or safety coefficient, and the ultimate goal of risk management is to guarantee that the system is always below this threshold.

One should wonder about the rationality behind a fixed threshold for the system, independently of other aspects, such as the social perception of risk. For instance, let's assume a transport system in a city impacted by an important earthquake with a low probability of occurrence and high consequences, and on the other hand, the same system suffering from a strike with a high probability of occurrence and low consequences, resulting in the same risk level.

The final goal of the science of resilience is not avoiding the failure itself, but guaranteeing specific functions under any disrupting scenario. The system requirements will vary according to the situation, e.g., a traffic network has different critical functions during an earthquake or a strike. In the first case, the goal is to guarantee the safety and security of people and goods; in the second case, the aim is to assure a certain level of reliability. If the last goal is established as a fixed threshold under any possible situation, the required effort and cost to guarantee that the system is always below this threshold would be absolutely disproportionate.

Nevertheless, an upper bound or critical state to be avoided, can be considered. For example, Nogal et al. (2016b) consider a system breakdown point, which is defined as the limit state associated with the failure of the traffic network due to the extreme over-cost generated by a strong perturbation. That is, although the system could theoretically recover, it would imply an unacceptable effort by the system. Freckleton et al. (2012) assume that the breakdown is the phase taking place when the network experiences a failure due to loss of transportation facility or reduced access to portions of the servicing network.

11.2.4 Temporal dimension

In contrast to the risk perspective, resilience has a temporal component, because it considers not only the system at a given moment, i.e., when the hazard occurs, but how it responds to, and how it recovers from, the impact. In other words, as indicated, when evaluating the resilience of a transport system, its critical functions have to be considered, and their corresponding level of functioning at different stages, that is, in a pre-disaster stage, during the disaster, and in the post-disaster stage. In that regard, Young and Leveson (2014) note that a resilient system should ensure continuity in critical functions and services with minimal disruption during its lifetime. Nogal and O'Connor (2017) appreciate that the critical function of a transport system is to enable the movement of people and goods, and to guarantee the supply chain, in terms of safety and security at the core level, in terms of reliability and sustainability at an intermediate level, and in terms of efficiency at an outer level.

The consideration of the temporal dimension has profound implications. The pre-disaster stage is characterized by the analysis of the proactive attitude and system state. As the hazard affecting the system is completely unknown in this stage, a functional approach covering preparation, prevention, and protection, independent of the potential hazard, should be considered. The second phase, during the hazardous event, the analysis is focused on the reactive attitude and system states. In this case, the type of hazard is known, but not necessarily its intensity, duration, or consequences. Therefore, a functional approach covering the immediate response is suggested. Finally, the last phase, after the hazardous event, is characterized by the complete knowledge of the hazard, and the assessment of the resilience is based on the recovery process.

This division has previously presented by other authors, such as Henry and Ramirez-Marquez (2012), who consider the original state, the disrupted state, and the recovered state.

11.3 Assessment of transport resilience

The characteristics described above motivate the development of specific methods for the resilience assessment. Indeed, evaluation of all aspects related to system resilience is completely impossible, thus, identification of the most important defining attributes of the resilience of any system becomes very relevant. Therefore, the selection of indicators to measure the capabilities of the system over time is the most practical way to address the problem. The way in which this selection is addressed will depend on the final objective of the analysis. If we are interested in a holistic approach where all the domains (e.g. physical, operational, and management) are included, it is very likely that many of the indicators chosen will be qualitative. In the case that the aim is objective comparison of different systems, or even fair evaluation of different actions upon the system, quantitative indicators are required. This idea allows classification of methodologies for resilience assessment as qualitative, semi-qualitative, and quantitative. A detailed description of these methods is presented below.

11.3.1 Qualitative assessment

The qualitative methods use indicators that cannot be objectively estimated. The main challenge of these methods is the selection of the most relevant indicators, which should be chosen in such a way that they cover all the domains of the study, namely, the physical, operational, and organizational domains. In addition, the indicators should be also classified according to temporal stages.

The time-ordered approach allows complete characterization of system behaviour in the advent and in case of anticipated and unanticipated threats. The proposed approach pays attention to potential loss of functionality of the system and its consequences, regardless of the probabilities of occurrence of events and without quantifying their risks.

The main challenge here is identification of the indicators that resilience depends on. Given that a complete scrutiny of all related indicators is unapproachable, the identification of the most relevant ones describing the resilience is important. The larger the number of indicators included, the more difficult and time consuming the methodology will be. Therefore, an adequate selection implies considering a subset of them, which, when combined, explains a high percentage of the system resilience.

Table 11.2 summarizes some examples of indicators (second column) classified according to their temporal dimension. Each indicator can be evaluated based on a number of attributes, organized per domains (columns 3, 4, and 5). Some of these indicators and attributes have been proposed by Taylor (2004) (accessibility), Murray-Tuite (2006) (adaptability), Freckleton et al. (2012) (goods and material access), Reggiani et al. (2015) (connectivity) and Serulle et al. (2011) (intermodality).

203

Table 11.2 Classification of indicators and some of the attributes related to them

STAGE	INDICATOR	ATTRIBUTES INCLUDED		
		Physical level	Operational level	Management level
PREVIOUS HAZARD	Performance during normal operation	Physical description of the transport infrastructure, such as number of lanes, width of the lanes, etc.	Traffic composition (freight, individual and collective road passenger transport, motorcycles, bicycles, etc.)	Network management (administration, maintenance, and provision of network)
			Travel cost, delays, speed, congestion	Management of the information, control and communication systems
	Adaptability	Dual carriageways	Driver and Passenger Information Systems	Inter-company co-operation between transport operators
			Behavioral patterns of users, such as route choices and mode choice decisions	Adaptive logistics (freight transport)
			Use of information systems (age of users, foreign users)	
	Redundancy	Infrastructure redundancy (within mode and between modes)	Use of inter-modality	Management of inter-modal systems
	Resourcefulness	Emergency stations, existence and distribution	Workers and labouring hours	Economic policies
		Goods and material access		
		Fuel and energy access		
	Vulnerability	Accessibility and connectivity	Traffic composition	Communication among stakeholders
		Topography	Demography	
		Geography	Dependence of telecommunication systems, power systems, etc.	
		Infrastructure condition		
	Preparedness	Pre-positioning resources Reinforcing network components	Early warning systems Previous experiences	Management of the early warning systems Previous experiences
				Qualification of agents involved (from the top management to lower staff levels)
				Legislation
				Emergency plans
				Mitigation plans (reducing the frequency and severity of risk)
DURING HAZARD	Serviceability	Loss of accessibility and connectivity	Emergency warning systems	Management of the emergency warning systems
		Infrastructure condition	Information services; control, monitoring and communication systems	Management of the information, control and communicating risk (road administrations with and within countries-, contractors, communication with stakeholders)
			Stress of users and operators	
POST HAZARD	Recovery	Distribution and intensity of damage	Adaptation capacity of users	Resources available
		Rapidity of the recovery		Adaptation capacity of managers

Then, the indicators can be estimated by means of their associated attributes. Nevertheless, many of these attributes are not numerically measurable (e.g. communication among stakeholders). In such cases, subjective evaluation should be used. Note that the indicated attributes in the previous-hazard stage are independent of the type and intensity of impact, allowing assessment of system resilience at that stage before a given hazardous event occurs, that is, without considering the probabilities of occurrence and the consequences of the event.

Nogal et al. (2018b) proposes a Delphi panel to select 50 attributes from a larger list of attributes based on a state-of-the-art literature review to assess the resilience. They are classified according to the social, economic, infrastructural, and institutional dimensions. Planning of ad hoc mitigation activities and identification of infrastructural assets needing upgrading as means of mitigation/prevention are examples of the chosen attributes.

Because of the simplicity of these methods, non-high technical skills are required, and multiple disciplines and perspectives can be easily combined, resulting in a more holistic evaluation. In addition, a generalization of the approach allows its application to different type and scales of systems.

11.3.2 Semi-qualitative assessment

In order to provide the assessment with some objectivity, the selecting set of attributes to evaluate the indicators should be measurable. Some of them, such as travel time, are clearly quantifiable, nevertheless, other attributes, such as the infrastructure condition, can be scaled from very good to very bad condition, which can be mathematically formalized by means of fuzzy logic.

Once the indicators are evaluated, one can wonder to which extent those indicators explain the resilience of the system. In other words, the challenge here is to determine the most suitable weights to combine the selected indicators. It is also relevant to avoid selected indicators overlapping information, to prevent final assessment from consideration of the same aspects several times, overweighting their importance.

To establish the contribution of any single indicator to resilience, Nogal et al. (2018a) proposes to study the probabilistic dependence among the indicators, and between the indicators and the descriptor (e.g. resilience). It is noted that probabilistic dependence modelling is a very complex issue. It requires identifying the subspace of possible dependence structures, which can be defined through copula-type functions, that is, positive monotonic functions in the range [0,1], conforming to a compatible multidimensional cdf. With this aim, statistical samples of joint observations of realizations are needed; however, they are usually scarce or just do not exist, as happens in the case of resilience of transportation networks. Under this perspective, the practical solution implies the structured expert elicitation, where experts are asked about dependence structures.

Traditionally experts' advice is required regarding judgments that go beyond well-established knowledge. Expert elicitation refers to the process of synthesis of subjective judgments of experts on a subject where there is uncertainty due to insufficient data because of physical constraints or lack of resources. Structured expert elicitation implies that the process is based on structured protocols that try to identify and to reduce potential sources of bias and error among experts (Nogal et al. 2016a).

As a proof of concept, Nogal et al. (2018a) evaluate to which extent accessibility and reliability, both quantifiable, explain the vulnerability of the Irish road network (see Figure 11.1). Through the proposed method, the conditional probability of the vulnerability, V, can be determined for different values of accessibility, A, and lack of reliability, R. For instance,

Figure 11.2 shows, for different Origin-Destination (OD) pairs, the conditional probability distribution of vulnerability for low values of accessibility (lower than its 25th percentile) and a high lack of reliability (larger than the 75th). The figure depicts that the OD pair 32−92 is the most vulnerable, followed by 32−69.

The structured expert elicitation of dependence modelling allows the dependence structure, removing the previously-referred problem of overlapping and eventually providing the adequate combination of indicators. For that reason the proposed method seems to be a sound approach for semi-qualitative analysis of the resilience.

11.3.3 Quantitative assessment

In quantitative methods, also called performance-based methods, resilience is estimated by measuring the performance of a system in a particular disturbing scenario. These last methods, though they present the advantage of providing a framework to objectively compare different cases, are usually less holistic approaches.

Dynamic restricted equilibrium model
The assessment of the traffic network resilience requires a dynamic approach as explained in Subsection 11.2.4. With this aim, Nogal et al. (2016b) propose a Dynamic Restricted Equilibrium (DRE) model that provides the behaviour of the traffic network over time when suffering a perturbation, from the beginning of the perturbation to the total recovery of the system.

Considering a connected traffic network defined by a set of nodes and a set of links, as the one presented in Figure 11.1, for certain OD pairs of nodes, there are given positive demands that create a link flow pattern when distributed through the network. The traffic flow governs network performance in terms of travel time, thus knowing how users select their routes according to traffic conditions is key when studying traffic network performance.

A dynamic *equilibrium-restricted* state can be obtained when, for each OD pair, the actual route travel cost experienced by travellers entering during the same time interval *tends to* be equal and minimal. Nevertheless, the system could be unable to reach this state in such a time interval. The reason that the system does not reach an optimal (or minimum cost) state in a given time interval is that traffic network behaviour is restricted by a system impedance to alter its previous state. This impedance is due to the actual capacity of adaptation of users to the changes, lack of knowledge of the new situation and lack of knowledge of the behaviour of other users.

When a perturbation occurs, travel costs tend to rise. However, the costs might not experience a large increase if users change their route choices, resulting in an increment of the stress level of the system. As this mechanism of response cost-stress is limited, the larger the disruption, the lower the remaining response capacity. Therefore, system behaviour when suffering a perturbation can be assessed by means of the exhaustion level of the transportation system (the portion of used resources), and its evolution over time. Figure 11.3 depicts the explained mechanism.

The advantages of this approach are: (a) it assesses the resilience of a traffic network suffering from a variable impact that progresses over time (see dashed line in Figure 11.4); (b) it provides information about the stress level of the system (Figure 11.4.a) and the extra cost generated by the perturbation (Figure 11.4.b), which are used to evaluate system resilience. Perturbation resilience is obtained as the normalized area over the exhaustion curve, between the initial and final time of the disruptive event (see Figure 11.4.c); (c) it includes aspects such as redundancy,

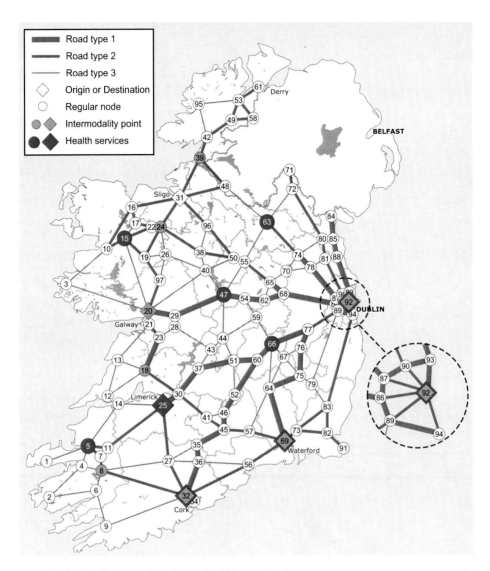

Figure 11.1   Traffic network under study; Irish case study.

adaptability, and ability to recover, which are some of the indicators considered by the qualitative approaches, as showed in Table 11.2; (d) it involves human response in the assessment, allowing the tradeoff between the level of users' information and stress level generated.

The last aspect is discussed in detail in Nogal et al. (2017). Nogal et al. conclude that an over informed society might generate larger stress levels and, on the contrary, a low degree of information might cause a slow, and inopportune, response. In addition to the impedance to changes, the traffic network resilience will depend to a large extent on perturbation degree (intensity and evolution), network congestion, and uneven characteristics of different connected areas. The response of a traffic system is highly nonlinear and determining the sensitivity to

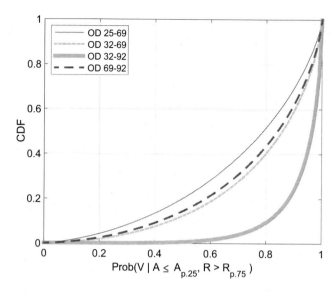

Figure 11.2 Conditional probability distribution of vulnerability given an accessibility ≤ its 25th quantile, and a reliability > its 75th quantile.

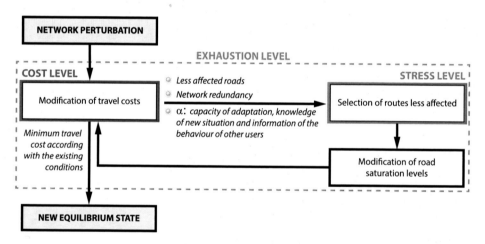

Figure 11.3 Diagrammatic representation of the traffic response of a traffic network suffering a perturbation.

these factors becomes tough. The influence of the users' impedance is larger when they play an active role, that is, when they can improve their situation by changing their routes. High congestions reduce the capacity of adaptation of the users, resulting in less resilient systems. In the case of networks with low saturation and low-to- moderate impact intensities, the response capacity of users takes relevance. On the other hand, users do not have many opportunities to improve their travel costs in networks with low redundancy, i.e. with few route choices, and/or when the whole network presents a similar degree of vulnerability to a given hazard. In such a case, system performance won't improve by providing users with more information and

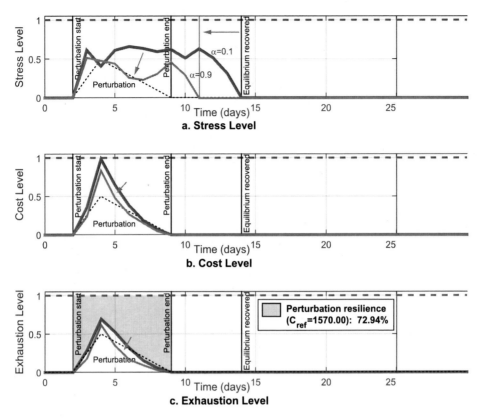

Figure 11.4 Resilience assessment for a traffic network suffering from the perturbation indicated by dashed line.

more response capacity. Thus, a redundant network with some stronger corridors is essential to improve system resilience.

For instance, Figure 11.4 exhibits how the resilience of a given traffic network can increase by improving the capacity of response of the users, α. An increment from $\alpha = 0.1$ (the darkest line) to $\alpha = 0.9$ (the lightest line) results in a reduction of the recovery time (from day 14 to day 11), and a decrease of stress level, cost level, and the resulting exhaustion level. Nevertheless, it is noted that on day 4, the stress level of the system is higher in the case of high response capacity, but still moderate.

Stochastic approach: Fragility curves
Analysing a specific scenario can provide very relevant information, mainly regarding the vulnerabilities of the system; however, the traffic system response will vary with every scenario created by different intensities, evolutions, durations, and extensions of hazards. In addition, important variables defining the system, such as traffic demand and adaptation capacity, may present a high uncertainty. In order to overtake these issues and assist in the decision-making process, Nogal et al. (2015) and Nogal et al. (2017) extend the deterministic DRE model through a stochastic approach, presenting the probabilistic response of the traffic network by means of fragility curves.

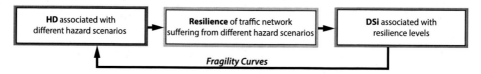

Figure 11.5   Definition of fragility curves. Work flow.

In the context of transportation systems, fragility curves are a representation of the conditional probability that a specific traffic network exceeds a given damage state, as a function of the hazard degree. Then, the fragility function is defined as

$$F_{DS_i}(HD) = P[DS > DS_i \mid HD],$$ (11.1)

where the parameters *DS* and *HD* indicate damage state and hazard degree, respectively.

To obtain this representation, the definition of three variables have to be addressed, that is, hazard degree, discrete Damage States, DS_i, and a variable that allows quantification of the response of the traffic network and is related to damage state, i.e. resilience. Thus, every resilience level will be related to a given discrete damage state (see Figure 11.5).

The fragility curves presented in Nogal et al. (2015) are applied in this case, to a traffic network situated in the east coast of Spain, affected by the extreme weather phenomenon called "cold drop", occurring almost annually in the western Mediterranean. It is characterized by rapid discharges, up to 500 litres per square metre, in extremely rapid rain episodes, causing serious flooding. It lasts from a few hours to a maximum of four days.

Figure 11.6 shows the daily precipitation in Valencia (Spain) from 1961 to 2010. It is assumed that flooding events occur when the capacity of drainage is exceeded by the rainfall amount. A comparison between the cumulative precipitation and cumulative drainage will show the intensity and duration of the hazard (see Figure 11.6). The capacity of drainage is calibrated by means of the historical flooding data.

Those important parameters involving uncertainty, i.e., demand, α and the uneven vulnerability of the system to the specific event, can be assumed as independent random variables. Samples of the variables are obtained by means of the Latin Hypercube, and combined to create different conditions of the traffic network. By means of Monte Carlo simulations, a number of conditions of the traffic network affected by the obtained weather events are analysed. In each case, its resilience is estimated using the DRE model.

In Nogal et al. (2015), four discrete damage states are defined, that is, negligible, light, light to moderate, and moderate, associated with the resilience levels 95%, 85%, 75%, and 65%, respectively. The values of the resilience obtained from the Monte Carlo simulations allow the calculation of the probability of exceeding the discrete damage states and the representation of fragility curves (see Figure 11.7). For a more detailed explanation, the reader is referred to Nogal et al. (2015) and Nogal et al. (2017).

Fragility curves in combination with resilience assessment are a powerful way of representing a realistic response of the traffic network under disturbing scenarios. The interpretation is straightforward; for instance, Figure 11.7 indicates that for a hazard of *HD* = 0.25, the probability that the damage state is worse than light to moderate is 40 percent, or a *HD* = 0.1 should not be neglected in 80 percent of cases.

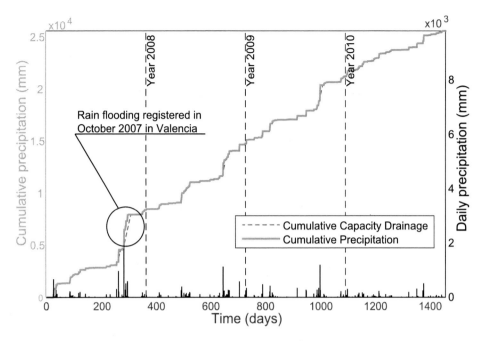

Figure 11.6 Identification of intensity and duration of the cold-drop events in Valencia (Spain) between 1961 and 2010.

11.4 Future of resilience science in the transportation field

The potential of resilience has barely been tapped in the transportation sector. Resilience should be understood and applied from bottom to top and from top to bottom. That implies not only to regulate, but also to educate in this perspective. Moreover, given the relevance of the transport systems in the developed world, an adequate resilience management implies the necessary involvement of many other sectors, such as industry and telecommunications.

A very challenging aspect of the resilience of transport systems is the understanding of human actors, such as users, operators, and managers, and how they interact with the built environment. They are a key component when dealing with resilience, as they represent the main capability of the system. Given the relevance of the human actors, they should be explicitly considered when assessing the resilience of transportation networks. Nevertheless, to quantify human behaviour is not an easy task, and only a few authors have tackled this issue. The methodologies presented in Section 11.3.3 include the capacity of adaptation of users to changes, their lack of knowledge of the new situation and their lack of knowledge of the behaviour of other users. Moreover, the assessment of traffic network resilience considers the stress of the users given by the amount of route changes.

On the other hand, it cannot be ignored how advances in telecommunication, and the introduction of more intelligent and interactive operations, have transformed the transport systems to the extent that some authors (Sadek et al. 2016; Nogal & O'Connor 2017) are now discussing the concept of Cyber-Transportation Systems, rather than the well-established concept of Intelligent Transportation Systems (ITS) coined at the end of the last century.

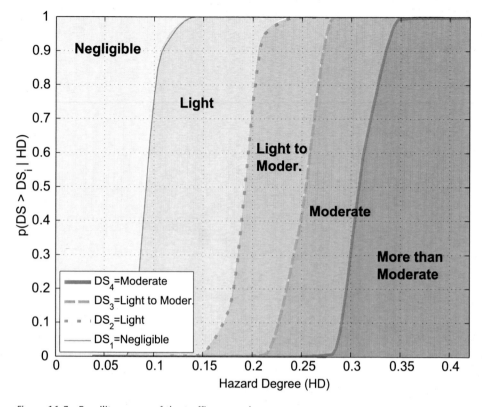

Figure 11.7 Fragility curves of the traffic network.

Cyber-Transportation Systems represent an opportunity for improving system performance in safety, sustainability, efficiency, and resilience. Nevertheless, they also imply new risks and threats. The complex interrelations of the cyber-transportation systems make the analysis of resilience especially difficult, given that it requires the consideration of combined interaction of human actors, physical system, and digital environment.

Studies on resilience considering physical and cyber systems as a unique system are uncommon, and most of them are applied to the case of smart energy grids. For instance, Arghandeh et al. (2016) and Eshghi et al. (2015) offer a good dissection of the components and domains of cyber-physical systems[1] to be considered, and Rao et al. (2013) capture the interactions among components through conditional probabilities. These papers motivate the analysis under the perspective of cyber-attacks, but none of them considers feedback loops where physical processes affect computations and vice versa.

First steps have been taken towards the consideration of interactions, dependencies and synergies in both directions, between transportation and cyber systems. Nogal and O'Connor (2017) analyse in detail these interactions (see Figure 11.8), and discuss how an adequate structure of dependence can generate redundancies, increasing the resilience of the whole system, instead of vulnerabilities. They conclude that dependencies among the human, physical, and digital world, and their evolution over time, play an important role into the resilience management. Understanding these relations results in an opportunity for improving the resilience

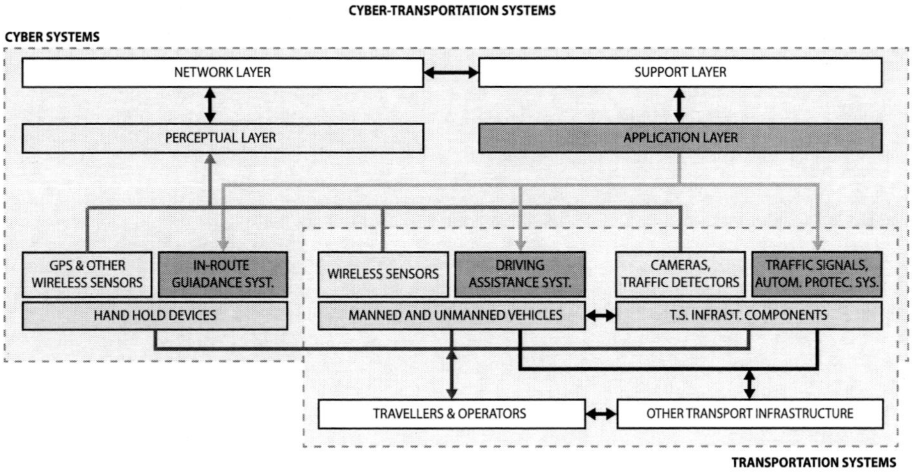

Figure 11.8 Diagrammatic representation of cyber-transportation systems at physical and operational levels.

Source: Nogal and O'Connor 2017.

of the cyber-transportation systems, which should be designed on the basis of non-critical dependencies.

11.5 Conclusions

Traditionally, the design and management of the engineering systems were addressed from a risk-based perspective. Risk-based approaches select and prioritize potential measures to prevent or mitigate impacts to the status quo based on an understanding of the threat. In contrast, resilience seeks to enhance the system's inherent capacity to respond throughout the process of inevitable change – both long and short duration, thus invoking a fundamentally temporal perspective (Roege et al. 2017). Additionally, the resilience approach implies considering not only the known hazards that might damage the system, but also those that have gone undetected or unpublicized.

Reaching a common understanding of the meaning of resilience and its associated properties will remove ambiguities and ensure coherent and agreed approaches across stakeholder disciplines. Furthermore, it will potentially impact upon the security and competitiveness of a critical sector. There is a need to raise transport efficiency, which implies making the best use of modern ICT and satellite-based technology, without dismissing safety and security. Enhancement strategies to increase infrastructure resilience should include both physical adaptations to the traffic network in conjunction with changes to management strategy (Nogal et al. 2016c).

Acknowledgement

The research leading to these results has received funding from the European Union's Horizon 2020 Research and Innovation Programme, under Grant Agreement no 653260.

Note

1 According to the Natural Science Foundation, Cyber-Physical Systems are smart networked systems with embedded sensors, processors and actuators that are designed to sense and interact with the physical world (including the human users), and support real-time, guaranteed performance in safety-critical applications.

References

Arghandeh, R., von Meier, A., Mehrmanesh, L., and Mili, L. (2016). "On the definition of cyber-physical resilience in power systems." *Renewable and Sustainable Energy Reviews*, 58, 1060–9.

BCI (2016). "Supply chain resilience report." *Report no.*, Business Continuity Institute, Caversham.

Bruneau, M., Chang, S.E., Eguchi, R.T., Lee, G.C., O'Rourke, T.D., Reinhorn, A.M., Shinozuka, M., Tierney, K., Wallace, W.A., and Von Winterfeldt, D. (2003). "A framework to quantitatively assess and enhance the seismic resilience of communities." *Earthquake Spectra*, 19(4), 733–52.

Doll, C., Ko¨hler, J., Klug, S., Papanikolaou, A., and Mitsakis, E. (2012). "WEATHER project summary and policy conclusions." Deliverable 7 of the research project WEATHER (Weather Extremes: Impacts on Transport Systems and Hazards for European Regions) funded under the 7th framework programme of the European Commission. Project co-ordinator: Fraunhofer ISI, Karlsruhe, 30.4.201. www.researchgate.net/profile/Evangelos_Mitsakis/publication/270571781_WEATHER_project_summary_and_policy_conclusions/links/56ec2f4908ae59dd41c4f689.pdf (last accessed September 8, 2018).

Eshghi, K., Johnson, B.K., and Rieger, C.G. (2015). "Power system protection and resilient metrics." *Resilience Week (RWS), 2015*, IEEE, 1–8.

Freckleton, D., Heaslip, K., Louisell, W., and Collura, J. (2012). "Evaluation of resiliency of transportation networks after disasters." *Transportation Research Record: Journal of the Transportation Research Board*, 2284, 109–116.

Henry, D. and Ramirez-Marquez, J.E. (2012). "Generic metrics and quantitative approaches for system re- silience as a function of time." *Reliability Engineering & System Safety*, 99, 114–22.

Linkov, I., Eisenberg, D., Bates, M., Chang, D., Convertino, M., Allen, J., Flynn, S., and Seager, T. (2013). "Measurable resilience for actionable policy." *Environmental Science & Technology*, 47, 10108–10.

Murray-Tuite, P. (2006). "A comparison of transportation network resilience under simulated system optimum and user equilibrium conditions." *Simulation Conference, 2006. WSC 06. Proceedings of the Winter*, 1398–1405.

Nogal, M. and O'Connor, A. (2017). Cyber-transportation resilience. Context and methodological framework. In I. Linkov and J.M. Palma-Oliveira (eds.), *Resilience and Risk: Methods and Application in Environment, Cyber and Social Domains*. New York: Springer, pp. 415–26.

Nogal, M., Martinez-Pastor, B., O'Connor, A., and Caulfield, B. (2015). "Dynamic restricted equilibrium model to determine statistically the resilience of a traffic network to extreme weather events." *Proceedings of the 12th International Conference on Applications of Statistics and Probability in Civil Engineering, ICASP12*, Vancouver (Canada).

Nogal, M., Morales-Napoles, O., and O'Connor, A. (2016a). "Understanding the vulnerability of traffic net- works by means of structured expert judgment elicitation." *Proceedings of the Irish Transport Research Network, ITRN2016*, Dublin (Ireland).

Nogal, M., O'Connor, A., Caulfield, B., and B., M.-P. (2016b). "Resilience of traffic networks: from pertur- bation to recovery via a Dynamic Restricted Equilibrium model." *Reliability Engineering & System Safety*, 156(1), 84–96.

Nogal, M., O'Connor, A., B., M.-P., and Caulfield, B. (2017). "Novel probabilistic resilience assessment framework of transportation networks against extreme weather events." *ASCE-ASME Journal of Risk and Uncertainty in Engineering Systems, Part A: Civil Engineering*, 04017003, 1–8.

Nogal, M., Morales-Napoles, O., and O'Connor, A. (2018a). "Structured expert judgment elicitation to assess the vulnerability of traffic networks." *Transportation Research Part A: Policy and Practice* (under revision).

Nogal, M., O'Connor, A., Caulfield, B., and Brazil, W. (2016c). "A multidisciplinary approach for risk analysis of infrastructure networks in response to extreme weather." *Transportation Research Procedia*, 14, 78–85.

Nogal, M., O'Connor, A., Groenemeijer, P., Prak, P., Luskova, M., Halat, M., Van Gelder, P., and Gavin, K. (2018b). "Assessment of the impacts of extreme weather events upon the pan-European infrastructure to the optimal mitigation of the consequences." *Transportation Research Procedia* (in press).

PhishMe (2016). "Phishing susceptibility and resilience report." *Report no.*, PhishMe.

Rao, N.S.V., Poole, S.W., Ma, C.Y.T., He, F., Zhuang, J., and Yau, D.K.Y. (2013). "Infrastructure resilience using cyber-physical game-theoretic approach." *Resilient Control Systems (ISRCS), 2013 6th International Symposium on*, IEEE, 31–6.

Reggiani, A., Nijkamp, P., and Lanzi, D. (2015). "Transport resilience and vulnerability: the role of connectiv- ity." *Transportation Research Part A: Policy and Practice*, 81, 4–15.

RESILENS (2016). Realising European Resilience for Critical Infrastructure, funded by the European Union, <http://resilens.eu/>.

Roege, P.E., Collier, Z.A., Chevardin, V., Chouinard, P., Florin, M.V., Lambert, J.H., Nielsen, K., Nogal, M., and Todorovic, B. (2017). Folding the digital world into resilience-building efforts. In I. Linkov and J.M. Palma-Oliveira (eds.), *Resilience and Risk. Methods and Application in Environment, Cyber and Social Domains*. New York: Springer, pp. 316–45.

Sadek, A.W., Park, B.B., and Cetin, M. (2016). "Special issue on cyber transportation systems and connected vehicle research." *Journal of Intelligent Transportation Systems*, 20(1), 1–3.

Serulle, N., Heaslip, K., Brady, B., Louisell, W., and Collura, J. (2011). "A case study of transportation network resiliency of Santo Domingo, Dominican Republic." *Transportation Research Record: Journal of the Transportation Research Board*, 2234, 22–30.

Taylor, M. (2004). "Critical infrastructure and transport network vulnerability: developing a method for diag- nosis and assessment." Ph.D. thesis, University of Canterbury New Zealand, University of Canterbury New Zealand.

Tierney, K. and Bruneau, M. (2007). "Conceptualizing and measuring resilience: A key to disaster loss reduc- tion." *TR News*, 250.

Young, W. and Leveson, N.G. (2014). "An integrated approach to safety and security based on systems theory." *Communications of the ACM*, 57(2), 31–5.

12

A framework for resilience assessment of highway transportation networks

Navya Vishnu,[1] *Sabarethinam Kameshwar,*[2] *and Jamie E. Padgett*[3]

[1] DEPARTMENT OF CIVIL AND ENVIRONMENTAL ENGINEERING, RICE UNIVERSITY, 6100 MAIN ST. MS-318, HOUSTON.TX-77005, USA

[2] SCHOOL OF CIVIL AND CONSTRUCTION ENGINEERING, OREGON STATE UNIVERSITY, 1491 SW CAMPUS WAY, CORVALLIS, OR 97331, USA

[3] DEPARTMENT OF CIVIL AND ENVIRONMENTAL ENGINEERING, RICE UNIVERSITY, 6100 MAIN ST. MS-318, HOUSTON.TX-77005, USA; JAMIE.PADGETT@RICE.EDU (CORRESPONDING AUTHOR)

12.1 Introduction

Extreme events such as earthquakes, hurricanes or floods not only have devastating impacts on life and property, but they also disrupt communities by forcing large scale displacement and evacuation of their population. Returning to normalcy for communities and societies can be, often times, slow and challenging as evidenced in past events such as Hurricane Katrina or the Northridge Earthquake. The ability of communities to prepare for, withstand, and recover from such disasters is termed as *resilience* (Bruneau et al. 2003; NIST 2015). A top-down approach to community resilience requires supporting infrastructure systems like transportation systems, utilities, and other lifelines to be resilient themselves. Particularly, rapid recovery and restoration of highway transportation systems are critical for emergency response, restoring other lifeline systems and accessing smaller communities. Additionally, functionality of the transportation system is essential for intermediate and long term recovery of a community, supporting transport of goods and access to businesses and schools.

Even though resilience is a broad and generic concept, it has been quantified as a measure of functionality with respect to time for bridges, bridge networks, and other transportation systems (Lounis & McAllister 2016; Bocchini & Frangopol 2012; Faturechi & Miller-Hooks 2014). The three main characteristics of resilient systems applied to road networks, are *preparedness* via mitigation of hazard risk, *withstanding* hazards via reduced consequences of failure and *recovery* via rapidity of restoration (Bruneau et al. 2003; Ghosn et al. 2016). Assessment of the three resilience characteristics for road networks require three main input models: (1) hazard performance assessment models of network components, (2) recovery and restoration models; and (3) network level performance assessment tools. Hazard vulnerability assessment of highway network components such as bridges or roads requires fragility models, which can provide the conditional probability of exceeding different damage states for given bridge characteristics and hazard intensity measures. With information on potential damage to bridges and roads obtained using the fragility models, recovery models can estimate restoration time. Based on these two inputs and network level performance assessment tools, the performance of the road network can be quantified, often by using a functionality metric like network connectivity or travel time.

For most performance metrics, the concept of resilience is tied to network functionality and recovery after a hazard event. Therefore, the ability to predict failures and possible recovery paths for a network subjected to a hazard scenario is important for identifying possible opportunities to improve the resilience of the network. For example, vulnerable components can be retrofitted before the hazard event and resource allocation can be optimized by prioritizing the recovery of critical components. Therefore, resilience assessment of road networks helps stakeholders and agencies in improving disaster preparedness and post-disaster recovery of communities, hence improving community resilience. In light of the importance of resilience assessment, this chapter provides a general resilience framework for road networks subjected to extreme events. Wherein, first, the concept of functionality and choice of different resilience metrics for transportation networks is explained followed by the details of vulnerability assessment, recovery models and functionality assessment for highway networks. The application of this framework to a case study highway network in Shelby County, Tennessee for seismic hazards concludes the discussion and highlights the opportunities and benefits of quantifying resilience metrics for infrastructure systems.

12.2 Framework for resilience assessment of highway transportation networks

Resilience, as defined in the previous section is quantified based on the time evolution of functionality of a transportation network. It is most commonly defined for engineering systems as the area under the functionality curve as and shown in Figure 12.1 and expressed in Equation 12.1:

$$R = \int_0^{t_r} F(0)\text{-}F(t)\,dt, \tag{12.1}$$

where R is the resilience, $F(0)$ is the pre-event or baseline functionality and $F(t)$ indicates the time dependent functionality of the system. Generally, the time period of interest for calculation of this area (t_r) is between the time of failure or hazard event – assumed to be time zero –and the time until target functionality is restored. If the value of t_r is very high or the reduction in functionality after the hazard event is very high, the area under the functionality curve increases, resulting in a higher value of the resilience metric. Hence, for transportation networks to be more resilient, the resilience metric computed according to Equation 12.1 must be low. However, low or high values of resilience are relative and are dependent on the choice of network functionality $F(t)$ as well. While area under the functionality curve is commonly adopted in literature, resilience has also been quantified as a ratio of post-event functionality to baseline functionality (Faturechi & Miller-Hooks 2014; Ouyang & Wang 2015).

The framework for quantifying resilience, using Equation 12.1, is explained in the flowchart shown in Figure 12.2. For a suitable network functionality and resilience metric, the first step is to model highway network components and identify possible hazard scenarios for the network's region.

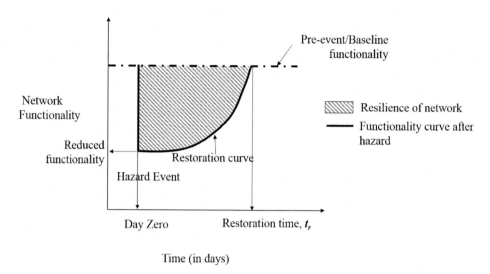

Figure 12.1 Resilience of a system.

Assuming the earthquake occurs at day 0, vulnerability assessment models inform damage states of highway components. For given component damages, the recovery models can esti-mate the time taken to restore component functionality. The network functionality is nega-tively impacted by component failures (bridges and roadways) and as different components are restored the network's performance improves with time. Therefore, network functionality assessment is carried out until the network functionality is restored to the pre-event condition or a desired functionality level. Thus, the time required to achieve the desired functionality after the earthquake (t_r) is obtained. The framework shown in Figure 12.2 can also be repeated for a suite of probabilistic scenarios to generate risk curves for the resilience of highway networks. These risk curves indicate the probability of exceeding target resilience and can be used for disaster planning and resource allocation for recovery.

12.2.1 Resilience and functionality metrics

The functionality of individual highway network components such as bridges and roads are closely tied to their operational condition and the ability to carry design traffic flow. Some models that map the relation between bridge damage states and traffic carrying cap-acities can be found in the literature (e.g. Mackie & Stojadinović 2006; Lee et al. 2010). However, it is more challenging to define functionality of a highway network because it is dependent on the objective for modeling the network. A brief review of common func-tionality metrics used by researchers to quantify the resilience of highway transportation networks is provided below:

(a) Connectivity
Connectivity in the network is often used to measure disruption in the network due to bridge or road failures after a hazard. The impact can be either measured as reliability or prob-ability of chosen origin and destination nodes being connected (Rokneddin et al. 2013; Kang et al. 2008) or as a percentage of network nodes that can be accessed after a hazard event

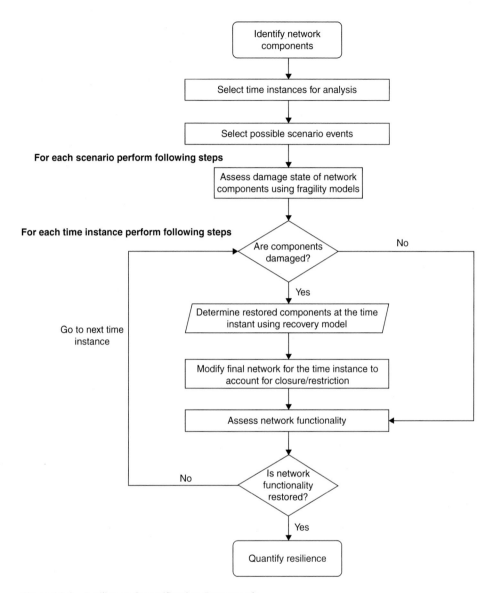

Figure 12.2 Resilience Quantification Framework.

(Bocchini & Frangopol 2011). Other metrics such as nodal diameter and efficiency have also been used to measure the connectivity in networks after extreme events (Guidotti et al. 2017).

(b) <u>Travel time</u>
Travel time across a highway network is one of the most commonly used metrics for functionality assessment (Bocchini & Frangopol 2011; Kiremidjian et al. 2007; Faturechi & Miller-Hooks 2014). Bridge or road failures may affect accessibility of highway segments, causing delays for users. Using travel time as the functionality metric in comparison to

connectivity has a few advantages. First, link restrictions such as partial closure or lane restrictions of bridges and roads can be captured in the network functionality level. Second, any congestion in links due to exceeding design traffic capacity is also captured as an increase in overall travel time.

(c) Economic or social impact

Network disruptions can also be represented as economic losses incurred due to the hazard event. Two types of economic losses can be considered in the network: repair costs of highway components and operational losses due to delays and detours in the network (Kiremidjian et al. 2007). For example, Zhou et al. (2010) considered social impacts in the form of driver delay in hours and "loss of opportunity" by accounting for missed work trips or other essential trips in addition to economic losses for defining network functionality.

(d) Other metrics

Besides the functionality metrics described above, many researchers have introduced newer performance metrics for transportation networks. Bocchini and Frangopol (2012) defined a performance metric that combines total travel time and total travel distance in the network. Miller-Hooks et al. (2012) consider the percentage of freight demand that is satisfied post-hazard as their functionality and resilience metric. A more detailed review of some common performance metrics used for spatial infrastructure networks and specifically transportation networks can be found in Ghosn et al. (2016).

12.2.2 Components of road networks

The two main components of any highway network are: Roads and Bridges. A realistic full-scale road network model might require fine resolution of roads, including the minor and local roads. However, this granularity has a disadvantage of increasing the size of the network, in turn, scaling up the computational cost of any network analysis. So, depending on the purpose of the network modeling and available computational resources, the road networks can vary from links just representing major highways to links for every road in the region. Bridges are another important component of a road network, including structures over waterways and highway segments.

A simple road network can be formed with nodes and links as shown in Figure 12.3. Nodes represent points of interest in a region, like essential facilities, residential buildings, or any place to be accessed before or after a hazard occurrence. Additionally, nodes may also be used to represent roadway intersections. Links represent the roadway segments that connect these points of interest, i.e. nodes. For modeling bridges as a part of highway networks, two main strategies, as shown for a fictional network in Figure 12.3, can be adopted:

(a) Model bridges as nodes

Modeling bridges as nodes in the network as shown in Figure 12.3(a) is a very common approach in the bridge engineering community (Liu & Frangopol 2005; Rokneddin et al. 2013). Such an assumption simplifies the network analysis and is more suitable for a connectivity based reliability problem.

(b) Model bridges as a part of a link

Modeling bridges as a part of a link, as shown in Figure 12.3(b), is a strategy that acknowledges that a highway segment can have multiple bridges between different points of interest and closure/failure of one bridge does not necessarily disrupt connectivity in the

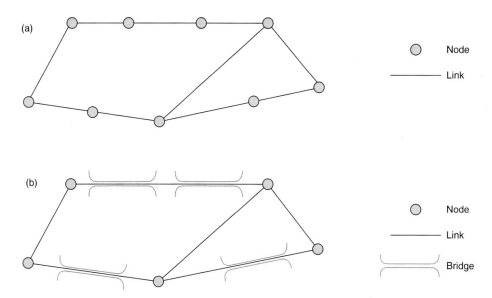

Figure 12.3 (a) Model bridges as nodes; (b) model bridges as part of link.

network. This type of assumption is better suited for a flow based model as trip start and end points are rarely highway bridges.

12.2.3 Vulnerability assessment of network components

The vulnerability in highway networks are captured through failures of its bridges and roads. Even though roads and bridges are both prone to damage due to a hazard, most research considers bridges to be the only vulnerable component of a network. Since roadway fragilities for different hazards are generally not available in the literature, this chapter focuses on failure of bridges in the network. However, as information on roadway failures becomes available, it can be readily incorporated into the framework following the approach used for bridges.

Response assessment of bridge components
Bridges are composed of several components such as abutments, bearings, deck, and columns. Under external loads from extreme events, the response of these bridge components is measured using engineering demand parameters (EDP) such as abutment displacement, bearing displacement, column curvatures, and column drift (Mackie & Stojadinović 2001; Gardoni et al. 2003; Nielson & DesRoches 2007b). Traditionally, for various hazards, component response models (also known as demand models) are developed by performing a large number of finite element (FE) simulations for a suite of hazard scenarios such as earthquake ground motions. Additionally, uncertainties in material and geometric properties may also be propagated during these simulations. Component demands obtained from FE simulations are often modeled with surrogate models ranging in complexity from simple univariate regression models in log-log space to complex multi-variate neural networks. Additional information on surrogate demand models for various hazards can be obtained from Kameshwar and Padgett (2014) and Kameshwar (2017).

Bridge component damage states and fragility assessment

The extent of damage to bridge components, i.e. their damage state, after an extreme event can be determined by comparing the demands on the components to their respective capacities. Typically, damage to bridge components is classified into one of five categories: no damage, slight, moderate, extensive, and complete damage (in order of severity from low to high). For each damage state, the capacity of the components should be defined in terms of one or more engineering demand parameters. For example, Berry and Eberhard (2004) and Panagiotakos and Fardis (2001) provide capacity estimates for columns in terms of drift capacity; Nielson (2005) and Ramanathan (2012) provide column capacity estimates using column curvature and Gardoni et al. (2002) use deformation to define flexural and shear capacity of columns. Seismic capacity limit states for other components can be obtained from Nielson (2005) and Padgett (2007). In contrast to earthquakes, hurricane damage to bridges is often classified into either complete or no damage state due to the most commonly observed deck unseating failure which renders bridges completely un-usable. Capacity limit states for deck unseating can be obtained using analytical methods (Ataei et al. 2010) or FE simulations (Ataei 2013; Kameshwar & Padgett 2014).

The conditional probability of a component exceeding a given damage state at various levels of hazard intensity measures can be depicted by a fragility curve. Often, component responses and capacity limits are assumed to follow a lognormal distribution – especially for earthquakes; therefore, the analytical fragility curves for bridges are usually expressed as a lognormal cumulative distribution function (CDF). While this enables one to use a continuous probability distribution that can be easily incorporated in risk assessment tools, the impact of aging of bridges and the effects of variations in bridge design and geometry on seismic performance are not captured by the traditional lognormal CDF. The impact of aging can be addressed by using a time-dependent median and dispersion for the lognormal CDF (Ghosh & Padgett 2010) or by using fragility increments (Gardoni & Rosowsky 2011). However, consideration of aging as well as variations of bridge design and geometry has paved way for "parameterized fragility curves" conditioned not only on intensity measures, but also on bridge parameters. Such fragility curves are developed for a portfolio of bridges and are better suited for a network analysis as explained in the subsequent section.

Parameterized response and fragility assessment for regional portfolio

Recent studies have modeled the response of bridge components using multi-dimensional polynomial response surfaces and machine learning techniques (Ghosh et al. 2013; Seo & Linzell 2013; Park & Towashiraporn 2014). These response and fragility models can be conditioned on hazard intensity measure as well as bridge parameters, such as column height and span length, or age dependent parameters, such as column rebar area and bearing pad stiffness. These recent developments enable hazard performance assessment of aging bridges spread across a region with variation in geometry and design details; additionally, the new models can be used for sensitivity analysis. Specific examples of parameterized fragilities using such algorithms for bridges is found in Ghosh et al. (2013); Kameshwar and Padgett (2014); Ataei and Padgett (2015); and Kameshwar (2017). A detailed review of highway bridge fragility models for different hazards can be found in Gidaris et al. (2017).

12.2.4 Restoration modeling

Restoration models are a key component to any resilience assessment framework. Restoration time not only depends on bridge or road damage states, but also on choice of repair or replacement action and availability of resources, such as funding, crews, material and equipment.

These uncertainties make restoration time estimation for a portfolio of bridges and roads challenging. However, some restoration models are available in the literature for bridges damaged during earthquakes, which use a combination of expert opinion surveys and engineering judgement. The HAZUS technical manual gives an expert opinion survey based discrete seismic restoration functions and smoothed normal restoration curves for bridges and roads for different damage states (FEMA 2015). Padgett and DesRoches (2007) conducted a web-based expert opinion survey to inform step-wise seismic restoration functions for different bridge damage states. Mackie et al. (2010) express repair times for seismic damage to reinforced concrete bridges in California in terms of working days of the repair crew. Zhou et al. (2010) use a uniform distribution with a minimum and maximum recovery time assigned for each damage state of a bridge. Bocchini et al. (2012) have proposed a generalized restoration function, which can be used for individual network components such as bridges or for an entire network. Their restoration model provides a general continuous function whose parameters can be modified to reflect duration, rapidity, and the shape of the recovery curve. Recovery models for other hazards are more limited and are detailed along with their scope and limitations in Gidaris et al. (2017). The restoration models discussed herein have been developed with various assumptions of repair actions or have been developed for bridges in a specific region. As such, using any of the above models has some drawbacks or limitations for resilience assessment. However, in absence of better suited models for a specific region and portfolio of bridges, these models can be judiciously applied.

12.2.5 Network performance: Functionality assessment

The functionality of road networks can be defined and quantified using several metrics discussed in Section 12.2.1. For each network performance metric, appropriate network level analysis is required. For this purpose, first, information on restoration of the network components, from the previous section, should be incorporated in the network modeling. For example, closure of a road should be reflected in the network by removing the corresponding link; similarly, links corresponding to roadways with closed bridges should also be removed from the network model. Additionally, effects of traffic restrictions, if available, should also be considered. Next, based on the chosen network functionality metric, appropriate network analysis tools should be used.

Network connectivity based functionality definitions require information on the availability of a path between nodes in a network. This information can be obtained by traversing the network using algorithms like depth first search or breadth first search (Newman 2010). These algorithms simply traverse the network node by node to determine connectivity. Inaccessibility of nodes during the traversal would imply disconnections in the network. These algorithms could also be used to determine connectivity to specific points, such as fire stations or hospitals.

Other resilience and functionality metrics discussed in Section 12.2.1 such as travel time, travel distance and economic losses due to network disruptions require analysis of traffic flow in a network. For this purpose, first, an estimate of travel demand, i.e. the number of trips between different origin and destination (O-D) pairs, within the road network must be obtained. Travel demand modeling is performed by regional metropolitan planning organizations (MPO) considering several factors such as demography, household income, employment, and business locations. Travel demand models are often publicly available, such as the one used by Memphis MPO (2016). Next, the traffic flow capacity of every roadway segment in the network is required to facilitate flow analysis. Traffic flow capacities for roads (f_{ijc}) between nodes i and j in a network can be obtained using the Highway Capacity Manual

N. Vishnu et al.

(2000). With information on travel demand and traffic flow capacity, traffic flow analysis can be performed. The literature has several traffic flow analysis methods; however, the user equilibrium traffic flow analysis methodology proposed by Evans (1976) has been used extensively for performance assessment of road networks (Stergiou & Kiremidjian 2010; Bocchini & Frangopol 2011). This user equilibrium model assumes that the cost of travel, usually travel time, on any route between an O-D pair cannot be improved for a single vehicle by choosing a different path. In other words, an equilibrium is reached with respect to travel time. The following briefly describes the iterative process for obtaining a user equilibrium solution for traffic flow in a road network.

The first step involves estimating travel cost, such as travel time or distance, for every roadway link, without considering any traffic; herein, travel time is used as a measure of travel cost. Travel time across a roadway segment without traffic (c_{ij0}) can be simply obtained as the ratio of roadway length to free flow speed. Next, using the travel time for each link, the shortest path in terms of travel time between all origin and destination nodes in the network is obtained. For all the links along a shortest path between an O-D pair, the number of trips between the O-D pair are added to the existing flow (f_{ij}) on the links. Next, the travel time across every link (c_{ij}) is updated for traffic and potential congestion using the following equation:

$$c_{ij} = c_{ij0}\left(1 + \alpha\left(\frac{f_{ij}}{f_{ijc}}\right)^{\beta}\right).$$ (12.2)

In Equation 12.2 shown above, α and β are constants which are usually assigned values 0.15 and 4 respectively (NCHRP 2012).

Using the updated travel time, the shortest paths and flow through the links are re-evaluated. Akin to line search algorithms in finite element analysis, a fraction of the updated flow estimate is added to the previous flow estimate, from the last iteration, to obtain the new flow estimates. The new flow values are provided to Equation 12.2 to determine new travel time and flow values, which are further used to obtain updated flow estimates. This process is repeated until the flow estimates converge.

12.3 Case study application to bridge system

The resilience assessment framework described above is demonstrated through a case study highway network located in Shelby County, Tennessee (Figure 12.4), a region of significant earthquake hazard due to its proximity to the New Madrid Seismic Zone. The detailed network can be found in the Mid-America Earthquake Center Seismic Loss Assessment System (MAEViz) database (Chang et al. 2010) and the IN-CORE modeling environment, maintained by the NIST Center for Risk-Based Community Resilience Planning. Four resilience metrics are quantified for this network based on four functionality metrics: connectivity, missed trips, travel time, and travel distance. The four different metrics highlight the importance of the choice of network functionality metric in affecting resilience quantification.

12.3.1 Network and hazard description

The network, shown in Figure 12.4, is formed of major highways and primary roads in Shelby County. The bridges are modeled as part of the links with highway intersections considered as nodes and any damage to bridges directly impacts the link's capacity to carry traffic. Four

224

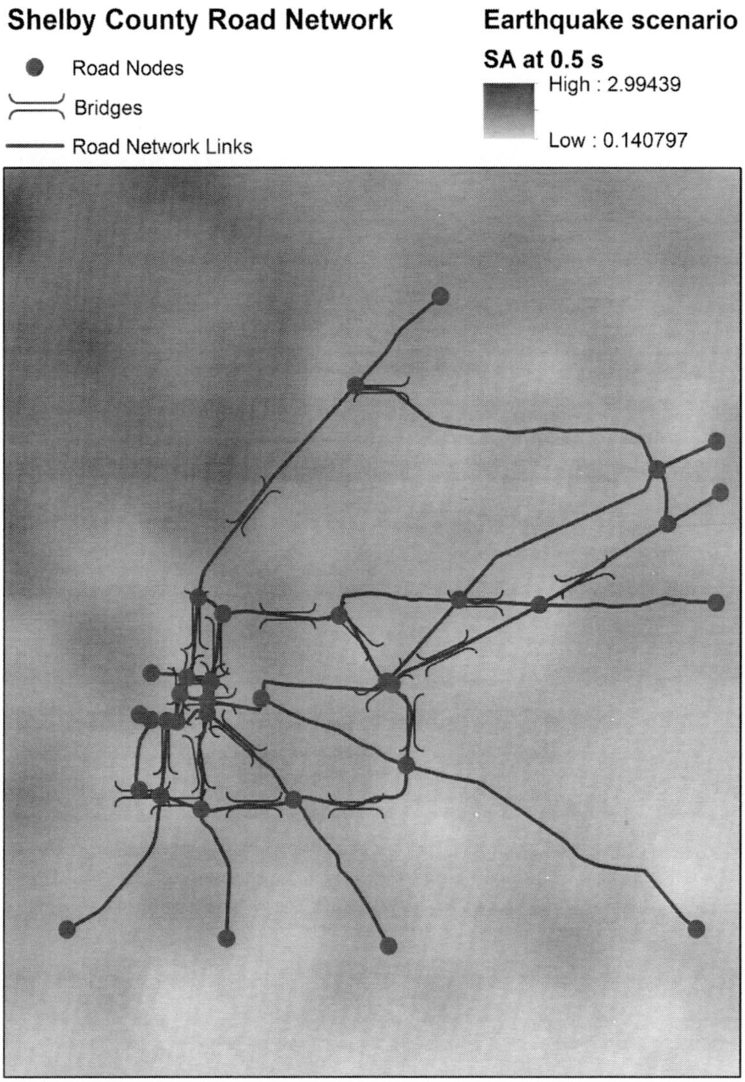

Shelby County Road Network

● Road Nodes

⌣ Bridges

── Road Network Links

Earthquake scenario

SA at 0.5 s

High : 2.99439

Low : 0.140797

Figure 12.4 Shelby County road network and a realization of the earthquake rupture scenario.

bridge classes are considered herein: Multi-Span Simply Supported (MSSS) Concrete, MSSS Steel, Multi-Span Continuous (MSC) Concrete and MSC Steel. For the earthquake scenario, a 7.5 moment magnitude scenario with the rupture site along the New Madrid Fault is chosen from the United States Geological Survey (USGS) catalog for the Memphis area. The particular rupture scenario was developed by the BSSC (2015) and corresponds to an intensity of IX on the Modified Mercalli Scale (MMI). The earthquake intensity used for analysis is Spectral Acceleration (SA) at 0.5 seconds. The propagation of the ground motions is performed using the USGS (Petersen et al. 2014) recommended ground motion prediction equations on the OpenQuake® engine. The aleatoric uncertainties in the ground motion as well as any uncertainties in the bridge demand models are propagated by using 1e5 realizations of the same rupture scenario. One of these realizations is shown in Figure 12.4.

12.3.2 Seismic fragility and restoration models

The response and fragility assessment procedure explained in Section 12.2 is used to develop parameterized seismic fragilities for bridge components such as columns, bearings and abutments. For each of the four bridge classes, a number of representative bridge samples with design and details following typical highway bridges in Central and Southeastern United States (CSUS) are modeled. The bridge response is assessed for a suite of synthetic ground motions developed for the CSUS region by Wen and Wu (2001) and Rix and Fernandez-Leon (2004) using the finite element software OpenSees®. Detailed analytical models of the bridges and bridge components can be found in Nielson (2005) and Kameshwar (2017). The bridge samples, representing a regional portfolio, account for uncertainties in material as well as geometric properties. Aging and deterioration with time is also considered to have impact on bridge behavior. The aging processes considered in this chapter include corrosion in super-structure and substructure and impact of thermal oxidation on rubber bearing pads. More details on modeling deterioration mechanisms for concrete and steel bridges can be found in Ghosh and Padgett (2010) as well as Ghosh (2013). The results of the FE simulations are used to fit polynomial response surface models to predict seismic demand for any bridge compo-nent belonging to the regional portfolio of bridges. Next, the component seismic demands are compared against their capacity limit states for various damage states and parameterized logistic regression models are developed to estimate the fragility of the bridge components.

With the information on bridge damage states, recovery models are next required. The bridge restoration functions tend to be discrete in nature with bridges opening only when they reach partial (e.g. 50%) or full (100%) functionality. The partial or 50 percent functionality can represent a bridge open with half of its original capacity; i.e. the traffic flow capacity of the bridges (number passenger cars that can pass the bridges in an hour) is reduced by 50 percent. Thus, given the practical nature of the step-wise recovery and relevance for the bridge classes of interest, the model proposed by Padgett and DesRoches (2007) is adopted herein, with infor-mation from HAZUS-MH (FEMA 2015) used to complete the stepwise restoration model. These models give three discrete functionality levels: 0 percent (closed), 50 percent (partially open) and 100 percent (open). The repair time estimation in days, counted after the earth-quake, for each damage state according to the hybrid restoration model adopted is detailed in Table 12.1. The restoration model is adopted in the network with the assumption that all bridges in similar damage states get restored on the same day. However, in reality, the order in which bridges get restored also depends on the availability of resources and any prioritization plan employed by stakeholders.

Table 12.1 Bridge functionality restoration model

Bridge Damage State	Functionality Restoration Time (Days)	
	50%	*100%*
Slight	1	3
Moderate	3	7
Extensive	75	180
Complete	240	400

12.3.3 Network flow model

The number of trips between each origin-destination pair in the network is obtained by using the travel demand model used by the Memphis MPO. This model estimates travel demand for an eight-county region around Memphis, across three states. Since the case study network only covers of a small portion of the entire eight-county region, the travel demands are condensed following the approach proposed used by Zhou et al. (2010) to obtain travel demands for the case study network. Network level travel demand and the network flow modeling approaches described in the previous section are used herein to assess the traffic flow in the network.

The traffic flow in the network before the earthquake is the baseline condition for comparing any changes observed in the post-event network functionality. Figure 12.5 shows the normal traffic flow in the network with the links numbered. The bulk of the traffic flow happens through the "Inner Beltway" of Memphis, which is formed by segments of I–40, I–69, and I–240, represented by links 27, 31, 9, 20, and 22 in the network.

Immediately after the earthquake, all the bridges with any damage are assumed to be closed. Bridges with slight damage regain 50 percent functionality on day 1 after the earthquake according to the restoration model in Table 12.1 and are assumed to be partially

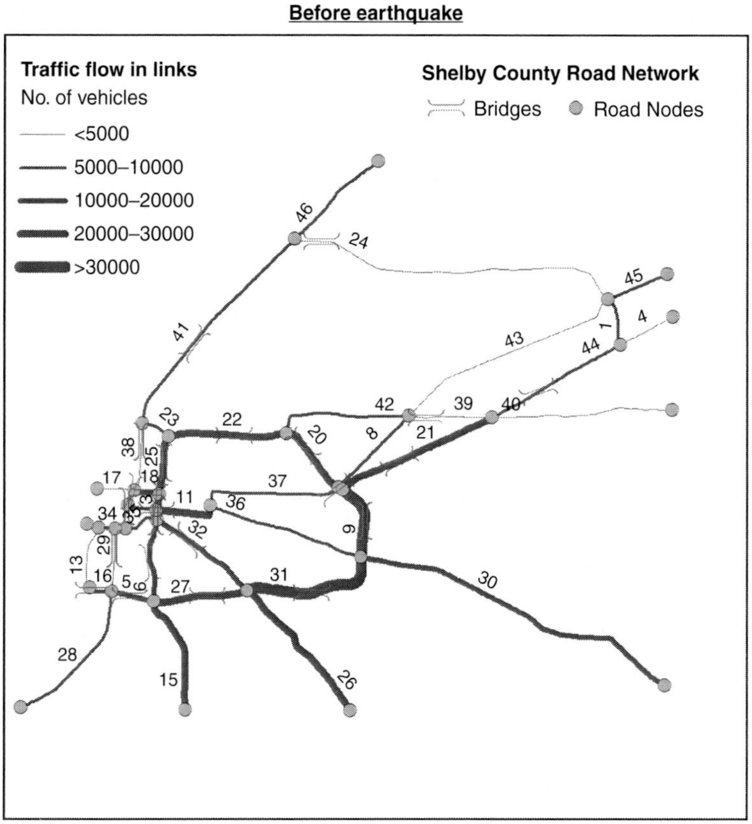

Figure 12.5 Network traffic flow before earthquake.

open. Bridges in all of the higher damage states remain closed on day 1. As the bridges in higher damage states get restored according to the restoration model, they are assumed to partially open at 50 percent functionality and fully open at 100 percent functionality. The rupture realization shown in Figure 12.4 is used as an example to demonstrate the impact of the earthquake scenario on the network traffic flow. Figure 12.6 shows the closure of bridges and network flow immediately after the earthquake. Due to the closure of most bridges on the highway segments along the "Inner Beltway," these links are inaccessible and have no flow of traffic. Hence, the travel demands from these nodes are not met, resulting in missed trips.

Figures 12.7 and 12.8 show how the network traffic flows evolve with the restoration of bridge functionality. By seven days, all bridges with slight and moderate damage have been restored to full functionality as seen in Figure 12.7. However, the bridges with extensive and complete damage are still closed. Some traffic flow along the "Inner Beltway" is restored and most of the travel demands are met, reducing the number of missed trips.

Day 1 after earthquake

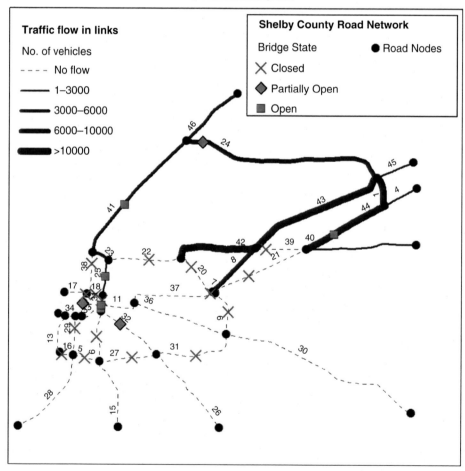

Figure 12.6 Change in network traffic flow after earthquake.

Day 7 after earthquake

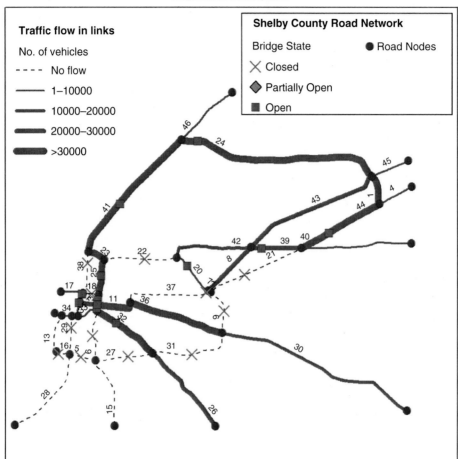

Figure 12.7   Network flow seven days after earthquake.

By day 240, all of the bridges are at least partially open and the network flow returns to nearly pre-earthquake condition as seen in Figure 12.8. With the network flow information for different time instances, resilience metrics can be quantified for this network for each of the 1e5 realizations of the scenario.

12.3.4 Resilience metrics

Before resilience can be quantified, the four network functionality metrics–connectivity, missed trips, travel time, and travel distance–have to be calculated. All the metrics can be assessed at each time interval as part of the network flow algorithm for each scenario realization. Figures 12.9 through 12.12 show the time evolution of the four network functionality metrics for each of the 1e5 realizations. The plots also show the mean values as well as the 25th and 75th percentile values across all scenarios realizations. Since the restoration model assumes that

Day 240 after earthquake

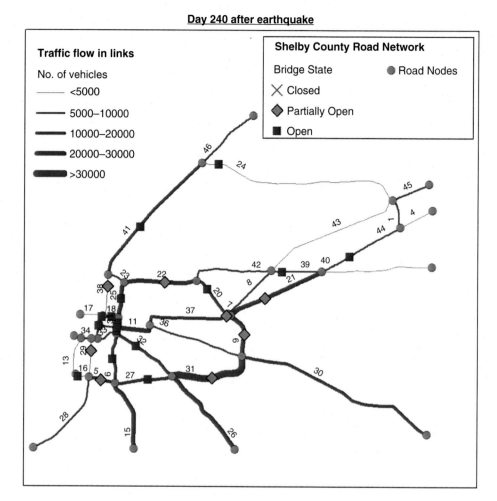

Figure 12.8 Network flow 240 days after earthquake.

all bridges are restored on the same day, changes in all the functionality metric figures can be observed around the same time instances like day 7 or day 75.

Connectivity analysis

The connectivity analysis is conducted by using the "Fully Connected Ratio (FCR)" as defined by Bocchini and Frangopol (2011). FCR is defined as a ratio of nodes disconnected after the event to total nodes in the network, as shown in Equation 12.3.

$$Fully\,Connected\,Ratio = \frac{No.\,of\,Disconnected\,Nodes}{Total\,Nodes}. \tag{12.3}$$

The total number of nodes in the network is 34. Before the earthquake, the network is fully connected as a path was always available to access each of the 34 nodes and hence the number

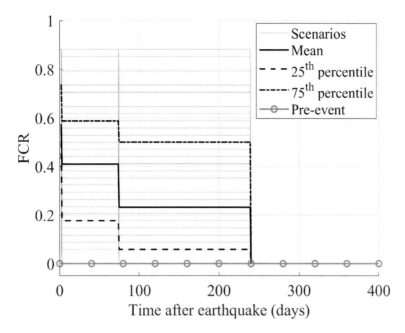

Figure 12.9   Time evolution of FCR for the earthquake scenarios.

of disconnected nodes and FCR are zero, which is the pre-event baseline case as shown in Figure 12.9. The mean FCR on day 1 is 0.6, indicating that 60 percent of nodes are disconnected on average across the network immediately after the earthquake. The changes in FCR happen at 3, 7, 75 days, which correspond to the days by when bridges get restored. By 240 days, even bridges in the complete damage state regain partial functionality and hence full connectivity in the network is restored. Hence, for FCR, the target restoration time, t_r is 240 days.

Missed trips
With the extent of disruption observed in the network due to a high intensity seismic rupture, a lot of travel demands are not met. These trips that could not be completed are counted as missed trips. Figure 12.10 shows that on an average 1e5 trips out of total 2.1e5 trips cannot be made on day 1. This metric can be interpreted as a proxy for social impact in the network due to the earthquake. The number of missed trips reduces with time as bridges get restored. The trends are similar to FCR with the mean and percentiles of missed trips converging to the pre-event zero missed trips at $t_r = 240$ days, as shown in Figure 12.10.

Travel time and distance analysis
The total travel time and total travel distance in the network are computed as the sum of travel time and distance on individual links. Generally, the network functionality with respect to travel time and travel distance in the network can be expected to be higher than the pre-event baseline case. However, due to the large number of missed trips caused by network changes because of bridge closures and restrictions, the number of trips are significantly reduced leading to low traffic flows, resulting in atypical evolution trends for travel time and distance as shown in Figures 12.11 and 12.12. Consequently, the total travel distance in the network is reduced, as

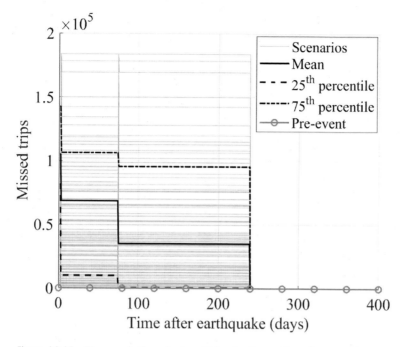

Figure 12.10   Time evolution of missed trips for the earthquake scenarios.

seen in Figure 12.12. Although fewer trips are realized in the network, the travel time in the network is higher than the pre-event travel times. This observation can be attributed to traffic congestion caused by partial bridge closures, which significantly reduce the traffic flow capacity of bridges and corresponding roadway links.

The travel time evolution in Figure 12.11 shows signs of congestion in the network between days 75 and 180. By day 75, bridges in the extensive damage state are partially open and by day 180, bridges in extensive damage are fully open. This partial functionality of bridges restores traffic flow to links, but causes congestion. As all bridges regain at least partial functionality by 240 days, the travel time decreases and by 400 days, the travel time is restored to the pre-event condition and hence t_r according to travel time analysis is 400 days.

The evolution of travel distance in the network after the earthquake is shown in Figure 12.12. Travel distance follows similar time evolution trends as travel time with changes observed at days 7, 75, 180, and 240. However, the impact of congestion between days 75 and 180 is not captured by the travel distance metric.

Resilience quantification
Based on the network functionality metrics calculated in the previous sub-section, resilience quantification can be carried out for the network as per Equation (12.1). Resilience is quantified as the area under the time evolution curves presented in Figures 12.9 through 12.12. A higher value of the resilience metric indicates greater loss in resilience and therefore the network is less resilient. If the functionality restoration time is large or the loss of functionality is high after the earthquake, the loss of resilience in the network will be higher. The resilience metrics are not computed here for travel time and travel distance because they are greatly impacted by the

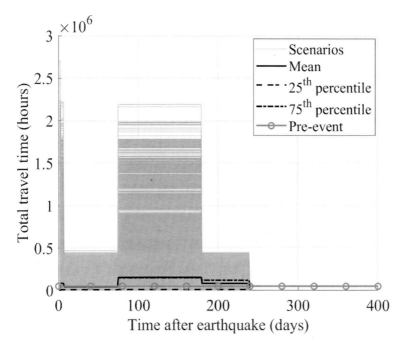

Figure 12.11 Time evolution of travel time for the earthquake scenarios.

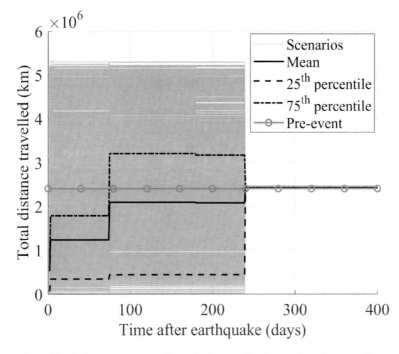

Figure 12.12 Time evolution of travel distance for the earthquake scenarios.

missed trips and the area under the functionality curves for these two metrics do not accurately represent the network resilience.

The resilience results are summarized in Table 12.2. Since there are 1e5 realizations available, the mean and standard deviations of the resilience metrics are reported here. Since the number of missed trips for most scenarios on day 1 are much larger than 1, the scale of the resilience metric computed for FCR and missed trips will differ. Hence missed trips for the purpose of resilience assessment is used as a ratio of missed trips as shown in Equation (12.4). The total number of trips in the network is 2.11e5 and the number of missed trips are as shown previously in Figure 12.10.

$$Missed\ Trips\ Ratio\ (MTR) = \frac{No.\ of\ Missed\ Trips}{Total\ Trips\ in\ Network}. \tag{12.4}$$

From Table 12.2, the network is less resilient with respect to regaining connectivity than it is with respect to meeting trip demands. However, both FCR and MTR metrics have the same mean target restoration time of 197 days. Whenever a node becomes accessible, the trip demands of that node may be met, resulting in a reduction of missed trips. Hence FCR and MTR are closely tied in terms of restoration time. However, the resilience metrics vary due to the varying levels of disruption for FCR and MTR in the network; the mean FCR on day 1 is around 0.57 and the mean MTR is around 0.5. From a connectivity perspective, all nodes have equal importance and failure of any one node impacts the FCR in the same way. However, if the failed node did not have many trips generating from it, the MTR metric will be low as majority of the trips in the network are not impacted by this failure. So, the MTR metric indirectly weighs the node according to its travel demand.

The travel time or travel distance based functionality assessments show that the target restoration time is 400 days. This agrees well with the network flow mainly because the flow optimization is carried out based on travel time in network links. From Table 12.2, it can be observed that the high standard deviation values for both travel time and travel distance values immediately after the earthquake shows the uncertainty in predicting them. While travel time increases in comparison to the baseline case, travel distance on day 1 decreases in comparison to the baseline. This is again due to the fact that many trips are not made in the network on day 1 and hence the distance traveled on many links becomes close to zero. In spite of this, travel time still shows an increase from the baseline case. This is often the case when travelers traverse the same link and hence the same distance to access a node; but there might be congestion

Table 12.2 Resilience metrics for the Shelby road network

Network Functionality Metric	Baseline (Pre-earthquake) value	Value on Day 1 after earthquake		Time to target restoration t_r (days)		Resilience Metric	
		Mean	Standard deviation	Mean	Standard deviation	Mean	Standard deviation
FCR	0	0.57	0.22	197.15	77.46	0.34	0.22
MTR	0	0.50	0.26	197.15	77.46	0.26	0.23
Travel Time (hours)	2.95 e6	3.05 e6	1.10 e7	400	–	N/A	N/A
Travel Distance (km)	2.41 e6	6.20 e5	8.23 e5	400	–	N/A	N/A

due to partial functionality of bridges and in turn links. Hence travel time is a good network functionality metric to capture congestion, but a more robust metric combining the impact of missed trips and travel time or distance may be required for such disruptive earthquake scenarios. Additionally, this issue arises mainly due to the sparsity of the network. In reality, there are smaller roads available as detours for travelers and hence the number of missed trips might be over-estimated. A finer resolution of the road network can be used to circumvent this issue. However, it is still worthwhile to compute travel time as it has the capability to capture congestion in the network better than any other metric explored herein. These comparisons underscore the fact that "resilience" can have different implications for different stakeholders depending on their choice of restoration metric.

12.4 Conclusions

Resilient transportation networks are essential for ensuring resilience of societies and communities and their return to normalcy after the occurrence of a natural hazard or extreme event. Resilience of a transportation network is intertwined with the performance of the network, and is often quantified as the area under the time-evolving network functionality curve for engineering systems. The choice of functionality metric influences both the time taken for the network to regain functionality as well as the measured resilience itself. Common resilience metrics are defined in terms of connectivity, missed trips, travel time and travel distance as described and illustrated herein, but may also assume the form of other associated loss metrics due to a hazard such as the freight flow through the network.

The resilience assessment framework presented in this chapter depends on three main input models: vulnerability models of network components, restoration models and network performance assessment models. The framework is demonstrated using a case study road network in Shelby County, Tennessee for earthquake hazard. For a chosen scenario, the resilience assessment is carried out in terms of four functionality metrics: connectivity, missed trips, travel time and travel distance. Connectivity based metrics are good if the resilience is measured in terms of accessibility to different parts of the network. Missed trips is a metric that combines connectivity as well as the social impact of network disruption. This metric takes into account both accessibility to a node and the number of trips generated to and from the node. If a hospital or emergency facility fall in a disconnected area, resilience based on connectivity or missed trips outweigh any concerns about travel time or distance. However, for meeting regular travel demand and returning to normalcy across the network, travel distance or travel time are more suited. Both metrics can capture impacts due to reduced functionality of network links due to partially open bridges, which is not captured by a connectivity or missed trip based metric. The complete picture of network disruption due to a hazard that collectively captures connectivity loss, congestion and reduced functionality is better summarized by the travel time metric. The network restoration time estimated according to the travel time based resilience metric also corresponds to the restoration of traffic flow in the network. However, the travel time and travel distance estimates in the network are conditional on all trip demands being met. Hence, a more holistic network functionality metric that combines travel time and missed trips might be required for robust resilience assessment of sparse networks.

The resilience metrics assessed and explained in this chapter are all sensitive to the input models, hazard scenario and network topology. Hence, it is imperative that vulnerability models and restoration models can capture properties of bridges and roads from the region accurately. There are many opportunities to improve existing or develop new input models for regional resilience assessment like improved implementation of restoration models that considers resource allocation; a new method to compute resilience for sparse networks; or a new functionality metric that weighs percentage of missed trips in travel time estimates. Performing the resilience assessment for a suite of probabilistic hazard scenarios can also be used to develop resilience based risk curves for a region. This not only helps identify potential weak links in the network, but also helps in better utilization of resources and planning immediately after an event. Improving the resilience of transportation networks has wide-reaching impacts on other lifeline systems dependent on transportation as well as on a community trying to recover after a devastating event.

Acknowledgements

The authors would like to gratefully acknowledge the support by the Center for Risk-Based Community Resilience Planning under National Institute of Standards and Technology (NIST) Financial Assistance Award Number: 70NANB15H044 for this research. The Center for Risk-Based Community Resilience Planning is a NIST-funded Center of Excellence; the Center is funded through a cooperative agreement between the US National Institute of Science and Technology and Colorado State University. In addition, this work was also supported in part by the Big-Data Private-Cloud Research Cyberinfrastructure MRI-award funded by National Science Foundation (NSF) under grant CNS-1338099 and by Rice University. Any opinions, findings, and recommendations presented in this work those of the authors, and may not represent the official position of the NIST, the NSF or the US Department of Commerce.

References

Ataei, N. 2013. *Vulnerability Assessment of Coastal Bridges Subjected to Hurricane Events.* Rice University.

Ataei, N. and Padgett, J. E. 2015. Fragility surrogate models for coastal bridges in hurricane prone zones. *Engineering Structures*, 103, 203–13.

Ataei, N., Stearns, M., and Padgett, J. 2010. Response sensitivity for probabilistic damage assessment of coastal bridges under surge and wave loading. *Transportation Research Record: Journal of the Transportation Research Board*, 93–101.

Berry, M.P. and Eberhard, M.O. 2004. *Performance models for flexural damage in reinforced concrete columns*, Pacific Earthquake Engineering Research Center.

Bocchini, P. and Frangopol, D.M. 2011. A stochastic computational framework for the joint transportation network fragility analysis and traffic flow distribution under extreme events. *Probabilistic Engineering Mechanics*, 26, 182–93.

Bocchini, P. and Frangopol, D.M. 2012. Restoration of bridge networks after an earthquake: Multicriteria intervention optimization. *Earthquake spectra*, 28, 426–55.

Bocchini, P., Decò, A., and Frangopol, D. 2012. Probabilistic functionality recovery model for resilience analysis. In: *Sixth International Conference on Bridge Maintenance, Safety and Management, 2012*. 8–12.

Bruneau, M., Chang, S.E., Eguchi, R.T., Lee, G.C., O'Rourke, T.D., Reinhorn, A.M., Shinozuka, M., Tierney, K., Wallace, W.A., and Von Winterfeldt, D. 2003. A framework to quantitatively assess and enhance the seismic resilience of communities. *Earthquake Spectra*, 19, 733–52.

Building Seismic Safety Council (BSSC). 2015. NEHRP recommended seismic provisions for new buildings and other structures, Volume 1: Part 1 Provisions, Part 2 Commentary, FEMA P-1050–1. Federal Emergency Management Agency, Washington, DC.

Chang, L., Elnashai, A.S., Spencer, B.F., Song, J., and Ouyang, Y. 2010. Transportations Systems Modeling and Applications in Earthquake Engineering. *Report of the Mid-America Earthquake Center*, University of Illinois at Urbana-Champaign, Champaign, IL.

Evans, S.P. 1976. Derivation and analysis of some models for combining trip distribution and assignment. *Transportation Research*, 10, 37–57.

Faturechi, R. and Miller-Hooks, E. 2014. Travel time resilience of roadway networks under disaster. *Transportation Research Part B: Methodological*, 70, 47–64.

Federal Emergency Management Agency (FEMA). 2015. HAZUS-MH MR4 Technical Manual. *Multi-hazard Loss Estimation Methodology Earthquake Model.* Washington, DC.

Gardoni, P. and Rosowsky, D. 2011. Seismic fragility increment functions for deteriorating reinforced concrete bridges. *Structure and Infrastructure Engineering,* 7(11), 869–79.

Gardoni, P., Der Kiureghian, A., and Mosalam, K.M. 2002. Probabilistic capacity models and fragility estimates for reinforced concrete columns based on experimental observations. *Journal of Engineering Mechanics,* 128(10), 1024–38.

Gardoni, P., Mosalam, K.M., and Der Kiureghian, A. 2003. Probabilistic seismic demand models and fragility estimates for RC bridges. *Journal of Earthquake Engineering,* 7, 79–106.

Ghosh, J. 2013. *Parameterized Seismic Fragility Assessment and Life-Cycle Analysis of Aging Highway Bridges.* Rice University.

Ghosh, J. and Padgett, J.E. 2010. Aging considerations in the development of time-dependent seismic fragility curves. *Journal of Structural Engineering,* 136, 1497–1511.

Ghosh, J., Padgett, J.E., and Dueñas-Osorio, L. 2013. Surrogate modeling and failure surface visualization for efficient seismic vulnerability assessment of highway bridges. *Probabilistic Engineering Mechanics,* 34, 189–99.

Ghosn, M., Dueñas-Osorio, L., Frangopol, D., McAllister, T., Bocchini, P., Manuel, L., Ellingwood, B., Arangio, S., Bontempi, F., and Shah, M. 2016. Performance indicators for structural systems and infrastructure networks. *Journal of Structural Engineering,* 142, F4016003.

Gidaris, I., Padgett, J. E., Barbosa, A. R., Chen, S., Cox, D., Webb, B., and Cerato, A. 2017. Multiple-hazard fragility and restoration models of highway bridges for regional risk and resilience assessment in the united states: State-of-the-art review. *Journal of Structural Engineering,* 143, 04016188.

Guidotti, R., Gardoni, P., and Chen, Y. 2017. Network reliability analysis with link and nodal weights and auxiliary nodes. *Structural Safety,* 65, 12–26.

Highway Capacity Manual. 2000. Transportation research board. National Research Council, Washington, DC.

Kameshwar, S. 2017. *Multi-hazard Fragility, Risk, and Resilience Assessment of Select Coastal Infrastructure.* Doctoral Dissertation, Rice University. http://hdl.handle.net/1911/96101 (last accessed August 31, 2018).

Kameshwar, S. and Padgett, J.E. 2014. Multi-hazard risk assessment of highway bridges subjected to earthquake and hurricane hazards. *Engineering Structures,* 78, 154–66.

Kang, W.-H., Song, J., and Gardoni, P. 2008. Matrix-based system reliability method and applications to bridge networks. *Reliability Engineering & System Safety,* 93, 1584–93.

Kiremidjian, A.S., Stergiou, E., and Lee, R. 2007. Issues in seismic risk assessment of transportation networks. *Earthquake Geotechnical Engineering.* Dordrecht: Springer.

Lee, Y. J., Song, J., Gardoni, P., and Lim, H.W. 2010. Post-hazard flow capacity of bridge transportation network considering structural deterioration of bridges. *Structure and Infrastructure Engineering,* 7, 509–21.

Liu, M. and Frangopol, D.M. 2005. Balancing connectivity of deteriorating bridge networks and long-term maintenance cost through optimization. *Journal of Bridge Engineering,* 10, 468–81.

Lounis, Z. and McAllister, T. P. 2016. Risk-based decision making for sustainable and resilient infrastructure systems. *Journal of Structural Engineering,* 142, F4016005.

Mackie, K. and Stojadinović, B. 2001. Probabilistic seismic demand model for California highway bridges. *Journal of Bridge Engineering,* 6, 468–81.

Mackie, K. and Stojadinović, B. 2006. Post-earthquake functionality of highway overpass bridges. *Earthquake Engineering & Structural Dynamics,* 35, 77–93.

Mackie, K.R., Wong, J.M., and Stojadinović, B. 2010. Post-earthquake bridge repair cost and repair time estimation methodology. *Earthquake Engineering & Structural Dynamics,* 39, 281–301.

Memphis Metropolitan Planning Organization (MPO). 2016. Travel Demand Model Documentation. *Livability 2040: Regional Transportation Plan* [Online], Appendix B.

Miller-Hooks, E., Zhang, X., and Faturechi, R. 2012. Measuring and maximizing resilience of freight transportation networks. *Computers & Operations Research,* 39, 1633–43.

National Cooperative Highway Research Program (NCHRP) 2012. *Travel Demand Forecasting: Parameters and Techniques,* Transportation Research Board & National Academies of Sciences, Engineering & Medicine Washington, DC, The National Academies Press. https://doi.org/10.17226/14665.

Newman, M. 2010. *Networks: An Introduction.* Oxford: Oxford University Press.

Nielson, B.G. 2005. *Analytical Fragility Curves for Highway Bridges in Moderate Seismic Zones.* Georgia Institute of Technology.

Nielson, B.G. and DesRoches, R. 2007a. Analytical seismic fragility curves for typical bridges in the central and southeastern United States. *Earthquake spectra*, 23, 615–33.

Nielson, B.G. and DesRoches, R. 2007b. Seismic fragility methodology for highway bridges using a component level approach. *Earthquake Engineering & Structural Dynamics*, 36, 823–39.

NIST 2015. Toward a more resilient community. *An Overview of the Community Resilience Planning Guide for Buildings and Infrastructure Systems*. Gaithersburg, MD: National Institute of Standards and Technology (NIST).

Ouyang, M. and Wang, Z. 2015. Resilience assessment of interdependent infrastructure systems: With a focus on joint restoration modeling and analysis. *Reliability Engineering & System Safety*, 141, 74–82.

Padgett, J.E. 2007. *Seismic Vulnerability Assessment of Retrofitted Bridges Using Probabilistic Methods*. Georgia Institute of Technology.

Padgett, J.E. and DesRoches, R. 2007. Bridge functionality relationships for improved seismic risk assessment of transportation networks. *Earthquake Spectra*, 23, 115–30.

Panagiotakos, T.B. and Fardis, M.N. 2001. Deformations of reinforced concrete members at yielding and ultimate. *Structural Journal*, 98, 135–48.

Park, J. and Towashiraporn, P. 2014. Rapid seismic damage assessment of railway bridges using the response-surface statistical model. *Structural Safety*, 47, 1–12.

Petersen, M.D., Moschetti, M.P., Powers, P.M., Mueller, C.S., Haller, K.M., Frankel, A.D., Zeng, Y., Rezaeian, S., Harmsen, S.C., and Boyd, O.S. 2014. Documentation for the 2014 update of the United States national seismic hazard maps. US Geological Survey.

Ramanathan, K.N. 2012. *Next Generation Seismic Fragility Curves for California Bridges Incorporating the Evolution in Seismic Design Philosophy*, Georgia Institute of Technology.

Rix, G. and Fernandez-Leon, J. 2004. Synthetic ground motions for Memphis, TN. www. ce. gatech. edu/ research/mae_ground_motionæ (last accesssed July 5, 2008).

Rokneddin, K., Ghosh, J., Dueñas-Osorio, L., and Padgett, J.E. 2013. Bridge retrofit prioritisation for ageing transportation networks subject to seismic hazards. *Structure and Infrastructure Engineering*, 9, 1050–66.

Seo, J. and Linzell, D.G. 2013. Use of response surface metamodels to generate system level fragilities for existing curved steel bridges. *Engineering Structures*, 52, 642–53.

Stergiou, E.C. and Kiremidjian, A.S. 2010. Risk assessment of transportation systems with network functionality losses. *Structure and Infrastructure Engineering*, 6, 111–25.

Wen, Y. and Wu, C.-L. 2001. Uniform hazard ground motions for mid-America cities. *Earthquake Spectra*, 17, 359–84.

Zhou, Y., Banerjee, S., and Shinozuka, M. 2010. Socio-economic effect of seismic retrofit of bridges for highway transportation networks: a pilot study. *Structure and Infrastructure Engineering*, 6, 145–57.

13

Physics-based fragility functions

Their mathematical formulation and use in the reliability and resilience analysis of transportation infrastructure

Fabrizio Nocera,[1] Armin Tabandeh,[2] Roberto Guidotti,[3] Jessica Boakye,[4] and Paolo Gardoni[5]

[1] DEPARTMENT OF CIVIL AND ENVIRONMENTAL ENGINEERING, MAE CENTER: CREATING A MULTI-HAZARD APPROACH TO ENGINEERING, UNIVERSITY OF ILLINOIS AT URBANA-CHAMPAIGN, URBANA, IL, USA; FNOCERA@ILLINOIS.EDU

[2] DEPARTMENT OF CIVIL AND ENVIRONMENTAL ENGINEERING, MAE CENTER: CREATING A MULTI-HAZARD APPROACH TO ENGINEERING, UNIVERSITY OF ILLINOIS AT URBANA-CHAMPAIGN, URBANA, IL, USA; TABANDE2@ILLINOIS.EDU

[3] DEPARTMENT OF CIVIL AND ENVIRONMENTAL ENGINEERING, MAE CENTER: CREATING A MULTI-HAZARD APPROACH TO ENGINEERING, UNIVERSITY OF ILLINOIS AT URBANA-CHAMPAIGN, URBANA, IL, USA; GUIDOTT2@ILLINOIS.EDU

[4] DEPARTMENT OF CIVIL AND ENVIRONMENTAL ENGINEERING, MAE CENTER: CREATING A MULTI-HAZARD APPROACH TO ENGINEERING, UNIVERSITY OF ILLINOIS AT URBANA-CHAMPAIGN, URBANA, IL, USA; BOAKYE3@ILLINOIS.EDU

[5] DEPARTMENT OF CIVIL AND ENVIRONMENTAL ENGINEERING, MAE CENTER: CREATING A MULTI-HAZARD APPROACH TO ENGINEERING, UNIVERSITY OF ILLINOIS AT URBANA-CHAMPAIGN, URBANA, IL, USA; GARDONI@ILLINOIS.EDU

13.1 Introduction

Ensuring the reliability and resilience of transportation infrastructure is critical for the public well-being. The consequences of past disasters around the world have raised concerns about the vulnerability of bridges to different natural hazards and have highlighted the significance of risk mitigation and management (Murphy & Gardoni 2006; Gardoni et al. 2016). The failure or closure of bridges disrupts regular residential and commercial activities, hinders the short-term emergency responses, and the ability of a community to recover (Guikema & Gardoni 2009; Lee et al. 2011). Thus, it is critical that bridges retain their traffic-carrying capacities after a hazard. The maintenance, mitigation, repair, or replacement of existing vulnerable or deteriorating bridges represents a significant investment. For example, restoring deteriorating bridges in the United States is estimated to require a $123 billion investment (ASCE 2017). To wisely invest the limited funding, it is crucial to use advanced risk and decision-analysis tools (Mori & Ellingwood 1993; Frangopol et al. 1997; Gardoni & Murphy 2008; Gardoni et al. 2016).

Fragility functions are commonly used to estimate the vulnerability of bridges subject to hazards (Gardoni et al. 2003; Padgett & DesRoches 2008). A fragility is defined as the conditional probability of attaining or exceeding a specified performance level given a (set of) hazard intensity measure(s) (Gardoni et al. 2002). Fragility functions are key elements in risk and resilience analysis, including life cycle analysis (LCA) (Kumar & Gardoni 2014a; Jia et al. 2017; Jia & Gardoni 2017) and retrofit decision-making (Williams et al. 2009; Bisadi et al. 2014). The development of the fragility functions for bridges has been the subject of much research. Empirical fragility functions are an early contribution. They were developed using observed damage data from past earthquake events (e.g., Basöz & Kiremidjian 1998). More recently, analytical fragility functions have been developed using the simulated response data obtained by the time-history analyses of specific bridge models (e.g., Choi et al. 2004). There are four common limitations with these two approaches, summarized as follows: (1) the fragility functions are structure-specific; thus, the fragility function developed for a specific bridge cannot generally be used for other bridges; (2) the fragility functions are typically developed at the structural system level (i.e., the full bridge); thus, they cannot take advantage of experimental test data, often available at the structural component level (i.e., individual members); (3) these approaches generally make assumptions on the shape of the fragility function, such as being a lognormal cumulative distribution function (CDF); thus, the parameters of the fragility function have no physical interpretation, cannot reflect the effects of deterioration, and include information from the field; and (4) these approaches typically do not account for the relevant sources of uncertainty (Gardoni et al. 2002; Murphy et al. 2011), including the statistical uncertainty due to limited data to calibrate the fragility function and model error due to simplifications in the mathematical models.

Gardoni et al. (2002, 2003) proposed a general formulation to develop fragility functions, named physics-based fragility functions, which captures the underlying physics of the problem and addresses these limitations. The formulation first develops probabilistic capacity and demand models based on first principles (i.e., rules of physics and mechanics) as well as information from computer simulations, laboratory tests and field data. Once the probabilistic capacity and demand models are developed, the fragility function can be obtained by conducting rigorous reliability analyses, rather than making assumptions on the shape of the fragility function. The physics-based fragility functions are parametric (i.e., functions of the physical properties of the structure); thus, once the capacity and demand models are developed, they can be used to obtain the fragility of other structures with characteristics that fall within the range of the data used for the calibration of the capacity and demand models. In addition, the parametric formulation also allows us to easily incorporate the effects of deterioration, improvement strategies, and the information from structural health monitoring (SHM) and non-destructive testing (NDT).

This chapter presents the general formulation for the physics-based fragility functions and the development of time-varying fragility functions that consider the effects of deterioration mechanisms and improvement strategies (which include maintenance, mitigation and recovery activities.) The chapter then discusses how to update the estimated fragility functions using SHM and NDT information. The formulation is general and applicable to different structures including, but not limited to, bridges. Furthermore, the chapter explains the integration of the fragility functions into time-varying network reliability analyses for regional risk and resilience analysis. Specifically, in relation to transportation infrastructure, the chapter reviews the state-of-the-art physics-based fragility functions for bridges subject to multiple hazards (seismic, wind, and collision hazards). We present specific models to capture the deterioration of bridges, which can be used to develop time-varying fragility functions. We also present common improvement strategies for bridges and their effects on the estimate of fragility functions. Furthermore, we review the approaches developed to update the fragility functions of bridges incorporating SHM and NDT information. Finally, the chapter illustrates the use of physics-based fragility and recovery functions for the reliability and resilience analysis of an example transportation infrastructure.

While the focus of this chapter is on transportation infrastructure, the presented formulations for developing physics-based fragility functions and conducting time-varying network reliability analysis are general and can be used for other infrastructure. Specifically, the formulation of physics-based fragility functions has been used also for buildings (Ramamoorthy et al. 2006, 2008; Zhu et al. 2006; Bai et al. 2011, 2015; Xu & Gardoni 2016; Elhami Khorasani et al. 2014, 2015, 2016), wind turbines (Mardfekri & Gardoni 2013, 2014; Mardfekri et al. 2015), mooring systems (Mousavi et al. 2013; Mousavi & Gardoni 2014), and rigid block-like elements (Bakhtiary & Gardoni 2016).

13.2 General formulation

Gardoni et al. (2002, 2003) proposed to develop fragility functions by conducting reliability analyses considering a limit-state function defined by the structural capacity of the individual infrastructure components and the corresponding demands imposed by a hazard. The capacity is defined as the maximum value of a physical quantity (e.g., a load or deformation) that a component can sustain without failure. The demand is the corresponding physical quantity imposed on the component by a hazard characterized by a (set of) intensity measure(s). The capacity and demand depend on a vector of basic variables that define the component and the characteristics of the hazard. To model such dependence, Gardoni et al. (2002, 2003) proposed a general formulation for probabilistic predictive models that accounts for the various sources of information (i.e., from the governing rules of physics and mechanics to the data from laboratory experiments and field measurements), as well as the different sources of uncertainty.

13.2.1 Probabilistic predictive models

The generic multivariate probabilistic predictive model can be written as (Gardoni et al. 2002, 2003)

$$T_k\left[Y_k(\mathbf{r},\boldsymbol{\Theta}_{T,k})\right] = T_k\left[\hat{y}_k(\mathbf{r})\right] + \gamma_k(\mathbf{r},\boldsymbol{\theta}_{T,k}) + \sigma_{T,k}\varepsilon_{T,k}, \quad k=1,\ldots,q, \tag{13.1}$$

where $T_k(\cdot)$ is a transformation function; $Y_k(\mathbf{r},\boldsymbol{\Theta}_{T,k})$ is the kth predicted quantity of interest (e.g., capacity or demand); $\hat{y}_k(\mathbf{r})$ is an existing deterministic model to predict Y_k (typically based on rules of physics and mechanics); $\gamma_k(\mathbf{r},\boldsymbol{\theta}_{T,k})$ is a correction term designed to improve the prediction and capture the bias in $\hat{y}_k(\mathbf{r})$ (also constructed in part based on the rules of physics and mechanics); $\mathbf{r}$ is a vector of basic variables that influence Y_k; $\boldsymbol{\Theta}_{T,k}=(\boldsymbol{\theta}_{T,k},\sigma_{T,k})$ is a vector of unknown model parameters that needs to be estimated; and $\sigma_{T,k}\varepsilon_{T,k}$ is the (additive) model error (additivity assumption), in which $\sigma_{T,k}$ is the standard deviation of the model error, assumed not to depend on $\mathbf{r}$ (homoskedasticity assumption), and $\varepsilon_{T,k}$ is a standard normal random variable (normality assumption). In general, $(\varepsilon_{T,1},\ldots,\varepsilon_{T,q})$ is a vector of dependent random variables.

Let $\mathbf{\Sigma}_T$ denote the covariance matrix of $(\sigma_{T,1}\varepsilon_{T,1},...,\sigma_{T,q}\varepsilon_{T,q})$. The collection of all unknown model parameters is then $\mathbf{\Theta}_T = (\mathbf{\theta}_T, \mathbf{\Sigma}_T)$, where $\mathbf{\theta}_T = (\mathbf{\theta}_{T,1},...,\mathbf{\theta}_{T,q})$. The transformation $T_k(\cdot)$ is used to (approximately) satisfy the additivity, homoskedasticity, and normality assumptions within the range of the data used to calibrate the model.

A distinctive feature of the predictive model in Equation (13.1) is that it takes advantage of both first principles (i.e., the governing rules of physics and mechanics) as well as empirical information. Statistical tools can then guide in tailoring the empirical portion of the model such that the calibrated model provides the most accurate predictions. For instance, Gardoni et al. (2002) proposed a stepwise deletion process to construct a parsimonious, yet accurate predictive model in which $\gamma_k(\mathbf{r}, \mathbf{\theta}_{T,k})$ includes only the terms that significantly contribute to the prediction of Y_k.

To estimate $\mathbf{\Theta}_T$, one can use a Bayesian approach that combines prior information about $\mathbf{\Theta}_T$ with the objective information from the observed data. In the Bayesian approach, the statistical uncertainty in the estimates of $\mathbf{\Theta}_T$ is captured through its posterior probability density function (PDF), $f(\mathbf{\Theta}_T)$. A Bayesian approach can be used to update the probabilistic models, as new data become available (Gardoni et al. 2003; Choe et al. 2007; Gardoni et al. 2007). Furthermore, Tabandeh and Gardoni (2015) developed a Bayesian hierarchical approach that accounts for the statistical dependence of clustered data.

To calibrate the probabilistic capacity and demand models, one can use both real data (i.e., data from laboratory tests or field measurements) (Gardoni et al. 2002, 2003; Zhong et al. 2009), and virtual data (i.e., computer simulations) (Gardoni et al. 2003; Zhong et al. 2008; Huang et al. 2010). An experimental design can be used to define the most informative cases to test or run (for a given number of tests/runs) and reduce the statistical uncertainty (Huang et al. 2010; Tabandeh & Gardoni 2015).

13.2.2 Formulation of fragility functions

After developing probabilistic capacity and demand models according to Equation (13.1), one can write the limit-state function for the kth failure mode, $g_k(\mathbf{r}, \mathbf{\Theta}_k)$, as (Gardoni et al. 2003; Gardoni 2017)

$$g_k(\mathbf{r}, \mathbf{\Theta}_k) = C_k(\mathbf{r}, \mathbf{\Theta}_{C,k}) - D_k(\mathbf{r}, \mathbf{\Theta}_{D,k}) \quad k = 1,...,q, \tag{13.2}$$

where $C_k(\mathbf{r}, \mathbf{\Theta}_{C,k})$ is the capacity model associated with the kth failure mode; $D_k(\mathbf{r}, \mathbf{\Theta}_{D,k})$ is the corresponding demand model; and $\mathbf{\Theta}_k = (\mathbf{\Theta}_{C,k}, \mathbf{\Theta}_{D,k})$. By partitioning $\mathbf{r}$ as $\mathbf{r} = (\mathbf{x}, \mathbf{s})$, where $\mathbf{x}$ is a set of variables that defines the system (e.g., member dimensions and material properties) called state variables, and $\mathbf{s}$ is a set of demand variables (e.g., hazard intensity measure(s)), we can write the fragility function as

$$F(\mathbf{s}, \mathbf{\Theta}) = \mathbf{P}\left\{\bigcup_k \left[g_k(\mathbf{x}, \mathbf{s}, \mathbf{\Theta}_k) \le 0\right] \middle| \mathbf{s}, \mathbf{\Theta}\right\}. \tag{13.3}$$

Depending on the treatment of uncertainty in $\mathbf{\Theta}$, one can obtain two estimates of fragility functions (Gardoni et al. 2002). The first option is to replace $\mathbf{\Theta}$ in Equation (13.3) with a fixed value $\hat{\mathbf{\Theta}}$ (e.g., the posterior mean or mode of $\mathbf{\Theta}$) and obtain a point-estimate of the fragility

$\hat{F}(\mathbf{s}) = F(\mathbf{s}, \hat{\Theta})$. The second option is to incorporate the uncertainty of in Θ by writing a predictive estimate as

$$\tilde{F}(\mathbf{s}) = \int F(\mathbf{s}, \Theta) f(\Theta) d\Theta. \tag{13.4}$$

Details on how to construct confidence intervals that explicitly capture the epistemic uncertainty in Θ can be found in Gardoni et al. (2002).

13.2.3 Incorporating the effects of deterioration and improvement strategies, and the information from SHM and NDT

This section explains how the effects of deterioration and improvement strategies, as well as the information from SHM and NDT, have been incorporated in the formulation of fragility functions.

Incorporating the effects of deterioration
The deterioration of engineering systems can adversely impact their serviceability and safety (Mori & Ellingwood 1993; Frangopol et al. 1997). Deterioration can occur both gradually over time due to for example corrosion, alkali-silica reaction, or delayed ettringite formation, as well as a shock due to damaging events like earthquakes (Choe et al. 2008, 2009; Kumar & Gardoni 2012, 2014a,b; Kumar et al. 2009). To incorporate the effects of deterioration, Choe et al. (2008) proposed to model the variation of $\mathbf{x}$ over time (i.e., $\mathbf{x} = \mathbf{x}(t)$) due to deterioration processes and use the estimate of $\mathbf{x}(t)$ at a given time t in the formulation of physics-based fragility functions. Kumar et al. (2015) proposed a stochastic formulation to model the deterioration of engineering systems (e.g., bridges) as a combination of gradual and shock deterioration processes. Kumar et al. (2015) also derived semi-analytical solutions for stochastic performance measures such as the time to failure and number of shocks to failure. Jia and Gardoni (2017, 2018a) generalized the stochastic formulation in Kumar et al. (2015) and proposed a general state-dependent stochastic formulation that also captures the possible interaction among different deterioration processes. For the estimation of the stochastic performance measures, Jia and Gardoni (2018b) proposed a general simulation-based approach that allows the consideration of the uncertainties associated with the external conditions, deterioration models, and performance evaluation models.

Following Jia and Gardoni (2017, 2018a), we can write the vector of state variables, $\mathbf{x}(t)$, as

$$\mathbf{x}(t) = \mathbf{x}(0) + \int_0^t \dot{\mathbf{x}}(\upsilon) d\upsilon, \tag{13.5}$$

where $\mathbf{x}(0)$ is the vector of state variables at time $t = 0$; and $\dot{\mathbf{x}}(\cdot)$ is the instantaneous rate of state change due to different gradual and shock deterioration processes. The model for $\dot{\mathbf{x}}(\upsilon)$ is generally expressed as $\dot{\mathbf{x}}(\upsilon) = \dot{\mathbf{x}}[\upsilon, \mathbf{x}(\upsilon^-), \mathbf{z}(\upsilon), \Theta_{\mathbf{x}}]$, where $\mathbf{x}(\upsilon^-)$ is the vector of the state variables immediately before time υ (i.e., υ^-); $\mathbf{z}(\upsilon)$ is the vector of external conditions at time υ (including both environmental conditions and shock intensity measures); and $\Theta_{\mathbf{x}}$ is a vector of model parameters. Xu and Gardoni (2018) extended the state-dependent formulation in Equation (13.5) to model the effects of deterioration on state variables considering their spatial variabilities. Section 13.4 reviews specific models developed for the deterioration of bridges.

To reduce the computational cost associated to the solution of Equations (13.3) and (13.4), Choe et al. (2010) and Gardoni and Rosowsky (2011) proposed fragility increment functions that directly provide the fragility of a system at any time t without requiring additional reliability analyses, given the fragility of the system at a reference time (typically $t = 0$.) The fragility increment function for the kth failure mode, $G_{F,k}$, are written as

$$G_{F,k} = \frac{F_k(t)}{F_k(0)} \quad k = 1, \ldots, q, \tag{13.6}$$

where $F_k(t)$ is the fragility estimate for the kth failure mode at time t, and $F_k(0)$ is the corresponding fragility estimate at time $t = 0$. The model for $G_{F,k}$ is generally expressed as $G_{F,k} = G_{F,k}[\mathbf{x}(0), t, \mathbf{s}(t), \mathbf{\Theta}_{G,k}]$, where $\mathbf{s}(t)$ is the vector of hazard intensity measures at time t; and $\mathbf{\Theta}_{G,k}$ is a vector of model parameters. The fragility increment functions can be developed also for a system reliability problem considering any subset of the q modes of failure.

Incorporating the effects of improvement strategies and definition of recovery functions
Improvement strategies include maintenance, mitigation, and recovery activities that might be implemented as preventive measures, or to reverse the effects of deterioration or refurbish an engineering system after damage. To incorporate the effects of improvement strategies, Sharma et al. (2018) proposed a general state-dependent stochastic formulation that models the recovery of state variables over time as a function of the relevant improvement influencing factors such as the component initial state and improvement resources. Following Sharma et al. (2018), we can model state variables during the implementation of the improvement strategies as

$$\mathbf{x}(\tau) = \sum_{i=1}^{\infty} \mathbf{x}(\tau_{i-1}) \mathbf{1}_{\{\tau_{i-1} \leq \tau < \tau_i\}} + \sum_{i,j=1}^{\infty} \Delta\mathbf{x}(\tau_j) \mathbf{1}_{\{\tau_{i-1} < \tau < \tau_i, \tau_{i-1} < \tau_j \leq \tau\}}, \tag{13.7}$$

where $\mathbf{x}(\tau)$ is the vector of state variables at relative time τ, measured from the beginning of the improvement; $\mathbf{x}(\tau_{i-1})$ is the vector of state variables after implementing the improvement step $(i-1)$ at time τ_{i-1}, as a special case $\mathbf{x}(\tau_0)$ is the vector of state variables at the beginning of implementing the improvement strategy, whose probability distribution is obtained from the deterioration models (i.e., Equation (13.5)); $\mathbf{1}_{\{A\}}$ is an indicator function, defined such that $\mathbf{1}_{\{A\}} = 1$, if A is a true statement, and $\mathbf{1}_{\{A\}} = 0$, otherwise; and $\Delta\mathbf{x}(\tau_j)$ is the state change due to the occurrence of the jth possible disrupting shock at time $\tau_j \in (\tau_{i-1}, \tau_i)$.

Recovery functions describe the state of a structure during the recovery process as a function of time. To develop physics-based recovery functions, Sharma et al. (2018) proposed to use the estimate of $\mathbf{x}(\tau)$ during the recovery in the formulation of physics-based fragility function. The functionality of the system can then be determined in terms of the estimate of the fragility function.

Incorporating the information from SHM and NDT
An effective way to reduce the uncertainty in the reliability analysis is to incorporate the information from a field inspection using SHM and NDT (Zheng & Ellingwood 1998). The information from field inspection using SHM and NDT at time t_{insp} can be used to obtain more accurate estimates of the fragility functions at time t_{insp} by providing more accurate estimates

of $\mathbf{x}(t_{\text{insp}})$ (Gardoni et al 2007; Gardoni & Rosowsky 2011; Huang et al. 2011). The information can also be used to update the models for $\mathbf{x}(t)$ $(t > t_{\text{insp}})$ and, hence, $G_{F,k}(t)$, so that better predictions can be made for future times.

To incorporate the information from field inspections, Huang et al. (2015) proposed an Adaptive Reliability Analysis (ARA) that includes the following steps: (1) use SHM to find the potential locations of deterioration, (2) estimate $\mathbf{x}(t)$ at specific locations from the results of NDT, and (3) incorporate the local estimates of $\mathbf{x}(t)$ in the estimates of fragility functions. Huang et al. (2012) proposed a probabilistic SHM approach to determine the potential deterioration location(s) based on the changes in the dynamic characteristics of the structure. In such an approach, Huang et al. (2012) used the damage index method (DIM) (Stubbs & Kim 1996) to identify the potential deterioration locations. You et al. (2014) also proposed an iterative damage index method that improves the accuracy of DIM. As for the second step, Huang et al. (2011) developed probabilistic models for the variables in $\mathbf{x}(t)$ as functions of the results of NDT, following the general form in Equation (13.1).

13.2.4 Integrating fragility functions into network reliability analysis

We consider a network as the mathematical representation of a critical infrastructure (e.g., transportation, water, or electrical power infrastructure). To assess the reliability and resilience of infrastructure, we need to integrate the fragility functions of individual components into a time-varying network reliability analysis (Guidotti et al. 2017a). As discussed in Guidotti and Gardoni (2018) and Guidotti et al. (2018), network capacity and demand models can be developed for topology-based or flow-based analyses. Such capacity and demand models are functions of the state of the individual components in the network (determined by the component fragility and recovery functions) as well as the network connectivity state and flow. For example, a specific component (e.g., a bridge in a transportation network) may be in a collapse damage state, but, because of the network redundancy, this may not compromise the overall functionality of the network.

In addition, the components in a network may lose their functionality due to the failure or functionality loss of supporting components that are part of either the same network or different networks. Guidotti et al. (2017b, 2018) proposed a multi-layered heterogeneous network model to assess the cascading effects due to the multiple classes of (inter)dependency (e.g., physical or geographical) among infrastructure.

13.3 Developing fragility functions for bridges considering multiple hazards

This section presents some examples of physics-based fragility functions for bridges subject to multiple hazards, developed following the general formulation in Section 13.2. Table 13.1 gives a summary of the discussed physics-based fragility functions.

13.3.1 Seismic hazard

Bridges are the most vulnerable components to seismic hazards in transportation infrastructure (Gardoni et al. 2003; Gardoni & LaFave 2016). Gardoni et al. (2002) developed probabilistic deformation and shear capacity models for reinforced concrete (RC) bridge columns

Table 13.1 Contributions to the development of physics-based fragility functions for bridges

Hazard	*Description*	*Author*	*Year*
Seismic	General capacity models for RC columns	Gardoni et al.	2002
	General demand models for RC bridges	Gardoni et al.	2003
	Demand models specific for RC bridges with one single-column bent	Huang et al.	2010
	Demand models specific for RC bridges with two-column bents	Zhong et al.	2008
	Bayesian updating of demand models for RC bridges with two-column bents	Zhong et al.	2009
	Closed-form fragility for RC bridges with single-column bents	Choe et al.	2007
	Demand models for base isolated RC bridges	Gardoni and Trejo	2013a
	Capacity models for FRP-retrofitted RC bridges	Tabandeh and Gardoni	2014
	Demand models for FRP-retrofitted RC bridges	Tabandeh and Gardoni	2015
	Capacity models for elevated RC bridges	Bisadi et al.	2011
	Demand models for elevated RC bridges	Bisadi et al.	2013
Wind	Capacity models for long-span bridges	Sun et al.	2016
Collision	Performance-based analysis	Sharma et al.	2012
	Demand model for RC columns	Sharma et al.	2014
	Capacity models for RC columns	Sharma et al.	2015

and obtained the corresponding fragility functions conditioning on the deformation and shear demands. To predict the fragility of RC bridges subject to a seismic hazard, Gardoni et al. (2003) developed probabilistic seismic demand models for deformation and shear. The demand models were first calibrated using a Bayesian approach with experimental data on single-column bents tested on a shake-table, and then updated using virtual data from finite element analyses of a curved RC bridge. The stepwise deletion process used in developing the demand models indicated the significance of the spectral acceleration, S_a, at the natural period of the structure among different candidate earthquake intensity measures. Using the developed capacity and demand models, the seismic fragility functions were obtained conditioning on S_a.

Based on the general formulation in Section 13.2, Huang et al. (2010) developed probabilistic seismic demand models specific for RC bridges with one single-column bent and obtained the corresponding seismic fragility functions. Likewise, Zhong et al. (2008, 2009) developed probabilistic seismic demand models for two-column bents RC bridges. To estimate the corresponding capacity of columns in multiple-column bents, Zhong et al. (2008) modified the probabilistic capacity models for single-column bents in Choe et al. (2007). Using the probablistic capacity and demand models, Zhong et al. (2008) obtained the seimic fragility functions for two-column bents RC bridges.

Developing closed-form fragility functions can facilitate their use in practice and are particularly convenient in regional risk analyses (Gardoni et al. 2016) and reliability-based optimizations (Mathakari et al. 2007; Liu et al. 2016a,b). To derive closed-form fragility functions, Choe et al. (2007) proposed to reduce the number of random variables in the limit-state function through an importance analysis. As an illustration of how to derive a closed-form fragility function, Choe et al. (2007) derived an approximate closed-form expression for the point-estimate fragility function of single-column bent RC bridges.

13.3.2 Wind hazard

For long and flexible structures, such as cable-stayed bridges, wind resistance design is critical (Xu 2013). Experimental data on the performance of cable-stayed bridges subject to wind are scarce and detailed finite element analyses that replicate the actual conditions are computationally expensive and might not be accurate (Sun et al. 2016). Developing simple yet accurate physics-based probabilistic models is important both to provide insights about the physics/mechanics of the problem and to facilitate the reliability analysis of such complex structures. Two common failure modes of cable-stayed bridges are the flutter and aerostatic instability of the deck. To obtain the fragility functions for these two modes of failure, Sun et al. (2016) developed probabilistic capacity models in terms of wind speed. For some of the rather complex inputs to the capacity models (i.e., natural frequencies in bending and torsion) Sun et al. (2016) also developed nested probabilistic models that predict the quantities of interest as functions of more easily measurable variables. Sun et al. (2016) then developed the fragility functions conditioning on the wind speed demand.

13.3.3 Collision hazard

Vehicle collisions on bridges is one of the most common causes of bridge failure in the US (Briaud et al. 2007). Sharma et al. (2012) proposed a performance-based approach for the response evaluation of RC columns subject to vehicle collisions. Specifically, Sharma et al. (2015) developed probabilistic shear capacity models for three performance levels while Sharma et al. (2014) developed a probabilistic shear demand model. Using the probabilistic capacity and demand models, Sharma et al. (2014) obtained the corresponding fragility functions by conditioning on the mass and velocity of the impacting vehicle.

13.4 Incorporating the effects of deterioration and improvement strategies, and the information from SHM and NDT into the fragility functions of bridges

In this section, we review some examples of models developed for incorporating the effects of deterioration and improvement strategies, and the information from SHM and NDT into the fragility functions specifically of bridges. Table 13.2 gives a summary of the presented models.

13.4.1 Effects of deterioration

A common gradual deterioration of bridges is due to corrosion (Vu & Stewart 2000). Once the corrosion initiates, the chemical reactions result in the loss of reinforcement steel. Choe et al. (2008, 2009) developed probabilistic models for the corrosion initiation time and reduction of the effective reinforcement diameter over time in RC bridges. Using these models in existing capacity and demand models, Choe et al. (2008, 2009) also obtained time-varying seismic fragility functions for RC bridges. The corrosion in RC components can also cause cracks in the concrete cover (Zhong et al. 2010). To account for this effect, Simon et al. (2010) estimated the seismic fragility functions of RC bridges considering both reinforcement corrosion and spalling of the concrete cover, while Zhong et al. (2012) included the effects of the stiffness degradation of the concrete cover.

Table 13.2 Models for incorporating the effects of deterioration and improvement strategies, and the information from SHM and NDT into the fragility functions of bridges

Author	Description	Year
Kumar et al.	Cumulative seismic damage	2009
Kumar and Gardoni	Low-cycle fatigue damage due to earthquakes	2012
Kumar and Gardoni	Renewal theory-based LCA	2014a
Kumar and Gardoni	Seismic degradation of push-over curve	2014b
Kumar et al.	Stochastic formulation for deterioration processes	2015
Jia et al.	Integrating stochastic deterioration and recovery models into LCA	2017
Jia and Gardoni	Stochastic Life-Cycle Analysis	2017
Jia and Gardoni	Stochastic formulation for state-dependent deterioration processes	2018a
Jia and Gardoni	Simulation-based approach for estimating stochastic performance measures	2018b
Choe et al.	Reinforcement corrosion and its effect of fragility	2008
Choe et al.	Reinforcement corrosion and its effect of fragility	2009
Choe et al.	Fragility increment functions	2010
Zhong et al.	Stiffness degradation of cover concrete	2010
Simon et al.	Reinforcement corrosion and spalling of the cover concrete	2010
Zhong et al.	Reinforcement corrosion and spalling of the cover concrete	2012
Huang et al.	RC columns affected by ASR	2014
Briaud et al.	Scour deterioration	2014
Bolduc et al.	Scour deterioration	2008
Gardoni and Trejo	Reliability analysis of PT bridges subject to corrosion	2013b
Gardoni et al.	Capacity models for unstressed strands subject to corrosion	2009
Pillai et al.	Capacity models for stressed strands subject to corrosion	2010a
Pillai et al.	Service reliability subject to corrosion	2010b
Pillai et al.	Ultimate reliability subject to corrosion	2014
Gardoni and Rosowsky	Fragility increment functions	2011
Huang et al.	Capacity models incorporating NDT data	2009
Huang et al.	Compressive strength of concrete	2011
Huang et al.	Probabilistic SHM approach	2012
Huang et al.	Adaptive Reliability Analysis	2015

Typical structures that may experience a significant reduction in capacity due to corrosion are post-tensioned (PT), segmental concrete bridges (Gardoni & Trejo 2013a). In PT bridges, the strands play a fundamental role in the load transferring mechanism. To prevent corrosion, strands are protected from the external environmental conditions using plastic ducts and grout. However, the presence of air voids in the grout, and moisture and chlorides in the environment might result in early age corrosion of PT strands (Poston & Wouters 1998; FDOT 2001). Gardoni et al. (2009) developed probabilistic capacity models for unstressed strands in PT bridges subject to corrosion, considering different void, moisture, and chloride concentration conditions. Pillai et al. (2010a) then extended the probabilistic models to account for the effects of stress. The models at the strand level were then used in a formulation to evaluate the time-varying capacity and demand of the mid-span cross-section (critical for flexure), which were used to assess the service and ultimate reliability of PT bridges (Pillai et al. 2010b, 2014).

Another gradual deterioration mechanism is due to alkali-silica reactions in RC components. Alkali-silica reactions are associated with internal volumetric expansion, which can result in cracking of the concrete (Eck Olave et al. 2015a,b). The development of such cracks at the interface of steel reinforcement and concrete can weaken their bond and eventually reduce the structural capacity (Bracci et al. 2011). Huang et al. (2014) developed a probabilistic model for the bond behavior of reinforcement-concrete that considers the effects of ASR. Such model can be used to estimate the impact of Alkali-silica reactions on the fragility of bridges.

Another common deterioration mechanism is scour at the bridge pier foundation. Scour might lead to a reduction of the load carrying capacity of the foundation, which might lead to bridge failure (Briaud et al. 2014). Bolduc et al. (2008) developed probabilistic models to assess the probability that a specified threshold depth is exceeded at a bridge pier for given hydrologic variables. Such models can be used to assess the reliability of bridges experiencing a reduction in the load carrying capacity of the foundation.

A common instance of shock deterioration is due to earthquakes. In seismic regions, bridges are likely to experience several damaging earthquakes during their service lives (Kumar & Gardoni 2012, 2014b). The damage from each earthquake accumulates over time and degrades the reliability of the bridge (Kumar et al. 2009). Kumar and Gardoni (2014b) developed probabilistic models that predict the degradation of the static pushover curve of RC bridges caused by damaging earthquakes. Furthermore, Kumar and Gardoni (2014b) developed a model for the degradation of the deformation capacity of RC bridge columns due to the low-cycle fatigue damage from consecutive earthquakes and obtained the corresponding impact on the estimates of the fragility functions of RC bridges.

Considering multiple deterioration mechanisms, Kumar et al. (2009) modeled the cumulative effects of corrosion and seismic damage on the reliability of bridges. Jia and Gardoni (2017, 2018a) developed a formulation for state-dependent models of deterioration that considers the possible interaction among different deterioration processes.

As examples of fragility increment functions, Choe et al. (2010) and Gardoni and Rosowsky (2011) developed fragility increment functions for RC bridges, considering deformation and shear modes of failure. The developed fragility increment functions capture the loss of reinforcement due to corrosion. Using the developed fragility increment functions, Choe et al. (2010) obtained the time-varying fragility estimates of a deteriorating RC bridge column, conditioned on the deformation and shear demands. Likewise, Gardoni and Rosowsky (2011) obtained the time-varying seismic fragility estimates of a deteriorating RC bridge, conditioned on S_a.

13.4.2 Effects of improvement strategies

Two common improvement strategies for bridges are base isolating the bridge deck and externally confining the bridge columns (e.g., with fiber reinforced polymer (FRP) composites.) To quantify the benefits of these two mitigation strategies, Gardoni and Trejo (2013b) developed probabilistic capacity and seismic demand models for RC bridges with base isolation and obtained the corresponding fragility functions, and Tabandeh and Gardoni (2014, 2015) developed probabilistic capacity and seismic demand models for FRP-retrofitted RC bridges and obtained the corresponding seismic fragility functions.

In addition to the strategies intended to mitigate the seismic hazard, steel pedestals have been used to elevate bridges and reduce the likelihood of collisions of overheight vehicles. However, the use of steel pedestals may increase the probability of damage or failure of bridges subject to seismic hazard (Bisadi et al. 2014). To quantify the seismic vulnerability of elevated bridges, Bisadi et al. (2011, 2013) developed probabilistic capacity and demand models and the corresponding fragility functions for elevated RC bridges.

Furthermore, Jia et al. (2017) coupled the state-dependent deterioration models with a selected mitigation strategy and the corresponding recovery function from Sharma et al. (2018) to propose a Stochastic Life-Cycle Analysis (SLCA) of bridges based on renewal theory.

13.4.3 Information from SHM and NDT

Huang et al. (2015) developed the Adaptive Reliability Analysis (ARA) to update the seismic fragility functions of bridges incorporating field information. The ARA uses information from both global and local damage detection methods and accounts for measurement and modeling errors. The information from global damage detection is used to define the global/equivalent structural properties of the bridge and detect potential damage locations. The information from the local damage detection is used to define the local characteristics of the bridge at selected locations (Huang et al. 2011). The identified structural properties are then used in probabilistic deformation and shear capacity models for RC bridge columns (Huang et al. 2009), and probabilistic deformation and shear seismic demand models for RC bridges (Huang et al. 2010) that account for the nonuniform distribution of $\mathbf{x}(t)$ along the column height. The capacity and demand models are then used in a reliability analysis to estimate the reliability of RC bridges incorporating the field information.

13.5 Reliability and resilience analysis of transportation infrastructure

In this chapter, we focus on a topology-based analysis to assess the network reliability and resilience. Applications of the topology-based analysis to physical networks subject to natural events can be found, for example, in Kang et al. (2008), Guikema and Gardoni (2009), and Kurtz et al. (2015). The topology-based analysis captures the reliability and resilience of infrastructure through measures of network connectivity. The measures of network connectivity and their variation over time have been proposed in Boakye et al. (2018) to assess specific community resilience goals. The common measures of network connectivity are the diameter, δ, and efficiency, η (Latora & Marchiori, 2001; Guidotti et al. 2017a). They describe the connectivity of a specific component (or set of components) to other components in the network (local connectivity) or the overall network connectivity as an average of all local connectivity measures (global connectivity).

The nodal diameter, δ_i, is the average length of the shortest paths between component i and the rest of the network. Considering a set of components $\mathbf{i}$, the local diameter $\delta_\mathbf{i}$ is defined as the average length of the shortest paths between each component $i \in \mathbf{i}$ and the rest of the network. The global diameter δ is a measure of the general connectivity of the network, defined as the average length of the shortest paths between each pair of components in the network. If at least one pair of components is disconnected, the value of δ is infinite, not capturing the number of disconnections. To capture the extent of the connectivity loss, we can use the efficiency η. Similarly to the diameter, nodal η_i, local $\eta_\mathbf{i}$, and global efficiency η are given by the average of the inverse of the shortest paths between pairs of considered components, at the nodal, local or global level, respectively. To describe the variability in diameter and efficiency (i.e., pairs of components may be in close proximity, and other at large distance), Guidotti et al. (2017a) proposed two second order measures of connectivity: the eccentricity, ξ, and the heterogeneity, ζ, defined as the standard deviation of the shortest paths between each pair of considered components and of their inverse, respectively.

13.6 Example reliability and resilience analysis considering the transportation infrastructure of Seaside, Oregon

This section illustrates the use of physics-based fragility and recovery functions in the reliability and resilience analysis of a transportation infrastructure by analyzing the transportation infrastructure of Seaside, Oregon subject to a seismic hazard. Seaside is a coastal community with 6,440 inhabitants, based on the 2010 decennial census data (Rosenheim et al. 2017, 2018). Seaside is in a seismic zone, as it is located near the Cascadia Subduction Zone. The city has been selected as a testbed by the Center for Risk-Based Community Resilience Planning funded by the National Institute of Standards and Technology (NIST), with the purpose of testing procedures and methodologies developed within the Center. In this illustration, Seaside is subjected to a hypothetical earthquake of magnitude M_W 7.0, located 25 km southwest of Seaside (offshore the Oregon coast, on the Cascadia subduction zone.) We use a ground motion prediction model (Boore & Atkinson 2008) to estimate the seismic intensity (in terms of peak ground values and spectral accelerations at the characteristic period of the structures). Figure 13.1 shows the model of the transportation infrastructure, developed for this example. The model consists of 377 (origin-destination) nodes, 11 bridges, and 7 assembly points (e.g., shelters, schools or gyms and large open areas.) The location of assembly points has been retrieved from available evacuation maps (www.oregongeology.org/.)

In this example, we consider bridges as the only vulnerable components of the transportation infrastructure. We estimate the damage state and the corresponding recovery duration using the physics-based fragility and recovery functions presented in this chapter. Table 13.3 summarizes the structural characteristics of the 11 bridges. Figure 13.2 shows the probabilities that each of the considered bridges is closed in the immediate aftermath of the seismic event. We consider a bridge to be closed when its damage state is either moderate, or heavy, or complete. Different damage states are defined according to Simon et al. (2010). To find the time for a bridge to re-open, we developed physics-based recovery functions for each of the moderate, heavy, and complete damage states following the procedure in Sharma et al. (2018).

Table 13.4 shows individual recovery activities for the repair of a bridge in the complete damage state. The duration of each activity is according to Mackie et al. (2007); however, we adjust the values based on the specific geometry of each bridge. In addition to the most likely duration of each activity, the table reports the lower and upper bounds of the duration that represent the variability in their estimates. The table also shows the set of predecessors of each activity (recovery activities needed before a specific activity can start).

We assess the performance of the transportation infrastructure, considering the variation of the connectivity measures in the immediate aftermath of the seismic event and during the recovery. We consider the four local connectivity measures, previously introduced, δ_i, ξ_i, η_i, and ζ_i, where i is the set of the seven assembly points. We use as the benchmark the values of the connectivity measures in the pre-disturbance scenario (i.e., $\delta_{i,0}$, $\xi_{i,0}$, $\eta_{i,0}$, and $\zeta_{i,0}$). Figure 13.3 shows the estimate of time-varying connectivity measures, standardized to the corresponding pre-disturbance value, during the recovery. The symmetric bands in the figure show a variation of one standard deviation from the estimated connectivity measures. To capture the uncertainties in the damage states of bridges, we perform a Monte Carlo Simulation (MCS) with a convergence criterion based on the coefficient of variation (COV) of the connectivity measures

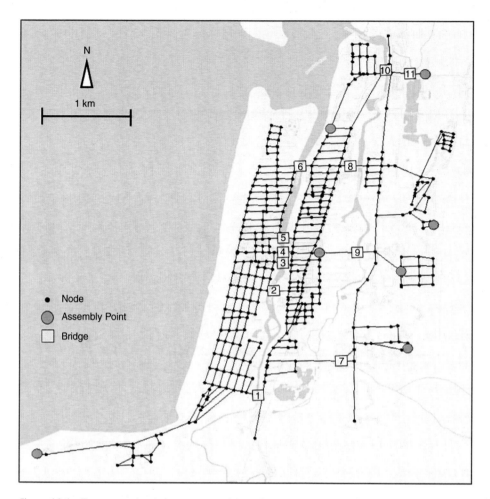

Figure 13.1 Transportation infrastructure of Seaside, Oregon.

with a threshold value of $COV = 0.02$. As for the recovery durations of the bridges, we modeled each activity (e.g., those in Table 13.4) as a random variable following a Beta distribution. In this example, the recovery duration for a closed bridge is obtained from the expected values of the required recovery activities. The treatment of the uncertainty in the recovery activities and, consequently, in the recovery duration of the bridge can be found in Sharma et al. (2018). As for the recovery sequence of bridges, for each run of the MCS, we choose to recover sequentially the bridges in the order that maximizes the increase of efficiency η. Though δ is not defined for disconnected networks, η is always defined and it ensures the fastest recovery of network connectivity. Figure 13.3 shows that in the immediate aftermath of the seismic event, there is 14.5 percent reduction in the value of η and 17.3 percent increase in δ; after about 18 months, the network almost restores the pre-disturbance state in terms of the connectivity measures.

In case bridge failures separate an assembly point from the rest of the network, we have a disconnected network. Figure 13.4 shows the probability that the network is connected in the

Table 13.3 Structural characteristics of the bridges of the transportation infrastructure of Seaside

Bridge ID	Year Built	Material	Design Type	Deck Structure	Deck Width [m]	Column Diameter [cm]	Column Height [m]	Spans Number	Columns Number	Skew [°]
1	1957	CC	G	CCP	105	60.96	3.353	3	8	0
2	1952	C	G	CCP	110	60.96	3.353	7	4	0
3	1963	PC	S	O	146	60.96	3.353	6	5	0
4	1924	CC	AD	N/A	163	–	–	3	–	0
5	2001	PC	S	O	141	60.96	3.353	3	8	0
6	2003	PC	Co	O	176	60.96	3.353	4	12	0
7	1975	PC	S	O	110	60.96	3.353	3	8	0
8	2001	PC	S	O	141	60.96	3.353	3	8	0
9	2002	PC	S	O	141	60.96	3.353	3	7	0
10	1957	S	Cu	N/A	–	–	–	3	–	30
11	2005	PC	S	CPP	98	60.96	3.353	1	6	0

Material: PC = Prestressed Concrete; CC = Continuous concrete; C = Concrete; S = Steel.
Design Type: G = Girder; S = Slab; AD = Arch Deck; Co = Concrete; Cu = Culvert.
Deck Structure: CCP = Concrete Cast-in Place; CPP = Concrete Precast Panels; O= Other; N/A = Not Available;

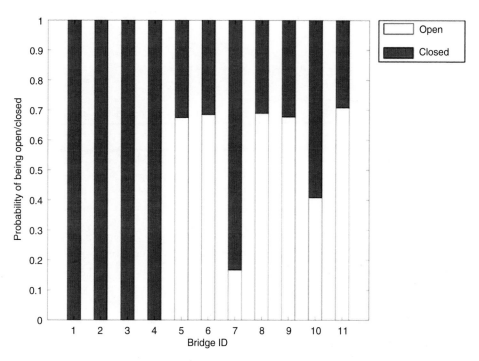

Figure 13.2 The probability of being open/closed for the bridges in the transportation infrastructure in the immediate aftermath of the seismic event.

Table 13.4 List of activities for recovery for a generic RC bridge in a complete damage state

Number	Activity	Duration (Days)			Predecessor(s)
		Lower Bound	Most Likely	Upper Bound	
1	Inspection	2	3	5	–
2	Bidding	15	20	30	1
3	Mobilization	5	7	15	2
4	Structure excavation	0.5	1	1	3
5	Erection of temporary support (Column)	1	2	3	3
6	Erection of temporary support (Abutment)	1	2	3	3
7	Remove existing column	0.5	1	2	5 and 6
8	Place reinforcement (Column)	1	2	3	7
9	Place column forms	0.5	1	2	8
10	Pour concrete (Column)	0.5	1	2	9
11	Curing (Column)	7	10	15	10
12	Demo existing shear key (Abutment)	1	1	3	6
13	Install reinforcement (Abutment)	0.5	1	2	12
14	Install forms (Abutment)	0.5	1	2	13
15	Pour concrete (Abutment)	0.5	1	2	14
16	Curing concrete (Abutment)	7	10	15	15
17	Strip forms (Abutment)	0.5	1	2	16
18	Install replacement bearings (Abutment)	0.5	1	2	17
19	Remove of temporary support (Abutment)	0.5	1	2	18
20	Repair cracks with epoxy (Abutment)	0.5	1	2	19
21	Repair spalls (Abutment)	0.5	1	2	19
22	Install joint seal assembly (Abutment)	0.5	1	2	20 and 21
23	Remove forms (Column)	0.5	1	2	11
24	Removal of temporary support (Column)	0.5	1	2	23
25	Structure backfill	1	2	4	24

aftermath of the seismic event as a function of time. The figure shows the confidence band (between 15% and 85% quantiles) due to the uncertainty in the damage state of the bridges in the immediate aftermath of the seismic event. We can observe that the full network connectivity is restored after about six months. The figure also shows the estimate of resilience metrics, according to Sharma et al. (2018), $\rho = \int_0^{T_R} \tau dQ(\tau) / \int_0^{T_R} dQ(\tau)$ and $\chi = \sqrt{\int_0^{T_R} \tau dQ(\tau) / \int_0^{T_R} dQ(\tau)}$, where $Q = P(\delta_i < \infty)$; ρ is the center of resilience that captures the recovery pace; T_R is the recovery duration; and χ is the resilience bandwidth that captures the recovery spread.

13.7 Conclusions

The chapter presented the theory of physics-based fragility functions. Fragility functions estimate the conditional probability of reaching or exceeding a performance level given a (set of) hazard intensity measure(s). To formulate physics-based fragility functions, capacity, and demand models are developed based on rules of physics and mechanics as well as information from computer simulations, laboratory tests, and field data. Using the probabilistic capacity and demand models, fragility functions are obtained by performing a rigorous reliability

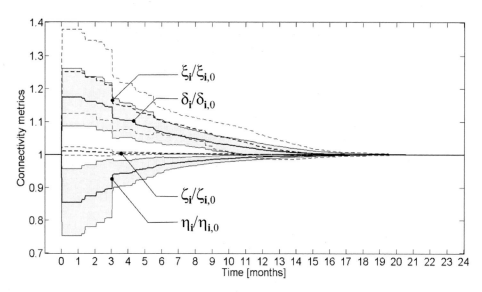

Figure 13.3 The recovery curve of the transportation infrastructure in terms of topology-based connectivity measures.

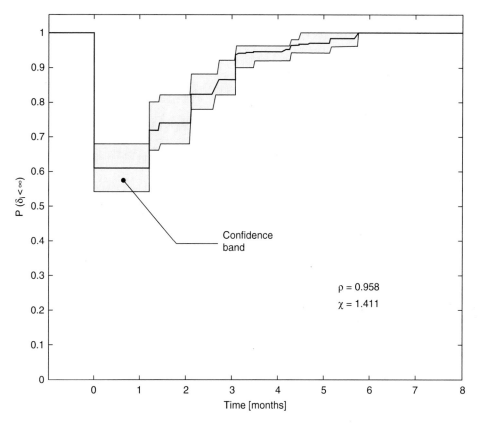

Figure 13.4 The time-varying probability of a connected transportation infrastructure during the recovery.

analysis. The chapter presented the formulation of time-varying fragility functions that consider the effects of deterioration mechanisms and improvement strategies. The chapter also presented how to incorporate the information from structural health monitoring and non-destructive testing in the fragility and recovery functions. After reviewing the general theory, the chapter discussed the state-of-the-art physics-based fragility and recovery functions for bridges subject to multiple hazards. Recovery functions describe the change in the state or performance of a structure as it is subject to an improvement strategy (maintenance, mitigation, repair, or replacement.) The chapter then showed how to use fragility and recovery functions for the reliability and resilience analysis of transportation infrastructure. As an illustration, the chapter showed a reliability and resilience analysis of the transportation infrastructure of Seaside, Oregon subject to a seismic hazard.

Acknowledgements

This work was supported in part by the National Science Foundation (NSF) under Award No. 1638346 and by the National Institute of Standards and Technology (NIST) through the Center for Risk-Based Community Resilience Planning under Award No. 70NANB15H044. Opinions and findings presented are those of the authors and do not necessarily reflect the views of the sponsor.

References

ASCE (2017) Infrastructure Report Card: A Comprehensive Assessment of America's Infrastructure.

Bakhtiary E. and Gardoni P. (2016) "Probabilistic seismic demand model and fragility estimates for rocking symmetric blocks," *Engineering Structures* 114, 25–34.

Bai J.W., Gardoni P,. and Hueste M.B.D. (2011) "Story-specific demand models and seismic fragility estimates for multi-story buildings," *Structural Safety* 33, 96–107.

Bai J.W., Hueste M.B.D., and Gardoni P. (2015) "Seismic vulnerability assessment of tilt-up concrete structures," *Structure and Infrastructure Engineering* 11, 1131–46.

Basöz N.I. and Kiremidjian. A.S. (1998) "Evaluation of bridge damage data from the Loma Prieta and Northridge, California earthquakes," Technical Report MCEER No. 98-0004 US Multidisciplinary Center for Earthquake Engineering Research (MCEER) Buffalo, NY.

Bisadi V., Gardoni P., and Head M. (2011) "Probabilistic capacity models and fragility estimates for steel pedestals used to elevate bridges," *Journal of Structural Engineering* 137, 1583–92.

Bisadi V., Gardoni P., and Head M. (2013) "Probabilistic demand models and fragility estimates for bridges elevated with steel pedestals," *Journal of Structural Engineering* 139, 1515–28.

Bisadi V., Gardoni P., and Head M. (2014) "Decision analysis for elevating bridge decks with steel pedestals," *Structure and Infrastructure Engineering* 10, 1059–67.

Boakye J., Guidotti R., Gardoni P., and Murphy C. (2018) "The role of critical infrastructure on the societal impact of natural hazards," *Nature Sustainability* (in preparation).

Bolduc L.C., Gardoni P., and Briaud J.-L. (2008) "Probability of exceedance estimates for scour depth around bridge piers," *Journal of Geotechnical and Geoenvironmental Engineering* 134, 175–84.

Boore D.M. and Atkinson G.M. (2008) "Ground-motion prediction equations for the average horizontal component of PGA, PGV, and 5%-damped PSA at spectral periods between 0.01 s and 10.0 s," *Earthquake Spectra* 24(1), 99–138.

Bracci J.M., Gardoni P., Trejo D., and Eck K. (2011) "Performance of lap splices in large scale column specimens affected by ASR and/or DEF," TxDOT Report No. 0-5722. Texas Transportation Institute, Texas Department of Transportation Austin, Texas, USA.

Briaud J.-L., Brandimarte L., Wang J., and D'Odorico P. (2007) "Probability of scour depth exceedance owing to hydrologic uncertainty," *Georisk: Assessment and Management of Risk for Engineered Systems and Geohazards* 1, 77–88.

Briaud J.-L., Gardoni P., and Yao C. (2014) "Statistical, risk, and reliability analyses of bridge scour," *Journal of Geotechnical and Geoenvironmental Engineering* 140, 04013011.

Choe D., Gardoni P., and Rosowsky D. (2007) "Closed-form fragility estimates, parameter sensitivity and Bayesian updating for RC columns," *Journal of Engineering Mechanics* 133, 833–43.

Choe D., Gardoni P., Rosowsky D., and Haukaas T. (2008) "Probabilistic capacity models and seismic fragility estimates for RC columns subject to corrosion," *Reliability Engineering and System Safety* 93, 383–93.

Choe D., Gardoni P., Rosowsky D., and Haukaas T. (2009) "Seismic fragility estimates for reinforced concrete bridges subject to corrosion," *Structural Safety* 31, 275–83.

Choe D., Gardoni P., and Rosowsky D. (2010) "Fragility increment function for deteriorating reinforced concrete bridge columns," *Journal of Engineering Mechanics* 136, 969–78.

Choi E., DesRoches R., and Nielson B. (2004) "Seismic fragility of typical bridges in moderate seismic zones," *Engineering Structures* 26, 187–99.

Eck Olave M.K., Bracci J.M., Gardoni P., and Trejo D. (2015a) "Performance of RC columns affected by ASR. I: Accelerated exposure and damage," *Journal of Bridge Engineering* 20, 04014069.

Eck Olave M.K., Bracci J.M., Gardoni P., and Trejo D. (2015b) "Performance of RC columns affected by ASR. II: Experiments and assessment," *Journal of Bridge Engineering* 20, 04014070.

Elhami Khorasani N., Garlock, M., and Gardoni P. (2014) "Fire load: Survey data, recent standards, and probabilistic models for office buildings," *Engineering Structures* 58, 152–65.

Elhami Khorasani N., Gardoni P., and Garlock M. (2015) "Probabilistic fire analysis: Material models and evaluation of steel structural members," *Journal of Structural Engineering* 141, 04015050.

Elhami Khorasani N., Garlock M., and Gardoni P. (2016b) "Probabilistic performance-based evaluation of a tall steel moment resisting frame under post-earthquake fires," *Journal of Structural Fire Engineering* 7, 193–216.

FDOT (2001) Mid-bay bridge post-tensioning evaluation Final Report prepared for Florida Department of Transportation Tallahassee, Florida, USA.

Frangopol D.M., Lin K.-Y., and Estes, A.C. (1997) "Life-cycle cost design of deteriorating structures," *Journal of Structural Engineering* 123, 1390–1401.

Gardoni P. ed. (2017) *Risk and Reliability Analysis: Theory and Applications.* New York: Springer.

Gardoni P. and LaFave J.M. eds. (2016) *Multi-hazard Approaches to Civil Infrastructure Engineering.* New York: Springer.

Gardoni P. and Murphy C. (2008) "Recovery from natural and man-made disasters as capabilities restoration and enhancement," *International Journal of Sustainable Development and Planning* 3(4), 1–17.

Gardoni P. and Rosowsky D. (2011) "Seismic fragility increment functions for deteriorating reinforced concrete bridges," *Structure and Infrastructure Engineering* 7, 869–79.

Gardoni P. and Trejo D. (2013a) "Seismic reliability of deteriorating reinforced concrete (RC) bridges," in Tesfamariam S. and Goda K. eds, *Handbook of Seismic Risk Analysis and Management of Civil Infrastructure Systems*, Woodhead Publishing Ltd.

Gardoni P. and Trejo, D. (2013b) "Probabilstic seismic demand models and fragiltiy estimates for reinforced concrete bridges with base isolation," *Earthquakes and Structures* 4, 525–55.

Gardoni P., Der Kiureghian A., and Mosalam K.M. (2002) "Probabilistic capacity models and fragility estimates for reinforced concrete columns based on experimental observations," *Journal of Engineering Mechanics* 128, 1024–38.

Gardoni P., Mosalam K.M., and Der Kiureghian A. (2003) "Probabilistic seismic demand models and fragility estimates for RC bridges," *Journal of Earthquake Engineering* 7, 79–106.

Gardoni P., Reinschmidt K.F., and Kumar R. (2007) "A probabilistic framework for Bayesian adaptive forecasting of project progress," *Computer-Aided Civil and Infrastructure Engineering* 22(3), 182–96.

Gardoni P., Pillai R.G., Hueste M.B.D, Reinschmidt K., and Trejo D. (2009) "Probabilistic capacity models for corroding posttensioning strands calibrated using laboratory results," *Journal of Engineering Mechanics* 135, 906–16.

Gardoni P. Murphy C., and Rowell A. eds. (2016) *Risk Analysis of Natural Hazards.* New York: Springer.

Guidotti R. and Gardoni, P. (2018) "Modeling of interdependent critical infrastructure for regional risk and resilience analysis," in Gardoni P. ed., *Handbook of Sustainable and Resilient Infrastructure.* Routledge.

Guidotti R., Gardoni P., and Chen Y. (2017a) "Network reliability analysis with link and nodal weights and auxiliary nodes," *Structural Safety* 65, 12–26.

Guidotti R. Gardoni P., and Chen Y. (2017b) "Multi-layer heterogeneous network model for interdependent infrastructure systems," *12th International Conference on Structural Safety & Reliability (ICOSSAR 2017).* TU Wien, Vienna (Austria) 2947–56.

Guidotti R., Gardoni P., and Rosenheim N. (2018) "Integration of physical infrastructure and social systems in communities' reliability and resilience analysis," *Reliability Engineering and System Safety* (under review).

Guikema S. and Gardoni P. (2009) "Reliability estimation for networks of reinforced concrete bridges," *Journal of Infrastructure Systems* 15, 61–9.

Huang Q., Gardoni P., and Hurlebaus S. (2009) "Probabilistic capacity models and fragility estimates for reinforced concrete columns incorporating NDT data," *Journal of Engineering Mechanics* 135, 1384–92.

Huang Q., Gardoni P., and Hurlebaus S. (2010) "Probabilistic seismic demand models and fragility estimates for reinforced concrete highway bridges with one single-column bent," *Journal of Engineering Mechanics* 136, 1340–53.

Huang Q., Gardoni P., and Hurlebaus S. (2011) "Predicting concrete compressive strength using combined ultrasonic pulse velocity and rebound number data," *ACI Materials Journal* 108, 403–12.

Huang Q., Gardoni P., and Hurlebaus S. (2012) "A probabilistic damage detection approach using vibration-based nondestructive testing," *Structural Safety* 38, 11–21.

Huang Q., Gardoni P., Trejo D., and Pagnotta, A. (2014) "Probabilistic model for steel-concrete bond behavior in bridge columns affected by alkali silica reactions," *Engineering Structures* 71, 1–11.

Huang Q., Gardoni P., and Hurlebaus S. (2015) "Adaptive reliability analysis of reinforced concrete bridges subject to seismic loading using nondestructive testing," *Journal of Risk and Uncertainty in Engineering Systems Part A: Civ. Eng.* 1, 04015014.

Jia G. and Gardoni P. (2017) "Stochastic life-cycle analysis: renewal-theory life-cycle analysis with state-dependent deterioation stochastic models," *Reliability Engineering & System Safety* (under review).

Jia G. and Gardoni P. (2018a) "State-dependent stochastic models: A general stochastic framework for modeling deterioration engineering systems considering multiple deterioration processes and their interactions," *Strucural Safety* 72, 99–110.

Jia G. and Gardoni P. (2018b) "Simulation-based approach for estimation of stochastic peformances of deteriorating engineering systems," *Probabilistic Engineering Mechanics* 52, 28–39.

Jia G., Tabandeh A., and Gardoni P. (2017) "Life-cycle analysis of engineering systems: Modeling deterioration, instantaneous reliability, and resilience," in Gardoni P ed., *Risk and Reliability Analysis: Theory and Applications.* New York: Springer.

Kang W.-H., Song J., and Gardoni P. (2008) "Matrix-based system reliability method and applications to bridge networks," *Reliability Engineering and System Safety* 93, 1584–93.

Kumar R. and Gardoni P. (2012) "Modeling structural degradation of RC bridge columns subjected to earthquakes and their fragility estimates," *Journal of Structural Engineering* 138, 42–51.

Kumar R. and Gardoni P. (2014a) "Renewal theory-based life-cycle analysis of deteriorating engineering systems," *Structural Safety* 50, 94–102.

Kumar R. and Gardoni P. (2014b) "Effect of seismic degradation on the fragility of reinforced concrete bridges," *Engineering Structures* 79, 267–75.

Kumar R., Gardoni P., and Sanchez-Silva M. (2009) "Effect of cumulative seismic damage and corrosion on life-cycle cost of reinforced concrete bridges," *Earthquake Engineering and Structural Dynamics* 38, 887–905.

Kumar R., Cline D.B.H., and Gardoni P. (2015) "A stochastic framework to model deterioration in engineering systems," *Structural Safety* 53, 36–43.

Kurtz N., Song J., and Gardoni P. (2015) "Seismic reliability analysis of deteriorating representative US West Coast bridge transportation networks," *ASCE Journal of Structural Engineering.* 10.1061/(ASCE) ST.1943-541X.0001368, C4015010.

Latora V. and Marchiori M. (2001) "Efficient behavior of small-world networks," *Physical Review Letters* 87(19), 198701.

Lee Y.J., Song L., Gardoni P., and Lim H.W. (2011) "Post-hazard flow capacity of bridge transportation network considering structural deterioration of bridges," *Structure and Infrastructure Engineering* 7, 509–21.

Liu K., Paulino G., and Gardoni P. (2016a) "Segmental multi-point linearization for parameter sensitivity approximation in reliability analysis," *Structural Safety* 62, 101–15.

Liu K., Paulino G., and Gardoni P. (2016b) "Reliability-based topology optimization using a new method for sensitivity approximation – application to ground structures," *Journal of Structural and Multidisciplinary Optimization* 54, 553–71.

Mackie K.R., Wong J.M., and Stojadinovic B. (2007) "Integrated probabilistic performance-based evaluation of benchmark reinforced concrete bridges," Technical Report PEER 2007/09 Pacific Earthquake Engineering Research Center University of California, Berkeley, California.

Mardfekri M. and Gardoni P. (2013) "Probabilistic demand models and fragility estimates for offshore wind turbine support structures," *Engineering Structures* 52, 478–87.

Mardfekri M. and Gardoni P. (2014) "Multi-hazard reliability assessment of offshore wind turbines," *Wind Energy* 18, 1433–50.

Mardfekri M., Gardoni P., and Bisadi V. (2015) "Service reliability of offshore wind turbines," *International Journal of Sustainable Energy* 34, 468–84.

Mathakari S., Gardoni P., Agarwal P., and Raich A. (2007) "Reliability-based optimal design of electrical transmission towers using multi-objective genetic algorithms," *Computer-Aided Civil and Infrastructure Engineering* 22, 282–92.

Mori Y. and Ellingwood B.R. (1993) "Reliability-based service-life assessment of aging concrete structures," *Journal of Structural Engineering* 119, 1600–21.

Mousavi M.E. and Gardoni P. (2014) "A simplified method for reliability- and integrity-based design of engineering systems and its application to offshore mooring systems," *Mar. Struct.* 36, 88–104.

Mousavi M.E., Gardoni P., and Maadooliat M. (2013) "Progressive reliability method and its application to offshore mooring systems," *Engineering Structures* 56, 2131–8.

Murphy C. and Gardoni P. (2006) "The role of society in engineering risk analysis: A capabilities-based approach," *Risk Analysis* 26, 1073–83.

Murphy C., Gardoni P., and Harris C.E. (2011) "Classification and moral evaluation of uncertainties in engineering modeling," *Science and Engineering Ethics* 17(3), 553–70.

Padgett J.E. and DesRoches R. (2008) "Methodology for the development of analytical fragility curves for retrofitted bridges," *Earthquake Engineering & Structural Dynamics* 37(8), 1157–74.

Pillai R.G., Gardoni P., Trejo D., Hueste M.B.D., and Reinschmidt K.F. (2010a) "Probabilistic models for the tensile strength of corroding strands in post-tensioned, segmental concrete bridges," *Journal of Materials in Civil Engineering* 22, 967–77.

Pillai R.G., Hueste M.B.D., Gardoni P., Trejo D., and Reinschmidt K.F. (2010b) "Time-variant service reliability of post-tensioned, segmental, concrete bridges exposed to corrosive environments," *Engineering Structures* 32, 2596–2605.

Pillai R.G., Trejo D., Gardoni P., Hueste M.B.D., and Reinschmidt K.F. (2014) "Time-variant flexural reliability of post-tensioned, segmental concrete bridges exposed to corrosive environments," *Journal of Structural Engineering* 140, A4014018.

Poston R.W. and Wouters J.P. (1998) Durability of precast segmental bridges 20–7/Task 92, National Cooperative Highway Research Program (NCHRP) Washington, DC, USA.

Ramamoorthy S.K., Gardoni P., and Bracci J.M. (2006) "Probabilistic demand models and fragility curves for reinforced concrete frames," *Journal of Structural Engineering* 132, 1563–72.

Ramamoorthy S.K., Gardoni P., and Bracci J.M. (2008) "Seismic fragility and confidence bounds for gravity load designed reinforced concrete frames of varying height," *Journal of Structural Engineering* 134, 639–50.

Rosenheim N., Guidotti R., and Gardoni P. (2017) "Integration of detailed household characteristic data with critical infrastructure and its implementation to post-hazard resilience modeling," *2nd International Workshop on Modelling of Physical, Economic and Social Systems for Resilience Assessment*, Ispra (Italy).

Rosenheim N., Guidotti R., and Gardoni P. (2018) "Integration of household characteristic data with critical infrastructure and its implementation to post-hazard resilience modeling," *Sustainable and Resilient Infrastructure* (in preparation).

Sharma H., Hurlebaus S., and Gardoni P. (2012) "Performance-based response evaluation of reinforced concrete columns subject to vehicle impact," *International Journal of Impact Engineering* 43, 52–62.

Sharma H., Gardoni, P., and Hurlebaus S. (2014) "Probabilistic demand model and performance-based fragility estimates for RC column subject to vehicle collision," *Engineering Structures* 74, 86–95.

Sharma H., Gardoni P., and Hurlebaus S. (2015) "Performance–based probabilistic capacity models and fragility estimates for RC columns subject to vehicle collision," *Computer-Aided Civil and Infrastructure Engineering* 30, 555–69.

Sharma N., Tabandeh A., and Gardoni P. (2018) "Resilience analysis: a mathematical formulation to model resilience of engineering systemsm," *Sustainable and Resilient Infrastructure* 3, 49–67.

Simon J., Bracci J.M., and Gardoni P. (2010) "Seismic response and fragility of deteriorated reinforced concrete bridges," *ASCE Journal of Structural Engineering* 136, 1273–81.

Stubbs N. and Kim J.H. (1996) "Damage localization in structures without baseline modal parameters," *Am Inst. Aeronaut. Astronaut.* 34, 1644–9.

Sun B., Gardoni P., and Xiao R. (2016) "Probabilistic aerostability capacity models and fragility estimates for cable-stayed bridge decks based on wind tunnel test data," *Engineering Structures* 126, 106–20.

Tabandeh A. and Gardoni P. (2014) "Probabilistic capacity models and fragility estimates for RC columns retrofitted with FRP composites," *Engineering Structures* 74, 13–22.

Tabandeh A. and Gardoni P. (2015) "Empirical Bayes approach for developing hierarchical probabilistic predictive models and its application to the seismic reliability analysis of FRP-retrofitted RC bridges," *Journal of Risk and Uncertainty in Engineering Systems Part A: Civ. Eng.* 1, 04015002.

Vu K.A.T. and Stewart M.G. (2000) "Structural reliability of concrete bridges including improved chloride-induced corrosion models," *Structural Safety* 22, 313–33.

Williams R.J., Gardoni P., and Bracci J.M. (2009) "Decision analysis for seismic retrofit of structures," *Structural Safety* 31, 188–96.

Xu H. and Gardoni P. (2016) "Probabilistic capacity and seismic demand models and fragility estimates for reinforced concrete buildings based on three-dimensional analyses," *Engineering Structures* 112, 200–14.

Xu H. and Gardoni P. (2018) "Improved latent space approach for modelling non-stationary spatial-temporal random fields," *Spatial Statistics* 23, 160–81.

Xu Y.L. (2013) *Wind Effects on Cable-Supported Bridges.* Singapore: John Wiley & Sons.

You T., Gardoni P., and Hurlebaus S. (2014) "Iterative damage index method for structural health monitoring," *Struct. Monit. Maint.* 1, 89–110.

Zheng R.H. and Ellingwood B.R. (1998) "Role of non-destructive evaluation in time-dependent reliability analysis," *Structural Safety* 20, 325–39.

Zhong J., Gardoni P., Rosowsky D., and Haukaas T. (2008) "Probabilistic seismic demand models and fragility estimates for reinforced concrete bridges with two-column bents," *Journal of Engineering Mechanics* 134, 495–504.

Zhong J., Gardoni P., and Rosowsky D. (2009) "Bayesian updating of seismic demand models and fragility estimates for reinforced concrete bridges with two-column bents," *Journal of Earthquake Engineering* 13, 716–35.

Zhong J., Gardoni P., and Rosowsky D. (2010) "Stiffness degradation and time to cracking of cover concrete in reinforced concrete structure subject to corrosion," *Journal of Engineering Mechanics* 136, 209–19.

Zhong J., Gardoni P., and Rosowsky D. (2012) "Seismic fragility estimates for corroding reinforced concrete bridges," *Structure and Infrastructure Engineering* 8, 55–69.

Zhu L., Elwood K.J., Haukaas T., and Gardoni P. (2006) "Application of a probabilistic drift capacity model for shear-critical columns," *ACI Special Publication* 236, 81–102.

Part III
Resilience of different systems

Electric and power infrastructure

14

Modeling the time-varying performance of electrical infrastructure during post disaster recovery using tensors

Neetesh Sharma[1] and Paolo Gardoni[2]

[1] DEPARTMENT OF CIVIL AND ENVIRONMENTAL ENGINEERING, MAE CENTER: CREATING A MULTI-HAZARD APPROACH TO ENGINEERING, UNIVERSITY OF ILLINOIS AT URBANA-CHAMPAIGN, URBANA, IL, USA; NSHARM11@ILLINOIS.EDU

[2] DEPARTMENT OF CIVIL AND ENVIRONMENTAL ENGINEERING, MAE CENTER: CREATING A MULTI-HAZARD APPROACH TO ENGINEERING, UNIVERSITY OF ILLINOIS AT URBANA-CHAMPAIGN, URBANA, IL, USA; GARDONI@ILLINOIS.EDU

14.1 Introduction

Modern societies depend on critical infrastructure to function (Corotis 2009; Ellingwood et al. 2016; Gardoni et al. 2016). Critical infrastructure enable individuals to fulfill their needs (Murphy & Gardoni 2006, 2007, 2011; Gardoni & Murphy 2008, 2009). For example, mobility and having access to energy are directly dependent on transportation and power infrastructure, while food availability and access to education can be indirectly affected by infrastructure performance (Tabandeh et al. 2018). Infrastructure are vulnerable to a variety of natural and anthropogenic hazards (Gardoni and LaFave 2016). Infrastructure is also interdependent, where service disruptions in one infrastructure can lead to widespread impact and additional disruptions in other infrastructure (Guidotti et al. 2017; Gardoni & Murphy 2018). When facing disruptive events, a timely recovery of infrastructure becomes cardinal in supporting socio-economic well-being, i.e. resilient infrastructure help communities be resilient (Sharma et al. 2018a, 2018b).

The need of mitigating and managing the risk to critical infrastructure has been advocated by researchers in the past (e.g.; Kang et al. 2008; Gardoni & Murphy 2008; Guikema & Gardoni 2009). Modeling the risk and resilience of critical infrastructure requires a general framework that combines different infrastructure and captures their dependencies and interdependencies, while considering their deterioration and recovery processes. However, developing a rigorous and comprehensive mathematical framework for risk and resilience analysis still remains challenging with several underlying unresolved issues pertaining to the modeling of individual infrastructure and their interdependencies. Specifically, for the electrical infrastructure three of the most significant challenges are the following: (1) the information on privately owned electrical infrastructure is often not available or incomplete; (2) electrical infrastructure has non-linear failure mechanisms pertaining to power flow (e.g., voltage collapse and dynamic instability), which gives rise to cascading failures and also makes processes such as service recovery non-trivial and computationally expensive to analyze; (3) electrical infrastructure typically has large geographic footprints and complexity, which require information and subsequent modeling of regions potentially significantly larger than the region of immediate interest and the boundaries of the modeled portion of the infrastructure are not always easy to define.

Birchfield et al. (2017) discussed the challenge of data availability and provided a methodology to generate synthetic power flow networks. Baldick et al. (2008), Papic et al. (2011), and Vaiman et al. (2012) provided reviews of the literature on cascading failures in electrical infrastructure using different power flow models. Song et al. (2016) broadly categorized the power flow models into quasi steady state direct current (DC) power flow, quasi steady state alternating current (AC) power flow, hybrid models, statistical models, and topological models. Disaster impact studies on electric infrastructure tend to favor the simpler models such as topological connectivity, maximum flow algorithm, and DC power flow to monitor power infrastructure performance (Adachi & Ellingwood 2008; Duenas-Osorio et al. 2007). The challenge of selecting boundaries for the power network analysis has not been well discussed in literature. Past studies typically implicitly select the boundaries such that the footprint of the electrical infrastructure is identical to the region of interest (Dong et al. 2004; Shinozuka et al. 2007; Unnikrishnan & van de Lindt 2016).

This chapter presents a general framework that addresses these challenges using a tensor based representation (Sharma & Gardoni 2018a). In this framework, we model the infrastructure as a collection of mathematical network objects. We characterize each of the networks using the general performance measures of capacity, demand and supply as well as derived performance measures for different functionalities. We provide a glossary of terms including network, capacity, demand, supply, performance, and interface, to clarify their meanings in the context of infrastructure. The mathematical framework then explains how to estimate each of the defined measures using the state variables (material properties, boundary conditions, etc.) of the infrastructure components. We then use the presented framework to model the electrical infrastructure. We characterize the electrical infrastructure using available data and the approach presented in Birchfield et al. (2017). The boundary and resolution selection depends on several factors such as the control characteristics and the hazard footprint. We use a steady state AC power flow model (Glover et al. 2008) to estimate the electric supply measure. For each component we develop a derived performance measure and then use an aggregated measure to capture the infrastructure performance. Finally, we analyze the infrastructure resilience by obtaining a stochastic recovery curve and measuring the infrastructure resilience in terms of the partial descriptors of the recovery curve (Sharma et al. 2018a).

The chapter is organized into six sections. The next section presents the glossary for infrastructure. Section 14.3 presents the mathematic representation of infrastructure. Section 14.4 describes the power infrastructure model for a given region of interest. Section 14.5 illustrates the proposed framework using the example of Shelby County, Tennessee as the region of interest under a post-earthquake recovery scenario. Finally, the last section summarizes the chapter and draws some conclusions.

14.2 Glossary for infrastructure

This section formalizes the definitions of some of the basic terms related to infrastructure.

Capacity: Capacity of an infrastructure is defined as a measure of its ability to generate or transmit the specific resources or services pertaining to the purpose of the specific infrastructure. Capacity of an infrastructure is typically distributed both spatially over its various components and temporally. An infrastructure may have multiple capacity measures necessary for capturing a variety of needs for resource/service generation and maintaining safety of operation.

Control system: A control system is defined as a system that manages the behavior of an infrastructure (Dorf & Bishop 2011). Control systems in an infrastructure manage the portion of capacity which is mobilized by the system at any given time.

Demand: Demand for an infrastructure is defined as the measure of the needs of its consumers in terms of the resources and services provided by the specific infrastructure (Gardoni et al. 2003; Suganthi & Samuel 2012). Similar to capacity, demand for an infrastructure may also be distributed spatially over its various components and temporally. An infrastructure may have multiple demand measures corresponding to the various capacities. A failure can be considered to occur when the demand on an infrastructure is more than its capacity (Gardoni et al. 2002; Gardoni 2017). When the demand on an infrastructure is less than its capacity, the system should only use a portion of its capacity.

Deterioration: Deterioration in an infrastructure is defined as a process by which its components decline in quality over time. Deterioration may include several processes depending upon the vulnerabilities of the infrastructure. Deterioration can be continuous over time or occur suddenly due to exposure to a damaging event (Kumar & Gardoni 2014a).

Infrastructure: Shishko and Aster (1995) defined a system as "[t]he combination of elements that function together to produce the capability to meet a need. The elements include all hardware, software, equipment, facilities, personnel, processes, and procedures needed for this purpose." We adopt the same definition also for infrastructure, as they serve basic needs of modern society.

Interface: An interface is defined as a boundary over which infrastructure or networks (defined below) interact. Dependencies among infrastructure or networks exist at the interfaces. Interface functions are mathematical mappings which modify the base measures of capacity and demand of individual infrastructure or networks to include the effects of dependencies (Sharma & Gardoni 2018a).

Network: A network is defined as a set of pairwise related objects where each of those objects have attributes other than the topology of their relations (Newman 2003). Infrastructure can be mathematically represented by multiple interdependent network layers where individual network layers have specific capacity and demand measures, which serve a specific need in collectively attaining the purpose of the infrastructure. For example, structural network layer for physical integrity and flow network layer for a general commodity exchange.

Performance: Performance of an infrastructure is defined as a measure of how well the infrastructure is fulfilling the needs of the stakeholders. Different stakeholders such as the owners, the regulators, and the consumers may have different requirements and measures for infrastructure performance. The owners typically prioritize profitability and efficiency. The regulators represent the collective societal interests and thus prioritize measures concerning quality, reliability, environmental protection, and economic justice. The consumers are typically concerned with the impact of the infrastructure services on their individual socio-economic activities which is measured in terms of functionality.

State variables: State variables are defined as the variables that describe the dynamic state of an infrastructure. State variables represent physical quantities that are specific to the individual network layers for specific infrastructure, such as material properties and geometry for structural components, and voltage and frequency for electrical components. The state variables that can be modified using the control system of the infrastructure are called the control state variables (e.g., voltage and active power at the generators in power infrastructure). Capacity and demand measures of an infrastructure can be estimated as functions of the state variables and other parameters that have uncertainty associated with them. Life-cycle processes such as deterioration and recovery affect the state variables, and, through the state variables, the quantities and measures derived from them (Jia & Gardoni 2018; Guidotti et al. 2016).

Supply: Supply is defined as the portion of the capacity that is mobilized by an infrastructure to meet an imposed demand. The supply for a particular capacity and demand is not unique, and depends on the control state variables. Different infrastructure may present different challenges to control supply. Control challenges may arise from infeasibility, inefficiency, cost, computation issues, legality, and ethics (Housner et al. 1997; Kundur et al. 1994). The supply of an infrastructure (along with its capacity and demand) is needed to measure the infrastructure performance in terms of derived measures such as efficiency, reliability, and functionality.

Tolerance: Tolerance of an infrastructure can be defined as its ability to avoid the deterioration of its components (sustain its capacity) and be functional while serving in an unbalanced demand-supply condition (Sharma & Gardoni 2018a). An unbalanced/low-quality supply may increase the rate of deterioration.

14.3 Mathematical representation of infrastructure

A general mathematical representation of infrastructure should (1) allow using different underlying models for the various infrastructure categories (electrical, water, sewerage, transportation); and (2) maintain a consistent framework to handle their interfaces (used in modeling dependencies/interdependencies.) A representation based on graph theory is a natural choice in this regard. Sharma and Gardoni (2018a) proposed such a framework, which is succinctly explained here specifically for electrical infrastructure.

Graph theory deals with the study of graphs, which are defined as mathematical structures or diagrams amounting from pairwise related objects. The objects that make the graph are called vertices (points or nodes) and the relation between a pair of nodes is called an edge (arc, line or link.) A graph can be written as $G = (V, E)$, where V is the set of nodes and E is the set of links. A network is defined as a graph in which the nodes and links have attributes other than their topological identities (e.g., names, hierarchy, functions, and type.) Thus infrastructure can be represented as a collection of network layers. Each of the network layers have nodes and links with their respective state variables as attributes.

14.3.1 Models for network capacity, demand, and supply

The topology of any directed graph with $|V|$ number of nodes can be represented as a $|V| \times |V|$ node adjacency matrix, $\mathbf{A}$, where $\mathbf{A}_{ij} = \mathbf{1}_{\{(i,j) \in E\}}$ (Watts & Strogatz 1998; Guidotti et al. 2016). Thus we need at most $|V|^2$ place holders to represent any quantities of interest for a network with the topology graph $G = (V, E)$. If a tensor is chosen to represent a general physical quantity for the network, the first two indices (i,i) refer to a nodal component and (i, j), $i \neq j$, refer to a link component.

The ordered set of state variables of a typical component indexed (i, j) can be written as the vector $\mathbf{x}_{i,j}$. The state of the whole network at any time τ can then be represented by a $|V| \times |V| \times \max_{\forall (i,j)}(|\mathbf{x}_{i,j}|)$ third order tensor $\mathbf{x}(\tau)$, where the mode-3 (tube) fibers represent the respective state variables for the individual components. Among the state variables there are control state variables, $\mathbf{x}_{:,:,\forall k \in \kappa}(\tau)$, and non-control state variables, $\mathbf{x}_{:,:,\forall k \notin \kappa}(\tau)$ (where κ is the index set of the control state variable types such that $\mathbf{x}_{:,:,k}(\tau)$ is the kth frontal slice of the tensor $\mathbf{x}$).

The base (i.e., interface-independent) capacity of the network, which depends on the $\mathbf{x}(\tau)$ alone, can then be written as

$$\mathbf{C}(\tau) = \mathbf{C}\big[\mathbf{x}(\tau), \mathbf{\Theta}_C\big], \tag{14.1}$$

where $\mathbf{C}[\cdot]$ is the capacity tensor field, i.e. a second order tensor of functions where each element is a capacity model, and $\mathbf{\Theta}_C$ is a third order tensor containing the parameters for the respective capacity models. Similarly the base demand for the individual components can be represented as a tensor field of demand models such as

$$\mathbf{D}(\tau) = \mathbf{D}\big[\mathbf{x}(\tau), \mathbf{IM}(\tau), \mathbf{\Theta}_D\big], \tag{14.2}$$

where $\mathbf{IM}(\tau)$ is the third order tensor where the mode-3 fibers are the intensity measures for each of the component demand models in $\mathbf{D}[\cdot]$, and $\mathbf{\Theta}_D$ contains the parameters for the respective demand models.

The supply tensor field $\mathbf{S}[\cdot]$, is a measure of the control state of the network components. For example, if the supply measure is in term of flow, $\mathbf{S}[\cdot]$ gives the flow generation or consumption at the individual nodes and the flow transmitted through the individual links. In such a case, positive nodal terms represent the generated flow and negative terms represent the consumed flow. For off diagonal terms, the sign of the flow indicates the direction with respect to the order of the indices. Supply at a given time τ is a function of $\mathbf{C}(\tau)$, $\mathbf{D}(\tau)$, $\mathbf{x}_{:,:,\forall k \in \kappa}(\tau)$, and the supply parameters $\mathbf{\Theta}_S$

$$\mathbf{S}(\tau) = \mathbf{S}\big[\mathbf{x}(\tau), \mathbf{C}(\tau), \mathbf{D}(\tau), \mathbf{\Theta}_S\big]. \tag{14.3}$$

The control state variables of the network and consequently the supply for a given capacity and demand are not unique. Ascertaining the control state and the supply for a system is an optimization problem described in Section 14.3.4.

14.3.2 Infrastructure performance at the component level

A general performance measure at a time τ for the individual infrastructure components can be represented in the form of a second order tensor field

$$\mathbf{Q}(\tau) = \mathbf{Q}\left[\mathbf{C}(\tau), \mathbf{D}(\tau), \mathbf{S}(\tau)\right]. \tag{14.4}$$

For example, in a power flow network, the capacity utilization factor (plant load factor) of the generators is an important performance measure for owners, which can be written as $[\mathbf{S}(\tau) \oslash \mathbf{C}(\tau)] \odot \mathbf{1}_{\{\mathbf{C}_{i,j}(\tau) \succ 0, i=j\}}$, where $\oslash$ and $\odot$ denote respectively the elementwise division and multiplication. Similarly, the ratio of the nodal demand served is an important measure for regulators and customers and can be written as $[\mathbf{S}(\tau) \oslash \mathbf{D}(\tau)] \odot \mathbf{1}_{\{\mathbf{D}_{i,j}(\tau) \succ 0, i=j\}}$. The ratio of supply to capacity for the transmission lines is an important performance measure regarding operational safety and can be written as $[\mathbf{S}(\tau) \oslash \mathbf{C}(\tau)] \odot \mathbf{1}_{\{\mathbf{C}_{i,j}(\tau) \succ 0, i \neq j\}}$.

14.3.3 Infrastructure interfaces

The dependencies across an interface can either be with supporting networks or supported networks. The supporting networks affect the base capacity of the network under consideration while the supported networks affect the base demand on the considered network. Sharma and Gardoni (2018a) take into account the (inter)dependencies using interface functions by writing

$$\begin{cases} \mathbf{C}'(\tau) = \mathbf{C}(\tau) \odot \mathcal{M}_C(\tau) \\ \mathbf{D}'(\tau) = \mathbf{D}(\tau) \odot \mathcal{M}_D(\tau), \end{cases} \tag{14.5}$$

where $\mathbf{C}'_k(\tau)$ are the modified capacity estimates for the components of G at time τ. If we use the subscript α to indicate quantities with supported interface (forward) interactions and the subscript β to indicate supporting interface (backward) interactions, then we can write the modifying tensor field for the capacity measures as $\mathcal{M}_C(\cdot) = \mathcal{M}_C(\{\mathbf{Q}_\alpha^{[l_\beta]} : G^{[l_\beta]} \in \pi_D(G)\})$, in which $\mathbf{Q}_\alpha^{[l_\beta]}$ indicates the relevant performances of the capacity side parents $\pi_D(G)$ (i.e., supporting network layer(s) of G). Similarly $\mathbf{D}'(\tau)$ are the modified demand estimates; and $\mathcal{M}_D(\cdot) = \mathcal{M}_D(\{\mathbf{Q}_\beta^{[l_\alpha]} : G^{[l_\alpha]} \in \pi_D(G)\})$ is the modifying tensor field for the demand measures, in which $\mathbf{Q}_\beta^{[l_\alpha]}$ indicates the relevant performances of the demand side parents $\pi_D(G)$ (i.e., supported network layer(s) of G.) The modified estimates of the supply measure, $\mathbf{S}'(\tau)$, and the derived performance measures $\mathbf{Q}'(\tau)$ can then be obtained using $\mathbf{C}'(\tau)$ and $\mathbf{D}'(\tau)$ in Equation (14.3). It follows that network G itself modifies the sets of base capacities $\{\mathbf{C}^{[l_\alpha]} : G^{[l_\alpha]} \in \pi_D(G)\}$ of the supported networks and base demands $\{\mathbf{D}^{[l_\beta]} : G^{[l_\beta]} \in \pi_C(G)\}$ of the supporting networks via the relevant performances $\mathbf{Q}'_\alpha(\tau)$ and $\mathbf{Q}'_\beta(\tau)$, respectively. Thus the interdependent infrastructure with two way interactions needs to be solved for convergence.

Figure 14.1 shows how the various quantities explained above interact to model one individual network layer. The arrows indicate the dependencies among different quantities, the grey colored box for $\mathbf{S}(\tau)$ and $\mathbf{x}_{:,:,\forall k \in \kappa}(\tau)$ indicates the mutual dependence and scope for supply optimization. We show the supporting interface on the left of the network layer where $\mathbf{C}(\tau)$ (via $\mathcal{M}_C(\tau)$) and $\mathbf{Q}_\beta(\tau)$ model the incoming and outgoing interactions with the supporting interface. Similarly $\mathbf{D}(\tau)$ (via $\mathcal{M}_D(\tau)$), and $\mathbf{Q}_\alpha(\tau)$ model the incoming and outgoing interactions with the supported interface.

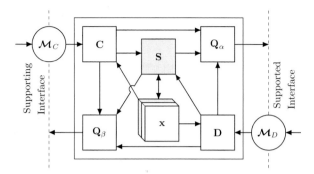

Supporting Interface

Supported Interface

Figure 14.1 The mathematical model for a general network layer and its interfaces.
Source: Sharma and Gardoni 2018a.

14.3.4 Supply optimization

Following from the discussion in Section 14.3.1, $\mathbf{S}'(\tau)$ for a network can be optimized by control-ling the state variables $\mathbf{x}_{.;:,\forall k \in \mathbf{\kappa}}(\tau)$. The objective of the supply optimization can generally be to minimize a loss function $\ell[\cdot]$ over a set of network performance measures $\{\mathbf{Q}'_{\alpha_i}(\tau), i \in \{1,2,...\}\}$. The optimization problem can be written as

$$\text{minimize} \quad \ell\left[\left\{\mathbf{Q}'_{\alpha_i}; \mathbf{w}_i, i \in \{1,2,...\}\right\}\right]$$
$$\text{subject to} \quad \mathbf{S}'(\tau) \preceq \mathbf{C}'(\tau), \tag{14.6}$$

where $\ell[\cdot]$ is the loss function defined for the chosen set of performances $\{\mathbf{Q}'_{\alpha_i}; \mathbf{w}_i, i \in \{1,2,...\}\}$, in which $\mathbf{w}_i$ is a weight vector that captures the relative importance of different components for the specific performance measure $\mathbf{Q}'_{\alpha_i}(\tau)$; and $\mathbf{S}'(\tau) \preceq \mathbf{C}'(\tau)$ are the traditional capacity constraints for flow networks. Additionally, variants of the continuity constraints such as power balance equations are applicable to $\mathbf{x}_{.;:,\forall k \in \mathbf{\kappa}}(\tau)$ for the power flow network (Glover et al. 2008).

14.4 Modeling of the electrical infrastructure

We model the electric infrastructure as two separate layers, namely the structural network and the power flow network. The structural network serves the purpose of providing the physical supporting infrastructure as well as maintaining the physical integrity whereas the power flow net-work serves the purpose of power transmission. The structural components (such as transmission towers, transformer casings, and powerhouse buildings) need to be in a functional state for the power flow capacities of the respective components to be available. This section starts with a dis-cussion on the selection of the boundaries and the resolution for the models, then provides details on the individual network layers, and finally discusses the modeling of deterioration and recovery.

14.4.1 Boundaries and resolution

Electric power infrastructure typically have large geographic footprint and complexity. For example, the whole North America is powered by five wide area synchronous grids (interconnections) where the Eastern, Western, and the Texas interconnection serve the contiguous United States. A major fault at any location in an interconnection can impact the whole interconnection with cascading failures (Song et al. 2016). The large footprint makes modeling an entire interconnection computationally challenging and requires a significant amount of input data often not available. However, because the region of interest in a risk or resilience analysis is often smaller than the footprint of an interconnection, such as a city or county, we can consider a network footprint that is smaller than a full interconnection. The selection of the boundaries of the network footprint and the resolution of the model are then important aspects in modeling of the power infrastructure serving the region of interest.

The boundary and resolution of the model depend on the following factors: (1) the footprint of the region of interest, (2) the footprint of the hazard impact, (3) the boundaries of the operation and regulatory control authorities such as balancing authorities, and reliability corporations (Hoff 2016), (4) the availability of data, (5) the type of network analysis, and (6) the interdependence characteristics of the modeled infrastructure. The electrical infrastructure of the region of interest needs be modeled with high resolution and accuracy to reduce the propagation of errors to other supported networks and to accurately capture the spatial variability of the service provided within the region of interest. The hazard impact footprint and the control boundaries define the portion of the infrastructure required for an accurate power flow analysis and recovery modeling. The resolution of the model may decrease as we consider locations farther from the region of interest. Additional details about deciding the resolution of the network flow model for critical infrastructure can be found in Guidotti et al. (2017).

14.4.2 Modeling of the physical network

The nodal and link components of the structural network layer may belong to several classes. The structural components classes depend on the hazard type and the resolution of the network modeling. We start with identifying the components based on their vulnerability to the hazard and availability of relevant capacity and demand models, or fragility estimates (see Gardoni et al. (2002) and Gardoni (2017) for a formal definition of fragility estimates). For example, FEMA (2014) provides seismic fragility estimates for transformers, disconnect switches, circuit breakers, and distribution circuits. FEMA (2014) also provides the combined fragility estimates for substations as a collection of different components. Thus one can choose to model the individual component classes for circuit breakers, disconnect switches, etc., or model a substation as a component class. This choice depends on the desired resolution of the models.

We define the structural network, $G^{[1]}$, as the first network layer of the electric infrastructure, where the superscript square bracket indicates the layer index. Thus the structural network at a time τ has state variables $\mathbf{x}^{[1]}(\tau)$ with capacity $\mathbf{C}^{[1]}(\tau)$, and demand $\mathbf{D}^{[1]}(\tau)$. The individual elements of $\mathbf{C}^{[1]}(\tau)$ and $\mathbf{D}^{[1]}(\tau)$ are the respective capacity and demand models for each component class. The supply tensor $\mathbf{S}^{[1]}(\tau)$ is defined as $\mathbf{S}^{[1]}(\tau) = \mathbf{D}^{[1]}(\tau) \odot \mathbf{1}_{\{\mathbf{D}^{[1]}(\tau) \leq \mathbf{C}^{[1]}(\tau)\}}$. Typically we can assume that there are no control state variables in the structural network i.e. $\kappa^{[1]} = \varnothing$. The structural performance $\mathbf{Q}_{\alpha}^{[1]}(\tau)$ affecting the supported network layers can then be written as the instantaneous reliability of each of the components defined as $Q_{\alpha,(i,j)}^{[1]}(\tau) = P[C_{i,j}^{[1]}(\tau) - D_{i,j}^{[1]}(\tau) > 0 \mid IM_{i,j}] \cdot \mathbf{1}_{\{C_{i,j}^{[1]}(\tau_0) > 0\}}$ (Gardoni et al. 2002).

A network may have capacity side or demand side interdependencies. The capacity side of the structural network is self-supporting and only depends on the state variables $\mathbf{x}^{[1]}(\tau)$ and the parameters $\mathbf{\Theta}_C$. Thus the capacity side interface function, $\mathcal{M}_C^{[1]}(\tau)$ is the second order tensor

Structural layer

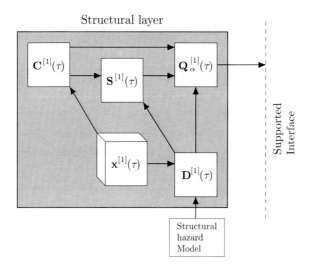

Figure 14.2 Structural network layer and its interfaces.

of ones. The demand side interdependency for the structural network would be present in a case the structural demand depends on the performance of the supported networks. Since the structural demand experienced by the structural components is generally independent of the operation of electric infrastructure, the demand side interface function $\mathcal{M}_D^{[1]}(\tau)$ for the structural layer is also a second order tensor of ones.

Figure 14.2 shows the specific model of the structural network layer following the general model described in Figure 14.1. Here, $\mathcal{M}_C^{[1]}(\tau)$ and $\mathcal{M}_D^{[1]}(\tau)$ are not shown because they are both tensor of ones. The specific definition of the $\mathbf{S}^{[1]}(\tau) = \mathbf{D}^{[1]}(\tau) \odot \mathbf{1}_{\{\mathbf{D}^{[1]}(\tau) \preceq \mathbf{C}^{[1]}(\tau)\}}$ makes $\mathbf{S}^{[1]}(\tau)$ explicitly dependent on $\mathbf{C}^{[1]}(\tau)$ and $\mathbf{D}^{[1]}(\tau)$, which also eliminates the optimization sub-problem.

14.4.3 Modeling of the power flow network

The set of component classes in the power flow network depend on the hazard, the resolution of network modeling, the type of network analysis, and the control characteristics. The effect of hazard and resolution is already discussed in the structural network layer modeling. The type of network analysis requires certain component classes and their state variables to be defined explicitly. For example, if we chose to run a power flow analysis using a steady state AC power flow, the flow network layer of the electrical infrastructure would contain the component classes of buses, lines, generators, transformers, loads, and shunts. On the contrary, a network connectivity analysis may only need the topological information where the components classes of substations and transmission lines would be enough.

We define the flow network layer of the electric infrastructure as $G^{[2]}$ with state variables $\mathbf{x}^{[2]}(\tau)$, base flow Capacity $\mathbf{C}^{[2]}(\tau)$ and base demand $\mathbf{D}^{[2]}(\tau)$. The supply $\mathbf{S}^{[2]}(\tau)$ can then be solved using a desired power flow algorithm. State variables such as active power input and voltage set points at the generators are control state variables (Glover et al. 2008); thus the solution for $\mathbf{S}^{[2]}(\tau)$ becomes an optimization problem as explained in Section 14.3.4.

The power flow network layer has both capacity side and demand side interdependencies. The modified capacity $\mathbf{C}'^{[2]}(\tau)$ for the power flow network layer is dependent on the structural

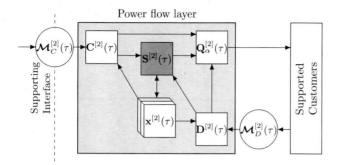

Figure 14.3 Power flow network layer and its interfaces.

network performance $\mathbf{Q}_{\alpha}^{[1]}(\tau)$ via $\boldsymbol{\mathcal{M}}_{C}^{[2]}(\tau)$. In this case, $\boldsymbol{\mathcal{M}}_{C}^{[2]}(\tau)$ is a second order tensor of system reliability problems that map the state of the structural component classes to the binary multipliers to obtain the modified flow network capacity tensor $\mathbf{C}'^{[2]}(\tau)$. Similarly, the modified demand $\mathbf{D}'^{[2]}(\tau)$ on the power flow network layer is dependent on the performance of the supported customer networks, which may be considered in an interdependent infrastructure analysis (as in Guidotti et al. 2018). In general, $\boldsymbol{\mathcal{M}}_{D}^{[2]}(\tau)$ takes into account the time varying power demand by modifying $\mathbf{D}^{[2]}(\tau)$ to obtain $\mathbf{D}'^{[2]}(\tau)$.

Figure 14.3 shows the specific model of the power flow layer following the general model described in Figure 14.1. Here, $\boldsymbol{\mathcal{M}}_{C}^{[2]}(\tau)$ and $\boldsymbol{\mathcal{M}}_{D}^{[2]}(\tau)$ respectively take into account the capacity and demand side interdependencies. Solving for $\mathbf{S}'^{[2]}(\tau)$ and $\mathbf{x}_{:,:,\forall k \in \kappa}(\tau)$ is an optimization problem. The power flow network does not affect the demand on the structural network layer, thus there is no $\mathbf{Q}_{\beta}^{[2]}(\tau)$ for this layer, which is the only difference with the general model in Figure 14.1.

To study the aggregated performance of the infrastructure we define an aggregated performance measure $Q_{\alpha,agg}^{[2]}(\tau)$ as

$$Q_{\alpha,agg}^{[2]}(\tau) = \sum_{sarea=1}^{n_{sarea}} w_{sarea} Q_{\alpha,(sarea)}^{\prime[2]}(\tau),\tag{14.7}$$

where *sarea* represents a unique service area, which corresponds to the index of a particular load bus in the power flow network. Based on Equation (14.7), $Q_{\alpha,agg}^{[2]}(\tau)$ gives the weighted average performance across all service areas as a function of time.

14.4.4 Modeling of the deterioration and recovery

Deterioration and recovery models describe the changes in the state variables $\mathbf{x}_{:,:,\forall k \in \kappa}(\tau)$ over the service life of infrastructure. Deterioration adversely impact the serviceability, safety, and resilience of infrastructure (Jia et al. 2017; Jia & Gardoni 2018). Deterioration can either be gradual (due to environmental exposure or regular use) or caused by shocks (earthquakes, hurricanes, floods, and blasts) (Kumar & Gardoni 2014a). Kumar and Gardoni (2014b), Kumar et al. (2015) and Jia and Gardoni (2018) developed a general state-dependent stochastic formulation that models the variation in the state variables over time due to deterioration mechanisms. Jia and Gardoni (2018) specifically considered the likely interaction among different deterioration mechanisms.

Recovery processes during the service life of infrastructure, correct the effects of deterioration during planned or forced interventions. The deteriorated state of the infrastructure defines the scope of the recovery process, and target performances define the recovery objectives (Sharma et al. 2018a). Recovery schedules specify the recovery activities and their respective durations, precedence, and resource requirements (Sharma et al. 2018a; Jia et al. 2017). Sharma et al. (2018a) developed a general state dependent stochastic formulation to model the variation of state variables over time during a recovery process while considering shocks potentially disrupting the recovery.

Jia et al. (2017) developed an integration of the deterioration and recovery processes, which can be used to model the whole life cycle of infrastructure components based on renewal theory (Kumar & Gardoni 2014b). Sharma and Gardoni (2018b) provided a spatial extension of the recovery modeling by modeling network recovery for interdependent infrastructure. Sharma et al. (2018b) proposed a framework to maximize infrastructure resilience by optimizing the recovery planning and execution strategies. Sharma et al. (2018a) also provided metrics to measure the resilience associated with various recovery curves. Sharma et al. (2018c) provides a brief review of the above listed works, so we refrain from repeating it here.

For the purpose of this chapter, it is enough to understand the following three points: (1) there are deterioration and recovery models compatible with the current approach, which model the time evolution of $\mathbf{x}(\tau)$ for interdependent infrastructure (Sharma et al. 2018a; Jia et al. 2017; Jia & Gardoni 2018), (2) given $\mathbf{x}(\tau)$ we can use the current framework to obtain general performance measures over time (Sharma & Gardoni 2018b), $\mathbf{Q}(\tau)$, which when considering their time evolution in a recovery process are commonly known as the recovery curves, and (3) we can measure the resilience associated with a recovery curve using resilience metrics such as ρ_Q (the center of resilience) and χ_Q (the resilience bandwidth), which are defined by Sharma et al. (2018a) as partial descriptors of the recovery curve $\mathbf{Q}(\tau)$.

Figure 14.4 provides a graphical representation of the complete model of electric infrastructure for a hazard affecting the structural layer. Effects of the hazard are propagated according to the proposed framework closely modeling reality. There is a one-way dependency among the two layers. Interface functions in one-way dependencies reduce the computational cost, because the probabilistic analysis of the structural layer and the power flow layer can be easily decoupled (Sharma & Gardoni 2018a).

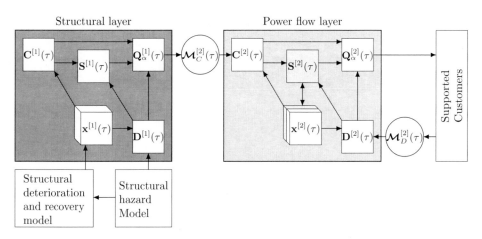

Figure 14.4 Electric power infrastructure model.

14.5 A benchmark example

We illustrate the framework presented in this chapter by modeling the performance of the electric power infrastructure in Shelby County, TN, USA as the region of interest. Shelby County has a population of about 1,000,000, out of which about 70 percent reside in the city of Memphis. Shelby County could experience an earthquake event from the New Madrid Seismic Zone (NMSZ).

14.5.1 Hazard model

In this example, we consider a scenario earthquake with moment magnitude $M_w = 7.7$ and epicenter at 35.93°N and 89.92°W. To capture the near-field effects, we use the three-dimensional (3D) physics-based model of the earthquake hazard developed by Guidotti et al. (2018) for the NMSZ. This model includes an accurate representation of the fault system, the rupture mechanism, and the basin, as well as a layered representation of the soil with its mechanical characteristics. For the far-field, we use GMPEs developed for the Central and Eastern US (Steelman et al. 2007).

14.5.2 Boundaries and resolution

Electrical power infrastructure in Shelby County is managed by the Memphis Light, Gas, and Water (MLGW). The balancing authority of the region is the Tennessee Valley Authority (TVA), who also owns and operates the generators and transmission lines providing power to MLGW owned infrastructure. We use the boundary of the power flow network generated by Birchfield et al. (2017) as the boundary of the power network model. This network covers the entire state of Tennessee that encompasses the region of interest and most part of the balancing authority. The data over Tennessee have enough attributes to run a steady state nonlinear Newton Raphson power flow analysis. The generator data is obtained for the actual generators in the region while the transmission line topology and attributes are designed synthetically as a realistic representation of the power infrastructure in the region.

Network topology for the region of interest (i.e., the MLGW portion of the infrastructure) is available at a relatively higher resolution in Shinozuka et al (1998). However the data attributes required to run a flow analysis were not published. We obtained the missing data from general research, analyzing satellite imagery and designing the rest based on industry practices. We also added the generators in the Shelby County portion of the network, which were not found in the original datasets. In total, there are 229 buses, 37 generator units, 253 transmission lines, 113 loads out of which 36 are in Shelby County, 2 capacitor bank shunts, and 94 transformers. Overall the network has a hybrid resolution. Figure 14.5(a) shows the topology and service areas of the electric power network in Shelby County, and Figure 14.5(b) shows the topology of the network in Tennessee. Detailed information about the network can be found in Sharma et al. (2018b).

14.5.3 Modeling of the physical network

We model the following three component classes that are vulnerable to earthquakes: transformers, circuit breakers, and disconnect switches (FEMA 2014). The structural capacities $\mathbf{C}^{[1]}(\tau)$ of these components are in terms of log-normally distributed random variables of parameters corresponding to state variables such as voltage level and foundation type. The demand tensor, $\mathbf{D}^{[1]}(\tau)$ is directly equal to $\mathbf{IM}$, which in this example is a deterministic value for

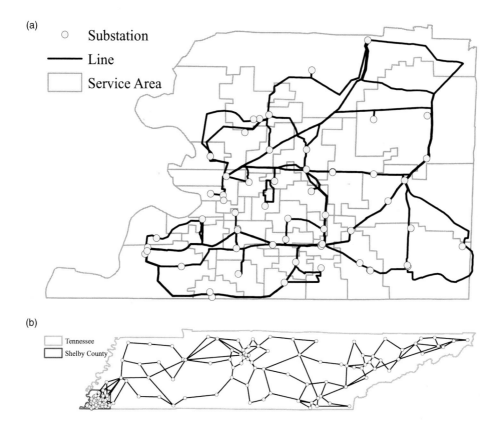

Figure 14.5 Electric power network (a) in Shelby County, and (b) in Tennessee.

the scenario earthquake in terms of the peak ground acceleration (PGA). The supply is $\mathbf{S}^{[1]}(\tau) = \mathbf{D}^{[1]}(\tau) \odot \mathbf{1}_{\{\mathbf{D}^{[1]}(\tau) \leq \mathbf{C}^{[1]}(\tau)\}}$ as defined in Section 14.4.2. The elements of the forward interacting performance tensor $\mathbf{Q}_\alpha^{[1]}(\tau)$ are $Q_{\alpha,(i,j)}^{[1]}(\tau) = \mathrm{P}[C_{i,j}^{[1]}(\tau) - D_{i,j}^{[1]}(\tau) > 0 \,|\, IM_{i,j}] \cdot \mathbf{1}_{\{C_{i,j}^{[1]}(\tau_0) > 0\}}$.

14.5.4 Modeling of the power flow network

As discussed in Section 14.5.2, the power network has the following component classes: buses, generators, lines, shunts, loads, and transformers. Capacities $\mathbf{C}^{[2]}(\tau)$ of these components are deterministic quantities obtained from the power infrastructure dataset. A deterministic demand $\mathbf{D}^{[2]}(\tau)$ on the network is available at the loads based on the population and activities/ zoning (e.g., residential, commercial, or industrial) of the service area. The demand is in terms of active and reactive power flow. So, demand $\mathbf{D}^{[2]}(\tau)$ is a second order tensor of complex numbers representing the apparent power. The state variables $\mathbf{x}^{[2]}(\tau)$ is a third order tensor, where the state variables include voltages, phase angles, impedances, active power, and reactive power. The supply $\mathbf{S}^{[2]}(\tau)$ is obtained by running a non-linear power flow analysis, where the power set points at each generator are obtained by solving a linear optimum dispatch algorithm while also accounting for line capacity constraints. The supply $\mathbf{S}^{[2]}(\tau)$ is in terms of

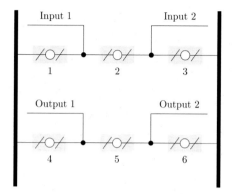

Figure 14.6 Schematic representation of a typical node in a substation.
Source: Adapted from Shinozuka et al. 1998.

active and reactive power consumed or generated at each node, or transmitted through each line, i.e. again a second order tensor of complex numbers. We use the Python package PyPSA (Brown et al. 2018) to run the dynamic flow analyses. The forward interacting performance $\mathbf{Q}'^{[2]}_{\alpha}(\tau)$ is a probability measure depicting whether the demand and supply are balanced, i.e. $Q'^{[2]}_{\alpha,(i,j)}(\tau) = \mathbb{P}[\,|S'^{[2]}_{i,j} - D'^{[2]}_{i,j}(\tau)| < \varepsilon_{\text{tol}} \,|\, \mathcal{M}^{[2]}_C(\tau), \mathcal{M}^{[2]}_D(\tau)].\mathbf{1}_{\{D^{[2]}_{i,j}(\tau)>0\}}$, and relevant state variables (voltages and phase angles) are in a tolerable range. Here ε_{tol} is the tolerable range (usually defined as some percentage of rated values of respective quantities).

The capacity side interface function $\mathcal{M}^{[2]}_C(\tau)$ is a system reliability problem. The probability of $\mathcal{M}^{[2]}_{C,i,i}(\tau)$ being zero for a bus in the power network layer corresponds to the disconnection of input from output in Figure 14.6 (Shinozuka et al. 1998). We can write $\mathbb{P}[\mathcal{M}^{[2]}_{C,i,i}(\tau) = 0] = \mathbb{P}[F^{[2]}_{(i,i)} \,|\, IM_{i,i:}]$ for the bus with index (i,i) in the power network layer, where

$$F^{[2]}_{(i,i)} = \left(F^{[1]}_1 F^{[1]}_3\right) \cup \left(F^{[1]}_4 F^{[1]}_6\right) \cup \left(F^{[1]}_1 F^{[1]}_6\right) \cup \left(F^{[1]}_3 F^{[1]}_4\right), \tag{14.8}$$

which represents the failure event of a bus with index (i,i) in the power flow network. In Equation (14.8), $F^{[1]}_i$ are the failure events of the compound components in a series system of two disconnect switches and one circuit breaker in the structural layer, i.e. $F^{[1]}_i = F^{[1]}_{CB_i} \cup F^{[1]}_{DS_i} \cup F^{[1]}_{DS_i}$. Also for the set of transformers {TRANS}, $\mathcal{M}^{[2]}_{C,i,j}(\tau), (i,j) \in$ {TRANS} being zero corresponds to the structural failure event of the corresponding transformer component in the structural layer, i.e. $\mathbb{P}[\mathcal{M}^{[2]}_{C,i,j}(\tau) = 0] = \mathbb{P}[F^{[1]}_{\text{TRANS}_{(i,j)}} \,|\, IM_{i,j:}]$.

14.5.5 Analyzing the time-varying performance during recovery

For this example, we consider the case of one uninterrupted recovery process for the electric infrastructure. We adopt the recovery schedule and recovery resources for electric infrastructure recovery in Sharma et al. (2018c). For any initial damage to the structural components the state variables at any time τ are provided by the recovery model also in Sharma et al. (2018c).

For the purpose of the probabilistic analysis we use a simulation approach where we sample damage scenarios from $\mathbf{x}^{[1]}(\tau_{0+})$. For each damage scenario of the structural network, we run a stochastic recovery process as in Sharma et al. (2018c). We update the state variables hourly and estimate the infrastructure performance in terms of $\mathbf{Q}'^{[2]}_{\alpha}(\tau)$ and $Q^{[2]}_{\alpha,agg}(\tau)$ by running a

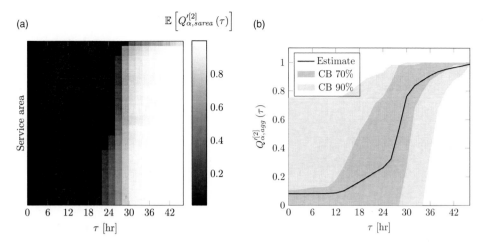

Figure 14.7 Predicted performance measure for the electric power network: (a) mean performance for each service area, and (b) mean aggregate performance with 70 and 90 percent confidence bands.

power flow analysis every hour after the occurrence of the scenario earthquake up-to the time to complete recovery. We run the simulation until the resilience metrics ρ_Q and χ_Q converge.

Figure 14.7 shows the recovery of the electric power network in terms of the performance measure $\mathbf{Q}_\alpha^{[2]}(\tau)$ over a period of 48 hours in the aftermath of the scenario earthquake. Figure 14.7(a) shows the mean of $Q_{\alpha,sarea}'^{[2]}(\tau)$, and Figure 14.7(b) shows the estimate of $Q_{\alpha,agg}^{[2]}(\tau)$, i.e. the aggregate recovery of the whole power infrastructure. In Figure 14.7(a), we observe that most of the service areas recover fairly quickly and around the same time. However, one service area tends to lag behind. This is because we used a set priority for the recovery scheduling that affects when the recovery work for individual service area starts. In Figure 14.7(b) we observe that the aggregated performance recovers fairly quickly (as expected given the quick recovery of the individual service areas.)

Figure 14.8 show the histograms for the values of resilience metrics for the obtained recovery curves for each run in the simulations. The mean and standard deviation of $\rho_{Q_{\alpha,agg}^{[2]}}$ are 29.25 hours and 5.71 hours respectively. The mean and standard deviation of $\chi_{Q_{\alpha,agg}^{[2]}}$ are 2.78 hours and 2.12 hours respectively. From the two histograms we can say that the rate of recovery of electric infrastructure is centered around 30 hours with approximately 85 percent of the electric infrastructure recovering in 32 hours (i.e., $\rho_{Q_{\alpha,agg}^{[2]}} + \chi_{Q_{\alpha,agg}^{[2]}}$).

14.6 Conclusions

This chapter presented a novel framework to model the time varying performance of electric infrastructure. The chapter provided a glossary for infrastructure which expanded some current definitions and introduced new definitions for physical quantities required to model critical infrastructure. A general mathematical framework for infrastructure modeling was presented. The framework is capable of representing regional infrastructure by explicitly modeling their various capacities, demands, and corresponding supply measures. Specifically, the framework was used to model the electrical infrastructure as a power flow network dependent on a structural network. The dependency was considered using interface functions. A steady state AC

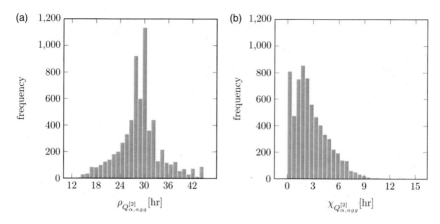

Figure 14.8 Histograms of measured resilience metrics: (a) Center of resilience, and (b) Resilience bandwidth.

power flow analysis with optimal power dispatch was used to estimate the supply measure in the power flow layer. Considering a benchmark example, the performance of the electrical infrastructure was estimated, considering the uncertainty in the initial damage and the recovery process. The resilience metrics for the recovery curves of the infrastructure performance were calculated capturing the prominent features of the recovery curve. The presented framework is general yet highly compatible with a variety of existing network analysis and life cycle modeling formulations, which can be incorporated in the presented framework. Future work should focus on developing more accurate component models and integrating other infrastructure such as communications and transportation as well socio-economic systems.

Acknowledgements

The research presented in this paper was supported in part by the Center for Risk-Based Community Resilience Planning funded by the US National Institute of Standards and Technology (NIST Financial Assistance Award Number: 70NANB15H044) and by the Critical Resilient Interdependent Infrastructure Systems and Processes (CRISP) Program of the National Science Foundation (Award Number: 1638346). The views expressed are those of the authors, and may not represent the official position of the sponsors.

References

Adachi, T. and Ellingwood, B. R. (2008). "Serviceability of earthquake-damaged water systems: Effects of electrical power availability and power backup systems on system vulnerability." *Reliability Engineering & System Safety*, 93(1), 78–88.

Baldick, R., Chowdhury, B., Dobson, I., Dong, Z., Gou, B., Hawkins, D., and Li, J. (2008, July). "Initial review of methods for cascading failure analysis in electric power transmission systems IEEE PES CAMS task force on understanding, prediction, mitigation and restoration of cascading failures." *Power and Energy Society General Meeting-Conversion and Delivery of Electrical Energy in the 21st Century, 2008 IEEE* (pp. 1–8). IEEE.

Birchfield, A.B., Gegner, K.M., Xu, T., Shetye, K.S., and Overbye, T.J. (2017). "Statistical considerations in the creation of realistic synthetic power grids for geomagnetic disturbance studies." *IEEE Transactions on Power Systems*, 32(2), 1502–10.

Brown, T., Hörsch, J., and Schlachtberger, D. (2018). "PyPSA: Python for Power System Analysis." *Journal of Open Research Software*, 6(1), DOI:10.5334/jors.188.

Corotis, R. (2009). "Societal issues in adopting life-cycle concepts within the political system." *Structure and Infrastructure Engineering*, 5(1), 59–65.

Dong, X., Shinozuka, M., and Chang, S. (2004). "Utility power network systems." *13th World Conference on Earthquake Engineering*, Vancouver, B.C., August 1–6.

Dorf, R.C. and Bishop, R.H. (2011). *Modern Control Systems*. London: Pearson.

Dueñas-Osorio, L., Craig, J.I., and Goodno, B.J. (2007). "Seismic response of critical interdependent networks." *Earthquake Engineering and Structural Dynamics*. 36(2), 285–306.

Ellingwood, B.R., Cutler, H., Gardoni, P., Peacock, W.G., van de Lindt, J.W., and Wang, N. (2016). "The Centerville Virtual Community: a fully integrated decision model of interacting physical and social infrastructure systems." *Sustainable and Resilient Infrastructure*, 1(3–4), 95–107.

Federal Emergency Management Agency (FEMA). (2014). *Multi-hazard Loss Estimation Methodology: Earthquake Model HAZUS-MH 2.1 Technical Manual*, Washington, DC.

Gardoni, P., (ed.), (2017). *Risk and Reliability Analysis: Theory and Applications*, Springer.

Gardoni, P., and LaFave, J.M. (eds.) (2016). *Multi-hazard Approaches to Civil Infrastructure Engineering*. New York: Springer.

Gardoni, P. and Murphy, C. (2008). "Recovery from natural and man-made disasters as capabilities restoration and enhancement." *International Journal of Sustainable Development and Planning*, 3(4), 1–17.

Gardoni, P. and Murphy, C. (2009). "Capabilities-based approach to measuring the societal impacts of natural and man-made hazards in risk analysis." *ASCE Natural Hazards Review*, 10(2), 29–37.

Gardoni, P. and Murphy, C. (2018). "Society-based design: Developing sustainable and resilient communities." *Sustainable and Resilient Infrastructure*, DOI: 10.1080/23789689.2018.1448667.

Gardoni, P., Der Kiureghian, A., and Mosalam, K.M. (2002). "Probabilistic capacity models and fragility estimates for reinforced concrete columns based on experimental observations." *Journal of Engineering Mechanics*, 128(10), 1024–38.

Gardoni, P., Mosalam, K.M., & der Kiureghian, A. (2003). "Probabilistic seismic demand models and fragility estimates for RC bridges." *Journal of Earthquake Engineering*, 7(spec01), 79–106.

Gardoni, P., Murphy, C., and Rowell, A. (eds.) (2016). *Societal Risk Management of Natural Hazards*. New York: Springer.

Glover, J.D., Sarma, M.S., and Overbye, T. (2008). *Power System Analysis & Design, 4th ed.* Toronto, ON, Canada: Thomson.

Guidotti, R., Chmielewski, H., Unnikrishnan, V., Gardoni, P., McAllister T., and Van de Lindt, J. (2016). "Modeling the resilience of critical infrastructure: the role of network dependencies." *Sustainable and Resilient Infrastructure*, 1(3–4), 153–168, DOI: 10.1080/23789689.2016.1254999.

Guidotti, R., Gardoni, P., and Chen, Y. (2017). "Multi-layer heterogeneous network model for interdependent infrastructure systems." *12th International Conference on Structural Safety & Reliability (ICOSSAR 2017)*, TU Wien, Vienna (Austria).

Guidotti, R., Gardoni, P., and Rosenheim, N. (2018a). "Integration of physical infrastructure and social systems in communities' reliability and resilience analysis." *Reliability Engineering & System Safety* (under review).

Guidotti, R., Tian, S., and Gardoni, P. (2018b). "Simulation of seismic wave propagation in the Metro Memphis Statistical Area (MMSA)" (in preparation).

Guikema, S. and Gardoni, P. (2009). "Reliability estimation for networks of reinforced concrete bridges." *ASCE Journal of Infrastructure Systems*, 15, 61–9.

Hoff, S. (2016, July). "U.S. electric system is made up of interconnections and balancing authorities. Today in energy." *Today In Energy*, EIA. www.eia.gov/todayinenergy/detail.php?id=27152 (last accessed August 18, 2018).

Housner, G.W., Bergman, L.A., Caughey, T.K., Chassiakos, A.G., Claus, R.O., Masri, S.F., ... and Yao, J.T. (1997). "Structural control: past, present, and future." *Journal of Engineering Mechanics*, 123(9), 897–971.

Jia, G. and Gardoni, P. (2018). "State-dependent stochastic models: A general stochastic framework for modeling deteriorating engineering systems considering multiple deterioration processes and their interactions." *Structural Safety*, 72, 99–110.

Jia, G., Tabandeh, A., and Gardoni, P. (2017). "Life-cycle analysis of engineering systems: Modeling deterioration, instantaneous reliability, and resilience." In *Risk and Reliability Analysis: Theory and Applications* (pp. 465–94). Springer, Cham.

Kang, W.-H., Song, J., and Gardoni, P. (2008). "Matrix-based system reliability method and applications to bridge networks." *Reliability Engineering and System Safety*, 93, 1584–93.

Kumar, R. and Gardoni, P. (2014a). "Effect of seismic degradation on the fragility of reinforced concrete bridges." *Engineering Structures*, 79, 267–75.

Kumar, R., and Gardoni, P., (2014b). "Renewal theory-based life-cycle analysis of deteriorating engineering systems." *Structural Safety*, 50, 94–102.

Kumar, R., Cline, D., and Gardoni, P. (2015). "A stochastic framework to model deterioration in engineering systems." *Structural Safety*, 53, 36–43.

Kundur, P., Balu, N.J., and Lauby, M.G. (1994). *Power System Stability and Control* (Vol. 7). New York: McGraw-Hill.

Murphy, C. and Gardoni, P., (2006). "The role of society in engineering risk analysis: A capabilities-based approach." *Risk Analysis*, 26(4), 1073–83.

Murphy, C. and Gardoni, P. (2007). "Determining public policy and resource allocation priorities for mitigating natural hazards: A capabilities-based approach." *Science and Engineering Ethics*, 13(4), 489–504.

Murphy, C. and Gardoni, P. (2008). "The acceptability and the tolerability of societal risks: A capabilities-based approach." *Science and Engineering Ethics*, 14(1), 77–92.

Murphy, C. and Gardoni, P. (2011). "Evaluating the source of the risks associated with natural events." *Res Publica*, 17(2), 125–40.

Newman, M.E. (2003). "The structure and function of complex networks." *SIAM Review*, 45(2), 167–256.

Papic, M., Bell, K., Chen, Y., Dobson, I., Fonte, L., Haq, E., and Samaan, N. (2011). "Survey of tools for risk assessment of cascading outages." *Power and Energy Society General Meeting, 2011 IEEE* (pp. 1–9). IEEE.

Sharma, N. and Gardoni, P. (2018a). "Mathematical modeling of interdependent infrastructure: An object oriented approach for generalized network-system analysis." *Reliability Engineering & System Safety* (in preparation).

Sharma, N. and Gardoni, P. (2018b). "Promoting resilient interdependent infrastructure: the role of strategic recovery scheduling." *Computer-Aided Civil and Infrastructure Engineering* (in preparation).

Sharma, N., Tabandeh, A., and Gardoni, P. (2018a). "Resilience analysis: A mathematical formulation to model resilience of engineering systems," *Sustainable and Resilient Infrastructure*, 3(2), 49–67.

Sharma, N., Tabandeh, A., and Gardoni, P. (2018b). "Resilience- informed recovery optimization: a multi-scale formulation for interdependent infrastructure," *Computer- Aided Civil and Infrastructure Engineering* (in preparation).

Sharma, N., Tabandeh, A., and Gardoni, P. (2018c). "Regional resilience analysis: A multi-scale approach to model the recovery of interdependent infrastructure." *Handbook of Sustainable and Resilient Infrastructure*, P. Gardoni (ed.), New York: Routledge.

Shinozuka, M., Rose, A., and Eguchi, R.T. (1998). "Engineering and socioeconomic impacts of earthquakes." *Monograph 98-MN02*, Multidisciplinary Center for Earthquake Engineering Research (MCEER), Buffalo, NY.

Shinozuka M., Dong X., Chen T.C., and Jin X., (2007). "Seismic performance of electric transmission network under component failures." *Earthquake Engineering and Structural Dynamics*, 36(2), 227–44.

Shishko, R. and Aster, R. (1995). *NASA Systems Engineering Handbook*. NASA Special Publication, 6105.

Song, J., Cotilla-Sanchez, E., Ghanavati, G., and Hines, P.D. (2016). "Dynamic modeling of cascading failure in power systems." *IEEE Transactions on Power Systems*, 31(3), 2085–95.

Steelman, J., Song, J., and Jerome, F. (2007). "Integrated data flow and risk aggregation for consequence-based risk management of seismic regional losses." Report of the Mid-America Earthquake Center, University of Illinois at Urbana-Champaign, Champaign, IL.

Suganthi, L. and Samuel, A.A. (2012). "Energy models for demand forecasting – A review." *Renewable and sustainable energy reviews*, 16(2), 1223–40.

Tabandeh, A., Gardoni, P., and Murphy, C. (2018). "Reliability-based capability approach: A system reliability formulation for the capability approach." *Risk Analysis*, 38(2), 410–24.

Unnikrishnan, V.U. and van de Lindt, J. W. (2016). "Probabilistic framework for performance assessment of electrical power networks to tornadoes." *Sustainable and Resilient Infrastructure*, 1(3–4), 137–52.

Vaiman, M., Bell, K., Chen, Y., Chowdhury, B., Dobson, I., Hines, P., and Zhang, P. (2012). "Risk assessment of cascading outages: Methodologies and challenges." *IEEE Transactions on Power Systems*, 27(2), 631.

Watts, D.J. and Strogatz, S.H. (1998). "Collective dynamics of 'small-world' networks." *Nature*, 393(6684), 440.

Part III

Resilience of different systems

Potable water and wastewater infrastructure

15

A holistic framework to evaluate water availability for post-earthquake firefighting

Negar Elhami Khorasani,[1] Maxwell Coar,[2]
Amir Sarreshtehdari,[3] and Maria Garlock[4]

[1] DEPT. OF CIVIL, STRUCTURAL AND ENVIRONMENTAL ENGINEERING,
UNIVERSITY AT BUFFALO, BUFFALO, NY, USA; NEGARKHO@BUFFALO.EDU

[2] DEPT. OF CIVIL AND ENVIRONMENTAL ENGINEERING, PRINCETON UNIVERSITY,
PRINCETON, NJ, USA; MCOAR@PRINCETON.EDU

[3] DEPT. OF CIVIL, STRUCTURAL AND ENVIRONMENTAL ENGINEERING,
UNIVERSITY AT BUFFALO, BUFFALO, NY, USA; AMIRSARR@BUFFALO.EDU

[4] DEPT. OF CIVIL AND ENVIRONMENTAL ENGINEERING, PRINCETON UNIVERSITY,
PRINCETON, NJ, USA; MGARLOCK@PRINCETON.EDU

15.1 Introduction

Earthquake is a potential hazard for communities in seismically active regions, and fire following earthquake (FFE), a cascading multi-hazard event, can cause major social and economic losses in a community. A study of 20 previous earthquakes from seven countries, where 15 of which occurred between 1971 and 2014, shows that fire events that followed the earthquakes caused considerable damage to the communities (Elhami Khorasani et al. 2017). The likelihood of a fire event is typically amplified following seismic events due to ruptured utility lines or toppled appliances. In addition, firefighter intervention can be hampered due to ruptured water lines, loss of water pressure, inadequate water supply due to widespread firefighting efforts or loss of electricity at water pumping stations, and inaccessible roadways due to damaged bridges, roadways, and debris. Further, active and passive fire protection systems in buildings, such as sprinkler systems and spray-applied materials or compartmentation partitions, can be compromised by earthquake. Wind condition can play an important role on fire spread, while the key to control fire spread is the available water supply.

As an example, there have been approximately 110 earthquake-related fires following the 1994 Northridge earthquake with magnitude 6.7 (Scawthorn et al. 2005). The earthquake caused significant damage to the Los Angeles water system including water supply and transmission systems (Davis et al. 2012). The loss of electric power in the Van Norman complex, that

283

lasted about 24 hours after the earthquake, interrupted the service in the largest water pumping station in the city system (O'Rourke 2007). In another example, in the report published in 2016, one of the priority recommendations after studying impacts of the 2014 South Napa earthquake is related to water supplies for firefighters, initiated from the vulnerability of water systems and the highlighted finding on "the additional fire hazards that earthquake-related water-system failures can pose …". (Johnson & Mahin 2016).

Fire following earthquake consists of three phases: ignition, spread, and suppression. Elhami Khorasani et al. (2017) have previously developed an ignition model to assess the likelihood of fire ignitions after an earthquake across a community. This chapter, in continuation of the ignition model, targets required inputs for modeling the spread and suppression phases of FFE. One of the key factors in suppressing fire is the availability of water flow and water pressure, given the level of damage to the water network after an earthquake (Coar et al. 2016). In addition, availability of electric power at the pumping stations is necessary for a functioning water network. The existing spread and suppression models in the literature (FEMA 2014; Li & Davidson 2013a) make a number of simplifying assumptions on the availability of water and firefighting resources at the fire location. The importance of such parameters is acknowledged in the studies, but neglect of these parameters can lead to unconservative results.

This chapter proposes an efficient and systematic framework to evaluate availability of water pressure and flow after an earthquake, as an input to a post-earthquake fire suppression model. The framework incorporates dependency of water and electric networks. In doing so, the first step is to investigate post-earthquake functionality of each network individually, and then adjust performance of the water network based on availability of power in the region of study. The proposed approach quantifies damage at the component level using fragilities and a capacity index parameter that measures operability. System level network analysis is then completed to measure and compare power flow before and after the earthquake. The results will determine the availability of water as an input to the suppression model for post-earthquake fire analysis, that can be used for informed decision-making related to mitigation, preparedness, and response of fire department and communities to earthquake events.

15.2 Background: Existing tools and models for fire following earthquake

Summary of existing tools: There are two available programs for economic loss estimation with the capability to perform FFE analysis, HAZUS (FEMA 2014) and MAEViz (2014). HAZUS is a GIS-based software that is developed to estimate potential losses from earthquakes, floods, and hurricanes and is developed by the Federal Emergency Management Agency (FEMA). HAZUS is well known in the USA and can be used for both mitigation and preparedness as well as response and recovery. MAEViz is an open-source platform for earthquake hazard risk management developed by the Mid-America Earthquake Center at the UIUC. MAEViz is developed for estimating potential earthquake damages including effects on transportation networks and socio-economic systems.

The HAZUS earthquake model includes FFE as one of the potential hazards. The module evaluates the extent of fire in terms of the number of fire ignitions and fire spread, given the general building stock inventory, available firefighting trucks, and speed and direction of wind. The FFE model outputs the number of ignitions, the area that is burnt, the population that is exposed to fire, and the dollar value of inventory that is exposed to fire. Although the FFE module in HAZUS covers all three phases of fire ignition, spread, and suppression, the technical manual states that the module is based on limited research and as a result, losses due to fire are not included in total potential losses from an earthquake event.

Yildiz and Karaman (2013) investigated the post-earthquake ignition vulnerability of a region in Turkey by only implementing an ignition model in MAEViz (the module is called HAZTURK), without looking at the spread or suppression phases. Their implemented ignition model uses an analytical approach that is based on a logical occurrence of events after an earthquake, having ignitions from damages to internal gas, electrical distribution systems, and overturning of appliances. The model calculates probability of ignition for every building in a region of interest, and provides the means to compare probability of ignition for different buildings in the region; however, the total predicted number of ignitions in the region is not realistic, and the results are not validated against historical FFE events. The model is good for comparative purposes (sensitivity studies) but not for predicting loss estimation from an FFE event.

Summary of existing analytical models: Lee et al. (2008) collected 17 fire spread and suppression models from the literature, 12 of which were published after late 1990's. Similarly confirmed by Li and Davidson (2013a), many of the recent spread models developed in the past few years can be categorized as semi-empirical with inclusion of physics-based modeling of spread such as branding and radiation (Himoto & Tanaka 2008; Iwami et al. 2004; Lee & Davidson 2010a, 2010b; Li and Davidson 2013b; Nussle et al. 2004; Otake et al. 2003). One of the well-established models is the formulation by Hamada (1975), which considers the effect of wind, building density, building plan dimensions, and building separation. The model outputs the length of fire in downwind and upwind directions from the initial ignition location and assumes that the fire spreads in an elliptical shape. The speed of fire advancement depends on the direction of spread (upwind or downwind), wind velocity, fire resistance of structures (e.g. fire in wood advances twice as fast as steel or concrete), and the suppression efforts by the firefighters.

Suppression is related to discovery time of fire, report time, arrival time, control time, and mop-up time. For realistic results, the effectiveness of suppression should be incorporated in the spread model at every time step during the analysis. The suppression model is mainly related to the number of available fire engines and the available amount of water to fight the fire. The main issues that are not considered in the existing models are (1) accurately incorporating the effects of damage to water supply systems and (2) road accessibility for firefighting operations. Li and Davidson (2013a) state that all existing models recognize the importance of water availability (flow volume and pressure at a hydrant) and road accessibility, but they use simplified approaches. For example, the available flow in HAZUS is calculated using a reduction factor for typical discharge of water. This reduction factor is not based on the true performance of the water network at the region of study but it is calculated based on studies on the overall system performance for water networks in Oakland, Tokyo, and San Francisco (FEMA 2014). The truck speed for firefighting measures is also based on simplified assumptions, such as doubling the arrival time during normal operation.

Li and Davidson (2013a) have developed a comprehensive spread and suppression model. The spread model considers fire evolution within a room, from room-to-room in a building, and from building-to-building by flame spread through different mechanism such as radiation, surface vegetation, branding, etc. The suppression model is primarily based on the number of engines needed for each fire, status of each available engine, and the water allocated for each fire. A case study by Li and Davidson (2013a) suggests that the availability of water and fire engines, parameters that are controllable as opposed to the wind speed, can mitigate the loss. However, their study makes similar simplifying assumptions for both parameters.

Sample of existing community level studies: The performance of a community under FFE involves great level of uncertainty and depends on the behavior of buildings, water and electric networks, and their interaction with each other. Such considerations are not represented in exiting FFE models and simplifying assumptions, as discussed above, can lead to unconservative results, but even so the existing models and studies indicate serious FFE consequences. For example, the US Geological Survey led a group of scientists and engineers to study consequences of a potential earthquake in California that resulted in "the Shakeout Scenario" (Scawthorn 2008). The study investigated the effects of a hypothetical 7.8 magnitude earthquake that occurred on the southern San Andreas Fault at 12 pm on a breezy day with relatively low humidity in the month of November. The total affected population by the earthquake was 20 million. It was found that such an earthquake could cause approximately 1600 fire ignitions, out of which 1200 would spread over large areas, and a few would grow into conflagrations (Scawthorn 2008). Another study conducted by the New York City Area Consortium for Earthquake Loss Mitigation (NYCEM 2003) showed that a moderate earthquake could result in an estimated 1100–1200 deaths, and ignitions up to 900 fires simultaneously in the NY–NJ–CT area.

15.3 Methodology

Figure 15.1 provides a schematic of the overall methodology for integrating water and electric network performance for fire following earthquake analysis. A summary of different parts of the methodology is described in the text to follow.

Earthquake hazard and intensity: The hazard level is quantified by the parameter *intensity measure.* The intensity measure used to quantify the effect of an earthquake should be selected carefully. Previous studies have considered different parameters such as peak ground acceleration (*PGA*), pseudo displacement (*S_d*), permanent ground deformation (*PGD*), etc. However, the intensity measure that most effectively characterizes the earthquake damage depends on the infrastructure type. For example, previous research shows that *PGD* is most suited to relate earthquake intensity and damage for underground components of water systems such as underground pipes (Maria et al. 2010). In addition to *PGD*, transient ground deformation (*TGD*) and peak

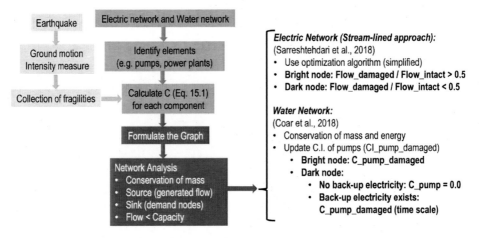

Figure 15.1 Schematic of the methodology for explicitly integrating water and electric network performance for FFE analysis.

ground velocity (*PGV*) effects should also be considered in evaluating water supply performance (FEMA 2014). On the other hand, components of an electric network can be evaluated based on *PGA* or *PGD* (FEMA 2014).

Fragility curves are typically used to quantify the probability of exceeding a damage state for a given intensity measure of a given earthquake (Elnashai 2003; Pan et al. 2007). The damage states (or limit states) are generally related to the performance level and can be grouped into different categories such as *no damage, slight, moderate, extensive,* and *complete.* The accuracy of fragility functions and the parameter that is used as the intensity measure are critical to obtain a reliable assessment of the community performance. Any bias in a fragility function can result in incorrect assessment and improper planning policies. The European collaborative research project on systematic seismic vulnerability of civil infrastructure systems SYNER-G (Pitilakis et al. 2013) collected and created a database of fragility curves for infrastructure systems. HAZUS (FEMA 2014) that is developed by the Federal Emergency Management Agency for applications in the US also includes a collection of fragility functions for infrastructure systems incorporating knowledge on performance of structures in historical earthquakes such as the 1994 Northridge earthquake. MAEViz, the open-source platform for earthquake risk management, also contains a set of fragility functions for different infrastructures.

Component level analysis: Water and electric network components must be identified considering (a) the inventory data that is available to the authorities to run the analysis and (b) the level of detail that is required to obtain a realistic output after the analysis. At the minimum, the water network will include treatment plants, storage tanks, pumping stations, and pipes/valves, while the electric network will include power plants/generators, substations and transmission/distribution lines. For a given component, a set of fragilities for different damage states is available (such as slight, moderate, collapse, etc.), which can be used to measure the functionality of a component in probabilistic terms after an earthquake. One approach to combine the fragilities for different damage states is the use of capacity index to arrive at one value that would represent the level of functionality, which is defined as the expected operability of a component, and is calculated as the following:

$$C = \sum_{i=1}^{n+1} c_i \times p_i,$$

(15.1)

where $p_i = (P_i - P_{i-1})$ and $P_0 = 0, P_{n+1} = 1.0,$

p_i in Equation (15.1) is the probability of the damage state i, c_i is a coefficient that measures the expected operability of a component if damage state i occurs, and $n+1$ is the number of considered damage states (n is the number of fragility curves). The p_i value is calculated from the fragilities defined by the lognormal distribution function with associated median and standard deviation parameters. The capacity index C is essentially the available functionality of a component after an earthquake, and is a number between zero and one. Therefore, the capacity of a component after an earthquake is quantified by multiplying the capacity index by the original output of the component. The capacity index in Equation (15.1), relies on the values of c_i to quantify the level of operability for a given damage state. This concept has been often used for buildings to assess structural damage due to earthquakes. Bai et al. (2009) extends the concept and performs probabilistic assessment to estimate losses due to structural damage, with a similar formulation to Equation (15.1) as the basis where a total damage factor for a building is calculated given an intensity measure. In order to determine the associated damage factors for the damage states from fragility functions, Bai et al. (2009) adopt, with some adjustments, the proposed damage factor ranges by ATC-13 Earthquake Damage Evaluation Data for California. A similar concept is applied to the components of the electric network and details can be found in Sarreshtehdari et al. (2018).

System level analysis: A lifeline system, such as water or electric system, is a network that can be modeled using the graph theory where the overall performance of a network is analyzed by *flow network.* A *Digraph* or a directed graph is defined as a graph, or set of vertices connected by edges, where the vertices have a direction associated with them. Flow network (Deo 1974) is a simple, connected, weighted, digraph *G* when the weight associated with every directed edge in *G* is a nonnegative number. In a flow network analysis, this number represents the capacity of the edge and is designated as c_{ij} for the edge directed from vertex *i* to vertex *j*. The capacity c_{ij} of an edge (*i,j*) can be thought of as the maximum amount of a certain service, such as electricity or water, that can be transported from station/node *i* to station/node *j*, along the connecting edge (*i,j*) per unit of time. For a given flow network in which a vertex has a specified capacity (for example a pump handles a certain flow level in a water system), the total flow into a vertex *v* must not exceed its capacity $c(v)$. Based on a theorem in graph theory (Deo 1974), for a given flow network *G*, *flow* is the assignment of a non-negative number f_{ij} to every directed edge (*i,j*) such that the conditions in Table 15.1 are satisfied.

Streamlined approach for electric network: The literature on analyzing an electric network can be grouped into two categories, (a) those who characterize performance based on topology of the network (e.g., Adachi & Ellingwood 2008; Albert et al. 2004; Duenas-Osorio et al. 2007; Unnikrishnan & van de Lindt 2016), and (b) those who perform power flow analysis (e.g, Dong et al. 2004; Shinozuka et al. 2007; Vanzi 1996). The first group quantifies change in performance, based on the change in topologic characteristics of the network, such as loss of connectivity after an earthquake, without taking the physical behavior of the system into account. The second approach would inherently take the topology structure into account while performing the flow analysis. It is apparent that the second approach is more rigorous, involves a higher level of complexity, and typically requires a specific tool or software for the analysis of electric circuits. In this work, rather than using topological properties or rigorous analysis of the electric network, the proposed methodology uses the comparison of the maximum flow before and after

Table 15.1 Conditions and equations of graph theory

Condition	Equation	
1. For every directed edge (*i,j*) in *G*, flow is less than the capacity.	$f_{ij} < c_{ij}$	(15.2)
2. There is a specified vertex *s* in *G*, called the source, for which Equation (15.3) holds. The summations are taken over all vertices entering and leaving the source *s*. Quantity *w* is called the generated value of flow, which is equivalent to the generated flow from a source in the lifeline systems (e.g. generated electricity in a power plant).	$\sum_i f_{si} - \sum_i f_{is} = w$	(15.3)
3. There is a specified vertex *t* in *G*, called the sink, for which Equation (15.4) holds. The sink vertices are equivalent to neighborhoods in a community that receive and consume the flow.	$\sum_i f_{ti} - \sum_i f_{it} = -w$	(15.4)
4. All other vertices in the graph *G* are called intermediate vertices (such as transformers, pumps, etc.). For each intermediate vertex *j* Equation (15.5) holds. Equation (15.5) is based on the continuity equation in physics.	$\sum_i f_{ji} - \sum_i f_{ij} = 0$	(15.5)

an earthquake as a metric for the performance of the network. This way, damage after earthquake is quantified with grid capacity for the undamaged network as the benchmark, while the network characteristics are captured in the flow analysis. The ratio of power flow, calculated before and after the earthquake for all the nodes in the network, denoted as α, provides a measure of reduction in operability. In this study, the flows are obtained using the Boykov and Kolmogorov (2004) algorithm for the maximum flow. The factor α provides an indication of whether a node is operable (bright) or not (dark). Different limiting values of α can be assigned depending on the problem statement, network characteristics, and performance expectations, while in this work a fixed value of 0.5 is proposed for α. The methodology is discussed in detail in Sarreshtehdari et al. (2018) where two validated case studies are presented.

Analysis of water network: The aim of water network analysis is to identify whether fire hydrants across the network have enough pressure, or *head*, to allow firefighters to suppress the flames. As described in the NFPA Handbook (Wenzel 2008), the American Water Works Association (AWWA 1989) defines the required fire fighting flow as "the rate of water flow, at a residual pressure of 20 psi and for a specified duration that is necessary to control a major fire in a specific structure." There are a number of different methodologies to quantify the required water flow rate. Table 15.2 provides typical required water flow rates found in the literature based on different occupancy types (Bhardwaj 2001).

In order to obtain flow and pressure at a given hydrant, one must solve the entire water network. Solving a network implies finding the flow in each pipe and the head at each node. The methodology applied in this work is based on the *hybrid method*. The method, described by (Boulos et al. 2006), is notable because unlike other methods, it solves for both head at nodes and flow in the pipes simultaneously. In addition, it is not necessary to identify independent loops in the system, which makes automation of the method simpler. The hybrid method, like all other water network solvers, is based on two underlying principles: (a) the conservation of mass, which asserts that the total flow of water entering any pipe junction, or a *node*, is equal to the total flow of water exiting that node; (b) conservation of energy equation, implying that the head loss between any two nodes is constant, regardless of the path taken. The equations for conservation of mass and energy are formulated and solved using the Newton-Raphson method, which is an efficient numerical solver. The details of the methodology are provided in Coar et al. (2018).

Modeling dependency: Guidotti et al. (2016) developed a framework for modeling dependent and interdependent infrastructure networks in a multi-step probabilistic procedure with the ultimate goal of estimating system recovery as a function of time. The procedure used an augmented adjacency table to capture dependencies. Monte Carlo Simulation was applied to capture uncertainties and the framework was applied to study cascading effects of damage to electric network on potable water distribution. In this chapter, to explicitly account for the dependencies, the capacity index is adjusted for components in the water network that are dependable on power. In doing so, the electric network is first analyzed. The availability of

Table 15.2 Typical storage requirements for fire fighting

Occupancy type	Demand rate	Storage volume (gallons)
Residential	2 hrs at 1000 gpm (2.2 cfs)	120,000
Light Commercial	4 hrs at 2000 gpm (4.45 cfs)	480,000
Commercial or industrial	4 hrs at up to 8000 gpm (17.82 cfs)	1,920,000

electricity in regions where water-pumping stations are located is checked. If a pumping station is in a region without electricity, the capacity index for pumping stations are adjusted depending on back-up electricity sources. In the absence of back-up electricity, the pumping station will have zero capacity. If back-up electricity is foreseen, the capacity is kept the same for as long as the back-up electricity functions.

15.4 Case study: effect of dependency on performance

This section investigates the effect of modeling explicit dependence of water network on power for performance evaluation following an earthquake. The modeling approach is based on the methodology described in the previous section. The selected case study is a large-sized water network, shown in Figure 15.2, and is derived from the "Trace Lake" benchmark study distributed with the EPANET water system analysis software package (Rossman 2000). The network was designed as an analysis problem to determine the percentage of water in the system coming from one of the sources and how that percentage changes over time. Made of 115 pipes and 92 nodes, it is a hybrid grid/branched-type network with demands ranging from

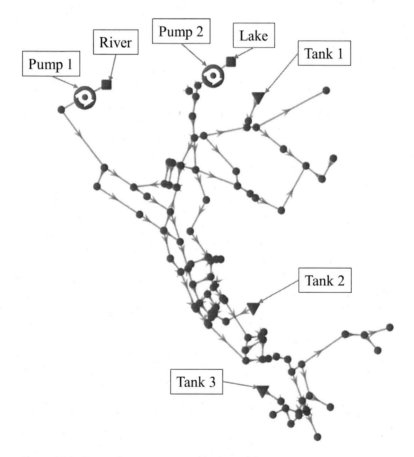

Figure 15.2   Large size water network, adopted from EPANET.
Source: Rossman, 2000.

residential to light industry. Two pumps feed the network from a river and a lake, located to the north of the network, and are supplemented by three elevated tanks distributed throughout the network.

In this case study, the performance of the water network is studied under four different levels of seismic intensity based on the peak ground acceleration (PGA) parameter – the primary intensity measure for nodal components: low intensity with a PGA of 0.1g, medium-low intensity with a PGA of 0.3g, medium-high intensity with a PGA of 0.5g, and high intensity with a PGA of 0.7g. It is acknowledged that the earthquake intensity would vary spatially across a distributed water network. However, for the purposes of comparison and investigating effects of modeling explicit dependence, all nodes in the network are subjected to the same PGA value. In order to investigate whether or not explicit dependence should be considered, the dependency of the water network on the electric network is modeled in three different ways: no dependency, implicit dependency, and explicit dependency.

The "None" dependency scenario does not consider dependency of the water network on the electric network and is intended to provide a reference state for the Implicit and Explicit scenarios that will be discussed next. This method uses the source data from Hazus (FEMA, 2014), which is also used in the Implicit method, to analyze performance of water network components, but assumes that there is no possibility of failure in water network component due to loss of commercial or backup power. Computationally, the backbone data from HAZUS is used and component level fragilities are re-generated for which failure branches related to power in the associated fault trees are not included.

The "Implicit" method uses the current industry standard as suggested by FEMA and implemented in HAZUS. This method does not directly observe the topography and perform-ance of the electric network. Instead, each water network component that may rely on com-mercial or backup (generator) power includes in its operational fault tree a branch for power. The parameters of this logic tree branch depend on the water network component size and typology (e.g., water treatment plants, pumping stations, and the source of water), and do not depend on any information about the specific power network. Because no information from the electric network is taken into account, the uncertainty parameter (lognormal deviation β of the fragility function) for this fault tree branch is relatively large. This method is denoted "Implicit" because the dependence on the electric network is implied in the water network component fault trees.

The "Explicit" method is based on the methodology discussed in the previous section and studies the electric network explicitly before analyzing the water network. However, for the purpose of this study, a more general approach is adapted and different combinations of bright or dark cases (operable or non-operable) are used to determine whether power will be avail-able to pumps or not. To this end, the case study is analyzed for each of the assumed PGAs (0.1g, 0.3g, 0.5g, and 0.7g), and for all the possible combinations of bright or dark nodes, to gain an understanding of general network performance for each of these earthquakes. As a benchmark, it is noted that, based on Sarreshtehdari et al.'s approach (2018), 8, 48, 75, and 87 percent reduction in electric network flow can be expected following a 0.1g, 0.3g, 0.5g, and 0.7g seismic scenario, respectively. If a pump does not receive power from a commercial source, it still may receive power from a backup generator. A set of fragility curves based on generator size and seismic design have been developed to determine the operability of such a generator following an earthquake.

Table 15.3 provides a summary of the considered scenarios and the shorthand nomenclature that will be used to refer to each scenario. There are three explicit dependency scenarios, which can be differentiated based on availability of power to the water network components. One

Table 15.3 Study scenarios and nomenclature

PGA	Dependence	Pump 1	Pump 2	Name
0.1 g	None	-	-	L-1-N
	Implicit	-	-	L-1-I
	Explicit	Bright	Dark	L-1-E1
	Explicit	Dark	Bright	L-1-E2
	Explicit	Dark	Dark	L-1-E3
0.3 g	None	-	-	L-3-N
	Implicit	-	-	L-3-I
	Explicit	Bright	Dark	L-3-E1
	Explicit	Dark	Bright	L-3-E2
	Explicit	Dark	Dark	L-3-E3
0.5 g	None	-	-	L-5-N
	Implicit	-	-	L-5-I
	Explicit	Bright	Dark	L-5-E1
	Explicit	Dark	Bright	L-5-E2
	Explicit	Dark	Dark	L-5-E3
0.7 g	None	-	-	L-7-N
	Implicit	-	-	L-7-I
	Explicit	Bright	Dark	L-7-E1
	Explicit	Dark	Bright	L-7-E2
	Explicit	Dark	Dark	L-7-E3

should note that the explicit scenario where both pumps are bright would be identical to the "No Dependency" scenario and is therefore not included separately in Table 15.3. Figure 15.3 shows the performance of the water network under the twenty scenarios. The results are provided in terms of percentage of distribution nodes at or above firefighting pressure (20 psi). It is observed that, regardless of dependency scenario, an increase in PGA results in a decrease in the number of operable nodes. This intuitively makes sense – more intense earthquakes cause more damage and results in less water availability. It is also observed that, regardless of the PGA, the no dependency and implicit dependency scenarios are almost identical – this shows that the industry-standard implicit method doesn't always fully capture the effects of the water network's dependency on the electric network. On the other hand, the different possible explicit scenario results differ significantly from the none and implicit scenarios, and from each other. Additionally, it can be seen that the -E3 scenario (both pumps inoperable) always underperforms the -E1 and -E2 scenarios (one pump inoperable), so the more damaged the electric network, the worse performance one can expect from the water network. In general, a stronger understanding of electric network performance leads to a stronger understanding of the water network performance.

15.5 Conclusions

Previous studies by the authors demonstrated that the cascading dependency between power and water networks after an extreme event, where pumps require power, is the most documented dependency among the lifelines, and the power network seems to be the most critical network. Meanwhile, the availability of water pressure and flow is the key parameter for suppressing fire ignitions after an earthquake, and to prevent conflagration. This work provided a framework

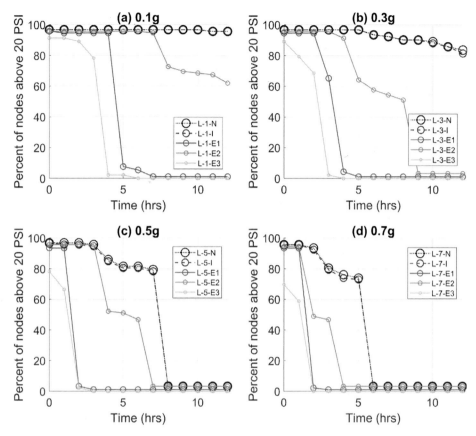

Figure 15.3 Effect of different earthquake intensity and dependency modeling on available water pressure for firefighting purposes.

to evaluate post-earthquake performance of a water network, considering its dependency to power, for fire following earthquake applications. As part of the framework, fragility curves were used to measure post-earthquake damage at the component level. The parameter, capacity index, was defined to quantify operability of a component following an earthquake. A probabilistic formulation could be applied to incorporate uncertainty in determining the capacity index parameters. In case of the electric network, a streamlined approach with graph theory-based maximum flow analysis was employed to build and analyze system level performance of the network. The drop in power flow after the earthquake, compared to the grid capacity for the intact condition, provided a "flow ratio" which was evaluated against a limiting value to identify "bright" vs. "dark" regions in the community. In case of the water network, a hybrid-method with conservation of mass and energy was applied to quantify water flow and pressure across the network.

This study investigated whether explicit dependence modeling of water pressure on availability of power is needed or not. The results suggest that ignoring explicit dependence of the water network on the electric network may provide inaccurate and unconservative predictions of available water pressure at fire hydrants. This is true for all seismic scenarios (0.1 PGA through 0.7 PGA). The results of this study can be incorporated for better informed emergency planning for firefighters and other first responders by being able to estimate the likelihood that water will be available considering dependency on electric network, evaluate if back up water supply is necessary, and identify the critical infrastructure elements, such as pump stations, for which their damage can lead to major losses and cascading failures.

References

Adachi, T. and Ellingwood, B.R. (2008). "Serviceability of earthquake-damaged water systems: Effects of electrical power availability and power backup systems on system vulnerability." *Reliability Engineering and System Safety*, 93(1): 78–88.

Albert, R., Albert, I., and Nakarado, G.L. (2004). "Structural vulnerability of the North American power grid." *Physical Review E*, 69: 1–4.

AWWA M31 (1989). *Distribution System Requirements for Fire Protection*, American Water Works Association, Denver, CO.

Bai, J.W., Hueste, M.B.D., and Gardoni, P. (2009). "Probabilistic assessment of structural damage due to earthquakes for buildings in Mid-America." *Journal of Structural Engineering*, 135(10), 1155–63.

Bhardwaj, V. (2001). *Tech Brief: Reservoirs, Towers, and Tanks*, the National Drinking Water Clearinghouse Fact Sheet.

Boulos, P.F., Lansey, K.E., and Karney, B.W. (2006). Comprehensive water distribution systems analysis handbook for engineers and planners. *Network*, 1–92. http://books.google.co.cr/books?id= ZLfgAAAAMAAJ (last accessed August 18, 2018).

Boykov, Y. and Kolmogorov, V. (2004). "An experimental comparison of min-cut/max-flow algorithms for energy minimization in vision." *IEEE Transactions on Pattern Analysis and Machine Intelligence*, 26(9): 1124–37.

Coar, M., Elhami Khorasani, N., and Garlock, M. (2016). "Integrating water and electric system in post-earthquake fire analysis." *Proceeding of the International Symposium on Sustainability and Resiliency of Infrastructure*. Taipei, Taiwan: National Taiwan University of Science and Technology.

Coar, M., Elhami Khorasani, N., and Garlock, M. (2018). "Effects of water network dependency on the electric network for post-earthquake fire suppression." *Sustainable and Resilient Infrastructure* (submitted).

Davis, C.A., O'Rourke, T.D., Adams, M.L., and Rho, M.A. (2012). "Case study: Los Angeles water services restoration following the 1994 Northridge earthquake." *Proceedings of 15th World Conference on Earthquake Engineering*, Lisboa, Portugal.

Deo, N. (1974). *Graph Theory with Applications to Engineering and Computer Science*. New York: Prentice-Hall.

Dong, X., Shinozuka, M., and Chang, S. (2004). "Utility power network systems." Proceedings of the 13th World Conference on Earthquake Engineering, Vancouver, B.C., August 1–6.

Duenas-Osorio, L., Craig, J.I., and Goodno, B.J. (2007). "Seismic response of critical interdependent networks." *Earthquake Engineering and Structural Dynamics*, 36: 285–306.

Elhami Khorasani, N. and Garlock, M.E.M. (2017). "Overview of fire following earthquake: Historical events and community responses." *International Journal of Disaster Resilience in the Built Environment*. 8(2): 158–74.

Elhami Khorasani, N., Gernay, T., and Garlock, M.E.M. (2017). "Data-driven probabilistic post-earthquake fire ignition model for a community." *Fire Safety Journal*, 94: 33–44.

Elnashai, A.S. (2003). "Next generation vulnerability functions for RC structures." *Proc., Response of Structures to Extreme Loading*. Toronto: Elsevier.

FEMA (2014). *Hazus: MH 2.1 Technical Manual – Earthquake Model*. Developed by the Department of Homeland Security. Federal Emergency Management Agency. Mitigation Division. Washington, DC.

Guidotti, R., Chmielewski, H., Unnikrishnan, V., Gardoni, P., McAllister, T., and van de Lindt, J. (2016). "Modeling the resilience of critical infrastructure: The role of network dependencies." *Sustainable and Resilient Infrastructure*, 1(3–4): 153–68, DOI: 10.1080/23789689.2016.1254999.

Hamada, M. (1975). *Architectural Fire Resistant Themes*. No 21. Kenchikugaku Taikei, Shokokusha, Tokyo.

Himoto, K. and Tanaka, T. (2008). "Development and validation of a physics-based urban fire spread model." *Fire Safety Journal* 43: 477–94.

Iwami, T., Ohmiya, Y., Hayashi, Y., Kagiya, K., Takahashi, W., and Naruse, T.N. (2004). "Simulation of city fire." *Fire Science and Technology*, 23(2): 132–40.

Johnson L.A. and Mahin, S.A. (2016). "The Mw 6.0 South Napa earthquake of August 24, 2014: A wake-up call for renewed investment in seismic resilience across California." California Seismic Safety Commission, Pacific Earthquake Engineering Research Center (PEER), CSSC Publication 16-03, PEER Report No. 2016/04.

Lee, S. and Davidson, R. (2010a). "Application of a physics-based simulation model to examine post-earthquake fire spread." *Journal of Earthquake Engineering*, 14(5): 688–705.

Lee, S. and Davidson, R. (2010b). "Physics-based simulation model of post-earthquake fire spread." *Journal of Earthquake Engineering* 14(5): 670–87.

Lee, S., Davidson, R., Ohnishi, N., and Scawthorn, C. (2008). "Fire following earthquake – reviewing the state-of-the-art of modeling." *Earthquake Spectra*. 24: 933–67.

Li, S. and Davidson, R.A. (2013a). "Parametric study of urban fire spread using an urban fire simulation model with fire department suppression." *Fire Safety Journal*, 61: 217–25.

Li, S. and Davidson, R. (2013b). "Application of an urban fire simulation model." *Earthquake Spectra*, 29(4): 1–21.

MAEViz. (2014). Hosted by the National Center for Supercomputing Applications, at the University of Illinois, Urbana: http://mae.cee.illinois.edu/software/software_maeviz.html (last accessed September 8, 2018),

Maria, A., Pitilakis, K., and Souli, A. (2010). *Fragility Functions for Water and Waste-Water System Elements*. SYNER-G deliverable 3.5.

Nussle, T., Kleiner, A., and Brenner, M. (2004). *Approaching Urban Disaster Reality: The ResQ Fire Simulator*. *Proceedings of RoboCup 2004: Robot Soccer World Cup VIII*, pp. 474–82.

NYCEM: The New York City Area Consortium for Earthquake Loss Mitigation. (2003). *Earthquake Risks and Mitigation in the New York, New Jersey, Connecticut Region*. Report Number MCEER-03-SP02.

O'Rourke, T.D. (2007). "Critical infrastructure, interdependencies, and resilience," *The Bridge – Linking Engineering and Society*, 37(1): 22–30.

Otake, H., Huang, H., Ooka, Y., Kato, S., and Hayashi, Y. (2003) "Simulation of flames and thermal plume in urban fire under windy condition." *Proceedings of the 17th Japan Society of Fluid Mechanics Symposium*, paper E.2-2 (in Japanese).

Pan, Y., Agrawal, A.K., and Ghosn, M. (2007). "Seismic fragility of continuous steel highway bridges in New York State." *J. Bridge Eng.*, 12(6), 689–99.

Pitilakis, K., Argyroudis, S., Kakderi, K., and Argyroudis, A. (2013). "Systemic seismic vulnerability and risk analysis for buildings, lifeline networks and infrastructures safety gain." *SYNER-G Synthetic Document*, JRC Scientific and Policy Reports.

Rossman, L.A. (2000). *EPANET 2 Users Manual*. US Environmental Protection Agency, Washington, DC, EPA/600/R-00/057.

Sarreshtehdari, A., Elhami Khorasani, N., and Coar, M. (2018). "A stream-lined approach for evaluating post-earthquake performance of an electric network." *Sustainable and Resilient Infrastructure* (in press).

Scawthorn, C. (2008). *The ShakeOut Scenario – Fire Following Earthquake*, Prepared for United States Geological Survey, Pasadena, CA and California Geological Survey, Sacramento, CA.

Scawthorn, C., Eidinger, J.M., and Schiff, A.J. (2005), *Fire Following Earthquake*. Technical Council on Lifeline Earthquake Engineering, Monograph No. 26, Published by the American Society of Civil Engineers, Reston.

Shinozuka M., Dong X., Chen T.C., and Jin X. (2007). "Seismic performance of electric transmission network under component failures." *Earthquake Engineering and Structural Dynamics*, 36(2), 227–44.

Unnikrishnan, V.U. and van de Lindt, J. (2016). "Probabilistic framework for performance assessment of electrical power networks to tornadoes." *Sustainable and Resilient Infrastructure*, 1(3–4): 137–52.

Vanzi, I. (1996). "Seismic reliability of electric power networks: methodology and application." *Structural Safety*, 18(4), 311–27.

Wenzel, L.J. (2008). *Water Supply Requirements for Public Supply Systems*, NFPA Handbook, 20th Edition, Section 15, Chapter 2, Quincy, MA.

Yildiz, S.S. and Karaman, H. (2013). "Post-earthquake ignition vulnerability assessment of Kucukcekmece District". *Journal of Natural Hazards and Earth System Sciences*. 13: 3357–68.

16

Risk and life cycle cost based asset management framework for aging water supply system

Solomon Tesfamariam[1], Golam Kabir,[2] and Rehan Sadiq[3]

[1,3] SCHOOL OF ENGINEERING, UNIVERSITY OF BRITISH COLUMBIA (UBC), 3333 UNIVERSITY WAY, KELOWNA, BC, CANADA, V1V1V7

[2] DEPARTMENT OF MECHANICAL, AUTOMOTIVE & MATERIALS ENGINEERING, UNIVERSITY OF WINDSOR, 401 SUNSET AVENUE, WINDSOR, ON, CANADA, N9B 3P4

[1] SOLOMON.TESFAMARIAM@UBC.CA

[2] GOLAM.KABIR@UBC.CA

[3] REHAN.SADIQ@UBC.CA

16.1 Introduction

Core public infrastructures (CPIs), including roads, bridges, transit, and water and wastewater systems are essential to ensure the health, safety, economic security, and maintaining the overall quality of life in an urban environment (Francisque et al. 2014; Lounis et al. 2010). The water supply systems (WSSs) are among the most important and expensive municipal infrastructure assets. Canada's first and second National Infrastructure Report Card (2016, 2012) showed that significant proportions of the WSS are in "fair" to "very poor" condition. The WSS is subject to failure due to aging and deterioration due to stressors from operational and environmental loads, and due to random traffic loads (Friedl & Fuchs-Hanusch 2011; Francisque et al. 2009; Rajani & Tesfamariam 2004; Yan & Vairavamoorthy 2003). Moreover, water main failure affects other existing nearby infrastructures such as sewer, stormwater, pavement, and gas pipes that may lead to cascading failures (USEPA 2010; Christodoulou et al. 2009). For this, the water main maintenance, repair or replacement (M/R/R) program has transformed from reactive to preventive actions plans and an effective asset management framework is necessary for proper planning, development, and management of the aging WSS (Francisque et al. 2014; Rogers 2006; Kleiner et al. 2004).

Decisions on the water main renewal are challenging for most municipalities. However, it is economically prohibitive to replace all damaged and aged water mains simultaneously (Shi et al. 2013; Kleiner et al. 2006). For this, the identification of critical and sensitive water mains and the selection of cost effective method(s) is vital for determining when to repair, renovate, or replace a section of water main (Friedl & Fuchs-Hanusch 2011; Jafar et al.

2010; Yan & Vairavamoorthy 2003). It is required to develop a comprehensive framework or effective tool, which will not only identify the sensitive and the risky pipes of the water distribution network but also determine the cost-effective maintenance, repair, and replacement action plan and prioritize them accordingly (Francisque et al. 2014; Lim et al. 2006; Engelhardt et al. 2003).

In this chapter, risk-based prioritization and life cycle cost (LCC)-based M/R/R decision action for buried infrastructure management is presented. The risk assessment entails the integration of system vulnerability to various hazards that lead to adverse consequences and the risk management guide the decision-maker select the effective alternative, which can reduce (control) risk (Kabir et al. 2015a; Francisque et al. 2014; Christodoulou et al. 2009; Kleiner et al. 2006). The proposed decision support tool is combined with the Geographic Information System (GIS) map of the utilities for developing risk map and identify the most critical and vulnerable pipes within the distribution network. On the other hand, the LCC provides decision makers with relevant information that helps them select a cost-effective design or management strategy for the rehabilitation of a damaged infrastructure system or for a new construction (Francisque et al. 2017; Ambrose et al. 2008; Rahman & Vanier 2004; Engelhardt et al. 2003; Kleiner et al. 2001). The proposed framework will enable municipalities and other authorities to build long- and short-term management plans.

The remainder of this chapter is structured as follows. In Section 16.2, the integrated water distribution asset management framework is described. The proposed risk and LCC based asset management framework for the aging WSS are described in the following section. After that, the utility of the proposed framework is illustrated with the Glenmore-Ellison Improvement District (GEID) water supply network. Finally, the summary, conclusions, limitations of the chapter and scope for further research are discussed.

16.2 Integrated water distribution asset management framework

This research was part of a five-year research program with medium- and small-sized municipalities located in the Okanagan region. As part of this project, a comprehensive integrated water distribution asset management framework was developed (Figure 16.1). Figure 16.1 shows the framework incorporates database management for condition and performance assessment, operation and maintenance for project level decision making, and finally asset accounting framework for network level decision making. The focus of this chapter is on risk assessment and life cycle cost framework. In this section, a general overview of this framework is discussed. The authors, in a separate chapter, will expound on key performance indicators and establish level of service.

16.2.1 Condition and performance assessment

Water distribution infrastructure is a complex network of pipes and appurtenances constructed of different materials and vintages, and manufacturing processes. 'Integrity' of water distribution infrastructure refers to its ability to transport water efficiently and effectively. The integrity of a water main can be described by a surrogate qualitative "condition," which dictates that the asset can perform its intended purpose, which in our case is providing water continuously to the public with desired quality and quantity. The condition of the water mains depends on numerous factors (Francisque et al. 2014). The asset database enables operators to maintain an up-to-date register of the existing assets. This research theme defined and established key

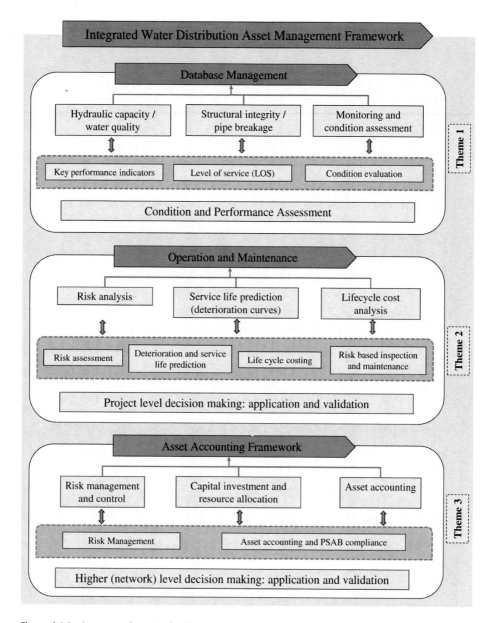

Figure 16.1 Integrated water distribution asset management framework.

performance indicators (KPIs), establish the level of service and conduct condition and performance assessment for the water system (Tesfamariam et al. 2013). The information collated and synthesized under this theme entails, network hydraulic capacity, distributed water quality, and historical pipe breakage and structural integrity database. The asset database enables operators to maintain an up-to-date register of the existing assets.

Key performance indicators

The integrity of a water main can be described by a surrogate qualitative "condition," which dictates that the asset can perform its intended purpose which in our case is providing water continuously to the public with desired quality and quantity. Lounis et al. (2010) highlighted that the performance of the water distribution system depends on numerous quantitative and qualitative key performance indicators (KPIs) like structural integrity, network hydraulic capacity, and water quality (Table 16.1). In this study, Haider et al. (2013) presented a comprehensive literature review on the performance indicators for small- and medium-sized water supply systems. Haider et al. (2014) identified 114 potential performance indicators (PIs) in operational, physical, water resources and environment, personnel, quality of service, water quality, and financial categories, and evaluated them using multicriteria decision analysis method. The developed method will support the utility manager or authorities to identify the most suitable or important Pis for their utility based on data availability and specific needs.

Level of service (LOS)

The level of service reflects social and economic goals of the community and may include many of performance objectives like safety, customer satisfaction, quality, quantity, capacity, reliability, responsiveness, environmental acceptability, cost, and availability (Lounis et al. 2010). Each KPI may have different threshold values that are dictated by the demand for services by the stakeholders and/or driven by regulatory requirements. The LOS is affected by both external and internal targets. External LOS targets typically are strategic or KPIs outcomes that are driven by customer's demand and set by the appropriate regulatory body. On the other hand, the internal LOS targets typically are tactical and geared toward focusing activities and strategic direction of the water utilities. The overall LOS for water distribution system is estimated based on individual KPIs (Haider et al. 2013, 2014). In this study, a multi-criteria decision-making model is developed to estimate overall LOS for water distribution system

Table 16.1 KPIs for water distribution system

Failure Criteria	Sub Criteria	Example: Performance Indicator
System Integrity	1) Minimize # and duration of interruptions	1) # of breaks (normalized)
	2) Minimize response time	2) # of leaks (normalized)
	3) Minimize non-revenue water loss	3) Amount of non-revenue water
	4) Maximize efficiency	4) # Service interruptions
	5) …	5) …
Hydraulic and Quantity of Flow	1) Adequate pressure	1) Flow velocity (max)
	2) Fire fighting capability	2) Pressure (min/max)
	3) Emergency storage	3) Water age (> 1 day)
	4) Adequate capacity	4) Demand (average, peak)
	5) Customer satisfaction	5) Pumps and storage capacity
	6) …	6) Water consumption/capita
		7) Low pressure complaints
		8) …
Water Quality	1) Point of entry (POE) and distribution guidelines	1) Residual chlorine
	2) Customer satisfaction	2) Customer complaints (#)
	3) …	3) Boil water advisories (#/time)
		…

Source: Lounis et al. 2010.

by aggregating information based on short-listed KPIs and acceptance criteria (Haider et al. 2015b, 2016a). The fuzzy rule-based technique has been employed to deal with uncertainty issues due to data limitations and vagueness in expert knowledge in small to medium-sized water utilities. The developed model can assess the performance of the utility as a whole, and/or different water supply systems, individually, operating within a utility for any assessment period (Haider et al. 2015b, 2016a).

Condition evaluation

Condition assessment or evaluation is the core component of asset management. The condition should not only relate to the "structural integrity," of the pipe rather it refers to "readiness of a component to serve its purpose" that includes more than structural or physical integrity (Sadiq et al. 2010a). The condition of the assets can be obtained by mapping or translating the observed and measured distresses onto a rating scale that describes the type, severity, and extent of different types of distresses. In this step, a multilevel performance management framework has been developed to evaluate the condition of the asset at a given time and identify the components that need M/R/R based on deficiencies in the desired level of service (Haider et al. 2015c, 2016b). At the beginning, the framework identifies and select the suitable performance indicators for SMWU, and to use them for inter-utility performance benchmarking. The following module can be used for detailed performance management at the utility, system, and sub-component levels (Haider et al. 2016c). Finally, a risk-based framework is developed for improving customer satisfaction through system reliability in small-sized to medium-sized water utilities (Haider et al. 2016b). This framework will provide the critical information needed to identify the underperforming functional components, to assess the remaining useful life and can rationally take corrective actions, and address customer satisfaction with efficient inventory management and data analyses (Haider et al. 2015c, 2016b).

16.2.2 Project level decision-making

This theme will deal with the development of models that evaluate failure probabilities and associated consequences based on established performance indicators and determine a risk of failure over the service life of water mains. It will provide a decision-making platform for inspection frequency, prioritization spending, and resource allocation to reduce risks to acceptable levels for a given water main.

Risk assessment

The risk is a combination of likelihood of failure of an asset and its associated consequences (Sadiq et al. 2004). The pipe fails generally through the gradual loss of mechanical strength due to deterioration processes (Rajani & Tesfamariam 2004). The exception to this is where there is a sudden catastrophic failure due to external factors such as subsidence or seismic activity (USEPA & WaterRF 2010). An asset considered failed when the consumers do not receive the quality of services at expected functionality, reliability and at an acceptable cost. Risk assessment helps to improve the quality of information that the decision-makers may utilize for decision-making. The risk assessment entails the integration of system vulnerability to various hazards that lead to adverse consequences. The GIS is integrated to document geographically factors/parameters related to asset vulnerability, and hazards to which the assets are exposed to determine the likelihood of failure and the consequences of pipe failure (Tesfamariam et al. 2015b; Francisque et al. 2014). More detail discussion is provided in Section 16.3.2.

Deterioration and service life prediction

The deterioration of pipes can be classified into two categories: (i) structural deterioration, which diminishes the pipe's structural integrity and its ability to withstand the various types of stresses; and (ii) deterioration of the inner surface of the pipe, resulting in diminished hydraulic capacity, degradation of water quality and even diminishing structural integrity in case of severe internal corrosion. The structural deterioration of water mains and their subsequent failure are complex processes, which are affected by both static (e.g., pipe material, size, age, soil type) and dynamic (e.g., climate, cathodic protection, pressure zone changes) (Kleiner & Rajani 2002) factors. In this study, statistical models are developed for predicting the deterioration of water mains considering pipe characteristic data (e.g., material, size, installation year, length), historical data based on physical integrity assessment (e.g., past failures, type, repair type, operability), environmental data (e.g., soil conditions, freezing index), and operational data (e.g., flow, pressure, water quality monitoring data) (Francisque et al. 2014; Tesfamariam et al. 2014).

As an outcome of this section, Gizachew et al. (2015) developed a Bayesian belief network (BBN) based model to predict the remaining service life of metallic pipes. Soil parameters that represent the corrosivity of the soil environment were used for prediction of corrosion pit depth, corrosion initiation time, time to failure and prediction of remaining service life. The BBN model considers the causal relationships and interdependencies between the soil parameters.

Life cycle cost

Water mains like any other CPI, age and deteriorate over time, which in turn leads to the reduction in its capacities. It is important to consider the life cycle cost (LCC) and especially the residual (remaining) life of the water mains in the management of its assets and particularly for risk management (Rahman & Vanier 2004). LCC provides decision makers with relevant information that helps them select a cost-effective design or management strategy for a new construction or for the rehabilitation of a damaged infrastructure system. The predicted deterioration helps to plan M/R/R strategies for assets in future based an acceptable threshold performance (condition state) or as low as reasonably practicable (ALARP) risk (Engelhardt et al. 2003). Information from the previous steps to develop and/or adapt models will enable to determine the remaining service life of each asset to help managers to improve their M/R/R decision-making process. More detail discussion is provided in Section 16.3.3.

Risk-based inspection and maintenance

Increasing complexity of water supply systems, coupled with growing public awareness for the need of higher levels of safety, exert additional pressure on decision-makers to find innovative solutions to ensure reliable but economical solutions. Risk-based inspection and maintenance (RBIM) can be used to identify critical component where inspections will pro-vide the most benefit in reducing the overall risk (Khan et al. 2004). If the periodic inspection is not carried out, the condition of a component may deteriorate over a period of time (Kleiner et al. 2006). Longer inspection intervals incur lower maintenance cost but may produce higher failure rates. Conversely, shorter inspection intervals may incur higher maintenance cost but produce lower failure rates. Trade-offs between the frequency of inspections (maintenance cost) and the risk resulting from higher failure rates can be achieved through the ALARP principle. This sub-theme of the framework developed an RBIM tool to determine the critical location, which requires immediate attention.

16.2.3 Network level decision-making and asset accounting

Over the years, the backlogs of M/R/R of aging water infrastructure are causing financial stress on local government which is jeopardizing the sustainability as well as the affordability of services. The main objective of this theme aims to make network level decision-making and developing asset accounting framework for water utilities including the calculation of future liabilities and life-cycle cost associated with alternative courses of action.

Risk management
Risk management helps to maintain risk within an acceptable (regulatory or otherwise) level and avoid any serious adverse effect on the public and environment. Risk management at the network level will facilitate decision-making related to questions (i) which water main to fix first, (ii) what are the consequences of "doing nothing"; and (iii) which water main is vital for the overall network reliability (Kleiner et al. 2006). Appropriate risk mitigation and control strategies for structural failure risk, hydraulic capacity risk, water quality risk, and overall risk are integrated with the risk assessment model developed in Theme 2 (Francisque et al. 2014). The risk-informed decision-making will provide utility managers the ability to reduce budgetary uncertainty when allocating limited monetary resources among competing for operational, repair, maintenance, and expansion activities within the realm of existing water distribution system.

Asset accounting and PSAB compliance
Public Sector Accounting Board requires local government to present information about the complete stock of tangible capital assets and amortization in the summary financial statements (PSAB 2007). Within this sub-theme, an asset accounting model is developed for small to medium-sized water utilities (Tesfamariam et al. 2015a). The developed model is a blend of single asset approach and component approach. The both approaches have their own benefits and are helpful in decision making and reporting purpose. The asset value, amortization rate, and current asset value may be obtained by selecting each component individually. This model will provide information about the full costs of services, help managers to assess future revenue requirements, performance and sustainability of existing programs and the likely cost and affordability of proposed future activities and services. This will eventually help managers understand the impact of using capital assets in the delivery of services and encourages them to consider alternative ways of managing costs and delivering services.

16.3 Proposed risk and LCC-based framework

In this chapter, the risk assessment and life cycle cost methods are integrated to develop risk and LCC based asset management framework, respectively. For rest of the models of Figure 16.1, interested readers are referred to Francisque et al. (2017, 2014), Haider et al. (2015a, 2015b), and Kabir et al. (2015a, 2015b). The proposed risk and LCC based asset management framework for the buried infrastructure is shown in Figure 16.2. The main components of the framework are described in the following sections.

16.3.1 Data collection

The pipe characteristics data, soil information, pipe breakage data, environmental, hydraulics, and consequence data will be collected from the water utility's GIS database, hydraulic database,

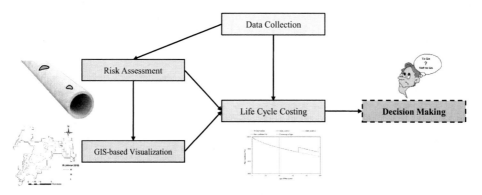

Figure 16.2 Risk and LCC based asset management framework.

Table 16.2 Data collection for the risk and LCC based asset management framework

Pipe Specific	*Soil Specific*	*Environmental*	*Water Quality*
Material	Soil Type	Temperature	Turbidity
Diameter	Soil Resistivity	Rain Deficit	Water Age
Age	Soil pH	Freezing Index	Water pH
Length	Moisture Content	Type of Traffic	Free Residual Cl
Thickness	Sulphide Content	Type of Road	Color
Cathodic Protection	Redox Potential		
Hydraulics	**Consequence**	**Breakage History**	
Water Pressure	Land Use	Previous Failures	
Water Velocity	Population	Break Type	
	Stream Flow		

water quality sampling station, environmental database, and other databases (Table 16.2). The data will be used for the next steps.

16.3.2 Risk assessment of WSS

Table 16.3 summarizes contributing risk factors and different water main risk assessment models have been reported in the different literature. Yan and Vairavamoorthy (2003) consider six factors and classified them into pipe physical and environmental factors. Francisque et al. (2009) grouped the factors into hydraulics, structural integrity, and water quality parameters. Despite some differences, the performance objectives of these water mains failure models can broadly be categorized as structural integrity index, hydraulic capacity index, water quality index, and consequences index (Kabir et al. 2015a; Francisque et al. 2014).

To quantify risk factors of water main failure and infrastructure deterioration, different hierarchical-based and network-based models are proposed. The weighted sum and product method (Studziński & Pietrucha-Urbanik 2012; Tchórzewska-Cieslak 2012; Friedl & Fuchs-Hanusch 2011) and analytic hierarchy process (AHP) (Francisque et al. 2014) are the most widely used hierarchical-based methods. Artificial neural network (ANN) (Jafar et al. 2010; Amaitik &Amaitik 2008; Najafi & Kulandaivel 2005; Christodoulou et al. 2003) based network

Table 16.3 Summary of water main risk assessment studies

Reference	Factors considered	Case study	Method
O'Day 1982	Pipe age, geographic location, diameter	Binghamton, N.Y, Nottingham, England, Severn-Trent, England	LDF[1] analysis
Kettler & Goulter 1985	Pipe breakage, time, diameter	New York, St. Catharines, Winnipeg, Philadelphia	Regression analysis
Christodoulou et al. 2003	Number of previous breakage, diameter, length, material, vicinity to highways, subway system, residential and industrial areas	District of Queens, New York City	ANN[2]
Jafar et al. 2003	Number of failures, length, materials, age, soil type, diameter, localization, thickness, pressure	North of France	Multiple linear regression, ANN
Yan &Vairavamoorthy 2003	Pipe age, diameter, material, road loading, soil condition, surroundings environmental conditions	Harbin, China	Fuzzy composite programming
Kleiner et al. 2004	Age, condition state, deterioration rate	Hypothetical example	Fuzzy rule-based NHMP[3]
Vanrenterghem-Raven et al. 2003	Material, length, diameter and break history, existence of ancient water zone	New York City	PHM[4]
Najafi & Kulandaivel 2005	Length, size, material, age, depth of cover, slope, sewer type	City of Atlanta	ANN
Kleiner et al. 2006	Age, condition state, deterioration rate	Hypothetical example	Fuzzy rule-based NHMP
Rogers & Grigg 2008	Break causes, break history, diameter, material, age, pressure, soil resistivity, soil type	Laramie (Wyoming) water; Colorado Spring	MCDA[5]
Rogers 2006	Break causes, break history, diameter, material, age, pressure, soil resistivity, soil type	Laramie (Wyoming) water; Colorado Spring	MCDA
Gorji-Bandpy & Shateri 2008	Pipe diameter, age, length, soil type, material, land use	Behshahr, Sari, Ramsar, Iran	Survial analysis
Amaitik & Amaitik 2008	Monitoring period, pipe age, soil resistivity, pressure, soil density, soil cover, wire wrap, wire diameter, wire pitch	Great Man-made River Project, Benghazi, Libya	ANN
Christodoulou et al. 2009	Number of previous breakage, diameter, length, material, vicinity to highways, subway system, residential and industrial areas	New York City, USA, City of Limassol, Cyprus	Neurofuzzy decision-support
Francisque et al. 2009	Pipe material, pipe age, water age, free residual chlorine, water temperature, population (children, elders and hospitalized individuals	Quebec City, Canada	Fuzzy synthetic evaluation, fuzzy rule-base
Jafar et al. 2010	Material, length, diameter, thickness, age, type of soil, location in the street, pressure and protection	North of France	ANN

Reference	Input parameters	Study	Method
Friedl & Fuchs-Hanusch 2011	Pipe segment, vintage, pipe joint, impact of ground water, operating pressure, installation location, future influences, diameter, supply redundancy, area designation, vulnerability and exposure, water losses, quality and time interval of asset inspection	Austrian water distribution system	Weighted method
Singh 2011	Cause of break, age at failure, pipe diameter; type of soil at the location	Honolulu, Hawaii	Bayesian network
Tchórzewska-Cieslak 2011	Failure probability; loss due to failure	Hypothetical study	Fuzzy logic
Studziński & Pietrucha-Urbanik 2012	Pipe length, failure rate, water shortage, substandard supply minutes, equivalent resident	South – eastern Poland	Weighted method
Tchórzewska-Cieslak 2012	Type of network, depth, pressure, age, material, hydrological conditions, location, number of failures	Hypothetical study	Weighted sum method
Pietrucha-Urbanik & Valis 2013	Probability of lack of water, population affected	Hypothetical study	Fuzzy logic
Shi et al. 2013	Age, diameter, material, temperature	Hong Kong	GIS cluster analysis
Francisque et al. 2014	Material, diameter, age, length, soil type, soil resistivity, soil pH, moisture content, sulphide content, freezing index, turbidity, water age, water pH, free residual Cl, color, water pressure, water velocity, land use, population	City of Kelowna, BC, Canada	AHP[6]
Kabir et al. 2015a	Material, diameter, age, length, thickness, soil type, soil resistivity, soil pH, moisture content, sulphide content, freezing index, turbidity, water age, water pH, free residual Cl, color, water pressure, water velocity, land use, population	City of Kelowna, BC, Canada	Bayesian belief network

[1] LDF: Linear Discriminate Function.
[2] ANN: Artificial Neural Network.
[3] NHMP: non-homogeneous Markov process.
[4] PHM: Proportional Hazards Model.
[5] MCDA: Multicriteria Decision Analysis.
[6] AHP: Analytic Hierarchy Process.

method is the widely used whereas some authors also proposed Neurofuzzy decision-support (Christodoulou et al. 2009), and Bayesian network (Kabir et al. 2015a; Singh 2011) for risk assessment of water mains.

To handle the vagueness and ambiguity, fuzzy expert system methods like fuzzy synthetic evaluation (Francisque et al. 2009), fuzzy rule-based nonhomogeneous Markov process (Kleiner et al. 2004), Hierarchical fuzzy expert system (Sadiq et al. 2004), fuzzy composite programming (Yan & Vairavamoorthy 2003), and fuzzy logic (Pietrucha-Urbanik & Valis 2013) are also proposed. Some of the authors also highlighted other methods like multiple linear regression (Jafar et al. 2003), proportional hazards model (PHM) (Vanrenterghem-Raven et al. 2003), multicriteria decision analysis (MCDA) (Rogers & Grigg 2008), linear discriminate function (LDF) analysis (O'Day 1982), survival analysis (Gorji-Bandpy & Shateri 2008), and GIS cluster analysis (Shi et al. 2013). However, the majority of these studies only evaluate the risk of water mains within the distribution network without discussing how to handle these sensitive and the risky pipes and to prioritize them for maintenance, repair, and replacement cost effectively.

As the pipe failure modes vary significantly based on the pipe materials, three different conceptual risk frameworks are considered for metallic, cementitious, and plastic pipes. Figure 16.3 shows the risk framework for the metallic pipes. For a cementitious-based pipe (i.e., asbestos-cement, concrete pipe), the soil corrosivity index (SCI) is calculated using soil pH, moisture content, and soil percentage of fines (% Fines) whereas water hardness and alkalinity have been added to water pH to determine the aggressiveness index (AI) (Tesfamariam et al. 2015b).

For the plastic pipe, the structural integrity index (SII) calculated using the SCI and structural failure index (Str.FI). The percentages of fines (% Fines) and gravel (% Gravel) are used as input factors for the SCI. The pipe vulnerability index (VI) or likelihood of failure and consequence index (CI) are integrated to determine the final risk index (RI) of each pipe and water quality index (WQI) od each pipe is associated to improve or support the decision-making process. For more details about the risk framework, interested readers are referred to Francisque et al. (2014) and Tesfamariam et al. (2014). Based on the risk index, the risk ranking of the each pipe will be performed and the result will be integrated with the GIS map of the water utility to identify critical pipes in the distribution system for repair or replacement plan or further decision making.

16.3.3 Life cycle cost of WSS

The life cycle cost studies for water mains are summarized in Table 16.4. The majority of the authors used net present value (NPV) based deterministic LCC models for decision-making issues for water mains (Francisque et al. 2017; Thomas et al. 2016; Ambrose et al. 2008; Rajani & Kleiner 2004; Engelhardt et al. 2003; Kleiner et al. 2001). Some of the other proposed deterministic methods are dynamic programming (Kleiner et al. 2001), activity based cost (Engelhardt et al. 2003), and benefit estimations (Lim et al. 2006). Shahata (2006) also presented Monte Carlo simulation based probabilistic LCC models.

The majority of the LCC studies of water main considered an average agency cost for M/R/R (Ambrose et al. 2008; Lim et al. 2006; Rajani & Kleiner 2004; Engelhardt et al. 2003) which are highly uncertain. Moreover, repair and rehabilitation costs depend highly on the land use and topographical condition of the location where the pipe is buried. For example, if one pipe is buried under a concrete pavement and another pipe is buried under an open or agricultural field or native soil, the repair cost of the former will be much higher than the latter one. However, if we consider only an average cost, then the repair cost for both these pipes will

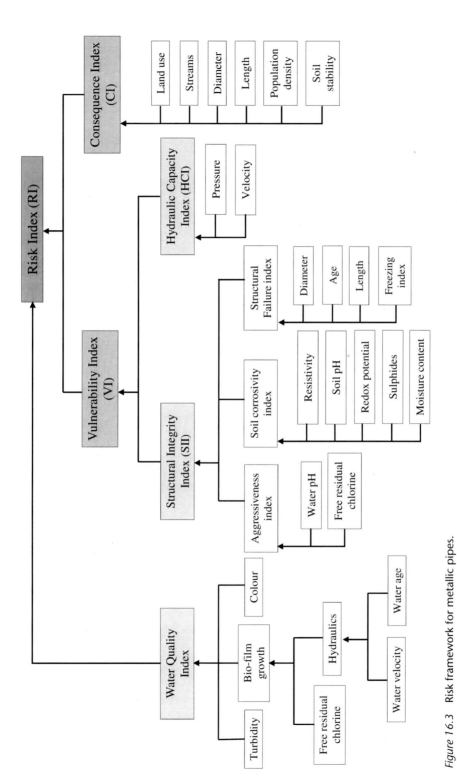

Figure 16.3 Risk framework for metallic pipes.

Table 16.4 Summary of life cycle costing studies for water mains

Reference	Different costs	Methods	Techniques	Applications
Kleiner et al. 2001	Rehabilitation, maintenance cost	Deterministic	Dynamic programming	Pipe rehabilitation alternatives selection
Engelhardt et al. 2003	Total cost, private cost, social cost, operating costs, capital expenditure, regulatory penalties	Deterministic	Activity based costing	Whole life costing of water distribution network
Rajani & Kleiner 2004	Renewal mitigation cost	Deterministic	NPV[1]	Failure management of transmission pipelines
Lim et al. 2006	Engineering & supervision, construction, O&M, disposal	Deterministic	NPV Cost & Benefit analysis	Economic feasibility evaluation of water network system
Shahata 2006	Operation &maintenance, repair, renovation, replacement	Probabilistic	Monte Carlo simulation	Stochastic LLC for water mains
Ambrose et al. 2008	Installation cost, repair cost, leakage cost, replacement cost	Deterministic	NPV	Whole life costing of water distribution network
Lim et al. 2008	Design & supervision, construction expenses, operations & maintenance, disposal	Deterministic	NPV	Environmental & economic performance of a water network system
McPherson et al. 2009	Capital cost, operational cost, maintenance cost	Deterministic	NPV	Evaluation of PVC and DI pipeline material in design
Du et al. 2012	Capital, operation & maintenance	Deterministic	Life cycle analysis	LCA for water & wastewater pipe materials
Thomas et al. 2016	Installation, operation and maintenance	Deterministic	NPV	To evaluate the life cycle costs and environmental impacts of water pipelines
Francisque et al. 2017	Maintenance, repair, renovation, replacement	Deterministic	NPV	To predict suitable new installation &/or rehabilitation programs

[1] NPV: Net present value.

be the same which is not practical and highly uncertain for effective decision-making. Most of these studies did not mention how to select the appropriate water mains to perform the LCC analysis and determine the cost-effective actions, as it is not feasible to perform the LCC analysis for all the water mains in the distribution network.

In order to optimize the usage of available funds for the cost-effective M/R/R action program of the critical pipes, an LCC framework is developed. Figure 16.4 provides the proposed life cycle cost analysis framework for the critical water mains. The break frequency curve and deterioration curves for water mains of different materials and sizes will be developed using Bayesian regression analysis based on pipe characteristics (i.e., age, length, and diameter), soil parameter (i.e., soil corrosivity index), hydraulic factors (i.e., velocity and pressure), and aggressiveness index.

For more details about the Bayesian regression analysis, interested readers have referred to Kabir et al. (2015b). After that, the pipe deterioration curves are developed using the

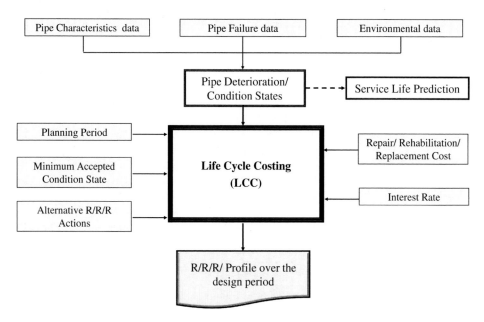

Figure 16.4 Proposed methodology for LCC of small to medium-sized water utilities.

methodology proposed by Banciulescu and Sekuler (2010). The service life of a pipe or structure is a time period at the end of which the pipe stops performing the functions it is designed and built for (Rahman & Vanier 2004). The developed deterioration curves will provide an overview of the remaining service life of each group of the pipe if the observed break patterns remain unchanged and basic break repair is carried out. Next, the different repair, rehabilitation, and replacement techniques and their corresponding costs will be collected. After determining the timing of future activities, set of scenarios combined of repair, renovation, and replacement alternatives can be suggested and generate the LCC profile of each pipe. The NPV for each suggested scenario is expressed using the following formula (Engelhardt et al. 2003):

$$TLCC = \sum_{t=0}^{l} \frac{C_t}{(1+r)^t},$$

where *TLCC* is the present value of the total life cycle cost, C_t is the sum of maintenance, repair, replacement/rehabilitation costs and salvage value, *r* is the discounted rate and *l* is the service life of the water mains or the planning period.

16.4 Case study

The proposed risk and LCC based asset management framework is applied to the water distribution network of the GEID, BC, Canada. The GEID is located in British Columbia, Canada and is one of the five water purveyors in the City of Kelowna and in a portion of the Regional District Central Okanagan (RDCO) (Tesfamariam et al. 2014, 2015b). The water distribution network of GEID consists 1,328 individual pipes and 152.17km length of pipe. C900 (1,071 pipes for a total length of 90.15km) and asbestos-cement (AC) (199 pipes for 45.73km of total length) pipes are the most frequent water mains. Other than that the network consists of the concrete cylinder (18 pipes), ductile iron (DI) (29 pipes), galvanized (2 pipes), steel (4 pipes), polyvinyl chloride (PVC) (3 pipes) and high-density polyethylene (HDPE) (2 pipes).

The pipe characteristics data (e.g., material, diameter, length, installation year, number of previous failures) are collected from GIS databases of GEID. Monthly water quality data have been collected (for 2003 to 2012) from GEID water quality monitoring stations. Free residual chlorine, water turbidity, and color have been collected from 14 water quality monitoring stations/sampling points whereas hardness and field temperature are also measured at some of these locations. As the starting point, the year 2012 data is used in this chapter. To consider seasonal variations, the average parameter value has been calculated for summer (May to October) and winter (November to April). The average pressure and average velocity inside the water main of the network are calculated using the EPANET model of GEID.

The soil properties (e.g., soil resistivity, redox potential, soil sulfide content, pH, percentage fines) are collected from Pacific Agri-Food Research Centre(Agricultural and Agrifood Canada, Summerland, BC), Ministry of Agriculture (Abbotsford, BC), and Ministry of Environment (Kelowna, BC). The soil corrosivity index of metallic pipes is determined using a 10-point scoring method introduced by the Cast Iron Pipe Research Association (CIPRA) and recommended by American Water Work Association (AWWA 1999). The values, characteristics, and points of soil resistivity, soil pH value, redox potential, sulfides content, and moisture content (according to drainage condition and classified as soil type) are shown in Table 16.5. Similarly, the soil corrosivity index of cementitious pipes is determined considering soil pH, the percentage of clay, and soil sulfide content (Table 16.5). For plastic pipes, there is no specific guideline to assess the external soil effects. The percentage of gravel and percentage of clay are considered for the soil corrosivity index assessment as backfill materials, potentially injurious bedding soil (e.g., rock soil, gravel) are the main concern for plastic pipes (Table 16.5). Figure 16.5 shows the soil corrosivity index (SCI) map for GEID water mains.

To determine the impact of a water main failure for different territory, 48 types of land uses (e.g., agricultural, school, hospital, roads) have been considered in this chapter (Tesfamariam et al. 2014). However, a water main can be under various land uses. To assess the consequence of land use in case of this water main failure, the final land use value is determined by normalizing the sum of the product of the weight of each intersected land use by the length of the portion of the water main that intersects this land use with respect to the total length of the water main. The relative weights to each land use are attributed using the analytic hierarchy process (AHP) developed by Saaty (1988). Figure 16.6 indicates the final land use calculation of a sample water main GEID_0012. The GEID_0012 intersects four land uses A1S (weight = 0.01048), P3 (weight = 0.010482), and RU5 (weight = 0.021063) twice. The final land use value (FLU) of GEID_0012 is 0.018174. For a qualitative approach, three classes or granularities such as Low (0–0.3), Medium (0.31–0.7), and High (0.71–1) have been used.

To determine the population density, a population distribution map named "Census2006_DisseminationArea" was collected from the City of Kelowna, which shows the total population distribution in 2006 for various dissemination areas. A dissemination area (DA) is a small, relatively stable geographic unit composed of one or more adjacent dissemination blocks. Based on the data, the density of population (Persons/Km^2) for each DA has been calculated by dividing

Table 16.5 Soil corrosiveness scoring system for metallic, cementitious, and plastic pipes

Material	Soil property	Values and characteristics	Points
Metallic	Soil resistivity (Ω-cm)	<1,500	10
		≥1,500–1,800	8
		>1800–2,100	5
		>2,100–2,500	2
		>2,500–3,000	1
		>3,000	0
	Soil pH	0–2	5
		2–4	3
		4–6.5	0
		6.5–7.5	0
		7.5–8.5	0
		>8.5	3
	Redox potential (mV)	> +100	0
		(+) 50 to (+)100	3.5
		0 to +50	4
	Soil sulphide content	Positive	3.5
		Trace	2
		Negative	0
	Moisture content	Poor drainage(continually wet)	2
		Fair drainage (generally moist)	1
		Good drainage (generally dry)	0
Cementitious	Soil pH	< 5.5	2
		5.5 – 6.5	3
		≥ 7	3
	% of clay	≥ 40	3
		30.0 – 35.0	2
		20.0 -30.0	1
		< 20	0
	Soil sulphide content	Positive	0
		Trace	1
		Negative	3
Plastic	% of gravel	> 30.0	5
		15.0 – 30.0	3
		8.0 – 14.0	2
		< 8.0	0
	% of clay	≥ 40.0	3
		30.0 – 35.0	2
		20.0 – 30.0	1
		< 20.0	0

the number of persons of each DA by its size in square kilometer. The population distribution in GEID service area is shown in Figure 16.7.

Based on the data, a Risk-based Life Cycle Asset Management tool for water Pipes (RiLCAMP) tool is developed for the prioritization of the water main repair or replacement program of the GEID (Figure 16.8). The RiLCAMP tool has two modules (1) Risk Analysis and (2) Life Cycle Cost Analysis. The developed framework and RiLCAMP tool are briefly discussed with appropriate examples.

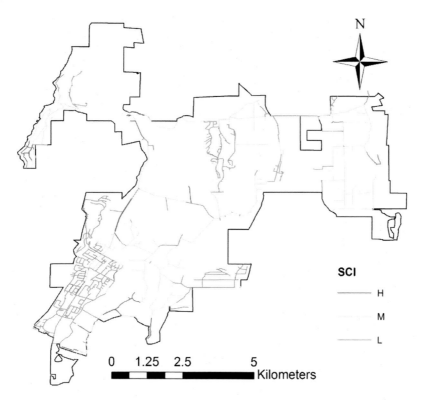

Figure 16.5   Soil corrosivity index (SCI) map for GEID water mains.

To prioritize the replacement and rehabilitation of water mains of GEID, the Risk Analysis module of RiLCAMP tool is used. To aggregate the sub-index values shown in Figure 16.3, a relative weight has been assigned to each parameter using the analytic hierarchy process (AHP) developed by Saaty (1998). Table 16.6 summarizes the index computation showing the input factors for each index and the way they are aggregated, and if required their weight, to produce the index. For further details about the transformation functions and weight computation, the reader can consult Francisque et al. (2014).

The developed risk framework for GEID is described with a sample pipe (ID: GEID_0392). The pipe characteristics, soil, hydraulics, and water quality information of GEID_0392 is shown in Table 16.7. According to the Figure 16.3 and Table 16.7, the StrFI, SCI, AI, SII, HCI, CI, WQI, and RI of the GEID_0392 is shown in Figure 16.9. The risk rank of GEID_0392 is 23. According to the risk index and risk rank, the GEID_0392 required immediate action. Similarly, the risk index of the other pipes is determined.

The developed framework is also able to determine the overall indices of the water distribution system (Figure 16.10). According to the analysis, almost 57 percent and 39 percent water mains are in low and medium risk levels whereas 4 percent of water mains are at high risk. The utility managers must direct very special attention to those pipes and take after inspection appropriate action (e.g., maintenance, replacement) to avoid their failure. To improve risk distribution spatial comprehension and favor utility managers' appropriate intervention, the

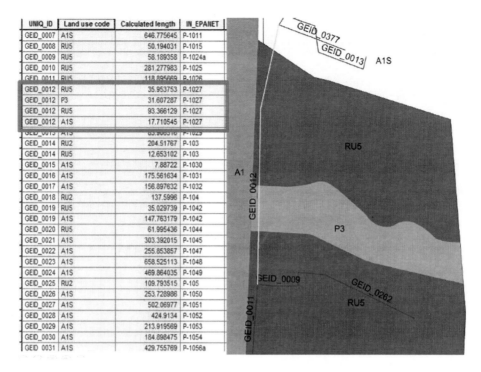

UNIQ_ID	Land use code	Calculated length	IN_EPANET
GEID_0007	A1S	646.775645	P-1011
GEID_0008	RU5	50.194031	P-1015
GEID_0009	RU5	58.189358	P-1024a
GEID_0010	RU5	281.277983	P-1025
GEID_0011	RU5	118.895669	P-1026
GEID_0012	RU5	35.953753	P-1027
GEID_0012	P3	31.607287	P-1027
GEID_0012	RU5	93.366129	P-1027
GEID_0012	A1S	17.710545	P-1027
GEID_0013	A1S	63.900310	P-1029
GEID_0014	RU2	204.51767	P-103
GEID_0014	RU5	12.653102	P-103
GEID_0015	A1S	7.88722	P-1030
GEID_0016	A1S	175.561634	P-1031
GEID_0017	A1S	156.897632	P-1032
GEID_0018	RU2	137.5996	P-104
GEID_0019	RU5	35.029739	P-1042
GEID_0019	A1S	147.763179	P-1042
GEID_0020	RU5	61.995436	P-1044
GEID_0021	A1S	303.392015	P-1045
GEID_0022	A1S	255.853857	P-1047
GEID_0023	A1S	658.525113	P-1048
GEID_0024	A1S	469.864035	P-1049
GEID_0025	RU2	109.793515	P-105
GEID_0026	A1S	253.728986	P-1050
GEID_0027	A1S	502.06977	P-1051
GEID_0028	A1S	424.9134	P-1052
GEID_0029	A1S	213.919569	P-1053
GEID_0030	A1S	184.898475	P-1054
GEID_0031	A1S	429.755769	P-1056a

Figure 16.6 Land use calculation of a sample water main (ID GEID_0012).

developed risk framework is integrated with the GIS map for developing a risk map of GIED (Figure 16.11).

The Life Cycle Cost Analysis module of RiLCAMP tool is used to prioritize M/R/R recommendations for water mains in high risk. To develop the pipe deterioration curves, the pipes have been grouped into five: Metallic (Diameter ≤ 200mm and Diameter > 200mm), Cementitious (Diameter ≤ 200mm and Diameter > 200mm) and Plastic. Bayesian regression analysis was performed for each pipe group (cementitious, metallic, and plastic pipes) (Tesfamariam et al. 2015b). The mean and standard deviation (SD) of the Bayesian regression coefficient for different models are used to generate the break frequency curves (Table 16.8). The break frequency curves are converted to pipe deterioration curves using the methodology proposed by Banciulescu and Sekuler (2010).

Currently, the GEID is using only open trench repair action. They did not consider any type of trenchless renewal methods. As there was no reliable information on the costs of water mains breaks, the average repair costs for different site (i.e., gravel, concrete pavement and agricultural/ no pavement/native soil) and location (same side or road crossing) conditions are shown in Table 16.9 based on the discussion with the authorities of GEID. According to the Table 16.9, if the asset is in road crossing, the average repair costs will be double compared to the asset on the same side. Moreover, due to the conflict with the other utilities like sewer, internet, gas, the average repair costs will be higher than the normal condition. For example, if a water main lay under a concrete pavement road crossing and it also conflicts with other utilities, then the total average R/R costs will be

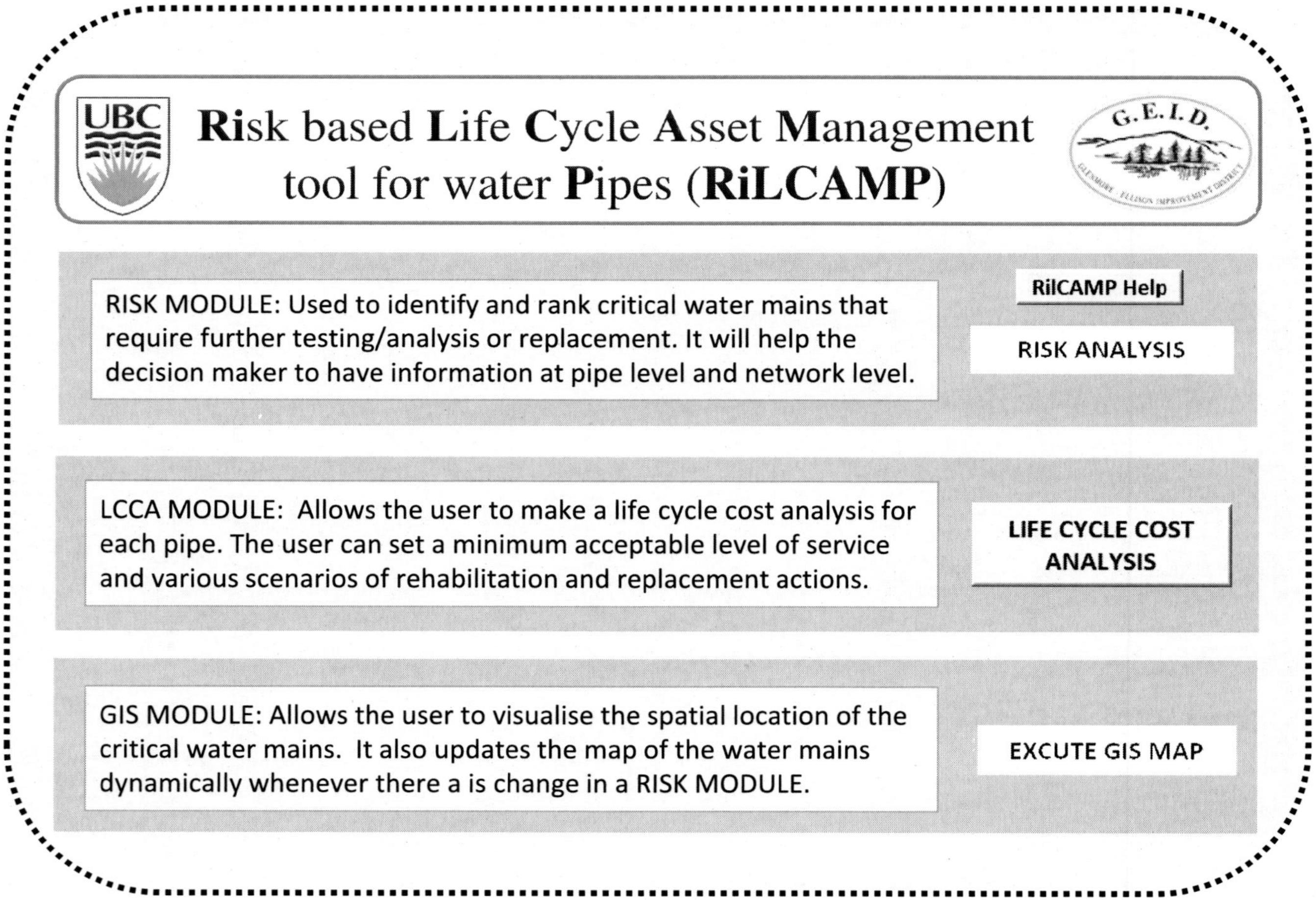

Risk based Life Cycle Asset Management tool for water Pipes (**RiLCAMP**)

G.E.I.D.

RilCAMP Help

RISK ANALYSIS

LIFE CYCLE COST ANALYSIS

EXCUTE GIS MAP

RISK MODULE: Used to identify and rank critical water mains that require further testing/analysis or replacement. It will help the decision maker to have information at pipe level and network level.

LCCA MODULE: Allows the user to make a life cycle cost analysis for each pipe. The user can set a minimum acceptable level of service and various scenarios of rehabilitation and replacement actions.

GIS MODULE: Allows the user to visualise the spatial location of the critical water mains. It also updates the map of the water mains dynamically whenever there is change in a RISK MODULE.

Figure 16.7 Distribution of population density by dissemination area (DA) in GEID.

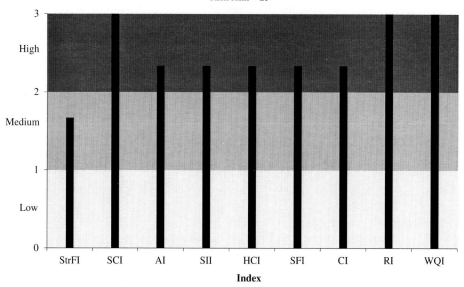

Figure 16.8 RiLCAMP tool for risk and LCC analysis.

Table 16.6 Index computation approach for risk framework

Level 4	Level 3	Level 2	Level 1
Str. FI^a = $f(a + bD + cA + dL + eD^2 + fA^2 + gL^2 + hD{*}A + iA{*}L + jL{*}D)$	SII = 0.5*Str.FI + 0.3*SCI + 0.2*AI SII$_{\text{plastic pipes}}$ = 0.5*Str. FI + 0.5*SCI	VI = 0.6*SII + 0.4*HCI	RI = 0.7*VI + 0.3*CI
SCI$_{\text{Metallic pipes}}$ = R$_{\text{score}}$ + pH$_{\text{score}}$ + RP$_{\text{score}}$ + Sc$_{\text{score}}$ + Mc$_{\text{score}}$ SCI$_{\text{plastic pipes}}$ = %Fines$_{\text{score}}$ + %Gravel$_{\text{score}}$ SCI$_{\text{Cementitious pipes}}$ = pH$_{\text{score}}$ + %Fines$_{\text{score}}$ + Sc$_{\text{score}}$			
AI$_{\text{Metallic pipes}}$ = 0.5*pH + 0.5* FRC^c AI$_{\text{Cementitious pipes}}$ = pH + log[AH]^c			
	HCI = 0.8*Pressure + 0.2*Velocity		
		CI = 0.35*LU + 0.35*PD + 0.2*D + 0.1*L	
			WQI^d = 0.22*T + 0.52*FRC + 0.04*C + 0.13*A$_W$ + 0.09*V

^{a} D = Diameter, A = Age, L = Length; a, b, c, d, e, f, g, h, i, and j = regression coefficients, LU = Land Use, PD = Population density.
^{b} R_{score} = soil resistivity score, $pHscore$ = soil pH score, RP_{score} = Redox Potential score, Sc_{score} = soil sulfure content score, Mc_{score} = soil moisture content score.
^{c} FRC = Free residual chlorine, $[AH]$ = [total alkalinity (mg/L CaCO$_3$)* calcium hardness H (mg/L CaCO$_3$)].
^{d} T = water Turbidity, C = Colour, A_w = water Age, V = water Velocity.

Table 16.7 Pipe characteristics, soil, hydraulics, and water quality information of GEID_0392

Pipe information		Unit	Hydraulic data		Unit
Installation year	1971	Year	Average Pressure	90.72	m
Diameter	100	mm	Average Velocity	0.00	m/s
Length	365.40	m			
Material	AC	Unit less			
Soil properties data		**Unit**	**Water quality data (Winter)**		**Unit**
Zone		Unit less	Water hardness	131.75	mg/L
Soil pH	7.4	Unit less	Water alkalinity	125.48	mg/L
Moisture content	Fair drainage	Unit less	Water pH	6.89	Unit less
Percent fines		(%)	Residual chlorine	1.61	mg/L
Percent gravel		(%)	Turbidity	1.85	NTU
Redox potential	630	(mV)	Colour	36.47	ACU
Sulphides	Negative	Unit less	Water age	65.31	Hr
Resistivity	1000	Ohm-cm	Water velocity	0.00	m/s

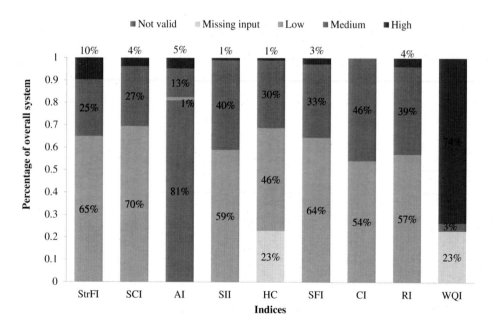

Figure 16.9 Overall indices for the GEID_0392 pipe.

$11,000.00 ($5,000.00 × 2 + $1,000.00). This will help to reduce the uncertainty in decision making. The pipe replacement or new pipe installation costs (including fitting and valves) is also presented in Table 16.9.

The deterioration of the GEID_0392 over the planning period can be shown in Figure 16.12. The pipe will follow the dotted deterioration profile if no intervention is selected over the planning period. However, if the decision makers want to keep very good LOS, then the pipe condition will be 75 percent and certain action or intervention is required after 67 years to

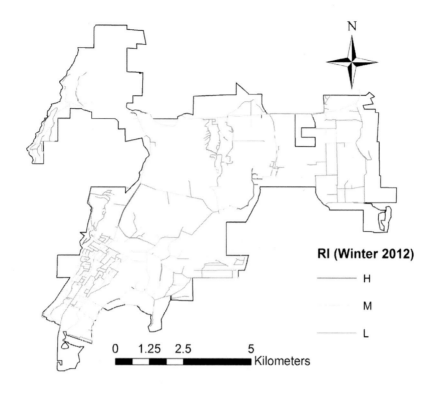

Figure 16.10 Percentage of overall indices of the water distribution system of GEID.

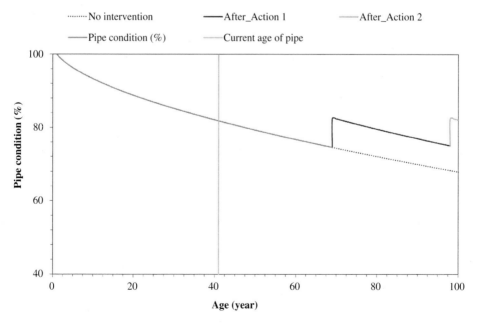

Figure 16.11 Risk map for GEID water mains.

Table 16.8 Mean and SD of the Bayesian regression coefficient for different models

| | Metallic | | | | Cementitious | | | | Plastic | |
| | Dia ≤ 200mm | | Dia > 200mm | | Dia ≤ 200mm | | Dia > 200mm | | | |
	Mean	SD	Mean	SD	Mean	SD	Mean	SD	Mean	SD
ln(AGE)	0.2005	0.0899	0.3880	0.1337	0.5765	0.0927	0.1881	0.1598	0.2510	0.1580
ln(LENGTH)	−0.8526	0.0618	−0.8197	0.1023	−0.7654	0.0554	−0.4989	0.1170	−0.5292	0.1899
SCI	0.0000	0.0000	0.0398	0.2837	−0.1867	0.1236	0.0000	0.0000	0.0000	0.0000
AI	2.7956	0.4398	0.0000	0.0000	0.0000	0.0000	0.0000	0.0000	0.0000	0.0000
PRESSURE	0.0000	0.0000	0.0087	0.0019	0.0016	0.0015	0.0000	0.0000	0.0000	0.0000
VELOCITY	0.0000	0.0000	0.1887	0.0019	0.0000	0.0000	0.0000	0.0000	0.0000	0.0000

Table 16.9 Replacement or new pipe installation cost for different actions for GEID

Water Main Repair Cost		Water Main Replacement Cost	
Site condition	Unit Cost	Diameter (mm)	Unit Cost/m
Gravel	$ 2,000.00	50	$ 65.00
Concrete pavement	$ 5,000.00	100	$ 70.00
Agricultural/No pavement/Native soil	$ 1,500.00	150	$ 80.00
		200	$ 110.00
Same side	1	250	$ 135.00
Road crossing	2	300	$ 150.00
		350	$ 200.00
Utility conflict	$ 1,000.00	400	$ 250.00
		450	$ 300.00
		500	$ 350.00
		600	$ 400.00

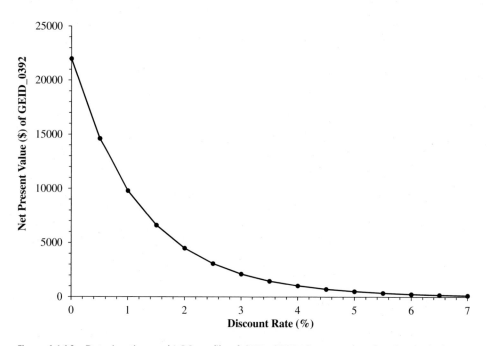

Figure 16.12 Deterioration and LCC profile of GEID_0392 pipe over the planning period.

Table 16.10 GEID_0392 pipe condition after each M/R/R actions over the planning period

Actions	LoS Threshold	Pipe Condition	Possible Interventions	Increase of pipe condition	New Pipe Condition
Action 1	Very Good	75 %	Repair	10 %	82.5 %
Action 2	Very Good	75 %	Repair	10 %	82.5 %

Table 16.11 GEID_0392 pipe cost after each M/R/R actions over the planning period

Actions	Site condition	Utility conflict	Road Condition	Repair Cost	NPV Repair	Replacement Cost	NPV Replacement
Action 1	Concrete pavement	Yes	Road crossing	$11,000.0	$1,518.1	$25,550	$3,526.11
Action 2	Concrete pavement	Yes	Road crossing	$11,000.0	$607.22	$25,550	$1,410.40
			Total	$22,000.0	$2,125.32	$511,00.0	$4,936.51

maintain or improve the LOS (Table 16.10). The decision maker can choose repair as an action which will improve the pipe condition by 10 percent. The new pipe condition will be 82.5 percent and the pipe will start deteriorating from there (Table 16.10). However, it is quite challenging to determine the percentage of improvement of pipe condition after any intervention or action due to the involvement of multiple factors (Engelhardt et al. 2003). For this, the decision makers can easily change the percentage of improvement of pipe condition after any intervention based on their judgment and experience. Similarly, the decision makers can choose other actions to maintain a satisfactory LOS or pipe conditions by selecting appropriate interventions shown in Figure 16.12. For the selection of different actions to improve the pipe condition, the pipe deterioration profile will also change. Figure 16.12 shows the deterioration profile of GEID_0392 pipe after selecting different actions.

The corresponding repair and replacement costs of GEID_0392 for Action 1 and 2 at 67 and 98 years respectively, total cost over the planning period and the net present value considering 3 percent discount rate are presented in Table 16.11. According to Table 16.11, the NPV of the repair costs of GEID_0392 after Action 1 at 2038 and Action 2 at 2069 are less compare to the replacement costs. Therefore, it is better to repair GEID_0392 than replacement. The NPV of the total LCC of GEID_0392 pipe is $2,125.32. The developed LCC module will help the decision makers to take the practical decision regarding their assets.

The discount rate is another important element for the M/R/R decision making. The discount rate represents the investor's minimum acceptable rate of return. Different province of Canada follows different discount rate for the decision making. For British Columbia province, prescribed rates changed from 2.5 percent to 1.5 percent for income loss and 3.5 percent to 2.0 percent for future care effective April 30, 2014 (www.collinsbarrow.com/ uploads/offices/ toronto/ Litigation_ Accounting_ and_Valuation_Services/Discount_Rates_2016.pdf). In this RiLCAMP tool, the discount rate is considered 3 percent by default although the decision makers can change or update the discount rate based on the location and other factors. The developed module is also capable of handling multiple discount rates. Figure 16.13 shows the net present value ($) of the LCC of GEID_0392 pipe for different discount rate (%). This will help the decision makers to take appropriate decision.

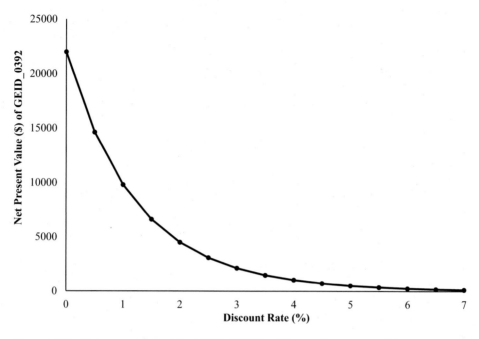

Figure 16.13   Net present value ($) of GEID_0392 for different discount rate (%).

16.5 Conclusions

In this chapter, a risk and LCC based decision support framework is developed to prioritize M/R/R recommendations for buried infrastructure. The developed risk assessment module can provide information at pipe level and network level, able to visualize the most "vulnerable" and the "highest risk" pipes within the distribution network. The developed LCC module will aid utility engineers and managers to predict the suitable new installation and/or rehabilitation programs as well as their corresponding costs for effective and proactive decision-making and thereby avoiding any unexpected and unpleasant surprises.

Water distribution network of Glenmore-Ellison Improvement District (GEID) is investigated to demonstrate the applicability of the proposed framework. The user-friendly and effective *RiLCAMP* tool will support the utility authorities to make an informed decision. In this research, the Bayesian regression model is proposed for the water main failure prediction or break frequency models due to its superior prediction capabilities compared to normal linear regression. A combination of M/R/R techniques is integrated into the model to develop different scenarios for rehabilitation of water mains. The M/R/R costs of the water mains provided by the decision makers based site and road conditions also reduce the uncertainty and unexpected expenses. Although, the *RiLCAMP* tool is developed for the WDN of GEID, any type of WDN can use the developed risk and LCC framework. The proposed framework is a unique tool for small to medium sized utilities because of their data/information scarcity, inadequate financial and technical resources, and limited experience.

In the proposed risk assessment framework, more emphasis was provided on the likelihood than a consequence of water main failure. For the future research, more parameter and detail analysis can be performed for better knowledge of water mains' condition and the magnitude of their potential consequences for consumers, business, and socio-economic activities. Due to the lack of economic data availability, average repair costs for different site locations and pipe replacement or new pipe installation costs were considered in the proposed framework. In future, user cost (e.g., loss of private property) and social cost (e.g., loss taxes, number of pedestrians, vehicles affected etc.) can be considered in life cycle cost analysis to reduce the uncertainty of decision-making.

Acknowledgments

The financial support through NSERC Collaborative Research and Development (CRD) Grant (Number: CRDPJ 434629-12) is acknowledged.

References

Amaitik, N.M. and Amaitik, S.M. (2008). Development of PCCP wire breaks prediction model using artificial neural networks. In *Pipelines 2008: Pipeline Asset Management: Maximizing Performance of our Pipeline Infrastructure* (pp. 1–11), July 22–27, Atlanta, Georgia, USA.

Ambrose, M., Burn, S., DeSilva, D., and Rahilly, M. (2008). Life cycle analysis of water networks. In *Plastics Pipe XIV: Plastics Pipes Conferences Association*, Budapest.

AWWA (1999). American National Standard for Polyethylene Encasement for Ductile-Iron Pipe Systems. American Water Works Association, Denver, CO.

Banciulescu, C. and Sekuler, L. (2010). Developing a CIP using a deterioration modeling and field sampling approach. *Proceedings of the Water Environment Federation, 2010*(1), 645–61.

Canadian Infrastructure Report Card. (2016, 2012). www.canadainfrastructure.ca (last accessed August 18, 2018).

Christodoulou, S., Aslani, P., and Vanrenterghem, A. (2003). Risk analysis framework for evaluating structural degradation of water mains in urban settings using neurofuzzy systems and statistical modeling techniques. In *Proceedings of World Water and Environmental Resources Congress*, ASCE, Reston, Va., USA, June 23–26, pp. 1–9.

Christodoulou, S., Deligianni, A., Aslani, P., and Agathokleous, A. (2009). Risk-based asset management of water piping networks using neurofuzzy systems. *Computers, Environment and Urban Systems, 33*(2), 138–49.

Demissie, G., Tesfamariam, S., and Sadiq, R. (2015). Considering soil parameters in prediction of remaining service life of metallic pipes: Bayesian belief network model. *Journal of Pipeline Systems Engineering and Practice, 7*(2), 04015028.

DIPRA (Ductile Iron Pipe Research Association) (2000). Polyethylene Encasement – Effective, Economical Protection for Ductile Iron Pipe in Corrosive Environments. www.dipra.org/ductile-iron-pipe-resources/technical-publications/corrosion-control?download=23:polyethylene-encasement-effective-economical-protection-for-ductile-iron-pipe-in-corrosive-environments (last accessed September 8, 2018).

Du, F., Woods, G.J., Kang, D., Lansey, K.E., and Arnold, R.G. (2012). Life cycle analysis for water and wastewater pipe materials. *Journal of Environmental Engineering, 139*(5), 703–11.

Engelhardt, M., Savic, D., Skipworth, P., Cashman, A., Saul, A., and Walters, G. (2003). Whole life costing: Application to water distribution network. *Water Science and Technology: Water Supply, 3*(1–2), 87–93.

Francisque, A., Rodriguez, M.J., Sadiq, R. Miranda, L.F., and Proulx, F. (2009). Prioritizing monitoring locations in a water distribution network: a fuzzy risk approach. *Journal of Water Supply: Research and Technology-AQUA, 58*(7), 488–509.

Francisque, A., Shahriar, A., Islam, N., Betrie, G., Siddiqui, R.B. Tesfamariam, S., and Sadiq, R. (2014). A decision support tool for water mains renewal for small to medium sized utilities: a risk index approach. *Journal of Water Supply Research and Technology: AQUA, 63*(4), 281–302.

Francisque, A., Tesfamariam, S., Kabir, G., Haider, H., Reeder, A., and Sadiq, R. (2017). Water mains renewal planning framework for small to medium sized water utilities: a life cycle cost analysis approach. *Urban Water Journal, 14*(5), 493–501.

Friedl, F., and Fuchs-Hanusch, D. (2011). Risk assessment of transmission water mains to support efficient rehabilitation decisions. In *First IWA Danube-Black Sea Regional Young Water Professional Conference*, Bukarest, Romania, 14(15), 270–9.

Gorji-Bandpy, M. and Shateri, M. (2008). Analysis of pipe breaks in urban water distribution network, *GMSARN International Journal, 2*(3), 117–24.

Haider, H., Sadiq, R., and Tesfamariam, S. (2013). Performance indicators for small-and medium-sized water supply systems: a review. *Environmental Reviews, 22*(1), 1–40.

Haider, H., Sadiq, R., and Tesfamariam, S. (2015a). Selecting performance indicators for small and medium sized water utilities: Multi-criteria analysis using ELECTRE method. *Urban Water Journal, 12*(4), 305–27.

Haider, H., Sadiq, R., and Tesfamariam, S. (2015b). Inter-utility performance benchmarking model for small-to-medium-sized water utilities: Aggregated performance indices. *Journal of Water Resources Planning and Management, 142*(1), 04015039.

Haider, H., Sadiq, R., and Tesfamariam, S. (2015c). Multilevel performance management framework for small to medium sized water utilities in Canada. *Canadian Journal of Civil Engineering, 42*(11), 889–900. www.collinsbarrow.com/uploads/offices/toronto/Litigation_Accounting_and_Valuation_Services/ Discount_Rates_2016.pdf (last accessed August 18, 2018).

Haider, H., Sadiq, R., and Tesfamariam, S. (2016a). Intra-utility performance management model (InUPM) for the sustainability of small to medium sized water utilities: Conceptualization to development. *Journal of Cleaner Production, 133*, 777–94.

Haider, H., Sadiq, R., and Tesfamariam, S. (2016b). Risk-based framework for improving customer satisfaction through system reliability in small-sized to medium-sized water utilities. *Journal of Management in Engineering, 32*(5), 04016008.

Jafar R., Eisenbeis P., and Shahrour, I. (2003). Modeling of the structural degradation of an urban water distribution system. In *Proceeding of the 17th (EJSW) on Rehabilitation Management of Urban Infrastructure Networks*, Dresden, Germany, pp 57–65.

Jafar, R., Shahrour, I., and Juran, I. (2010). Application of artificial neural networks (ANN) to model the failure of urban water mains, *Mathematical and Computer Modelling, 51*(9–10), 1170–80.

Kabir, G., Tesfamariam, S., Francisque, A., and Sadiq, R. (2015a). Evaluating risk of water mains failure using a Bayesian belief network model. *European Journal of Operational Research, 240*(1), 220–34.

Kabir, G., Tesfamariam, S., Loeppky, J., and Sadiq, R. (2015b). Integrating Bayesian linear regression with ordered weighted averaging: Uncertainty analysis for predicting water main failures. *ASCE-ASME Journal of Risk and Uncertainty in Engineering Systems, Part A: Civil Engineering, 1*(3), 04015007.

Kettler, A.J. and Goulter, I.C. (1985). An analysis of pipe breakage in urban water distribution networks. *Canadian Journal of Civil Engineering, 12*(2), 286–93.

Khan, F.I., Sadiq, R., and Haddara, M.M. (2004). Risk-based inspection and maintenance (RBIM): multiattribute decision-making with aggregative risk analysis. *Process Safety and Environmental Protection, 82*(6), 398–411.

Kleiner, Y. and Rajani, B. (2002). Forecasting variations and trends in water-main breaks. *Journal of Infrastructure Systems, 8*(4), 122–31.

Kleiner, Y., Adams, B.J., and Rogers, J. S. (2001). Water distribution network renewal planning. *Journal of Computing in Civil Engineering, 15*(1), 15–26.

Kleiner, Y., Sadiq, R., and Rajani, B. (2004). Modeling failure risk in buried pipes using fuzzy Markov deterioration process. In *Proceedings of Pipeline Engineering and Construction: What's on the Horizon?* ASCE, Reston, Va., pp. 1–12.

Kleiner, Y., Rajani, B., and Sadiq, R. (2006). Failure risk management of buried infrastructure using fuzzy-based techniques. *Journal of Water Supply Research and Technology: AQUA, 55*(2), 81–94.

Lim, S.R., Park, D., Lee, D.S., and Park, J.M. (2006). Economic evaluation of a water network system through the net present value method based on cost and benefit estimations. *Industrial & Engineering Chemistry Research, 45*(22), 7710–18.

Lim, S.R., Park, D., and Park, J.M. (2008). Analysis of effects of an objective function on environmental and economic performance of a water network system using life cycle assessment and life cycle costing methods. *Chemical Engineering Journal, 144*(3), 368–78.

Lounis, Z., Vanier, D.J., Daigle, L., Sadiq, R., and Almansor, H. (2010). Framework for Assessment of State, Performance and Management of Canada's Core Public Infrastructure. Infrastructure Canada, Ottawa, ON., pp. 422.

McPherson, D.L. (2009). Choice of pipeline material: PVC or DI using a life cycle cost analysis. In *Pipelines 2009: Infrastructure's Hidden Assets* (pp. 1342–54).

Najafi, M. and Kulandaivel, G. (2005). Pipeline condition predicting using neural network models. In *Proceedings of Pipelines 2005: Optimizing Pipeline Design, Operations, and Maintenance in Today's Economy*, ASCE, New York, pp. 767–81.

O'Day, D.K. (1982). Organizing and analyzing leak and break data for making main replacement decisions. *Journal of AWWA*, *74*(11), 588–94.

Pietrucha-Urbanik, K. and Valis, D. (2013). Application of fuzzy logic for failure risk assessment in water supply system management. In *Proceedings of the 13th International Conference of Environmental Science and Technology*, Athens, Greece, September 5–7.

PSAB (2007). Guide To Accounting for and Reporting Tangible Capital Assets: Guidance for Local Governments And Local Government Entities That Apply The Public Sector Handbook, p. 107. www.psab-ccsp.ca/other-non-authoritative-guidance/item14603.pdf (last accessed September 2012).

Rahman, S. and Vanier, D.J. (2004). Life cycle cost analysis as a decision support tool for managing municipal infrastructure. *CIB 2004 Triennial Congress*, Toronto, Ontario, May 2–9, 2004, pp. 1–12.

Rajani, B. and Kleiner, Y. (2004). Alternative strategies for pipeline maintenance/renewal. *AWWA 2004 Annual Conference*, Orlando, Florida, June 13–17, pp. 1–16.

Rajani, B. and Tesfamariam, S. (2004). Uncoupled axial, flexural, and circumferential pipe soil interaction analyses of partially supported jointed water mains. *Canadian Geotechnical Journal*, *41*(6), 997–1010.

Rogers, P. (2006). *Failure assessment model to prioritize pipe replacement in water utility asset management* (Doctoral dissertation, Colorado State University), Colorado, USA.

Rogers, P.D. and Grigg, N.S. (2008). Failure assessment model to prioritize pipe replacement in water utility asset management. In *Water Distribution Systems Analysis Symposium 2006* (pp. 1–17), Cincinnati, Ohio, USA, August 27–30.

Saaty, T.L. 1988 *Multicriteria Decision-Making: The Analytic Hierarchy Process*. University of Pittsburgh, Pittsburgh, PA.

Sadiq, R., Kleiner, Y., and Rajani, B. (2004). Aggregative risk analysis for water quality failure in distribution networks. *Journal of Water Supply: Research and Technology-AQUA*, *53*(4), 241–61.

Sadiq, R., Rodríguez, M.J., and Tesfamariam, S. (2010). Integrating indicators for performance assessment of small water utilities using ordered weighted averaging (OWA) operators. *Expert Systems with Applications*, *37*(7), 4881–91.

Shahata, K. (2006). *Stochastic life cycle cost modeling approach for water mains* (Doctoral dissertation, Concordia University), Montreal, Quebec, Canada.

Shi, W.Z., Zhang, A.S., and Ho, O.K. (2013). Spatial analysis of water mains failure clusters and factors: a Hong Kong case study. *Annals of GIS*, *19*(2), 89–97.

Singh, A. (2011). Bayesian analysis for causes of failure at a water utility. *Built Environment Project and Asset Management*, *1*(2), 195–210.

Studziński A. and Pietrucha-Urbanik K. (2012) Risk indicators of water network operation. *Chemical Engineering Transactions*, 26, 189–94.

Tchórzewska-Cieslak, B. (2011). Matrix method for estimating the risk of failure in the collective water supply system using fuzzy logic. *Environment Protection Engineering*, *37*(3), 111–18.

Tchórzewska-Cieslak, B. (2012). Model of failure risk analysis in the water pipe network. *International Journal of Performability Engineering*, *8*(4), 379–88.

Tesfamariam, S., Sadiq, R., Haider, H., and Kabir, G. (2013). Risk-based asset management for small to medium-sized water utilities: Condition and Performance Assessment (Theme 1) (RBAM/FR-2014/GEID-T1), Glenmore Ellison Improvement District (GEID), BC, Canada.

Tesfamariam, S., Sadiq, R., Haider, H., Kabir, G., Demissie, G.A., and Iqbal, H. (2014). Risk based Life Cycle Asset Management tool for water Pipes (RiLCAMP): Risk Assessment (Theme 2) (RBAM/FR-2014/GEID-T2), Glenmore Ellison Improvement District (GEID), BC, Canada.

Tesfamariam, S., Sadiq, R., Iqbal, H., Demissie, G.A., Kabir, G., and Haider, H. (2015a). Risk based Life Cycle Asset Management tool for water Pipes (RiLCAMP): Asset Accounting and implementation of PSAB (Theme 3) (RiLCAMP/DPSAB-2015/GEID-T3), Glenmore Ellison Improvement District (GEID), BC, Canada.

Tesfamariam, S., Sadiq, R., Kabir, G., Demissie, G.A., Haider, H., and Iqbal, H. (2015b). Risk based Life Cycle Asset Management tool for water Pipes (RiLCAMP): Life Cycle Cost Analysis (Theme 3) (RiLCAMP/FR-2015/GEID-T3), Glenmore Ellison Improvement District (GEID), BC, Canada.

Thomas, A., Mantha, B.R., and Menassa, C.C. (2016). A framework to evaluate the life cycle costs and environmental impacts of water pipelines. In *Pipelines 2016* (pp. 1152–63).

USEPA and WaterRF (2010). Final Priorities of the Distribution System Research and Information Collection Partnership.: www.epa.gov/sites/production /files /2015-09/documents /finalprioritieso fdistributionsystemricpmay2010.pdf (last accessed December 2012).

Vanrenterghem-Raven, A., Eisenbeis, P., Juran, I., and Christodoulou, S. (2003). Statistical modeling of the structural degradation of an urban water distribution system: case study of New York City. In *World Water & Environmental Resources Congress 2003* (pp. 1–10).

Yan, J.M., and Vairavamoorthy, K. (2003). Fuzzy approach for pipe condition assessment. *Conf. Proc., 2003 Int. Conf. on Pipeline Engineering and Construction*, ASCE, New York, 466–76.

17

Resilience of potable water and wastewater networks

Max Didier,[1] *Simona Esposito,*[2] *and Božidar Stojadinović*[3]

[1] DEPARTMENT OF CIVIL, ENVIRONMENTAL AND GEOMATIC ENGINEERING (D-BAUG), ETH ZURICH, STEFANO-FRANSCINI-PLATZ 5, 8093 ZURICH, SWITZERLAND; DIDIERM@ETHZ.CH

[2] SWISS RE MANAGEMENT LTD., 8022 ZURICH, SWITZERLAND; SIMONA_ESPOSITO@SWISSRE.COM

[3] DEPARTMENT OF CIVIL, ENVIRONMENTAL AND GEOMATIC ENGINEERING (D-BAUG), ETH ZURICH, STEFANO-FRANSCINI-PLATZ 5, 8093 ZURICH, SWITZERLAND; STOJADINOVIC@IBK.BAUG.ETHZ.CH

17.1 Introduction

Water supply and water distribution networks are among the oldest civil infrastructure systems. The ancient Romans developed the technical knowledge to build water supply and distribution systems more than 2000 years ago (Gallo 2015; Monteleone et al. 2007). The Roman systems consisted of covered channels (made of masonry or concrete); aqueducts; underground (pressurized and non-pressurized) ceramic, lead or stone pipes; dams; water reservoirs; and settling basins. They had many similarities with today's modern water systems. The main purposes of the systems were to assure a constant flow of high-quality potable water to Roman cities (for hygiene, health, and leisure), to increase agricultural production through irrigation and to provide water for industrial use (e.g. flour mills and mining). The water was often transported via long channels from fresh sources outside of the cities and distributed by a large network of pipes of different sections to the individual houses, baths, and public fountains in the cities. Historic remains of impressive structures like the Pont du Gard (Nîmes, France) or the aqueduct of Gier (Lyon, France) still testify to the high importance of these systems for the Roman society. To collect and evacuate the wastewater, the Romans built sewage systems, usually discharging the wastewater into a river. While the Roman systems relied on gravity to assure the flow of the water, the first US water system built in 1754 in Pennsylvania already relied on horse-driven pumps (Haestad Methods 2015).

Today, the supply of water remains a key feature of modern societies and communities. A constant and reliable supply of potable water, and a reliable evacuation of wastewater, is needed to assure healt and living standards. Potable water is an essential resource for human existence and it is needed to satisfy the demand for drinking water consumption, and to guarantee the quality of sanitary conditions, hygiene, and health standards. Additionally, it is important to provide sufficient water flow and pressure for fire protection, industrial purposes, and irrigation in agriculture. It is, thus, a key for sustainable economic and social development, and a constant investment of money and resources is required to assure a reliable service level.

Resilient potable water and wastewater systems are characterized by robust system components and a resourceful recovery and adaptation in the case of damage (e.g. caused by a disaster). In fact, a resilient system is characterized by its "ability to anticipate, absorb and adapt to events potentially disruptive to its function, and to recover either back to its original state or to an adjusted state based on new post-event conditions" (Bruneau et al. 2003; NIAC 2009; USPPD 2013; Didier et al. 2017c). New post-event conditions may include degradation and damage of system components as well as emergence of new demand patterns. Demand for (potable) water can decrease, for example, after a disaster, due to damage to the community infrastructure and due to population movement. On the other hand, demand for water can increase as well during or after disasters, especially if fire hazard is of concern (e.g. outbreak of large fires in San Francisco after the 1906 earthquake, Ellsworth et al. 1981). A holistic resilience assessment needs, thus, to consider both the post-event evolution of demand and of supply.

In the following sections, the components of water supply and distribution systems and wastewater systems are first described. Possible environmental stressors and damage to these systems observed during past disasters, more precisely during past earthquakes, are discussed next. Finally, a methodology to quantify the resilience of a water distribution or wastewater system is presented and its application is shown on the case study of the water supply and distribution systems of the Kathmandu Valley in Nepal, submitted to a scenario earthquake. The methodology can be easily extended to other hazards and to water supply and distribution systems or wastewater systems of other cities or regions.

17.2 Components of water supply and distribution systems and wastewater systems

Modern water supply and distribution systems and wastewater systems have been built and extended over multiple years and decades and have become a main capital asset of many communities. In general, three different types of water supply and distribution systems can be distinguished (Arasmith 2009): watering point systems (e.g. local wells), haul systems (e.g. water supply via water tanker trucks) and traditional piped systems. Watering point and haul systems are often used to complement piped systems, if those are not able to supply the needed water quantity and/or quality, or to supply customers at far distances from the pipe network. In the following, the focus is on traditional piped systems. Such systems are usually composed of point-like facilities and a spatially distributed pipe and channel system of a variety of different components and materials. The prinicpal types of point-like facilities are (ALA 2001; Arasmith 2009; Kakderi & Argyroudis 2014; Wikimedia 2015):

(i) For the water supply system:
   - Water collection points or intake sources (above or below ground): intakes of raw (untreated) water from lakes, rivers, springs, aquifers, etc.
   - Water treatment and purification facilities to treat raw water.
   - Water storage facilities to store water: above, underground or elevated reservoirs (e.g. steel, concrete, or wood reservoirs), water tanks, water towers or cisterns used, for example, to maintain pressure on the system, or to cover peak or fire demand.
   - Water pumping stations/pumps assuring a pressurized water flow, to cover height differences, or to fill reservoirs.

- Water flow mechanisms (valves, gates) controlling the water flow quantities and pressure.
- Connections to consumers providing access to water supply to the consumers for end use (e.g. taps, fire hydrants).

(ii) For the wastewater system:
- Water treatment and purification facilities to treat used water (wastewater).
- Sewage lift stations to move wastewater from lower to higher elevation.

Usually, pipe and channel networks transport the water from sometimes distant sources or remote areas to the local distribution systems in urban areas, through which the water is distributed to the end consumers. Long distance transportation often happens through aqueducts, tunnels or covered channels or large-diameter pipes. Local distribution is then assured by an underground pipe network. The local pipe networks usually have a grid, loop, or tree-like network structure. In many regions and cities, the water distribution network has been constructed and extended over decades, often following the growth of the population and have a large variety of pipe and joint materials, as well as many different pipe diameters. Due to a lack of documentation, it is, however, often quite difficult to determine the exact pipe location and material, especially in some older parts of the networks. Lead pipes were often used in old systems but are not used anymore due to the adverse effects on water quality. Materials employed in recent systems include gray cast iron (CI) pipes (in use for over 100 years); ductile cast iron (DI) pipes; asbestos cement (AC) pipes; concrete or steel pipes (used especially for large-diameter water mains); high-density polyethylene (HDPE) pipes; and polyvinyl chloride (PVC) pipes (Arasmith 2009). PVC pipes are corrosion-free and, therefore, PVC is used nowadays as a main material for new pipes.

The used or abundant water is collected and evacuated by a wastewater system. The wastewater system usually consists of a wastewater transmission pipe network (consisting of pipes, channels, or aboveground ditches) assuring the evacuation of wastewater from customer service connections (sewage collection). The wastewater is treated in a treatment plant for reuse or for disposal into a river or the sea. Water treatment includes clarification (separation of particles and dirt), filtration (removal of smaller particles) and disinfection (killing bacteria and viruses) of the wastewater.

17.3 Degradation and damage of water distribution and supply systems and wastewater systems

Water distribution and supply systems are, similar to other civil infrastructure systems, submitted to permanent environmental stressors, e.g. corrosion and wear and tear. They are also submitted to severe stressors imposed by natural disasters, like earthquakes, floods or landslides. This leads to degradation of and damage to the water and wastewater system components (e.g. breaks or leaks in pipes). In fact, water loss due to leakage is a significant issue in some systems: up to 30 percent of the potable water supply capacity is sometimes lost due to leakage (this is, for example the case in the water distribution system of the Kathmandu Valley in Nepal, KUKL 2015). Factors contributing to pipe breaks (and therefore leakage) include the pipe age, diameter, material, number of observed previous breaks, as well as the network's operating pressure and water flow (Fragiadakis et al. 2013). A regular maintenance is, thus, necessary to assure and preserve the reliability and operability of the systems, including regular cleaning, inspection to find and repair leaks, and retrofitting and maintenance of storage and other point-like facilities. In the United States alone, the necessary investment to maintain and replace old facilities and to cover the increases in demand is estimated to be as high as 125.9 billion USD in the year 2020 (ASCE 2011).

Major past earthquakes, e.g. the 1994 Northridge (California, United States) earthquake, the 2009 L'Aquila (Italy) earthquake, the 2010–11 Canterbury (New Zealand) earthquake sequence, and the 2015 Gorkha (Nepal) earthquake, had an adverse impact on the availability of potable water. During the moment magnitude (M_w) 6.7 1994 Northridge earthquake, the water distribution and supply systems of Los Angeles, California were severely damaged (Davis 2014). Damage to the raw water supply conduits, the transmission and distribution pipes, the service connections, and the reservoirs and treatment plant service was observed after the earthquake. In particular, the aqueducts extending more than 500km to the north of Los Angeles that supply the northern part of the city with water got damaged and the water supply was interrupted. Additionally, ground water pumping, service at some transmission pumping stations and remote monitoring and control systems were adversely affected due to electric power outages. Ground settlement damaged power conduits, leading to a major loss of operability of the main treatment plant. The seismically retrofitted chlorination stations to disinfect water and the retrofitted pumping stations of the distribution system did not subsist any damage, or showed only minor damage, respectively. However, several pipelines and tanks of the distribution system were damaged, with some tanks removed from service for an extended time. Damage included draining of tanks and breaks to pipes, leading to water leakage.

While system redundancy (e.g. several supply conduits serving the same area) allowed to maintain water delivery in most parts of Los Angeles, several areas in the northern part lost complete water supply after the earthquake (Davis 2014). In fact, water delivery service dropped to about 78 percent of the pre-disaster level immediately after the earthquake. Quantity of water for consumption and for the fire protection services dropped to almost 70 percent of the pre-earthquake serviceability level. The loss of fire protection service was, however, limited to smaller areas. A large drop was observed in the quality service, which dropped immediately to 0 percent after the 1994 Northridge earthquake. In fact, boil-water notices were issued in the hours after the disaster for the whole supply area. Finally, the functionality of the system dropped to an estimated 30 percent of the pre-disaster level.

Restoration of the services of the water distribution network began shortly after the earthquake (Davis 2014). Water delivery service was restored in the whole city to the pre-disaster level after about 7 days, due to rapidly initiated recovery measures. Water quantity and fire services were recovered after about 8 days and water quality service after about 12 days after the occurrence of the earthquake. The main goals were to restore water delivery and quality service as fast as possible. Repairs to transmission and distribution pipes as well as to damaged tanks continued for months and some damage reducing system reliability was repaired over a period of several years. In fact, system functionality returned to the pre-disaster level only about 4.5 to 5 years after the earthquake.

The water distribution network of the area affected by the M_w 6.3 L'Aquila earthquake consisted of relatively old cast iron and steel pipes (Dolce et al. 2009; Kongar et al. 2015). Only one main transmission pipeline was damaged during the earthquake: the steel joint of a major pipeline slipped-off, causing a violent escape of water. The delivery of potable water to consumers was again possible 24 hours after the earthquake as the incurred damage was temporarily repaired. Further repair action was necessary on the temporary repaired transmission pipe, as the welded joint broke a few days later. Even though the transmission network performed relatively well, it was decided to not restore the water distribution in the most affected villages. A multitude of breaks of cast iron pipes and slips of the joints was expected to have occurred in the minor water distribution system. Provision of water was reinstated gradually to these areas in the weeks after the earthquake. Some severely damaged areas were evacuated and the water network in these zones was shut down for a long time. Instead, a new water distribution network was designed and constructed to deliver water to the sites of temporary housing, thus accounting for the changes in the water demand and supply patterns.

Most treatment plants of the L'Aquila region were only slightly damaged and remained almost fully functional after the earthquake. Damage included cracks on walls of distribution traps and operation buildings. One treatment plant needed to be fed with electric power from a backup generator for three days, as the electric power supply system failed. Only a single treatment plant subsisted larger damage due to the partial collapse of one RC digestion tank, this plant was partially closed. The disposal capacity of the plant was reduced to about 60 percent, which was, however, still sufficient to satisfy the entire demand.

The 2010 M_w 7.1 Darfield (Canterbury, New Zealand) and the 2011 M_w 6.3 Christchurch (New Zealand) earthquakes had a major impact on the water distribution and the wastewater systems of the city of Christchurch, serving almost 400,000 people (Cubrinovski et al. 2011; Giovinazzi et al. 2011; Eidinger & Tang 2012 ; Ministry of Health 2012; Kongar et al. 2015). In many areas, large ground movements and deformations related to liquefaction caused extensive damage to the underground pipe networks of the water supply and wastewater system (Cubrinovski et al. 2011). Cumulatively over three major earthquake events (including the June 2011 M_w 6.0 aftershock), 250km (7.5 percent of the total network) water mains and submains needed to be renewed, 60 out of 160 wells needed to be repaired and several water tanks and reservoirs were damaged (Eidinger & Tang 2012). Infiltration of sand and silt into the broken pipes of the sewage system hampered the functioning of the major treatment plant serving Christchurch, damaging clarifiers and settling basins. Damage to the wastewater system included as well damage to sewage lift stations, manholes and sanitary sewers (Eidinger & Tang 2012).

Approximately 50 percent of the city had no access to water during the first days after the 2011 Christchurch earthquake, and 30 percent had no access for over a week. After one month, water access was reassured for 95 percent of the city (Giovinazzi et al. 2011). Water supply for customers without access to the water supply network was assured with potable water trucks and using bottled water. A large part of the raw sewage was discharged directly into rivers in the aftermath of the earthquake and households were requested to apply water conservation measures to prevent a complete collapse of the wastewater system. Portable and chemical toilets were installed for households that had no sewage service anymore (Eidinger & Tang 2012).

The water in Christchurch did not need treatment before the earthquake. However, boil water notices needed to be issued after the earthquake. To prevent waterborne disease outbreaks due to possible inflow of sewage into the potable water system, chlorination of the system was necessary, and chlorinators had to be installed in the weeks after the earthquake (Ministry of Health 2012).

The main priority of the system operator in Christchurch was to repair the broken buried pipes of the water supply network. Over 300 pipe repair crews completed 3000 repairs of damaged pipes within 6 weeks after the earthquake. Within six months, most of the components of the water supply system could be repaired. Only after reinstating potable water to all customers, the focus of the repairs shifted to the wastewater systems, of which significant parts were still out of service three months after the 2011 Christchurch earthquake. It was estimated that it would take several years to completely recover the water and wastewater systems from earthquake damage.

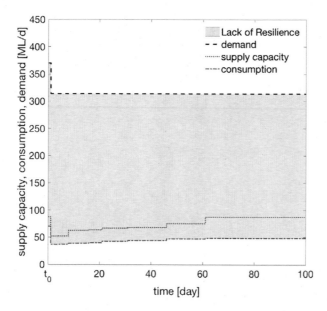

Figure 17.1 Resilience of the water supply and distribution system of the Kathmandu Valley after the 2015 Gorkha earthquake.

Source: Adapted from Didier et al. 2018a.

The damage to the water supply and distribution systems of the Kathmandu Valley due to the 2015 M_w 7.8 Gorkha earthquake was significant (Didier et al. 2018a; Figure 17.1). The systems were already unable to cover the water demand before the earthquake: a large part of the demand of the community was instead delivered by water tanker trucks or not covered at all. Additionally, the quality of the water supplied by the water distribution system was insufficient due to the low operable capacity of the treatment plants. The 2015 Gorkha earthquake included damage to sources and water intakes, pumping houses, water storage tanks, and to the local distribution pipe system. Sources were running dry after the earthquake due to ground deformation and landslides. Damage to water tanks included, for example, cracks in shear walls of the reservoirs. Supply losses related to leakage were estimated to about 20 percent of the total system supply capacity before the earthquake. According to the local system operators, almost every pipe of the distribution system was damaged during the earthquake. The supply capacity, water demand, and consumption decreased after the earthquake as consequence of the damage to the point-like facilities, the distribution system, and the community building stock. The supply capacity of the water supply system was recovered about 60 days after the occurrence of the earthquake. However, more than 100 days after the earthquake numerous pipes remained broken, and, consequently, the demand and the consumption remained at low levels.

17.4 Resilience of water supply systems

Given the importance of a reliable supply of (potable) water for modern communities, it is not surprising that the performance assessment of water and wastewater systems after natural disasters has been the topic of numerous past studies (e.g. related to the impacts of earthquakes,

Hwang et al. 1998; Adachi & Ellingwood 2006; Fragiadakis et al. 2013; Didier et al. 2018a). Most of the metrics proposed in recent literature are mainly focused on the evaluation of the reliability of the system, or on the functional performance expressed in terms of connectivity (level of customer connections immediately after an earthquake) or serviceability (expressing the quality of service that the connected customers are experiencing).

However, recent disastrous events such as the 2009 L'Aquila and the 2015 Gorkha earthquakes have shown that in addition to considering the vulnerability of these systems to degradation effects and natural hazards, it is essential to also consider the recovery of the systems and the evolution of the service demand. In fact, financial and social losses due to natural hazards, e.g. earthquakes or floods, include not only losses due to direct damage to the system components, but also indirect losses due to (persisting) service unavailability, having an additional adverse impact on the society and the economy. The time to recover and/or adapt the service supply and to meet new demand criteria is, thus, equally important and needs to be included in a holistic resilience assessment of a civil infrastructure-community system.

In the following, a methodology to assess the resilience of water supply and distribution and wastewater systems using the Re-CoDeS framework is introduced using the example of the water supply and distribution system of the Kathmandu Valley in Nepal submitted to a scenario seismic event. A more detailed overview of the Re-CoDeS framework is given by Didier et al. 2017c. The detailed modeling assumptions used in the case study are presented in Didier et al. 2018b.

17.5 The Re-CoDeS resilience quantification framework

The Re-CoDeS framework is a compositional demand/supply resilience quantification framework. It allows to consider not only the performance of civil infrastructure systems after a disaster, but to also include the evolution of the community demand for the services of civil infrastructure systems. It is adapted in the following case study to model the demand and supply evolution of the (potable) water service to a community, more specifically to the Kathmandu Valley (Nepal). The main components of the proposed Re-CoDeS framework, adapted for the water supply and distribution systems, are:

- the evolution of the water supply, given essentially by the vulnerability and the recovery of the components of the water distribution and supply system (i.e. water intakes, water pumps, etc…);
- the evolution of the community demand for (potable) water, given essentially by the vulnerability and the recovery of the community built inventory (e.g. industries, hospitals, residencies…);
- the system service model that determines the distribution and the allocation of the water supply to the consumers in order to cover their water demand.

The water consumption at a given node i at time t is, then, the minimum of the available water supply and the water demand at that node at time t:

$$C_i(t) = \min\left(S_i^{av}(t), D_i(t)\right),$$

where $C_i(t)$ is the consumption at node i at time t, $S_i^{av}(t)$ is the available supply at node i at time t, and $D_i(t)$ is the water demand at node i at time t.

The Lack of Resilience of the water supply and distribution system, LoR_{sys}, is computed in a bottom-up approach, considering the Lack of Resilience at the individual demand nodes $i \in \{1,...,I\}$, where I is the total number of demand nodes. A Lack of Resilience at a given node i, LoR_i, is observed if the water demand cannot be fully supplied, i.e. if the available supply, and consequently the consumption, is smaller than the water demand at that node. LoR_i is then the total service deficit at node i over the resilience assessment period $t_0 \leq t \leq t_f$, with t_0 and t_f the starting and ending time of the resilience assessment. LoR_{sys} is the aggregated service deficit over all the demand nodes of the system:

$$LoR_i = \int_{t_0}^{t_f} \langle D_i(t) - S_i^{av}(t) \rangle dt = \int_{t_0}^{t_f} \left(D_i(t) - C_i(t) \right) dt$$

$$LoR_{sys} = \sum_{i=1}^{I} \int_{t_0}^{t_f} \langle D_i(t) - S_i^{av}(t) \rangle dt = \sum_{i=1}^{I} \int_{t_0}^{t_f} \left(D_i(t) - C_i(t) \right) dt = \int_{t_0}^{t_f} \left(D_{sys}(t) - C_{sys}(t) \right) dt,$$

where $\langle \cdot \rangle$ is the singularity function, $D_{sys}(t)$ is the water demand of the entire community and $C_{sys}(t)$ is the water consumption in the system. The resilience of a single node i, R_i, and of the water supply and distribution system, R_{sys}, can, finally, be computed using the normalized metrics of the nodal and system Lack of Resilience, $\widehat{LoR}_i$ and $\widehat{LoR}_{sys}$, respectively:

$$R_i = 1 - \widehat{LoR}_i = 1 - \frac{\int_{t_0}^{t_f} \langle D_i(t) - S_i^{av}(t) \rangle dt}{\int_{t_0}^{t_f} D_i(t) dt} = 1 - \frac{\int_{t_0}^{t_f} \left(D_i(t) - C_i(t) \right) dt}{\int_{t_0}^{t_f} D_i(t) dt}$$

$$R_{sys} = 1 - \widehat{LoR}_{sys} = 1 - \frac{\sum_{i=1}^{I} LoR_i}{\sum_{i=1}^{I} \int_{t_0}^{t_f} D_i(t) dt} = 1 - \frac{\sum_{i=1}^{I} \int_{t_0}^{t_f} \langle D_i(t) - S_i^{av}(t) \rangle dt}{\sum_{i=1}^{I} \int_{t_0}^{t_f} D_i(t) dt} = 1 - \frac{\int_{t_0}^{t_f} \left(D_{sys}(t) - C_{sys}(t) \right) dt}{\int_{t_0}^{t_f} D_{sys}(t) dt}.$$

17.6 Determining the seismic resilience of the water supply and distribution system of the Kathmandu Valley

In order to use the Re-CoDeS framework to assess the resilience of the water supply and distribution system of the Kathmandu Valley, the components of the Re-CoDeS framework need to be defined and modeled to facilitate the desired resilience assessment. The seismic resilience is of interest in this case study. In fact, the Kathmandu Valley region is at high seismic risk and experienced many earthquakes in the past (EERI 2016). Historic earthquakes in Nepal include, for example, the 1934 earthquake, causing almost 17,000 deaths and destruction of 300,000 houses, and the 2015 Gorkha earthquake, causing approximately 9,000 deaths, damaging more than 500,000 buildings and causing large damage to civil infrastructure systems.

A simplified topology of the water supply and distribution system of the Kathmandu Valley is shown in Figure 17.2. The topology of the network has been simplified due to the lack of complete data and to reduce the complexity of the resilience assessment (see Didier et al. 2018a; Didier et al. 2018b). Most of the water intakes are sources located outside of the city

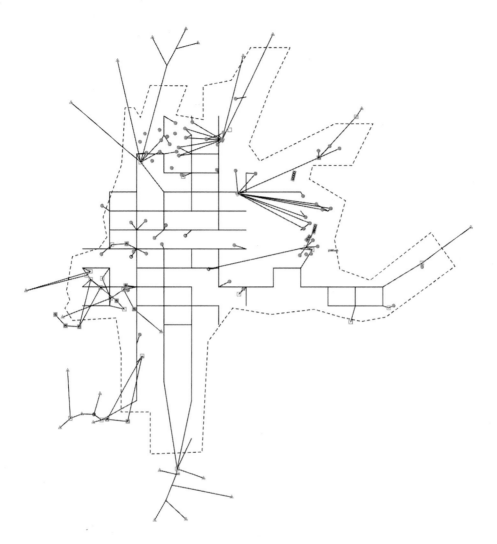

Figure 17.2 Topology of the water supply and distribution system of the Kathmandu Valley (simplified).

Source: Adapted from Didier et al. 2018a.

of Kathmandu. Water is, then, transported via water mains to the Kathmandu Valley, where it is temporarily stored (e.g. in overhead water tanks) and distributed to the demand nodes via the distribution pipe network. Due to the poor quality of the water supplied by the water distribution system of the Kathmandu Valley, the quality of service in terms of water potability is supposed to be at 0 percent and is disregarded for the following analysis, which focuses only on the quantities of water supply and demand.

The seismic vulnerability and the recovery of the point-like facilities of the water supply and distribution system, of the pipe network, and of the demand nodes need to be modeled to assess the seismic resilience of the system. For the point-like facilities of the water distribution and supply system, existing component seismic fragility and recovery functions can be employed to model their seismic behavior (see, for example the overview given in FEMA 2013 or Kakderi & Argyroudis 2014). Component seismic fragility functions give the probability of failure of a component, or of observing or exceeding a certain damage state, for a given earthquake ground motion intensity measure. Intensity measures usually used for the evaluation of seismic fragility functions include ground motion intensity parameters such as the peak ground velocity (PGV), the peak ground acceleration (PGA) or the spectral acceleration (Sa). Higher damage states have often an adverse effect on the ability of a component to fulfill its function: pumps are not operating anymore, water tanks leak water, etc. A large number of components in high damage states leads, therefore, to a decrease of the supply capacity of the water supply and distribution system. Fragility functions for the components of the water supply and distribution systems available in FEMA 2013 are employed in this case study. In a conservative approach, fragility functions for unanchored components are selected.

The recovery of the components can be modeled using lognormal or Weibull component recovery functions conditioned on the initial post-disaster damage state (Didier et al. 2015). Such recovery functions return the probability that a damaged component has been recovered after a given amount of time after a disaster, depending on the initial post-disaster damage state. In fact, it takes longer to recover an extensively damaged component than one that only needs minor repair. The probabilistic nature of the recovery curves allows to account for the uncertainties in the recovery process and variability of the recovery times: while some damaged components might have been already repaired shortly after the earthquake, the repair of others takes more time, for example, due to a lack of specialized workforce. Some mean recovery durations are provided by FEMA 2013 for different components. The recovery time often depends on the region or country in which the disaster happened. Developing countries have, for example, a weaker economy and a limited availability of financial resources, leading to a restricted stock of spare parts for components. Such factors can delay recovery. Therefore, the parameters of the component recovery functions should, if possible, be computed using empirical recovery data from past disasters in the same or similar countries. For this case study, recovery parameters based on the observed recovery of the point-like components of the water supply and distribution system after the 2015 Gorkha earthquake are employed (Didier et al. 2018a, 2018b).

The evolution of the water demand can be determined using the performance of the building stock (composed of its residential and office buildings, industrial building stock and critical facilities, e.g. schools and hospitals) as a proxy (Didier et al. 2017e). In fact, the water distribution system delivers the water to the end consumers via connections which are often located in buildings. These include, for example, water taps and connections to appliances like toilets, bathtubs, washing machines, or industrial production lines, etc. If the building is damaged or destroyed, the access to the connections is, generally, limited as well, and the con-sumption of water decreases. To assess the seismic performance of the building stock, seismic fragility functions are again employed in this case study. The building stock of the Kathmandu Valley is divided into different occupancy categories (i.e. residential, industrial, commercial, and critical) and building types (e.g. adobe, brick in mud, brick in cement, reinforced concrete, etc...), each represented by a corresponding fragility function (see Didier et al. 2017b) specific to Nepal. Fragility functions representative of the building stock of other countries can be found, for example, in Pitilakis et al. 2014. The water demand associated with the different building types is estimated using demand, consumption, and supply data from KUKL 2015 and CBS 2012. It is supposed that the water demand associated to the concerned building decreases with an increasing damage level. The decrease is modeled using demand reduction factors for the different occupancy categories (Didier et al. 2017e). Water demand data for other countries is usually available from local agencies, for example in the US, USGS 2014 provides water demand and consumption data. Existing fragility functions obtained from literature can also be updated to include empirical damage data available after past disasters. A methodology for updating, based on the data acquired through rapid visual damage assessments after the 2015 Gorkha earthquake, is shown in Didier et al. 2017a. A more elaborated approach to assess the water demand of a community, considering a multitude of community characteristics, can be found in Guidotti et al. 2018.

Similar to the components of the water supply and distribution system, component recovery functions are employed to estimate the recovery of the elements of the building stock, and, simultaneously, the evolution of the post-disaster water demand. Usually, it takes longer for the building recovery process to start, compared to the recovery of the components of civil infrastructure systems. Therefore, Weibull component recovery functions, which allow a variable skewness, are employed (Didier et al. 2015). For the building stock, it is again supposed that it takes longer to rebuild a collapsed building than to repair a slightly damaged one. The recovery curves allow to account for the variability of the recovery process: while one damaged building might have been repaired after a certain time after the disaster, the neighboring one might still remain unrepaired, for example, due to a lack of financial resources. The parameters of the employed recovery functions for the Nepalese building stock can be based on building recovery data available from the 2005 Kashmir earthquake (ERRA 2015): the actual building stock recovery process after the 2015 Gorkha earthquake remains slow even more than two years after the event, resulting in a small number of data points to base an empirical assessment of building recovery duration.

To evaluate the fragility functions chosen to model the seismic vulnerability of the components of the water supply and distribution system and of the building stock of the Kathmandu Valley, the expected PGA and PGV need to be evaluated at the different locations for the particular earthquake scenario. For this case study, a scenario earthquake of moment magnitude M_w 8.0 with an epicenter located northwest of the Kathmandu Valley is selected. In fact, earthquakes of M_w 8 and higher are expected in the Kathmandu Valley (Wesnousky et al. 2017). For a more sophisticated resilience analysis, more scenario earthquakes can be chosen or a probabilistic seismic hazard analysis can be implemented. The PGV and the PGA in this case study are evaluated using the attenuation relations for Nepal given by Aman et al. 1995. These relations estimate the horizontal PGV and the PGA at a given location depending on the moment magnitude of the (scenario) earthquake and the distance to the epicenter of the earthquake.

Water pipes are geographically distributed elements, covering often long distances between two point-like facilities of the water supply or distribution system. Pipes are, however, especially susceptible to damage due to peak ground deformation (PGD). PGD is caused, for example, by landslides or by liquefaction of the soil. To assess the seismic vulnerability of pipes due to PGD, the liquefaction and landslide potential has to be evaluated. The soil type, groundwater depth, and slope angles have a large influence on a potential PGD observed during earthquakes. For the Kathmandu Valley, the geographic distribution of the different soil classes is given by JICA and MoHA 2002a. JICA and MoHA 2002c provide data on the groundwater level, which varies substantially between dry and wet seasons (during which the water level will raise considerably) in Nepal. In a conservative approach, the groundwater level of the wet season is assumed in this case study. The liquefaction probability can, then, be estimated using the liquefaction susceptibility (JICA & MoHA 2002b), the map of the groundwater depth, soil type, and level of ground shaking (in this case given by the PGV). The PGD related to lateral spreading and ground settlement due to liquefaction can then be estimated. Landslide susceptibility categories, allowing to determine the critical acceleration of the slope stability, can be computed using the slope angle and the geological and hydrological conditions (FEMA 2013). The displacement expected from landslides can be obtained, for example, from the empirical model from Saygilli and Rathje 2008, which expects the critical acceleration and the earlier computed PGA as input. Finally, the PGD is the maximum of the ground deformation due to liquefaction and due to landslides. The detailed procedure is explained in more details in Bellagamba 2015, Eicher 2015 and Didier et al. 2018b.

Damage to the pipes of the water supply and distribution system of the Kathmandu Valley is estimated using the pipe repair rates given by ALA 2001 and the estimated PGD and PGV. The pipe repair rates depend on the material, the diameter, the connection type and the age of the pipes. In fact, different types of pipes and joints have a markedly varying seismic performance. Historical data on pipe breaks can be used to produce survival curves estimating the pipe's survival rate over time in function of the pipe's age (Fragiadakis et al. 2013). Such effects can, then, be considered in the resilience assessment by combining the survival curves compiled from the historical records of the operators with the employed ALA curves, which have been estimated using the repair numbers of damaged pipes reported after several past earthquakes. In this case study, it is assumed that 80 percent of the damage induced by PGD are breaks and 20 percent leaks. For transient ground deformation, 80 percent of the damage is supposed to be leaks and 20 percent breaks (FEMA 2013). Finally, a section is considered as broken (i.e. no water flow is possible through that pipe anymore, until it has been repaired), if it contains at least one break or more than five leaks (Bellgamba 2015). For the recovery of the pipe network, a random recovery process is assumed in this case study. Optimized recovery processes are, for example, presented in Fang and Sansavini 2017.

Finally, a system service model determining the allocation of the water supply to cover the water demand needs to be defined for the undamaged and the damaged networks, obtained during the multiple post-disaster repair steps. The resilience of a system does not solely depend on the performance of its components but is also governed by system dynamics imposed by the topology and system service model. In fact, after the recovery of a point-like facility or a pipe of the network, the topology and configuration of the system change, new demand and supply situations can be observed, and the system needs to adapt to them. For the purpose of the resilience assessment of this case study, a simple distribution model was used. Due to the large supply deficit present before the occurrence of the scenario earthquake, it is supposed that the entire water supply capacity that is still deliverable to a consumer after the earthquake will be consumed. Connectivity between the different nodes, still operable after the earthquake, is determined using the Floyd-Warshall algorithm (Adachi & Ellingwood 2006). If it is of interest, more elaborated hydraulic flow models can be included in the resilience assessment. The EPANET software (Rossman 2000) allows, for example, to track the flow of water in the individual pipes, the pressure at each node, etc.

The results of the resilience assessment of the water supply and distribution system of the Kathmandu Valley for the chosen scenario earthquake are shown in Figure 17.3. The supply capacity, water consumption, and demand decrease after the scenario earthquake, similar to the observations after the 2015 Gorkha earthquake (Figure 17.1). The supply capacity and the consumption decrease to almost 0 immediately after the disaster. In fact, almost every pipe was damaged during the scenario earthquake as well as many water intakes. The observed Lack of Resilience can be quantified as $LoR_{sys} = 0.85$ and the resilience as $R_{sys} = 0.15$. Based on this

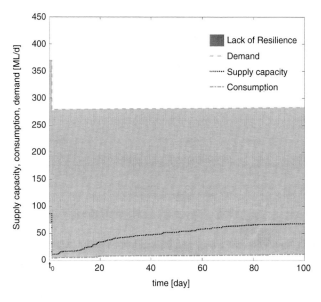

Figure 17.3 Computed mean Lack of Resilience of the water supply and distribution system of the Kathmandu Valley, considering a M_w 8.0 scenario earthquake.

analysis, the system can be characterized as having a classical resilience-related configuration (Didier et al. 2017d). As can be observed, the supply deficit of the system decreased following the earthquake. In fact, the decrease in water demand exceeded the decrease in the water supply.

17.7 Conclusion

Resilient water supply and distribution systems are essential for the functioning of modern communities. They provide (potable) water required to guarantee public health, irrigation in agriculture and for industrial production. Wastewater systems are needed to evacuate the used water. However, these systems are vulnerable to environmental stressors and to disasters. In order to limit possible adverse effects of damage to the systems on the community, not only robust components and systems are needed, but a resourceful recovery and adaptation is also important. A general methodology for a resilience assessment using the Re-CoDeS framework has been introduced and used in a case study to assess the seismic resilience of the water supply and distribution system of the Kathmandu Valley (Nepal). The Re-CoDeS framework allows to include the evolution of the demand to the resilience assessment. Challenges, such as a growing population over time, or displacement of population after disasters, can create new demand patterns and can have adverse effects on the resilience of the water systems. Mitigating the adverse effects of the inability to satisfy the demand for water may necessitate significant investments over long periods of time combined with public policy measures, such as voluntary or mandatory water conservation.

The Re-CoDeS framework can be adapted to assess the resilience of other civil infrastructure systems (e.g. wastewater systems, electric power supply systems, ...), or of systems of other regions (e.g. of a city in the United States), or towards other disasters (e.g. hurricanes or floods).

The employed fragility and recovery functions of the components, the system service model, and the topology of the networks can be adapted to be representative for the system and hazard(s) of interest. The influence of environmental stressors can be additionally included in the assessment. The resilience assessment can as well be extended to a more detailed micro component level, considering, for example, the behavior of the individual valves, etc. at the expense of the computational effort needed for such detailed information.

Additionally, to assess the resilience of the water supply and distribution system considering the demand/supply interactions between the community demand and the water supply and distribution system, the interdependencies with other civil infrastructure systems can be included in the Re-CoDeS framework (Didier et al. 2018c). After past earthquakes, it has been observed that the water distribution system relies on electric power to operate, for example, pumping and treatment plants. In a holistic community resilience assessment, the effect of damage to the electric power supply system needs, thus, to be considered as well. Finally, the demand/supply equilibrium obtained at the different steps of the pre- and post-disaster assessment do not necessarily correspond to an economic demand/supply equilibrium. Pricing models can be combined with the water demand and supply model to include the price influences on both quantities and to assess the resilience from an economic point of view (Didier et al. 2018c).

References

Adachi T. and Ellingwood B.R. (2006) "Serviceability of earthquake-damaged water systems: Effects of electrical power availability and power backup system on system vulnerability," *Reliability Engineering and System Safety*, *93*, 78–88.

Aman A., Singh U.K., and Singh R.P. (1995) "A new empirical relation for strong seismic ground motion for the Himalayan region," *Current Science*, *69*, 10.

American Lifelines Alliance (ALA) (2001) Seismic Fragility Formulations for Water Systems.

American Society of Civil Engineers (ASCE) (2011) *Failure to act – The economic impact of current investment trends in water and wastewater treatment infrastructure.* Washington DC, USA.

Arasmith S. ed. (2009) *Introduction to Small Water System: A Course for Level I Operators* Albany, Oregon, USA.

Bellagamba X. (2015) Seismic Resilience of a Gas Distribution Network. Master Thesis ETH Zurich, Switzerland.

Bruneau M., Chang S.E., Eguchi R.T., Lee G.C., O'Rourke T.D., Reinhorn A.M., Shinozuka M., Tierney K., Wallace W.A., and Von Winterfeldt D. (2003) "A framework to quantitatively assess and enhance the seismic resilience of communities," *Earthquake Spectra*, *19*(4), 733–52.

Central Bureau of Statistics (CBS) Government of Nepal (2012) *National Population and Housing Census 2011* Kathmandu, Nepal.

Cubrinovski M., Bradley B., Wotherspoon L., Green R., Bray J., Wood C., Pender M., Allen J., Bradshaw A., Rix G., Taylor M., Robinson K., Henderson D., Giorgini S., Ma K., Winkley A., Zupan J., O'Rourke T., DePascale G., and Wells D. (2011) "Geotechnical aspects of the 22 February 2011 Christchurch earthquake," *Bulletin of the New Zealand Society for Earthquake Engineering*, *44*, 4.

Davis C.A. (2014) "Resiliency of water, wastewater, and inundation protection systems." *Encyclopedia of Earthquake Engineering.* Berlin, Heidelberg: Springer-Verlag.

Didier M., Sun L., Ghosh S., and Stojadinovic B. (2015) "Post-earthquake recovery of a community and its electrical power supply system," *COMPDYN 2015, Crete Island, Greece, 25–27 May 2015.*

Didier M., Baumberger S., Tobler R., Esposito S., Ghosh S., and Stojadinovic B. (2017a) "Improving post-earthquake building safety evaluation using the 2015 Gorkha earthquake rapid visual damage assessment data," *Earthquake Spectra*, 33, S1, S415–S434.

Didier M., Grauvogl B., Steentoft A., Ghosh S., and Stojadinovic B. (2017b) "Seismic resilience of the Nepalese power supply system during the 2015 Gorkha earthquake," *16th World Conference on Earthquake Engineering, 16WCEE 2017, Santiago Chile, January 9th to 13th 2017.*

Didier M., Broccardo M., Esposito S. and Stojadinovic B. (2017c) "A compositional demand/supply framework to quantify the resilience of civil infrastructure systems (Re-CoDeS)," *Sustainable and Resilient Infrastructure*, *3*(2): 86–102.

Didier M., Broccardo M., Esposito S., and Stojadinovic B. (2017d) "Resilience-related configurations of civil infrastructure and community systems," *2nd International Workshop on Modelling of Physical, Economic and Social Systems for Resilience Assessment*. Ispra, Italy, December 12–14, 2017.

Didier M., Grauvogl B., Steentoft A., Broccardo M., Ghosh S., and Stojadinovic B. (2017e) "Assessment of post-disaster community infrastructure services demand using Bayesian networks." *16th World Conference on Earthquake Engineering, 16WCEE 2017, Santiago Chile, January 9 to 13 2017*.

Didier M., Baumberger S., Tobler R., Esposito S., Ghosh S., and Stojadinovic B. (2018a) "Seismic resilience of the water distribution and the cellular communication systems after the 2015 Gorkha earthquake," *Journal of Structural Engineering*, *144*(6): 04018043-1–04018043-11.

Didier M., Broccardo M., Esposito S. and Stojadinovic B. (2018b) "Seismic Resilience of the Water Distribution Network", *16th European Conference on Earthquake Engineering (16ECEE)*, Thessaloniki (Greece), June 18–21, 2018.

Didier M., Broccardo M., Esposito S., and Stojadinovic B. (2018c) "Seismic resilience interdependent civil infrastructure systems", *11th National Conference on Earthquake Engineering (11NCEE)*, Los Angeles, USA, June 25–29, 2018.

Dolce M., Giovinazzi S., Iervolino I., Nigro E., and Tang A. (2009) "Emergency management for lifelines and rapid response after L'Aquila earthquake," *Effects on Structures and Infrastructures*, *2*(12), 209–17.

Earthquake Engineering Research Institute (EERI) (2016) EERI Earthquake Reconnaissance Team Report: M7.8 Gorkha, Nepal Earthquake on April 25, 2015 and its Aftershocks, Oakland, CA, USA.

Earthquake Reconstruction & Rehabilitation Authority (ERRA) Pakistan (2015) ERRA Sectoral Update, Islamabad, Pakistan.

Eicher C. (2015) Seismic Resilience of a Water Supply Network Master Thesis ETH Zurich, Switzerland.

Eidinger J. and Tang A.K. ed. (2012) *Christchurch, New Zealand earthquake sequence of Mw 7.1 September 04, 2010 Mw 6.3 February 22, 2011 Mw 6.0 June 13, 2011 Lifeline Performance*, Reston, Virginia.

Ellsworth W.L., Lindh A.G., Prescott W.H., and Herd D.G. (1981) The 1906 San Francisco earthquake and the seismic cycle. *Earthquake Prediction: An International Review*, Washington, USA.

Fang Y. and Sansavini G. (2017) "Emergence of antifragility by optimum postdisruption restoration planning of infrastructure networks" *J. Infrastruct. Syst.* *23*(4), 04017024-1–04017024-13.

Federal Emergency Management Agency (FEMA) – Department of Homeland Security (2013) *Hazus MH 2.1 – Technical Manual*, USA.

Fragiadakis M., Christodoulou S.E., and Vamvatsikos D. (2013) "Reliability assessment of urban water distribution networks under seismic loads," *Water Ressour. Manage. 27*.

Gallo I.M. (2015) "Roman water supply systems, new approach," *De Aquaeductu atque Aqua Urbium Lyciae Pamphyliae Pisidiae*, The Legacy of Sextus Julius Frontinus, Anatalya (Turkey).

Giovinazzi S., Wilson T., Davis C., Bristow D., Gallagher M., Schofield A., Villemure M., Eidinger J., and Tang A. (2011) "Lifelines performance and management following the 22 February 2011 Christchurch earthquake, New Zealand: highlights of resilience," *Bulletin of the New Zealand Society for Earthquake Engineering*, *44*(4): 402–17.

Guidotti, R., Rosenheim, N., and Gardoni, P. (2018) "Integration of Physical Infrastructure and Social Systems in Communities' Reliability and Resilience Analysis," *Reliability Engineering & System Safety* (under review).

Haestad Methods 2015 A brief history of water distribution technology https://pierderideapa.wordpress.com/2015/07/26/a-brief-history-of-water-distribution-technology/ (last accessed October 20, 2017).

Hwang H., Lin H., and Shinozuka M. (1998) "Seismic performance assessment of water delivery systems," *Journal of Infrastructure Systems*, *4*(3), 118–25.

Japan International Cooperation Agency (JICA) and Ministry of Home Affairs (MoHA), HMG of Nepal (2002a) *The Study of Earthquake Disaster Mitigation in the Kathmandu Valley Volume 1*. Kingdom of Nepal.

Japan International Cooperation Agency (JICA) and Ministry of Home Affairs (MoHA), HMG of Nepal (2002b) *The Study of Earthquake Disaster Mitigation in the Kathmandu Valley Volume 2*. Kingdom of Nepal.

Japan International Cooperation Agency (JICA) and Ministry of Home Affairs (MoHA), HMG of Nepal (2002c) *The Study of Earthquake Disaster Mitigation in the Kathmandu Valley Volume 3*. Kingdom of Nepal.

Kakderi K. and Argyroudis S. (2014) Fragility functions of water and waste-water systems, *SYNER-G: Typology Definition and Fragility Functions for Physical Elements at Seismic Risk, eds Pitilakis, Crowley, Kaynia*, Dordrecht.

Kathmandu Upatyaka Khanepani Limited (KUKL) (2015) *Annual Report, 2071 Falgun* Kathmandu, Nepal.

Kongar I., Esposito S., and Giovinazzi S. (2015) "Post-earthquake assessment and management for infrastructure systems: learning from the Canterbury (New Zealand) and L'Aquila (Italy) earthquakes," *Bull. of Earthquake Eng.*, 15, 589–620.

Ministry of Health (2012) Annual Report on Drinking-Water Quality 2010–2011, Wellington, New Zealand.

Monteleone M.C., Yeung H., and Smith R. (2007) "A review of Ancient Roman water supply exploring techniques of pressure reduction," *Water Science & Technology: Water Supply*, 7(1), 113–20.

National Infrastructure Advisory Council (NIAC) (2009) Critical Infrastructure Resilience Final Report and Recommendations, 1–43.

Pitilakis K., Crowley H., and Kaynia A.M. ed. (2014) *SYNER-G: Typology Definition and Fragility Functions for Physical Elements at Seismic Risk*, Dordrecht, Springer.

Rossman L.A. (2000) *EPANET 2 Users Manuel* Cincinnati, OH, USA.

Saygili G. and Rathje E. (2008) "Empirical predictive models for earthquake-induced sliding displacements of slopes," *Journal of Geotechnical and Geoenvironmental Engineering, 134*(6), 790–803.

US Geological Survey (2014) *Estimated Use of Water in the United States in 2010* Reston, Virginia, USA.

US Presidential Policy Directive (USPPD) 21 (2013) Critical Infrastructure Security and Resilience, The White House Office of the Press Secretary.

Wesnousky S.G., Kumahara Y., Chamlagain D., Pierce I.K, Karki A., and Gautam D. (2017) "Geological observations on large earthquakes along the Himalayan frontal fault near Kathmandu, Nepal," *Earth and Planetary Science Letters* 457, 366–75.

Wikimedia (2015) Water supply network. https://en.wikipedia.org/wiki/Water_supply_network (last accessed October 20, 2017).

18

Population dynamics and the resiliency of water and wastewater infrastructure

Kasey M. Faust[1] and Jessica A. Kaminsky[2]

[1] CIVIL, ARCHITECTURAL AND ENVIRONMENTAL ENGINEERING, THE UNIVERSITY OF TEXAS AT AUSTIN, AUSTIN, TEXAS, 301 E. DEAN KEATON C1700, AUSTIN, TEXAS 78712, USA; FAUSTK@UTEXAS.EDU (CORRESPONDING AUTHOR)

[2] CIVIL AND ENVIRONMENTAL ENGINEERING, THE UNIVERSITY OF WASHINGTON, SEATTLE, WASHINGTON, 201 MORE HALL, SEATTLE, WASHINGTON 98195, USA; JKAMINSK@UW.EDU

18.1 Introduction

Resiliency for the built environment refers to the ability to respond or adapt to extreme events or changing operating conditions (Fiksel 2003; Marchese & Linkov 2017; Matthews 2016; Opdyke et al. 2017b; IRGC 2016). This definition of resiliency includes identifying (1) the thresholds at which critical infrastructure systems fail to provide adequate services under extreme conditions that differ significantly from the environment the system was designed to operate within, (2) the length of time the system needs to recover from such events, and (3) if the system is able to adapt to such events to mitigate impacts. If critical infrastructure systems fail, utilities, decision-makers, and regulating governments are challenged to restore critical infrastructure services as quickly as possible to avoid negative impacts to public health and safety. In the civil engineering community, conversations about resiliency have often centered around those infrastructure systems that have been physically damaged or destroyed by extreme events (e.g. Sun & Xu 2010; El-Anwar & Chen 2012; Opdyke et al. 2017a). In contrast, in this chapter we consider a different category of infrastructure impacts from extreme events. These impacts arise from extreme population dynamics that significantly change the demand for infrastructure services from those intended during design. In this type of extreme event, either increases or decreases of population can mean that civil infrastructure systems are operating outside of these design tolerances and are accordingly at risk of failure.

The negative impacts of extreme events typically fall inequitably on the vulnerable members of society least equipped to shoulder the burdens (Wisner at al. 2003); the impacts of extreme population dynamics are no different (Faust et al. 2016). Those most susceptible to disasters, and therefore most likely to be displaced, have been found to be the most vulnerable populations within our communities due to a combination of political, social, and economic factors (Wisner et al. 2003). For example, housing located in areas prone to floods or subpar construction that cannot withstand extreme weather more commonly impact low-income communities. In another example, utilities in once vibrant cities experiencing chronic population decline over multiple decades have fewer customers and thus, a reduced tax base to pay for existing civil infrastructure. In shrinking cities, this issue is compounded by a high proportion (often reaching 40 percent) of the remaining taxpayer population falling below the poverty line (Faust et al. 2016). More generally, and as discussed here, changes in the number of consumers or in the socio-demographics of the population served by utilities can impact both the performance and management of infrastructure systems. For example, frontend planning or physical system modifications may not meet the need due to factors such as implementation time constraints (in the case of rapid population increase in communities hosting displaced populations) or lack of financial resources (in the case of chronic population decline).

Extreme population dynamics may occur suddenly, such as rapid population increases due to post-disaster migrations out of damaged areas to hosting communities. They may also occur over decades, such as the chronically declining populations seen in shrinking cities worldwide. While these two scenarios are the examples discussed in this chapter, other types of extreme population change such as rapid rural-to-urban migration may also have this kind of impact on infrastructure systems. Similarly, and although this chapter discusses extreme population dynamics that result in a drastic net change in population, cities may experience resiliency challenges due to movement *within* the city. For example, growth of the downtown with corresponding decline of other areas of the city and no net population change results in a different spatial distribution of demands than the system was originally designed for, posing potential resiliency gaps. Still, regardless of the causal triggers of extreme population dynamics, and despite the scale and frequency of occurrence, to date this analytic category of extreme event has been largely missing from the infrastructure resiliency conversation. As such, this chapter discusses the ways in which two kinds of extreme population dynamics impact water and wastewater systems, beginning with rapid population growth due to disaster displacements and then moving to the case of shrinking cities. Finally, it presents a comparison of strategies that may be used to mitigate the identified impacts of both (Tables 18.2 and 18.3).

18.2 Rapid influx of population

Disaster events are increasing in frequency and severity. In August and September 2017, Hurricanes Harvey/Irma/Maria hit the Caribbean and United States, causes billions of dollars in damage (Horowitz 2017). The impacts of these events are far reaching, causing many secondary impacts. For the built environment, one of these secondary impacts is triggered by large post-event migration of the impacted populations to otherwise undamaged locations. This kind of post-disaster population displacement may be temporary or permanent, but at scale either can have serious impacts to infrastructure systems. Providing critical infrastructure services post-disaster, both in undamaged communities hosting displaced populations and at the disaster impacted location itself, is a challenge for civil engineers. Still, although there has been considerable research in the domain of providing critical infrastructure services at the immediate location of the disaster event, there has been considerably less work exploring the impacts of disaster migration on the resiliency of critical infrastructure services in hosting communities (Faust & Kaminsky 2017).

A recent example of large-scale disaster migration is the ongoing European refugee situation. Since 2015, millions of displaced persons sought asylum due to instability in the Middle East. This situation is ongoing through at least 2017 (UNHCR 2015, 2017). In 2015 alone, approximately 1.3 million first-time applicant asylum seekers arrived in Europe (Eurostat 2016). The challenges associated with providing refuge to this magnitude of displaced persons with limited to no frontend planning have become increasingly evident; European Union President Donald Tusk stated that, in 2016, "the practical capabilities of Europe to host new waves of refugees, not to mention irregular economic migrants, are close to the limits" (Ap 2016). Further exacerbating the questions of how to provide such infrastructure services to displaced persons (e.g. temporary or permanent expansion of infrastructure) is the uncertainty associated with how many displaced persons will remain in Europe, and how long they will do so.

As the displacement continues to present day (2018) in Europe, the resiliency of the hosting communities' built environment has been tested. Accordingly, the engineering community has become increasingly aware of the impacts of suddenly increased populations on critical infrastructure services. Notably, due to contextualized factors such as non-uniform population distributions and system capacities in cities, the technical impacts of population decline can be either positive or negative (Faust & Kaminsky 2017). There are also financial challenges with providing services to aslyum seekers who are circumstantially temporarily unable to pay for water and wastewater services. To maintain the European status quo performance of virtually universal clean water and sanitation coverage (shown by the dashed line in Figure 18.1) the hosting population and utility must provide adequate water and wastewater services to the vulnerable, displaced population. Otherwise, system performance would drop (as shown by the solid line in Figure 18.1) until the displaced population is able to pay for infrastructure services. Indeed, a survey sent to the German public (Kaminsky & Faust 2017) indicate that the public perceives a collective, societal responsibility to provide water and wastewater services to displaced persons who do not have the financial capability to pay for such services (viewing the provision of services as a human right, at least for a period of time). However, this collective expectation to provide water and wastewater services to asylum seekers regardless of the ability to pay is a challenge for engineers, policy makers, and water utility staff, and suggest a potential resilience gap during this transition time (Figure 18.1; Kaminsky & Faust 2017).

In a first step towards quantifying this resilience gap, survey results indicated that a majority of the German public believes water and wastewater services should be provided to vulnerable

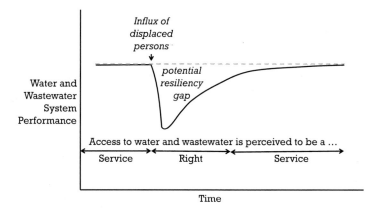

Figure 18.1 System resiliency and the transition from a right to a service.
Source: Kaminsky and Faust 2017.

displaced populations upon arrival. During this timeframe, then, the provision of water and sanitation to the disadvantaged population tends to be perceived as an issue of human rights (Kaminsky & Faust 2017). Indeed, 13 percent of survey respondents viewed the provision of water and wastewater services as a human right that should be provided *indefinitely* to displaced persons. In contrast, 21.3 percent of respondents did not identify a collective responsibility to provide services to those unable to pay for any time at all, viewing water and wastewater as just another service to be paid for. However, the majority of survey respondents (65.2 percent) viewed the provision of water and wastewater services to displaced persons as something that transitions from a question of human rights to a question of the provision of an infrastructure service after a period of time (Kaminsky & Faust 2017). In other words, they were willing to pay for services to vulnerable others for a while, but not forever. Most respondents (88 percent) in this group believed that water and wastewater should be provided for the same amount of time, and expected these services to be provided to disaster migrants who were unable to pay for these services for an average of 2.9 years (Kaminsky & Faust 2017). This is a substantial length of time that the German utilities are expected to provide services to a large, vulnerable, and unexpected population. In other words, this is a substantial challenge to infrastructure resiliency, or a potential *resiliency gap*.

Other contexts with highly developed utilities – such as the US – would reasonably also be expected to provide services to disaster displaced populations. This has been the case in the past; for example, in 2017 individuals sheltering from Hurricane Harvey in Dallas were provided with water and wastewater services (Cowan 2017). As such, to explore the potential for resiliency gaps or system benefits in the US resulting from extreme population displacements, Faust and Kaminsky (2017) surveyed 25 water and wastewater utilities nationwide to explore the hypothetical impacts of this kind of extreme event on water and wastewater infrastructure systems. The final respondent pool represented 19 US states and gathered knowledge from 32 subject matter experts (SMEs) with backgrounds as utility directors, managers, supervisors, chief engineers, superintendents, and city engineers. These respondents represented 17 urbanized areas (population of 50,000+) and eight urbanized clusters (populations between 2,500 and 50,000) (US Census 2017). Both positive and negative hypothetical impacts of mass displacements anticipated by survey respondents were coded to technical, managerial and financial categories, which together are thought to determine the utility's ability to meet relevant standards and regulations (US EPA 2016a; WADOH 2013). Respondents identified both positive and negative hypothetical impacts arising from a rapid population influx in the technical and financial categories. In addition, additional categories of hypothetical impacts emerged, including Personnel, Temporary Infrastructure, New Infrastructure, and Coordination, Design, and Construction. Each of these categories and the knowledge gained from this body of research is discussed below (see Faust & Kaminsky 2017). A common theme throughout this discussion is that the potential impacts to infrastructure from a suddenly increased population may be positive or negative depending on how the situation is handled. This is in contrast to the challenges of population dynamics in shrinking cities, where it is rarely if ever possible to control where population decline occurs.

18.2.1 Technical system capacity

Population dynamics can impact a system's technical performance and the resultant level of service it can provide (Faust et al. 2016; Ap 2016). For example, increased demands can only be met given sufficient source water volume, an issue compounded by droughts that climate change is increasing in severity and frequency. Indeed, even when the raw water supply can meet increased demands in the short term, it may not be sustainable to do so in the long term. Similarly, there may be challenges associated with the technical capacity of the existing infrastructure to deliver increased flows, even if a utility has sufficient preexisting supply and sufficient existing treatment capacity to handle the new population. Capital improvement needs (e.g. alterations to pump stations, increased tank volume, or pipeline sizes) may be necessary to deliver the water. For example, Varis et al. (2006) has found that population growth from rapid urbanization can result in inequitable levels of service. Technical capacity concerns related to the water system include meeting fire flow regulations and sufficient fire flow supply, indicating a cascading impact into the emergency service critical infrastructure sector. Notably, many utilities respondents in Faust and Kaminsky (2017) foresaw insufficient capacities as a greater concern for the wastewater system, with potential issues including wastewater discharges exceeding permitting thresholds. In the longer term, increasing physical infrastructure capacity to meet increased water or wastewater demands can result in underutilized infrastructure if the migrant population does not remain.

For water infrastructure, even when utilities can meet increased demands for volume the spatial distribution of the new demands throughout the city are a critical factor. Demand distribution impacts the available capacity in the system at locations throughout the system as well as influencing water quality. In an example of the importance of demand distribution, older infrastructure is more easily stressed by a demand surge than is newer infrastructure, meaning it is more difficult to meet increased demands using older assets. In contrast, when increased populations are placed in an area with system redundancy, ample capacity, or previously low demands, new demands can more likely be met. However, areas of the systems may still experience problems during peak flows, or may experience newly increased flows during previously off-peak times. In sum, unless there is coordination with utilities regarding placement of new populations, there is the potential for detrimental impacts. However, with coordination of placement decisions, the new population and related demands can bring benefits to the water system, such as reducing water age. Similarly, previously underutilized areas of water systems may see improvements in metrics such as nitrification, disinfection by-product formation, temperature increases, or sediment deposition.

Only one utility that responded to the survey issued by Faust and Kaminsky (2017) foresaw challenges to the wastewater system in regards to water quality. This utility was concerned about increased wastewater effluent violations due to the treatment plant capacity. Other potential issues might reasonably include conveyance system overflows, backups, or changed loadings. As for the water system, these and other impacts to the wastewater infrastructure would be heavily influenced by the placement of the new demands in the infrastructure system.

Finally, suddenly increased demands could also cause operational challenges, including needed changes in the operation of water sources, storage tank(s), pumps, or reservoirs. Correspondingly, an increase in main break frequency due to additional loads might result in new construction/maintenance needs and temporarily increased nonrevenue water loss. In the context of maintenance, anticipated challenges include less time for preventive maintenance, the inability to defer maintenance and replacement, and increased fragility resulting from increased maintenance costs without the revenues to support such costs. At treatment plants, expected operational issues include changes to treatment processes. Beneficial operational impacts can also result from increased demand for services. For example, these could include an improved match between design capacity and demand. Notably, utilities tend to see operational challenges as manageable (Faust & Kaminsky 2017), and broadly antici-pate providing services regardless to the potential financial limitations of disaster displaced populations.

18.2.2 Financial capacity

In the long term, additional customers means additional revenue and increased financial capacity for utilities. When utilities have sufficient existing system capacity to meet the new demands, they can enjoy increased revenues without additional capital costs. These increased revenues may improve levels of service by funding system upgrades, or may even reduce con-sumer rates through reducing per capita fixed costs. Other utilities are in locations with policies for increasing the density of development and the new demands could aid in meeting the infill and densification goals of the city. In addition, providing services to disaster migrants may involve emergency federal or state funding that can provide a long-term benefit to the infra-structure systems through the creation of new or improved assets.

However, these long-term benefits of new customers arrive coupled with the concern that many disaster displaced persons may not initially have the ability to pay for infrastruc-ture services. As such, immediate revenue gains are unlikely to meet the immediate costs necessary to accommodate the growth. This suggests that in the short term the hosting community and ratepayers could see surcharges or increased rates due to increased water and wastewater flows, network extenuations, or expansion of capacity. Needless to say, this is a serious concern for host communities to manage. Indeed, funding investments for the provision of water and wastewater is a concern for many utilities even under status quo conditions; this difficulty would almost certainly be exacerbated with the arrival of a large number of displaced persons. Bonding would likely be required for the scale of investment needed in many instances. It is also possible that state or federal emergency funding would be made available to meet these demands. However, because hosting communities are geo-graphically distinct from the location of the physical damage from the disaster, there is a great deal of uncertainty regarding the availability of such funds. Based on current US policy, federal emergency funding is directed at the area impacted by the disaster or for support at emergency shelters (FEMA 2016a; US EPA 2016b). Notably, funding may be available for meeting housing needs, but currently there is no mechanism to direct funds to utilities to reduce strain placed on systems from disaster displaced populations (Faust & Kaminsky 2017).

18.2.3 Personnel

Workforce or personnel challenges are also a concern under disaster migration conditions (Faust & Kaminsky 2017). For example, increased demands would likely require increased personnel for operations and maintenance of existing facilities or (as discussed in the section below) for the construction of new or expanded assets. Additional personnel would be needed to handle new non-technical needs such as new customer accounts. Similarly, it is possible that there would be new personnel needs for education and outreach regarding the use and limitations of the water and wastewater infrastructure. Depending on the origin of the displaced population, language barriers may present a significant challenge to meeting these types of multilingual customer service needs. However, members of the displaced population itself could help meet this need, as well as providing a resource that can help the utilities to understand and meet any differing, culturally based water use needs of the new population. Finally, and regardless of language or cultural knowledge, a larger and more diverse hiring pool can only benefit utilities.

18.2.4 Temporary and new infrastructure

There are important differences between providing infrastructure services on temporary or permanent bases. Existing legislation assigns responsibilities to various levels of the government and utilities for emergency services post disaster and disruption to infrastructure systems (AWWA 2011). For example, existing plans range from water transport to coordination with various response partners (AWWA 2011). With this in mind, it is likely that these plans may be applied to provide off-grid service to displaced persons in the host communities in the short-term, especially when displaced persons first arrive, or if it is anticipated that the displaced persons will only remain for a limited period of time. For example, this could mean tanker truck water delivery or the provision of portable toilets. In contrast, when new populations are expected to stay, there is a need for longer term solutions. These solutions may include the expansion and upsizing of both the water and wastewater networks such as water/sewer main extensions, lift stations, elevated storage, additional wells, and physical changes the water distribution system. It is possible this circumstance could force deferred capital improvements, ultimately providing a benefit to the community regardless of how long the displaced population remains.

18.2.5 Coordination, design, and construction

The limited time available for the construction of new infrastructure and at least temporarily limited new revenue streams suggest real challenges for engineering and construction. Even utilities with sufficient capacity would need to plan and update existing long-range plans that would have to be expedited. In the context of construction, multiple years are often needed to complete planning, design, permitting, and construction. However, under the emergency situations of disaster migration there is a clear need to construct infrastructure as quickly as possible. With the declining workforce throughout the US (e.g. Federle et al. 1993; Burleson et al. 1998; Gomar et al. 2002; Chih et al. 2016), hosting communities would likely face obstacles in quickly meeting any infrastructure needs that require construction. Further exacerbating these issues is that during recovery, there is a surge in demands for construction workforce in disaster impacted areas (Arneson et al. 2016). These workforce issues would be a significant challenge for utilities as they seek to upsize, expand, or construct new infrastructure while continuing to provide adequate levels of service.

18.3 Chronic decline of population

Worldwide, cities such as Gary, IN, Detroit, MI, and Leipzig, Germany, are experiencing chronic urban decline – a paradigm of population life-cycle trajectories not often considered in infrastructure management. In these cities, the size of the built infrastructure footprint has not contracted with the corresponding population decline, but has remained relatively constant, resulting in underfunded and underutilized infrastructure systems (Faust et al. 2016). Notably, approximately 75–80 percent of water sector infrastructure costs are fixed costs for addressing capital and operational needs (Herz 2006; Hummel & Lux 2007; Schlör et al. 2009).

These fixed costs must still be recovered regardless of changes in population (Faust et al. 2016). Within shrinking cities, there are fewer taxpayers and consumers, and often, a high proportion (upwards of 40 percent) of the population falls below the poverty line (Faust et al. 2016). As a result, the cost of water sector infrastructure service can become prohibitively expensive (Herz 2006; Rybczynski & Linneman 1999; Beazley et al. 2011; Butts & Gasteyer 2011; Faust et al. 2016). This financial strain on the utility provider is further exacerbated due to requirements for meeting increasingly stringent regulations (Roberson 2011). In addition to financial challenges, problems associated with aging (ASCE 2013) and underutilized water infrastructure system exist, such as increased water age from the declining demands (Rink et al. 2010, Barr 2013).

Although each shrinking city is unique, many common threads may be found spanning this classification of cities (Faust et al. 2016). Of these common challenges, this section discusses issues in the resiliency of water and wastewater infrastructure in medium and large shrinking cities in US. Cities falling in this classification are those that have experienced at least 30 percent population loss, chronically, over multiple decades, from a peak population of at least 100,000. Circumstances discussed here challenging the resiliency of these cities comes from semi-structured interviews with personnel in Gary, IN, Akron, OH, Saginaw, MI, and Flint, MI (see Faust et al. 2016 for more details). These cities, although all shrinking, have different yet representative water and wastewater supply infrastructure management approaches – public vs. private, regional management vs. bounded by the city – and span multiple states, allowing for generalization across local policies.

18.3.1 Technical system capacity

Water and wastewater infrastructure systems have finite lives. Without intervention the condition of these systems deteriorates over time toward failures, decreased performance, and decreased levels of service. As such, maintenance and reinvestment in infrastructure is necessary to extend their service lives (NAE 2009). However, underinvesting in infrastructure is common nationwide (ASCE 2013), resulting in reactive approaches to maintenance and operations. Nevertheless, many cities are attempting to transition to more efficient, proactive approaches (e.g., Durrans et al. 2004; US EPA 2013). Needless to say, this difficult task is only exacerbated by the operating environment in shrinking cities.

In this context, due to the fiscal constraints and reduced personnel characteristic of shrinking cities, proactive maintenance may become prohibitively difficult, and consequentially often occurs on a reactive, as-needed basis (Faust et al. 2016). For example, water mains may only receive attention if they fail, and are only replaced when absolutely necessary due associated costs. While this approach maximizes the service life of the infrastructure, it also guarantees infrastructure failures and resultant reductions in levels of service that may impact public health. Indeed, few shrinking cities have shifted to proactive attempts to identify solutions to manage and maintain excess infrastructure (Faust et al. 2016). In an exception to this trend, the personnel interviewed from one shrinking city indicated that their municipal department has spent time and resources to explore addressing infrastructure issues through decommissioning and are actively looking for ways to resize their infrastructure for the current population. This reduction in physical footprint could potentially save maintenance costs and improve level of services end users received. However, interviews with SMEs indicate that this appears to be the exception rather than common practice.

In the context of wastewater systems in shrinking cities, the presence of combined sewer systems (CSS) and the sheer number of impervious surfaces present particular challenges. Vacant properties and brownfields leave behind concrete and asphalt foundations, parking lots, and other surfaces that impede groundwater infiltration during rainfall. Run-off enters the stormwater or combined sewer systems, ultimately contributing to discharges as the systems reach and exceed capacity. During wet weather events, the systems can exceed their storage capacity or the capacity of the treatment plant, discharging untreated wastewater into surrounding streams, rivers, lakes, and oceans; depending on the CSS capacity, as little as 0.1 inch of precipitation may result in overflows (Lijklema & Tyson 1993). This untreated wastewater impacts the water quality and environment, can present public health threats, and reduce aesthetics, due to the consequential introduction of pathogens and pollutants into the receiving water. Further exacerbating these issues posed by CSS in shrinking cities is that during dry periods solids in wastewater may settle within the system due to low flows arising from underutilization of the systems from reduced customer demands that are subsequently discharged during the aforementioned overflows (Faust et al. 2016). Commonly suggested methods for mitigating overflows include increasing the capacity of the CSS, separating sewer and stormwater systems, and implementing stormwater management alternatives to reduce runoff entering the CSS (US EPA 2009). Still, these proactive approaches are particularly difficult in the context of shrinking revenue streams in shrinking cities (Faust et al. 2016).

It should be noted that in the presence of extensive impervious surfaces, it is difficult to reduce stormwater runoff with solely green infrastructure (Baker 2011). In these shrinking cities, similar to the water sector infrastructure, underutilized impervious surfaces from reduced populations generate runoff. In order to reduce the area of these surfaces – as opposed to replacing already underutilized areas with pervious pavement that is often fiscally infeasible in shrinking cities – cities must commit to re-zoning areas of the city (Faust et al. 2016). Thus, a combination of strategies may be appropriate depending on the severity of the overflow problem in the city and the severity of challenges from local population decline.

18.3.2 Financial capacity

In shrinking cities, the cost of maintaining the aging infrastructure intended for use by larger populations remains constant or increases, while the tax base and number of customers declines (Rybczynski & Linneman 1999; Beazley et al. 2011; Butts & Gasteyer 2011). For instance, Detroit has an excess of aging water infrastructure, some of which is over two centuries old and was originally intended to support over twice the current population and a water-intensive manufacturing industry. However, since the 1950s, Detroit's population and manufacturing industry have been shrinking, leaving the city with far fewer people who utilize the water infrastructure and fewer water ratepayers.

In order for water and wastewater systems in shrinking cities to be self-sustaining, financial challenges must be met by either decreasing utility operation and maintenance costs or by increasing rates to consumers (Faust et al. 2016). The high fixed costs of water sector infrastructure (Herz 2006; Hummel & Lux 2007; Schlör et al. 2009), coupled with the financial burden of capital replacements, treatment, and regulatory compliance, therefore falls upon the remaining residents. In other words, the recovery of costs in the event of shrinking city populations results in municipal services becoming more expensive per capita (Rybczynski & Linneman 1999; Herz 2006; Beazley et al. 2011; Butts & Gasteyer 2011; Faust et al. 2016).

Of course, rate increases to meet financial challenges may not be uniform across all water users; different classes of consumers may be billed differently due to wholesale agreements between utilities and municipalities (Faust et al. 2016). For instance, in Akron the water rates for suburban customers are higher than those for residents within the city boundaries. In Saginaw, the rates for both residential and wholesale customers are derived based on the distance required to transport the water. Gary's regional rates are derived based on a "cost of service study," to determine the appropriate billing for wholesale and residential customers. Previous studies (Schlör et al. 2009; Butts & Gasteyer 2011) indicate these increased costs for both water and wastewater are not insignificant. As such, in regions where population decline has been the highest and the incomes are the lowest (see Table 18.1), there is significant social inequity of impacts occurring due to population decline patterns. In addition, the cities discussed here use broadly representative water supply and infrastructure management regimes typical in cities throughout the US, and span multiple states. This illustrates that the inequity challenges are not isolated to select geographies or management approaches. Given these empirically observed relationships between population decline, increasing per capita rates for water and wastewater services, and low incomes, shrinking cities not only face a decline in customers but also the inability of the existing customers to afford drastically increasing rates, as the cost of services is a higher percentage of the residents' average income. A similar impact is seen on revenues coming from tax bases rather than individual ratepayers. In other words, the lower average incomes linked with urban decline result in a tax base that is not only decreasing in size due to the shrinking population, but is also decreasing due to lower average incomes of the remaining residents.

As a result of the decreased number of consumers, utilities in shrinking cities have taken measures such as the continual reduction of personnel and reactive maintenance, in order to operate on reduced funds and lessen the need for rate increases (Faust et al. 2016). These decisions, made under the present-day financial constraints characteristic to utilities in shrinking cities, may result in the inability to maintain the previously existing level of service (Faust et al. 2016). However, contrary to many shrinking city utilities' perceptions, a majority of users indicated that they are willing to pay increased rates for water and wastewater service if they understood the benefits or had a perceived increase in reliability, defined as the perceived improved quality or operational characteristics associated with the level of service provided (Faust et al. 2016). A majority (70–75 percent) of the survey respondents from shrinking cities indicated that they would be willing to pay for improved reliability (e.g. fire flows, pressures, reduced disruption of service) of water and wastewater service (Faust et al. 2016). The willingness to pay for improved services demonstrates public support to shift towards management alternatives that would improve the efficiency and operations of the systems, which is a need readily identified by utility providers. Approximately

Table 18.1 Incomes in select shrinking cities

	Percent of population in poverty	2016 Population estimate	Per capita money income in past 12 months (2015 dollars)	Median household income 2006–2010 (2015 dollars)
Flint, MI	41.2 percent (Michigan: 15 percent)	97,386	$14,765 (Michigan: $26,607)	$24,862 (Michigan: $49,576)
Saginaw, MI	35.9 percent (Michigan: 15 percent)	48,984	$14,697 (Michigan: $26,607)	$27,990 (Michigan: $49,576)
Gary, In	37.1 percent (Indiana: 14.1 percent)	76,424	$16,305 (Indiana: $25,346)	$28,020 (Indiana: $49,255)
Akron, OH	26.5 percent (Ohio: 14.6 percent)	197,633	$20,872 (State: $26,953)	$34,512 (Ohio:49,429)

Source: US Census Bureau 2017.

50 percent of all respondents stated that they would be willing to pay 1–10 percent more for their service for these improvements (with 20–25 percent willing to pay more than a 10 percent increase), which may come in the form of maintenance or reinvestment in the infrastructure system (Faust et al. 2016). Although there is often a disconnect between perceived system performance and actual system performance, it is nonetheless important to consider the end users' – i.e. consumers in the context of water service – views of the service provided due to the intrinsic relationship between policies and public perceptions (Burstein 2003; Soroka & Wlezien 2004; Gray et al. 2004).

18.3.3 Personnel

Due to the dramatic decrease in available funds within shrinking cities, one of the common cost saving strategies taken in many shrinking cities has been a reduction in personnel (Faust et al. 2016). However, completing non-urgent repairs, providing system upgrades, and pursuing long-term planning is difficult with a reduced level of staffing. Indeed, necessary maintenance may simply not be feasible with reduced personnel resources. For instance, in an attempt to provide services with reduced personnel, one city recruits members of the public to flush the neighborhood hydrants annually (Faust et al. 2016). Further straining the fiscal operations of these systems is the retirement of personnel and the ensuing obligations to pay retirement benefits. For example, one city was paying retirement to approximately four times more people than were currently working (Faust et al. 2016). Detroit's Chapter 9 bankruptcy filing in July 2013 included the fiscal burdens associated with retired personnel across municipal departments (Helms & Guillen 2013). One private, regional water provider did not cite personnel reductions due to declining funds within shrinking cities as a major problem (Faust et al. 2016). Instead, it reported a need to reallocate personnel to disconnecting and reconnecting services, as nonpayment rates in the shrinking city were higher than in other cities within the region. Unfortunately, this increased expense for new personnel increased operation costs across the entire system.

18.3.4 Regulatory requirements

Water and wastewater providers must constantly meet increasing standards set by the state and federal government. These standards, put in place for consumer safety, have become increasingly stringent throughout the years (Roberson 2011) and are known to have resulted in significant public and environmental health benefits. Still, in order to maintain the safety of the public and continue to meet federal and state requirements, investments and regular maintenance that require financial capital are necessary. The cost of meeting more stringent regulations is difficult for water and wastewater systems within shrinking cities due to issues of declining numbers of ratepayers and other fiscal constraints as discussed previously. For instance, in order to obtain a National Pollutant Discharge Elimination System (NPDES) permit, the US Environmental Protection Agency requires any municipality with a population greater than 100,000 to have separate storm sewer systems (US EPA 2013). However, many shrinking cities have CSS, and constructing a separate storm water management program requires extensive financial resources that is often beyond the reach of many cities experiencing population decline (Faust et al. 2016).

18.4 Infrastructure alternatives to meet to address the resiliency gaps in the water and wastewater system

The examples provided here suggest the need for cities to consider both technical and managerial methods to proactively address water and wastewater infrastructure resiliency challenges

Table 18.2 Water infrastructure system alternatives to aid in resiliency gap arising from population dynamics

Alternative	Rapid Influx of Population	Urban Decline
Do Nothing	Face potential reductions in the level of service for both the hosting and the displaced community	Face potential reductions in the level of service and further financial constraints
Increase rates	Increase rates or surcharges on hosting community	Inability of residents to shoulder the burden of increased rates
	Possible resistance faced by hosting community to pay for services that they do not (seemingly) directly benefit from	Possible resistance from community due to increased rates
Location of demands	Consult with utilities on the placement of new populations to areas of the network with excess capacity or areas that could benefit from infill and densification	Relocate sparsely populated residences to more densely populated areas of the city for infill and densification for improved water age and allow system to function closer to design capacities
Trucking water in/ tanks	Temporary solution if population is thought to be transient or while permanent alternations to physical network is made	Remove residents from the network and bring in water separately in sparsely populated areas to offset operational costs
Water ATM	Temporary solution if population is thought to be transient or while permanent alternations to physical network is made	Remove residents from the network and have a stand-alone system in sparsely populated areas offset operational costs
Wells (New, currently used, out of service)	If quality groundwater and treatment methods are available, can offset supply challenges	If quality groundwater and treatment methods are available, can offset operational costs by removing residents from network
Water loss programs (decrease water loss, withdrawals, and maintenance costs; US EPA 2010)	Ultimately reduce strain on water supply and costs for the utility due to possibly lack of financial aid/ratepayers supporting system	Reduce system wide operation and maintenance costs to aid in stabilizing/ reducing costs passed on to community.
Energy management conservation program (25–30 percent of operation and maintenance costs are energy; US EPA 2012)	Reduce system costs to offset financial burden of potential non-paying consumers	Reduce system wide operation and maintenance costs to aid in stabilizing/ reducing costs passed on to community
Physical alternation of network	Extend or upsize pipelines in network to meet new demands System interconnections	Decommission underutilized portions of the network to reduce system footprint and associated operation and maintenance costs while improving level of service

resulting from population dynamics. The location of changing demands is a key challenge for utilities that are either hosting displaced populations (Faust & Kaminsky 2017) or experiencing population decline (Faust et al. 2016). For instance, the spatial patterns of changing demands change the viability of solutions due to issues in – for example – connectivity of the network, fire flow demands, or available capacity. Financial constraints are another common consideration

Table 18.3 Wastewater infrastructure system alternatives to aid in resiliency gap arising from population dynamics

Alternative	Rapid Influx of Population	Urban Decline
Do Nothing	Face potential reductions in the level of service for both the hosting and the displaced community	Face potential reductions in the level of service and further financial constraints
Increase rates	Increase rates or surcharges on hosting community	Inability of residents to shoulder the burden of increased rates
	Possible resistance faced by hosting community to pay for services that they do not (seemingly) directly benefit from	Possible resistance from community to increased rates
Greywater collection and onsite use (e.g., irrigation)	Reduce demands placed on system through greywater reuse; cascading impact into water system by reduction of water demands	For cities with CSS, greywater reuse may reduce demands placed on system – however, cascading impacts into water systems through reduced demands in already underutilized portions of the system
Individual septic systems or septage hauler, Onsite sewage facility	Reduce strain on network in areas that lack capacity if feasible	Reduce strain on network in areas that lack capacity if feasible in location
	High typical rates of groundwater pollution from failed onsite systems	High typical rates of groundwater pollution from failed onsite systems
Energy management conservation program (30 percent of operation and maintenance costs are energy; US EPA 2012)	Reduce system costs to offset financial burden of potential non-paying consumers	Reduce system wise operation and maintenance costs to aid in stabilizing/reducing costs passed on to community
Contract excess wastewater treatment plant space to surrounding communities	If community has excess capacity at plant, this may be used a revenue generating stream	If community has excess capacity at plant, this may be used a revenue generating stream
Physical alternation of network	Extend or upsize pipelines in network to meet new demands	Decommission underutilized portions of the network to reduce system footprint and associated operation and maintenance costs while improving level of service
	System interconnections	

for utilities as they seek to implement alternatives to maximize public benefits while also minimizing financial burdens. Although population dynamics may manifest in various ways, common alternatives may meet both the short- and long-term needs and aid in addressing identified resiliency gaps. Tables 18.2 and 18.3 show possible, generalized alternatives that may address the resiliency gaps faced by extreme population dynamics occurring *at both ends of the spectrum*.

18.5 Conclusions

Common to the two cases presented in this chapter – rapid urban population growth arising from disaster displaced populations, and chronic urban population decline – is the need for alternatives to address the resiliency gap presently faced by utilities in the instance of extreme and unexpected population dynamics. No matter the driver of population dynamics, the absence of this category of extreme events from the conversation regarding the resiliency of our built environment leaves communities without the tools and knowledge they need to adapt to changing conditions in both the short and long term. Questions certainly remain regarding the scale and timing of resources it is appropriate to spend mitigating consequences of disaster events that may never occur; the answers to these questions are certainly deeply contextual. However, if this type of extreme event is ignored during utility planning efforts we may miss easy opportunities for adding flexibility and resilience. At the very least, by having the conversation we move the technical community towards the kind of robust and rational decision-making that is the hallmark of good design and construction practice.

References

American Society of Civil Engineers. (2013) *Failure to act: The impact of current infrastructure investment on America's economic future* (www.asce.org/uploadedFiles/ Issues_and_Advocacy/Our_Initiatives/ Infrastructure/Content_Pieces/failure-to-act-economic-impact-summary-report.pdf)

Ap, T. (2016) "Europe 'close to limit' on refugee numbers, EU president says – CNN.com." *CNN Online*.

Arneson, E., Javernick-Will, A., Hallowell, M., and Thomas, W. (2016) "Construction capacity: The role of regional construction supply chain resources in post-disaster rebuilding," *Engineering Project Organization Society*, Cle Elum, Washington.

AWWA. (2011) *Planning for an Emergency Drinking Water Supply – emergencywater.pdf*. USEPA, Washington, DC.

Baker, L. (2011) "New strategies for controlling stormwater overflows," *Governing: The States and Localities: Energy and Environment*. www.governing.com/topics/transportation-infrastructure/New-Strategies-Controlling-Stormwater-Overflows.html (last accessed August 31, 2018).

Barr, D. (2013) "Dealing with high water age in a water distribution system," *Ohio AWWA Southeast District Fall Meeting*, Everal Barn at Heritage Park, Westerville, OH.

Beazley, M., Wilkowski, K., Eckert, J., and Wuest, S. (2011) *A state of inequity in Ohio: Funding and service disparities between municipalities and townships in Montgomery County, Ohio*. Toledo, OH: University of Toledo Urban Affairs Center for the Greater Dayton Mayors and Managers Association.

Burleson, R.C., Haas, C.T., Tucker, R.L., and Stanley, A. (1998) "Multiskilled labor utilization strategies in construction," *Journal of Construction Engineering and Management*, 124(6), 480–9.

Burstein, P. (2003) "The impact of public opinion on public policy: A review and an agenda," *Political Research Quarterly*, *56*(1), 29–40.

Butts, R. and Gasteyer, S. (2011) "Environmental reviews and case studies: More cost per drop: Water rates, structural inequality, and race in the United States – The case of Michigan" *Environmental Practice*, *13*, 386–95.

Chih, Y.-Y., Kiazad, K., Zhou, L., Capezio, A., Li, M., and Restubog, S.L.D. (2016) "Investigating employee turnover in the construction industry: A psychological contract perspective" *Journal of Construction Engineering and Management*, 142(6), 4016006.

Cowan, J. (2017) "As Hurricane Harvey evacuees make Dallas home, what Katrina taught us about how D-FW may change" *DallasNews*. www.dallasnews.com/news/harvey/2017/10/12/hurricane-harvey-evacuees-making-dallas-home-katrina-taught-us (last accessed August 18, 2018).

Durrans, S., Graettinger, A., Tucker, B., and Supriyaslip, T. (2004) *A Maintenance System for Storm Water Infrastructure*. Government Engineering (www.govengr.com).

El-Anwar, O. and Chen, L. (2012) "Computing a displacement distance equivalent to optimize plans for postdisaster temporary housing projects," *Journal of Construction Engineering and Management*, *139*(2), 174–84.

Eurostat. (2016) "Asylum statistics – statistics explained." http://ec.europa.eu/eurostat/statistics-explained/index.php/Asylum_statistics (last accessed August 18, 2018).

Faust, K. and Kaminsky, J. (2017) "Building water and sanitation resilience to disaster migration: utility perspectives," *Journal of Construction Engineering Management*, 143(87). With permission from ASCE. This material may be downloaded for personal use only. Any other use requires prior permission of the American Society of Civil Engineers.

Faust, K., Abraham, D., and McElmurry, S. (2016) "Sustainability of water and wastewater infrastructure in shrinking cities," *Journal of Public Works Management and Policy*, 21, 128–56.

Federle, M., Rowings Jr, J., and DeVany, T. (1993) "Model of career choice for craftworkers." *Journal of Construction Engineering and Management*, 119(1), 105–14.

FEMA. (2016a) "Resources to Plan for Post-Disaster Recovery | FEMA.gov." www.fema.gov/resources-plan-post-disaster-recovery (last accessed August 18, 2018).

Fiksel, J. (2003) "Designing resilient, sustainable systems," *Environ. Sci. Technol. 37*(23), 5330–9.

Gomar, J., Haas, C., and Morton, D. (2002) "Assignment and allocation optimization of partially multiskilled workforce," *Journal of Construction Engineering and Management*, 128(2), 103–9.

Gray, V., Lowery, D., Fellowes, M., and McAtee, A. (2004) "Public opinion, public policy, and organized interests in the American states," *Political Research Quarterly* 57(3), 411–20.

Helms, M., and Guillen, J. (2013) "Financial manager: Detroit "dysfunctional, wasteful" *USA Today*. https://eu.usatoday.com/story/money/business/2013/05/13/detroit-emergency-financial-manager-report/2155081/ (last accessed August 18, 2018).

Herz, R. (2006) "Buried infrastructure in shrinking cities," *International Symposium: Coping with City Shrinkage and Demographic Change-Lessons from Around the Globe*, Dresden. http://archiv.schader-stiftung.de/docs/herz_presentation.pdf (last accessed August 18, 2018).

Horowitz, J. (2017) "Hurricanes Irma and Harvey have racked up billions in damages. Who pays?" *CNNMoney*. http://money.cnn.com/2017/09/15/news/economy/irma-harvey-damage-who-pays/index.html (last accessed August 18, 2018).

Hummel, D. and Lux, A. (2007) "Population decline and infrastructure: The case of the German water supply system" *Vienna Yearbook of Population Research, 5*, 167–91.

IRGC. (2016) *IRGC Resource Guide on Resilience*; Linkov, I., Florin, M.-V., Series Eds.; doi:10.5075/epfl-irgc-228206; EPFL International Risk Governance Council (IRGC): Laussane, Switzerland.

Kaminsky, J. and Faust, K. (2017) "Transitioning from a human right to an infrastructure service: Water, wastewater, and displaced persons in Germany" *Environmental Science and Technology*, DOI: 10.1021/acs.est.7b03594 <http://pubs.acs.org/doi/abs/10.1021%2Facs.est.7b03594>, Further permissions related to the material excerpted should be directed to the ACS.

Lijklema, L. and Tyson, J.M. (1993) "Urban water quality: Interactions between sewers, treatment plants, and receiving waters" *Water Science and Technology*, 27(5), 29–33.

Marchese, D. and Linkov, I. (2017) "Can you be smart and resilient at the same time?" *Environ. Sci. Technol., 51* (11), 5867–8.

Matthews, J. (2016) "Disaster resilience of critical water infrastructure systems" *J. Struct. Eng, 142* (8), C6015001.

(NAE) National Academy of Engineering. (2009) *NAE Annual Report 2009*. www.nae.edu/About/ 43339/ 43347.aspx (last accessed August 18, 2018).

Opdyke, A., Javernick-Will, A., and Koschmann, M. (2017a) "Infrastructure hazard resilience trends: an analysis of 25 years of research," *Nat. Hazards, 87*(2), 773–89.

Opdyke, A., Lepropre, F., Javernick-Will, A., and Koschmann, M. (2017b) "Inter-organizational resource coordination in post-disaster infrastructure recovery," *Construction Management and Economics*, 35(8–9), 514–30.

Rink, D., Haase, A., Bernt, M., and Grobmann, K. (2010) *Addressing Urban Shrinkage Across Europe-Challenges and Prospects* Shrink Smart Research Brief No. 1. www.ufz.de/export/data/400/39030_D9_Research_Brief_FINAL.pdf (last accessed August 31, 2018).

Roberson, A. (2011) "What's next after 40 years of drinking water regulations?" *Environmental Science and Technology. 45*(1), 154–60.

Rybczynski, W. and Linneman, P. (1999) "How to save our shrinking cities," *Public Interest, 135*, 30–44.

Schlör, H., Hake, J.-H., and Kuckshinrichs, W. (2009) "Demographics as a new challenge for sustainable development in the German Wastewater Sector," *International Journal of Environmental Technology and Management, 10*, 327–52.

Soroka, S.N. and Wlezien, C. (2004) "Opinion representation and policy feedback: Canada in comparative perspective," *Canadian Journal of Political Science* 37(3), 531–59.

Sun, C. and Xu, J. (2010) "Estimation of time for Wenchuan earthquake reconstruction in China," *Journal of Construction Engineering and Management, 137*(3), 179–87.

UNHCR. (2015) "Worldwide displacement hits all-time high as war and persecution increase." *UNHCR*. www.unhcr.org/558193896.html (last accessed August 18, 2018).

UNHCR. (2017) "Forced displacement worldwide at its highest in decades." *UNHCR*. www.unhcr.org/afr/news/stories/2017/6/5941561f4/forced-displacement-worldwide-its-highest-decades.html (last accessed August 18, 2018).

US Census Bureau. (2017) "State and County QuickFacts." www.census.gov/quickfacts/fact/table/US/PST045217 (last accessed August 31, 2018).

(US EPA) US Environmental Protection Agency. (2009) "NPDES home." http://water.epa.gov/polwaste/npdes/ (last accessed August 18, 2018).

(US EPA) US Environmental Protection Agency. (2010) "Control and mitigation of drinking water losses in distribution systems." *Office of Water* http://water.epa.gov/type/drink/pws/smallsystems/upload/Water_Loss_Control_508_FINALDEc.pdf (last accessed August 18, 2018).

(US EPA) US Environmental Protection Agency. (2012) "Solar energy for water and wastewater utilities: Step-by-step project implementation and funding approaches" (Webinar). www.epa.gov/sites/production/files/2016-01/documents/solar-energy-for-water-and-wastewater-utilities-step-by-step-project-implementation-and-funding-approaches.pdf (last accessed August 31, 2018).

(US EPA) US Environmental Protection Agency. (2013) "Asset management 101." www.epa.gov/sites/production/files/2015-10/documents/assetmgt101.pdf (last accessed August 31, 2018).

(US EPA) US Environmental Protection Agency. (2016a) "Technical, Managerial and Financial (TMF) capacity resources for small drinking water systems," *Collections and Lists.* www.epa.gov/dwcapacity/technical-managerial-and-financial-tmf-capacity-resources-small-drinking-water-systems (last accessed August 18, 2018).

(US EPA) US Environmental Protection Agency. (2016b) "Federal funding for water and wastewater utilities in national disasters (Fed FUNDS)." *Collections and Lists.* www.epa.gov/fedfunds (last accessed August 18, 2018).

Varis, O., Biswas, A., Tortajada, C., and Lundqvist, J. (2006) "Megacities and water management," *Water Resources Development*, 22(2), 377–94.

WADOH. (2013) *Water System Capacity.* Washington State Department of Health, Spokane, WA.

Wisner, B., Blaikie, P., Cannon, T., and Davis, I. (2003) *At Risk: Natural Hazards, People's Vulnerability, and Disasters*, 2nd ed. London; New York: Routledge.

Part III

Resilience of different systems

Cyber infrastructure

19

Cyber threat on critical infrastructure

A growing concern for decision makers

Omar Kammouh[1] and Gian Paolo Cimellaro[2]

[1] DEPARTMENT OF CIVIL ENGINEERING, 307 W ILLINOIS ST, URBANA, IL, 61801, USA;
OMAR.KAMMOUH@POLITO.IT

[2] DEPARTMENT OF STRUCTURAL, BUILDING & GEOTECHNICAL ENGINEERING (DISEG), POLITECNICO DI TORINO,
CORSO DUCA DEGLI ABRUZZI 24, 10129 TURIN, ITALY; GIANPAOLO.CIMELLARO@POLITO.IT

19.1 Introduction

Cyber-security nowadays is of paramount importance: there is an industry built around it, with people spending their lives securing systems, and other people spending theirs trying to get into those very same systems. It is a never-ending process that requires both parties to always think ahead of the opponent and, as time passes, the stakes get higher and higher. With the advent of the digital era, where more people and devices are connecting together, cybercrime is becoming one of the main focuses for security. According to United Nations estimate, cybercrime represents one of the biggest illegal economies in the world, reaching a value of 445 billion dollars.

To a certain degree, it has always been like that: back in the 1960s, when the first password-protected shared computers (specifically, the CTSS, the Compatible Time-Sharing System) showed up, groups of hackers thought that this sort of limitation was unacceptable. Because of that, they decided to get familiar enough with the system to be able to bypass the login request and be free to use the system in whatever way they wanted (Levy 1984). This kind of breach was not exactly worthy of concern: those hackers may have found a way around the login procedure, but they were acting out of frustration with the sole goal of using that computer. Things started to get more serious when people decided to store important information on their computers, and malicious users (or crackers) realized how profitable it could be to have access to this sort of sensible data. This got only worse with time: today, we are on the blurred line between this previous "data-centered" security concern and the much more serious "life-centered" one. Figure 19.1 shows the evolution of cyber threats with time. It used to be that crackers could steal one's money and identity without directly endangering the victim's life. In the years to come, and even now to some extent, the ubiquity of connected

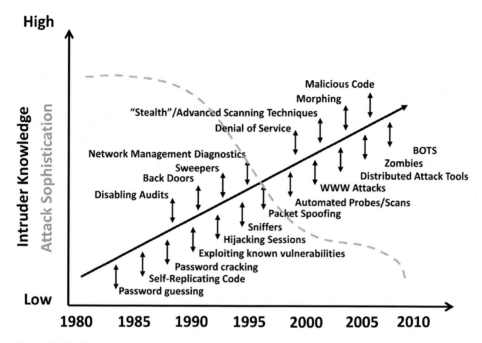

Figure 19.1 The increasing complexity of cyber threats for industrial agents.
Source: Adapted from IAEA 2011.

devices will make IT systems exploitable by crackers, and this brings cyber-security to a whole new level.

Pinpointing the exact moment cyber-security started representing a life threat is hard, if not impossible. We have transitioned towards a connected world smoothly, not fully realizing the implications of such a change. So now, the mid-sixties man with a wireless pacemaker implanted is completely oblivious to the fact that crackers could take full control of the device that keeps them alive (Rubin 2011). Nor does anybody expect traffic lights to behave any differently than they did ten years ago; yet, this is exactly the case as traffic lights are starting to be connected to the Internet with all the implications that come with it. In other words, we are not ready for the consequences of a connected world; the bad news is, attackers are.

This chapter deals with cybersecurity and the risk it poses to the current infrastructure. Infrastructure can be roughly described as the facilities and systems serving the population, such as roads, bridges, sewers, electrical grids, telecommunications, etc. The comprehensive list not only includes these facilities but also the operating procedures, management practices, and development policies that interact together with the societal demand and the physical world (Fulmer 2009).

19.2 Risk and threats on physical infrastructure

Cyberattacks have been intensively researched and discussed in the literature; however, it is somewhat challenging to systematize all threats in one typology. Nong et al. (2005) proposed a "System-Fault-Risk Framework" that describes a cyberattack with cause and effect attributes. Even though all known cyberattacks can be classified through this framework, it appears too hefty to provide a general overview. Shiva et al. (2009) suggested a comprehensive "cause, action, defense, analysis, and target" taxonomy to circumscribe a cyberattack, labeled AVOIDIT. It clusters the attack in five stages: Attack Vector, Operational Impact, Defense, Information Impact, and Target. The AVOIDIT framework seems to represent a powerful tool to cluster any cyberattack, but is hardly understandable without at least intermediate IT knowledge. Choo (2008; 2011) applied a more hands-on approach, by listing the various types of cyberattacks (or "computer security incidents") experienced by organizations or individuals. However, it does not differentiate in which way the target has been attacked. Table 19.1 lists several types of cyber threats with descriptions about the threat itself and the means the threat can be delivered. It is worth to point out that some threats represent a first step for an even bigger threat. For instance, an attacker first gains access to a computer through a computer intrusion "hacking into the computer" and then installs malware on it.

It is crucial to understand that there is no full protection against cybercrime (Hall 2015), which is why the term cyber threat prevention does not correctly describe the idea of cyber resilience or cybersecurity. In order to lower the risk of a successful attack, it is important to understand what factors increase the possibility of a cybercrime. As mentioned earlier, cybercrime follows a similar decision-making process as a general crime. Beside the motivation to commit a crime, two more factors raise the possibility of a successful cyberattack: the presence of an opportunity to commit a crime and the absence of a guardian to prevent it (Cohen & Felson 1979). Figure 19.2 illustrates the three factors visually.

Table 19.1 Cyber threat landscape

Cyber threat	Description	Delivery Means
Malware	Short for malicious software and refers to any software or algorithm that is developed to cause damage to a computer or network. Malware includes Trojans, Virus, Worms, Key loggers and Ransomware which has become the most used cybercrime threat recently.	Email or local installation, if the attacker gained access before.
Spam	Unsolicited emails aiming to persuade targets to purchase scam products, invest in bad stocks or similar deceptive marketing practices.	Emails or messages using iMessage / WhatsApp.
Phishing	The attacker is pretending to be someone else (usually a legitimize organization with a broad customer base such as big banks, telecommunication operators, etc.) and trying to convince targets to disclose sensitive information.	Usually emails or internet pages that appear like the legitimate one (for instance a scam internet site that resembles an online bank interface).
Computer or Network intrusions	Access on computer or networks with malicious intents. Once a computer or network is accessible, malware can be installed.	Remote hacking or even local if the device is physically accessible. A local intrusion can be carried out through identifying fraud and through workforce or contractors with granted access.
Identity Fraud	Using another identity to gain access onto the targets financial or to sensitive information of organizations.	Theft (e.g. credit card theft). It is also possible to purchase identities online (through the Darknet). In the latter case, the data is often collected through phishing attacks.

Source: Created by the authors.

Figure 19.2 The three factors that support committing a crime.
Source: Based on Cohen and Felson 1979.

19.2.1 From critical infrastructure to cyber interdependency

It is reasonable to think that there are some infrastructures that are more likely to be attacked by prowlers than others since the damage they would produce is higher. Such critical infrastructures, in case of collapse, could start a domino effect. A critical infrastructure can be defined as a system that includes all elements necessary to provide a sustainable service, such as the nation's power plant, transportation network, waste management, water network, telecommunication facilities, etc. These entities, together with the welfare and the financial system, create a network of externalities, also called interdependencies, in which all the other infrastructures and services are involved. Interdependency is defined as a bidirectional relationship between two infrastructures where the state of one influences or is correlated to the state of the other, and the collapse of one would produce a knock-on effect on all the network (Cimellaro 2016). Since the risk is the product of the likelihood of an event and the impact of the event, we can affirm that the risk of an element being failed is a function of the risk of other elements in the system being failed:

$$R(I_i) = f(C_i, R(I_j)), \forall j \neq i$$

$$(19.1)$$

where $R(I_i)$ is the risk function related to the element i, C_i accounts for any contingency (i.e. a future event or circumstance that is possible but cannot be predicted with certainty). However, such implicit and strongly non-linear function often reveals itself only after a disruptive event, where the higher the interdependency, the higher the impact. To plan a system that is resilient against hazards, awareness should be raised towards the interdependency among infrastructures.

19.2.2 The Stuxnet case study

An example of the impact that cyberattacks can induce to the infrastructure comes from the Stuxnet worm. A worm is something similar to a virus, but has the possibility to sneak better under the enemies' cyber-defenses, and if correctly supported can interact with many devices linked to the infected one. In the Stuxnet case, the worm was made by the USA and Israel Intelligence in 2010, and interacted with the SCADA systems that controlled

Siemens' devices. Such devices were also largely employed in the Iranian nuclear proliferation program carried along by President Ahmadinejad. Since there were very strong economic and political interests, the Stuxnet worm had an extremely high degree of complexity and exploited more than one zero day vulnerability, unknown even to Microsoft, and thus it was able to sneak in the nuclear power plants and make a Man-In-The-Middle attack. These kind of attacks, also known as MITMs, are based on a system that takes place between two communicating systems and passes misleading information from one to another without being caught. The USA and Israel were able to hijack the centrifuges that controlled the separation of Uranium, the necessary fuel for the fission reaction, and to delay the power production until it was discovered two years afterwards. The energy sector is considered as one of the most critical infrastructures since it ties interdependencies with almost every sector of community. Therefore, the following sections focus on the cyber threats of electrical and nuclear plants.

19.3 Cyber threats on electrical power networks

19.3.1 Areas of vulnerability of electric power networks

One of the greatest cause of increased vulnerability is the constantly increasing interconnectivity of the systems around the world. In (Arvind 2015), the following macro categories of vulnerability causes are identified:

- Internet-connected energy management systems: when energy management systems are connected to the Internet, they are subject to the most serious cybersecurity threats. An attacker that gets the control of such systems is able to change the physical settings of the grid components.
- Human factors: as in every security system, a great part of the vulnerability area is given by the people involved in the organization (everyone that basically interacts with the asset). Usually, employees are trained only to deal with the system and not its security, and this raises the possibility of successful attacks.
- Smart meters: the energy management systems nowadays exploit the newest IoT technology for the decentralized measurement and control. These "smart meters" expose another vulnerability surface and, if hacked, they can leak user data or report unreal meter readings.

To have a clear view of the risk of cyber-attacks on the power network, we need first to describe the main components of a power grid system. The North American grid (MSC 2016) is taken as a reference. We can identify three main components in this huge architecture:

- Generation: electricity is initially generated by fuel sources, usually via turbines. This phase relies on local control loops which include sensors that send monitoring data to a control room. The control room manages the generation equipment. Usually, this kind of control systems have a pretty small attack surface due to their locality (they are not part of a fully connected network).
- Transmission: after generation, the electricity is increased in voltage and then transported. The electricity grid is composed by nodes, which are substation transformers whose purpose is to increase or decrease the voltage to efficiently transport energy across large distances. High voltage transformers are surely the most valuable and impactful, both for the cost

of replacement and the long time of fixing. The risk increases when there are no alternative delivery paths or there is no access to spare transformers in the transmission utilities. The main attack surface in substations are the controllers and the other devices used for its automation.

- Distribution: the last phase of the process. The electricity is conveyed to the different users. This is usually not considered part of the architecture, which means the security standards and their implementation can vary significantly, usually depending on the kind of user. It must be noted that in some cases an attack on the distribution facilities can affect also the rest of the architecture.

19.3.2 Threatening cyber attacks

Attacks can target single points like critical substations, transmission controllers, and metering device, or multiple components with the intension of breaking down the regional grids or the wide network supply. The first one, named isolated attack, is less sophisticated than the second. In the following, a list of some important attacks on the power systems is provided:

- Data integrity attacks: this type of attack is made using false signal values. Those attacks can lead to wrong decisions since the data received is wrong.
- Denial of service (DoS) attacks: it blocks the communication among the sensors and the control center. DoSs attack can also damage the physical system.
- Replay attacks: this attack (also called playback attack) is a type of system attack in which a substantial information transmission is maliciously or falsely repeated or delayed.
- Timing attacks: cause delay in signal transmission.
- Spoofing: this attack occurs when an attacker impersonates another device or user on a network. From this attack, the attacker can steal data, spread malware, etc. But spoofing is prevented from some cryptographic authentication because the attacker should sign or encrypt the message with a shared or private key in order to verify its integrity.
- Authentication issues: several devices in smart grids do not use strong methods to authenticate users. Devices are arranged by default or with weak passwords. This can give access to unauthorized users to have access and do changes to the system.
- Malware, or malicious software: any program or record that is destructive to a PC client. Malware incorporates PC viruses, worms, Trojan horses and spyware. These malicious projects can play out an assortment of capacities, including stealing, encoding or erasing delicate information, adjusting or hijacking core computing capacities, and observing users PC action without their consent.

19.4 Cyber threats on nuclear plants

The importance of cyber security in the nuclear sector is growing due to the spread of digital technology over the analogue one. Cyber-attack on the Instrumentation and Control System (I&CS) can cause system malfunctions and data alterations, which may cause the reactor core to melt down. Cyber-attack can also induce radiation leakages that can cause a large-scale life threatening disaster. In addition, the nuclear power plant supervisors may be blackmailed and they may give up to the extortion in order to avoid a disaster. In these circumstances, the cyber security of I&CS is an urgent issue. Those responsible for the safety of the nuclear power plants have realized that such threats should not be overlooked any longer.

Table 19.2 Potential impacts of cyber-attacks on different digital systems that are present within nuclear facilities

Compromised Nuclear Facility Digital System	Potential impact of the specific attack on the facility
Physical access control system	HIGH: Access given to unauthorized persons. Authorized persons prevented from gaining access to areas they are required to access
Potential impact of the specific attack on the	LOW: Administrative burdens. Daily operations made more difficult
Work permit and work order system	MEDIUM: Wrong actions on components. Disruption of normal operation and maintenance
Document management system	MEDIUM: Information used to plan more severe attacks
Process control system	HIGH: Plant operation compromised
Reactor protection system	CRITICAL: Plant safety compromised, radiological release

Source: Extracted and adapted from IAEA 2011.

19.4.1 Potential impact of a cyber-attack on different nuclear facility elements

The cyber-attack may be conducted against different digital systems within a nuclear facility, and the potential impact of the resulting consequences could be strongly different. Table 19.2 lists different digital systems within the nuclear plant with the potential impacts they may suffer in case of a cyber-attack.

19.4.2 The attack against South Korean facilities

In December 2014, South Korea's nuclear plant operator (Korea Hydro and Nuclear Power KNHP) declared that its computer systems had been violated. The attack resulted in the leak of personal details of 10 000 KHNP workers, designs and manuals for two reactors, electricity flow charts, and estimates of radiation exposure among local residents. Therefore, KHNP supervisors together with the government conducted an investigation to understand the actual relevance of the data leak. In the meantime, anxiety began to spread among the population because it was feared that the cyber- attack had been conducted by the North Korean government to gain control on the nuclear plants of South-Korea with the aim of causing a catastrophe. Adding fuel to the fire, an unidentified hacker threatened on Twitter to release further information unless the government shut three reactors by Thursday. The message warned people living nearby to avoid the area for the next few months. At the end, no evidence that the nuclear control systems had been hacked was found, but this is a clear example of how a cyber-attack against national nuclear facilities could represent a threat for the population and the stability of the country.

19.4.3 Current legislations: The US context

In the USA, the nuclear energy industry began dealing with the cyber security issue after the terrorist attacks of September 11, 2011. The Nuclear Regulatory Commission (NRC) had mandated the companies that operate nuclear power plants to increase the security level in many areas and as a consequence codified the new obligations in 2009 in the document 10 CFR 73.54 "Protection of digital computer and communication systems and networks."

As part of these requirements, the NRC established new cyber security rules. Every company operating nuclear power plants must have an NRC-approved cyber security program.

19.5 Cyber threat mitigation methods

19.5.1 Countermeasures against cyber-attack

SANS (System Administration, Networking, and Security Institute) provides a complete list of possible cyber-attack countermeasures based on five main goals (CCS 2015):

1) Identify
2) Protect
3) Detect
4) Respond
5) Recover

Each of the countermeasures can be used properly under certain circumstances. Table 19.3 provides a list of the countermeasures that should be taken by the decision making authority under certain circumstances.

In Korman (2016), the following additional measures are reported:

• Network segmentation and DMZs between networks: DMZ stands for demilitarized zone, and in computer systems stands for an exposed network created to add an additional layer of security.

Table 19.3 SANS cyber-attack countermeasures

Counter measure	Goal
Inventory of authorized and unauthorized devices	Identify
Inventory of authorized and unauthorized software	Identify
Secure configuration of end-user devices	Protect
Continuous vulnerability assessment & remediation	Identify, Detect, Respond
Controlled use of administrative privileges	Protect
Maintenance, monitoring, and analysis of audit logs	Detect, Despond
Email and web browser protections	Protect
Malware defense	Protect, Detect
Limitation & control of network ports, protocols, and service	Protect
Data recovery capability	Recover
Secure configuration of network devices	Protect
Boundary defense	Detect
Data protection	Protect
Controlled access based on need to know	Protect
Wireless access control	Protect
Account monitoring and control	Protect, Detect
Security skills assessment and appropriate training	Protect
Application software security	Protect
Incident response and management	Detect, Respond
Penetration tests and red team exercises	Respond, Recover

Source: CCS 2015.

- Firewalls
- Connection tracking and network access control
- Blacklisting
- Intrusion detection (both based on signatures and models of normal behavior)
- Honeypots: "A honeypot consists of data (for example, in a network site) that appears to be a legitimate part of the site, but is actually isolated and monitored, and that seems to contain information or a resource of value to attackers, who are then blocked" (Wu et al. 2008).

In Bolzoni et al. (2016), a framework based on SAN (Situational Awareness Network) to monitor the network and assess threats was proposed, and consistent metrics to evaluate it were identified. In Ntalampiras (2016), an algorithm for automatic detection of integrity attacks is developed based on pattern recognition. Cho et al. (2016) introduced Petri networks to assess nuclear power plants vulnerability. Finally, Li et al. (2016) proposed a bi-level model to assess coordinated attacks on power systems.

Many authors and experts point out that the vulnerability is the result of neglecting the risk that is posed. Once the vulnerabilities are identified, relative policies and actions can be determined. There are various tools to perform security risk assessment, such as:

- Risk watch, which is an automated tool to perform qualitative and quantitative risk analysis and vulnerability assessments.
- OCTAVE (Operationally Critical Threat, Asset, and Vulnerability Evaluation) is a framework for identifying and managing information security risks, developed at Carnegie Mellon University.
- CORAS is a tool-supported methodology for model-based risk analysis of security-critical systems developed under the European Information Society Technologies Program.

19.5.2 Need for coordinating the cyber security methods

Critically, there appears to be insufficient information sharing and coordination of actions in the sector. There is a need for some major steps to be taken to implement cross-sector strategies and platforms to address the above-mentioned issues. The situation requires us to rethink the minimum standards, to ensure the development of capabilities through audits and sanctions, and to encourage cross-border information sharing, which would address the diversity and inconsistency at a sectoral level.

19.5.3 Need for change in legislation

At the end of the day, empowering the security systems can be done with proper regulations to implement the standards. Suggestions might include appointing a central authority for the cyber security to do the following duties:

- Reporting security incidents;
- Provisions to enable the information sharing;
- Establishment of a certification board;
- Development of security standards;
- Harmonization of security requirements across the country;
- Promoting the consumer awareness and engagement;
- Establishment of a stakeholder network for the security.

19.5.4 Public and private contribution for innovation

In addition to policy and legislation instruments, efforts of public and private organizations to develop innovative solutions and approaches are required to improve the overall state and functionality of the cyber security. Areas requiring innovation can be broadly classified into three categories based on their function (Healey et al. 2016):

- Analytical function: analyzing existing cyber security protection and standardization practices to identify gaps in the framework and provide strategic suggestions.
- Technological function: introducing new technological solutions for cyber security enhancement.
- Collaborative function: bringing together multiple stakeholders and foster cooperation and information sharing amongst them.

19.6 Decision making

When a system is attacked, it is very important to have an immediate control over the situation to avoid the consequences. This section analyzes different models present in literature to investigate cybercrimes. They are rather useful for standardizing terminologies, defining requirements, and supporting the development of new techniques and tools for decision makers. They are a sort of decision making model to define how to behave after a crime. It is important to note that the decision making process also depends on the type of crime committed and on the stakeholder that is affected, since there is a difference between small individuals, firms, and governments.

Libicki (2007) proposed a model for cybercrime investigation with four main steps: recognition, identification, individualization, and reconstruction (Figure 19.3). During the recognition phase, the investigator looks for all items of potential evidence through a process of documentation and collection, which are then classified and compared with some standards in the identification step. Then, the items are individualized whether they are unique so that they may be linked to a particular event. Finally, during the reconstruction phase, all the outputs of the previous steps are brought together to provide a detailed account of the events and actions at the crime scene. This model emphasizes that the investigation of a crime scene must be systematic and methodical.

Other models present in literature seemed to adopt the same logic. For example, the first Digital Forensics Research Workshop (Palmer 2001) developed an analysis procedure in a linear process: identification, preservation, collection, examination, analysis, presentation, and decision. The main lack of models with this common structure is that they do not cover all aspects of cybercrime investigation. They focus mainly on the processing of digital evidence. What is more, they do not lead to the definition of tools and techniques for investigation. Ciardhuáin

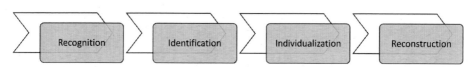

Figure 19.3 A model for cybercrime investigation.
Source: Created by the authors.

(2004) proposed a refined model that allows a systematic approach for the decision making process after an emergency condition. It consists of 13 activities that have to be followed mainly in a "waterfall" fashion (in sequence).

In this work, more attention is given to the OODA loop and its application to cybersecurity. The OODA loop was developed by the military strategist Colonel John Boyd and applied to combat operations process. According to Boyd, decision-making occurs in a cycle of observe-orient-decide-act that can be infinitely repeated. The quicker this cycle is followed, the quicker can be the reaction to an event, which allows gaining advantage over the opponent. Even for cybersecurity, the ability to observe and react to threats more rapidly than the attacker can significantly enhance the network security of the user. Taking the OODA loop one step further and overlaying the NIST based security controls, it is possible to create an effective Cybersecurity plan (Protiviti 2015). Figure 19.4 introduces the different phases of the OODA loop with a brief explanation for each of them.

- OBSERVE: the observation phase includes the monitoring and collection of data within the network. It is the detection of malicious activities through internal monitoring tools or external services. Nowadays, one can find several tools that monitor the performance of devices in a network and control firewalls to check the incoming and outgoing network traffic through data packet inspections. These tools are provided by many firms in the cybersecurity field.
- ORIENT: orientation is the moment at which the real-time collection and correlation of performance information is executed. To be more specific, one can correlate network traffic with device and application log data to identify the sources, destinations, and generators of intrusions.

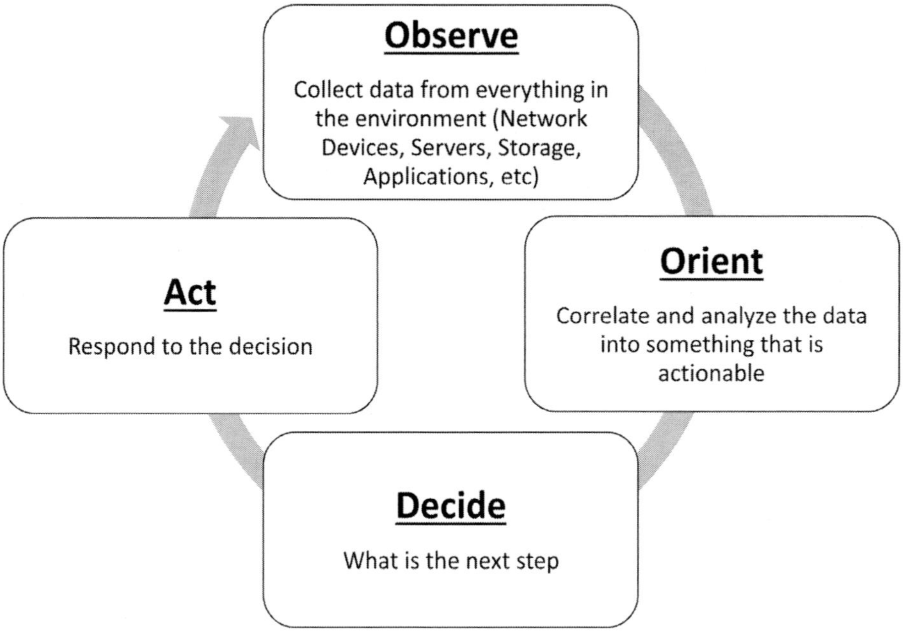

Figure 19.4 OODA loop for cyber security.
Source: Created by the authors.

- DECIDE: the decision is usually based on the previous steps and on the overall risk management profile of the organization. The environment is constantly changing and new threats and vulnerabilities emerge every day. At this stage, the lower the available information and the trust level of the information, the higher the risk of irrational decision because when the information is not available or trusted, counterproductive behavior due to emotional bias, expectation bias, cost fallacy, risk aversion bias, and past fixation becomes more common (Kuhn & Mueller 2015). Decision outcomes, according to Hale (Protiviti 2015), typically fall into one of four categories: (1) risk assumption: accept risk and continue operating; (2) risk avoidance: avoid the risk by eliminating the risk cause and/or consequence; (3) risk limitation: limit the risk by assigning controls that minimize the impact; (4) risk transference: transfer the risk by using other options to compensate for the loss.
- ACT: the final objective is the action to be taken. In cybersecurity, if the acting process can be automated, it can speed up the reaction moving closer to risk avoidance. Even in this case, there are different tools that allow us to respond to security and operational issues and track and isolate users and devices.

Figure 19.5 illustrates the OODA loop for a typical cyberattack (malware). Once the email is received, the recipient may open the attached document without any scrutiny. This can dangerously pass the malware to the computer, bypassing the virus detection system causing damage. As a result, steps 2 and 3 of the OODA loop are skipped.

Fostering a culture of security is essential to avoid such threats. Educating individuals about the danger of email attachments would be a fast and rather cheap solution. However, this is not enough to mitigate the risk effectively. It is often suggested to install a more mature and robust network so that when the individual fails, further protection measures take place. In addition,

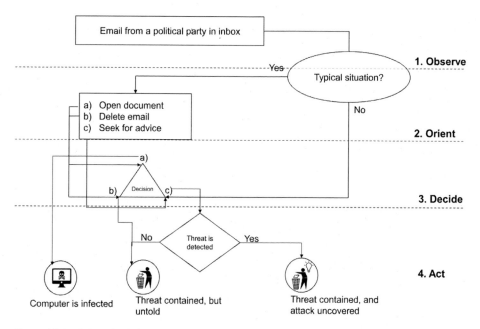

Figure 19.5 OODA loop for a typical cyberattack.
Source: Created by the authors.

proper segmentation of the network's components so that infected computers just infect a small part of a network can be very effective to decrease the vulnerability.

19.7 Case study: Cyberattack on the Ukraine power grid

19.7.1 The attack

The vast majority of cyber-attacks yield an important lesson: if you realize that the attack is going on, it is already too late. There is no way an already-happening attack can result in no harm being done: even when no tangible damage has occurred, the target of the attack will suffer from "credibility" issues. In many cases, damaging the credibility of a company, or a government, is the sole purpose of the attackers. This may have been the case with the Ukraine power grid cyber-attack that took place on December 23, 2015: the attack resulted in 230,000 people being left without electricity for a period of up to 6 hours (Zetter 2016). Many, including the Security Service of Ukraine and US cyber intelligence firm iSight Partners, believe the attack originated from Russia: either the nation or a Russian hacking group, or a combination of the two (Finkle 2016). If this was a Russian attack, one of the goals could have been to "weaken the Ukrainians' trust in the Ukrainian power companies and government." Given the difficult political situation in Ukraine, it is not hard to believe that this attack would have represented a hard blow to the nation, despite the limited entity of the actual damage (while the attack was indeed extremely serious, no fatalities have occurred because of it. In light of the catastrophic outcomes that this attack might have resulted in, the entity of the damage should be considered as limited). This attack is particularly worthy of attention for three different reasons:

- The attack is the first known cyber-attack targeting a nation's power grid: targeting a critical infrastructure is precisely the kind of life-threatening attacks we should be expecting to happen more and more frequently in the years to come
- The attackers were not aiming to profit from this attack. Other cyber-threats, such as ransomware (Boatman 2014), are solely aimed at making a profit.
- The attack was crafted elegantly, leaving few loose ends and using a series of complex techniques to achieve the final result of mayhem. This is not the case with most cyber-attacks that make it to the news: these are mostly Denial of Service (DoS) attacks (or their distributed counterpart, DDoS), whereby attackers flood the target servers with requests (e.g. for a webpage), until these servers are unable to serve actual users (thus, denying the service). This kind of attack is relatively harmless, incredibly simplistic, and actionable by anybody with the right amount of bandwidth. Because of that, and because the media likes to pick up on "hacking" stories, DoS attacks have become the perfect way to discredit large companies (which then are reported as having been "hacked", while no real breach of security has occurred).

19.7.2 Six short months before the power outage

Most actions performed by the attackers have been logged and have been used after the attack to understand exactly what happened. The technical aspects of the attacks are not relevant in this study, but may be found in a report by E-ISAC (Lee et al. 2016).

The reconstruction of the attack shows that the attack started at least six months prior to the actual power outage. This is representative of the fact that well-laid plans do not unfold overnight. The attackers started with a spear phishing campaign, which consisted in sending emails with a malicious attachment to the companies' employees and, with a false pretense, they lured some victims into opening the file.

After that, a series of sophisticated exploits and six months of time allowed the attackers to take down three companies' stations. Once again, the system administrators' work (done well before the beginning of the attack) made it hard for crackers to carry out the attack.

19.7.3 When you notice it, it's too late

On December 23, neither employees nor system administrators could do much to handle the situation because it was already too late. This case shows how in cyber-security taking an action after the attack is completed is not the best of strategies. The situation does not improve when the result of a cyber-attack is the theft of sensible data; in this case, chances are that nobody will notice the attack for a long time.

Cyber-security is all about prevention: problems should be fixed before crackers have a chance of even considering carrying out an attack. This gives companies the opportunity of taking the time to take all the necessary measures, which can be summed up in two points: securing the IT infrastructure, and training all employees. While the Ukrainian companies successfully took care of the first point, they obviously failed to handle the latter: employees should, for starters, be trained to recognize phishing and social engineering attempts and under no circumstance should they engage in behaviors that could jeopardize the security of the company. This would have prevented the energy company employees from opening an executable attachment that allowed the attackers to access the internal network.

In order to assess a company's overall robustness to external attacks, penetration tests can be carried out by security specialists (Northcutt et al. 2006). These are "controlled attacks" done with the permission of the owner of the computing resources, but without letting anybody else within the company know about it (in order to avoid biasing the outcome). The result of a pen-testing session is a report highlighting a list of vulnerabilities found on all levels (from the janitor's willingness to let someone access a restricted area without proper identification to the SQL injection vulnerability that allows accessing all database records using a well-crafted URL). The report can then be used by the company to improve their security and be better prepared to handle real attacks.

19.7.4 The OODA loop in the Ukraine case study context

This section highlights the importance of prevention in cyber-security, showing how last-minute decisions can do little to mitigate the problems. While the OODA loop can be applied just as well to cyber-security, it is most effective when done with prevention in mind (Sager 2015):

- Observe: keeping track of recently disclosed vulnerabilities (security bulletins and advisories) is the first step to keeping an IT system healthy. Only a fraction of vulnerabilities exploited are "zero-day" (i.e. vulnerabilities discovered by crackers and exploited before a fix is released by the developers), the rest are vulnerabilities that have been sitting around for months (or years) without anybody ever bothering updating the software.
- Orient: not all patches and fixes are equally applicable. The "orientation" phase consists in assessing the level of risk in leaving the system exposed.
- Decide: based on the previous assessment, easy-to-fix and/or highly dangerous vulnerabilities should be prioritized.

- Act: apply all the patches required and make sure (through the system logs) that no attacker exploited the problem during the window of vulnerability (i.e. the time window between the vulnerability disclosure and the successful application of the patch).

The OODA loop should be accompanied by a slow decision-making process concerned with building and updating the architecture of the IT system and the way it interfaces with the rest of the company.

19.8 Conclusions

This chapter highlights the ever-growing importance of cyber-security due to the ubiquity of Internet-connected devices. Special attention has been given to critical infrastructure, such as the power networks. Several methods to mitigate or even prevent the consequences of cyberattacks have been introduced. As a case study, the famous 2015 Ukraine power grid cyber-attack was considered: this showed how attacks are actually planned many months in advance, making it hard if not impossible to contain the damages when the attack actually happens. This led to the observation that cyber-security should be mostly concerned with prevention.

References

Arvind, H.M.Z., Azizi, A., and Anwar, K. (2015) *Cyber Security for Power Systems (Draft Report)*.

Boatman, K. (2014) "Beware the Rise of Ransomware." http://in.norton.com/yoursecurityresource/detail.jsp?aid=rise_in_ransomware (last accessed August 17, 2014).

Bolzoni, D., Leszczyna, R., and Wróbel, M.R. (2016) *Situational Awareness Network for the Electric Power System: The Architecture and Testing Metrics*, translated by IEEE, 743–49.

CCS (2015) *The Critical Security Controls for Effective Cyber Defense*, Council on Cyber Securit-SANS institute.

Cho, C.-S., Chung, W.-H., and Kuo, S.-Y. (2016) "Cyberphysical security and dependability analysis of digital control systems in nuclear power plants," *IEEE Transactions on Systems, Man, and Cybernetics: Systems*, 46(3), 356–69.

Choo, K.K.R. (2008) 'Organised crime groups in cyberspace: a typology', *Trends in organized crime*, 11(3), 270–295.

Choo, K.K.R. (2011) "Cyber threat landscape faced by financial and insurance industry," *Trends and Issues in Crime and Criminal Justice*, 408 (1).

https://search.informit.com.au/documentSummary;dn=711489616728119;res=IELHSS (last accessed August 31, 2018).

Ciardhuáin, S.Ó. (2004) 'An extended model of cybercrime investigations', *International Journal of Digital Evidence*, 3(1), 1–22.

Cimellaro, G.P. (2016) *Urban Resilience for Emergency Response and Recovery*. New York: Springer.

Cohen, L. and Felson, M. (1979) "Social change and crime rate trends: A routine activity approach," *American Sociological Review*, 44(4), 588–608.

Finkle, J. (2016) "U.S. firm blames Russian 'Sandworm' hackers for Ukraine outage." www.reuters.com/article/us-ukraine-cybersecurity-sandworm-idUSKBN0UM00N20160108 (last accessed January 8, 2016).

Fulmer, J. (2009) "What in the world is infrastructure," *PEI Infrastructure Investor*, 1(4), 30–2.

Hall, K. (2015) "Protecting against cyber attacks." https://home.kpmg.com/xx/en/home/insights/2015/06/protecting-against-cyber-attacks.html (last accessed June 15, 2015).

Healey, D., Meckler, S., Antia, U., and Cottle, E. (2016) *Cyber Security Strategy for the Energy Sector*, Brussels: Policy Department A: Economic and Scientific Policy European Parliament.

IAEA (2011) *Computer Security at Nuclear Facilities, Technical Guidance Reference Manual*, Vienna: International Atomic Energy Agency.

Korman, M. (2016) *Cyber Security in Power Systems*, 3, Industrial Information and Control Systems, KTH.

Kuhn, J. and Mueller, L. (2015) "The Dyre Wolf campaign: Stealing millions and hungry for more." https://securityintelligence.com/dyre-wolf/ (last accessed April 2, 2015).

Lee, R.M., Assante, M.J., and Conway, T. (2016) *Analysis of the Cyber Attack on the Ukrainian Power Grid*, SANS Industrial Control Systems.

Levy, S. (1984) *Hackers: Heroes of the Computer Revolution*. New York: Anchor Press/Doubleday.

Li, Z., Shahidehpour, M., Alabdulwahab, A., and Abusorrah, A. (2016) "Bilevel model for analyzing coordinated cyber-physical attacks on power systems," *IEEE Transactions on Smart Grid*, 7(5), 2260–72.

Libicki, M.C. (2007) *Conquest in Cyberspace: National Security and Information Warfare*. Cambridge: Cambridge University Press.

MSC (2016) *Cyber Threat and Vulnerability Analysis of the U.S. Electric Sector*, Mission Support Center, Idaho National Laboratory.

Nong, Y., Newman, C., and Farley, T. (2005) "A system-fault-risk framework for cyber attack classification," *Information Knowledge Systems Management*, 5(2), 135–51.

Northcutt, S., Shenk, J., Shackleford, D., Rosenberg, T., Siles, R., and Mancini, S. (2006) *Penetration Testing: Assessing Your Overall Security before Attackers Do*, SANS Institute.

Ntalampiras, S. (2016) "Automatic identification of integrity attacks in cyber-physical systems," *Expert Systems with Applications*, 58, 164–73.

Palmer, G. (2001) *A Roadmap for Digital Forensic Research (Technical Report DTR-T001–01)*, Utica, NY: Air Force Research Laboratory.

Protiviti (2015) "Managing cyber threats with confidence." www.protiviti.com/VE-es/node/6696 (last accessed August 18, 2018).

Rubin, A. (2011) "All your devices can be hacked," *TED Talks*,

Sager, T. (2015) *The Cyber OODA Loop: How Your Attacker Should Help You Design Your Defence*, Computer Security Resource Center.

Shiva, S., Simmons, C., Ellis, C., Dasgupta, D., and Roy, S. (2009) "AVOIDIT: A cyber attack taxonomy." *University of Memphis*, Tech. Rep., August.

Wu, T.-C., Lei, C.-L., and Rijmen, V. (2008) *Information Security: 11th International Conference ISC 2008*, translated by Taipei, Taiwan: Springer Science & Business Media.

Zetter, K. (2016) "Inside the cunning, unprecedented hack of Ukraine's power grid." www.wired.com/2016/03/inside-cunning-unprecedented-hack-ukraines-power-grid/ (last accessed March 3, 2016).

Part IV

Sustainable materials, design, and construction

20

Low CO$_2$ cement for sustainable concrete

Maria C.G. Juenger

UNIVERSITY OF TEXAS AT AUSTIN, 301 E. DEAN KEETON ST., C1748,
AUSTIN, TX 78712, USA; MJUENGER@MAIL.UTEXAS.EDU

20.1 Introduction

Portland cement is the heart and soul of concrete, the world's most used building material. The statistics for global cement production and its consequences are staggering: 4.2 billion metric tons of portland cement were produced in 2016 (USGS 2017), 1.6 times the production in 2006, just ten years earlier, of 2.55 billion metric tons (USGS 2008). Portland cement manufacturing is responsible for high CO$_2$ emissions, with 0.86 tons of CO$_2$ produced per ton of cement (WBCSD 2009; Barcelo et al. 2014). It is commonly estimated that cement manufacturing is responsible for 5 percent of anthropogenic CO$_2$ emissions (IEA 2009), contributing significantly to global warming. However, in order to meet the demands of new global development and repair of existing infrastructure, there remains no better material than portland cement concrete for cost and durability. Finding a substitute material at this scale would be difficult, so instead efforts are better placed at improving the material we have.

The Cement Technology Roadmap 2009 (IEA 2009), published by the International Energy Agency and the World Business Council for Sustainable Development, anticipates that the cement industry can reduce direct CO$_2$ emissions by 18 percent by 2050. It identifies four "carbon emission reduction levers" to achieve this:

1. Thermal and electric efficiency;
2. Alternative fuels;
3. Clinker substitution;
4. Carbon capture and storage.

The Eisenhower Decision Matrix (Covey 2004) is a method of time management that is derived from a quote from former US President Dwight D. Eisenhower: "I have two kinds of problems, the urgent and the important. The urgent are not important, and the important are never urgent." In the decision matrix, tasks can be assigned to quadrants depending on their importance and urgency, as shown in Figure 20.1. Tasks in the upper right quadrant are both urgent and important, while tasks in the lower left are neither urgent nor important. In order to prioritize efforts, we can qualitatively assign the four carbon emission reduction levers to

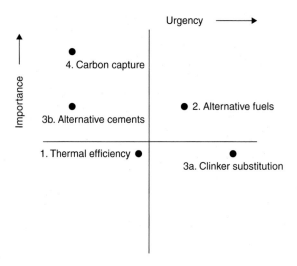

Urgency

Importance

- 4. Carbon capture
- 3b. Alternative cements
- 2. Alternative fuels
- 1. Thermal efficiency
- 3a. Clinker substitution

Figure 20.1   Eisenhower decision matrix for carbon emission reduction levers.

these quadrants. In this exercise, importance is defined by how much carbon reduction can be achieved by the lever, and urgency is defined by how quickly or easily the reduction can be feasibly achieved. The definition chosen for urgency here deviates from the intention of the Eisenhower Decision Matrix in that it is not about how quickly something *should* be done, but how quickly it *can* be done. Using the definition chosen here, problems that are urgent can indeed be important, and problems that are important can indeed be urgent. The highest priorities are still those with high urgency and high importance.

The Cement Technology Roadmap (IEA 2009) acknowledges that the first lever, improving thermal and electric efficiency, can only really contribute 10–15 percent to the total anticipated reduction of CO_2 emissions from using all four levers listed earlier. Schneider (2015) further explained that this is because the newest kiln technologies are already above 80 percent of theoretical thermal efficiency. So, it can be assumed that improving thermal efficiency is not particularly "important," since the benefits are limited. Further, improving thermal efficiency is not particularly "urgent," since the primary obstacle to implementation is the retrofitting or rebuilding of older kilns, which requires significant capital investment (IEA 2009) with little other associated benefit. Improvements in thermal efficiency should not be altogether dismissed, however, as slow and incremental improvements can still have significant rewards.

Cement plants typically burn coal to heat the kiln. Approximately 40 percent of the CO_2 produced during cement manufacturing comes from the burning of coal. Alternative fuels are gaining traction in the industry, including natural gas, biomass, and wastes (e.g., solvents, tires, municipal waste, and sewage sludge). Alternative fuels can be combined with coal to produce a mixed fuel, and substitutions for coal in some plants can reach 98 percent, with 10–50 percent being more typical in countries where alternative fuels are used (IEA 2009). The importance of alternative fuel use is high, since fuel burning contributes significantly to CO_2 emissions from cement plants. The Roadmap (IEA 2009) estimates that 24 percent of projected CO_2 reductions by 2050 can come from using more alternative fuels. Switching to alternative fuels can also be considered urgent, since the technology is already available. In some cases, alternative fuels may be lower cost than coal. The obstacles to implementation are identification of locally available sources, treatment (e.g. de-watering or crushing), and ensuring that the fuels don't interfere with clinker composition by selecting appropriate fuel sources or installing a gas bypass (Schneider 2015).

Cement kilns produce clinker, which is then ground with gypsum to make portland cement. The CO$_2$ emissions from cement production come primarily from the clinker production, with 40 percent associated with the burning of fuel, as mentioned earlier, and 60 percent from the calcination of limestone, since calcite in limestone (CaCO$_3$) decomposes to lime (CaO) in the kiln, releasing CO$_2$ (WBCSD 2009). The concept of clinker substitution can be considered to encompass two strategies, which will be referred to as Levers 3a and 3b. The first (Lever 3a), by far the most prevalent, is to make cement from a combination of clinker, gypsum, and a supplementary cementitious material (SCM) and/or a filler. For example, a cement may contain 70 percent clinker, 5 percent gypsum, 5 percent limestone filler, and 20 percent fly ash, a by-product of coal burning. Since this cement contains less clinker than a cement without SCMs or fillers, its associated CO$_2$ emissions are lower. Accordingly, the global average clinker content of cement in 2006 was 78 percent (IEA 2009). There is room to reduce this number, but the importance of such a move is limited, as the Roadmap suggests that this strategy will likely only contribute to 10 percent of projected CO$_2$ reductions by 2050. The urgency is high, however, as the technology already exists and is relatively easy to implement. The second clinker substitution strategy (Lever 3b) is to replace portland cement clinker entirely with a different type of cement. Alternatives, such as calcium sulfoaluminate cements, alkali-activated materials, and super-sulfated cements, for example, can achieve similar mechanical performance to portland cement with a smaller CO$_2$ footprint (Juenger et al. 2011). However, these materials have been slow to gain acceptance in the industry for a variety of reasons, including concerns about cost and long-term durability, and are, therefore, of lower urgency, though of potentially high importance.

Carbon capture and storage, Lever 4, is truly an emerging technology in the cement industry. The concept is to capture the post-production CO$_2$ using chemical absorption, membranes, or carbon looping (using the captured CO$_2$ to make CaCO$_3$) (IEA 2009). These technologies are being used in pilot plants (Schneider 2015) and are considered to be quite important, contributing 54 percent to the projected CO$_2$ reductions by 2050. The obstacles are large, however, considering there is a need for investment into the development of the technologies as well as the implementation industrially, resulting in a relatively low urgency.

From Figure 20.1, it can be concluded that the most important carbon emission reduction lever is carbon capture, while the most urgent is clinker substitution. Given the small body of literature on carbon capture, as it is such a new technology, and the relatively vast body of literature on clinker substitution, the focus of this chapter is on the "lowest hanging fruit" for reducing CO$_2$ emissions from cement manufacturing, clinker substitution. Finally, it should be noted that the Cement Technology Roadmap referenced in this discussion was written in 2009 and based its projections for carbon emission reductions on an estimate that cement production in 2050 would reach 4.5 billion tons. However, this value is a serious underestimate, given that in 2016 production was already quite close to that value (4.2 billion tons). Nonetheless, the strategies targeted in the Roadmap are still quite relevant, likely even more so.

20.2 Supplementary cementitious materials and fillers

A supplementary cementitious material (SCM) is defined by the American Concrete Institute (ACI) as "inorganic material such as fly ash, silica fume, metakaolin, or slag cement that reacts pozzolanically or hydraulically" (ACI 2016). As such, these materials can substitute a portion of clinker in cement and still provide the concrete with mechanical strength. A filler, on the other hand, is "a finely divided, relatively inert material (such as pulverized limestone, silica, or colloidal substances) added to portland cement…" (ACI 2016). Fillers are generally assumed to be chemically inert and only contribute to mechanical strength through enhancing the hydraulic reactions of the clinker phases (Lothenbach et al. 2011). Therefore, when considering clinker substitution strategies, it is understood that SCMs can substitute a larger proportion of clinker in cement than fillers.

Clinker substitution by SCMs and fillers is handled differently in different regions of the world. In Europe, for example, both fillers and SCMs are combined with clinker in the cement plant. In the US, on the other hand, limestone fillers are combined with clinker and gypsum in the cement plant, while SCMs are commonly added during concrete mixing, replacing a portion of the cement used. The end result is effectively the same, with less clinker being used in concrete when SCMs and fillers are used.

The dominant SCMs used globally are fly ash, a by-product of coal burning in power plants, and ground granulated blast furnace slag, a by-product of steel manufacturing. Both are considered to be low-CO_2 alternatives to clinker because they are wastes from other industries (Juenger & Siddique 2015). A concern as we try to reduce the clinker factor in cement, however, is that the supply of these SCMs is limited, varies depending on region, and cannot meet the demand of the cement industry. As stated earlier, the USGS estimates that 4.2 billion tons of cement was produced globally in 2016. In order to reduce the clinker content of the cement produced in the future, we have to utilize increasing amounts of SCMs. However, 2010 data show that only 780 million tons of coal combustion products were produced in 2010 (Heidrich et al. 2013), approximately 85 percent of which (663 million tons) was fly ash, and 415 million tons were already being utilized. This means that there may be only about 250 million metric tons of fly ash available to further reduce clinker factors (about 6% of the 4.2 billion tons of cement being produced); this is not enough to enable significant increases in the use of fly ash SCMs. Considering environmental restrictions that are changing the landscape for coal burning power production, it's unlikely that this number will increase much. The USGS (2016) estimated that "global iron slag output in 2015 was on the order of 300 to 360 million tons, and steel slag about 170 to 250 million tons." Again, considering that some of this material is unsuitable as a clinker substitute, the supply of slag is not sufficient to enable significant increases in clinker substitution. Therefore, there is increasing interest in exploring and developing new sources of SCMs, as will be discussed in the following sections.

20.3 Reclaimed and remediated fly ash

One option to enable the continuation of using well-proven and accepted SCMs as clinker substitutes is to reclaim and remediate landfilled material to render it suitable for use. China may have 2.5 billion tons of fly ash in reserve (Lan & Yuansheng 2007). The US has over 180 acres (0.73 km²) of fly ash in landfills and impoundments, 20–40 feet (6–12 m) deep, in more than 1000 sites (EPA 2017). The fly ash stored in impoundments is wet, while that in landfills is mostly dry. Generally, these have not been combined with other wastes, so the sources are not contaminated and can be physically and chemically stable. While some of this fly ash is understandably unusable, some fly ash can be processed (e.g. dried and ground) to make it useful as a clinker substitute. Research is showing that this is a viable option, in some cases, as the properties and performance of the reclaimed and treated material can be comparable to as-produced fly ash (Berry et al. 1989, Cheerarot & Jaturapitakkul 2004, Diaz-Loya et al. 2017, McCarthy et al. 2017, Ranganath et al. 1998). Comparable performance leads to comparable use in concrete, meaning that the reclaimed material can be used in all aspects of concrete construction where fly ash is currently used, including pavements, buildings, bridges, etc.

Table 20.1 Chemical and physical characteristics of production (FA-G) and reclaimed (RC-G) fly ashes from the same power plant

	SiO₂ (%)	*Al₂O₃* (%)	*Fe₂O₃* (%)	*CaO* (%)	*MgO* (%)	*SO₃* (%)	*Na₂O* (%)	*K₂O* (%)	*Moisture* (%)	*LOI* (%)	*d₅₀* (μm)
FA-G	50.88	22.79	5.01	10.60	2.45	0.47	0.13	0.86	0.54	0.39	26.9
RC-G	51.50	21.34	4.92	11.33	2.08	2.72	0.17	0.78	3.89	0.87	22.2

As an example, a current production fly ash (FA-G) from the US is compared here against a reclaimed, landfilled fly ash from the same power plant (RC-G) (Al-Shmaisani 2017). The primary difference in oxide composition in these two fly ashes is in their sulfate content, Table 20.1, which is likely a result of different emission controls used in the power plants at the time of the fly ash production. The reclaimed fly ash was ground and dried before testing, and the median particle diameter (d$_{50}$) are similar is similar to the production fly ash, but the moisture contents are very different. The reclaimed fly ash has retained a higher moisture content, demonstrating that more extensive drying is needed. Loss on ignition (LOI) values are quite similar, though.

Examples of the performance of these fly ashes are shown in Figure 20.2. Figure 20.2a shows the compressive strength development of a portland cement (OPC) mortar and mortars with 20 percent substitution of the cement with the fly ashes (FA-G and RC-G). Strength was tested at 1, 7, 28, and 56 days; error bars indicate the range in measured values, and lines are provided on the plot to guide the eye. Figure 20.2a shows that strength development was quite similar between the two fly ashes; both increase the long-term strength of mortar compared to the cement-only control, as is expected with SCMs.

Fly ash is also known to improve many long-term durability characteristics of concrete, including resistance to expansions due to alkali-silica reaction (Thomas 2007). Both the production and the reclaimed fly ash performed well in this regard, as shown in Figure 20.2b, which shows results from an accelerated test for alkali-silica reaction. In this test, 20 percent of cement (OPC) was replaced by the fly ashes, and expansion of the mortars was measured over a 14 day period of immersion in a 1 N NaOH solution at 80°C. Expansions greater than 0.1 percent of the length of the specimens indicate poor performance, as exhibited by the cement-only control. Both fly ashes controlled expansion to below to 0.1 percent threshold, proving that they both improve performance.

It is clear that the vast reserves of fly ash worldwide can be tapped as resources for clinker reduction in concrete. The constraints are economic, as the material needs to be processed before use. However, the costs of building treatment facilities may be balanced by the costs of disposal for plants that are still actively producing coal ash (Fedorka et al. 2015).

20.4 Natural pozzolans, calcined clays, and fillers

The original supplementary cementitious materials were the volcanic ashes used by the Romans. Volcanic ashes and other natural minerals were common in concrete mixtures until the low cost of fly ash and slag gave them dominance, starting in the second half of the twentieth century. Natural SCMs, or pozzolans, include both volcanic minerals, such as pumicites and pearlites, and sedimentary minerals, such as clays and shales. Typically, clays and shales are heated to high temperatures (calcined) prior to use. A common example is the metakaolin mentioned in the ACI definition of SCMs provided earlier, which is a calcined kaolinite clay.

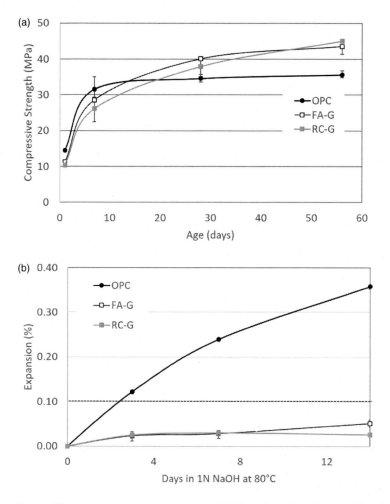

Figure 20.2 Performance of production (FA-G) and reclaimed (RC-G) fly ashes from the same power plant: (a) compressive strength of cement mortars following ASTM C109 with 20 wt% replacement of cement with fly ash and a water-to-cementitious materials ratio of 0.45; (b) control of alkali-silica reaction following ASTM C1567 using 20 wt% fly ash replacement of cement and a reactive sand.

The ability to effectively use natural pozzolans as SCMs is typically limited by two factors, regional availability and cost. The minerals must be quarried and ground to a fine powder, which increases the price relative to a waste material like fly ash. In the case of calcined clays, the calcination process also adds to the cost. Nonetheless, natural pozzolans contribute favorably to the performance of concrete, as demonstrated in Figure 20.3 for a pearlite and pumicite of US origin. Like fly ash, they increase the long-term compressive strength of concrete compared to a cement-only control (Figure 20.3a). Also like fly ash, they can protect against deterioration from alkali silica reaction (not shown) and from sulfate attack (Figure 20.3b) (Seraj et al. 2014). Suppression of sulfate attack is measured through the ability to control expansion to less than 0.1 percent during long-term exposure to a sodium sulfate solution, with measurements taken at periodic intervals and lines provided in the plot to guide the eye.

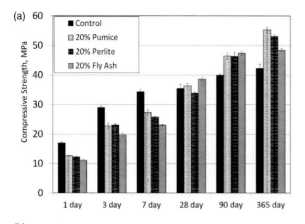

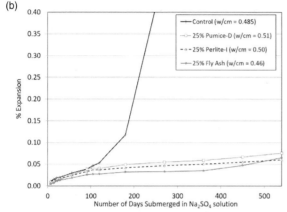

Figure 20.3 Performance of a pumicite and pearlite SCM compared to fly ash: (a) compressive strength of cement mortars following ASTM C109 with 20 wt% replacement of cement with SCM and a water-to-cementitious materials ratio of 0.5; (b) resistance to sulfate attack following ASTM C1012 using a 25 wt% SCM replacement of cement, with expansion limits to "pass" the test shown on the plot. (ACI 201 2008).

Metakaolin has a higher cost than other SCMs; in US dollars, metakaolin is approximately $300–$500/ton compared to $100–$120/ton for cement and $40–$50/ton for fly ash. This limits its use in concrete, though performance can be quite good. Recently, there has been a strong push toward exploring other clay minerals and low purity kaolinite bearing-minerals (Fernandez et al. 2011; Taylor-Lange et al. 2015; Alujas et al. 2015; Hollanders et al. 2016), with an interest in expanding availability and reducing cost. Results have shown that calcined smectic (montmorillonite/bentonite) clays are pozzolanic, though less so than calcined kaolinitic clays. Blends of clays containing kaolinite and some montmorillonite also show promising performance.

An interesting observation of a synergistic effect between aluminosiliceous SCMs (such as fly ash and metakaolin) and limestone fillers has led to research into a combined SCM-filler material as a low-cost, high availability solution. The synergy comes in the form of enhanced compressive strength in cementitious systems (Figure 20.4) due to the formation of

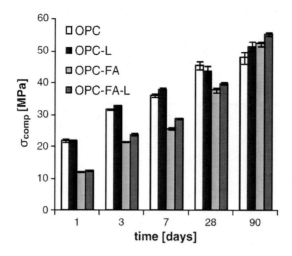

Figure 20.4 Synergistic effect of SCMs and fillers on compressive strength of mortars where OPC is portland cement, FA is fly ash, and L is limestone.

Source: Reproduced with permission from De Weerdt et al. 2011.

a mono- and hemicarbonate phases in addition to the other cementitious hydration products (De Weerdt et al. 2011; Antoni et al. 2012). The so-called LC[3] system (Limestone + Calcined Clay + Clinker) was developed to combine impure clays with limestone to improve performance and provide a low-cost, low CO_2 cement. A 2:1 ratio of metakaolin to limestone has been suggested as optimal for strength enhancement in this type of system (Antoni et al. 2011), and such limestone-calcined clay blends have been used to successfully replace up to 50 percent of clinker in cement (Martirena Hernandez & Scrivener 2015; Krishnan & Bishnoi 2015). Full scale industrial trials in India (Maity et al. 2015) and Cuba (Vizcaíno-Andrés et al. 2015) have shown promising results for impure clays, even when processed in large quantities. Economic and environmental assessments of the system have also demonstrated that the system can provide a low-cost, low carbon solution for clinker replacement (Sánchez Berriel et al. 2016). In fact, it was estimated that the LC[3] cement can provide a 30 percent reduction in both CO_2 production and cost.

We should expect to see increasing interest in the use of natural pozzolans and combined pozzolan-filler systems as the available supply of well-known SCMs is consumed. Both volcanic minerals and calcined clays will contribute to the supply chain, depending on regional resources and the economics of use.

20.5 Conclusions

In summary, there are several means to reducing greenhouse gas emissions from cement and concrete production, and all of these are likely to be explored and further implemented in the coming years to accommodate increasing demand while simultaneously reducing emissions. The industry will continue to make improvements to thermal efficiency of cement kilns, and it is likely that the use of alternative fuels will increase. Alternative cements and carbon capture and storage are promising strategies and will be worth keeping an eye on as technology improves and successful case studies emerge. The simplest strategy remains that of partial clinker substitution, and we should expect increasing, widespread use of SCMs and fillers to the extent that discovery of new sources is critical. Current research into reclaimed waste materials (e.g. fly ash) and impure natural pozzolans, calcined clays and otherwise, is providing a promising opportunity for the future, long-term supply of SCMs.

References

Al-Shmaisani, S. (2017) *Evaluation of Reclaimed and Remediated Fly Ashes as a Substitute for Class F Fly Ash in Concrete*, Thesis, University of Texas at Austin.

Alujas A., Fernandez R., Quintana R., Scrivener K.L., and Martirena, F. (2015) "Pozzolanic reactivity of lowgrade kaolinitic clays: Influence of calcination temperature and impact of calcination products on OPC hydration," *Applied Clay Science, 108*, 94–101.

American Concrete Institute (ACI) (2008) *Guide to Durable Concrete*, ACI 201.2R-08, American Concrete Institute, Farmington Hills, Michigan.

American Concrete Institute (ACI) (2016) *ACI Concrete Terminology ACI CT-16*, Farmington Hills, Michigan.

Antoni M., Rossen J., Martirena F., and Scrivener K. (2012) "Cement substitution by a combination of metakaolin and limestone," *Cement and Concrete Research, 42*, 1579–89.

ASTM C109/C109M-16a (2016) *Standard Test Method for Compressive Strength of Hydraulic Cement Mortars (Using 2-in. or [50-mm] Cube Specimens)*, ASTM International, West Conshohocken, Pennsylvania.

ASTM C1012/C1012M-15 (2015) *Standard Test Method for Length Change of Hydraulic-Cement Mortars Exposed to a Sulfate Solution*, ASTM International, West Conshohocken, Pennsylvania.

ASTM C1567-13 (2013) *Standard Test Method for Determining the Potential Alkali-Silica Reactivity of Combinations of Cementitious Materials and Aggregate (Accelerated Mortar-Bar Method)*, ASTM International, West Conshohocken, Pennsylvania.

Barcelo L., Kline J., Walenta G., and Gartner E. (2014) "Cement and carbon emissions," *Materials and Structures, 47*, 1055–65.

Berry E.E., Hemmings R.T., Langley W.S., and Carette G.G. (1989) "Beneficiated fly ash: Hydration, microstructure, and strength development in portland cement systems." In V.M. Malhotra (ed.), ACI Special Publication SP-114 (pp. 241–273). Trondheim, Norway: American Concrete Institute.

Cheerarot R. and Jaturapitakkul C. (2004) "A study of disposed fly ash from landfill to replace Portland cement," *Waste Management, 24*, 701–9.

Covey, S.R. (2004) *The 7 Habits of Highly Effective People: Powerful Lessons in Personal Change*. Free Press. New York.

De Weerdt K., Ben Haha M., Le Saout G., Kjellsen K.O., Justnes H., and Lothenbach B. (2011) "Hydration mechanisms of ternary portland cements containing limestone powder and fly ash," *Cement and Concrete Research, 41*, 279–91.

Diaz-Loya I., Juenger M., Seraj S., and Minkara R. (2017) "Extending supplementary cementitious material resources: reclaimed and remediated fly ash and natural pozzolans," *Cement and Concrete Composites*, in press.

EPA (2017) *Frequent Questions about the Coal Ash Disposal Rule.* www.epa.gov/coalash/frequent-questions-about-coal-ash-disposal-rule#2 (last accessed July 15, 2017).

Fedorka W.F., Knowles J., and Castleman, J. (2015) "Reclaiming and recycling coal fly ash for beneficial reuse with the STAR^{TM} process." World of Coal Ash (WOCA) Conference, Nashville, Tennessee.

Fernandez R., Martirena F., and Scrivener K.L. (2011) "The origin of the pozzolanic activity of calcined clay minerals: A comparison between kaolinite, illite and montmorillonite," *Cement and Concrete Research, 41*, 113–22.

Heidrich C., Feuerborn H.-J., and Weir A. (2013) "Coal combustion products: a global perspective," World of Coal Ash (WOCA) Conference, Lexington, Kentucky.

Hollanders S., Adriaens, R., Skibsted J., Cizer O., and Elsen J. (2016) "Pozzolanic reactivity of pure calcined clays," *Applied Clay Science, 132–3*, 552–60.

International Energy Agency (IEA); World Business Council for Sustainable Development (WBCSD) (2009) *Cement Technology Roadmap 2009: Carbon Emissions Reductions up to 2050.* IEA Publications, Paris.

Juenger M.C.G., Winnefeld F., Provis J.L., and Ideker, J.H. (2011) "Advances in alternative cementitious binders," *Cement and Concrete Research, 41*, 1232–43.

Juenger M.C.G. and Siddique R. (2015) "Recent advances in understanding the role of supplementary cementitious materials in concrete," *Cement and Concrete Research, 78*, 71–80.

Krishnan S. and Bishnoi, S. (2015) "High level clinker replacement in ternary limestone-calcined clay-clinker cement," *Advances in Structural Engineering*, 1725–31. https://doi.org/10.1007/978-81-322-2187-6_131

Lan W. and Yuansheng C. (2007) "The application and development of fly ash in China," World of Coal Ash (WOCA), Northern Kentucky, USA.

Lothenbach B., Scrivener K., and Hooton R.D. (2011) "Supplementary cementitious materials," *Cement and Concrete Research, 41*, 1244–56.

Maity S., Bishnois S., and Kumar A. (2015) "Field application of limestone-calcined clay cement in India," *Calcined Clays for Sustainable Concrete*. New York: Springer, pp. 435–41.

Martirena Hernandez J.F. and Scrivener K. (2015) "Development and introduction of a low clinker, low carbon, ternary blend cement in Cuba," *Calcined Clays for Sustainable Concrete*. New York: Springer, pp. 323–9.

McCarthy M.J., Robl T., and Csetenyi L.J. (2017) "Recovery, processing, and usage of wet-stored fly ash." In T. Robl, A. Oberlink, and R. Jones (eds.), *Coal Combustion Products (CCP's): Characteristics, Utilization and Beneficiation* (pp. 343–367). Duxford, UK: Woodhead Publishing.

Ranganath R., Bhattacharjee B., and Krishnamoorthy, S. (1998) "Influence of size fraction of ponded ash on its pozzolanic activity," *Cement and Concrete Research, 28*, 749–61.

Sánchez Berriel A., Favier A., Rosa Domínguez E., Sánchez Machado I.R., Heierli U., Scrivener K., Martirena Hernández F., and Habert G. (2016) "Assessing the environmental and economic potential of limestone calcined clay cement in Cuba," *Journal of Cleaner Production, 124*, 361–9.

Schneider M. (2015) "Process technology for efficient and sustainable cement production," *Cement and Concrete Research, 78*, 14–23.

Seraj S., Cano R., Liu S., Whitney D., Fowler D., Ferron R., Zhu J., and Juenger M. (2014) *Evaluating the Performance of Alternative Supplementary Cementing Material in Concrete*, Technical Report 0-6717-1, Center for Transportation Research, The University of Texas at Austin, Austin, Texas.

Taylor-Lange S.C., Lamon E.L., Riding K.A., and Juenger, M.C.G. (2015) "Calcined kaolinite–bentonite clay blends as supplementary cementitious materials," *Applied Clay Science, 108*, 84–93.

Thomas M. (2007) *Optimizing the Use of Fly Ash in Concrete*, Portland Cement Association, Skokie, Illinois.

US Geological Survey (USGS) (2008) Mineral Commodity Summaries: Cement. https://minerals.usgs.gov/minerals/pubs/commodity/cement/mcs-2008-cemen.pdf (last accessed September 7, 2017).

US Geological Survey (USGS) (2016) Mineral Commodity Summaries: Iron and Steel Slag. https://minerals.usgs.gov/minerals/pubs/commodity/iron_&_steel_slag/mcs-2016-fesla.pdf (last accessed September 7, 2017).

US Geological Survey (USGS) (2017) Mineral Commodity Summaries: Cement. https://minerals.usgs.gov/minerals/pubs/commodity/cement/mcs-2017-cemen.pdf (last accessed September 7, 2017).

Vizcaíno-Andrés L.M., Sánchez-Berriel S., Damas-Carrera S., Pérez-Hernández A., Scrivener K.L., and Martirena-Hernández J.F. (2015) "Industrial trial to produce a low clinker, low carbon cement," *Materiales de Construcción, 65*(317): e045.

World Business Council for Sustainable Development (WBCSD) (2009) *Cement Industry Energy and CO2 Performance: "Getting the Numbers Right."* WBCSD Cement Sustainability Initiative (CSI), Geneva.

21

The need for standardized testing for service life prediction of reinforced concrete

Ensuring sustainable systems

David Trejo

DEPT. OF CIVIL AND CONSTRUCTION ENGINEERING, OREGON STATE UNIVERSITY, USA

21.1 Introduction

Sustainability is broadly defined as the ability of some resource to be maintained at a certain level. The Brundtland Report of 1987 defined sustainable development as the development that meets the needs of the present without compromising the ability of future generations to meet their own needs. From a construction perspective, the Brundtland definition has generated much interest in assessing resources used to construct facilities and systems. Pearce and Atkinson (1993) reported that the definition "aims at assuring the on-going productivity of exploitable natural resources..." The commercial sector of the construction industry has emphasized constructing with solar, wind, and geothermal sources to minimize energy use, has incorporated methods to re-use rainwater (e.g., rain gardens, rooftop gardens, green roofing technologies and onsite storm water reclamation systems), has promoted using pervious pavers and concrete for runoff control, promotes the use of recycled materials, recommends the use of skylights, daylighting, and photo and motion sensors to minimize energy use, and also promotes the use of low-flow water systems. The Federal Highway Administration (FHWA), which is more focused on heavy construction, has emphasized minimizing fuel consumption during material transport to and from and within the construction site, minimizing exhaust and particulate emissions from equipment and jobsites, minimizing construction impacts on traffic, minimizing noise generated during construction, and producing a product (e.g., pavements) with constructed characteristics that maximize sustainability. The FHWA does identify pavement performance and overall life as a sustainable challenge but identify construction factors that impact pavement system sustainability over the life cycle as being construction-related energy consumption, effect of construction on the surrounding area, and economics of construction practices, including user costs. Although the construction industry has made significant advances in sustainable development, one critical component of sustainability that has received less emphasis from owners and trade groups is how to reliably assess the serviceable life of a structure.

Assuming the same initial investment, a structure that could last 100 years would be more economical than a structure that last only 10 years, considering both have minimal maintenance costs. But do we need 100 years of service life? In 2017 the American Society of Civil Engineering reported that 1 in 8 bridges are functionally obsolete, meaning that the deficiency is a result of inadequate design standards for current use, not that the materials and system have performed inadequately (ASCE Report Card 2016). If high-performing materials and/or systems were used and these influenced the initial construction cost, the value of these materials and systems was not realized. Designing a system for a service life that is beyond the functional service life provides no value. However, very little information is known about functional service life and research is needed to better predict this for infrastructure systems. Although research has been performed on predicting service life, most work has focused on modeling the service life. Limited research has focused on standardizing testing for input variables and research is needed. If standardized testing can be developed so that service life models can be used to reasonably predict the in-service life of a structural system, decisions can be made to use materials and/or systems that result in a service lives similar to that of the predicted functional service life (which we currently have no process to assess). This chapter will focus on the need for developing standardized input data for predicting the service life of reinforced concrete (RC) systems exposed to chlorides (i.e., corrosion induced deterioration). Note that other deterioration mechanisms do occur in RC systems but models for these deterioration mechanisms are in earlier development stages and in many cases, necessary input variables are not well defined.

Models for predicting service life of RC exposed to chlorides are readily available. The chapter will provide an overview of methods used to predict the service life, will identify challenges with existing methods, will identify data and/or methods used in the literature to predict the predict, and will show results from service life models using data from the literature. It will be shown that using data from literature results in wide variability in service life predictions and there is a critical need to standardize testing for predicting service lives, which is a critical component of sustainable systems.

21.2 Background

Much research attention has been given to deterioration of RC systems and these systems are generally very durable. The challenge is that when these systems do deteriorate, there can be significant disruption and costs. One specific cause of deterioration is the corrosion and resulting damage caused by salts, more specifically chlorides. Chlorides can be present in the constituent materials used to make the concrete or can enter concrete from the exposure environment. These chlorides can lead to early corrosion of the reinforcing steel, resulting in premature deterioration and reduced service-lives. Many researchers have developed theoretical and empirical models with the objective of predicting the time-to-corrosion and service-life of reinforced concrete structures constructed with chlorides and exposed to chloride environments. The rate at which these chlorides are transported into the concrete to the steel reinforcing surface is an influencing variable for predicting the service life. Determining this transport rate requires solving partial differential equations that have no closed form solutions and can only be solved using numerical methods, such as finite element or finite difference analyses. However, these calculations can be simplified by making assumptions regarding the boundary conditions and the interactions of the RC with its environment. For example, if it is assumed that chlorides are predominantly transported through concrete via diffusion, Fick's second law of diffusion can be used to model the transport of these chlorides.

The movement of chlorides into the hardened concrete from the environment occurs via diffusion, migration, permeation, sorption, convection, and/or wicking action. The actual transport mechanisms depend on the exposure environment and the physical and chemical characteristics of the concrete. Depending on these environmental conditions and material characteristics, several transport mechanisms likely occur simultaneously. Even though several mechanisms may occur simultaneously, the transport of chlorides in concrete is commonly modeled assuming a general diffusion process. Diffusion is the movement of a solute (e.g., chlorides or other ions) in a stationary solvent (e.g., concrete pore solution) under the influence of a concentration gradient, with movement of the ions occurring from higher ionic concentrations to lower ionic concentrations. Steady-state diffusion is modeled using Fick's first law of diffusion, but this assumes steady state systems where the concentration is constant (i.e., the flux does not vary with time). For concrete systems exposed to chlorides, the concentration and the flux of ions change with time and as a result, Fick's second law of diffusion is commonly used to model the diffusion chlorides over time as follows:

$$\frac{\partial C}{\partial t} = -\frac{\partial}{\partial x}\left(D\frac{\partial C}{\partial x}\right), \tag{21.1}$$

where D is the diffusion coefficient (length^2/time), $\frac{\partial C}{\partial x}$ is the concentration gradient, and x is distance from the exposure face (length). In the form shown, Equation (21.1) does not have an analytical solution. However, if it is assumed that D is constant and independent of location, which is a reasonable assumption for structures that are exposed to chlorides after the concrete has been nearly fully hydrated, Equation (21.1) can be written in the form of:

$$\frac{\partial C}{\partial t} = -D\frac{\partial^2 C}{\partial x^2}, \tag{21.2}$$

where the negative sign indicates the direction of the flux is from higher to lower concentrations. The diffusion coefficient, D, is unique for each solute and solvent combination and can be determined using Einstein's relation. As would be expected, the diffusion coefficient for chlorides in concrete would be significantly lower than the diffusion coeficient of chlorides in water. This is a result of the denser and more tortuous microstructure of the concrete system. Therefore, D in Equations (21.1) and (21.2), when applied to concrete systems, should be replaced with an effective diffusion coefficient, D_e, as follows:

$$D_e = \frac{D_{cl,ps}}{F}, \tag{21.3}$$

where $D_{Cl,ps}$ is the diffusion coefficient of chloride ions in the pore solution and F is the formation factor. The formation factor is the ratio of the pore solution electrical conductivity, σ_p, and the bulk concrete conductivity (solid and pore solution), σ_{bc}, determined as follows (Snyder et al. 2003):

$$F = \frac{\sigma_p}{\sigma_{bc}}. \tag{21.4}$$

The formation factor has been reported to characterize the solid microstructure of the concrete and relates the tortuosity of concrete to the electrical resistivity of concrete (Shen and Chen 2007). Crank (1979) proposed a closed form solution for Equation 21.2 by defining the concentration of chlorides, C, at the surface of the concrete as C_s and the chloride concentration of the bulk concrete at time 0 as C_i as follows:

$$C(x,t) = C_s - (C_s - C_i) \cdot erf\left(\frac{x}{\sqrt{4D_e t}}\right),$$

(21.5)

where $C(x,t)$ is the chloride concentration at depth x and time t, erf is the error function, and the other variables have been defined. Note that the porosity, tortuosity, and density of the concrete system are dependent on the type and proportions of the constituent materials used to make the concrete and D_e will be different for different constituent materials and proportions.

As chlorides enter the concrete, these chlorides can be present as free chlorides, weakly bound chlorides (physically bound), and strongly bound chlorides (chemically bound) (Puyate et al. (1998); Baroghel-Bouny et al. 2012; Azad & Isgor 2016). Chlorides can chemically bind with aluminates (C_3A) and ferrites (C_4AF) to form Friedel's and Kuzel's salts, respectively, and can physically bind with the calcium silicate hydrates (CSH) as a result of electrostatic forces between the chlorides and CSH. The relationship between the bound chlorides (C_b) and free chlorides (C_{free}) is commonly modeled using either the Langmuir or Freundlich isotherms as shown in Equations (21.6) and (21.7), respectively, as follows:

$$C_{b, Langmuir} = \frac{\alpha C_{free}}{1 + \beta C_{free}}$$

(21.6)

$$C_{b, Freundlich} = \alpha C_{free}^{\beta},$$

(21.7)

where α and β are constants. It can be assumed that only the free chlorides (C_{free}) in the concrete system contribute to the corrosion of reinforcing steel and therefore Equation (21.2) can be rewritten as:

$$\frac{\partial C_{free}}{\partial t} = -D_a \frac{\partial^2 C_{free}}{\partial x^2}$$

(21.8)

where D_a is given by:

$$D_a = \frac{\dfrac{D_{cl,ps}}{F}}{1 + \dfrac{1}{w_e} \dfrac{\partial C_b}{\partial C_{free}}},$$

(21.9)

where w_e is the evaporable water content. Equations (21.2) and (21.8) are similar and the closed form solution for Equation (21.8) is:

$$C(x,t) = C_s - (C_s - C_i) erf\left(\frac{x}{\sqrt{4D_a t}}\right).$$

(21.10)

To solve for the time to corrosion initiation, t_i, the chloride concentration at the depth of the reinforcement (i.e., depth x) at some time can be set to the amount of chlorides that result in active corrosion, referred to as the critical chloride threshold, C_{crit}, as follows:

$$t_i = \frac{1}{1.2614 \times 10^8 \times D_a} \times \left(\frac{x}{inverf \left(\dfrac{C_{crit} - C_s}{C_i - C_s} \right)} \right)^2. \tag{21.11}$$

Marchand and Samson (2009) reported that although this equation is theorectically limited, this equation is commonly used to predict the service life of structures exposed to chlorides. Because of this, it is important that the equation provide reasonable and relatively accurate measures of service lives for RC structures. To reasonably and more accurately assess service life, the input variables must be measurable and the quantification of these variables must be standardized. Yet limited research has been performed to standardize testing for the input variables and limited research has been performed on how to adjust these input variables for different materials, proportions, and environmental exposure conditions. The remainder of this chapter will address the challenges asssociated with not standardizing testing for input variables and will identify a clear need for standardizing testing to more accurately quantify these input variables. By standardizing the testing for input variables, the service life prediction should be more representative of actual field performance, thereby making RC systems more sustainable.

21.3 A critical need for standardization of input variables: The current practice

Equation 21.11 provides an estimate of the time to corrosion of steel reinforcement embedded in concrete exposed to chlorides. This equation requires deterministic input variables necessary to predict the service life of reinforced concrete structures. As with any prediction tool, the accuracy of the input variables determine the reasonableness and reliability of the prediction equation. Because concrete is a heterogeneous material, some variability in these input variables would be expected. However, when various methods and definitions are used to quantify these key variables, the value of the equation to predict actual service is reduced. Unfortunately, there has been limited research efforts in developing standardizing testing for these input variables. Because of this, the reasonableness of the service lives predicted with this equation is commonly questioned. The following sections provide a review of input variables from the literature and address some issues associated with each. This information from the literature is then used to predict the service life by randomly selecting values for each variable from the reported values. The wide range of service life values determined from the values reported ion the literature clearly show that standardized testing for input variables is critical for reasonable and reliable assessment of service life.

21.3.1 The apparent diffusion coefficient, D_a

Unlike other input variables, there are some standardized approaches to assessing the apparent diffusion coefficient, D_a, for concrete systems. It is common practice to expose a concrete specimen in the lab to chloride solution for some time period to assess D_a. Another approach is to obtain a sample from an existing field structure that has been exposed to chlorides and use this sample to assess D_a. These samples can then be sectioned as a function of depth, crushed, and then tested (commonly using titration) to determine the chloride content of each sectioned layer. The D_a is then determined by fitting a best fit curve to the data (layer depth versus chloride concentration) using Equation (21.10) and the method of least squares. Several factors can influence the D_a. For example, Page et al. (1981) reported that chloride diffusion increases with the increase in water-to-cement-ratio (w/c) and temperature. The authors also reported that moist curing can significantly reduce the diffusivity of concrete when compared with air curing. Dhir et al. (2004) reported similar findings for w/c and also reported that increasing the cement content decreases the D_a. In an earlier study by Dhir et al. (1993), the authors reported that increasing the volume of supplementary cementing material (SCM) can result in a reduction in D_a. The authors attributed this reduction to the pozzolonic reaction and improvement in the pore structure, which resulted in a denser concrete matrix.

The research on factors affecting the transport of chlorides in concrete has led to the advent of empirical models for chloride diffusion. For example, Mangat and Limbachiya (1999) reported that there is an inverse relationship between chloride diffusion and time and proposed a power function for predicting the diffusion coefficient as follows:

$$D_e = D_i t^{-m}, \tag{21.12}$$

where the authors reported that D_i is the effective diffusion coefficient at time t equal to one second and m is an empirical constant. Bentz et al. (2001) proposed a time dependent model for the apparent diffusion coefficient as follows:

$$D_a = \frac{D_i}{1-m} t^{-m}, \tag{21.13}$$

where the variables have already been defined. Visser et al. (2004) proposed another variation of the diffusion model introduced by Mangat and Limbachiya (1999) as:

$$D(t) = D_0 \left(\frac{t_0}{t}\right)^n, \tag{21.14}$$

where D_0 is the reference diffusion coefficient at 28 days (reference time t_0) and n is an age exponent. Ehlen et al. (2009) incorporated the effects of temperature on diffusion coefficient as follows:

$$D(t) = D_{ref} \cdot \exp\left[\frac{U}{R}\left(\frac{1}{T_{ref}} - \frac{1}{T}\right)\right], \tag{21.15}$$

where D_{ref} is the diffusion coefficient at time t_{ref} equal to 28 days, U is activation energy of diffusion process (35,000 J/mol), R is gas constant, T_{ref} is 293K, and T is the temperature. Petcherdchoo (2013) proposed a more complex time-variant for D_a given as:

$$D_a = \frac{D_{ref}}{1-m}\left[\left(1 + \frac{t_{ex}}{t}\right)^{1-m} - \left(\frac{t_{ex}}{t}\right)^{1-m}\right]\left(\frac{t_{ref}}{t}\right)^m, \tag{21.16}$$

Table 21.1 Distribution of D_a reported in the literature

#.	Distribution	Unit	Mean	COV	Reference
1	Lognormal	cm²/s	$10^{-10+4.66\,w/c}$	0.75	(Stewart & Rosowsky 1998)
2	Normal	mm²/year	158	0.10	(Edvardsen & Mohr 1999)
3	Lognormal	cm²/s	1.62×10^{-8}	0.80	(Lounis & Mirza 2001)
4	Normal	m²/s	8.87×10^{-12}	0.25	(Bentz 2003)
5	Normal	m²/s	4.75×10^{-12}	0.15	(Schiessl 2005)
6	Lognormal	m²/s	3.87×10^{-12}	0.52	(Kwon et al. 2009)
7	Lognormal	m²/s	3×10^{-11}	0.20	(Bastidas-Arteaga et al. 2011)

COV: coefficient of variation

where D_{ref} is diffusion coefficient at 28 days, t_{ex} is defined as the age of concrete at the start of exposure, t is the time after exposure, and m is an empirical age factor proposed by Ehlen et al. (2009) as follows:

$$m = 0.2 + 0.4\,(\%FA\,/\,50), \tag{21.17}$$

where %FA is the amount of fly ash replacement.

It is important to note that the closed form solution to Fick's second law of diffusion is obtained assuming D is constant and independent of location. Because of this, the time dependent diffusion coefficients cannot be used with the closed form solution to Fick's second law. Using a time dependent diffusion coefficient requires either solving the governing partial differential equation for diffusion with new boundary conditions or using numerical methods such as finite difference or finite elements.

Although much of the equations for predicting the diffusion coefficient as a function of time were deterministic, probabilistic modeling has been performed. In probabilistic service life modeling, it is often assumed that D_a follows a certain distribution function with some parameters that are generally selected subjectively. Table 21.1 lists some of the commonly used distributions published in the literature. Table 21.1 shows that there is no standardization for determining or estimating D_a. and considerable variation exists. In some cases, the mean value of D_a can vary by several orders of magnitude, which can have a significant impact on the estimates of service life models. Standardization is needed.

21.3.2 The background chlorides, C_i

As discussed earlier, chlorides can be present in concrete as a result of being in the constituent materials (cement, water, aggregates, and/or admixtures), added intentionally, or from exposure to a chloride-laden environment. Chlorides from the concrete constituent materials or chlorides that have been intentionally added contribute to the background chlorides, C_i, which can influence the time to corrosion initiation. Equation 21.11 (the time to corrosion equation) indicates that an increase in C_i, with other parameters kept constant and $C_s > C_T > C_i$, increases the value of $inverf((C_T - C_s)/(C_i - C_s))$, thereby decreasing the time to corrosion initiation. To minimize the risk of chloride-induced reinforcement corrosion, US organizations, including the American Concrete Institute (ACI) and most state highway agencies (SHAs), limit the amount of chlorides that can be included in fresh concrete. These limits are commonly referred to as the allowable chloride (C_A) limits. The value of C_i can be less than or equal to the allowable limit value of C_A and the value of C_A should be significantly lower than critical chloride threshold value, C_T (the chloride concentration that results in active corrosion). For probabilistic modeling of time to corrosion, the value of C_i in Equation 21.11 can be replaced by C_A to represent a worst-case scenario. That is, all admixed chlorides can be assumed to be free chlorides (Shakouri et al. 2017).

The published C_A limits in most ACI documents are specific to the structure type (reinforced or prestressed concrete), exposure condition (dry, wet, and wet plus chloride), and the type of test method used for determining chloride content (acid-soluble and water-soluble). SHAs also limit chlorides for the constituent materials used to prepare concrete. Whether ACI or SHA limits, there is no consensus among the different standard documents on how to justify the C_A limits (Trejo et al. 2016; Shakouri et al. 2017). Shakouri et al. (2017) conducted a comprehensive review of C_A limits published by SHA in specification documents. For a concrete system containing 356 kg/m³ (600 lb/yd³) of portland cement and a w/c of 0.55, the authors reported that C_A limits published by the SHAs can differ by several orders of magnitude, ranging from 0.04 kg/m³ (0.067 lb/yd³) to 0.53 kg/m³ (0.9 lb/yd³). Trejo et al. (2016) reported similar variation in the C_A limits specified by ACI. Irrespective of organization, it seems that specified C_A limits are set based on "gut instinct" with limited scientific data or process used to determine these limits. A standardized and scientific approach in specifying C_A is needed.

21.3.3 The surface chloride concentration, C_s

Researchers have used the closed form solution to Fick's second law to predict the service life of concrete structures. When doing this, many researchers assume the concentration of chlorides at the concrete surface (C_s) is constant. However, this is not the case for field structures exposed to chlorides. From a physics point of view, time-dependence of the build-up of chlorides on the surface of the concrete is more realistic and representative.

Several researchers have recommended that the time-variant properties of C_s should be incorporated into the service life models (Maheswaran & Sanjayan 2004; Nokken et al. 2006; Luping & Gulikers 2007; Song et al. 2008; Petcherdchoo 2013). Although several theoretical time-variant models for C_s have been proposed, there is little empirical evidence available to validate such models and field studies are needed. Thus, there is a need to study the time-dependency of C_s and propose a model that is accurate and properly accounts for the key parameters influencing the C_s.

Research indicates two main factors can influence the C_s value: these factors include the exposure conditions and concrete mixture proportions (Bamforth & Price 1993). In a longitudinal study Uji et al. (1990) reported that the C_s of concrete in the tidal zone was higher than the C_s values in the splash or atmospheric zones. The authors reported that this was a result of the regular wetting and drying cycles that resulted in higher chloride build-up at the surface of the concrete in the tidal zone. In addition to the effects of exposure and location, several researchers reported that the use of SCMs in the concrete mixture can result in an increase in C_s values (Bentz et al. 1996; Mohammed et al. 2002). This has been reported to be a result of the denser microstructure of concrete containing SCMs, which decelerate the ingress of chlorides and results in a higher chloride build-up at the surface.

In a recent study, Shakouri and Trejo (2017) developed an improved model for C_s that is a function of time and other influencing factors. The researchers reported that w/c, time to exposure, the concentration of chlorides in the exposure environment, and exposure duration influence C_s. By performing a short-term research study and using long-term data from the literature, Shakouri and Trejo (2017) reported that C_s values asymptotically approach equilibrium

Table 21.2 Probabilistic parameters used in the literature to predict surface chloride

#	*Distribution*	*Unit*	*Mean*	*COV*	*Ref.*
1	Lognormal	kg/m³	3.5	0.50	(Stewart & Rosowsky 1998)
2	Normal	% wt. concrete	2.33	0.51	(Edvardsen & Mohr 1999)
3	Lognormal	kg/m³	1.27	0.40	(Lounis & Mirza 2001)
4	Normal	% wt. concrete	0.63	0.10	(Ferreira 2004)
5	Normal	kg/m³	3.05	0.74	(Stewart & Mullard 2007)
6	Normal	kg/m3	13.1	0.10	(Kwon et al. 2009)
7	Lognormal	kg/m³	1.15	0.50	(Nogueira & Leonel 2013)

with the chlorides in the exposure environment with time. It is important to note that similar to time-variant diffusion coefficients, using time-variant C_s functions require solving Fick's second law with new boundary conditions using finite difference or finite elements methods.

In probabilistic service life modeling, there is no consensus among researchers on an "appropriate" C_s value. Table 21.2 lists some of the reported distributions of C_s in the literature. It can be seen that reported units are not standardized and mean and coefficient of variation (COV) values vary significantly. Although mean values should be dependent on exposure environment, a standard methodology is needed on how to select a representative C_s value (or functions).

21.3.4 The critical chloride threshold, C_T

Regardless of how chlorides are introduced into concrete, when chlorides exceed a certain concertation at the surface of reinforcing steel, known as the critical chloride threshold (C_T), corrosion will initiate. Factors that contribute to the epistemic uncertainty in C_T are, but not limited to, the following:

i. the lack of a standard definition for corrosion initiation;
ii. the lack of a standard test criterion to measure corrosion initiation;
iii. the lack of a standardized test method to measure C_T;
iv. the lack of a single specified test method to measure chloride content and the lack of a standard unit to express C_T; and
v. the heterogeneous nature of cementitious materials and reinforcement systems.

A review of the literature indicates that many researchers use distributions for quantifying C_T and these C_T distributions vary significantly. Results from the review are presented in Table 21.3. Note that distribution type, mean values, and COV exhibit wide variation and that values are commonly assumed, as there is no standardized test to assess C_T (although ACI has currently formed a subcommittee to develop a standard test).

21.3.5 Concrete cover depth, x

Depending on the type of structure and the quality of construction, the depth of the concrete cover can vary significantly throughout a structure. There is published information regarding the variability of concrete depth for different structures. In probabilistic service life modelling either a nominal concrete depth with some variation is often assumed or the service life is estimated for a range of cover thicknesses. Table 21.4 shows some of the distributions used for

Table 21.3 Probabilistic parameters used in the literature to predict chloride threshold

#	Distribution	Unit	Mean	COV	Ref.
1	Uniform	kg/m³	0.6	0.19	(Stewart & Rosowsky 1998)
2	Normal	% wt. concrete	0.9	0.16	(Edvardsen & Mohr 1999)
3	Lognormal	kg/m³	0.72	0.1	(Lounis & Mirza 2001)
4	Triangular	kg/m³	5	0.29	(Kirkpatrick et al. 2002)
5	Normal	kg/m³	1	0.2	(Han & Kooiman 2003)
6	Normal	kg/m³	0.5	0.2	(Stewart & Mullard 2007)
7	Normal	% wt. cement	0.5	0.2	(Val & Trapper 2008)
8	Normal	% wt. concrete	0.1	0.2	(Ryan & O'Connor 2013)

Table 21.4 Probabilistic parameters used in the literature to predict concrete depth

#	Distribution	Unit	Mean	COV	Ref.
1	Normal	mm	50	0.07	(Stewart & Rosowsky 1998)
2	Lognormal	mm	75	0.13	(Edvardsen & Mohr 1999)
3	Normal	mm	36.5	0.45	(Lounis & Mirza 2001)
4	Normal	mm	60	0.25	(Bentz, 2003)
5	Normal	mm	50	0.10	(Schiessl 2005)
6	Normal	mm	50	0.18	(Stewart & Mullard 2007)
7	Normal	mm	40	0.25	(Val & Trapper 2008)
8	Normal	mm	70	0.07	(Srubar 2015)

modelling concrete depth found in the literature. Although different mean depths are expected for different structures, there seems to be no correlation between depth and COV. Other than specified cover depth, there is no scientific basis behind the selection of these distributions (especially the normal distribution, which includes negative values, which is physically not possible for a chloride transport scenario) and COV. Further investigations are needed to assess if a relationship exists between specified cover depth and COV and data are needed to justify this distribution.

21.4 The influence of documented input variables on service life

As presented in the previous sections, the literature contains a wide range of data for the different input values required for estimated time to corrosion and service life. This range of values is a result of a lack of standardized testing methods and a lack of standardized framework for selecting these values. Because of this, there are significant drawbacks and concerns associated with the current approach to probabilistic service life modeling. These drawbacks can be shown with an example. For this purpose, a hypothetical concrete structure made with concrete containing ordinary portland cement, with a w/c of 0.53, and cement content of 450 kg/m³ (759 lb/yd³) is assumed. The service life is calculated using Equation (21.11) using random input values from the values reported in the literature and shown in Tables 21.1 through 21.4. For simplicity, all the C_T and C_s values were converted to percent by weight of concrete, assuming the weight of concrete to be 2400 kg/m³ (4045 lb/yd³). Ten thousand simulations were performed and the results from the service life predictions are shown in Figure 21.1. The figure shows the time to corrosion for each simulation. Although a large portion of predicted service lives fall within the first 25 years, there is significant scatter among

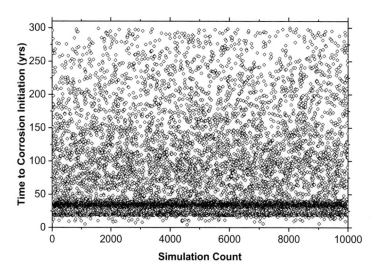

Figure 21.1 Simulated probabilistic service life predictions.

the predictions, with values ranging from 1 to over 300 years. The important take-away here is that when using variables published in the literature, almost any length of service life can be calculated using Equation (21.11). This wide variation in service life prediction provides limited value to users, owners, and owners representatives and more importantly provides limited trust in the procedure for predicting service life. Significant advances have been made in predicting the service life of reinforced concrete structures but more advances are needed. As presented, the literature includes a wide range of values for input variables needed to predict the service life of RC structures. Standardize testing and standardized frameworks are needed for these more reasonably determining these input variables for better and more accurate predictions.

21.5 The need for standardized testing

One of the most common equations used to predict the service life of RC structures is based on Fick's second law. Fick's second law includes 5 input variables: D_a, x, C_T, C_i, and C_s. With the exception of cover depth, x, which is specified in the design, the literature contains a wide range of mean values, distributions, and COV for the remaining input variables. The assumed distributions and reported COV values for the cover depth also vary. Using the values reported in the literature can result in a wide range of times to corrosion and service life prediction values. Such a wide range of prediction values devalues the process of predicting these service lives and limits the perceived sustainability of RC structures. Owners are requiring defined service lives and with time, if these service lives are not achieved, the process and value of predicting the life of a structure will be questioned. Standardized testing and frameworks are needed to provide realistic representation of the input variables such that realistic service lives can be predicted. Once predicted, these values should be compared with anticipated functional service lives to maximize anticipated sustainability. Research is needed to quantify and estimate functional service life. A summary of needs follows.

The cover depth is a design parameter determined by the design engineer and this design value can be used for service life prediction. What is not clear regarding cover depth is the distribution of the cover depths and the COV of these cover depths. Does COV vary with cover depth or is the COV fixed with depth? Is it a function of structure type, installer, bar size, location of construction, or other variables? A comprehensive study of existing structures could provide valuable information on cover depth parameters and should be performed. Testing of concrete cover should follow a standard testing protocol.

Unlike the case for many input variables used for service life prediction, standardized testing is available for predicting apparent chloride diffusion coefficients (ASTM C1556). However, the standard states that the method is applicable for mixtures that "have not been exposed to external chloride ions" prior to performing the test. In addition, the method is applicable only for samples that are continuously submerged in sodium chloride solution. The author believes that this is an adequate start for developing a standard test but additional factors are needed to correlate differing exposure conditions to the test condition. Exposure conditions can significantly influence the rate at which chlorides are transported into concrete must be considered. It has been well established that introducing wetting and drying cycles introduces different transport mechanisms, but factors may be applicable to reduce the wide range of values reported in the literature. A significant body of research has been performed to assess D_a values but unfortunately additional information is needed to correlate the current standard test procedure, which assesses one exposure condition, with field performance.

Standardized testing for determining C_i is available. However, several test methods are allowed to determine the chloride concentration and correlation between the results from these test methods has not been well defined. Current research at Oregon State University indicates little correlation between acid-soluble chloride (ASC) test results and water-soluble chloride (WSC) test results, as shown in Figure 21.2. ACI documents allow both test methods. At issue is that ACI documents assume the ratio of water to acid-soluble test results (WSC/ASC) is between 0.75 and 0.8. Figure 21.2 clearly shows that this is not the case for many mixtures. The ratio of water- to acid-soluble test results range from 0.04 to 0.79, depending on mixture proportions and constituent materials (Trejo et al. 2018). In fact, less than 3 percent of the 243 data points have WSC-ASC ratios between 0.75 and 0.80. Chloride binding varies for different systems and reasonable correlations between WSC and ASC have yet to be quantified.

Lastly, significant discussion evolves around whether the water- or acid-soluble chloride testing should be required for testing. Water-soluble testing likely better represents the free chlorides in the system and acid-soluble testing is more representative of total chlorides in the system. But it has been documented that bound chlorides in the concrete can be freed during the life of a structure and as such, acid-soluble testing would provide a more conservative limit. However, all chlorides may not be able to be unbound and using acid soluble testing may be too conservative. Although standardized tests methods are available, the concrete community needs to reach consensus on which test method best represents field conditions and risk of corrosion.

The last input variable for predicting service life shown in Equation (21.11) is the surface chloride concentration, C_s. The simple boundary conditions associated with the "standard" solution to Fick's Second Law is not applicable to non-constant surface chloride concentrations: finite element or finite difference analyses are needed. Research is needed to assess errors associated with a constant chloride surface concentration. In addition, recent models have been developed to estimate the time-variant surface chloride build-up as a function of concrete proportion and material type. Therefore, the assessment of surface chloride concentrations for RC structures has two challenges: first, what standard testing should be used for determined surface chloride build-up and second, should the surface concentration be evaluated with water- or acid-soluble testing?

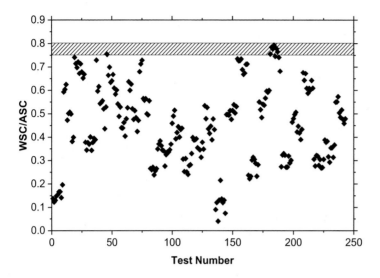

Figure 21.2 Distribution of water-soluble to acid soluble chloride ratios for 27 different mixtures (hatched region is ratio assumed in ACI documents).

Where standardized testing is available, having more than one testing option can result in confusion and increased variability of service life prediction outcome. Unfortunately, standardized testing is not available for all input variables needed for estimating the time to corrosion and service life prediction. Although significant advances have been made with modeling chloride transport and corrosion initiation, until input parameters can be better represented with standardized and uniform testing, significant variation in service life prediction will occur.

21.6 Conclusions

One of the early meetings to address the development of service life prediction of reinforced concrete structures occurred in 1998 (Frohnsdorff 1998). Significant progress has been made in developing more models to predict the service life of these structures since this early meeting. Service life relationships, such as that shown in Equation (21.11), are being used to predict the life expectancies of major structures. Unfortunately, less efforts have focused on developing standardized tests to reasonably represent the input variables for these service life models. Standardizing these tests is essential for owners and the concrete community at large so that the scientific and engineering communities can better trust the output of these service life models. Due to the lack of reliable information on these input parameters, the sustainability of RC systems can be questioned. In fact, by not having a good and reliable measure of service life, the potential value of these systems is not being maximized. The engineering and scientific communities must standardize testing and clearly specify uniform standardized testing so that service life models accurately represent field performance of concrete structures exposed to salt solutions. This will optimize sustainability of these systems, enhancing the confidence within the communities of scholars, engineers, owner representatives, and owners of RC structures. If standardized and uniform testing is not rigorously pursued, the significant progress made over the past 20 years could be for naught. It is time for the development of specific standardized tests to reliably assess input variables needed for service life prediction of sustainable RC structures.

References

American Society of Civil Engineering (2016). *Failure to Act: Closing the Infrastructure Investment Gap for America's Economic Future.* Reston, VA.

ASTM C1556-11 (2016). Standard Test Method for Determining the Apparent Chloride Diffusion Coefficient of Cementitious Mixtures by Bulk Diffusion, ASTM International, West Conshohocken, PA, 2016.

Azad, V.J. and Isgor, O.B. (2016). "A thermodynamic perspective on admixed chloride limits of concrete produced with SCMs," *Special Publication*, 308: 1–18.

Bamforth, P., and Price, W. (1993). "Factors influencing chloride ingress into marine structures," *Economic and Durable Construction through Excellence*, Dundee, UK.

Baroghel-Bouny, V., Wang, X., Thiery, M., Saillio, M., and Barberon, F. (2012). "Prediction of chloride binding isotherms of cementitious materials by analytical model or numerical inverse analysis," *Cement and Concrete Research*, 42(9): 1207–24.

Bastidas-Arteaga, E., Chateauneuf, A., Sánchez-Silva, M., Bressolette, P., and Schoefs, F. (2011) "A comprehensive probabilistic model of chloride ingress in unsaturated concrete," *Engineering Structures*, 33(3): 720–30.

Bentz, D.P., Feng, X., and Hooton, R.D. (2001). "Time-dependent diffusivities: possible misinterpretation due to spatial dependence." Paper presented at the *Proceedings of the 2nd International RILEM Workshop on Testing and Modelling the Chloride Ingress into Concrete*, pp. 225–33.

Bentz, E. (2003). "Probabilistic modeling of service life for structures subjected to chlorides," *ACI Materials Journal*, 100(5): 391–7.

Bentz, E., Thomas, M., and Evans, C. (1996). "Chloride diffusion modelling for marine exposed concretes," *Special Publication, Royal Society of Chemistry*, 183: 136–45.

Dhir, R., Jones, M., and Elghaly, A. (1993). "PFA concrete: exposure temperature effects on chloride diffusion," *Cement and Concrete Research*, 23(5): 1105–14.

Dhir, R., McCarthy, M., Zhou, S., and Tittle, P. (2004). "Role of cement content in specifications for concrete durability: cement type influences," *Proceedings of the Institution of Civil Engineers-Structures and Buildings*, 157(2): 113–27.

Edvardsen, C. and Mohr, L. (1999). "DURACRETE – a guideline for durability-based design of concrete structures," Prague, October.

Ehlen, M.A., Thomas, M.D., and Bentz, E.C. (2009). "Life-365 service life prediction model™ Version 2.0," *Concrete International*, 31(05): 41–6.

Ferreira, R.M. (2004). "Probability-based durability analysis of concrete structures in marine environment,"

Frohnsdorff, G. (1998). "Modelling service life and life-cycle cost of steel-reinforced concrete." Report from the NIST/ACI/ASTM Workshop held in Gaithersburg, MD, November 9–10.

Han, N. and Kooiman, A. (2003). "Performance and reliability based service life design for the Green Heart Tunnel," Paper presented at the *(Re) claiming the Underground Space: Proceedings of the ITA World Tunneling Congress 12–17 April 2003*, Amsterdam, The Netherlands.

Kirkpatrick, T.J., Weyers, R., Anderson-Cook, C., Sprinkel, M., and Brown, M. (2002). "A Model to Predict the Impact of Specification Changes on Chloride-induced Corrosion Service Life of Virginia Bridge Decks," Virginia Center for Transportation Innovation and Research.

Kwon, S.J., Na, U.J., Park, S.S., and Jung, S.H. (2009). "Service life prediction of concrete wharves with early-aged crack: Probabilistic approach for chloride diffusion," *Structural Safety*, 31(1): 75–83.

Lounis, Z. and Mirza, M. (2001). "Reliability-based service life prediction of deteriorating concrete structures."

Luping, T. and Gulikers, J. (2007). "On the mathematics of time-dependent apparent chloride diffusion coefficient in concrete," *Cement and Concrete Research*, 37(4): 589–95.

Maheswaran, T. and Sanjayan, J. (2004). "A semi-closed-form solution for chloride diffusion in concrete with time-varying parameters," *Magazine of Concrete Research*, 56(6): 359–66.

Mangat, P. and Limbachiya, M. (1999). "Effect of initial curing on chloride diffusion in concrete repair materials," *Cement and Concrete Research*, 29(9): 1475–85.

Marchand, J. and Samson, E. (2009). "Predicting the service-life of concrete structures: Limitations of simplified models," *Cement and Concrete Composites*, 31(8): 515–21.

Mohammed, T.U., Yamaji, T., and Hamada, H. (2002). "Chloride diffusion, microstructure, and mineralogy of concrete after 15 years of exposure in tidal environment," *ACI Materials Journal*, 99(3): 256–63.

Nogueira, C.G. and Leonel, E.D. (2013). "Probabilistic models applied to safety assessment of reinforced concrete structures subjected to chloride ingress," *Engineering Failure Analysis*, 31: 76–89.

Nokken, M., Boddy, A., Hooton, R., and Thomas, M. (2006). "Time dependent diffusion in concrete—three laboratory studies," *Cement and Concrete Research*, 36(1): 200–7.

Page, C., Short, N., and El Tarras, A. (1981). "Diffusion of chloride ions in hardened cement pastes," *Cement and Concrete Research*, 11(3): 395–406.

Pearce, D. and Atkinson, G.D. (1993). "Capital theory and the measurement of sustainable development: an indicator of 'weak' sustainability," *Ecological Economics*, 8(2): 103–8.

Petcherdchoo, A. (2013). "Time dependent models of apparent diffusion coefficient and surface chloride for chloride transport in fly ash concrete," *Construction and Building Materials*, 38: 497–507.

Puyate, Y., Lawrence, C., Buenfeld, N., and McLoughlin, I. (1998). "Chloride transport models for wick action in concrete at large Peclet number," *Physics of Fluids*, 10(3): 566–75.

Report of the World Commission on Environment and Development (1987). *Our Common Future* (commonly referred to as the Brundtland Report), United Nations.

Ryan, P.C. and O'Connor, A.J. (2013). "Probabilistic analysis of the time to chloride induced corrosion for different self-compacting concretes," *Construction and Building Materials*, 47: 1106–16.

Schiessl, P. (2005). "New approach to service life design of concrete structure," *Asian Journal of Civil Engineering (Building and Housing)*, 6(5): 393–407.

Shakouri, M. and Trejo, D. (2017). "A time-variant model of surface chloride build-up for improved service life predictions," *Cement and Concrete Composites*, 84: 99–110.

Shakouri, M., Trejo, D., and Gardoni, P. (2017). "A probabilistic framework to justify allowable admixed chloride limits in concrete," *Construction and Building Materials*, 139: 490–500.

Song, H.W., Lee, C.H., and Ann, K.Y. (2008). "Factors influencing chloride transport in concrete structures exposed to marine environments," *Cement and Concrete Composites*, 30(2): 113–21.

Srubar, W.V. (2015). "Stochastic service-life modeling of chloride-induced corrosion in recycled-aggregate concrete," *Cement and Concrete Composites*, 55: 103–11.

Stewart, M.G., and Mullard, J.A. (2007). "Spatial time-dependent reliability analysis of corrosion damage and the timing of first repair for RC structures," *Engineering Structures*, 29(7): 1457–64.

Stewart, M.G. and Rosowsky, D.V. (1998). "Structural safety and serviceability of concrete bridges subject to corrosion," *Journal of Infrastructure Systems*, 4(4): 146–55.

Trejo, D., Isgor, O.B., and Weiss, W.J. (2016). "The allowable admixed chloride conundrum," *Concrete International*, 38.

Trejo, D, Vaddey, N.P., and Shakouri, M. (2018). "Factors influencing the chloride test outcome of cementitious systems," *ACI Materials Journal* (in review).

Uji, K., Matsuoka, Y., and Maruya, T. (1990). "Formulation of an equation for surface chloride content of concrete due to permeation of chloride," *Elsevier Applied Science*, 258–67.

Val, D.V. and Trapper, P.A. (2008). "Probabilistic evaluation of initiation time of chloride-induced corrosion," *Reliability Engineering and System Safety*, 93(3): 364–72.

Visser, J., Andrade, C., and Kropp, J. (2004). "Time dependency of chloride diffusion coefficients in concrete." Paper presented at *The Third International RILEM Workshop on Testing and Modelling Chloride Ingress into Concrete*, RILEM Publications SARL, pp. 423–33.

22

The long-term ageing trends of asphalt binders in highway pavements

Yuhong Wang,[1] Kecheng Zhao,[2] and Fangjin Li[3]

[1] DEPARTMENT OF CIVIL AND ENVIRONMENTAL ENGINEERING, THE HONG KONG POLYTECHNIC UNIVERSITY, ZS921, HUNG HOM, KOWLOON, HK; TEL: 852-2766-4489; FAX: 852-2334-6389; CEYHWANG@POLYU.EDU.HK (CORRESPONDING AUTHOR)

[2] DEPARTMENT OF CIVIL AND ENVIRONMENTAL ENGINEERING, THE HONG KONG POLYTECHNIC UNIVERSITY, ZS917 HUNG HOM, KOWLOON, HK, TEL: 852-6477-1307; KC.ZHAO@CONNECT.POLYU.HK

[3] DEPARTMENT OF CIVIL AND ENVIRONMENTAL ENGINEERING, THE HONG KONG POLYTECHNIC UNIVERSITY, ZN906 HUNG HOM, KOWLOON, HK, TEL: 852-6477-1307; FJ.LI@CONNECT.POLYU.HK

22.1 Introduction

The transport sector has significant impacts on the three pillars of sustainable development. Using environmental impacts as an example, approximately 14 percent of global greenhouse gas (GHG) emissions are estimated from transport sector, and 72 percent of the GHG emissions from this sector are associated with road construction, rehabilitation, maintenance, service, and usage (ASTAE 2017; Edenhofer et al. 2014; Chong & Wang 2017). Although the majority of GHG emissions from road transportation are generated by vehicles, the emissions are affected by road pavements. Particularly, road roughness (Chatti & Zaabar 2012) and traffic congestions due to road closures are found to significantly affect vehicles' fuel consumption as well as GHG emissions (Chong & Wang 2017). In addition to environmental impacts, the other two pillars of sustainability, i.e., economy and society, are also heavily influenced by road design, construction, and management decisions, and their relationships have also been extensively discussed and documented (e.g., Fwa et al. 2000; Venner 2004). Durable road pavements generally lead to enhanced sustainability at different dimensions.

The majority of highways worldwide are made of flexible pavements surfaced with hot-mix asphalt (HMA). Flexible pavement durability is not only affected by its overall structural capacity, but also the durability of pavement materials. As an organic material, asphalt binder in hot-mix asphalt (HMA) pavement is subject to ageing, especially oxidative ageing (Petersen 2009). Asphalt binder ageing causes an increase in binder stiffness and reduction in binder ductility (Petersen 2009), which further cause the behavioral and performance changes of HMA pavement. In addition, because the fluidity of asphalt binder is reduced due to ageing, micro cracks in aged pavements become more difficult to be healed as compared with new pavements. Ageing is the driving force behind the long-term deterioration of HMA pavements.

Although the effects of asphalt binder ageing have been long recognized and regularly examined in engineering practices, existing practices are mainly focused on the ageing susceptibility of asphalt binders. It remains unclear how asphalt binder ages in field pavements. In fact, early studies suggest that long-term asphalt binder ageing in field HMA pavements is limited to pavement surface (Coons 1965; Mirza & Witczak 1995). Therefore, HMA pavements may be potentially renewed by periodically replacing the surface layers (resurfacing).

Recent studies by Glover and colleagues (Al-Azri et al. 2006; Glover et al. 2009), however, suggest that HMA pavement ages relentlessly throughout the asphalt pavement layers. Mechanistic-based, intricate ageing models have been proposed by their team. For instance, Prapaitrakul (2009; Prapaitrakul et al. 2009) developed an oxygen transport and reaction model, where oxygen was modeled to be transported in air voids (AV) channels and diffused into asphalt binder shells, and the average size and distribution of AV are used to predict binder oxidative ageing. Han (2011) further refined the model by including temperature and the number of AV in binder oxidation prediction. The model assumes that the oxygen content in the entire pavement structure is the same as that in the atmosphere. Consequently, HMA pavement ageing is a function of pavement temperature at a certain depth as well as the voids characteristic of HMA mixtures. The variations of HMA pavement ageing with time, cross-sectional location, and pavement depth are also reported by a few other researchers based on field data (Wang et al. 2014).

With recent advancement in understanding HMA ageing mechanisms and more data being collected from field pavements, it becomes necessary to re-examine how asphalt binder ages in field pavements. After all, the ageing states of HMA in different pavement layers affect the fundamental engineering properties and performance of both new and rehabilitated pavements. The objective of this chapter is to examine the trends of long-term ageing in highway asphalt pavements. The rest of the chapter is organized as follows. In the second section, the current asphalt ageing prediction methods used in the mechanistic-empirical pavement design guide (ME-PDG) are introduced. In the third section, analysis methods and field data on asphalt pavement ageing are presented. The analysis results are summarized and discussed in the fourth section. Conclusions and future research needs are discussed in the last section. It is anticipated that the findings will paint a realistic picture on how asphalt pavement ages and help develop improved ageing prediction models in the future.

22.2 The empirical pavement ageing prediction

Highway agencies around the world are moving from the traditional empirical pavement design methods toward methods that incorporate mechanistic principles. The mechanistic-empirical pavement design guide (ME-PDG) represents one of the major initiatives in this direction. In ME-PDG, asphalt binder ageing during the design or analysis period is a necessary step and it is predicted by a procedure named as the Global Ageing System (Mirza & Witczak 1995). The ageing states of asphalt binders at different time are predicted by four models, including: original (binder) to mix/lay-down model, (pavement) surfacing ageing model, air void adjustment, and viscosity-depth model. Because these models are closely related to this study, for easy reference, they are introduced as follows (Mirza & Witczak 1995; ARA 2004):

The mix/lay-down model is used to predict the change of binder viscosity during mixing and construction (Mirza & Witczak 1995):

$$\log\log\left(\eta_{t=0}\right) = a_0 + a_1 \log\log\left(\eta_{orig}\right)$$

$$a_0 = 0.054405 + 0.004082 \times code \tag{22.1}$$

$$a_1 = 0.972035 + 0.010886 \times code,$$

where

$\eta_{t=0}$ = the mix/lay-down viscosity (cP) at temperature T_R (Rankine),
η_{orig} = the original binder viscosity (cp) at temperature T_R (Rankine),
code = the hardening ratio of the binder (code = 0 for average).

The long-term ageing model is used to predict the ageing evolution of the binder at surface pavement at a certain time point t (Mirza & Witczak 1995):

$$\log\log\left(\eta_{aged}\right) = \frac{\log\log\left(\eta_{t=0}\right) + At}{1 + Bt}, \tag{22.2}$$

where

$A = -0.004166 + 1.41213\ C + C\log\left(Maat\right) + D\log\log\left(\eta_{t=0}\right)$
$B = 0.197725 + 0.068384\log C$
$C = 10^{274.4946 - 193.831\log(T_R) + 33.9366\log(T_R)^2}$
$D = -14.5521 + 10.47662\log(T_R) - 1.88161\log(T_R)^2,$

where

η_{aged} = the viscosity of aged binder, cP;
$\eta_{t=0}$ = viscosity at mix/lay-down, cP;
Maat = mean annual air temperature, °F;
T_R = temperature in Rankine;
t = time in months.

To account for the effects of air voids, an adjustment factor may be applied to the predicted binder viscosity for field pavement ageing (Mirza & Witczak 1995):

$$\log\log\left(\eta_{aged}\right)' = F_v \log\log\left(\eta_{aged}\right)$$

$$F_v = \frac{1 + 1.0367 \times 10^{-4}\left(VA\right)(t)}{1 + 6.1798 \times 10^{-4}(t)} \tag{22.3}$$

$$VA = \frac{VA_{orig} + 0.011(t) - 2}{1 + 4.24 \times 10^{-4}(t)(Maat) + 1.169 \times 10^{-3}\left(\dfrac{t}{\eta_{orig,77}}\right)} + 2,$$

where

VA_{orig} = initial air voids;
t = time in months;
Maat = mean annual air temperature, °F;
$\eta_{orig,77}$ = original binder viscosity at 77 °F, 10^6 Poise.

The last component in the Global Ageing System is the ageing-depth model, which takes the form (Mirza & Witczak 1995):

$$\eta_{t,z} = \frac{\eta_t(4+E) - E(\eta_{t=0})(1-4z)}{4(1+Ez)},$$

(22.4)

where

$\eta_{t,z}$ = Aged viscosity at time t, and depth z, 10^6 Poise

η_t = Aged surface viscosity, 10^6 Poise

z = Depth, in

E = $23.83e^{(-0.0308 \, Maat)}$

Maat = Mean annual air temperature, °F.

Based on Equations (22.1)–(22.4), a sensitivity analysis of pavement ageing variations with time and pavement depth is performed. The pavements are assumed to be located in three climate zones with mean annual air temperature of 5 °C, 12 °C, and 20 °C, respectively. The asphalt binder is assumed to have an initial viscosity of 1.4 10^6 poise at 25 °C (corresponding to a penetration value of 70 at 25 °C). The changes of asphalt binder ageing states with time and location are shown in Figure 22.1.

Figure 22.1 indicates that asphalt binder ageing is sensitive to the mean annual air temperature. Under the same climate condition, the ageing of asphalt binder decreases with pavement depth. Such decrease becomes more significant as pavement gets older and in warmer climate conditions. At the same pavement depth, the rate of asphalt binder ageing apparently decreases with time. According to Figure 22.1, asphalt binder at the bottom of a thick pavement may not be severely aged. Since the ageing states of asphalt binders play a key role in pavement design and analysis, actual ageing data from field pavements were collected and analyzed, as shown in the next section.

22.3 Long-term asphalt binder ageing in field pavements

Data from three sources were used to investigate the long-term asphalt binder ageing in field pavements. The first source is cored samples from two expressways in Hong Kong. The two expressways have been used longer than 25 years. They provide information on long-term ageing trend in asphalt pavements in a subtropical climate. The second source of data is from the long-term pavement performance (LTPP) program, which provides information on both the original asphalt binders and those extracted from a large number of test sections. The third source of data is from the MnRoad experimental program conducted in Minnesota, US. It provides information on long-term ageing trend in a cold climate. The research methods are discussed in more details as follows.

22.3.1 Field experiments

HMA pavement sample cores were obtained from two expressways in Hong Kong: Tuen Mun Road and Tolo Highway. Tuen Mun Road was opened to traffic in 1977 and has a total of six lanes. The asphalt layers consist of a 30 mm open-graded friction course (OGFC) that was added in recent years, 40 mm wearing course (WC), 60 mm base course (BC), and 150 mm roadbase (RB). Since initial construction, several resurfacing activities have been performed in various locations of the roads, but the BC and RB layers were not replaced. Cores were retrieved from

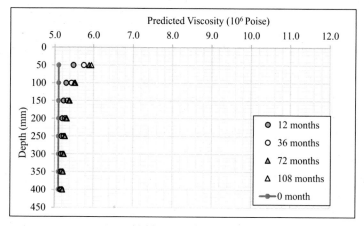

(a) Mean annual air temperature=5 °C

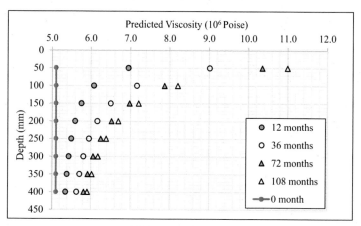

(b) Mean annual air temperature=12 °C

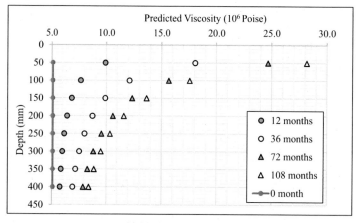

(c) Mean annual air temperature=20 °C

Figure 22.1 The changes of asphalt binder ageing with time and pavement depth at three climate conditions.

Figure 22.2 One of the sample cores used for binder extraction.

the roads in 2013 and asphalt binders were extracted subsequently for analysis. Tolo Highway, opened to traffic in 1987, also consists of six traffic lanes. Sample cores were taken from the road in 2016 and were subsequently tested. Because Tolo Highway was constructed at a later time, the thickness of the RB layer was increased to about 300 mm. It was designed as a "perpetual" pavement, i.e., a pavement for which the structural layer will not be damaged by cumulative traffic loads. The structure of the pavement in Tolo Highway is shown in one of the extracted cores in Figure 22.2. For each road, a same asphalt binder was used for each layer.

The sample cores obtained from the field were cut into thin slices, including WC, BC, and 3–5 slices of RB depending on RB thickness. WC data was not included for analysis in this study because it had been resurfaced. The slices were stored in an air-conditioned environment before binder extraction. Asphalt binders were extracted using an extraction unit bowl in accordance with the ASTM standard D2171/D2172M-11 and the solvent is dichloromethane. The extracted solution was placed in a sample tube and was clarified by using a centrifuge machine according to the European Standard EN 12697-3:2005. Before the clarification process, a small amount of silica gel passing the 0.063 mm sieve size was added to the solution to remove the residual water. Asphalt binder was recovered from the clarified solution by using a

Table 22.1 The LTPP SPS 1 test sites used in this study

	Freeze	*Non-Freeze*	*Total*
Wet	AR(5) DE(10) IA(19) KS(20) MI(26) NE(31) OH(39) WI (55)	AL(1) FL(12) LA(22) OK(40) TX(48) VA(51)	14
Dry	MT(30) NV(32)	AZ(4) NM(35)	4
Total	10	8	18

Note (14):
a. Wet Regions — Average Annual Rainfall > 20 inches (508 mm).
b. Dry Regions — Average Annual Rainfall < 20 inches (508 mm).
c. Freeze Regions — Average Annual Freezing Index > 83.3 °C-day (150 °F-day).
d. Non-Freeze Regions — Average Annual Freezing Index < 83.3 °C-day (150 °F-day).

rotary evaporator according to EN 12697-3:2005. The recovered asphalt binders were tested by using a dynamic shear rheometer (DSR) for rheological properties and Fourier transform infrared spectroscopy (FTIR) for chemical properties.

22.3.2 LTPP data and MnRoad data

Binder test data from the LTPP program and MnRoad were also used. Although multiple experiments in the LTPP program contain information on extracted asphalt binders, it was found that the SPS 1 experiment (Strategic Study of Structural Factors for Flexible Pavements) has the most complete information on both pavement structures and extracted binders. In addition, test sections at each road in the SPS 1 experiment were built at the same time using the same type of asphalt binders, and sample cores were also taken at approximately the same time. This facilitates the comparison of ageing variations with pavement depth. The main table used for extracted binder information is "TST_AE05." The reported binder test data includes kinematic viscosity (centistokes) at 275°F (135°C) and absolute viscosity (poise) at 140°F (60°C). The test roads from the SPS 1 experiments are summarized in Table 22.1, which shows that the roads cover different climate zones.

MnROAD test program is located near Albertville, Minnesota (Mndot 2017). It is "one of the most sophisticated, independently operated pavement test facilities of its type in the world (Mndot 2017)." The data collection from the MnROAD program has started since 1993 (Mndot 2017). MnROAD data release 1.0 (2012) was used for analysis. The table "hma ageing" was used to obtain information on the ageing states of asphalt binders extracted from different pavement layers. According to the table, samples were taken from the test cells in September 2002. The ageing indicator provided in the table is high-temperature performance grade (PG). The high-temperature PG grade is based on the value of $G^*/\sin \delta$ from the dynamic shear test using a DSR. Asphalt binder ageing leads to an increase in the high-temperature PG grade. In contrast to data in Hong Kong, the MnROAD data sheds lights on ageing trends of asphalt pavements in a cold region.

22.4 Results and discussion

22.4.1 Results from field experiments

Frequency sweep test using DSR was performed on the extracted binders from the field experiments. The G* master curve and the FTIR spectra of a sample from the 29-year-old

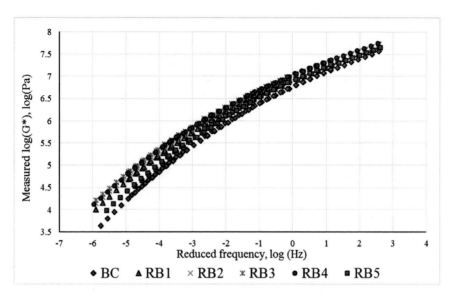

Figure 22.3 Master curves of extracted asphalt binders from one sample core at the 29-year-old Tolo highway pavement.

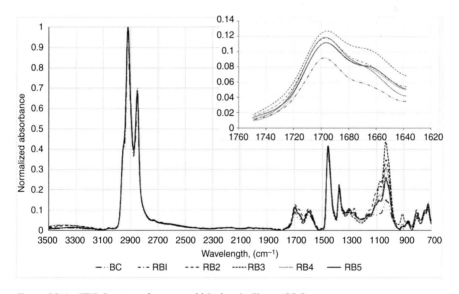

Figure 22.4 FTIR Spectra of extracted binders in Figure 22.3.

pavement are shown in Figure 22.3 and Figure 22.4, respectively. Figure 22.3 indicates that the ageing states of the extracted binders from different layers of pavements are different, and the ageing severity is not necessarily reduced with pavement depth. Infrared spectrometry is extensively used to study the chemical changes of asphalt binder with ageing (Petersen 2009). The wave length at about 1695 cm⁻¹ corresponds to the characteristic peak of a major oxidation product – ketones, which are well related to binder's physical ageing properties (Petersen 2009).

In this study, the ratios between the absorbance peak height at about 1695 cm⁻¹ to that at about 1455 cm⁻¹ (saturated C-C band) were used to eliminate variation caused by sample preparation (Negulescu et al. 2006). The magnitude of the ratio indicates the severity of ageing. Figure 22.4 clearly indicates the different ageing states of asphalt binders extracted from different layers.

The LTPP data reports viscosity values of the extracted binders. To be comparable, the DSR measurements were converted to viscosity at 60°C using the following equation (Bari & Witczak 2007):

$$\eta = \left(\frac{|G_b^*|}{\omega} \right) \left(\frac{1}{\sin\delta_b} \right)^{a_0 + a_1\omega + a_2\omega^2}, \tag{22.5}$$

where:

η = viscosity, P (Note: The viscosity unit may be mistakenly written as cP in the original equation. It has been changed to Poise in this paper);
$|G_b^*|$ = binder complex shear modulus, Pa;
δ_b = binder phase angle, degree;
ω = angular frequency, rad/s;
a_0, a_1, a_2 = fitting parameters, 3.639, 0.1314, and –0.0009, respectively.

The physical and chemical ageing depth relationships for the samples from the two roads are shown in Figure 22.5 and Figure 22.6, respectively. Although there are variations in the data, both Figure 22.5 and Figure 22.6 show that the ageing severity of base course (BC, layer beneath the wearing course) is lower than that of the adjacent Roadbase (RB). For the same RB mixtures, ageing severity generally decreases with pavement depth. Because temperature of the BC layer is higher than that of the RB layer and higher temperature accelerates binder ageing, it is likely that mixture characteristics (air voids, gradation, etc). cause the different ageing susceptibility of the two mixture types. For the same type of asphalt mixture (Roadbase), the ageing severity generally decreases with pavement depth, following the temperature gradient of the pavement.

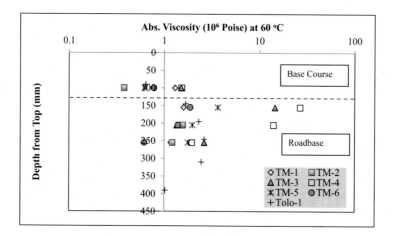

Figure 22.5 The change of binder viscosity with pavement depth for seven samples (TM: Tun Mun Rd; Tolo: Tolo Highways).

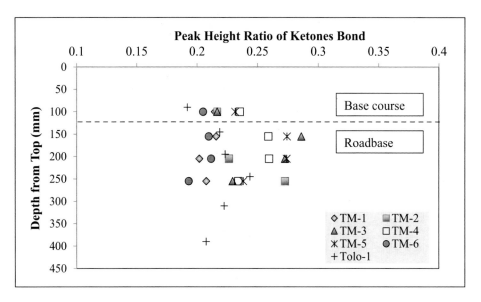

Figure 22.6 The change of peak height ratio of ketones bond with pavement depth for seven samples (TM: Tun Mun Rd; Tolo: Tolo Highways).

The changes of binder viscosity with pavement depth at the LTPP sites are shown in Figures 22.7, 22.8, and 22.9. Because there are 18 roads, they are organized into three figures according to different climate conditions for better presentation: wet and non-freeze (Figure 22.7), wet and freeze (Figure 22.8), and dry (including both freeze and non-freeze, Figure 22.9). The figures clearly indicate that binder viscosity does not uniformly change with pavement depth. In fact, for many sites, the ageing state of the base course is higher than that of the adjacent binder course. Moreover, the data shows great variations of binder ageing with pavement depth. In view of the same type of binder used in construction, the binder in different depth must be subjected to different ageing environment. Such variations in binder ageing states will generate profound impacts on the properties of HMA mixtures and their responses to traffic induced loads.

Figure 22.10 indicates the change of ageing states of the four samples retrieved from the MnROAD experiment. The high-temperature PG grade indicates the severity of ageing. Similarly, the data indicates that ageing does not continuously decay with pavement depth. Instead, the trend generally follows a parabola curve: The ageing severity of the top layers is generally high, but it first decreases with pavement depth and then increases with pavement depth. The bottom of the base layer records the higher ageing severity. The pattern is in general repetitive among the four samples; therefore, it must reveal a general trend of ageing in the pavement. Interestingly, compared with the trends in Hong Kong roads (Figures 22.5–22.6), the direction of the ageing-depth curve is just the opposite.

22.4.2 Discussion

The Global Ageing System in ME-PDG always generates a consistent prediction of the trend of asphalt binder ageing with pavement depth. According to the prediction, the ageing severity of the asphalt binder decreases with pavement depth. The effects of climate conditions and

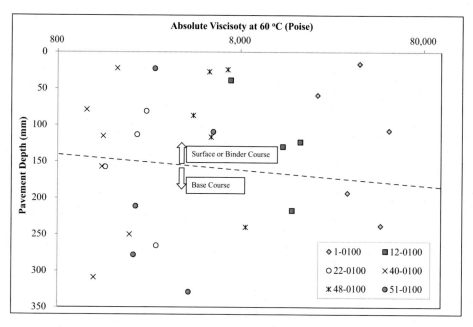

Figure 22.7 The change of binder viscosity with pavement depth in LTPP sites (wet and non-freeze climate).

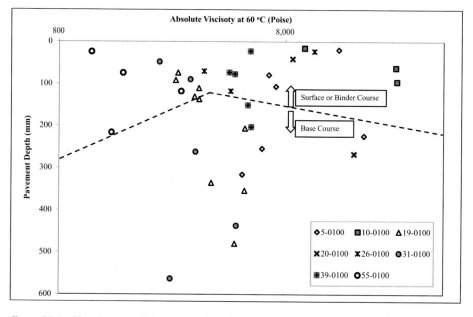

Figure 22.8 The change of binder viscosity with pavement depth in LTPP sites (wet and freeze climate).

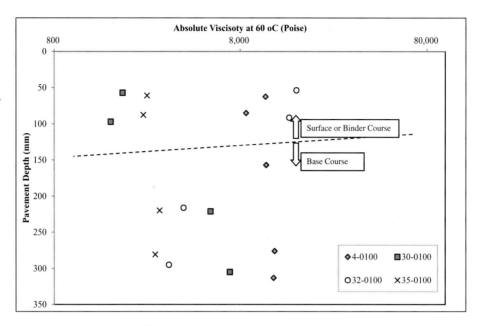

Figure 22.9 The change of binder viscosity with pavement depth in LTPP sites (dry climate).

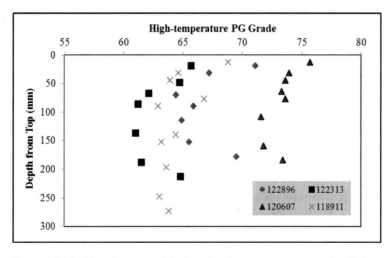

Figure 22.10 The change of binder viscosity with pavement depth in samples from the MnROAD experiment.

pavement materials on asphalt binder ageing are manifested at the surface layers. Actual pavement ageing data as shown above, however, clearly indicate that asphalt binder ageing varies greatly. This variation cannot be explained by random or experimental errors, as the data from Hong Kong and MnRoad show consistent trends in multiple samples at each respective location.

To understand the asphalt binder ageing in field pavements, the ageing mechanisms have to be taken into consideration. A large number of studies have been performed on the mechanisms of asphalt binder ageing (e.g., Al-Azri et al. 2006; Glover et al. 2009; Petersen 2009; Prapaitrakul 2009; Prapaitrakul, Han et al. 2009). The predominant long-term ageing mechanism of asphalt binder is found to be oxidative ageing (e.g. Petersen 1986; Lau et al. 1992). Laboratory studies show that the long-term oxidative ageing of asphalt binders can be divided into two stages: an initial jump period that occurs within a relatively short time period and a continuous ageing stage with a constant hardening rate (Petersen 2009). The second stage is the main cause of asphalt binder ageing in the field. The hardening rate during the second stage can be expressed as (Petersen & Harnsberger 1998; Ruan et al. 2003):

$$r_\eta = HS \times r_{CA}, \tag{22.6}$$

where r_η is the hardening rate after the "initial jump", HS is the hardening susceptibility of a particular type of asphalt binder, r_{CA} is the growth rate of the carbonyl area in the infrared spectrum of the asphalt binder with time; and

$$r_{CA} = \partial CA / \partial t = AP^{\pm\alpha}e^{-E/RT}, \tag{22.7}$$

where A, E, and α are coefficients that are dependent on asphalt binder type, R is the gas constant, P is oxygen pressure, and T is the absolute temperature. E was also found to be a function of oxygen pressure (Ruan et al. 2003).

As indicated in Equations (22.6) and (22.7), the age hardening of an asphalt binder is essentially determined by four factors: hardening susceptibility of the asphalt binder which is binder-specific, temperature of the in-situ asphalt mixture, and the oxygen content and void characteristics of the in-situ asphalt mixtures. Several studies have been attempted to incorporate the fundamental mechanisms of asphalt binder ageing in the prediction of asphalt binder ageing. A realistic prediction of asphalt pavement ageing at different depth and time is dependent on: (1) the realistic prediction of the ageing influencing factors, and (2) a model (or models) that predicts asphalt binder ageing in a mixture environment. Although pioneering work has been done in this direction (e.g., Al-Azri et al. 2006; Glover et al. 2009), more research is still needed.

22.5 Conclusions

The ageing of asphalt is a main factor that affects the long-term durability of highway pavements, which further affects the sustainability of the pavements in different dimensions. The evolution of asphalt pavement ageing is investigated in this chapter. Asphalt ageing predicted in the Global Ageing System in ME-PDG was examined. A total of 21 roads from different experiments were then used to investigate the trends of asphalt binder ageing with pavement depth, including two roads in Hong Kong, 18 roads from the LTPP SPS1 program, and one road from the MnROAD experiment. The data clearly show that asphalt binder ageing does not necessarily continuously decrease with pavement depth. In fact, only on one road asphalt binder ageing severity apparently decreases with pavement depth. The detailed experimental programs in Hong Kong and MnROAD show that ageing-depth trend follows a parabola curve, but the direction of the curve is opposite for the roads in two different climates.

Binder ageing is an essential issue for mechanistic-based pavement design and analysis. The variations shown from the different roads investigated in this study indicate that the relationship between asphalt binder ageing and pavement depth cannot be captured by a uniform empirical equation. Therefore, it is recommended that a mechanistic-based asphalt ageing equation be developed in the future. Existing studies suggest that asphalt binder ageing in asphalt mixtures is governed by several factors: the ageing susceptibility of a specific asphalt binder, temperature, and oxygen exposure. The first two factors can be well quantified through laboratory tests and thermodynamic computation based on climate conditions, while the third factor is affected by mixture design and may be quantified indirectly. Several studies have used X-ray computed tomography (CT) to characterize asphalt mixtures and use the obtained information to estimate the effects of asphalt mixtures on asphalt binder ageing. X-ray CT, however, is not commonly used in routine engineering practices. Therefore, more studies are needed in the future to develop an asphalt pavement ageing prediction procedure based on commonly measured parameters.

Acknowledgements

The authors would like to thank the LTPP program and the MnROAD program for providing the research data. The authors would also like to thank the Highways Department in Hong Kong for facilitating taking sample cores from two expressways. This study is financially supported by a research project from the Research Grant Council of Hong Kong Special Administrative Region Government (Project Number: PolyU 152222/15E).

References

Al-Azri, N., S. Jung, K. Lunsford, A. Ferry, J. Bullin, R. Davison, and C. Glover (2006). "Binder oxidative ageing in Texas pavements: hardening rates, hardening susceptibilities, and impact of pavement depth." *Transportation Research Record: Journal of the Transportation Research Board*(1962): 12–20.

Applied Research Associates, Inc. (ARA). ERES Consultants Division. (2004). Guide for Mechanistic-Empirical Design of New and Rehabilitated Pavement Structures, National Cooperative Highway Research Program, Transportation Research Board, National Research Council, Washington, DC.

ASTAE (2017). *Greenhouse Gas Emission Mitigation in Road Construction and Rehabilitation | Asia Sustainable and Alternative Energy Program*. www.astae.net/content/greenhouse-gas-emission-mitigation-road-construction-and-rehabilitation (last accessed October 28, 2017).

Bari, J. and M. Witczak (2007). "New predictive models for viscosity and complex shear modulus of asphalt binders: for use with mechanistic-empirical pavement design guide." *Transportation Research Record: Journal of the Transportation Research Board* (2001): 9–19.

Chatti, K. and I. Zaabar (2012). *Estimating the effects of pavement condition on vehicle operating costs*, Transportation Research Board.

Chatti, K., N. Buch, S. Haider, A. Pulipaka, R.W. Lyles, D. Gilliland, and P. Desaraju (2005). "LTPP data analysis: Influence of design and construction features on the response and performance of new flexible and rigid pavements." *Final Report. NCHRP Project*: 20–50.

Chong, D. and Y. Wang (2017). "Impacts of flexible pavement design and management decisions on life cycle energy consumption and carbon footprint." *The International Journal of Life Cycle Assessment* 22(6): 952–71.

Coons, R. F. (1965). *An Investigation of the Hardening of Asphalt Recovered from Pavements of Various Ages*. Georgia Institute of Technology.

Edenhofer, O., R. Pichs-Madruga, Y. Sokona, E. Farahani, S. Kadner, K. Seyboth, A. Adler, I. Baum, S. Brunner, and P. Eickemeier (2014). "Climate change 2014: mitigation of climate change." *Contribution of Working Group III to the Fifth Assessment Report of the Intergovernmental Panel on Climate Change* 5.

Fwa, T., W. Chan, and K. Hoque (2000). "Multiobjective optimization for pavement maintenance programming." *Journal of Transportation Engineering* 126(5): 367–74.

Glover, C.J., A.E. Martin, A. Chowdhury, R. Han, N. Prapaitrakul, X. Jin, and J. Lawrence (2009). "Evaluation of binder ageing and its influence in ageing of hot mix asphalt concrete: literature review and experimental design." Texas Transportation Institute, Texas, Rep. 0-6009-1, February 2009.

Han, R. (2011). *Improvement to a transport model of asphalt binder oxidation in pavements: Pavement temperature modeling, oxygen diffusivity in asphalt binders and mastics, and pavement air void characterization*, Texas A&M University.

Lau, C., K. Lunsford, C. Glover, R. Davison, and J. Bullin (1992). "Reaction rates and hardening susceptibilities as determined from pressure oxygen vessel ageing of asphalts." *Transportation Research Record* (1342): 50–7.

Mirza, M.W. and M.W. Witczak (1995). "Development of a global ageing system for short and long term ageing of asphalt cements (with discussion)." *Journal of the Association of Asphalt Paving Technologists* 64: 393–430.

Mndot (2017). MnROAD. www.mndot.gov/mnroad (last accessed October 25, 2017).

Negulescu, I., L. Mohammad, W. Daly, C. Abadie, R. Cueto, C. Daranga, and I. Glover (2006). "Chemical and rheological characterization of wet and dry ageing of SBS copolymer modified asphalt cements: Laboratory and field evaluation (with discussion)." *Journal of the Association of Asphalt Paving Technologists* 75: 267–96.

Petersen, J. and P. Harnsberger (1998). "Asphalt ageing: dual oxidation mechanism and its interrelationships with asphalt composition and oxidative age hardening." *Transportation Research Record: Journal of the Transportation Research Board* (1638): 47–55.

Petersen, J.C. (1986). "Quantitative functional group analysis of asphalts using differential infrared spectrometry and selective chemical reactions – theory and application." *Transportation Research Record* (1096): 1–11.

Petersen, J.C. (2009). "A review of the fundamentals of asphalt oxidation: chemical, physicochemical, physical property, and durability relationships." *Transportation Research E-Circular* (E-C140): 1–62.

Prapaitrakul, N. (2009). *Toward an Improved Model of Asphalt Binder Oxidation in Pavements*, Texas A&M University.

Prapaitrakul, N., R. Han, X. Jin, and C.J. Glover (2009). "A transport model of asphalt binder oxidation in pavements," *Road Materials and Pavement Design* 10(sup1): 95–113.

Ruan, Y., R. Davison, and C. Glover (2003). "An investigation of asphalt durability: Relationships between ductility and rheological properties for unmodified asphalts." *Petroleum Science and Technology* 21(1–2): 231–54.

Venner, M. (2004). "Environmental stewardship practices, procedures, and policies for highway construction and maintenance." Technical Report, Part of NCHRP Project 25-25 Project. Transportation Research Board, Washington DC.

Wang, P.Y., Y. Wen, K. Zhao, D. Chong, and A.S. Wong (2014). "Evolution and locational variation of asphalt binder ageing in long-life hot-mix asphalt pavements." *Construction and Building Materials* 68: 172–82.

Part V

Merging sustainability and resilience

23

Bridging the gap between sustainability and resilience of civil infrastructure using lifetime resilience

David Y. Yang and Dan M. Frangopol[1]

DEPARTMENT OF CIVIL AND ENVIRONMENTAL ENGINEERING, ATLSS ENGINEERING
RESEARCH CENTER, LEHIGH UNIVERSITY, BETHLEHEM, PA, USA

[1] DAN.FRANGOPOL@LEHIGH.EDU (CORRESPONDING AUTHOR)

23.1 Introduction

Civil infrastructure, the backbone of modern society, has a huge impact on sustainability. On the one hand, it serves as the physical foundation for human and commodity communications that can boost economic growth and reinforce social justice. On the other hand, construction and operation of civil infrastructure consume large amounts of energy and natural resources and may also incur or exacerbate social and environmental problems such as community degradation (Stromberg 2016), poverty (Semuels 2016), climate change, desertification, deforestation, and pollution (Kibert 2016).

According to the Brundtland report (Brundtland 1987), sustainable development is defined as "development that meets the needs of the present without compromising the ability of future generations to meet their own." This definition first highlights the inter-generational consideration for sustainable development. The Brundtland definition is sometimes criticized by its anthropocentric viewpoint. An alternative definition states that sustainable development should be able to "improve the quality of human life" while "conserving vitality and diversity of the Earth" by living within the "carrying capacity of the supporting ecosystem" (IUCN/UNEP/WWF 1991). This statement indicates the supply–demand relation in sustainability and emphasizes the environmental aspect of sustainable development.

In general, sustainability in civil engineering can be interpreted from two perspectives: functional integrity and structural longevity (Thompson 2010). The former encourages a holistic and multidimensional standpoint rather than the current cost-driven practice for construction projects; namely, in order to achieve functional integrity, sustainable development should consider economic, social, and environmental aspects of a project, which, in the context of sustainability, are usually referred to as the three pillars (United Nations General Assembly 2005) or triple bottom lines (LEED 2009). The latter stresses

419

the capability of infrastructure to withstand deterioration and to adapt to hazards and demand changes so that it can meet the needs of future generations. Overall, structural longevity deals mainly with the infrastructure itself during its life-cycle, while the functional integrity takes into account the community and ecosystem where the infrastructure is located. The two perspectives of sustainability suggest that sustainable development should be discussed on basis of comprehensive life-cycle assessment that encompasses all the three pillars. In addition, the supply–demand relation underneath the concept of sustainability indicates that reliability analysis and risk assessment, which quantify the probability and consequences of exceeding functional capacities, are important tools for the evaluation of sustainability of civil infrastructure.

Compared to other engineered systems, civil infrastructure has a much longer service life. To achieve structural longevity, sustainable infrastructure systems are expected to withstand and recover quickly from progressive deterioration due to aggressive environments as well as sudden functionality drop due to natural and man-made hazards. Both progressive and sudden deterioration are likely to compromise the longevity and functional integrity of civil infrastructure. In addition, post-hazard recovery plays an equally important role in the sustainability-informed life-cycle assessment, because both the lack of full functionality and the actions taken for recovery can have tremendous economic, social, and environmental impacts (Gardoni & Murphy 2008). Recently, studies on post-hazard recovery have drawn ever increasing attention under the name of resilience (Bocchini et al. 2014). Adapted from Timmerman's (1981) initial definition, infrastructure resilience can be defined in the context of sustainability as the ability of communities and ecosystems to withstand external shocks or perturbations to the infrastructure and to recover from such events. A complete sustainability assessment should bring in resilience considerations to reduce adverse impacts of hazards and manage post-hazard recovery in a sustainable manner (Bocchini et al. 2014; Dong & Frangopol 2015; Basu et al. 2015; Alibrandi & Mosalam 2017; Grabowski & Miller 2017). In order to include resilience in a sustainability-informed life-cycle assessment, it is necessary to introduce novel indicators for resilience from the life-cycle perspective.

In this chapter, existing studies on sustainability-informed life-cycle assessment are first reviewed. Tools to perform such assessment are then presented in detail. Specifically, multi-attribute utility theory is introduced for the functional integrity perspective of sustainability, while generic probabilistic models of deterioration and resilience are provided for sustainability-informed life-cycle assessment. To bridge the gap between sustainability and resilience, a novel concept referred herein as *lifetime resilience* (LR) is proposed considering lifetime hazards of a structure. Based on MAUT and LR, an integrated framework is proposed for probabilistic life-cycle optimization of civil infrastructure considering both sustainability and resilience.

23.2 Literature review

Since the early advocacy of sustainability, researchers and practitioners worldwide have made significant contributions to the sustainability of civil infrastructure, with both technological and methodological innovations. This chapter focuses primarily on methodological approaches for sustainability assessment and management. Current methods for sustainability assessment are largely based on rating systems developed in public and private sectors (e.g. the British Building Research Establishment Environmental Assessment Method (BREEAM) in the UK (Building Research Establishment 1990); the American Leadership in Energy and Environmental Design (LEED) system in the US (LEED 2009); the German Sustainable Building Council (DGNB) system (DGNB 2007); and the sustainable project appraisal routine (SPeAR) by ARUP (2000)). These rating systems are mainly for building structures and adopt qualitative indicators designed primarily for comparing different project proposals in the initial phase of development. A majority of these rating systems are targeted at the environmental aspect of sustainability, while few of them provide insights into the life-cycle performance of a project.

Due to the insufficiency of the aforementioned rating systems in reflecting the intrinsic characteristic of sustainability, a number of studies have been conducted to better assess and manage the sustainability of civil infrastructure. For highway bridges, sustainability-informed life-cycle assessment was conducted by Dong et al. (2013, 2014c), who monetized social and environmental consequences and incorporated them into a risk assessment framework for bridges and bridge networks under seismic hazards. Based on this sustainability assessment method, the same authors further developed a multi-objective decision support tool for pre-earthquake retrofit optimization of bridge networks (Dong et al. 2014b). For sustainability assessment, not all social and environmental factors can be converted to economic values. The utilities of these factors are largely dictated by the risk attitudes and risk perceptions of stakeholders. It has been shown that projects optimized based on economic and environmental criteria can have very different outlooks in terms of life-cycle performance (García-Segura et al. 2017). To this end, Sabatino et al. (2015) introduced the multi-attribute utility theory (MAUT) into sustainability assessment and proposed a MAUT-based framework for sustainability-informed maintenance optimization of highway bridges. This MAUT framework has proved to be a powerful tool to harmonize the three pillars of sustainability (Dong et al. 2015; Sabatino et al. 2016; Alibrandi & Mosalam 2017). Besides bridge structures, sustainability-informed life-cycle assessment has also been widely used in other types of civil infrastructure such as pavement systems (FHWA 2015) and geotechnical projects (Basu et al. 2015). Based on the previous discussion, sustainability-informed life-cycle assessment should underpin the methodology for sustainability assessment and management of civil infrastructure.

As mentioned previously, civil infrastructure suffers from both progressive and sudden deterioration in their service life. Nevertheless, most of the existing studies on sustainability assessment did not consider the adverse impacts of hazards that result in sudden drops of structural performance (Dong & Frangopol 2016a). Although some studies did include hazards in sustainability assessment and management (Dong et al. 2013, 2014b, 2014c), they dealt mainly with pre-event mitigation measures instead of post-event recovery, i.e. resilience.

Despite the close relation between sustainability and resilience, only a few studies have been conducted in the pursuit of an integrated framework for sustainability and resilience. The first holistic framework trying to unify sustainability and resilience was proposed by Bocchini et al. (2014), who assimilated the method for multi-hazard risk assessment and proposed the use of weighted impacts to consider both sustainability and resilience. Based on MAUT, Alibrandi and Mosalam (2017) presented a conceptual decision support tool for sustainable and resilient design of building structures. Although resilience was formulated as an attribute of the overall utility, the economic, social, and environmental impacts due to recovery actions were not taken into account. Details on how sustainability and resilience are coupled were not provided either. Additionally, most of the existing studies on resilience are built on "what-if" scenarios, namely, the resilience performance is based on an assumed hazard scenario. As the occurrence of a hazard is usually a stochastic process, the resilience performance at certain specified points-in-time cannot fit into the overall life-cycle performance of a structure. This chapter is aimed at solving this misalignment of sustainability and resilience studies using the concept of lifetime resilience.

23.3 Three pillars of sustainability assessment

Economic, social, and environmental impacts of a project constitute the three pillars for sustainable development. Only through this multidimensional consideration can the functional integrity associated with an infrastructure project be preserved. From the economic aspect, sustainability assessment in a life-cycle context should include the initial cost, the intervention cost incurred during the service life, and salvage value (if exists, e.g. through recycle and reuse). From the social aspect, failure of civil infrastructure may impact local communities in various fronts (e.g. fatalities, displaced households, or shelter requirements under hazards (Wei et al. 2016)). From the environmental aspect, gaseous/pollution emissions, and energy consumption are widely used for sustainability assessment, while various other metrics are proposed in the literature, e.g. global warming potential, carbon footprint, embodied carbon dioxide, and embodied energy (Basu et al. 2015).

For bridge structures, quantification of economic, social, and environmental impacts has been conducted in various studies (Dong et al. 2013, 2014c, 2015; Sabatino et al. 2016). If the salvage value is ignored, the life-cycle economic cost of a structure can be evaluated by the following equation (Sabatino et al. 2016)

$$C_{ec} = \sum_{j=0}^{m} \frac{r_j c_{reb} \cdot WL}{(1+r)^{t_j}},$$

(23.1)

where c_{reb} is the (re)building cost per square meter; r_j is the ratio of the j-th intervention action at time t_j to c_{reb} ($j = 0$ indicates that values are associated with initial construction time or cost); W and L are the bridge width and length, respectively; r is the discount ratio of money; and m is the total number of intervention actions.

For social impacts, bridge failure or intervention indicates extra travel time and distance that traffic users must endure, in addition to any fatalities that may occur. In the service life of a bridge, extra travel time (T_{tr}) and distance (D_{tr}) can be expressed as (Sabatino et al. 2015):

$$T_{tr} = \sum_{j=1}^{m} \left[O_{car} \cdot (1-\alpha_v) + O_{truck} \cdot \alpha_v \right] \frac{L_D \cdot A(t_j) \cdot d_j}{v_D}$$

(23.2)

and

$$D_{tr} = \sum_{j=1}^{m} L_D \cdot A(t_j) \cdot d_j,$$

(23.3)

where O_{car} and O_{truck} are the vehicle occupancies for cars and trucks, respectively; α_v is the ratio of average daily truck traffic to average daily traffic; L_D is the detour length; $A(t_j)$ is the average daily traffic in year t_j; d_j is the duration in days of the j-th intervention action; v_D is the speed on detour. Equations (23.2) and (23.3) can be expressed in economic terms as follows (Dong et al. 2014b; García-Segura et al. 2017):

$$C_{tr,T} = \sum_{j=1}^{m} \left[c_{AW} O_{car} \cdot (1-\alpha_v) + \left(c_{ATC} O_{truck} + c_{good} \right) \cdot \alpha_v \right] \cdot \frac{L_D \cdot A(t_j) \cdot d_j}{v_D} \cdot \frac{1}{(1+r)^{t_j}}$$

(23.4)

$$C_{tr,D} = \sum_{j=1}^{m} \left[c_{run,car} \cdot (1-\alpha_v) + c_{run,truck} \cdot \alpha_v \right] \cdot L_D \cdot A(t_j) \cdot d_j \cdot \frac{1}{(1+r)^{t_i}}, \tag{23.5}$$

where $C_{tr,T}$ and $C_{tr,D}$ are the extra travel expenses associated with extra travel time and distance, respectively; c_{AW} is the average wage of car drivers; c_{ATC} is the average compensation for truck drivers; c_{good} is the time value of a cargo; $c_{run,car}$ and $c_{run,truck}$ are the running costs for cars and trucks, respectively. As both costs (i.e. $C_{tr,T}$ and $C_{tr,D}$) are incurred by traffic users due to detour, they can be added up to represent the total extra travel expenses (C_{tr}) of travel users, i.e. $C_{tr} = C_{tr,T} + C_{tr,D}$. For fatality estimation, the following equation can be used given bridge failure (Sabatino et al. 2015):

$$N_{fl} = \left(\frac{L}{d_f} + 1 \right) \cdot \left[O_{car} \cdot (1-\alpha_v) + O_{truck} \cdot \alpha_v \right], \tag{23.6}$$

where N_{fl} is the estimated number of fatalities given bridge failure; d_f is the safe following distance.

Construction and intervention, as well as extra travel distance, have environmental impacts. For highway bridges, the environmental impact from these activities can be estimated in a similar manner to economic and social impacts presented previously. For construction and intervention, environmental consequences can be expressed as (Dong et al. 2014b; Sabatino et al. 2015)

$$E_{en} = \sum_{j=1}^{m} \varepsilon_j E_{reb} \cdot WL, \tag{23.7}$$

where E_{en} is the environmental metrics of interest (e.g., CO_2 emissions or energy consumption); E_{reb} is the unit environmental cost measured in the environmental metrics per square meter. For environmental consequences associated with detour, the following equation can be formulated similar to Equation (23.5) (Dong et al. 2014b; Sabatino et al. 2015):

$$E_{tr,D} = \sum_{j=1}^{m} \left[E_{car} \cdot (1-\alpha_v) + E_{truck} \cdot \alpha_v \right] \cdot D \cdot A(t_j) \cdot d_j, \tag{23.8}$$

where E_{car} and E_{truck} are the environmental metrics of interest associated with car and truck operations, respectively. By comparing Equations (23.7) and (23.8) to Equations (23.1) and (23.5), it can be found that the environmental impact differs from economic and social impacts in the sense that time value is not considered for the environmental impact. This feature can lead to changes in sustainability management strategies (García-Segura et al. 2017).

23.4 Multi-attribute utility theory

The most direct way to consider all three aspects of sustainability is to monetize all impacts and convert the sustainability-informed life-cycle assessment to life-cycle cost analysis (Dong et al. 2013, 2014b, 2014c). However, such an endeavor to consider sustainability is subjected to many limitations and pitfalls. First of all, not all quantities in social and environmental aspects can or should be monetized in sustainability assessment and management. For instance, is it ethical to monetize fatalities purely based on insurance data and/or lifetime incomes? Is the reduction of CO_2 emissions a moral obligation or a profitable business? These moral concerns in social and environmental aspects, once entering market domain, can dramatically alter the behavior of stakeholders (Ariely 2008), leading to unexpected consequences such as the infringement of social justice (e.g. exploitation of residents with little political and economic capital) and the failure of environmental goals (e.g. degradation of the emission reduction goal to a zero-sum game). Even for quantities that can be modeled reasonably in economic terms, simply adding economic costs together means the neglect of different risk attitudes and risk perceptions of different stakeholders. For instance, extra travel expenses are incurred by all traffic users. These expenses can be several orders higher than economic costs to bridge managers. Therefore, extra travel expenses, if added to construction/intervention costs directly, may distort the importance of social impacts.

In order to reconcile different aspects of sustainability, multi-attribute utility theory (MAUT) can be used (Sabatino et al. 2016). Herein, utility indicates the desirability of a decision alternative to a decision-maker. Utility theory provides a powerful tool to decision-makers for rationally comparing different decision alternatives. In the context of sustainable development, an attribute can be the economic, social, or environmental dimension of a project. For multiple attributes, MAUT is used to combine different attributes so that trade-offs can be obtained (Keeney & Raiffa 1993). Overall, MAUT used for sustainability assessment can be summarized by the flowchart in Figure 23.1. This general procedure includes: (a) selection of attributes and sub-attributes; (b) quantification of risk attitudes and risk perceptions of the decision maker; (c) selection of utility functions for single-attribute utilities; (d) selection of weighting factors to combine multiple attributes; (e) calculation of multi-attribute utilities of different decision alternatives. It is worth mentioning that each

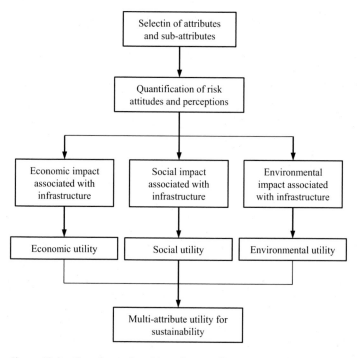

Figure 23.1   Flowchart of multi-attribute utility assessment of sustainability.
Source: Adapted from Sabatino et al. 2015.

single-attribute can also include sub-attributes. For instance, extra travel expenses and fatalities can be considered as two sub-attributes of the social impact, while CO_2 emissions and energy consumption can be two sub-attributes of the environmental impact. Scaling up from sub-attributes to single-attribute can follow similar procedures from single-attribute to multi-attribute (i.e. Figure 23.1).

Once single-attribute values are determined, risk attitudes and risk perceptions of the decision maker are quantified. Risk attitudes describe whether the decision maker is risk-averse, risk-seeking, or risk neutral, whereas risk perceptions provide the boundary values of different attributes from the decision maker's perspective. The determination of risk attitudes and risk perceptions dictates the form of utility functions. Generally, two types of utility functions exist: (a) one where utilities increase with attribute values, and (b) one where utilities decrease with attribute values (Sabatino et al. 2016). For the former, the utility function can be represented as

$$u_{a,inc} = \frac{1}{1-\exp(-\gamma)} \cdot \left[1-\exp\left(-\gamma \cdot \frac{a-a_{min}}{a_{max}-a_{min}} \right) \right],$$ (23.9)

where a, a_{min}, and a_{max} are the attribute value and its lower and upper bounds, respectively; $u_{a,inc}$ is the utility ($u_{a,inc}=0$ for $a \leq a_{min}$, and $u_{a,inc}=1$ for $a \geq a_{max}$); γ is the risk attribute of the decision maker ($\gamma>0$, $\gamma<0$, and $\gamma=0$ indicate risk aversion, risk seeking, and risk neutrality, respectively). Decreasing utility functions can be expressed as

$$u_{a,dec} = \frac{1}{1-\exp(-\gamma)} \cdot \left[1-\exp\left(-\gamma \cdot \frac{a_{max}-a}{a_{max}-a_{min}} \right) \right],$$ (23.10)

where $u_{a,dec}$ is the utility ($u_{a,dec}=0$ for $a \geq a_{max}$, and $u_{a,dec}=1$ for $a \leq a_{min}$). Figure 23.2 shows schematically the shape of both types of utility functions with respect to different values of gamma.

For multi-attribute utilities, weighting factors reflect the relative importance of different attributes from the decision maker's perspective. Assuming independent attributes, a simple additive formulation shown in the following equation can be utilized (Stewart 1996):

$$u_m = w_{ec}u_{ec} + w_{so}u_{so} + w_{en}u_{en},$$ (23.11)

where u_m is the overall utility; u_{ec}, u_{so}, and u_{en} are the utilities associated with the economic, social, and environmental impacts, respectively; w_{ec}, w_{so}, and w_{en} are the weighting factors for u_{ec}, u_{so}, and u_{en}, respectively; $0 \prec [w_{ec}, w_{so}, w_{en}] \prec 1$ and $w_{ec} + w_{so} + w_{en} = 1$. Usually, weighting factors are difficult to quantify. In cases where the decision maker has an estimated range of the weighting factor for each attribute, Jiménez et al. (2003) proposed the following equation to determine weighting factors:

$$w_i = \frac{w_i^L + w_i^U}{\sum_{i=1}^3 \left(w_i^L + w_i^u \right)},$$ (23.12)

where w_i^L and w_i^U are the lower and upper bounds of the i-th attribute; for sustainability assessment, there are three attributes in total, associated with economic, social, and environmental aspects respectively.

It should be noted that the use of linear combination (Equation (23.11)) suggests independence of different attributes, which may sometimes be invalid. For example, embodied energy and cost are usually correlated (Jiao et al. 2012), resulting in possible correlation between u_{ec}

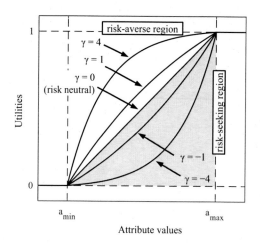

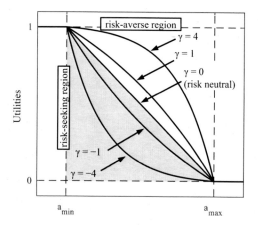

Figure 23.2 Exponential utility functions: utilities (a) increase and (b) decrease with attribute values.

Source: Adapted from Sabatino et al. 2016.

and u_{en}. In this case, other forms of combination are recommended (Stewart 1996). Usually, utility estimation contains uncertainties. Hence, probabilistic MAUT should be used to compare expected utilities of different decision alternatives (Ang & Tang 1984). In high-uncertainty domains, the assumption of human rationality, underpinning the use of expected utilities for decision-making, may be in question (Tversky & Kahneman 1992). In this case, other methods can be considered, such as the prospect theory (Cha & Ellingwood 2012, 2013) and the life profitability method (Gardoni et al. 2016).

23.5 Generic models of deterioration and resilience

MAUT discussed previously is targeted at the functional integrity perspective of sustainability. The other perspective, structural longevity, should be assessed in the context of life-cycle civil engineering. Civil infrastructure is expected to serve for a relatively long time, even across several generations. During the service life, a structure is subjected to progressive deterioration due to environmental stressors (e.g. corrosion) and long-term effects (e.g. fatigue) as well as sudden performance drops from natural and man-made hazards (e.g. earthquakes, floods, fires, and explosions). All these detrimental events, progressive or sudden, would reduce the safety and serviceability of structures. In the following discussion, generic models of deterioration and resilience are presented. Herein, the former refers strictly to progressive deterioration, while the latter deals with structural response and recovery of deteriorating infrastructure under hazards. As many uncertainties are involved in performance prediction, reliability indices are used to represent structural performance (Frangopol 2011). As stated at the beginning of this chapter, the use of structural reliability analysis also underlines the supply–demand relation in sustainability assessment.

23.5.1 Generic model of deterioration

Many mechanisms can lead to the deterioration of structural performance, including corrosion, fatigue, and their coupling effects (Ellingwood 2005; Frangopol & Soliman 2016; Frangopol et al. 2017; Jia & Gardoni 2018). All these mechanisms can reduce the load-carrying capacities of structures, compromise structural reliability, and even lead to catastrophic structural failure. Various models have been proposed to predict the effects of different deterioration mechanisms during the service life of structures (Biondini & Frangopol 2016). In order to ensure structural safety and serviceability, multiple intervention actions are usually made during the structure's service life to prevent, reduce, and/or reverse adverse effects from deterioration. As illustrated in Figure 23.3, both deterioration and intervention involve many uncertainties including those arising from (a) initial performance; (b) time of damage initiation; (c) deterioration rate without intervention; (d) intervention time; (e) improvement due to intervention; (f) deterioration rate under intervention effects; (g) duration of intervention effects; and (h) deterioration rate after intervention effects (Frangopol et al. 2001). As a result, the generic model for structural performance deterioration can be expressed in terms of the reliability index $\beta(t)$ as:

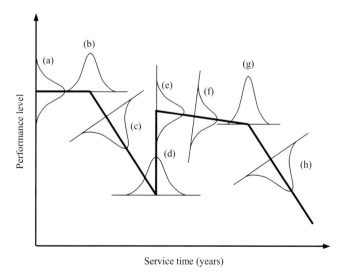

Figure 23.3 Uncertainties in the structural life-cycle.
Source: Adapted from Frangopol et al. 2001.

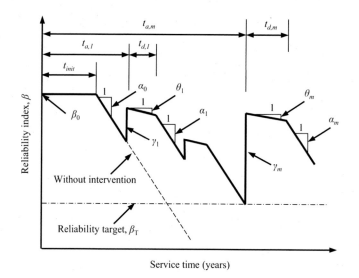

Figure 23.4 Generic model of deterioration in terms of reliability indices.
Source: Adapted from Frangopol et al. 2001.

$$\beta(t) = \begin{cases} \beta(t_{a,m}) - (t_{a,m} + t_{d,m} - t) \cdot \theta_m & \text{if } t \le t_{a,m} + t_{d,m} \\ \beta(t_{a,m}) - t_{d,m} \cdot \theta_m - (t - t_{a,m} - t_{d,m}) \cdot \alpha_m & \text{if } t > t_{a,m} + t_{d,m} \end{cases} \tag{23.13}$$

and

$$\beta(t_{a,m}) = \begin{cases} \beta_0 & \text{if } m = 0 \\ \beta_0 + \sum_{i=0}^{m-1} \gamma_i - t_{d,i} \cdot \theta_i - (t_{a,i+1} - t_{a,i} - t_{d,i}) \cdot \alpha_i & \text{if } m \ge 1, \end{cases}$$

where β_0 is the initial reliability index; $\beta(t_{a,m})$ is the reliability index after the most recent intervention actions; $t_{a,i}$ $(i = 1, 2, \dots, m)$ is the time for the ith intervention; $t_{d,i}$ $(i = 1, 2, \dots, m)$ is the duration of the intervention effects associated with the ith intervention; γ_i $(i = 1, 2, \dots, m)$ is the improvement of reliability indices due to the ith intervention; θ_i $(i = 1, 2, \dots, m)$ is the deterioration rate under the intervention effects associated with the ith intervention; α_i $(i = 1, 2, \dots, m)$ is the deterioration rate before the $(i+1)$th intervention but after the intervention effects associated with the ith intervention; parameters in Equation (23.13) are illustrated in Figure 23.4. If a group of structures is under consideration, reliability profiles of all structures can be represented by random variables (Frangopol et al. 2001). Despite the linear deterioration assumption, Equation (23.13) has been widely used in reliability-based infrastructure management (Van-Noortwijk & Frangopol 2004).

23.5.2 Generic model of resilience

The resilience model presented herein reflects the recovery of structural functionality under hazards. Various analytical definitions of resilience exist in the literature (Bocchini & Frangopol 2011; Frangopol & Bocchini 2011). Herein, resilience is defined by the following equation (Bocchini & Frangopol 2011):

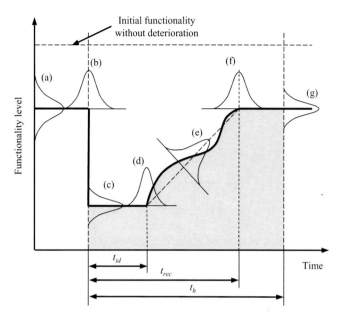

Figure 23.5 Uncertainties in a resilience process.
Source: Adapted from Decò et al. 2013.

$$R = \frac{\int_{t_0}^{t_0 + t_h} Q(t)\,dt}{t_h \cdot Q_{init}}, \tag{23.14}$$

where $Q(t)$ is the time-variant functionality of a structure under a hazard; t_0 is the time of hazard occurrence; t_h is the time horizon under consideration; Q_{init} is the initial functionality. Schematically, the numerator in Equation (23.14) represents the area under the functionality recovery path, as represented by the shaded area in Figure 23.5. The model is generic in the sense that the definition is independent of the hazard that causes the functionality drop. Therefore, the same definition can be used for various hazards such as earthquakes, floods, and hurricanes. Similar to structural deterioration, various uncertainties are associated with resilience, including those of (a) initial functionality; (b) time of hazard occurrence; (c) residual functionality; (d) idle time; (e) recovery path; (f) recover duration; and (g) functionality after recovery (Decò et al. 2013). These uncertainties are illustrated in Figure 23.5. It should be noted that structural functionality is a general concept, for which various indicators are applicable. By using reliability indices and linear approximation, the generic model for resilience can be expressed as (Decò et al. 2013)

$$R = \begin{cases} \dfrac{(\beta_c - \xi) \cdot t_{id} + 0.5 \cdot (\beta_r - \beta_c + \xi) \cdot t_h^2 / t_{rec} + (\beta_c - \xi) \cdot t_h}{t_h \cdot \beta_0} & \text{if } t_h < t_{rec} \\[4mm] \dfrac{(\beta_c - \xi) \cdot t_{id} + 0.5 \cdot (\beta_c + \beta_r - \xi) \cdot t_{rec} + \beta_r \cdot (t_h - t_{rec})}{t_h \cdot \beta_0} & \text{if } t_h \geq t_{rec}, \end{cases} \tag{23.15}$$

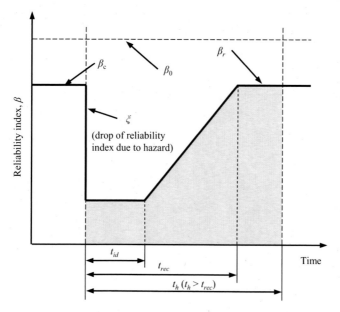

Figure 23.6 Generic model of resilience in terms of reliability indices.
Source: Adapted from Decò et al. 2013.

where β_0, β_c, and β_r are the initial reliability index without deterioration, current reliability index prior to hazards, recovered reliability index after hazards $(\beta_r \leq \beta_0)$; ξ is the immediate reliability drop due to hazards; t_{id} and t_{rec} are the duration of idle time and the duration of recovery, respectively; t_h is the time horizon under consideration. The model is shown schematically in Figure 23.6.

23.5.3 Interaction between sustainability and resilience

Sustainability and resilience have drastically different time horizons under consideration. Sustainability, from the structural longevity perspective, considers the entire life-cycle of a structure, which may span generations; resilience, defined based on a "what-if" scenario, focuses primarily on the period from the hazard occurrence to the completion of recovery. Only a few models tried to combine sustainability and resilience. Bocchini et al. (2014) proposed a method to unify sustainability and resilience based on their impacts. Despite being simple and effective, the interaction between sustainability and resilience is neglected. In fact, resilience of a structure is affected by its performance upon hazard occurrence (Dong et al. 2014a; Biondini et al. 2015; Dong & Frangopol 2016b), whereas hazards in general cause severe and sudden functionality drops that may overshadow progressive deterioration and dominate the life-cycle performance of the structure. Therefore, it should be recognized that events with sustainability impacts (e.g. structural deterioration) may change the resilience performance of structures under hazards and vice versa. The interaction between sustainability (structural longevity perspective) and resilience can be well illustrated by Figure 23.7. This interaction indicates that sustainability and resilience should be analyzed in an integrated manner.

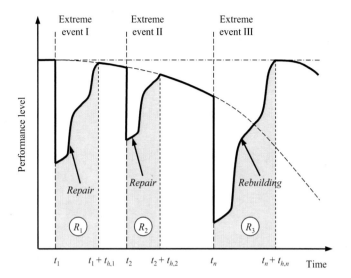

Figure 23.7 Interaction between sustainability (structural longevity perspective) and resilience.
Source: Adapted from Dong et al. 2014; Biondini et al. 2015; Dong and Frangopol 2016b.

23.6 Integrated framework for sustainability-resilience assessment and management

23.6.1 Expected lifetime resilience

As mentioned previously, an important obstacle that gaps the sustainability and resilience assessment is their different time horizons of interest. During the service life of a structure, hazards can occur at different points-in-time (see Figure 23.7) and, thus, different resilience performance for each hazard has to be considered. In order to bridge the gap, the concept of *lifetime resilience* is introduced herein. For a sequence of hazards occurred during the structure's service life, the resilience associated with each hazard can be evaluated based on the generic deterioration and resilience models. Herein, two types of recovery are differentiated. For the first type, the structure under a hazard is considered less severely damaged so that quick recovery can put back the structural performance to its pre-hazard level, which, nevertheless, is still lower than the initial performance due to previous deterioration. For the second type, the hazard is considered to have caused severe damage to the structure to such an extent that rebuilding is triggered. In this scenario, the structure, by rebuilding, recovers to a prescribed performance level (e.g. initial performance). To distinguish the two types of recovery, the former is referred to herein as "recovery," while the later "restoration." Suppose that the time horizon for resilience (t_h in Equation (23.15)) is the same for all hazard occurrences, lifetime resilience can be defined by the following equation:

$$R_L = \frac{\sum_{i=1}^{n_h} R_i \cdot t_h}{n_h \cdot t_h} = \frac{\sum_{i=1}^{n_h} R_i}{n_h}, \tag{23.16}$$

where n_h is the number of hazards; R_i is the resilience associated with hazard i. If the arrival of hazards is regarded as a stochastic process, lifetime resilience becomes a random value.

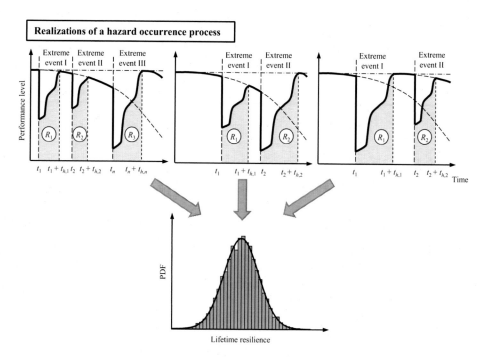

Figure 23.8 Illustration of probabilistic lifetime resilience.

Figure 23.8 shows that the concept of probabilistic lifetime resilience schematically. Probabilistic lifetime resilience can then be converted to utility values based on upper and lower limits of R_L and an increasing utility function (i.e. Equation 23.9). Lifetime resilience is an important indicator of the life-cycle resilience performance of a structure, which can also bridge the gap between sustainability and resilience assessment.

23.6.2 Framework formulation

Based on MAUT and lifetime resilience, an integrated framework is proposed herein for probabilistic optimization of civil infrastructure considering sustainability and resilience. The proposed framework considers the three attributes of sustainability (i.e. economic, social, and environmental aspects) using MAUT. Multi-attribute utilities are used to evaluate the sustainability performance associated with lifetime risk, intervention actions, and lifetime resilience. These three facets of sustainability performance are then used as the three objectives in multi-objective optimization to maximize the utilities associated with risk, intervention, and resilience. Based on the results of multi-objective optimization, a series of solutions representing optimal trade-offs of objectives can be obtained. The proposed framework is represented by the flowchart in Figure 23.9.

The risk of a structure is defined as the product of the failure probability and the failure consequences:

$$\rho = P_f \cdot \mathcal{X},$$

(23.17)

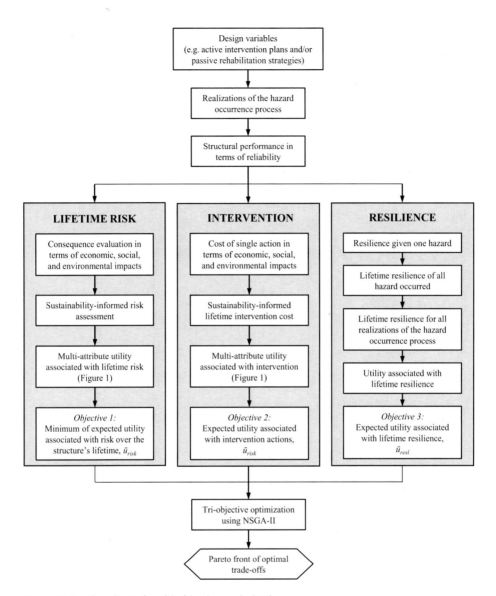

Figure 23.9 Flowchart of multi-objective optimization.

where P_f is the failure; $\mathcal{X}$ is the value of consequences evaluated in terms of economic, social, and environmental impacts, which can be calculated using Equations (23.1) to (23.8). It should be noted that, in most cases, the time horizon associated with a hazard is much shorter than that for life-cycle assessment. Therefore, the variation of failure risk within the time horizon associated with a hazard is neglected in risk assessment. As the decision-maker always prefers minimizing the lifetime risk, Equation (23.11) is used to obtain the multi-attribute utility values associated with lifetime risk. Intervention actions can affect the life-cycle performance of a structures (e.g. lifetime failure risk and lifetime resilience) and incur costs in economic, social, and environmental terms. These costs can be evaluated using Equations (23.1) to (23.8). Similar to risk, costs associated with intervention actions can be converted to utility values using Equation (23.11). Different rehabilitation methods for recovery and restoration actions under hazards can also be treated in a similar manner to that for intervention actions. In fact, rehabilitation methods can be considered as reactive intervention actions that are triggered by hazards. Therefore, the costs of these actions should also be included in the cost of intervention actions. It should be noted that recovery and restoration actions can deliver different lifetime resilience performance, which can be converted to utility values using Equation (23.9). Overall, the proposed framework can be summarized by the following optimization formulation:

Given:
- The consequence models, multi-attribute utility models, and models of deterioration and resilience as well as the parameters for all these models;

Find:
- The optimal plan for proactive intervention (i.e. intervention actions without consideration of hazards) and reactive actions under hazards;

So that:
- The expected value of the minimum utility associated with risk over the structure's lifetime is maximized;
- The expected value of the utility associated with proactive and reactive intervention actions is maximized;
- The expected value of the utility associated with lifetime resilience is maximized;

Subjected to:
- Reliability constraints in the structure's service life;
- Other constraints applicable.

23.6.3 Illustrative example

The proposed framework is illustrated using a bridge that is assumed to be newly constructed. The basic information of the bridge is summarized in Table 23.1. The functional integrity perspective of sustainability is considered using MAUT. Among the possible sub-attributes in each single-attribute, the example takes into account only one sub-attribute for each single-attribute, namely, intervention costs for economic impacts (Equation (23.1)), extra travel expenses for social impacts (Equations (23.4) and (23.5)), and CO_2 emissions for environmental impacts (Equations (23.7) and (23.8)). It should be mentioned that multiple sub-attributes are possible in the proposed framework by following the same procedure used to construct multi-attribute utilities from single-attribute utilities. The parameters used to calculate single-attribute values are listed in Table 23.2. In order to obtain multi-attribute utilities in terms of sustainability, lower and upper attribute values are selected for risk, intervention, and resilience respectively, as shown in Table 23.3. For all three attributes, it is assumed that the decision-maker is risk-averse with $\gamma = 2$ in Equations (23.9) and (23.10). In addition, weighting factors are selected to be $1/3$ for all three attributes.

The structural longevity perspective of sustainability is evaluated with sustainability-informed life-cycle assessment. In order to obtain the life-cycle performance of the bridge, the generic models in Equations (23.13) and (23.15) are used. In this example, intervention actions planned beforehand are referred to as proactive intervention actions, which are planned to ensure that the reliability level of the bridge is always higher than a prescribed threshold, i.e. $\beta_T = 1$.

Table 23.1 Bridge information

Notation	Description	Mean	COV	Distribution*	References
W	Bridge width	10.4 (m)	—	Det.	Sabatino et al. (2016)
L	Bridge length	64.5 (m)	—	Det.	Sabatino et al. (2016)
A	Average daily traffic (ADT)	100,000	—	Det.	Dong, Frangopol & Saydam (2014b)
α_p	Average daily truck traffic to ADT	0.12	0.2	LN	Dong, Frangopol & Saydam (2014b)
L_{detour}	Detour length	10 (km)	—	Det.	Sabatino et al. (2016)
v_{detour}	Speed on detour	30 (km/h)	0.15	LN	Dong, Frangopol & Saydam (2014b)

Note: Det. = Deterministic; LN = Lognormal

Table 23.2 Parameters for consequence evaluation

Notation	Description	Mean	COV	Distribution*	References
c_{reb}	Rebuilding	1292 (USD/m²)	0.2	LN	Dong, Frangopol & Saydam (2014)
c_{rep}	Repair	258.4 (USD/m²)	0.2	LN	Assumed
c_{truck}	Compensation for truck drivers	29.28 (USD/h)	0.31	LN	Dong et al. (2014)
c_{car}	Average wage of car drivers	23.36 (USD/h)	0.28	LN	Dong et al. (2014)
O_{car}	Vehicle occupancies for cars	1.5	0.15	LN	Dong et al. (2014)
O_{truck}	Vehicle occupancies for trucks	1.05	0.15	LN	Dong et al. (2014)
$c_{run,car}$	Running costs for cars	0.40 (USD/km)	0.2	LN	Dong et al. (2014)
$c_{run,truck}$	Running costs for trucks	0.56 (USD/km)	0.2	LN	Dong et al. (2014)
c_{good}	Time value of a cargo	3.81 (USD/h)	0.2	LN	Dong et al. (2014)
L_D	Detour length	10 (km)	-	Det.	Sabatino et al. (2016)
A	Average daily traffic	100,000	-	Det.	Assumed
v_D	Speed on detour	30 (km/h)	0.15	LN	Dong et al.(2014)
T_{reb}	Rebuilding time $(T_{reb} \geq 2/3)$	1 (year)	1/3	Shifted Exp. $(\lambda = 3)$	Assumed
E_{reb}	CO2 emissions w/ rebuilding	159 (kg/m²)	0.2 (assumed)	LN	Sabatino et al. (2016)
E_{car}	CO2 emissions of cars	0.22 (kg/km)	0.2	LN	Dong et al. (2014, 2015)
E_{truck}	CO2 emissions of trucks	0.56 (kg/km)	0.2	LN	Dong et al. (2014, 2015)
T_{rep}	Repair time	0.33 (year)	0.2	LN	Assumed

Note: Det. = Deterministic; LN = Lognormal; Shifted Exp. = Shifted exponential

Table 23.3 Lower and upper bounds of single-attribute values

Objective	Single-attribute	Minimum	Maximum	Utility function
Risk	Economic (USD)	0	5.0×10^4	Equation (23.10)
	Social (USD)	0	2.5×10^7	Equation (23.10)
	Environmental (kg)	0	1.0×10^4	Equation (23.10)
Intervention	Economic (USD)	2.0×10^5	5.0×10^5	Equation (23.10)
	Social (USD)	1.2×10^8	4.5×10^8	Equation (23.10)
	Environmental (kg)	2.0×10^7	7.0×10^7	Equation (23.10)
Resilience	—	0.4	1.0	Equation (23.9)

For the deterioration model (Equation (23.13)), the initial reliability index is assumed to be 5.0 (i.e. $\beta_0 = 5.0$); the deterioration rate $\alpha_i = \alpha = 0.1$ per year; proactive actions are assumed to be able to restore the load-carrying capacity (i.e. γ_i will increase the reliability level back to β_0) but not effective in stopping further deterioration (i.e. $t_{d,i} = 0$). The occurrence of hazards is assumed to be a Poisson process with parameter $\lambda = 0.02$, i.e. the period between two adjacent hazards follows an exponential distribution with the mean value of $1 / \lambda = 50$ years. It is also assumed that the occurrence of each hazard will lead to a unit drop of reliability index, i.e. $\alpha = 1.0$. The recovery and restoration actions triggered by hazards are herein referred to as reactive intervention actions. The effect of a recovery action on the structural reliability is considered to be the same as that of a proactive intervention action. A restoration action (i.e. rebuilding) is only triggered when the reliability index after a hazard drops below the threshold β_T. This action can not only restore the load-carrying capacity but also re-exert a damage initial period. It is also assumed that if a hazard occurs in a year with planned proactive intervention, a restoration action is triggered no matter if the reliability index reaches the threshold.

With the proposed framework, various variables related to the structural life-cycle can be optimized, including the time and type of proactive intervention actions as well as the form of recover/restoration actions (reactive intervention actions). For illustration purposes, only the times for proactive intervention actions are scheduled with multi-objective optimization considering three objectives: utilities associated with risk, intervention cost, and lifetime resilience. Therefore, the multi-objective optimization problem can be formulated as follows.

Given:
- Equations (23.1), (23.4), (23.5), (23.7), and (23.8) as consequence models and their parameters in Tables 23.1 and 23.2;
- Equations (23.9) and (23.10) with $\gamma = 2$ as utility models and upper and lower limits in Table 23.3;
- Equations (23.13) and (23.15) as deterioration and resilience models, respectively;
- Structural service life $t_L = 100$ years;

Find:
- The number of proactive intervention actions and the time for their implementation, i.e. m and $t_{int} = \left[t_{a,1}, t_{a,2}, \ldots, t_{a,m} \right]$;

So that:
- The expected values of u_{risk}, u_{intv}, and u_{res} (as shown in Figure 23.9) are maximized;

Subjected to:
- Reliability index threshold $\beta(t) > \beta_T = 1.0$;
- $m \in \{2, 3, 4\}$ and $t_{int,i+1} - t_{int,i} \geq 1$ year.

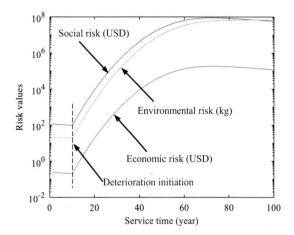

Figure 23.10 Lifetime risk values without intervention actions.

Table 23.4 Solutions on Pareto front

Solution	Time of active Intervention (years)	Expected utilities		
		Risk ($\bar{u}_{risk}$)	Resilience ($\bar{u}_{resil}$)	Intervention ($\bar{u}_{intv}$)
A	[40, 70]	0.951	0.727	0.571
B	[31, 55, 75]	0.992	0.824	0.490
C	[27, 46, 64, 80]	0.998	0.872	0.436

For the bridge under consideration, lifetime risk values without intervention actions are shown in Figure 23.10 in terms of economic, social, and environmental risks, respectively. It is worth mentioning that the discount rate has a significant effect on the shape of risk evolution. Because of discount rate, monetary risk values decrease before deterioration initiation, while environmental risk with non-monetary consequences stays the same. Without any intervention actions, failure probabilities will approach to one in the later stage of service life. As a result, the discount rate again leads to slight decreases for economic and social risks. It should also be noted that the unit of environmental risk is different from that of economic and social risks, while the social risk, which is imposed on all traffic users, is much higher than the economic risk posed to stakeholders. Therefore, MAUT provides a feasible tool to combine all three aspects rationally. For two proactive intervention actions at years 40 and 70 (i.e. $t_{int} = [40, 70]$), distributions of utilities associated with risk, intervention and resilience (i.e. u_{risk}, u_{intv}, and u_{resl}) are obtained using Monte Carlo simulation with 10,000 samples and are shown in Figure 23.11. The expected utility values are also denoted in Figure 23.11. The Pareto front of the multi-objective optimization problem is attained using nondominated sorting genetic algorithm II (Deb et al. 2002) and is presented in Figure 23.12. For points A, B, and C located on the Pareto front in Figure 23.12a, Table 23.4 summarizes the expected utilities associated with risk, resilience, and intervention, respectively. As expected, with more proactive intervention actions, the utilities associated with intervention actions decrease, while the utilities associated with risk and resilience increase.

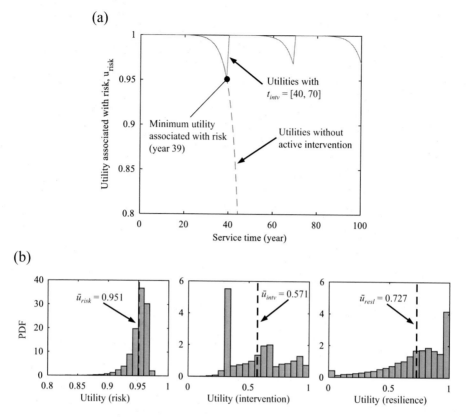

Figure 23.11 Sustainability-informed life-cycle assessment: (a) lifetime utilities associated with risk; (b) distributions of utilities associated with risk, intervention, and resilience.

It should be noted that, with certain simplifications, utilities associated risk, intervention, and lifetime resilience may be modeled as renewal-reward stochastic processes (Sanchez-Silva et al. 2011; Jia et al. 2017), for which closed-form solutions for objective functions may exist. Such closed-form solution should be able to significantly improve the computational efficiency of the proposed framework.

23.7 Conclusions

Sustainable and resilient civil infrastructure is of paramount importance for future-oriented development. Despite the similar scope of impacts on economy, society, and environment, existing studies and practices regarding sustainability and resilience differ greatly in research focuses, time horizons of interest, and methods adopted. This chapter is aimed to merging the differences between the two by first clarifying the two perspectives of sustainability and then proposing a new concept termed as lifetime resilience to be embedded in sustainability-informed life-cycle assessment. The work presented in this chapter advances towards an integrated approach for sustainable and resilient civil infrastructure by virtue of sustainability-informed life-cycle management considering structural resilience under lifetime hazards. Conclusions derived from the present study are summarized as follows:

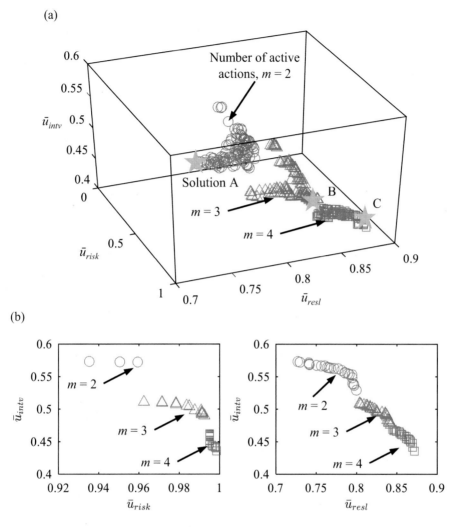

Figure 23.12 Pareto front of multi-objective optimization: (a) tri-objective Pareto front; (b) bi-objective Pareto fronts with intervention utilities.

1. Sustainability of civil infrastructure can be interpreted from two perspectives: functional integrity and structural longevity. The former requires an overall consideration of economic, social, and environmental impacts of a project, whereas the latter demands life-cycle assessment and management. Multi-attribute utility theory (MAUT), which provides a holistic and balanced consideration of economic, social, and environmental impacts, represents an effective tool to assess sustainability from the functional integrity perspective. Also, sustainability-informed life-cycle assessment (LCA) is enabled by the use of MAUT. LCA considers sustainability from the structural longevity perspective and lays the foundation for incorporating resilience into sustainability assessment.

2. Resilience of civil infrastructure to lifetime hazards are needed to be analyzed for a comprehensive understanding of the structural life-cycle performance in terms of sustainability. Nevertheless, existing studies on resilience, which adopt a "what-if" approach, cannot represent the interactions between sustainability and resilience. To this end, a novel concept, referred to as *lifetime resilience*, is proposed to grasp a full understanding of the life-cycle performance of a structure in terms of resilience. By combining life-cycle and resilience analyses, resilience is embedded into sustainability-informed life-cycle assessment and management.

3. As many uncertainties are involved in MAUT and LCA, a holistic probabilistic framework is proposed for multi-objective life-cycle performance optimization considering multi-attribute utilities of lifetime risk, intervention actions, and lifetime resilience. The application of the framework is illustrated through an example using a bridge structure. The framework presented herein relies on Monte Carlo simulation to obtain values of different objectives. However, the formulation of the framework implies the potential of using stochastic process theories for more efficient computations. This outlines a possible path for future studies.

Acknowledgements

The support by grants from (a) the National Science Foundation (NSF) Award CMMI-1537926, (b) the US Federal Highway Administration (FHWA) Cooperative Agreement Award DTFH61-07-H-00040, and (c) the US Office of Naval Research (ONR) Awards N00014-08-1-0188, N00014-12-1-0023, and N00014-16-1-2299 is gratefully acknowledged. Opinions presented in this paper are those of the authors and do not necessarily reflect the views of the sponsoring organizations.

References

Alibrandi, U. and Mosalam, K.M. (2017). A decision support tool for sustainable and resilient building design. In P. Gardoni, ed. *Risk and Reliability Analysis: Theory and Applications*. 509–36.

Ang, A.H.-S. and Tang, W.H. (1984). *Probability Concepts in Engineering Planning and Design, Vol. 2: Decision, Risk, and Reliability*, New York, NY: Wiley.

Ariely, D. (2008). *Predictably Irrational*, New York: HarperCollins.

ARUP (2000). Sustainable project appraisal routine: Flexible and robust sustainability decision-making tool. www.arup.com/projects/spear (last accessed July 27, 2017).

Basu, D., Misra, A., and Puppala, A.J. (2015). Sustainability and geotechnical engineering: Perspectives and review. *Canadian Geotechnical Journal*, 52(1): 96–113.

Biondini, F. and Frangopol, D.M. (2016). Life-cycle performance of structural systems under uncertainty. *Journal of Structural Engineering*, 142(9): F4016001.

Biondini, F., Camnasio, E., and Titi, A. (2015). Seismic resilience of concrete structures under corrosion. *Earthquake Engineering & Structural Dynamics*, 44: 2445–66.

Bocchini, P. and Frangopol, D.M. (2011). Resilience-driven disaster management of civil infrastructure. In M. Papadrakakis, M. Fragiadakis, and V. Plevris, eds. *ECCOMAS Thematic Conference on Computational Methods in Structural Dynamics and Earthquake Engineering*. Corfu, Greece, 11 pp. on CD-ROM.

Bocchini, P., Frangopol, D.M., Ummenhofer, T., and Zinke, T. (2014). Resilience and sustainability of civil infrastructure: Toward a unified approach. *Journal of Infrastructure Systems, ASCE*, 20(2): 4014004.

Brundtland, G.H. (1987). Our common future—call for action. *Environmental Conservation*, 14(4): 291–94.

Building Research Establishment (1990). BREEAM: Why BREEAM. www.breeam.com/why-breeam (last accessed July 27, 2017).

Cha, E.J. and Ellingwood, B.R. (2012). Risk-averse decision-making for civil infrastructure exposed to low-probability, high-consequence events. *Reliability Engineering and System Safety*, 104: 27–35.

Cha, E.J. and Ellingwood, B.R. (2013). Seismic risk mitigation of building structures: The role of risk aversion. *Structural Safety*, 40: 11–19.

Deb, K., Pratap, A., Agarwal, S., and Meyarivan, T. (2002). A fast and elitist multiobjective genetic algorithm: NSGA-II. *IEEE Transactions on Evolutionary Computation*, 6(2): 182–97.

Decò, A., Bocchini, P., and Frangopol, D.M. (2013). A probabilistic approach for the prediction of seismic resilience of bridges. *Earthquake Engineering and Structural Dynamics*, 42(10): 1469–87.

DGNB (2007). German Sustainable Building Council (DGNB). www.dgnb.de/en/council/dgnb/ (last accessed July 27, 2017).

Dong, Y. and Frangopol, D.M. (2015). Risk and resilience assessment of bridges under mainshock and aftershocks incorporating uncertainties. *Engineering Structures*, 83: 198–208.

Dong, Y. and Frangopol, D.M. (2016a). Performance-based seismic assessment of conventional and base-isolated steel buildings including environmental impact and resilience. *Earthquake Engineering & Structural Dynamics*, 45: 739–56.

Dong, Y. and Frangopol, D.M. (2016b). Probabilistic time-dependent multihazard life-cycle assessment and resilience of bridges considering climate change. *Journal of Performance of Constructed Facilities, ASCE*, 30(5): 4016034.

Dong, Y., Frangopol, D.M., and Saydam, D. (2013). Time-variant sustainability assessment of seismically vulnerable bridges subjected to multiple hazards. *Earthquake Engineering & Structural Dynamics*, 42: 1451–67.

Dong, Y., Frangopol, D.M., and Sabatino, S. (2014a). Risk-informed decision making for disaster recovery incorporating sustainability and resilience. In *Proceedings of the 3rd International Conference on Urban Disaster Reduction (3ICUDR), EERI*. Boulder, Colorado, 4 pp. on USB stick.

Dong, Y., Frangopol, D.M., and Saydam, D. (2014b). Pre-earthquake multi-objective probabilistic retrofit optimization of bridge networks based on sustainability. *Journal of Bridge Engineering*, 19(6): 4014018.

Dong, Y., Frangopol, D.M., and Saydam, D. (2014c). Sustainability of highway bridge networks under seismic hazard. *Journal of Earthquake Engineering*, 18(1): 41–66.

Dong, Y., Frangopol, D.M., and Sabatino, S. (2015). Optimizing bridge network retrofit planning based on cost-benefit evaluation and multi-attribute utility associated with sustainability. *Earthquake Spectra*, 31(4): 2255–80.

Ellingwood, B.R. (2005). Risk-informed condition assessment of civil infrastructure: state of practice and research issues. *Structure and Infrastructure Engineering*, 1(1): 7–18.

FHWA (2015). *Towards Sustainable Pavement Systems: A Reference Document – FHWA-HIF-15-002*, Federal Highway Administration (FHWA).

Frangopol, D.M. (2011). Life-cycle performance, management, and optimisation of structural systems under uncertainty: Accomplishments and challenges. *Structure and Infrastructure Engineering*, 7(6): 389–413.

Frangopol, D.M. and Bocchini, P. (2011). Resilience as optimization criterion for the bridge rehabilitation of a transportation network subject to earthquake. In D. Ames, T.L. Droessler, and M. Hoit, eds. *Proceedings of the ASCE Structures Congress 2011*. Las Vegas, Nevada, 2044–55.

Frangopol, D.M. and Soliman, M. (2016). Life-cycle of structural systems: Recent achievements and future directions. *Structure and Infrastructure Engineering*, 12(1): 1–20.

Frangopol, D.M., Kong, J.S., and Gharaibeh, E.S. (2001). Reliability-based life-cycle management of highway bridges. *Journal of Computing in Civil Engineering, ASCE*, 15(1): 27–34.

Frangopol, D.M., Dong, Y., and Sabatino, S. (2017). Bridge life-cycle performance and cost: analysis, prediction, optimisation and decision-making. *Structure and Infrastructure Engineering*, 13(10): 1239–57.

García-Segura, T., Yepes, V., Frangopol, D.M., and Yang, D.Y. (2017). Lifetime reliability-based optimization of post-tensioned box-girder bridges. *Engineering Structures*, 145: 381–91.

Gardoni, P. and Murphy, C. (2008). Recovery from natural and man-made disasters as capabilities restoration and enhancement. *International Journal of Sustainable Development and Planning*, 3(4): 317–33.

Gardoni, P., Guevara-Lopez, F., and Contento, A. (2016). The life profitability method (LPM): A financial approach to engineering decisions. *Structural Safety*, 63: 11–20.

Grabowski, Z.J. and Miller, T. (2017). Infrastructures as socio-eco-technical systems: Five considerations for interdisciplinary dialogue. *Journal of Infrastructure Systems, ASCE*, 23(4): 1–9.

IUCN/UNEP/WWF (1991). *Caring for Earth: A Strategy for Sustainable Living*. New York: Routledge.

Jia, G. and Gardoni, P. (2018). State-dependent stochastic models: A general stochastic framework for modeling deteriorating engineering systems considering multiple deterioration processes and their interactions. *Structural Safety*, 72: 99–110.

Jia, G., Tabandeh, A. and Gardoni, P. (2017). Life-cycle analysis of engineering systems: Modeling deterioration, instantaneous reliability, and resilience. In P. Gardoni, ed. *Risk and Reliability Analysis: Theory and Applications*. 465–94.

Jiao, Y., Lloyd, C.R., and Wakes, S.J. (2012). The relationship between total embodied energy and cost of commercial buildings. *Energy and Buildings*, 52: 20–7.

Jiménez, A., Ríos-Insua, S., and Mateos, A., 2003. A decision support system for multiattribute utility evaluation based on imprecise assignments. *Decision Support Systems*, 36(1): 65–79.

Keeney, R.L. and Raiffa, H. (1993). *Decisions with Multiple Objectives – Preferences and Value Tradeoffs*. Cambridge: Cambridge University Press.

Kibert, C.J. (2016). *Sustainable Construction: Green Building Design and Delivery*, 2nd ed. New York: John Wiley & Sons.

LEED, 2009. *LEED Reference Guide for Green Building Design and Construction*. Washington, DC: US Green Building Council.

Sabatino, S., Frangopol, D.M., and Dong, Y. (2015). Sustainability-informed maintenance optimization of highway bridges considering multi-attribute utility and risk attitude. *Engineering Structures*, 102: 310–21.

Sabatino, S., Frangopol, D.M., and Dong, Y. (2016). Life cycle utility-informed maintenance planning based on lifetime functions: optimum balancing of cost, failure consequences and performance benefit. *Structure and Infrastructure Engineering*, 12(7): 830–47.

Sanchez-Silva, M., Klutke, G.A., and Rosowsky, D. (2011). Life-cycle performance of structures subject to multiple deterioration mechanisms. *Structural Safety*, 33(3): 206–17.

Semuels, A. (2016). The role of highways in American poverty: They seemed like such a good idea in the 1950s. *The Atlantic*. www.theatlantic.com/business/archive/2016/03/role-of-highways-in-american-poverty/474282/ (last accessed July 27, 2017).

Stewart, T.J. (1996). Robustness of additive value function methods in MCDM. *Journal of Multi-Criteria Decision Analysis*, 5(June 1995): 301–9.

Stromberg, J. (2016). Highways gutted American cities. So why did they build them? *Vox*. www.vox.com/2015/5/14/8605917/highways-interstate-cities-history (last accessed July 27, 2017).

Thompson, P.B. (2010). What sustainability is (and what it isn't). *Pragmatic Sustainability: Theoretical and Practical Tools* 16–29.

Timmerman, P. (1981). Vulnerability, resilience and the collapse of society: A review of models and possible climatic applications. *Environmental Monograph*, 1: 1–45.

Tversky, A. and Kahneman, D. (1992). Advances in prospect theory: Cumulative representation of uncertainty. *Journal of Risk and Uncertainty*, 5(4): 297–323.

United Nations General Assembly (2005). Resolution adopted by the General Assembly 2005 World Summit Outcome. www.un.org/womenwatch/ods/A-RES-60-1-E.pdf (last accessed July 27, 2017).

Van-Noortwijk, J.M. and Frangopol, D.M. (2004). Two probabilistic life-cycle maintenance models for deteriorating civil infrastructures. *Probabilistic Engineering Mechanics*, 19(4): 345–59.

Wei, H.-H., Shohet, I.M., Skibniewski, M.J., Shapira, S., and Yao, X. (2016). Assessing the lifecycle sustainability costs and benefits of seismic mitigation designs for buildings. *Journal of Architectural Engineering*, 22(1): 4015011.

24

Tradeoffs between sustainable and resilient buildings

Abbie B. Liel[1] and Sarah J. Welsh-Huggins[2]

[1] DEPARTMENT OF CIVIL, ENVIRONMENTAL AND ARCHITECTURAL ENGINEERING, UNIVERSITY OF COLORADO BOULDER, USA; ABBIE.LIEL@COLORADO.EDU

[2] AAAS SCIENCE & TECHNOLOGY POLICY FELLOW, SERVING AT THE US AGENCY FOR INTERNATIONAL DEVELOPMENT, USA; SJWELSHHUGGINS@GMAIL.COM

24.1 Introduction

Principles of green building design and hazard-resistant design are often employed separately to enhance performance of buildings and other infrastructure, but with a focus on different objectives and employing different units of measurement. Green building practices aim to mitigate threats from building construction and operations to human health, and degradation of the natural environment, through more efficient uses of water, energy, and material resources (Bokalders & Block 2010). Engineering for green buildings encompasses a wide range of design choices, from decisions about structural features, to energy-saving technologies, to building orientation. The green building initiative is part of the larger sustainable development movement, which recognizes the need to reduce present-day negative environmental impacts to sustain resources for future generations (Berke 1995; Bokalders & Block 2010; Schwab & Brower 1999). Green building rating systems, such as LEED in the US (USGBC 2009), or BREEAM in Europe (BREEAM 2015), have become popular tools to evaluate "greenness" and to recognize buildings where owners and operators have taken steps towards sustainable design and operations.

Hazard-resistant design has traditionally involved quantification of extreme loads, and probabilistic representation of those loads through load resistance factor designs to generate relatively simple calculations (e.g., static loads) for use in design codes. More recently, performance-based engineering (PBE) methodologies have been developed and adopted in an effort to create design procedures that satisfy performance objectives for design-level hazard events *a priori*. In this context, performance is generally related to different levels of post-disaster functionality (Porter 2003). Proponents of PBE believe that this methodology can enable a paradigm shift toward construction of more robust, redundant structures that experience low levels of hazard-induced damage and limit loss of post-event functionality (Bruneau et al. 2003). Yet, most building design is still carried out according to prescriptive design procedures that specify code-defined minimum levels of hazard resistance.

443

Although still considered as separate concerns by many building professionals, hazard resistant and green philosophies of building design are motivated by shared principles, and can be evaluated with shared assessment tools. Both design approaches require long-term decision horizons to balance upfront impacts or costs, with uncertain future environmental, societal, and safety benefits (Berke 1995; Mileti & Peek-Gottschlich 2001; Schwab & Brower 1999). In addition, recent work has demonstrated that a structure's hazard-resistance can impact its life-cycle environmental impacts. For example, when buildings, and their components, are less likely to experience damage in a hazard event (i.e., they are more resilient), short and long-term economic costs and environmental impacts from repair and replacement activities may be reduced. Moreover, reducing hazard-induced building repairs enables diversion of material and financial resources from restoration of individual buildings towards community-scale efforts for emergency response, relief, and community recovery. On the other hand, incorporating green building design technologies in the interest of sustainability may have unintended positive or negative consequences in terms of hazards resistance.

This chapter explores tradeoffs between sustainable and resilient buildings using a life-cycle assessment (LCA) methodology that incorporates PBE. Successful integration of these two design philosophies requires development of techniques that integrate hazard performance in quantification of a building's life-cycle impacts (Comber & Poland 2013; Gromala et al. 2010; Portland Cement Association 2012). The next section describes LCA methods that can be used to quantify a building's environmental and economic life-cycle, considering a hazard event, like an earthquake. The chapter then focuses on two studies illustrating application of this methodology. The first study addresses the question "Are resilient buildings sustainable?", by investigating how structural design principles for hazard resistance influence life-cycle environmental impacts of a building. The second study addresses the question "Are sustainable buildings resilient?", and explores how green materials can potentially influence building hazard-resistance. Both studies are based on the life-cycle environmental impacts and seismic performance of a series of code-conforming, reinforced concrete office buildings in Los Angeles, varied with respect to nonstructural green building features, structural frame and member configurations, and structural concrete properties.

24.2 Methods

24.2.1 Life-cycle assessment

To explore the tradeoffs between sustainable and resilient building design, we employ the comparative LCA methodology, following the ISO 14040 framework (ISO 2006). Here, this method is applied to a comparison of environmental impacts of the production and performance of various modern reinforced concrete buildings in Southern California that are intended to provide usable office space for 50 years; in LCA terminology, a single reinforced concrete building is considered the "functional unit" of analysis. The primary life-cycle stages of a building are: construction, service life or operation (including maintenance), and end-of-life. These studies focus on the construction and service life stages, which are the most relevant to seismic performance, and, consequently, to hazard resilience. The construction stage is referred to here as the "upfront" life-cycle stage. Service life is defined to encompass the potential for earthquake hazard events and any associated repairs (e.g., Bocchini et al. 2014; Court et al. 2012; Padgett & Li 2016; Rodriguez-Nikl 2015; Welsh-Huggins & Liel 2017). In general, life-cycle stages and unit processes that are equivalent between the building alternatives have been excluded, since they will not significantly change the relative environmental impacts or overall conclusions about the comparisons of interest (ISO 2006).

The LCA in these studies considers unit processes for production of concrete, structural rebar and all nonstructural components in the building. In the first study, the LCA boundary for structural concrete considers a pre-defined unit impact for a single concrete mix design, without quantifying variations in material sources or transportation distances. In the second study, the LCA boundary for concrete production is expanded to account explicitly for: (1) cement production; (2) sand production for use as fine aggregate; (3) granite production for use as coarse aggregate; (4) transportation of materials from each extraction/processing site to the concrete mix plant; and (5) energy production to power the concrete mix plant.

In both studies, nonstructural components considered include partitions, windows, ceiling tiles, and other mechanical and architectural equipment. These components are: concrete roof tiles; staircases; exterior concrete cladding; exterior glazed curtain walls; suspended ceiling tiles; carpeted floor tiles; interior wall partitions; heating, ventilation, and air conditioning (HVAC) systems; and water service piping systems. The inventory of nonstructural components, although not exhaustive, is representative of those components most likely to be damaged in an earthquake and, thus, most likely to contribute to post-earthquake losses and environmental impacts (Ramirez et al. 2012).

For both structural and nonstructural material quantities, calculation of the amount and type of each material for the functional unit is based on the architectural and structural design of the building. The environmental impacts associated with each unit process (materials and energy) are accounted for primarily with data from the Ecoinvent v3 database (Swiss Centre for Life-cycle Inventories 2014). The *SimaPro* LCA software is used to apply the US EPA's impact assessment method, *Tool for the Reduction and Assessment of Chemical and Other Environmental Impacts* (TRACI) (Bare 2012), to translate all the relevant life-cycle environmental emissions into environmental impacts. The primary environmental assessment metric considered here is life-cycle greenhouse gas emissions, expressed as CO_2 equivalents. This quantity is sometimes referred to (and is referenced herein) as "embodied carbon".

24.2.2 Seismic performance assessment

Dynamic analysis of nonlinear simulation models

The seismic performance assessment requires, first, nonlinear simulation of the dynamic response of the buildings of interest. All of the building models described in the studies described below are modeled in the *OpenSEES* nonlinear seismic analysis program (PEER, 2014) in two dimensions. These models utilize a plastic hinge approach to represent structural elements, such that elastic elements represent beams and columns, with plasticity confined to hinge elements whose properties are assigned using the hysteric model presented in Ibarra et al. (2005). This approach has been described in detail elsewhere (e.g., Haselton et al. 2011). The models capture P-Δ effects, and are assigned 5 percent Rayleigh damping at the first and third modes.

Dynamic analysis is conducted with a set of 30 California acceleration recordings of strong ground motions at firm sites with site-to-source distances ranging from 15 to 33 km and from earthquakes with magnitudes between 6.5 and 6.9 (Vamvatsikos & Cornell 2006). These records are generally representative of the crustal ground motions that may occur in Southern California. The dynamic analysis is organized with incremental dynamic analysis (Vamvatsikos & Cornell 2002), wherein structural response, including story drifts and floor accelerations, is simulated under each recorded ground motion at multiple intensity (or scale) levels of interest.

Collapse is defined to occur if drifts greater than 12 percent are recorded at any story (Haselton et al. 2011). The analysis is repeated for all 30 recordings to capture record-to-record variability in response.

Seismic loss analysis

Performance-based earthquake engineering provides a framework for linking structural response (e.g., drifts and accelerations) to decision variables more aligned with goals for resilience, such as economic and environmental costs. Probabilistic seismic loss analysis quantifies building performance under seismic loading in terms of building damage and associated seismic losses. The losses of interest here are both *economic* (dollar value of loss incurred from earthquake-induced damage and repairs) and *environmental*. The environmental losses are quantified, in the first study, as the embodied carbon or CO_2 equivalents released by material manufacturing for repairs and replacement of damaged components and structure, and, in the second study, as embodied carbon produced both by material manufacturing and from transportation of materials to the presumed case study site.

The seismic loss assessment here follows the FEMA P-58 seismic performance and probabilistic loss-estimation procedures (ATC 2012a), which determines the level of damage in each building component as a function of dynamic analysis results to estimate possible earthquake-induced repair costs. Total losses represent the sum of repair and replacement costs for all building components. The level of damage in each component is determined from component-specific "fragility curves" defined in FEMA P-58, and the seismic demand on the structure, as quantified through peak floor accelerations or story drifts calculated in the dynamic analysis described above (ATC, 2012a, 2012b). Here, the FEMA P-58 component-based loss methodology has been implemented using the SP3 software (Haselton Baker Risk Group 2016). Actions needed to replace or repair a component to its initial, undamaged, pre-earthquake state, and associated costs, are defined as functions of the severity of damage in the SP3 software.

The losses are initially computed conditioned on a particular ground motion intensity level (IM), defined here in terms of the spectral acceleration at the first-mode period of the building of interest, $Sa(T_1)$. The expected seismic loss at each intensity level, $E[SL|IM]$, shown in Equation (24.1), is computed as the sum of expected non-collapse building repair costs and total building replacement cost in the case of collapse, considering the collapse probability at that intensity level (ATC 2012a):

$$E[SL\,|\,IM] = [1 - P(C\,|\,IM)]E[SL\,|\,NC, IM] + P(C\,|\,IM)E[SL\,|\,C] \qquad (24.1)$$

In Equation (24.1), $P(C|IM)$ is the probability of collapse at the IM level of interest. $E[SL|NC, IM]$ is the sum of seismic losses associated with repairing all damaged structural and nonstructural components to restore the building to its initial undamaged state, given that the structure does not collapse. $E[SL|C]$ is the expected seismic loss from collapse, corresponding to total building replacement. This value is assumed to be the same as the cost (or embodied carbon) of initial construction for each building, based on typical construction economic costs.

The loss analysis calculations incorporate several thousand Monte Carlo realizations of potential damage outcomes for each structural and nonstructural building component at each intensity level. Each individual realization represents a different level of acceleration and drift, level of damage in each component, and thus varying outcomes for expected building repairs costs (ATC 2012a).

Adding a further step to the seismic performance assessment, Welsh-Huggins and Liel (2017) developed an approach for translating damaged component quantities into material volumes for repair actions at each intensity level. That study cataloged each nonstructural and structural repair action recommended in FEMA P-58 (ATC 2012b) by material needs and quantities, following typical construction practices described in Ching (2014). Thus, repair actions are identified for each component in the building, and then the embodied carbon impact from the required repair or replacement materials (e.g., structural steel, glass, etc.) is computed (Welsh-Huggins & Liel 2017). We assume that building repairs and replacement will use the same materials/components as in the original construction (i.e., no post-hazard event upgrades).

24.3 Are resilient buildings sustainable?

24.3.1 Problem statement

In one recent study, we investigate the idea that "green" buildings should be designed to withstand higher extreme loads (i.e., loads associated with earthquakes or other hazards) (Welsh-Huggins & Liel 2018). A number of authors have advocated for increasing design forces for earthquakes, snow loads, and other extreme loads for green buildings, arguing that designing buildings for higher loads will reduce environmental impacts associated with post-hazard repairs (Chiu et al. 2013; PCA 2012; Wei et al. 2016a, 2016b). However, this claim has not been systematically investigated.

To explore the potential environmental tradeoffs of resilient design, we therefore assess the seismic performance and associated environmental impact of 30 modern reinforced concrete frame buildings with varying lateral strengths and ductility capacities, considering 4- and 12-story space and perimeter frames. As described in the Methods section above, seismic performance is assessed probabilistically using nonlinear dynamic analysis and seismic losses – economic (dollars) and environmental (equivalent CO_2 emissions) – quantified for earthquake-induced damage. The life-cycle environmental impacts are then compared between code designed buildings and buildings designed above or below code either in terms of strength or ductility capacity.

We vary the lateral strength by varying the response modification factor used in design, as described in ASCE 7 (2010), R, which is inversely correlated to building strength. Figure 24.1a presents the pushover results for the 4-story buildings with varying lateral strengths, showing that increased design earthquake loads lead to greater base shear capacity, while ductility capacity remains similar. We vary the ductility capacity by varying the design column-to-beam strength (SCWB) ratio; columns are required to be 1.2 times stronger than the beams in current codes (ACI 2011). Higher values of the column-to-beam-strength ratio provide more system-level ductility, due to distribution of deformations and damage over multiple stories (Sattar & Liel 2017). Increasing the column-to-beam strength ratio substantially enhances ductility capacity, as well as base shear strength, as shown in Figure 24.1b.

The results presented here focus on the 4-story space frame buildings, but findings are similar for the 12-story structures and the 4-story perimeter frame buildings.

24.3.2 Key findings

Increasing the lateral strength or ductility of buildings increases upfront embodied carbon, compared to code-level designs, due to larger structural material demands and increased member sizes.

Figure 24.2a shows how embodied carbon associated with the buildings' initial production and construction (the so-called "upfront" emissions) varies with lateral strength, indicating that

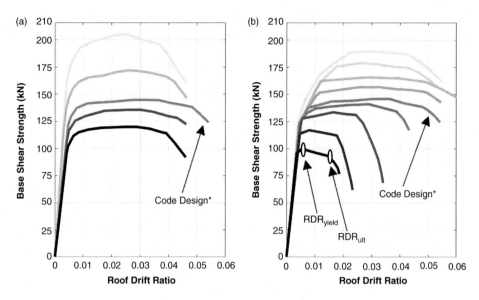

Figure 24.1 Nonlinear static pushover results (per frame line) for 4-story buildings: (a) with varying strength and (b) with varying ductility capacities (measured through SCWB ratio). The labels RDR$_{yield}$ and RDR$_{ult}$ in (b) illustrate the points used to calculate the ductility capacity for a selected building.

Source: Reproduced from Welsh-Huggins and Liel 2018, with permission of ASCE.

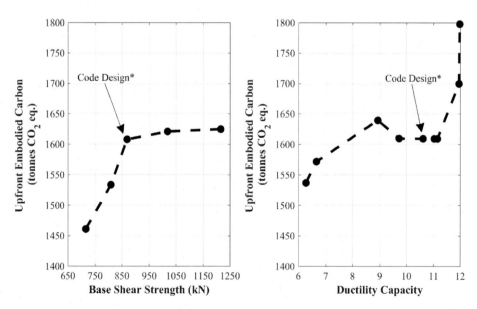

Figure 24.2 Influence of seismic design on upfront embodied carbon for 4-story buildings showing effect of: (a) lateral base shear strength and (b) ductility capacity.

Source: Reproduced from Welsh-Huggins and Liel 2018, with permission of ASCE.

stronger buildings are associated with greater upfront embodied carbon. In a building, the production of structural materials is associated with higher levels of greenhouse gas and other emissions than production of nonstructural component materials, due to types of materials and the volumes used for the structural design (this finding is consistent with others (e.g., Guggemos & Horvath 2005). However, levels of embodied carbon do not correlate linearly with enhanced lateral strength due to other design requirements (gravity loads, drift limits, etc.) that also impact member sizes.

In Figure 24.2b, the below-code ductility design buildings have similar levels of upfront embodied carbon to the code-design building. Changes in design ductility capacity at this level are mainly associated with redistribution of material from columns to beams, without significant changes in the total amount of material. However, Figure 24.2b also demonstrates a notable increase in embodied carbon for buildings to achieve above-code ductility capacities. This increase is due to the increase in member size and amount of steel required to achieve larger column-to-beam strength ratios and, hence, larger ductility capacities.

Increasing lateral strength lowers seismic economic and environmental losses compared to weaker building designs.

Figure 24.3 shows the median earthquake-induced ("post-EQ") economic losses at each intensity level considered in the dynamic analysis. In Figure 24.3a, the buildings with varying strengths illustrate an inverse correlation between lateral strength and economic losses at most intensity levels, indicating that, in general, stronger buildings (lower R buildings) experience less damage and, hence, lower repair costs/losses. The few exceptions to this trend (i.e., where stronger buildings have higher losses) occur because of changes in fundamental period, which come with changes in strength, because stronger buildings tend to also be stiffer. These period changes can intensify story drifts and floor acceleration demands under certain ground motions. Although not shown in the figures, the results also indicate that increasing lateral strength reduces damage especially to structural members and leads to lower probabilities of collapse; hence, larger percent contributions of the losses at all intensity levels are associated with damage and losses in nonstructural components. The trends presented here are consistent with general observations made in previous studies of the same buildings and other similar designs (Goulet et al. 2007; Ramirez et al. 2012).

Figure 24.3b reveals similar trends between strength and environmental (embodied carbon) losses as those observed with economic losses; increased strength of the building is generally associated with lower repair needs and, hence, lower environmental impacts.

As expected, when the life-cycle losses (considering all intensities of shaking and their probabilities of exceedance) are computed, there is a clear trend between stronger buildings and reductions in life-cycle economic and environmental losses. These results are presented in Figure 24.4 For example, the strongest building has life-cycle embodied carbon losses that are 63 percent lower than the code-compliant design.

Enhancing ductility capacity does not reduce, and can increase, seismic economic and environmental losses.

Increasing ductility capacity generally does not reduce economic seismic losses (Figures 24.5 and 24.6). The greater a building's ductility capacity, the more uniform the distribution of lateral deformation and damage that develops. This uniform distribution is beneficial for energy dissipation and, hence, collapse performance and life safety, but increases the damage

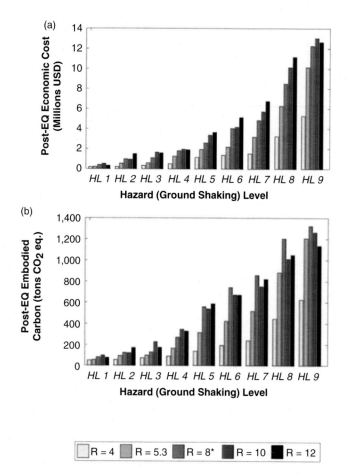

Figure 24.3 Median post-earthquake: (a) economic and (b) embodied carbon losses for 4-story buildings with varying strengths at each of nine ground shaking intensity levels (* denotes code-compliant designs).

to structural and nonstructural components over the height of the building. Figure 24.5 shows that enhanced ductility capacity increases losses, even though the risk of collapse decreases, due to the enhanced percent contribution and magnitude of nonstructural losses. Here, the more ductile building (i.e., SCWB = 2.5) has significantly lower collapse loss contributions than a below-code, less ductile building (i.e., SCWB = 0.6). However, the below-code building has lower total seismic economic losses at each hazard level. Trends were slightly different for the 12-story buildings (not shown here). Due to p-delta effects in the 12-story buildings, increased ductility capacity is not sufficient to substantially change the distribution of damage over the height of the building. In this case, larger ductility capacity can be associated with reduced losses.

The results for all ductility variations of the 4-story buildings are provided in Figure 24.6. The most ductile design has 19 percent higher life-cycle embodied carbon than the code-level design. For the 12-story buildings, there is a very small reduction in life-cycle embodied carbon associated with some, but not all, of the higher ductility designs.

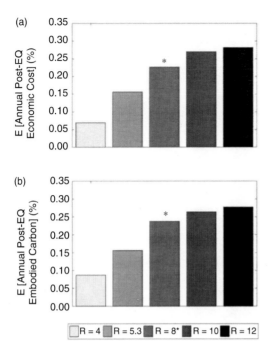

Figure 24.4 Life-cycle earthquake: (a) economic and (b) embodied carbon losses for 4-story buildings with varying strengths, quantified as annuities and expressed as percentage of total building replacement values (* denotes code-compliant designs).

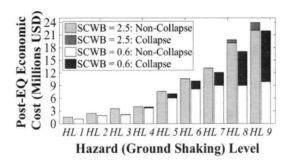

Figure 24.5 Median post-earthquake economic losses for selected 4-story buildings with varying ductility capacities, at each of nine ground shaking intensity levels. Each bar is deaggregated by non-collapse and collapse contributions.

In summary, these results show that enhancing ductility capacity can in fact increase life-cycle embodied carbon and environmental impacts. Although more ductile buildings have higher lateral strength and collapse capacities, the effect of large drifts on nonstructural component damage can result in less desirable seismic loss outcomes, particularly when these drift demands are well-distributed over the height of the building. In fact, these results suggest that above-code ductility designs can increase both upfront embodied carbon (from larger structural

451

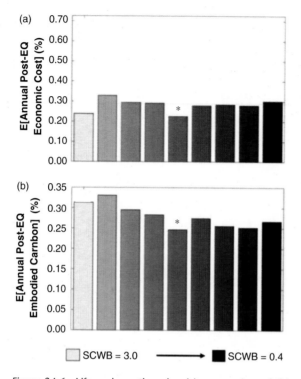

Figure 24.6 Life-cycle earthquake: (a) economic and (b) embodied carbon losses for 4-story buildings with varying ductility capacities, quantified as annuities and expressed as percentage of total building replacement values (* denotes code-compliant designs).

member sizes to achieve enhanced ductility) and life-cycle embodied carbon from earthquakes (due to greater distribution of damage). Even in cases where the life-cycle seismic embodied carbon losses decrease with enhanced ductility in the design, this reduction is not sufficient to counteract the additional upfront carbon necessary to produce the above-code designs.

> **For high seismic regions, enhanced lateral strength can reduce life–cycle embodied carbon losses by reducing seismic environmental impacts sufficiently to offset the higher upfront embodied carbon from constructing larger structural members.**

The results suggest that enhancements to lateral strength will increase upfront embodied carbon, but that these carbon emissions can be offset over a building's life-cycle by large reductions in seismic losses, achieving a net environmental benefit from savings in embodied carbon. In this study, upfront material production for the strongest 4-story building releases 16 more metric tonnes of CO_2 equivalents than that of the code-level design. However, at the site considered, post-earthquake repair activities for these above-code design changes are associated with 121 fewer metric tonnes of CO_2 equivalents than the code-compliant design, resulting in a life-cycle net reduction when both upfront and seismic CO_2 are considered. This finding supports the idea proposed by the Portland Cement Association (PCA) and others that one tool for achieving "greener" buildings is to design for higher seismic forces than required by current standards (PCA 2012). Specifically, the 20 percent increase in design forces proposed by the PCA is associated with significant savings in avoided embodied carbon due to lower seismic losses, compared to the original code-compliant design. In summary, these results (which are also generalizable to the other 4-story and 12-story buildings analyzed) show that enhancing lateral strength will increase upfront embodied carbon, but this increase can be offset by lower future seismic losses that significantly reduce post-earthquake levels of embodied carbon.

Of course, the tradeoffs between upfront strength (an additional cost of embodied carbon) and earthquake performance (a reduction in embodied carbon) depend on the regional seismicity of the site of interest. As expected, at sites with lower seismic hazard, carbon savings associated with building stronger are reduced. In Welsh-Huggins and Liel (2018), we examined three different sites with different levels of seismicity: Los Angeles (the site considered in the results above), Pasadena and Reno. At the selected Pasadena site, which has higher seismicity than the Los Angeles site, enhanced lateral strength greatly reduces earthquake embodied carbon and environmental impacts compared to the code-level designed building. In Reno, which has lower seismicity than the Los Angeles site, there is a much smaller difference in post-earthquake embodied carbon between the above-code and code-level designs.

These results suggest that enhanced lateral strength can produce more resilient (higher collapse capacities and lower economic seismic loss) and more sustainable (lower seismic loss embodied carbon) outcomes than a strictly code-compliant design. Moreover, upfront increases in embodied carbon can be offset by avoided post-earthquake impacts, i.e., a net reduction in life-cycle embodied carbon, compared to the code-compliant design. However, the total benefits will depend on the regional seismic risk of a site of interest.

The building components that contribute most to economic seismic losses may not be the same components that contribute most to environmental seismic losses.

To illustrate this effect, seismic losses are deaggregated at each of the intensity levels with respect to the contributing component, or so-called "performance groups." Figure 24.7 shows component contributions to seismic loss for a selected 4-story building at each of the considered hazard levels. The results show that the dominant building components contributing to seismic loss at each hazard level vary with the analysis metric of interest. For example, some components may be relatively inexpensive (in dollar terms) to repair, but these repairs may be relatively CO_2-intensive; two such components are ceiling tiles and interior partitions. On the other hand, repairing structural concrete with epoxy can be expensive, but does not require a large volume of materials or associated emissions.

Use of a discount rate to calculate life-cycle embodied carbon de-emphasizes the significance of environmental impacts in the future.

As the results of this study show, seismic design decisions affect economic and environmental outcomes over many years. Calculating the present value of future uncertain seismic losses helps to value present-day decisions. In engineering economic calculations, the time value of money is typically accounted for using equations that apply a discount (or interest) rate to future losses (Cowing et al. 2004). However, applying a discount rate to environmental impacts assumes that environmental impacts will be less burdensome on future generations than on present generations. When calculating total life-cycle environmental impacts, therefore, climate change economists question the ethics of applying discount factors to non-economic metrics

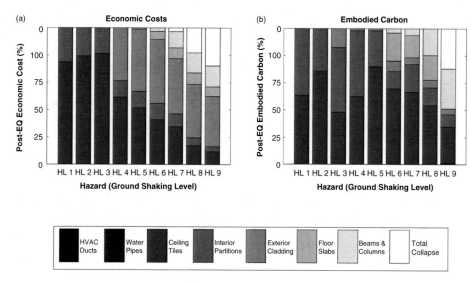

Figure 24.7 Seismic losses deaggregated by component contributions: (a) in terms of economic costs and (b) in terms of embodied carbon. Results are shown for the strongest 4-story building with R = 4.

like carbon emissions. As a result, many scholars recommend a zero or very low discount rate for life-cycle analysis of environmental impacts (Jacquet et al. 2013; Schelling 1995; Tol 2011). A 0 percent discount rate corresponds to summing the embodied carbon annuities over the lifespan of a structure of interest, here over 50 years.

Using the annuities presented in Figure 24.4 and Figure 24.6, we can calculate the present value environmental impact associated with earthquake repairs, considering a range of discount rates from 0 to 5 percent. Three percent is a typical value used in engineering economics for dollar losses (Pate-Cornell 1984). As expected, higher discount rates decrease the value placed on future societal impacts from embodied carbon. In some cases, the range of discount rates assessed can change in estimated life-cycle embodied carbon of about 30 percent. For the ethical reasons, all the results presented above considered no discounting.

24.4 Are sustainable buildings resilient?

24.4.1 Problem statement

In another recent study, we investigate whether new materials that are green (or "sustainable") support or conflict with resilience goals (Welsh-Huggins 2017). Because concrete is one of the most widely consumed materials in the world, and its production is energy-intensive and environmentally-impactful (Flower & Sanjayan 2007; Worrell et al. 2001), we focus in this study on alternative, potentially green, concretes that can replace conventional materials with repurposed waste or recycled materials. Two categories of concretes are considered: (1) concretes in which fly ash, a byproduct of coal combustion, is used to replace some of the cement; and (2) concretes in which some of the gravel (coarse aggregate) is replaced with recycled concrete aggregate (RCA).

There is substantial literature on the mechanical properties, environmental impacts, and long-term durability of these alternative materials (see Welsh-Huggins 2017 for a more detailed review of this literature). The environmental impacts of fly ash concretes are generally found to be lower than conventional concretes, largely due to the reduction in cement needs when cement is replaced with fly ash. However, RCA concretes are more porous than conventional concretes, and their mix designs may require additional cement to ensure that design strengths can be achieved. As a result, RCA concretes may actually increase embodied carbon, due to the larger cement requirements, while reducing demands for mining of virgin materials. However, few studies have been conducted on the performance of buildings in extreme events, like an earthquake, when built using these alternative materials for structural concretes. An analytical study of a reinforced concrete bridge by Rodriguez-Nikl et al. (2012) seemed to indicate a conflict between resilience and sustainability objectives for variations of a bridge designed with RCA concretes. Likewise, shake table tests conducted by Changqing and Jianzhuang (2013) showed potentially worse performance of an RCA building than a conventional concrete building, due to development of a weak story mechanism.

This section explores how the adoption of alternative materials may impact resilience positively or negatively using a code-conforming building, designed and assessed with both conventional and alternative concretes. The study examines a 4-story code-compliant reinforced concrete frame building in Los Angeles, designed with conventional concrete and three fly ash concretes (with varying percentages of cement replacement with fly ash) and three RCA concretes (with varying percentages of coarse aggregate replacement with RCA). We evaluate "resilience" in terms of the structure's capacity to withstand extreme events, examining how alternative concretes change the damage experienced by the building during earthquakes, as well as associated repair needs and environmental impacts. We assess the life-cycle seismic performance and environmental impacts of this RC building through nonlinear dynamic simulation, probabilistic environmental impact accounting, in term of embodied carbon, and probabilistic seismic loss analysis, in terms of economic and environmental metrics, as described above.

The mix design of our conventional concrete contains cement, water, and virgin coarse (gravel) and fine (sand) aggregate. All concrete mixes are designed to reach the same 28-day strength of 35.8 MPa (5,200 psi). In defining the LCA boundary for assessing these alternative concrete materials, we exclude the environmental impacts from the coal plant operations that generate fly ash and material extraction and those impacts from the production processes for the original concrete materials that are eventually recycled to form RCA. However, we consider the processing and transportation impacts that result from converting these waste products (fly ash and RCA) into usable materials (for more details, see Welsh-Huggins 2017). The analysis does not consider the different porosities and durability levels of the concretes, nor their impacts on chloride intrusion and time-dependent material properties.

24.4.2 Key findings

The use of fly ash concrete as a structural concrete in a seismic region can reduce life-cycle environmental impacts of a building, without compromising resilience.

We first present results on the environmental impacts associated with constructing a building with fly ash structural concrete. Our study indicates that the embodied carbon – or equivalent CO_2 emissions – from producing a volume of fly ash is approximately 92 percent lower than that from the production of the same volume of cement. Therefore, replacing even 20 percent of cement with fly ash will reduce the emissions associated with concrete production (by 15%).

This calculation considers the environmental impacts of capturing, milling, and refining the fly ash waste product for use in structural concrete mixes (Flower & Sanjayan 2007), and of transporting the fly ash from a coal-fired power plant to a concrete plant (considering that the coal plants currently closest to Southern California are in Utah).

The main input to the upfront embodied carbon of the entire 4-story reinforced concrete frame building (i.e., the functional unit of analysis) is the CO_2 emissions associated with production of each alternative concrete. As expected, the total upfront environmental impact of the building decreases when the structural concrete has more fly ash, due to the reductions in environmental impacts associated with the concrete. For the most fly ash-heavy concrete, the building's upfront embodied carbon is 87 percent of that of the conventional concrete building.

To construct nonlinear simulation models of the 4-story building with alternative concretes, we first estimated the stress-strain response of the alternative concretes with added fly ash. Our analysis of over 100 articles examining the stress-strain response of fly ash concretes (Welsh-Huggins 2017) showed virtually no difference in response when fly ash was added to mixes (when the fly ash and conventional concrete mixes targeted the same design strength). Preliminary analyses subsequently showed that, although replacing cement with fly ash in concrete slightly enhances compressive strength, these gains are insufficient to substantially alter the collapse capacity, seismic demand, or earthquake-induced losses of an entire building. As a result, the seismic performance predictions for the buildings with fly ash structural concrete are assumed to be identical to those from the building with conventional concrete (Figure 24.8).

Given that the replacement of cement with fly ash does not change the structural response or seismic performance assessment, the differences in earthquake-related environmental impacts in Figure 24.9 are those associated with repairs or replacement of cement/concrete materials. Here, we assume that each building is repaired with the same type of concrete used in its original construction. Thus, the fly ash concrete buildings have lower seismic environmental impacts because the production of the concrete material for repairs and replacement

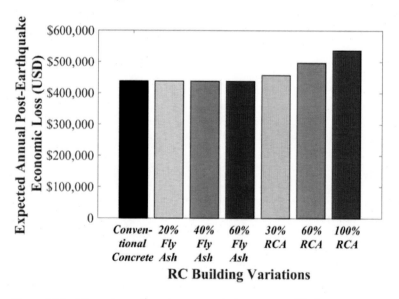

Figure 24.8 Life-cycle earthquake economic losses, quantified as an annuity, for the 4-story reinforced concrete building with alternative structural concretes.

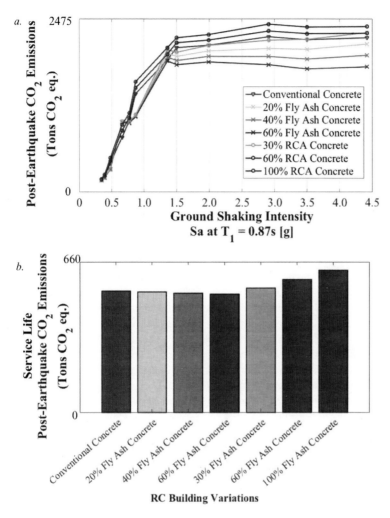

Figure 24.9 Life-cycle earthquake embodied carbon losses for case study building constructed with conventional and alternative concretes: (a) as a function of ground shaking intensity level and (b) totaled over the entire 50-year service life.

is less impactful. At low levels of shaking (corresponding to roughly $Sa(T_1 = 0.87s) < 1.4g$ in Figure 24.9), nonstructural components dominate repair actions, meaning that earthquake repairs for all buildings are similar, since repairs to concrete materials are minimal. However, the lower emissions associated with fly ash concretes offer improved earthquake environmental impacts when structural damage begins to occur at higher shaking intensities. Therefore, the life-cycle earthquake CO_2 emissions decrease with increasing amounts of fly ash. Replacement of 60 percent of cement with fly ash decreases life-cycle earthquake CO_2 emissions by 7.5 percent, relative to the building with conventional concrete.

The total life-cycle impacts of the alternative materials are a function of both the upfront and service life earthquake environmental impacts. Relative to the building with conventional concrete, the fly ash concrete buildings have lower upfront emissions (by up to 13%) and lower service life earthquake-related emissions (by 7.5%). Thus, the positive seismic performance (lower earthquake-related emissions) of the fly ash concretes contributes to overall lower life-cycle environmental impacts. Despite this benefit, use of fly ash concrete in the future may be limited by continued divestment from coal plant power in the US. At present, however, adoption of fly ash concretes in design of reinforced concrete buildings supports goals for both green building outcomes and hazard resistant objectives, in terms of reducing both upfront and post-earthquake embodied carbon.

The use of RCA concretes as a structural concrete may increase environmental impacts associated with embodied carbon in a seismic region, and may also worsen seismic performance.

Again, we first present results on the environmental impacts associated with constructing a building with an alternative concrete, this time focusing on the RCA concrete buildings. The CO_2 emissions associated with processing waste concrete into RCA is 30 percent lower than those generated from producing the same volume of virgin coarse aggregate. This calculation considers the impacts of crushing and sorting of waste concrete to form RCA, as well as impacts from transportation of materials. However, replacing virgin coarse aggregate with RCA also requires higher volumes of the most carbon-intensive material (cement) in a mix design to achieve the targeted strength. As a result, the environmental impact of the RCA concretes is very similar to that of the conventional concretes, because the benefits from using RCA as coarse aggregate are balanced by the negative effects from using additional cement. As a result, the upfront life-cycle stage embodied carbon impacts of a 4-story building with RCA concretes is virtually unaltered from the building with conventional concrete.

As a concrete's virgin coarse aggregate is replaced with RCA, existing literature (summarized in Welsh-Huggins 2017) indicates a slight decrease in peak strength, an increase in flexibility, and an increase in the ultimate strain in the stress-strain response, even when the mix design targets the same compressive strength. The impact of this change in the material response on earthquake-induced economic losses is shown in Figure 24.10. The collapse capacity of a building increases slightly with higher percentages of RCA concrete, due to its somewhat more ductile material level response. However, RCA concrete buildings also experience slightly higher drift and acceleration demands, resulting in more (and costlier) repair actions and higher nonstructural component losses. These losses outweigh the benefits from improved collapse resistance. The effect of these losses over the entire building life-cycle indicate about a 20 percent increase in losses between the building with conventional concrete and that with 100 percent replacement of coarse aggregate by RCA. Therefore, this study suggests that seismic losses associated with the constructing a building with RCA concrete increase with greater aggregate replacement percentage.

Overall, the CO_2 equivalent emissions associated with constructing an RCA concrete building are almost identical to the conventional concrete case, but the earthquake impacts are higher. Therefore, the benefits of reducing the use of virgin aggregate seem to come at the expense of earthquake-induced losses or resilience, due to moderately worse seismic performance. Furthermore, this loss of resilience can have negative environmental impacts not apparent in analysis of the initial building construction, at least in terms of embodied carbon. In the coming years, it is likely that there will continue to be a steady supply of demolished existing structures providing a source of RCA. For use in high seismic areas, work is needed to develop concrete mix designs that utilize this aggregate without potentially compromising seismic performance.

a.

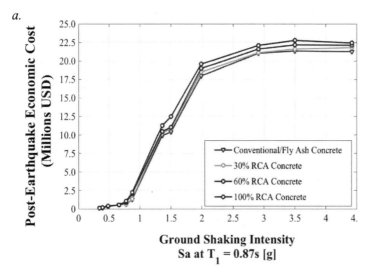

b.

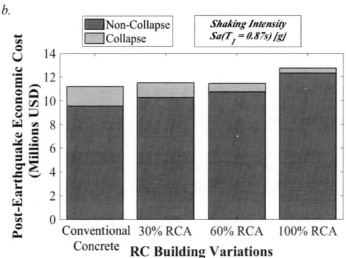

Figure 24.10 Life-cycle earthquake economic losses for case study building constructed with conventional and alternative concretes showing: (a) economic losses as a function of ground shaking intensity, and (b) economic losses deaggregated by collapse and non-collapse losses.

24.5 Conclusions

This chapter identifies and assesses tradeoffs between goals to build buildings that are more sustainable and more resilient. Although the studies presented use reinforced concrete buildings in a high seismic region of Southern California as the focus of the analysis, a number of the identified tradeoffs shed light on building and infrastructure design and assessment more broadly, and especially in earthquake prone areas.

The key findings are as follows:

- **The manufacturing and repair of some nonstructural components (i.e. architectural, mechanical, and electrical systems) are associated with significant embodied carbon.** As a result, our analyses showed that buildings with less robust structural systems (i.e. higher collapse risk) can incur smaller environmental impacts than buildings with more robust structural systems in which there are significant drift and acceleration demands on nonstructural components. As a practical matter, this finding suggests that there is an opportunity to design and invest in more resilient nonstructural component systems, to reduce their potential damage in future hazard events. These changes could produce positive payoffs in terms of both sustainability and resilience objectives.
- **Increasing building ductility capacity, while important for life safety and collapse resistance in earthquake prone areas, can have negative environmental impacts.** Our studies show that these negative impacts can accumulate from both the upfront design changes that occur to provide the additional ductility capacity, as well as the correlation between ductility, and damage and repairs. To advance sustainability and resilience goals, it is important to consider building designs holistically, accounting for not only collapse risk (the focus of building codes), but also on earthquake-induced repair requirements. In many cases, it may be fruitful for designers to provide the requisite deformation capacity to achieve life safety goals, but to focus further investments on enhancing other aspects of building performance.
- **Increasing building lateral strength generally is associated with improvements in resilience that translate into improvements in sustainability.** Our results suggest that designing stronger requires greater member sizes that have additional costs (environmental and otherwise). However, in earthquake-prone regions, these costs can be more than offset by the improvements in outcomes for the stronger building, and this finding is likely applicable regardless of structure type or material choice. While we focused on earthquake-resistant design, these benefits of strength are likely also applicable in regions where other hazards (such as hurricanes or landslides) may be significant.
- **The impacts of green building technologies on resilience vary.** Of the two classes of alternative structural concretes considered, one – the fly ash concretes – appears to improve sustainability metrics without compromising seismic resilience. The other – concretes with recycled concrete aggregate – may, in fact, amplify environmental impacts when the cement content is increased to achieve design concrete strengths, and when the repair impacts of this material in an earthquake event are considered. An earlier study by the authors (Welsh-Huggins & Liel 2017) of green roof systems likewise showed that green roofs can reduce operational energy costs, but may worsen building response under seismic loads and require upsizing of structural members. These findings encourage engineers to assess other green building features, like solar panels, or other alternative building materials, like modular timber construction, in the context of resilience objectives. Designing for sustainability goals need not compromise a structure's hazard resistance, but it may introduce conflicts that should be addressed in design.

The longevity of infrastructure in the twenty-first century will depend on harmonious, not harmful, interactions with the natural environment. The findings of this research suggest that design goals to promote resilient and sustainable buildings need not be at odds and can, in fact, be mutually reinforcing. However, in other cases, careful consideration is needed to identify, quantify, and evaluate the impacts of each design objective (whether for resilience or sustainability) on building life-cycle outcomes to support holistic decision making. The analysis approach and findings presented here encourage inclusion of green building ideals in hazard-resilient design practices and vice versa. In addition, the study shows that earthquake and other hazard impacts can be incorporated seamlessly in life-cycle cost and environmental assessments.

Acknowledgments

This research was made possible through the support of the National Science Foundation (NSF), Grant #1234503. Any opinions, findings, and recommendations expressed are those of the authors and do not necessarily reflect the views of NSF. The authors gratefully acknowledge the Haselton Baker Risk Group for providing access to the SP3 software. Discussions with Sherri Cook, Joseph Kasprzyk, Tona Rodriguez-Nikl, and Wil Srubar were particularly helpful in developing the ideas herein.

References

ACI (2011). *Building code requirements for structural concrete (ACI 318-11) and commentary (ACI 318R-11)*. Farmington Hills, MI: American Concrete Institute.

ASCE (2010). *Minimum design loads for buildings and other structures: ASCE/SEI 7–10*. Reston, VA: American Society of Civil Engineers.

ATC (2012a). *Seismic performance assessment of buildings. Volume 1 – Methodology* (Vol. 1). Redwood City, CA: Applied Technology Council.

ATC (2012b). *Seismic performance assessment of buildings. Volume 2 – Implementation guide* (Vol. 2). Redwood City, CA: Applied Technology Council.

Bare, J. (2012). "Tool for the Reduction and Assessment of Chemical and Other Environmental Impacts (TRACI): Version 2.1 User's Manual." http://nepis.epa.gov/Adobe/PDF/P100HN53.pdf (last accessed August 18, 2018).

Berke, P.R. (1995). Natural-hazard reduction and sustainable development: a global assessment. *Journal of Planning Literature*, *9*(4), 370–82.

Bocchini, P., Frangopol, D.M., Ummenhofer, T., and Zinke, T. (2014). Resilience and sustainability of civil infrastructure: toward a unified approach. *Journal of Infrastructure Systems*, *4014004*, 1–16.

Bokalders, V. and Block, M. (2010). *The Whole Building Handbook*. London: Earthscan.

BREEAM. (2015). What is BREEAM? www.breeam.org

Bruneau M., Chang, S.E., Eguchi, R.T., Lee, G.C., O'Rourke, T.D., Reinhorn, A.M., Shinozuka, M., Tierney, K, Wallace, W., and von Winterfledt, D. (2003). A framework to quantitatively assess and enhance the seismic resilience of communities. *Earthquake Spectra*, *19*(4), 733–52.

Changqing, W. and Jianzhuang, X. (2013). Study of the seismic response of a recycled aggregate concrete frame structure. *Earthqquake Engineering and Engineering Vibration 12*(4), 669–80.

Ching, E. (2014). *Building Construction Illustrated*. Hoboken, New Jersey: Wiley.

Chiu, C.K., Chen, M.R., and Chiu, C.H. (2013). Financial and environmental payback periods of seismic retrofit investments for reinforced concrete buildings estimated using a novel method. *Journal of Architectural Engineering*, *19*(2), 112–18.

Comber, M. V., & Poland, C. D. (2013). Disaster resilience and sustainable design: quantifying the benefits of a holistic design approach. Structures Congress 2013, 2717–28.

Comber, M.V., Poland, C., and Sinclair, M. (2012). Environmental impact seismic assessment: Application of performance-based earthquake engineering methodologies to optimize environmental performance. *Structures Congress 2012*, 910–21.

Court, A., Simonen, K., Webster, M., Trusty, W., and Morris, P. (2012). Linking next-generation performance-based seismic design criteria to environmental performance (ATC-86 and ATC-58). In *Structures Congress 2012* (pp. 922–8).

Cowing, M.M., Pate, M.E., and Glynn, P.W. (2004). Dynamic modeling of the tradeoff between productivity and safety in critical engineering systems. *Reliability Engineering and System Safety*, *86*, 269–84.

Flower, D.J.M. and Sanjayan, J.G. (2007). Green house gas emissions due to concrete manufacture. *International Journal of Life Cycle Assessment*, *12*(5), 282–8.

461

Goulet, C.A., Haselton, C.B., Mitrani-reiser, J., Beck, J.L., Deierlein, G.G., Porter, K. A., and Stewart, J.P. (2007). Evaluation of the seismic performance of a code-conforming reinforced-concrete frame building — from seismic hazard to collapse safety and economic losses. *Earthquake Engineering and Structural Dynamics*, *36*, 1973–97.

Gromala, D.S., Kapur, O., Kochkin, V., Line, P., Passman, S., Reeder, A., and Trusty, W. (2010). *Natural Hazards and Sustainability for Residential Buildings*. FEMA P-798.

Guggemos, A.A. and Horvath, A. (2005). Comparison of environmental effects of steel- and concrete-framed Buildings. *Journal of Infrastructure Systems*, 11(2), 93–101.

Haselton, C.B., Liel, A.B., Deierlein, G.G., Dean, B.S., and Chou, J.H. (2011). Seismic collapse safety of reinforced concrete buildings. I: Assessment of ductile moment frames. *Journal of Structural Engineering*, *137*(4), 481–91.

Haselton Baker Risk Group. (2016). Seismic Performance Prediction Program. www.hbrisk.com/

Ibarra, L.F., Medina, R.A., and Krawinkler, H. (2005). Hysteretic models that incorporate strength and stiffness deterioration. *Earthquake Engineering & Structural Dynamics*, *34*(12), 1489–1511.

International Organization for Standardization (ISO). 2006. "ISO 14040-Environmental Management – Life-cycle Assessment – Principles and Framework." *International Organization for Standardization* 3: 20. doi:10.1016/j.ecolind.2011.01.007.

Jacquet, J., Hagel, K., Hauert, C., Marotzke, J., Röhl, T., and Milinski, M. (2013). Intra- and intergenerational discounting in the climate game. *Nature Climate Change*, *3*(12), 1025–8.

Mileti, D.S. and Peek-Gottschlich, L. (2001). Hazards and sustainable development in the United States. *Risk Management*, *3*(1), 61–70.

Pacific Earthquake Engineering Research Center (PEER). (2014). The open system for earthquake engineering simulation. www.opensees.berkeley.org.

Padgett, J. and Li, Y. (2016). Risk-based assessment of sustainability and hazard resistance of structural design. *Journal of Performance of Constructed Facilities* 30(2), 04014208. https://ascelibrary.org/doi/pdf/10.1061/%28ASCE%29CF.1943-5509.0000723 (last accessed September 8, 2018).

Pate-Cornell, M.E. (1984). Discounting in risk analysis: capital vs. human safety. In M. Grigoriu (ed.), *Risk, Structural Engineering and Human Error*. Waterloo, Canada: University of Waterloo.

Porter, K.A., 2003. An overview of PEER's performance-based earthquake engineering methodology. *Proc. Ninth International Conference on Applications of Statistics and Probability in Civil Engineering (ICASP9) July 6–9, 2003, San Francisco, CA.* Civil Engineering Risk and Reliability Association (CERRA), http://spot.colorado.edu/~porterka/

Portland Cement Association (PCA). (2012). Functional resilience: prerequisite for green buildings. www.sustainableconcrete.org.

Ramirez, C.M., Liel, A.B., Haselton, C.B., Mitrani-Reiser, J., Haselton, C.B., Spear, A.D., … Miranda, E. (2012). Expected earthquake damage and repair costs in reinforced concrete frame buildings. *Earthquake Engineering & Structural Dynamics*, *41*(11), 1455–75.

Rodriguez-Nikl, T. (2015). Linking disaster resilience and sustainability. *Civil Engineering and Environmental Systems*, 32(1–2), 157–69.

Rodriguez-Nikl, T., Christiansen, J.W., and Walters, K. (2012). Reliability-based life cycle assessment of green concrete structures. *American Concrete Institute: Special Publication*, *289*, 1–13.

Sattar, S. and A.B. Liel (2017). "Collapse indicators for existing nonductile concrete buildings with varying column and frame characteristics," *Engineering Structures*, 152, 188–201.

Schelling, T.C. (1995). Intergenerational discounting. *Energy Policy*, *23*(4–5), 395–401.

Schwab, A.K. and Brower, D.J. (1999). *Sustainable Development and Natural Hazards Mitigation*. Raleigh, North Carolina: North Carolina Division of Emergency Management.

Swiss Centre for Life-cycle Inventories (2014). "Ecoinvent Database" 3.1 (July). Düebendorf, Switzerland.

Tol, R.S.J. (2011). The social cost of carbon. *Annual Review of Resource Economics*, *3*, 419–43.

USGBC (2009). *Green Building and LEED Core Concepts*. Washington, DC.

Vamvatsikos, D. and Cornell, C.A. (2002). Incremental dynamic analysis. *Earthquake Engineering & Structural Dynamics*, *31*(3), 491–514.

Vamvatsikos, D. and Cornell, C.A. (2006). Direct estimation of the seismic demand and capacity of oscillators with multi-linear static pushovers through IDA. *Earthquake Engineering and Structural Dynamics*, *35*(9), 1097–1117.

Wei, H., Shohet, I.M., Skibniewski, J., and Shapira, S. (2016a). Assessing the lifecycle sustainability costs and benefits of seismic mitigation designs for buildings. *J. Archit. Eng.*, *22*(1), 1–13.

Wei, H., Skibniewski, J., Shohet, I.M., and Yao, X. (2016b). Lifecycle environmental performance of natural-hazard mitigation for buildings. *Journal of Performance of Constructed Facilities*, *30*(3), 1–13.

Welsh-Huggins, S. (2017) *Evaluating Tradeoffs Between Hazard-Resistance and Environmental Impacts: A Multi-Criteria Approach to Building Design and Life-cycle Performance*. Ph.D. Dissertation, University of Colorado Boulder.

Welsh-Huggins, S.J. and Liel, A.B. (2017). A life-cycle framework for integrating green building and hazard-resistant design: examining the seismic impacts of buildings with green roofs. *Structure and Infrastructure Engineering*, 13(1), 19–33.

Welsh-Huggins, S.J. and Liel, A.B. (2018). Evaluating multi-objective outcomes for hazard resilience and sustainability from enhanced building seismic design decisions. *Journal of Structural Engineering*, In press.

Worrell, E., Price, L., Martin, N., Hendriks, C., and Meida, L.O. (2001). Carbon dioxide emissions from the global cement industry. *Annual Review of Energy Environment*, *26*, 303–29.

Part VI

The role of dependencies/ interdependencies

25

The role of interdependencies in infrastructure modeling and community resilience

Dorothy A. Reed and Shuoqi Wang

CIVIL AND ENVIRONMENTAL ENGINEERING, UNIVERSITY OF WASHINGTON, SEATTLE, WA, USA

25.1 Introduction

The resilience of communities following natural disasters has been the focus of much attention in recent years. In particular, the lack of post-hurricane resilience in Texas, Florida, and Puerto Rico in 2017 has had profound effects on US society. The type of devastation wreaked by hurricanes Harvey, Irma, and Maria has illustrated the importance of durable civil infrastructure especially in urban areas. First and foremost, in any natural disaster, the safety of residents in buildings and other structures is paramount. Secondly, although many residents may be able to find shelter from storms and flooding, they need basic human services after the storm passes. Civil infrastructure systems provide these basic services for the proper functioning of modern society. In this chapter, "infrastructure" is comprised of "human," "green," and "gray" systems. All aspects of these civil infrastructure systems must be examined to provide a complete picture of community resilience.

The interactions among the infrastructure systems have been labeled as "interdependencies." The simplest characterization is that interdependencies represent *relationships* among the various systems of the infrastructure. For engineering models, the numerical simulation of the performance of the various subsystems provides a framework for assessing and evaluating the inherent correlations. In the context of this chapter, resiliency models will be employed as a means to characterize the interdependent relationships. Infrastructure resiliency models will be presented in this section before the relationships among them are discussed.

25.1.1 Infrastructure definitions

Types: Green, gray, and human
Human infrastructure systems, also known as human resources or capital, are the social organization of a community. They include the activities and behaviors of individuals, families, neighborhoods, etc. They also include governmental and non-governmental organizations that provide vital services.

Green infrastructure systems are the natural areas or green spaces that provide essential services for the community. Rottle (2013) defined *urban green infrastructure* as five systems that provide integrated multiple benefits. These five systems, also referred to as "dimensions," are *social, biological, hydrological, circulatory,* and *metabolic.* The social dimension is comprised mainly of public outdoor spaces. The biological dimension includes green belts and trees, which provide biological diversity. The hydrological dimension includes storm water, urban drainage, and swales; the metabolic dimension includes solar panel arrays and building integrated cladding, and efficient building heating-ventilation and air-conditioning or HVAC; and the circulatory dimension includes transportation systems such as bike paths and pedestrian trails.

Gray or built infrastructure systems are defined here as a set of 11 networked interdependent systems often referred to as "lifelines." In the formulation derived by (Chang et al. 2005), the 11 lifelines are

1. Electric power delivery with subsystems of distribution, transmission and generation;
2. Telecommunications with subsystems of cable, broadband, cell towers and associated equipment, and media;
3. Transportation, with subsystems of roadways connected via bridges; airports, mass transit, and port facilities;
4. Utilities, with subsystems of water supply and treatment, oil and natural gas delivery;
5. Building support, with subsystems of HVAC, elevators, security, and plumbing;
6. Business, with computer and other subsystems;
7. Emergency services, with subsystems of 911, ambulance, fire, police, and shelters;
8. Financial systems, with subsystems of ATM, banks, credit cards, and stock exchange;
9. Food supply, with subsystems of distribution, storage, preparation, and production;
10. Government, with subsystems of offices and services; and
11. Health care, with subsystems of hospitals and public health.

Influence of space and time scales on properties

Community resiliency models may be derived using network theory, geo-spatial statistical systems theory, time series analysis, input–output models, or combinations of these approaches, e.g. NIST (Center for Risk-Based Community Resilience); Bruneau et al. (2003); Oregon Seismic Safety Policy Commission (2013); Lewis (2006). Model selection and composition are based upon the space and time scales required for analysis. Figure 25.1 provides a simple sketch of the influence of the spatial scale on the numerical modeling of infrastructure systems as it compares selected green, gray, and purple spatial scales.

For example, macro-level hazard modeling is required for national physical infrastructure performance assessment; human systems [purple] infrastructure at the federal level is important to recovery efforts nationally. At the community level, local transportation [gray] and wetlands [green] infrastructure are important.

Figure 25.2 illustrates the influence of the time and space scales for infrastructure systems subject to natural hazards such as hurricanes, floods, and fire. The life span for buildings in the US is about the same as a human life span (50–100 years). Forests (green infrastructure) and power lifelines (gray infrastructure) may be characterized by similar space and time scales. Climate change occurs over a century whereas individual hurricanes are a "blip" in time. Large-scale storms and major earthquakes can affect large regions, e.g. Hurricane Maria physically destroyed the built environment and severely damaged the natural environment of a significant number of islands in the Caribbean. The 2017 earthquake in Mexico affected millions of people. Because the infrastructure system models change over space and time, it is hypothesized that the associated interactions among the systems will vary also.

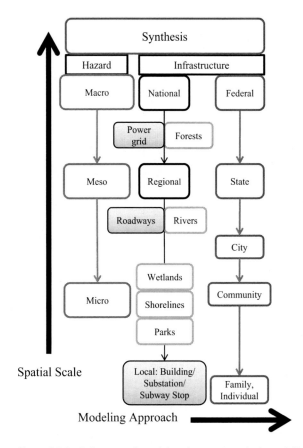

Figure 25.1   Influence of spatial scale on numerical modeling of infrastructure.

25.2 Interdependency definitions

The Infrastructure Assurance Center of Argonne National Laboratory (Pederson et al. 2006) provides the following broad definition of interdependency for civil infrastructure:

> the multi or bi-directional reliance of an asset, system, network, or collection thereof, within or across sectors, on input, interaction, or other requirement from other sources in order to function properly.

Rinaldi et al. (2001) delineated four major types of interdependencies: *physical, cyber, geographic* and *logical*. "Physical" involves the transfer among assets or users of goods or services; "cyber", the transfer of data or information; "geographic", the co-location of assets; and "logical", influences through human factors, policies or financial markets. Pederson et al. (2006) identified the categories of interdependencies as *physical, informational, geospatial, policy and procedural*, and *societal*. Petit & Lewis (2015) focused on *logical* interdependencies, which are perhaps the most challenging to delineate and model numerically. Logical dependencies are those which are not physical, cyber, or geographic in nature. They are part of the management of dependent systems. They include laws and policies that affect infrastructure operations. They also include

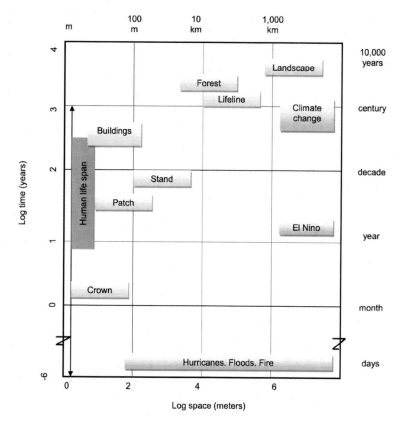

Figure 25.2 Time-space overlap of infrastructure.
Source: After Gunderson and Holling 2002.

the influence of supply chains, taxes and incentives, and other business and economic factors. Social influences of access and cost are also called logical dependencies.

25.2.1 Relationship-based

Normal or pre-event conditions
In his analysis of interdependent relationships, (Peerenboom 2007) created a database framework that synthesized information on linkages among community systems. His database model of interdependency among infrastructure systems under "normal" operating conditions required knowledge in many categories, including the following:

- Dependencies through direct reliance on other infrastructure, indirect reliance through supply chains, and reliance on vendors who supply goods and services;
- Cascading impacts from disruptions;
- If back-up systems are in place, and if so, how long will they last; and
- Information about infrastructure restoration priorities and timelines.

One of the most challenging aspects of identifying internal and external assets and networks is the desire for many service providers to maintain security, especially where data confidentiality

Table 25.1 Disruption scale

Disruption Scale		
6 = Very disruptive to many people		
5 = Very disruptive to a few people		
4 = Moderately disruptive to many people		
3 = Moderately disruptive to a few people		
2 = Minor inconvenience to many people		
1 = Minor inconvenience to a few people		
Definitions		
Many people =		*Few people =*
More than 100,000 people		Less than 100,000 people
Very disruptive	*Moderately disruptive*	*Minor inconvenience*
Requires significant modifications in daily routine or plans and causes considerable hardship to the person or entity	Requires a few modifications in daily routine or plans and causes some hardship to the person or entity	Requires minor modifications in daily routine or plans and causes negligible hardship to the person or entity

Source: After Chang et al. 2005.

is concerned. In addition, many businesses do not appreciate government oversight. However, establishing communication about public–private interdependencies before disasters occur can be very beneficial to everyone in the community.

Trans and post-event conditions

The interdependent behavior of infrastructure during and after extreme events has received the most attention by the research community. Table 25.1 provides a disruption scale for the effect of a natural hazard on civil infrastructure. The degree of disruption is defined in terms of the population affected. The table provides a somewhat subjective relationship between infrastructure loss of functionality and social disruption.

The type of interdependencies and the assessment of consequences are given in Table 25.2 for gray and green infrastructure. Table 25.2 provides the constituent elements of a broad framework for describing how the loss of functionality of one infrastructure system affects others and the consequences of the losses in society. The table provides attributes of the dimensions of "outage" events and "interactions" with other systems. The consequences may be far-reaching in part due to the interactions. The framework is equally appropriate for green and gray infrastructure.

Characteristics of green and human infrastructure system interactions have been investigated by Gunderson and Holling (2002) and others, e.g. Tzoulas (2007). These characteristics include heterogeneity, predictability, resilience, decomposability, productivity, and extent in space and time. The ability to relate the two systems at the community level in a resilience analysis has been undertaken; however, the typical engineering approach has been to identify the green services required and to model behaviors when outages occur to assess interdependencies through acceptance levels (e.g. Nojima & Sugito 2005; Terpstra & Lindell 2013).

25.2.2 Subjective versus objective metrics in decision-making

Objective measurement of all of the attributes discussed in Section 25.2.1 is not possible, particularly in terms of the impacts. Some researchers and practitioners have used scales of "small,"

Table 25.2 Attributes of interdependent systems failures

Dimension	Attributes	Example Values for (Gray) Power Delivery Systems	Example Values for (Green) Urban Swales
Inoperability	Initiating Event	Internal to the electric power delivery system, External	Internal to water drainage system, External
	Spatial extent	Local, Regional, National, International	Local, Regional
	Duration	Minutes, Hours, Days, Weeks	Minutes, Hours, Days, Weeks
	Weather	Moderate, Extreme	Moderate, Extreme
	Temperature	Cold, Mild, Hot	Cold, Mild, Hot
Interactions	Type of dependency	Physical, Geographic, Cyber, Logical	Physical, Geographic, Logical
	Type of interdependent failure	Cascading, Escalating	Cascading, Escalating
	Order	Direct, Second, Higher	Direct, Second
	Complexity	Linear, Complex	Linear, Complex
	Feedback to electric power	Yes, No	No
	Operational state of dependent system	At capacity at time of event, Near capacity, Below capacity	At capacity at time of event, Near capacity, Below capacity
	Potential for adaptive response	High, Low	High, Low
	Restart time for dependent system	Minutes, Hours, Days, Weeks	Hours, Days, Weeks, Months
Consequence	Severity of impact	Minor inconvenience, Moderate disruption, Major disruption	Minor inconvenience, Moderate disruption, Major disruption
	Type of impact	Economic, Environmental, Health, Safety, Social	Environmental, Health, Safety, Social
	Spatial extent of impact	Local, Regional, National, International	Local, Regional
	Number of people impacted in spatial extent	Few, Many, Most	Few, Many, Most
	Duration of impact	Minutes, Hours, Days, Weeks	Hours, Days, Weeks, Months

Source: After Chang et al. 2005; McDaniels et al. 2007.

"medium," and "high" to characterize the relationship between the outage of one system and another dependent system (e.g. Oregon Seismic Safety Policy Commission 2013). This approach, while useful in establishing influences, does not provide enough information for engineering approaches. Engineers rely on numerical models for simulation of networked system services, as well as weighting factors and measures, which can be verified and calibrated. In this regard, the use of influence diagrams and Bayes nets are important for evaluating numerical weights and combinations. In addition, it is noted that levels of community acceptance of infrastructure service outages have been investigated by Nojima for earthquake events in Japan (Nojima et al. 1995). In this chapter, outage models will be derived, which may then be employed by urban planners and others to predict acceptability and possible post-event behaviors.

25.3 Resilience models using inoperability

The emphasis of the Argonne National Laboratory definition on the ability of the assets to "function properly" provides a starting point for numerical modeling of interdependency. That is, the *reliance* of one asset on another is best described through the *function* of the asset or system. Because of interdependent *relationships*, one lifeline may not be able to function properly without the input of another. In the context of this chapter, the ability of an asset to *function* is described as the *operability* of the asset: Is it operating at capacity, or has its ability to operate been compromised in some way?

Operability is tied to the notion that each infrastructure system provides a service, or services, and its ability to provide that service without interruption is its function. This leads to the list of services that are required for society to function properly. It is noted that the words "service" and "functionality" are used here as opposed to the word "serviceability" because it has a different structural engineering connotation in ASCE7-16 (American Society of Civil Engineers 2016). This formulation makes green and gray systems interdependent, rather than separate (Holling 2001). Table 25.3 illustrates the equivalent services provided by green and gray infrastructure. Additionally, this green-gray formulation encompasses the idea that negative consequences of this relationship can occur. For example, trees may contribute to water filtration, CO_2 sequestration, and slope stability, but individual failure, especially at the base (root), may exacerbate the failure of electric power distribution lines.

The characterization of the *operability*, or conversely the *inoperability*, of each lifeline to provide services is through resilience modeling, with the dimensions of "robustness," "rapidity," "redundancy," and "resourcefulness," as designated by Bruneau et al. (2003). Figure 25.3 illustrates these concepts.

In this figure, the inoperability $X(t)$ is zero percent when the system is fully functional, and then after landfall of the hurricane, it increases. A completely failed system would result in $X(t) = 100\%$. The robustness and vulnerability of the system are identified in the plot. In this formulation, robustness is the complement of "vulnerability." In the structural engineering community, the "vulnerability" is often called a "fragility." That is, it represents the probability of damage or failure of a component or system for a certain level of hazard intensity. The time at which the impact of the hazard is felt according to Figure 25.3 is at time t equals zero. The rest of the curve shows the recovery of the system or component. "Rapidity" describes how quickly the recovery occurs. At a system level, "redundancy" contributes to the "robustness" and reduces the "vulnerability." The "rapidity" of recovery is affected by the degree of "resourcefulness" of a community. Numerical modeling of the resiliency will be discussed in detail in subsections of Section 25.4.

25.4 Assessment of interdependency through inoperability resilience modeling

25.4.1 Influence diagrams

Community resilience may be evaluated through post-event numerical modeling of infrastructure systems using influence diagrams. An influence diagram is a decision-making technique

Table 25.3 Green and gray infrastructure equivalent services

Green	Gray	Service
Forests and wetlands	Water filtration facility	Clean drinking water
Mangroves	Seawalls	Shoreline protection
Natural floodplains	Dikes and canals	Flood prevention
Wetlands, including swales	Tertiary water treatment facility	Clean effluent from municipal or industrial processes

Source: After Talberth and Hanson (n.d.).

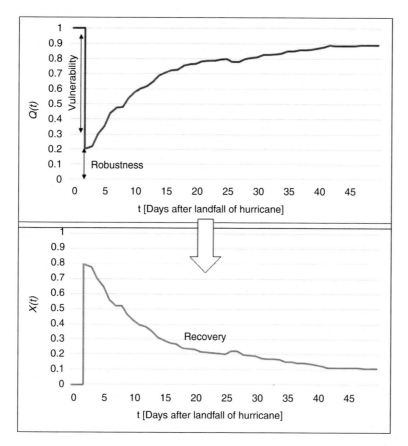

Figure 25.3 Examples of operability Q(t) and inoperability X(t) for a hurricane.

for combining events in a causal manner (e.g. Clemen & Reilly 2001). The diagram is acyclical, with deterministic, probabilistic, and decision nodes connected in a causal manner, terminating in a decision, or the diagram may only illustrate the relationships among the various assets of a system. The degree of disruption to a community post event may be visually assessed through the influence diagram. An example is provided in Figure 25.4 for the gray infrastructure system post-landfall for Hurricane Rita in affected Louisiana parishes. In this diagram, there is no decision node, but rather circular nodes of the infrastructure system inoperabilities $X_i(t)$ are connected in a causal fashion. The rectangular boxes represent specific instances of outage related damages.

The initiating event is shown in the center of the diagram (electric power delivery X_1) with the power delivery system becoming *inoperable* due to the storm. The influence of the power outage is linked to the other ten gray systems delineated in the first subsection of Section 25.1.1. The diagram may be used to assess the influence of the power system on the recovery of other systems through a_{ij} values representing the influence of one system upon another. It is noted that the storm itself has an influence on the community in addition to the infrastructure problems as shown in a simple form in Figure 25.5. The extreme weather has an effect on the population directly, such as the temperature being very high or low. The extreme weather

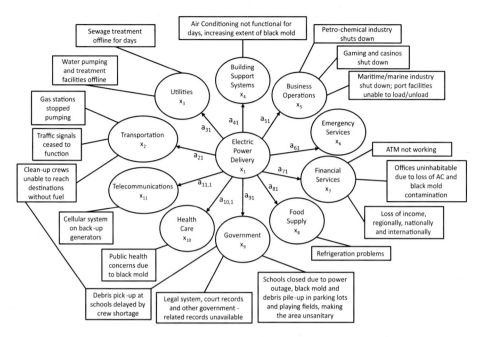

Figure 25.4 Simple influence diagram for Louisiana parishes following Hurricane Rita. The diagram has an initiating event "electric power outage" which influences other infrastructure systems. The a_{ij} weights are influence coefficients.

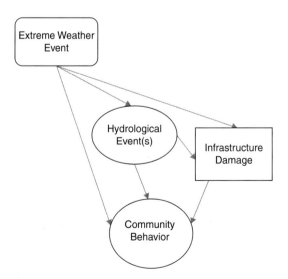

Figure 25.5 Simple influence diagram for a community following an extreme weather event.

also indirectly affects the population through flooding (hydrological event) and infrastructure damage (loss of power, loss of transportation systems, etc.).

Assessment of dependency

Influence diagrams have been used in the decision analysis community to assess "causality" in the form of conditional probabilities. While the notion of "causality" is a philosophical construct (Pearl 2007), for the purposes of the interdependency analysis, the conditional probability formulation is used as a means to model numerically the influence of one node upon another in a larger network. The assessment of conditional probabilities for the Rita storm may be undertaken by evaluating conditional probabilities as stated in Equation (25.1):

$$a_{ij} = \text{probability of infrastructure component inoperability } X_j \qquad (25.1)$$
$$\text{conditional on inoperability } X_i$$

The network model using these types of relationships is a "causal" or "Bayes" network.

Basis for scale of causal network models

Simple causal networks are possible for interdependency modeling, but the assessment of the multiple probabilities required in a realistic setting can be formidable, even in such a simple diagram as in Figure 25.5. That is, if a node y is conditional upon "n" nodes X_r, where $r = 1, 2, \ldots n$, the assessment of conditional probabilities requires 2^n probability assessments. For this case, an approximation called the noisy OR is used, as given in Equation (25.2):

$$p(y \mid X_1, X_2, \ldots X_n) = 1 - \prod_{r=1}^{n} \left(1 - p(y \mid X_r)\right) \qquad (25.2)$$

Alternatively, larger spatial scales may be employed to simplify the number of nodes and links required to formulate an actual network model for infrastructure such as power delivery.

25.4.2 Input–output models: Time series

Input–output models have been selected for further study in this chapter because of their similarity to the influence diagram formulation of post-event behavior of infrastructure as discussed in Section 25.4.1 (Haimes 2004) made significant modifications to Leontief's input–output models for economic relationships (e.g. Leontief 1951) to characterize infrastructure system performance when subject to disruptions. Reed et al. (2009) removed the economic data from the Haimes formulation and replaced the "disruption" parameter with the fragility to obtain the following input–output relationships for lifeline operabilities denoted as X_1-$X_n(t)$:

$$\{X\} = [A]\{X\} + [B]\{\dot{X}\} + \{F\}$$

$$\{X\} = \begin{Bmatrix} X_1 \\ \vdots \\ X_n \end{Bmatrix}; \text{ where } X_i = \text{inoperability for the } i-th \text{ infrastructure system or lifeline:}$$

$\dot{X}_i$ = the derivative of the inoperability $X_i(t)$ with respect to time t;

$$[A] = \begin{bmatrix} a_{11} & \cdots & a_{1n} \\ \vdots & \ddots & \vdots \\ a_{n1} & \cdots & a_{nn} \end{bmatrix}$$

influence coefficient a_{ij} = the influence of $X_i(t)$ on $X_j(t)$;

$$[B] = \begin{bmatrix} b_{11} & \cdots & b_{1n} \\ \vdots & \ddots & \vdots \\ b_{n1} & \cdots & b_{nn} \end{bmatrix}$$

(25.3)

dynamic influence coefficient b_{ij} = the influence of $\dot{X}_i(t)$ on $\dot{X}_j(t)$;

$$\{F\} = \begin{Bmatrix} F_1 \\ \vdots \\ F_n \end{Bmatrix}; \text{ where } F_i = \text{fragility of system } i.$$

The diagonal values of the A matrix are equal to zero. The off-diagonal values may be derived from a causal approach as discussed in Section 25.4.1, or using linear regression approaches on post-event in situ data e.g. (Reed, Kapur, & Christie, 2009) as will be discussed in the following sections. The B matrix is not as easily modeled as the data sets required are not readily available for computing the inoperability derivatives.

It is noted that the input–output formulation of Equation (25.3) has been expanded greatly outside the world of economics to characterize many engineering relationships and systems (e.g. Box & Jenkins 1970). For example, random vibration theory employs the input–output formulation to describe the dynamic behavior of structures subject to input loadings such as earthquakes and hurricanes. Because knowledge of the $X(t)$ variables is required, we explore the time series models derived from combining the Bruneau et al. (2003) definitions of resilience with empirical in situ post-event data.

Figure 25.6 shows the relationship between the inoperability $X(t)$ time series and a single degree of freedom system (SDOF) mechanical analog. At the initial point of the response, i.e. $X(t)$ when $t = 0$, the vulnerability can best be determined from a fragility analysis. The "fragility" is defined here as a conditional probability function. The rapidity with which the system recovers depends in part upon the system redundancies, as well as upon the resourcefulness of the community to repair the damaged systems. It has been shown that $X(t)$ for wind and seismic events is best fit using the mechanical analog of the free vibration of an overdamped SDOF as given in Equation (25.4) below (Reed et al. 2015).

The SDOF system free vibration equation is

$$\ddot{X} + 2\zeta\omega\dot{X} + \omega^2 X = 0$$

(25.4)

The solution for an overdamped system is as follows:

$$X(t) = e^{-\alpha t}\left(\frac{X_0(\alpha+\beta)+\dot{X}_0}{2\beta}e^{\beta t} + \frac{X_0(\beta-\alpha)-\dot{X}_0}{2\beta}e^{-\beta t} \right)$$

where
$\ddot{X}$ = second derivative of X with respect to time t;
$\dot{X}$ = first derivative of X with respect to time t;
$X(t=0) = X_0; \dot{X}(t=0) = \dot{X}_0$;
ω = the natural frequency;
ζ = critical damping factor;
$\alpha = \omega\zeta$;
$\beta = \omega\sqrt{\zeta^2 - 1}$.

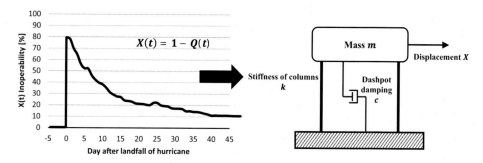

Figure 25.6 Illustration of the inoperability function and the SDOF mechanical model.

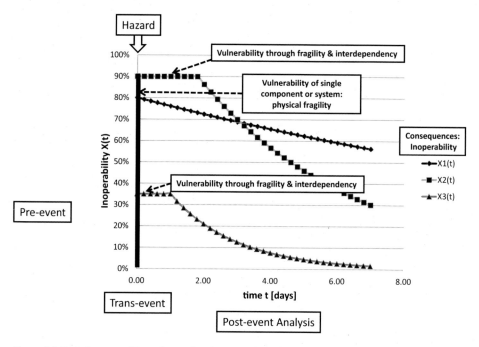

Figure 25.7 Influence of interdependencies over time through resilience assessment.

The SDOF system response is controlled by the stiffness parameter ω and the damping parameter ζ. These two parameters have been determined at various spatial scales for hurricanes, winter storms, and earthquakes (e.g. Reed et al. 2015; Wang 2017; Wang & Reed 2017). These results will be presented in detail in the "Recovery" section below.

It is noted that interdependencies are important pre-event, trans-event, and post-event in a resiliency analysis as shown in Figure 25.7, also noted by Peerenboom (2007). Resiliency analysis also incorporates the vulnerability of infrastructure and consequences following hazard events. Figure 25.7 shows an idealized formulation of inoperability for three different systems, $X_1(t)$, $X_2(t)$ and $X_3(t)$. Pre-event, the inoperability is assumed to be zero; that is, the system is operating at full capacity. Trans-event, when the loading occurs, the vulnerability is shown through the fragility of the individual systems, as well as affected through their interdependent relationships.

Finally, as recovery occurs, the systems recover at rates, with varying degrees of rapidity, affected by the resources available for repair, as well as the influence of other interdependent systems. For example, power cannot be restored until repair crews can travel to damaged facilities; roadway travel is affected by the structural status of the roads and bridges. Figure 25.7 also illustrates that time lags occur in the initiating recovery time for various systems due to dependencies.

In the following sections, resiliency formulations for electric power delivery, telecommunications and water supply for hurricane, winter storm, and seismic hazards will be compared. Interdependency metrics will be formulated and compared with similar work by others using time series data for interdependency modeling (e.g. Duenas-Osorio & Kwasinski 2012; Cimellaro et al. 2014).

Fragilities

Fragility models in civil engineering have been constructed for individual components, buildings, bridges, and other systems using Monte Carlo techniques as well as in situ empirical derivation. Recent formulations of fragilities for structures have been based upon logistic regression models (e.g. Kameshwar & Padgett 2014; Mardfekri & Gardoni 2014; Rokneddin et al. 2014; Reed et al. 2016). Hurricane-based models have been examined in detail (e.g. Reed et al. 2016). The fragility function F corresponding to inoperability $X_i(t)$, for hurricane events is given by

$$X_i(t=0) = (X_0)_i \approx F\left((X_{max})_i | V, W, R\right).$$

F is the conditional cumulative probability function;
X_{max} is the largest value of $X(t)$, usually it is equal to the initial value X_0; $\qquad$ (25.5)
V = wind speed or intensity;
W = storm surge intensity;
R = rainfall intensity.

For a single hazard H, the logistic response function F (here also called the fragility) has the form

$$F = P(X | H) = \frac{\exp(\beta_0 + \beta_1 H)}{1 + \exp(\beta_0 + \beta_1 H)} \qquad (25.6)$$

where β_0 and β_1 are parameters of the logistic regression model and $P(*/**)$ is the probability of * conditional on ***

The logit transformation of F is given by e.g. Hosmer & Lemeshow (2000):

$$y = \beta_0 + \beta_1 H_1. \qquad (25.7)$$

For multiple interactive hazards, $H_1 \ldots H_n$, Equation (25.7) becomes

$$y = \beta_0 + \beta_1 H_1 + \beta_2 H_2 + \ldots + \beta_m H_m + \sum_{1 \le j \ne k \le m}^{m} \beta_{jk} H_j H_k \qquad (25.8)$$

Combining Equations (25.5)–(25.8) yields

$$F_i((X_0)_i | H_1, H_2, \ldots H_n) = \frac{\exp(\beta_0 + \beta_1 H_1 + \ldots)}{1 + \exp(\beta_0 + \beta_1 H_1 + \ldots)} \qquad (25.9)$$

for each inoperability $X_i(t)$.

Combining Equation (25.9) with Equation (25.3) provides a complete vector of fragilities, F_i.

Recovery

Recovery is modeled using the single degree of freedom free vibration mechanical analog discussed earlier. In this formulation, the inoperability may be modeled at the component, locality, parish, or county, and state or larger levels. The model stays the same, but the parameters of ω and ζ change. In situ models have shown that ζ values for power delivery are close to 1 to 1.5 percent whereas the frequency parameter ω shows greater variation. In some instances, the community does not return to its pre-event state, but reaches a "new normal." The "new normal" infrastructure represents adaptations in the community population; and over time, this change may lead to others in the community overall. For example, the subway line from Manhattan to Brooklyn, which failed during Hurricane Sandy, took two years to restore. The closure affected commuting behavior and resulted in neighborhood modifications on both ends of the line (The City of New York 2013; Zimmerman 2014).

Restoration

Restoration is defined here as "long term recovery." Restoration models have not been examined in detail in the engineering research community as the time scale expands for months and sometimes years. Examples include the restoration of the port facilities in Kobe, Japan 1995 post-earthquake (Chang 2010), the Ninth Ward neighborhood in New Orleans, Louisiana post-Katrina in 2005, and the previously mentioned Manhattan subway system post-Sandy in 2012 (Zimmerman 2014). In addition to the physical rebuilding and population migration, the disaster survivors often adapt to new conditions, which are challenging to quantify.

Examples

Electric power delivery

Electric power delivery during and post hurricanes has been examined in detail by many researchers (e.g. He & Cha 2016; Lopez et al. 2009; Lee II et al. 2007; Reed et al. 2010; Lee II 2006). Investigations of power delivery time series data in situ post-earthquake have been conducted by Duenas-Osorio and Kwasinski (2012); Cimellaro et al. (2014) and Nojima and Kato (2014). The numerical characterization for hurricanes and seismic events is discussed in this section.

HURRICANES

Figure 25.8 illustrates the inoperability behavior of power delivery systems post-hurricane at the state level for a normalized time scale. This performance has been modeled using Equation (25.4) for 11 hurricane systems, primarily in the Gulf of Mexico. Table 25.4 provides the range of ζ and ω values for performance under hurricanes at the state level; at the parish level for Hurricane Isaac; and at the locality level for Hurricane Sandy.

The influence of the spatial scale on X_0 (fragility) values is also given in Table 25.4. It seems reasonable that the X_0 values are larger for the smaller regions investigated, as the percentage of residents affected would be higher than for the larger regions.

The fragility functions for Isaac and Sandy have been investigated, using the logistic regression model of Equation (25.9) for the multiple hurricane hazards of wind speed, rainfall and inundation due to storm surge (Reed et al. 2016). Given that the inoperability data were available for several hurricanes, fragilities using combined data sets for wind speed and storm surge, respectively, were investigated (e.g. AEP Texas 2017; CenterPoint Energy 2017; Entergy 2017;

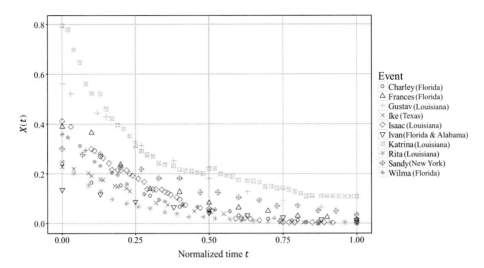

Figure 25.8 Comparison of inoperability curve for power delivery using normalized time.
Source: After Wang 2017.

Table 25.4 Inoperability resiliency model parameters

Region	Range of ω	Range of ζ	Range of R^2	Range of X_0
Locality	0.419–1.281	1.001(constant)	80.5–93.2	0.199–1.00
Parish	0.32–3.1	1.001–1.273	91.2–99.9	0.154–0.961
State	0.249–0.879	1.001–2.00	90.0–99.9	0.135–0.795

HWind Scientific 2012–2016). The best-fit models based upon these preliminary results are given in Equations (25.10) and (25.11).

$$F(X_1 \mid V[m/s]) = \frac{\exp(-4.58 + 0.187V[m/s])}{1 + \exp(-4.58 + 0.187V[m/s])}$$

(25.10)

where V is the wind speed in m/s.

The wind speed data are for standard conditions as determined through H*Wind (HWind Scientific 2012–2016).

$$F(X_1 \mid W[m]) = \frac{\exp(-4.0 + 1.82W[m])}{1 + \exp(-4.0 + 1.82W[m])}$$

(25.11)

where W is the storm surge inundation in meters.'

TREES
In our formulation, trees are considered part of the green infrastructure lifeline "forests" as they perform important community services and they contribute to water drainage systems (Rottle 2013; Holling 2001; Tzoulas 2007). Therefore, they are not treated as a hazard, but rather an

interdependent system that can initiate a cascading failure in power delivery under certain circumstances. Fragility functions for trees may be derived using the cantilever-based physics models employed in the forestry literature, or through post event in situ analysis (e.g. Reed 2008). Anecdotally, trees fail more readily after significant rainfall, as shallow root systems no longer hold.

SEISMIC

Power delivery systems perform well in the US for minor and moderate seismic events, so most derivations of fragilities and recovery have been determined using data from outside the US. The two events discussed in this chapter are the 2010 Chilean Earthquake and the Tohoku 2011 Earthquake and Tsunami in Japan. The USGS shakemap adapted for grayscale using ArcGIS for instrumental intensity is shown for the 2010 Chile Earthquake in Figure 25.9. Infrastructure damage data were available from Duenas-Osorio and Kwasinski (2012) for the two regions of Maule (Region VII) and Bio-Bio (Region VIII).

Because the outage data were limited to two regions, fitting fragility functions was not possible. The inoperability data for power, mobile, and fixed (landline) phones are shown in Figures 25.10 and 25.11 for Regions VII and VIII, respectively.

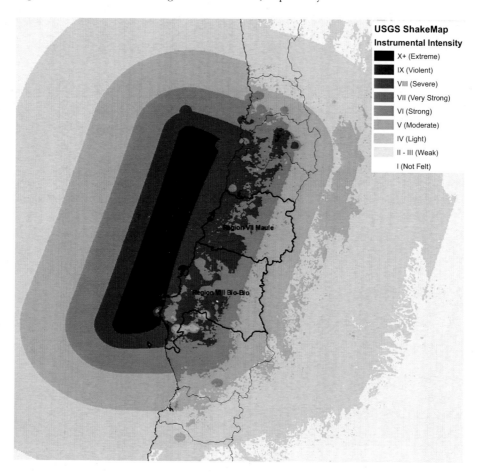

Figure 25.9   USGS shakemap for the 2010 Chile Earthquake.
Source: Earthquake Hazards Program Office 2011.

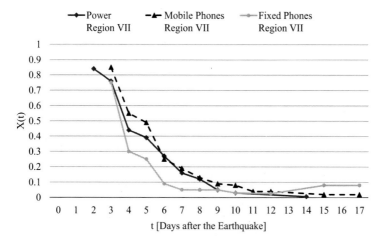

Figure 25.10 Region VII or Maule, Chile X(t) data for the February 27, 2010 Chilean earthquake.
Data source: Duenas-Osorio and Kwasinski 2012.

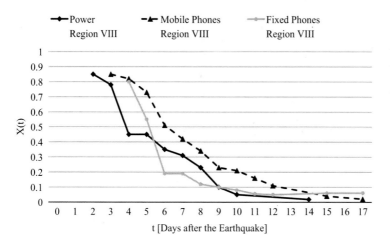

Figure 25.11 Region VIII or Bio-Bio, Chile X(t) data for the February 27, 2010 Chilean earthquake.
Data source: Duenas-Osorio and Kwasinski 2012.

The parameters for the power inoperability models are given in Table 25.5. The fixed and mobile phone data will be discussed in the Telecommunications section.

On March 11, 2011, the Tohoku earthquake struck Japan with devastating consequences. The USGS Shakemap adapted for grayscale using ArcGIS is shown in Figure 25.12 for selected prefectures. A "prefecture" is similar in size to a US "county."

Outage data were obtained from Nojima and Kato (2014) and converted into inoperabilities. The resulting electric power delivery inoperability data are shown in Figure 25.13.

The aftershock on day 27 after the main event did not affect the majority of the prefectures because they were still in recovery, so the data were fitted without this disruption. The parameter

483

Table 25.5 Electric power delivery inoperability data for the 2010 Chile Earthquake

Region	X_0	ω	ζ	$R^2[\%]$
VII Maule	0.84	0.174	1.004	97.6
VIII Bio-Bio	0.85	0.121	1.027	96.5

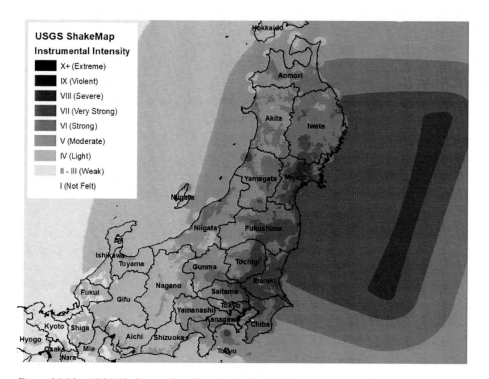

Figure 25.12 USGS Shakemap for the March 11, 2011 Tohoku earthquakes. Prefectures are outlined on the map.

Source: Earthquake Hazards Program Office 2011.

estimates for the models are given in Table 25.6, arranged in order of highest to lowest X_0 values.

The best fit fragility model for power denoted as (X_0) for system "1" or simply X_1 based upon peak ground acceleration (PGA) in "g" was

$$F(X_1 \mid PGA[g]) = \frac{\exp(-4.0 + 2.832 PGA[g])}{1 + \exp(-4.0 + 2.832 PGA[g])}. \tag{25.12}$$

For the tsunami run-up water height H in meters, the best-fit fragility was

$$F(X_1 \mid H[m]) = \frac{\exp(-4.0 + 0.204 H[m])}{1 + \exp(-4.0 + 0.204 H[m])}. \tag{25.13}$$

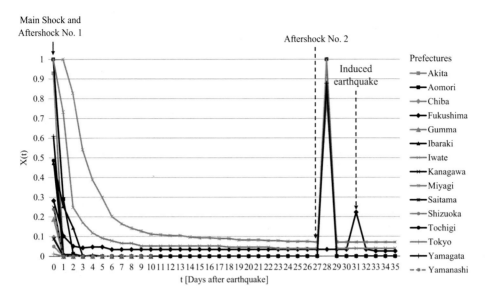

Figure 25.13 Electric power inoperability data for selected prefectures for the March 11, 2011 Tohoku earthquake.

Table 25.6 Inoperability model parameters for selected prefectures in Japan for the Tohoku earthquake of 2011

Prefecture	X_0	Ω	ζ	$R^2[\%]$
Electric Power Delivery				
Aomori	1.000	2.40	1.01	99.88
Iwate	1.000	1.34	1.27	94.58
Miyagi	1.0000	0.58	1.38	94.44
Akita	0.929	7.03	1.01	99.99
Yamagata	0.610	7.03	1.01	99.99
Tochigi	0.486	3.56	2.66	99.99
Ibaraki	0.473	1.16	1.01	98.60
Fukushima	0.283	*0.08*	*8.24*	*99.64*
Kanagawa	0.250	7.03	1.01	99.99
Yamanashi	0.238	6.65	1.05	99.99
Gumma	0.188	7.04	1.01	99.99

Data source: Nojima and Kato 2014.

Telecommunications

The term "telecommunications" encompasses many types of communication devices and systems. In this chapter, landlines, cell towers and customer outages are investigated. The data for examining telecommunications outages are not always available. Correlations between landline and electric power outages are easier to evaluate than for cell phones since most landlines and broadband lines employ the same poles as electric power distribution systems. In 2016, the Federal Communications Commission (FCC) provided cell tower outage data over time for Hurricane Matthew in the North Carolina region (Federal Communications Commission 2016). The FCC has since provided similar information for Hurricanes Harvey, Irma and

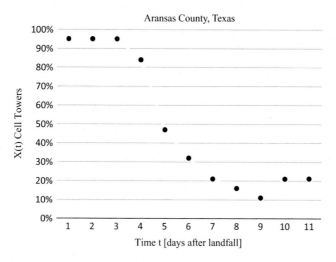

Figure 25.14 Cell tower inoperability for Aransas County, Texas after Harvey landfall.

Maria (Federal Communications Commission 2017). The cell tower outage data, while useful, are not easily matched with other systems, in the same way that customer outages are.

HURRICANES

Landline customer outage data were available for Hurricane Katrina in Louisiana. The inoperability outage data were $X_0 = 0.44$, $\omega = 0.126$, $\zeta = 1.01$, with a goodness of fit R^2 of 86.1 percent.

After the FCC data became available, inoperability models were fit to county-level cell tower outage data per county for Texas for Hurricane Harvey (Federal Communications Commission 2017). Landfall first occurred near Corpus Christi, Texas, and then Harvey shifted to the Houston area. Inoperability over time is shown for Aransas County in Figure 25.14 with $X_0 = 0.95$, $\omega = 0.386$, $\zeta = 1.01$, and $R^2 = 90.6$ percent.

The best fit fragility relationships at the county level for Texas for the FCC cell tower data X_2 are as follows:

For wind speed V:

$$F(X_2 | V[m/s]) = \frac{\exp(-4.23 + 0.107V[m/s])}{1 + \exp(-4.23 + 0.107V[m/s])} \tag{25.14}$$

For storm surge inundation W:

$$\tag{25.15}$$

$$F(X_2 | W[m]) = \frac{\exp(-3.02 + 1.005W[m])}{1 + \exp(-3.02 + 1.005W[m])}.$$

Initial analysis of the cell tower and maximum rainfall data did not prove promising. Either the peak rainfall is not the appropriate metric, or a combination of other physical factors is important.

SEISMIC

For the 2010 Chile earthquake, the inoperability models for mobile and landline phones are given in Table 25.7. The mobile phone model is similar to that for electric power whereas the landline

Table 25.7 Inoperability parameters for mobile and fixed phones for the 2010 Chilean Earthquake

Region	X_0	ω	ζ	$R^2[\%]$
Mobile Phone				
VII Maule	0.85	0.305	1.015	98.7
VIII Bio-Bio	0.85	0.520	1.206	99.5
Fixed Phone (Landline)				
VII Maule	0.75	0.195	2.382	97.2
VII Bio-Bio	0.80	0.069	4.484	97.4

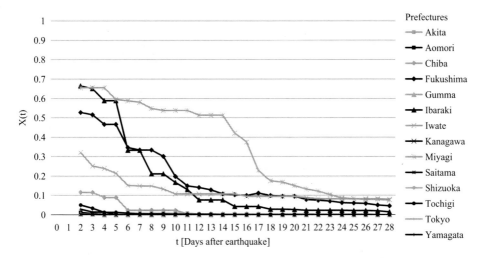

Figure 25.15   Water service recovery after the 2011 Japan earthquake.
Data source: Nojima and Kato 2014.

parameters differ. This result implies that the cell tower system consisting mainly of towers acts independently and similar to the distribution system of poles and towers of power delivery.

Water supply
Water supply data were only available for the two earthquakes. The 2010 Chile earthquake data set for water supply for Conception consisted of four data points, so model fitting was not undertaken. However, for the Tohoku earthquake in Japan, inoperability models were fit to the water service recovery data shown in Figure 25.15. The model parameters are given in Table 25.8.

The best-fit logit regression fragility models for the water system $X_3(t)$ for the peak ground acceleration *PGA* in "g" and the tsunami runup water height *H* in meters are respectively

$$F(X_3 \mid PGA[g]) = \frac{\exp(-3.639 + 1.781 PGA[g])}{1 + \exp(-3.639 + 1.781 PGA[g])} \tag{25.16}$$

$$F(X_3 \mid H[m]) = \frac{\exp(-4.0 + 0.113 H[m])}{1 + \exp(-4.0 + 0.113 H[m])}. \tag{25.17}$$

Table 25.8 Water supply inoperability models for the Tohoku earthquake

Water Supply and Delivery X_3				
Prefecture	X_0	ω	ζ	$R^2 [\%]$
Ibaraki	0.665	0.439	1.191	98.7
Miyagi	0.656	0.156	1.007	92.9
Fukushima	0.528	0.027	2.490	96.9
Iwate	0.321	0.059	2.509	98.2
Chiba	0.116	0.160	1.098	93.9
Tochigi	0.050	0.373	1.172	98.6
Yamagata	0.029	0.337	1.113	94.6
Aomori	0.012	0.513	1.112	97.3
Akita	0.008	0.220	1.067	88.7
Gumma	0.004	0.653	1.098	84.8
Saitama	0.002	0.360	1.097	84.8

Transportation

Transportation infrastructure encompasses a wide variety of services that are challenging to define and model. Roadway service data are often based upon the analysis of traffic movement. Inoperabilities exist between power and transportation in many ways that are difficult to model. For roadways, traffic lights, signage, and gasoline pumps often require power sources. Additionally, GPS systems for traffic directions may not function properly after extreme events. Conversely, power lines may not be repaired if roadways for crew travel are not accessible.

In large cities, subway systems typically have dedicated power sources for trains, lights, air ventilation in stations, and signage. Ridership in subways would be a useful metric post-event to understand recovery but it is challenging to obtain. (Zimmerman 2014) used the opening of subway lines in New York City as a metric to assess recovery of the subway system after Hurricane Sandy as shown in Figure 25.17. The power recovery is plotted in the same figure to illustrate a qualitative relationship to recovery. It is noted that subway systems recovered more slowly than power because of the significant flooding in lower Manhattan.

The resilience metric employed in many post-emergency situations for transportation is the "accessibility" metric (Chang 2003; Taylor & Susilawati 2012). "Accessibility" is defined as "the ease with which services and facilities can be reached within a specified region by using the transportation network" (Taylor & Susilawati 2012). It applies most easily to roadways. The IEEE 1366 Standard employs reliability metrics that incorporate the time to repair which implicitly includes the accessibility (IEEE 2001).

Derivation of interdependency relationships using resiliency models

Given the inoperability data models derived earlier, it is straightforward to obtain interdependency values for a two system scenario involving X_1 (power) and X_2 (telecommunications) or X_3 (water supply). The recovery data allow for inoperability models and fragilities. These input models can be used to describe the two system infrastructure for either hazard.

Hurricane analysis

Using data sets for Hurricanes Katrina and Wilma (Reed et al. 2015) found that the A matrix values were much higher for landlines and electric power than for wireless (mobile)

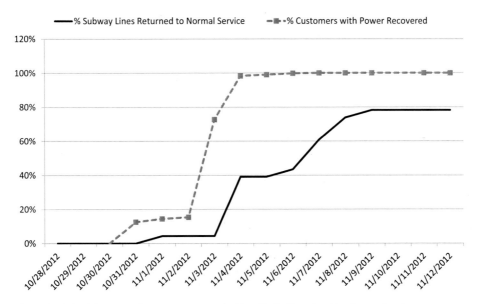

Figure 25.16 Subway and power recovery in New York City after Hurricane Sandy.
Data source: Zimmerman 2014.

telecommunications systems. Specifically, if power is represented by inoperability X_1, and telecommunication X_2, then a_{21} for landlines was in the range of 0.685–0.738, and for cell towers alone, $a_{21} = 0.208$. These values, which are based on customer outages, are not meant to represent a complete "fit," but rather the influence of the power recovery on the landline and cell phone systems, with a time lag of several days. The higher correlation of landline with power is due to the use of the same distribution poles, as mentioned previously. Analysis of Hurricane Harvey data has shown no interactions of power and cell tower damage in Texas. The power outages were severe, mostly due to flooding, and they were not restored for several weeks whereas the cell towers were repaired in a few days for most counties.

Seismic
For the 2010 Chile earthquake, linear regression was employed to assess the off-diagonal terms for the A matrix of Equation (25.3) for power and telecommunications as shown in Figure 25.17 and Table 25.9 for the telecommunications data.

For the Tohoku Earthquake of 2011, more extensive data sets were available. For electric power and water supply, the correlations were small, or did not fit at all, as for prefectures Fukushima and Ibaraki, in agreement with reports by others (e.g. Cimellaro et al. 2014). An in-depth analysis of water pumping stations may be useful in understanding the results. The comparison also suggests that interdependency cannot be reduced to a single coefficient, but must be investigated in more dimensions, in a manner similar to resilience.

Comparisons
Duenas-Osorio and Kwasinski (2012) employed a cross-correlation function (CCF) approach to their modeling of the Chile 2010 data. Their CCF values are compared with the derived influence coefficients for the same data set. The results are similar, but not equivalent.

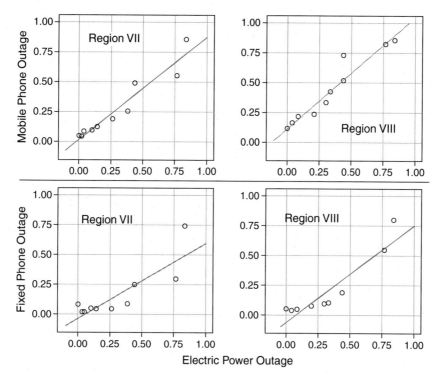

Figure 25.17 Linear regression results for the Chile 2010 earthquake.

Table 25.9 A matrix values for the 2010 Chile earthquake

Region	System "1"	System "2"	a_{21}	R^2 [%]
VII Maule	Electric power	Mobile Phones	0.866	91.1
VII Maule	Electric power	Fixed Phones [Landlines]	0.637	69.4
VIII Bio-Bio	Electric power	Mobile Phones	0.931	91.0
VIII Bio-Bio	Electric power	Fixed Phones	0.810	81.7

Table 25.10 Coefficient comparison for the Chile 2010 data

Region	System "1"	System "2"	a_{21}	CCF weight (Duenas-Osorio & Kwasinski, 2012)
VII Maule	Electric power	Mobile Phones	0.866	0.83
VII Maule	Electric power	Fixed Phones [Landlines]	0.637	0.94
VIII Bio-Bio	Electric power	Mobile Phones	0.931	0.73
VIII Bio-Bio	Electric power	Fixed Phones	0.810	0.84

25.5 Conclusions

The chapter has focused on the use of an infrastructure-based input–output model combined with a SDOF mechanical analog of inoperabilities to examine interdependency. The resulting metrics are useful in ultimately predicting recovery in future hurricanes and to a lesser extent, earthquakes. It has been shown that the input-output formulation of select infrastructure can provide accurate interdependency characterization at various spatial scales. Because the exact nature of the interdependency is not always easy to assess, or can be formidable to model numerically, the degree to which the interdependency can be implemented for predictive modeling is somewhat challenging. "Time-lag" recovery modeling may be the best bet for recovery and restoration models.

Unfortunately, the present input–output models cannot assess the degree to which interdependencies increase or decrease overall resilience. As a general principle, redundancy is a desired characteristic of any system, but the degree and type is often a design challenge. Indeed, the "load path" is required when assessing the strength of the system, and in a similar manner, the path of failure for coupled infrastructure would be interesting to analyze for various scenarios. Unfortunately, the infrastructure in the US was constructed in an ad hoc manner and it is challenging to predict how systems may fail. In some ways, it may be more instructive to ascertain how to harden the underlying power and telecommunication systems before undertaking an 11 system overhaul. Greater robustness can be achieved through structural hardening as well as more redundancy. An example of power redundancy creating greater robustness is the addition of green energy systems such as on-site renewable power generation coupled with storage batteries at the building or community level. Micro-grids may also add robustness through redundancy rather than hardening of the existing power grid.

Implicit in the chapter's formulation of interdependency is the *type* of relationship that exists among various entities. The terms "influence," "conditional," "correlated," and "dependent" are frequently used in interdependency discussions. "Influence" best describes our use of the term "interdependent" when describing the relationship between two or more systems, components or assets. "Influence" is broad enough to incorporate objective and subjective assessments. The changing of the relationships over time should be investigated in greater detail. Methods for improved prediction of performance should lead to a better understanding of the community infrastructure systems. Only then will society be able to create a more robust, sustainable environment.

References

AEP Texas (2017). *AEP Texas Outage Tracker*. http://outagemap.aeptexas.com.s3.amazonaws.com/extrenal/default.html (last accessed September 26, 2017).

American Society of Civil Engineers (2016). Minimum Design Loads for Buildings and Other Structures. Washington, DC: ASCE.

Box, G. and Jenkins, G.M. (1970). *Time Series Analysis*. New York: Wiley.

Bruneau, M. et al. (2003). A framework to quantitatively assess and enhance seismic resilience of communities. *EERI. Earthquake Spectra, 19*(4): 733–52.

Center for Risk-Based Community Resilience (2015). *IN-CORE Interdependent Network-Based Community Resilience* (NCSA). http://resilience.colostate.edu (last accessed December 10, 2017).

CenterPoint Energy (2017). *Center Point Energy Outage Tracker*. http://gis.centerpointenergy.com/outagetracker/?WT.ac=OC Image Callout (last accessed September 26, 2017).

Chang, S. (2003). Transportation planning for disasters: An accessibility approach. *Environment and Planning A, 35*(6), 1051–72.

Chang, S.E. (2010). Urban disaster recovery: A measurement framework and its application to the 1995 Kobe earthquake. *Disasters, 34*(2), 303–27.

Chang, S., McDaniels, T., and Reed, D.A. (2005). Mitigation of extreme events: Electric power outage and infrastructure failure interactions. In H.W. Richardson, P. Gordon, and J.E. Moore II (eds.), *The Economic Impacts of Terrorist Attacks* (pp. 70–90). Cheltenham, UK: Edward Elgar Publishing.

Cimellaro, G.P., Solari, D., and Bruneau, M. (2014). Physical infrastructure interdependency and regional resilience index after the 2011 Tohoku Earthquake in Japan. *Earthquake Engineering & Structural Dynamics, 43*, 1763–84.

Clemen, R.T. and Reilly, T. (2001). *Making Hard Decisions*. Pacific Grove, CA: Thomson Learning.

Duenas-Osorio, L. and Kwasinski, A. (2012). Quantification of lifeline system interdependencies after the 27 February 2010 Mw 8.8 Offshore Maule, Chile Earthquake. *Earthquake Spectra, 8*(5), 5581–5603.

Earthquake Hazards Program (2010). *M8.8 offshore Bio-Bio, Chile.* https://earthquake.usgs.gov/earthquakes/eventpage/official20100227063411530_30#shakemap (last accessed August 19, 2018).

Earthquake Hazards Program (2011). *M9.1 – near the east coast of Honshu, Japan.* https://earthquake.usgs.gov/earthquakes/eventpage/official20110311054624120_30#shakemap (last accessed August 19, 2018).

Eidinger, J., and Kempner, Jr., L. (2012). Reliability of transmission towers under extreme wind and ice loading. *CIGRE*. Paris, France.

Entergy (2017). *Entergy Storm Center.* http://stormcenter.entergy.com (last accessed October 1, 2017).

Federal Communications Commission (2016). *Hurricane Matthew Outage Data.* www.fcc.gov/matthew (last accessed January 20, 2017).

Federal Communications Commission (2017). *Communications Status for Areas Impacted by Post-tropical Storm Harvey.* www.fcc.gov/harvey (last accessed September 5, 2017).

Gunderson, L., and Holling, C.S. (eds.) (2002). *Panarchy: Understanding Transformations in Human and Natural Systems.* Washington, DC: Island Press.

Haimes, Y.Y. (2004). *Risk Modeling, Assessment, and Management.* Hoboken, NJ: John Wiley & Sons.

He, X., and Cha, E.J. (2016). Modeling the operability of interdependent critical infrastructure systems for quantification of the integrated network resilience. *EMI 2016 and PMC 2016 Conference.* Nashville: ASCE.

Holling, C. (2001). Understanding the complexity of economic, ecological, and social systems. *Ecosystems, 4*, 390–405.

Hosmer, D., and Lemeshow, S. (2000). *Applied Logistic Regression.* New York, NY: Wiley.

HWind Scientific. (2012–2016). *Hwind scientific real-time hurricane impact data.* www.hwind.co (last accessed July 22, 2015).

IEEE (2001). *IEEE 1366 Standard Guide for Electric Power Distribution Reliability Indices.* IEEE.

Kameshwar, S. and Padgett, J.E. (2014). Multi-hazard risk assessment of highway bridges subjected to earthquake and hurricane hazards. *Engineering Structures, 78*: 154–66.

Lee II, E.E. (2006). *Assessing Vulnerability and Managing Disruptions to Interdependent Infrastructure Systems: A Network Flows Approach.* Troy New York: Rensselaer Polytechnic Institute.

Lee II, E.E., Mitchell, J.E., and Wallace, W.A. (2007). Restoration of services in interdependent infrastructure systems: A network flows approach. *IEEE Transactions on Systems, Man and Cybernetics: Part C, 37*(6), 1303–17.

Leontief, W. (1951). Input/output economics. *Scientific American, 185*(4): 15–21.

Lewis, T.G. (2006). *Critical Infrastructure Protection in Homeland Security: Defending a Networked Nation.* Hoboken, NJ: John Wiley & Sons.

Lopez, A.L., Rocha, L.P., Black, C.M., Corona, J.C., and Escobedo, D.L. (2009). Reliability and damage analysis for seismic and wind hazards of latticed frame structures for electrical substations in Mexico. *11th Americas Wind Engineering Conference.* San Juan, Puerto Rico.

Mardfekri, M., and Gardoni, P. (2014). Multi-hazard reliability assessment of offshore wind turbines. *Wind Energy, 18*(8): 1433–50.

McDaniels, T., Chang, S.E., Peterson, K., Mikawoz, J., and Reed, D.A. (2007, Sept. 1). Empirical framework for characterizing infrastructure failure interdependencies. *Journal of Infrastructure Systems, 13*(3). doi:10.1061/(ASCE)1076-0342(2007)13:3(175).

NIST (2016). *PEOPLES Resilience Framework.* http://peoplesresilience.org/ (last accessed January 6, 2017).

Nojima, N. and Kato, H. (2014). Modification and validation of an assessment model of post-earthquake lifeline serviceability based on the Great East Japan Earthquake disaster. *Journal of Disaster Research, 9*(2), 108–20.

Nojima, N. and Sugito, M. (2005). Probabilistic assessment model for post-earthquake serviceability of utility lifelines and its practical application. *Proceedings of ICOSSAR: Safety and Reliability of Engineering Systems and Structures*, Rome, Italy, June 19–23, 2005.

Nojima, N., Kameda, H., and Hayashi, H. (1995). Assessment of users' response and inconvenience caused by earthquake-induced malfunction of lifeline systems. *Proceedings of the 4th Japan US Workshop on Urban Earthquake Hazard Reduction*. Osaka, Japan.

Oregon Seismic Safety Policy Commission (2013). *The Oregon Resilience Plan*. Salem: Oregon Department of Geology and Mineral Industries.

Panteli, M., Mancarella, P., Wilkinson, S., Dawson, R., and Pickering, C. (2015). Assessment of the resilience of transmission networks to extreme wind events. *PowerTech IEEE*. Eindhoven, The Netherlands.

Park, J., Nojima, N., and Reed, D.A. (2006). Nisqually earthquake electric utility analysis. *Earthquake Spectra*, 22(2), 491–509.

Pearl, J. (2007). *Causality: Models, Reasoning and Inference* (7th ed.). Cambridge, England: Cambridge University Press.

Pederson, P., Dudenhoeffer, D., Hartley, S., and Permann, M. (2006). *Critical Infrastructure Interdependency Modeling: A Survey of US and International Research*. Idaho National Labaoratory, US Dept. of Energy, National Laboratory operated by Battelle Energy Alliance. Idaho Falls, Idaho: Idaho National Laboratory.

Peerenboom, J. (2007). PNWER. *Regional Critical Infrastructure Interdependencies Seminar*, December 13. Redmond, WA.

Petit, F., and Lewis, L.P. (2015). Critical infrastructure logical dependencies and interdependencies. *The 2nd National Symposium on Resilient Critical Infrastructure*. Philadelphia.

Pitilakis, K., Crowley, H., and Kaynia, A.M. (eds.). (2014). *SYNER-G: Typology Definition and Fragility Functions for Physical Elements at Seismic Risk*. Springer Science-Business Media. Retrieved from www.springer.com/series/6011.

Plumer, B. (2017). Why getting the power back on in Florida could take weeks. *New York Times*, September 12. https://nyti.ms/2eSZGB9 (last accessed August 19, 2018).

Reed, D. (2008). Electric utility distribution analysis for winter storms. *Journal of Wind Engineering and Industrial Aerodynamics*, 96, 123–40.

Reed, D., Friedland, C.J., Wang, S., and Massarra, C. (2016). Multi-hazard system-level logit fragility functions. *Engineering Structures*, 122: 14–23.

Reed, D., Kapur, K.C., and Christie, R.D. (2009). Methodology for assessing the resilience of networked infrastructure. *IEEE System Journal*, 3(2), 174–80.

Reed, D., Powell, M.D., and Westerman, J. (2010a). Energy infrastructure damage for Hurricane Rita. *Natural Hazards Review, ASCE*, 11(3), 102–9.

Reed, D., Powell, M.D., and Westerman, J.M. (2010b). Energy supply system performance for Hurricane Katrina. *Journal of Energy Engineering*. doi:10.1061/(ASCE)EY.1943-7897.0000028.

Reed, D., Wang, S., Kapur, K., and Zheng, C. (2015). Systems-based approach to interdependent electric power delivery and telecommunications infrastructure resilience subject to weather-related hazards. *Journal of Structural Engineering*. doi:10.1061/(ASCE)ST.1943-541X.0001395.

Rinaldi, S.M., Peerenboom, J.P., and Kelly, T.K. (2001). Identifying, understanding and analyzing critical infrastructure interdependencies. *IEEE Control Systems Magazine*, 21(6), 11–25.

Rokneddin, K., Ghosh, J., Duenas-Osorio, L., and Padgett, J.E. (2014). Seismic reliability assessment of aging highway bridge networks with field instrucmentation data and correlated failures, II: Application. *Earthquake Spectra*, 30(2), 819–43.

Rottle, N.D. (2013). Urban green infrastructure for climate benefit: Global to local. *Nordic Journal of Architectural Research*, 25(2): 43–66.

Talberth, J. and Hanson, C. (n.d.). *WRI Insights: Green vs. Gray Infrastructure*. http://insights.wri.org/news/2012/06 (last accessed November 11, 2012).

Taylor, M.A. and Susilawati. (2012). Remoteness and accessibility in the vulnerability analysis of regional road networks. *Transportation Research Part A: Policy and Practice*, 46(5), 761–71.

Terpstra, T. and Lindell, M.K. (2013). Citizens' perceptions of flood hazard adjustments: An application of the protective action decision model. *Environment and Behavior*, 45(8), 993–1018.

The City of New York (2013). *A Stronger, More Resilient New York*. The City of New York. www1.nyc.gov/site/sirr/report/report.page (last accessed August 19, 2018).

Tzoulas., K. et al. (2007). Promoting ecosystem and human health in urban areas using green infrastructure: A literature review. *Landscape and Urban Planning*, 81, 167–78. doi:10.1016/j.landurbplan.2007.02.001.

Wang, S. (2017). *Integrated Approach and Analysis of Reliability, Robustness, Resilience and Infrastructure Applications.* Seattle, WA: University of Washington.

Wang, S. and Reed, D.A. (2017). Vulnerability and robustness of civil infrastructure systems to hurricanes. *Frontiers in Built Environment, 3*(60). doi:10.3389/fbuil.2017.00060.

Zimmerman, R. (2014). Planning restoration of vital infrastructure services following Hurricane Sandy: Lessons learned for energy and transportation. *Journal of Extreme Events, 1*(1), 38. doi:10.1142/S2345737614500043.

26

Probabilistic modeling of interdependencies for resilient infrastructure systems

Iris Tien

SCHOOL OF CIVIL AND ENVIRONMENTAL ENGINEERING, GEORGIA INSTITUTE OF TECHNOLOGY,
790 ATLANTIC DRIVE, ATLANTA, GA 30332–0355, USA; ITIEN@CE.GATECH.EDU

26.1 Introduction

Infrastructure systems are critical for a functioning society. These include water, power, gas, communication, and transportation networks, providing the products and services that support the health, safety, and growth of communities (Johansen et al. 2017). These systems, however, are subject to an increasing number of hazards. These include both natural disaster events and targeted anthropogenic attacks. System-level risk and reliability analyses are required to assess the vulnerabilities of these critical systems, as well their resilience – "the ability to prepare for and adapt to changing conditions and withstand and recover rapidly from disruptions" (White House 2013).

In these analyses, the complexities of infrastructure systems must be considered. Specifically, many of these systems are interdependent, with the functioning of one system dependent on the states of the components in others. For example, a power generating system may require water for cooling, with the water provided by a water pump, which relies on electricity for operation. Therefore, while previous studies on infrastructure reliability have focused on single systems, the interdependencies between systems must be modeled to provide a comprehensive view of infrastructure resilience (Tien 2018). Further, with the uncertainties associated with the hazards that infrastructures are subjected to, expected system performance, and our knowledge about a given network, a probabilistic approach is required.

This chapter presents a probabilistic framework for modeling interdependencies for critical infrastructure systems to assess and improve resilience. In the chapter, first, three general, comprehensive types of interdependencies are defined. These capture the functional, geographic, and recovery dependencies between multiple infrastructure systems serving a given community. Each of these is then modeled using a probabilistic Bayesian network framework. This enables the dependencies between components both within a system and across systems to be quantitatively modeled. It also enables rapid updating of system assessments with new information. The framework is applied to an example interdependent water, power, and gas network to demonstrate its use. Inference results are provided to show the types of analyses possible using the proposed method to assess and improve the resilience of infrastructure systems.

26.2 Background

The study of infrastructure systems and their functioning under different scenarios is a growing area of research. Due to the complexities of infrastructure systems, however, previous studies of infrastructure performance have typically focused on only one or a few systems, e.g. only the water and power networks (Duenas-Osorio et al. 2007), transportation systems (Kang et al. 2008; Lee et al. 2011; Zhang & Peeta 2011), or just the power grid (Korkali et al. 2014). However, with the increasing connections between infrastructures, it is important to consider the interdependencies between systems to form a comprehensive view of infrastructure performance (Guidotti et al. 2016). This is particularly true when considering infrastructure vulnerabilities and recovery for resilience.

There are many approaches to modeling interdependencies between critical infrastructure systems, including empirical, agent-based, system dynamics-based, economic theory-based, and network-based approaches (Ouyang 2014). Network-based approaches in particular are effective at evaluating the ability of the network to prevent events that lead to large consequences, determining the effects of improving the capacities of critical infrastructure components to absorb shocks, and analyzing the ability of the network to support design decisions to quickly find restoration priorities.

This chapter presents a network-based approach for interdependent infrastructure modeling using Bayesian networks (BNs). Compared to static approaches, e.g., Haimes (2008), BNs are able to be dynamically updated in light of new information collected about any part of system (Jensen & Nielsen 2007). While static approaches describe the state of a system at one point in time, BNs allow for updating as the states of the components and of the system change. Specifically, the BN framework incorporates both prior and updating information into assessments of system performance. Prior knowledge about components in the network is incorporated into the BN during construction of the network model. Updating information, such as measurements and observations about a specific component, is integrated by updating the state of the component. Information entered at any node in the BN propagates to all nodes in the network through inference to provide up-to-date system assessments based on the new information.

Previously, four classes of critical infrastructure interdependencies have been proposed (Rinaldi et al. 2001): physical, where the state of a component is dependent on the material output of another; cyber, where the state of a component is dependent on information transmitted from another; geographic, where local environmental variables affect the states of multiple components; and logical, any other interdependency. The three types of interdependencies defined in this chapter are related to these. However, they are defined to specifically and comprehensively address infrastructure resilience. How each of the newly defined interdependencies – service provision, geographic, and access for repair – is probabilistically modeled is also described.

26.3 Method

26.3.1 Bayesian network model of interdependent infrastructure systems

A BN is a directed acyclic graph composed of nodes and links. Nodes represent random variables, and links the dependencies between them. In a BN model of an infrastructure system, the nodes represent infrastructure components, and the links the dependencies between component states. The addition of system nodes in the BN models overall infrastructure system performance. The nodes are defined by the states of the components and systems. These can be binary states such as working or failed (Tien and Der Kiureghian 2016), or multiple states such as a level of flow of 0%, 25%, 50%, 75%, or 100% of maximum flow capacity through the node (Tong & Tien 2017). Links in the BN occur both within systems to model functionality of a single system, e.g., the state of a distribution node in the network relying on the state of its supplying node, and across systems to model interdependencies between multiple systems, e.g., the state of a water distribution node depending on the state of the node modeling its power supply.

Each node in the BN is defined by the probability distribution for the random variable it represents. Nodes, called children, that are dependent upon others, called parents, are defined by conditional probability distributions. Nodes without parents are defined by marginal distributions. For BNs with random variables represented by discrete states, the distributions are defined by values in conditional probability tables (CPTs). Each entry in the CPT provides the probability of the node being in the state given the mutually exclusive states of its parent nodes. As the number of parent nodes increase, the size of the CPT increases exponentially. Therefore, BN models are often limited in the size of the system they can tractably represent (Boudali & Dougan 2005). For the BN modeling of critical infrastructure, the exponentially increasing computational demands for the model as the number of components in the system increases limits the size of systems that have been able to be studied (Tien 2017).

To reduce the number of parent nodes of any given node in the network, in this modeling framework, intermediate minimum link set (MLS) nodes are introduced. All components in a MLS must function for the MLS to function. If any one MLS survives, the system survives and is able to provide the infrastructure service. In the BN, the components composing a MLS are modeled as parents of the MLS node. MLS nodes are then modeled as parents of a system output node. MLSs capture the functionality of the network through its flow paths. In addition, to further reduce computational complexity of the network model, component nodes that exist in series are grouped together as single "supercomponent" nodes (Song & Ok 2010; Tien & Der Kiureghian 2017). All nodes in such a supercomponent must function for the supercomponent to function. As knowing the states of the components in the supercomponent determines the state of the supercomponent, this remains an exact representation of the system and reduces the number of parent nodes in the network without making any approximations.

Figure 26.1 shows an example BN model of an infrastructure system. n total individual infrastructure components are indicated, $C_1,...,C_i,C_j,C_k,...C_n$. In the example, components $C_1,...,C_i$ compose the supercomponent denoted Sup. Multiple supercomponents are possible. The supercomponent and components up to C_j compose the MLS node denoted MLS. Finally, the overall system performance modeled by the node Sys is a function of the MLSs and components $C_k,...,C_n$. It is noted that the computational limits of a BN model are a function of the number of parents for any given node in the network. With the typical BN configuration, this will be a function of the number of component nodes that are parents of a system function node. The MLS and supercomponent modeling is a way to reduce this number. Alternatively, topology optimization (Bensi et al. 2013) and compression (Tien & Der Kiureghian 2016) algorithms have been proposed. In the example provided in this chapter, an interdependent system of 127 nodes is able to be modeled using the described framework. The topology optimization and compression algorithms may be used to further reduce the computational demands of the model. The BN shown in Figure 28.1 is provided as an example of the network structure. For a given infrastructure system, the configuration of components, supercomponents, and MLSs will differ based on the topology and connectivity of the nodes in the network.

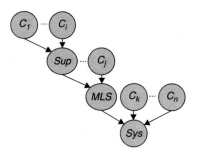

Figure 26.1 Example BN of infrastructure system, including component, supercomponent, MLS, and system nodes.

26.3.1 Interdependency types

The BN shown in Figure 28.1 is for a single infrastructure system. To model the interdependencies between infrastructures, three general, comprehensive types of interdependencies are defined. These are: service provision, geographic, and access for repair interdependencies (Johansen & Tien 2018). Each of these is described in the following sections along with the generalized probabilistic BN methodology developed to model them. Together, these comprehensively describe the relationships that occur between critical infrastructures to enable full risk and reliability analyses of these systems. Performing inference over the system model under different scenarios facilitates assessment of interdependent infrastructure systems and supports recommendations to improve their resilience.

26.3.2 Modeling service provision interdependencies

Service provision interdependencies are defined as the case where the functioning of one component of an infrastructure system is dependent on the service outputs of a component from another system. For example, several components in the water system, e.g., treatment plants and pumping stations, require power to function. Other examples include the power system depending on the outputs of the water system for cooling, or any infrastructure control system relying on a working communication network to carry out its functions. This type of interdependency combines both the physical and cyber relationships proposed in Rinaldi et al. (2001). In the author's view, whether the output that a component depends on is physical in nature or based on information, it is the provision of services from another system, both physical and cyber, which is needed for functioning. These relationships are captured as service provision interdependencies.

Within the BN framework, we model service provision interdependencies using a direct dependence in the network as shown in Figure 26.2, where C_i^p represents the component in the power system and C_j^w its dependent component in the water network. sys^p and sys^w represent the performance of the power and water system outputs, respectively. The states of the system nodes indicate the ability of the system to provide a given service. These system nodes can be defined by service area in a community. The dependency across systems as shown in Figure 26.2 models the fact that the performance of component C_i^p affects not only the performance of the power system, but the water system as well. Additional dependencies of this type would be similarly modeled.

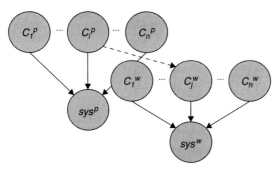

Figure 26.2 Service provision interdependency modeled between C_i^p and C_j^w.

Table 26.1 Conditional probability table for interdependent power and water components C_i^p and C_j^w to remove cyclical dependence in graph

	C_i^p working	C_i^p failed
C_j^w working	$\dfrac{p\left(C_j^w = working, C_i^p = working\right)}{p\left(C_i^p = working\right)}$	$\dfrac{p\left(C_j^w = working, C_i^p = failed\right)}{p\left(C_i^p = failed\right)}$
C_j^w failed	$\dfrac{p\left(C_j^w = failed, C_i^p = working\right)}{p\left(C_i^p = working\right)}$	$\dfrac{p\left(C_j^w = failed, C_i^p = failed\right)}{p\left(C_i^p = failed\right)}$

In modeling service provision interdependencies, there is one specific case that must be specially considered. This is the case where components in multiple systems are each dependent on the other. For example, in the scenario where power generation requires water for cooling, and the water pump in turn requires electric power to function, if the BN model includes a power supply node and a water supply node, the functioning of the power supply node may be dependent on the state of the water supply node, while the functioning of the water supply node may be dependent on the state of the water supply node. Within the BN framework, this creates a cycle in the network. As BNs are acyclic graphs, this potential cyclic dependency relationship between components in multiple systems must be addressed. The presented methodology is able to model this scenario through the use of joint distributions to define the conditional probability distributions required to build the CPTs for the BN.

An example CPT for the power and water supply scenario is shown in Table 26.1. In it, the elements of the CPT for the power and water components C_i^p and C_j^w are defined using the joint distribution values and based on the definitions of possible component states. Specifically, if the water component is defined as requiring the power component to function, the joint probability that C_j^w is working and C_i^p is failed is 0. Defining the conditional distribution for a node in terms of the joint distribution enables one of the dependency relationships between nodes to be removed, resolving the cycle in the network while still accounting for the bidirectional dependency in the BN formulation.

26.3.3 Modeling geographic interdependencies

Geographic interdependencies are defined as the case where the functioning of one infrastructure is related to the functioning of another due to physical similarity or geographic proximity.

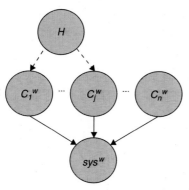

Figure 26.3 Geographic interdependency modeled between $C_1^w, \ldots, C_j^w$ with common hazard node H.

For example, many components in an area may be similar in terms of materials, age, or physical design. Therefore, if one component has been observed to fail, it is more likely that the other similarly designed components have failed. In addition, many infrastructures are collocated. This is particularly true for buried infrastructure, e.g., pipes, cables, and fiber lines located in trenches along the same street or routed along the same bridge. In these cases, given a hazard event, the collocated infrastructures are more likely to fail together. The increased likelihood of failure of one component given failure of a nearby component must be modeled.

Within the BN framework, geographic interdependencies are modeled by adding common parent hazard nodes to the network as shown in Figure 26.3. In this case, similar or proximate components represented as $C_1^w, \ldots, C_j^w$ would share a common parent hazard node H, modeling the dependence between their component states. It is noted that while the relationship here may be viewed as a unidirectional dependency rather than a bidirectional interdependency, unless the state of the component affects the hazard, for consistency in language, the interdependency terminology is used here.

26.3.4 Modeling access for repair interdependencies

Access for repair interdependencies specifically address post-disaster recovery for resilience. They refer to the case where the ability of one infrastructure to be repaired is affected by the access provided by another infrastructure. This is particularly relevant for analyses of system resilience, where not just the reliability of the system, but also the ability of the infrastructure to recover after a damage event, is of interest. Access for repair interdependencies include components for both physical and cyber access. For example, open roads may be required to physically access an infrastructure asset for repair. Or, a functioning communication network may be required to enable diagnostics to be run on a piece of equipment or facilitate remote repairs. These requirements for access result in access for repair interdependencies with both transportation and communication networks in particular.

An additional element that must be considered in defining access for repair interdependencies is the temporal aspect of infrastructure damage and repair processes. Systems evolve over time, and only when a component has failed does access become important. Specifically, if an infrastructure component is working, then its state is independent of the ability to access the component for repair. It is only when the component fails that the state of the component and

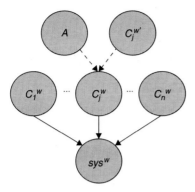

Figure 26.4 Access for repair interdependency modeled for C_j^w with access node A and previous state node $C_j^{w'}$.

its ability to be repaired become dependent on the states of its routes for access. Therefore, in defining this type of interdependency in the BN framework, a dynamic time component is added to the model. To do this, an additional node is introduced in the BN that represents the state of the dependent component in the previous time step. The state of the component in the current time step is then dependent on both the access node and previous state node.

This is shown in Figure 28.4 for an example water system component C_j^w, which has both access node A and previous state node $C_j^{w'}$ as parents. Incorporating access for repair interdependencies enables us to move beyond infrastructure risk and reliability assessment to model system resilience. Access nodes provide a measure of component remoteness and redundancy in the paths to reach a component. This provides the ability to account for the factors, including paths for access and resources, necessary to recover infrastructure systems to pre-event service levels or better after a disaster event.

26.4 Example application

The probabilistic framework for interdependent infrastructure modeling is now applied to an example application to demonstrate its use. The application system comprises the interdependent power, water, and gas networks in Shelby County, Tennessee, USA. The full system consists of 60 components and 74 links, 49 components and 78 links, and 16 components and 17 links, for the power, water, and gas networks, respectively. The nodes are classified as supply, transshipment, and distribution nodes. Flow proceeds from supply or production station nodes, to transshipment nodes where several lines meet, to final distribution nodes. The system overlaid onto a map of the county is shown in Figure 26.5.

For the purposes of showing the full BN model, the focus here is on the power, water, and gas output nodes closest to the city of Memphis, Tennessee, as shown in Figure 26.6, which we assume provide services to this largest city in the county.

The resulting BN is shown in Figure 26.7. The BN includes all system interdependencies. Geographic interdependencies are modeled with the indicated hazard nodes. Access for repair interdependencies are modeled with the indicated access nodes, as well as shaded nodes representing the state of the component in the previous time step. Service provision interdependencies between components are shown. Nodes corresponding with supercomponents and MLSs are indicated, as well as nodes representing individual components and links. Finally,

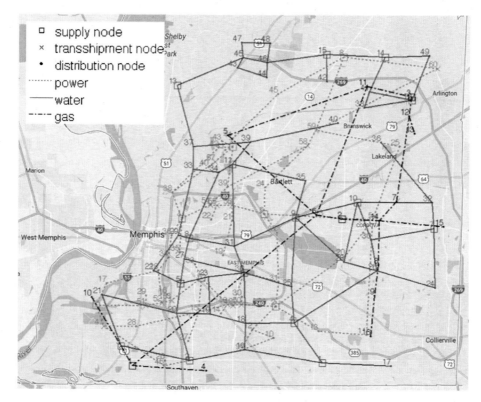

Figure 26.5 Example application of interdependent power, water, and gas networks with supply, transshipment, and distribution nodes shown.

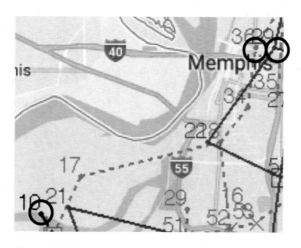

Figure 26.6 Power, water, and gas nodes (circled) closest to the city of Memphis.

these nodes combine to provide critical infrastructure services to the terminal distribution node indicated. The BN captures all interdependency relationships to probabilistically model and assess interdependent infrastructure resilience.

26.5 Inference results

With the network model built and conditional probability distributions for the BN model as shown in Figure 26.7 defined, inferences across the system are possible. For example, if one component is observed to have failed, inputting that information into the BN will propagate through the network to update probabilities of failure for dependent components as well as probabilities of system-level service provision. Assessing system reliability outputs at the infrastructure system nodes under a variety of component performance scenarios enables identification of critical components and prioritization of components for repair or retrofit to increase overall system performance.

As an example of inference to assess service provision interdependencies, Table 26.2 provides the conditional probability distribution for the power node given the binary states of the water node providing resources for cooling in electricity generation. In the BN, components are initialized with conditional probabilities of failure given varying earthquake magnitudes based on fragility curves for the components (Gonzalez et al. 2015) under earthquakes of moment magnitudes six, seven, eight, and nine. Prior conditional probabilities of failure for the

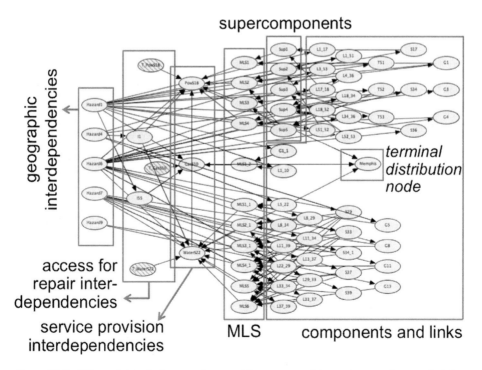

Figure 26.7 BN model including service provision, geographic, and access for repair interdependencies; supercomponent, minimum link set (MLS), component, link, and terminal distribution nodes.

Table 26.2 Example inference for service provision interdependency providing conditional probabilities for power node

	water node working	water node failed
power node working	0.996	0.000
power node failed	0.004	1.000

Table 26.3 Example inference for geographic interdependency providing node survival probabilities under earthquake hazard of varying moment magnitudes M_w

	no hazard	$M_w = 6$	$M_w = 7$	$M_w = 8$	$M_w = 9$
power node working	1.000	0.976	0.833	0.457	0.136
water node working	1.000	0.985	0.920	0.738	0.495
gas node working	1.000	0.831	0.639	0.401	0.207

Table 26.4 Example inference for access for repair interdependency providing node survival probabilities under varying conditions of interstates I1 and I55 for access

	I1 working, I55 working	I1 failed, I55 working	I1 working, I55 failed	I1 failed, I55 failed
power node working	0.965	0.942	0.965	0.942
water node working	0.968	0.965	0.968	0.965
gas node working	0.932	0.932	0.920	0.920

individual components range from 0.02 to 0.08 for earthquake moment magnitude six, up to 0.25 to 0.5 for earthquake moment magnitude nine. In general, these initial component state marginal or conditional probability distributions can be defined according to varying information sources, including empirical data, mechanical properties such as material and age, historical data, updated fragility curves, expert opinion, etc.

An example of inference to assess geographic interdependencies is shown in Table 26.3. In it, the conditional probabilities of survival for the power, water, and gas nodes under geographic hazard scenarios, represented by varying earthquake moment magnitudes, are provided. The survival probability of 1.000 under the no hazard scenario is due to rounding of the inference result.

To assess access for repair interdependencies, the infrastructure required to provide physical access to failed components is considered. The interstates representing the two highest functional classifications of roads in the area, I-1 and I-55, are overlaid on the Memphis power, water, and gas nodes to assess performance under different conditions of access. It is assumed that if the interstate section closest to a node is failed, there is no access to be able to repair the failed component. If access is available, the component is repaired. The effect of the states of the two interstates on the performance of the power, water, and gas nodes is shown in Table 26.4.

With the transportation infrastructure components required for access integrated into the BN, inferences over the network with functioning or non-functioning transportation components enable the impacts of the access network on the ability for a system to recover after an event to be quantified. Further, with the updating capabilities of the BN model, if new measurements or observations are made on any part of the network, that information can be input into the model to update assessments of all nodes across the BN.

In general, with the full model, inference over the network enables assessment of system performance incorporating all interdependencies. By performing analyses for specific components and observing the resulting performance of the interdependent systems, it enables quantification of cascading effects beyond initial disruptions to a single network. Comparing system outcomes based on varying component behaviors facilitates evaluation of the network and identification of the critical nodes.

For pre-hazard planning, critical components can be identified and retrofitted or replaced to prevent or minimize damage from future disruptions. During a disaster event, rapid updating of the states of all components using the built BN model facilitates recovery decisions. For example, a decision-maker can determine the impact of the repair of each of the components that failed during the disaster event. Impact can be measured by the effect on system performance, e.g., the ability to provide service to a critical facility such as a hospital or based on an overall system service metric. Those components with the largest effects would be prioritized for repair over less impactful components. For post-disaster planning and response, running analyses over multiple recovery scenarios supports identification of critical components for repair or replacement to minimize the risk of cascading failures, facilitate recovery, and increase resilience.

26.6 Conclusions

This chapter presents a generalized probabilistic methodology for modeling interdependencies in critical infrastructure systems. Three comprehensive types of interdependencies are defined, including service provision, geographic, and access for repair. Service provision interdependencies are modeled using direct dependencies in the network model. The case of two components each being dependent on the other is addressed through the definition of joint probability distributions. Geographic interdependencies are modeled using common hazard parent nodes to quantify correlations between dependent component states. Access for repair interdependencies are modeled by adding nodes representing the access infrastructure and the state of the component at the previous time step to indicate the relevance of the access dependency. The Bayesian network model that is created that includes each of these interdependencies provides a comprehensive view of system performance. It enables probabilistic analyses of interdependent infrastructures across a range of scenarios to predict system outcomes and support decisions in the design, management, and rehabilitation of these critical networks to increase infrastructure resilience.

References

Bensi, M., Kiureghian, A., and Straub, D. (2013). Efficient Bayesian network modeling of systems. *Reliability Engineering & System Safety*, 112, 200–13.

Boudali, H. and Dugan, J.B. (2005). A discrete-time Bayesian network reliability modeling and analysis framework. *Reliability Engineering and System Safety*, 87, 337–49.

Dueñas-Osorio, L., Craig, J.I., and Goodno, B. (2007). Seismic response of critical interdependent networks. *Earthquake Engineering and Structural Dynamics*, 36, 285–306.

González, A.D., Dueñas-Osorio, L., Sánchez-Silva, M., and Medaglia, A.L. (2015). The interdependent network design problem for optimal infrastructure system restoration. *Computer-Aided Civil and Infrastructure Engineering*, 31, 334–50.

Guidotti, R., Chmielewski, H., Unnikrishnan, V., Gardoni, P., McAllister, T., and van de Lindt, J. (2016) Modeling the resilience of critical infrastructure: The role of network dependencies. *Sustainable and Resilient Infrastructure*, 1(3–4), 153–68.

Haimes, Y.Y. (2008). Models for risk management of systems of systems. *International Journal of System of Systems Engineering*, 1, 222–36.

Jensen, F.V. and Nielsen, T.D. (2007). *Bayesian Networks and Decision Graphs*. 2nd ed., New York: Springer.

Johansen, C. and Tien, I. (2018). Probabilistic multi-scale modeling of interdependencies between critical infrastructure systems for resilience. *Sustainable and Resilient Infrastructure*, 3(1), 1–15, doi: 10.1080/23789689.2017.1345253.

Johansen, C., Horney, J., and Tien, I. (2017). Metrics for evaluating and improving community resilience. *Journal of Infrastructure Systems*, 23(2), 1–11.

Kang, W.-H., Song, J., and Gardoni, P. (2008). Matrix-based system reliability method and applications to bridge networks. *Reliability Engineering and System Safety*, 93, 1584–93.

Korkali, M., Veneman, J.G., Tivnan, B.F., and Hines, P.D.H. (2014). Reducing cascading failure risk by increasing infrastructure network interdependency. https://arxiv.org/abs/1410.6836 (last accessed August 19, 2018).

Lee, Y.-J., Song, J., Gardoni, P., and Lim, H.-W. (2011). Posthazard flow capacity of bridge transportation network considering structural deterioration of bridges. *Structure and Infrastructure Engineering*, 7, 509–521.

Ouyang, M. (2014). Review on modeling and simulation of interdependent critical infrastructure systems. *Reliability Engineering and System Safety*, 121, 43–60.

Rinaldi, S.M., Peerenboom, J.P., and Kelly, T. (2001). Identifying, understanding, and analyzing critical infrastructure interdependencies. *IEEE Control Systems Magazine*, 11–25.

Song, J., and Ok, S.Y. (2010). Multi-scale system reliability analysis of lifeline networks under earthquake hazards. *Earthquake Engineering and Structural Dynamics*, 39, 259–79.

Tien, I. (2017). Bayesian network methods for modeling and reliability assessment of infrastructure systems. *Risk and Reliability Analysis: Theory and Applications*, Springer: Springer Series in Reliability Engineering, 417–52.

Tien, I. (2018). Resilient by design: the case for increasing resilience of buildings and their linked food-energy-water systems. *Elementa: Science of the Anthropocene*, 6(18), 1–12.

Tien, I. and Der Kiureghian, A. (2016). Algorithms for Bayesian network modeling and reliability assessment of infrastructure systems. *Reliability Engineering and System Safety*, 156, 134–47.

Tien, I. and Der Kiureghian, A. (2017). Reliability assessment of critical infrastructure using Bayesian networks. *ASCE Journal of Infrastructure Systems*, 23(4): 1–11.

Tong, Y. and Tien, I. (2017). Algorithms for Bayesian network modeling, inference, and reliability assessment for multistate flow networks. *ASCE Journal of Computing in Civil Engineering*, 31(5): 1–10.

White House (2013). Presidential Policy Directive/PPD 21 – Critical Infrastructure Security and Resilience.

Zhang, P., and Peeta, S. (2011). A generalized modeling framework to analyze interdependencies among infrastructure systems. *Transportation Research Part B: Methodological*, 45(3), 553–79.

27

Modeling of interdependent critical infrastructure for regional risk and resilience analysis

Roberto Guidotti[1] *and Paolo Gardoni*[2]

[1] DEPARTMENT OF CIVIL AND ENVIRONMENTAL ENGINEERING, MAE CENTER: CREATING A MULTI-HAZARD APPROACH TO ENGINEERING, UNIVERSITY OF ILLINOIS AT URBANA-CHAMPAIGN, URBANA, IL, USA; GUIDOTT2@ILLINOIS.EDU

[2] DEPARTMENT OF CIVIL AND ENVIRONMENTAL ENGINEERING, MAE CENTER: CREATING A MULTI-HAZARD APPROACH TO ENGINEERING, UNIVERSITY OF ILLINOIS AT URBANA-CHAMPAIGN, URBANA, IL, USA; GARDONI@ILLINOIS.EDU

27.1 Introduction

Critical infrastructure (such as water and wastewater, electric power, transportation, telecommunication, and gas and liquid fuel networks) constitute the backbone of modern society. They provide essential goods and services to the community, supporting the population well-being. Critical infrastructure are exposed to low-probability, high-consequence hazard events. When hazard events threaten the functionality of one or more infrastructure, the resilience of a community is called into play, where resilience has been defined as the "ability to prepare for and adapt to changing conditions and withstand and recover rapidly from disruptions" (PPD-21 2013). Any interruption or disruption in the functionality of critical infrastructure may result in considerable losses, and impacts on the economy and the well-being of society (Gardoni & LaFave 2016; Gardoni et al. 2016, 2017; Gardoni & Murphy 2018). Several reports and presidential policy directives (e.g., PCCIP 1997; PPD-21 2013; ATC 2016) underscored the strategic importance of critical infrastructure and the importance of understanding the societal needs in disaster recovery. A prompt recovery of the critical infrastructure leads to a prompt recovery of the economic vitality and the general well-being of the impacted communities. In addition, (inter)dependencies increase the vulnerability of critical infrastructure. In the case of a damaging event, (inter)dependencies may propagate the impact of failure or reduction of functionality of one infrastructure to other supported infrastructure, often resulting in widespread disruption (Rinaldi et al. 2001; Vespignani 2010; Chang 2014; Franchin & Cavalieri 2015; Guidotti et al. 2016a).

This chapter presents network-based models of interdependent critical infrastructure for regional risk and resilience analysis. With respect to other methods available in the literature (see e.g., Ouyang 2014), network-based methods offer the important advantage of allowing the extension of well-established mathematical tools of graph theory to civil engin-eering applications. They are suitable to model interdependencies by introducing links among different infrastructure and by removal and addition of networks components, they allow the modeling of the failure and restoration processes of interdependent critical infrastructure. Following Guidotti et al. (2016a, 2018a), the models are based on the following four steps for regional risk and resilience analysis: (i) definition of the infrastructure in the region, (ii) defin-ition of the initial damage state for the infrastructure, (iii) assessment of cascading effects due to interdependencies, and (iv) assessment of reduction or loss of functionality over time for each damaged infrastructure. The chapter applies the presented network-based models to two example testbeds.

27.2 Definition of the infrastructure and of the state variables of its components

In this section, we introduce a mathematical representation of critical infrastructure as networks, based on the concepts of the graph theory. We then propose a taxonomy of infrastructure and networks components to capture their heterogeneity. The proposed taxonomy leads to define category-specific state variables models. These models are used to define the state of each com-ponent and to capture the response of an infrastructure during its entire service life (including the impact of a damaging event and its recovery).

27.2.1 Networks as mathematical representation of infrastructure

Network-based methods represent mathematically a generic infrastructure, or multiple systems of infrastructure, as networks. Referring to the same object, in this chapter, the term infra-structure is used for its physical representation, while the term network is used for its math-ematical representation. Based on the concepts of the graph theory (e.g., Ruohonen 2013), a generic network $G = (V, E)$ can be defined by the set V of N nodes or vertices, $V = (v_1, v_2, ..., v_N)$, and by the set E of M links or edges that connect the nodes, $E = (e_1, e_2, ..., e_M)$. A generic link e_m, $1 \leq m \leq M$ connecting two nodes v_i and v_j ($1 \leq i \leq N$, $1 \leq j \leq N$, $i \neq j$) can be represented as $e_{ij} = (v_i, v_j)$. Generally, nodes v_i and v_j are connected if there exists a finite sequence of nodes and links from v_i to v_j. If all of the nodes of the network are connected to each other, we have a connected network. Networks are typically represented in a matrix form through adja-cency tables (Guidotti et al. 2016a, 2017a, 2017b). The adjacency table of network G is an $N \times N$ matrix $\mathbf{A}^{(G)} = [a_{ij}]$, ($1 \leq i \leq N$, $1 \leq j \leq N$), where $a_{ij}^{(G)}$ ($i \neq j$) is either 1 if $e_{ij} = (v_i, v_j) \in E$, or 0 otherwise, and $a_{ii}^{(G)} = 0$. The adjacency table provides information on the connectivity of the network. In civil engineering applications, physical infrastructure and systems of infrastructure under regular operational conditions can typically be modeled as connected networks.

27.2.2 Taxonomy of infrastructure and network components

The components of a civil infrastructure can be classified into three main categories, based on their function: generation, transportation, and distribution components. Generation (or source) components originate the essential goods and services. Distribution (or sink) components use the goods and services. Transmission component ensure the flow of goods and services from the gen-eration components to the distribution components. In addition to these three main categories, some infrastructure may have components that allow the storage of goods, as for example tanks in a water system. The geographic area served by each distribution component is defined as tributary area. Based on this taxonomy, we can define the following sets: $V_G = (v_{G,1}, v_{G,2}, ..., v_{G,N_G})$, $V_T = (v_{T,1}, v_{T,2}, ..., v_{T,N_T})$, $V_D = (v_{D,1}, v_{D,2}, ..., v_{D,N_D})$ and $V_S = (v_{S,1}, v_{S,2}, ..., v_{S,N_S})$ for the generation, transmission, distribution, and storage nodes, respectively. We then write the set V of $\mathcal{N} = (N_G + N_T + N_D + N_S)$ heterogeneous nodes of network G as the union of those sets $V = V_G \cup V_T \cup V_D \cup V_S$. The components of civil infrastructure can also be classified topologically in point elements (e.g., reservoirs, tank, pumping stations, junctions in a potable water network) and linear elements (e.g., pipelines, channels, and flumes). The set V has heterogeneous nodes consisting in both point and linear elements. The links in the set E connect nodes in set V and represent connections between couples of typically heterogeneous nodes.

27.2.3 Definition of the state variables of the network components

Following the approach in Jia et al. (2017) and Jia and Gardoni (2018), to model the response of an infrastructure during its entire service life (including the impact of a damaging event and its recovery), let us define the vector of state variables $\mathbf{x}(v_i, t)$ of node v_i at time t for each element of set V as the set of basic variables that define the node. For example, $\mathbf{x}(v_i, t)$ might include material properties, member dimensions, structural properties, and imposed boundary conditions. Following Jia and Gardoni (2018), the state variables can be modeled as

$$\mathbf{x}(v_i, t) = \mathbf{x}\left[\mathbf{x}_0(v_i), t, \{\mathbf{Z}(t)\}; \mathbf{\Theta}_x\right], \tag{27.1}$$

where $\mathbf{x}_0(v_i) = \mathbf{x}(t = 0)$ is the vector of the state variables of node v_i at a reference time $t = 0$, $\mathbf{\Theta}_x$ is a vector of model parameters of the state model, and $\{\mathbf{Z}(t)\}$ is the sequence of vectors of external conditions or variables $\mathbf{Z}(t)$ occurring from time $t = 0$ to time t. The vector $\mathbf{Z}(t)$ might be portioned into environmental conditions or variables that influence the gradual deterioration over time of $\mathbf{x}$, denoted as $\mathbf{E}(t)$, and shock intensity measures (e.g., the characteristic of possible damaging events) that influence the shock deterioration, denoted as $\mathbf{S}(t)$. More details about the definition of gradual and shock deterioration can be found in Kumar et al. (2009, 2015), and Kumar and Gardoni (2012, 2013, 2014a, 2014b). Hazard-specific models can be used to generate maps of the intensity measures of interest. At time $t = 0$ (e.g., the time of completion of the construction/installation process), the initial values of the state variables of the generation, storage, transmission, and distribution nodes are typically defined. Information on the population living in the tributary areas served by each node is also included as a state variable for the distribution nodes V_D to obtain the initial amount of goods and services requested to the infrastructure. The amount of goods and services is proportional to the population served by the infrastructure, namely the population living in the tributary areas. More details on the procedure to assign the population to a specific tributary area can be found in Rosenheim et al. (2018).

Following the taxonomy previously defined, we can classify the state variables according to the category of the node, resulting in category-specific state variables models, defined as follows:

$$\forall \lambda \in \Lambda \,\exists\, \mathbf{x}_\lambda(v_{\lambda,i}, t) : \mathbf{x}_\lambda(v_{\lambda,i}, t) = \mathbf{x}_\lambda\left[\mathbf{x}_{\lambda,0}(v_{\lambda,i}), t, \{\mathbf{Z}_{\lambda,i}(t)\}; \mathbf{\Theta}_{\mathbf{x}_\lambda}\right], \tag{27.2}$$

where $\mathbf{x}_{\lambda,0}(v_{\lambda,i})$ is the vector of the state variables of node $v_{\lambda,i}$ of category $\lambda \in \Lambda$, at a reference time $t = 0$, the set Λ includes the categories of the node (i.e., generation, storage, transmission, and distribution), $\{\mathbf{Z}_{\lambda,i}(t)\} = \{\mathbf{E}_{\lambda,i}(t); \mathbf{S}_{\lambda,i}(t)\}$ is the sequence of vectors of external conditions or variables occurring from time $t = 0$ to time t that have an impact specifically at the site of node $v_{\lambda,i}$, and $\Theta_{\mathbf{x}_\lambda}$ is the vector of the parameters of the state variables model for nodes of category λ.

27.3 Definition of the initial state for the considered infrastructure

In this section, based on the state variables previously introduced, we propose models for the capacity and demand at the component and network level. Capacity and demand models are used to develop fragility functions, and repair rate curves. For a given set of intensity measures at the site, fragility functions and repair rate curves are used to express the likelihood of damage or failure of point and linear components, respectively.

27.3.1 Models for the capacity and demand at the component level

Based on the state variables $\mathbf{x}(v_i, t)$, we can model the structural capacity and demand of each component. The capacity of a component is defined as the maximum value of load or deformation that the component can sustain without failure. The demand of a component is defined as actual value of load or deformation applied to the considered component. Capacity and demand models for each category of nodes can be written as

$$\begin{cases} c_\lambda(t) := c_\lambda\left[\mathbf{x}_\lambda\left(v_{\lambda,i}, t\right); \Theta_{c,\lambda}\right] \\ d_\lambda(t) := d_\lambda\left[\mathbf{x}_\lambda\left(v_{\lambda,i}, t\right), \mathbf{S}_\lambda(t); \Theta_{d,\lambda}\right], \end{cases} \tag{27.3}$$

where $c_\lambda[\mathbf{x}_\lambda(v_{\lambda,i}, t); \Theta_{c,\lambda}]$ and $d_\lambda[\mathbf{x}_\lambda(v_{\lambda,i}, t), \mathbf{S}_\lambda(t); \Theta_{d,\lambda}]$ are the category-specific capacity and demand models, $\Theta_{c,\lambda}$ and $\Theta_{d,\lambda}$ are their vectors of model parameters, and $\mathbf{S}_\lambda(t)$ is the vector of category-specific shock intensity measures. The capacity and demand models in Equation (27.3) can follow the general forms proposed by Gardoni et al. (2002, 2003). Examples of capacity and demand models for components of transportation networks can be found in Gardoni et al. (2002, 2003); Choe et al. (2009, 2010); Huang et al. (2010, 2014); Bisadi et al. (2011, 2012); Kumar and Gardoni (2012, 2014b); Sharma et al. (2014, 2015); Tabandeh and Gardoni (2014, 2015); examples of models for components of power network can be found in Mardfekri and Gardoni (2013) and Mardfekri et al. (2015).

27.3.2 Fragility functions and repair rate curves

Fragility functions and repair rate curves are used to express the likelihood of damage or failure of components (Gardoni 2017). For point elements, fragility functions give the conditional probability of attaining or exceeding a prescribed performance level for given shock intensity measures at the site (Gardoni et al. 2002, 2003), which are included in $\mathbf{S}_{\lambda,i}(t)$. For linear elements, repair rate curves provide the number of expected repairs per unit length of the linear element as a function of the intensity measures at the site. Gardoni et al. (2002) and (2003) defined physics-based fragility functions by introducing a limit-state function $g_\lambda(t) = c_\lambda(t) - d_\lambda(t)$. Different nodes in each category λ have, in general, different limit-state function $g_\lambda(t)$. The model form is generally the same, but the models of capacity $c_\lambda(t)$ and demand $d_\lambda(t)$ include node-specific information from the values of the state variables $\mathbf{x}(v_i, t)$, which are function of $\{\mathbf{Z}_{\lambda,i}(t)\}$. A reliability analysis (Ditlevsen & Madsen 1996; Gardoni 2017) can then be carried out to estimate the conditional probability of failure (fragility) at time t as

$$F\left[\mathbf{S}_\lambda(t); \Theta_\lambda\right] = P\left[g_\lambda(t) \le 0 \middle| \mathbf{S}_\lambda(t)\right], \tag{27.4}$$

where $\Theta_\lambda = (\Theta_{\mathbf{x}_\lambda}; \Theta_{c,\lambda}; \Theta_{d,\lambda})$ includes the parameters of the state variables model and of the corresponding capacity and demand models and $\mathbf{S}_\lambda(t)$ is the vector of external conditions or variables occurring at time t that have an impact specifically on nodes of category λ. Following the approach in Gardoni et al. (2002), we can compute the point estimate of the fragility as $\hat{F}[\mathbf{S}_\lambda(t)] = F[\mathbf{S}_\lambda(t); \hat{\Theta}_\lambda]$ where $\hat{\Theta}_\lambda$ is a fixed value of Θ_λ (e.g., a point estimate like the posterior mean and the maximum likelihood estimate). To account for the uncertainties in Θ_λ, Gardoni et al. (2002) also defined a predictive estimate of the fragility as $\tilde{F}[\mathbf{S}_\lambda(t)] = \int F[\mathbf{S}_\lambda(t); \Theta_\lambda] f(\Theta_\lambda) d\Theta_\lambda$, where $f(\Theta_\lambda)$ is the probability density function (PDF) of Θ_λ. To explicitly express the effect of the statistical uncertainty in the model parameters, approximate confidence bounds can be computed by first order analysis (Gardoni et al. 2002). From the fragility functions, we can obtain the probability of failure at time t as a point estimate as shown in Equation (27.5) or a predictive estimate as shown in Equation (27.6) (Jia et al. 2017; Jia & Gardoni 2018)

$$\hat{P}_f(t) = \int \hat{F}\big[\mathbf{S}_\lambda(t)\big] f\big[\mathbf{S}_\lambda(t)\big] d\mathbf{S}_\lambda(t),$$

(27.5)

$$\tilde{P}_f(t) = \int \tilde{F}\big[\mathbf{S}_\lambda(t)\big] f\big[\mathbf{S}_\lambda(t)\big] d\mathbf{S}_\lambda(t).$$

(27.6)

Repair rate curves have been used to estimate the number of leaks and breaks in linear elements, e.g. pipelines (e.g., ALA 2001; O'Rourke & Ayala 1993; O'Rourke & Deyoe 2004). However, the number of ruptures in a linear element depends on the location and on the spatially variable external conditions and does not have stationary increments along the linear element; therefore, at a given time t and for a given segment of length Δs, we propose to model the number of ruptures R as a nonhomogeneous Poisson process

$$P_R\big\{R(s \leq \varsigma \leq s + \Delta s, t) = r\big\} = \frac{\left[\int_s^{s+\Delta s} \omega(\varsigma, t) d\varsigma\right]^r}{r!} e^{-\int_s^{s+\Delta s} \omega(\varsigma,t) d\varsigma}, \quad r = 0,1,2,\dots$$

(27.7)

where $\omega = \omega(s,t)$ is the temporal and spatial dependent repair rate, r is the realization of the random variable R and s is the local coordinate along the linear element. The number of ruptures in any spatial interval along the linear element depends on the location of the interval, as

$$R(s + \Delta s, t) - R(s, t) \sim Poisson\left(\int_s^{s+\Delta s} \omega(\varsigma, t) d\varsigma\right).$$

(27.8)

Repair rates provide an estimate of the expected number of ruptures per unit length, given the occurrence of certain intensity measures $\mathbf{S}_\lambda(t,s)$, for the given set of state variables $\mathbf{x}_\lambda$ of the considered node $v_{\lambda,i} \in V$. Mathematically we can write

$$\omega(s,t) = \omega\Big\{\mathbf{S}_\lambda(t,s); \mathbf{x}_\lambda\big[\mathbf{x}_{\lambda,0}(v_{\lambda,i}), t, \{\mathbf{Z}_\lambda(t,s)\}; \Theta_{\mathbf{x}_\lambda}\big]\Big\}.$$

(27.9)

where $\mathbf{S}_\lambda(t,s)$ and $\{\mathbf{Z}_\lambda(t,s)\}$ show the dependency of $\omega(s,t)$ on the vector of external conditions or variables occurring at time t at location s of the linear element of category λ. Following the formulation in Gardoni et al. (2002) for the definition of point and predictive fragilities, we can define point and predictive repair rates as

$$\hat{\omega}(s,t) = \omega\left\{\mathbf{Z}_\lambda(t,s); \mathbf{x}_\lambda\left[\mathbf{x}_{\lambda,0}(v_{\lambda,i}), t, \{\mathbf{Z}_\lambda(t,s)\}; \hat{\mathbf{\Theta}}_{x_\lambda}\right]\right\}. \tag{27.10}$$

$$\tilde{\omega}(s,t) = \int \omega\left\{\mathbf{Z}_\lambda(t,s); \mathbf{x}_\lambda\left[\mathbf{x}_{\lambda,0}(v_{\lambda,i}), t, \{\mathbf{Z}_\lambda(t,s)\}; \mathbf{\Theta}_{x_\lambda}\right]\right\} f(\mathbf{\Theta}_{x_\lambda}) d\mathbf{\Theta}_{x_\lambda}. \tag{27.11}$$

Once the repair rate has been defined, the probability of failure of the node consisting in a linear element can be calculated expressing capacity and demand of the node $v_{\lambda,i} \in V$ as a function of the numbers of ruptures in the considered node $v_{\lambda,i}$. For example, considering a pipeline in a water system, the occurrence of at least one break results in the failure of the considered pipeline.

27.3.3 Models for the capacity and demand at the network level

The models in Equation (27.3) are at the single component level. Capacity and demand models at the network level are needed to assess the reliability and resilience of the entire infrastructure. We express the capacity of the entire network as

$$C(t) := C\left[\mathbf{X}(t); \mathbf{\Theta}_C\right], \tag{27.12}$$

where $C[\mathbf{X}(t); \mathbf{\Theta}_C]$ is the network capacity model, $\mathbf{X}(t) = [\mathbf{x}(v_1,t), \mathbf{x}(v_2,t), ..., \mathbf{x}(v_N,t)]$ is the vector of the state variables of the N nodes of the network G, and $\mathbf{\Theta}_C = [\mathbf{\Theta}_{c,1}, \mathbf{\Theta}_{c,2}, ..., \mathbf{\Theta}_{c,\Lambda}]$ is the vector of the model parameters of the Λ capacity models. Similarly, we express the demand imposed by a damaging event on the system as

$$D(t) := D\left[\mathbf{X}(t), \mathbf{S}(t); \mathbf{\Theta}_D\right], \tag{27.13}$$

where $D[\mathbf{X}(t), \mathbf{S}(t); \mathbf{\Theta}_D]$ is the demand model, and $\mathbf{\Theta}_D = [\mathbf{\Theta}_{d,1}, \mathbf{\Theta}_{d,2}, ..., \mathbf{\Theta}_{d,\Lambda}]$ is the vector of the model parameters of the Λ demand models. The capacity and demand models in Equation (27.12) and Equation (27.13) can follow the general forms proposed by Gardoni et al. (2002, 2003). The models presented here take as input the states variables of all the nodes $v_i \in V$ of the considered network G and include the time dependency. These models can be used in the network reliability analysis to predict the reduction or loss of functionality of a network, as described in Section 27.5.

27.4 Assessment of cascading effects due to (inter)dependencies among critical infrastructure

In this section, we first introduce five classes of (inter)dependency: physical, cyber, geographic, logical, and social. We then adopt a multi-layered heterogeneous network model (in the remaining of this chapter indicated as MHN model) (Guidotti et al. 2017b, 2018b) to assess the cascading effects due to the multiple classes of (inter)dependency among critical infrastructure, taking into account the heterogeneity of their components.

27.4.1 Classes of dependency/interdependency

The models presented in the previous section allow us to evaluate the physical state and effect of the direct damage to isolated network. However, critical systems of infrastructure are interconnected and a disruption in one infrastructure may cause cascading effects, resulting in disruptions of dependent infrastructure and, more generally, degrading their functionality (Vespignani 2010; Chang 2014; Guidotti et al. 2016b). This section integrates the physical infrastructure as well as the social systems considering multiple dependencies and interdependencies.

Rinaldi et al. (2001) defined four types of dependencies: physical, cyber, geographic, and logical. Physical dependency is when the state of one infrastructure system is dependent on the material outputs of another infrastructure system. Cyber dependency is when the state of one infrastructure system depends on information transmitted through the information infrastructure. Geographic dependency is when a local environmental event can create state changes in two or more infrastructure systems. Logical dependency is when the state of one infrastructure system depends on the state of others via a mechanism that is not physical, cyber, or geographic. Going beyond the dependencies of physical infrastructure, Guidotti et al. (2018a) also introduced a fifth type of dependency: social dependency. The population served by each distribution node $v_{D,i} \in V_D$ may change because of the human response to damaging events. As examples of human response models, Lin (2009) and Rosenheim et al. (2017, 2018) obtained the probability of household dislocation due to the structural damage of residential buildings by a logistic regression model that also required demographic information. Changes in the population lead to changes in the service demand at the corresponding distribution node with a direct impact on the state variable $\mathbf{x}_D(v_{D,i}, t)$ of the distribution nodes of the infrastructure. We can also differentiate between internal and external population dislocation to determine the change in population size and spatial distribution. External dislocation results in a reduction of the population size of a community; internal dislocation results in an increase of the population size at given assembly points, keeping a constant overall population.

27.4.2 Multi-layered heterogeneous network model

A MHN model was proposed by Guidotti et al. (2017b, 2018b) to assess the probability of failure of a dependent node given the failure of a supporting node (of any category λ and belonging to any network) considering different classes of dependency/interdependency. The main conceptual shift of an MHN model with respect to current approaches is that all of the different components of the considered networks are modeled on the same conceptual "plane", with different levels describing the different classes of interdependencies (Figure 27.1). An MHN model takes into account in the same model that the network components are of different categories; and captures the fact that different classes of dependency are possible between the same nodes. The remaining of this section briefly summarizes the main elements of a MHN model.

Augmented adjacency table
The MHN model builds on the concept of adjacency table, introducing an augmented adjacency table. In the case of K networks, each network k can be represented by a symmetric $n^{(k)} \times n^{(k)}$ adjacency table $\mathbf{A}^{(k)} = [a_{ij}^{(k)}]$, $k = 1,..., K$, $(i, j \in k; i, j = 1,..., n^{(k)})$. The augmented adjacency table $\mathbf{A}$ has the K adjacency tables arranged along its diagonal. Out-of-diagonal tables are used to represent pairwise connections between nodes of different networks. For example, considering two generic networks y and w, the connections between nodes of the two networks is represented by the generally rectangular $n^{(y)} \times n^{(w)}$ table $\mathbf{A}^{(y,w)} = [a_{ij}^{(y,w)}]$, where $a_{ij}^{(y,w)}$, $(y, w = 1,..., K)$, is either 1, if node i of network y is connected to node j of network w, or 0 otherwise. The connections are mutual, thus $a_{ij}^{(y,w)} = a_{ji}^{(w,y)}$ and the augmented adjacency table is symmetric.

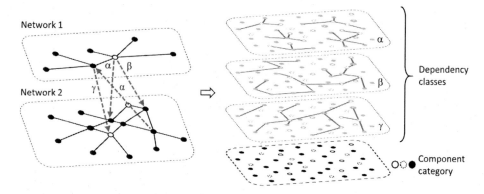

Figure 27.1   Pictorial representation of the multi-layered heterogeneous network (MHN) model.

Multi-layered dependency tables

Guidotti et al. (2017b, 2018b) also introduced a dependency table **D** to capture relations of dependency and interdependency between pairs of nodes of the same network or of different networks. Considering a system of K networks, we have along the diagonal the dependencies within a given network k: $\mathbf{D}^{(k)} = [d_{ij}^{(k)}]$, $k = 1,...,K$, $(i, j \in k; \ i, j = 1,...,n^{(k)})$ where $d_{ij}^{(k)}$ $(i \neq j)$ is either 1, if nodes i of network k depends on node j of the same network k, or 0 otherwise, and $d_{ii}^{(k)} = 0$. The terms out of the diagonal represent the dependency between nodes of different networks: $\mathbf{D}^{(y,w)} = [d_{ij}^{(y,w)}]$, $y, w = 1,...,K$, $(i, j \in k; \ i, j = 1,...,n^{(k)})$, where $d_{ij}^{(y,w)} = 1$, $(i \neq j)$, indicates a dependency relation between node i of network y and node j of network w. Under this definition, the symmetry of **D** holds true only when $d_{ij}^{(y,w)} = d_{ji}^{(w,y)} = 1$, i.e., a mutual dependency (interdependency) exists between all the couples of nodes having a relation of dependency. Table **D** is different from table **A** since: (i) a connection between two nodes in table **A** does not necessarily corresponds to a relation of dependency between them; and (ii) a relation of dependency in table **D** may link two nodes even if they are not connected in table **A** (e.g., the dependency may be not only physical).

Multiple classes of dependency/interdependency are possible among the components of systems of infrastructure. Each class establishes a different relation between pairs of nodes of the same network and between nodes of different networks. In that sense, we have a multi-layered model (Paul & Chen 2016) and each class of interdependency can be represented as a different layer, with its own dependency table. Let α be a generic class of dependency/interdependency, Guidotti et al. (2017b) proposed a multi-layered dependency table where, along the main diagonal, there are the tables $\mathbf{D}^{(k),\,\alpha} = [d_{ij}^{(k),\,\alpha}]$, $k = 1,...,K$, $\alpha = 1,...,\Omega$, $(i, j \in k; \ i, j = 1,...,n^{(k)})$ with $d_{ij}^{(k),\,\alpha}$ $(i \neq j)$ that is either 1, if there is a dependency of class α between nodes i and j of network k, or 0 otherwise, and $d_{ii}^{(k),\,\alpha} = 0$. Out of the diagonal, there are the generally rectangular $n^{(y)} \times n^{(w)}$ tables $\mathbf{D}^{(y,w),\,\alpha} = [d_{ij}^{(y,w),\,\alpha}]$, where $d_{ij}^{(y,w),\,\alpha}$ is either 1, if there is a dependency of class α between node i of network y and node j of network w, or 0 otherwise.

Heterogeneity in multi-layered likelihood tables

Focusing on the role of (inter)dependencies, we are interested in the conditional probability of failure of a node given the failure of a supporting node (cascading effect). Let us consider K different networks, each one having Λ different categories of nodes. For a class α of dependency, we introduce the $K \times K$ likelihood table $\mathbf{L}^{\alpha}$. Table $\mathbf{L}^{\alpha}$ has along its main diagonal the

Λ likelihood tables $\mathbf{L}^{\lambda),\ \alpha} = [l_{yw}^{(\lambda),\ \alpha}]$, where $y, w = 1,...,K$, $\lambda = 1,...,\Lambda$, $\alpha = 1,...,\Omega$ and $l_{yw}^{(\lambda),\ \alpha}$ is the conditional probability of the failure of a node belonging to network y given the failure of a supporting node of the same category λ belonging to network w, for dependency class α. Out of diagonal, there are the tables $\mathbf{L}^{\lambda,\vartheta),\ \alpha} = [l_{yw}^{(\lambda,\vartheta),\ \alpha}]$, where $y, w = 1,...,K$, $\lambda, \vartheta = 1,...,\Lambda$, $\alpha = 1,...,\Omega$, and $l_{yw}^{(\lambda,\vartheta),\ \alpha}$ is the conditional probability of failure of a node of category λ belonging to network y given the failure of a supporting node of category ϑ belonging to network w, for dependency class α. In practical applications, the most challenging part is to calculate the entries of table $\mathbf{L}^{\alpha}$. The conditional probability of failure of a node given the failure of another one may depend on the categories of both nodes, on the respective network of belonging, and on the class of dependency. Moreover, the entries of table $\mathbf{L}^{\alpha}$ are functions of time. Values in $\mathbf{L}^{\alpha}$ could vary with time, capturing the fact that the dependency could vary (e.g., due to deteriorations or other changes over time of the network connections).

Probability dependency tables

Each node of a network has its own probability of failure, as discussed in Section 27.3. For a generic class α of interdependency, we define a probability dependency table $\mathbf{P}^{\alpha}$ by attributing to each dependency of table $\mathbf{D}^{\alpha}$ the conditional probability of failure resulting from the likelihood table $\mathbf{L}^{\alpha}$. The entries of table $\mathbf{P}^{\alpha}$ are $p_{ij}^{(y,w),\alpha}$, $(i, j \in k; i, j = 1,...,n^{(k)})$, namely the conditional probability of failure of a node i of network y given the failure of node j of network w, taking into account the node categories and the class of dependency. Tables $\mathbf{D}^{\alpha}$ and $\mathbf{L}^{\alpha}$ have different dimensions. Following the approach in Sengupta and Chen (2015) to combine them, we use a N by $\Lambda \times K$ membership table $\mathbf{M} = [m_{i,\lambda \times k}]$, $i = 1,...,N$, $\lambda = 1,...,\Lambda$, $k = 1,...,K$ with $m_{i,\lambda \times k} = 1$ if node i is of category λ and belongs to network k; N in this case is given by the sum of the nodes of all the K different networks. The membership table is used to map the $\Lambda \times K$ by $\Lambda \times K$ likelihood table into the N by N extended likelihood table $\mathbf{L}^{\alpha\prime} = \mathbf{M} \cdot \mathbf{L}^{\alpha} \cdot \mathbf{M}^{T}$.

Between the same two nodes, multiple classes of dependency may exist. Defined, for a generic entry $p_{ij}^{(y,w),\alpha}$ of table $\mathbf{P}^{\alpha}$, B^{α} as the event of failure of a node i of network y given the failure of node j of network w, for class of dependency α, we can write $p_{ij}^{(y,w),\alpha} = P(B^{\alpha})$, that is the probability of event B^{α}. The elements of the probability dependency table $\mathbf{P} = [p_{ij}^{(y,w)}]$, considering Ω possible classes of interdependency, can be obtained by the inclusion-exclusion rule of the union of events

$$p_{ij}^{(y,w)} = P\left(\bigcup_{\alpha=1}^{\Omega} B^{\alpha}\right) = \sum_{\alpha=1}^{\Omega} P(B^{\alpha}) - \sum_{\alpha=1}^{\Omega-1}\sum_{\beta=\alpha+1}^{\Omega} P(B^{\alpha}B^{\beta}) + ... + (-1)^{\Omega-1} \cdot P(B^{\alpha}B^{\beta}...B^{\Omega}) \quad (27.14)$$

Under the assumption that failures due to different classes of dependency are statistically independent events, we write Equation (27.14) as

$$p_{ij}^{(y,w)} = \sum_{\alpha=1}^{\Omega} p_{ij}^{(y,w),\alpha} - \sum_{\alpha=1}^{\Omega-1}\sum_{\beta=\alpha+1}^{\Omega} p_{ij}^{(y,w),\alpha} \cdot p_{ij}^{(y,w),\beta} + ... + (-1)^{\Omega-1} \cdot p_{ij}^{(y,w),\alpha} \cdot p_{ij}^{(y,w),\beta} \cdot ... \cdot p_{ij}^{(y,w),\Omega} \quad (27.15)$$

Moreover, the same node may have more than one supporting node, of different categories and from different networks, and its failure may depend on the status of each one of them. In the case of failure of multiple supporting nodes, the entries of table $\mathbf{P}$ can be obtained by the inclusion-exclusion rule of the union of events in a similar way as in Equation (27.14) and Equation (27.15).

27.5 Assessment of reduction or loss of functionality over time for each damaged physical infrastructure

In this section, we present topology-based and flow-based methods to assess the reduction or loss of functionality over time for each damaged physical infrastructure. The topology-based method relies on measures of connectivity, whereas the flow-based method requires the modeling of the network-specific flow of goods and services. In both cases, system network fragilities are introduced to assess the response of the damaged infrastructure, at the time of the considered shock event $\mathbf{S}(t)$ and throughout the entire recovery time.

27.5.1 Topology-based method

In a topology-based analysis, the failure of a component (both directly and indirectly, by propagation of the cascading effects) corresponds to a possible change in the network connectivity between some nodes and the rest of the network. It is possible to assess the reliability of the entire network by considering measures of network connectivity in the definition of the limit-state function defined by $C(t)$ and $D(t)$. The topology-based method is typically used with technological and social networks, focusing on the state of the network subject to a random or targeted attack (e.g., Albert et al. 1999, 2000; Crucitti et al. 2003; Lusseau et al. 2003; Arianos et al. 2009; Schneider et al. 2011; Zhang & Chen 2013, 2015). Recently, applications of the topology-based method to physical networks subject to natural events have also gained relevance (e.g., Pitilakis et al. 2006; Dueñas-Osorio et al. 2007; Adachi & Ellingwood 2008; Kang et al. 2008; Guikema & Gardoni 2009; Frangopol & Bocchini 2012; Kurtz et al. 2015; Guidotti et al. 2017a, 2017b).

Measures of connectivity
The information on the connectivity within each network and between nodes of different networks is provided by the augmented adjacency table $\mathbf{A}$, previously defined. The occurrence of a damaging event may result in the removal (failure) of certain nodes. Removal, reduction in functionality and restoration of nodes imply a variation over time in the networks connectivity, and a change in the augmented adjacency table, $\mathbf{A} = \mathbf{A}(t)$.

Two typical measures of network connectivity are the diameter δ and the efficiency η (Latora & Marchiori 2001; Guidotti et al. 2017a). Both describe the connectivity of a specific node to the other nodes in the network (in the case of the nodal diameter and nodal efficiency) or the overall network connectivity as an average of all of the nodal connectivity (in the case of global diameter and global efficiency). Considering a generic network k and $d_{ij}^{(k)}$ as the shortest path between node i and j, the nodal diameter $\delta_i^{(k)}$ is the average length of the shortest path between node i and the rest of the network. The nodal diameter $\delta_i^{(k)}$ ranges from 1 to $+\infty$. It is equal to 1 in the ideal case of a complete network, which is a network with a link between each pair of nodes. Higher values of $\delta_i^{(k)}$ indicate loss of connectivity with respect to the optimal case. Once $\delta_i^{(k)}$ has been defined, the global diameter $\delta^{(k)}$ is a measure of the general connectivity of the network. It is defined as the average length of the shortest path between each pair of nodes in the network k. If node i is disconnected from node j, it is not possible to find a path of finite length between the two nodes. As a result, the diameter is equal to ∞. In that case, we do not have information on the extent of the loss of connectivity (e.g., whether just one node or a larger number of nodes lost their connection with node i). The efficiency η addresses this issue. For a generic network k the nodal efficiency $\eta_i^{(k)}$ is defined as the average of the inverse of the shortest path between node i and the other nodes of the network where $h_{ij}^{(k)} = 1/d_{ij}^{(k)}$ for $i \neq j$ and $h_{ij} = 0$ otherwise. The value of $\eta_i^{(k)}$ is between 0 (no links between node i and the other nodes) and 1 (in the case of a complete network). The efficiency metric provides information on the extent of the loss of connectivity: when node i is disconnected from node j, $h_{ij}^{(k)} = 1/d_{ij}^{(k)} = 1/\infty = 0$. Similarly to the global diameter, once $\eta_i^{(k)}$ has been defined, the global efficiency $\eta^{(k)}$ can be defined as the average length of the inverse of the shortest path between each pair of nodes in the network k, that is

$$
\begin{cases}
\delta^{(k)}(t) = \dfrac{1}{N^{(k)}\left(N^{(k)}-1\right)} \displaystyle\sum_{i=1}^{N^{(k)}} \sum_{\substack{j=1 \\ j \neq i}}^{N^{(k)}} d_{ij}^{(k)}(t) \\[4mm]
\eta^{(k)}(t) = \dfrac{1}{N^{(k)}\left(N^{(k)}-1\right)} \displaystyle\sum_{i=1}^{N^{(k)}} \sum_{\substack{j=1 \\ j \neq i}}^{N^{(k)}} \dfrac{1}{d_{ij}^{(k)}(t)}
\end{cases}
\tag{27.16}
$$

Guidotti et al. (2017a) proposed a modification of the connectivity measures to account for the importance of different nodes and their variability across the network. Specifically, Guidotti et al. (2017a) included nodal weights (to take into account the importance of the nodal components), and two second order measures of connectivity, namely the eccentricity $\xi^{(k)}$ and the heterogeneity $\zeta^{(k)}$ (to describe the variability in the connectivity measures), defined in Equation (27.17).

$$
\begin{cases}
\xi^{(k)}(t) = \sqrt{\dfrac{1}{N^{(k)}\left(N^{(k)}-1\right)} \left[\displaystyle\sum_{i=1}^{n} \sum_{\substack{j=1 \\ j \neq i}}^{n} \left(d_{ij}^{(k)} - \delta^{(k)}\right)^2 \right]} \\[6mm]
\zeta^{(k)}(t) = \sqrt{\dfrac{1}{N^{(k)}\left(N^{(k)}-1\right)} \left[\displaystyle\sum_{i=1}^{n} \sum_{\substack{j=1 \\ j \neq i}}^{n} \left(h_{ij}^{(k)} - \eta^{(k)}\right)^2 \right]}
\end{cases}
\tag{27.17}
$$

The eccentricity $\xi^{(k)}$ is defined as the standard deviation of the shortest paths between each pair of nodes in the network (standard deviation of elements $d_{ij}^{(k)}$). The diameter $\delta^{(k)}$ provides a measure of the distance between each pair of connected nodes; the eccentricity $\xi^{(k)}$ captures the fact that there may be pairs of nodes in close proximity, and other ones at large distance. The heterogeneity $\zeta^{(k)}$ is defined as the standard deviation of the inverse of the shortest paths between each pair of nodes in the network (standard deviation of elements $h_{ij}^{(k)}$). The efficiency $\eta^{(k)}$ provides a measure of the network connectivity in even disconnected network; the heterogeneity $\zeta^{(k)}$ captures the fact that there may be pairs of nodes in close proximity, with $h_{ij}^{(k)}$ close to one, and other at large distance or disconnected, with small or null values of $h_{ij}^{(k)}$, respectively.

Assessment of the loss or reduction of functionality
The topology-based method assesses the reliability of the network considering in the definition of the limit-state function, as capacity and demand models, measures of network connectivity (like those previously described). These measures can be deterministically calculated in the pre-disturbance scenario based on the actual state of the elements in the network and become random variables when we look at the future. The uncertainty comes from the unknown state

of the individual component that might fail or not due to deterioration and the occurrence of a disturbance. System network fragilities can be developed to estimate the conditional probabilities of the following four events, given $\mathbf{S}(t)$: i) $\delta^{(k)}(t)$ is larger than or equal to a given threshold $\delta_{Tr}^{(k)}(t)$; ii) $\eta^{(k)}(t)$ is smaller than or equal to a given threshold $\eta_{Tr}^{(k)}(t)$; iii) $\xi^{(k)}(t)$ is larger than or equal to a given threshold $\xi_{Tr}^{(k)}(t)$; and iv) $\zeta^{(k)}(t)$ is larger than or equal to a given threshold $\zeta_{Tr}^{(k)}(t)$. Percentage variations from the initial values in the undamaged scenario can be considered as thresholds. At a network level, Guidotti et al. (2017a) proposed the following system network fragilities:

$$
\begin{aligned}
F\left[\mathbf{S}(t);\Theta\right] &= P\left[g(t) \leq 0 \big| \mathbf{S}(t)\right] = \\
&= P\left\{\left[\delta^{(k)}(t) \geq \delta_{Tr}^{(k)}(t)\right] \cup \left[\xi^{(k)}(t) \geq \xi_{Tr}^{(k)}(t)\right] \Big| \mathbf{S}(t), \delta_{Tr}^{(k)}(t), \xi_{Tr}^{(k)}(t)\right\}
\end{aligned}
\tag{27.18}
$$

$$
\begin{aligned}
F\left[\mathbf{S}(t);\Theta\right] &= P\left[g(t) \leq 0 \big| \mathbf{S}(t)\right] = \\
&= P\left\{\left[\eta^{(k)}(t) \leq \eta_{Tr}^{(k)}(t)\right] \cup \left[\zeta^{(k)}(t) \geq \zeta_{Tr}^{(k)}(t)\right] \Big| \mathbf{S}(t), \eta_{Tr}^{(k)}, \zeta_{Tr}^{(k)}\right\}
\end{aligned}
\tag{27.19}
$$

$$
\begin{aligned}
F\left[\mathbf{S}(t);\Theta\right] &= P\left[g(t) \leq 0 \big| \mathbf{S}(t)\right] = \\
&= P\left\{\left[\delta^{(k)}(t) \geq \delta_{Tr}^{(k)}(t)\right] \cup \left[\xi^{(k)}(t) \geq \xi_{Tr}^{(k)}(t)\right] \cup \ldots \right. \\
&\left. \ldots \cup \left[\eta^{(k)}(t) \leq \eta_{Tr}^{(k)}(t)\right] \cup \left[\zeta^{(k)}(t) \geq \zeta_{Tr}^{(k)}(t)\right] \Big| \mathbf{S}(t), \delta_{Tr}^{(k)}(t), \xi_{Tr}^{(k)}(t), \eta_{Tr}^{(k)}(t), \zeta_{Tr}^{(k)}(t)\right\},
\end{aligned}
\tag{27.20}
$$

where $\Theta = (\Theta_{\mathbf{x}}; \Theta_C; \Theta_D)$. These system network fragilities are defined as the conditional probability of attaining or exceeding a combination of first and second order connectivity measures thresholds.

27.5.2 Flow-based method

The flow-based method considers the specific flow of goods and services delivered by the considered infrastructure (Lee et al. 2011). In a flow-based analysis, the failure of the network is not only a function of the network connectivity. More generally, the failure of the network is associated to a reduction or loss of functionality, i.e. the damaged network is not able to provide a requested amount of goods and services from the generation nodes to the distribution nodes. The flow-based method tracks metrics of interest related to the flow of goods and services within the network. For example, in the case of potable water infrastructure, a hydraulic analysis is conducted to obtain the values of the water pressure at the distribution nodes as a metric of interest.

Models of network flow
We define for the nodes of a network G a mapping $(w_V : V \to \mathbb{R})$ that associates to each node desired values or weights. In civil engineering applications, these values may provide information that capture a characteristic of interest for the specific node, as, for example, the population served by a distribution node (Guidotti et al. 2018a), or to the physical characteristics of a transmission node, such as length, material and diameter, in the case of a transmission node (e.g., a pipeline). Similarly, we define for links a mapping $(w_E : E \to \mathbb{R})$ that associates to each link desired values. In civil engineering applications, the mapping w_E may correspond to the flow of goods and services from one node to the other.

Let us define for each link of G the flow ψ with the following mapping:

$$\{\psi : E \to \mathbb{R} | \forall e_m \in E, \ \forall t \in [t_0, t_R] \ \exists \ \psi_{e_m, t} \Rightarrow \psi_{e_m, t} = \psi(e_m, t)\}. \tag{27.21}$$

The flow $\psi(e_m, t)$ of the generic link e_m from node v_i to node v_j can be expressed as $\psi[(v_i, v_j), t]$, specifying the input (v_i) and output (v_j) node. At each transmission node, and for each time step considered, the flow ψ satisfies the conservation condition: the sum of the flows afferent to a node is equal to the sum of the flows efferent from that node

$$\forall v_{T,i} \in V_T, \forall t \in [t_0, t_R] : \sum \psi[(\cdot, v_{T,i}), t] = \sum \psi[(v_{T,i}, \cdot), t]. \tag{27.22}$$

The value of the generated flow, given by the sum of the flows efferent from the generation nodes and from the storage nodes, if any, at time t, is equal to the distributed flow, given by the sum of the flows afferent to the distribution nodes and to the storage nodes, if any (equilibrium condition)

$$\left\{ \sum_{i=1}^{N_G} \left\{ \sum \psi[(v_{G,i}, \cdot), t] \right\} + \sum_{i=1}^{N_S} \left\{ \sum \psi[(v_{S,i}, \cdot), t] \right\} \right\} + \cdots$$
$$- \left\{ \sum_{i=1}^{N_S} \left\{ \sum \psi[(\cdot, v_{S,i}), t] \right\} + \sum_{i=1}^{N_D} \left\{ \sum \psi[(\cdot, v_{D,i}), t] \right\} \right\} = 0. \tag{27.23}$$

Under normal conditions, civil infrastructure ensure the equilibrium condition, being able to satisfy the requested demand of goods and services, which may be daily or seasonally variable (e.g., considering the daily variability of the water demand in a potable water system; or of the traffic in a transportation system; or the electric power demand in an electric power system).

Assessment of the loss or reduction of functionality
In the aftermath of a damaging event, or due to aging and deterioration, the ability of the network to ensure the satisfaction of the imposed demands may be reduced. The network may not be able to provide to the distribution nodes the requested amount of goods and services, even if generation and distribution nodes are connected. For a generic distribution node $v_{D,i}$, we do not meet a target flow $\psi_{D,Tr}(v_{D,i}, t)$ if the sum $\psi_D(v_{D,i}, t)$ of the flows afferent to the distribution node $v_{D,i}$ is lower than the target flow

$$\psi_D(v_{D,i}, t) = \sum \psi[(\cdot, v_{D,i}), t] < \psi_{D,Tr}(v_{D,i}, t), \tag{27.24}$$

where $\psi_{D,Tr}(v_{D,i}, t)$ ensures the amount of goods and services requested at the given distribution node. In the aftermath of a damaging event, a generic distribution node might have a flow below its target because of any combination of the following reasons:

i) A reduction or loss of functionality (due to direct damage or to cascading effects) of the generation or storage nodes may reduce the generated flow and, by equilibrium condition, the distributed flow;
ii) A reduction or loss of functionality of the transmission nodes $v_{T,i}$ may result in a localized loss of flow $\Delta \psi_{T,i}$ (e.g., a leak); and
iii) The requested amount of goods and services at a specific distribution node may change not only as a function of the direct or indirect damage to the node, but also based on,

for example, the population served by that node. People assigned to a specific node may decide to dislocate or to relocate to a different node, changing the requested amount of demand flow, or target flow, $\psi_{D,Tr}(v_i,t)$ at a specific node.

The variations in the generated and distributed flow depend on the generation, storage, transmission, and distribution nodes of the network, and in particular on their state variables. The reliability of the entire network can be assessed through system network fragilities, considering as the definition of the limit-state function the union of the events in which the distributed flow of goods and services at node $v_{D,i} \in V_D$ at time t is lower than the target value (that is, at least one distribution node is not able to provide the target value of goods and services):

$$F\left[\mathbf{S}(t);\mathbf{\Theta}\right]=P\left[g(t)\leq 0\big|\mathbf{S}(t)\right]=P\left[\bigcup_{i=1}^{N_D}\left\{\psi_D\left(v_{D,i},t\right)-\psi_{D,Tr}\left(v_{D,i},t\right)\leq 0\right\}\bigg|\mathbf{S}(t)\right].\qquad(27.25)$$

27.5.3 Recovery of the physical infrastructure

As different components recover after a damaging event that calls for repairs or reconstruction, the entire network also recovers. For each time step and for each considered component, the vector $\mathbf{X}(t)=\left[\mathbf{x}(v_1,t),\mathbf{x}(v_2,t),...,\mathbf{x}(v_N,t)\right]$ of the state variables of the N nodes of network G is updated following specified recovery functions. The values of $\mathbf{X}(t)$ during the recovery can be used in the component and network capacity $C(t)$ and demand $D(t)$ in both the topology- and flow-based methods. In doing so, we obtain the recovering network functionality. The recovery of physical components can be estimated with empirical recovery functions (e.g., FEMA 2003). However, empirical recovery functions are typically based on significant assumptions, do not reflect the actual construction phases of a recovery, and consider the recovery of a single component without accounting for the overall regional recovery. Sharma et al. (2017) and Sharma and Gardoni (2018) developed physics-based recovery functions that address the above limitations.

Physics-based recovery functions are developed on the basis of the actual sequence of recovery activities, taking into account the available resources, and the rate and prioritization of their mobilization. As shown in Gardoni et al. (2007), physics-based recovery functions can also be updated with a Bayesian approach to incorporate field data as they might become available. External and internal people dislocation might result in different scenarios in the aftermath of a disrupting event and lead to different recovery processes. Also, the lack of essential goods and services for an extended period may induce further population dislocation. This may result in an additional change in the population size served by the distribution nodes $v_{D,i} \in V_D$. Additional details about the modeling of the interdependency between physical networks and social systems during the recovery process can be found in Guidotti et al. (2018a) and Rosenheim et al. (2018).

27.6 Applications to testbeds

In this section, the models presented in this chapter are used to analyze two example testbeds. First, the topology-based method is used to analyze two generic interdependent physical networks, considering physical and geographical dependency and two categories for the nodes (generation and distribution). Then, the flow-based method is used to analyze a water network (consisting in generation, storage, transmission, and distribution nodes), considering its physical dependency on the electric power network.

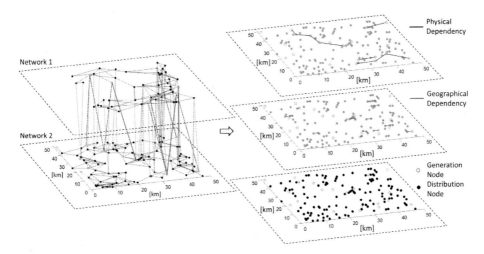

Figure 27.2 3D illustration of the networks with representation of their interdependencies on a plane.

27.6.1 Topology-based method applied to two interdependent physical networks

First we apply the topology-based method discussed in Section 27.5.1 to two interdependent hypothetical physical networks, having respectively 50 and 100 nodes. The nodes of each network are of two categories, with 15 percent of the nodes belonging to generation category and the remaining 85 percent belonging to distribution category. Two different classes of interdependency are considered: physical, between generation nodes of the two networks, and geographical, based on the location of the nodes. As a result, the model includes 13 physical and 76 geographical dependencies. Two nodes have dependencies of both classes (physical and geographical). Figure 27.2 provides a three-dimensional (3D) illustration of the networks. We consider the same likelihood table $\mathbf{L}$ for the two classes of dependency with the following values for the nodes of the two categories and belonging to the two networks:

$$
\mathbf{L} = \begin{bmatrix} \mathbf{L}^{(1)} & \vdots & \mathbf{L}^{(1,2)} \\ \text{---} & \text{+} & \text{---} \\ \mathbf{L}^{(2,1)} & \vdots & \mathbf{L}^{(2)} \end{bmatrix} = \begin{bmatrix} 0 & 0.95 & \vdots & 0 & 0.25 \\ 0.95 & 0 & \vdots & 0.25 & 0 \\ \text{---} & \text{---} & \text{+} & \text{---} & \text{---} \\ 0 & 0.90 & \vdots & 0 & 0.75 \\ 0.90 & 0 & \vdots & 0.75 & 0 \end{bmatrix}
\tag{27.26}
$$

We simulate the network damage by a random removal of nodes. Removing a node from a network impact its connectivity and likely its functionality. Direct removal of nodes triggers the removal of depending nodes, according to the probabilities from table $\mathbf{P}$. The removal of the depending nodes may, in turn, triggers the removal of nodes that are supported by them, according to the probabilities from table $\mathbf{P}$, and so on, until equilibrium is reached, in a iterative process that captures the cascading effect among and within critical infrastructure. In this example, we halt the cascading effect to the first iteration, focusing on the effects of the additional failures induced by the initial direct removal of nodes only. To quantify the impact of the removal on the network, we use the first order connectivity metrics previously introduced. Figure 27.3 shows the variation of the two metrics, diameter $\delta^{(k)}$ and efficiency $\eta^{(k)}$,

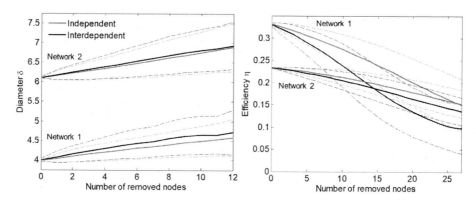

Figure 27.3 Variation of the connectivity metrics as a function of the number of removed nodes.

as a function of the number of removed nodes, comparing the case of the two interdependent networks system with the case of independent networks. The continuous lines refer to the mean value while the dotted lines to the one-standard deviation confidence bands. The statistics of $\delta^{(k)}$ and efficiency $\eta^{(k)}$ are obtained by Monte Carlo simulations with a convergence criterion based on the coefficient of variation (COV) of the connectivity metrics; we used a threshold value of $COV = 0.02$ in the calculation. The confidence band reflects the uncertainty in the order of removal of the nodes and in the probability of failure of dependent nodes, as from table **P**. The interdependency results in smaller values of efficiency and higher values of diameter, for the same number of removed nodes.

27.6.2 Flow-based method applied to two dependent physical networks

We now apply the flow-based method presented in Section 27.5.2 to the Centerville testbed. The Centerville testbed was developed by the Center of Excellence for Risk-Based Community Resilience Planning, funded by the US National Institute of Standards and Technology. Centerville is a virtual community developed to test the modeling and linkages between relatively simple representations of urban infrastructure systems and develop algorithms to estimate damage and recovery patterns, essential for disaster resilience (Ellingwood et al., 2016).

We consider the physical dependency of the water network (WN) of Centerville on the power network (EPN). The water network consists in 14 distribution nodes $V_D^{(WN)}$, including small diameter distribution lines receiving water from trunk lines and distributing it to customers of the tributary area served by each node; 29 transmission nodes $V_T^{(WN)}$, corresponding to the large diameter pipelines; two generation nodes $V_G^{(WN)}$, consisting in a reservoir that provides water to the system and a backup source of water (northeastern well); and two storage nodes $V_S^{(WN)}$, consisting in two tanks. This system depends on the electric power network, which consists in 24 distribution nodes $V_D^{(EPN)}$, constituted by towers/poles, 29 transmission nodes $V_T^{(EPN)}$, consisting in 5 transmission lines, 4 distribution lines and 20 sub-distribution lines; and 8 generation nodes $V_G^{(EPN)}$, consisting in a power plant, a transmission substation, a main grid substation, two distribution substations and three sub-distribution substations (Figure 27.4).

For each node of each network we define the vector of state variables $\mathbf{x}(v_i, t)$, used in the category-specific capacity and demand models. For example, in the case of the transmission nodes of the water network, the state variables include geometric characteristics of the pipe,

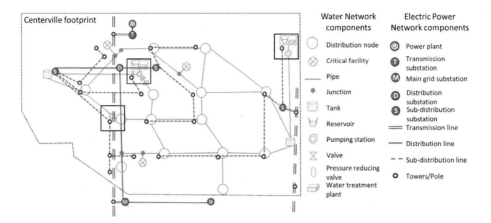

Figure 27.4 Centerville's electrical power network superimposed to the potable water network, with highlighted dependency areas.

Source: Adapted from Guidotti et al. 2016a.

material, and year of installation. In the example, we consider the response of the two networks under a seismic event, namely a M_W 6.5 earthquake located 25 km southwest of Centerville. The Fernandez and Rix (2006) ground motion prediction equations are used to obtain the vector of the intensity measures of interest $S(t)$ for the different categories of nodes. The topologies of the water and power networks provide the adjacency tables along the main diagonal of the augmented adjacency table, $A^{(WN)}$ and $A^{(EPN)}$, respectively. We identify the areas of Centerville that need energy supply (square boxes in Figure 27.4). These areas include the nodes of the water network with a physical dependency on supporting nodes of the electric power network. This information is used to obtain the out-of-diagonal tables of the augmented adjacency table, $A^{(WN,EPN)}$ and $A^{(EPN,WN)}$, and the dependency tables $D^{(WN,EPN)}$ and $D^{(EPN,WN)}$. We are considering the dependency of the water network on the power network only, therefore $D^{(EPN,WN)}$ is a null matrix and the dependency table D is not symmetric. We model two extreme cases: the first one with independent (isolated) networks, the second one with perfect dependency, with the entries of the probability dependency table P corresponding to the dependent nodes of the water network equal to 1 (i.e., a failure of a supporting node of the electric power network implies a failure of the depending node).

A flow-based network analysis is performed with the software IN-CORE (Gardoni et al. 2018). The software calculates the flow of potable water ψ in the damaged network, in the two extreme cases. To assess the loss or reduction of functionality of the water network we used a network specific metric, i.e. the percentage of nodes attaining or exceeding a pressure threshold of at least 138 kPa (20 psi). This threshold is typically used to prevent cross-contamination and as a measure of fire protection capacity (e.g., Davis et al. 2012). The status of the network components is updated at each time step using restoration curves (FEMA 2003). Figure 27.5 shows at each hour and day of the recovery process the functionality metric of interest. The minimum values of the functionality metric is lower for the dependent water network than for the isolated one. In addition, we observe a more rapid recovery of the isolated water network, compared to the dependent one, consistently with the fact that two networks need to recover from the event, instead of only one network. In particular, in the case of an independent water network after the fourth day of recovery more than 90 percent of the nodes attain or exceed

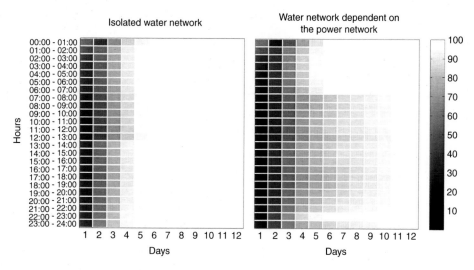

Figure 27.5 Percentage of nodes attaining or exceeding the pressure threshold during the recovery process.

the pressure threshold. In the case with dependency, this condition is reached only after the tenth day of recovery. A higher water demand in the central hours of day results in a periodic reduction of the number of nodes able to attain the pressure threshold. We used a Monte Carlo simulation to capture the uncertainties in the problem, with a termination criterion based on the COV of the described metric; we used a threshold value of $COV = 0.15$ in the calculation. The uncertainties accounted for in this application are in the assessment of the physical damage of the network components, in the dependencies, and the recovery time for network functionality. More details on the presented application and on the modeling of the resilience of water system can be found in Guidotti et al. (2016a, 2016b) and Chmielewski et al. (2016).

27.7 Conclusions

Infrastructure play a central role in regional risk and resilience analysis. This chapter presents network-based models for critical infrastructure. Infrastructure are mathematically represented by networks and a taxonomy is proposed to characterize their components, typically heterogeneous and with different functions. State variables of network components are introduced to develop models of capacity and demand. These models are used to obtain fragility functions and repair rate curves to define the damage state for the considered infrastructure. To understand and model the complex interdependencies among critical infrastructure, we present multiple classes of dependency/interdependency and include them in a multi-layered heterogeneous network model. The model considers all of the networks on the same conceptual "plane," with the different classes of interdependencies described by different planes. Topology-based and flow-based methods are discussed. They provide an assessment of the reduction or loss, and subsequent recovery of functionality of critical infrastructure based on measures of connectivity and models of flow of goods and service, respectively. The chapter applies the network-based models to two example testbeds. The first application applies the concepts of the topology-based method to two interdependent generic physical networks. The second application uses the flow-based method to model the dependency of the water network of the virtual city of Centerville on the power network.

Results of the presented applications show the following:

1) considering interdependencies in the topology-based method results in changes of the metrics of connectivity that may lead to the failure of the dependent/interdependent network for a lower number of damaged components than in independent network; and

2) the flow-based method applied to two physical networks demonstrates that the recovery time following a hazard event increases when network dependencies/interdependencies are considered. The additional failures in the dependent network due to damage to the supporting network cause a faster decline in the network functionality, resulting in a greater overall loss of service.

Acknowledgements

This work was funded by the Center of Excellence for Risk-Based Community Resilience Planning, funded by the US National Institute of Standards and Technology (NIST Financial Assistance Award Number: 70NANB15H044).

References

Adachi T. and Ellingwood B.R. (2008) "Serviceability of earthquake-damaged water systems: effects of electrical power availability and power backup systems on system vulnerability," *Reliability Engineering and System Safety*, 93, 78–88.

ALA (2001) "Seismic fragility formulations for water Systems: Part 1 – guideline," American Lifelines Alliance, April, ASCE.

Albert R., Jeong H., and Barabási A.L. (1999) "Internet: Diameter of the world-wide web," *Nature*, 401(6749), 130.

Albert R., Jeong H., and Barabási A.L. (2000) "Error and attack tolerance of complex networks," *Nature*, 406(6794), 378.

Applied Technology Council (2016) "Critical assessment of lifeline system performance: understanding societal needs in disaster recovery," Prepared for US Department of Commerce, National Institute of Standards and Technology, Engineering Laboratory, Gaithersburg, MD, NIST GCR 16-917-39.

Arianos S., Bompard E., Carbone A., and Xue F. (2009) "Power grid vulnerability: A complex network approach," *Chaos: An Interdisciplinary Journal of Nonlinear Science*, 19(1), 013119.

Bisadi V., Gardoni P., and Head M. (2011) "Probabilistic capacity models and fragility estimates for steel pedestals used to elevate bridges," *ASCE Journal of Structural Engineering*, 137(12), 1583–92.

Bisadi V., Gardoni P., and Head M. (2012) "Probabilistic demand models and fragility estimates for bridges elevated with steel pedestals," *ASCE Journal of Structural Engineering*, 139(9), 1515–28.

Chang S.E. (2014). "Infrastructure resilience to disasters," *The Bridge*, 44(3), 36–41.

Chmielewski H., Guidotti R., McAllister T.P., and Gardoni P. (2016) "Response of water systems under extreme events: a comprehensive approach to modeling water network resilience," *World Environmental & Water Resources Congress, 2016 EWRI-ASCE*, West Palm Beach, Florida (USA).

Choe D., Gardoni P., Rosowsky D., and Haukaas T. (2009) "Seismic fragility estimates for reinforced concrete bridges subject to corrosion," *Structural Safety*, 31, 275–83.

Choe D., Gardoni P., and Rosowsky D. (2010) "Fragility increment functions for deteriorating reinforced concrete bridge columns," *ASCE Journal of Engineering Mechanics*, 136(8), 969–78.

Crucitti P., Latora V., Marchiori M., and Rapisarda A. (2003) "Efficiency of scale-free networks: Error and attack tolerance," *Physica A: Statistical Mechanics and its Applications*, 320, 622–42.

Davis C.A., O'Rourke T.D., Adams M.L., and Rho M.A. (2012) "Case study: Los Angeles water services restoration following the 1994 Northridge earthquake," 15 WCEE.

Ditlevsen O. and Madsen, H.O. (1996) *Structural Reliability Methods*. New York: Wiley.

Dueñas-Osorio L., Craig J.I., and Goodno B.J. (2007) "Seismic response of critical interdependent networks," *Earthquake Engineering & Structural Dynamics*, 36, 285–306.

Ellingwood B.R., Cutler H., Gardoni P., Peacock W.G., van de Lindt J.W., and Wang N. (2016) "The Centerville Virtual Community: a fully integrated decision model of interacting physical and social infrastructure systems," *Sustainable and Resilient Infrastructure*, 1(3–4), 95–107.

FEMA (2003) "Multi-hazard loss estimation methodology, earthquake model," *HAZUS-MH 2.1 Technical Manual*, 1–699. Federal Emergency Management Agency, Washington, DC.

Fernandez J.A. and Rix G.J. (2006) "Soil attenuation relationships and seismic hazard analyses in the Upper Mississippi Embayment," *Proceedings of the 8th US National Conference on Earthquake Engineering*, San Francisco, California, April, 18–22. http://doi.org/Paper No. 521.

Franchin P. and Cavalieri F. (2015) "Probabilistic assessment of civil infrastructure resilience to earthquakes," *Computer-Aided Civil and Infrastructure Engineering*, 30(7), 583–600.

Frangopol D.M. and Bocchini P. (2012) "Bridge network performance, maintenance and optimisation under uncertainty: accomplishments and challenges," *Structure and Infrastructure Engineering*, 8(4), 341–56.

Gardoni P. (ed.) (2017) *Risk and Reliability Analysis: Theory and Applications*. New York: Springer.

Gardoni P. and LaFave J. (eds.) (2016) *Multi-hazard Approaches to Civil Infrastructure Engineering*. New York: Springer.

Gardoni P. and Murphy C. (2018) "Society-based design: promoting societal well-being by designing sustainable and resilient infrastructure," *Sustainable and Resilient Infrastructure*, DOI: 10.1080/23789689.2018.1448667.

Gardoni P., Der Kiureghian A., and Mosalam K.M. (2002) "Probabilistic capacity models and fragility estimates for RC columns based on experimental observations," *ASCE Journal of Engineering Mechanics*, 128(10), 1024–38.

Gardoni P., Mosalam K.M., and Der Kiureghian A. (2003) "Probabilistic seismic demand models and fragility estimates for RC bridges," *Journal of Earthquake Engineering*, 7 (Special Issue 1), 79–106.

Gardoni, P., Reinschmidt, K.F., and Kumar, R. (2007) "A probabilistic framework for Bayesian adaptive forecasting of project progress," *Computer-Aided Civil and Infrastructure Engineering*, 22 (3), 182–96.

Gardoni, P., Murphy C., and Rowell A. (eds.) (2016) *Societal Risk Management of Natural Hazards*. New York: Springer.

Gardoni, P., van de Lindt, J., Ellingwood, B., McAllister, T., Lee, J.S., Cutler, H., Peacock, W., and Cox, D. (2018) "The interdependent networked community resilience modeling environment (IN-CORE)," In *Proceeding of the 16th European Conference on Earthquake Engineering*, Thessaloniki, Greece.

Guidotti R., Chmielewski H., Unnikrishnan V., Gardoni P., McAllister T., and van de Lindt J. (2016a) "Modeling the resilience of critical infrastructure: the role of network dependencies," *Sustainable and Resilient Infrastructure*, 1(3–4), 153–68.

Guidotti R., Chmielewski H., Gardoni P., and McAllister T.P. (2016b) "Modeling resilient infrastructure combining physical damage and loss and restoration of functionality: The case of a water network," *Engineering Mechanics Institute/ Probabilistic Mechanics and Reliability Conference (EMI/PMC 2016)*, Vanderbilt University, Nashville, Tennessee (USA).

Guidotti R., Gardoni P., and Chen Y. (2017a) "Network reliability analysis with link and nodal weights and auxiliary nodes," *Structural Safety*, 65, 12–26.

Guidotti R., Gardoni P., and Chen Y. (2017b) "Multi-layer heterogeneous network model for interdependent infrastructure systems," *12th International Conference on Structural Safety & Reliability (ICOSSAR 2017)*, TU Wien, Vienna (Austria), 2947–56.

Guidotti R., Rosenheim N., and Gardoni P. (2018a) "Integration of physical infrastructure and social systems in communities' reliability and resilience analysis," *Reliability Engineering & System Safety* (under review).

Guidotti R., Gardoni P., and Chen Y (2018b) "Multi-layer heterogeneous network model for interdependent infrastructure systems," *Structural Safety* (in preparation).

Guikema S. and Gardoni P. (2009) "Reliability estimation for networks of reinforced concrete bridges," *Journal of Infrastructure Systems*, 15(2), 61–9.

Huang Q., Gardoni P., and Hurlebaus S. (2010) "Probabilistic seismic demand models and fragility estimates for reinforced concrete highway bridges with one single-column bent," *ASCE Journal of Engineering Mechanics*, 136 (11), 1340–53.

Huang Q., Gardoni P., Trejo D., and Pagnotta A. (2014) "Probabilistic model for steel-concrete bond behavior in bridge columns affected by alkali silica reactions," *Engineering Structures*, 71, 1–11.

Jia G. and Gardoni P. (2018) "State-dependent stochastic models: A general stochastic framework for modeling deteriorating engineering systems considering multiple deterioration processes and their interactions," *Structural Safety*, 72, 99–110.

Jia G., Tabandeh A., and Gardoni P. (2017) "Life-cycle analysis of engineering systems: modeling deterioration, instantaneous reliability, and resilience," In Paolo Gardoni (ed.), *Risk and Reliability Analysis: Theory and Applications*. New York: Springer.

Kang W.-H., Song J., and Gardoni P. (2008) "Matrix-based system reliability method and applications to bridge networks," *Reliability Engineering and System Safety*, 93, 1584–93.

Kumar R. and Gardoni P. (2012) "Modeling structural degradation of RC bridge columns subject to earthquakes and their fragility estimates," *ASCE Journal of Structural Engineering*, 138(1), 42–51.

Kumar R. and Gardoni P. (2013) "Stochastic modeling of structural deterioration in infrastructure systems," in Solomon Tesfamariam and Katsu Goda (eds.) *Handbook of Seismic Risk Analysis and Management of Civil Infrastructure Systems*. Woodhead Publishing Ltd, Cambridge, UK, pp. 410–32.

Kumar R. and Gardoni P. (2014a) "Renewal theory-based life-cycle analysis of deteriorating engineering systems," *Structural Safety*, 50, 94–102.

Kumar R. and Gardoni P. (2014b) "Effect of seismic degradation on the fragility of reinforced concrete bridges," *Engineering Structures*, 79, 267–75.

Kumar R., Gardoni P., and Sanchez-Silva M. (2009) "Effect of cumulative seismic damage and corrosion on life-cycle cost of reinforced concrete bridges," *Earthquake Engineering and Structural Dynamics*, 38(7), 887–905.

Kumar R., Cline D., and Gardoni P. (2015) "A stochastic framework to model deterioration in engineering systems," *Structural Safety*, 53, 36–43.

Kurtz N., Song J., and Gardoni P. (2015) "Seismic reliability analysis of deteriorating representative US West Coast bridge transportation networks," *ASCE Journal of Structural Engineering*, 10.1061/(ASCE) ST.1943-541X.0001368, C4015010.

Latora V. and Marchiori M. (2001) "Efficient behavior of small-world networks," *Physical Review Letters*, 87(19), 198701.

Lee Y.-J., Song J., Gardoni P., and Lim H.-W. (2011) "Post-hazard flow capacity of bridge transportation networks considering structural deterioration of bridges," *Structure and Infrastructure Engineering*, 7(7), 509–21.

Lin Y.S. (2009) "Development of algorithms to estimate post-disaster population dislocation – a research-based approach," *PhD Thesis*, Texas A&M University.

Lusseau D., Schneider K., Boisseau O.J., Haase P., Slooten E., and Dawson S.M. (2003) "The bottle-nose dolphin community of Doubtful Sound features a large proportion of long-lasting associations," *Behavioral Ecology and Sociobiology*, 54(4), 396–405.

Mardfekri M. and Gardoni P. (2013) "Probabilistic demand models and fragility estimates for offshore wind turbine support structures," *Engineering Structures*, 52, 478–87.

Mardfekri M., Gardoni P., and Bisadi V. (2015). "Service reliability of offshore wind turbines," *International Journal of Sustainable Energy*, 34(7), 468–84.

Murphy C., Gardoni P., and Harris C.E. (2011) "Classification and moral evaluation of uncertainties in engineering modeling," *Science and Engineering Ethics*, 17(3), 553–70.

O'Rourke M.J. and Ayala G. (1993) "Pipeline damage due to wave propagation," *Journal of Geotechnical Engineering*, 119, 1490–8.

O'Rourke M.J. and Deyoe E. (2004) "Seismic damage to segmented buried pipe," *Earthquake Spectra*, 20, 1167–83.

Ouyang M. (2014) "Review on modeling and simulation of interdependent critical infrastructure systems," *Reliability Engineering & System Safety*, 121, 43–60.

Paul S. and Chen Y. (2016) "Consistent community detection in multi-relational data through restricted multi-layer stochastic blockmodel," *Electronic Journal of Statistics*, 10(2), 3807–70.

PCCIP (1997) "Critical Foundations: Protecting America's Infrastructures," The Report of the President's Commission on Critical Infrastructure Protection, October. www.fas.org/sgp/library/pccip.pdf (last accessed August 19, 2018).

Pitilakis K., Alexoudi M., Argyroudis S., Monge O., and Martin C. (2006) "Earthquake risk assessment of lifelines," *Bulletin of Earthquake Engineering*, 4(4), 365–90.

PPD-21 (2013) Presidential Policy Directive/PPD-21, Critical Infrastructure Security and Resilience. The White House, February 12, 2013.

Rinaldi S.M., Peerenboom J.P., and Kelly T.K. (2001) "Identifying, understanding, and analyzing critical infrastructure interdependencies," *IEEE Control Systems Magazine*, 21(6), 11–25.

Rosenheim N., Guidotti R., and Gardoni P. (2017) "Integration of detailed household characteristic data with critical infrastructure and its implementation to post-hazard resilience modeling," *2nd International Workshop on Modelling of Physical, Economic and Social Systems for Resilience Assessment*, Ispra (Italy).

Rosenheim N., Guidotti R., and Gardoni P. (2018) "Integration of household characteristic data with critical infrastructure and its implementation to post-hazard resilience modeling," *Sustainable and Resilient Infrastructure* (in preparation).

Ruohonen K. (2013) "Graph theory," Originally titled Graafiteoria, lecture notes translated by Tamminen, J., Lee, K.C. and Piché, R. http://math.tut.fi/~ruohonen/GT_English.pdf (last accessed December 2017).

Schneider C.M., Moreira, A.A., Andrade J.S., Havlin S., and Herrmann H.J. (2011) "Mitigation of malicious attacks on networks," *Proceedings of the National Academy of Sciences*, 108(10), 3838–41.

Sengupta S. and Chen Y. (2015) "Spectral clustering in heterogeneous networks," *Statistica Sinica*, 25(3), 1081–1106.

Sharma N. and Gardoni P. (2018) "Promoting resilient interdependent infrastructure: the role of strategic recovery scheduling," *Computer-Aided Civil and Infrastructure Engineering* (in preparation).

Sharma H., Gardoni P., and Hurlebaus S. (2014) "Probabilistic demand model and performance-based fragility estimates for RC column subject to vehicle collision," *Engineering Structures*, 74, 86–95.

Sharma H., Gardoni P., and Hurlebaus S. (2015) "Performance–based probabilistic capacity models and fragility estimates for RC columns subject to vehicle collision," *Computer-Aided Civil and Infrastructure Engineering*, 30, 555–69.

Sharma N., Tabandeh A., and Gardoni P. (2017) "Resilience analysis: a mathematical formulation to model resilience of engineering systems," *Sustainable and Resilient Infrastructure*, 3(2), 49–67.

Tabandeh A. and Gardoni P. (2014) "Probabilistic capacity models and fragility estimates for RC columns retrofitted with FRP composites," *Engineering Structures*, 74, 13–22.

Tabandeh A. and Gardoni P. (2015) "Empirical Bayes approach for developing hierarchical probabilistic predictive models and its application to the seismic reliability analysis of FRP-retrofitted RC bridges," *ASCE-ASME Journal of Risk and Uncertainty in Engineering Systems, Part A: Civil Engineering*, 1(2), 04015002.

Vespignani A. (2010) "Complex networks: The fragility of interdependency," *Nature*, 464(7291), 984–5.

Zhang J. and Chen Y. (2013) "Sampling for conditional inference on network data," *Journal of the American Statistical Association*, 108(504), 1295–1307.

Zhang J. and Chen Y. (2015) "Exponential random graph models for networks resilient to targeted attacks," *Statistics and Its Interface*, 8(3), 267–76.

28

Regional resilience analysis

A multi-scale approach to model the recovery of interdependent infrastructure

Neetesh Sharma,[1] Armin Tabandeh,[2] and Paolo Gardoni[3]

[1] DEPARTMENT OF CIVIL AND ENVIRONMENTAL ENGINEERING, MAE CENTER: CREATING A MULTI-HAZARD APPROACH TO ENGINEERING, UNIVERSITY OF ILLINOIS AT URBANA-CHAMPAIGN, URBANA, IL, US; NSHARM11@ILLINOIS.EDU

[2] DEPARTMENT OF CIVIL AND ENVIRONMENTAL ENGINEERING, MAE CENTER: CREATING A MULTI-HZARD APPROACH TO ENGINEERING, UNIVERSITY OF ILLINOIS AT URBANA-CHAMPAIGN, URBANA, IL, USA; TABANDE2@ILLINOIS.EDU

[3] DEPARTMENT OF CIVIL AND ENVIRONMENTAL ENGINEERING, MAE CENTER: CREATING A MULTI-HAZARD APPROACH TO ENGINEERING, UNIVERSITY OF ILLINOIS AT URBANA-CHAMPAIGN, URBANA, IL, USA; GARDONI@ILLINOIS.EDU

28.1 Introduction

The prosperity of modern societies and public well-being depend on critical infrastructure to deliver essential resources and services such as potable water, electric power, and transportation to communities (Corotis 2009; Ellingwood et al. 2016; Gardoni et al. 2016). Because of infrastructure interdependencies, disruptions can propagate within and across infrastructure and result in widespread, catastrophic consequences (Guidotti et al. 2016). A well-known example of such cascading disruptions is the Northeastern blackout in the United States (US) and Canada in 2003 (NERC 2004). The spatial extent and duration of infrastructure service disruptions are determinant factors in characterizing regional resilience (Guidotti et al. 2016). In this chapter, the resilience of a system (e.g., an infrastructure or society) is understood as a performance measure of the system subject to external stressors (i.e., a disruptive event) in relation to its residual performance immediately after the occurrence of the stressor(s) and the subsequent recovery. The recovery modeling of infrastructure generally consists of (Jia et al. 2017; Sharma et al. 2018a): (1) developing a recovery schedule for the repair or replacement of damaged components, and (2) predicting the performance of infrastructure under the developed recovery schedule and estimating the corresponding implication on the recovery objectives (e.g., incurred costs, recovery duration, and resilience).

In recent years, there has been a growing interest in the recovery modeling of interdependent infrastructure (e.g., Alderson et al. 2014; Ouyang 2014; Guidotti et al. 2016). The focus of current approaches is to schedule the recovery sequence of damaged components such that the incurred cost is minimized (Lee et al. 2007; Nurre et al. 2012; Cavdaroglu et al. 2013; González 2016). The incurred cost typically includes the operational and recovery cost as well as the cost of unmet demand during the recovery (Cavdaroglu et al. 2013; González et al. 2016). There are two common approximations to estimate the cost of unmet demand. The first approximation is about the duration of unmet demand, where an ordered index set is used as a proxy for the actual time to estimate the duration of unmet demand. The second approximation is about the extent of service disruptions, which is limited to the service areas of damaged components; depending on the definition of service areas, the cost of unmet demand might be under- or over-estimated.

Despite recent advances, developing mathematical models and optimization algorithms for the recovery of interdependent infrastructure remains a daunting task. The fundamental challenges that remain to address include (1) developing mathematical models for the recovery of individual components as explicit functions of the recovery influencing factors (e.g., component damage level, recovery resources); (2) integrating the recovery of individual components into a workable recovery schedule for interdependent infrastructure; and (3) developing a computationally manageable approach for the recovery modeling/optimization. The first challenge refers to the fact that the recovery modeling/optimization is about exploring and quantifying the effects of the recovery influencing factors on the recovery objective(s). The second challenge requires that the development of the recovery schedule for repetitive recovery activities considers the prevalent physical and logical constraints (e.g., activities precedence, crew and material availability, work continuity) such that the resulting schedule is feasible to implement and easy to communicate. Finally, the last challenge highlights the need for a computationally manageable approach that allows us to genuinely model the dynamics of interdependent infrastructure under developed recovery schedules.

This chapter presents a novel multi-scale approach to model the recovery of interdependent infrastructure (Sharma and Gardoni 2018a). The multi-scale approach breaks down the recovery scheduling of interdependent infrastructure into (1) the *Zonal Scale Recovery*, which defines a set of recovery zones, based on, for example, existing urban planning land-use and community neighborhoods, and prioritizes the zones to implement the recovery; and (2) the *Local Scale Recovery*, which develops specific schedules for the recovery activities in each zone. The multi-scale approach contributes, both at the zonal and local scales, to the development of a recovery schedule that is feasible to implement as well as easy to manage and communicate. At the zonal scale, all the recovery activities in a (set of) working zone(s) need to be completed before starting the next (set of) zone(s) in the sequence, rather than allowing selective recovery in a neighborhood. At the local scale, we develop the recovery schedule for components as a function of the recovery influencing factors (Sharma et al. 2018a), while considering the constraints arising from repetitive recovery activities on multiple components (Sharma and Gardoni 2018a). The multi-scale approach also addresses the computational challenge by reducing the size of the optimization problem from scheduling the recovery of individual components to scheduling the sequence of the recovery zones (Sharma et al. 2018b).

To model the performance of infrastructure under a developed recovery schedule, we use the mathematical formulation proposed by Sharma and Gardoni (2018b). In this formulation, we characterize the performance of infrastructure in terms of capacity, demand, and supply measures, defined for individual components. Several capacity measures can be defined for components with respect to the demand placed on them. For example, we can define capacity measures for water pipelines relative to structural failure modes in shear and tension, and relative to functionality as the maximum water flow. For each capacity measure, there is a corresponding demand measure due to the occurrence of an extreme event or regular service conditions. Furthermore, the supply measure captures the ability of the infrastructure to serve the demand placed on the components. The estimates of capacity, demand, and supply measures are functions of state variables that define infrastructure components such as material properties, member dimensions, and imposed boundary conditions (Jia & Gardoni 2018). For each component, we model the variations of the state variables over time due to the completion of the respective recovery activities (Jia et al. 2017; Sharma et al. 2018a). We then use the estimate of the state variables at any time during the recovery in the predictive models for capacity and demand measures to model their recovery (Jia & Gardoni 2018; Sharma et al. 2018a). Eventually, to model the recovery of (commodity) supply measure, we use the capacity and demand estimates for components in the network flow analyses. A main source of computational difficulty in the performance analysis is to keep track of interdependencies among different sets of capacity, demand, and supply measures for each infrastructure as well as with those for other infrastructure during the recovery. The solution approach in this chapter employs the formulation proposed by Sharma and Gardoni (2018b). The formulation decouples different sets of capacity, demand, and supply measures by conditioning on the estimate of supporting performance measures and develops separate models for the recovery of the conditioned performance measures. For the regional resilience analysis, we develop derived performance measures to model the recovery of disrupted services (i.e., model the recovery curve). Following Sharma et al. (2018a), we define the resilience metrics as partial descriptors of the predicted recovery curve.

The rest of the chapter is organized into six sections. The next section discusses multi-scale recovery modeling. Section 28.3 presents time-varying performance analysis of interdependent infrastructure. Section 28.4 discusses resilience analysis. Section 28.5 illustrates the multi-scale approach to model the recovery of the potable water and electric power infrastructure in Shelby County, Tennessee (TN), US subject to seismic hazards. Finally, the last section summarizes the chapter and draws some conclusions.

28.2 Multi-scale recovery modeling

Infrastructure are generally modeled as a collection of networks, where each network represents the topological relationships among a set of components (Sharma & Gardoni 2018b; Guidotti & Gardoni 2018). Specifically, one can define a finite set of component classes, sub-dividing the nodes and links in a network, based on attributes such as hierarchy, function, or material. The definition of component classes is affected by several factors, such as hazard type, modeling resolution, and the type of network analysis (e.g., connectivity-based or dynamic flow-based analysis). For a given hazard type, the set of vulnerable components can be modeled as a separate class from those that are not vulnerable to the specific hazard type. Considering the modeling resolution, components below a certain resolution level or in close proximity can be grouped into a class. The type of network analysis determines what component classes need to be modeled explicitly for the desired analysis. For example, a connectivity-based analysis may require only the basic topology, whereas a dynamic flow-based analysis may require a larger set of component classes to be defined, since the component functionality is also important. The set of component classes, number of components in each class, and their topology determine the complexity of networks and their recovery modeling (Sharma & Gardoni 2018b). In this section, we first explain the recovery modeling of individual infrastructure components (e.g., a bridge in a transportation infrastructure) and then discuss the multi-scale approach to generalize the recovery of individual components to the recovery of interdependent infrastructure.

28.2.1 Recovery modeling of infrastructure components

The scope of the recovery is defined by the magnitude and nature of the sustained damage. For a given damage level, the recovery schedule specifies the required recovery activities (i.e., their types and numbers). Activities in a recovery schedule have precedence, constraints, and planned durations that collectively create a network of activities (Jia et al. 2017; Sharma et al. 2018a). The duration of the recovery is a function of factors such as the level of damage, accessibility of damaged members of the component (e.g., a bridge column), availability of resources (i.e., budget, materials, and skilled workforce), and weather condition (Jia et al. 2017; Sharma et al. 2018a).

The completion of the repair of damaged members, at discrete (random) points in time during the recovery, marks changes in the state variables. For the recovery modeling of infrastructure components, Sharma et al. (2018a) developed a general state-dependent stochastic formulation that models the variation of the state variables during the recovery due to the (1) repair of damaged members, and (2) occurrence of potential disrupting shocks during the recovery. According to Sharma et al. (2018a), we can write the following general expression for the state variables during the recovery:

$$\mathbf{x}(\tau) = \sum_{i=1}^{\infty} \mathbf{x}\left(\tau_{r,i-1}\right)\mathbf{1}_{\left\{\tau_{r,i-1} \le \tau < \tau_{r,i}\right\}} + \sum_{i,j=1}^{\infty} \Delta\mathbf{x}\left(\tau_{s,j}\right)\mathbf{1}_{\left\{\tau_{r,j-1} < \tau < \tau_{r,j}, \tau_{r,j-1} < \tau_{s,j} \le \tau\right\}}, \tag{28.1}$$

where $\mathbf{x}(\tau)$ is the vector of state variables at the relative time τ during the recovery ($\tau = 0$ is the time of occurrence of the external stressor that caused the sustained damage); $\mathbf{x}(\tau_{r,i-1})$ is the vector of state variables after completing the repair of a damaged member (i.e., a recovery step) at time $\tau_{r,i-1}$; by convention, $\mathbf{x}(\tau_{r,0})$ denotes the vector of state variables at the beginning of the recovery process, whose probability distribution is obtained from the deterioration models (Jia et al. 2017; Jia & Gardoni 2018); $\mathbf{1}_{\{A\}}$ is an indicator function, defined such that $\mathbf{1}_{\{A\}} = 1$, if A is a true statement, and $\mathbf{1}_{\{A\}} = 0$, otherwise; $\Delta\mathbf{x}(\tau_{s,j})$ is the state change due to the occurrence of a disrupting shock at time $\tau_{s,j} \in (\tau_{r,i-1}, \tau_{r,i})$.

In Equation (28.1), the number of recovery steps completed by a given time τ is modeled as a stochastic point process, the rate of which is a function of the recovery influencing factors (Sharma et al. 2018a). Furthermore, the model for $\Delta\mathbf{x}(\tau_{s,j})$ is generally expressed as $\Delta\mathbf{x}(\tau_{s,j}) = \Delta\mathbf{x}[\tau_{s,j}, \mathbf{x}(\tau_{s,j}^-), \mathbf{IM}(\tau_{s,j}), \mathbf{\Theta_x}]$, where $\mathbf{x}(\tau_{s,j}^-)$ is the vector of state variables immediately before time $\tau_{s,j}$ (i.e., $\tau_{s,j}^-$); $\mathbf{IM}(\tau_{s,j})$ is the vector of intensity measures of the shock at time $\tau_{s,j}$; and $\mathbf{\Theta_x}$ a vector of model parameters.

The estimate of $\mathbf{x}(\tau)$ can be used in capacity and demand models (e.g., those developed by Tabandeh and Gardoni 2014, 2015 for reinforced concrete (RC) bridges, retrofitted with Fiber Reinforced Polymer (FRP) composites) to predict the corresponding capacity and demand measures during and after the recovery activities. The performance of infrastructure components can then be modeled in terms of quantities such as the reliability or functionality at any given time (Sharma et al. 2018a). A recovery curve represents the path of such quantities over the recovery duration. Further discussions to develop specific recovery models and implement this formulation can be found in Jia et al. (2017) and Sharma et al. (2018a).

28.2.2 Recovery modeling of interdependent infrastructure

The recovery modeling of interdependent infrastructure builds upon that of individual components. However, we need to consider the additional constraints arising from the repetitive recovery activities on multiple components, including crew availability, work continuity, and access to damaged components (El-Rayes & Moselhi 2001). Furthermore, the sequence in which components are recovered affects the recovery of disrupted services as well as the recovery cost and duration. Scheduling the recovery sequence of damaged components is generally a combinatorial optimization problem. The direct solution is to search over the permutations of the recovery sequence and evaluate the corresponding recovery objective(s). The direct solution results in complexity $\mathcal{O}(n!)$, where n is the number of damaged components. The evaluation of the recovery objective(s) often involves the performance analyses of inter-dependent infrastructure, which further increases the difficulty of the problem. Furthermore, there is a need to exclude impractical recovery schedules and promote simple schedules that are easy to manage and communicate at different levels of detail.

To overcome these challenges, Sharma and Gardoni (2018a) proposed a multi-scale approach that develops a hierarchical recovery model. At the zonal scale, the region of interest is partitioned into a set of recovery zones, where the damaged components in each zone recover with the same zonal priority (which can be decided at the higher management level). Figure 28.1 shows a schematic representation of the recovery zones, developed for the repair of damaged infrastructure components. The solid and dashed lines in the figure show the intact and damaged line components, respectively, whereas the open and filled circles show the intact and damaged nodal components, respectively. The thick (curly) lines in the figure define the boundary of the recovery zones. Here, we use $\mathbf{z}_k = (z_{\sigma(1)}, \ldots, z_{\sigma(n_k)})$ to denote the tuple of the recovery zones, where $(\sigma(1), \ldots, \sigma(n_k))$ is a permutation of $(1, \ldots, n_k)$. The definition of zones can be based on, for example, the functional logic and geographical location. The hierarchy of the components (primary and secondary components) and the location attributes (land use zone, social neighborhood, and population demographic) are also useful to define the recovery zones. For example, we can define each substation in the electric power infrastructure and the corresponding service area as a recovery zone. At the local scale, we identify the set of recovery activities for the repair of damaged components in a zone (e.g., dashed lines and filled circles in zone $z_{\sigma(1)}$ in Figure 28.1), assign the identified recovery activities to available crews, and develop a schedule for the crews to perform the set of assigned activities (which can be decided at the lower management level). The multi-scale approach avoids impractical schedules and facilitates

zone $z_{\sigma(1)}$

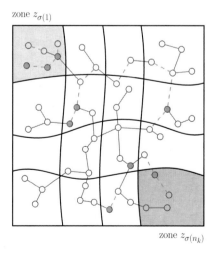

zone $z_{\sigma(n_k)}$

Figure 28.1   Recovery zones for the repair of damaged infrastructure components.

the recovery management. This is because the recovery zones enable a natural way to schedule and implement the recovery and monitor the recovery progress for a large area, where different authorities can manage the recovery at different levels of detail. It also decreases the computational cost, because the number of zones is significantly smaller than the number of damaged components (i.e., reducing n in $\mathcal{O}(n!)$).

To develop the zonal and local scale recovery schedules, we consider the availability of resources, crews, and the scheduling constraints. We divide the crews (i.e., workforce and equipment resources) into multiple teams, where each team works in a single zone and the respective crews in the team finish their assigned recovery activities according to the developed local scale recovery schedule. The crews working in a zone move on to the next available zone in the zonal sequence after completing their assigned activities, whereas multiple teams can work in parallel in different zones. For example, Figure 28.2 shows the recovery schedule developed for the repair of damaged substations of electric power infrastructure. In the figure, the set of recovery activities for the first and last substations (in zones $z_{\sigma(1)}$ and $z_{\sigma(n_k)}$) are in colored boxes. The recovery activities which are not in a box are in common for all substations. The dashed arrows in the figure indicate the sequel of the zonal recovery from the first zone to the last one. We can observe that the recovery of each substation is shaped by a set of repetitive activities (two repetitions in Figure 28.2). Each recovery team, working on a single substation, consists of two sets of crews as follows: (1) the diagnostic crews, who detect components' faults, before the recovery starts, and certify the completion of the recovery (i.e., commissioning); and (2) the repair crews, who perform the recovery of transformers, circuit breakers, and disconnect switches. The crews in a team can move on to the next zone in the sequence, upon completing the assigned activities in a working zone. For example, the dashed arrow in Figure 28.2 shows that the diagnostic crews can start fault detection in a zone only after completing the commissioning in an earlier zone in the sequence.

We obtain the base productivity rate for each crew from available databases (e.g., the RS Means database (Means 2018)). We then modify the base productivity rates, considering specific influencing factors such as weather condition, skilled working force, and working hours in a day as well as correction for the crew congestion in a team, beyond the minimum required. To model the variations of the state variables for each infrastructure component, as the result of completing the respective recovery steps, we rewrite Equation (28.1) as follows:

$$\mathbf{x}(\tau) = \sum_{i=1}^{\infty} \mathbf{x}\left(\xi_{r,i-1}\right)\mathbf{1}_{\left\{\xi_{r,i-1} \leq \tau < \xi_{r,i}\right\}} + \sum_{i,j=1}^{\infty} \Delta\mathbf{x}\left(\tau_{s,j}\right)\mathbf{1}_{\left\{\xi_{r,i-1} < \tau < \xi_{r,i}, \, \xi_{r,i-1} < \tau_{s,j} \leq \tau\right\}}, \tag{28.2}$$

where $\xi_{r,i}$ is the completion time of the recovery step i for the specific component. We can generally write $\xi_{r,i} = \tau_{r,z} + \tau_{r,l} + \tau_{r,i}$, where $\tau_{r,z}$ is the starting time of the recovery in the zone; $\tau_{r,l}$ is the starting time of the recovery on the component, relative to the respective $\tau_{r,z}$; and $\tau_{r,i}$ is the completion time of the component recovery step, relative to the respective $\tau_{r,l}$. For each component, this setup models the number of the recovery steps completed by a given time τ as the sum of three stochastic point processes, representing zonal, local, and component recovery. As discussed next, we use $\mathbf{x}(\tau)$ in the models for the capacity and demand measures of components in different networks to predict the performance of interdependent infrastructure.

28.3 Time-varying performance analysis

In structural reliability theory (Gardoni 2017a), a simple beam with possible failure modes in flexure, shear, and torsion is a system with three components. The mathematical expressions

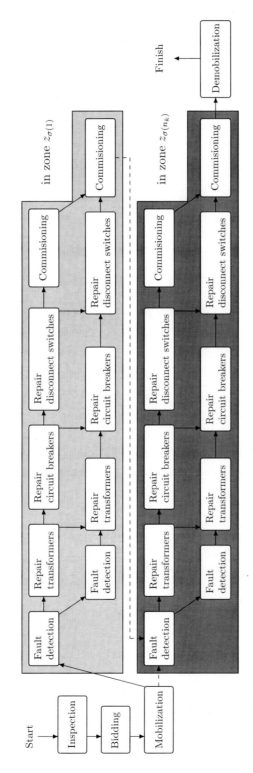

Figure 28.2 Recovery schedule for the repair of damaged substations.

describing the failure modes in flexure, shear, and torsion represent the components of the system. Likewise, following the formulation proposed by Sharma and Gardoni (2018b), we model each infrastructure using multiple networks, where each network is a mathematical representation characterized by a unique set of capacity, demand, and supply measures. For example, we can model the electric power infrastructure with two networks, where one network models the structural state of the infrastructure (i.e., measures are defined relative to a structural failure mode) and the other network models the functionality state. Though the two networks represent the same infrastructure, the topologies of the two networks are not necessarily the same. Specifically, the components of the structural network can include transformers, disconnect switches, and circuit breakers, whereas the components of the flow network include buses, generators, loads and shunts as nodal components, and transmission lines and transformers as line components. In this section, we first explain the mathematical modeling of individual networks and then generalize the discussion to the performance analysis of infrastructure comprised of interdependent networks.

28.3.1 Individual networks

Let $\mathcal{G} = \{G^{[k]} = (V^{[k]}, E^{[k]}) : k = 1,...,K\}$ denote the collection of all networks, where each network k is a graph $G^{[k]}$, composed of a set of vertices, $V^{[k]}$, and a set of edges, $E^{[k]} \subset (V^{[k]} \times V^{[k]})$. The vertices in a graph are nodal components (e.g., water tanks), and the edges are line components (e.g., water pipelines). Following Gardoni et al. (2002), we can write the general expression for the component capacity model as

$$C(\tau) = C\left[\mathbf{x}(\tau), \mathbf{\Theta}_C\right], \tag{28.3}$$

where $C[\mathbf{x}(\tau), \mathbf{\Theta}_C]$ is the predicted capacity measure (or a suitable transformation thereof) at time τ during the recovery; $\mathbf{x}(\tau)$ is the vector of state variables for the component at time τ; and $\mathbf{\Theta}_C$ is the vector of parameters for the capacity model. Likewise, following Gardoni et al. (2003), we can write the general expression for the demand on a component due to a shock as

$$D(\tau) = D\left[\mathbf{x}(\tau), \mathbf{IM}(\tau), \mathbf{\Theta}_D\right], \tag{28.4}$$

where $D[\mathbf{x}(\tau), \mathbf{IM}(\tau), \mathbf{\Theta}_D]$ is the predicted demand measure (or a suitable transformation thereof) at time τ, due to a shock with intensity measure(s) $\mathbf{IM}(\tau)$; and $\mathbf{\Theta}_D$ is the vector of parameters for the demand model. For example, based on the general expressions in Equations (28.3) and (28.4), Tabandeh and Gardoni (2014, 2015) developed probabilistic capacity and demand models for RC bridges, retrofitted with FRP composites (as a repair strategy for damaged RC bridges). Likewise, Iannacone and Gardoni (2018) developed probabilistic capacity and demand models for water pipelines. For nonstructural demands (i.e., demands for different commodities), one can predict $D(\tau)$ from the information available on the consumption rates for the specific commodities.

Let $\mathbf{C}^{[k]}(\tau)$ and $\mathbf{D}^{[k]}(\tau)$ denote the vector of capacity and demand estimates for the components of $G^{[k]}$ at time τ. To quantify the ability of a network to serve the requested demand at time τ, we define the supply measure for $G^{[k]}$ as a function of $\mathbf{C}^{[k]}(\tau)$ and $\mathbf{D}^{[k]}(\tau)$. Following Sharma and Gardoni (2018b), we write the general expression for the supply measure of $G^{[k]}$ as

$$\mathbf{S}^{[k]}(\tau) = \mathbf{S}^{[k]}\left[\mathbf{x}^{[k]}(\tau), \mathbf{C}^{[k]}(\tau), \mathbf{D}^{[k]}(\tau), \mathbf{\Theta}_S^{[k]}\right], \tag{28.5}$$

where $\mathbf{S}^{[k]}[\mathbf{x}^{[k]}(\tau), \mathbf{C}^{[k]}(\tau), \mathbf{D}^{[k]}(\tau), \Theta_S^{[k]}]$ is the predicted supply measures (or a suitable transformation thereof) at time τ; $\mathbf{x}^{[k]}(\tau)$ is the vector of control state variables (e.g., voltage and frequency in power flow network or pressure and velocity in water flow network); and $\Theta_S^{[k]}$ is the vector of parameters for the supply model. For networks corresponding to structural performance measures (i.e., structural networks), we can rewrite Equation (28.5) as $\mathbf{S}^{[k]}(\tau) = \mathbf{D}^{[k]}(\tau) \odot \mathbf{1}_{\{\mathbf{D}^{[k]}(\tau) \preceq \mathbf{C}^{[k]}(\tau)\}}$, where $\odot$ denotes the elementwise product of vectors $\mathbf{D}^{[k]}(\tau)$ and $\mathbf{1}_{\{\mathbf{D}^{[k]}(\tau) \preceq \mathbf{C}^{[k]}(\tau)\}}$, and $\preceq$ denotes elementwise inequality. For networks corresponding to nonstructural performance measures (i.e., flow networks), Equation (28.5) represents a network flow analysis. The network flow analysis allows us to translate the recovery of infrastructure to the recovery of disrupted services. In the network flow analysis, it is crucial to consider the stability of the flow, in addition to the connectivity of the network. The service areas that are physically connected to the flow network may still experience service disruption, if specific flow constraints are violated (e.g., voltage/frequency stability in electric power infrastructure).

Using the triplet $(\mathbf{C}^{[k]}, \mathbf{D}^{[k]}, \mathbf{S}^{[k]})$ as the basic performance measures for $G^{[k]}$, we can write the following general expression for derived performance measures (Sharma & Gardoni 2018b):

$$\mathbf{Q}^{[k]}(\tau) = \mathbf{Q}^{[k]}\left[\mathbf{C}^{[k]}(\tau), \mathbf{D}^{[k]}(\tau), \mathbf{S}^{[k]}(\tau)\right]. \tag{28.6}$$

For instance, one can define $\mathbf{Q}^{[k]}(\tau)$ as the time-varying failure probability of components. Let $g(\tau) = C(\tau) - D(\tau)$ denote the limit-state function for a component at time τ, such that $\{g(\tau) \le 0\}$. indicates a failure event. We can write the time-varying failure probability as $P_F(\tau, \Theta) = P[\Omega_F(\tau, \Theta)]$, where $\Omega_F(\tau, \Theta) = \{[\mathbf{x}(\tau), \mathbf{IM}(\tau), \varepsilon_C, \varepsilon_D] : g(\tau) \le 0\}$ is the failure domain at time τ, in which ε_C and ε_D are the model errors for the capacity and demand estimates; and Θ includes all the parameters used in the models for the state variables, capacity, and demand measures (Gardoni 2017a). Depending on the treatment of uncertainty in Θ, we can obtain two estimates for $P_F(\tau, \Theta)$ (Gardoni et al. 2002). We can obtain a point estimate $\hat{P}_F(\tau) = P_F(\tau, \hat{\Theta})$, where $\hat{\Theta}$ is a fixed value (e.g., the mean or mode of Θ). Alternatively, we can obtain a predictive estimate as $\tilde{P}_F(\tau) = \int P_F(\tau, \Theta) f(\Theta) d\Theta$, where $f(\Theta)$ is the PDF of Θ. Furthermore, to capture the recovery of disrupted services, we can define the performance measure as the fraction of demand served at any time as $\mathbf{Q}(\tau) = [\mathbf{S}(\tau) \oslash \mathbf{D}(\tau)] \odot \mathbf{1}_{\{\mathbf{D}(\tau) \succ 0\}}$, where $\oslash$ denotes the elementwise division and $\mathbf{1}_{\{\mathbf{D}(\tau) \succ 0\}}$ is to ensure that the performance measure is defined only for components that place a demand on the network (i.e., $\mathbf{D}(\tau) \succ 0$).

28.3.2 Interdependent networks

Given the performance measures for individual networks, we introduce interface functions to account for the interdependencies among their capacity and demand estimates. Following Sharma and Gardoni (2018b), we write the modified capacity and demand estimates as

$$\begin{cases} \mathbf{C}'^{[k]}(\tau) = \mathbf{C}^{[k]}(\tau) \odot \mathcal{M}_c^{[k]}(\tau), \\ \mathbf{D}'^{[k]}(\tau) = \mathbf{D}^{[k]}(\tau) \odot \mathcal{M}_b^{[k]}(\tau), \end{cases} \tag{28.7}$$

where $\mathbf{C}'^{[k]}(\tau)$ is the modified capacity estimates for the components of $G^{[k]}$ at time τ; $\mathcal{M}_c^{[k]}(\cdot) = \mathcal{M}_c^{[k]}(\{\mathbf{Q}^{[l]}(\cdot) : G^{[l]} \in \pi_C(G^{[k]})\})$ is the vector of interface functions for the capacity measures, in which $\pi_C(G^{[k]})$ indicates the parent(s) (or, supporting network(s)) of $G^{[k]}$, for the

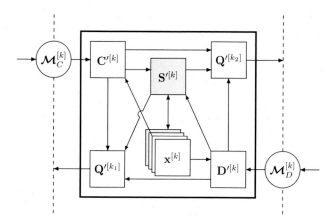

Figure 28.3 Dynamics of interdependent networks.
Source: Adapted from Sharma and Gardoni 2018b.

capacity measures; $\mathbf{D}'^{[k]}(\tau)$ is the modified demand estimates for the components of $G^{[k]}$ at time τ; and $\mathcal{M}_D^{[k]}(\cdot) = \mathcal{M}_D^{[k]}(\{\mathbf{Q}'^{[l]}(\cdot) : G^{[l]} \in \pi_D(G^{[k]})\})$ is the vector of interface functions for the demand measures, in which $\pi_D(G^{[k]})$ indicates the parent(s) of $G^{[k]}$, for the demand measures. For instance, we can write the interface function for an electric power transmission line $e = (v_i, v_j)$, connecting components v_i and v_j in the flow network, as $\mathcal{M}_C(\tau) \propto P[\bar{\Omega}_{F,v_i}(\tau) \cap \bar{\Omega}_{F,v_j}(\tau)]$, where $\bar{\Omega}_{F,v_i}(\tau)$ and $\bar{\Omega}_{F,v_j}(\tau)$ are the complementary of the failure domains $\Omega_{F,v_i}(\tau)$ and $\Omega_{F,v_j}(\tau)$ (i.e., the safe domains) for the components v_i and v_j in the structural network at time τ. Figure 28.3 shows a schematic representation of interdependent networks. The figure illustrates the interaction among the performance measures of a network, which are separated from other networks through the network boundary, shown with thick lines. The interactions of the network with its parents and children networks occur through the interface functions, shown on the dashed lines in the figure.

The direction of the parent–child relation between any two networks can change for the capacity and demand measures. For example, when considering the interdependency for the capacity measure, the power flow network is a parent to the water flow network, insofar as the electric power infrastructure provides power for water pumps to operate; instead, when considering the interdependency for the demand measure, the potable water flow network is a parent to the electric power flow network, insofar as the water pumps are placing demands on the electric power infrastructure. Using $\mathbf{C}'^{[k]}(\tau)$ and $\mathbf{D}'^{[k]}(\tau)$ in Equations (28.5) and (28.6), we can obtain the modified estimates of the supply measure, $\mathbf{S}'^{[k]}(\tau)$, and the derived performance measures, $\mathbf{Q}'^{[k]}(\tau)$ (see Figure 28.3). To model the overall regional recovery of disrupted services, we can define an aggregate measure as $Q'^{[agg]}(\tau) = Q'^{[agg]}(\{\mathbf{Q}'^{[k]}(\tau) : k = 1,\dots,K\})$. For example, Tabandeh et al. (2018a,b) proposed a system reliability formulation to model $Q'^{[agg]}(\tau)$ in the context of societal risk and resilience analysis.

28.4 Resilience analysis

The (predicted) recovery curve, $Q'^{[agg]}(\tau)$, contains all the required information to quantify the associated resilience. Sharma et al. (2018a) proposed a general mathematical approach

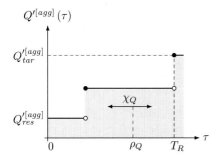

Figure 28.4 Schematic recovery curve and the associated resilience metrics.

for resilience analysis in which resilience metrics are defined as partial descriptors of the recovery curve. The resilience metrics are defined in analogy with the definitions of the statistical moments in the probability theory. Following Sharma et al. (2018a), we call $Q'^{[agg]}(\tau)$ the Cumulative Resilience Function (CRF) in analogy with the Cumulative Distribution Function (CDF) of a random variable. Figure 28.4 shows a schematic recovery curve, where $Q'^{[agg]}_{res}$ is the residual performance level in the immediate aftermath of a disruptive event; $Q'^{[agg]}_{tar}$ is the target/desired performance level after completing the recovery; and $T_R = \inf\{\tau : Q'^{[agg]}(\tau) \geq Q'^{[agg]}_{tar}\}$ is the recovery duration, defined as the earliest time that the performance level meets/exceeds $Q'^{[agg]}_{tar}$ (i.e., first passage time).

Accordingly, we can define the resilience metrics ρ_Q and χ_Q as follows:

(1) The Center of Resilience, ρ_Q, combines the residual performance and recovery duration into a single metric (see Figure 28.4). Mathematically, we can write ρ_Q in analogy with the mean of a random variable as

$$\rho_Q = \frac{\int_0^{T_R} \tau dQ'^{[agg]}(\tau)}{\int_0^{T_R} dQ'^{[agg]}(\tau)}.$$

(28.8)

(2) The Resilience Bandwidth, χ_Q, is a measure of dispersion of the recovery (see Figure 28.4). Mathematically, we can write χ_Q in analogy with the standard deviation of a random variable as

$$\chi_Q = \sqrt{\frac{\int_0^{T_R} \left[\tau - \rho_Q\right]^2 dQ'^{[agg]}(\tau)}{\int_0^{T_R} dQ'^{[agg]}(\tau)}}.$$

(28.9)

The treatment of the epistemic uncertainty due to Θ in the estimates of the resilience metrics is similar to that of $P_F(\tau, \Theta)$, discussed earlier. The definition of the resilience metrics is general (i.e., applicable to characterize the resilience of any infrastructure), and we can systematically extend these metrics to higher order metrics to fully characterize the CRF. Furthermore, the resilience metrics are simple and have tangible interpretations which facilitate the communication of resilience among researchers, decision-makers, and public.

28.5 Resilience-informed infrastructure recovery: A benchmark example

We illustrate the multi-scale approach for the recovery modeling of interdependent electric power and potable water infrastructure in Shelby County, TN, US. The population of Shelby County is about 1 million people, out of which about 70 percent centers in the city of Memphis. The region of interest could experience a damaging earthquake originated from the New Madrid Seismic Zone (NMSZ). In this example, we consider a (historical) scenario earthquake with magnitude $M_w = 7.7$ and epicenter at 35.93°N and 89.92°W (north of Shelby County).

To accurately model the impact of the scenario earthquake on the components of the considered infrastructure, distributed over a large area, it is important that the hazard model captures the spatial variabilities of the earthquake intensity measures (Gardoni 2017b; Gardoni & Murphy 2018). For example, in a region within 30–50 km from the earthquake source (near-field), directivity effects may induce higher values of intensity measures along specific directions. Also, the shape of the basin and the specific topography may result in the amplification of the seismic waves at certain locations (Guidotti et al. 2011, 2018). Furthermore, the characteristics of the soil and scattering phenomena may change the propagation path of the seismic waves (Guidotti et al. 2011, 2018). These factors generally limit the accuracy of common ground motion prediction equations (GMPEs), when used in the near-field. Instead, we can consider three-dimensional (3D) physics-based models that consider the effects of source kinematics, basin configuration, and local site topographic and geologic conditions on the estimate of the earthquake intensity measures. In this example, we use a 3D physics-based model for the near-field of NMSZ, developed by Guidotti et al. (2018). For the far-field, we use GMPEs developed for the Central and Eastern US (Steelman et al. 2007).

28.5.1 Description of electric power and potable water infrastructure

The majority of the US critical infrastructure are owned and operated by private companies; as a result, the complete information on infrastructure topology and operation often remains confidential and publicly unavailable. In Shelby County, both the electrical power and potable water infrastructure are managed by the Memphis Light, Gas, and Water (MLGW) Division. Starting from general information available from past research (e.g., Chang et al. 1996), we collected additional data and designed the missing parts of each infrastructure in accordance with then/current design practice (Su et al. 1987; Birchfield et al. 2017).

For the region of interest (i.e., Shelby Country), we considered a detailed model of the electric power infrastructure that captures the variability of the initial impact and recovery of different areas of Shelby County (Sharma & Gardoni 2018c). The electric power infrastructure in Shelby County is operated by MLGW which sources its power from the Tennessee Valley Authority (TVA). TVA constitutes its own balancing authority in the eastern interconnection of the continental US power transmission grid. We modeled the power infrastructure of TVA with sufficient details to be able to run a power flow analysis (Sharma and Gardoni 2018c). Figure 28.5(a) shows the topology and service areas of the electric power infrastructure in Shelby County, as explained in Chang et al. (1996), and Figure 28.5(b) shows the topology of the infrastructure in Tennessee. The TVA operated infrastructure in Figure 28.5(b) is synthetically generated but it is representative in accordance with the data provided by Birchfield et al. (2017). To estimate the hourly power demand at different service areas, we used the MLGW annual fact sheet (MLGW 2015) and the per capita power demand provided by Birchfield et al. (2017). We also added the generators from Allen and Southaven power plant, located near Memphis, which were not included in past studies.

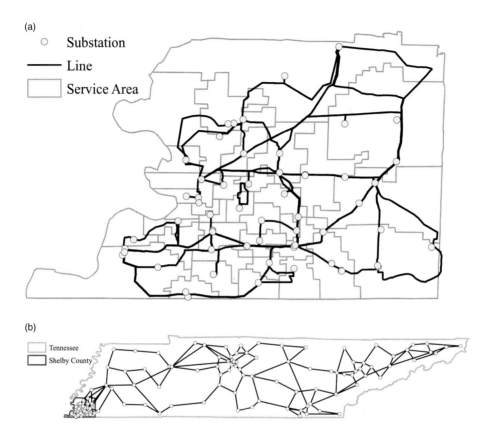

(a)

○ Substation

—— Line

☐ Service Area

(b)

☐ Tennessee
☐ Shelby County

Figure 28.5 Electric power infrastructure: (a) in Shelby County, and (b) in Tennessee.

Figure 28.6 shows the topology of the potable water infrastructure in Shelby County. The solid lines in the figure show the portion of the infrastructure that we developed in a Geographic Information System (GIS) based on existing maps (Chang et al. 1996). The dotted lines in the figure show the portion of the infrastructure that we added based on street maps and buildings access (Sharma & Gardoni 2018c) to complete the water infrastructure. To identify low- and high-pressure zones, we also overlaid the elevation contour map in the figure. The infrastructure consists of 10 pumping stations, 9 booster pumps to connect low- and high-pressure zones, and 6 elevated tanks in the high-pressure zones. The water flow network model includes 965 demand nodes, and 1,346 pipes. To model hourly demands, we first estimated the total daily consumption for residential, commercial, and industrial buildings, using the residential population data, consumption data for different commercial and industrial sectors, and the annual fact sheet published by MLGW (2015). We then introduced specific patterns for residential, commercial, and industrial consumptions to capture the hourly variation of demands (Guidotti et al. 2016). Furthermore, we designed the individual pipe diameters, location of valves, and pump curves to satisfy working pressure and pipe velocity constraints through iterative flow analyses.

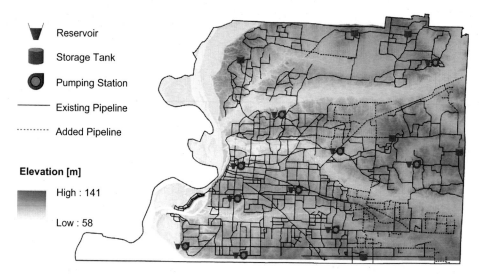

Figure 28.6 Potable water network in Shelby County.

28.5.2 Multi-scale recovery modeling

The components in the electric power infrastructure that are vulnerable to the seismic excitation are the transformers, circuit breakers, and disconnect switches. Figure 28.7 (adapted from Shinozuka et al. 1998) shows a schematic diagram of a typical node in a substation (several such nodes may exist in a substation). In the figure, open circles and slashes represent circuit breakers and disconnect switches. The shaded boxes in the figure are compound components, each consists of a circuit breaker and two disconnect switches. The failure of a node is the event where the input and output lines are disconnected. To determine the connection state of a node, we first determine the state (failure/survival) of individual components, using for this example the fragility curves in the HAZUS-MH Technical Manual (FEMA 2014). We then write the failure event for a compound component as $F_{[i]} = F_{CB_i} \cup F_{DS_i} \cup F_{DS_i}$, for $i = 1, 2, \ldots, 6$, where F_{CB_i} is the failure event for a circuit breaker CB_i, and F_{DS_i} is the failure event for a disconnect switch DS_i. Eventually, we can write the failure event for the node as

$$F_{node} = \left(F_{[1]}F_{[3]}\right) \cup \left(F_{[4]}F_{[6]}\right) \cup \left(F_{[1]}F_{[6]}\right) \cup \left(F_{[3]}F_{[4]}\right). \tag{28.10}$$

The connected nodes and transformers in a substation form a series system. We label the nodes which are damaged and lost their functionalities (i.e., disconnected) as critical nodes, while the ones which are damaged but are still functional as non-critical nodes.

We define each substation in the electric power infrastructure and the corresponding service area as a recovery zone, resulting in 36 recovery zones in Shelby County. Due to the large footprint of the electric power infrastructure in this example and the fact that two different agencies manage the power infrastructure inside and outside Shelby County, we define four different recovery projects as follows: (1) MLGW critical repairs, required to recover non-functional substations in Shelby County; (2) MLGW non-critical repairs, required to recover the functional but damaged substations in Shelby County; (3) TVA critical repairs, required to recover

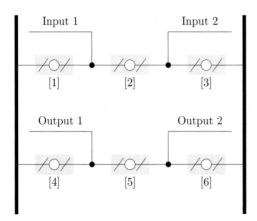

Figure 28.7 Schematic representation of a typical node in a substation.
Source: Adapted from Shinozuka et al. 1998.

non-functional substations in Tennessee; and (4) TVA non-critical repairs, required to recover the functional but damaged substations in Tennessee. We assign different recovery teams for each of these four projects that work in parallel.

Figure 28.2 shows the recovery schedule developed for the repair of damaged substations. To estimate the recovery duration, Table 28.1 summarizes the base productivity rate for the activities in Figure 28.2, according to RS Means (2018). To account for the specific situation of the post-disaster recovery, we modify the base rate by increasing the working hours per day to

Table 28.1 Base productivity rate for the recovery activities to repair damaged substations

Activity	Unit	Mean productivity [units/crew/8 hrs.]
Inspection	–	–
Bidding	Number	–
Mobilization	–	–
Fault detection	Number	8
Transformer repair	Number	0.5
Circuit breaker repair	Number	2
Disconnect switch repair	Number	4
Commissioning	Number	8
Demobilization	–	–

Table 28.2 Formation of the recovery teams for the repair of damaged substations

Operator	Team	Fault detection	Transformer repair	Circuit breaker repair	Disconnect switch repair	Commissioning
MLGW	1	2	4	4	4	2
	2	2	4	4	4	2
	3	2	4	4	4	2
TVA	1	5	10	10	10	5
	2	5	10	10	10	5
	3	5	10	10	10	5

24 hrs (MLGW 2017a). Furthermore, Table 28.2 shows the formation of the recovery teams for critical and non-critical repairs in MLGW and TVA operated infrastructure, required to estimate $\{\xi_{r,i}\}$ in Equation (28.2). Each recovery team for the repair of MLGW operated infrastructure consists of 2 diagnostic crews and 4 repair crews, whereas each team for the repair of TVA operated infrastructure consists of 5 diagnostic crews and 10 repair crews.

The vulnerable components to seismic excitations in the potable water infrastructure are the pumping stations, booster pumps, tanks, and pipelines. In this example, we use the seismic fragility and repair rate curves in HAZUS-MH Technical Manual (FEMA 2014) to estimate the damage levels of different component. For the capacity of pumping stations in Shelby County, we use the (median) values reported by Hwang et al. (1998) from a field inspection. Furthermore, for a pipeline of length l_e, we can obtain the number of leaks/breaks, $N(l_e)$, according to a Poisson process as

$$P\left[N\left(l_e\right)=m\right]=\frac{\left(v_e l_e\right)^m}{m!}e^{-v_e l_e}, \quad \text{for } m=0,1,2,\ldots \tag{28.11}$$

where m is the number of leaks/breaks; v_e is the repair rate (i.e., number of leaks/breaks per unit length of the considered pipeline). Given the limited number of damaged pumping stations, booster pumps, and tanks, as well as their criticalities, we assume that separate crews are assigned for the recovery of these components, where the respective recovery durations in this example are obtained from HAZUS-MH Technical Manual (FEMA 2014). For the repair of damaged pipelines, we define the recovery zones based on the geographical location, land-use, and functional hierarchy. We first use the k-means clustering algorithm (Hastie et al. 2009) to group the pipelines into 8 different geographical zones. We further cluster pipelines in each of the 8 zones into industrial, open, residential and commercial zones, according to the land-use. We also define explicit zones for the main pipelines based on diameter to reach a list of 18 different recovery zones.

Figure 28.8 shows the recovery schedule developed for the repair of damaged pipelines. The figure shows the set of recovery activities for the first zone, $z_{\sigma(1)}$, and the last zone, $z_{\sigma(n_k=18)}$, in colored boxes. The rest of recovery activities (i.e., not in a colored box) are in common for all the recovery zones. We can observe that the recovery in each zone is shaped by a set of repetitive activities (two repetitions in Figure 28.8) for different segments of the damaged pipeline. Each recovery team, working in a single zone, consists of four sets of crews as follows: (1) the earthwork crews, that perform excavation and backfill; (2) the shoring crews, that install temporary shoring systems to support the sides of excavated trenches; (3) the repair crews, that perform the repair of breaks and seal of leaks; and (4) the testing crews, that perform final inspection and certify the recovery completion. The crews in a team can move on to the next zone in the sequence, upon completing the assigned activities in a working zone.

To estimate the recovery duration, Table 28.3 summarizes the base productivity rate for the activities in Figure 28.8, according to RS Means (2018). To account for the specific situation of the post-disaster recovery, we modify the base rate by increasing the working hours per day to 16 hrs (PlaNYC 2014). Furthermore, Table 28.4 shows the formation of the teams to perform the recovery activities. Each team consists of 4 earthwork crews, 3 shoring crews, 4 repairs crews, and 1 test crew. We assign the 3 teams to work in parallel in 3 different zones.

28.5.3 Time-varying performance analysis

To model the performance of the electric power infrastructure, we develop one structural and one flow network. The components of the structural network include transformers, disconnect

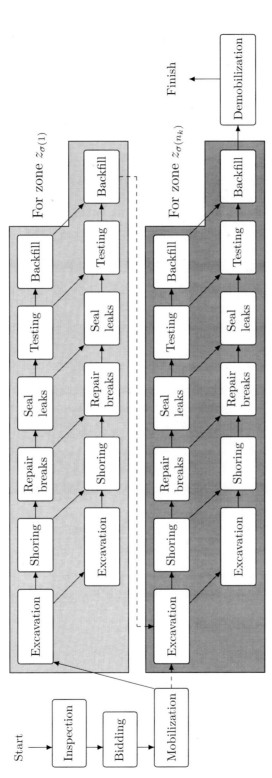

Figure 28.8 Recovery schedule for the repair of damaged water pipelines.

Table 28.3 Base productivity rate for the recovery activities to repair damaged pipelines

Activity	Unit	Mean productivity [crew / 8 hrs.]
Inspection	–	–
Bidding	Number	–
Mobilization	–	–
Excavation	Cubic yard	300
Shoring	Square foot	330
Repair leaks	Number	4
Seal leaks	Number	16
Testing	Number	4
Backfill	Cubic yard	1500
Demobilization	–	–

Table 28.4 Formation of the recovery teams for the repair of damaged pipelines

Team	Excavation	Shoring	Repair breaks	Seal leaks	Testing	Backfill
1	4	3	4	4	1	4
2	4	3	4	4	1	4
3	4	3	4	4	1	4

switches, and circuit breakers. The structural capacity and demand are in terms of the hazard intensity measures (i.e., $C(\mathbf{x}, \Theta_C)$ is taken as the maximum value of the peak ground acceleration (PGA) that a component can sustain and $D(\mathbf{x}, \mathbf{IM}, \Theta_D)$ as the PGA for the scenario earthquake). The components of the flow network include buses, generators, loads, and shunts as nodal components and transmission lines and transformers as line components. The capacity and demand for the components of the electric power flow network (indicated with the superscript *epn*) are estimated using the relevant state variables, $\mathbf{x}^{[epn]}$, in terms of power (active, reactive, and apparent). For example, we estimate the base transmission capacity of a line using conductor type and line geometry, or the base demand at the loads, using per capita consumption values. The capacity of the flow network components is dependent on the state of the structural network. To estimate $\mathbf{S}'^{[epn]}(\tau)$ for the power flow network, we use the Python package PyPSA (Brown et al. 2018). We also incorporate the effects of voltage collapse in the estimate of $\mathbf{S}'^{[epn]}(\tau)$, where the value of $\mathbf{S}'^{[epn]}(\tau)$ tends to zero at load buses whose voltage ($\in$ $\mathbf{x}^{[epn]}$) falls out of the range [0.9,1.1] per unit. To model the recovery of disrupted services, we define the performance measure, for load buses, as the fraction of demand served at any time (i.e., $\mathbf{Q}'^{[epn]}(\tau) = [\mathbf{S}'^{[epn]}(\tau) \oslash \mathbf{D}'^{[epn]}(\tau)] \odot \mathbf{1}_{\{\mathbf{D}'^{[epn]}(\tau) \succ 0\}}$).

To model the performance of the potable water infrastructure, we develop structural and flow networks, as for the electric power infrastructure. However, in the potable water infrastructure, the components of the two networks are identical. Each network consists of junctions, tanks, and reservoirs as nodal components, and pipelines and pumps as the line components. The structural capacity and demand are in terms of the hazard intensity measures (similar to the power structural network). We also estimate the base flow capacity and demand measures, using the designed value of $\mathbf{x}^{[pwn]}$ for the components of the potable water network (indicated with the superscript *pwn*). For instance, we estimate the discharge capacity of pipelines, using the section area and design velocity, and the corresponding discharge demand based upon the information on water consumption rate under normal operating condition. The performance of the flow network is dependent on the damage state of the structural network and the performance of the electric power flow network. Furthermore, the estimate of $\mathbf{S}'^{[pwn]}(\tau)$ for the water flow network requires a pressure-dependent flow analysis such that when the pressure at a (demand) junction drops below a threshold, the value of $\mathbf{S}'^{[pwn]}(\tau)$ at the junction tends to zero (Wagner et al. 1988). We developed a model for the pressure-dependent flow analysis, using the Python package WNTR (Klise et al. 2017). The treatment of the network interdependencies in WNTR consists of replacing the non-functional tanks and pumps (extensively damaged or not having power) during the recovery with a pipe that allows water to flow through with no additional pressure head. The pipe leaks/breaks are also modeled as additional demands (the demand for the pipe break is such that to drain the pipe). To model the recovery of disrupted services, we define the performance measure, for demand junctions, as the fraction of demand met at any time (i.e., $\mathbf{Q}'^{[pwn]}(\tau) = [\mathbf{S}'^{[pwn]}(\tau) \oslash \mathbf{D}'^{[pwn]}(\tau)] \odot \mathbf{1}_{\{\mathbf{D}'^{[pwn]}(\tau) \succ 0\}}$.

28.5.4 Resilience analysis

In this example, we define the aggregate performance measure for the regional recovery of disrupted services and resilience analysis as follows:

$$Q'^{[agg]}(\tau) = \sum_{cell=1}^{n_{cell}} w_{cell} Q_{cell}'^{[epn]}(\tau) Q_{cell}'^{[pwn]}(\tau), \tag{28.12}$$

where a *cell* is a geographical region served by a unique pair of nodes in the electric power and potable water networks; w_{cell} is a weight for the recovery *cell*, defined in terms of the service area such that $\sum_{cell=1}^{n_{cell}} w_{cell} = 1$; $Q_{cell}'^{[epn]}(\tau)$ is the fraction of the electric power demand met for the *cell* at time τ; and $Q_{cell}'^{[pwn]}(\tau)$ is the fraction of the potable water demand met for the *cell* at time τ. The performance measure $Q'^{[agg]}(\tau)$ considers the recovery of disrupted services provided by both the electric power and potable water infrastructure.

28.5.5 Results and discussion

The scenario earthquake causes damage to the components of the electric power infrastructure in 17 out 36 zones managed by MLGW, which require critical repairs, whereas all the 18 zones of the potable water infrastructure include damaged components. For the zonal scale recovery, we need to prioritize the recovery zones for the networks $\mathcal{Z} = \{\mathbf{z}_1, \mathbf{z}_2, \mathbf{z}_3, \mathbf{z}_4\}$, where $\mathbf{z}_1 = \mathbf{z}_2 = (z_{\sigma(1)}, \ldots, z_{\sigma(17)})$ is the vector of recovery zones for the two electric power networks, and $\mathbf{z}_3 = \mathbf{z}_4 = (z_{\sigma(1)}, \ldots, z_{\sigma(18)})$ is the vector of recovery zones for the two potable water networks. We develop the zonal scale recovery schedule based on the current recovery practice. Specifically, MLGW (2017b) sets the priorities for the recovery of the electric power infrastructure in order of importance as follows: (1) damaged substations along with primary circuits serving hospitals, water pumping stations, and sewer treatment plants; (2) damaged circuits associated with the greatest number of customers without power; (3) damaged components in areas that restore power to the most number of customers per repair; and (4) individual service lines from transformers on a pole to customers houses. Using these priorities, we develop a representative recovery schedule for the electric power infrastructure. For the potable water infrastructure, we also develop a recovery schedule, representative of current practice, according to the following prioritization: (1) mainlines, (2) damaged components in residential and commercial areas, (3) damaged components in industrial areas, and (4) damaged components in open areas.

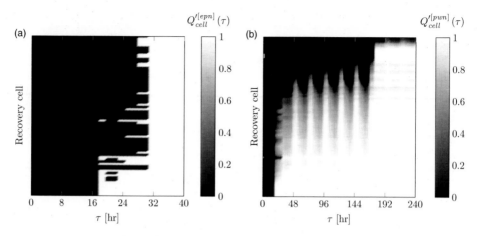

Figure 28.9 Predicted recovery of disrupted services provided by: (a) electric power, and (b) potable water infrastructure across Shelby County.

Figure 28.9 shows the recovery of the electric power and potable water infrastructure in terms of the performance measures $Q'^{[epn]}_{cell}(\tau)$ and $Q'^{[pwn]}_{cell}(\tau)$. Figure 28.9(a) shows the estimate of $Q'^{[epn]}_{cell}(\tau)$ for the electric power infrastructure over a period of 40 hours in the aftermath of the scenario earthquake. The recovery of the electric power infrastructure is associated to the critical repairs. Non-critical repairs continue even after completing the critical repairs but do not cause further changes in $Q'^{[epn]}_{cell}(\tau)$ due to redundancy. In the figure, we observe that $Q'^{[epn]}_{cell}(\tau)$ for some recovery cells shows a fluctuating pattern over time. This is because as the recovery advances, redistribution of loads on operating buses can result in voltage collapse. The recovery schedule for the electric power infrastructure results in $\rho_Q = 18.1$ hours and $T_R = 34$ hours for the critical repairs. To estimate ρ_Q, we obtain $Q'^{[agg]}(\tau)$ from Equation (28.12) and set $Q'^{[pwn]}_{cell}(\tau) = 1$ for all $cell = 1, \ldots, n_{cell}$. Likewise, Figure 28.9(b) shows the estimate of $Q'^{[pwn]}_{cell}(\tau)$ for the potable water infrastructure over a period of 240 hours (i.e., 10 days) in the aftermath of the scenario earthquake. The fluctuation of $Q'^{[pwn]}_{cell}(\tau)$ in the figure is due to the hourly variations in the water demand. The results indicate that the initial power outage affects the water service recovery. The recovery schedule results in $\rho_Q = 69.6$ hours and $T_R = 457$ hours. To estimate ρ_Q, we obtain $Q'^{[agg]}(\tau)$ from Equation (28.12) and set $Q'^{[epn]}_{cell}(\tau) = 1$ for all $cell = 1, \ldots, n_{cell}$.

Figure 28.10 shows the recovery of disrupted services (i.e., electric power and potable water) in terms of the aggregate performance measure $Q'^{[agg]}_{cell}(\tau)(= Q'^{[epn]}_{cell}(\tau)Q'^{[pwn]}_{cell}(\tau))$ over a period of 240 hours (i.e., 10 days) in the aftermath of the scenario earthquake. The recovery schedule results in $\rho_Q = 60.6$ hours and $T_R = 457$ hours. Because the recovery of disrupted services after $\tau \approx 34$ hours is controlled by the potable water infrastructure, both the recovery patterns and durations for the recovery cells are similar to those of the water infrastructure. The resilience metric ρ_Q approximately corresponds to the time at which 50 percent of the demand on both flow networks can be served (i.e., the time at which $Q'^{[agg]}(\tau) \approx 0.5$). Hence, targeting ρ_Q to improve the recovery of disrupted services may result in faster recovery in an average sense over the region. Considering χ_Q besides ρ_Q also allows us to control the variations of the recovery duration across the region (i.e., increasing or decreasing the difference in the recovery durations of different cells). Finally, to highlight the significance of the recovery scheduling, we note that for Shelby County, with a population of about 1 million

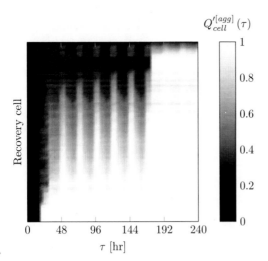

$$Q_{cell}^{\prime[agg]}(\tau)$$

Figure 28.10 Predicted recovery of disrupted services in terms of the aggregate performance measure across Shelby County.

people, 1-hour improvement in the recovery duration implies 1 million people-hours more access to essential services.

28.6 Conclusions

This chapter presented a novel multi-scale approach for the recovery modeling of interdependent infrastructure. The multi-scale approach builds upon the development of physics-based recovery models for individual components that account for the effects of the recovery influencing factors such as components damage level and recovery resources. The multi-scale approach integrates the recovery models for individual components into a workable recovery schedule for infrastructure, typically distributed over a large area. To promote a recovery schedule that is both feasible to implement and easy to communicate, the multi-scale approach accounts for the prevalent physical and logical constraints to implement repetitive recovery activities on multiple components, such as activities precedence, crew and material availability, and work continuity. An integral part of the recovery modeling is the performance analysis of interdependent infrastructure under a developed recovery schedule. This chapter presents a mathematical formulation that models infrastructure as a collection of interdependent networks, where each network is characterized by a unique set of capacity, demand, and supply measures. Derived performance measures are also developed in terms of capacity, demand, and supply measures to model the recovery of disrupted services. The developed recovery schedule informs the variations of the performance measures over the course of the recovery. Furthermore, the formulation develops interface functions to decouple the performance analyses of interdependent networks; hence, allows different analysts and computing resources to work on different networks at the same time. The chapter further introduced the regional resilience analysis to monitor the recovery of disrupted services. The multi-scale approach is explained through a large-scale problem for the post-disaster recovery modeling of electric power and potable water infrastructure in Shelby County, TN with a service population of one million people. The recovery schedules for each of the electric power and potable water infrastructure are developed based on the current practice of the recovery prioritization. The recovery models are developed for the repair of damaged components and the impact on the recovery of disrupted services is modeled through network flow analyses for both the electric power and potable water infrastructure. The results indicate that the post-disaster recovery of the electric power infrastructure is faster than the recovery of the potable water infrastructure. As a result, the recovery of the potable water infrastructure controls the overall duration of the recovery of the region.

Acknowledgements

This work was supported in part by the National Institute of Standards and Technology (NIST) through the Center for Risk-Based Community Resilience Planning under Award No. 70NANB15H044 and by the National Science Foundation (NSF) under Award No. 1638346. Opinions and findings presented are those of the authors and do not necessarily reflect the views of the sponsor.

References

Alderson, D.L., Brown, G.G., and Carlyle, W.M. (2014). "Assessing and improving operational resilience of critical infrastructures and other systems." *Tutorials in Operations Research: Bridging Data and Decision*, A. Newman and J. Leung, (eds.), Institute for Operations Research and Management Science, Hanover, MD, 180–215.

Birchfield, A.B., Gegner, K.M., Xu, T., Shetye, K.S., and Overbye, T.J. (2017). "Statistical considerations in the creation of realistic synthetic power grids for geomagnetic disturbance studies," *IEEE Transactions on Power Systems*, 32(2), 1502–10.

Brown, T., Hörsch, J., and Schlachtberger, D. (2018). "PyPSA: Python for power system analysis," *Journal of Open Research Software*, 6(1), DOI:10.5334/jors.188.

Cavdaroglu, B., Hammel, E., Mitchell, J.E., Sharkey, T.C., and Wallace, W.A. (2013). "Integrating restoration and scheduling decisions for disrupted interdependent infrastructure systems," *Annals of Operations Research*, 203(1), 279–94.

Chang, S.E., Seligson, H.A., and Eguchi, R.T. (1996). "Estimation of the economic impact of multiple lifeline disruption: Memphis light, gas and water division case study," *Technical Report No. NCEER-96-0011*, Multidisciplinary Center for Earthquake Engineering Research (MCEER), Buffalo, NY.

Corotis, R. (2009). "Societal issues in adopting life-cycle concepts within the political system," *Structure and Infrastructure Engineering*, 5(1), 59–65.

Ellingwood, B.R., Cutler, H., Gardoni, P., Peacock, W.G., van de Lindt, J.W., and Wang, N. (2016). "The Centerville Virtual Community: a fully integrated decision model of interacting physical and social infrastructure systems," *Sustainable and Resilient Infrastructure*, 1(3–4), 95–107.

El-Rayes, K. and Moselhi, O. (2001). "Optimizing resource utilization for repetitive construction projects," *Journal of Construction Engineering and Management*, 127(1), 18–27.

Federal Emergency Management Agency (FEMA). (2014). Multi-hazard Loss Estimation Methodology: Earthquake Model HAZUS-MH 2.1 Technical Manual, Washington, DC.

Gardoni, P. (ed.), (2017a). *Risk and Reliability Analysis: Theory and Applications*. Cham: Springer.

Gardoni, P. (2017b). "Promoting societal well-being by designing sustainable and resilient infrastructure," *Proceedings of the 12th International Conference on Structural Safety & Reliability (ICOSSAR 2017)*, TU Wien, Vienna (Austria).

Gardoni, P. and Murphy, C. (2018). "Society-based design: Developing sustainable and resilient communities," *Sustainable and Resilient Infrastructure*, DOI: 10.1080/23789689.2018.1448667.

Gardoni, P., Der Kiureghian, A., and Mosalam, K.M. (2002). "Probabilistic capacity models and fragility estimates for reinforced concrete columns based on experimental observations," *Journal of Engineering Mechanics*, 128(10), 1024–38.

Gardoni, P., Mosalam, K.M., and Der Kiureghian, A. (2003). "Probabilistic seismic demand models and fragility estimates for RC bridges," *Journal of Earthquake Engineering*, 7(spec01), 79–106.

Gardoni, P., Murphy, C., and Rowell, A. (eds.) (2016). *Societal Risk Management of Natural Hazards*. Cham: Springer.

Gonzalez, A.D., Duenas-Osorio, L., Sanchez-Silva, M., and Medaglia, A.L. (2016). "The interdependent network design problem for optimal infrastructure system restoration," *Computer-Aided Civil and Infrastructure Engineering*, 31(5), 334–50.

Guidotti, R. and Gardoni, P. (2018). "Modeling of interdependent critical infrastructure for regional risk and resilience analysis," in *Handbook of Sustainable and Resilient Infrastructure*, P. Gardoni (ed.). New York: Routledge.

Guidotti, R., Stupazzini, M., Smerzini, C., Paolucci, R., and Ramieri, P. (2011). "Numerical study on the role of basin geometry and kinematic seismic source in 3D ground motion simulation of the 22 February 2011 MW 6.2 Christchurch earthquake," *Seismological Research Letters*, 82(6), 767–82.

Guidotti, R., Chmielewski, H., Unnikrishnan, V., Gardoni, P., McAllister, T., and van de Lindt, J. (2016). "Modeling the resilience of critical infrastructure: The role of network dependencies," *Sustainable and Resilient Infrastructure*, 1(3–4), 153–68.

Guidotti, R., Tian, S., and Gardoni, P. (2018). "Simulation of seismic wave propagation in the Metro Memphis Statistical Area (MMSA)" (in preparation).

Hastie, T., Tibshirani, R., and Friedman, J. (2009). *The Elements of Statistical Learning*, 2nd Edition. New York: Springer.

Hwang, H.H., Lin, H., and Shinozuka, M. (1998). "Seismic performance assessment of water delivery systems," *Journal of Infrastructure Systems*, 4(3), 118–25.

Iannacone L. and Gardoni P. (2018). "Physics-based repair rates for pipelines subject to seismic excitations," *Proceedings of 16th European Conference on Earthquake Engineering*, Thessaloniki, Greece.

Jia, G. and Gardoni, P. (2018). "State-dependent stochastic models: A general stochastic framework for modeling deteriorating engineering systems considering multiple deterioration processes and their interactions," *Structural Safety*, 72, 99–110.

Jia, G., Tabandeh, A., and Gardoni, P. (2017). "Life-cycle analysis of engineering systems: Modeling deterioration, instantaneous reliability, and resilience," *Risk and Reliability Analysis: Theory and Applications*, P. Gardoni (ed.). Cham: Springer, 465–94.

Klise, K.A., Hart, D., Moriarty, D., Bynum, M.L., Murray, R., Burkhardt, J., and Haxton, T. (2017). "Water Network Tool for Resilience (WNTR)," *User Manual (No. SAND2017--8883R)*, Sandia National Laboratories (SNL-NM), Albuquerque, NM.

Lee II, E.E., Mitchell, J.E., and Wallace, W.A. (2007). "Restoration of services in interdependent infrastructure systems: A network flows approach," *IEEE Transactions on Systems, Man, and Cybernetics, Part C (Applications and Reviews)*, 37(6), 1303–17.

Memphis Light, Gas and Water (MLGW). (2015). Facts and figures for years ending December 31, 2015. www.mlgw.com/images/content/files/pdf/FactsFigures.pdf (last accessed March 30, 2018).

Memphis Light, Gas and Water (MLGW). (2017a). MLGW crews working 24/7 to restore power [Press release]. www.mlgw.com/news/mlgw-crews-working-24-7-to-restore-power-2017 (last accessed August 19, 2018).

Memphis Light, Gas and Water (MLGW). (2017b). How MLGW restores power [Press release]. www.mlgw.com/news/how-mlgw-restores-power-5-2017 (last accessed August 19, 2018).

NERC Steering Group. (2004) Technical analysis of the August 14, 2003, blackout: What happened, why, and what did we learn. report to the NERC Board of Trustees.

Nurre, S.G., Cavdaroglu, B., Mitchell, J.E., Sharkey, T.C., and Wallace, W.A. (2012). "Restoring infrastructure systems: An integrated network design and scheduling (INDS) problem," *European Journal of Operational Research*, 223(3), 794–806.

Ouyang, M. (2014). "Review on modeling and simulation of interdependent critical infrastructure systems," *Reliability Engineering & System Safety*, 121, 43–6.

PlaNYC (2014). "PlaNYC Progress Report: Sustainability and Resiliency 2014." New York City, NY. www.nyc.gov/html/planyc/downloads/pdf/140422_PlaNYCP-Report_FINAL_Web.pdf (last accessed August 19, 2018).

RS Means (2018). *Building Construction Costs Book*, 76th Edition. Construction publishers and consultants, Kingston, MA.

Sharma, N. and Gardoni, P. (2018a). "Promoting resilient interdependent infrastructure: The role of strategic recovery scheduling," *Computer-Aided Civil and Infrastructure Engineering* (in preparation).

Sharma, N. and Gardoni, P. (2018b). "Mathematical modeling of interdependent infrastructure: An object-oriented approach for generalized network-system analysis," *Reliability Engineering & System Safety* (in preparation).

Sharma, N. and Gardoni, P. (2018c). "Modeling the time-varying performance of electrical infrastructure during post disaster recovery using tensors," *Handbook of Sustainable and Resilient Infrastructure*, P. Gardoni (ed.), New York: Routledge.

Sharma, N., Tabandeh, A., and Gardoni, P. (2018a). "Resilience analysis: A mathematical formulation to model resilience of engineering systems," *Sustainable and Resilient Infrastructure*, 3(2), 49–67.

Sharma, N., Tabandeh, A., and Gardoni, P. (2018b). "Resilience- informed recovery optimization: a multi-scale formulation for interdependent infrastructure," *Computer- Aided Civil and Infrastructure Engineering* (in preparation).

Shinozuka, M., Rose, A., and Eguchi, R.T. (1998). "Engineering and socioeconomic impacts of earthquakes," *Monograph 98-MN02*, Multidisciplinary Center for Earthquake Engineering Research (MCEER), Buffalo, NY.

Steelman, J., Song, J., and Jerome, F. (2007). "Integrated data flow and risk aggregation for consequence-based risk management of seismic regional losses," Report of the Mid-America Earthquake Center, University of Illinois at Urbana-Champaign, Champaign, IL.

Su, Y.C., Mays, L.W., Duan, N., and Lansey, K.E. (1987). "Reliability-based optimization model for water distribution systems," *Journal of Hydraulic Engineering*, 113(12), 1539–56.

Tabandeh, A. and Gardoni, P. (2014). "Probabilistic capacity models and fragility estimates for RC columns retrofitted with FRP composites," *Engineering Structures*, 74, 13–22.

Tabandeh, A., and Gardoni, P. (2015). "Empirical Bayes approach for developing hierarchical probabilistic predictive models and its application to the seismic reliability analysis of FRP-retrofitted RC bridges," *ASCE-ASME Journal of Risk and Uncertainty in Engineering Systems, Part A: Civil Engineering*, 1(2), 04015002.

Tabandeh, A., Gardoni, P., and Murphy, C. (2018a). "A reliability-based capability approach," *Risk Analysis*, 38(2), 410–24.

Tabandeh, A., Gardoni, P., Murphy, C., and Myers, N. (2018b). "Societal risk and resilience analysis: Dynamic bayesian network formulation of a capability approach," *ASCE-ASME Journal of Risk and Uncertainty in Engineering Systems, Part A: Civil Engineering*, DOI: 10.1061/AJRUA6.0000996.

Wagner, J.M., Shamir, U., and Marks, D.H. (1988). "Water distribution reliability: Simulation methods," *Journal of Water Resources Planning and Management*, 114(3), 276–94.

Part VII

The role and impact of aging and deterioration, and life-cycle analysis

29

Deterioration models for engineered systems

Javier Riascos-Ochoa[1] and Mauricio Sánchez-Silva[2]

[1] DEPARTAMENTO DE CIENCIAS BÁSICAS Y MODELADO, FACULTAD DE CIENCIAS NATURALES E INGENIERÍA, UNIVERSIDAD JORGE TADEO LOZANO, BOGOTÁ, COLOMBIA; JAVIER.RIASCOS@UTADEO.EDU.CO

[2] DEPARTMENT OF CIVIL AND ENVIRONMENTAL ENGINEERING, UNIVERSIDAD DE LOS ANDES, BOGOTÁ, COLOMBIA; MSANCHEZ@UNIANDES.EDU.CO

JULY 26, 2018

29.1 Introduction

The assessment of the mechanical performance of infrastructure systems is central for project evaluation and decision making; particularly in the case of large infrastructure. It is the main input for life-cycle cost analysis and plays an important role in defining operational (mainten-ance) strategies (Santander & Sánchez-Silva 2008). Performance refers to the evolution of a set of system control parameters (e.g., reliability, system state). In particular, the main concern in infrastructure is related with the decay in performance, also referred to as *deterioration* (Sánchez-Silva & Klutke 2016). Modeling deterioration is necessary to define design parameters and oper-ational strategies that maximize the benefits derived from the project. It is also important as an input to provide the flexibility necessary for future changes to the system (Sánchez-Silva 2018). This chapter presents a review of reliability assessment methods for systems that deteriorate.

Deterioration is a time-dependent problem whose modeling requires understanding the sto-chastic nature of the physical processes and the evolution of uncertainty with time. Common deterioration processes in infrastructure include progressive continuous loss of capacity due to, for example, corrosion, fatigue, creep, and aging; or sudden and unexpected damages caused by extreme events such as overloads or natural phenomena. Currently, most existing models tackle these phenomena separately. However, recent studies have shown the need for new and more general models, which also provide easy-to-evaluate expressions for reliability and various related quantities. This chapter discusses a specific class of stochastic processes known as *additive process*, being the *Lévy process* particularly relevant (Riascos-Ochoa et al. 2014; Sánchez-Silva & Klutke 2016). Through this approach it is easy to combine various deterioration mechanisms and to obtain numerically the main reliability quantities required for better life-cycle analysis.

The chapter is structured as follows. The basic reliability problem of deteriorating systems is described and discussed in Section 29.2. Afterwards, two basic deterioration mechanisms (i.e., shock-based and progressive) are defined; specifically, shock-based models are presented in Section 29.3; and progressive deterioration models in Section 29.4. Furthermore, the case of combined mechanisms (shock-based and progressive) is presented in Section 29.5. The theoretical basis of *additive processes* arepresented in Section 29.6; and the numerical considerations in Section 29.7. Finally, in Section 29.8 a detailed example of additive processes is presented and discussed.

29.2 Reliability problem for deteriorating systems

29.2.1 Basic reliability formulation

Any engineered system is designed and built to accomplish a specific function during a specified time window; usually referred to as *time mission* t_m. However, once in operation, the ability to satisfy its function diminishes reaching eventually a *failure state*, where its intended function is not satisfied. The time-dependent reliability, $R(t)$, is the probability that the system has survived beyond time t; i.e., $P(L > t)$, where L is the time to failure. Thus, the probability that the system is capable to fulfill its function beyond the time mission is defined as (Sánchez-Silva & Klutke 2016):

$$R(t_m) = P(L > t_m).$$
(29.1)

In the case of systems that deteriorate, the negative variation of the system's *performance* or *condition* has a direct impact on the reliability assessment. In general, the system state (condition) at time t can be described by a stochastic process $\{V_t\}_{t\geq 0}$, where V_t is a n-dimensional random variable. It may represent the performance of one or several physical quantities of the system, such as the stiffness, the structural capacity/resistance or residual ductility to collapse (e.g., in infrastructures or mechanical components, (Sánchez-Silva et al. 2011; Iervolino et al. 2013); it can be defined as a composite index like the pavement condition index for roads (ASTM 2008); or it can be any other indicator describing the functionality of the system.

In this chapter we consider only a one dimensional (1d) process, $\{V_t\}_{t\geq 0}$ (Figure 29.1). Without maintenance or recovery, V_t is assumed to be monotonically decreasing with time; which is consistent with the nature of deterioration. Therefore, the expression for reliability presented in Equation (29.1) can be also written as Sánchez-Silva and Klutke (2016):

$$R(t_m) = P(V_{t_m} > k^*),$$
(29.2)

where k^* is a performance threshold that separates the safe and failure regions. It represents a performance *limit state*; then, failure occurs when V_t falls bellow k^* (i.e., $V_t < k^*$). For any time t, the *time-dependent reliability* or *reliability function*, $R(t)$, can be written as:

$$R(t) = P(V_t > k^*),$$
(29.3)

from which other quantities of interest such as the lifetime distribution $f(t)$ or the mean time to failure $\mathbb{E}[L]$ (MTTF) can be defined:

$$f(t) = -\frac{d}{dt} R(t)$$
(29.4)

$$\mathbb{E}[L] = \int_0^\infty t f(t) dt.$$
(29.5)

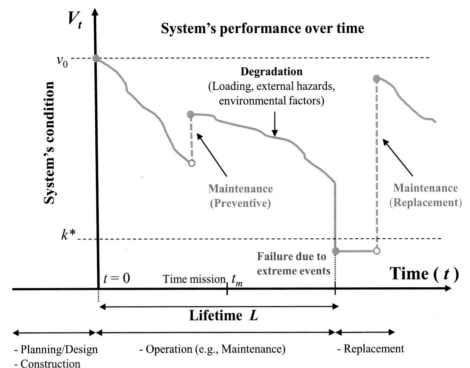

Figure 29.1 Sample path of the performance indicator (system's condition) V_t over time t, and actions involved during the life-cycle of an engineered system.

29.2.2 Reliability modeling alternatives

Depending upon the knowledge and understanding of the system performance, there are different modeling alternatives for evaluating reliability; they are (Nicolai et al. 2007):

- Statistical-based lifetime methods or black-box models.
- Stochastic-based or grey-box models.
- Physics-based or white-box models.

The focus of this chapter is on the second case; i.e., a stochastic-based approach in which the variation of the system's condition with time is described as a stochastic process. Thus, let's define deterioration – the reduction in the system's condition with time – as a stochastic process $\{D_t\}_{t\geq0}$. Furthermore, consider that the system initial condition is known, i.e., $V(0) = v_0$ (state at time $t = 0$); then, the system condition at time t will be:

$$V_t = v_0 - D_t, \tag{29.6}$$

noting that D_t has increasing sample paths (given that there is no maintenance/updating). Therefore, the system reliability (Equation (29.3)) takes the form:

$$R(t,z) = \mathrm{P}(D_t \leq z), \tag{29.7}$$

557

with $z = v_0 - k^*$ called the *acceptable operational range*; and k^* the limit state threshold. Note that we have made explicit the dependence of the reliability function on z.

29.2.3 Deterioration mechanisms

Deterioration models describe the damage accumulation process over time, i.e., $\{D_t\}_{t \geq 0}$, as a result of its dynamic interaction with external (environmental) demands or internal changes in the system structure. Frequently, deterioration models are divided into two basic mechanisms (Sánchez-Silva et al. 2011):

1. **Shock-based deterioration**: where the system condition is subject to sudden changes (decays) at specific points in time. This problem can be observed in a wide range of engineering problems; e.g., structures subjected to earthquakes or blasts, or electric systems. This chapter will focus on the case where the damage caused by shocks accumulates over time (Nakagawa 2007; Riascos-Ochoa et al. 2014).
2. **Progressive deterioration**: where the system condition decreases continuously and slowly over the time. Most of these problems are observed as a consequence of the interaction between the system and its environment; e.g., aging, wear or corrosion (Pandey et al. 2009; van Noortwijk 2009; Sánchez-Silva et al. 2011; Sánchez-Silva & Klutke 2016).

In reality, any system is subjected to these two deterioration mechanisms; thus, a comprehensive deterioration model should include the effect of both sudden changes and continuous removal of the system condition. This case is known as *combined deterioration* mechanism. The following sections present and discuss the most common models to characterize D_t.

29.3 Models for shock-based deterioration

29.3.1 Basic formulation

Shock-based deterioration is a process in which the system's condition, V_t, is reduced by sudden events (i.e., jumps) occurring at discrete points in time. Let's first define T_i as a random variable describing the time to the ith shock and $\Delta T_i := T_i - T_{i-1}$ the *inter-arrival time* between two consecutive shock events; i.e., between the $(i-1)^{th}$ and the ith shocks, for $i \geq 1$. Consider further that each shock reduces the system condition by a random amount Y_i; also called the *shock size*. Thus, total deterioration S_t in a (cumulative) shock-based model can be expressed as (Klutke & Yang 2002b; Sánchez-Silva et al. 2011; Iervolino et al. 2013; Nakagawa 2007; Sumita & Shanthikumar 1983; Wortman et al. 1994) (see Figure 29.2):

$$S_t = \sum_{i=1}^{N_t} Y_i, \tag{29.8}$$

with N_t the number of shocks that have occurred by time t. Hence, the system's remaining capacity by time t (Equation (29.6)) can be expressed as:

$$V_t = v_0 - S_t = v_0 - \sum_{i=1}^{N_t} Y_i, \tag{29.9}$$

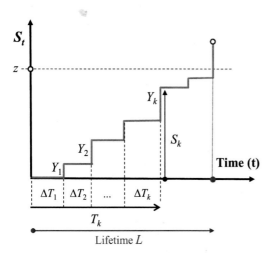

Figure 29.2 Cumulative deterioration caused by shocks.

and the reliability function in Equation (29.7) becomes:

$$R(t,z) = P\left(\sum_{i=1}^{N_t} Y_i < z\right) = P(S_t < z).$$

(29.10)

In order to formulate explicitly the reliability function, it is important to distinguish between two cases. Models where deterioration caused by one shock depends on the history of the process up to that point; and those where the damage caused by every shock accumulates in an independent manner. Regarding the former, there are three possible dependencies:

- between shock sizes and arrival times (i.e., between T_k and Y_k). A particular case is when the damage Y_k depends on the previous inter-arrival time ΔT_{k-1}, like in the δ-shock model (Lam et al. 2004; Lam 2009).
- between the k-th shock size, Y_k, and the accumulated damage until the immediate previous event, i.e., $Y_1 + \cdots + Y_{k-1}$ (Junca & Sanchez-Silva 2012, 2013) – this is also called *state-dependent* shock model –; and
- between inter-arrival times, where T_k depends on the time history up to T_{k-1}.

In general, the reliability estimation of these models is numerically expensive, and requires the evaluation of expressions in terms of infinite sums and convolution integrals (Sumita & Shanthikumar 1983). Therefore, they are of limited value in most practical applications. In the rest of this chapter, we will focus only on the case of independent shock models.

29.3.2 Independent shock models

A common assumption is that the set of inter-arrival times $\{\Delta T_i\}_{i\geq 1}$ and shock sizes $\{Y_i\}_{i\geq 1}$ are mutually independent, and that the random variables ΔT_i are independent among them, as well as the Y_i (Sánchez-Silva et al. 2011). This can be the case of earthquakes with large inter-arrival times, whose occurrences and magnitudes are assumed to be uncorrelated. To

J. Riascos-Ochoa and M. Sánchez-Silva

this class belongs: the Compound Poisson Process (CPP), the Renewal Process shock model, and the Phase-type (PH) shock model (Sánchez-Silva & Klutke 2016; Riascos-Ochoa et al. 2014).

Let us assume that shock sizes Y_i and inter-arrival times ΔT_i are independent and identically distributed random variables; with distributions F_{Y_i} and $F_{\Delta T_i}$, respectively. Thus, conditioning out the number of shocks N_t in Equation (29.10), the system reliability can be written as:

$$R(t,z) = P\left(N_t = 0\right) + \sum_{k=1}^{\infty} P\left(\sum_{i=1}^{k} Y_i < z\right) P(N_t = k)$$

$$= P\left(N_t = 0\right) + \sum_{k=1}^{\infty} \bar{P}_k(z) P\left(N_t = k\right),$$

(29.11)

where $\bar{P}_k(z)$ is the probability of survival until the kth shock (for a failure threshold z), given by the distribution of the cumulated damage until the kth shock, $S_k = \sum_{i=1}^{k} Y_i$ (Figure 29.2):

$$\bar{P}_k(z) = P\left(\sum_{i=1}^{k} Y_i < z\right) = P\left(S_k < z\right) = F_{S_k}(z),$$

(29.12)

where, the distributions $F_{S_k}(x)$ is the k-fold convolution of the distributions of the shock sizes Y_i. Note also that the term $P(N_t = k)$ is the probability of having exactly k shocks by time t:

$$P(N_t = k) = P\left(T_k < t\right) - P\left(T_{k+1} < t\right) = F_{T_k}(t) - F_{T_{k+1}}(t).$$

(29.13)

In this case, the distribution $F_{T_k}(t)$ is the k-fold convolution of the inter-arrival time ΔT_i; i.e, $F_{T_k} = F_{\Delta T_1} * F_{\Delta T_2} * \ldots * F_{\Delta T_k}$. Note that, the distribution of S_k (i.e., $F_{S_k}(x)$) and T_k (i.e., $F_{T_k}(t)$) could be written as a two-fold convolution as follows:

$$F_{S_k}(y) = \int_0^{\infty} F_{S_{k-1}}(y-x) dF_{Y_k}(x)$$

(29.14)

$$F_{T_k}(t) = \int_0^{\infty} F_{T_{k-1}}(t-\tau) dF_{\Delta T_k}(\tau).$$

(29.15)

The analytical solution of these convolutions only exists for some special distributions such as the normal, exponential, gamma, or Phase-Type (van der Weide & Pandey 2011; Iervolino et al. 2013; Riascos-Ochoa et al. 2014). However, even in these cases, in order to compute the reliability it is necessary the evaluation of an infinite number of convolutions; which are necessary to solve the infinite series in Equation (29.11). This is a very expensive numerical and computational task.

In summary, two main problems arise in the previous shock-based models:

1. find the appropriate probabilistic model for the random variables: inter-arrival times ΔT_i and shock sizes Y_i; and
2. numerically compute the reliability function $R(t,z)$, from which the rest of reliability quantities are deduced.

560

The first problem can be addressed by identifying and modeling the physical phenomena. This information combined with field data can be used to fit probabilistic models; although in general, in many engineered systems (e.g., large civil infrastructure systems) there is a significant lack of dependable deterioration data. The second problem is the complexity associated with the numerical computations of the distributions of the variables S_k and T_k, i.e., the convolutions in Equations (29.14) and (29.15).

The compound Poisson process (CPP)

Let's consider that shock sizes Y_i and inter-arrival times ΔT_i are *iid* (independent and identically distributed) and exponentially distributed with rate λ. Therefore, the arrival of shocks constitutes a Poisson Process (PP) and the shock-based deterioration process D_t, as described in Equation (29.8), forms a Compound Poisson Process (CPP). In this case, the term $P(N_t = k)$ in (29.11) takes the form:

$$P(N_t = k) = e^{-\lambda t} \frac{(\lambda t)^k}{k!}. \tag{29.16}$$

and in case where the shock's arrival process follows a Non-Homogeneous Poisson Process (NHPP),

$$P(N_t = k) = e^{-\Lambda(t)} \frac{\Lambda(t)^k}{k!}, \tag{29.17}$$

with $\lambda(t)$ the time-dependent rate and $\Lambda(t)$ the *mean value function* defined by:

$$\Lambda(t) = \int_0^t \lambda(s)ds. \tag{29.18}$$

The resulting process with *iid* shock sizes, and shock arrivals that follow a NHPP, is called in this chapter the *Non-Homogeneous Compound Poisson Process* (NHCPP). It has been applied to model aftershock sequences (Iervolino et al. 2013; Utsu et al. 1995) and crack growth (Bogdanoff & Kozin 1985), among others. Note that with the expressions derived for $P(N_t = k)$ in Equations (29.16) or (29.17), the problem of computing the convolutions in Equation (29.15) is resolved. However, the convolutions required to calculate the distribution of the cumulated damage F_{S_k}, in Equation (29.14), are still a problem. Both CPP and NHCPP models will be further investigated as part of the Lévy deterioration models proposed in this chapter in Section 29.6.

The renewal process (RP) shock model

This model assumes that inter-arrival times ΔT_i and shock sizes Y_i are *iid* but not necessarily exponentially distributed. In other words, $\{\Delta T_i\}$ and $\{Y_i\}$ constitute renewal a processes (Sánchez-Silva & Klutke 2016). The same difficulty arises in this model with respect to the convolutions.

The Phase-type (PH) shock model

This model, which was proposed by Riascos-Ochoa et al. (2014), assumes that inter-arrival times ΔT_i and shock sizes Y_i are distributed Phase-type (PH). In this case both ΔT_i and

Y_i are not necessarily *iid*; therefore, this model is more general than the RP shock model (Section 29.3.2). The advantage of the PH shock model is that it does not require the computation of convolutions because PH distributions are closed under convolution. Moreover, closed-form expressions for the reliability function (Equation 29.7) and the lifetime density are available, and are relatively easy to compute. Finally, another advantage of PH distributions is that they are dense in the set of distributions with positive support (Latouche & Ramaswami 1999; Neuts & Meier 1981; Neuts 1981). Therefore, it is possible to find PH distributions as close as desired to any positive distribution or to empirical data. For this purpose a wide set of fitting algorithms have been proposed (Osogami & Harchol-Balter 2003; Bobbio et al. 2005; Kharoufeh et al. 2010; Telek & Heindl 2002; Thummler et al. 2006).

29.4 Models for progressive deterioration

Progressive deterioration is the (almost) continuous reduction of the system's condition V_t over time. This is the case of wear-out, fatigue, corrosion, or deterioration of pavements (Sánchez-Silva et al. 2011; Iervolino et al. 2013). This section presents the main stochastic processes used for modeling progressive deterioration; these are: the *random variable* (RV) model, the *gamma process* (GP) and the *inverse Gaussian processes* (IGP). A model that is frequently used is the *Gaussian process*, despite the fact that it does not have *monotone increasing sample paths*; for that reason, it is not presented and discussed in this chapter.

At first sight, computing the reliability using these models is relatively easier compared with shock-based models. However, if different progressive deterioration models occur simultaneously and must be combined into a single progressive model, the complexity of the solution increases substantially. For example, this is the case of the sum of a deterministic process and a GP or IGP, or the sum of a GP and an IGP. For these cases the probabilistic description becomes extremely complicated because convolutions are involved again.

29.4.1 Random variable (RV) model

A popular approach for progressive deterioration assumes that the functional form of deterioration is known, but the parameters are uncertain (i.e., random); these parameters may represent, for example, physical properties of the process such as material characteristics, geometry, environmental conditions, etc. These models are known in the literature as random variable (RV) models, and their solution conveys to a parameter estimation problem or to an statistical regression to obtain the probability distributions of these parameters.

There are two basic approaches to these models. The first consists on defining a deterministic function that depends on time and some other set of random parameters **p** (*random vector parameter*) to be defined. Thus, the deterioration P_t of such a RV models is given by:

$$P_t = \Upsilon_{\mathbf{p}}(t). \tag{29.19}$$

The function $\Upsilon_{\mathbf{p}}(t)$ is increasing in t, and may take any functional form depending on the physics of the problem. It is important to notice that RV models are not strictly stochastic processes. As pointed out by Pandey and van Noortwijk (Pandey et al. 2009) the sample paths of these RV models are curves whose future behavior can be predicted beforehand with a single inspection at any time. That is, the temporal variability of these models is lost.

The second modeling alternative is to define the process in terms of a deterioration rate $\delta_p(t)$ for $t \geq 0$. Thus, the deterioration process at time t can be computed as:

$$P_t = \int_0^t \delta_p(t) d\tau. \tag{29.20}$$

Since these two models do not fully capture the temporal variability, the stochastic process approach provides a better representation of the uncertain nature of these deterioration process. Two models are of particular importance: the *gamma* process and the *inverse gaussian* process; they will be presented in the following sections.

29.4.2 The gamma process

The gamma process has been successfully used in many engineering disciplines as a model for deterioration; specially after the works of Abdel-Hammed (1975), Çinlar (1977, 1980) and Dykstra et al. (1981); and more recently, van Noortwijk in e.g. van Noortwijk (2009), among others (Nicolai et al. 2007; Lawless & Crowder 2004; Pandey et al. 2009).

A process process $\mathcal{Z} = \{\mathcal{Z}_t\}_{t \geq 0}$ is said to be a non-stationary gamma process (GP) with shape function $\Lambda(t) > 0$ and scale parameter $\beta > 0$ – denoted as $\Gamma(\Lambda(t), \beta)$ (van Noortwijk 2009) –, if:

1. $\mathcal{Z}_0 = 0$ with probability one.
2. $\mathcal{Z}_t$ has independent increments.
3. $\mathcal{Z}_\tau - \mathcal{Z}_t \sim Ga(\Lambda(\tau) - \Lambda(t), \beta)$ for all $\tau > t \geq 0$, with Ga the gamma distribution.

These conditions describe the probability density of a GP:

$$P(\mathcal{Z}_t \in dx) = \frac{\beta^{\Lambda(t)}}{\Gamma(\Lambda(t))} x^{\Lambda(t)-1} \exp(-\beta x) dx, \quad x \geq 0, \tag{29.21}$$

where $\Gamma(a) = \int_0^\infty z^{a-1} e^{-z} dz$ is the gamma function for $a > 0$. The mean $\mathbb{E}[\mathcal{Z}_t]$, second central moment (variance) $\mu_{2,t}$, and third central moment $\mu_{3,t}$ of a GP are given by:

$$\mathbb{E}[\mathcal{Z}_t] = \frac{\Lambda(t)}{\beta}, \qquad \mu_{2,t} = \frac{\Lambda(t)}{\beta^2}, \qquad \mu_{3,t} = \frac{2\Lambda(t)}{\beta^2}. \tag{29.22}$$

The reliability function $R(t, z)$ is obtained by integrating Equation (29.21); i.e.,

$$R(t, z) = 1 - \int_z^\infty P(\mathcal{Z}_t \in dx) = 1 - \frac{\Gamma(\Lambda(t), \beta z)}{\Gamma(\Lambda(t))}, \tag{29.23}$$

where $\Gamma(a, x) = \int_x^\infty z^{a-1} e^{-z} dz$ is the incomplete gamma function for $x \geq 0$ and $a > 0$. Note that the lifetime distribution has an increasing failure rate as long as $\Lambda'(t) > 0$. The amenability of the gamma process isthat it accounts for temporal variability and also can resemble any functional form for its deterioration trend $\mathbb{E}[P_t]$ by varying the shape function $\Lambda(t)$. Moreover, Equation (29.23) provides an easy-to-evaluate expression for the reliability function. Figure 29.3 shows

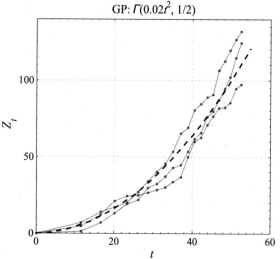

Figure 29.3 Sample paths of a gamma process $\Gamma(0.02t^2, 1/2)$.

three sample paths of a GP with shape function $\Lambda(t) = 0.02t^2$ and scale parameter $\beta = 1/2$. The mean of this process is $\mathbb{E}[Z_t] = 0.5t$.

29.4.3 The inverse Gaussian process

Recently, the inverse Gaussian process (IGP) has gained attention as an alternative model due to its closed-form expressions for the reliability quantities (as with the GP) (Wang & Xu 2010; Ye & Chen 2014; Zhang et al. 2013). The usual definition of an IGP $Z = \{Z_t\}_{t \geq 0}$ with mean function $\Lambda(t)$ and scale parameter η – denoted IGP($\Lambda(t), \eta$) – is:

1. $Z_0 = 0$ a.s.
2. The increments of Z_t are independent
3. The increments are distributed Inverse Gaussian: $Z_\tau - Z_t \sim IG(\Lambda(\tau) - \Lambda(t), \eta(\Lambda(\tau) - \Lambda(t))^2)$ for all t, τ such that $0 < t \leq \tau$.

Recall that the density of an Inverse Gaussian distribution $IG(\mu, \theta)$ with mean μ and variance μ^3 / θ is defined by:

$$f_{IG}(x; \mu, \theta) = \sqrt{\frac{\theta}{2\pi x^3}} \exp\left(-\frac{\theta(x - \mu)^2}{2\mu^2 x}\right), \quad x \geq 0. \tag{29.24}$$

which provides an easy-to-evaluate formula for the reliability function $R(t, z)$. The mean $\mathbb{E}[Z_t]$, second central moment (variance) $\mu_{2,t}$, and third central moment $\mu_{3,t}$ of an IGP are given by:

$$\mathbb{E}[Z_t] = \Lambda(t), \quad \mu_{2,t} = \frac{\Lambda(t)}{\eta}, \quad \mu_{3,t} = \frac{3\Lambda(t)}{\eta^2}. \tag{29.25}$$

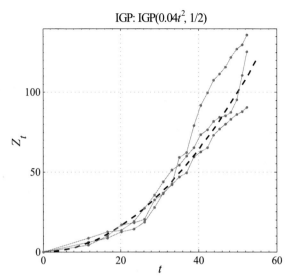

Figure 29.4 Sample paths of an inverse Gaussian process IGP $(0.04t^2, 1/2)$.

Figure 29.4 shows three sample paths of an IGP($0.04t^2, 1/2$). Note that the mean of this process is also $\mathbb{E}[\mathcal{Z}_t] = 0.5t$, as for the GP in Figure 29.3.

29.5 Combined deterioration models

A combined deterioration process accounts for the effect of both shock-based and progressive deterioration. Under the assumption that these two mechanisms are independent, total deterioration can be written as:

$$D_t = \sum_{i=1}^{N_t} Y_i + P_t. \tag{29.26}$$

Several proposals to solve this problem have been made under specific restrictions. For example, in Sánchez-Silva et al. 2010, 2011) the cumulative shock model has arbitrary distributions for inter-arrival times and shock's sizes, and progressive deterioration is a deterministic function $\Upsilon(t)$. In Klutke and Yang (2002a) a more tractable expression for the mean of the lifetime L is obtained, considering a linear deterministic model for P_t and a cumulative shock model with occurrences as a PP and shock sizes distributed arbitrarily. In Kumar et al. (2015) a similar model is proposed with linear progressive deterioration and shocks as CPP, but considering dependence between the capacity thresholds and shocks. Finally, in Iervolino et al. (2013), deterioration is a combination of a gamma process and a shock-based model with occurrences following a PP and shock magnitudes distributed gamma (and exponential as an special case). Easy-to-evaluate solutions were obtained for the probability of failure (and consequently, the reliability function). In summary, in most cases, in this formulation the mathematical expression for the reliability quantities cannot be solved numerically as convolutions and multiple improper integrals are involved. In fact, there are no references that account for combinations of a GP and a CPP with shock sizes different of gamma, a GP with any NHCPP, or the combination of an IGP with any CPP or NHCPP. The difficulties arise in the convolutions present in their reliability estimation.

The next section presents a recent approach to overcome these difficulties, by modeling deterioration as a general additive process.

29.6 Modeling deterioration using additive processes

29.6.1 Additive processes and subordinators

Consider a filtered probability space $(\Omega, \mathcal{F}, \mathbb{F}, \mathrm{P})$; and adapted process $X = \{X_t\}_{t \geq 0}$ that takes values on $\mathbb{R}$, with $X_0 = 0$ almost surely (a.s.), and with right-continuous sample paths and left limits. the process X is an *additive process* if (Abdel-Hameed, 2014; Sato, 1999; Cont & Tankov 2004):

1. X has increments independent of the past; that is, $X_t - X_s$ is s-independent of $\mathcal{F}_s$, for all s, t such that $0 \leq s < t < \infty$;
2. X is continuous in probability; that is, $\lim_{t \to s} \mathrm{P}(X_t \in \cdot) = \mathrm{P}(X_s \in \cdot)$.

Note that an additive process is not necessarily stationary, i.e., the distribution of $X_t - X_s$ may not be equal to the distribution of X_{t-s}, and can depend on both s and t (Sato 1999; Cont & Tankov 2004). When the process is stationary it is called a *Lévy process*. Besides, if the additive process X has increasing sample paths (i.e., X_t is increasing as a function of t a.s.), it is called an *additive subordinator*, and if it is increasing and stationary it is a *subordinator*.

29.6.2 Modeling deterioration as an additive process

A deterioration process, D_t, can be modeled as an additive process X if the following conditions are satisfied:

1. The deterioration process D_t has independent increments with monotone increasing sample paths a.s.
2. The mean of D_t is finite for all $0 \leq t < \infty$.
3. The deterioration that results from multiple sources (mechanisms) can be expressed as the sum of the constitutive additive deterioration processes, as long as they are mutually independent.

Condition (1) comes from the assumption of no maintenance, and makes D_t an *additive subordinator*; condition (2) contains the physical requirement of finite deterioration (in the mean) for t finite; and condition (3) guarantees that deterioration from multiple sources is still an additive process.

29.6.3 Characteristic function, characteristic exponent, and moments

For a random variable X, its characteristic function is defined as:

$$\phi_X = \mathbb{E}[e^{i\omega X}], \quad \omega \in \mathbb{R}. \tag{29.27}$$

The characteristic function of an additive deterioration process D_t, i.e., $\phi_{D_t}(\omega)$, plays a funda-mental role in the reliability evaluation. If D_t is an additive subordinator, $\phi_{D_t}(\omega)$ takes a special form (Sato 1999; Cont & Tankov 2004):

$$\phi_{D_t}(\omega) = e^{-\Psi_{D_t}(\omega)}, \tag{29.28}$$

where

$$\Psi_{D_t}(\omega) = \int_{(0,\infty)} (1 - e^{i\omega x}) \Pi_t(dx) - i\Upsilon(t)\omega \tag{29.29}$$

is known as the *characteristic exponent* of D_t. The function $\Upsilon(t)$ is nonnegative and continuous, with $\Upsilon(0) = 0$; and Π_t is called the *Lévy measure* and determines the jumps ΔD of D_t.

Furthermore, the moments of D_t can be evaluated from its characteristic function by the well-known formula (Riascos-Ochoa et al. 2016; Durret 2010):

$$\mathbb{E}[D_t^n] = (-i)^n \phi_{D_t}^{(n)}(0), \tag{29.30}$$

where $\phi_{D_t}^{(n)}(0)$ denotes the nth derivative of $\phi_{D_t}(\omega)$ with respect to ω evaluated at $\omega = 0$. From Equations (29.28) and (29.30), the mean $\mathbb{E}[D_t]$ and n-central moments $\mu_n(t) = \mathbb{E}[(D_t - \mathbb{E}(D_t))^n]$ ($n = 2, 3$) of an additive process D_t, can be deduced:

$$\mathbb{E}[D_t] = i\,\Psi'_{D_t}(0), \qquad \mu_2(t) = \Psi_{D_t}^{(2)}(0), \qquad \mu_3(t) = -i\,\Psi_{D_t}^{(3)}(0). \tag{29.31}$$

29.6.4 Deterioration mechanisms in an additive process

Based on Equation (29.29), it can be shown that an additive deterioration process D_t can be expressed as:

$$D_t = \sum_{i=1}^{N_t} \Upsilon(T_i) + Z_t + \Upsilon(t). \tag{29.32}$$

The first term corresponds to the shock deterioration process, with N_t (i.e., the number of shock's by time t) described as a NHPP (or as a PP in the Lévy case); and $\Upsilon(T_i)$ the shock size at time T_i. Assuming independence between shock sizes and their occurrence times, and considering the particular case in which shock sizes are identically distributed, the first process becomes a NHCPP (or as a CPP in the Lévy case). This means that $\sum_{i=1}^{N_t} \Upsilon(T_i)$ is a pure-jump process characterized by a finite Lévy measure; i.e., finite number of jumps happen in any finite time-interval.

Progressive deterioration can be associated with the sum $P_t = Z_t + \Upsilon(t)$ in Equation (29.32). Thus, the process Z_t represents the random contribution, explicitly a pure-jump process with infinite Lévy measure; that is, infinite number of jumps happen in any finite time interval. This property is suitable to model the effect of progressive deterioration. Examples of this process are the GP and the IGP. Finally, the function $\Upsilon(t)$ is the deterministic contribution to deterior-ation (also known as the *drift* of the process).

Table 29.1 Characteristic exponent $\Psi_{D_t}(\omega)$ and mean $\mathbb{E}[D_t]$ for deterioration models as additive subordinators D_t. For shock-based models, $\Lambda(t)$ is the mean value function (Equation (29.18)), and ϕ_Y is the characteristic function of the shock size Y_i

Additive Deterioration Model:	$\Psi_{D_t}(\omega)$	$\mathbb{E}[D_t]$
Shock-based: S_t	$\Psi_{S_t}(\omega)$	$\mathbb{E}[S_t]$
NHCPP	$\Lambda(t)(1-\phi_Y(\omega))$	$\Lambda(t)\mathbb{E}[Y]$
Progressive: P_t	$\Psi_{P_t}(\omega)$	$\mathbb{E}[P_t]$
Deterministic: $\Upsilon(t)$	$-i\Upsilon(t)\omega$	$\Upsilon(t)$
Pure Jump: Z_t	$\Psi_{Z_t}(\omega)$	$\mathbb{E}[Z_t]$
GP: $GP(\Lambda(t),\beta)$	$\Lambda(t)\ln(1-i\omega/\beta)$	$\dfrac{\Lambda(t)}{\beta}$
IGP: $IGP(\Lambda(t),\eta)$	$\Lambda(t)\left[\sqrt{\eta^2-2i\eta\omega}-\eta\right]$	$\Lambda(t)$
General: $\Upsilon(t)+Z_t$	$-i\Upsilon(t)\omega+\Psi_{Z_t}(\omega)$	$\Upsilon(t)+\mathbb{E}[Z_t]$
Combined: K_t	$\Psi_{K_t}(\omega)$	$\mathbb{E}[K_t]$
General: $S_t+\Upsilon(t)+Z_t$	$\Psi_{S_t}(\omega)-i\Upsilon(t)\omega+\Psi_{Z_t}(\omega)$	$\mathbb{E}[S_t]+\Upsilon(t)+\mathbb{E}[Z_t]$
Multiple sources of deterioration:	$\Psi_{D_t}(\omega)$	$\mathbb{E}[D_t]$
$D_t^{\{1\}}+\ldots+D_t^{\{n\}}$	$\Psi_{D_t^{\{1\}}}(\omega)+\ldots+\Psi_{D_t^{\{n\}}}(\omega)$	$\mathbb{E}[D_t^{\{1\}}]+\ldots+\mathbb{E}[D_t^{\{n\}}]$

Therefore, a general additive subordinator (as given by Equation (29.32)) has the form of a combined deterioration model (Equation (29.26)). Moreover, as a general case, it is also possible to account for multiple sources of deterioration whose process is given by the independent sum of constitutive processes of the form given by Equation (29.32). Tables 29.1 and 29.2 show the characteristic exponent of several examples of additive deterioration models, along with the expressions of their mean, second and third central moments. Because of the independence property, the characteristic exponents, mean and central moments of combined and multiple sources of deterioration are given by the sum of the constitutive exponents and moments.

To illustrate the previous point, let us compute the characteristic exponent of a deterioration process D_t given by the sum of two independent additive deterioration processes $D_t^{\{1\}}$ and $D_t^{\{2\}}$. By Equation (29.27):

$$\phi_{D_t}=\mathbb{E}\left[e^{i\omega D_t}\right]=\mathbb{E}\left[e^{i\omega\left(D_t^{\{1\}}+D_t^{\{2\}}\right)}\right]=\mathbb{E}\left[e^{i\omega D_t^{\{1\}}}\cdot e^{i\omega D_t^{\{2\}}}\right]. \tag{29.33}$$

By independence the following holds:

$$\phi_{D_t}=\mathbb{E}\left[e^{i\omega D_t^{\{1\}}}\right]\cdot\mathbb{E}\left[e^{i\omega D_t^{\{2\}}}\right]=e^{-\Psi_{D_t^{\{1\}}}(\omega)}\cdot e^{-\Psi_{D_t^{\{2\}}}(\omega)}=e^{-\left(\Psi_{D_t^{\{1\}}}(\omega)+\Psi_{D_t^{\{2\}}}(\omega)\right)}, \tag{29.34}$$

Table 29.2 Central moments $\mu_{n,D}(t)$, $n = 2,3$ for several additive deterioration models D_t

Additive Deterioration Model:	$\mu_{n,D}(t)$
Shock-based: S_t	$\mu_{n,S}(t)$
NHCPP	$\Lambda(t)\mathbb{E}[\Upsilon^n]$
Progressive: P_t	$\mu_{n,P}(t)$
Deterministic: $\Upsilon(t)$	0
Pure Jump: $\mathcal{Z}_t$	$\mu_{n,\mathcal{Z}}(t)$
GP: GP$(\Lambda(t), \beta)$	$(n-1)\dfrac{\Lambda(t)}{\beta^n}$
IGP: IGP$(\Lambda(t), \eta)$	$n!\dfrac{\Lambda(t)}{2\eta^{n-1}}$
General: $\Upsilon(t) + \mathcal{Z}_t$	$\mu_{n,\mathcal{Z}}(t)$
Combined: K_t	$\mu_{n,K}(t)$
General: $S_t + \Upsilon(t) + \mathcal{Z}_t$	$\mu_{n,S}(t) + \mu_{n,\mathcal{Z}}(t)$
Multiple sources of deterioration:	$\mu_{n,D}(t)$
$D_t^{\{1\}} + \ldots + D_t^{\{n\}}$	$\mu_{n,D^{\{1\}}}(t) + \cdots + \mu_{n,D^{\{n\}}}(t)$

therefore, the characteristic exponent $\Psi_{D_t}(\omega)$ associated to D_t is given by the sum of the characteristic exponents of the constitutive processes:

$$\Psi_{D_t}(\omega) = \Psi_{D_t^{\{1\}}}(\omega) + \Psi_{D_t^{\{2\}}}(\omega). \tag{29.35}$$

It is easily deduced from Equations (29.31) and (29.35) that the mean, second and third central moments of D_t are given by the sum of the respective moments of $D_t^{\{1\}}$ and $D_t^{\{2\}}$.

29.7 Reliability estimation and sample paths simulation of additive deterioration processes

The main objective of this chapter is to obtain the reliability function $R(t,z)$ and lifetime density $f(t,z)$ of an arbitrary additive deterioration process. This requires the use of numerical methods; in particular the inversion formula (Gil-Pelaez 1951), which is used to compute $R(t,z)$ in terms of the characteristic function $\phi_{D_t}(\omega) = e^{-\Psi_{D_t}(\omega)}$ of the process. Thus, to obtain a numerical approximation in terms of an easy-to-evaluate sum involving complex numbers, rules of discretization and truncation are necessary (Section 29.7.1). From the distribution of D_t ($P(D_t \leq z) = R(t,z)$) is possible to simulate sample paths of general additive subordinators, with an algorithm presented in Section 29.7.2.

29.7.1 Inversion formula and numerical approximations

For notational simplicity in this section the characteristic exponent of D_t will be denoted as Ψ_t. The probability distribution of D_t, $P(D_t \leq z)$, (i.e., reliability function $R(t,z)$; Equation (29.7)) can be obtained from its characteristic function $\phi_{D_t}(\omega)$ via the inversion formula (Gil-Pelaez 1951; Shephard 1991); this is,

$$R(t,z) = \mathrm{P}(D_t \leq z) = \frac{1}{2} - \frac{1}{2\pi i} \int_{-\infty}^{\infty} \frac{e^{-i\omega z}}{\omega} e^{-\Psi_t(\omega)} d\omega. \tag{29.36}$$

Also, the density of the lifetime can be computed as:

$$f(t,z) = -\frac{1}{2\pi i} \int_{-\infty}^{\infty} \frac{e^{-i\omega z}}{\omega} \left(\frac{d}{dt} \Psi_t(\omega) \right) e^{-\Psi_t(\omega)} d\omega. \tag{29.37}$$

The improper integrals presented in Equations (29.36) and (29.37) can be approximated to infinite sums by discretizing the domain. Explicitly, evaluate the integrand at discrete points $\omega_m = (m-1/2)h$, for $-\infty < m < \infty$ with h the discretization step size. Then, the infinite sum is truncated outside the range $[-M, M]$, with $M > 0$. The selection of the truncation level M depends on the tail behavior of the integrands. For progressive processes such as the GP and the IGP there is absolute convergence to 0 as $\omega \to \pm\infty$. However, for shock-based processes there is no convergence which makes the distribution $\mathrm{P}(D_t \leq z)$ discontinuous. In the discontinuity points the truncation produces the so-called Gibbs phenomenon, consisting in oscillations near these points (Waller et al., 1995). The truncation level M must be selected empirically to reduce this effect. In general, a value of $M = 10^4$ or greater lead to accurate results (Riascos-Ochoa et al. 2016; Waller et al. 1995; Feng & Lin 2013). Then the approximation to the reliability and the lifetime density can be computed as:

$$R(t,z) \approx R(t,z;h,M) \tag{29.38}$$

$$:= \frac{1}{2} - \frac{1}{2\pi i} \sum_{m=-M}^{M} \frac{e^{-iz(m-1/2)h}}{(m-1/2)} e^{-\Psi_t((m-1/2)h)}$$

$$f(t,z) \approx f(t,z;h,M) \tag{29.39}$$

$$:= -\frac{1}{2\pi i} \sum_{m=-M}^{M} \frac{e^{-iz(m-1/2)h}}{(m-1/2)} \left(\frac{d}{dt} \Psi_t((m-1/2)h) \right) e^{-\Psi_t((m-1/2)h)}.$$

For the numerical solution, the discretization step size can be selected as follows:

$$h = h(z,t) = \frac{1}{20} \frac{2\pi}{z + \mathbb{E}[D_t]}, \tag{29.40}$$

which takes into account the main variations of the integrands in (29.38) and (29.39) (Riascos-Ochoa et al. 2016).

From the numerical approximations presented in Equations (29.38) and (29.39) for the distribution $\mathrm{P}(D_t \leq z)$ and lifetime density $f(t,z)$, can be easily obtained. Furthermore, these approximations can be used to construct sample paths and to obtain the lifetime moments; more details can be found in Riascos-Ochoa et al. (2016).

29.7.2 Simulation of sample paths

From the numerically computed distribution of deterioration $P(D_t \le z)$ (Equation 29.36), it is possible to simulate sample paths of additive subordinators. In Riascos-Ochoa et al. (2016) an algorithm is presented to simulate sample paths of subordinators (increasing Lévy processes), but for the more general case of additive deterioration processes the algorithm changes slightly. Instead of dividing the time range, we divide the deterioration range in appropriate equally spaced intervals and find the corresponding set of times. This is done to avoid small or large values of deterioration increments for numerical efficiency. The complete procedure is described as follows:

1. Set N the number of deterioration data points to be simulated.
2. Select a maximum value z of the expected total deterioration and set $t_0 = 0$. Define $\Delta \bar{D} = z / N$.
3. Find the set of times $\{t_n\}_{n=1,\ldots,N}$ such that the defined time intervals have mean deterioration equal to $\Delta \bar{D}$. That is, $\mathbb{E}[D_{t_n}] - \mathbb{E}[D_{t_{n-1}}] = \Delta \bar{D} = z / N$, for $n = 1,\ldots,N$. As $\mathbb{E}[D_{t_0}] = 0$ we have $\mathbb{E}[D_{t_n}] = nz / N$, which is solved for t_n.
4. Define ΔD_n as the deterioration increment in the nth time interval $[t_{n-1}, t_n)$. Its characteristic exponent is $\Psi_{t_{n-1},t_n}(\omega) = \Psi_{t_n}(\omega) - \Psi_{t_{n-1}}(\omega)$.
5. For each time interval define N_x equally spaced values x_i at which the CDF of ΔD_n will be evaluated, ranging from $x_1 = 0$ to $x_{N_x} = \Delta \bar{D} + 6\sqrt{\mu_2(t_{n-1},t_n)}$, where $\mu_2(t_{n-1},t_n)$ is the second central moment (variance) of ΔD_n. This value of x_{N_x} is set to assure the complete coverage of the range of the CDF, i.e., from 0 to 1. Good results are obtained with $N_x = 200$.
6. Calculate the CDF of ΔD_n, given by $P(\Delta D_n < x_i)$ for each x_i, with Equation (29.38) using $\Psi_{t_{n-1},t_n}(\omega)$ as the characteristic exponent.
7. Apply an inverse transform sampling from the CDF of ΔD_n to generate the nth random increment $\Delta \hat{D}_n$.
8. The sample path $\{D_{t_n}\}_{n=1,\ldots,N}$ is obtained by summing the random increments generated for each time interval: $\hat{D}_{t_n} = \sum_{i=1}^n \Delta \hat{D}_i$.

29.8 Illustrative examples

This section presents some examples of additive deterioration processes for the three deterioration cases presented in Section 29.2.3. In all cases, the mean and moments are computed, simulation is used to evaluate sample paths, and the reliability function is obtained.

29.8.1 Shock-based additive deterioration

Consider a system subjected to two shock-based deterioration processes $S_t^{\{1\}}$ and $S_t^{\{2\}}$ as described in Section 29.6.4. The shock sizes, Y_i, for both processes are uniformly distributed within the range $[a,b] = [15,25]$ (in suitable units), for all $t \ge 0$. That is, $Y_i \sim U(a,b)$ with mean $\mathbb{E}[Y] = 20$ and characteristic function:

$$\phi_Y(\omega) = \frac{e^{i\omega b} - e^{i\omega a}}{i\omega(b-a)},$$

(29.41)

with $a = 15$, $b = 25$.

The shock's arrival rates for each process are given by:

$$\lambda_1(t) = \frac{6}{200}, \quad \lambda_2(t) = \frac{12}{200^2}\, t. \tag{29.42}$$

Note that while $S_t^{\{1\}}$ is a CPP, because its constant arrival rate, the process $S_t^{\{2\}}$ is a strictly NHCPP with increasing (linear) rate. The mean value functions $\Lambda_j(t) = \int_0^t \lambda_j(s)ds; \; j = 1, 2,$ for the shock's arrival processes are:

$$\Lambda_1(t) = \frac{6}{200}\, t, \quad \Lambda_2(t) = \frac{6}{200^2}\, t^2. \tag{29.43}$$

Then, according to Table 29.1, the expected value $\mathbb{E}\left[S_t^{\{j\}}\right] = \Lambda_j(t)\, \mathbb{E}[Y]; \; j = 1, 2,$ of each deterioration process are:

$$\mathbb{E}\left[S_t^{\{1\}}\right] = 20\frac{6}{200}\, t, \quad \mathbb{E}\left[S_t^{\{2\}}\right] = 20\frac{6}{200^2}\, t^2, \tag{29.44}$$

where it is clear the linear nature of the expected value of $S^{\{1\}}$ and the nonlinear (quadratic) nature of $S^{\{2\}}$. Notice also that $\mathbb{E}\left[S_{200}^{\{j\}}\right] = 120$ for both.

According to Table 29.1, the characteristic exponents for $S_t^{\{1\}}$ and $S_t^{\{2\}}$ are:

$$\Psi_{S_t^{\{1\}}}(\omega) = \Lambda_1(t)\left(1 - \phi_Y(\omega)\right)$$

$$= \frac{6}{200}t\left(1 - \frac{e^{25i\omega} - e^{15i\omega}}{10 i\omega}\right) = 0.03t\left(1 + i\frac{e^{25i\omega} - e^{15i\omega}}{10\omega}\right) \tag{29.45}$$

$$\Psi_{S_t^{\{2\}}}(\omega) = \Lambda_2(t)\left(1 - \phi_Y(\omega)\right)$$

$$= \frac{6}{200^2}t^2\left(1 - \frac{e^{25i\omega} - e^{15i\omega}}{10 i\omega}\right) = 0.00015t^2\left(1 + i\frac{e^{25i\omega} - e^{15i\omega}}{10\omega}\right). \tag{29.46}$$

The reliability function $R(t, z)$ and lifetime density $f(t, z)$ of both processes, for a failure threshold of $z = 100$, are shown in Figures 29.5 and 29.6. These are obtained by their numerical approximations in Equations (29.38) and (29.39) assuming the truncation level $M = 10^4$, with $\Psi_t(\omega) = \Psi_t^{S^{\{j\}}}(\omega)$, in either Equation (29.45) or (29.46); and with the discretization step size from Equation (29.40):

$$h_{S_1}(t) = \frac{1}{20}\frac{2\pi}{z + \mathbb{E}[D_t]} = \frac{1}{20}\frac{2\pi}{100 + 20\frac{6}{200}t} = 0.05 \cdot \frac{2\pi}{100 + 0.6t} \tag{29.47}$$

$$h_{S_2}(t) = \frac{1}{20}\frac{2\pi}{100 + 20\frac{6}{200^2}t^2} = 0.05 \cdot \frac{2\pi}{100 + 0.003t^2} \tag{29.48}$$

We also apply the algorithm in Section 29.7.2 to generate four sample paths for each process (Figure 29.7). Note that the deterioration paths are distributed around their theoretical mean.

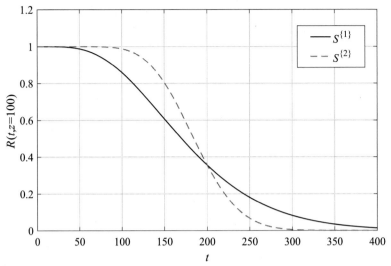

Figure 29.5 Reliability function of the additive shock-based models , $j = 1,2$, with shock sizes $Y_i \sim U(15,25)$ and shock's arrival rates $\lambda_1(t)$ and $\lambda_2(t)$ given in (29.42).

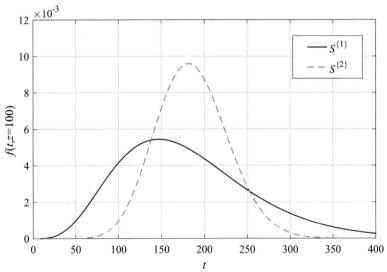

Figure 29.6 Lifetime density of the additive shock-based models $S^{\{j\}}$, $j = 1,2$, with shock sizes $Y_i \sim U(15,25)$ and shock's arrival rates $\lambda_1(t)$ and $\lambda_2(t)$ given in (29.42).

The process $S^{\{1\}}$ has mean lifetime $\mathbb{E}[L] = 179$ days and coefficient of variation of lifetime equal to 0.43, while $S^{\{2\}}$ has $\mathbb{E}[L] = 186$ days and coefficient of variation of 0.22. The smaller variation of $S^{\{2\}}$ can be explained by the fact that the sample paths of $S^{\{2\}}$ grow quadratically, with lower increments near $t = 0$ and faster increments after around $t = 100$. This produces an almost certain failure after $t = 100$, which is also evident in the lifetime density (distribution more concentrated around the mean).

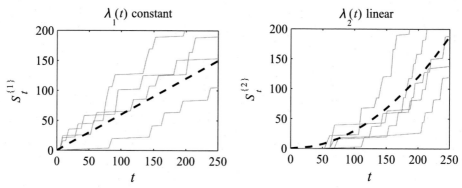

Figure 29.7 Paths of the additive shock-based models $S^{\{j\}}$, $j=1,2$, with shock sizes $Y_i \sim U(15,25)$ and rates $\lambda_1(t)$ and $\lambda_2(t)$ given in (29.42).

29.8.2 Combined additive deterioration

Consider the shock-based process $S^{\{2\}}$ defined Section 29.8.1. The purpose of this example is to combine this process with two progressive deterioration processes $P^{\{j\}}$, $j=1,2$ to obtain a new process $K^{\{j\}}$; i.e.,

$$K^{\{j\}} = S^{\{2\}} + P^{\{j\}}. \tag{29.49}$$

The characterization of every progressive deterioration process $P^{\{j\}}$ is shown in Table 29.3. The parameters that describe these processes were selected to have the same mean deterioration for all $t \geq 0$, i.e., $\mathbb{E}[P_t^{\{j\}}] = 0.5t$; and the same coefficient of variation at time $t = 100$, i.e., $cov_{100}^{\{j\}} = \sqrt{\mu_{2,P^{\{j\}}}(100)} \, / \, \mathbb{E}[P_{100}^{\{j\}}] = 1$.

The characteristic exponent of the first combined process (i.e., $K^{\{1\}} = S^{\{2\}} + P^{\{1\}}$) can be computed as:

$$\Psi_{K^{\{1\}}} = \Psi_{S_t^{\{2\}}}(\omega) + \Psi_{P_t^{\{1\}}}(\omega)$$

$$= \Lambda_2(t)\left(1 - \phi_Y(\omega)\right) + \lambda_1 t \ln\left(1 - \frac{i\omega}{\beta}\right)$$

$$= \Lambda_2(t)\left(1 - \frac{e^{i\omega b} - e^{i\omega a}}{i\omega(b-a)}\right) + \lambda_1 t \ln\left(1 - \frac{i\omega}{\beta}\right) \tag{29.50}$$

$$= \frac{6}{200^2}t^2\left(1 - \frac{e^{25i\omega} - e^{15i\omega}}{10i\omega}\right) + 0.01t \ln\left(1 - \frac{i\omega}{0.02}\right) \tag{29.51}$$

$$= 0.00015t^2\left(1 + i\frac{e^{25i\omega} - e^{15i\omega}}{10\omega}\right) + 0.01t \ln\left(1 - 50i\omega\right) \tag{29.52}$$

and for the second process $K^{\{2\}} = S^{\{2\}} + P^{\{2\}}$:

Table 29.3 Progressive additive deterioration models $P^{\{j\}}$

Progressive Model	Characteristic exponent $\Psi_{P_t^{\{j\}}}(\omega)$	Parameters
$P^{\{1\}}$: GP$(\lambda_1 t, \beta)$	$\lambda_1 t \ln\left(1 - \dfrac{i\omega}{\beta}\right)$	$\lambda_1 = 0.01, \ \beta = 0.02$
$P^{\{2\}}$: IGP$(\lambda_2 t, \eta)$	$\lambda_2 t\left[\sqrt{\eta^2 - 2i\eta\omega} - \eta\right]$	$\lambda_2 = 0.5, \ \eta = 0.02$

Table 29.4 Combined additive deterioration models $K^{\{j\}}$, with their characteristic functions, mean and second and third central moments

Combined Model	Characteristic exponent $\Psi_{K_t^{\{j\}}}(\omega)$	Expected value $\mathbb{E}\left[K_t^{\{j\}}\right]$	2nd moment of the combined process $\mu_{2,K^{\{j\}}}(t)$	3rd moment of the combined process $\mu_{3,K^{\{j\}}}(t)$
$K^{\{1\}}$	$\Psi_{S_t^{\{2\}}}(\omega) + \Psi_{P_t^{\{1\}}}(\omega)$	$0.003t^2 + 0.5t$	$0.06125t^2 + 25t$	$1.275t^2 + 2500t$
$K^{\{2\}}$	$\Psi_{S_t^{\{2\}}}(\omega) + \Psi_{P_t^{\{2\}}}(\omega)$	$0.003t^2 + 0.5t$	$0.06125t^2 + 25t$	$1.275t^2 + 3750t$

$$\Psi_{K_t^2} = \Lambda_2(t)\left(1 - \frac{e^{i\omega(b)} - e^{i\omega(a)}}{i\omega(b-a)}\right) + \lambda_2 t\left[\sqrt{\eta^2 - 2i\eta\omega} - \eta\right] \tag{29.53}$$

$$= \frac{6}{200^2}t^2\left(1 - \frac{e^{25i\omega} - e^{15i\omega}}{10i\omega}\right) + 0.5t\left[\sqrt{0.02^2 - 2\cdot 0.02 i\omega} - 0.02\right] \tag{29.54}$$

$$= 0.00015t^2\left(1 + i\frac{e^{25i\omega} - e^{15i\omega}}{10\omega}\right) + 0.5t\left[\sqrt{0.02^2 - 0.04i\omega} - 0.02\right] \tag{29.55}$$

and are also shown in Table 29.4. The table also presents the mean, second and third central moments of the combined processes $K^{\{j\}}$; $j = 1, 2$. For example, the expected value of the two process can be computed simply as:

$$\mathbb{E}[K^{\{1\}}] = \mathbb{E}[S^{\{2\}}] + \mathbb{E}[P^{\{1\}}] = \Lambda_1(t)\mathbb{E}[Y] + 0.5t = 20\frac{6}{200^2}t^2 + 0.5t = 0.003t^2 + 0.5t \tag{29.56}$$

$$\mathbb{E}[K^{\{2\}}] = \mathbb{E}[S^{\{2\}}] + \mathbb{E}[P^{\{2\}}] = 20\frac{6}{200^2}t^2 + 0.5t = 0.003t^2 + 0.5t. \tag{29.57}$$

The reliability function and lifetime densities for both combined processes $K^{\{j\}}$; $j = 1, 2$, with failure threshold $z = 100$, are shown in Figures 29.8 and 29.9. Note that the curves of

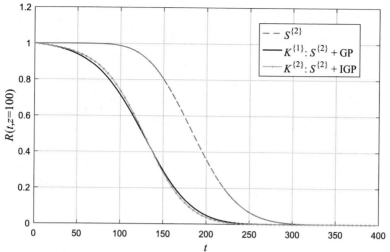

Figure 29.8 Reliability function for the combined models $K^{\{j\}}$ in Table 29.4.

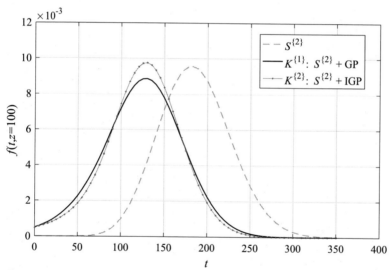

Figure 29.9 Lifetime density for the combined models $K^{\{j\}}$ in Table 29.4.

the combined processes are located to the left of that of the shock-based process $S^{\{2\}}$; this is expected, because we are adding two additional sources of deterioration, and therefore, the lifetime decreases. The two combined processes have the same mean lifetime: $\mathbb{E}[L] = 125$ days, and their reliability and lifetime densities are similar. This can be explained because the constitutive progressive processes $P^{\{1\}}$ (GP) and $P^{\{2\}}$ (IGP) were fitted to have the same mean and second central moment of deterioration for all $t \geq 0$ (Table 29.3). However, they differentiate in their third central moment, which explains the little differences in the curves.

29.9 Conclusions

This chapter presents a summary of the state-of-the-art of stochastic deterioration models for infrastructure systems. Deterioration was divided into two basic mechanisms: progressive and shock-based. Some examples of progressive deterioration are corrosion, fatigue, creep, and aging; and examples of shock-based deterioration include sudden and unexpected damages caused by extreme events such as overloads or natural phenomena. It is argued in this chapter that most existing models tackle these mechanisms separately, although in reality they occur simultaneously (e.g., corrosion and earthquake damage). Besides, the analytical complexity of dealing with two or more simultaneous mechanisms requires the search for new modeling alternatives. Thus, the central model presented in this chapter is a specific class of stochastic process known as *additive process*, which was formulated and discussed in detail. Through this approach, it is easy to combine various deterioration mechanisms and to obtain, numerically, the main reliability quantities. The details of the numerical approach were presented and described. Two step-by-step examples were also included to illustrate the proposed approach. In summary, this chapter provides the tools to carry out better reliability models, which are essential for decision-making within life-cycle analyses.

References

Abdel-Hameed, M. (1975) A gamma wear process. *IEEE Transactions on Reliability*, 24: 152–3.

Abdel-Hameed, M. (2014) *Lévy Processes and Their Applications in Reliability and Storage*. New York: Springer.

Bobbio, A., A. Horváth, and M. Telek (2005) Matching three moments with minimal acyclic phase type distributions. *Elsevier Science B.V.*, 210(1): 303–26.

Bogdanoff, J.L. and F. Kozin (1985) *Probabilistic Models of Cumulative Damage*. New York: John Wiley Sons.

Çinlar, E. (1980) On a generalization of gamma processes. *Journal of Applied Probability*, 170 (2): 467–80.

Çinlar, E., Z.P. Bazant, and E. Osman (1977) Stochastic process for extrapolating concrete creep. *Journal of the Engineering Mechanics Division*, 103: 1069–88.

Cont, R. and P. Tankov (2004) *Financial Modelling with Jump Processes*. USA: Chapman & Hall/CR.

Durret, R. (2010) *Probability: Theory and Examples*. USA: Cambridge University Press.

Dykstra, R.L. and P. Laud (1981). A Bayesian nonparametric approach to reliability. *The Annals of Statistics*, 90(2): 356–67.

Feng, L. and X. Lin (2013) Inverting analytic characteristic functions and financial applications. *Scand. Actuarial J.*, 40(1): 372–98.

Gil-Pelaez, J. (1951) Note on the inversion theorem. *Biometrika Trust*, 380 (3/4): 481–2.

Iervolino, I., M. Giorgio, and E. Chioccarelli (2013) Gamma degradation models for earthquake-resistant structures. *Structural Safety*, 45: 48–58.

International ASTM (2008) Designation: D 6433 â€" 07, Standard Practice for Roads and Parking Lots Pavement Condition Index Surveys. Technical report, ASTM International, West Conshohocken, PA 19428-2959, United States.

Junca, M. and M. Sanchez-Silva (2012) Optimal maintenance policy for a compound poisson shock model. *IEEE – Transactions on Reliability* (to appear).

Junca, M. and M. Sánchez-Silva (2013) Optimal maintenance policy for permanently monitored infra-structure subjected to extreme events. *Probabilistic Engineering Mechanics*, 33: 1–8.

Kharoufeh, J.P., C.J. Solo, and M.Y. Ulukus (2010) Semi-markov models for degradationbased reliability. *IIE Transactions*, 420(8): 599–612.

Klutke, G.-A. and Y. Yang (2002a) The availability of inspected systems subject to shocks and graceful degradation. *IEEE Transactions on Reliability*, 51(3): 371–4.

Klutke, G-A. and Y. Yang (2002b) The availability of inspected systems subject to shocks and graceful deterioration. *IEEE Transactions on Reliability* 51(3): 371–4.

Kumar, R., D.B.H Cline, and P. Gardoni (2015) A stochastic framework to model deterioration in engineering systems. *Structural Safety*, 53: 36–43.

Lam, Y. (2009) A geometric process-shock maintenance model. *IEEE Transactions on Reliability*, 580(2): 389–96.

Lam, Y., L. Zhu, J.S.K. Chan, and Q. Liu (2004) Analysis of data from a series of events by a geometric process model. *Acta Mathematicae Applicatae Sinica*, 200(2): 263–82.

Latouche, G. and V. Ramaswami (1999) *Introduction to Matrix Analytic Methods in Stochastic Modeling*. Philadelphia: Society for Industrial and Applied Mathematics.

Lawless, J. and M. Crowder (2004) Covariates and random effects in a gamma process model with application to degradation and failure. *Lifetime Data Analysis*, 10: 213–27.

Nakagawa, T. (2007) *Shock and Damage Models in Reliability*. London: Springer.

Neuts, M.F. (1981) *Matrix-geometric Solutions in Stochastic Models: An Algorithmic Approach*. New York: Courier Dover Publications.

Neuts, M.F. and K.S. Meier (1981) On the use of phase type distributions in reliability modelling of systems with two components. *OR Spektrum*, 2: 227–34.

Nicolai, R.P., R. Dekkerb, and J.M. van Noortwijk (2007) A comparison of models for measurable deterioration: An application to coatings on steel structures. *Reliability Engineering and System Safety*, 92: 1635–50.

Osogami, T. and M. Harchol-Balter (2003) A closed-form solution for mapping general distributions to minimal ph distributions. *Computer Performance Evaluation. Modelling Techniques and Tools*, 630(6): 200–17.

Pandey, M.D., X.X. Yuan, and J.M. van Noortwijk (2009) The influence of temporal uncertainty of deterioration on life-cycle management of structures. *Structure and Infrastructure Engineering* 50(2): 145–56.

Riascos-Ochoa, J., M. Sanchez-Silva, and R. Akhavan-Tabatabaei (2014) Reliability analysis of shock-based deterioration using phase-type distributions. *Probabilistic Engineering Mechanics*, 38: 88–101.

Riascos-Ochoa, J., M. Sánchez-Silva, and G-A. Klutke (2016) Modeling and reliability analysis of systems subject to multiple sources of degradation based on Lévy processes. *Probabilistic Engineering Mechanics*, 45: 164–76.

Sánchez-Silva, M. (2018) Managing infrastructure system through changeability. (under review).

Sánchez-Silva, M. and G-A. Klutke (2016) *Reliability and Life-Cycle Analysis of Deteriorating Systems*. Switzerland: Springer International Publishing.

Sánchez-Silva, M., G-A. Klutke, and D.V. Rosowsky (2010) Optimisation of the design of infrastructure components subject to progressive deterioration and extreme loads. *Structure and Infrastructure Engineering*, 8: 655–67.

Sánchez-Silva, M., G-A. Klutke, and D.V. Rosowsky (2011) Life-cycle performance of structures subject to multiple deterioration mechanisms. *Structural Safety*, 33: 206–17.

Santander, C.F. and M. Sánchez-Silva (2008) Design and maintenance-program optimization for large infrastructure systems. *Structure and Infrastructure Engineering*, 40(4): 297–309.

Sato, K-I. (1999) *Lévy Processes and Infinitely Divisible Distributions*. Cambridge: Cambridge University Press.

Shephard, N.G. (1991) From characteristic function to distribution function: a simple framework for the theory. *Econometric Theory*, 70(04): 519–29.

Sumita, U. and J.G. Shanthikumar (1983) A class of correlated cumulative shock models. *Advances in Applied Probability*, 170(2): 347–66.

Telek, M. and A. Heindl (2002) Matching moments for acyclic discrete and continuous phase-type distributions of second order. *I. J. of Simulation*, 30(3–4).

Thummler, A., P. Buchholz, and M. Telek (2006) A novel approach for phase-type fitting with the em algorithm. *IEEE Transactions on Dependable and Secure Computing*, 30(3): 245–58.

Utsu, T., Y. Ogata, and R.S. Matsu'ura (1995) The centenary of the omori formula for a decay law of aftershock activity. *J. Phys. Earth*, 43: 1–33.

van der Weide, J.A.M. and M.D. Pandey (2011) Stochastic analysis of shock process and modeling of condition-based maintenance. *Reliability Engineering and System Safety*, 96: 619–26.

van Noortwijk, J.M. (2009) A survey of the application of gamma processes in maintenance. *Reliability Engineering and System Safety*, 94: 2–21.

Waller, L.A., B.W. Turnbull, and J.M. Hardin (1995) Obtaining distribution functions by numerical inversion of characteristic functions with applications. *The American Statistician*, 490(4): 346–50.

Wang, X. and D. Xu. (2010) An inverse gaussian process model for degradation data. *Technometrics*, 520(2): 188–97.

Wortman, M.A., G-A. Klutke, and H. Ayhan (1994) A maintenance strategy for systems subjected to deterioration governed by random shocks. *IEEE Transactions on Reliability*, 430(3): 439–45.

Ye, Z-S. and N. Chen (2014) The inverse gaussian process as a degradation model. *Technometrics*, 560(3): 302–11.

Zhang, S., W. Zhou, and H. Qin (2013) Inverse gaussian process-based corrosion growth model for energy pipelines considering the sizing error in inspection data. *Corrosion Science*, 730(3): 309–20.

30

Stochastic life-cycle analysis and performance optimization of deteriorating engineering systems using state-dependent deterioration stochastic models

Gaofeng Jia,[1] and Paolo Gardoni[2]

[1]DEPARTMENT OF CIVIL AND ENVIRONMENTAL ENGINEERING, COLORADO STATE UNIVERSITY, FORT COLLINS, CO 80523, USA

[2]DEPARTMENT OF CIVIL AND ENVIRONMENTAL ENGINEERING, UNIVERSITY OF ILLINOIS AT URBANA-CHAMPAIGN, URBANA, IL 61801, USA

30.1 Introduction

Engineering systems are typically designed for a certain service life. Recently, there has been an increasing attention toward sustainability (Bocchini et al. 2014; Gardoni & Murphy 2008; Gardoni et al. 2016b), which calls for engineering systems to have longer service lives. However, the service life may be adversely impacted by different deterioration processes to which a system might be subject (e.g., deterioration over time due to either aging, regular operation, or extreme loading/environmental conditions (Choe et al. 2009, 2010; Ellingwood 2005; Kumar et al. 2015). Life-Cycle Analysis (LCA) (Barone & Frangopol 2014a, 2014b; Biondini & Frangopol 2016; Bocchini et al. 2013) provides a rigorous framework to plan and evaluate candidate designs and mitigation strategies (e.g., maintenance actions, and interventions) for engineering systems (Gardoni 2017; Gardoni & LaFave 2016) and can be used to promote the sustainable use of the existing resources (e.g., life-cycle performance based optimization of mitigation strategies) (Dong et al. 2014; Gardoni et al. 2016b; Jia et al. 2017; Joanni & Rackwitz 2008; Kumar & Gardoni 2014b; Kurtz et al. 2016; Pandey & van der Weide 2017; van Noortwijk & Frangopol 2004; van Noortwijk & van der Weide 2008).

During a system service life, due to various deteriorations, the system performance (e.g., measured in terms of capacity, reliability, or functionality) degrades over time. When the performance falls below a prescribed acceptable threshold an intervention (e.g., repair or replacement) is typically triggered (Sharma et al. 2017; Tabandeh & Gardoni 2014). Therefore, a deteriorating system typically experiences alternating phases of being in use and down. For a complete LCA of engineering systems, it is critical to model and incorporate the deterioration processes and the associated uncertainties (Cheng & Pandey 2012; Choe et al. 2009; Ciampoli

& Ellingwood 2002; Ellingwood & Yasuhiro 1993; Jia et al. 2017; Kumar & Gardoni 2014b; Mori & Ellingwood 1994; Sanchez-Silva et al. 2011). In general two types of deterioration mechanisms can be identified for most engineering systems (Kumar et al. 2009, 2014a, 2014b, 2015): (1) gradual (or progressive) deterioration (e.g., due to corrosion (Choe et al. 2009; Gardoni & Rosowsky 2011; Gardoni & Trejo 2013; Vu & Stewart 2000; Zhong et al. 2010), Alkali-Silica reaction (Eck Olave et al. 2015a, 2015b), fatigue and crack growth (Guida & Pulcini 2011)); and (2) shock (sudden) deterioration (e.g., due to damages from extreme events like earthquakes, hurricanes, floods, blasts and other natural or anthropogenic hazards) (Kumar et al. 2015; Sanchez-Silva et al. 2011).

This chapter discusses the estimation and optimization of stochastic life-cycle performances of deteriorating engineering systems. The general formulation of state-dependent stochastic models (SDSMs) proposed in Jia and Gardoni (2018b) is used to model the deterioration due to multiple deterioration processes. The SDSMs predict the system performance as a function of the values of the state variables that vary with time due to multiple deterioration processes and explicitly consider the possible interaction among different deterioration processes. The SDSMs are then integrated into the renewal-theory life-cycle analysis (RTLCA) proposed in Kumar and Gardoni (2014b) to evaluate life-cycle performance quantities such as age, instantaneous probability of being in service, availability, costs of operation, total cost, and benefits. A stochastic simulation-based approach is adopted to estimate the time-variant performance indicators needed to inform intervention activities (i.e., whether intervention is needed at any time instant) for life-cycle analysis. To efficiently estimate and optimize the life-cycle performances (i.e., selection of optimal value of intervention criterion), a novel sampling and kernel density estimation (KDE) based approach is presented for the efficient approximation of the probability density functions (PDFs) in RTLCA for any selected value of intervention criterion. The sampling and KDE based approach requires simulation of only one set of samples, which are used to establish the information for evaluating the life-cycle performance for any selected value of the intervention criterion. This approach has a significant computational efficiency. To illustrate the sampling and KDE based approach, the proposed approach is used to evaluate and optimize the life-cycle performances of an example reinforced concrete (RC) bridge subject to deterioration due to corrosion and seismic loading.

The rest of the chapter is organized as follows. Section 30.2 presents the estimation and optimization of life-cycle performance quantities, including the general formulation of SDSMs, their implementation in RTLCA, and the sampling and KDE based approach for efficient estimation and optimization of life-cycle performance quantities. Section 30.3 uses the sampling and KDE based approach to assess and optimize the life-cycle performance of an example RC bridge. The last section summarizes the chapter and draws a few conclusions.

30.2 Life-cycle analysis and optimization of deteriorating engineering systems

30.2.1 State-dependent stochastic models (SDSMs)

To model the impact of deterioration on the life-cycle performance quantities, we adopt the general formulation for SDSMs in Jia and Gardoni (2018b). The SDSMs describe the change of the properties of engineering systems using a state-dependent formulation, which allows us to consider multiple deterioration processes and their interactions. This formulation is briefly reviewed here.

State change due to deterioration

In the general formulation of SDSMs, the modeling starts with the vector of the external conditions/variables at time t, $\mathbf{Z}(t)$. The vector $\mathbf{Z}(t)$ can be partitioned into environmental conditions/variables denoted as $\mathbf{E}(t)$ (e.g., temperature, atmospheric pressure, and relative humidity), and shock measures denoted as $\mathbf{S}(t)$ (e.g., external loadings and intensity measures). The vector $\mathbf{Z}(t)$ influences the deterioration processes to which the system might be subjected. Let the vector $\mathbf{X}(t) = [X_1(t) \cdots X_j(t) \cdots X_{n_s}(t)]^T$ denote the state variables of the system at time t, including a set of basic variables such as material properties, member dimensions, and imposed boundary conditions (Gardoni et al. 2002, 2003). Let $\mathbf{X}_0 = \mathbf{X}(t=0)$ be the initial state variables at reference time $t = 0$. Due to the impacts of various deterioration processes (with potential interactions between them), starting from $\mathbf{X}_0$, the system state variables change to $\mathbf{X}(t)$ at time t. In this formulation, the vector of state variables at time t is written as $\mathbf{X}(t) = \mathbf{X}_0 + \int_0^t \dot{\mathbf{X}}(\xi)d\xi$ where $\dot{\mathbf{X}}(\xi)$ is the instantaneous rate of state change at time ξ due to the deterioration processes. Suppose the system is subject to m deterioration processes, the overall rate $\dot{\mathbf{X}}(t)$ can be written as the sum of the rates associated to individual deterioration processes as $\dot{\mathbf{X}}(t) = \sum_{k=1}^{m} \dot{\mathbf{X}}_k[t, \mathbf{X}(t), \mathbf{Z}_k(t); \Theta_{\mathbf{x},k}]$

where $\dot{\mathbf{X}}_k(t) = \dot{\mathbf{X}}_k[t, \mathbf{X}(t), \mathbf{Z}_k(t); \Theta_{\mathbf{x},k}]$ denotes the rate of state change due to the kth deterioration process. Note that this rate includes the dependency not only on t and the external conditions, $\mathbf{Z}_k(t)$ (i.e., the external conditions that have an impact on the kth deterioration process), but also on the state variables of the system at time t, $\mathbf{X}(t)$. The rate $\dot{\mathbf{X}}_k(t)$ also depends on $\Theta_{\mathbf{x},k}$ which is a vector of model parameters related to the impact of the kth deterioration process. This formulation results in what Jia and Gardoni called state-dependent deterioration models (Jia & Gardoni 2018b). This formulation is different from other formulations in the literature, where $\dot{\mathbf{X}}_k(t)$ only depends on time. More specifically, we can write $\dot{\mathbf{X}}_k(t) = \dot{\mathbf{X}}_k[t, \mathbf{X}(t), \mathbf{E}_k(t); \Theta_{\mathbf{x},k}]$ for gradual deterioration processes, and $\dot{\mathbf{X}}_k(t) = \Delta\mathbf{X}_k[\mathbf{X}(t_{k,i}^-), \mathbf{S}_k(t_{k,i}); \Theta_{\mathbf{x},k}]\delta(t - t_{k,i})$ for $t_{k,i}^- < t \le t_{k,i+1}^-$ for shock deterioration processes, where $\Delta\mathbf{X}_k[\cdot]$ is the change of state variables due to the ith shock occurring at time t_i (i.e., $\mathbf{X}(t_{k,i}^+) = \mathbf{X}(t_{k,i}^-) + \Delta\mathbf{X}_k[\cdot]$), $\mathbf{X}(t_{k,i}^-)$ is the state variable at time $t_{k,i}^-$ (i.e., right before $t_{k,i}$), and $\delta(\cdot)$ is the Dirac delta function.

To implement this formulation in a life-cycle analysis, we need to establish specific models for the changes of the state variables for each deterioration process. For shock deterioration, first we need to model the characteristics of the shocks (e.g., the occurrence rate/frequency and the intensity). Stochastic models such as Poisson processes are typically used to model the random occurrence of shocks. Then we need to model the change of the state variables for a given shock. To predict $\dot{\mathbf{X}}_k(t)$'s, analytical models can be used, if available, or probabilistic predictive models like those in Kumar and Gardoni (2012, 2014a) can be developed.

Stochastic capacity and demand models

The changes in $\mathbf{X}(t)$ lead to changes in the capacity $\mathbf{C}(t)$ (the ability of the system to sustain an imposed condition) as well as in the demand $\mathbf{D}(t)$ (the condition imposed on the system by external event/shock). In general, the capacity and demand are vectors (e.g., consisting of different capacities and demands corresponding to different modes of failure). Given the state variables at time t, $\mathbf{X}(t)$, the time-variant capacity of the system can be estimated using a capacity model, e.g., $\mathbf{C}(t) = \mathbf{C}[\mathbf{X}(t); \Theta_C]$, where $\mathbf{C}[\mathbf{X}(t); \Theta_C]$ is a capacity model that take $\mathbf{X}(t)$ as input and Θ_C is a set of parameters of the capacity model (Choe et al. 2010, 2009; Gardoni et al. 2013). Similarly, the demand that a shock characterized by intensity measure(s) $\mathbf{S}(t)$ imposes on the system can be estimated using a demand model, e.g., $\mathbf{D}(t) = \mathbf{D}[\mathbf{X}(t), \mathbf{S}(t); \Theta_D]$, where $\mathbf{D}[\mathbf{X}(t), \mathbf{S}(t); \Theta_D]$ is a demand model and Θ_D is a set of parameters of the demand model. As an example, the capacity and demand models can follow the general forms proposed by Gardoni et al. (2002, 2003). Note that any appropriate capacity and demand models that take the state variables as input can be adopted in the formulation.

Time-variant system performance indicators

Once $\mathbf{X}(t)$, $\mathbf{C}(t)$ and $\mathbf{D}(t)$ are modeled, they can be used to predict time-variant system performances measured in terms of a performance indicator $Q(t)$ (e.g., reliability, or functionality). One commonly used performance indicator is the failure probability (Jia et al. 2017). For a given realization of $\mathbf{X}(t)$ at time t, i.e., $\mathbf{x}(t)$, the conditional failure probability can be established by propagating the uncertainties in the capacity and demand models and the intensity measure as

$$P_f\left[t\big|\mathbf{x}(t)\right] = \int_{\Theta, \mathbf{S}(t)} I_F\left[\Theta, \mathbf{s}(t), \mathbf{x}(t)\right] f_\Theta(\Theta) f_{\mathbf{S},t}\left[\mathbf{s}(t)\right] d\Theta d\mathbf{s}(t). \tag{30.1}$$

The unconditional failure probability at time t can be obtained by further propagating the uncertainties in the deterioration paths (i.e., different realizations of $\mathbf{X}(t)$ at time t), i.e., $P_f(t) = \int_{\mathbf{X}(t)} P_f\left[t\big|\mathbf{x}(t)\right] f_{\mathbf{X},t}\left[\mathbf{x}(t)\right] d\mathbf{x}(t)$, where $\Theta = [\Theta_C, \Theta_D]$, $\mathbf{s}(t)$ and $\mathbf{x}(t)$ are realizations of the random variables $\Theta = [\Theta_C, \Theta_D]$, $\mathbf{S}(t)$ and $\mathbf{X}(t)$, $I_F[\Theta, \mathbf{s}(t), \mathbf{x}(t)]$ is the indicator function (defined as 1 if $C[\mathbf{x}(t); \Theta_C] \le D[\mathbf{x}(t), \mathbf{s}(t); \Theta_D]$ and 0 otherwise). $f_\Theta(\Theta)$ is the PDF for Θ, $f_{\mathbf{S},t}[\mathbf{s}(t)]$ is the PDF of the shock intensity measure at time t, and $f_{\mathbf{X},t}[\mathbf{x}(t)]$ is the PDF of the state variables at time t (Jia & Gardoni 2018a).

Simulation-based estimation of time-variant performance indicator

To estimate the performance indicators, we need to consider the various uncertainties associated with the deterioration processes, the state dependence in the deterioration processes, the time-variant characteristics of stochastic loads, the dependence between deterioration and the load occurrences. To address these needs, the simulation-based approach proposed in Jia and Gardoni (2018a) can be adopted. A simulation-based approach puts no constraints on the complexity of the adopted models (e.g., deterioration models, capacity, and demand model) and input probability models, and is generally well-suited for this estimation.

For example, take $Q(t) = P_f[t|\mathbf{x}(t)]$ for a given realization of the state variables at time t, $\mathbf{x}(t)$. Then $Q(t)$ can be estimated as follows. First for an efficient estimation for small failure probabilities, which are typical in early stages of the life-cycle of a system, we adopt a Monte Carlo Simulation (MCS) with Importance Sampling (IS) (Au & Beck 2003). Parameters in the deterioration models are also considered in the IS. Using importance sampling densities $q_\Theta(\Theta)$ and $q_{\mathbf{S}}(\mathbf{s})$ for Θ and $\mathbf{S}(t)$, $P_f[t|\mathbf{x}(t)]$ can be estimated as

$$\hat{P}_f\left[t\big|\mathbf{x}(t)\right] = \frac{1}{N} \sum_{k=1}^{N} R_{IS}^k I_F^k \tag{30.2}$$

where $I_F^k = I_F[\Theta^k, \mathbf{s}(t)^k, \mathbf{x}(t)]$, $R_{IS}^k = \{f_\Theta(\Theta^k) f_{\mathbf{S},t}[\mathbf{s}(t)^k]\} / \{q_\Theta(\Theta^k) q_{\mathbf{S}}[\mathbf{s}(t)^k]\}$, and Θ^k, $\mathbf{s}(t)^k$ are samples from $q_\Theta(\Theta)$ and $q_{\mathbf{S}}(\mathbf{s})$, respectively.

To generate realizations for state variables at time t (i.e., $\mathbf{x}(t)$) or to simulate samples from the PDF $f_{\mathbf{X},t}[\mathbf{x}(t)]$, we need to consider both gradual deterioration and potential shock deterioration for all shocks that might have occurred before time t as well as the associated uncertainties in the random occurrence of shocks and deterioration path of the state variables. For the random shock occurrence, if it is modeled as homogeneous Poisson process, then the number of shocks before time t, N_t, is a random variable following a Poisson distribution. For given realizations of $N_t = n_t$, to simulate samples from the PDF $f_{\mathbf{X},t}[\mathbf{x}(t)]$, we need to simulate the sequence of state variables $\mathbf{M}_t = [\mathbf{X}(t_0^+), \mathbf{X}(t_1^-), \mathbf{X}(t_1^+), \mathbf{X}(t_2^-), \cdots, \mathbf{X}(t_{n_t}^+), \mathbf{X}(t)]^T$ (with $\lambda_t = [\mathbf{x}(t_0^+), \mathbf{x}(t_1^-), \mathbf{x}(t_1^+), \mathbf{x}(t_2^-), \cdots, \mathbf{x}(t_{n_t}^+), \mathbf{x}(t)]^T$ being its corresponding realization). For a given sequence of shocks occurring at time instants/sequence $T_{\{n_t\}} = t_{\{n_t\}} = \{t_1, \cdots, t_{n_t}\}$ with intensities $\mathbf{S}_{\{n_t\}} = \mathbf{s}_{\{n_t\}} = \{\mathbf{s}(t_1), \mathbf{s}(t_2), \cdots, \mathbf{s}(t_{n_t})\}$, the deterioration path is typically uncertain considering the uncertainties in the deterioration models for the change of the state variables due to both gradual and shock deteriorations. Therefore, considering the uncertainties in the random shock occurrence, the shock intensity, and the deterioration paths, we need to simulate samples from the PDF $f(\lambda_t, t_{\{n_t\}}, \mathbf{s}_{\{n_t\}})$, which can be written as $f(\lambda_t, t_{\{n_t\}}, \mathbf{s}_{\{n_t\}}) = f(\lambda_t \mid t_{\{n_t\}}, \mathbf{s}_{\{n_t\}}) f(\mathbf{s}_{\{n_t\}} \mid t_{\{n_t\}}) f(t_{\{n_t\}})$. Here $f(\lambda_t \mid t_{\{n_t\}}, \mathbf{s}_{\{n_t\}})$ can be further expanded as

$$f\left(\lambda_t \mid t_{\{n_t\}}, \mathbf{s}_{\{n_t\}}\right) = f\left[\mathbf{x}\left(t_0^+\right)\right] \left\{ \prod_{i=1}^{n_t} f\left[\mathbf{x}\left(t_i^-\right) \mid \mathbf{x}\left(t_{i-1}^+\right)\right] f\left[\mathbf{x}\left(t_i^+\right) \mid \mathbf{x}\left(t_i^-\right), \mathbf{s}(t_i)\right] \right\} f\left[\mathbf{x}(t) \mid \mathbf{x}\left(t_{n_t}^+\right)\right] \quad (30.3)$$

More specifically, the PDF $f[\mathbf{x}(t_i^-) \mid \mathbf{x}(t_{i-1}^+)]$ is the transition probability from $\mathbf{x}(t_{i-1}^+)$ to $\mathbf{x}(t_i^-)$ considering gradual deterioration, which can be established based on the adopted gradual deterioration model. The PDF $f[\mathbf{x}(t_i^+) \mid \mathbf{x}(t_i^-), \mathbf{s}(t_i)]$ corresponds to the conditional PDF of $\mathbf{x}(t_i^+)$ given $\mathbf{x}(t_i^-)$ and shock intensity $\mathbf{s}(t_i)$, which can be established based on the adopted shock deterioration model. In Equation (30.3), $f(\mathbf{s}_{\{n_t\}} \mid t_{\{n_t\}})$ is the joint instantaneous PDF of $\mathbf{S}$ at $t_{\{n_t\}} = \{t_1, \cdots, t_{n_t}\}$. The joint PDF $f(t_{\{n_t\}})$ corresponds to the PDF for the shock occurrence times and depends on the shock occurrence model. Therefore, the PDF $f(\lambda_t, t_{\{n_t\}}, \mathbf{s}_{\{n_t\}})$ or samples from this PDF can now be established. In the end, samples from the PDF $f_{\mathbf{X},t}[\mathbf{x}(t)]$ can be obtained as well.

30.2.2 Renewal-theory life-cycle analysis (RTLCA) using SDSMs

Renewal-theory life-cycle analysis (RTLCA)
The time-variant performance quantities obtained with SDSMs can be used in the RTLCA to estimate various life-cycle performance quantities. Because of the use of stochastic models, Jia et al. (2017) named such formulation of the life-cycle analysis: stochastic life-cycle analysis (SLCA).

Figure 30.1 illustrates the life-cycle of a deteriorating system in terms of a performance indicator $Q(t)$ as a function of time t. During its life-cycle, a system experiences alternating phases of being in use and down. Typically, within each cycle, $Q(t)$ degrades due to either gradual deterioration (leading to continuous changes in performance) or shock deterioration (leading to sudden changes in performance). When $Q(t)$ falls below a prescribed acceptable threshold (i.e., $Q(t_{I_i}) \le Q_{acc}$), an intervention is triggered, and the system undergoes a recovery process, i.e., repair or replacement, corresponding to being down (Sharma et al. 2017). Let I_i denote the ith intervention event (triggered at time t_{I_i}), and L_i denote the ith renewal cycle, and T_{L_i} denote the length of the ith renewal cycle, also called renewal interval, which can be written as $T_{L_i} = T_{I_i} + T_{D_i}$, where T_{I_i} is the period that the system is in use and T_{D_i} is period that the system is down (i.e., down time). To account for the possible lag period between the intervention time and the time to initiate the recovery (i.e., repair or replacement), T_{D_i} can be further written as $T_{D_i} = T_{l_i} + T_{R_i}$, where T_{l_i} is the lag period (during which $Q(t)$ may further degrade, e.g., from t_{I_i} to $t_{I_i} + T_{l_i}$ as shown in Figure 30.1) and T_{R_i} is the recovery time.

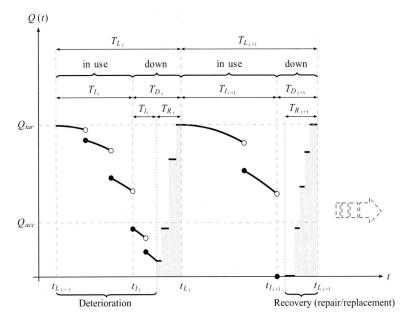

Figure 30.1 Illustration of the life-cycle performance of a system.
Source: Adapted from Jia et al. 2017.

A renewal event, L_i, can be either a repair event L_R or a replacement due to failure L_F, with probabilities $P(L_R)$ and $P(L_F)$, respectively. Also, we have $P(L_F) = 1 - P(L_R)$ given that a renewal event does occur. Specifically, in terms of information on the first renewal event, we need the PDFs of T_L and T_I (including the corresponding PDFs conditional on failure, which are needed for the calculation of failure losses). The PDF of T_L, $f_{T_L}(t)$, can be written as $f_{T_L}(t) = f_{T_L|L_R}(t \mid L_R)P(L_R) + f_{T_L|L_F}(t \mid L_F)P(L_F)$, where $f_{T_L|L_R}(t \mid L_R)$ is PDF of T_L conditional $L_i = L_R$; and $f_{T_L|L_F}(t \mid L_F)$ is the PDF of T_L conditional on $L_i = L_F$. Similarly, for T_I, we have $f_{T_I}(t) = f_{T_I|L_R}(t \mid L_R)P(L_R) + f_{T_I|L_F}(t \mid L_F)P(L_F)$.

RTLCA assumes that any intervention (i.e., repair or replacement) results in a complete renewal of the system (i.e., restore it to the as-built state). Under the assumption of the renewal theory, $\{T_{L_i}\}_{i \in N}$ forms a sequence of statistically independent and identically distributed (*s.i.i.d*) random variables. This means that only information on the first renewal event (which is the same as that for any other renewal cycles) is needed for estimating life-cycle performance quantities. Next, we briefly review the estimation equations for different life-cycle performance quantities in a renewal theory formulation, including age, availability, cost of operation, failure losses, and benefits. Additional details can be found in (Kumar & Gardoni 2014b).

Estimation of life-cycle performance quantities
The age at time t, $\Lambda(t)$, is defined as the time elapsed since the last renewal given that the system is in use at t (the age is zero if the system is down at t). The expected age can be written as

$$E\big[\Lambda(t)\big] = t\big[1 - F_{T_I}(t)\big] + \int_0^t E\big[\Lambda(t - \xi)\big] f_{T_L}(\xi) d\xi \tag{30.4}$$

where $F_{T_I}(t)$ is the cumulative distribution function (CDF) for T_I. The availability of a system during a time interval $[0,t]$ is defined as the fraction of the time for which the system is available (or in use), i.e., $A(t) = \int_0^t 1_{\{in\ use\ at\ \xi\}}(\xi)d\xi/t$. The expected availability is simply $E[A(t)] = \int_0^t P_S(\xi)d\xi/t$, where $P_S(t)$ is the instantaneous probability that the system is in use at time t and can be calculated according to

$$P_S(t) = \left[1 - F_{T_I}(t)\right] + \int_0^t P_S(t-\xi) f_{T_L}(\xi)d\xi \tag{30.5}$$

The operation cost, $C_{Op}(t)$, includes the total cost of repairs and replacement of the system in order to operate it up to time t. The expected value of $C_{Op}(t)$ can be expressed as

$$E[C_{Op}(t)] = \int_0^t \left\{ \bar{c}_{Op}(\xi) + E[C_{Op}(t-\xi)] \right\} e^{-\gamma\xi} f_{T_L}(\xi)d\xi \tag{30.6}$$

where $\bar{c}_{Op}(\xi) = E[c_{Op_h} | T_{L_1} = \xi]$ and c_{Op_h} is the cost of the repair or replacement occurring between events I_1 and L_1, and γ is the discount rate to calculate the net present value of the cost. Additional costs incurred during the life-cycle of the system include the failure losses, $C_L(t)$ (e.g., injuries, deaths, or damage to properties etc.). The expected failure losses can be written as

$$E[C_L(t)] = P(L_F) c_L e^{\gamma T_{DF}} \int_0^{t+T_{DF}} e^{-\gamma\xi} f_{T_I|L_F}(\xi|L_F)d\xi + \int_0^t E[C_L(t-\xi)] e^{-\gamma\xi} f_{T_L}(\xi)d\xi \tag{30.7}$$

where c_L is the loss corresponding to the event I_1, and T_{DF} is the down-time after an ultimate failure. Then the expected total cost is simply $E[C_{total}(t)] = E[C_{Op}(t)] + E[C_L(t)]$.

In addition to the costs, the benefit of operating a system, $B(t)$, is another important performance quantity in LCA (Gardoni et al. 2016a). Let b denote the benefit of operating the system (i.e., having the system in use) for a unit time, the expected benefit can be obtained as

$$E[B(t)] = b \int_0^t P_S(\xi) e^{-\gamma\xi} d\xi \tag{30.8}$$

Then the expected net benefit can be established as $E[B_{net}(t)] = E[B(t)] - E[C_{total}(t)] - C_C$, where C_C is the construction cost for the system.

To estimate the life-cycle performance quantities in Equations (30.4)–(30.8), the following strategy can be adopted. Take $E[\Lambda(t)]$ for example, considering Equation (30.4), first, discretize the time as $0, \Delta t, 2\Delta t, \cdots k\Delta t$ with $t = k\Delta t$; then rewrite the integral $\int_0^t E[\Lambda(t-\xi)] f_{T_L}(\xi)d\xi$ in a summation form. Given the initial condition $E[\Lambda(t)] = 0$, the values of $E[\Lambda(t)]$ at subsequent time instants, i.e. $E[\Lambda(\Delta t)]$, $E[\Lambda(2\Delta t)]$, $\cdots$, $E[\Lambda(k\Delta t)]$ can then be solved sequentially. The same solution approach can be used to evaluate also all of the other life-cycle performance quantities.

To obtain the relevant PDFs in the above estimation, we need to model the deterioration and recovery processes, and estimate the time-variant performance indicator $Q(t)$. For this purpose, the SDSMs discussed in Section 30.2.1 can be adopted. However, estimation of time-variant performance and establishing the required PDFs in this context are nontrival tasks. Therefore, we adopt the simulation-based approach proposed in Jia and Gardoni (2018a) to estimate the time-variant performance indicator needed to inform the intervention, and a sampling-based approach to establish the required PDFs (as discussed next).

Sampling-based estimation of PDFs in RTLCA

To carry out the solution strategy on p. 578, we need to establish the corresponding PDFs in the estimation equations. Once we can establish the required PDFs, the estimation of the life-cycle performance quantities is relatively easy. Typically, there are no analytical expressions for these PDFs. The sampling-based approach in Jia and Gardoni (2018a) can be adopted for this purpose. The approach first simulates samples from these PDFs and then based on these samples uses either parametric approaches (e.g., fitting a distribution) or nonparametric approaches (e.g., kernel density estimation) to approximate the PDFs.

Suppose the intervention criterion corresponds to the failure probability conditional on a given realization $\mathbf{x}(t_i^+)$ (after a shock) being larger than a prescribed threshold p_a, i.e., $Q(t_i^+) = P_f[t_i^+ \,|\, \mathbf{x}(t_i^+)] \geq p_a$ and failure/replacement (L_F) corresponds to $Q(t_i^+) = 1$. Once the intervention criterion is decided, the sampling-based approach involves the following steps (Jia & Gardoni 2018a):

(1) Generate n_s realizations for $(T_{\{n\}}, \mathbf{S}_{\{n\}})$ (where n is a sufficiently large number);
(2) For the jth realization $(t_{\{n\}}^j, \mathbf{s}_{\{n\}}^j)$, first, generate a realization for the deterioration path of the state variables $\mathbf{X}(t)$ using the adopted models for state change due to gradual and shock deterioration, giving $[\mathbf{x}(t_0^+), \mathbf{x}(t_1^+), \cdots, \mathbf{x}(t_n^+)]^T$; then (a) estimate the conditional failure probability $P_f[t_i^+ \,|\, \mathbf{x}^j(t_i^+)]$ using the simulation-based approach discussed on p. 575 (in this case, the state is deterministic, i.e., $\mathbf{x}^j(t_i^+)$); (b) repeat the estimation in (a) for i from 1 to n and stop when the criterion $P_f[t_i^+ \,|\, \mathbf{x}^j(t_i^+)] \geq p_a$ is satisfied; keep the corresponding t_i, which corresponds to a sample from $f_{T_I}(t)$; and
(3) Repeat Step (2) for each of the n_s realizations.

In the end, we can generate n_s samples from the distribution $f_{T_I}(t)$ and out of these samples, the ones that correspond to a repair intervention are distributed according to $f_{T_I|L_R}(t \,|\, L_R)$ while the rest of the samples are distributed according to $f_{T_I|L_F}(t \,|\, L_F)$. The percentages of the number of samples out of the n_s samples corresponding to L_R and L_F are the estimates of $P(L_R)$ and $P(L_F)$, respectively. The PDFs of T_I can be estimated based on the samples. To establish the PDFs of T_L, we need to know the distribution of T_D since $T_L = T_I + T_D$. As shown in Figure 30.1, T_D is the sum of the lag time and the recovery time, both of which are typically related to the type of intervention. More details on the modeling of T_D can be found in Sharma et al. (2017). Once we have $f_{T_I}(t)$ and the distribution of T_D, the distribution for T_L can be derived accordingly. Then the solution strategy on p. 578 can be used to esimate life-cycle performance quantities. The main computational cost comes from obtaining the PDFs using the sampling-based approach discussed above, which requires the modeling of the deterioration processes and simulation-based estimation of the performance indicator (e.g., failure probability) at different time instants.

30.2.3 Optimization of life-cycle performances

Formulation of optimization of life-cycle performances

This section discusses the selection of the optimal performance threshold p_a so that a certain life-cycle performance during a desired period is optimized. Let $H(p_a)$ denote the objective function, which could be any of the life-cycle performance quantities during a desired life-cycle time period $(0, t_{lca}]$, e.g., the expected total cost $E[C_{\text{total}}(t_{lca}) \,|\, p_a]$ for a selected p_a. The optimization can be formulated as

$$\text{Find } p_a \text{ such that } H(p_a) \text{ is optimized} \tag{30.9}$$

An intuitive approach to solve this optimization is to simply consider different values of p_a, for each value use the approaches on pp. 575 and 578 to evaluate the life-cycle performance (i.e., the objective function), and then select the value of p_a that gives the most desirable value of $H(p_a)$. However, it is obvious that this straightforward approach is computationally expensive, since we would need to repeat the sampling-based approximation of the PDFs (which involves the deterioration modeling and simulation-based estimation of performance indicators) for each p_a. To alleviate the computational effort and facilitate efficient optimization, a sampling and KDE based approach is presented here.

Sampling and KDE based approach for efficient life-cycle performance optimization
The PDFs and probabilities shown on pp. 577 and 578 are for a given p_a (or conditional on a given p_a) although p_a is not explicitly written in the expressions. For the following discussions, p_a is explicitly included in the expressions for the related PDFs and probabilites for a clear explanantion of the proposed approach. As mentioned earlier, the main computational effort comes from simulating samples from $f_{T_l}(t)$ for a given p_a, which can be denoted as $f_{T_l}(t|p_a)$. The idea here is to decouple (a) the sampling (to approximate $f_{T_l}(t|p_a)$ for given p_a), and (b) the estimation and optimization of the objective function. More specifically, first a new sampling and KDE approach is proposed to establish the PDF $f_{T_l}(t|p_a)$ for any given p_a. Then, once we can evaluate the PDFs $f_{T_l}(t|p_a)$ for any p_a, the estimation and optimization of the objective function can be carried out directly. Next, we discuss in detail the sampling and KDE based approach to establish the required PDFs and probabilities.

If we treat p_a as a random variable with PDF $f_{P_a}(p_a)$, we can write

$$f_{T_l}(t|p_a) = \frac{f_{T_l,P_a}(t,p_a)}{f_{P_a}(p_a)} \tag{30.10}$$

For convenience, we can assume p_a as a uniformly distributed random variable in the domain of $[p_{a,l}, p_{a,u}]$; then $f_{P_a}(p_a) = 1/(p_{a,u} - p_{a,l})$, which is a constant. If there is prior information (e.g., engineering judgement) on which region the optimal p_a might be, a PDF that has higher values in this region can be defined. Therefore, using Equation (30.10) once we estimate the joint PDF $f_{T_l,P_a}(t,p_a)$, we can obtain $f_{T_l}(t|p_a)$ for any given p_a. The new approach relies on generating samples from the joint PDF $f_{T_l,P_a}(t,p_a)$ and then approximating it using KDE. This leads to $f_{P_a}(p_a)f_{T_l}(t|p_a) = \tilde{f}_{T_l,P_a}(t,p_a)/f_{P_a}(p_a)$ where $\tilde{f}_{T_l,P_a}(t,p_a)$ is the KDE approximation of $f_{T_l,P_a}(t,p_a)$ based on the samples. For $f_{P_a}(p_a) = 1/(p_{a,u} - p_{a,l})$, we have that $f_{T_l}(t|p_a) = \tilde{f}_{T_l,P_a}(t,p_a) \cdot (p_{a,u} - p_{a,l})$.

As the key step in this approach, we need to generate samples from $f_{T_l,P_a}(t,p_a)$. This can be done through a modification of the sampling approach on p. 579. The generation of samples from $f_{T_l,P_a}(t,p_a)$ involves the following steps:

(1) Generate n_s realizations for $(p_a, T_{\{n\}}, \mathbf{S}_{\{n\}})$ (where n is a sufficiently large number and p_a is generated from uniform distribution in $[p_{a,l}, p_{a,u}]$);
(2) For the jth realization $(p_a^j, t_{\{n\}}^j, s_{\{n\}}^j)$, first, generate a realization for the deterioration path of the state variables $\mathbf{X}(t)$ using the adopted models for state change due to gradual and shock deterioration, giving $[\mathbf{x}(t_0^+), \mathbf{x}(t_1^+), \cdots, \mathbf{x}(t_n^+)]^T$; then (a) estimate the conditional failure probability $P_f[t_i^+|\mathbf{x}^j(t_i^+)]$ using the simulation-based approach discussed on p. 575 (in this case, the state is deterministic, i.e., $\mathbf{x}^j(t_i^+)$); (b) repeat the estimation in (a) for i from 1 to n and stop when the criterion $P_f[t_i^+|\mathbf{x}^j(t_i^+)] \geq p_a^j$ is satisfied; keep the corresponding t_i and p_a^j, which correspond to a sample from $f_{T_l,P_a}(t,p_a)$; and

(3)   Repeat Step (2) for each of the n_s realizations.

In the end, we can generate n_s samples from the joint distribution $f_{T_I,P_a}(t, p_a)$. Out of these samples, the ones that correspond to repair intervention are distributed according to $f_{T_I|L_R,P_a}(t, p_a \mid L_R)$ while the rest of the samples are distributed according to $f_{T_I|L_F,P_a}(t, p_a \mid L_F)$; and the corresponding samples for p_a are distributed according to $f(p_a \mid L_R)$ and $f(p_a \mid L_F)$, respectively.

Based on the samples from $f_{T_I,P_a}(t, p_a)$, KDE can be used to establish an approximation $\tilde{f}_{T_I,P_a}(t, p_a)$. This approximation can be plugged into Equation (30.10) to approximate the conditional PDF $f_{T_I}(t \mid p_a)$ as

$$f_{T_I}(t \mid p_a) = \frac{\tilde{f}_{T_I,P_a}(t, p_a)}{f_{P_a}(p_a)} = \tilde{f}_{T_I,P_a}(t, p_a) \cdot (p_{a,u} - p_{a,l}), \tag{30.11}$$

which can be used to approximate $f_{T_I}(t \mid p_a)$ for any given p_a. Similarly, the conditional PDF $f_{T_I|L_F}(t \mid L_F, p_a)$ and $f_{T_I|L_R}(t \mid L_R, p_a)$ can be approximated as

$$f_{T_I|L_F}(t \mid L_F, p_a) = \frac{\tilde{f}_{T_I|L_F,P_a}(t, p_a \mid L_F)}{\tilde{f}(p_a \mid L_F)}$$
$$f_{T_I|L_R}(t \mid L_R, p_a) = \frac{\tilde{f}_{T_I|L_R,P_a}(t, p_a \mid L_R)}{\tilde{f}(p_a \mid L_R)}, \tag{30.12}$$

where $\tilde{f}(.)$ are KDE approximation of the PDF based on the corresponding samples. In terms of PDFs for T_L, we simply need to add the values of corresponding T_D to T_I (since $T_L = T_I + T_D$) and again use KDE to establish approximations of PDFs for T_L. Therefore, we can establish approximations for all the required PDFs.

In addition to these PDFs, another probability is needed, which is $P(L_F \mid p_a)$ for a given p_a. Based on $f_{T_I}(t \mid p_a) = f_{T_I|L_R}(t \mid L_R, p_a)P(L_R \mid p_a) + f_{T_I|L_F}(t \mid L_F, p_a)P(L_F \mid p_a)$ and $P(L_F \mid p_a) = 1 - P(L_R \mid p_a)$, $P(L_F \mid p_a)$ can be written as

$$P(L_F \mid p_a) = \frac{f_{T_I}(t \mid p_a) - f_{T_I|L_R}(t \mid L_R, p_a)}{f_{T_I|L_F}(t \mid L_F, p_a) - f_{T_I|L_R}(t \mid L_R, p_a)}. \tag{30.13}$$

Therefore, for a given p_a, to estimate $P(L_F \mid p_a)$, we need to know $f_{T_I}(t \mid p_a)$, $f_{T_I|L_R}(t \mid L_R, p_a)$, and $f_{T_I|L_F}(t \mid L_F, p_a)$, all of which can be established using the expressions discussed earlier. Plugging the approximations for these PDFs into Equation (30.13) gives

$$P(L_F \mid p_a) = \frac{\dfrac{\tilde{f}_{T_I,P_a}(t, p_a)}{f_{P_a}(p_a)} - \dfrac{\tilde{f}_{T_I|L_R,P_a}(t, p_a \mid L_R)}{\tilde{f}(p_a \mid L_R)}}{\dfrac{\tilde{f}_{T_I|L_F,P_a}(t, p_a \mid L_F)}{\tilde{f}(p_a \mid L_F)} - \dfrac{\tilde{f}_{T_I|L_R,P_a}(t, p_a \mid L_R)}{\tilde{f}(p_a \mid L_R)}}. \tag{30.14}$$

The probability $P(L_F \mid p_a)$ can be estimated using any value of t in Equation (30.14). In the following example, the average of $P(L_F \mid p_a)$ estimated for several values of t is used.

In the end, all of the PDFs and probabilities required in the estimation of life-cycle perform-ance can be established based on the same set of generated samples. Once we can evaluate the PDFs and probabilities for any given p_a, the estimation of the objective funciton and the optimization in Equation (30.9) can be carried out directly.

In terms of the computational effort, the approach proposed here for the evaluation of the life-cycle performance for any p_a requires a computational effort comparable to the one for the evaluation of the life-cycle performance for one particular p_a (i.e., as on p. 579). This is realized through sampling from the joint PDF $f_{T_l, P_a}(t, p_a)$, and the KDE approximation of all relevant PDFs. Overall, the proposed approach is very efficient. Note that in addition to KDE (which is nonparametric), other parametric PDF approximation approaches can also be used to approxi-mate the PDFs based on the generated samples.

30.3 Example: Stochastic life-cycle analysis and performance optimization of a deteriorating RC bridge

This section illustrates the proposed life-cycle analysis and optimization approach considering an example RC bridge under gradual deterioration due to chloride-induced corrosion and shock deterioration due to earthquakes.

30.3.1 Example bridge and site

We consider the RC bridge with one single-column bent in Jia and Gardoni (2018b). Figure 30.2 shows the bridge and a schematic layout of the hypothetical site of the bridge with respect to a seismic fault.

30.3.2 SDSMs for deterioration processes

For the deterioration due to corrosion, we model the reduction of the diameter of the reinforce-ment steel and its impacts on the resulting structural properties of the RC bridge column including moment curvature characteristics and pushover characteristics (Choe et al. 2008, 2009, 2010). For deterioration due to seismic loading, we model the stiffness reduction and damage

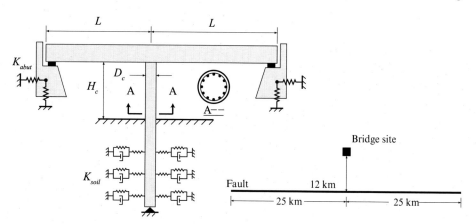

Figure 30.2 Example RC bridge.

Source: Adapted from Jia and Gardoni 2018b.

accumulation due to low-cycle fatigue (Kumar & Gardoni 2014a). Overall, both the impact on the state variables $\mathbf{X}$ (e.g., reinforcement steel diameter) and the resultant impact on structural properties (e.g., ultimate curvature capacity, stiffness, damage index), which are functions of the state variables $\mathbf{X}$, are modeled. One convenience in modeling the structural properties directly is that they serve as direct inputs to the capacity and demand models used later.

To model the interaction between corrosion and seismic damage, the initiation and the rate of corrosion of the reinforcement steel are modified considering the fact that the formation of cracks caused by past earthquakes may initiate corrosion and accelerate the corrosion rate (Jia & Gardoni 2018b). Such interaction is supported by the finding in Otieno et al. (2010) that found that even small cracks may significantly impact the initiation and rate of corrosion, and the fact that seismic loading might create cracks, widen existing cracks and reopen self-healed cracks, all of which may accelerate the corrosion process. The modeling discussed in Section 30.2.1 allows us to incorporate this interaction. Next, we briefly review the modeling of deterioration due to corrosion and earthquakes. More details can be found in Jia and Gardoni (2018b).

Deterioration due to corrosion

To consider the impact of seismic damage on the corrosion initiation, the corrosion initiation time is modeled as $T_{corr} = \min(t_{corr}, t_1)$ where t_{corr} is a random variable representing the corrosion initiation time without considering the impact of seismic damages, and t_1 is the time of the first damaging earthquake (e.g., an earthquake such that $S_a > s_{a0}$, where s_{a0} is a specified threshold beyond which cracks form in the concrete). The distribution of t_{corr} can be obtained using the formula in Choe et al. (2008), which is a function of the environmental exposure conditions (e.g., submerged, tidal, splash, atmospheric) that affect the chloride concentration on the surface and also the chloride transport characteristics related to the concrete. So, such exposure conditions have to be included in $\mathbf{E}(t)$. Essentially, the selection of $T_{corr} = \min(t_{corr}, t_1)$ means that a damaging earthquake initiates the corrosion (because of the formation of cracks) if corrosion has not started. Compared to t_{corr}, the use of T_{corr} tends to shift the corrosion initiation time towards lower values as the rate of earthquakes increases.

For the corrosion, we model the uniform reduction of the diameter of the reinforcement steel. To consider the impact of earthquakes on the corrosion rate, the time-dependent model in Jia and Gardoni (2018b) for the reduction in diameter of the reinforcement steel is adopted, which introduces a constant acceleration factor r_a for the corrosion rate (i.e., the ratio between corrosion rate after and before the damaging shock),

$$d_b(t, T_{corr}) = d_b(t_{N_{iD}}, T_{corr}) - (r_a)^{N_{iD}} \frac{1.0508(1 - w/c)^{-1.64}}{d_c} \left[(t - T_{corr})^{0.71} - (t_{N_{iD}} - T_{corr})^{0.71} \right] \quad (30.15)$$

where $d_b(t, T_{corr})$ is the diameter at time t for a given T_{corr}, N_{iD} is the number of damaging shocks before time t, $t_{N_{iD}}$ is the time of occurrence of the N_{iD}th damaging shock, and w/c is the water-to-cement ratio, d_c is the concrete cover depth. For $r_a = 1$, the corrosion rate is not accelerated after the earthquake, i.e., Equation (30.15) is equivalent to the rate in Choe et al. (2008, 2009). In this example, we assume a tidal zone exposure condition and for corrosion acceleration we assume $s_{a0} = 0.1g$ and $r_a = 1.2$. These values are assumed to illustrate the formulation presented in this chapter. Additional studies should assess the most appropriate values of s_{a0} and r_a for a specific structure and site.

The changes in d_b lead to changes in the structural properties such as the ultimate curvature capacity of the RC section, ϕ_u, and the pushover characteristics such as pre-yield lateral stiffness, K, and the displacement at yield, Δ_y. State-dependent regression models in Jia and Gardoni (2018b) are adopted in this example to predict the changes of these structural properties due to changes in d_b.

Deterioration due to earthquakes

For the deterioration due to seismic loading, the random occurrence of damaging earthquakes and the PDF of their intensity measure (i.e., the spectral acceleration S_a in this example) are modeled as follows. Following Kumar and Gardoni (2012), a homogeneous Poisson process is used to model the occurrence of earthquake mainshocks while a non-homogeneous Poisson process is used to model the occurrence of aftershocks between the mainshocks. For mainshocks, the rate is $\lambda_m = 10^{\upsilon_{m0} - \upsilon_1 M}$ with parameters υ_{m0} and υ_1. The time-varying rate of aftershocks is modeled as $\lambda(t_a, M; m_m) = 10^{\upsilon_0 + \upsilon_1 (m_m - M)} / (t_a + \upsilon_2)^{\upsilon_3}$ where $\lambda(t_a, M; m_m)$ is the mean daily rate of aftershocks with magnitude M or larger at time t_a, following a mainshock of magnitude m_m; υ_0, υ_1, υ_2, and υ_3 are model parameters and are related to the regional seismicity. For this example we take $\upsilon_{m0} = 3.8$, $\upsilon_0 = -1.67$, $\upsilon_1 = 0.91$, $\upsilon_2 = 0.05$, and $\upsilon_3 = 1.08$. These values are typical of seismically active regions. Given the occurrence rates and the site layout with respect to the seismic fault (shown in Figure 30.2), the distribution of S_a at the site can be obtained by performing a probabilistic seismic hazard analysis for the mainshock-aftershocks sequence (Kramer 1996; Yeo & Cornell 2009).

For a shock with given intensity, we need to estimate the amount of deterioration. More specifically, the corresponding changes in $\mathbf{X}$ (e.g., $\Delta \mathbf{X}_k [\mathbf{X}(t_{k,i}^-), \mathbf{S}_k(t_{k,i}); \boldsymbol{\Theta}_{\mathbf{x},k}]$ as discussed in Section 30.2.1) or in the structural properties need to be modeled. In this example, we adopt the probabilistic models developed in Kumar and Gardoni (2014a) that predict the degradation of the static pushover properties of RC columns as a function of $\mathbf{X}$ and S_a. When the drift demand $\delta_D(t_i)$ caused by the shock with intensity $\mathbf{S}(t_i) = S_a$ is such that $\delta_D(t_i) / \delta_y(t_i^-) \geq 1$ where $\delta_y(t_i^-)$ is the drift at yield, the probabilistic models for the reduction in K and the change in Δ_y are written as (Kumar & Gardoni 2014a)

$$\ln\left[K\left(t_i^+\right)/K\left(t_i^-\right)\right] = \left[\theta_{K,1} + \theta_{K,2} P_u /\left(f_c' A_g\right) + \theta_{K,3} T_n\left(t_i^-\right)\right] \ln\left[\delta_D\left(t_i\right)/\delta_y\left(t_i^-\right)\right] + \sigma_K \varepsilon_K \quad (30.16)$$

$$\ln\left[\Delta_y\left(t_i^+\right)/\Delta_y\left(t_i^-\right)\right] = \theta_{\Delta,1} \ln\left[K\left(t_i^+\right)/K\left(t_i^-\right)\right] + \sigma_\Delta \varepsilon_\Delta, \quad (30.17)$$

where $\theta_{K,1}, \theta_{K,2}, \theta_{K,3}$ and $\theta_{\Delta,1}$ are uncertain models parameters, σ_K and σ_Δ are constants representing the standard deviations of the model errors, ε_K and ε_Δ are bivariate normal random variables with correlation coefficient $\rho_{K,\Delta}$. If $\delta_D(t_i) / \delta_y(t_i^-) < 1$ there is no change in K and Δ_y. Posterior distributions for these parameters are listed in Table 30.1, and additional details and justifications for these probabilistic models can be found in Kumar and Gardoni (2014a).

To capture the reduction in the ultimate curvature capacity of the RC section due to accumulation of low-cycle fatigue damage in the reinforcing steel, the following probabilistic model established in Kumar and Gardoni (2014a) is adopted

$$\phi_u\left(t_i^+\right) = \phi_u\left(t_i^-\right) \times \begin{cases} 1.0 & 0 \leq DI\left(t_i\right) \leq DI_{tr}\left(t_i^-\right) \\ \left[\dfrac{1 - DI\left(t_i\right)}{1 - DI_{tr}\left(t_i^-\right)}\right]^\alpha + \sigma_\phi \varepsilon_\phi & DI_{tr}\left(t_i^-\right) < DI\left(t_i\right) < 1 \end{cases} \quad (30.18)$$

Table 30.1 Posterior statistics of the parameters in the probabilistic degradation models

Parameters	$\theta_{K,1}$	$\theta_{K,2}$	$\theta_{K,3}$	$\theta_{\Delta,1}$	σ_Δ	σ_K	$\rho_{K,\Delta}$
Mean	−0.735	0.347	0.124	−0.967	0.050	0.120	0.070
St. dev.	0.018	0.25	0.033	0.003	0.005	0.005	0.066
Correlations							
$\theta_{K,1}$	1.00						
$\theta_{K,2}$	−0.45	1.00					
$\theta_{K,3}$	−0.37	−0.61	1.00				
$\theta_{\Delta,1}$	0.28	−0.06	−0.14	1.00			
σ_Δ	−0.03	−0.02	0.062	0.20	1.00		
σ_K	0.16	−0.01	−0.15	0.01	0.09	1.00	
$\rho_{K,\Delta}$	−0.09	−0.13	0.21	−0.17	−0.03	−0.15	1.00

Table 30.2 Posterior statistics of the parameters in the probabilistic curvature capacity degradation model

Parameters	$\theta_{\phi1}$	$\theta_{\phi2}$	$\theta_{\phi3}$	$\theta_{\phi4}$	α	σ_ϕ
Mean	0.690	−30.2	0.031	−0.002	0.266	0.168
St. dev.	0.014	3.28	0.007	0.0002	0.021	0.010
Correlations						
$\theta_{\phi1}$	1.00					
$\theta_{\phi2}$	−0.65	1.00				
$\theta_{\phi3}$	−0.71	0.81	1.00			
$\theta_{\phi4}$	−0.71	0.82	0.85	1.00		
α	0.10	−0.10	0.68	−0.11	1.00	
σ_ϕ	−0.46	0.26	0.10	0.26	−0.20	1.00

where $DI(t_i)$ is the damage index after the ith earthquake (i.e., sum of low-cycle fatigue damage ΔDI over past earthquakes, from 1 to i), and $DI_{tr}(t_i^-)$ is a threshold value above which the low-cycle fatigue would lead to reduction of ϕ_u and takes the form $DI_{tr}(t_i^-) = \theta_{\phi1} + \theta_{\phi2}\varepsilon_{cu}(t_i^-) + \theta_{\phi3}\rho_{sl}(t_i^-) + \theta_{\phi4}[\phi_u(t_i^-)/\phi_y](f_y/f_c')$. To estimate ΔDI for a given earthquake, the probabilistic model $\Delta DI(t_i) = \theta_{DI,1} + \theta_{DI,2}\ln[\delta_D(t_i)] + \theta_{DI,3}\ln[T_n(t_i^-)] + \sigma_{DI}\varepsilon_{DI}$ in Kumar and Gardoni (2014a) is adopted, with $\theta_{DI,1}$, $\theta_{DI,2}$, $\theta_{DI,3}$, and σ_{DI} the uncertain model parameters. The posterior statistics for the model parameters are listed in Table 30.2 and Table 30.3.

Stochastic capacity and demand models

To estimate the life-cycle performance quantities and carry out the optimization, the intervention criterion is chosen as $P_f[t_i^+ \mid \mathbf{x}(t_i^+)] \geq p_a$, which means the bridge is repaired after the ith earthquake if the failure probability $P_f[t_i^+ \mid \mathbf{x}(t_i^+)]$ for the given realization of the state variable $\mathbf{x}(t_i^+)$ is larger than a prescribed threshold p_a. Failure is defined in this example as deformation demand, $D(t)$, exceeding the deformation capacity $C(t)$. To estimate the time-variant capacity and demand, the predicted time-variant state variables and structural properties (through the deterioration models) are plugged into the probabilistic capacity model in Gardoni et al. (2002) and the probabilistic demand model in Gardoni et al. (2003). Specifically, considering the damage index DI, when its value is larger than 1, the longitudinal reinforcement steel is expected to fail due to low-cycle fatigue (Kumar & Gardoni 2012, 2014a), and the deformation capacity in this case is taken as zero.

Table 30.3 Posterior statistics of the parameters in the probabilistic low-cycle fatigue damage accumulation model

Parameters	$\theta_{DI,1}$	$\theta_{DI,2}$	$\theta_{DI,3}$	σ_{DI}
Mean	5.81	2.40	−2.07	1.44
St. dev.	0.270	0.080	0.110	0.076
Correlations				
$\theta_{DI,1}$	1.00			
$\theta_{DI,2}$	0.93	1.00		
$\theta_{DI,3}$	−0.22	−0.52	1.00	
σ_{DI}	0.01	0.02	−0.01	1.00

Time-variant system performance indicators

Using the formulation on p. 574 and the simulation-based approach on p. 575, we can estimate $P_f[t_i^+ \mid \mathbf{x}(t_i^+)]$. It is expected that due to deterioration caused by both corrosion and seismic excitations, the failure probability increases over time.

30.3.3 Renewal-theory life-cycle analysis and optimization

Renewal-theory life-cycle analysis (RTLCA)

In terms of repair and recovery time, in this example, we make the same simplifying assumptions as those in Kumar and Gardoni (2014b) since here the focus is on integrating SDSMs in RTLCA. A more detailed modeling of recovery processes can be found in Jia et al. (2017) and Sharma et al. (2017). Specifically, the lag period T_l to initiate repairs is assumed to be 0.25 years, and the time to replace the bridge is assumed to be 2 years. Further, it is assumed that the time to repair a damaged bridge is a fraction of the 2 years depending on the extent of damage which is measured in terms of the failure probability at the time when repair is initiated (i.e., $t_{l_i} + 0.25$), given by $P_f[t_{l_i} + 0.25 \mid \mathbf{x}(t_{l_i} + 0.25)] \times 2$. Because the recovery is not instantaneous, it is important to consider the likely extra damage to the bridge due to aftershocks during the lag period. The adoption of P_f at $(t_{l_i} + 0.25)$ for determining the repair time reflects this consideration. The operation cost is assumed to be proportional to the bridge's replacement value with $\bar{c}_{Op} = 0.2 C_C$ (Jia et al. 2017). Additionally, the following values are chosen for the current example: $c_L = 2C_C$, $\gamma = 0.04$ year^{-1}, and $b = 0.1 C_C$ year^{-1}.

Optimization of life cycle performances

As mentioned earlier, the selection of p_a impact the life-cycle performances. For optimization of life-cycle performances, the optimization approach in Section 30.2.3 is used. To implement the sampling approach, we assume p_a is uniformly distributed in $[p_{a,l}, p_{a,u}]$ with $p_{a,l} = 10^{-3}$, and $p_{a,u} = 0.08$. The actual range can be decided for example by asset managers or decision makers. Also, $n_s = 2{,}500$ is used, i.e., 2,500 samples are generated to approximate the joint PDF $f_{T_l,P_a}(t, p_a)$. In this example, we consider $H(p_a) = E[C_{\text{total}}(t_{lca}) \mid p_a] / C_c$ (i.e., the expected total cost for selected p_a during a desired time period $(0, t_{lca}]$ normalized by C_c), where $t_{lca} = 50$ years.

Approximation of required PDFs and probabilities

Figure 30.3(a) shows the samples from the joint PDF $f_{T_l,P_a}(t, p_a)$, and Figure 30.3(b) shows an approximation of $f_{T_l,P_a}(t, p_a)$ by KDE based on the samples (i.e., $\tilde{f}_{T_l,P_a}(t, p_a)$). Based on

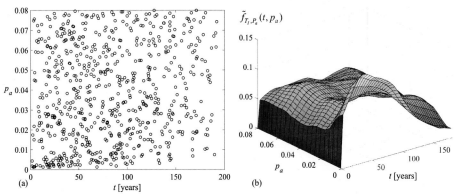

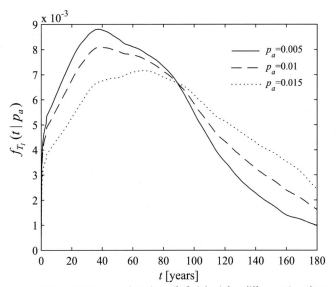

Figure 30.3 (a) Samples from the joint PDF $f_{T_I,P_a}(t,p_a)$, and (b) KDE approximation of $f_{T_I,P_a}(t,p_a)$ based on samples.

Figure 30.4 KDE approximation of $f_{T_I}(t\,|\,p_a)$ for different p_a values.

$f_{T_I}(t\,|\,p_a)=\tilde{f}_{T_I,P_a}(t,p_a)\cdot(p_{a,u}-p_{a,l})$, we can estimate $f_{T_I}(t\,|\,p_a)$ for any given value of p_a. Figure 30.4 shows $f_{T_I}(t\,|\,p_a)$ for several values of p_a. As expected, larger p_a, which means less frequent repairs, leads to larger values of T_I.

From the samples in Figure 30.3(a), we can identify the samples from the conditional PDF $f_{T_I|L_F,P_a}(t,p_a\,|\,L_F)$, while the rest of the samples correspond to samples from the conditional PDF $f_{T_I|L_R,P_a}(t,p_a\,|\,L_R)$. These samples are plotted in Figure 30.5(a) and Figure 30.5(c). As expected, for $f_{T_I|L_F,P_a}(t,p_a\,|\,L_F)$, more samples are observed in regions with larger p_a values, since larger p_a means less frequent repairs and the system is more likely to experience failure. On the other hand, for $f_{T_I|L_R,P_a}(t,p_a\,|\,L_R)$, more samples are observed in regions with smaller p_a values,

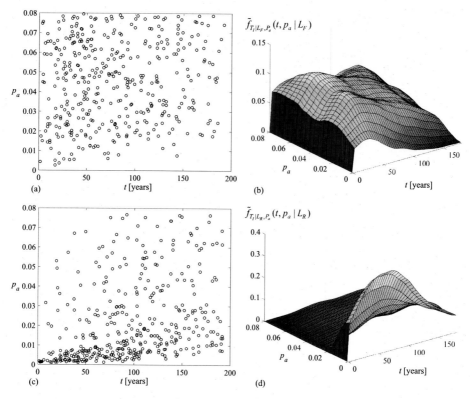

Figure 30.5 Samples from and KDE approximations of the conditional PDFs $f_{T_I|L_F,P_a}(t, p_a | L_F)$ and $f_{T_I|L_R,P_a}(t, p_a | L_R)$, (a) samples from $f_{T_I|L_F,P_a}(t, p_a | L_F)$, (b) $\tilde{f}_{T_I|L_F,P_a}(t, p_a | L_F)$, (c) samples from $f_{T_I|L_R,P_a}(t, p_a | L_R)$, and (d) $\tilde{f}_{T_I|L_R,P_a}(t, p_a | L_R)$.

since for smaller p_a values the system is more likely to experience repair interventions. The p_a components of these samples are then samples from the conditional PDFs $f(p_a | L_F)$ and $f(p_a | L_R)$, both of which can be estimated as well using KDE. Figure 30.5 also shows the corresponding KDE approximations of the PDFs, i.e., $\tilde{f}_{T_I|L_F,P_a}(t, p_a | L_F)$ and $\tilde{f}_{T_I|L_R,P_a}(t, p_a | L_R)$. Then based on these PDFs and Equation (30.12), the conditional PDFs $f_{T_I|L_F}(t | L_F, p_a)$ and $f_{T_I|L_R}(t | L_R, p_a)$ can be estimated for any given p_a. Figure 30.6 shows these conditional PDFs for several values of p_a (the same p_a values as in Figure 30.4).

Therefore, for given p_a, we can estimate $f_{T_I}(t | p_a)$, $f_{T_I|L_R}(t | L_R, p_a)$, and $f_{T_I|L_F}(t | L_F, p_a)$, and also $f(p_a | L_F)$ and $f(p_a | L_R)$. Then using Equation (30.14), we can calculate $P(L_F | p_a)$ for any given p_a. As expected, $P(L_F | p_a)$ tends to increase as p_a increases, since larger value of p_a means less frequent repairs and larger value for $P(L_F | p_a)$. In terms of PDFs for T_L, we simply need to add the values of corresponding T_D to T_I (since $T_L = T_I + T_D$) and again use KDE to establish approximations of PDFs for T_L. In this example, the contribution of T_I to T_L dominates and the marginal and conditional PDFs of T_L are close to those of T_I, and are not shown here. Therefore, we can establish approximations for all the required PDFs. In the end, all of the PDFs and probabilities required in the estimation of life-cycle performance can be established based on the same set of samples generated.

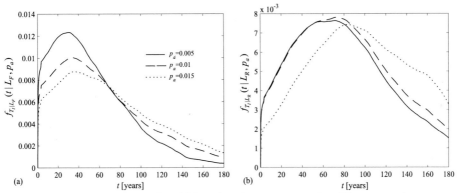

Figure 30.6 Conditional PDFs $f_{T_i|L_F}(t\,|\,L_F,p_a)$ and $f_{T_i|L_R}(t\,|\,L_R,p_a)$ for different p_a values.

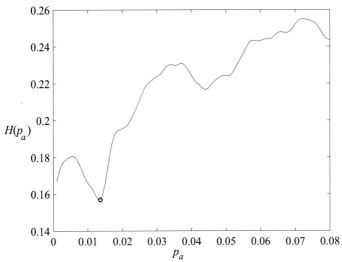

Figure 30.7 Variation of objective function $H(p_a)=E[C_{\text{total}}(t_{lca})\,|\,p_a]\,/\,\mathrm{C}_c$ as a function of p_a.

Life-cycle performance optimization results

Once we can evaluate the PDFs and the probabilities for any given p_a, the estimation of the objective funciton can be carried out directly as discussed on p. 582, then the optimization in Equation (30.9) can be solved directly as well. Figure 30.7 shows the variation of objective function $H(p_a)$ as a function of p_a. The p_a that minimizes $H(p_a)$ (i.e., the expected total cost) is 0.0136. For p_a values lower than the optimal value, which means more frequent repairs, the system is less likely to experience failure. However, the more frequent repairs also increase the operation cost, which leads to higher total cost in the current example. On the other hand, for p_a values higher than the optimal value, which means less frequent repairs, the system is more likely to experience failure resulting in higher failure loss, which leads to a higher total cost.

Other selections of objective functions and t_{lca} can be considered as well without additional simulations, since the required PDFs and probabilities have been established. For example,

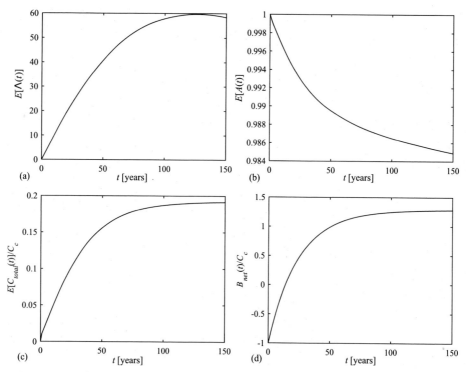

Figure 30.8 Variation of life-cycle performance quantities over time for the selection of optimal p_a: (a) expected age, (b) expected availability, (c) expected total cost, (d) expected net benefit.

we can consider $H(p_a)=E[B_{net}(t_{lca})\mid p_a]/C_c$. In this example, since $E[B(t_{lca})\mid p_a]$ has little variation for different values of p_a, the variation of the net benefit $E[B_{net}(t_{lca})\mid p_a]$ is dominated by the variation of $E[C_{total}(t_{lca})\mid p_a]$, and the same optimal p_a as for the previous optimization is observed.

Figure 30.8 shows the variation of life-cycle performance quantities over time for the selection of optimal p_a. From Figure 30.8(a) we can see that the expected age $E[A(t)]$ first increases and then reaches a plateau after a certain time. The leveling behavior is because of the renewal of the system after the intervention and repair/replacement. In Figure 30.8(b), it is observed that $E[A(t)]$ decreases initially and then gradually increases toward an asymptotic value. The initial decrease can be attributed to the fact that the system deteriorates as it operates over time and becomes more likely to be down (out of service) due to a repair or replacement. In Figure 30.8(c), it is observed that $E[C_{total}(t)]$ increases with time and after about $t = 80$ years it becomes almost constant. This leveling behavior is because of the discount rate, which makes the costs associated with the events occurring after a long period irrelevant to the decision made at $t = 0$. When comparing the values of $E[C_{Op}(t)]$ and $E[C_L(t)]$, it is found that $E[C_L(t)]$ is significantly larger and dominates in the expected total cost $E[C_{total}(t)] = E[C_{Op}(t)] + E[C_L(t)]$ (i.e., the values and trend of $E[C_{total}(t)]$ are similar to those of $E[C_L(t)]$). In Figure 30.8(d), it is observed that $E[B_{net}(t)]$ increases with time and after about $t = 100$ years it saturates. The reason for this saturation is similar to that of considering long term expected total costs.

30.4 Conclusions

This chapter discussed the estimation and optimization of stochastic life-cycle performances of deteriorating engineering systems. State-dependent stochastic models (SDSMs) were used to model the deterioration due to multiple deterioration processes and include their interactions. The SDSMs were then integrated into the renewal-theory life-cycle analysis (RTLCA) to evaluate life-cycle performance quantities. The time-variant system state variables (modeled using the SDSMs) were used to calculate time-variant performance indicators (such as the failure probability) using a stochastic simulation-based approach to inform the repair or replacement interventions. For the estimation of the life-cycle performances, the main computational effort comes from generating samples from the relevant PDFs in RTLCA, since the simulation of samples requires modeling of the deterioration processes and estimating the performance indicator at many different time instants. To alleviate the computation cost and allow for an efficient optimization of the life-cycle performances (i.e., selection of optimal value of intervention criterion), a novel sampling and kernel density estimation (KDE) based approach was proposed. The sampling and kernel density estimation (KDE) based approach efficiently approximates the PDFs in RTLCA for any selected value of intervention criterion. The proposed approach first treats the value of intervention criterion (i.e., p_a) as a random variable instead of a deterministic value, and then it relies on generating samples from the joint PDF $f_{T_I, P_a}(t, p_a)$ for the intervention time (i.e., T_I) and the value of intervention criterion (i.e., p_a). In the end, KDE is used to approximate $f_{T_I, P_a}(t, p_a)$ for any given value of T_I and p_a based on the generated samples without the need for additional simulations. This faciliates the estimation and optimiziton of life-cycle performances for any selection p_a values. Overall, the proposed approach requires simulation of only one set of samples. These samples are used to establish the information needed to evaluate the life-cycle performance for any selected value of the intervention criterion. Therefore, the proposed approach has a significant computational efficiency. In the illustrative example, the proposed formulation was applied to estimate and optimize the life-cycle performance of an example RC bridge considering deteriorations due to corrosion and seismic loading. The results showed that the proposed approach can efficiently identify the optimal intervention criterion that minimizes the expected total cost over a given time period.

Acknowledgement

The research herein was supported in part by the Center for Risk-Based Community Resilience Planning funded by the US National Institute of Standards and Technology (NIST Financial Assistance Award Number: 70NANB15H044). The views expressed are those of the authors and may not represent the official position of the National Institute of Standards and Technology or the U.S. Department of Commerce.

Note

1   Corresponding author.
    E-mail addresses: GaofengJia@colostate.edu (G. Jia), gardoni@illinois.edu (P. Gardoni).

References

Au, S.K. and Beck, J.L. (2003). Important sampling in high dimensions. *Structural Safety*, 25(2), 139–63.
Barone, G. and Frangopol, D.M. (2014a). Life-cycle maintenance of deteriorating structures by multi-objective optimization involving reliability, risk, availability, hazard and cost. *Structural Safety*, 48, 40–50.

Barone, G. and Frangopol, D.M. (2014b). Reliability, risk and lifetime distributions as performance indicators for life-cycle maintenance of deteriorating structures. *Reliability Engineering and System Safety*, *123*, 21–37.

Biondini, F. and Frangopol, D.M. (2016). Life-cycle performance of structural systems under uncertainty. *Journal of Structural Engineering*, *142*(9), F4016001.

Bocchini, P., Saydam, D., and Frangopol, D.M. (2013). Efficient, accurate, and simple Markov chain model for the life-cycle analysis of bridge groups. *Structural Safety*, *40*, 51–64.

Bocchini, P., Frangopol, D.M., Ummenhofer, T., and Zinke, T. (2014). Resilience and sustainability of civil infrastructure: Toward a unified approach. *Journal of Infrastructure Systems*, *20*(2), 04014004.

Cheng, T. and Pandey, M.D. (2012). An accurate analysis of maintenance cost of structures experiencing stochastic degradation. *Structure and Infrastructure Engineering*, *8*(4), 329–39.

Choe, D.-E., Gardoni, P., Rosowsky, D., and Haukaas, T. (2008). Probabilistic capacity models and seismic fragility estimates for RC columns subject to corrosion. *Reliability Engineering and System Safety*, *93*(3), 383–93.

Choe, D.-E., Gardoni, P., Rosowsky, D., and Haukaas, T. (2009). Seismic fragility estimates for reinforced concrete bridges subject to corrosion. *Structural Safety*, *31*(4), 275–83.

Choe, D.-E., Gardoni, P., and Rosowsky, D. (2010). Fragility increment functions for deteriorating reinforced concrete bridge columns. *Journal of Engineering Mechanics*, *136*, 969–78.

Ciampoli, M. and Ellingwood, B.R. (2002). Probabilistic methods for assessing current and future performance of concrete structures in nuclear power plants. *Materials and Structures*, *35*(1), 3–14.

Dong, Y., Frangopol, D.M., and Saydam, D. (2014). Pre-earthquake multi-objective probabilistic retrofit optimization of bridge networks based on sustainability. *Journal of Bridge Engineering*, *19*(6), 04014018.

Eck Olave, M.K., Bracci, J.M., Gardoni, P., and Trejo, D. (2015a). Performance of RC columns affected by ASR. I: Accelerated exposure and damage. *Journal of Bridge Engineering*, *20*(3), 04014069.

Eck Olave, M. K., Bracci, J. M., Gardoni, P., and Trejo, D. (2015b). Performance of RC Columns Affected by ASR. II : Experiments and Assessment. *Journal of Bridge Engineering*, *20*(3), 04014070.

Ellingwood, B.R. (2005). Risk-informed condition assessment of civil infrastructure: State of practice and research issues. *Structure and Infrastructure Engineering*, *1*(1), 7–18.

Ellingwood, B.R., and Yasuhiro, M. (1993). Probabilistic methods for condition assessment and life prediction of concrete structures in nuclear power plants. *Nuclear Engineering and Design*, *142*, 155–66.

Gardoni, P. (2017). *Risk and Reliability Analysis: Theory and Applications*. (P. Gardoni, ed.). New York: Springer.

Gardoni, P. and LaFave, J.M. (2016). *Multi-hazard Approaches to Civil Infrastructure Engineering*. (P. Gardoni and J. M. LaFave, eds.). New York: Springer.

Gardoni, P. and Murphy, C. (2008). Recovery from natural and man-made disasters as capabilities restoration and enhancement. *International Journal of Sustainable Development and Planning*, *3*(4), 317–33.

Gardoni, P. and Rosowsky, D. (2011). Seismic fragility increment functions for deteriorating reinforced concrete bridges. *Structure and Infrastructure Engineering*, *7*(11), 1–11.

Gardoni, P. and Trejo, D. (2013). Seismic reliability of deteriorating reinforced concrete (RC) bridges. In S. Tesfamariam and K. Goda (eds.), *Handbook of Seismic Risk Analysis and Management of Civil Infrastructure Systems* (pp. 514–35). Cambridge, UK: Woodhead Publishing Ltd.

Gardoni, P., Der Kiureghian, A., and Mosalam, K.M. (2002). Probabilistic capacity models and fragility estimates for reinforced concrete columns based on experimental observations. *Journal of Engineering Mechanics*, *128*(10), 1024–38.

Gardoni, P., Mosalam, K. M., and Der Kiureghian, A. (2003). Probabilistic Seismic Demand Models and Fragility Estimates for RC Bridges. *Journal of Earthquake Engineering*, *7*(1), 79–106.

Gardoni, P., Trejo, D., and Kim, Y.H. (2013). Time-variant strength capacity model for GFRP bars embedded in concrete. *Journal of Engineering Mechanics*, *139*(10), 1435–45.

Gardoni, P., Guevara-Lopez, F., and Contento, A. (2016a). The Life Profitability Method (LPM): A financial approach to engineering decisions. *Structural Safety*, *63*, 11–20.

Gardoni, P., Murphy, C., and Rowell, A. (eds.) (2016b). *Risk Analysis of natural hazards: Interdisciplinary challenges and integrated solutions*. New York: Springer.

Guida, M. and Pulcini, G. (2011). A continuous-state Markov model for age- and state-dependent degradation processes. *Structural Safety*, *33*(6), 354–66.

Jia, G. and Gardoni, P. (2018a). Simulation-based approach for estimation of the stochastic performances of deteriorating engineering systems. *Probabilistic Engineering Mechanics*, *52*(April), 28–39.

Jia, G. and Gardoni, P. (2018b). State-dependent stochastic models: A general stochastic framework for modeling deteriorating engineering systems considering multiple deterioration processes and their interactions. *Structural Safety*, *72*, 99–110.

Jia, G., Gardoni, P., and Trejo, D. (2017a). Stochastic modelling of deterioration of reinforced concrete structures considering joint effects of earthquakes, corrosion and ASR. In *ICOSSAR 2017: 12th International Conference on Structural Safety and Reliability*. Vienna, Austria.

Jia, G., Tabandeh, A., and Gardoni, P. (2017b). Life-cycle analysis of engineering systems: Modeling deterioration, instantaneous reliability, and resilience. In P. Gardoni (ed.), *Risk and Reliability Analysis: Theory and Applications*. New York: Springer.

Joanni, A. and Rackwitz, R. (2008). Cost-benefit optimization for maintained structures by a renewal model. *Reliability Engineering and System Safety*, 93(3), 489–99.

Kramer, S.L. (1996). *Geotechnical Earthquake Engineering* (Vol. 6). New York: Prentice-Hall, Inc.

Kumar, R. and Gardoni, P. (2012). Modeling structural degradation of RC bridge columns subjected to earthquakes and their fragility estimates. *Journal of Structural Engineering*, 138(1), 42–51.

Kumar, R. and Gardoni, P. (2014a). Effect of seismic degradation on the fragility of reinforced concrete bridges. *Engineering Structures*, 79, 267–275.

Kumar, R. and Gardoni, P. (2014b). Renewal theory-based life-cycle analysis of deteriorating engineering systems. *Structural Safety*, 50, 94–102.

Kumar, R., Gardoni, P., and Sanchez-Silva, M. (2009). Effect of cumulative seismic damage and corrosion on the life-cycle cost of reinforced concrete bridges. *Earthquake Engineering and Structural Dynamics*, 38(7), 887–905.

Kumar, R., Cline, D.B.H., and Gardoni, P. (2015). A stochastic framework to model deterioration in engineering systems. *Structural Safety*, 53, 36–43.

Kurtz, N., Song, J., and Gardoni, P. (2016). Seismic reliability analysis of deteriorating representative U.S. west coast bridge transportation networks. *Journal of Structural Engineering*, 142(8), 1–11.

Mori, Y. and Ellingwood, B.R. (1994). Maintaining reliability of concrete structures. II: Optimum inspection/repair. *Journal of Structural Engineering*, 120(3), 846–62.

Otieno, M.B., Alexander, M.G., and Beushausen, H.-D. (2010). Corrosion in cracked and uncracked concrete – influence of crack width, concrete quality and crack reopening. *Magazine of Concrete Research*, 62(6), 393–404.

Pandey, M.D. and van der Weide, J.A.M. (2017). Stochastic renewal process models for estimation of damage cost over the life-cycle of a structure. *Structural Safety*, 67, 27–38.

Sanchez-Silva, M., Klutke, G.A., and Rosowsky, D.V. (2011). Life-cycle performance of structures subject to multiple deterioration mechanisms. *Structural Safety*, 33(3), 206–17.

Sharma, N., Tabandeh, A., and Gardoni, P. (2017). Resilience analysis: A mathematical formulation to model resilience of engineering systems. *Sustainable and Resilient Infrastructure*, 3(2), 49–67.

Tabandeh, A. and Gardoni, P. (2014). Probabilistic capacity models and fragility estimates for RC columns retrofitted with FRP composites. *Engineering Structures*, 74, 13–22.

van Noortwijk, J.M., and Frangopol, D.M. (2004). Two probabilistic life-cycle maintenance models for deteriorating civil infrastructures. *Probabilistic Engineering Mechanics*, 19(4), 345–59.

van Noortwijk, J.M., and van der Weide, J.A.M. (2008). Applications to continuous-time processes of computational techniques for discrete-time renewal processes. *Reliability Engineering and System Safety*, 93(12), 1853–60.

Vu, K.A.T. and Stewart, M.G. (2000). Structural reliability of concrete bridges including improved chloride-induced corrosion models. *Structural Safety*, 22(4), 313–33.

Yeo, G.L. and Cornell, C.A. (2009). A probabilistic framework for quantification of aftershockground-motion hazard in California. *Earthquake Engineering and Structural Dynamics*, (38), 45–60.

Zhong, J., Gardoni, P., and Rosowsky, D. (2010). Stiffness degradation and time to cracking of cover concrete in reinforced concrete structures subject to corrosion. *Journal of Engineering Mechanics*, 136(2), 209–19.

Part VIII

The role and impact
of climate change

31

Infrastructure and climate change

*Mikhail Chester, Samuel Markolf, Andrew Fraser, Daniel Burillo,
Emily Bondank, Yeowon Kim, and Christopher Hoehne*

SCHOOL OF SUSTAINABLE ENGINEERING AND THE BUILT ENVIRONMENT,
SCHOOL OF SUSTAINABILITY, ARIZONA STATE UNIVERSITY, USA

31.1 Introduction

Climate change creates new challenges for those who design, manage, and use infrastructure in the form of both gradual changes in environmental conditions and extreme events. There is increasing evidence that our civil infrastructure are vulnerable to climate change. While extreme events have always posed a risk to infrastructure, the increasing frequency and intensity of events that may exceed the safe design thresholds of infrastructure are of particular concern. There is a growing body of knowledge on the potential risks of climate change. These risks vary by region and their severity may very well be determined by the aggressiveness (or lack thereof) of policies, technologies, and behavioral changes that reduce greenhouse gas emissions. The challenge for infrastructure designers and managers is that they must now build and operate their infrastructure with climate change in mind. In the past, standard practice was to design infrastructure based on historical weather conditions (climate can be thought of as long term weather patterns). Now, knowing that weather is changing, infrastructure must remain functional in a future with an uncertain climate. This creates a fundamental new challenge. Infrastructure are obdurate, they are typically long lasting (often on the order of many of decades) and the technologies that define them do not change quickly (the basic materials, structure, and technologies that are used for roads, water networks, and power systems have not changed in any major way in decades). Certainly new technologies have been implemented in infrastructure but for the most part their core structures and functions have not changed in the long-term. This is largely because the demand for the services and resources that infrastructure facilitate don't change on short time scales. The obdurate nature of infrastructure creates a major challenge for climate change planning. Given that infrastructure is intended to last a long time, and the uncertainty in the frequency and intensity of future events, new models of design and construction may be needed to ensure resiliency.

The changing frequencies and intensities of precipitation, heat, cold, wind, flooding, and wildfires predicted with climate change are each of concern when it comes to infrastructure. These changes can be both gradual (e.g., slow increase in average temperatures over decades) or in the extremes (e.g., the changing return periods of precipitation) (Hunt & Watkiss 2011; Dominguez et al. 2012). One problem is that infrastructure are designed assuming a normative future. That is, designers are typically required to size infrastructure components to be able to withstand a particular intensity event (often a 100 year event, meaning that there is a

1 percent chance that that intensity of the event will occur each year). This practice is essentially an acceptance of a particular level of risk. While infrastructure could possibly be designed to withstand even more intense events (e.g., a 500 year rainstorm), in the past these more robust implementations have not been selected, largely because the greater costs are deemed to exceed the benefits. But as climate change progresses, what was historically a 500 year event may now become a 100 year event, and what was a 100 year event may now become a 20 year event (Gilroy & McCuen 2012; Tramblay et al. 2013). A more significant problem may be our inability to predict the normative future to change design goals. The uncertainty in climate change is not simply from our greenhouse gas emissions changes but from the complexities and nonlinearities that define many Earth systems.

With climate change two fundamental problems arise for infrastructure. First, infrastructure hardware may not be designed to function in weather conditions that exceed design thresholds, leading to increasing numbers of failures that may directly or indirectly impact people, services, and economies. Second, the design of infrastructure may contribute to people's environmental exposure or fail to protect people from exposure. For example, deploying walkable streets without sufficient shade or refuge may result in increased exposure as temperatures rise (the authors are not arguing against walkable streets but that changing climates must be central to their design). And the deployment of new housing stock should include considerations for passive or active cooling systems for increasing temperatures. Infrastructure are our front line of defense against climate change and to continue providing the basic services and protections that they've enabled in the past we must plan around the uncertainties of a climate-impact future.

In this chapter we summarize emerging literature on infrastructure and climate change, and then discuss how we can shift our approach to preparing infrastructure for climate change, from risk-based to resilience-based.

31.2 Infrastructure and climate change

The United States Department of Homeland Security identifies 16 critical infrastructure sectors that are considered vital to the "security, national economic security, and national public health or safety" of the country (DHS 2015). These critical infrastructure sectors include chemicals, commercial facilities, communications, critical manufacturing, dams, defense, emergency services, energy, financial services, food and agriculture, government facilities, healthcare and public health, information technology, nuclear, transportation, and water and wastewater systems (DHS 2015). Across these infrastructure sectors, there is increasing evidence that climate change will impact physical assets, operations, and use (Field et al. 2014; Melillo et al. 2014). There are too many effects to characterize across all of these infrastructure and we choose electricity, water, and transportation to provide some context for how climate change may affect our critical infrastructure systems.

Each of the aforementioned infrastructure systems are vulnerable to unique and shared pathways of disruption from climate change as a result of physical component design, processes, and managing institutions. It is important to recognize that failure of infrastructure is often the result of many processes happening concurrently or sequentially. The 2003 Northeast blackout, for example, started with a single overloaded transmission line shorting after coming into contact with a tree. However, sufficient redundancy existed to move power through other circuits. Unfortunately, FirstEnergy in Ohio did not have the organizational capacity to know what was happening due to a bug in their alarm system (NERC 2004). The blackout left approximately 55 million people without electricity in the peak of the summer (some for prolonged periods of time) and resulted in significant economic losses. The example illustrates how multiple smaller failures must occur for a large-scale failure to occur because we have instituted significant extra capacity and redundancies into our systems. Because infrastructure are agglomerations of physical and institutional processes, often built, added to or modified over decades, predicting how infrastructure will fail when components or processes are affected by climate change is difficult. As such, the study of infrastructure resilience to climate change represents a new frontier for research and management. Yet substantial evidence has emerged as to the vulnerability of infrastructure to a number of climate related hazards. The remainder of this section focuses on power, water, and transportation systems, and describes how vulnerabilities to climate change manifest within these systems. For each section we tend to focus on a subset of hazards in our discussion but provide tables and overviews of challenges associated with a broad suite of hazards.

31.2.1 Electric power systems

Electric power infrastructure broadly consists of three systems: generation, delivery, and demand. Climate change can affect electricity systems in a number of ways. A shortage of electric power generation, or sequence of faults in the delivery network, can result in an interruption in service at any second. Table 32.1 provides a summary of major climate variables and their associated impacts on the power sector.

Generation is vulnerable to flooding, reduced streamflow, and warmer water and air temperatures which can all cause a shortage of power supply in the system (van Vliet et al. 2016; Miara et al. 2017). There are many ways to physically generate electrical power, but to evaluate the effects of climate change it is helpful to broadly categorize them as those that use water, and those that do not. Conventional hydroelectric and water-cooled turbine generators (e.g. nuclear, coal-fired, and some natural gas) use water, and so are vulnerable to changes in hydrology in three ways. First, flooding can damage physical hardware of above and below ground equipment if that hardware is not sufficiently shielded (Hollnagel & Fujita 2013). For example, sea level is projected to rise by 1–1.4m by the end of the century, and if that were the case, then 25 coastal plants in California would be at risk of flooding during 1-in-100 year high-tide events (Sathaye et al. 2012). Second, if the water levels in natural sources are too low (e.g. low river flow during droughts), then production capacity can be dependent upon priority level in access rights or reduced to zero if the water level physically goes below the intake pipe (Wagman 2013), see Figure 31.1. Third, once-through generators are vulnerable to increases in water temperature (e.g. some coastal plants), as a certain amount of temperature rise is necessary to cool the generators, but environmental regulations prevent expelling of water that is too hot to be safe for the ecosystem (EEA 2008). In August 2015, the Pilgrim Nuclear Power Station in Massachusetts cut its power because the temperature of sea water used as influent was too high (Abel 2015). Power generators that do not use water include dry combustion natural gas and solar photovoltaics. These types of "dry" power generators are generally inland, and could also be at risk to flooding. Dry power generators also operate less efficiently under higher ambient air temperatures, which means they also have lower production capacity to meet peak demand. Dry generators are also vulnerable to changes in humidity that can affect their air circulation systems, as well as flooding and storm-gusty winds in general (ADB 2012).

Delivery systems can be affected by climate change due to higher temperatures causing higher demand, reduced capacity, and congestion; wildfires that can render power lines inoperable due to ionized air; and large storms that can cause physical damage via flooding and high winds that make trees fall on lines (Campbell 2012). Delivery systems physically consist

Table 31.1 Summary of key climate drivers and possible impacts to power systems

Climate Hazard	Key Impacts	Impacted Segment	Adaptation Strategies
Increased Air Temperatures	• Lower generation efficiency • Decreased coal-to-gas conversion efficiency • Decreased combined cycle gas turbine efficiency • Decreased solar PV efficiency	Generation	• Implement air chillers or more efficient chillers • Site new generation in cooler locations
	• Reduced carrying capacity of lines and transformers • Increased losses in lines and transformers	Delivery – Transmission & Distribution	• Underground hardware • Use more heat-resistant materials • Implement more effective cooling for transformers
	• Increased peak demand and total energy demand for cooling	Demand – End Use	• AC energy efficiency • Building thermal efficiency • Peak load shifting
Increase in precipitation	• Reduced combustion efficiency due to increased moisture content of coal	Generation	• Protect coal stockpiles Switch to fuel that is more moisture resistant (e.g. natural gas)
	• Damaged power lines from snow and ice • Flooding of underground infrastructure • Damaged towers due to erosion	Delivery – Transmission & Distribution	• Improved flood protection for equipment at ground level • Use covered and/or insulated conductors • Include lightning protection (e.g., earth wires, spark gaps) in the distribution network
Decrease in precipitation	• Decreased availability of freshwater for thermal cooling	Generation	• Switch to recirculating or dry cooling • Switch to more "water-efficient" fuels (e.g. natural gas, wind, solar) • Increase volume of water treatment system • Restore/reforest land
Sea Level Rise/ Increased storm surge during hurricanes and tropical storms/ Increased nuisance flooding during high tides	• Flooding/damage to coastal/ low-lying infrastructure	Generation/ Delivery - Transmission & Distribution Demand – End use	• Implement flood control (dams, dikes, reservoirs, polders, etc.) • Improve coastal defenses (seawalls, bulkheads, etc.) • Build in and/or relocate to less exposed locations • Raise structure levels • Improved drainage systems • Protect fuel storage

Table 31.1 (Cont.)

Climate Hazard	Key Impacts	Impacted Segment	Adaptation Strategies
More frequent/severe extreme events (floods, typhoons, drought, high winds, etc.)	• Damaged infrastructure • Disrupted supply chains and offshore activity • Damage to facilities related to soil erosion	Generation Delivery - Transmission & Distribution	• Same as above • Concrete-sided buildings instead of metal • Implement more rigorous structural standards • Implement porous materials for better wind flow • Increased decentralized energy generation • Cite infrastructure away from heavily wooded areas/ rigorously prune trees

Source: Adapted from ADB 2012.

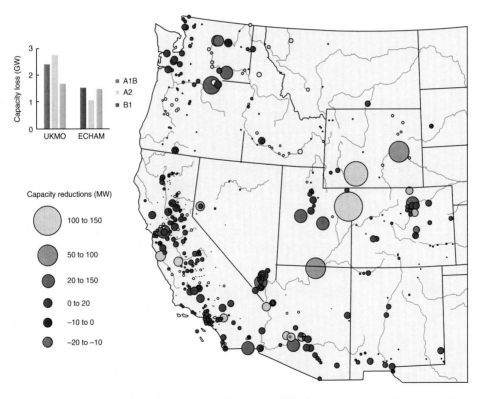

Figure 31.1 Estimated average reductions in western US electricity summertime generation capacity by mid-century.
Source: Bartos and Chester 2015.

of various types of power lines that transport energy, transformers which convert the power to different voltage levels, quality devices for efficiency and reliability, and protection devices that interrupt power flows during hazardous conditions. Climate change can cause failures via physical hardware damage, or create operational conditions that exceed hardware tolerances. Higher temperatures can cause individual components to become inoperable because protection devices will cut them off if power flow is too high for the weather conditions (IEEE 2012). Additionally, higher temperatures may mean that the amount of power that lines can safely carry may need to be reduced, see Figure 31.2 (Bartos et al. 2016). If too many components are offline or the capacity of the system is significantly reduced, then power may not be available when it is needed causing cascading failures and blackouts as happened in the US in 2003 and 2011 (NERC 2004; FERC/NERC 2012). Alternatively, if protection devices are not properly calibrated, then components can overheat. This has happened to hundreds of distribution-level transformers during recent record breaking heat waves in the US southwest (Jerod MacDonald-Evoy 2016). Moreover, lines can sag to the point that deformation is irreversible. Not coincidentally, during these record-breaking heat waves, the air is very dry, and the risk of wildfires is high. If wildfires burn under power lines, then those components can fail as well due to air ionization. Like generators, substations are vulnerable to rising sea levels and storm floods near the coast and in basin-like land areas (Sathaye et al. 2012). Flooding can erode or short the hardware in substations and underground power lines (ADB 2012). Lastly, severe storms can blow trees and other objects into power lines and cause outages.

Electric power demand is primarily susceptible to higher air temperatures, which can increase both total energy consumption and the peak demand in regions with significant electric air conditioning (Burillo et al. 2017; Reyna et al. 2017; Bartos et al. 2016; Auffhammer et al. 2017). Demand is typically planned for at city- and state-level geographies based on seasonal weather usage patterns, daily weather usage patterns, and local use patterns. In warm to hot climates, the peak electricity demand is usually in the late afternoon during the summer when businesses are still operating and people are coming home and turning on air

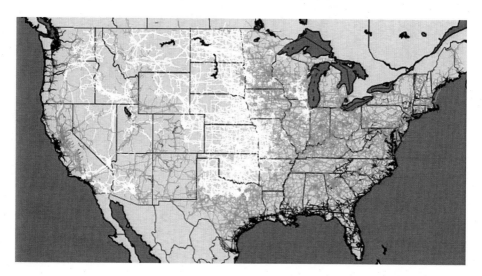

Figure 31.2 Transmission capacity reduction (percentage) relative to 1990–2010 by 2060 under RCP4.5. Darker (Gulf Coast) is around 1–2% and lighter (Midwest) is around 7.5%.
Source: Bartos et al. 2016.

conditioners (EIA 2016). Historically, preparing for higher peak demand means building additional generation and delivery capacity, but policies aimed at natural resource conservation have targeted building and appliance energy efficiency standards which also offset increases in peak demand (Burillo et al. 2017). In terms of climate change, higher average temperatures and higher maximum temperatures mean more demand for AC usage, which could mean more energy usage over time, higher power demand for ACs to operate at hotter temperatures, and more installations of ACs total in moderately warm climates. The combined effects could be a significant increase in per capita demand. This may be more than local delivery infrastructure are capable of supporting without systemic (network-wide) investments (Willis et al. 2001).

31.2.2 Water and wastewater systems

Extreme temperatures, drought, frequency of freeze and thaw cycles, extreme precipitation, sea level rise, and increased frequency and extent of wildfires are hazards for water, wastewater, and stormwater infrastructure. These hazards can contribute to water supplied at insufficient quantity and/or quality, or flooding from overflows of stormwater and wastewater. An summary of the effects of climate change on the different water systems is shown in Table 31.2.

The availability of bulk water resources is sensitive to drought and sea level rise. Increased levels of drought causes decreased annual snowfall and precipitation, and sea level rise causes saltwater intrusion into groundwater aquifers (Melillo et al. 2014). With simultaneous increases in population and reduction of water supply, both surface water and groundwater could be insufficient to meet demands in some desert regions (Melillo et al. 2014). Additionally, increased bulk water temperatures can cause increased growth of pathogens in stagnant reservoirs that are difficult to treat at treatment plants (Clark et al. 2011). Common elements across all water systems are pumps and pipes which facilitate transport, facilities including treatment plants, and the operators who manage the infrastructure. Heat exposure can cause pumps to overheat and increase corrosion of thermoplastic, metal, and concrete materials in canal linings and pipes (Banerjee et al. 2008; Cowern 2000; Csanyi 2015; Rockwell Automation 1998; Kreeley & Coulton 2012; Hoffman 2017; Whittle & Stahmer 2005; Volk et al. 2000; Toshiba 2017). The freezing of water in pipes in any of the infrastructural systems leads to blockages and outages, and an increased frequency of freeze and thaw cycles causes increased cracking of pipes (Gauffre et al. 2014; Gilpin 1977; Goulter & Kazemi 1989). In places where temperatures will increase in the winter, climate change could beneficially decrease freeze-thaw cycles. Additionally, increased amounts of standing water and infiltration from extreme precipitation events can cause stress loads to underground pipes from soil expansion, causing an increase in cracking (Hudak et al. 1998). Sea level rise threatens to affect both pumps and pipes along with treatment facilities as summarized in Figure 31.3. Salt water intrusion into soil causes increased corrosion and degradation of pipes and increased fracturing of pipes from land subsidence. Salt water intrusion could also cause flooding of pumping stations, sewers, treatment plants, and wastewater sewage backup (Azevedo de Almeida & Mostafavi 2016). From a human physiological perspective, extreme heat is known to increase water demand, and cause heatstroke in water system operators (Guhathakurta & Gober 2007; USA Blue Book 2013).

Each water infrastructure system also has unique physical, chemical, and biological sensitivities to climate change events. Increasing duration and intensity of precipitation events could cause an exceedance of detention basin and sewer inlet capacity in the stormwater drainage system, leading to flooding of rural and urban areas (Melillo et al. 2014). Increases in frequency and expanse of wildfires can cause erosion, contaminating runoff and resulting in flooding (Smith et al. 2011). As populations have grown, cities where stormwater sewers are

Table 31.2 Summary of key climate drivers and possible impacts to water systems

Climate Hazard	Key Impacts	Impacted Segment	Potential Adaptation Strategies
Drought	• Decreased amount of fresh water	Bulk surface water	Water banking, groundwater management, conservation policy, constructing new intakes, implementing direct reuse desalination
Sea level rise	• Salt water intrusion • Contamination from pipe corrosion	Bulk ground water	Improve water treatment processes, raising pumping stations, constructing and/or elevating dikes and seawalls, groundwater recharge with fresh water
	• Changes in utility gradient causing pipe fracture • Corrosion and degradation of pipes	Water distribution, storm water, wastewater	constructing and/or elevating dikes and seawalls
	• Overflow of inlets	Storm water	Enhancing pumping capacity
	• Flooding of wastewater treatment plants	Wastewater treatment	Constructing green infrastructure, constructing and/or elevating dikes and seawalls
	• Sewage backup	Wastewater conveyance	constructing and/or elevating dikes and seawalls
Increased air temperatures	• Pump overheating • Pipe corrosion and degradation • Increased water demand • Increased heat fatigue of operators	Bulk surface water, bulk water conveyance, water treatment, water distribution, wastewater conveyance, wastewater treatment	Cooling mechanisms, corrosion inhibitors
	• Growth of pathogens	Bulk surface water, water distribution	Improving water treatment processes, aerating water, sampling distribution water more frequently, decreasing water residence times
	• Residual disinfectant decay	Water distribution	Decreasing water residence times, increasing disinfectant dosage
Increasing Freeze-thaw cycles	• Underground pipe fracture	Water treatment, water distribution, wastewater conveyance, wastewater treatment	Preventatively repair pipes, monitor pipe condition
Extreme Precipitation Events	• Soil expansion and underground pipe cracking	Water distribution, wastewater and storm water conveyance	Avoiding placing pipes in clay soils, increasing pipe diameters, preventatively repair pipes, monitor pipe condition
	• Overflow of sewer inlets	Wastewater and storm water conveyance	Increasing capacity, installing grey and green infrastructure to reduce flooding

Table 31.2 (Cont.)

Climate Hazard	Key Impacts	Impacted Segment	Potential Adaptation Strategies
	• Canal breach	Bulk water conveyance	Preventative repair of canals, moving canals outside of floodplain
	• Bulk water high turbidity and low pH	Water treatment	Improving pre-treatment processes, preparing a quick switch to another water source or water utility, treating water with alum
	• Infrastructure and facility flooding and damage	Bulk surface water, water treatment, water distribution, wastewater conveyance, wastewater treatment	Reinforcing dams, improving dam standards, preventative repair of assets, increasing redundancy, moving components above ground
Wildfires	• Bulk water high turbidity and low pH	Bulk water conveyance, water treatment	Dredging dams, Improving water pre-treatment processes

Source: Adaptation strategies are from Hu et al. 2010; Heyn and Winsor 2015; and Azevedo de Almeida and Mostafavi 2016.

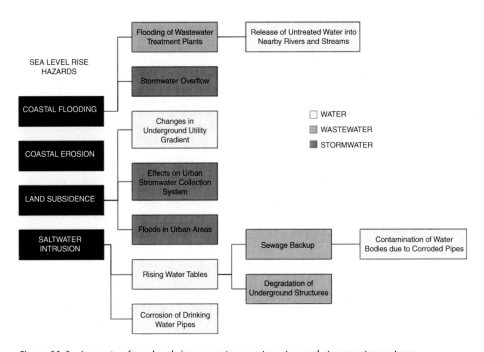

Figure 31.3 Impacts of sea level rise on water, wastewater and stormwater systems.
Source: Azevedo de Almeida and Mostafavi 2016.

combined with wastewater conveyance have seen increasing incidences of even mild precipitation events causing exceedances of sewer capacity, resulting in the release of waste to natural and urban systems (Semadeni-Davies et al. 2008). Increases in the frequency or intensity of precipitation events are a major risk for these systems (Semadeni-Davies et al. 2008). The infrastructure used to transport water to treatment plants is at risk to extreme precipitation events and heat exposure. The flooding of canals from precipitation and sewer infrastructure failure causes high turbidity and low pH levels which could exceed treatment capacity due to the lower-turbidity and higher-pH design of the treatment processes. This could lead to temporary outages of treated water to consumers (Yordanova 2015; Barrett 2014; ParkPioneer. net 2012). Additionally, concrete canals with jointed panels can breach, leading to a shutdown of the larger system (ParkPioneer.net 2012). The chemical and biological treatment processes within water and wastewater treatment plants are sensitive to water temperature as well as from levels of turbidity from high precipitation events. Water temperature correlates to the speed of chemical reactions and microbial growth. Higher water temperatures are generally beneficial for quickening the speed of reactions and growth of microbes that consume organic material and convert harmful chemicals into harmless ones (Kim 1995). If water temperatures become colder the treatment efficiency could be reduced. In contrast, increased chemical reaction rates in the distribution system are harmful, causing an increased decay of the disinfectant residual, formation of disinfection byproducts, nitrification rates, and the growth of harmful bacteria like Mycobacterium Avium Complex and Legionella (Hua et al. 1999; Toroz & Uyak 2005; Graham et al. 2009; Wadowsky et al. 1985; Rogers et al. 1994; Torvinen et al. 2004; Archuleta et al. 2002; Pintar & Slawson 2003; Wild et al. 1971; Lipponen et al. 2002; AWWA 2002). A combination of strategic and coordinated preventative and response actions of water managers has the potential to mitigate risk from climate change events.

Adaptation strategies for water systems emphasize increasing source options and conserving existing supply, armoring and strengthening hardware to minimize the effects of climate hazards, preventative maintenance to address more frequent hardware failures, and changing treatment processes in response to increasing temperature and extreme precipitation effects on water quality. Adaptation strategies often emphasize protecting and maintaining the existing infrastructure and its structure.

31.2.3 Transportation systems

Given the spatial reach and technological diversity of transportation systems and their infrastructure, there are many potential consequences of climate change that may impact the transportation sector. Severe weather can impact mobility, accessibility, public safety, and the health of travelers. Additionally, increased frequency and severity of extreme weather events (e.g. heat and precipitation), increased freeze-thaw cycles, and sea level rise can impact the planning, design, construction, performance, and maintenance of transportation infrastructure. Table 31.3 provides a summary of some of the ways that climate change may affect transportation infrastructure. Compared to historical weather and climate averages, the relative effects of climate change are predicted to vary by region – so too will the variety and scale of impacts on the transportation sector.

Transportation infrastructure (roads, bridges, airport runways, shipping ports, canals, etc.) have planned lifetimes measured in decades and may be susceptible to premature degradation or increased risk of failure under climate change. While not exhaustive, the following discussion highlights several potential pathways for transportation infrastructure failure due to predicted

Table 31.3 Summary of key climate drivers and possible impacts to road and rail transportation infrastructure

Climate Hazard	Key Impacts	Impacted Network	Adaptation Strategies
Increase in maximum temperatures and extreme heat events	• Asphalt cracking • Asphalt aging/oxidation • Migration of liquid asphalt • Asphalt softening • Failed expansion joints	Road Network	• Heat-resistant paving materials • Alter asphalt composition • Switch from asphalt to concrete • More frequent maintenance/replacement • Increase albedo • Increased natural and artificial shading
	• Railway buckling • Catenary wire sag	Rail Network	• More frequent maintenance/replacement • Heat-resistant materials (i.e. rails and wires) • Increased vegetation near infrastructure • Increased natural and artificial shade
Seasonal shift in temperatures (e.g., later freeze/earlier thaw)	• Increased damage from freeze-thaw cycles • More frequent landslide/mudslides • Degraded structural integrated from lost permafrost (in places like Alaska)	Road Network Rail Network	• More frequent maintenance/replacement • Additional/fortified slope retention structures • Alter design standards for more variance • Alter asphalt composition
Increased rainfall/extreme precipitation events	• Flooding of roadways/railways • Overloading of drainage systems • Roadway/Railway washout • Bridge scour/washout • Reduced structural integrity due to increased soil moisture • More frequent landslides/mudslides	Road Network Rail Network	• Upgrade drainage systems • Increase culvert capacity • Increase pumping capacity for tunnels/low-lying areas • Modify design storm criteria • Fortify bridge piers and abutments • Add green infrastructure/storm retention basins
More intense/frequent drought	• Increased likelihood of wildfire • Road/rail closure due to wildfire & reduced visibility • Increased flooding in areas deforested by wildfire • More debris in storm water management system once rain occurs • Increased likelihood of landslide • Reduced structural integrity due to ground shrinking	Road Network Rail Network	• Vegetation management • Upgrade/expand drainage system • Additional/fortified slope retention structures

(continued)

Table 31.3 (Cont.)

Climate Hazard	Key Impacts	Impacted Network	Adaptation Strategies
Sea level rise/ Storm surge/ Coastal flooding	• More frequent/intense floods in low-lying areas • Erosion of road/rail base • Erosion if bridge supports/ bridge scour • Land subsidence	Road Network Rail Network	• Expand drainage near low-lying infrastructure • Elevate/protect tunnel openings & low-lying areas • Increase pumping capacity for bridges/tunnels/roads/rails • Relocation/retreat of roads and infrastructure • Add/strengthen levees, seawalls, dikes, etc.

Source: Adapted from TRB 2008; FHA 2012; Meyer and Weigel 2011; Rattanachot et al. 2015; Taylor and Philp 2015; Markolf et al. 2017; FTA 2011; Meyer et al. 2014.

climate change impacts. Direct climate change impacts may raise capital costs, increase repair and maintenance expenditures, and create public safety hazards (e.g. bridge collapse, unsafe levels of pavement quality). An increase in annual average temperatures and the frequency and severity of heatwaves may exceed the thermal tolerance of materials used in transportation infrastructure (Anderson et al. 2015; Winguth et al. 2015). Increased heat in colder climates may also increase freeze-thaw cycles, requiring accelerated maintenance, rehabilitation, or reconstruction (Mills et al. 2009). Notable effects of heat on transportation infrastructure include pavement softening and rutting, pavement buckling, bleeding asphalt, and railway track buckling (Miller et al. 2008). Despite projected warming due to climate change, pavement engineers commonly design asphalt mixtures based on historical temperatures that may no longer be pertinent. As such, roadways being deployed today may experience accelerated deterioration due to climate change (see Figure 31.4). Sea-level rise and storm surge from hurricanes and tropical storms can threaten coastal transportation assets. Gradual sea-level rise is expected to damage coastal infrastructure and could render the lowest-lying infrastructure permanently inaccessible (Koetse & Rietveld 2009). Storm surges associated with powerful hurricanes and tropical storms may inundate large areas of coastal communities and severely damage critical assets (Jacob et al. 2011). The most susceptible infrastructure to storm surges are bridges (erosion, scour, slab and span displacement, and collapse) and tunnels (flooding). Damage to these assets can be highly disruptive to regional transportation systems. Increased frequency and intensity of precipitation events may increase urban flooding by overwhelming drainage systems, damage bridges and culverts, damage rail-bed support structures, and cause landslides and mudslides that damage or inundate transportation infrastructure.

Beyond infrastructure, climate change may have significant impacts on transportation operations, mobility, travel behavior, and traveler health and safety. Adverse weather conditions are associated with service disruptions, congestion, and accidents that can reduce traffic speed and volume, increase delays, and decrease capacity (Cools et al. 2010). Such conditions often contribute to variations in traveler behavior such as changing destination, departure time, mode, or forgoing non-essential trips all together. The increasing frequency, severity, and duration of heatwaves and precipitation events will impact the viability of active modes (walking, biking, and transit) that expose travelers potentially dangerous or unconfutable conditions. In addition, some travelers may be disproportionately exposed to environmental stressors (such as those with low income and the elderly), and have increased risk of health issues associated with exposure and reduced mobility or accessibility (Karner et al. 2015).

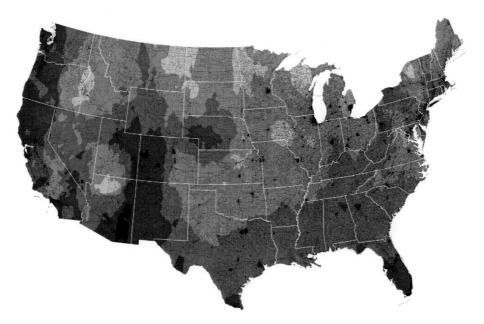

Figure 31.4 Change in pavement fatigue cracking by 2040–2060 with RCP 8.5 temperature rise. Darker (Southwest) is around 0–2% and lighter patches are around 10–12%.
Source: Gudipudi et al. 2017.

Beyond surface transport, climate change creates several vulnerabilities for aviation, both air
travel and airports (Eurocontrol 2014). Precipitation change may disruption operations, cause
ground subsidence, reduce airport throughput, cause flooding, affect airport access and egress,
and disrupt utilities. Temperature change can affect aircraft performance, damage runways
and taxiways, require changes in heating and cooling at airports, and increase utility costs. Sea
level rise threatens coastal airports and nearby services. Changes in wind may affect operations
and turbulence.

It is important to note that climate change may also prove beneficial to transportation
systems in certain locations and circumstances. For example, a warming climate in may reduce
material damage caused by winter conditions and freeze-thaw cycles, reduce the burden of
snow and ice removal, and create safer winter travel conditions for vehicles. Milder winters may
also increase the attractiveness of cycling, walking and transit use and reduce the dependency
on automobiles (Saneinejad et al. 2012).

31.3 Adaptation: From risk to resilience

Before discussing the tradeoffs of adaptation options for protecting infrastructure from climate
change, it is necessary to take a step back and explore how our systems have been designed and
operated. Infrastructure design for climate and weather has largely centered on the risk-based
approach of storm intensity design criteria (e.g. 100-year event). In this case, risk is a function
of exposure to a given hazard, the probability of hazard occurrence, and the severity of the
impacts should the event occur. This definition is analogous to expected value. It should be
noted that risk frequently takes on a negative connotation, but this does not have to be the
case – the impacts of the event being analyzed could just as easily refer to a positive outcome.

Risk analysis further recognizes *vulnerability* as a function of the complex interactions between the magnitude of the hazard to which one is exposed, the technical capacity/integrity of the system, the social capacity/integrity of the system, the amount of time and resources devoted to preparation and planning before the exposure, and the level of experience (or lack thereof) with similar types of exposure in the past. Nearly all infrastructure systems are designed (either implicitly or explicitly) to reduce identified vulnerabilities based on specified risk threshold. The value of this threshold is defined by codes, laws, physical limits, practice standards or rules-of-thumb.

The design of infrastructure for a particular risk threshold can broadly be defined as *robustness* – a risk-based approach to estimating the likelihood of a certain threshold being exceeded (e.g. 100-year storm event) and an emphasis on strengthening/armoring infrastructure. Increasingly, robustness has been treated as synonymous with *resilience*. However, this is likely a flawed and overly limited understanding of resilience for two reasons: (1) several factors can inhibit the level of certainty with which we can predict various events and outcomes, and (2) even under a regime of limited uncertainty, there may still be physical, economic, or political constraints that inhibit the effectiveness of robustness strategies.

One of the main factors limiting our ability to form reasonable uncertainty estimates, and thus effectively implement robustness, *is non-stationarity*. At a high level, non-stationarity is the inability to accurately predict current and future conditions based on historical data/trends. Climate non-stationarity implies that historically observed temperature and precipitation values and trends may become increasingly less predictive of future conditions (Milly et al. 2008). The challenge presented by climate non-stationarity is exacerbated by the fact that infrastructure systems are often planned on decadal scales, are highly centralized, and are highly rigid. As a result, uncertainty surrounding the climatic and meteorological conditions in which the infrastructure are expected to operate can make it very difficult to assess the severity of a potential extreme event. This hinders the effectiveness of design decisions related to safety thresholds and system robustness.

Robustness certainly has a place as an adaptation strategy, but there remains increasing challenges for using it as the sole strategy. Despite historical and ongoing efforts, robustness should not be considered to be synonymous with resilience. Instead, we argue that *resilience* is a series of non-mutually exclusive adaptation regimes (described below), and *adaptive capacity* is the ability to successfully and effectively move between these regimes as different challenges, threats, and vulnerabilities arise. Following are some proposed regimes of resilience (Woods 2015; Eisenberg et al. 2017; Seager et al. 2017). Ultimately, the form that infrastructure takes – e.g., safe-to-fail (described below) or an emphasis on green components – should be in response to enhancing adaptive capacity and the ability to move across these regimes.

> *Rebound* – The ability to restore conditions and/or systems that have been damaged or disrupted. For example, in anticipation of an extreme weather event, back-up fuel and water supplies may be stockpiled, vehicles may be moved to "safer" locations, etc. Implementation of these types of strategies are all aimed at maintaining some level of service (e.g. water, power, food, etc.) after a major disruption and/or aiding in the return to "normal" service levels as quickly as possible.

> *Robustness* – The capacity to prevent disruptions from occurring by emphasizing control, armoring, strengthening, and/or redundancy. For example, after the devastation of Hurricane Katrina, roughly $15 billion has been spent strengthening 350 miles of hurricane barriers, installing new flood gates (including the $1.1 billion West Closure Complex that is nearly as long as a football field), and updating pumping stations (Burnett 2015).

Graceful extensibility – The ability to extend performance and mitigate the consequences of surprising events to avoid sudden and catastrophic failure. For example, during Hurricane Harvey in 2017, the U.S. Army Corps of Engineers deliberately released water from two overfilled reservoirs in the west side of Houston. The release of the water inundated certain parts of downtown with flood waters, but prevented the collapse (and subsequent catastrophic flooding) of the reservoirs' dams (Jervis et al. 2017).

Sustained Adaptability – The ability to transform, balance, and trade multiple system dimensions in response to a continually changing system and environmental conditions over the long-term. Iterative learning from past mistakes (and successes) and evolution are critical elements of sustained adaptability

One potential approach for enhancing the movement among various resilience regimes is to expand beyond the fail-safe approach commonly applied to infrastructure, i.e., infrastructure designed to prevent any level of failure up to a certain (predetermined) risk threshold. Thus, when failure does occur (during low probability, high impact events), the consequences to human life, property, and other infrastructure systems can be catastrophic. In contrast, a *safe-to-fail* design approach still manages risk, but also recognizes consequences that arise from uncertainties within the risk calculation, and focuses on strategies that do not necessarily compromise the entire urban system upon failure (Kim et al. 2017). Rather than focusing exclusively on reducing the probability of a certain failure occurring, safe-to-fail facilitates resilience strategies by acknowledging the wide range of possible mechanisms and consequences of infrastructure failure beyond the calculated risks thresholds. The "Room for the River" strategy used in the Netherlands is a good example of safe-to-fail infrastructure design for flooding (Zevenbergen et al. 2013). Communities intentionally expand flood-prone areas into nearby farmland. By using the farmland as floodways and developing a subsidy for affected farmers for lost crop production, local flood management districts are able to redirect urban damages to less socially and economically vital regions and reduce the impact of flooding in the region (i.e., managed consequences).

31.4 Towards climate resilient infrastructure

A robustness only approach to resilience appears insufficient to address the complex, emergent, and evolving challenges facing our infrastructure systems. Instead, as discussed in Section 31.4, robustness should be thought of as one of several complementary, non-mutually exclusive resilience regimes (rebound, robustness, graceful extensibility, and sustained adaptability), and the movement between these regimes is enabled by the *adaptive capacity* of the system(s). Adaptive capacity can be described as the ability of the system to perceive and respond to stimuli as determined by various system competencies and properties. Naturally, this leads to the question: how can we effectively increase the adaptive capacity of urban infrastructure systems, and thus enhance our ability to move between different resilience regimes as needed?

One potential avenue for increasing the adaptive capacity of infrastructure systems is to incorporate elements of *flexibility* and *agility* into their design, implementation, management, and governance. Broadly speaking, *flexibility* can be thought of as the ability to reconfigure or alter system parameters to absorb and/or respond to foreseeable changes and uncertainties. *Agility* describes the ability to adapt and evolve in an environment of continuous and unanticipated changes (Chester & Allenby 2017; Bernardes & Hanna 2009; Richards 1996). Although flexibility and agility are comparable on many levels, two important distinctions should be made: (1) flexibility relates to changes that are able to be anticipated or expected, while agility relates to changes that are completely unexpected, unanticipated, or unforeseen; (2) flexibility is enabled (or hindered) by the existing set of systems and protocols, while agility is enabled by a fundamental transformation of the existing systems and protocols (or even the creation of new systems and protocols altogether).

We propose the following methods for potentially increasing the flexibility and agility of infrastructure systems (Chester & Allenby 2017): (i) *Roadmapping* – continually re-evaluating how climate is changing, re-assessing how those changes influence infrastructure design and operations, and identifying when/where it might no longer make sense to invest in overly long-lasting and rigid components; (ii) *Planned obsolescence* – Planning for changes in function, profitability, and/or other dimensions of performance that result in a greater capacity to alter, substitute, or decommission components in order to more efficiently meet changing demands (Lemer 1996); (iii) *Compatibility* – The ability to share information and functions across different technological components; (iv) *Connectivity* – The ability of any technology to communicate with other components inside and outside of the system – it enhances shareability and allows for resources to be used for new functions (Duncan 1995); (v) *Modularity* – The ability to easily modify, remove, or add components to a system without needing to alter other modules and subsystems – often enhanced by standardization (Duncan 1995); (vi) *Organic institutional structure* – Organizations with authority tied to tasks instead of position, shifts in authority as dictated by tasks, fewer levels of hierarchy, informal and changing lines of authority, open and networked communication, loose boundaries among function and units, distributed decision making, and fluid role definitions (Sherehiy al. 2007; Weick & Quinn 1999). A good example of the merits of an organic institutional/communication structure is the volunteer rescue efforts undertaken by the "Cajun Navy" and others during the flooding that followed Hurricane Harvey in Southeast Texas in 2017 (Fernandez 2017; Fountain & Gabriel 2017); (vii) *Cultures of change* – Organizations that encourage innovation, learning, experimentation, and awareness of changes in the operating environment (Sherehiy et al. 2007);

The obdurate, fixed, and long-standing nature of many infrastructure systems may prove to be particularly strong barriers to the introduction of concepts of flexibility and agility. These barriers are further strengthened by *lock-in* where past conditions (financial, political, codes and standards, social and cultural values, and technological forces) significantly impact (and often limit) future trajectories. Thus, infrastructure designers and managers will need to be cognizant of the challenges presented by lock-in, and will need to be innovative in developing ways to address these challenges.

31.5 Conclusions

This chapter has highlighted the challenges of climate change and extreme weather events for our infrastructure systems. Initial responses to these challenges have achieved varying levels of success, but it appears that the traditional risk and robustness based approach to infrastructure management may not be sufficient to meet the increasing difficulties presented by a changing climate, increased complexity and interconnectedness across infrastructure systems, and uncertain human behavior, preferences, and decision making. As a result, we argue for the inclusion of flexibility and agility into the design and implementation of infrastructure systems. More broadly, we propose moving away from a paradigm solely reliant on risk and robustness toward a paradigm of resilience in which flexibility and agility enhance the adaptive capacity of the system, which in turn facilitates the movement between different regimes (e.g., rebound, robustness, graceful extensibility, or other) based on environmental and systemic cues. In other words, flexibility and agility (driven by concepts like roadmapping, planned obsolescence, compatibility, connectivity, modularity, organic institutional structure, and cultures of change) increase adaptive capacity, which in turn enhances a system's ability to perceive various stimuli and respond by facilitating the movement between various infrastructure regimes. Ultimately, the goal should not necessarily be to rebound as quickly possible or be as robust as possible, but to move across and among those different resilience regimes based on the magnitude and type of threat facing the system. In doing so, we can transform our infrastructure systems to be capable of handling both the probabilistic and the "possibilistic."

References

Abel, D. 2015. "Pilgrim Facility Cuts Its Power: Sea Water Used by Plant Was Warmer than Is Allowed." *Boston Globe*, August 11. www.bostonglobe.com/metro/2015/08/11/high-water-temperatures-forced-power-cut-pilgrim-nuclear-plant/fMgG6VtRmadnVcuacbPpGI/story.html (last accessed August 19, 2018).

ADB. 2012. "Climate Risk and Adaptation in the Electric Power Sector." Mandaluyong, Philippines. www.adb.org/publications/climate-risk-and-adaptation-electric-power-sector (last accessed August 31, 2018).

Anderson, T., C. Beck, K. Gade, and S. Olmsted. 2015. "Extreme Weather Vulnerability Assessment." Arizona Department of Transportation.

Archuleta, R., P. Mullens, and T.P. Primm. 2002. "The Relationship of Temperature to Desiccation and Starvation Tolerance of the Mycobacterium Avium Complex." *Archives of Microbiology* 178 (4): 311–14.

Auffhammer, M., P. Baylis, and C.H. Hausman. 2017. "Climate Change Is Projected to Have Severe Impacts on the Frequency and Intensity of Peak Electricity Demand across the United States." *Proceedings of the National Academy of Sciences of the United States of America* 114 (8). National Academy of Sciences: 1886–91.

AWWA. 2002. "Offfice of Ground Water and Drinking Water Distribution System Issue Paper: Nitrification." Denver, CO.

Azevedo de Almeida, B. and A. Mostafavi. 2016. "Resilience of Infrastructure Systems to Sea-Level Rise in Coastal Areas: Impacts, Adaptation Measures, and Implementation Challenges." *Sustainability.* doi:10.3390/su8111115.

Banerjee, A., A. Tiwari, J. Vico, and C. Wester. 2008. "Motor Protection Principles." *2008 61st Annual Conference for Protective Relay Engineers*, 215–31.

Barrett, B. 2014. "CAP on Skunk Creek Flooding." *Azcentral*, August 19. www.azcentral.com/videos/news/local/phoenix/2014/08/19/14296545/.

Bartos, M. and M. Chester. 2015. "Impacts of Climate Change on Electric Power Supply in the Western United States." *Nature Climate Change* 5 (8): 748–52.

Bartos, M., M. Chester, N. Johnson, B. Gorman, D. Eisenberg, I. Linkov, and M. Bates. 2016. "Impacts of Rising Air Temperatures on Electric Transmission Ampacity and Peak Electricity Load in the United States." *Environmental Research Letters* 11 (11). IOP Publishing

Bernardes, E.S. and M.D. Hanna. 2009. "A Theoretical Review of Flexibility, Agility and Responsiveness in the Operations Management Literature." *International Journal of Operations & Production Management* 29 (1): 30–53.

Bondank, E., M. Chester, and B. Ruddell. 2018. "Water Distribution System Failure Risks." *Environmental Science & Technology.* 52 (17), pp 9605–9614. doi: 10.1021/acs.est.7b01591

Burillo, D., M. Chester, B. Ruddell, and N. Johnson. 2017. "Electricity Demand Planning Forecasts Should Consider Climate Non-Stationarity to Maintain Reserve Margins during Heat Waves." *Applied Energy* 206. doi:10.1016/j.apenergy.2017.08.141.

Burnett, John. 2015. "Billions Spent On Flood Barriers, But New Orleans Still A 'Fishbowl.'" *NPR.* www.npr.org/2015/08/28/432059261/billions-spent-on-flood-barriers-but-new-orleans-still-a-fishbowl (last accessed August 19, 2018).

Campbell, R.J. 2012. "Weather-Related Power Outages and Electric System Resiliency." *Congressional Research Service Report.* August 28.

Chester, M. and B. Allenby. 2017. "Towards Adaptive Infrastructure: Flexibility and Agility in a Non-Stationarity Age." *Sustainable and Resilient Infrastructure.* In review.

Clark, R.M., Z. Li, and S.G. Buchberger. 2011. "Adapting Water Treatment Design and Operations to the Impacts of Global Climate Change." *Frontiers of Earth Science* 5 (4): 363–70.

Cools, M., E. Moons, L. Creemers, and G. Wets. 2010. "Changes in Travel Behavior in Response to Weather Conditions." *Transportation Research Record: Journal of the Transportation Research Board* 2157: 22–8.

Cowern, E. 2000. "The Hot Issue of Motor Temperature Ratings." *EC and M: Electrical Construction and Maintenance* 99 (9): 104–6.

Csanyi, E. 2015. "Heat as One of the Most Common Cause of Motor Failure Service Life." *Electrical Engineering Portal.* https://electrical-engineering-portal.com/heat-as-one-of-the-most-common-cause-of-motor-failure (last accessed August 31, 2018).

DHS. 2015. "Presidential Policy Directive 21 Implementation." Washington, DC.

Dominguez, F., E. Rivera, D.P. Lettenmaier, and C.L. Castro. 2012. "Changes in Winter Precipitation Extremes for the Western United States under a Warmer Climate as Simulated by Regional Climate Models." *Geophysical Research Letters* 39 (5): 1–7.

Duncan, N.B. 1995. "Capturing Flexibility of Information Technology Infrastructure: A Study of Resource Characteristics and Their Measure." *Journal of Management Information Systems* 12(2): 37–57.

EEA. 2008. "Energy and Environment." Vol. 6/2008.

EIA. 2016. "U.S. Electric System Operating Data – Hourly." www.eia.gov/beta/realtime_grid/#/data/graphs?end=20160916T00&start=20160909T00 (last accessed August 19, 2018).

Eisenberg, D.A, T.P. Seager, M.M. Hinrichs, Y. Kim, B.A. Wender, S.A. Markolf, J.E. Thomas, et al. 2017. "Robustness and Extensibility in Infrastructure Systems." *Reliability Engineering and System Safety.* https://repository.asu.edu/attachments/189265/content/Robustness and Extensibility in Inf Sys_watermark_07282017.pdf (last accessed August 19, 2018).

Eurocontrol. 2014. "Adapting Aviation to Climate Change." Brussels, Belgium.

FERC/NERC. 2012. *Arizona-Southern California Outages on September 8 2011.* Washington, DC. www.ferc.gov/legal/staff-reports/04-27-2012-ferc-nerc-report.pdf (last accessed August 31, 2018).

Fernandez, M. 2017. "On Roads Turned Waterways, Volunteers Improvise to Save the Trapped and Desparate." *The New York Times,* August 29. www.nytimes.com/2017/08/29/us/volunteer-rescue-crews-hurricane-harvey-houston.html (last accessed August 19, 2018).

FHA. 2012. "Climate Change and Extreme Weather Vulnerability Assessment Framework." *US Development of Trasportation.* Washington, DC.

Field, C., V. Barros, D.J. Dokken, K. Mach, M. Mastrandrea, T.E. Bilir, M. Chatterjee, et al. 2014. "Technical Summary." *Climate Change 2014: Impacts, Adaptation, and Vulnerability. Part A: Global and Sectoral Aspects. Contribution of Working Group II to the Fifth Assessment Report of the Intergovernmental Panel on Climate Change.*

Fountain, E.D. and T. Gabriel. 2017. "'Cajun Navy' Brings Its Rescue Fleet to Houston's Flood Zone." *The New York Times,* August 30. www.nytimes.com/2017/08/30/us/cajun-navy-brings-its-rescue-fleet-to-houstons-flood-zone.html (last accessed August 19, 2018).

FTA. 2011. "Flooded Bus Barns and Buckled Rails: Public Transportation and Climate Change Adaptation." Washington, DC. http://trid.trb.org/view.aspx?id=1133763 (last accessed August 19, 2018).

Gauffre, P. Le, J-B. Aubin, S. Bruaset, R. Ugarelli, C. Benoit, F. Trivisonno, and K. Van den Bliek. 2014. "Impacts of Climate Change on Maintenance Activities: A Case Study on Water Pipe Breaks." Prepared Program: Seventh Framework Programme.

Gilpin, R.R. 1977. "The Effects of Dendritic Ice Formation in Water Pipes." *International Journal of Heat and Mass Transfer* 20 (6): 693–99.

Gilroy, K.L. and R.H. McCuen. 2012. "A Nonstationary Flood Frequency Analysis Method to Adjust for Future Climate Change and Urbanization." *Journal of Hydrology* 414–415: 40–8.

Goulter, I.C. and A. Kazemi. 1989. "Analysis of Water Distribution Pipe Failure Types in Winnipeg, Canada." *J. Transp. Eng.* 115 (2): 95–111.

Graham, N.J.D., C.D. Collins, M. Nieuwenhuijsen, and M.R. Templeton. 2009. "The Formation and Occurrence of Haloacetic Acids in Drinking Water." DWI report. http://dwi.defra.gov.uk/research/completed-research/reports/DWI70_2_194.pdf (last accessed August 31, 2018).

Gudipudi, P., B.S. Underwood, and A. Zalghout. 2017. "Impact of Climate Change on Pavement Structural Performance in the United States." *Transportation Research Part D: Transport and Environment* In press.

Guhathakurta, S. and P. Gober. 2007. "The Impact of the Phoenix Urban Heat Island on Residential Water Use." *Journal of the American Planning Association* 73 (3): 317–29.

Heyn, K. and W. Winsor. 2015. "Climate Risks to Water Utility Built Assets and Infrastructure." Organization: City of Portland Water Bureau. www.wucaonline.org/assets/pdf/pubs-asset-infrastructure.pdf (last accessed August 31, 2018).

Hoffman. 2017. "Thermal Management: Heat Dissipation in Electrical Enclosures." Equipment Protection Solutions Spec – 00488 E. Anoka, MN, Hoffman. www.hoffmanonline.com/stream_document.aspx?rRID=233309&pRID=162533 (last accessed August 31, 2018).

Hollnagel, E. and Y. Fujita. 2013. "The Fukushima Disaster-Systemic Failures as the Lack of Resilience." *Nuclear Engineering and Technology* 45 (1). Korean Nuclear Society: 13–20.

Hu, Y., D. Wang, K. Cossitt, and R. Chowdhury. 2010. "AC Pipe in North America: Inventory, Breakage, and Working Environments." *Journal of Pipeline Systems Engineering and Practice* 1 (November): 156–72.

Hua, F., J.R. West, R.A. Barker, and C.F. Forster. 1999. "Modelling of Chlorine Decay in Municipal Water Supplies." *Water Research* 33 (12): 2735–46.

Hudak, P.F., B. Sadler, and B. Hunter. 1998. "Analyzing Underground Water-Pipe Breaks in Residual Soils." *Water Engineering and Management* 145 (12): 15–20.

Hunt, A. and P. Watkiss. 2011. "Climate Change Impacts and Adaptation in Cities: A Review of the Literature." *Climatic Change* 104 (1): 13–49.

IEEE. 2012. "IEEE Std C37.30.1–2011 IEEE Standard Requirements for AC High-Voltage Air Switches Rated Above 1000 V 2.00."

Jacob, K., G. Deodatis, J. Atlas, M. Whitcomb, M. Lopeman, O. Markogiannaki, Z. Kennett, A. Morla, R. Leichenko, and P. Vancura. 2011. "Transportation." In *Responding to Climate Change in New York State (ClimAID)*, 299–362.

Jervis, R., D. Rice, and J. Bacon. 2017. "Release of Reservoir Could Affect Thousands in Houston Area." *USA Today*, August 28. www.usatoday.com/story/news/nation-now/2017/08/28/controlled-release-water-houston-reservoirs/607594001/ (last accessed August 19, 2018).

Karner, A., D.M. Hondula, and J.K. Vanos. 2015. "Heat Exposure during Non-Motorized Travel: Implications for Transportation Policy under Climate Change." *Journal of Transport and Health* 2 (4). Elsevier: 451–9.

Kim, Y., D. Eisenberg, E. Bondank, M. Chester, G. Mascaro, and S. Underwood. 2017. "Fail-Safe and Safe-to-Fail Adaptation: Decision-Making for Urban Flooding under Climate Change." *Climatic Change. In press.*

Kim, Y.H. 1995. *Coagulants and Flocculants: Theory and Practice.* Tall Oaks Pub.

Koetse, M.J. and P. Rietveld. 2009. "The Impact of Climate Change and Weather on Transport: An Overview of Empirical Findings." *Transportation Research Part D: Transport and Environment* 14 (3). 205–21.

Kreeley, B., and S. Coulton. 2012. "Increasing the Lifespan and Reliability of Electrical Components." Kooltronic, Inc. www.kooltronic.com/downloads/K1182.pdf (last accessed August 31, 2018).

Lemer, A.C. 1996. "Infrastructure Obsolescence and Design Service Life." *Journal of Infrastructure Systems* 2 (4): 153–61.

Lipponen, M.T.T., M.H. Suutari, and P.J. Martikainen. 2002. "Occurrence of Nitrifying Bacteria and Nitrification in Finnish Drinking Water Distribution Systems." *Water Research* 36 (17): 4319–29.

MacDonald-Evoy, J. 2016. "Power Outages Impact Thousands around Arizona." *The Arizona Republic.* www.azcentral.com/story/news/local/mesa-breaking/2016/06/05/1900-mesa-homes-lose-power-record-breaking-heat/85464650/ (last accessed August 19, 2018).

Markolf, S.A., C. Hoehne, A. Fraser, M.V. Chester, and B.S. Underwood. 2017. "Transportation Resilience to Climate Change and Extreme Weather Events – Beyond Risk and Robustness." *Transport Policy.* https://repository.asu.edu/attachments/189264/content/Markolf et al_Transportation Resilience Beyond Risk and Robustness.pdf (last accessed August 19, 2018).

Melillo, J.M., T.C. Richmond, and G.W. Yohe (eds.) 2014. *Climate Change Impacts in the United States Climate Change Impacts in the United States.* doi:10.7930/j0z31WJ2.

Meyer, M. and B. Weigel. 2011. "Climate Change and Transporation Engineering: Preparing for a Sustainable Future." *Journal of Transportation Engineering* 137 (6): 393–403.

Meyer, M., M. Flood, J. Keller, J. Lennon, G. McVoy, C. Dorney, K. Leonard, et al. 2014. *Climate Change, Extreme Weather Events, and the Highway System: Practitioner's Guide and Research Report. Transportation Research Board.* Vol. 2. doi:10.17226/22473.

Miara, A., J.E. Macknick, C.J. Vörösmarty, V.C. Tidwell, R. Newmark, and B. Fekete. 2017. "Climate and Water Resource Change Impacts and Adaptation Potential for US Power Supply." *Nature Climate Change* 7 (11). Nature Publishing Group: 793–98.

Miller, D., A. Kanafani, R. Skinner, B. Barker, A. Biehler, J. Bowe, D. Butler, W. Clark, and R, Van Antwerp. 2008. "Potential Impacts of Climate Change on US Transportation." *Transportation Research Board*, Special Report 290.

Mills, B.N., S.L. Tighe, J. Andrey, J.T. Smith, and K. Huen. 2009. "Climate Change Implications for Flexible Pavement Design and Performance in Southern Canada." *Journal of Transportation Engineering* 135 (October): 773–82.

Milly, P.C.D., J. Betancourt, M. Falkenmark, R.M. Hirsch, Z.W. Kundzewicz, D.P. Lettenmaier, and R.J. Stouffer. 2008. "Stationarity Is Dead: Whither Water Management?" *Science* 319 (5863): 573–74.

NERC. 2004. "Technical Analysis of the August 14, 2003, Blackout." www.nerc.com/docs/docs/blackout/NERC_Final_Blackout_Report_07_13_04.pdf (last accessed August 31, 2018).

ParkPioneer.net. 2012. "Canal Breaks near Bouse." *ParkerPioneer.net*, October 1. www.parkerpioneer.net/news/article_2ebf4370-b83e-54e3-abde-d2f68454151a.html.

Pintar, K.D.M. and R.M. Slawson. 2003. "Effect of Temperature and Disinfection Strategies on Ammonia-Oxidizing Bacteria in a Bench-Scale Drinking Water Distribution System." *Water Research* 37 (8): 1805–17.

Rattanachot, W., Y. Wang, D. Chong, and S. Suwansawas. 2015. "Adaptation Strategies of Transport Infrastructures to Global Climate Change." *Transport Policy* 41: 159–66.

Reyna, J.L. and M.V. Chester. 2017. "Energy Efficiency to Reduce Residential Electricity and Natural Gas Use under Climate Change." *Nature Communications* 8 (May). Nature Publishing Group: 14916.

Richards, C.W. 1996. "Agile Manufacturing: Beyond Lean?" *Production and Inventory Management Journal* 37 (2): 60.

Rockwell Automation. 1998. "Basics for Practical Operation Motor Starting." Rockwell Automation.

Rogers, J., A.B. Dowsett, P.J. Dennis, J.V. Lee, and C.W. Keevil. 1994. "Influence of Temperature and Plumbing Material Selection on Biofilm Formation and Growth of Legionella Pneumophila in a Model Potable Water System Containing Complex Microbial Flora." *Applied and Environmental Microbiology* 60 (5): 1585–92.

Saneinejad, S., M.J. Roorda, and C. Kennedy. 2012. "Modelling the Impact of Weather Conditions on Active Transportation Travel Behaviour." *Transportation Research Part D: Transport and Environment* 17 (2): 129–37.

Sathaye, J., L. Dale, P. Larsen, G. Fitts, K. Koy, S. Lewis, and A. Lucena. 2012. "Estimating Risk To California Energy Infrastructure From Projected Climate Change." Berkeley, CA. Lawrence Berkeley National Laboratory for the California Energy Commission.

Seager, T.P., S. Spierre Clark, D.A. Eisenberg, J.E. Thomas, M.M. Hinrichs, R. Kofron, C. Nørgaard Jensen, L.R. McBurnett, M. Snell, and D.L. Alderson. 2017. "Redesigning Resilient Infrastructure Research." In *Resilience and Risk*, Dordrecht: Springer, 81–119.

Semadeni-Davies, A., C. Hernebring, G. Svensson, and L.G. Gustafsson. 2008. "The Impacts of Climate Change and Urbanisation on Drainage in Helsingborg, Sweden: Combined Sewer System." *Journal of Hydrology* 350 (1–2): 100–13.

Sherehiy, B., W. Karwowski, and J.K. Layer. 2007. "A Review of Enterprise Agility: Concepts, Frameworks, and Attributes." *International Journal of Industrial Ergonomics* 37 (5): 445–60.

Smith, H.G., G.J. Sheridan, P.N.J. Lane, P. Nyman, and S. Haydon. 2011. "Wildfire Effects on Water Quality in Forest Catchments: A Review with Implications for Water Supply." *Journal of Hydrology* 396 (1–2): 170–92.

Taylor, M.A.P. and M.L. Philp. 2015. "Investigating the Impact of Maintenance Regimes on the Design Life of Road Pavements in a Changing Climate and the Implications for Transport Policy." *Transport Policy* 41: 117–35.

Toroz, I. and V. Uyak. 2005. "Seasonal Variations of Trihalomethanes (THMs) in Water Distribution Networks of Istanbul City" 176: 127–41.

Torvinen, E., S. Suomalainen, M.J. Lehtola, T. Ilkka, O. Zacheus, L. Paulin, M-l. Katila, P.J. Martikainen, and I.T. Miettinen. 2004. "Mycobacteria in Water and Loose Deposits of Drinking Water Distribution Systems in Finland," *Applied and Environmental Microbiology* 70 (4): 1973–81.

Toshiba. 2017. "Application Guideline # 05 Temperature Rise – Insulation." Vol. 5. http://toshont.com/wp-content/uploads/2017/06/Motor-Temperature-Rise.pdf (last accessed August 19, 2018).

Tramblay, Y., L. Neppel, J. Carreau, and K. Najib. 2013. "Non-Stationary Frequency Analysis of Heavy Rainfall Events in Southern France." *Hydrological Sciences Journal* 58 (2): 280–94.

TRB. 2008. "Potential Impacts of Climate Change on U.S. Transportation." Washington, DC: National Academy of Sciences.

USA Blue Book. 2013. *USABlueBook Operator's Companion.* 10th ed. USABlueBook. www.usabluebook.com/p-307561-operators-companion.aspx (last accessed August 19, 2018).

Vliet, M.T.H. van, D. Wiberg, S. Leduc, and K. Riahi. 2016. "Power-Generation System Vulnerability and Adaptation to Changes in Climate and Water Resources." *Nature Climate Change* 6 (4): 375–80.

Volk, C., E. Dundore, J. Schiermann, and M. Lechevallier. 2000. "Practical Evaluation of Iron Corrosion Control in a Drinking Water Distribution System." *Water Research* 34 (6): 1967–74.

Wadowsky, R.M., R. Wolford, A.N. McNamara, and R.B. Yee. 1985. "Effect of Temperature Ph and Oxygen Level on the Multiplication of Naturally Occurring Legionella-Pneumophila in Potable Water." *Applied and Environmental Microbiology* 49 (5): 1197–1205.

Wagman, D. 2013. "Water Issues Challenge Power Generators." www.powermag.com/water-issues-challenge-power-generators/ (last accessed August 19, 2018).

Weick, K.E. and R.E. Quinn. 1999. "Organizational Change and." *Annual Review of Psychology* 50: 361–86.

Whittle, A. and M. Stahmer. 2005. "Temperature Derating of PVC Pipes for Pressure Applications." Organization: Plastics Industry Pipe Association of Australia Limited. Chatswood, NSW, Australia.

Wild, H.E., C.N. Sawyer, and T.C. McMahon. 1971. "Factors Affecting Nitrification Kinetics." *Water Pollution Control Federation* 43: 10. www.jstor.org/stable/25037179 (last accessed August 19, 2018).

Willis, H.L., G.V. Welch, and R.R. Schrieber. 2001. *Aging Power Delivery Infrastructures.* Marcel Dekker, Inc.

Winguth, A., J.H. Lee, and Y. Ko. 2015. "Climate Change / Extreme Weather Vulnerability and Risk Assessment for Transportation Infrastructure in Dallas and Tarrant Counties." North Central Texas Council of Governments.

Woods, D.D. 2015. "Four Concepts for Resilience and the Implications for the Future of Resilience Engineering." *Reliability Engineering and System Safety* 141: 5–9.

Yordanova, L. 2015. "Phoenix Historic September Monsoon Rainstorm Causes Unique Treatment Scenario at Tempe Water Treatment Plant." In *88th AZ Water Annual Conference.*

Zevenbergen, C, Tuijn, J. van, Rijke, J., Bos, M., Herk, S. van, Douma, J., et al. 2013. "Rijkswaterstaat Room for the River. Tailor made collaboration: A clever combination of process and content." http://alfa-project.eu/en/news/5/new-publication-tailor-made-collaboration-a-clever-combination-of-process-and-content (last accessed August 31, 2018).

32

Climate change impact on RC structures subjected to chloride ingress and carbonation-induced corrosion

Emilio Bastidas-Arteaga[1] and Mark G. Stewart[2]

[1] RESEARCH INSTITUTE IN CIVIL AND MECHANICAL ENGINEERING, UMR CNRS 6183, UNIVERSITÉ DE NANTES, 2 RUE DE LA HOUSSINIÈRE BP 92208, 44322 NANTES CEDEX 3, FRANCE; TEL: +(33)2-51-12-55-24, WWW.UNIV-NANTES.FR/BASTIDASARTEAGA-EE; EMILIO.BASTIDAS@UNIV-NANTES.FR

[2] CENTRE FOR INFRASTRUCTURE PERFORMANCE AND RELIABILITY, SCHOOL OF ENGINEERING, THE UNIVERSITY OF NEWCASTLE, NEWCASTLE NSW 2308 AUSTRALIA; TEL. +61 2 49216027; WWW.NEWCASTLE.EDU.AU/PROFILE/MARK-STEWART; MARK.STEWART@NEWCASTLE.EDU.AU

32.1 Introduction

Reinforced concrete (RC) structures are subjected to environmental actions affecting their performance, serviceability and safety. Among these actions, chloride ingress and carbonation lead to corrosion of reinforcing bars that reduces the service life of RC structures. Experimental evidence indicates that carbonation and chloride ingress are highly influenced by environmental and climatic conditions of the surrounding environment – i.e. atmospheric CO_2 concentration, temperature, and humidity (Saetta et al. 1993). According to the International Panel of Climate Change (IPCC), the environmental CO_2 concentration could increase from 379 ppm in 2005 to nearly 1,000 ppm by the year 2100 (IPCC 2007). The changes in environmental temperature, relative humidity, and carbon dioxide concentration can increase corrosion risks resulting in more widespread corrosion damage and loss of structural safety. Consequently, the effect of atmospheric CO_2 concentration change and global warming on both chloride ingress and carbonation should be considered for long-term sustainable and resilient management of RC structures.

Climate change could affect directly or indirectly human communities and ecosystems in different ways – e.g., sea-level rise, increase in frequency and/or intensity of many extreme climate events, more frequent heat waves, increases in rainfall, etc. The impact of climate change on the performance of structures is becoming an important research issue from an engineering point of view. Moreover, risk-based methods are highly suited to assess the cost-effectiveness of climate adaptation measures (e.g. Stewart & Deng 2015). For instance, Bastidas-Arteaga et al.

(2010) proposed a stochastic approach to study the influence of global warming on chloride ingress, but this study only focused on the effect of climate change on the corrosion initiation stage. Stewart and Peng (2010) carried out a preliminary risk and cost-benefit study on adaptation measures to mitigate the effects of carbonation of RC structures. Other studies also focused on the assessment of climate change on the durability of concrete structures in specific locations. Stewart et al. (2011, 2012) and Wang et al. (2012) studied the impact of climatic change on corrosion-induced damage in Australia. They proposed a probabilistic approach to asses corrosion damage (cracking and spalling) taking into account the influence of climate change on areas characterized by different geographical conditions. Talukdar et al. (2012) estimated the effects of climate change on carbonation in Canadian cities (Toronto and Vancouver). They found potential increases in carbonation depths over 100 years of approximately 45 per cent. However, this work did not consider the uncertainties related to climate, materials and models, nor did it predict the effect of carbonation on damage and safety of concrete infrastructure.

The main objectives of this chapter are:

- to propose chloride ingress and carbonation models able to account for climate change variations;
- to present and discuss the IPCC climate change scenarios and related parameters that could affect the durability of corroding RC structures; and
- to assess the effects of increasing CO_2 concentrations and global warming induced changes in temperature and humidity on the durability and safety of RC structures.
- to illustrate how climate change may significantly reduce the resilience and reliability of RC infrastructure.

32.2 Time-dependent performance of corroding RC structures

The assessment of corrosion effects on RC structures is a difficult task because several deterioration mechanisms interact in the process; ingress of the corroding agent – i.e., chlorides or carbon dioxide, corrosion of reinforcing steel and concrete cover cracking. The ingress of the corroding agent induces corrosion of the reinforcing bars. Corrosion reduces the structural capacity and the accumulation of corrosion products in the steel/concrete interface generates concrete cover cracking. The corrosion process is divided into two stages namely 'corrosion initiation' and 'corrosion propagation'.

32.2.1 Time to corrosion initiation induced by chloride ingress

The adopted chloride ingress model considers the interaction between three physical processes: *chloride ingress*, *moisture diffusion*, and *heat transfer*. Each phenomenon is represented by a partial differential equation (PDE) expressed in the following general form (Bastidas-Arteaga et al. 2011; Nguyen et al. 2017):

$$\zeta \frac{\partial \psi}{\partial t} = \underbrace{\operatorname{div} \mathcal{J}}_{\text{diffusion}} + \underbrace{\operatorname{div} \mathcal{J}'}_{\text{convection}}, \tag{32.1}$$

where ζ represents the studied parameter, t is the time and the correspondence between ψ, $\mathcal{J}$, $\mathcal{J}'$ and the terms for the physical problem is presented in Table 32.1.

Table 32.1 Correspondence between Equation (32.1) and the governing differential equations

Physical Process	ψ	ζ	$\vec{j}$	$\vec{j}'$
Chloride ingress	C_{fc}	1	$D_c^*\vec{\nabla}C_{fc}$	$C_{fc}D_h^*\vec{\nabla}h$
Moisture diffusion	h	$\partial w_e/\partial h$	$D_h^*\vec{\nabla}h$	0
Heat transfer	T	$\rho_c\,c_q$	$\lambda\vec{\nabla}T$	0

For chloride ingress, C_{fc} is the concentration of free chlorides, h is the relative humidity and D_c^* and D_h^* represent the apparent chloride and humidity diffusion coefficients, respectively:

$$D_c^* = \frac{D_{c,ref}\,f_1(T)f_2(t)f_3(h)}{1+(1/w_e)(fC_{bc}/fC_{fc})} \tag{32.2}$$

$$D_h^* = \frac{D_{h,ref}\,g_1(h)g_2(T)g_3(t_e)}{1+(1/w_e)(fC_{bc}/fC_{fc})}, \tag{32.3}$$

where $D_{c,ref}$ and $D_{h,ref}$ are reference diffusion coefficients measured at standard conditions (Saetta et al. 1993), w_e is the evaporable water content, and f_i and g_i are correction functions to account for the effects of temperature, relative humidity, ageing, and degree of hydration of concrete. These functions are detailed in (Bastidas-Arteaga et al. 2011). The term $\partial C_{bc}/\partial C_{fc}$ represents the binding capacity of the cementitious system which relates the free and bound chlorides concentration at equilibrium. A Langmuir isotherm is used in this work.

For moisture diffusion, the humidity diffusion coefficient D_h is estimated by accounting for the influence of the parameters presented in Equation (32.3). The term $\partial w_e/\partial h$ (Table 32.1) represents the moisture capacity which relates the amount of free water, w_e, and the pore relative humidity, h. For a given temperature this relationship has been determined experimentally by adsorption isotherms. According to the Brunauer-Skalny-Bodor (BSB) model considered herein, the adsorption isotherm depends on temperature, water/cement ratio, w/c, and the degree of the hydration attained in the concrete, t_e.

Finally, for heat transfer (Table 32.1), ρ_c is the concrete density, c_q is the concrete specific heat capacity, λ is the thermal conductivity of concrete, and T is the temperature inside the concrete after time t.

The numerical approach used to solve the coupled system of PDEs combines a finite element formulation with finite difference to estimate the spatial and temporal variation of C_{fc}, h and T. Then, the time to corrosion initiation, t_{ini}, is estimated by comparing the chloride concentration at the cover depth, c_t, with a threshold concentration for corrosion initiation C_{th}.

32.2.2 Time to corrosion initiation induced by carbonation

The coupled drying and carbonation model of concrete detailed in (de Larrard et al. 2013) assumes that the main phenomena involved in carbonation are water migration through the connected porosity, and diffusion of carbon dioxide in the gaseous phase and its subsequent interactions with the hydrated phases initially present to produce calcium carbonate (calcite). Accordingly, it is governed by two coupled mass conservation equations for water (Equation (32.4)) and carbon dioxide in gas phase (Equation (32.5)):

$$\frac{\partial(\rho_l \phi S_r)}{\partial t} = \nabla\left[K(\phi)\frac{\rho_l}{\eta} k_r(S_r)\nabla(P_l)\right] + W_{H_2O} \tag{32.4}$$

$$\frac{\partial((1-S_r)\phi P_{\bar{c}})}{\partial t} = \nabla\left[f(\phi, S_r) D_{\bar{c}}\nabla(P_{\bar{c}})\right] + W_{CO_2}. \tag{32.5}$$

Equation (32.4) implicitly assumes that the main transport process for moisture results from gradients of partial pressure of water in the liquid phase P_l (permeation), i.e. the migration of vapor in gas phase is neglected (Bary & Sellier 2004; Mainguy et al. 2001). Moreover, the pressure of the gas phase is neglected with respect to the liquid phase, such that $P_c \approx -P_l$, where P_c is the capillary pressure. Equation (32.4) is also driven by P_c in the desorption isotherm that accounts for the relationships between the saturation degree S_r and P_c (Van Genuchten 1980):

$$S_r = \left[1 + (P_c/P_0)^{1/(1-m)}\right]^{-m}, \tag{32.6}$$

where P_0 and m are calibration parameters. Other parameters involved in Equation (32.4) are: $K(\phi)$ is the intrinsic permeability coefficient that depends on the initial porosity ϕ and the initial intrinsic permeability K_0 (Van Genuchten 1980); ρ_l and η are the density and dynamic viscosity of water, respectively; $k_r(S_r)$ is the relative permeability for liquid that depends on the saturation degree S_r (Van Genuchten 1980); and W_{H_2O} is the rate of water formation.

Equation (32.5) is driven by the partial pressure of CO_2 in the gaseous phase denoted as $P_{\bar{c}}$. $f(\phi, S_r)$ and $D_{\bar{c}}$ are the reduction factor (Millington 1959) and the diffusion coefficient of CO_2 in gas phase, respectively, such that their product can be considered as the effective diffusion coefficient of CO_2 through the porous material. W_{CO_2} is the rate of CO_2 dissolution. The coupling between Equations (32.4) and (32.5) appears through (i) the saturation degree S_r, and (ii) the rates of water formation and carbon dioxide dissolution.

The model has been modified to take into account the influence of temperature variations on carbonation. These modifications, detailed in (de Larrard et al. 2014), consider the influence on the following thermo-activated parameters/phenomena: (i) the CO_2 diffusion coefficient, (ii) the dissolution of portlandite and other hydrates, (iii) the constant of Henry, and (iv) the sorption-desorption isotherms. The dependency of temperature of all these parameters/phenomena is modeled with Arrhenius functions. According to Yuan and Jiang (2011), we assume that temperature inside concrete is constant and equal to the atmospheric temperature. This carbonation model was implemented in the finite element code Cast3M (www-cast3m.cea.fr), and the equations solved successively and iteratively with a fully implicit numerical scheme.

32.2.3 Corrosion propagation

After corrosion initiation, the diameter reduction of reinforcing bars induced by corrosion can be estimated in terms of a change in the volumetric rate by using Faraday's law:

$$d_u(t) = d_0 - 0.0232\int_{t_{ini}}^t i_{corr}(t)dt \text{ and } p(t) = 0.0116\alpha\int_{t_{ini}}^t i_{corr}(t)dt, \tag{32.7}$$

where $d_u(t)$ is the residual diameter of the reinforcing bar at time t for uniform corrosion in mm, d_0 is the initial diameter of the bar in mm, and $p(t)$ is the pit depth at time t in mm, α is the ratio between pitting and uniform corrosion depths, and $i_{corr}(t)$ is the time-variant corrosion rate ($\mu A/cm^2$). The remaining cross-sectional area of steel for pitting corrosion is computed herein considering the relationships proposed by Val and Melchers (1997). Given the complexity of the corrosion process, i_{corr} depends on many factors such as concrete pH and availability of oxygen, and water in the corrosion cell. For instance, the optimum relative humidity for corrosion is 70–80 per cent. This study considers the following time-variant corrosion rate model that takes into account the effect of temperature changes (DuraCrete 2000a,b):

$$i_{corr}(t) = i_{corr,20}\left[1 + K_c\left(T(t) - 20\right)\right],$$

(32.8)

where $i_{corr,20}$ is the corrosion rate at 20 °C, $T(t)$ is the temperature at time t (in °C) and K_c is a factor that depends on the value of $T(t)$. For instance, $K_c = 0.025$ if $T(t) < 20$°C or $K_c = 0.073$ if $T(t) > 20$°C. Corrosion rates are obtained from various sources (DuraCrete 1998). For more details of carbonation-induced corrosion due to a changing climate see Stewart et al. (2011); Stewart and Peng (2010); Peng and Stewart (2014).

32.3 Modeling climate change actions

32.3.1 IPCC climate change scenarios

The future climate is projected by defining carbon emission scenarios in relation to changes in population, economy, technology, energy, land use, and agriculture, represented by a total of four scenario families, i.e., A1, A2, B1 and B2 (IPCC 2007). The A1 scenario describes a future world of very rapid economic growth, global population that peaks in mid-century and declines thereafter, and the rapid introduction of new and more efficient technologies. This scenario family is divided into three groups distinguished by different technological emphasis: fossil-intensive (A1FI), non-fossil energy sources (A1T) or a balance across all sources (A1B). The A2 scenario describes a very heterogeneous world with continuously increasing population. The economic development is primarily regionally oriented and technological change more fragmented and slower. The B1 scenario is similar to the A1 scenario respecting to population growth, but with rapid change in economic structures toward a service and information economy, with reductions in material intensity and the introduction of clean and resource-efficient technologies. The B2 scenario describes a world in which the emphasis is on local solutions to economic, social, and environmental sustainability. The population growth pattern is similar to the scenario A2 but with a lower rate. It also includes more diverse technological solutions. In addition, scenarios of CO_2 stabilization at 450 and 550 ppm by 2150 were also introduced to consider the effect of policy intervention (Wigley et al. 1996). Hence, the A1FI or A2, A1B and 550 ppm stabilization scenarios represent high, medium emission scenarios, and policy intervention scenarios, respectively. The IPCC Fifth Assessment Report (AR5) (IPCC 2013) uses Representative Concentration Pathways (RCPs) where RCP 8.5, RCP 6.0 and RCP 4.5 are roughly equivalent to A1FI or A2, A1B, and A1B to B1 emission scenarios, respectively (Inman 2011).

32.3.2 Uncertainties for climate projections

Climate projections are subject to considerable uncertainty that depend on CO_2 emission scenarios and accuracy of general circulation models (GCM). These uncertainties can be classified into three types (Hawkins & Sutton 2009; Madsen 2013):

- Internal uncertainty is related to the natural variability of the climate system without considering any anthropogenic climate change effect. There are weather disturbances of different duration, size and location that turn climate into a chaotic system. Consequently, it is currently impossible to predict future climate at different scales (daily, monthly, yearly, etc.) even for the more complete climate models and short-time windows.
- Model uncertainty (also known as response uncertainty) is associated to the fact that GCMs simulate different changes in climate in response to a given radiative forcing. This kind of uncertainty depends mainly on the simplifications and assumptions that are implemented for each GCM to simulate natural systems.
- Scenario uncertainty is related to the assumptions made to define each climate change scenario that determine the future radiative forcing used in climate projections (e.g., future emissions of greenhouse gases, population growth, introduction of clean technologies, changes in land use, etc.).

Figure 32.1 illustrates how these uncertainties interact over time for surface temperature projections and two different scales: global (earth) and regional (British isles) (Hawkins & Sutton 2009). At a global scale, it is observed that model and internal uncertainties are initially predominant (Figure 32.1a). However, scenario uncertainties grow considerably and become the most important source of uncertainties after 50 years. A regional scale changes the relative importance of uncertainties. Internal uncertainty has initially the largest importance because regional weather is largely affected by random weather and climate fluctuations. Model uncertainties have the largest importance from 20 to 70 years. The importance of scenario uncertainties grows significantly during the latter part of the century (after 70 years).

The complexity of these uncertainties implies several considerations for the assessment of climate change impacts on civil infrastructure:

- Use of several climate trajectories from the same GCM to account for internal uncertainty.
- Use of several climate trajectories for various GCMs to account for model uncertainty.

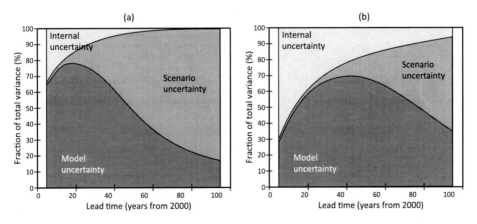

Figure 32.1 Relative importance of uncertainty sources over time for decadal mean surface air temperature projections: (a) global (earth) and (b) British Isles.

Source: Adapted from Hawkins and Sutton 2009.

- Consider several climate change scenarios to account for scenario uncertainty. A scenario of no change in climate may make economic sense as a 'no regrets' policy even if climate predictions are wrong.
- Verify that climate change projection be representative of climate at the scale of the study (local, regional, global). For instance, downscaling is required to represent climate at a local scale.

Exchanges with climate scientists are paramount for selecting appropriate climate parameters for specific problems. Special attention should be paid to the assessment of climate change effects related to rare climate events (extreme temperatures, wind, precipitations, etc.).

32.3.3 Effects on climate: Temperature and humidity

As mentioned previously, chloride penetration and carbonation are governed by diffusion coefficients that depend, among other factors, on the surrounding humidity and temperature. Therefore, it is necessary to implement a comprehensive model of weather (humidity and temperature). However, given the difficulties of integrating a fully coupled model of weather with chloride ingress and carbonation phenomena, a simplified model of climate is presented in this section. It accounts for the following aspects:

- influence of global warming,
- seasonal variations, and
- random nature of weather within a season.

The change of temperature and humidity produced by global warming for the upcoming years is modeled by a linear time-variant function. By denoting θ_w as the weather parameter (humidity or temperature), the annual mean value of θ_w for a period of analysis t_a (i.e., $t_a = 100$ years) is:

$$\overline{\theta}_w(t) = \theta_{w0} + \left(\theta_{wa} - \theta_0\right)t / t_a,$$

(32.9)

where θ_{w0} and θ_{wa} are the values of the annual means of humidity or temperature at the beginning of the analysis ($t = 0$ yr) and at the end of the reference period ($t = t_a$ yr), respectively. To take seasonal variations of humidity and temperature into consideration, the model divides the year into two seasons: hot and cold for temperature, and wet and dry for humidity. Actual forecasts of global warming also indicate that the droughts increase the length of hot (or wet) seasons, L_h, with respect to the length of cold (or dry) seasons, L_c (IPCC 2007). By defining R_0 as the normalized duration of the cold (or dry) season for $t=0$, i.e. $R_0 = L_c/(1 \text{ year})$, and R_a as the normalized duration of the cold or dry season for $t=t_a$ (L_c in yr); it is possible to linearly estimate the normalized duration of the cold or dry season R for a given t:

$$R(t) = R_0 + \left(R_a - R_0\right)\lfloor t \rfloor / t_a,$$

(32.10)

where $\lfloor t \rfloor$ represents the floor function. Thus by using a sinusoidal formulation to simulate the seasonal variation of θ_w around the linear trend (Equation (32.9)), the seasonal mean of θ_w for hot of wet seasons is:

$$\overline{K}(t) = \overline{\theta}_w(t) + \frac{\theta_{w,max} - \theta_{w,min}}{2} \sin\left(\frac{t - \lfloor t \rfloor}{1 - R(t)}\pi\right)$$

(32.11)

and for cold or dry seasons:

$$\overline{\kappa}(t) = \overline{\theta}_w(t) - \frac{\theta_{w,\max} - \theta_{w,\min}}{2} \sin\left(\frac{t - \lfloor t \rfloor}{1 - R(t)}\pi\right), \tag{32.12}$$

where $\theta_{w,\max}$ and $\theta_{w,\min}$ are respectively the maximum and minimum values taken by θ_w during one year and t is expressed in years.

To further improve the predictability of the assessments, it is important to implement a model that reproduces realistically temperature and humidity. The Karhunen-Loève expansion is appropriate to represent the weather variables. Let $\kappa(t, \theta)$ be a random process, which is a function of time t and defined over the domain $\mathbf{D}$ with θ belonging to the space of random events Ω; $\kappa(t, \theta)$ can thus be expanded as follows (Ghanem and Spanos 1991):

$$\kappa(t, \theta) \simeq \overline{\kappa}(t) + \sum_{i=1}^{n_{KL}} \sqrt{\lambda_i}\,\xi_i(\theta)f_i(t), \tag{32.13}$$

where $\overline{\kappa}$ is the mean of the process (Equations (32.11) and (32.12)), $\xi_i(\theta)$ is a set of normal random variables, n_{KL} is the number of terms of the truncated discretization, $f_i(t)$ are a complete set of deterministic orthogonal functions, and λ_i are the eigenvalues of the covariance function $C(t_1, t_2)$. Since closed-form solutions for $f_i(t)$ and λ_i are obtained for an exponential covariance (Ghanem & Spanos 1991), this study assumes that the processes of temperature and humidity have this kind of covariance.

This climate model can be used to represent the temperature or relative humidity for a given location. However, on real structures, structural components could be exposed to different climate exposures (solar radiation, wind, etc.) that will also affect deterioration. Further work is required to account for these microclimatic variations.

32.3.4 Increase of carbon dioxide emissions

Following the current patterns, studies have estimated that environmental CO_2 concentration could increase from 379 ppm in 2005 to up to 1000 ppm by the year 2100 (IPCC 2007). The increase of atmospheric CO_2 concentration is difficult to estimate because it depends on several socio-technical and political factors such as different assumptions in terms of population growth, economical development, transfer of clean technologies, etc. Figure 32.2 presents a projection from 2000 of CO_2 concentrations for A2, A1B, and B1 global warming scenarios. These scenarios were selected because they represent pessimistic, medium and optimistic climate change scenarios, respectively. These values were computed using the MAGICC software (Model for Assessment of Greenhouse-gas Induced Climate Change) (Wigley et al. 1996).

32.4 Numerical example 1: Climate change effects for RC structures subjected to chloride ingress

This example evaluates the influence of realistic environmental conditions including global warming on the structural reliability of a simply supported RC girder placed in various chloride-contaminated environments. A detailed description of this example is found in (Bastidas-Arteaga et al. 2013; Bastidas-Arteaga 2018). The girder has a span of 10 m and is subjected to a point (concentrated) wheel load placed in the middle of the span. Figure 32.3 presents the characteristics of the cross-sectional section that has been designed according to Eurocode 2

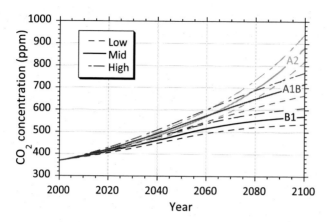

Figure 32.2 CO₂ concentrations for various global warming scenarios.

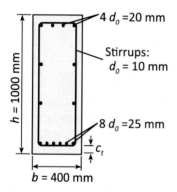

Figure 32.3 Configuration of the bridge girder.

(European standard 2004). Its material design properties are described in Table 32.2 and the climatic conditions are defined by:

- two environments: oceanic and tropical (Table 32.3);
- three levels of corrosion aggressiveness: low, moderate and high (Table 32.4), and
- three scenarios of global warming: without, expected and pessimistic (Table 32.5).

The time to corrosion initiation considers flow of chlorides in one dimension where the Langmuir isotherm is used to account for chloride binding. The constants of the isotherm are $\alpha_L = 0.1185$ and $\beta_L = 0.09$.

32.4.1 Climate change scenarios

This analysis defines three possible scenarios of global warming: *without*, *expected*, and *pessimistic* global warming. A complete description of these considerations is given in (Bastidas-Arteaga et al. 2010). Each scenario is defined in terms of:

Table 32.2 Design load and material constants

Variable	Value
Characteristic design load, P_k	150 kN
Elastic modulus of steel, E_{st}	200 GPa
Characteristic concrete compression strength, f'_{ck}	30 MPa
Characteristic steel strength, f_{yk}	500 MPa
Concrete Poisson ratio, v_c	0.2

Table 32.3 Description of the studied environments

Climate	Latitude	T_{min}	T_{max}	h_{min}	h_{max}
Oceanic	Middle	5°C	25°C	60%	80%
Tropical	Equatorial	20°C	30°C	70%	90%

Table 32.4 Corrosion aggressiveness levels

Corrosion Level	C_{env}	$i_{corr,20}$
Low	0.35 kg/m³	0.5 μA/cm²
Moderate	1.15 kg/m³	2.0 μA/cm²
High	2.95 kg/m³	5.0 μA/cm²

Table 32.5 Scenarios of global warming for 100 years

Scenario	ΔT (°C)	Δh (%)	ΔR (%)
Without: climate change is neglected	0	0	0
Expected: Use of alternative and fossil sources of energy, birth-rates follow the current patterns and there is no extensive deployment of clean technologies	2.5	5	–10
Pessimistic: Vast utilisation of fossil sources of energy, appreciable growth of population and there are no policies to develop and extend the use of clean technologies	6.5	10	–20

- the difference between the annual means of temperature for the initial year $T(t_0)$ and the year of the end of the forecast $T(t_a)$, ΔT,
- the difference between the annual mean of relative humidity for $h(t_0)$ and $h(ta)$, Δh, and
- the difference between the normalized durations of cold seasons for $R(t_0)$ and $R(t_a)$, ΔR.

By taking as reference a period of analysis of 100 years –i.e., $t_a = 100$ yr, the features and the values of ΔT, Δh and ΔR for each scenario are given in Table 32.5.

32.4.2 Reliability analysis

The integration of the deterioration models presented earlier into a suitable probabilistic framework is necessary to perform efficient probabilistic lifetime assessments and reliability analysis. The cumulative distribution function (CDF) of the time to failure, t_f, is:

$$F_{t_f}(t) = \Pr\{t_f \le t\} = \int_{t_f \le t} f(\underline{x})d\underline{x},$$

(32.14)

where $\underline{x}$ is the vector of random variables to be taken into account, and $f(\underline{x})$ is the joint probability density function (PDF) of $\underline{x}$. The cumulative failure probability, p_f, is then estimated by integrating the PDF of $\underline{x}$ over the failure domain as:

$$p_f = \int_{g(\underline{x},t) \le 0} f(\underline{x})d\underline{x},$$

(32.15)

where $g(\underline{x}, t)$ is the limit state function. Defining failure in terms of the limit state of bending, $g(\underline{x}, t)$ becomes:

$$g(\underline{x},t) = M_f(A_s(t),\underline{x}) - M_e(P,\underline{x}),$$

(32.16)

where $A_s(t)$ is the residual cross-sectional area of reinforcement at time t, P is the applied load, $\underline{x}$ is the vector of random variables (i.e. concrete compressive strength, f'_c, yield stress, f_y, etc.), M_f $(A_s(t), \underline{x})$ is the bending moment capacity, and $M_e(P, \underline{x})$ is the bending moment due to the load P.

Closed-form solutions for both the CDF of the time to failure and the failure probability are very difficult to obtain. Therefore, Monte Carlo simulations and Latin hypercube sampling are used herein to deal with this problem. The probabilistic models used to estimate both failure probability and PDF of the time to failure are presented in Table 32.6. It is assumed that all the random variables are statistically independent. Loading P is modeled by a random wheel load placed at the middle of the span.

For illustrative purposes, this example focuses on the study of the effects of climate change under several environmental conditions defining failure only in terms of the limit state of bending. However, the results of the evaluation of the effects of climate change could change when the limit state function is defined in terms of other failure modes, such as cracking and spalling of the concrete cover (Bastidas-Arteaga et al. 2010; Stewart et al. 2011, 2012; Wang et al. 2012; Peng & Stewart 2014). Therefore, although similar trends could be obtained for

Table 32.6 Probabilistic models of the random variables

Variable	Units	Distribution	Mean	COV	Reference
$D_{c,ref}$	m²/s	log-normal	$3 \cdot 10^{-11}$	0.20	(DuraCrete 2000a; Saetta et al. 1993; Val and Trapper 2008)
C_{env}	kg/m³	log-normal	Table 33.4	0.20	(DuraCrete 2000a; Vu and Stewart 2000)
C_{th}	wt% cem.	normal[a]	0.5	0.20	(DuraCrete 2000a)
c_t	Mm	normal[b]	50	0.25	(Val and Stewart 2003)
$D_{h,ref}$	m²/s	log-normal	$3 \cdot 10^{-10}$	0.20	(Saetta et al. 1993; Val and Trapper 2008)
λ	W/(m°C)	beta on [1.4;3.6]	2.5	0.20	(Neville 1981)
c_q	J/(kg°C)	beta on [840;1170]	1000	0.10	(Neville 1981)
ρ_c	kg/m³	normal[a]	2400	0.04	(JCSS (Joint committee of structural safety) 2001)
α		gumbel	5.65	0.22	(Val and Stewart 2003)
P	kN	log-normal	115	0.20	(Bastidas-Arteaga et al. 2009, Bastidas-Arteaga, 2018)
f'_c	MPa	normal[a]	40	0.15	(Pham 1985)
f_y	MPa	normal[a]	600	0.10	(Mirza et al. 1979)

[a] truncated at 0, [b]truncated at 10mm

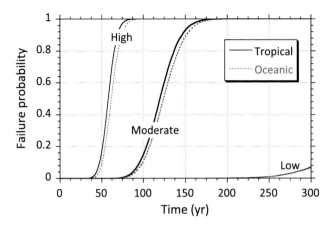

Figure 32.4   Failure probability for various levels of corrosion aggressiveness.

other failure modes, it is important to highlight that the findings herein are only valid for the limit state function presented by Equation (32.16).

32.4.3 Results and discussion

Figure 32.4 shows the failure probability of the RC beam for the tropical and the oceanic environments, and the three levels of corrosion aggressiveness for the stochastic weather model ignoring global warming. It is observed that the failure probability increases, in all cases, when the level of corrosion aggressiveness is higher. This increment is caused by higher concentrations of chlorides and corrosion rates in aggressive environments. If failure probabilities are evaluated for a lifecycle length of 50 years, the structural reliabilities are very low for the high level of corrosion aggressiveness. By considering that the failure probability should be lower than a critical value to ensure a safety level – i.e., $p_f < p_{fl} = 10^{-4}$, the studied structural configuration only guarantees this condition for moderate and low levels of aggressiveness. These results are not surprising because in real structures close to the sea as ports or quays, appreciable levels of deterioration have been reported after only 15 or 20 years of exposure. The results are similar for both environments. However, the failure probabilities are lower for the oceanic environment where the lower temperature and humidity delay corrosion initiation. This behaviour indicates that a sophisticated model of chloride ingress calibrated with experimental observations and monitored with inspections should be included in the management of structures to assure appropriate levels of serviceability and safety during its lifecycle.

The effects of weather and global warming on the PDF of time to failure are then evaluated. Table 32.7 presents the computed mean and standard deviation of the time to failure for the studied cases, for three climate scenarios using the stochastic weather model. It is observed that the mean time to failure decreases for more aggressive environments. The mean time to failure is lower for tropical than for oceanic environments. This behaviour seems logical because tropical environments are characterized by higher temperature and humidity that accelerate chloride ingress reducing corrosion initiation time. By taking as reference the scenarios without global warming, it is also noted that the effect of global warming is more important for structures located in oceanic environments. While for the tropical environment global warming induced reductions varying from 2 per cent to 20 per cent in the mean time to failure, for the oceanic

Table 32.7 Mean (μ_{t_f}) and standard deviation (σ_{t_f}) of the time to failure for the tropical environment

Corrosion aggressiveness	Climate Scenario	Tropical environment			Oceanic Environment		
		μ_{t_f} (yr)	σ_{t_f} (yr)	Reduction (%)	μ_{t_f} (yr)	σ_{t_f} (yr)	Reduction (%)
High	without	41.3	12.4	0	55	18	0
	expected	40.6	11.9	1.7	53.4	16.8	3
	pessimist	39.8	11.4	3.7	51.5	15.4	6.5
Moderate	without	84.9	26.4	0	115.2	37.3	0
	expected	82.1	24	3.3	107.7	31.5	6.6
	pessimist	78.9	21.4	7.1	100.3	27	12.9
Low	without	292.8	69.5	0	406.5	97.2	0
	expected	269.3	56.6	8.1	326.3	64.6	19.7
	pessimist	234.5	43.3	19.9	280.6	48.4	31

environment this reduction ranges between 3 per cent and 31 per cent. It can be concluded that climate change has more influence in environments where humidity and temperature are characterized by important seasonal variations.

This example showed that climate change could lead to considerable reduction to the predicted time to failure. In other words, how climate change may significantly reduce the resilience and reliability of RC infrastructure. The following section focuses on the assessment of climate change risks on RC structures subjected to carbonation.

32.5 Numerical example 2: Climate change effects for RC structures subjected to carbonation

The objective of this example is to estimate the effects of several scenario of climate change on the carbonation of a RC structure placed in several cities in France. This example only focuses on the stage of corrosion initiation due to carbonation. Then the methodology and results could be associated to any kind of RC structure (bridge, building, etc.) built with a CEM I concrete with a water/cement ratio equal to 0.42 and 68 per cent aggregate volume fraction. The material is initially set to a saturation degree corresponding to the year before 2000, and exposed to drying, carbonation, and temperature variations according to climate change scenarios for each city. It is also supposed that carbonation takes place in one dimension. The material properties as well as the model parameters were chosen equivalent to those proposed in de Larrard et al. (2013). A detailed description of this example is also found in de Larrard et al. (2014).

Table 32.8 presents the random variables considered in this study. Concrete cover corresponds to a global structural uncertainty related to a variability introduced by the building process. The initial porosity of the cement paste has a significant influence on the kinetics of the diffusion processes studied here, as it appears in every term of the governing equations. Two other variables concern the drying process: the intrinsic permeability K_0 and the m parameter from the van Genuchten model, which governs the desorption isotherm. The last random variable is the diffusion coefficient for CO_2. Their 'randomness' stands for the natural uncertainty and spatial variability of the materials properties, even for the same concrete formulation. These random variables follow independent normal distributions. Their means

Table 32.8 Statistical parameters of the random variables for the carbonation model

Variable	Unit	Distribution	Mean	COV
concrete cover, c_t	cm	Normal	2	5%
Initial porosity, ϕ_0	%	Normal	30	5%
Intrinsic permeability, K_0	m^2	Normal	1.8×10^{-22}	5%
Parameter, m (eqn. (33.6))		Normal	0.532	5%
Diffusion coefficient, D_c	m^2/s	Normal	1.9×10^{-8}	5%

Source: de Larrard et al. 2010, 2013.

and COVs are among the values observed for a given concrete formulation (de Larrard et al. 2010, 2013).

32.5.1 Climate change scenarios

This work focused on the study of the effects of climate change on six locations in France: Marseille, Paris, Toulouse, Strasbourg, Clermont-Fd., and Nantes (Figure 32.5). These cities correspond to different types of climate: Nantes has a temperate oceanic climate; Toulouse has continental, oceanic, and Mediterranean influences; Marseille has a Mediterranean climate which is hot and dry; Strasbourg has a northern continental climate; Paris has an intermediate continental climate; and Clermont-Fd. is in the mountains of 'Massif Central', in elevated south-central France and has a continental climate.

The effect of climate change on weather will change depending on the geographical and meteorological characteristics of the studied location. The impact of climate change on the future weather of the selected locations was estimated by using data computed by the French general circulation model SCRATCH-ARPEGE-V4-RETIC (Déqué et al. 1994). This model was selected because it is able to account for climate projections at a regional scale with a 8 km grid. For instance, Figure 32.6 presents the yearly projections of temperature and RH for the city of Nantes and the selected climate change scenarios. It is noted that climate change projections show a temperature increase and RH decrease for all scenarios. The most important changes in temperature and RH are related to the larger emissions scenarios described in previous section. Concerning consequences on climate change, it is possible to define A2 as a pessimistic scenario, A1B as a medium impact scenario, and B1 as an optimistic scenario. For this study, it has been decided to take into account only the mean (mid) CO_2 emissions for each climate change scenario according to Figure 32.2.

32.5.2 Reliability analysis

As the carbonation depth is not directly accessible numerically, the failure function for the carbonation model presented earlier is based on the quantity of portlandite dissolved at the steel/concrete interface. The carbonation depth, as defined by the widely used phenolphthalein test, is simply estimated from the portlandite profile for a threshold value of dissolution. For instance, if the remaining volume fraction of portlandite is less than 33 per cent of the initial value after dissolution at the cover depth, it is considered that corrosion starts. This threshold is among the values reported in the literature (Chang & Chen 2006; de Larrard et al. 2013; Park 2008). Thus, for this threshold value, the limit state function becomes:

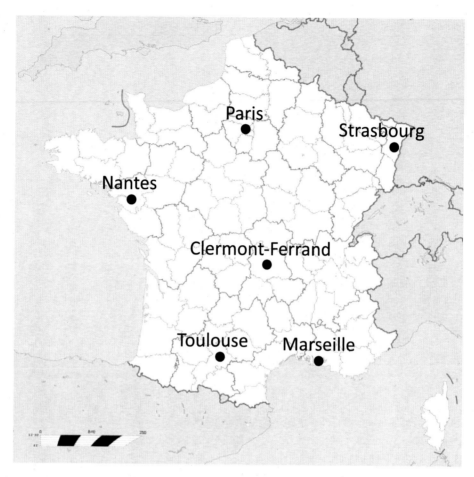

Figure 32.5   Studied locations in France.

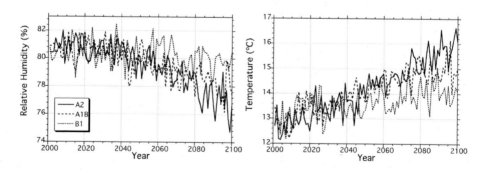

Figure 32.6   Temperature and RH projections for Nantes.

$$G(\underline{\mathbf{x}}) = V_p\left(\underline{\mathbf{x}}, c_t(\underline{\mathbf{x}}), t_{fin}\right) - 0.33 V_p\left(\underline{\mathbf{x}}, c_t(\underline{\mathbf{x}}), t_0\right), \tag{32.17}$$

where V_p is the volume fraction of portlandite, depending on c_t, being the concrete cover thickness from the exposed face, and the time. V_p is calculated with the FE model presented earlier t_{fin} is the final time of the simulations (100 years), and t_0 is the initial time (0 year). It is clear that the choice of the dissolved portlandite threshold will affect the assessment of reliability index. However, for a comparative study of climate change effects on various climates, the global trends will be the same for all the studied cases if the threshold is fixed.

According to design codes, $G(\underline{\mathbf{x}})$ defines a limit-state function, which is expected to be continuous. In the carbonation model considered in this study, the limit state function G is computed by using the finite element method. Therefore, the reliability index (β) is computed according to the gradient projection algorithm in the standardized space (Duprat et al. 2010). The result of the reliability analysis could therefore provide β over the lifetime t_{fin}.

32.5.3 Results and discussion

By using the outputs of the French atmosphere model, Table 32.9 describes the mean temperature and RH for the first decade of the study (2001–10). It is observed that Marseille is the hottest and driest city, Strasbourg is the most cold and Nantes is the most humid. Table 32.9 also summaries the effects of climate change by comparing the mean values of the first (2001–10) and the last decade (2091–2100) for each climate change scenario.

Table 32.10 presents the reliability indexes for these climate change scenarios over a period of 100 years. It is observed that there is a large variation of the reliability index from $\beta < 0$ ($p_f > 0.5$) to $\beta > 8$ ($p_f < 10^{-15}$). Let us specify here that a negative reliability index refers to a situation where the probability of corrosion initiation is higher than 50 per cent. This implies a larger difference in the safety issues for the extreme cases. This larger variability is due to the fact that the same material has been tested for cities with different climates (Table 32.9). For instance, the climate is very different in Nantes and Marseille. Since the exposure conditions are not the same, we should design a specific formulation for a concrete or select a different concrete cover adapted for each city. Considering the same concrete mix design for such different exposure conditions was required only for the needs of the comparison within the framework of this study. The reliability index for Marseille was $\beta < 0$, indicating that the probability of corrosion initiation is very high in a period of 100 years. The lower values of β for Marseille

Table 32.9 Mean temperature and RH over the period 2001–10 and predicted changes for B1, A1B, and A2 climate change scenarios

City	Mean temperature and RH over the period 2001–2010		Change in temperature (°C) over the period 2001–2100			Change in relative humidity (%) over the period 2001–2100		
	Temp. (°C)	RH (%)	B1	A1B	A2	B1	A1B	A2
Marseille	14.75	68.78	1.16	2.21	3.04	−0.21	−1.1	−2.61
Paris	13.04	74.22	1.33	2.56	3.59	−1.14	−3.44	−4.92
Toulouse	14.08	77.36	1.18	2.29	3.23	−0.93	−2.79	−4.79
Strasbourg	11.53	77.02	1.4	2.58	3.63	−1.11	−2.87	−4.64
Clermont–Ferrand	11.66	75.44	1.28	2.39	3.43	−0.79	−2.33	−4.59
Nantes	12.76	80.65	1.14	2.23	3.22	−0.59	−2.75	−3.96

Table 32.10 Reliability indexes for the different climate change scenarios

City	B1	A1B	A2
Marseille	< 0	< 0	< 0
Paris	6.55	3.68	1.70
Toulouse	6.91	3.90	2.09
Strasbourg	> 8	> 8	7.51
Clermont-Ferrand	> 8	> 8	> 8
Nantes	> 8	> 8	> 8

are explained, on the one hand, because the temperature is more important and carbonation is thermo-activated. On the other hand, RH varies between 65 per cent and 70 per cent by accelerating carbonation. These results could justify the implementation of an adaptation measure for this type of climate that could consist of increasing the concrete cover or the strength grade (Bastidas-Arteaga & Stewart 2015, 2016).

On the opposite, corrosion initiation risks are very low for Strasbourg, Clermont-Fd., and Nantes. The lower temperatures and higher RH for these cities slowdown the carbonation process. For example, the RH in Nantes remains between 80 per cent and 85 per cent which corresponds to a 'retarding effect,' modeled by the function presented in Equation (33.4) (Millington 1959): when RH is larger (RH > 80%), there is not enough gaseous phase in the pores for the diffusion process to occur efficiently. This 'natural safety' due to a higher RH appears mainly because only carbonation is studied here, but the opposite effect would appear if the corrosion process were considered instead (because its kinetics is driven by water saturation).

Climate change could have important effects in structures in Paris and Toulouse. Although Paris has lower temperatures than southern cities, the value of RH for the decade 2001–10 is within the optimal interval for accelerating carbonation (Table 32.9). Climate changes also accelerate carbonation in Paris by a significant decrease of RH (Table 32.9). Toulouse has a similar behaviour to that of Paris. On the one hand, the higher temperature in Toulouse accelerates the carbonation effects; but the larger RH reduces them. It is therefore possible to conclude that, for the studied locations, carbonation is more sensitive to RH than temperature. It is to be noted that, except for Marseille, the reliability index is higher to the 1.5 value given for a serviceability limit state in Eurocode 0. The reliability index calculated here only takes into account the carbonation process, and not the oxygen transfer for instance which is linked to the corrosion process kinetics. Therefore, no conclusion concerning actions required on the RC elements considered here can be drawn directly from these results.

Concerning the effects of different climate change scenarios, it appears that the reliability index decreases when temperature increases and RH decreases. The impact of the scenario is significant for Paris and Toulouse. For instance in Paris, according to B1-scenario, the reliability index is close to 6.6, which corresponds to a rather safe area, but according to A2-scenario, it is reduced to 1.7. This means that, under A2-scenario, the RC structures should be surveyed with care or adaptation measures implemented, because the risk of carbonation around the steel rebar (and corrosion initiation) is significant.

32.6 Conclusions

This chapter presented some considerations to assess the effects of climate change on the durability of corroding RC structures subjected to chloride ingress or carbonation. The first part of this chapter described the deterioration models that can be used for modeling this interaction. Afterwards, the discussion focused on presenting and modeling the effects of global warming on the environmental factors that could alter the kinematics of the deterioration process (temperature, humidity and CO_2 concentrations).

The proposed methodology is illustrated with numerical examples that study the effects of climate change on the resiliency and reliability of RC structures. For chloride-induced corrosion, the results showed that global warming could reduce the time to failure by up to 31 per cent, or shorten service life by up to 15 years for moderate levels of aggressiveness. Concerning carbonation-induced corrosion, this study has shown that carbonation is very sensitive to local climate and climate change scenarios. For example, carbonation risks are lower for an optimistic climate change scenario for Paris and Toulouse but could be significantly increased for the most pessimistic scenario. To enhance resiliency, specific design improvement and/or adaptation strategy should therefore consider exposure and specific climate of each structural location.

References

Bary, B. and Sellier, A. (2004). 'Coupled moisture—carbon dioxide—calcium transfer model for carbonation of concrete'. *Cement and Concrete Research*, 34(10), 1859–72.

Bastidas-Arteaga E. (2018) 'Reliability of reinforced concrete structures subjected to corrosion-fatigue and climate change'. *International Journal of Concrete Structures and Materials*, 12: 1–13.

Bastidas-Arteaga, E., and Stewart, M.G. (2015). 'Damage risks and economic assessment of climate adaptation strategies for design of new concrete structures subject to chloride-induced corrosion'. *Structural Safety*, 52, 40–53.

Bastidas-Arteaga E, and Stewart M G. (2016). 'Economic assessment of climate adaptation strategies for existing RC structures subjected to chloride-induced corrosion'. *Structure and Infrastructure Engineering* 12(4), 432–49.

Bastidas-Arteaga, E., Bressolette, P., Chateauneuf, A., and Sánchez-Silva, M. (2009). 'Probabilistic lifetime assessment of RC structures under coupled corrosion–fatigue deterioration processes'. *Structural Safety*, 31(1), 84–96.

Bastidas-Arteaga, E., Chateauneuf, A., Sánchez-Silva, M., Bressolette, P., and Schoefs, F. (2010). 'Influence of weather and global warming in chloride ingress into concrete: A stochastic approach'. *Structural Safety*, 32(4), 238–49.

Bastidas-Arteaga, E., Chateauneuf, A., Sánchez-Silva, M., Bressolette, P., and Schoefs, F. (2011). 'A comprehensive probabilistic model of chloride ingress in unsaturated concrete'. *Engineering Structures*, 33(3), 720–30.

Bastidas-Arteaga, E., Schoefs, F., Stewart, M.G., and Wang, X. (2013). 'Influence of global warming on durability of corroding RC structures: A probabilistic approach'. *Engineering Structures*, 51, 259–66.

Chang, C.-F. and Chen, J.-W. (2006). 'The experimental investigation of concrete carbonation depth'. *Cement and Concrete Research*, 36(9), 1760–7.

Déqué, M., Dreveton, C., Braun, A., and Cariolle, D. (1994). 'The ARPEGE/IFS atmosphere model: A contribution to the French community climate modelling'. *Climate Dynamics*, 10(4–5), 249–66.

Duprat, F., Sellier, A., Nguyen, X.S., and Pons, G. (2010). 'The projection gradient algorithm with error control for structural reliability'. *Engineering Structures*, 32(11), 3725–33.

DuraCrete. (1998). *Modelling of Degradation, DuraCrete – Probabilistic Performance based Durability Design of Concrete Structures, EU – Brite EuRam III*, Contract BRPR-CT95-0132, Project BE95-1347/R4-5.

DuraCrete. (2000a). *Statistical quantification of the variables in the limit state functions, DuraCrete – Probabilistic Performance based Durability Design of Concrete Structures, EU – Brite EuRam III*, Contract BRPR-CT95-0132, Project BE95-1347/R9.

DuraCrete. (2000b). *Probabilistic calculations. DuraCrete—probabilistic performance based durability design of concrete structures. EU—brite EuRam III*. Contract BRPR-CT95-0132. Project BE95-1347/R12-13.

European Standard. (2004). *Eurocode 1 and 2: Basis of design and actions on structures and design of concrete structures.*

Ghanem, R.G., and Spanos, P.D. (1991). *Stochastic Finite Elements: A Spectral Approach*. New York: Springer.

Hawkins, E., and Sutton, R. (2009). 'The potential to narrow uncertainty in regional climate predictions'. *Bulletin of the American Meteorological Society*, 90(8), 1095–1107.

Inman, M. (2011). 'Opening the future'. *Nature Climate Change*, Nature Publishing Group, 1(1), 7–9.

IPCC. (2007). *Climate Change 2007: The Physical Science Basis. Contribution of Working Group I to the Fourth Assessment Report of the Intergovernmental Panel on Climate Change.* (S. Solomon, D. Qin, M. Manning, Z. Chen, M. Marquis, K.B. Averyt, M. Tignor, and H. L. Miller, eds.), Cambridge and New York: Cambridge University Press.

IPCC. (2013). *Climate Change 2013: The Physical Science Basis. Contribution of Working Group I to the Fifth Assessment Report of the Intergovernmental Panel on Climate Change.* (T.F. Stocker, D. Qin, G.-K. Plattner, M. Tignor, S.K. Allen, J. Boschung, A. Nauels, Y. Xia, V. Bex, and P.M. Midgley, eds.), Cambridge and New York: Cambridge University Press.

JCSS (Joint Committee of Structural Safety). (2001). *Probabilistic Model Code.*

de Larrard, T., Benboudjema, F., Colliat, J.B., Torrenti, J.M., and Deleruyelle, F. (2010). 'Concrete calcium leaching at variable temperature: Experimental data and numerical model inverse identification'. *Computational Materials Science*, 49(1), 35–45.

de Larrard, T., Bary, B., Adam, E., and Kloss, F. (2013). 'Influence of aggregate shapes on drying and carbonation phenomena in 3D concrete numerical samples'. *Computational Materials Science*, 72, 1–14.

de Larrard, T, Bastidas-Arteaga, E, Duprat, F, and Schoefs, F. (2014). 'Effects of climate variations and global warming on the durability of RC structures subjected to carbonation'. *Civil Engineering and Environmental Systems* 31(2): 153–64.

Madsen, H. (2013). 'Managing structural safety and reliability in adaptation to climate change'. *11th International Conference on Structural Safety & Reliability*, G. Deodatis, B.R. Ellingwood, and D. Frangopol, eds., New York: CRC Press, 81–8.

Mainguy, M., Coussy, O., and Baroghel-Bouny, V. (2001). 'Role of air pressure in drying of weakly permeable materials'. *Journal of Engineering Mechanics*, American Society of Civil Engineers, 127(6), 582–92.

Millington, R.J. (1959). 'Gas diffusion in porous media'. *Science (New York, N.Y.)*, American Association for the Advancement of Science, 130(3367), 100–2.

Mirza, S.A., Hatzinikolas, M., and MacGregor, J.G. (1979). 'Statistical descriptions of strength of concrete'. *Journal of the Structural Division*, 105, 1021–37.

Nguyen P-T., Bastidas-Arteaga, E., Amiri, O., and El Soueidy, C-P. (2017). 'An efficient chloride ingress model for long-term lifetime assessment of reinforced concrete structures under realistic climate and exposure conditions'. *International Journal of Concrete Structures and Materials* 11(2): 199–213.

Neville, A. (1981). *Properties of Concrete* (3rd ed.). Harlow: Longman Scientific & Technical.

Park, D.C. (2008). 'Carbonation of concrete in relation to $CO2$ permeability and degradation of coatings'. *Construction and Building Materials*, 22(11), 2260–8.

Peng, L. and Stewart, M.G. (2014), 'Spatial time-dependent reliability analysis of corrosion damage to concrete structures under a changing climate'. *Magazine of Concrete Research*, 66(22): 1154–69.

Pham, L. (1985). 'Reliability analysis of reinforced concrete and composite column sections under concentric loads'. *Civil Engineering Transactions*, 1, 68–72.

Saetta, A., Scotta, R., and Vitaliani, R. (1993). 'Analysis of chloride diffusion into partially saturated concrete'. *ACI Materials Journal*, 90(5), 441–51.

Stewart, M.G. and Peng, J.X. (2010). 'Life-cycle cost assessment of climate change adaptation measures to minimise carbonation-induced corrosion risks'. *International journal of Engineering Under Uncertainty*, 2, 35–46.

Stewart, M.G. and Deng, X. (2015), 'Climate Impact Risks and Climate Adaptation Engineering for Built Infrastructure'. *ASCE-ASME Journal of Risk and Uncertainty in Engineering Systems, Part A: Civil Engineering*, 1(1), 04014001.

Stewart, M.G., Wang, X., and Nguyen, M.N. (2011). 'Climate change impact and risks of concrete infrastructure deterioration'. *Engineering Structures*, 33(4), 1326–37.

Stewart, M.G., Wang, X., and Nguyen, M.N. (2012). 'Climate change adaptation for corrosion control of concrete infrastructure'. *Structural Safety*, 35, 29–39.

Talukdar, S., Banthia, N., Grace, J. R., and Cohen, S. (2012). 'Carbonation in concrete infrastructure in the context of global climate change: Part 2, Canadian urban simulations'. *Cement and Concrete Composites*, 34(8), 931–5.

Val, D.V. and Melchers, R.E. (1997). 'Reliability of deteriorating RC slab bridges'. *Journal of Structural Engineering ASCE*, 123(12), 1638–44.

Val, D.V. and Stewart, M. G. (2003). 'Life-cycle analysis of reinforced concrete structures in marine environments'. *Structural Safety*, 25, 343–62.

Val, D.V. and Trapper, P.A. (2008). 'Probabilistic evaluation of initiation time of chloride-induced corrosion'. *Reliability Engineering and System Safety*, 93, 364–72.

Van Genuchten, M.T. (1980). 'A closed-form equation for predicting the hydraulic conductivity of unsaturated soils'. *Soil Science Society of America Journal*, 44(5), 892–8.

Vu, K.A.T. and Stewart, M.G. (2000). 'Structural reliability of concrete bridges including improved chloride-induced corrosion'. *Structural Safety*, 22, 313–33.

Wang, X., Stewart, M.G., and Nguyen, M. (2012). 'Impact of climate change on corrosion and damage to concrete infrastructure in Australia'. *Climatic Change*, 110(3–4), 941–57.

Wigley, T.M.L., Richels, R., and Edmonds, J.A. (1996). 'Economic and environmental choices in the stabilization of atmospheric CO2 concentrations'. *Nature*, 379, 240–3.

Yuan, Y., and Jiang, J. (2011). 'Prediction of temperature response in concrete in a natural climate environment'. *Construction and Building Materials*, 25(8), 3159–67.

33

Hazard-based hurricane loss estimation including climate change impacts

Sea surface temperature change

David V. Rosowsky

UNIVERSITY OF VERMONT, 85 SOUTH PROSPECT STREET, BURLINGTON,
VT, 05405, USA; DAVID.ROSOWSKY@UVM.EDU

33.1 Introduction

As evidenced by this year's major landfalling US hurricanes (Harvey and Irma), hurricanes are among the most devastating natural hazards impacting coastal communities. With improvements in data recording, simulation, and modeling, and experimental wind tunnel studies, there have been considerable advances in hurricane hazard modeling and risk analysis over the last two decades, including advances in structure and infrastructure system vulnerability analysis, damage/loss estimation, and community-wide resiliency. Vickery et al. (2000a,b) developed a hurricane simulation framework, including hurricane genesis, tracking, intensity, decay, and terrain models, based on historical hurricane data. This framework was adopted in the hurricane genesis module of the loss estimation software HAZUS_MH (FEMA, 2012). Emanuel et al. (2006) and Lee and Rosowsky (2007) also developed hurricane simulation frameworks with elements similar to those in Vickery's model. The model by Lee and Rosowsky (2007) was later used by Mudd et al. (2014) and Liu (2014) to generate synthetic hurricane wind speed databases. A summary of the evolution of the model and its application is provided by Rosowsky et al. (2016).

As mesoscale meteorological events, hurricanes may be affected by climate change, resulting (according to some models) in larger, more intense and/or more frequent storms. Considering landfalling events, the result would be more widespread and more severe damage (and greater losses) to coastal zones in particular. In order for current design codes and standards to adapt to reflect projected global climate change (should that be a goal), it is essential that the impact of climate change on hurricane hazards be quantitatively evaluated. Recent studies (Mudd et al. 2014; Liu 2014) have investigated the effect of climate change on hurricane hazard along the East Coast and Gulf Coast of the United States. In this study, we adopted the Mudd et al.

(2014) methodology in which changes in sea surface temperature (SST), the driving parameter in most hurricane models, are explicitly considered.

Five general types of structural vulnerability models were summarized by Pita et al. (2014) as: (1) models using only post-disaster building loss data; (2) models using damage data enhanced with engineering and scientific knowledge; (3) heuristic models using only expert opinion; (4) models built upon an estimation of physical damage on key resisting components and supplementary expert opinion, and (5) simulation-based models that better estimate the interaction between the wind and the building. Most simulation-based models used in recent studies include a wind-induced load (pressure) model, estimation of wind-load effects on building geometries, and a probabilistic physical structural damage model that simulates the component strength, interactions, and damage.

Loss estimation studies generally employ some form of empirical loss function, often expressed in terms of a building loss ratio (building and contents losses divided by the total building and content values) versus the peak gust wind speed. The loss to the building is estimated from the state of building damage using empirical cost estimation techniques considering cost of building repair and replacement. The loss to the contents is often estimated from an empirical model that relates contents damage to building envelope damage, based largely on both insurance loss data and engineering judgment. Further details, as well as examples, can be found in Vickery et al. (2006b) and FEMA (2012).

Such models been incorporated into complete hurricane loss/risk estimation frameworks and software, perhaps most widely known being HAZUS_MH (FEMA, 2012). The HAZUS_MH Hurricane Model (HM) is based on the "hazard-load-resistance-damage-loss" methodology developed by Vickery et al. (2006a,b). The hurricane event is first simulated based on the historical hurricane information from the HURDAT database. The wind loads (pressure coefficient) from numerous laboratories' wind tunnel tests on different types of structures were then determined. The structural resistance model was developed (again using extensive test data from various laboratories) for structural component and cladding elements/systems including roof covering, roof sheathing, windows, joints, and walls. Five structural damage states, ranging from "No Damage" to "Destruction," were defined. Finally, the loss function (mean loss ratio versus peak gust wind speed) was developed and validated using insurance loss data from three historical hurricane events, Hurricane Andrew (1992), Erin (1995) and Hugo (1989) (Bhinderwala 1995). Damage (loss) from water intrusion was estimated using a hurricane rainfall model (Rogers et al. 1994). A similar framework (Hamid et al. 2010) was used to develop the Florida Public Hurricane Loss Model (FPLHM).

Performance-based assessment concepts and techniques also have evolved rapidly in the last ten years, perhaps most notably for seismic applications. Performance-based engineering (PBE) tools for both wind and seismic applications may be especially useful for disaster preparedness (assessment) and hazard mitigation (decision), and more broadly to ensure that the performance of structures and infrastructure systems meet the expectations of owners, occupants, and the public. PBE approaches typically define several performance requirements levels corresponding to different hazard levels. The hazard level is described as an exceedance probability in N years (e.g., 2%/50 years). The total potential loss for a given region (e.g., state-wide) subjected to a specified hazard event could then be statistically characterized. For example, such an approach could be used to answer the question: what is the exceedance probability of a particular regional loss target amount, such as $5 billion, for a specified hazard event (e.g., 2%/50 year)?

Although HAZUS_MH HM allows for an embedded probabilistic hurricane scenario, only the N-year Mean recurrence interval (MRI) hurricane event in terms of total losses can be identified. Therefore, the probabilistic loss estimation under a specific hurricane hazard level (e.g., 2%/50 year) described in terms of hazard metrics (such as wind speed), which is the case for defining the hazard in performance-based engineering, could not conducted explicitly in HAZUS_MH. Also, the hurricane hazard is usually defined using only maximum wind speed (e.g., the Saffir-Simpson Hurricane Scale). No information about storm size (spatial extent or energy) is included. Recent studies (Shen 2006; Irish et al. 2008) have also demonstrated the importance of including storm size when estimating spatial extent of potential damage (i.e., regional loss). For purposes of regional loss estimation and studies of community-wide resiliency, therefore, considering maximum wind speed alone may not be adequate. In other words, a storm with larger size but lower intensity might result in more damage and hence greater total loss than a smaller, more intense storm. In this study, the maximum wind speed (intensity) and the radius of maximum winds (spatial extent) were selected as the two dominant indicators (variables) characterizing the hurricane hazard. The resulting bivariate hazard model was then used as input to a regional loss estimation model to illustrate a potential application.

In this chapter, we present a methodology for estimating regional hurricane loss based on the "hazard-load-resistance-damage-loss" methodology in HAZUS_MH HM and a bivariate hurricane hazard characterization considering both wind speed and size. We also consider the impact of climate change, specifically projected SST change. A study region comprising several South Carolina (SC) coastal counties was considered, as this region was used in previous studies validating the loss model using actual insurance loss data (Bhinderwala 1995). Here we consider only the damage and loss caused by wind and water intrusion; collateral flood and storm surge damage is not considered.

33.2 Overview of methodology

In this study, a total of 100,000 years of hurricane events were first simulated using the framework developed by Lee and Rosowsky (2007). Two critical parameters, the maximum gradient wind speed, V_{max} (at the eye-wall), and the radius to maximum wind speed, R_{max} (at the time of landfall), were recorded for each landfalling hurricane. These extracted data were then used to characterize the joint (V_{max}, R_{max}) hazard. Specifically, the joint (V_{max}, R_{max}) histogram and joint exceedance probability surface (i.e., complementary joint CDF) were developed for the location of landfall. Bivariate hazard contours were then able to be constructed for different hazard levels. Complete details about this approach can be found elsewhere (Rosowsky et al. 2016; Rosowsky 2017; Wang & Rosowsky 2012).

Characteristic hurricane parameter (V_{max}, R_{max}) combinations were next identified along a given bivariate hazard contour. The nearest simulated hurricane event to the selected (V_{max}, R_{max}) parameter combination was selected and the complete time history of that event was used as input to the loss-estimation module. The time history was manually imported into HAZUS_MH. The terrain model, wind loading model, resistance model, damage model, and loss model are embedded in HAZUS_MH as a package. Information about building stock and inventory also is embedded in HAZUS_MH. A "fast-running" (Vickery et al. 2006b) loss estimation was then performed to obtain an estimate of the total regional loss for the study region subjected to each selected hurricane event at the given hazard level (e.g., 2%/50 years). Once the regional direct economic loss is obtained for each selected hurricane event, the results were rank-ordered and a non-parametric loss distribution curve was constructed.

33.3 Hurricane hazard simulation and characterization

33.3.1 Hurricane hazard modeling and simulation

The occurrence of hurricane events is modeled as a Poisson process with an annual occurrence rate in the Atlantic basin of 8.4 per year (Lee & Rosowsky 2007). A simulated hurricane starts in the Atlantic basin with parameters based on information in the historical HURDAT database (i.e. initial location, heading angle, translational speed, and central pressure). The simulated hurricane is then moved along a track defined by an empirical tracking model first developed by Vickery et al. (2000a,b):

$$\begin{cases} \Delta \ln c = a_1 + a_2 \psi + a_3 \lambda + a_4 \ln c_i + a_5 \theta_i + \varepsilon \\ \Delta \theta = b_1 + b_2 \psi + b_3 \lambda + b_4 c_i + b_5 \theta_i + b_6 \theta_{i-1} + \varepsilon, \end{cases} \tag{33.1}$$

where c = translational wind speed; θ = heading angle; c_i = translational wind speed at the previous time-step i; θ_i = heading angle at the previous time-step i; θ_{i-1} = heading angle at the previous time-step i-1; $a_i (i=1,2,\ldots)$ = coefficient for translational wind speed; $b_i (i=1,2,\ldots)$ = coefficient for heading angle; ψ and λ = storm latitude and longitude; and ε = random error term. The entire Atlantic basin was divided into $5° \times 5°$ grid blocks and the coefficients a_i and b_i for each grid location were determined through regression analysis of the HURDAT data at 6-hour intervals. Each grid block therefore has its own grid-based parameters (coefficients a_i and b_i) which are used to determine the translational wind speed and heading angle at the next time-step. In this way, the hurricane eye's position, translational wind speed, and heading angle at each time-step (6-hour interval) can be determined using Equation (33.1) and the entire hurricane track can be simulated.

At each time-step, the hurricane intensity is described by a hurricane central pressure model initially proposed by Vickery et al. (2000b) based on the relative intensity concept (Darling 1991). The hurricane eye central pressure P_c can be expressed in terms of relative intensity I, and vice versa. Details can be found in the appendix of Darling's original paper (Darling 1991). In this central pressure model, the hurricane eye central pressure is calculated as:

$$\ln(I_{i+1}) = c_0 + c_1 \ln(I_i) + c_2 \ln(I_{i-1}) + c_3 \ln(I_{i-2}) + c_4 T_s + c_5 \Delta T_s + \varepsilon, \tag{33.2}$$

where I_{i+1} = relative intensity at the next time-step i+1; I_i, I_{i-1}, I_{i-2} = relative intensity at the previous time-steps i, i-1 and i-2; c_i = the grid-based coefficient for relative intensity; T_s = sea surface temperature (°K); ΔT_s = difference in sea surface temperatures at time-steps i and i+1 (°K); and ε = random error term. Similar to the tracking model coefficients, the coefficient parameters c_i for each grid location were determined by regression analysis of the relative intensity values calculated from the HURDAT central pressure data at each grid location.

After the hurricane makes landfall, its energy and intensity (central pressure) decay due to being cut off from its heat source (the ocean) and increased surface friction. The relative intensity approach (Equation (33.2)) is therefore no longer applicable and central pressure is assumed to decay following the exponential function as proposed by Vickery and Twisdale (1995):

$$\Delta p(t) = \Delta p_0 \exp(-at), \tag{33.3}$$

where $\Delta p(t)$ = central pressure deficit (mb) at time t after landfall; Δp_0 = central pressure deficit (mb) at landfall; a = site-specific decay parameter (constant); and t = time after landfall. Using historical hurricane central pressure data from HURDAT, statistical analyses of decay constant a were performed by Rosowsky et al. (1999), Vickery (2005), Liu and Pang (2011), and Wang and Rosowsky (2012) for different geographical regions. The probabilistic decay constant for the North Carolina region was adopted here.

Once the hurricane eye central pressure P_c is determined by Equation (33.2) (at sea) and Equation (33.3) (after landfall), the air pressure $P(r)$ at a distance r from the hurricane eye at each time-step can be calculated by Vickery et al. (2000b):

$$P(r) = P_c + \Delta p \exp[-(\frac{R_{max}}{r})^B], \tag{33.4}$$

where P_c = central air pressure at the hurricane eye; Δp = the central pressure deficit (mb) = 1013- P_c (mb); R_{max} = radius of maximum winds; and B = pressure profile parameter. Details about the calculation of R_{max} and B can be found in Vickery et al. (2000b). Once the air pressure $P(r)$ is determined for the entire wind field, the rotational vortex shape of hurricane at each time-step can then be described using the Georgiou's wind field model (Georgiou 1985):

$$V_g^2(r, \alpha) = \frac{r}{\rho} \cdot \frac{\partial P}{\partial r} + V_g(r, \alpha) \cdot (V_T \sin \alpha - fr) \tag{33.5}$$

where V_g = gradient wind speed; r = distance from hurricane eye; α = angle from hurricane heading direction (counter-clockwise +); ρ = air density; V_T = translational wind speed; f = coriolis parameter; and P = surface air pressure (= $P(r)$ determined by Equation (33.4). By substituting Equation (33.4) into Equation (33.5), the gradient wind speed V_g can be calculated as (Vickery et al. 2000b):

$$V_g = \frac{1}{2}(c \sin \alpha - fr) + \sqrt{\frac{1}{4}(c \sin \alpha - fr)^2 + \frac{B \Delta p}{\rho}(\frac{R_{max}}{r})^2 \exp[-(\frac{R_{max}}{r})^2]}. \tag{33.6}$$

Finally the gradient wind speed from Equation (33.6) can be converted to a surface wind speed using gradient-to-surface wind speed conversion factors (Lee & Rosowsky 2007). If the simulated hurricane produces a significant maximum 10-min surface wind speed (defined in this study as 15 m/s or greater) at any zip code location, this value is recorded for that zip code. Following the procedures described above, a total of 100,000 years of simulated hurricane events are generated and synthetic hurricane wind speed records are developed for each zip-code in the study region.

33.3.2 Bivariate hurricane hazard characterization

Using the 100,000 years of simulated hurricane events, we can statistically characterize the hurricane (event) hazard considering both hurricane wind speed and storm size, specifically using the V_{max} and R_{max} descriptors (Wang & Rosowsky 2012). The joint histogram of V_{max} and R_{max} at the time of landfall is first constructed, from which the joint exceedance probability surface (i.e., the joint complementary CDF) of V_{max} and R_{max} can be determined. Bivariate hazard contours were then able to be constructed for different hazard levels.

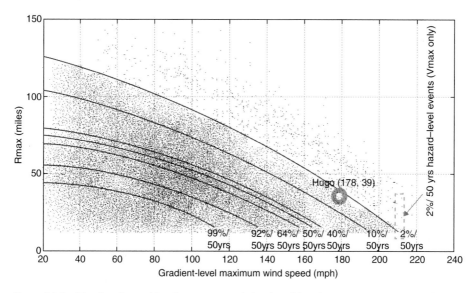

Figure 33.1 Bivariate hazard level contours and simulated hurricane events at time of landfall for SC coastal study region (1 mile = 1609 meters; 1 mph = 0.447 m/s).

The simulated data pairs of V_{max} and R_{max} at the time of landfall are plotted in Figure 33.1. The bivariate contours corresponding to hazard levels of 2%/50 years, 10%/50 years, 40%/50 years, 50%/50 years, 64%/50 years, 92%/50 years, 99%/50 years (with corresponding mean recurrence intervals or MRI's of 2475, 475, 100, 71, 50, 20, 10 years, respectively; or annual exceedance probabilities of 0.04%, 0.2%, 1%, 1.4%, 2%, 5% and 10%, respectively) also are shown in Figure 33.1. Simulated hurricane events described by (V_{max}, R_{max}) data pairs that falls on (or close to) a given contour would have the same joint annual exceedance probability. A suite of hazard-consistent hurricane events can therefore be determined by selecting appropriate combinations of (V_{max}, R_{max}) along a given hazard-level contour. For example, for the 2%/50 year hazard level, 237 (V_{max}, R_{max}) simulated data pairs are identified along the contour. Thus, we have 237 characteristic landfalling hurricane events for this study region associated with 2%/50 year hazard level. Note that, the (V_{max}, R_{max}) data pair at time of landfall for the most damaging historical hurricane event Hugo (1989) for the study region (178 mph, 39 miles) is very close to the 2%/50 year joint hazard contour. This suggests, based on our bivariate analysis, that hurricane Hugo was approximately a 2%/50 year event.

In this study, although two dominant parameters, V_{max} and R_{max}, were selected to characterize the bivariate hurricane (event) hazard, the uncertainty and variability in other parameters (heading angle, landfall location, and translational speed) were assumed to be captured by the database of simulated hurricane events.

33.4 Probabilistic hurricane loss estimation

33.4.1 Loss function

In this study, losses are estimated using the loss estimation module in the HAZUS_MH software (FEMA 2012) developed jointly by the Federal Emergency Management Agency (FEMA) and the National Institute of Building Sciences (NIBS). In the HAZUS_MH, the "hazard-load-resistance-damage-loss" described previously, is employed.

Loss functions for different building types are embedded in the HAZUS_MH database to enable quick damage and loss estimation for a given peak gust wind speed. For each structural type and specific building configuration, a corresponding loss function (from which mean loss ratio is obtained), developed by FEMA and NIBS, is embedded in HAZUS_MH. The direct economic loss can then be calculated as the product of the loss ratio and the total value of the building and its contents. The building-related direct economic loss includes: (1) costs of repair, replacement, content, and inventory; and (2) costs resulting from loss of use, such as rental income loss, daily production output loss, etc. Further details can be found in Vickery et al. (2006a,b) and FEMA (2012).

33.4.2 Probabilistic regional aggregated loss estimation procedure

Once the 237 (V_{max}, R_{max}) data pairs were identified along 2%/50 year bivariate hazard contour, a suite of 237 corresponding simulated landfalling hurricane events (time-histories) were extracted from the database. The time history of each hurricane event scenario is then imported manually into the HAZUS_MH. Five key parameters, latitude, longitude, V_{max}, R_{max} (or pressure profile parameter B (see Equation (33.4))), and central pressure P_c, are required as input to completely define the hurricane wind field at each time-step. Using Equation (33.6) and surface roughness information, the surface wind speeds at each census block in the study region can be calculated. Note that the surface wind speeds as the input for the loss function is calculated in HAZUS_MH, based on the method in Vickery et al. (2000a,b; 2006a,b), while the wind speeds used to generate the bivariate hazard contours in Figure 33.1 are from the database of 100,000 years simulated hurricane events, based on the method in Lee and Rosowsky (2007). Differences exist between the boundary layer model and the gradient-to-surface conversion factor in these two modeling approaches. However, the maximum wind speeds produced using these two methods were compared for this study region and were found to be broadly consistent (Lee & Rosowsky 2007; Liu 2014). Thus, the hurricane events, identified by (V_{max}, R_{max}) combinations shown in Figure 33.1, would result in consistent peak gust wind speeds calculated using these two methods.

The study region considered in our study comprises 13 coastal counties in South Carolina, all located within 50 miles of the coastline and including the most populated county, Charleston. Embedded in HAZUS, there are 649,149 buildings in this study region. The building stock (inventory) is listed in Table 33.1 by both occupancy and building type.

Table 33.1a Building number counts in occupancy classes of study region

Occupancy	Number counts	Percentage of total buildings (%)
Residential	603,014	92.9
Commercial	30,664	4.72
Industrial	7,918	1.22
Religion	3,596	0.55
Agriculture	1,945	0.30
Education	1,111	0.17
Government	900	0.14

Table 33.1b Building number counts in building types of study region

Building type	Number counts	Percentage of total buildings (%)
Wood	441,923	68.1
Manufactured Homes	122,540	18.9
Masonry	57,864	8.92
Steel	21,201	3.26
Concrete	5,377	0.83

Once the time history of each hurricane event scenario is imported manually into the HAZUS_MH, total (aggregate) direct economic loss for the entire study region can then be estimated by running the loss model for the entire building stock (based on loss models embedded in HAZUS_MH) in the study region. In the next section, we describe the construction of probabilistic loss distribution curves using the results of this procedure.

33.5 Results and discussion

33.5.1 Direct economic loss distribution curve

Once the direct economic loss for each hurricane scenario is calculated using the loss analysis embedded in HAZUS_MH, the results can be rank-ordered to create a probabilistic characterization of hurricane loss (wind and rain induced) for the given study region. Specifically, an empirical cumulative distribution function (CDF) of loss conditioned on the non-zero loss events was first constructed by rank-ordering the non-zero loss data for each hurricane scenario. Such a loss distribution curve can be plotted for any bivariate hazard level. Using a loss threshold value of $100M ($0.1B), 139 non-zero loss events out of 237 total simulated events along the 2%/50 year bivariate hazard contour were identified (a ratio of 59% non-zero loss events). Then, the (unconditional) loss exceedance probability is calculated by multiplying the complementary conditional CDF value by the ratio of non-zero loss events to the total number of landfalling events (i.e., 59% for the case of 2%/50 year bivariate hazard). Figure 33.2 shows both conditional and unconditional loss distribution curves (CDF of direct economic loss in US $B) for the 2%/50 year bivariate hazard for this SC coastal region. For example, as shown in the Figure 33.2, the probability of total direct economic loss for the study region exceeding $5B conditioned on a non-zero loss event is approximately 40% (1–0.6), therefore, the unconditional probability of total loss for the study region exceeding $5B under a specified 2%/50 year event is approximately 40%*0.59 = 0.24. Note that the most destructive hurricane to have impacted this study region was Hugo (1989), which caused $7.1B (converted to present value) in losses. This estimate is calculated by the loss module within HAZUS_MH, rather than based on a post-disaster survey or actual insurance loss data. From Figure 33.2, this corresponds to about a 20 percent exceedance probability, or an 80th-percentile event in terms of loss.

Loss distribution curves such as these can be used for performance-based assessments of infrastructure portfolios, regional planning, disaster preparedness, and risk-informed decision-making and mitigation. As an example, take the question: what is the exceedance probability of a particular regional loss target (threshold amount) of $5B, for a specified hazard-level event (e.g., 2%/50 year)? From Figure 33.2, the exceedance probability is approximately 0.24. This suggests that a 2%/50 year hurricane event has 24 percent probability of inducing a total direct economic loss in excess of $5B.

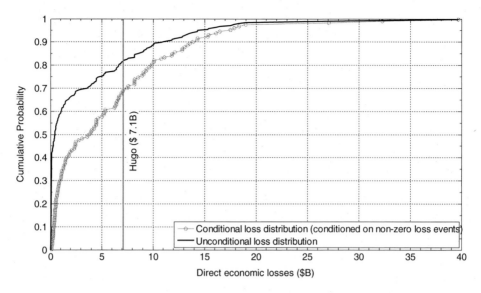

Figure 33.2 Conditional and unconditional direct economic loss distribution under 2%/50 year bivariate hazard for SC coastal study region.

Such loss distribution curves also can be used to determine whether mitigation strategies are needed to contain the expected regional loss to within some acceptable level (with some tolerable level of risk). For example, if a community, owner or agency determines that the maximum acceptable probability for a loss in excess of $5B at the 2%/50 year hazard level is (e.g.) 10%, Figure 33.2 (which shows a 24% exceedance probability) would suggest some combination of mitigation strategies (structural, e.g., retrofit; or policy, e.g., codes) will be needed to reduce vulnerability and therefore expected losses.

In order to compare expected losses at the (e.g., 2%/50 year) bivariate hazard level with these at the 2%/50 year V_{max} (single variable) hazard level, the loss distribution considering the 2%/50 year V_{max} only hazard was developed. A total of nine non-zero loss events out of 18 simulated events close to the 2%/50 year V_{max} value ($\approx$ 210 mph) (see dashed box in Figure 33.1) were indentified. These nine non-zero loss hurricane events were then used as input to HAZUS_MH and the same procedure was used to construct the conditional and unconditional empirical loss CDFs. This loss distribution curve (single variable hazard characterization) was constructed using only nine points for illustrative purposes only. Clearly the shape (and information content and hence the utility) of this distribution function would change when a larger number of data points are included. This could be achieved either by widening the selection region (indicated by the dashed box at $V_{max} \approx$ 210 mph in Figure 33.1), or by generating a larger database (more than 100,000 years) of synthetic hurricane events. We present the distribution developed using only the nine points to illustrate how a comparison can be made to the single-variable hazard characterization case.

Both 2%/50 year (unconditional) loss distribution curves are shown in Figure 33.3. These two loss distribution curves generally agree with each other at losses less than about $5B. However, for losses greater than $10B, the loss distribution curves diverge, and the figure suggests the bivariate hazard results in a lower exceedance probability at a given target loss amount. For example, the exceedance probability of $10B for the 2%/50 year bivariate hazard

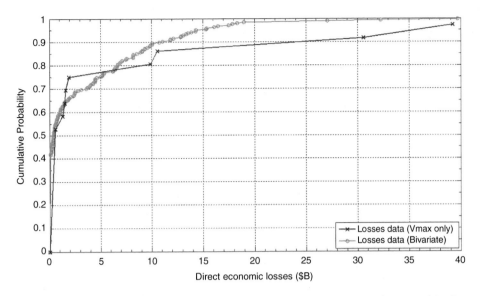

Figure 33.3 Comparison of (unconditional) loss distributions under 2%/50 year bivariate hazard and 2%/50 year Vmax only hazard for the SC coastal study region.

event is 10% (1–0.9), which is lower than the 20% (1–0.8) exceedance probability for the 2%/50 year V_{max} only hazard event. Therefore, for this study region and considering only the nine data points (for illustration), using the 2%/50 year V_{max} only hazard becomes more conservative as the loss estimates increase.

Note that the study region considered herein is a coastal area with having only one densely populated county, Charleston County. The rest of the study region includes smaller communities separated by more sparsely populated areas. While there is considerable development located along the coast in this region, the population (and hence infrastructure) density is concentrated in the Charleston area. The extent of a storm's impact (damage, losses) is a function of (a) storm intensity, (b) storm size, and in the case of non-uniformly high-density population, (c) storm track. Sensitivity to storm track, for example, decreases as population density becomes more uniform throughout the region. The issues of population (infrastructure) density or uniformity (or lack thereof) are not addressed herein, as we consider only one geographic region; however, it points to the need to perform such site-specific event-based hurricane simulation studies when characterizing expected regional losses (e.g., loss distribution curves). Note also that losses resulting from storm surge and flooding were not considered in the present study. These, too, would be affected by storm intensity and storm size.

33.5.2 Climate change impact on the loss distribution curve

The IPCC Fifth Assessment Report (IPCC AR5) (IPCC 2014) provides climate change projections in the form of Representative Concentration Pathways (RCP) scenarios. The RCPs are projections of the radiative forcing in the year 2100 and have served as input for climate and atmospheric modeling studies and assisted climate modelers in developing their own projections and scenarios. Four such RCPs, increasing in severity, are referred to as RCP

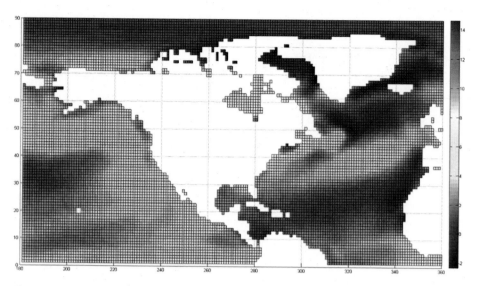

Figure 33.4 Sea surface temperature change under climate change scenario RCP 8.5.

3-PD, RCP 4.5, RCP 6.0, and RCP 8.5. For our study, we consider only the worst-case scenario having the most dramatic radiative forcing (RCP 8.5), a radiative forcing level of 8.5 watt/m² in the year 2100. By comparison, the 2005 radiative forcing level, according to the IPCC Fourth Assessment Report (IPCC, 2007), was 1.6 watt/m². The projected monthly average Sea Surface Temperature (SST) values in the year 2100 under the RCP 8.5 scenario were developed by scientists at the National Center of Atmospheric Research using the Community Earth System Model. The difference between the actual SST in August 2005 and the projected SST in August 2100 (historically the most active month for hurricanes in the US) is shown in Figure 33.4.

Note that the largest increase in SST is along the northeast US/Canadian coast, suggesting significant increase in hurricane risk (due to strengthening prior to landfall) and expected damage in some of the most densely populated US cities along the east coast. It was for this reason that Mudd et al. (2014) chose this region for their analysis of changing hurricane hazard as a result of projected climate change. However, Figure 33.4 also suggests a more moderate increase in SST in much of the Atlantic basin over which most US landfalling storms form and travel. While the increase is not as dramatic as that seen along the northeast coast, the region of warming SST extends across the entire Atlantic, thereby providing significant opportunity for storms to intensify (across a longer fetch, even if at a slower rate). Our study provided an opportunity to confirm that even such modest projected increases in SST would result in significant changes to the hurricane hazard along the hurricane-prone Carolina coast.

It might be reasonable to assume that SST increase could impact (1) storm genesis, (2) storm tracking, and (3) storm intensity and size, all of which impacts the landfalling hurricane hazard. Mudd et al. (2014) investigated historic hurricane genesis frequency and suggested it might be possible to extrapolate an increase in genesis frequency over the next century. An earlier study (Mudd 2014) considering only historic hurricanes making landfall on the eastern US seaboard, however, revealed no such trend in the frequency of landfalling storms. Mudd et al. decided to focus only on the simulation of landfalling hurricane events, saving significant computational time, and therefore assumed a stationary rate (i.e., not influenced by increase in SST). Mudd et al. also were unable to identify changes in tracking parameters with increase in SST. Since the probabilistic tracking model parameters in our event-based simulation procedure are based on the 150 years of historic storm data in the HURDAT database, we assume that inherent variability in tracking (heading angle, landfalling location, directional changes, etc.) are captured therein. Any changes in tracking parameters over time that were unable to be identified by Mudd et al. or others would therefore also be captured if they existed. Thus, in the present study, only the impacts on central pressure and hence storm intensity and size (see Equation (33.2)) due to increases in SST are considered, adopting a worst-case future climate scenario. We acknowledge the limitation of this tracking parameter stationarity assumption and recognize this as an area for future study.

Using the same hurricane simulation procedure described previously, 100,000 years of synthetic hurricane events were simulated based on the RCP 8.5 climate change scenario, considering the SST change projections shown in Figure 33.4. The joint hurricane hazard (V_{max} and R_{max}) at landfall was then re-characterized and bivariate hazard contours corresponding to different annual exceedance probabilities (or MRIs) were identified. A comparison of the bivariate hazard contours under both the current and projected (RCP8.5) future climate scenario is shown in Figure 33.5. Compared to the increase in hurricane intensity for the northeast US coast (see Mudd et al. 2014), the increase in hurricane intensity for SC coast is moderate because the SST increase in mid-Atlantic area is moderate compared to that in northeast US/ Canadian coast (see Figure 33.4). Although the SST increase in and approaching the mid-Atlantic area is moderate, an increase in hurricane intensity for each hazard level can still be seen in Figure 33.5 for the SC coast. This confirms that modest SST change in the Atlantic basin, over which the landfalling storms travel and intensify, results in more severe landfalling hurricane events.

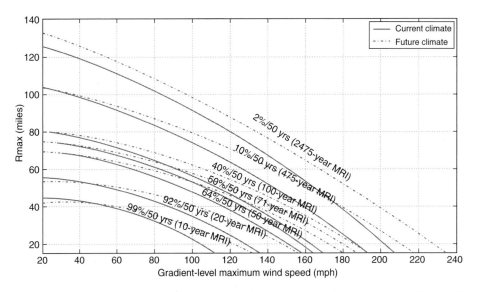

Figure 33.5 Comparison of bivariate hazard level contours under both current and future climate scenarios for SC coastal study region (1 mile = 1609 meters; 1 mph = 0.447 m/s).

As was done previously, the (V_{max}, R_{max}) data pairs (a total of 275 in this case) were identified along or close to the target 2%/50 year bivariate hazard contour. The 275 corresponding simulated landfalling hurricane events were then extracted from the database. The time history of each hurricane event was then imported manually into HAZUS_MH and an estimation of the direct economic loss was obtained. The total direct economic loss for the entire study region was obtained by aggregating results from the entire building stock in the study region for each hurricane scenario. Note that the embedded loss estimation module in HAZUS assumes stationarity in the building stock. Thus, no changes in density of buildings, relative distribution of structural types, structural age or condition are considered herein. This, too, would be a good area for future study.

Finally, the results of total loss for each non-zero hurricane event were rank-ordered to create an empirical CDF of loss for the study region (under the RCP8.5 climate change scenario) conditioned on non-zero loss events. Using the same threshold value for loss of $100M ($0.1B) that was used for the current climate scenario, 129 non-zero loss events (of 275 total simulated events) along the 2%/50 year bivariate hazard contour were identified (a ratio of 47% non-zero loss events). Then the (unconditional) loss distribution curve was generated using the same procedure described for the case of 2%/50 year bivariate hazard under the current climate scenario. Figure 33.6 shows the (unconditional) loss distribution (CDF of direct economic loss in US$B) for this projected climate change scenario. For comparison, the (unconditional) loss distribution for the 2%/50 year bivariate hazard under the current scenario also is shown in Figure 33.6.

As would be expected, the loss distribution curve shifts to the right when changing from the current (2005) climate scenario to the projected (2100) climate scenario, suggesting a higher exceedance probability for any given loss amount. For example, for an aggregated loss in this study region of $10B, the exceedance probability for a 2%/50 year hazard event resulting in this amount of loss under the future climate scenario is 25 percent (1–0.75), while the

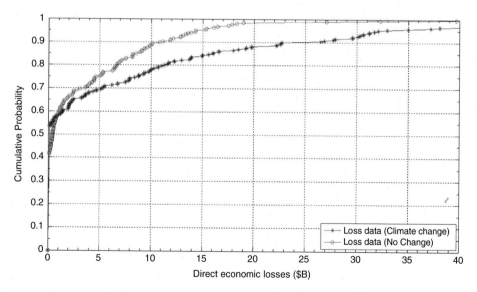

Figure 33.6 Comparison of (unconditional) loss distributions for 2%/50 year bivariate hurricane hazard under both current and future climate scenarios for SC coastal study region.

comparable exceedance probability under the current climate scenario is only 10 percent (1–0.90). Indeed the results in Figure 33.6 are quite compelling in making the case that the projected climate change scenario significantly impacts expected losses at high hazard levels (e.g., 2%/50 years) in this study region. Similar figures could be prepared showing results at lower hazard levels.

Note that the loss distributions presented in this study were developed using the loss estimation methodology (and implicit loss functions and building inventory data) in HAZUS_MH. The assumption is made that the building inventory information is, therefore, stationary throughout the period of study. It would be reasonable to expect that (and therefore attempt to explicitly model) the building inventory changes over time. Buildings age; building condition, integrity, and vulnerability changes; buildings are renovated, altered, or strengthened; buildings are demolished; and buildings are added. Further, building codes could change, as could code enforcement, building materials, and construction techniques evolve. Clearly the assumption of building stock stationarity is one that could be considered in future work.

33.6 Conclusions

This chapter proposes a methodology to evaluate regional economic loss distributions associated with hurricane events at specified hazard levels. Unlike the probabilistic hurricane loss estimation embedded in HAZUS_MH, where the hurricane hazard is characterized in terms of the N-year expected losses, the methodology in this study constructs a distribution of expected losses using a suite of characteristic hurricane events at a specified hazard level. Whereas HAZUS uses a single variable (V_{max}) to characterize the hurricane hazard, this study uses a bivariate (V_{max}, R_{max}) characterization to account for both storm intensity and size.

The methodology proposed herein incorporates established event-based hurricane simulation techniques, a bivariate hurricane hazard characterization approach, and a deterministic loss estimation methodology embedded in HAZUS_MH. To further consider the impact of projected SST change on the hurricane hazard and resulting loss distribution, the analyses is extended by explicitly accounting for projected SST change in the Atlantic basin (using a worst-case scenario), over which storms affecting the study region form and strengthen. As an illustrative example, we consider a region of the SC coastline comprising 13 counties (with the building inventory embedded in HAZUS_MH) and the loss distribution curves at 2%/ 50 years bivariate hazard level are constructed for both current (2005) and projected (2100) climate scenarios. The results suggest a significant change in expected losses, especially at higher hazard levels, under the projected SST change scenario.

Loss distribution curves, such as those developed herein, can be used for performance-based assessment of building portfolios as well as disaster planning and mitigation decision-making purposes. They can inform communities, building owners, emergency managers, and insurers about vulnerability and expected losses associated with hurricane events at specified hazard levels (e.g., 2%/50 years). Since the framework described herein is modular, new damage models, new loss models, and new climate change scenarios all can be easily incorporated as they become available.

There are significant opportunities to extend and refine this work, making it more broadly applicable to other regions, more robust by accounting for other factors, more accessible to planners and decision-makers, and thus more directly useful in studies of community-wide resiliency. In particular, future work might consider (1) relative population density and infrastructure distribution, (2) building inventory non-stationarity, and (3) concomitant hazards (flood, surge).

33.7 Post-script

The US saw three very significant landfalling hurricane events in the weeks during which the author was completing this chapter, hurricanes Harvey (Texas), Irma (Florida), and Maria (Puerto Rico). These events were reported as extremely large and extremely powerful, and their landfalls occurred within weeks of one another. Complete damage assessments and loss estimates remain to be completed, but it is clear that each storm's losses will be in the tens of billions of US\$ and that rebuilding of the most hard hit communities will take years. While hindcast estimates of maximum wind speed (V_{max}), radius of maximum wind (R_{max}) values, and maximum rainfall rates (RR_{max}) for each of these massive storms as they came ashore have yet to be finalized, we know that Irma had maximum sustained wind speeds in excess of 180 mph and that Harvey dropped more than 50 inches of rain in some locations. Early reports indicate Maria had maximum sustained wind speeds of 170 mph and dropped 30 inches of rain over two days. All three storms set new records for Atlantic hurricanes impacting the US.

   While the study region in this chapter comprises several coastal counties in South Carolina, the author thought it would be of interest to the readers to consider where these hurricanes fall on the hazard curves (albeit for a different US coastal region). The maximum recorded wind speeds (when converted to gradient level wind speeds) are far beyond the maximum wind speeds plotted in Figures 33.1 and 33.5. Similarly, the maximum rainfall rates could not be plotted on the comparable figures in (Rosowsky et al. 2016; Rosowsky 2017). These set new maxima and, thus, represent new extreme data points that must be considered in the HURDAT database and the resulting statistical models. Regardless of whether or not these new maxima, occurring within the same year, are tied to a change in sea surface temperature or other climate-induced change, it is clear that the hurricane hazard in this region is, in fact, changing. – DVR, September 2017

References

Bhinderwala, S. (1995). "Insurance loss analysis of single-family dwellings damaged in Hurricane Andrew." M.S. thesis, Department of Civil Engineering, Clemson University, Clemson, SC.

Darling, R.W.R (1991). "Estimating probabilities of hurricane wind speeds using a large scale empirical model." *Journal of Climate*, 4 (10), 1035–46.

Emanuel, K., Ravela, S., Vivant E., and Risi C. (2006). "A statistical deterministic approach to hurricane risk assessment." *Bulletin of the American Meteorological Society*, 87(3), 299–314.

FEMA (2012). "Multi-hazard loss estimation methodology hurricane model technical manual," Department of Homeland Security, Federal Emergency Management Agency, Mitigation Divison, Washington, DC.

Georgiou, P.N. (1985). Design Wind Speeds in Tropical Cyclone-Prone Regions. Ph.D. Dissertation, Department of Civil Engineering, University of Western Ontario, Canada.

Hamid. S., Kibria, B.M., Gulati, S., Powell, M. Annane, B., Cocke, S. Pinelli J.P., Gurley, K., and Chen, S.C. (2010). "Predicting losses of residential structures in the state of Florida by the public hurricane loss evaluation moel." *Statistical Methodology*, 7(5), 552–73.

Intergovernmental Panel on Climate Change (IPCC) (2007). "Climate change 2007: Synthesis report." *Contribution of Working Groups I, II and III to the Fourth Assessment Rep. of the Intergovernmental Panel on Climate Change*, R.K. Pachauri and A. Reisinger (eds.), Geneva, Switzerland, 104 pp.

Intergovernmental Panel on Climate Change (IPCC). (2014). "Climate Change 2014: Synthesis Report." *Contribution of Working Groups I, II and III to the Fifth Assessment Report of the Intergovernmental Panel on Climate Change*, R.K. Pachauri and L.A. Meyer (eds.), Geneva, Switzerland, 151 pp.

Irish, J.L., Donald, T.R., and Jay, J.R. (2008). "The influence of storm size on hurricane surge." *Journal of Physical Oceanography*, 38(9): 2003–13.

Lee, K.H. and Rosowsky, D.V. (2007). "Synthetic hurricane wind speed records: Development of a database for hazard analysis and risk studies." *ASCE Natural Hazards Review*, 8 (2), 23–34.

Liu, F.Q. (2014). Projections of Future US Design Wind Speeds due to Climate Change for Estimating Hurricane Losses. Ph.D. Dissertation, Department of Civil Engineering, Clemson University, SC.

Liu, F.Q. and Pang, W.C. (2011). "Development and calibration of central pressure decay models for hurricane simulation." *Proceedings of the 11th International Conference on Applications of Statistics and Probability in Civil Engineering*, Zurich, Switzerland.

Mudd, L. (2014), "A multi-hazard assessment of climatological impacts on hurricanes affecting the northeast US: Wind and rain," Ph.D. Dissertation, Department of Civil and Environmental Engineering, Rensselaer Polytechnic Institute, Troy, NY.

Mudd, L., Wang, Y., Letchford, C., and Rosowsky, D.V. (2014). "Assessing climate change impact on the US East Coast hurricane hazard: Temperature, frequency, track," *ASCE Natural Hazards Review*, *15*(3): 04014001.

Pita, G., Pinelli, J.P., Gurley, K., and Mitrani-Reiser, J. (2014). "State of the art of hurricane vulnerability estimation methods: a review." *ASCE Natural Hazards Review*, *16*(2), 04014022.

Rogers, E., Chang, S., and Pierce, H. (1994). "A satellite observational and numerical study of precipitation characteristics in Western North Atlantic cyclones." *Journal of Applied Meteorology*, 33, 129–39.

Rosowsky, D.V. (2017), "Modeling to project the impact of climate change on hurricane hazard: wind and rain," *Proceedings*: International Conference on Structural Safety and Reliability, ICOSSAR 2017, Vienna, Austria.

Rosowsky D.V., Sparks P.R., and Huang Z. (1999). "Wind field modeling and hurricane hazard analysis," *Report to the South Carolina Sea Grant Consortium*, Department of Civil Engineering, Clemson University, SC.

Rosowsky, D.V., Mudd, L., and Letchford, C. (2016), "Assessing climate change impact on the joint wind-rain hurricane hazard for the northeastern U.S. coastline." In: Gardoni, P., Murphy, C., and Rowell, A. (eds.), *Societal Risk Management of Natural Hazards*. New York: Springer.

Shen, W. (2006). "Does the size of hurricane eye matter with its intensity?," *Geophysical Research Letters*, *33*(18).

Vickery, P.J. (2005). "Simple empirical models for estimating the increase in the central pressure of tropical cyclones after landfall along the coastline of the United States." *Journal of Applied Meteorology*, 44, 1807–1826.

Vickery, P.J. and Twisdale, L.A. (1995). "Wind-field and filling models for hurricane wind-speed prediction." *ASCE Journal of Structural Engineering*, 121(11), 1700–1209.

Vickery, P.J., Skerlj, P.F., Steckley, A.C., and Twisdale, L.A. (2000a). "Hurricane wind field model for use in hurricane simulations." *ASCE Journal of Structural Engineering*, 126(10), 1203–21.

Vickery, P.J., Skerlj, P.F., and Twisdale, L.A. (2000b). "Simulation of hurricane risk in the U.S. using empirical track model." *ASCE Journal of Structural Engineering*, 126 (10), 1222–37.

Vickery, P.J., Lin, J., Skerlj, P.F., Twisdale, L.A., and Huang, K. (2006a). "HAZUS-MH hurricane model methodology. I: Hurricane hazard, terrain, and wind load modeling." *ASCE Natural Hazards Review*, 7(2), 82–93.

Vickery, P.J., Skerlj, P.F., Lin, J., Twisdale, L.A. Yong, M.A., and Lavelle, F.M. (2006b). "HAZUS-MH hurricane model methodology, II: Damage and loss estimation." *ASCE Natural Hazards Review*, 7(2), 94–103.

Wang, Y. and Rosowsky, D.V. (2012). "Joint distribution model for prediction of hurricane wind speed and size." *Structural Safety*, 35, 40–51.

34

A physics-based transportable probabilistic model for climate change dependent storm surge

Alessandro Contento,[1] Hao Xu,[2] and Paolo Gardoni[3]

[1] DEPARTMENT OF CIVIL AND ENVIRONMENTAL ENGINEERING, MAE CENTER: CREATING A MULTI-HAZARD APPROACH TO ENGINEERING, UNIVERSITY OF ILLINOIS AT URBANA-CHAMPAIGN, URBANA, IL, USA; CONTENT2@ILLINOIS.EDU

[2] DEPARTMENT OF CIVIL AND ENVIRONMENTAL ENGINEERING, MAE CENTER: CREATING A MULTI- HAZARD APPROACH TO ENGINEERING, UNIVERSITY OF ILLINOIS AT URBANA- CHAMPAIGN, URBANA, IL, USA; HAOXU3@ILLINOIS.EDU

[3] DEPARTMENT OF CIVIL AND ENVIRONMENTAL ENGINEERING, MAE CENTER: CREATING A MULTI- HAZARD APPROACH TO ENGINEERING, UNIVERSITY OF ILLINOIS AT URBANA- CHAMPAIGN, URBANA, IL, USA; GARDONI@ILLINOIS.EDU

34.1 Introduction

Storm surge is one of the main causes of hurricane damage. Even hurricanes low in the Saffir-Simpson Hurricane Wind Scale (commonly used to communicate the power and the potential damage of a hurricane) can produce a high surge with devastating effects. For example, Hurricane Ike in 2008 was a category 2 hurricane but produced surges up to about 50 cm in the Galveston bay. In some cases, as for Hurricane Katrina in 2005, the flooding consequent to the storm surge led to a high number of fatalities. The potential increase in intensity of hurricanes consequent to climate change (Knutson et al. 2013; Gardoni et al. 2016) will result in an increase in the threat posed by storm surge occurrences. Consequently, long-term mitigation strategies against hurricanes should account for the results of storm surge analyses performed under different climate change scenarios.

Simulating hurricane occurrences is the first step of a storm surge analysis and the focus of many studies of the last couple of decades (Vickery et al. 2000a; 2000b; Emanuel et al. 2006; Lee & Rosowsky 2007). Traditionally, researchers in atmospheric science tried to understand and model this phenomenon as an effect of the global circulation patterns. Civil engineers approached this problem with the aim of defining the interactions between the strong winds generated by tropical storms and structures. After the devastating consequences of recent hurricanes, such as Katrina, storm modeling became important in several other fields (Gardoni et al. 2016). For example, hurricane events have been considered in studies on their economic impact as well as on societal adaptation and resilience (Murphy et al. 2018).

Moreover, remaining on the economic side of the problem, insurance and reinsurance are particularly interested in predictions of damage associated to hurricanes to define the risk of their contracts and price them correctly (Contento et al. 2017). In addition, the interest and concerns generated by climate change (Murphy et al. 2018) are pushing researchers to forecast the effects of climate change on tropical storms (Lin et al. 2012; Mudd et al. 2014).

Most researchers (e.g., Vickery et al. 2000a, Emanuel et al. 2006, Lee & Rosowsky 2007) focused on the modeling of the atmospheric part of the phenomenon, the primary interest being on the evaluation of the wind velocity and the amplitude of the storms. However, not only the wind but also the storm surge associated with the hurricane is responsible for a significant portion of the damage to structures and infrastructure as well as of the economic and societal impact. So, more attention is needed toward the modeling of the storm surge.

There are a few coupled hurricane-surge studies, as the one presented by Lin et al. (2012). Most of them use models such as the Advanced Circulation (ADCIRC) model (Westerink et al. 1994) and Sea, Lake, and Overland Surges from Hurricanes (SLOSH) model (Jelesnianski et al. 1992). Such models use shallow-water equations (SWEs) to model the hydrodynamics of the storm surge. The ADCIRC model numerically integrates the depth-integrated barotropic SWEs in spherical coordinates over an unstructured grid. The grid has a wide range of element sizes (Westerink et al. 2008) that are chosen to obtain an extremely fine resolution near the coast that becomes coarser and coarser moving toward the deeper ocean, according to the required accuracy. The high-resolution numerical grid used by ADCIRC captures the complex spatial variability of the phenomenon (Dietrich et al. 2011), yet it results in the model being computationally demanding. The SLOSH model was originally developed for real-time forecasting of hurricane storm surges on continental shelves. In the model, the SWEs are solved using the finite difference method over a grid (polar, elliptic, or hyperbolic) centered on the region of interest (Jarvinen & Lawrence 1985). The model requires the characteristics of the hurricane to derive a model of the wind field, which drives the storm surge. The main limit of the model is that the accuracy of the storm surge predictions is highly dependent on the accuracy of the meteorological input and the error in the estimate is about 20 percent using accurate hurricane predictions (Jelesnianski et al. 1992). Moreover, the model does not account for astronomical tides and wind waves.

Using accurate models, such as the ADCIRC model, the time requirement for a single run of a storm surge simulation is large; consequently, it is difficult to obtain a sufficient number of results to build probabilistic models, and almost impossible to use a simulation to forecast the storm surge promptly in the case of a real hurricane occurrence. For this reason, in the last few years, some metamodels have been used as surrogates for storm surge modeling.

Metamodels are developed using the results of the atmospheric part of the hurricane simulations and a limited amount of physics-based simulations of storm surge scenarios. As output they provide an estimate of storm surge at different selected points in the domain of the model (Irish et. al. 2008; Jia & Taflanidis 2013; Kim et al. 2015; Jia et al. 2016). In Irish et al. (2008), estimates of storm surge height are derived as functions of the central pressure, radius of maximum wind speed, and forward velocity of the hurricane. The model is calibrated using ADCIRC simulations where the storm surge is driven by synthetic hurricanes whose sustained near-surface winds are estimated using a coupled hurricane vortex–planetary boundary layer (PBL) model (Thompson & Cardone 1996). This metamodel presents a simplified formulation whose aim is not to obtain accurate estimates of storm surge but to show the dependence of the storm surge on the size of the hurricane. Jia et al. (2016) use a Kriging metamodel to predict storm surge over an extended coastal region. To improve the computational efficiency of the Kriging metamodel, they integrate the principal component analysis (Jolliffe 2002) in their formulation. The results presented in Jia et al. (2016) show that the metamodel is capable of providing accurate predictions of both storm surge and wave height. However, the metamodel is subject to a computationally demanding calibration that required 400 combined ADCIRC and SWAN (Dietrich et al. 2011) simulations. Artificial Neural Networks (ANNs) have also been used for storm surge predictions. An example can be found in Kim et al. (2015), where a time-dependent surrogate model for storm surge is built using an artificial neural network trained with high-fidelity simulations of two historical hurricanes. ANNs are a good option for highly nonlinear or large data problems but are usually best suited for deterministic applications and may not significantly reduce the computational expenses.

Common limitations of all the metamodels in the literature include: (i) they cannot include in the calibration data coming from historical records; and (ii) they can provide estimates of storm surge only at the same locations used for model calibration and consequently their use cannot be extended to regions different from those for which they have been calibrated.

This chapter presents a novel probabilistic model for storm surge prediction developed using the combination of a logistic regression and a physics-based non-stationary spatial random field (Contento et al. 2018). The logistic regression model estimates the probability of one location being wet (flooded). The non-stationary random field model estimates the distribution of the storm surge/water depths given that a location is wet. A spatial random field is a collection of random variables at different locations considering the spatial correlation (Vanmarcke 2010, Xu & Gardoni 2018). Non-stationarity means the statistics of a random field (e.g., mean and covariance) vary in space. The mean of a non-stationary random field is typically modeled as a deterministic function, while the covariance using a parametric spatial covariance function (Schmidt et al. 2011; Bornn et al. 2012; Fuglstad et al. 2015; Risser & Calder 2015). The presented probabilistic model uses an Improved Latent Space Approach (ILSA) developed by Xu and Gardoni (2018) to model the random field. Specifically, the ILSA considers physical regressors as latent dimensions in addition to the spatial dimensions, and models the variances and correlations as functions of such regressors. As a result, the ILSA-based random field model can describe and explain the non-stationarity based on the physical principles.

Differently from existing metamodels, the probabilistic model presented in this chapter can use not only data from high-fidelity simulations but also historical records. Moreover, the presented probabilistic model is able to give storm surge predictions at new locations where historical or simulation data are not available.

This chapter is organized into six sections. Following this introduction, Section 34.2 provides a description of the physical factors that affect storm surge. Section 34.3 describes the models for the logistic regression and random field. Section 34.4 provides the algorithms for the model selection, calibration and prediction. Section 34.5 implements the proposed model for the prediction of storm surge at the Tar River and Pamlico River area in North Carolina using climate change dependent data. The last section concludes the model and example presented in the chapter, and describes the possibility of using the presented model for different regions and climate change scenarios.

34.2 Physics of storm surges and their occurrences

Storm surge occurs when a storm generates an abnormal rise of water above the predicted astronomical tide (Resio & Westerink 2008). The wind circulation around the eye of a hurricane on the ocean surface produces a vertical circulation in the ocean. In shallow waters near the coast, the ocean bottom disrupts the vertical circulation, so the water rises and moves inland. As a result, storm surge is influenced by both the hurricane characteristics and the geomorphology of the site. Among the hurricanes characteristics those that play the major role are the storm intensity, the forward speed, the central pressure (pressure in the eye of the hurricane), the size of the storm, and the angle of approach to the coast. As to the site characteristics, both width and slope of the ocean bottom and local features that influence the flow of the water affect the storm surge.

34.3 Formulation of the probabilistic model for storm surge estimation and prediction

This section presents the formulation of the proposed probabilistic model for storm surge that considers the physics discussed in Section 34.2 (Contento et al. 2018). The model estimates the statistics of the spatially varying storm surge based on a set of observations $\mathbf{y}_o$ (that could be either recorded and/or simulated), and predicts the storm surge at new locations, $\mathbf{y}$. The storm surge observations are from n hurricane events (recorded or simulated), so that for each event there is an associated subset of observations $\mathbf{y}_{oi}$, $i = (1,\ldots,n)$. Each observation, y_{oij}, of the ith set, $\mathbf{y}_{oi}$, refers to a different location $j_i = (1,\ldots,m_i)$ so that $\mathbf{y}_{oi} = (y_{oi1},\ldots, y_{oij},\ldots, y_{oim_i})$. Because the formulation can use data at locations that are different for each storm surge scenario, differently from the other metamodels available in the literature (Jia & Taflanidis 2013; Kim et al. 2015; Jia et al. 2016), it is now possible to consider both recordings from historical records and results from high fidelity simulations (the latter typically providing data at a higher level of granularity than the former).

Independently from the source, each observation y_{oij} is associated with some characteristics of the measurement locations, $\mathbf{x}_o$, and of the associated hurricane, $\mathbf{s}_o$. The location characteristics include the longitude, x_{o1}, latitude, x_{o2}, and altitude, x_{o3}, of the observation location. The vector of the hurricane characteristics include six elements: the longitude and latitude of the hurricane landing point, s_{o1} and s_{o2}, the heading angle of the hurricane at landing, s_{o3}, the central pressure (pressure in the eye of the hurricane), s_{o4}, the forward velocity, s_{o5}, and the radius of maximum wind speed, s_{o6}. Table 34.1 shows a schematic representation of the format of the data. Figure 34.1 shows the location and hurricane geometric characteristics (i.e., those not related to the hurricane intensity). In the figure, points O and L denote the observation location and the landing point of the hurricane, respectively.

The storm surge is modeled as a function of the two sets of characteristics (regressors) $\mathbf{x}$ and $\mathbf{s}$

$$\mathbf{y} = \mathbf{y}(\mathbf{x},\mathbf{s},\Theta), \text{ or equivalently } y_{ij} = y_{ij}(\mathbf{x}_j,\mathbf{s}_i,\Theta) \tag{34.1}$$

Table 34.1 Format of the storm surge observations

Hurricane event	Storm surge observations $\mathbf{y}_o$	Location characteristics $\mathbf{x}_o$			Hurricane characteristics $\mathbf{s}_o$					
		$\mathbf{x}_{o1}$	$\mathbf{x}_{o2}$	$\mathbf{x}_{o3}$	$\mathbf{s}_{o1}$	$\mathbf{s}_{o2}$	$\mathbf{s}_{o3}$	$\mathbf{s}_{o4}$	$\mathbf{s}_{o5}$	$\mathbf{s}_{o6}$
1	y_{o11}	x_{o11_1}	x_{o21_1}	x_{o31_1}	s_{o11}	s_{o21}	s_{o31}	s_{o41}	s_{o51}	s_{o61}
	y_{o1j}	x_{o1j_1}	x_{o2j_1}	x_{o3j_1}						
	y_{o1m_1}	x_{o1m_1}	x_{o2m_1}	x_{o3m_1}						
i	y_{oi1}	x_{o11_i}	x_{o21_i}	x_{o31_i}	s_{oli}	s_{o2i}	s_{o3i}	s_{o4i}	s_{o5i}	s_{o6i}
	y_{oij}	x_{o1j_i}	x_{o2j_i}	x_{o3j_i}						
	y_{oim_i}	x_{o1m_i}	x_{o2m_i}	x_{o3m_i}						
n	y_{on1}	x_{o11_n}	x_{o21_n}	x_{o31_n}	s_{oln}	s_{o2n}	s_{o3n}	s_{o4n}	s_{o5n}	s_{o6n}
	y_{onj}	x_{o1j_n}	x_{o2j_n}	x_{o3j_n}						
	y_{onm_n}	x_{o1m_n}	x_{o2m_n}	x_{o3m_n}						

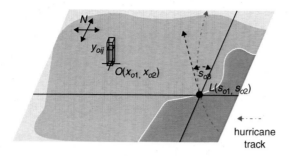

Figure 34.1 Graphic representation of location and hurricane characteristics.

Table 34.2 Explanatory functions

Function	Description
$h_0 = 1$	Intercept
$h_1 = g(x_1, s_1, s_2)$	Longitudinal distance between observation location and landing point
$h_2 = g(x_2, s_1, s_2)$	Latitudinal distance between observation location and landing point
$h_3 = x_3$	Altitude of the observation location
$h_4 = g(x_1, x_2, s_1, s_2)$	Distance between observation location and landing point
$h_5 = s_1$	Longitude of the landing point
$h_6 = s_2$	Latitude of the landing point
$h_7 = s_3$	Heading angle of the hurricane at landing
$h_8 = s_4$	Central pressure
$h_9 = s_5$	Forward velocity
$h_{10} = s_6$	Radius of maximum wind speed
$h_{11} = \cos[g(x_1, x_2, s_1, s_2)]$	Cosine of the angular distance between the direction of the heading angle and the direction connecting the observation point to the landing point (cosine of the angle h_{11}^{**} in Figure 34.2)
$h_{12} = s_4^2$	Second power of the central pressure
$h_{13} = s_4 \cdot s_6$	Cross product of central pressure and radius of maximum wind speed
$h_{14} = s_4 / s_6$	Ratio of central pressure and radius of maximum wind speed

where $\mathbf{x} = [\mathbf{x}_j] \, \forall j$, $\mathbf{s} = [\mathbf{s}_i] \, \forall i$, and $\boldsymbol{\Theta}$ are unknown model parameters. To find a suitable form for Equation (34.1), the regressors are combined into explanatory functions, $\mathbf{h}_{ij}^{+}(\mathbf{x}_j, \mathbf{s}_i)$, that are either physically meaningful or are shown to be relevant for the modeling of the storm surge in the literature (Irish et al. 2008). Such explanatory functions are then standardized, $\mathbf{h}(\mathbf{x}_j, \mathbf{s}_i)$, to be used in the model. The standardized explanatory functions are obtained by subtracting the sample mean and dividing by the sample standard deviation of the values of the actual explanatory functions. Table 34.2 shows the 15 standardized explanatory functions considered, and Figure 34.2 gives a visual representation of the actual explanatory functions related to locations, distances, and directions for a storm surge scenario.

The modeling of the storm surge is divided into two stages. The first stage evaluates the probability that a location is wet using a logistic regression model. The second stage models the distribution of storm surge with a random field developed using the Improved Latent Space Approach (ILSA) proposed by Xu and Gardoni (2018).

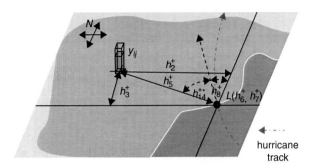

Figure 34.2 Graphic representation of selected explanatory functions.

34.3.1 Logistic regression model

The logistic regression model is used to estimate the probability of one location being wet. The wet locations are those where the storm surge has a value greater than zero, $y_{ij} > 0$. Let p_{ij} be the probability of a location j of being wet in the occurrence of a hurricane with characteristics $\mathbf{s}_i$. The p_{ij} is estimated with a logistic regression model where the logit is a polynomial function of the explanatory functions

$$\ln\left[\frac{p_{ij}\left(\mathbf{x}_j,\mathbf{s}_i,\boldsymbol{\theta}_l\right)}{1-p_{ij}\left(\mathbf{x}_j,\mathbf{s}_i,\boldsymbol{\theta}_l\right)}\right]=\boldsymbol{\theta}_l^{\mathrm{T}}\cdot\mathbf{h}^*\left(\mathbf{x}_j,\mathbf{s}_i\right), \tag{34.2}$$

where $\mathbf{h}^*(\mathbf{x}_j,\mathbf{s}_i)$ is the extended vector of the standardized explanatory functions. Such extended vector contains the original explanatory functions in $\mathbf{h}(\mathbf{x}_j,\mathbf{s}_i)$ as well as additional explanatory functions whose expression are obtained by taking the powers, from the 2nd to the 4th order, of the original explanatory functions. The term $\boldsymbol{\theta}_l$ is a vector of unknown model parameters. The model parameters $\boldsymbol{\theta}_l$ can be estimated with different approaches. Common approaches are Maximum Likelihood Estimation or Bayesian approach. A deletion process can be used to remove insignificant explanatory functions. The explanatory functions remaining after the deletion process give a good trade-off between accuracy and simplicity of the model. Knowing the expression for the logit, the probability p_{ij} can be expressed as

$$p_{ij}\left(\mathbf{x}_j,\mathbf{s}_i,\boldsymbol{\theta}_l\right)=\frac{\exp\left[\boldsymbol{\theta}_l^{\mathrm{T}}\cdot\mathbf{h}^*\left(\mathbf{x}_j,\mathbf{s}_i\right)\right]}{1+\exp\left[\boldsymbol{\theta}_l^{\mathrm{T}}\cdot\mathbf{h}^*\left(\mathbf{x}_j,\mathbf{s}_i\right)\right]}. \tag{34.3}$$

34.3.2 Non-stationary random field model based on the ILSA

The non-stationary random field model is used to estimate the water depths at the wet locations. The random field model is developed for the natural logarithm of the storm surge for the purpose of normalization,

$$\mathbf{z}=\ln\left(\mathbf{y}\right). \tag{34.4}$$

The random field $z_{ij}(\mathbf{x}_j,\mathbf{s}_i,\boldsymbol{\theta}_{IL})$ is defined as the sum of three contributions: a mean field, $m(\mathbf{x}_j,\mathbf{s}_i,\boldsymbol{\theta}_m)$, a zero mean correlated field, $v(\mathbf{x}_j,\mathbf{s}_i,\boldsymbol{\theta}_\Sigma,\boldsymbol{\theta}_\sigma)$, and a white noise, $\varepsilon(\mathbf{x}_j)$

$$z_{ij}\left(\mathbf{x}_j,\mathbf{s}_i,\boldsymbol{\theta}_{IL}\right)=m\left(\mathbf{x}_j,\mathbf{s}_i,\boldsymbol{\theta}_m\right)+v\left(\mathbf{x}_j,\mathbf{s}_i,\boldsymbol{\theta}_\Sigma,\boldsymbol{\theta}_\sigma\right)+\sigma\varepsilon\left(\mathbf{x}_j\right), \tag{34.5}$$

where $\boldsymbol{\theta}_{IL}=(\boldsymbol{\theta}_m,\boldsymbol{\theta}_\Sigma,\boldsymbol{\theta}_\sigma,\sigma)$ are the unknown model parameters of the different terms composing the random field, in which σ is the standard deviation of the white noise. The mean field, $m(\mathbf{x}_j,\mathbf{s}_i,\boldsymbol{\theta}_m)$, is a deterministic function. For this model, such function is taken as a linear combination of the standardized explanatory functions

$$m\left(\mathbf{x}_j,\mathbf{s}_i,\boldsymbol{\theta}_m\right)=\sum_k \theta_{mk}h_k\left(\mathbf{x}_j,\mathbf{s}_i\right), \tag{34.6}$$

where the $h_k(\mathbf{x}_j,\mathbf{s}_i)$ are the elements of $\mathbf{h}(\mathbf{x}_j,\mathbf{s}_i)$ that is augmented to include $h_{15}=s_4^2$ as suggested by Irish et. al. (2008). Such additional explanatory function is considered in all terms of the random field.

The covariance of the random field is obtained summing the contributions of the covariance of the zero mean correlated field, $v(\mathbf{x}_j,\mathbf{s}_i,\boldsymbol{\theta}_\Sigma,\boldsymbol{\theta}_\sigma)$, and the variance of the white noise, $\varepsilon(\mathbf{x}_j)$. The generic element of the covariance matrix reads

$$\begin{aligned}\left[\boldsymbol{\Sigma}_{\mathbf{zz}}\left(\mathbf{x},\mathbf{s},\boldsymbol{\theta}_\Sigma,\boldsymbol{\theta}_\sigma,\sigma\right)\right]_{rq}&=\left[\boldsymbol{\Sigma}_{\mathbf{vv}}\left(\mathbf{x},\mathbf{s},\boldsymbol{\theta}_\Sigma,\boldsymbol{\theta}_\sigma\right)\right]_{rq}+\sigma^2\cdot 1_{\{r=q\}}=\\&=\sigma_v\left(\mathbf{x}_j,\mathbf{s}_i,\boldsymbol{\theta}_\sigma\right)\cdot\sigma_v\left(\mathbf{x}_{j'},\mathbf{s}_{i'},\boldsymbol{\theta}_\sigma\right)\cdot\exp\left[-Q_{rq}\left(\mathbf{x}_j,\mathbf{s}_i,\mathbf{x}_{j'},\mathbf{s}_{i'},\boldsymbol{\theta}_\Sigma\right)\right]+\sigma^2\cdot 1_{\{r=q\}},\end{aligned} \tag{34.7}$$

where $\sigma_v(\mathbf{x}_j,\mathbf{s}_i,\boldsymbol{\theta}_\sigma)$ is the standard deviation of $v(\mathbf{x}_j,\mathbf{s}_i,\boldsymbol{\theta}_\Sigma,\boldsymbol{\theta}_\sigma)$, and $Q_{rq}(\mathbf{x}_j,\mathbf{s}_i,\mathbf{x}_{j'},\mathbf{s}_{i'},\boldsymbol{\theta}_\Sigma)$ is the generalized distance in the spatial correlation function, where the subscript r identifies the couple of indexes (i,j) and q identifies the couple of indexes (i',j'). Following the ILSA (Xu & Gardoni 2018), both $\sigma_v(\mathbf{x}_j,\mathbf{s}_i,\boldsymbol{\theta}_\sigma)$ and $Q_{rq}(\mathbf{x}_j,\mathbf{s}_i,\mathbf{x}_{j'},\mathbf{s}_{i'},\boldsymbol{\theta}_\Sigma)$ are also written as functions of the standardized explanatory functions, $\mathbf{h}(\mathbf{x}_j,\mathbf{s}_i)$. The standard deviation $\sigma_v(\mathbf{x}_j,\mathbf{s}_i,\boldsymbol{\theta}_\sigma)$ is written as the exponential of a linear combination of the components in $\mathbf{h}(\mathbf{x}_j,\mathbf{s}_i)$

$$\sigma_v\left(\mathbf{x}_j,\mathbf{s}_i,\boldsymbol{\theta}_\sigma\right)=\exp\left[\sum_k\theta_{\sigma k}h_k\left(\mathbf{x}_j,\mathbf{s}_i,\right)\right], \tag{34.8}$$

while the generalized distance $Q_{rq}(\mathbf{x}_j,\mathbf{s}_i,\mathbf{x}_{j'},\mathbf{s}_{i'},\boldsymbol{\theta}_\Sigma)$ is written as

$$Q_{rq}\left(\mathbf{x}_j,\mathbf{s}_i,\mathbf{x}_{j'},\mathbf{s}_{i'},\boldsymbol{\theta}_\Sigma\right)=\sqrt{\sum_k\frac{\left(h_k\left(\mathbf{x}_j,\mathbf{s}_i\right)-h_k\left(\mathbf{x}_{j'},\mathbf{s}_{i'}\right)\right)^2}{\theta_{\Sigma k}}}. \tag{34.9}$$

Based on Equations (34.6–34.9) we obtain the joint distribution of the natural logarithm transformations of storm surge, i.e.,

$$\begin{bmatrix}\mathbf{z}_o\left(\mathbf{x}_o,\mathbf{s}_o,\boldsymbol{\theta}_{IL}\right)\\\mathbf{z}\left(\mathbf{x},\mathbf{s},\boldsymbol{\theta}_{IL}\right)\end{bmatrix}\sim\mathcal{N}\left(\begin{bmatrix}\mathbf{m}\left(\mathbf{x}_o,\mathbf{s}_o,\boldsymbol{\theta}_m\right)\\\mathbf{m}\left(\mathbf{x},\mathbf{s},\boldsymbol{\theta}_m\right)\end{bmatrix},\begin{bmatrix}\boldsymbol{\Sigma}_{\mathbf{z}_o\mathbf{z}_o}\left(\mathbf{x}_o,\mathbf{s}_o,\boldsymbol{\theta}_\Sigma,\boldsymbol{\theta}_\sigma,\sigma\right)&\boldsymbol{\Sigma}_{\mathbf{zz}_o}^T\left(\mathbf{x},\mathbf{s},\mathbf{x}_o,\mathbf{s}_o,\boldsymbol{\theta}_\Sigma,\boldsymbol{\theta}_\sigma,\sigma\right)\\\boldsymbol{\Sigma}_{\mathbf{zz}_o}\left(\mathbf{x},\mathbf{s},\mathbf{x}_o,\mathbf{s}_o,\boldsymbol{\theta}_\Sigma,\boldsymbol{\theta}_\sigma,\sigma\right)&\boldsymbol{\Sigma}_{\mathbf{zz}}\left(\mathbf{x},\mathbf{s},\boldsymbol{\theta}_\Sigma,\boldsymbol{\theta}_\sigma,\sigma\right)\end{bmatrix}\right), \tag{34.10}$$

where $\mathbf{z}_o(\mathbf{x}_o,\mathbf{s}_o,\boldsymbol{\theta}_{IL})$ are the random variables corresponding to the observed storm surge, and $\mathbf{z}(\mathbf{x},\mathbf{s},\boldsymbol{\theta}_{IL})$ are the random variables corresponding to the storm surge to be predicted. Based on

Equation (34.10), the predictions $\mathbf{z}(\mathbf{x},\mathbf{s},\boldsymbol{\theta}_{IL}|\mathbf{z}_o)$ follow a conditional normal distribution given the observations of $\mathbf{z}_o(\mathbf{x}_o,\mathbf{s}_o,\boldsymbol{\theta}_{IL})$,

$$\mathbf{z}(\mathbf{x},\mathbf{s},\boldsymbol{\theta}_{IL}|\mathbf{z}_o) \sim \mathcal{N}\left[\boldsymbol{\mu}\left(\mathbf{x},\mathbf{s},\mathbf{x}_o,\mathbf{s}_o,\mathbf{z}_o,\boldsymbol{\theta}_{IL}\right),\boldsymbol{\Sigma}\left(\mathbf{x},\mathbf{s},\mathbf{x}_o,\mathbf{s}_o,\mathbf{z}_o,\boldsymbol{\theta}_{IL}\right)|\mathbf{x}_o,\mathbf{s}_o,\mathbf{z}_o,\boldsymbol{\theta}_{IL}\right], \tag{34.11}$$

where the explicit form of the mean is given by

$$\boldsymbol{\mu}\left(\mathbf{x},\mathbf{s},\mathbf{x}_o,\mathbf{s}_o,\mathbf{z}_o,\boldsymbol{\theta}_{IL}\right) = \mathbf{m}\left(\mathbf{x},\mathbf{s},\boldsymbol{\theta}_m\right) +$$
$$+ \boldsymbol{\Sigma}_{\mathbf{z},\mathbf{z}}\left(\mathbf{x},\mathbf{s},\mathbf{x}_o,\mathbf{s}_o,\boldsymbol{\theta}_\Sigma,\boldsymbol{\theta}_\sigma,\sigma\right)\boldsymbol{\Sigma}_{\mathbf{z}_o\mathbf{z}_o}^{-1}\left(\mathbf{x}_o,\mathbf{s}_o,\boldsymbol{\theta}_\Sigma,\boldsymbol{\theta}_\sigma,\sigma\right)\left[\mathbf{z}_o - \mathbf{m}\left(\mathbf{x}_o,\mathbf{s}_o,\boldsymbol{\theta}_m\right)\right] \tag{34.12}$$

and the covariance matrix has the form

$$\boldsymbol{\Sigma}\left(\mathbf{x},\mathbf{s},\mathbf{x}_o,\mathbf{s}_o,\boldsymbol{\theta}_{IL}\right) = \boldsymbol{\Sigma}_{\mathbf{z}\mathbf{z}}\left(\mathbf{x},\mathbf{s},\boldsymbol{\theta}_\Sigma,\boldsymbol{\theta}_\sigma,\sigma\right) +$$
$$- \boldsymbol{\Sigma}_{\mathbf{z},\mathbf{z}}\left(\mathbf{x},\mathbf{s},\mathbf{x}_o,\mathbf{s}_o,\boldsymbol{\theta}_\Sigma,\boldsymbol{\theta}_\sigma,\sigma\right)\boldsymbol{\Sigma}_{\mathbf{z}_o\mathbf{z}_o}^{-1} \tag{34.13}$$
$$\left(\mathbf{x}_o,\mathbf{s}_o,\boldsymbol{\theta}_\Sigma,\boldsymbol{\theta}_\sigma,\sigma\right)\boldsymbol{\Sigma}_{\mathbf{z},\mathbf{z}}^{T}\left(\mathbf{x},\mathbf{s},\mathbf{x}_o,\mathbf{s}_o,\boldsymbol{\theta}_\Sigma,\boldsymbol{\theta}_\sigma,\sigma\right).$$

After finding the statistics of $\mathbf{z}$ using Equations (34.12) and (34.13), the inverse transformation of Equation (34.4) can be used to find the prediction of the storm surge. Specifically, the random field of storm surge follows a joint lognormal distribution. The mean and median of the lognormal distribution are estimated as

$$\boldsymbol{\mu}_{\mathbf{y}}\left(\mathbf{x},\mathbf{s},\mathbf{x}_o,\mathbf{s}_o,\mathbf{z}_o,\boldsymbol{\theta}_{IL}\right) = \exp\left[\boldsymbol{\mu}\left(\mathbf{x},\mathbf{s},\mathbf{x}_o,\mathbf{s}_o,\mathbf{z}_o,\boldsymbol{\theta}_{IL}\right) + 0.5\sigma_\Sigma^2\left(\mathbf{x},\mathbf{s},\mathbf{x}_o,\mathbf{s}_o,\boldsymbol{\theta}_{IL}\right)\right] \tag{34.14}$$

and

$$\mathbf{M}_{\mathbf{y}}\left(\mathbf{x},\mathbf{s},\mathbf{x}_o,\mathbf{s}_o,\mathbf{z}_o,\boldsymbol{\theta}_{IL}\right) = \exp\left[\boldsymbol{\mu}\left(\mathbf{x},\mathbf{s},\mathbf{x}_o,\mathbf{s}_o,\mathbf{z}_o,\boldsymbol{\theta}_{IL}\right)\right], \tag{34.15}$$

where $\sigma_\Sigma^2\left(\mathbf{x},\mathbf{s},\mathbf{x}_o,\mathbf{s}_o,\boldsymbol{\theta}_{IL}\right)$ are the diagonal terms of $\boldsymbol{\Sigma}\left(\mathbf{x},\mathbf{s},\mathbf{x}_o,\mathbf{s}_o,\boldsymbol{\theta}_{IL}\right)$. The covariance matrix is estimated as

$$\boldsymbol{\Sigma}_{\mathbf{y}\mathbf{y}}\left(\mathbf{x},\mathbf{s},\mathbf{x}_o,\mathbf{s}_o,\mathbf{z}_o,\boldsymbol{\theta}_{IL}\right) = \boldsymbol{\mu}_{\mathbf{y}}\left(\mathbf{x},\mathbf{s},\mathbf{x}_o,\mathbf{s}_o,\mathbf{z}_o,\boldsymbol{\theta}_{IL}\right)\left[\boldsymbol{\mu}_{\mathbf{y}}\left(\mathbf{x},\mathbf{s},\mathbf{x}_o,\mathbf{s}_o,\mathbf{z}_o,\boldsymbol{\theta}_{IL}\right)\right]^{T}$$
$$\left\{\exp\left[\boldsymbol{\Sigma}\left(\mathbf{x},\mathbf{s},\mathbf{x}_o,\mathbf{s}_o,\boldsymbol{\theta}_{IL}\right)\right] - 1\right\}. \tag{34.16}$$

34.4 Model selection and calibration

Group 1 includes the observations where the altitude is positive, $x_{o3j} > 0$. Group 2 includes the observations where $x_{o3j} \leq 0$. While the model selection is performed only once, the logistic regression and the random field models are independently calibrated for each of the two groups of data. The reason is that locations with altitude $x_{o3j} \leq 0$ are more likely to be wet (most of them are on the riverbed) than the locations with altitude $x_{o3j} > 0$, and consequently developing two separate sets of models is more accurate than considering only one set of models.

34.4.1 Model selection

Logistic regression model
For the logistic regression, an initial model selection is performed using the Akaike Information Criterion (AIC) (Johansson 1993). Among the remaining candidate models, the final model

669

is chosen with a cross-validation technique that consists in comparing the prediction error of the different models similarly to the Lasso technique (Hastie et al. 2001). The prediction error is defined as total number of wrong predictions. The available observations are randomly split into two parts, a training set and a validation set, which contain approximately 80 percent and 20 percent of the total observations, respectively. All competing models are trained using the data in the train set. Then, multiple predictions are performed on test data sets obtained by resampling the initial validation data set. In this way, we obtain the mean value and the 95 percent confidence interval of the prediction error for each model. All of the models whose 95 percent confidence intervals of the prediction error include the value of the lowest mean prediction error among all of the models are considered as possible candidates for the final model. Among the candidate models, the simplest one (i.e., the one that has the smallest number of explanatory functions) is chosen as the final model. Additional details can be found in Contento et al. (2018).

Non-stationary random field model based on the ILSA

For the random field model, we consider different combinations of the explanatory functions as candidate models. Similar to the selection of the logistic regression model, we randomly take 80 percent data with non-zero storm surge observations as training data, and use the remaining 20 percent data for validation. The training data are used to fit each candidate model, and the validation data are used to compare the predictions obtained with each fitted model. Based on the predictions and actual observations of the validation data, we compute the AIC and the prediction error of each model. Among the models with the lowest AIC values, the one with the smallest prediction error is chosen as the final model.

34.4.2 Model calibration

For both the logistic regression model and the random field model, the joint distribution of the model parameters Θ is obtained using a Bayesian approach. With this approach, the posterior distribution of the parameters $f''(\Theta)$ can be written as

$$f''(\Theta) = aL(\Theta)f'(\Theta),$$

(34.17)

where a is a normalizing constant, $L(\Theta)$ is the likelihood function and $f'(\Theta)$ is the prior distribution of Θ. Specifically, $L(\Theta)$ contains the objective information from experimental or simulation data, while $f'(\Theta)$ captures the information available before the data are collected.

By combining the information coming from both $L(\Theta)$ and $f'(\Theta)$, $f''(\Theta)$ reflects all of the available knowledge on Θ. Since, in this case, there is no closed-form for $f''(\Theta)$, a Markov Chain Monte Carlo (MCMC) approach is adopted to numerically estimate $f''(\Theta)$. The next two subsections will discuss how to model $L(\Theta)$ and $f'(\Theta)$ in the logistic regression model and random field model, respectively.

Logistic regression model

For the logistic regression model, the likelihood function used in the Bayesian approach is written as

$$L(\theta_i) = \prod_{i=1}^{n} \prod_{j=1}^{m_i} \left[p_{ij}^{b_{ij}} \cdot \left(1 - p_{ij}\right)^{1-b_{ij}} \right],$$

(34.18)

where b_{oij} is an indicator function defined as $b_{oij} = 1_{\{y_{oij} > 0\}}$. Equation (34.18) is obtained under the simplifying assumptions of independent observations.

Non-stationary random field model based on the ILSA
For the random field, the likelihood function is written as

$$
L(\boldsymbol{\theta}_{IL}) \propto \left|\boldsymbol{\Sigma}_{\mathbf{z}_o\mathbf{z}_o}(\mathbf{x}_o, \mathbf{s}_o, \boldsymbol{\theta}_\Sigma, \boldsymbol{\theta}_\sigma, \sigma)\right|^{-1/2} \cdot
$$
$$
\exp\left\{-\frac{1}{2}\left[\mathbf{z}_o - \mathbf{m}(\mathbf{x}_o, \mathbf{s}_o, \boldsymbol{\theta}_m)\right]^{\mathrm{T}} \boldsymbol{\Sigma}_{\mathbf{z}_o\mathbf{z}_o}^{-1}(\mathbf{x}_o, \mathbf{s}_o, \boldsymbol{\theta}_\Sigma, \boldsymbol{\theta}_\sigma, \sigma)\left[\mathbf{z}_o - \mathbf{m}(\mathbf{x}_o, \mathbf{s}_o, \boldsymbol{\theta}_m)\right]\right\} \quad (34.19)
$$

In addition, assuming that the sets of model parameters appearing in each term of the model in Equation (34.5) are independent from each other, the prior distribution $f'(\boldsymbol{\theta}_{IL})$ can be written as the product of the prior distributions of the model parameters

$$
f'(\boldsymbol{\theta}_{IL}) = f'(\boldsymbol{\theta}_m) f'(\boldsymbol{\theta}_\Sigma) f'(\boldsymbol{\theta}_\sigma) f'(\sigma). \tag{34.20}
$$

Differently from the parameter estimation for the logistic regression model, both the model selection and the parameter estimation for the random field model make use only of the wet observations. Although including all observations in the model selection and parameter estimation of the random field model would simplify the modeling process, considering a large number of zero values would violate the normality assumption and lead to underestimate the storm surge values.

34.4.3 Predictions

Following Gardoni et al. (2002), it is possible to either consider a point estimate $\hat{\Theta}$ in Equations (34.3) and (34.11) to obtain point estimates of the probability $\hat{\mathbf{p}}$ and the conditional distribution of $\hat{\mathbf{z}}$, or to develop a predictive distribution that also accounts for the uncertainties in the model parameters as

$$
\tilde{f}_{\mathbf{d}} = \int_\Theta f_{\mathbf{d}}\left[\mathbf{d}(\mathbf{x}, \mathbf{s}, \Theta)\Theta\right] | f(\Theta) d\Theta, \tag{34.21}
$$

where $\mathbf{d}(\mathbf{x}, \mathbf{s}, \Theta)$ should be replaced with $\mathbf{p}(\mathbf{x}, \mathbf{s}, \boldsymbol{\theta}_l)$ for the logistic regression model, and with $\mathbf{z}(\mathbf{x}, \mathbf{s}, \boldsymbol{\theta}_{IL} | \mathbf{z}_o)$ for the random field model, respectively.

Since there is no analytical solution for the integral in Equation (34.21), a numerical approximation of its statistics is obtained by Monte Carlo sampling. The posterior distribution of Θ, $f''(\Theta)$, is used to generate n_s samples of the parameters, $\Theta_u, (u = 1, ..., n_s)$, that are replaced in the expressions of $\mathbf{d}(\mathbf{x}, \mathbf{s}, \Theta)$ (Equations (34.3) and (34.11)) to obtain the correspondent predictions $\mathbf{d}_u(\mathbf{x}, \mathbf{s}, \Theta_u)$. These predictions are used to obtain the mean prediction

$$
\tilde{\mathbf{d}}(\mathbf{x}, \mathbf{s}) = \frac{\displaystyle\sum_{u=1}^{n_s} \mathbf{d}_u(\mathbf{x}, \mathbf{s}, \Theta_u)}{n_s}. \tag{34.22}
$$

The $\alpha\%$ confidence interval for the prediction $\tilde{\mathbf{d}}$ is obtained by considering the relative quantiles of the n_s predictions, $0.5(100 - \alpha)\%$ and $[100 - 0.5(100 - \alpha)]\%$, for the lower and upper bounds, respectively. In the case of the random field, the median prediction $\tilde{\mathbf{y}}$ and its confidence interval are then obtained from $\tilde{\mathbf{z}}$ and its confidence interval using the inverse of Equation (34.4). The predictive estimate provides more exhaustive information about the uncertainties.

Water depth prediction

For each location and each hurricane, the storm surge prediction is obtained pairing the probability $\tilde{p}_{ij}(\mathbf{x}_j, \mathbf{s}_i)$ with the storm surge predicted by the random field model, $\tilde{y}_{ij}(\mathbf{x}_j, \mathbf{s}_i)$. Therefore, each prediction is constituted by a distribution of storm surge and a probability of the location of being wet. In order to provide a more intuitive representation of the risk due to the storm surge, we provide the results in terms of water depth, $k_{ij}(\mathbf{x}_j, \mathbf{s}_i)$, subtracting the altitude of the location of the prediction x_{3j}, as

$$\tilde{k}_{ij}(\mathbf{x}_j, \mathbf{s}_i | \mathbf{z}_o) = \tilde{y}_{ij}(\mathbf{x}_j, \mathbf{s}_i | \mathbf{z}_o) - x_{3j}, \qquad (34.23)$$

so that a prediction is given by the pairs of values $[\tilde{k}_{ij}(\mathbf{x}_j, \mathbf{s}_i), \tilde{p}_{ij}(\mathbf{x}_j, \mathbf{s}_i)]$.

34.5 Application to a case study area

To show the capability of the presented physics-based transportable probabilistic model, the model is used to estimate and predict storm surges (and water depths) accounting for climate change effects. The effects of climate change are embedded in the data used to train the model, as explained in the next section. Two kinds of predictions are made. The first kind predicts the storm surge due to hurricanes that have been used to calibrate the model but at different points (locations) in the same area (this is something that typical metamodels do by interpolating predictions obtained for locations used in the model calibration). The second kind of predictions provides the storm surge at the same locations used in the model calibration for different hurricanes whose observations are not used in the model calibration. The results of both predictions are presented in terms of water depth. Predictions are provided separately for locations whose altitude is above and below the mean sea level (i.e., $x_{o3} > 0$ and $x_{o3} \leq 0$).

34.5.1 Data

The storm surge observations used for the model calibration are located in North Carolina, in the area surrounding the Tar River and the Pamlico River, mostly in the stretch of river in between Washington and Greenville (see Figure 34.3).

The observations come from 238 simulations performed with the coupled model for hurricanes, storm surge and coastal flooding presented in Kendra et al. (2017). Each simulation has as input a synthetic hurricane whose track and characteristics are obtained taking into account the effects of climate change and, specifically, the climate change scenario obtained under the 8.5 Representative Concentration Pathway (RCP8.5). This scenario is the worst-case climate scenario described in the Intergovernmental Panel for Climate Change (IPCC) Fifth Assessment Report (AR5) (IPCC 2013), which assumes a radiative forcing level of 8.5 watt/m² in the year 2100.

Among the 238 sets of observations resulting from the simulations, 25 sets are randomly chosen for model selection and calibration. From these 25 sets, two groups of observations are selected. The first group, Group A, contains 60 observations per set, for a total of 1,500 observations (25×60). The 60 observation per set have the same location in all of the sets (i.e., only 60 different locations are considered). Among these initial group of 1,500 observations, 70% is used to calibrate both the logistic regression model and the random field model. The

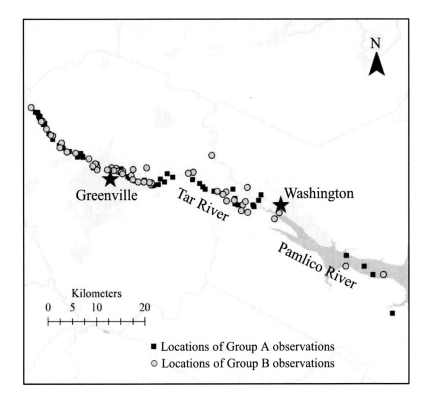

Figure 34.3 Area of the locations of the storm surge observations.

second group, Group B, contains 20 observations per set for a total of 500 observations (25×20). The locations of the 20 observations are the same in each set and are different from the 60 locations used before. These observations are used to make predictions of water depth in locations not considered in the model calibration (first kind of predictions). In addition, other four sets of observations, different from the 25 sets chosen before, are selected to be used for predictions. To avoid extrapolation in the predictions, these additional sets of storm surge observations are selected based on the characteristics of the hurricanes used for their simulations. The choice is made so that the values of such characteristics fall within the ranges of the hurricane characteristics used to train the models. For each of these four additional sets, the observations related to the 60 locations considered for the observations in Group A are selected (i.e., these 60 observations have the same locations of the observations of Group A but are generated by different hurricanes). These observations are used to make predictions for hurricane characteristics not considered in model calibration (second kind of predictions).

34.5.2 Model selection and parameter estimation

The first step in developing the predictions consists in the model selection, performed considering all of the 1,500 observations for the logistic regression model and all the wet observation (734 out of the 1,500) for the ILSA-based random field model.

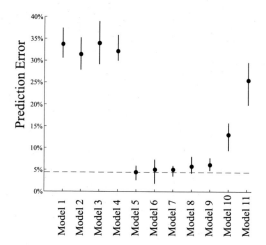

Figure 34.4 Mean values (dots) and 95 percent confidence intervals (bars) of the prediction error for the different models.

For the logistic regression, we consider all of the possible linear combinations from the 1st to the 4th order of the standardized explanatory functions as candidate models. Since no prior knowledge is available, we consider non-informative priors for the model parameters in the Bayesian updates. After an initial scrimmage, the models with the lowest AIC are compared using the model selection based on the prediction error discussed in Section 34.4. For such models, Figure 34.4 shows the mean value of the prediction error expressed as percentage of incorrect predictions on the total number of observations used for the validation step of the model selection.

In Figure 34.4, the vertical bars represent the 95 percent confidence intervals. Models 5–9 have similar prediction errors. However, only models 5–8 have a 95 percent confidence interval that includes the value of the smallest mean prediction error (the one of Model 5). Among these models, we select the one that includes the fewest explanatory functions (i.e., Model 5), which is written as

$$
\ln\left[\frac{p_{ij}\left(\mathbf{x}_j,\mathbf{s}_i,\theta_l\right)}{1-p_{ij}\left(\mathbf{x}_j,\mathbf{s}_i,\theta_l\right)}\right]=\theta_l^\Gamma\cdot\mathbf{h}^*\left(\mathbf{x},\mathbf{s}\right)=
$$
$$
=\theta_{l1}h_1^*+\theta_{l2}h_2^*+\theta_{l3}h_3^*+\theta_{l4}h_4^*+\theta_{l5}h_5^*+\theta_{l6}h_6^*+\theta_{l7}h_7^*+\theta_{l8}h_8^*+\theta_{l11}h_{11}^*+
$$
$$
+\theta_{l12}h_{12}^*+\theta_{l18}h_{18}^*+\theta_{l20}h_{20}^*+\theta_{l21}h_{21}^*+\theta_{l22}h_{22}^*+\theta_{l23}h_{23}^*+\theta_{l34}h_{34}^*+\theta_{l47}h_{47}^*.
\qquad(34.24)
$$

where $h_1^* - h_{14}^* = h_1 - h_{14}$, $h_{18}^* = g_1(x_1,x_2,s_1,s_2)^2$, $h_{20}^* = s_2^2$, $h_{21}^* = s_3^2$, $h_{22}^* = s_4^2$, $h_{23}^* = s_5^2$, $h_{34}^* = s_3^3$, and $h_{47}^* = s_3^4$. After the model selection, the storm surge observations are divided into the two groups, Group 1 and Group 2, as described in Section 34.4. The two groups are made of 1,178 and 322 observations, respectively. Group 1 is composed of 1,178 observations, of which 918 are wet and 260 are dry. While all of the observations in Group 2 are wet observations. The model parameters $\boldsymbol{\theta}_l$ are estimated using the Bayesian approach described in Section 34.4. Table 34.3 gives the posterior statistics of the model parameters.

Only the model for Group 1 is calibrated because all of the observations in Group 2 are wet (i.e., $y_{oij} > 0$). For both Group 1 and Group 2, Figure 34.5 shows the mean values of the

Table 34.3 Logistic regression model parameters

Parameters	Mean	Variance	Correlations coefficients																		
			θ_{l0}	θ_{l1}	θ_{l2}	θ_{l3}	θ_{l4}	θ_{l5}	θ_{l6}	θ_{l7}	θ_{l8}	θ_{l9}	θ_{l10}	θ_{l11}	θ_{l12}	θ_{l13}	θ_{l14}	θ_{l15}	θ_{l16}	θ_{l17}	θ_{l18}
θ_{l0}	-1.90	0.62	1.00																		
θ_{l1}	7.51	2.38	0.10	1.00																	
θ_{l2}	26.76	4.91	-0.12	0.60	1.00																
θ_{l3}	-7.03	0.21	0.04	-0.04	-0.62	1.00															
θ_{l4}	3.79	0.46	0.19	0.09	0.24	-0.26	1.00														
θ_{l5}	9.89	2.42	-0.84	0.08	0.24	-0.27	-0.23	1.00													
θ_{l6}	-2.73	0.46	-0.24	-0.10	-0.17	0.19	-0.97	0.33	1.00												
θ_{l7}	-4.43	0.75	0.72	-0.05	-0.20	0.22	0.40	-0.94	-0.54	1.00											
θ_{l8}	0.46	0.01	-0.34	0.06	0.22	-0.21	0.17	0.24	-0.13	-0.14	1.00										
θ_{l9}	-5.67	70.79	-0.06	-0.09	-0.04	0.04	-0.08	-0.07	0.07	0.03	-0.05	1.00									
θ_{l10}	-1.00	0.26	0.35	0.38	-0.22	0.06	-0.08	-0.10	0.00	0.12	-0.12	-0.11	1.00								
θ_{l11}	1.10	0.03	-0.19	-0.17	0.18	-0.30	0.10	0.16	-0.05	-0.10	0.17	0.00	-0.36	1.00							
θ_{l12}	7.97	2.34	-0.01	0.93	0.66	-0.05	0.09	0.12	-0.10	-0.07	0.15	-0.16	0.16	-0.14	1.00						
θ_{l13}	24.86	4.48	-0.07	0.62	0.97	-0.61	0.23	0.21	-0.16	-0.18	0.17	0.02	-0.13	0.18	0.58	1.00					
θ_{l14}	-1.09	0.06	-0.19	-0.27	0.02	0.22	-0.01	-0.09	0.03	0.03	-0.03	0.15	-0.66	-0.41	-0.11	-0.06	1.00				
θ_{l15}	-4.36	1.07	-0.10	-0.16	-0.16	0.21	-0.20	-0.13	0.19	0.04	-0.10	0.81	-0.13	-0.09	-0.25	-0.08	0.26	1.00			
θ_{l16}	2.60	0.47	0.11	0.12	0.13	-0.20	0.23	0.09	-0.23	0.01	0.02	-0.37	0.13	-0.01	0.19	0.07	-0.13	-0.76	1.00		
θ_{l17}	0.90	0.06	0.08	0.11	0.12	-0.19	0.24	0.09	-0.24	0.01	0.01	-0.30	0.13	-0.04	0.17	0.07	-0.10	-0.68	0.99	1.00	
θ_{l18}	6.22	78.73	0.06	0.09	0.04	-0.04	0.07	0.08	-0.07	-0.03	0.05	-1.00	0.11	0.00	0.16	-0.02	-0.15	-0.81	0.36	0.30	1.00

Sym

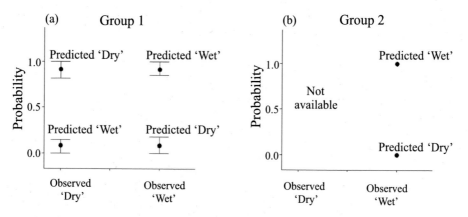

Figure 34.5 Predicted probabilities of dry and wet observations.

Table 34.4 Posterior statistics of the parameters in the random field model of Group 1

Parameter	Mean	Standard Deviation	Parameter	Mean	Standard Deviation	Parameter	Mean	Standard Deviation
θ_{m0}	0.63	0.02	σ^2	0.84	0.01	$\theta_{\sigma0}$	0.01	0.01
θ_{m1}	−0.88	0.20	$\theta_{\Sigma1}$	1.28	0.39	$\theta_{\sigma1}$	0.02	0.01
θ_{m2}	0.56	0.25	$\theta_{\Sigma2}$	0.87	0.54	$\theta_{\sigma2}$	0.01	0.01
θ_{m3}	0.31	0.03	$\theta_{\Sigma3}$	1.03	0.02	$\theta_{\sigma3}$	0.07	0.03
θ_{m4}	0.09	0.03	$\theta_{\Sigma4}$	1.10	0.96	$\theta_{\sigma4}$	−0.03	0.01
θ_{m5}	−3.65	3.21	$\theta_{\Sigma5}$	1.68	0.48	$\theta_{\sigma5}$	−0.01	0.00
θ_{m6}	0.02	0.01	$\theta_{\Sigma6}$	0.42	0.53	$\theta_{\sigma6}$	0.01	0.00
θ_{m7}	8.56	4.96	$\theta_{\Sigma7}$	1.64	0.68	$\theta_{\sigma7}$	−0.02	0.01
θ_{m8}	−0.14	0.02	$\theta_{\Sigma8}$	0.99	0.01	$\theta_{\sigma8}$	0.02	0.01
θ_{m9}	0.01	0.01	$\theta_{\Sigma9}$	7.63	2.99	$\theta_{\sigma9}$	−0.03	0.01
θ_{m10}	−0.84	0.20	$\theta_{\Sigma10}$	1.64	1.42	$\theta_{\sigma10}$	0.03	0.01
θ_{m11}	0.40	0.25	$\theta_{\Sigma11}$	10.57	2.24	$\theta_{\sigma11}$	0.01	0.01
θ_{m12}	4.08	3.55	$\theta_{\Sigma12}$	0.53	0.70	$\theta_{\sigma12}$	0.07	0.01
θ_{m13}	−8.89	5.10	$\theta_{\Sigma13}$	0.38	0.10	$\theta_{\sigma13}$	0.01	0.01
θ_{m14}	0.20	0.09	$\theta_{\Sigma14}$	1.02	0.84	$\theta_{\sigma14}$	−0.07	0.02

probabilities of being wet and dry for the wet and dry observations used in the training of the logistic regression model. The black dots denote such mean value while the bars represent the one standard deviation confidence interval. For the observations in Group 2 there are no confidence intervals because all the observation are wet.

For the random field model, we start with non-informative distributions for the prior distributions in Equation (34.16). After the model selection, all of the 15 explanatory functions are retained. The final model has 45 model parameters (15 arameters in both θ_m and θ_σ, 14 parameters in θ_Σ, and σ). Table 34.4 and 34.5 give the posterior statistics of θ_m, θ_σ, θ_Σ, and σ obtained using data in Group 1 and Group 2. Figure 34.6 shows the fitting of the training data for Group 1 and Group 2.

From Figure 34.6, we can see that the fitting of training data from both models are unbiased. The model obtained for the observations in Group 2 has a smaller variability in the prediction.

Table 34.5 Posterior statistics of the parameters in the random field model of Group 2

Parameter	Mean	Standard Deviation	Parameter	Mean	Standard Deviation	Parameter	Mean	Standard Deviation
θ_{m0}	0.40	0.15	σ^2	0.39	0.02	$\theta_{\sigma 0}$	−0.54	0.03
θ_{m1}	−0.18	0.03	$\theta_{\ell 1}$	391.63	30.01	$\theta_{\sigma 1}$	0.02	0.01
θ_{m2}	0.497	0.21	$\theta_{\ell 2}$	86.04	15.67	$\theta_{\sigma 2}$	0.07	0.04
θ_{m3}	−0.10	0.01	$\theta_{\ell 3}$	114.13	11.13	$\theta_{\sigma 3}$	0.06	0.01
θ_{m4}	0.053	0.02	$\theta_{\ell 4}$	728.43	36.90	$\theta_{\sigma 4}$	0.07	0.02
θ_{m5}	−11.67	4.01	$\theta_{\ell 5}$	296.82	11.65	$\theta_{\sigma 5}$	−0.12	0.03
θ_{m6}	−0.08	0.02	$\theta_{\ell 6}$	550.06	26.71	$\theta_{\sigma 6}$	0.05	0.01
θ_{m7}	27.66	6.81	$\theta_{\ell 7}$	128.27	62.09	$\theta_{\sigma 7}$	−0.20	0.09
θ_{m8}	−0.20	0.03	$\theta_{\ell 8}$	100.47	4.15	$\theta_{\sigma 8}$	−0.01	0.04
θ_{m9}	0.016	0.01	$\theta_{\ell 9}$	139.81	6.53	$\theta_{\sigma 9}$	−0.37	0.01
θ_{m10}	−0.13	0.04	$\theta_{\ell 10}$	2081.44	90.78	$\theta_{\sigma 10}$	0.25	0.03
θ_{m11}	0.20	0.10	$\theta_{\ell 11}$	1448.52	78.76	$\theta_{\sigma 11}$	0.06	0.03
θ_{m12}	13.39	4.46	$\theta_{\ell 12}$	270.28	16.67	$\theta_{\sigma 12}$	0.49	0.05
θ_{m13}	−28.72	7.00	$\theta_{\ell 13}$	638.31	32.74	$\theta_{\sigma 13}$	0.17	0.05
θ_{m14}	0.79	0.26	$\theta_{\ell 14}$	386.47	18.28	$\theta_{\sigma 14}$	−0.42	0.11

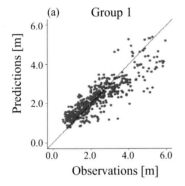 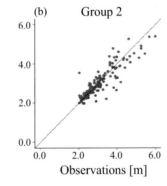

Figure 34.6 Fitting of the training data for the random field model.

This implies that the random field model tends to perform better for the locations whose altitude is below the sea level.

34.5.3 Predictions at different locations

Figure 34.7 shows the predictions of the water depth corresponding to 100 randomly sampled observations belonging to Group B, i.e., the observations with same hurricane characteristics but at different locations from the training data. For each location, the two plots in Figure 34.7 compare the observed water depth values to those predicted by the random field and show the probability of the location being wet provided by the logistic regression. The dots show the median predictions versus the actual observations, while the bars represent the one standard deviation confidence intervals. The color of each prediction fades as the probability of the location being wet approaches zero. The diagonal line is the 1:1 line that represents a perfect

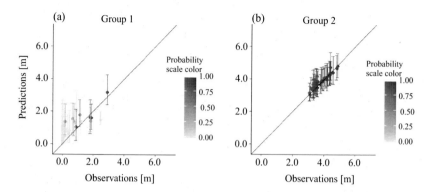

Figure 34.7 Predictions of water depth due to hurricanes used to calibrate the model (different locations).

Table 34.6 Hurricane characteristics

Hurricane	Hurricane characteristics					
	s_1 [°lon]	s_2 [°lat]	s_3 [rad]	s_4 [hpa]	s_5 [m/s]	s_6 [km]
1	−76.162	34.856	5.16	989.81	5.02	52.80
2	−75.518	35.112	5.75	986.83	3.13	47.77
3	−75.736	35.142	5.22	988.57	5.22	38.85
4	−75.695	35.156	5.16	994.82	5.94	36.29

prediction. For Group 1 we see that higher predictions of water depth generally correspond to higher probabilities of the locations of being wet. This entails that the locations that are subject to a higher surge risk are also those that are predicted with higher confidence of being indeed wet. As expected, for the predictions of the locations in Group 2 all of the locations are wet. The predictions for the locations in Group 2 are generally more accurate. Moreover, the values of water depth are higher than those in Group 1 since at these locations there is an initial water depth even before the occurrence of the storm surge.

34.5.4 Predictions for different hurricane characteristics

Figures 34.8 and 34.9 show the predictions of water depth for the four hurricanes selected for the second kind of predictions (i.e., predictions of the storm surge for hurricanes whose observations have not been used in the model calibration). Table 34.6 contains the characteristics of the four hurricanes.

Figure 34.8 presents the results obtained for Hurricanes 1 and 2, while Figure 34.9 shows those for hurricanes 3 and 4. Similarly to Figure 34.7, the two figures show the comparison between median predictions and observations; each median prediction is shown with a one standard deviation confidence interval and a color whose darkness is proportional to the probability of the location of being wet.

Figures 34.8 and 34.9 show a good agreement between predictions and observations and confirm the same trends shown by the previous kind of predictions (predictions at different locations) presented in Figure 34.7. The observations with higher values of storm surge

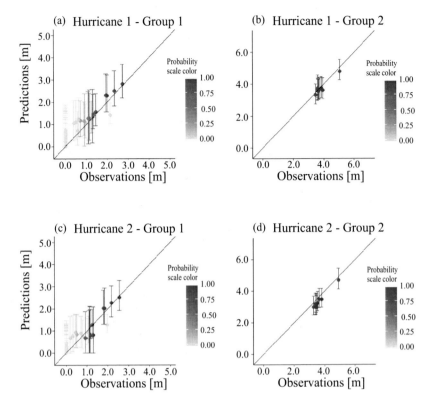

Figure 34.8 Predictions of water depth for different hurricanes characteristics (Hurricane 1 and 2).

are those that are predicted to have the highest probabilities of being wet. In addition, the locations of the observations belonging to Group 2 are all wet, and the values of water depth are predicted with higher accuracy.

The least accurate predictions are for water depths values lower than one meter. For these predictions the local geographical features, which are not accounted for in the model, have a significant influence. However, the likelihood of damage for low water depth is generally small and, in addition, the probability of these locations of being wet is usually low, as the logistic regression suggests.

34.6 Conclusions

The chapter presented the formulation of a physics-based transportable probabilistic model intended to replace existing model formulations that are either computationally demanding or have low accuracy. The model used for the predictions combines a logistic regression model and a random field model developed with the Improved Latent Space Approach. Differently from existing metamodels, a model developed with the presented formulation can be trained with both data from high-fidelity simulations and historical records. Moreover, the model is able to give storm surge predictions in locations different from those used for the model calibration. For each location considered for the predictions, the model provides the probability of

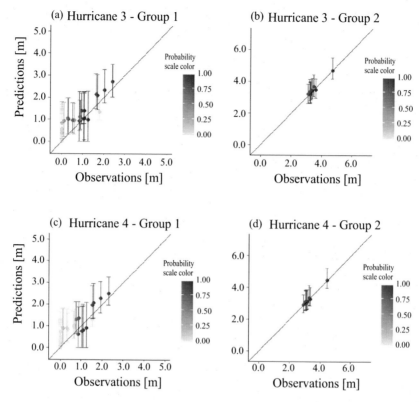

Figure 34.9 Predictions of water depth for different hurricanes characteristics (Hurricane 3 and 4).

the location of being wet and prediction of storm surge, or equivalently water depth. Also the model can give storm surge prediction for hurricanes different from those used for the model calibration.

As an example, a specific model is developed to predict the storm surge accounting for climate change effects. Observations obtained with a high-fidelity simulations for locations near the Pamlico River in North Carolina are used to train and test the model. The predictions show a good agreement with the observations, especially for the locations below the sea level and for high surge levels. The least accurate predictions are for water depths lower than one meter. The lower accuracy of these predictions can be explained noticing that for these predictions the local geographical features, which are not unaccounted for in the model, have a significant influence.

Since the proposed model captures the fundamental physics of the phenomena, it is possible to extend its use to different regions where simulation data are not available. For example, after training the model for a region with a sufficient amount of observations coming from high fidelity data, the model could be used for a different region by updating the model using only few local observations coming, for example, from historical records.

In addition, the probabilistic model can be used in an extended analysis of the consequences of climate change on storm surge. For a defined region, it is possible to train the model with observations related to the present climate and then update the parameters with a limited number of simulations for the different future climate change scenarios.

Acknowledgements

The research herein was supported in part by the Center for Risk-Based Community Resilience Planning funded by the US National Institute of Standards and Technology (NIST Financial Assistance Award Number: 70NANB15H044). The views expressed are those of the authors and may not represent the official position of the National Institute of Standards and Technology or the US Department of Commerce.

References

Bornn L., Shaddick, G., and Zidek J.V. (2012E "Modeling nonstationary processes through dimension expansion," *Journal of the American Statistical Association*, 107(497), 281–9.

Contento A., Chhabra T., Gardoni P., and Dierer S. (2017) "Analysis of the effects of climate change on insurance against hurricanes." In the *12th Int. Conference on Structural Safety & Reliability* (ICOSSAR2017), Vienna, Austria, August.

Contento A., Xu H., and Gardoni P. (2018) "Probabilistic formulation for climate change dependent predictions of storm surge," *Natural Hazard* (in preparation)

Dietrich J. C., Zijlema M., Westerink J. J., Holthuijsen L. H., Dawson C., Luettich R. A., Jensen R. E., Smith J. M., Stelling G. S. and Stone G. W. (2011) "Modeling hurricane waves and storm surge using integrally-coupled, scalable computations," *Coastal Engineering*, 58, 45–65

Emanuel K., Ravela S., Vivant E., and Risi C. (2006) "A statistical deterministic approach to hurricane risk assessment," *Bulletin of the American Meteorological Society*, 87(3), 299–314.

Fuglstad G.A., Simpson D., Lindgren F., and Rue H. (2015) "Does non-stationary spatial data always require non-stationary random fields?" *Spatial Statistics*, 14, 505–31.

Gardoni P., Der Kiureghian A., and Mosalam K.M. (2002). "Probabilistic capacity models and fragility estimates for RC columns based on experimental observations," ASCE *Journal of Engineering Mechanics*, 128(10), 1024–38.

Gardoni P., Murphy C., and Rowell A. eds. (2016) *Societal Risk Management of Natural Hazards*. Cham: Springer.

Hastie T., Friedman H J., and Tibshirani R. ed. (2001) *Elements of Statistical Learning*. Berlin: Springer.

IPCC (2013) "Climate change 2013: The physical science basis," *Contribution of Working Group I to the Fifth Assessment Report of the Intergovernmental Panel on Climate Change*, Stocker T.F., Qin D., Plattner G.-K., Tignor M., Allen S.K., Boschung J., Nauels A., Xia Y., Bex V. and Midgley P.M. eds., Cambridge and New York: Cambridge University Press.

Irish J.L., Resio D.T., and Ratcliff J.J. (2008) "The influence of storm size on hurricane surge," *Journal of Physical Oceanography*, 38, 2003–13.

Jarvinen B. and Lawrence M. (1985) "An evaluation of the SLOSH storm surge model," *Bulletin American Meteorological Society*, 66, 1408–11.

Jelesnianski C.P., Chen J., and Shaffer W.A. (1992) "SLOSH: Sea, Lake, and Overland Surges from Hurricanes." In: *NOAA Tech. Report NWS* 48.

Jia G. and Taflanidis A.A. (2013) "Kriging metamodeling for approximation of high-dimensional wave and surge responses in real-time storm/hurricane risk assessment." *Computer Methods in Applied Mechanics and Engineering*, 261–262, 24–38.

Jia G., Taflanidis A.A., Nadal-Caraballo N.C., Melby J.A., Kennedy A.B. and Smith J.M. (2016) "Surrogate modeling for peak or time-dependent storm surge prediction over an extended coastal region using an existing database of synthetic storms," *Natural Hazards*, 81(2), 909–38.

Johansson R. (1993) *System Modeling and Identification*. Englewood Cliffs, NJ: Prentice Hall.

Jolliffe I.T. (2002) *Principal Component Analysis*, Series: Springer Series in Statistics, 2nd ed. New York: Springer.

Kendra M.D., Xue X., Xu J., Wang N, Kolar R.L., and Geoghegan K.M. (2017) "A coupled model system for hurricanes, storm surge and coastal flooding to support community resilience planning under climate change." In the *12th Int. Conference on Structural Safety & Reliability* (ICOSSAR2017), Vienna, Austria, August.

Kim S.W., Melby J.A., Nadal-Caraballo N.C., and Ratcliff J. (2015) "A time-dependent surrogate model for storm surge prediction based on an artificial neural network using high-fidelity synthetic hurricane modeling," *Natural Hazards*, 76(1), 565–85.

Knutson T.R., Sirutis J.J., Vecchi G.A., Garner S., Zhao M., Kim H.-S., Bender M., Tuleya R.E., Held I.M., and Villarini G. (2013) "Dynamical downscaling projections of twenty-first-century Atlantic hurricane activity: CMIP3 and CMIP5 model-based scenarios," *Journal of Climate*, 26, 6591–6617.

Lee K.H. and Rosowsky D.V. (2007) "Synthetic hurricane wind speed records: Development of a database for hazard analysis and risk studies," *ASCE Natural Hazards Review*, 8(2), 23–34.

Lin N., Emanuel K., Oppenheimer M., and Vanmarcke E. (2012) "Physically based assessment of hurricane surge threat under climate change," *Nature Climate Change*, 2(6), 462–7.

Mudd L., Wang Y., Letchford C., and Rosowsky D. (2014) "Assessing climate change impact on the US East Coast hurricane hazard: Temperature, frequency, and track," *Natural Hazards Review*, 15(3), 1–11.

Murphy C., Gardoni, P., and McKim R. eds. (2018) *Climate Change and Its Impact: Risks and Inequalities.* Cham: Springer.

Resio D.T. and Westerink J.J. (2008) "Modeling the physics of storm surges," *Physics Today*, 61(9), 33–8.

Risser, M.D. and Calder C.A. (2015) "Regression-based covariance functions for nonstationary spatial modeling," *Environmetrics*, 26(4), 284–97.

Schmidt A.M., Guttorp P., and O'Hagan A. (2011) "Considering covariates in the covariance structure of spatial processes," *Environmetrics*, 22(4), 487–500.

Thompson E.F. and Cardone V.J. (1996) "Practical modeling of hurricane surface wind fields," *Journal of Waterway, Port, Coastal, and Ocean Engineering*, 122(4), 195–205.

Vanmarcke E. (2010) *Random Fields: Analysis and Synthesis.* Singapore: World Scientific.

Vickery P.J., Skerlj P.F., Steckley A.C., and Twisdale L.A. (2000a) "Hurricane wind field model for use in hurricane simulations," *ASCE Journal of Structural Engineering*, 126(10), 1203–21.

Vickery P.J., Skerlj P.F., and Twisdale L.A. (2000b) "Simulation of hurricane risk in the U.S. using empirical track model," *ASCE Journal of Structural Engineering*, 126(10), 1222–37.

Westerink J.J., Luettich R.A., Blain C.A., and Scheffner N.W. (1994) "ADCIRC: An advanced three-dimensional circulation model for shelves, coasts and estuaries." *Report 2: User's Manual for ADCIRC-2DDI*, Department of the Army, US Army Corps of Engineers.

Westerink J.J., Luettich R.A., Feyen J.C., Atkinson J.H., Dawson C., Roberts H.J., Powell M.D., Dunion J.P., Kubatko E.J., and Pourtaheri H. (2008) "A basin to channel scale unstructured grid hurricane storm surge model applied to Southern Louisiana," *Monthly Weather Review*, 136(3), 833–64.

Xu H. and Gardoni P. (2018) "Improved latent space approach for modelling non-stationary spatial–temporal random fields," *Spatial Statistics*, 23, 160–81.

Part IX

Smart cities and the role of information and communication technology in achieving sustainability and resilience

35

Exploiting smart technologies to build smart resilient cities

Emanuele Bellini and Paolo Nesi

UNIVERSITY OF FLORENCE, INFORMATION ENGINEERING DEPT., DISTRIBUTED SYSTEMS
AND INTERNET TECHNOLOGIES LAB; ITALY; EMANUELE.BELLINI@UNIFI.IT; PAOLO.NESI@UNFI.IT

35.1 Introduction

According to the United Nations Population Fund in 2014, 54 percent of the world's population were living in urban areas, which is approximately 3.3 billion people. By 2030, roughly 66 percent or 5 billion people will live in urban areas. Demand for services in urban areas is therefore increasing exponentially, and the capacity of local governments to manage this demand is challenging.

Moreover, cities are constantly competing with each other to attract new residents and businesses.[1] Between 2012 and 2013, 12 percent of US citizens (ca. 36M) moved to another city and one way to win this competition is by offering even better services to residents. Wi-Fi needs to be provided everywhere and hopefully for free. In winter climes, cities could offer information services such as where is the plow blade down, actively clearing snow? It is well known that there are apps that may help cities to find potholes, and now cities should detect problems *before* they become potholes, while they are still just cracks in the road. During disasters, situational awareness becomes essential. Smart cities are starting to enhance situational awareness by improving its sentient capacity, communication, connectivity, user interfaces, and data analytics. And, how can governments mobilize and take the initiative necessary to put all the innovative, emerging technologies to work, making cities safer, adaptive to unexpected changing conditions, and more responsive to the needs of residents? The answer is to operationalize city resilience theoretical concepts through the adoption of a systemic view able to drive a wide implementation of those enabling technologies offered by the latest Information and Communication Technology (ICT) solutions.

The fast growth of ICT has led to a widespread interconnection amongst people, which in turn has produced strong interdependencies among every human social and economic activity. In recent years, as ICT has become progressively embedded with automation solutions, the connectivity potential has rapidly extended to what is currently defined as the "Internet of Things" (Höller et al. 2014). This fact has generated numerous interdependency related phenomena, the impacts of which are most profoundly felt in most major urban areas worldwide. In fact, while such strong and large scale interdependencies enabled the pursuit of significant economic and social opportunities, they have also generated equally significant exposures to new threats, many of which remain poorly understood. Overall, the increased complexity and fast pace changing nature of urban systems are generating many emergent challenges, in the face of which most currently used management and operational practices have demonstrated many shortfalls. In particular:

a) the underspecified nature of operations in complex systems not only generates potential for unforeseeable failures and cascading effects, but it also creates unexpected opportunities for intentional and unlawful acts of disturbance;
(b) the existence of multiple and diverse sub-systems with complex, non-linear and sometimes hidden interactions, requires approaches able to cope with "unknown unknowns";
c) multiple dimensions and scales of analysis;
d) multiple stakeholders and institutions which are affected and which have different worldviews and competing opportunistic objectives.

Moreover, the global trend of smart city implementation has pushed major investments towards the deployment of smart technologies (e.g., environmental sensors, traffic sensors, public Wi-Fi) in the urban area trying to bridge the gap existing between the number of events occurred in the city and the level of awareness of the operators to manage them properly. However, even if the level of "smartness" is increased in many cities around the world making a number of events detectable (e.g., river level, pollution, wind speed, traffic flows, human movements), the actual ability of the city to prepare, respond, recover, and adapt in case of critical event, seems not to be enhanced as well. Often, examples of smart city solutions are actually examples of smart silos: areas where certain cities are particularly thriving, though they do not tie into a bigger picture. For instance Washington, DC has great water analytics; San Diego and Singapore have thousands of smart streetlights; Florence is developing IoT at city level installing a number of sensors and enhancing connectivity mostly covering the city with public Wi-Fi. All these initiatives need to be accommodated in a holistic view able to coherently drive ICT investments and deployments toward well defined goals, namely resilience and sustainability. Moreover, according to Walker and Salt (2006) the boost to efficiency and optimization of a part of a socio-eco-technical system that underline smart city implementation, for instance, fails to acknowledge secondary effects and feedbacks that cause changes in the system as a whole. Thus, while increasing efficiency is important for economic viability, when undertaken without considering the systemic response, it will not lead to sustainability but to economic collapse.

To this end, there is a call for a paradigm shift from the smart city (characterized by ICT leaded approach) to the smart resilient city (driven by the sustainable adaptability holistic view). Cities need to increase their knowledge base, and strengthening the science–policy interaction, to properly assess their current situation, the urban-regional metabolism dynamics, and to increase socio-ecological sustainability and resilience in facing global challenges. The transition from smart city to smart resilient city requires a transdisciplinary, complex, and systemic view, new strategies, decision support systems and frameworks, methodologies, tools, and evaluation procedures for multi-level governance; as well as the integration of risk-management, mitigation and adaptation, within a self-adaptive, pro-active, and participatory frame.

35.2 Smart resilient cities

The analysis of urban resilience is currently an open research field, for which there is no consensus or mainstreamed approach yet (Meerow et al. 2016); it is thereby necessary to build new conceptual approaches, rethinking the principles of urban resilience including ontological, epistemological, methodological, and axiological assumptions. The notion of "resilience thinking" (Walker & Salt 2006) offers a different way of understanding the world and a new approach to managing resources. It embraces human and natural systems as complex entities continually adapting through cycles of change, and seeks to understand the qualities of a system that must be maintained or enhanced in order to achieve sustainability. It explains why greater efficiency by itself cannot solve resource problems and offers a constructive alternative that opens up options rather than closing them down. Resilience is rapidly emerging as a viable path towards successfully coping with the complexity of the challenges faced by urban areas. According to Linkov et al. (2018), it has become prevalent among scientists, engineers, and policymakers in various socio-ecological fields (e.g., ecology, urban planning, flood protection, drought management) and across public domains (e.g., city managers, state, regional, and federal officials).

In fact, there are a number definitions related to resilience covering different disciplines and subjects (Gunderson et al. 2002; Jackson 2010; Vugrin et al. 2010; Boin et al. 2010; Cimellaro et al. 2010). In particular, resilience has emerged as an attractive perspective with respect to cities, often theorized as highly complex, adaptive systems (Batty 2008; Godschalk 2003).

The model of the adaptive cycle in urban context is derived from the panarchy theory (Holling et al. 2002) grounded on dynamics of ecosystems. In Harmon et al. (2013), it is an explicit reference to panarchic city – the dynamic set of urban adaptive cycles – that evolve, irreversibly and uniquely, as it adapts to new demands, disturbances, and crisis. Adaptive cycles are nested in a hierarchy across time and space which helps explain how adaptive systems can generate novel recombination that are tested during longer periods of capital accumulation and storage.

Thus, if a city is no longer considered to be a system that should perpetuate in a state of dynamic equilibrium, but rather a panarchy of urban adaptive cycles, which may descend into disequilibrium, then the city needs to be considered stochastic, unstable, and unpredictable (Harmon et al. 2011) by nature. Thus a measure of resilience must be in direct relation with how a system performs, and how capable it is in monitoring and controlling performance throughout a given period and in view of system purposes. In this sense, Hollnagel and Woods (2006) consider that only the potential (adaptive capacity) for resilience can be measured and not resilience itself. In fact the notion of city operation safety boundaries needed to define metrics, tends to be only metaphorical and thus, measuring a "deviation" between city operations and such limits becomes unrealistic.

The potential for urban resilience is expressed by the types and levels of resources that a system can secure and how it is able to allocate for sustaining urban adaptive cycle. Resources are by nature finite and no system (or sub-system) is self-sufficient in the pursuit of its purposes, even more in the face of continuous and ever changing operational pressures. The urban adaptability is targeted at both expected and unexpected system variability. Therefore, guidance as to what capabilities and how much is needed can be offered by foremost understanding and assessing the sources of operational variability in the system.

The direction towards the adaptive capacity concepts for urban resilience is also supported by the literature. In fact, according to Meerow et al. (2016) more than half of the urban resilience definitions retrieved in the their review, associate generic adaptability, flexibility, or adaptive capacity concepts to urban resilience.

In Hollnagel and Woods (2006) are highlighted three characteristics as fundamental capabilities of a resilient system. These characteristics are aligned with the three conditions of resilient situations approached by Westrum (2006):

- Being prepared provides the ability to avoid something bad from happening.
- Being flexible becomes fundamental to ensure survival under varying conditions and degraded modes.
- Being adaptive supports quick recovery from disruptions to regain desired performance.

Thus in the present work, we combine the holistic definition provided by the 100 Resilient Cities (100RC) – pioneered by The Rockefeller Foundation: "the capacity of individuals, communities, institutions, businesses, and systems within a city to survive, adapt, and grow no matter what kinds of chronic stresses and acute shocks they experience" with that derived from the Resilience Engineering domain: "the intrinsic ability of a system or organization to adjust its functioning prior to, during, or following changes, disturbances, and opportunities so that it can sustain required operations under both expected and unexpected conditions" (Hollnagel 2009). In fact the 100RC resilience definition not only addresses the impact of acute shocks, but also of chronic stresses, and identifies the multi-scalar nature of urban resilience as resting on capacity existing at a range of levels from individuals to macro systems (Flax et al. 2016). This aspect matches the resilience engineering perspective that considers the capability of adjusting its functioning on changing conditions (thus in both acute and chronic/daily stress) a key ability of a resilient system.

Moreover, in line with the resilience engineering approach, the potential for resilience to emerge from system performance is assessed based on the "four resilience cornerstones" (Hollnagel 2009):

- Knowing what to do (Respond)
- Knowing what to look for (Monitor)
- Knowing what to expect (Anticipate)
- Knowing what has happened (Learn).

Resilience is thus focused on sustaining the capacity of a complex system to adapt in the presence of continuous change. Generating, maintaining, and deploying adaptability processes rely upon the allocation of a wide range of resources and at many different system levels and time scales.

As such, adaptive capacities (see Figure 35.1) are intrinsically related to the level of resources that a system can allocate and its ability to manage these resources to sustain specific adaptive cycles.

Sustaining this adaptability requires overall enhanced operational efficiency, mainly by optimizing the allocation and utilization of available resources (organizational technical and human), whilst striving to continuously minimize incidents, accidents, and other operational failures. Within this context, resilience can be seen as an emergent property of a complex system and it is about managing high variability and uncertainty in order to continuously pursue successful performance of a system. Understanding the sources of operational variability, the mechanisms through which it may potentially propagate and the impact on the system performance, the resources and system capacities needed to manage and cope with operational variability, are the main ability of a resilient system. Thus rather than targeting continuous economic and financial growth of businesses and or ICT deployment, cities should develop the ability to continuously adjust to ever-changing operational environments. This can be performed by orienting the smart city trend towards those enabling technologies capable of enhancing the adaptive capacities of a city.

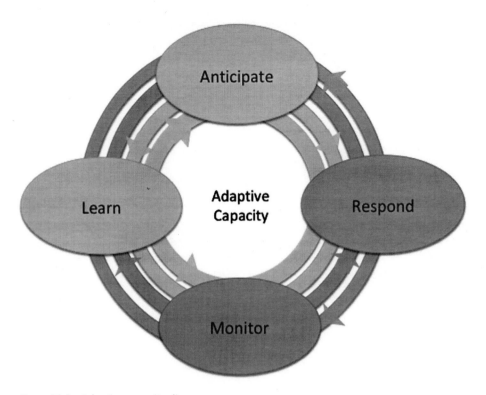

Figure 35.1 Adaptive capacity diagram.

35.2.1 Capacity building

There is a consensus around the importance of generating system capacities towards enhanced adaptability and on the fact that such capacities must be based on a more flexible management of available resources. The growing presence of technology at every system level pushed by the smart city trend, which is in turn supported by the Internet of Everything (IoE) propagation, renders Knowledge-Information-Data (KID) to generate one of the most critical resources and therefore, one of the key factors to be considered when addressing urban planning and resilience (Martelli & Bellini 2013). According to Lea (2017) smart city technologies can be grouped as:

Network and communications: The complexity of smart city technological and services ecosystems requires a holistic approach to networking and communications that offers support for a number of needs, from infrastructure monitoring to backbones for digital media enterprises and from household security to citywide transportation monitoring. These diverse needs require a mix of technologies ranging from low bandwidth wireless technologies (Bluetooth LE and ZigBee Low Power WAN) that use an unlicensed spectrum and focus on low power and cost, to dedicated fiber optics for backbone needs.

Internet of Things: City infrastructures are now being connected using open standard protocols such as IP and HTTP, and made accessible through web technologies such as REST call. Lower "hookup" costs are allowing the sensing to expand to more parts of the city infrastructure and enabling higher fidelity sensing. This allows a deep pervasiveness of monitoring systems implementing a true cyber-physical urban environment.

Cloud computing: Cloud computing is acting a key role in smart city implementation affecting the way cities manage and deliver services. Cloud computing, defined generally as the delivery of computing as a service, has offered organizations such as cities ways to reduce costs and increase efficiency. Due to legal and privacy concerns, cities have been reluctant to exploit the full benefits of public cloud services for core services, but many have used private cloud services and some have experimented with public/private or a hybrid cloud infrastructure.

Open data: Open data are related to government transparency that encourages public agencies to release data sets and make them freely accessible also to third parties. The evolution of open data represents a broadening of the information available related to city operations. There are several methods and formats (Excel, CSV, RDF, etc.) classified in stars by W3C to open these data. Indeed adopting the W3C 5 stars (maximum openness) approach means to make data available through open standards and link these data to others (Linked Open Data).

Big data: Smart cities continuously generate an impressive amounts of data in their daily operation. Mostly of them are in real time. These data exhibit high volume, velocity, and extreme heterogeneity in its sources, formats, and characteristics (variability). The technologies that capture, manage, and analyze big data are now based on cloud computing coupled with technologies like Hadoop/HDFS, Spark, Hive, and a plethora of proprietary tools.

In Table 35.1, the role of the smart technologies in developing adaptive capacities in a Smart Resilient City is reported:

Thanks to the adoption of smart ICT, the adaptive capacity (potential for resilience) of the urban system can be enhanced (Bellini et al. 2017a). Now it is possible to support decision makers in taking informed decisions, improving the availability, granularity, quality, comprehensiveness, and precision of the KID. Moreover, the citizens can now be reached through a 4R communication strategy (right person, at the right time, in the right place, with the right message) thanks to the pervasiveness of the smart technologies.

Thus decisions can be immediately translated in actions, while the feedback about the effects can immediately be detected through sensors and social media, so that adjustments aiming to reduce unwanted variability (e.g., people escaping in a wrong direction) can be actuated in time. Such a fast control loop, enabled by smart technologies and KID, may sustain the Evidence Driven Adaptive Cycle at city level.

35.3 Data strategy to sustain evidence driven adaptive cycle

However, the success of the data-driven approach is reliant upon the quality of the data gathered avoiding the risk of being overwhelmed and getting lost in the noise and hype of surrounding data. Thus in order to implement such an approach the following steps have been identified and accomplished:

(1) **Identify decision makers' informative needs to manage resilience:** By working out exactly what is needed to be known, focus can be on the data that is really needed. The data requirements, cost and stress levels are massively reduced when moving from "collect everything just in case" to "collect and measure x and y to answer questions z."

2) **Selecting/producing (big) data able to address the decision makers' informative needs to manage resilience:** Cities are generating tons of data and there is the risk of being overwhelmed and getting lost in the noise and hype of surrounding data. Starting with a strategy helps decision makers to ignore the hype and cut to what is going to make a difference for *resilience management*. Thus, instead of collecting everything "just in case" and/or considering data as given, it is necessary to start with what system aims to achieve.

Table 35.1 System capacity enhancement enabled by ICT

Capacity	Actions enabled by ICT
ANTICIPATE (knowing what to expect)	• Support resource allocation optimization • Appling ex-ante predictive analytics based on Big Data • Planning activities and restructuring on the basis of Big Data analytics • Continuously supporting the assessment of vulnerability and identifying when the system operates nearer to safety boundaries, • Predicting behaviours and event dynamics, • Supporting evidence based decisions at strategic, tactic and operation level, • Covering urban areas with multiple communication channels (Wi-Fi, 5/4/3G, LoRaWAN, etc.)
MONITOR (knowing what to looking for)	• Knowing how other operators are operating in normal and emergency status. • Detecting disruptions just when they occur with social media and sensors. • Turn citizens into proactive sensors with mobile devices • Improving the granularity and breadth of knowledge and awareness about the system status and dynamics using IoT, • Continuously collecting and processing RT data and Open Data from heterogeneous data sources/streams and sensors and aggregating them into a Big Data storage. • Early warning on the basis of anomaly detection models • Defining real time computable metrics
RESPOND (knowing what to do)	• Quickly getting a reliable overview of the disruptive situation through real time sensors and multimedia user (citizens/operators) reporting • Coordinate emergency respond through real time data sharing among operators • Supporting citizens as well as operators in their opportunistic decisions with mobile technologies • Delivering personalized, real time, context aware, and ubiquitous advices to the community; • Supporting reaction calculating possible activities and priorities to recover by simulation and on the basis of Big Data
LEARN (knowing what has happened)	• Applying advanced ex-post analysis on Big Data (e.g., identifying metrics and indicators which may allow you to set up of predictive models and models for early warning and/or anomaly detection and/or selecting suitable reactions; the data analytics performed by using statistic or machine learning approaches);

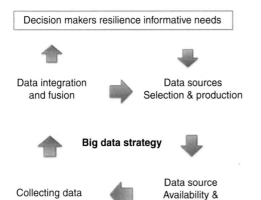

Figure 35.2 Big data management cycle for evidence driven adaptive cycle.

It's really important to understand that no data is inherently better or more valuable than others, in general. Moreover, the selection should not be stuck only on what is currently available. The missing data required to implement the strategy should be produced. In fact, the focus should be on those data that best fits the purpose: the data that could help answering the most pressing questions and deliver on strategic objectives.

3) **Identify (big) data availability and accessibility:** Once the data needed have been identified, it is necessary to start looking for online open datasets. If some critical datasets are not released with open license, specific agreement with the data providers should be put in place. For instance data generated within public utilities (energy, water, gas, etc.) like the GIS based pipeline positions or the operations data may be covered by security policy.

4) **Collecting data:** The kind of data needed to support resilience are very diverse and could be Open as well as Private, Static, and Real time data. Such complexity cannot be reduced and needs to be addressed through the implementation of tailored harvesting processes.

5) **Data integration and fusion:** In order to manage resilience, it is not only necessary to have a strategy but also an idea of what a city is, what are its entities and relationships. Adopting an ontology to model a city, the risk and resilience concepts represents a strong but necessary assumption that can reduce the risk of getting lost in the data.

35.3.1 Identify decision makers' informative needs to manage resilience

The Data-driven Resilience management starts by collecting the knowledge and informative needs of city operators (fire brigades, civil protection, mobility operators, etc.). A number of focus groups and workshops organized around critical scenarios (flash flooding, big floods, traffic jam, car accidents, large yards, etc.) have been organized to elicit the explicit and implicit operator knowledge about how the system works "*as imagined*" compared with the actual performance during the emergency (work-as done). The results of the work have identified several criticalities (Bellini et al. 2017b) that can be mitigated if some of the daily decisions taken by the operators are improved in terms of efficiency (timing, resource allocated, etc.) and effectiveness.

Most of these decisions require a rich and comprehensive informative layer behind to be reliable and produce a positive impact at systemic level. In particular analyzing scenarios like water bomb, yards, river and flash flooding, and bomb attack, emerged the need of managing static as well a dynamic/real time information to cope with unexpected events and support better decisions. Moreover, the zoom needs to be dynamically tuned according to the magnitude and geographical extension of the event avoiding any loss in data granularity and quality.

35.3.2 Identify the (big) data able to address the decision makers' informative needs to manage resilience

According to the informative stakeholder needs and strategy defined (bridging knowledge, alignment, and effect gaps) several class of datasets have been identified that can be exploited to enhance situational awareness and system resilience as a whole. In Tables 35.2 and 35.3, the datasets identified able to support event contextualization according to the operators requirements and specific informative needs to enhance the quality of the operator decisions have been mapped. Contextual information includes data needed to frame the context and that are useful for all kind of decision makers (cross-operators common information).

Table 35.2 Contextual information need

Contextual Information	Dataset
Geographic based city structure/entities	• streets and related civic numbers
	• street directions, type
	• squares
	• pedestrian areas
	• building
	• green areas
	• services
	• cycle paths
	• admission areas
	• waiting areas
	• gathering areas
Passengers/ civilians: position, number	• traffic flow sensors position
	• traffic flow sensors Real Time
	• people presence detection sensors Real Time
Weather information and alerting	• local weather forecast
	• civil protection alerting
Risk Maps	• GIS based (hydrogeological, seismic, etc.) risk maps
	• Flooding susceptibility areas
News/event (planned and unplanned) updates:	• Public events in the city – Real Time (e.g. exhibitions)
Traffic information (public transport)	• Traffic lights
	• UTC traffic lights
	• Tram traffic lights
	• Limited traffic area,
	• controlled Parking Zones
	• covered parking description
	• covered parking free place
	• traffic flow sensors position
	• traffic flow sensors data
	• mobility events (incidents)

The main challenges here is to understand what information and data are generated in the city making an extended recognition across multiple institution and organizations acting in the city such as mobility operators, energy operators, ambulance operators, fire brigades, civil protection etc.

35.3.3 Identify (big) data actual availability and accessibility

Information and data sources can be official and unofficial. Official information/data are those made available by institutions and organizations like city council, public transport operators, private transport operators, civil protection organizations, etc. Some of these datasets are available in Open Data according to e-gov trends while others that are more sensitive (e.g., position of the people on the ground) require specific agreements between the data owner/provider and the data aggregator (for instance www.km4cityaggregator, adopted in H2020-RESOLUTE European project www.resolute-eu.org). In particular, such agreements define reusability licenses, data privacy and security constraints, the commitment of owners in making data available according to a Service Level Agreement (SLA), etc. However, not all the data useful for

Table 35.3 Specific information needs

Specific Information needs	Datasets (IoT, Social media, GIS, etc.)
Magnitude and dynamic of the event	• anemometers lat/long &measure
	• rainfall lat/long & measure
	• hydrometers lat/long &measure
	• hygrometry lat/long &measure
	• twitter dedicated channel for user reporting
	• seismic sensors measurement
Real time impact estimation	• # of people present on the ground and close to the event
	• # of vehicles present on the ground and close to the event
	• People behaviour (direction movement) RT
	• Underpasses status – RT
	• Services status (e.g. open/close) – RT
	• Presences at school – RT
Number of qualified operators available	• # of volunteers available in RT
	• # of operators engaged
Means availability	• Triage – emergency rooms status RT
	• # of civil protection vehicles available
	• # of ambulances available in RT
	• # free parking
Critical Event prediction	• weather forecast
	• people present on the ground trend & forecast
	• river basin level trend & forecast
Energy supply status.	• planned maintenance schedule
	• Outage status – RT
Alternative transport means	• tramway map, schedule, position RT
	• taxi stops and positions RT
Position and behaviour dynamics of the people in the city	• covered parking description
	• traffic flow sensors position
	• traffic flow sensors data
	• people presence detection sensors
	• local public transport
	• variable message signs position
	• variable message signs status
	• Information related to Civil Protection (via Social Channels: Twitter)
	• Civil Protection Alert Messages
	• Wi-Fi connected devices
People sentiment/reports	• Twitter data (Natural Language Processing/Sentiment Analysis)

supporting informed decisions can be accessible because of business or security constraints; the data are not available in a digital and shareable format, etc. For instance, private organizations consider their data as a strategic asset for their business and tend to avoid sharing them. In other cases (e.g., critical infrastructures), data are covered by national security constraints (e.g., the energy network topology) and could be accessed only though public organizations like city council or civil protection.

This means that a specific political mandate needs to be assigned to the data aggregator in order to properly operate.

Unofficial data are generated by channels like social media that have an impressive message distribution speed. They can be detected and used to integrate official information sources.

Table 35.4 Metadata model for dataset survey

Field	Description
Name/ID	Name/ID associated to the dataset
Type:	Category, one or more taxonomy voices. It is useful to classify the datasets in an easy way.
Description	A free text to describe the content of the dataset
Dynamic	Field to classify the datasets as: static, periodic, real time
Frequency update period	It is connected to the 'Dataset dynamic' field and regards the frequency update period of the dataset. Specifying the unit measure (s, min, h, day, etc.)
Date	Date time of the dataset (in case of static or periodic)
Format	Format of the file related to the dataset (csv, html, JSON, SHP, XML, SOAP, etc.)
Data Provider	Name/URL related to who (Authority, Municipality, other Private/public provider, etc.) provide the dataset
Dataset URI	Actionable URI in which the dataset is available
Data fields description	Description of each field in case of tabular datasets
License/Condition	**License** of use (CC-By, etc.)

Unofficial data are usually highly available (e.g., Twitter data) through some given methods (APIs).

However, in order to better understand data availability, a preliminary survey using a dedicated metadata model is necessary. The fields are described in the Table 35.4:

35.3.4 Data collection

In general, all big data solutions must cope with data volume, variety, and veracity. Most of the big data problems connected to the (smart) city platform for resilience monitoring are related to real time data (e.g. vehicle and human mobility, energy consumption, IOT, etc.). The city level architecture should be capable of taking advantage of huge amount of data coming from several domains, at different generation rates for exploiting and analyzing them for computing integrated and multi domain information, making predictions, detecting anomalies for early warning, and for producing suggestions and recommendations to city users and operators. The RESOLUTE platform is a three-layer architecture model capable of managing such a complexity. It is organized as follows:

- The *big data management layer*, or data services layer, deals with data acquisition, aggregation, and fusion from various sources acting in the smart city. It addresses the computational and heterogeneity challenges of multi-source data collection and integration. It is decoupled respect to the upper level of the system making the data available in a standardized way to the applications.
- The *mission critical layer* consists of core system intelligence. This is the layer where developers can solve mission-critical business problems, enabling data sharing among sub-systems and achieving major productivity advantages. These components can be used to enforce business rules, such as business algorithms and legal or governmental regulations, and data rules, which are designed to keep the data structures consistent. This layer consumes the data aggregated and standardized by the lower level.
- The *presentation layer*, or user services layer, gives a user access to the application. This layer presents the results of the data analysis to multiple users through the resilience dashboard

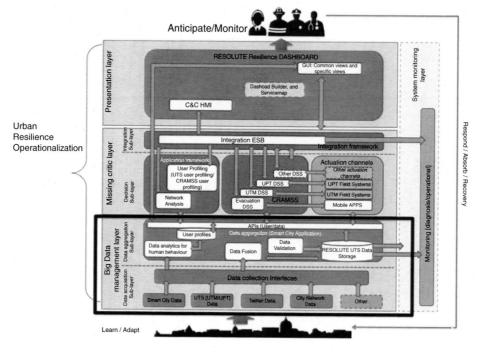

Figure 35.3 RESOLUTE platform.

and optionally permits data manipulation and data entry. The two main types of user inter-face for this layer are the traditional application and the web-based application.

Ingesting data issues from different kinds of sources can be partially solved by using spe-cific reconciliation processes to make these data interoperable with others ingested. Dataset transformation is necessary to realize the harmonization and the quality improvement of the datasets. To better understand this aspect, the following categories of data have been identified:

Smart city data: this consists of a collection of open and private data coming from the city and territory. The major part of this kind of information is published by governmental organizations as open data, in different file formats such as html, xml, csv, shp, etc., and typically provides information that may present links to web resources. Moreover, the information is usually static, but can also be distributed in real time or semi-real time modality (e.g. number of visitors in a museum, city tours that start at a specific time and make a guided visit of the city, weather forecasts for different municipalities, events in the city, etc.).

UTS (UTM/UTP) data: it consists of a collection of a wide set of data regarding mobility and transport aspects in a smart city. In particular:

- Intelligent Transportation Systems, ITS, for bus/train/ferry/tram/etc., management.
- Public Transport plans and real time status
- Traffic flows, people flows
- Parking, car sharing, movements of public vehicles, …
- etc.

City network data: represent a set of data coming from mobile network to calculate origin destination matrices, extrapolation on larger areas, etc. This kind of channel, in a smart city context, it is fundamental to take care of the people/citizen's presence and needs. It can be useful to receive real time information coming from:

- Cellular data collected from the mobile operators, that may collect data about the number of people connected to a quite large area in the city. The authorized amplitude of the telecommunication cell for monitoring is in the order of 1000 mt, and is thus too large for extracting detailed information about city user movement in medium and small cities; it can be used to understand wider movements.
- The Wi-Fi or sensors networks having information related to citizens' habits, collecting their activities and those that are fundamental. For example to study citizens' flows, to establish what are the citizens' preferred services, what can be improved for them, to collect their ideas and necessities, etc.
- Special apps that can be used to track user behaviour and to perform measures on the city such as *"Firenze dove cosa.."* in Florence are available on all devices. In this case, monitoring may be performed only on the population who have installed the "city app." The benefit would be to have a diffuse coverage and dense measurement.

Twitter data: data streams from Twitter will be collected and analyzed through the creation of dedicated thematic channels, which can be tuned to monitor one or more search queries on Twitter with a sophisticated and expressive syntax. The Twitter data module is realized thanks to the use of the following tools, already developed and at disposal for the RESOLUTE project:

- Twitter Vigilance (www.disit.org/tv): this continuously operates in two different working modalities at the same time (offline and real time www.disir.org/rttv). In the former mode, it accumulates Twitter data and performs different types of analysis, such as statistics and trends about messages and users, Natural Language Processing (NLP) and Sentiment Analysis (SA) of text messages, in order to provide analysis results, temporal trends and statistics (at level of channel and search, users etc.), sentiment polarity at channel and search level for keywords, adjectives, and verbs. In the latter mode, this component will perform a real-time analysis (both statistics/trends and NLP-SA) on specifically defined channels, in order to monitor and detect critical conditions and providing alert signals or other type of actions, suggestions, etc.
- Twitter Vigilance Real Time, allows a real time analysis of sentiments, trends, etc. in order to detect immediately if something is going wrong.
- Twitter Sensing Module for Evacuation DSS: sensing Twitter continuously to detect anomaly or emergency situations. The data collected are displayed as graphs using the k-partite method and the force directed method creating visual clusters where further analysis can be applied. For instance, root cause analysis of abnormal phenomena can be performed and/or even anomaly detection.

35.3.5 Data integration and fusion

In general, all smart city solutions must cope with big data related issues (Bellini et al. 2013) in particular in relation to their meanings.

A Semantic Aggregator and Reasoner (Figure 35.4) collects data and services from the data sources, to aggregate and integrate them in a unified and semantically interoperable model based on a multi-domain ontology. This approach allows re-conciling data and

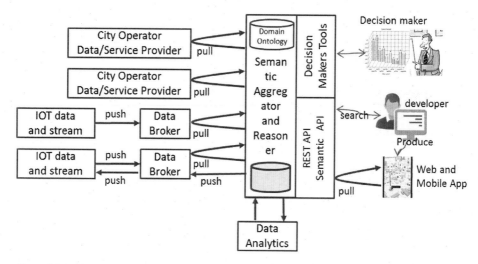

Figure 35.4 Data integration schema.

exploiting a coherent model to reduce errors, integrating data representing the same concept and coming from different structures, operators, and sources. The ontology can be used by the semantic aggregator to model city domains entities and their relationships. The usage of a multi-domain ontology allows the adoption of a model representing relationships of specialization among classes and relationships, aggregation, association, and similarity, that enable the inferential processes in the RDF Graph Database (Kotoulas et al. 2014; Bellini et al. 2014). Thus, the obtained knowledge base can be used for creating strategies for data quality improvement and for setting up algorithms and reasoning about several aspects and services belonging to multiple domains (prediction, early warning, etc.). Some solutions fit to this case: CitySDK[2] partially covering all features has been developed in an EC project involving major cities and providing specific REST API and grounded on OASC (Open & Agile Smart Cities) adopted the FIWARE NGSI API agnostic model;[3] and more widely covering features Km4City (Bellini et al. 2014b) exploited by Sii-Mobility Smart City project, providing Smarty City API of Km4City (Bellini et al. 2014b), and SPUD proposed by IBM in (Kotoulas et al. 2014) exploiting commercial non-open solutions via a non-accessible ontology. These kinds of solutions need mapping tools from data to ontology and to support reconciliation as performed by DataLift in (Scharffe et al. 2012) and by Km4City in Bellini et al. (2014). In both cases, vocabularies, algorithms, and dedicated languages have been used, as SILK (Jentzsch et al. 2010).

In order to create an ontology to support city resilience, a large number of data sets have been analyzed. The results of the analysis allowed to create an integrated ontological model comprise six main areas of macroclasses as depicted in Figure 35.5.

- *Administration*: includes classes related to the structuring of the general public administrations, namely PA, and its specifications, Municipality, Province and Region; also includes the class Resolution, which represents the ordinance resolutions issued by each administration that may change the traffic stream.
- *Street-guide*: formed by entities as Road, Node, RoadElement, etc., it is used to represent the entire road system of Tuscany, including the permitted maneuvers and rules of access to

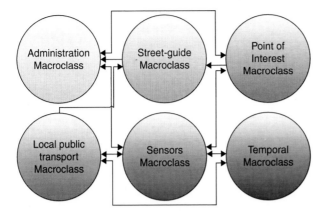

Figure 35.5 Km4City ontology macroclasses.

limited traffic zones. In this case, OTN vocabulary has been exploited to model traffic that is more or less a direct encoding of GDF (Geographic Data Files) in OWL.

- *Point of Interest*: includes all services, activities, which may be useful to the citizen who may have the need to seek and find them. In addition, this macro segment of the ontology may take advantage of reusing the Good Relation model of commercial offers.[4]
- *Local public transport*: includes data related to major TPL (Transport Public Local) companies' scheduled times, the rail graph, and data relating to real time passage at bus stops.
- *Sensors*: macroclass concerns data from sensors: ambient, weather, traffic flow, pollution, etc.
- *Temporal*: macroclass that puts concepts related to time (time intervals and instants) into the ontology, to associate a timeline to recorded events and to make forecasts. It may take advantage from time ontologies such as OWL-Time.

35.4 Ontology extension with resilience-related concepts

This generic structure has been extended with concepts dedicated to model risk and resilience at city level. The objective was to design a model able to support real time computing (queries) and to extract information related to the amount of damage occurring in a given urban area during an event whose magnitude is measured by georeferenced sensors. The impact is calculated considering different kinds of city asset exposers (services, assets, people, etc.) and their status (open/close, presence/absence, etc.) at the time of the event.

It is well known that the product of vulnerability for the value of the element exposed allows us to calculate the potential damage expected in relation to a critical event with a certain intensity/magnitude. The vulnerability depends on the type of asset, its location, its physical characteristics (materials, design), the threats considered. The value of the asset is dynamic and depends on its functionality in a certain instant t (presence of the people in a specific area), and may have an economic and/or social value.

The extention created models such aspects to allows a more precise estimation of the damage/disruption during an event (real time) or through simulated scenarions.

The operator can then make timely decisions in emergency or in planning phase regarding priorities for action in order to safeguard the security of goods and people involved, while

699

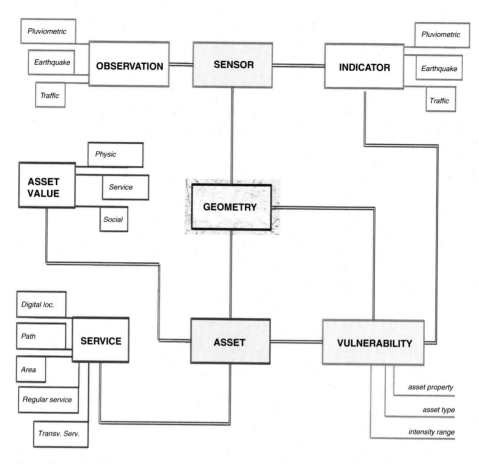

Figure 35.6 KM4City ontology extension for impact analysis.

simultaneously studying such areas that have greater potential harm to the occurrence of an event in order to implement preventive policies.

- **Observation** corresponding to class modeling sensor observations such as measurements;
  - *EarthQuakeObservation, PluviometricObservation, TrafficObservation* as subclass of km4city: Observation, created to catalog instances of observations received from the sensors;
- **Service (in KM4City)**, which catalogs the surveyed services in km4city
- **Geometry**: The GIS ontology[5] has been also used for the Geometry class, useful to catalog areas and points. A geometry is associated to a sensor to define its position.
- **Asset:** This class models the main elements considered in the city such as services, people, infrastructures, etc.
- **AssetValue:** models the values of the assets that can be expressed through a specific unit of measure (e.g. currency). It can be *PhysicAssetValue* used to model economic values/ importance for the population related to business/physical asset; *ServiceAssetValue* used to model economic values/importance for the population related to the type of service; *SocialAssetValue* to model the value and/or the social importance related to asset/service.

- **Vulnerability** to model the vulnerability values of assets; the vulnerability values are characterized by the following features:
  - it has a geographical area defined;
  - it is associated to an asset;
  - it is linked to a type of indicator.
- **Indicator** This class models a sensor indicator, and offers insight on what the sensor observes.

Through these classes it is possibile to study or monitor scenarios associated with each sensor in one or more geographic regions. The sensor observations will be used to estimate the damage occurring to the assets within these regions.

35.4.1 Data integration process phases

1. *Quality Improvement (QI)*: this is fundamental because the datasets ingested can contain a set of different errors and inaccuracies considering the following aspects: completeness, consistency, accuracy, absence of duplication, integrity, etc.
2. *Reconciliation:* this task solves the lack of coherence among indexed entities referring to the same concept but coming from different data sets. Entities may present a mismatch in semantics on names of the elements, dates, GPS coordinates, emails, telephone numbers, area codes, etc..
3. *Triple generation and aggregation*: this phase generates RDF triples that are stored in RESOLUTE Semantic Data Storage based on a model built on relationships defined within the City Ontology (which will be realized starting from the multi-domain and Open Source Ontology Km4City, www.disit.org/6506).
4. *Data validation:* this is created to apply validation and verification techniques that allow checking the correctness and consistencies of the system and its data. Given the complexity of structure implemented for each dataset, a SPARQL based validation of the triples has been performed, to verify that the realized RDF stored is well-formed.
5. *Dataset load/indexing into the knowledge base*: this loads the RDF triples on the RESOLUTE storage.

After these kinds of processes, the data enriched and aggregated is available though dedicated APIs, decoupling the data management from the data analysis.

Scenario analysis: Smart City vs Smart Resilient City
According to the Scenario Based Design technique (Carroll 1995) and with the support of domain experts, a comparison is conceived between the Smart City and Smart Resilient City on the capacity to respond in face of a critical event: flash flooding. Flash flooding is an extreme event that is going to be even more frequent in Florence because of climate changes.

The main characteristics of the flash flooding scenario are:

a) Impossibility to identify exactly the areas involved
b) Extremely intensity of rainfall
c) Abrupt reduction of temperature and visibility
d) Sudden rising of water on roads, underpasses, etc.

Table 35.5 analyzes how a smart city may support the emergency management with respect to a smart resilient city.

Table 35.5 Smart City vs Smart Resilient City Scenario analysis

Timeline	Smart City	Smart Resilient City
Flash Flooding Event Starting	Detection, by the rain gauge sensor, of the rapid increase in falling rain Rain gauge data visualization in the city council information system department.	Detection, by the rain gauge sensor, of the rapid increase in falling rain Rain gauge data visualization on the resilience dashboard via a geographic map that will indicate the area affected by the event, the vulnerabilities, the assets affected, the presence of the people Information enriched by social medial analysis tuned on dedicated channels Information shared with all operators in real time
Situational awareness enriched by people reporting (with mobile app) to the Civil Protection and fire brigades	Reports collected by Civil protection and fire brigades through their own channels.	Reports collected by Civil protection and fire brigades through their own channels and shared with the other operators in real time.
The rapid increase in falling rain causes a slowdown in traffic in the affected and adjacent areas.	UTM DSS system detects this condition and inform the mobility department that apply a pre-calculated mobility strategy that may include the closure of a part of the road network near the affected area, the modification of local road traffic (driving directions, traffic lights, etc.), as well as the publication of messages on the PMV to inform the population	UTM DSS system detects this condition and share the messages of the traffic events to all the city operators (civil protection, fire brigades, urban police, etc.), applies a pre-calculated mobility strategy, inform the population with the PMV and share all these actions among all the other operators.
The event affects the tramline operation	On the base of the few information available, the tramline operator decide to suspend the operation to protect its infrastructure/service.	On the base of the information available, the tram operator decides to degrade the services (instead of suspending it) since the actual magnitude of the event and the amount of people in the affected areas call for this decision. This action is displayed on the resilience dashboards.
Underpasses affected	Water sensor detects a water level over the safe threshold. No alerting is timely propagated because of the information is not directly managed by first responders.	Water sensor detects a water level over the safe threshold. Since local Police has a direct access to this information, sends units in the affected area to monitor the situation and to empty the underpasses
First responders send units to the most affected areas to aid population.	Operators do not properly staffed respect to the actual magnitude of the event, the status of the assets affected, the presence of other operators in the area. Need to wait more resources on the base of the reports provided by the operators arrived in the affected area.	Thanks to the data integration and sharing, operators are properly staffed respect to the actual magnitude of the event, to the status of the assets affected, to the presence of other operators in the area. Aid can be immediately provided.

Table 35.5 (Cont.)

Timeline	Smart City	Smart Resilient City
Local Police officers, present in the event area, send information about the traffic status and updates the Local Police DSS.		Local Police reports are shared among the other operators
People should be evacuated	Sms, telephone calls are sent to the citizens. The presence of first responders is needed to guide the evacuation.	Evacuation DSS, based on the status of the event propose an evacuation plan and send the evacuation path to be displayed on a map on the mobile application. People are enabled to save by themselves Evacuation paths are shared with all operators
Event concluded		Ex-post data analysis to identify aspects to be improved in the city to mitigate the impact of future events.

According to this analysis, the adoption of a resilient perspective in a smart city, allows a better exploitation of the smart technologies enhancing the capacity of the city to respond to critical events through knowledge, information, and data (KID) extraction and sharing according to a specific strategy.

35.5 Conclusions

The present chapter discussed how application of smart technologies (multiple communication networks as WiFi, Bluetooth, LTE, Smart Sensors, etc.) guided by a holistic view of urban resilience, is able to sustain the city adaptive cycle needed to cope with emerging threats (e.g. climate changes).

There is a call to move from the smart city to the smart resilient city paradigm, looking beyond the simple smart technology deployment. In this regard "Resilience thinking" offers a different way of understanding the city and a new approach to managing resources including ICT. It embraces urban systems as complex entities continually adapting through cycles of change (panarchy), and seeks to understand the qualities of a system that must be maintained or enhanced in order to achieve sustainability (Walker & Salt 2006). In this view the role of smart technologies and big data is crucial in developing the four adaptive capacities (anticipate, respond, monitor, learn) needed to sustain the Evidence Drive Adaptive Cycle of a city.

The analysis of a scenario of a critical event (flash flooding) offered us the opportunity to compare two different contexts: where smart technologies are deployed without a global strategy for resilience and where such a strategy governs smart technology implementation. The result shows that smart technologies combined with a global strategy for resilience can be more effective and valuable providing benefit at systemic level.

Thus the possibility of knowing when the event occurs, its magnitude, where people are concentrated in a specific moment, their behaviour as well as the possibility to reach them collectively or personally, every time, everywhere, with tailored information, if properly governed with a urban resilience holistic view, enhances decision makers in taking informed and coherent decisions to achieve the common goal of resilience and sustainability.

Notes

1 https://content.extremenetworks.com/extreme-networks-blog/the-very-latest-smart-city-trends-2
2 www.citysdk.eu/
3 http://oascities.org/
4 www.heppnetz.de/projects/goodrelations/
5 www.opengeospatial.org/standards/geosparql

References

Batty, M. (2008) "The size, scale, and shape of cities," *Science*, 319(5864), 769–71.

Bellini, E., Nesi, P., Pantaleo, G., and Venturi, A. (2016) Functional resonance analysis method based-decision support tool for urban transport system resilience management. In *Smart Cities Conference* (ISC2), *IEEE International*, September (pp. 1–7).

Bellini, E., Ceravolo P., and Nesi P. (2017a) Quantify Resilience Enhancement of UTS through Exploiting Connected Community and Internet of Everything Emerging Technologies, ACM Transactions on Internet Technology.

Bellini, E., Nesi, P., Ferreira, P., Simoes, A., Candelieri, A., and Gaitanidou E., (2017b) Towards resilience operationalization in urban transport system: The RESOLUTE project approach. DOI:10.1201/9781315374987-320, pp. 2110–17. In *Risk, Reliability and Safety: Innovating Theory and Practice*.

Bellini, P., Benigni, M., Billero, R., Nesi P., and Rauch, N. (2014) "Km4City ontology building vs data harvesting and cleaning for smart-city services," *International Journal of Visual Language and Computing*, 25(6), 827–39.

Bellini, P., Cenni, D., and Nesi, P. (2016) "AP positioning for estimating people flow as origin destination matrix for smart cities," *The 22nd International Conference on Distributed Multimedia Systems*, DMS.

Biggs, R., Schluter, M., Schoon, M.L. (2015) *Principle of Building Resilience: Sustaining Ecosystem Services in Social-Ecological Systems*. Cambridge: Cambridge University Press.

Boin, A., Comfort, L., and Demchak, C. (2010) "The rise of resilience." In Comfort, L., Boin, A., and Demchak, C. (eds.), *Designing Resilience: Preparing for Extreme Events*. The University of Pittsburgh Press.

Bungay S. (2010) *The Art of Action: How Leaders Close the Gaps between Plans, Actions and Results*. London: Nicholas Brealey.

Carroll, J.M. (1995) "Introduction: the scenario perspective on system development." In J.M. Carroll (ed.) *Scenario-based Design: Envisioning Work and Technology in System Development* (pp. 1–18). New York: John Wiley & Sons, Inc.

Cimellaro, G.P., Reinhorn, A. M., and Bruneau, M. (2010) "Framework for analytical quantification of disaster resilience," *Engineering Structures*, 32(11), 3639–49.

Flax, L., Armstrong, A., and Yee, L. (2016) "Measuring urban resilience as you build it: Insights from 100 resilient cities – resilience." In Florin, M.-V. and Linkov, I. (eds.). *IRGC Resource Guide on Resilience*. Lausanne: EPFL International Risk Governance Center (IRGC).

Godschalk, D. (2003) "Urban hazard mitigation: Creating resilient cities," *Natural Hazards Review*, 4, 136–43.

Gunderson, L., Holling, C., Pritchard, L., and Peterson, G. (2002) "Resilience of large-scale resource systems." In Gunderson, L. and Holling, C. (eds.), *Resilience and the Behaviour of Large-Scale System*. Washington, DC: Island Press.

Harmon, B.A., Goran, W.D., and Harmon R.S. (2013) "Military installations and cities in the twenty-first century: Towards sustainable military installations and adaptable cities." In *Sustainable Cities and Military Installations*. New York: Springer.

Höller, J., Tsiatsis, V., Mulligan, C., Avesand, S., Karnouskos, S., and Boyle, D. (2014) *From Machine-to-Machine to the Internet of Things: Introduction to a New Age of Intelligence*. Elsevier: Academic Press.

Holling, C.S., Gunderson, L., and Peterson, G. (2002) "Sustainability and panarchies." In L.H. Gunderson and C.S. Holling, eds., *Panarchy: Understanding Transformations in Human and Natural Systems*. Washington, DC: Island Press,, pp. 63–102.

Hollnagel, E. (2009) "The four cornerstone of resilience engineering." In C.P. Nemeth, E. Hollnagel, and S. Dekker (eds.), *Resilience Engineering Perspective, Vol. 2: Preparation and Restoration*. Aldershot: Ashgate.

Hollnagel, E. and Woods, D. (2006) "Epilogue: Resilience engineering precepts." In E. Hollnagel, D.D. Woods, and N. Leveson (eds.), *Resilience Engineering – Concepts and Precepts* (pp 347–58). Aldershot: Ashgate.

Howard, R.A. (1988) "Decision analysis: Practice and promise," *Management Science*, 34(6): 679–95.

Jackson, S. (2010) *Architecting Resilient Systems: Accident Avoidance and Survival and Recovery from Disruptions.* New York: John Wiley & Sons.

Jentzsch, A., Isele, R., and Bizer, C. (2010) Silk – Generating RDF links while publishing or consuming Linked Data. Poster at the International Semantic Web Conference (ISWC2010), Shanghai, November.

Kotoulas S., Lopez, V., Lloyd, R., Sbodio, M.L., Lecue, F., Stephenson,M., Daly, E., Bicer, V., Gkoulalas-Divanis, A., Di Lorenzo, G., Schumann, A., and Aonghusa, M. (2014) "SPUD – Semantic Processing of Urban Data." *Journal of Web Semantics: Science, Services and Agents on the World Wide Web*. DOI: 10.1016/j.websem.2013.12.003.

Lea, R. (2017) *Smart City: An Overview of the Technology Trends Driving Smart Cities.* IEEE.

Linkov, I., Fox-Lent, C., Read, L., Allen, C.R., Arnott, J.C., Bellini, E., Coaffee, J., Florin, M.-V. Hatfield, K., Hyde, I., Hynes, W., Jovanovic, A., Kasperson, R., Katzenberger, J., Keys, P.W., Lambert, J.H., Moss, R., Murdoc, P.S., Palma-Oliveira, J., Pulwarty, R.S., Sands, D. Thomas, E.A., Tye, M.R., and Woods, D. (2018) "Tiered approach to resilience assessment," *Risk Analysis Journal*. https://doi.org/10.1111/risa.12991.

Martelli, C. and Bellini E. (2013) "Using value network analysis to support data driven decision making in urban planning," *IEEE SITIS*, 998–1003.

Meerow, S., Newell, J.P., and Stults M. (2016) "Defining urban resilience: A review," *Landscape and Urban Planning*, 147, 38–49.

NAS (National Academy of Sciences) (2012) *Disaster Resilience: A National Imperative.* The National Academies Press, Washington, DC. www.nap.edu/catalog.php?record_id=13457 (last accessed August 20, 2018).

Park, J., Seager, T.P., Rao, P.S.C., Convertino, M., and Linkov, I. (2013) "Integrating risk and resilience approaches to catastrophe management in engineering systems," *Risk Analysis*, 33(3), 356–67.

Scharffe, F., Atemezing, G., Troncy, R., Gandon, F., Villata, S., Bucher, B., Hamdi, F., Bihanic, L., Kepeklian, G., Cotton, F., et al. (2012) "Enabling linked-data publication with the datalift platform." In: *Proc. AAAI Workshop on Semantic Cities. 26th Conference on Artificial Intelligence*, Toronto, Canada.

Vugrin, E., Warren, D., Ehlen, M., and Camphouse, C. (2010) "A framework for assessing resilience of infrastructure and economic systems." In Gopalakrishnan, K. and Peeta, S. (eds.), *Sustainable and Resilient Critical Infrastructure Systems: Simulation, Modelling and Intelligent Engineering.* (pp. 77–116). New York: Springer.

Walker, B. and Salt, D. (2006) *Resilience Thinking – Sustaining Ecosystems and People in a Changing World.* Washington, DC: Island Press.

Westrum, R. (2006) "A typology of resilience situations." In E. Hollnagel, D.D. Woods, and N. Leveson (eds.), *Resilience Engineering – Concepts and Precepts* (pp 55–65). Aldershot: Ashgate.

Woltjer, R. (2006) "Resilience assessment based on models of functional resonance." In *Proceedings of the 3rd Symposium on Resilience Engineering*.

36

Framework for improved indoor thermal comfort through personalized HVAC control

Da Li,[1] *Carol C. Menassa,*[2] *and Vineet R. Kamat*[3]

DEPT. OF CIVIL AND ENVIRONMENTAL ENGINEERING, UNIVERSITY OF MICHIGAN, USA;

[1] DLISEREN@UMICH.EDU; [2] MENASSA@UMICH.EDU; [3] VKAMAT@UMICH.EDU

36.1 Introduction

Thermal comfort of individuals is an important factor that affects occupant's overall satisfaction about the building indoor environment. According to a survey comprised of over 34,000 responses in 215 office buildings throughout North America and Finland, only 39 percent of respondents are satisfied with the thermal environment in their workspace (Huizenga et al. 2006). People's thermal sensation and preference depend not only on the environmental factors such as temperature and humidity, but also multiple aspects from human perspective including physiological factors (e.g., metabolic rate), psychological factors (e.g., stress, beliefs, and attitudes), and behavioral factors (e.g., activity, clothing level) (Brager & De Dear 2000; Goto et al. 2002; Parsons 2014). As a result, people's thermal sensation and satisfaction vary from one person to another. For example, gender has been proven to be closely related to thermal comfort where previous studies suggested that women prefer a relatively higher temperature than men in offices (Karjalainen 2007). Considering the interactions with buildings (e.g., turn on a fan, open the window), occupants can have diverse thermal sensations within the same room (Brager et al. 2004). Even for the same person, his/her thermal sensation and preference may vary significantly with temporal and spatial variations (Humphreys et al. 2015).

In typical office buildings, a centralized HVAC setpoint is usually chosen by facility managers based on industry guidelines such as American Society of Heating, Refrigeration, Air-Conditioning Engineers Standard (ASHRAE 55). However, this conventional strategy of maintaining the room temperature at a static value is unlikely to meet the thermal requirements of occupants in single or multi-occupancy spaces for several reasons. First, air temperature is non-uniform across the room where occupants sitting near the air outlets or in direct sunlight may have a different thermal sensation compared to others. Second, using room temperature as the only indicator of thermal comfort is inadequate to reflect an occupant's thermal state. For example, people who are doing heavy physical work may prefer a cooler environment than people at resting state due to their different metabolic rates (Fanger 1970). Furthermore, several studies suggested that even room temperature is set according to the recommended indoor conditions, there is still a high percentage of dissatisfaction among the occupants about the indoor thermal environment, which reveals the inconsistency of people's actual and predicted thermal sensations (Yang et al. 2015). In some cases where occupants don't have control over the thermostat, facility managers have to painfully deal with the frequent hot/cold complaints and constantly adjust the system to meet occupants' diverse thermal requirements (Friedman 2004).

The most widely used approach to evaluate occupant's thermal comfort is the Predicted Mean Vote (PMV) model developed by Fanger (1970) which is adopted by ASHRAE Standard 55. The PMV model considers four environmental factors: air temperature, relative humidity, air velocity, and mean radiant temperature, and two human factors: metabolic rate and clothing level to predict occupants' mean thermal sensation in a seven-point scale from -3 (cold) to 3 (hot). Predicted Percentage of Dissatisfied (PPD) is associated with PMV index which quantitatively describes the percentage of dissatisfied occupants under any given thermal conditions (Olesen & Brager 2004). However, Fanger's PMV model has several limitations. First, the PMV model is developed based on the feedback of a large group of people under steady state conditions in laboratory settings (influential factors maintain a constant condition over time). In addition, human factors in the PMV model are assumed the same across all human subjects without the consideration of personal variations. This can lead to discrepancies between the actual and predicted thermal sensation (Hwang et al. 2006; Yao et al. 2007; Van Hoof 2008). Second, the PMV model is originally developed for mechanically ventilated buildings and assumes the human body as a passive recipient of thermal stimuli (Yao el al. 2009). However, this approach doesn't truly reflect human conditions in naturally ventilated environments. For example, several field studies in naturally ventilated buildings suggested that occupants' adaptive behaviors (e.g., open the window) also play an important role in their thermal preferences. This behavioral adaption can result in a wider comfort range and indicates that the PMV model is not accurate for naturally ventilated buildings (De Dear et al. 1998; Brager & De Dear 2000; De Dear & Brager 2002; Feriadi et al. 2003).

To improve thermal comfort in indoor environments given occupants' diverse thermal preferences, several researchers investigated the "human-in-the-loop" approach which allows for human-based adjustments of the HVAC system (Feldmeier & Paradiso 2010; Daum et al. 2011; Bermejo et al. 2012; Nouvel & Alessi 2012; Erickson & Cerpa 2012; Purdon et al. 2013; Gao & Keshav 2013; Hang-yat & Wang 2013; Jazizadeh et al. 2013a; Jazizadeh et al. 2013b; Zhao et al. 2014a). "Human-in-the-loop" denotes the incorporation of human actual thermal sensation in the operation of HVAC system. However, these prior studies have several limitations such as lack of automatic control, low comfort prediction accuracy due to limited data sources, absence of natural ventilation in the HVAC control strategy. To address these limitations, this study proposes a personalized HVAC control framework which is capable of dynamically determining the optimum conditioning model (mechanical conditioning or natural ventilation) and HVAC settings (thermostat setpoint) with reduced human participation. To achieve this, personalized comfort prediction models are developed based on the environment and human data collected from various sources to evaluate each occupant's thermal comfort level over time. In mechanical conditioning mode, occupants' net votes (i.e., the average voting), as well as, the predicted preference from comfort models collectively determine the temperature setpoint. If comfort models suggest thermal comfort can be maintained in naturally ventilated conditions, occupants will be notified to open the window.

The chapter is organized to first provide a detailed review of existing research studies on the personalized control of thermal comfort, discuss their main limitations and outline the specific contributions of this work to this body of knowledge. Then the development of personalized HVAC control framework and comfort prediction model is explained in detail. Finally, two case studies (single occupancy and multi-occupancy) are presented to demonstrate the feasibility of the proposed framework and the results are discussed.

36.2 Related Work

This section will present a review of relevant literature. First, we review selected studies to illustrate the common approaches of personalized conditioning implemented thus far, as well as the limitations of each study. Then we discuss the findings from studies of thermoregulation which demonstrate the feasibility of predicting thermal comfort using human bio-signals. Third, we introduce the influences of natural ventilation on thermal comfort and the difficulties of selecting conditioning mode. In this study, we incorporate human bio-signals and conditioning model selection in the personalized HVAC control framework to address the limitations of prior studies as discussed in the first subsection.

36.2.1 Personalized conditioning through human participation

With the rapid development of wireless sensor network, mobile devices, and ubiquitous computing, researchers have explored various approaches to implement personalized control of indoor climate using various forms of human feedback (Feldmeier & Paradiso 2010; Daum et al. 2011; Bermejo et al. 2012; Erickson & Cerpa 2012; Gao & Keshav 2013; Purdon et al. 2013; Hang-yat & Wang 2013; Jazizadeh et al. 2013a; Jazizadeh et al. 2013b; Zhao et al. 2014a; Wang et al. 2016; Gupta et al. 2016). In these studies, indoor environment data and human feedback on the ambient conditions are used to assess the indoor thermal comfort level and thus adjust the HVAC system using different decision algorithms.

In general, these prior studies can be divided into two categories: the PMV-based approaches and non-PMV-based approaches. In the PMV-based approaches (e.g., Nouvel & Alessi 2012; Erickson & Cerpa 2012; Gao & Keshav 2013; Hang-yat & Wang 2013), researchers collected occupants' actual thermal sensations from phone applications to adjust the setpoint according to the PMV model. For example, Erickson and Cerpa (2012), Gao and Keshav (2013) and Hang-yat and Wang (2013) developed participatory sensing applications to collect occupant's thermal vote. The decision algorithms allowed real-time correction of setpoint based on occupants' overall thermal votes. However, these studies have the limitations inherited from the PMV model, such as the assumption of steady state conditions, lack of personal variations, and often times researchers have to estimate some parameters in the PMV model (e.g., mean radiant temperature, metabolic rate) which may significantly deviate from the real situation.

In the non-PMV-based approaches (e.g., Feldmeier & Paradiso 2010; Daum et al. 2011; Bermejo et al. 2012; Jazizadeh et al. 2013a; Jazizadeh et al. 2013b; Zhao et al. 2014a; Wang et al. 2016; Gupta et al. 2016; Purdon et al. 2013), researchers usually aimed to model occupants' thermal sensation using data collected from the indoor environment. For example, Feldmeier and Paradiso (2010) used a wrist-worn sensor to measure environment conditions such as ambient temperature and humidity, and to collect occupant's comfort state (hot, cold, and neutral) through voting. In this study, the authors trained a Fisher Discriminant classifier using two features (room temperature and humidity) to find the boundary of hot and cold sensations. Jazizadeh et al. (2013b) developed a smartphone application to collect occupants' thermal preferences (from cooler to warmer) under different ambient temperature conditions in mechanically conditioned offices. In this study, the fuzzy controller only applied the ambient temperature to predict comfort levels. Similarly, Zhao et al. (2014a) developed a complaint-driven control system which collects occupants' complaints (hot or cold) and environment conditions (air temperature and relative humidity) to determine their comfort state under both transient and steady state conditions. Wang et al. (2016) compared two HVAC control strategies (i.e., user satisfaction based control and empirical setpoint based control) and concluded that involving user feedback in the control loop can achieve a satisfied thermal environment. However, considering the diverse influential factors of thermal comfort from the human perspective, the lack of human data (e.g., skin temperature, activity level) in these studies may cause the model to be less representative under some circumstances (e.g., people with different workload can have diverse thermal comfort levels under the same room temperature).

Purdon et al. (2013) proposed a "model-free" approach which used only temperature data from the building management system (BMS) as environment inputs and avoided the cumbersome data collection required in the PMV model. For each control step, the temperature setpoint was directly changed by a fixed value according to occupants' overall net vote. However, as room temperature is the only factor collected to evaluate thermal comfort, this "model-free" approach is unable to predict thermal comfort if any factor from human or environment perspective changes. Thus, such a model-less system heavily relies on human reports during its operation, which can be cumbersome for its users.

In the market, some commercial products such as Comfy, CrowdComfort, Keen and Wally also adopted the idea of continuously collecting occupants' thermal votes and indoor conditions to maximize thermal comfort in the workplace through the optimization of temperature setpoint and air flow. Although these products involve human participation in the control loop, they have the same limitation as the model-less approach where the setpoint is adjusted according to the overall voting of thermal preference. As a result, the system is not able to dynamically adjust the indoor environment without continuous voting from users.

36.2.2 Thermal comfort prediction using bio-signals

Several studies have suggested the feasibility of using human bio-signals (e.g., skin temperature, heart rate) to evaluate people's thermal comfort level under laboratory conditions (Yao et al. 2007; Wang et al. 2007; Liu et al. 2008; Choi & Loftness 2012). For example, Yao et al. (2007) assessed participants' overall and local thermal sensations with respect to their mean skin temperature under three environment conditions (slightly cool, neutral, warm). This study suggested skin temperature is highly correlated with people's thermal sensation and thus developed comfort prediction formulas using linear regression models with skin temperature as an independent variable and overall/local thermal sensation as the dependent variable. Choi and Loftness (2012) measured skin temperature of multiple body parts at different room temperatures, clothing, and activity conditions in a climate chamber. The result showed that the gradient of temperature on hand, wrist, and upper arm is a good indicator to predict human thermal sensation.

On the other hand, as heart rate is closely related to the metabolic level and work intensity (Strath et al. 2000; Goto et al. 2002; Perini & Veicsteinas 2003), researchers have investigated the relationship between heart rate and thermal sensation and suggested a significant correlation between these two indexes (Choi et al. 2012; Liu et al. 2008). However, all these studies are conducted in laboratory conditions with controlled environment and human factors such as humidity, air velocity, clothing, and activity level. None of these studies have explored skin temperature and heart rate as predictors of thermal sensation in naturalistic settings.

36.2.3 Ventilation mode and thermal comfort

Prior studies of personalized conditioning discussed in the first subsection mainly focused on the HVAC strategy in pure mechanically conditioned buildings. For buildings with operable windows, natural ventilation is an effective approach to maintain indoor thermal comfort and good air quality (Santamouris & Allard 1998). Several field studies have suggested that the range of comfortable indoor temperature is wider in naturally ventilated buildings (Brager & De Dear 2000; De Dear & Brager 2002; Feriadi et al. 2003). For example, Feriadi et al. (2003) surveyed 300 households in naturally ventilated buildings and concluded that in reality people are more thermally comfortable compared to the prediction of the PMV model. In general, natural ventilation at a slightly higher outdoor temperature may still be perceived as comfortable due to several reasons, such as occupant's diverse control over the environment, behavioral adjustments, increased skin evaporation rate when wind passes human body, to name a few. On the other hand, natural ventilation can produce much higher ventilation rates than mechanical ventilation (Atkinson et al 2009; Schulze & Eicker 2013). Several studies investigated the concentration of air pollutants in naturally ventilated buildings and suggested that natural ventilation plays a significant role in removing indoor air pollutants and improving air quality (Santamouris et al. 2008; Hummelgaard et al. 2007).

According to a recent study carried out by Canada Green Building Council (CaGBC 2016), 69 percent of respondents revealed they have used mechanical conditioning strategies in office buildings compared to only 35 percent who have adopted natural ventilation. As pointed out by Brager and De Dear (2000), engineers often fail to distinguish when the building should solely rely on mechanical conditioning, and under what circumstances natural ventilation (or a mixed mode) outstands with equal, if not better, indoor environment but less energy consumption.

Considering the limitations of previous literature discussed in the first two subsections, as well as, the benefits of natural ventilation, we extend the current knowledge of personalized conditioning by incorporating human bio-signals and natural ventilation into the control loop which allows the HVAC system to dynamically determine the optimum conditioning mode and temperature setpoint based on the thermal comfort levels predicted from an integrated dataset, including both environment data (indoor/outdoor condition, window state) and human data (skin temperature, heart rate, activity, clothing level).

36.3 Objectives

This chapter presents a novel personalized HVAC control framework which is capable of improving occupants' overall thermal comfort using integrated human and environment data. The main objectives of this study are to: (1) evaluate the feasibility of using human and environment data to predict thermal comfort levels in naturalistic settings; (2) demonstrate how human and environment data from different sources are integrated in a phone application and applied in the control loop; and (3) illustrate the capabilities of the developed framework to improve overall thermal comfort in single and multi-occupancy spaces.

36.4 Methodology

36.4.1 Overview of the personalized control framework

The personalized control framework was developed based on our previous work (Li et al. 2017) which achieves the objectives by leveraging a range of new capabilities that have emerged in recent years such as: (1) portable and wearable health monitoring devices, (2) pervasiveness of smart mobile devices continuously available with the human occupants, and (3) efficient wireless sensing, actuation, and communication networks for distributed decision and control. An overview of the basic operating principle of the framework is shown in Figure 36.1. One of our important features of this approach that differentiates it from the previous studies is the integration of human bio-signals and behavioral data, thermal sensations, and preferences with environment data for decision making. To integrate data from various sources (e.g., human sensation and preference, human bio-signal data, indoor conditions, weather), we developed a smartphone application. The smartphone application fuses data collected through different approaches including (1) wrist-worn health monitoring devices (e.g., Microsoft band) which can measure human bio-signals and behavioral factors such as skin temperature, heart rate, and activity level; (2) wireless sensors and probes which can measure building indoor environment data (e.g., temperature, humidity, CO_2 level, window state); (3) weather station to get real-time outdoor conditions (e.g., temperature and humidity).

36.4.2 Main components of the personalized HVAC control framework

The personalized HVAC control framework includes five operating components (i.e., indoor sensors and wearable devices, phone application, central database, control script, and programmable thermostat) as shown in Figure 36.2. At the front-end, the phone application is paired

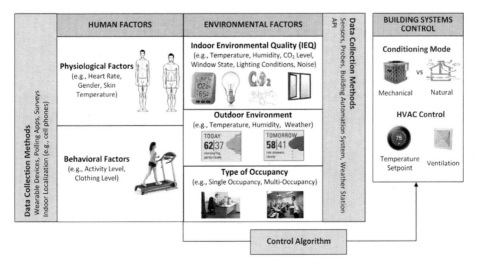

Figure 36.1 The operating principle of personalized control framework.

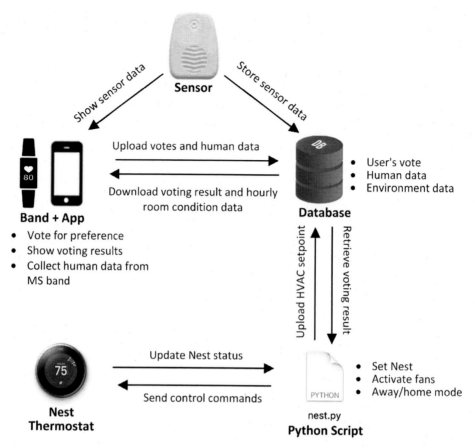

Figure 36.2 Data flow among the main components of personalized HVAC control framework.

with wearable health monitoring devices (e.g., Microsoft band) via Bluetooth to collect human bio-signal data (heart rate, skin temperature), behavioral data (clothing, activity level), and actual thermal sensations and preferences. Environment data which are collected from indoor sensors and weather station are displayed together with human data in the phone application.

The collected human and environment data are stored in the central database which communicates the phone application (front-end) and control script (back-end). At the back-end, the control script predicts each occupant's comfort level under different conditioning modes and setpoints. After running the control script, an adjustment is sent to the programmable thermostat to implement the new strategy.

In the following subsections, we will discuss the details of each component in the personalized HVAC control framework as shown in Figure 36.2, including the development of software (phone app, database, control script) and the specifications of hardware (sensor, wristband, thermostat). However, it should be noted that the main contribution of this study is to demonstrate a framework which uses various human and environment data to implement personalized HVAC control. Thus, the hardware we adopted in this study can be replaced by any other suitable devices with similar functionalities.

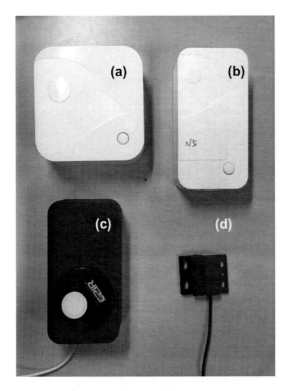

Figure 36.3 Sensors and probes for indoor environment data collection (a) gateway; (b) T/H sensor; (c) CO2 probe; (d) window contact probe.

Indoor sensors and wearable devices

Indoor environment data are collected from a set of sensors and probes as shown in Figure 36.3. In each room, the authors installed a Sensorist Wireless Pro T/H digital sensor (Figure 36.3b) to measure temperature (precision: ±0.2 °C) and relative humidity (precision: ±3%). To ensure adequate indoor air quality, a COZIR probe (precision: ±50 ppm, Figure 36.3c) is used to measure indoor CO_2 level, which is a good indicator of indoor air quality. Operable windows are equipped with contact probes (Figure 36.3d) to monitor their state (either open or close). All the sensors and probes communicate through the gateway (Figure 36.3a) which uploads the data to a web server for easy access.

To collect human bio-signals and behavioral data, the authors compared several portable fitness and health monitoring devices available in the market (e.g., Microsoft band 2, Fitbit, AIRO) which are popular due to powerful functionalities, affordable prices, and lightweight features. Considering our requirements on the comprehensiveness of human data, the wrist-worn Microsoft band 2 (see Figure 36.4) is adopted. Microsoft band 2 (hereinafter "MS band") embeds multiple sensors and is capable of tracking heart rate, skin temperature, light intensity, activity level, sleep quality, etc. Most importantly, all sensors in the MS band are accessible via the application programming interface (API).

Phone application

In Figure 36.2, the center of this personalized HVAC control framework is a smartphone application which enables human-building interaction. In this study, we developed an iOS

713

Figure 36.4   Microsoft band 2.

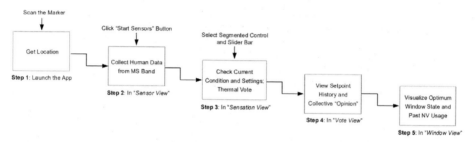

Figure 36.5   Steps of using phone application.

application which allows users to collect bio-signals and behavioral data, view room condition and HVAC settings, report actual thermal sensation and preference, check thermal votes of other occupants' sharing the room, acquire recommendation on the conditioning mode, and visualize their past efforts of using natural ventilation.

Figure 36.5 shows the steps of using a phone application (user required actions are in bold) and Figure 36.6 shows the application interfaces on an iPhone. To obtain a user's location and occupancy state (single or multi-occupancy), a marker with encoded location (e.g., office room 1) is strategically placed next to each user's desk in advance (see Figure 36.9). The phone app will first ask the user to scan this marker to get localized in the building. This is an improvement to prior studies where users need to manually select their location from a drop-down menu every time they use the application (Jazizadeh et al. 2013a; Erickson & Cerpa 2012). This is particularly helpful in large complex buildings as users can frequently move around multiple places.

Next, the phone app starts to collect bio-signals and behavioral data including heart rate, skin temperature, activity, and clothing level through the MS band sensor API (Figure 36.6a). The tab bar located at the bottom provides easy access to different views of the phone app. In the "sensation" view (Figure 36.6b), users can get the current room condition and HVAC data, as well as report their actual sensation and preference for the corresponding indoor environmental conditions through the segmented control. For the comfort scale, several designs have

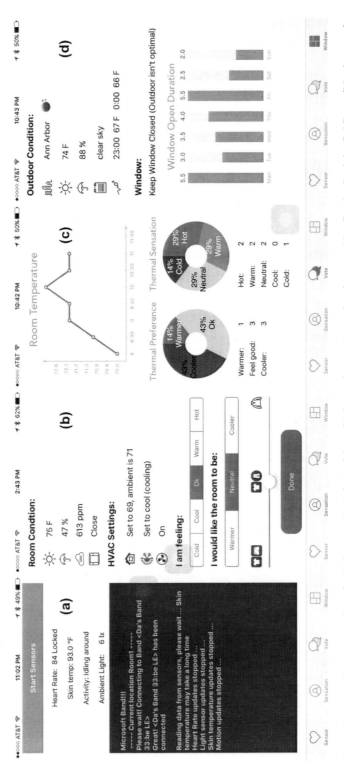

Figure 36.6 Application interfaces for (a) human physiological data; (b) thermal sensation and preference; (c) collective "opinion"; (d) conditioning mode.

Figure 36.7 Push notifications for two scenarios (left: setpoint is changed; right: time to use natural ventilation).

been proposed in previous studies (e.g., ASHRAE 5-point sensation scale, McIntyre 3-point preference scale, Bedford comfort scale). For example, Jazizadeh et al. (2013a) compared several design alternatives of comfort preference scale and recommended a combined preference and sensation scale with 10 intensity levels. However, people's thermal preference is not necessarily related to a certain sensation (e.g., people may consider a cooler sensation as comfortable) (Feriadi et al. 2003; Yao et al. 2007). Also, too many options may be confusing and thus hinder the human participation. Therefore, the authors adopted a 5-point sensation scale (cold, cool, ok, warm, hot) and a 3-point preference scale (warmer, neutral, cooler) in the phone app.

In the "vote" view (Figure 36.6c), the collaborative voting is shown using pie charts to represent user's "opinion" about indoor thermal environment in a multi-occupancy space. This feature allows users to view the unresolved cold/hot requests from their peers, which aims to promote mutual understanding of each other and mitigate the conflicts to some extent.

In the "window" view (Figure 36.6d), a bar chart displays the daily usage of natural ventilation. This feedback is anticipated to show users' efforts of adopting natural ventilation to promote long-term conservation. Users are notified by push notifications if there is an automatic adjustment of setpoint or natural ventilation is chosen as the optimum conditioning strategy (see Figure 36.7).

Database, comfort model and control script
In this study, we used MongoDB database to store and exchange information. In the database, data are arranged into three main collections. "UserInfo" collection manages each user's information (e.g., username, gender). "UserData" collection stores the time-stamped human and environment data, which are used to develop the comfort prediction model. "VoteResult" collection updates users' collective thermal votes during each decision cycle. Each time a new decision cycle starts, this collection will be reset for any future requests to represent users' dynamic "preferences".

As thermal preferences are categorical values (e.g., cooler and warmer), we adopted four common classification algorithms including Logistic Regression, K-nearest Neighbor, Support Vector Machine, and Random Forest. Given the data we collected in the case study, Random Forest classifier produces the highest classification accuracy. Therefore, only the result of Random Forest is discussed in the case study section. Random Forest is an ensemble method which classifies an object by averaging a large collection of decision trees and can reduce the overfitting problem originated from decision trees (Breiman 2001). In this study, we used this classifier to predict thermal preference from all other features collected from human and environment aspects.

To quantify thermal comfort level, we defined *"group comfort score"* (denoted as *group_comft* in Table 36.1 and 36.2) as "the total number of occupants who are comfortable in current conditions." The intuition of this metric is to find the optimum HVAC strategy that can maximize the overall thermal comfort in a multi-occupancy environment. Previous studies have

Table 36.1 Algorithm 1 – pseudo code for Mode Selection Algorithm

Input: *user_vote, human_data, envir_data, occupancy*
Output: mode (MC – mechanical conditioning, NV – natural ventilation)

for every *n* minutes **do**
    if non-operable window
      run **Algorithm_2**
      break
    end if

    group_comft_NV = 0
    for each occupant
      individual_comft_NV = comft_model(*human_data, envir_data, NV*)
      // 1- comfortable, 0 – uncomfortable
      group_comft_NV += *individual_comft_NV*
    end for
    group_comft_MC = run **Algorithm_2** // best condition achieved by MC
    if *group_comft_NV* >= *group_comft_MC*
      return Mode_Set(*NV*)
    else
      return Mode_Set(*MC*)
    end if
end for

Table 36.2 Algorithm 2 – pseudo code for Collective Decision Algorithm

Input: *user_vote, human_data, envir_data, occupancy, set_point*
Output: HVAC_Command, *group_comft*

if CO_2 > threshold **then**
    return HVAC_FanOn()
else
    return HVAC_FanOff()
end if

if *occupancy* = 1 **then** // single occupancy
    return HVAC_TempSet(*user_vote*)
else if *user_vote* < 0 (or if *user_vote* > 0)
    temp = *set_point* – 1 (or *temp* = *set_point* + 1)
    group_comft_MC = 0
    for each occupant
      individual_comft_MC = comft_model(*temp, human_data, envir_data, MC*)
      // 1- comfortable, 0 – uncomfortable
      group_comft_MC += *individual_comft_MC*
    end for
    if *group_comft_MC* > ½ *occupancy*
      HVAC_TempSet(*temp*)
    else
      HVAC_TempSet(*unchanged*)
    end if
    reset(*user_vote*)
    return *group_comft_MC*
end if

proposed several approaches on this issue. For example, Zhao et al. (2014b) implemented a geometrical solution which takes the convex hull of individual complaint regions as the group complaint region. Thus, a comfortable environment should be maintained within the compliment set of the group complaint region. However, this approach can fail if the individual hot and cold complaints have a significant overlap (i.e., the comfort state is uncertain in the overlapped region). In another study, Purdon et al. (2013) proposed to directly use the net vote to guide the temperature setpoint. If more votes of warmer environment are received, then the setpoint is increased by a fixed step and vice versa. However, this approach cannot handle the situation where some occupants do not vote because they feel comfortable in current condition.

To overcome these limitations, in this study we evaluated each occupant's comfort level by plugging the human and environment data into the individual comfort prediction model. If the predicted thermal preference is "neutral," then this occupant is regarded as comfortable. Otherwise (i.e., "warmer" or "cooler"), this occupant is regarded as uncomfortable. As occupants are more likely to report their uncomfortable state, we assumed that if no reports are received from an occupant, he/she is considered as comfortable in that period or has reached the comfortable state on his/her own by performing some adaptive behaviors (e.g., put on a jacket). Therefore, we divided the typical working hours (from 8 am to 6 pm) into 20 segments with 30 minutes for each interval. This 30-minute decision interval is also supported by Purdon et al. (2013) and Hang-yat and Wang (2013) as occupants may not feel any changes in a shorter duration. If more than one report from a single occupant is collected in a segment, only the last report is considered. This assumption guarantees that the comfort level of occupants with different report frequencies can be compared and computed using the same measure.

The authors wrote a Python script which continuously executes the decision algorithm to enable connections between the cloud data and physical HVAC system. The HVAC control loop includes two algorithms, namely the *Mode Selection Algorithm* and *Collective Decision Algorithm*. Python script first executes the *Mode Selection Algorithm* (see Table 36.1) to choose the optimum conditioning mode. In each decision cycle, the *Collective Decision Algorithm* (see Table 36.2) is implemented to evaluate the highest *group comfort score* that can be achieved in mechanical conditioning mode (the total number of occupants that are comfortable under the optimum setpoint). Then the *group comfort score* is evaluated again in the natural ventilation mode. The *Mode Selection Algorithm* selects natural ventilation as the optimum conditioning mode if it can produce a higher *group comfort score* compared to mechanical conditioning. Otherwise, if mechanical conditioning produces a higher *group comfort score* in the current situation or the window is non-operable, pure mechanical conditioning is chosen as the optimum strategy and the setpoint will be determined according to Algorithm 2. In this case, ventilation is automatically activated when indoor CO_2 level is higher than the 1000 ppm threshold specified in ASHRAE Standard 55 (ASHRAE 2010; Menassa et al. 2013).

Programmable thermostat

Unlike other studies which manage the BMS through the BACnet protocols (Pang et al. 2012; Jazizadeh et al. 2013b), we adopted a programmable Wi-Fi enabled thermostat (e.g., Nest) to operate the HVAC system; as well as, operable window sensors to allow for natural ventilation under certain conditions. By using Nest, we can directly control the HVAC system through the Python script we customized for this study without involving the details of the HVAC system (e.g., make, model). This approach requires no retrofits to the existing HVAC system, and most importantly, we can develop and test the decision algorithms before accessing the physical HVAC system in a building.

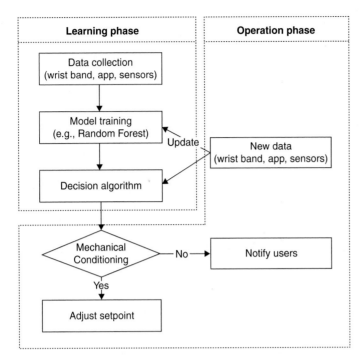

Figure 36.8 Overview of the workflow.

36.4.3 Workflow of the personalized HVAC control framework

In this study, the workflow of the proposed HVAC control framework consists of two stages (see Figure 36.8): the learning phase and the operation phase. In the learning phase, machine learning methods (e.g., Random Forest) are adopted to develop comfort prediction models using human and environment data. In the operation phase, the decision algorithm 1 and 2 are continuously executed to determine the optimum conditioning mode and HVAC setpoint (detailed in *Database, Comfort Model, and Control Script* section). If natural ventilation is the present optimum strategy, the script notifies users to open the window and turn off the HVAC system (if windows are operable). Otherwise, the script stays in mechanical conditioning mode and adjusts the thermostat setpoint by checking users' recent collective voting.

36.5 Case study

Two case studies of different types of occupancy were selected to demonstrate the proposed HVAC control framework. The first case study was conducted in single occupancy rooms to demonstrate the framework's capability of determining conditioning mode. The second case study evaluated the HVAC decision algorithm to improve overall comfort in a multi-occupancy space.

36.5.1 Single occupancy study

The first case study was conducted in three single-occupancy rooms. The test beds are regular residential housing units located in Ann Arbor, Michigan. Each room is equipped

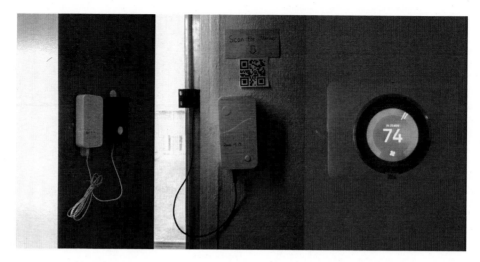

Figure 36.9 Temperature and CO_2 sensors (left); location marker and window sensor (middle); nest thermostat (right).

with operable windows and an individual HVAC unit. All participants have full control over the windows and thermostat. In each room, we placed a set of temperature and CO_2 sensor (Figure 36.9) near the desk to monitor a participant's work area. A contact probe was placed on the window frame to detect the window state. Each participant was assigned a location marker and received instructions on how to use the phone app and wristband before data collection.

The data collection took place during the cooling season from mid-June through July in 2016. The average daily highest and lowest temperatures are 28.9 °C and 16.7 °C respectively. Each participant was asked to provide a feedback through the phone app under two scenarios several times a day: (1) when they feel comfortable with the indoor thermal environment; (2) when they feel uncomfortable and are about to take actions to restore the comfortable state (e.g., close the window, change the thermostat, put on a jacket).

To obtain data in the natural ventilation mode, participants were asked to open the window (also set back HVAC system) twice per day when outdoor temperatures were deemed acceptable (once in the morning and once in the afternoon). If participants feel uncomfortable in natural ventilation mode, they are allowed to close the window and switch to mechanical conditioning (a feedback is made before switching the mode). Otherwise, the indoor environment can stay in natural ventilation until participants feel uncomfortable.

From the three participants, a total of 271 thermal comfort reports are considered valid after removing incomplete reports. A sample dataset and the frequency of reports for each level are shown in Table 36.3 and Table 36.4. The training data can be categorized into three main groups: (1) participant's thermal preference. This is the variable that will be used to obtain the comfort model; (2) human data, including clothing level (Clo, its value can be L – low, M – medium, H – heavy), heart rate (HR, beats/minute), skin temperature (T_{skin}, °C), activity level (activity, its value can be idling, walking, running); and (3) environment data, including room temperature (T_{room}, °C), room humidity (H_{room}, %), CO_2 level (ppm), window state (NV, 0 – close, 1 – open), outdoor temperature (T_{out}, °C), and outdoor humidity (H_{out}, %).

Table 36.3 Sample data collected in learning phase

Time	Sensation	Preference	Clo	HR	T_{skin}	Activity	T_{room}	H_{room}	CO_2	NV	T_{out}	H_{out}
06-24 17:46	Ok	Neutral	L	60	32	Idling	24	51	622	0	28	65
06-24 19:08	Hot	Cooler	L	60	33	Idling	28	54	585	0	30	72
06-24 20:14	Warm	Cooler	L	57	32	Idling	28	51	708	0	31	63
06-25 09:21	Cool	Neutral	L	70	28	Idling	24	40	1020	0	28	68
06-25 11:35	Warm	Cooler	M	80	31	Walking	25	44	827	0	29	75
06-25 16:18	Cool	Warmer	L	59	32	Idling	24	62	664	1	25	88
06-25 17:02	Ok	Neutral	L	55	32	Idling	24	65	643	1	26	73
06-26 11:37	Warm	Neutral	L	62	31	Walking	26	63	711	1	28	58
06-26 14:35	Hot	Neutral	L	62	34	Idling	27	54	425	1	32	39
06-27 10:27	Warm	Cooler	M	68	33	Idling	25	42	791	0	23	57

Table 36.4 Frequency of reports for each level of single occupancy testbed (ME – Mechanical conditioning, NV – Natural ventilation)

Subject ID	Number of Data Points for Each Level – ME			Number of Data Points for Each Level – NV		
	Cooler	Neutral	Warmer	Cooler	Neutral	Warmer
1	14	24	11	6	19	6
2	22	11	14	14	19	10
3	14	21	22	16	18	10
Total	50	56	47	36	56	26

A summary of reported room temperature and skin temperature is shown in Figure 36.10. In this figure, each row represents a participant's reports and the four columns represent participants' thermal preferences with respect to room temperature in mechanical conditioning, room temperature in natural ventilation, skin temperature in mechanical conditioning, and skin temperature in natural ventilation, respectively. A participant is considered comfortable if his/her preference is neutral. In general, participants tend to have a wider comfortable range in naturally ventilated conditions compared to mechanically conditioned spaces. This figure also confirms prior findings that people can have different preferences under the same room temperature which suggests the need of including other factors (such as human factors) when evaluating thermal comfort.

The personalized comfort prediction models are developed using Random Forest algorithm. Due to the lack of consensus on the appropriate dataset size, parameters are tuned to produce the highest cross-validation accuracy (we adopted the Python Scikit-learn package with the following parameters: n_estimators = 1000, criterion = "entropy", max_depth = 10). Oversampling of minority classes has been adopted to address the class imbalance problem. Three feature sets are adopted for each scenario: the first feature set only contains environment data (Envir Only), namely, room temperature, room humidity, window state, outdoor temperature, and outdoor humidity; the second feature set only contains human data (Human Only), namely, clothing level, heart rate, skin temperature, and activity level; the third feature set contains both environment and human data (Envir + Human). Using such configuration, we can compare the performances of prediction models with different feature sets and determine whether some features are influential in the comfort model.

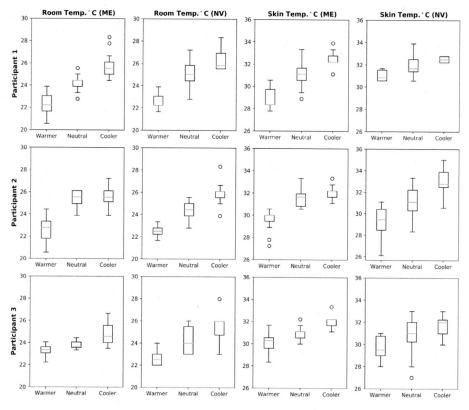

Figure 36.10 Three participants' reported room temperature and skin temperature of different thermal preference levels.

Ten-fold cross-validation is performed to evaluate the classification accuracy of three feature sets under six scenarios (see Table 36.5). The third feature set (Envir + Human) performs the best, which can achieve approximately 80 percent accuracy to classify three labels. Compared to the Envir Only and Human Only feature set, the Envir + Human feature set improves the classification accuracy by 24 percent and 39 percent respectively, indicating that having a feature set that incorporates both environment and human data can significantly improve the performance of comfort prediction model.

As participants' reports are continuously collected over time, the comfort prediction model can evolve as more reports are received. Figure 36.11 shows the classification accuracy with respect to the size of training data under six scenarios. Each subplot represents the prediction accuracy when 60 percent up to 100 percent training data are collected. In this case, the training data is segmented in chronological order to represent the data collected over time. For scenario (1), (2), and (3), classification accuracy is improving as the size of the training data is increasing, indicating the "learning" ability of the comfort model. For scenario (4), (5), and (6), classification accuracy of the whole training set is close to the accuracy when 60 percent of data are used. Overall, with a relatively small dataset (approximately 50 samples), the comfort model can achieve an acceptable classification accuracy. This result suggests that the proposed HVAC control framework does not heavily rely on human inputs and implies its ability to dynamically control the indoor environment without continuous voting from users.

Table 36.5 Classification accuracy for random forest classifier with different feature sets

Scenarios	$P1 - ME$	$P1 - NV$	$P2 - ME$	$P2 - NV$	$P3 - ME$	$P3 - NV$
Envir Only	0.595	0.635	0.700	0.654	0.602	0.667
Human Only	0.674	0.540	0.694	0.495	0.506	0.565
Envir + Human	**0.805**	**0.852**	**0.887**	**0.792**	**0.714**	**0.707**

Note: P1, P2, P3 – Participant ID; ME – Mechanical conditioning, NV – Natural ventilation

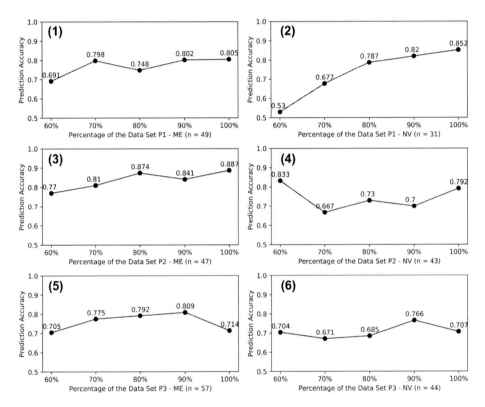

Figure 36.11 Classification accuracy of comfort prediction model with respect to data size (n represents the total number of samples in the dataset).

36.5.2 Multi occupancy study

Another case study was conducted in an office building located in Madison, Wisconsin which aims to evaluate the HVAC decision algorithm in a multi-occupancy space. The case study was conducted for three weeks from Nov.14 to Dec 2, 2016. The case study building has an open office area which accommodates twenty full-time employees (see Figure 37.12). A single programmable thermostat controls the thermal environment of this work area. During the test period, all windows were kept closed and only mechanical conditioning was considered in the decision algorithm.

Figure 36.12 Multi-occupancy test bed (photo courtesy of Seventhwave).

Seven participants joined in the data collection and used the phone app to report their thermal preferences and corresponding human data. Before data collection, the authors explained the importance of feedback and encouraged participants to vote multiple times per day. A total of 362 complete reports are collected during the test period and the frequency of reports for each level is summarized in Table 36.6. The comfort prediction model is trained and tested using the Random Forest algorithm as discussed in the single occupancy case study. The classification accuracy of three feature sets (Envir Only, Human Only, Envir + Human) for the seven participants are shown in Table 36.7. Overall, the model can achieve over 80 percent accuracy of predicting thermal comfort level.

Figure 36.13–36.15 demonstrate the room temperature and occupant responses across three weeks. As shown in each figure, the data is trimmed to weekdays from 8 am to 6 pm to represent typical working hours. In each day, the bold black curve represents the room temperature over time. Participants' thermal preference "Warmer", "Cooler", and "Neutral" are marked using vertical red, blue lines and black dots respectively. Each line or dot indicates that a participant reports his/her thermal sensation and preference at some point during the day. No reports are collected during Nov. 23–Nov. 25 due to the Thanksgiving holiday.

Room temperature in Figure 37.13–37.15 can vary by as much as 1.7 °C in a day. The lowest temperature usually occurs in the early morning (8 am) and gradually reaches the highest value at around 2 pm. The overlap of red, blue lines and black dots indicate the participants have diverse thermal preferences in a multi-occupancy space given the same environment condition. The frequent cold and hot reports (i.e., uncomfortable reports) represent a less than satisfactory thermal environment.

By interviewing with the participants, we found several reasons that lead to the unsatisfied thermal comfort. For example, participant 5 commented that "*Even though the thermostat is next to*

Table 36.6 Frequency of reports for each level of multi-occupancy testbed

Subject ID	1	2	3	4	5	6	7
Cooler	6	7	10	11	14	9	11
Neutral	21	12	28	34	30	14	14
Warmer	16	28	17	19	23	31	7
Total	43	47	55	64	67	54	32

Table 36.7 Prediction accuracy of the seven participants in the multi-occupancy room

Subject ID	1	2	3	4	5	6	7
Envir Only	0.634	0.739	0.655	0.185	0.554	0.529	0.483
Human Only	0.373	0.434	0.601	0.696	0.712	0.679	0.634
Envir + Human	**0.932**	**0.964**	**0.839**	**0.723**	**0.744**	**0.779**	**0.748**

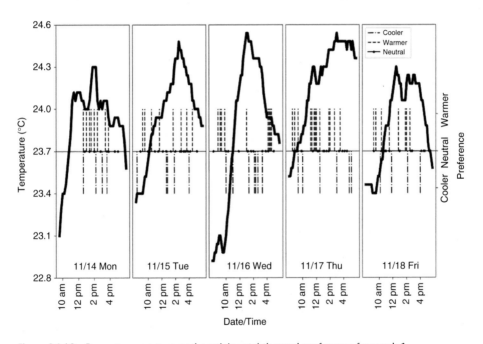

Figure 36.13 Room temperature and participants' thermal preference for week 1.

my table, *I never adjust it when I feel uncomfortable as I don't know if my colleagues have the same feelings as I do.*" Participant 6 commented that "*I always feel cold in the room, but I don't know how much I should change (if I am allowed to do so) the setpoint to make me feel comfortable.*" Participant 7 commented that "*I think it is a dummy thermostat as nobody ever touches it.*" Therefore, to improve thermal comfort in a multi-occupancy space, it is particularly important to engage building occupants in the control loop and enable the adjustment of setpoint based on the evaluation of overall comfort level instead of relying on the empirical judgement.

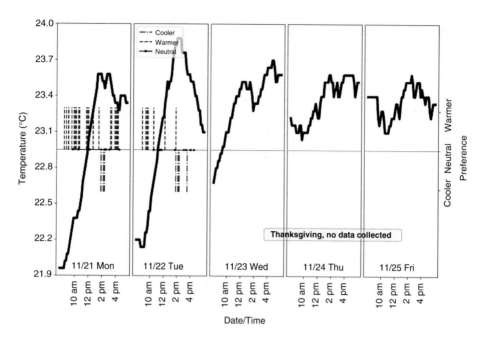

Figure 36.14 Room temperature and participants' thermal preference for week 2.

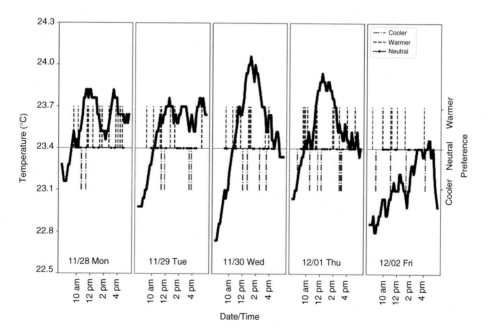

Figure 36.15 Room temperature and participants' thermal preference for week 3.

Table 36.8 Description of scheduled and dynamic environment

Scenario	Scheduled Environment	Dynamic Environment
Description	Total number of uncomfortable reports of this office is counted from the original reports as shown in Figures 36.13–36.15. This scenario represents the scheduled environment where the thermostat setpoint is fixed and no dynamic adjustments are made over time.	Total number of uncomfortable reports of this office is calculated based on the predicted responses after implementing the HVAC decision algorithm. The responses are predicted using each occupant's comfort model when the setpoint is adjusted. This scenario represents the environment where dynamic adjustments are made according to occupants' reports and comfort predictions.

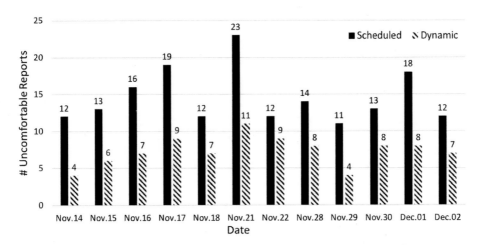

Figure 36.16 Number of uncomfortable reports of the scheduled and dynamic environment.

Two scenarios are compared to demonstrate the feasibility of our proposed framework in improving thermal comfort (see Table 36.8). The scheduled scenario represents the situation where the setpoint of thermostat follows a predefined fixed schedule (as the multi-occupancy office did in the data collection). The dynamic scenario represents the situation where the *Algorithm 2 – Collective Decision Algorithm* (discussed in *Database, Comfort Model and Control Script* section) has been implemented to dynamically adjust the temperature setpoint. In the dynamic environment, total number of uncomfortable reports (i.e., cooler or warmer reports) are calculated from the personalized comfort models.

The total number of uncomfortable reports of the scheduled and dynamic scenarios are shown in Figure 36.16. On average, the total number of uncomfortable reports have been reduced by as much as 53.7 percent after implementing the *Collective Decision Algorithm*. The reduced uncomfortable reports in the dynamic scenario indicates the improvement of overall thermal comfort in the case study office.

36.6 Discussion

Our work shows that the personalized comfort models with human and environment data can achieve approximately 80 percent accuracy in predicting thermal preference in both mechanical conditioning and natural ventilation. This result suggested the importance of incorporating human bio-signals and behavioral data in the HVAC control framework as environment data alone is inadequate to indicate people's thermal comfort due to the dynamic nature of human factors and adaptive behaviors. The data collected from the case study also confirmed prior studies that people can have diverse thermal preferences under the same environment condition (Brager & De Dear 2000; Yao et al. 2007).

The comfort models can evolve as more reports are collected. With a relatively small sample size (n=50), the Random Forest classifier can achieve an acceptable classification accuracy. However, we noted that the accuracy is not always monotonically increasing with respect to the size of the training data. There can be several possible reasons leading to this phenomenon: (1) even though the comfort model used several environment and human factors to jointly predict thermal comfort, there are other influential factors which are not considered in this study, such as the air velocity and time spent indoors. Future research will focus on investigating these "hidden" factors and how they affect the comfort model when they are dominant under some cases; (2) the data we collected are not always accurate. The inaccuracy can come from the inherent measurement error of devices (wristband, sensors, etc.), as well as, the improper use by the participants. For example, participants may not wear the wristband for at least five minutes before they report the comfort level. The skin temperature and heart rate collected in this case can vary significantly from the actual value; (3) The training data are collected in the naturalistic settings such that some parameters may be limited to a relatively narrow range due to participant's actual control or behavior. For example, one occupant may wear the same clothes and always maintain sedentary state during the data collection period, resulting in limited values of clothing and activity level. Later, if he/she changes the clothing and activity level, the pre-developed comfort model lacks data in the current scenarios and can therefore make wrong predictions.

To improve the prediction accuracy, future studies will focus on collecting data in a more "controlled" test bed and then evaluate the comfort model in naturalistic settings. In this case, all participants are exposed to the identical environment conditions including room temperature, humidity, air speed, window state, etc. during the same period of time. Three experimental scenarios, namely cold to cool environment, neutral environment, and warm to hot environment, can be evaluated to get a comprehensive dataset. In each experimental scenario, the potential influential factors should be identical for all participants (e.g., wear the same clothes, all stay in resting and then lightly active state) in both natural ventilation and mechanical conditioning environment.

Our proposed *Collective Decision Algorithm* determines the optimum setpoint by maximizing the *group comfort score*. Results from the case study show that for a large office room (where we have seven participants), it is possible to make more people feel comfortable by adjusting the setpoint. However, in small areas or some extreme cases (e.g., one occupant feels hot while the other feels cold), only adjusting the setpoint cannot improve the overall satisfaction. In this case, other interventions such as changing the clothing level or using space heater/fans should be considered. On the other hand, it is possible that participants didn't vote when they felt uncomfortable. This can be caused by two reasons: (1) participants may reach the comfortable level on their own by performing some adaptive behaviors (e.g., put on a jacket) rather than expecting the setpoint to be adjusted; (2) participants failed to vote due to heavy workload or frustration. In this case, our algorithm assumes them as comfortable and may not be able to improve the overall comfort as expected.

The proposed HVAC control framework can be adopted in different types of buildings and seasons. However, it is also worth noting that the personalized comfort model may not remain the same due to spatial and temporal variations, such as types of buildings, locations in the room, weather zones, different seasonal climates, etc. In this case, a new learning phase is needed to collect data and update personalized comfort models.

As demonstrated in the two case studies, the proposed HVAC control framework can notify occupants when natural ventilation is available and significantly reduce uncomfortable reports from occupants which indicates an improvement of overall thermal comfort. From the sustainability point of view, the personalized HVAC control framework can lead to energy savings in three scenarios: (1) as an occupant-driven approach, the HVAC system will be set back if the room is not occupied; (2) based on comfort predictions and occupants' requests, the HVAC system will provide "just-the-right" conditioning which avoids energy wastes due to over-heating/cooling; (3) this framework can remind users to open the window and set back the mechanical HVAC system when natural ventilation can maintain an acceptable thermal environment.

However, this study also has several limitations. First, the evaluation of natural ventilation is conducted in cooling seasons when the outdoor environment is relatively stable. The feasibility of adopting natural ventilation in shoulder seasons (i.e., the beginning of spring and fall when temperature can change significantly during a day) and heating seasons is unknown in the current study. Second, when natural ventilation is available, only notifications will be sent to user's phone as the windows are not mechanically operable. Whether following the instruction to open the window still relies on the decision of users. Third, the wrist temperature is used to predict the overall thermal comfort. However, thermal comfort of certain body parts can directly affect the overall thermal comfort in some cases. For example, some people may consider themselves as comfortable if their faces are comfortable. This requires more detailed investigations on building occupants when developing personalized comfort prediction models.

36.7 Conclusions

This study proposed an HVAC control framework which is capable of determining the optimum room conditioning mode (mechanical conditioning or natural ventilation) and HVAC settings (temperature setpoint) under different environment and human conditions. The main contribution of this study is the integration of human bio-signals and behavioral data in the HVAC control system. This additional human data can significantly improve the accuracy of predicting thermal preferences.

The main conclusions from this study include: First, it is particularly important to consider human bio-signals and behavioral factors when implementing a human-focused HVAC control system that can dynamically control the environment. Second, using the identified feature set and Random Forest model, an 80 percent classification accuracy can be achieved with a relatively small dataset (approximately 50 samples). Third, our results confirm findings from previous studies that occupants can have different thermal preferences in the same environment considering their diverse human factors (Brager & De Dear 2000; Parsons 2014), as well as, the fact that occupants' comfort state can change over time due to factors such as metabolic rate and workload (Yao et al. 2009), making a static setpoint unable to satisfy the conflicting and dynamic thermal requirement. As discussed in the case study, our proposed *Collective Decision Algorithm* can reduce the uncomfortable reports by as much as 53.7%. Lastly, room conditioning mode can be determined by evaluating human and environment factors identified in this study. The proposed mode selection capability in our HVAC control framework reveals the potential to reduce energy consumption while maintaining a satisfied indoor environment.

To summarize, in this chapter we first introduced the major components of the personalized HVAC control framework and demonstrated its operating principles. Then we discussed how various types of human and environment data are integrated in the decision loop, the specifications of supporting hardware (wristband, sensors, thermostat) and the development of software (smartphone application, database, control script), as well as, two HVAC control algorithms (*Mode Selection Algorithm* and *Collective Decision Algorithm*). Lastly, we demonstrated the prediction accuracy of comfort models developed from the case study and evaluated the overall thermal comfort conditions after implementing the decision algorithm.

This study introduced the foundations of the personalized HVAC control framework to determine optimum HVAC strategy using integrated human and environment data. Future research by the authors will focus on implementing "real" control in a multi-occupancy space. This will allow the research team to subsequently validate its capability to resolve actual thermal conflicts and evaluate corresponding energy consumptions. Moreover, if the windows are mechanically operable (i.e., equipped with motors), fully automatic window operation can be implemented in the test beds for a truly hybrid ventilation mode.

Acknowledgments

The authors would like to acknowledge the financial support for this research received from the US National Science Foundation (NSF) CBET 1407908 and 1349921. Any opinions and findings in this paper are those of the authors and do not necessarily represent those of the NSF. The authors would also like to thank Seventhwave for the help with data collection.

Copyright

References

ASHRAE Standard (2010). Standard 55–2010: "Thermal Environmental Conditions for Human Occupancy"; ASHRAE. *Atlanta USA*.

Atkinson, J., Chartier, Y., Silvia, C.L.P., Jensen, P., Li, Y., and Seto, W.H. (eds.). (2009). *Natural Ventilation for Infection Control in Health-Care Settings*. World Health Organization.

Bermejo, P., Redondo, L., de la Ossa, L., Rodríguez, D., Flores, J., Urea, C., ... and Puerta, J.M. (2012). Design and simulation of a thermal comfort adaptive system based on fuzzy logic and on-line learning. *Energy and Buildings*, 49, 367–79.

Brager, G. and de Dear, R. (2000). A standard for natural ventilation. *ASHRAE journal*, 42(10), 21.

Brager, G., Paliaga, G., and De Dear, R. (2004). Operable windows, personal control and occupant comfort. *ASHRAE Transactiobns, 11o:* 17–35.

Breiman, L. (2001). Random forests. *Machine learning*, 45(1), 5–32.

CaGBC, 2016. "Healthier buildings in Canada 2016: Transforming building design and construction." www.cagbc.org/cagbcdocs/Smart_Market_Report_Final_Web_PUBLIC.pdf (last accessed August 20, 2018).

Choi, J.H. and Loftness, V. (2012). Investigation of human body skin temperatures as a bio-signal to indicate overall thermal sensations. *Building and Environment*, 58, 258–69.

Choi, J.H., Loftness, V., and Lee, D.W. (2012). Investigation of the possibility of the use of heart rate as a human factor for thermal sensation models. *Building and Environment, 50,* 165–75.

Daum, D., Haldi, F., and Morel, N. (2011). A personalized measure of thermal comfort for building controls. *Building and Environment, 46*(1), 3–11.

De Dear, R.J., and Brager, G.S. (2002). Thermal comfort in naturally ventilated buildings: revisions to ASHRAE Standard 55. *Energy and Buildings, 34*(6), 549–61.

De Dear, R.J., Brager, G.S., Reardon, J., and Nicol, F. (1998). Developing an adaptive model of thermal comfort and preference/discussion. *ASHRAE Transactions, 104,* 145.

Erickson, V.L., and Cerpa, A.E. (2012, November). Thermovote: participatory sensing for efficient building hvac conditioning. In *Proceedings of the Fourth ACM Workshop on Embedded Sensing Systems for Energy-Efficiency in Buildings* (pp. 9–16). ACM.

Fanger, P.O. (1970). *Thermal Comfort. Analysis and Applications in Environmental Engineering.* Copenhagen: Danish Technical Press.

Feldmeier, M. and Paradiso, J.A. (2010, November). Personalized HVAC control system. In *Internet of Things (IOT), 2010* (pp. 1–8). IEEE.

Feriadi, H., Wong, N.H., Chandra, S., and Cheong, K. W. (2003). Adaptive behaviour and thermal comfort in Singapore's naturally ventilated housing. *Building Research and Information, 31*(1), 13–23.

Friedman, G. (2004). Too hot or too cold: Diagnosing occupant complaints. *ASHRAE Journal, 46*(1), S157.

Gao, P.X., and Keshav, S. (2013, January). SPOT: a smart personalized office thermal control system. In *Proceedings of the Fourth International Conference on Future Energy Systems* (pp. 237–246). ACM.

Goto, T., Toftum, J., Dear, R.D., and Fanger, P.O. (2002). Thermal sensation and comfort with transient metabolic rates. *Indoor Air, 1,* 1038–43.

Gupta, S.K., Atkinson, S., O'Boyle, I., Drogo, J., Kar, K., Mishra, S., and Wen, J.T. (2016). BEES: Real-time occupant feedback and environmental learning framework for collaborative thermal management in multi-zone, multi-occupant buildings. *Energy and Buildings, 125,* 142–52.

Hang-yat, L.A. and Wang, D. (2013, November). Carrying my environment with me: A participatory-sensing approach to enhance thermal comfort. In *Proceedings of the 5th ACM Workshop on Embedded Systems For Energy-Efficient Buildings* (pp. 1–8). ACM.

Huizenga, C., Abbaszadeh, S., Zagreus, L., and Arens, E.A. (2006). Air quality and thermal comfort in office buildings: Results of a large indoor environmental quality survey. *Proceeding of Healthy Buildings 2006, 3,* 393–7.

Hummelgaard, J., Juhl, P., Sæbjörnsson, K.O., Clausen, G., Toftum, J., and Langkilde, G. (2007). Indoor air quality and occupant satisfaction in five mechanically and four naturally ventilated open-plan office buildings. *Building and Environment, 42*(12), 4051–8.

Humphreys, M., Nicol, F., Roaf, S., and Sykes, O. (2015). *Standards for Thermal Comfort: Indoor Air Temperature Standards for the 21st Century.* New York: Routledge.

Hwang, R.L., Lin, T.P., and Kuo, N.J. (2006). Field experiments on thermal comfort in campus classrooms in Taiwan. *Energy and Buildings, 38*(1), 53–62.

Jazizadeh, F., Marin, F.M., and Becerik-Gerber, B. (2013a). A thermal preference scale for personalized comfort profile identification via participatory sensing. *Building and Environment, 68,* 140–9.

Jazizadeh, F., Ghahramani, A., Becerik-Gerber, B., Kichkaylo, T., and Orosz, M. (2013b). Human-building interaction framework for personalized thermal comfort-driven systems in office buildings. *Journal of Computing in Civil Engineering, 28*(1), 2–16.

Karjalainen, S. (2007). Gender differences in thermal comfort and use of thermostats in everyday thermal environments. *Building and environment, 42*(4), 1594–1603.

Li, D., Menassa, C.C., and Kamat, V.R. (2017). A personalized HVAC control smartphone application framework for improved human health and well-being. In *Computing in Civil Engineering 2017* (pp. 82–90).

Liu, W., Lian, Z., and Liu, Y. (2008). Heart rate variability at different thermal comfort levels. *European Journal of Applied Physiology, 103*(3), 361–6.

Menassa, C. C., Taylor, N., and Nelson, J. (2013). A framework for automated control and commissioning of hybrid ventilation systems in complex buildings. *Automation in Construction, 30,* 94–103.

Nouvel, R., and Alessi, F. (2012, September). A novel personalized thermal comfort control, responding to user sensation feedbacks. In *Building Simulation* (Vol. 5, No. 3, pp. 191–202). Tsinghua Press.

Olesen, B.W. and Brager, G.S. (2004). A better way to predict comfort. *ASHRAE Journal, 46*(8), 20.

Pang, X., Wetter, M., Bhattacharya, P., and Haves, P. (2012). A framework for simulation-based real-time whole building performance assessment. *Building and Environment, 54,* 100–8.

Parsons, K. (2014). *Human Thermal Environments: The Effects of Hot, Moderate, and Cold Environments on Human Health, Comfort, and Performance*. CRC Press.

Perini, R., and Veicsteinas, A. (2003). Heart rate variability and autonomic activity at rest and during exercise in various physiological conditions. *European Journal of Applied Physiology, 90*(3–4), 317–25.

Purdon, S., Kusy, B., Jurdak, R., and Challen, G. (2013, October). Model-free HVAC control using occupant feedback. In *Local Computer Networks Workshops (LCN Workshops), 2013 IEEE 38th Conference on* (pp. 84–92). IEEE.

Santamouris, M., and Allard, F. (eds.). (1998). *Natural Ventilation in Buildings: A Design Handbook*. Earthscan.

Santamouris, M., A. Synnefa, M. Asssimakopoulos, I. Livada, K. Pavlou, M. Papaglastra, N. Gaitani, D. Kolokotsa, and V. Assimakopoulos. (2008). Experimental investigation of the air flow and indoor carbon dioxide concentration in classrooms with intermittent natural ventilation. *Energy and Buildings, 40*(10), 1833–43.

Schulze, T., and Eicker, U. (2013). Controlled natural ventilation for energy efficient buildings. *Energy and Buildings, 56*, 221–32.

Strath, S.J., Swartz, A.M., Bassett Jr, D.R., O'Brien, W.L., King, G.A., and Ainsworth, B.E. (2000). Evaluation of heart rate as a method for assessing moderate intensity physical activity. *Medicine and Science in Sports and Exercise, 32*(9 Suppl), S465–70.

Van Hoof, J. (2008). Forty years of Fanger's model of thermal comfort: comfort for all?. *Indoor Air, 18*(3), 182–201.

Wang, D., Zhang, H., Arens, E., and Huizenga, C. (2007). Observations of upper-extremity skin temperature and corresponding overall-body thermal sensations and comfort. *Building and Environment, 42*(12), 3933–43.

Wang, F., Chen, Z., Feng, Q., Zhao, Q., Cheng, Z., Guo, Z., and Zhong, Z. (2016). Experimental comparison between set-point based and satisfaction based indoor thermal environment control. *Energy and Buildings, 128*, 686–96.

Yao, Y., Lian, Z., Liu, W., and Shen, Q. (2007). Experimental study on skin temperature and thermal comfort of the human body in a recumbent posture under uniform thermal environments. *Indoor and Built Environment, 16*(6), 505–18.

Yao, R., Li, B., and Liu, J. (2009). A theoretical adaptive model of thermal comfort–Adaptive Predicted Mean Vote (aPMV). *Building and Environment, 44*(10), 2089–96.

Yang, Y., Li, B., Liu, H., Tan, M., and Yao, R. (2015). A study of adaptive thermal comfort in a well-controlled climate chamber. *Applied Thermal Engineering, 76*, 283–91.

Zhao, Q., Zhao, Y., Wang, F., Jiang, Y., and Zhang, F. (2014a). Preliminary study of learning individual thermal complaint behavior using one-class classifier for indoor environment control. *Building and Environment, 72*, 201–11.

Zhao, Q., Cheng, Z., Wang, F., Jiang, Y., and Ding, J. (2014b, August). Experimental study of group thermal comfort model. In *Automation Science and Engineering (CASE), 2014 IEEE International Conference on* (pp. 1075–8). IEEE.

37

Reinforcement learning for intelligent environments

A tutorial

Zoltan Nagy,[1] June Young Park, and José Ramón Vázquez-Canteli

INTELLIGENT ENVIRONMENTS LABORATORY, DEPARTMENT OF CIVIL, ARCHITECTURAL AND
ENVIRONMENTAL ENGINEERING, THE UNIVERSITY OF TEXAS AT AUSTIN, AUSTIN, TX, USA

[1] NAGY@UTEXAS.EDU (CORRESPONDING AUTHOR)

37.1 Introduction

The built environment accounts for 30 percent of global final energy consumption and greenhouse gas emissions. At the same time, buildings have a 50–90 percent emission reduction potential using existing technologies and their widespread implementation (Lucon & Ürge-Vorsatz 2014). Some of these technologies, such as cost-effective monitoring and data acquisition equipment, were made possible by recent developments in information and communication technologies (ICT) (Park & Nagy 2018).

The promise is that monitoring and analysis of building data with high spatiotemporal resolution allows building owners and building managers to (a) understand their consumption patterns, and as a result (b) make informed decisions about reducing the energyconsumption of their building. Whether this is through active measures, i.e., updating the operation of their building systems (heating, ventilation, air conditioning, and lighting), or passive measures, i.e., upgrading the building envelope or fenestration, analyzing the monitored data is time-consuming, and typically requires specialized knowledge. Therefore, machine learning (ML) has been proposed to automate and inform the decision making process (Dounis & Caraiscos 2009; Krarti 2003; Miller et al. 2015, 2018; Reddy 2011), culminating in the idea of smart buildings and cities. Machine learning can be considered as the

> field of study that gives computers the ability to learn without being explicitly programmed.
> *(attributed to Arthur Samuel, 1959)*

Or, more formally

> A computer program is said to learn from experience E with respect to some class of tasks and performance measure P if its performance at tasks in T, as measured by P, improves with experience E.
> *(Mitchell 1997)*

733

As illustrated in Figure 37.1, ML techniques can be generally classified into three domains (Russell & Norvig 2010). In supervised learning, the learning agent receives a labelled dataset $\{x_1, x_2, ..., x_n, y_1, ..., y_m\}$, where x_i are called features, predictors, covariates, inputs, or independent variables, and the y_j are called targets, outputs, or dependent variables. Typically, the goal of the agent is to find a suitable mapping that will predict the output for an unknown feature vector. When the targets are numeric, the learning task is regression, while for categorical targets the agent performs classification. Examples include linear or logistic regression, support vector machines, or nearest neighbour classifiers.

In unsupervised learning, the agent receives an unlabeled dataset $\{x_1, x_2, ..., x_n\}$, which only contains features x_i. Its goal is then to discover *interesting patterns* in the data. This is typically achieved through grouping of the feature vectors into similar clusters. Examples include k-means clustering and self-organizing maps.

Reinforcement learning (RL) is the third, machine learning technique in which the learning agent learns the optimal set of actions through interaction with its environment. In contrast to supervised learning, the agent does not receive large amounts of labeled data to learn from. In contrast to unsupervised learning, the agent receives a delayed feedback from the environment. In brief, for a given input, the agent chooses to perform a certain action. It then observes an immediate or delayed reward signal from the environment, and uses it to modify its knowledge on which action is best to choose under given circumstances. Because the agent acts in and learns from its environment, RL can be considered at the intersection between machine learning, and control theory (Jordan & Mitchell 2015), and has elements of game theory.

This interactive aspect is a key feature for the development of intelligent environments for two reasons. For one, it allows the agent to operate, and make decisions without the need for a predefined model. This is particularly interesting for large-scale, complex systems, such as buildings, or groups of buildings, where it is not cost-effective to develop

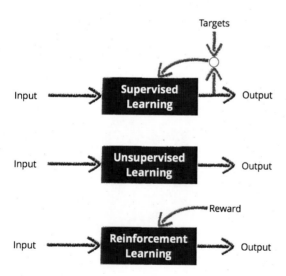

Figure 37.1 Overview of the three machine learning techniques.

Source: Modified from Wang 2012.

such a model (Prívara et al. 2013). Second, the learning agent interacts with its environment (and receives feedback from it), and part of this environment can be a person. Thus, RL provides a natural interface for occupants and facility managers to interact with the learning agent. Conversely, the learning agent can learn directly from the feedback provided by people.

The objective of this chapter is to review and discuss reinforcement learning in the context of the built environment to motivate further research in this direction. In Section 37.2, we introduce reinforcement learning, and highlight the most typical variants of the algorithm. In Section 37.3, we discuss the opportunities for RL and show application examples from building energy and environments, while Section 37.4 discusses the challenges of implementation and algorithm development. Finally, Section 37.5 concludes the chapter.

37.2 Reinforcement learning

In this section, we review the basics of reinforcement learning (RL). For a complete introduction, we refer the reader to standard textbooks (Sutton & Barto 1998). Figure 37.2 illustrates the basic principle of RL. It can be formalized using aMarkov Decision Process (MDP). An MDP is a tuple (S, A, P, R), where S is a set of states, A is a set of actions, P are the transition probabilities for taking an action $a \in A$ in a state $s \in S$, and $R : S \times A \mapsto \mathbb{R}$ is a reward function. The Markovian property refers to the fact that the probability of receiving a particular reward or transitioning from one state to another does not depend on the previous states or actions of the agent, but only on the current ones. The policy $\pi : S \mapsto A$ of the agent maps states to actions, and the value $V^\pi(s)$ of a state is the expected return for the agent when starting in that state and following the policy:

$$V^\pi(s) = E_\pi \left\{ \sum_{k=0}^{\infty} \gamma^k r(s_k, \pi(s_k)) \mid s_0 = s \right\}$$

$$= r(s, \pi(s)) + \gamma \sum_{s' \in S} P(s, \pi(s), s') \cdot V^\pi(s') \tag{37.1}$$

where $r \in R$ is the reward received for taking the action, and $\gamma \in [0,1]$ is a discount factor. As seen in (1), γ allows it to balance between an agent that considers only immediate rewards ($\gamma = 0$) and one that strives towards long term rewards ($\gamma \rightarrow 1$).

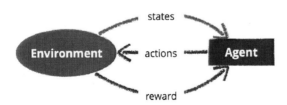

Figure 37.2 Basic structure of reinforcement learning.
Source: Sutton and Barto 1998.

Algorithm 37.1 Value iteration

Initialize $V(s)$ arbitrarily

repeat
    foreach $s \in S$ **do**
        foreach $a \in A$ **do**
$$Q(s,a) \leftarrow r(s,a) + \gamma \sum\nolimits_{s' \in S} P(s,a,s') V(s')$$
        end
        $V(s) \leftarrow \max_a Q(s,a)$
    end
until *policy good enough*

Algorithm 37.2 Policy iteration

Initialize to random policy π'
repeat
    $\pi \leftarrow \pi'$
    compute the value function of policy π
$$V^\pi(s) = r(s, \pi(s)) + \gamma \sum\nolimits_{s' \in S} P(s, \pi(s), s') \cdot V^\pi(s')$$
    improve policy:
$$\pi'(s) \leftarrow \arg\max_a \{ r(s,a) + \gamma \sum\nolimits_{s' \in S} P(s,a,s') V^\pi(s') \}$$
until $\pi = \pi'$

The goal of the learning agent is to determine the optimal policy, π^*, i.e., the policy that leads to the highest expected return. The approach for this, i.e., for solving the MDP, depends on whether or not the probability transitions P and the reward function R, i.e., the dynamics of the system or model are known. This is shown in Figure 37.3 and discussed in the next two subsections.

37.2.1 Model-based learning

If P and R are known, an optimal, or close to optimal, solution can be found through iterative methods, e.g., *value* or *policy iteration* as follows. First, for a given policy π, define the optimal value V^* of a state as (Kaelbling et al. 1996):

$$V^*(s) = \max_\pi E \left\{ \sum_{k=0}^{\infty} \gamma^k r(s_k, \pi(s_k)) \right\}. \tag{37.2}$$

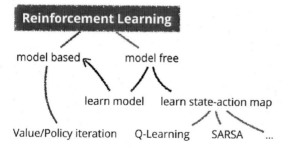

Figure 37.3 Types of reinforcement learning.

It can be shown that $V^*(s)$ is unique and the solution of the following iterative equation:

$$V^*(s) = \max_a \left\{ r(s,a) + \gamma \sum_{s' \in S} P(s,a,s')V^*(s') \right\},$$

(37.3)

and once the optimal value function, V^*, is found, the optimal policy can be determined as

$$\pi^*(s) = \arg \max_a \left\{ r(s,a) + \gamma \sum_{s' \in S} P(s,a,s')V^*(s') \right\}.$$

(37.4)

This is called *value* iteration, and shown in Algorithm 37.1. An alternative, called *policy* iteration, is shown in Algorithm 37.2, where instead of iterating over the value function, the policy is improved iteratively until convergence, and the resulting optimal value function is determined.

Algorithm 37.3 Tabular Q-learning

Initialize $Q(s; a)$ arbitrarily
Initialize s
Define α, γ
while *true* **do**
    Choose a from s using policy (e.g. ϵ-greedy, softmax)
    Take action a, observe r, and s'
    $Q(s,a) \leftarrow Q(s,a) + \alpha[r + \gamma \max_{a' \in A(s')} Q(s',a') - Q(s,a)]$
    $s \leftarrow s'$
end

37.2.2 Model-free learning

If the model dynamics are not known, one can distinguish between two approaches (see Figure 37.3). First, in the model-based approach, the probability transitions are first learned by observing the system, and then used in a planning procedure as mentioned above. Second, in the model-free approach, the agent learns to associate the optimal action for each state without explicitly determining transition probabilities between the states or the value of the states.

Q-Learning is the most widely used model-free reinforcement learning technique due to its simplicity (Watkins 1992). In simple tasks with small finite state sets, and discrete actions, all transitions can be represented using a table, hence the name *Tabular Q-Learning*, which stores the state-action values, i.e., Q-values (see Algorithm 37.3). Then, after taking an action a, given a state s, and observing the reward r, learning is achieved through updating $Q(s,a)$ as

$$Q(s,a) \leftarrow Q(s,a) + \alpha[r + \gamma \max_{a' \in A(s')} Q(s',a') - Q(s,a)],$$

(37.5)

where $\alpha \in [0,1]$ is the learning rate, which explicitly defines to what degree new knowledge overrides old knowledge: for $\alpha = 0$, no learning happens, while for $\alpha = 1$, all prior knowledge is lost. Notice that in contrast to the model-based learning, where the value of a state was determined, here, the $Q(s,a)$-value represents the value of taking a specific action a when being in a certain state s. The relationship between model based value iteration, and model free Q-learning is that

$$V^*(s) = \max_{a' \in A} Q^*(s,a),$$

(37.6)

and as a consequence

$$\pi^*(s) = \arg \max_{a \in A} Q^*(s,a). \tag{37.7}$$

In other words, the optimal policy, π^*, results from taking those actions a that maximize the respective Q-values in each state. In order for the algorithm (e.g., Algorithm 37.3) to converge to the optimal policy, the requirement is that each state-action pair (s,a) be visited infinitely many times, such that the Q-values have converged. In the following, we discuss important features and extensions of Q-learning.

Action selection In Q-learning, the process of accumulating knowledge happens through the trade-off between exploiting known, high-reward, actions, and exploring other, unknown, actions that have not been executed yet under that state. Two approaches are commonly used for this action selection. The first, called ϵ-greedy, selects a random action with probability ϵ (exploration), and the action with the highest expected return with probability $1-\epsilon$ (exploitation). This balancing allows the agent to avoid local minima (exploration), while striving towards convergence (exploitation). In practice, ϵ is set relatively large in the beginning of the learning process, and then reduced progressively. The choice of the initial value and the reduction strategy is domain specific and task of the designer.

Another method for action selection is Boltzmann exploration, which uses the softmax function to transform the Q-values into probabilities as

$$p(a) = \frac{\exp\{Q(a) / \tau\}}{\sum_{a' \in A} \exp\{Q(a') / \tau\}}, \tag{37.8}$$

where the parameter τ can be interpreted as an artificial temperature that controls exploration and exploitation. In the beginning, τ is initialized to a large value, such that all actions are equally probable ($p(a) = 1/|A|$), and efficient exploration can happen. Over time, τ is reduced (or annealed), and for $\tau \to 0$, the action with the highest value will have probability 1 (exploitation). In other words, for $\tau \to 0$, Boltzmann exploration is reduced to ϵ-greedy. The advantage over ϵ-greedy is that instead of taking the current best (greedy) or a completely random action (as in ϵ-greedy), the softmax approach selects the action probabilistically, such that the probability of taking actions with larger Q-values is higher.

Algorithm 37.4 Batch Q-learning

---

while *true* **do**

    Initialize experience set $\mathcal{D}$

    episodes ← 0

    repeat

        if new episode **then**

            episodes ← *episodes* + 1

        end

        Choose a from s using policy (e.g. ϵ-greedy)

        Take action a, observe r, and s'

        Add transition (s,a,r,s') in $\mathcal{D}$

    until *episodes* = m

    $Q \leftarrow UpdatePolicy(\mathcal{D})$

End

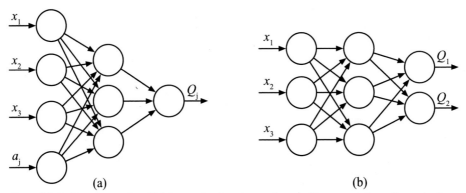

Figure 37.4 Two types of artificial neural networks can be used to map state-action pairs to Q values. Example for three states and two actions: (a) Input: 3 measurements (x_1, x_2, x_3) and 1 action (a_j). Output: $Q_j = Q(x_1, x_2, x_3, a_j)$. (b) Input: 3 measurements. Output $Q_1 = Q(x_1, x_2, x_3, a_1)$ and $Q_2 = Q(x_1, x_2, x_3, a_2)$.

Curse of dimensionality Tabular Q-Learning is affected by the curse of dimensionality: as the size of the state space increases due to, e.g., continuous sensor inputs, the size of the Q-table has to necessarily increase is well. In particular for building control, the curse of dimensionality is significant, considering the potentially large number of sensors measuring various quantities (temperature, humidity, energy consumption, illumination, etc.) continuously. This means that the agent has an exponentially increasing number of state-action pairs to explore before it can converge to an optimal solution. Function approximators, e.g., linear regression or artificial neural networks (Haykin 2009), have been proposed as solutions that allow generalization by directly mapping the state-action pairs, (s, a), to their respective Q-value, $Q(s, a)$.

Two neural network architectures are possible, both assuming a discrete action space (see Figure 37.4). In the first, Figure 37.4(a), the inputs to the network are continuous sensory data (x_i) and one action, and its output is the expected Q-value of the action. In the second version, Figure 37.4(b), only the states serve as inputs, and the output of the network are all the Q-values of all the possible actions. For large action spaces, the first version is more favorable as it allows to compute the Q-values of any possible continuous actions and states. On the other hand, the second version allows to compute the Q-values of any continuous states, but only of as many discrete actions as number of neurons in the output layer.

At the action-selection stage, it is necessary to compute the Q-values of many possible actions under a given state. This can be done by testing different possible combinations of actions in the neural network represented in Figure 37.4(a). For example, if a greedy action-selection is to be followed, an optimization algorithm can be implemented to find the action that, when applied as an input into neural network, maximizes the function of Q-values. This allows to find a continuous optimal action.

Batch reinforcement learning Q-learning using a neural network is performed through updating the weights in the network, typically through the back-propagation algorithm (Haykin 2009). To avoid oscillation of the weights, and achieve good learning behavior of the network, many, dissimilar examples have to be presented to the network in one setting, rather than individual samples. This means, that weight updates of the network should not be performed after each state transition, but rather after many, e.g., m transitions. From another perspective, notice how in Algorithm 37.3, only the Q-values of the previous time-step are used to update the policy, i.e., previous state transitions or experiences of the agent are not retained. However, faster learning could be achieved by retaining not only the last experience, but many experiences, and use those as well in the policy update process. The set of these experiences is called a *batch*, and, thus, this approach is known as *Batch Q-Learning* (Kalyanakrishnan & Stone 2007), and shown in Algorithm 37.4.

The policy update function *UpdatePolicy(D)* used in Algorithm 37.4, can be implemented in different ways. Two of the more prominent approaches are *Experience/Memory Replay* (Lin 1992) and *Fitted Q-Iteration* (Ernst et al. 2005). Experience replay is shown in Algorithm 37.5 (Kalyanakrishnan & Stone 2007), and essentially consists of applying the Q-value update of (5) repeatedly, k times, for all the experiences saved in $\mathcal{D}$. In contrast, Fitted Q Iteration approximates the Q-values successively in a supervised learning approach as shown in Algorithm 37.6.

Memory replay Finally, since in many real-life applications the data contain transitions that occur much more frequently than others, e.g., the diurnal variations of building energy demand, the network should be only presented with the most representative samples in order to avoid biasing the learning process towards the most frequent patterns. This is achieved by extending batch Q-learning with previous experience to a technique called *Batch Q-Learning with Memory Replay* (see Algorithm 37.7 with $\gamma = 0$). In brief, all transitions (s, a, r) experienced by the agent are stored in a data-set $\mathcal{D}$. Then, during learning, a random batch is drawn from $\mathcal{D}$ and used to train the neural network. This algorithm has been successfully applied for building systems (Yang et al. 2015), and is the basis of the recent Deep Learning breakthroughs in Artificial Intelligence (Mnih et al. 2013, 2015; Silver et al. 2017).

Algorithm 37.5 UpdatePolicy(D): Experience/Memory Replay

Initialize Q-values
for *iteration*=1 to k **do**

    foreach $(s, a, r, s') \in \mathcal{D}$ **do**

        $Q(s,a) \leftarrow Q(s,a) + \alpha[r + \gamma \max_{a' \in A(s')} Q(s',a') - Q(s,a)]$
    end

End

Algorithm 37.6 UpdatePolicy(D): Fitted Q-Iteration

---

for *epoch*=1 to E **do**

    foreach $(s, a, r, s') \in \mathcal{D}$ **do**

        $T_i \leftarrow r_i + \gamma_a \max_a Q_{epoch-1}(s_{i+1}, a)$
    end

    $Q_{epoch} \leftarrow Q_0$
    for *iteration*=1 to k **do**

        foreach $(s, a, r, s') \in \mathcal{D}$ **do**

            $Q_{epoch}(s_i, a_i) \leftarrow Q_{epoch}(s_i, a_i) + \alpha_{supervised}(T_i - T_{epoch}(s_i, a_i))$
        end

    end

end

37.3 Opportunities for smart buildings and cities

Consider the following two examples that are particularly interesting to transfer to the built environment. In the first example, Ng et al., over a series of papers have taught a helicopter to fly maneuvers autonomously using model-based RL (Coates et al. 2008; Ng et al. 2004). What is interesting is that no dynamic model has been used to design an optimal controller. Rather, the helicopter was flown manually by a pilot, and the recorded data (pilot commands, and resulting movement of the actuators) have been used to build a probabilistic model of the state transitions, which then have been used to solve the MDP.

Algorithm 37.7 Batch Q-Learning with Memory Replay

Initialize experience set $\mathcal{D}$
Initialize neural network (Q-values) with random weights
Initialize s
Define γ
while *true* **do**
        Choose a from s using policy (e.g. ε-greedy)
        Take action a, observe r, and s'
        Add transition (s, a, r, s') in $\mathcal{D}$
        Sample random batch of size N from $\mathcal{D}$
        Set neural network targets to

$$y_i = r_i$$
End

In the second example, Knox and Stone present the TAMER (Training an Agent Manually via Evaluative Reinforcement) framework, in which the reward signal is explicitly provided by a human (Knox & Stone 2010, 2015). They demonstrate its effectiveness by teaching an agent to learn the computer game Tetris solely by having a human provide it with feedback on individual moves (*good move, bad move, indifferent*) rather than preprogramming that the objective of Tetris is to complete lines. Thus, the learning agent does not need to know the objective explicitly, it is able to learn it from its interaction with the human.

These two examples illustrate that is possible to (a) learn complex dynamics and use them to derive optimal controllers, and (b) learn directly from simple human feedback. These two characteristics are interesting because they occur in building control on adaily basis. Buildings, especially commercial buildings, are inherently complex systems with an increasing number of sensors and actuators, resulting in a large number of states. Accurately modeling the energetic behavior and designing control systems for it is inherently complex and requires significant engineering efforts, which increases the costs.

Similarly, human–building interaction occurs on a daily basis, by way of how occupants use the building (occupancy, lights, blinds, windows, thermostats, etc.), and have a large influence on the energy consumption of the building (Gunay et al. 2013). In both cases, reinforcement learning is inherently suitable to offer an automatic, adaptive approach to increase energy efficiency and occupant comfort.

As an example, consider thermal comfort. Although models exists to understand the environmental conditions under which occupants will generally feel comfortable (ASHRAE 2012; Fanger 1970), to this date it is very challenging to predict the acceptable/comfortable environment for one particular person. Yet, the person typically knows whether or not he/she feels comfortable, and could give simple feedback ("I {am/am not} comfortable now"). In the formalized interactive approach of RL, this feedback becomes a reinforcement signal, which, together with environmental measurements, can be used by the agent to modify its knowledge of the environment, with the goal of potentially avoiding these situations in the future. Recently, Cheng et al. developed a satisfaction Q-learning algorithm for a lighting and blind control system. Using a graphical user interface to gather human comfort, their laboratory experiment demonstrated that Q-learning provided a more acceptable visual environment and energy saving control strategies (Cheng et al. 2016).

For pure energy optimization, De Somer et al. used reinforcement learning to increase the self-consumption of the PV production in six residential buildings by storing energy in domestic hot water (DHW) buffers. They almost tripled the solar energy captured by the domestic hot water buffers compared to the default thermostat controller, and increased the total self-consumption of the PV production by 25 percent (De Somer et al. 2017). Similarly, Kazmi and D'Oca used reinforcement learning to improve the energy efficiency of an air-source heat pump and a DHW storage vessel. They carried out simulations using data from 40 houses, and tested their controller in an actual house, achieving 27 percent energy savings (Kazmi & D'Oca 2017).

At the urban scale, it is important not only to balance the energy efficiency and comfort in individual buildings, but also to coordinate buildings amongst each other. Occupants tend to follow similar energy consumption patterns (e.g. people usually arrive home at similar times and create a peak in the electrical consumption), and buildings also tend to be more efficient at certain hours (e.g. when the indoor temperature is closest to the outdoor temperature). A lack of coordination can cause many buildings to consume electricity at the same hours, which would result in an inefficient management of the overall energy resources. Reinforcement learning would not just allow to learn from occupants and building energy systems, but it would also allow buildings to learn from each other in a multi-agent approach (Vázquez-Canteli et al. 2017).

Finally, notice that reinforcement learning is essentially the formalization of a trial-and-error approach, which is very human and can be expressed poetically as

Ever tried. Ever failed. No matter. Try again. Fail again. Fail better.

(Samuel Beckett, Worstward Ho, 1983)

And this human touch may actually increase its acceptance with the occupants, because the *smart* building or thermostat is not some obscure black-box system working in the background, but rather it works on the very familiar principles of trial-and-error, very much how humans train some animals.

37.4 Challenges

Despite the many advantages of RL for application in the built environment, many challenges remain. As RL is a relatively new and emerging field, there are no off-the-shelf implementations available that researchers could experiment with, in contrast to supervised or unsupervised methods. The reason for this is also that the application of RL depends heavily on the design of the state-action spaces and the reward signal, which are domain and application specific.

Further, as mentioned above, building systems and human–building interaction are highly complex systems. This results in many potential learning agents, which naturally constitute a multi agent system (MAS). Multi-agent RL has been recognized as the most suitable approach to tackle large scale complex real-world problems. However, the theoretical field is still in its infancy, and most available results are on stability and learning convergence for two agents. One of the main challenges here is the fact that the presence of multiple agents violates the stationary environment underlying most single agents learning approaches (Babuska et al. 2008; Tuyls & Weiss 2012). Here, research from the built environment can define clear goals and metrics by which the learning agents are to be evaluated to guide the theoretical developments.

One major challenge for reinforcement learning approaches in general is the relatively long learning time compared to model based approaches. This is typically the case for systems starting with zero prior knowledge. In buildings, however, a substantial prior and expert knowledge exists that can be leveraged to initialize the controllers and to guide them efficiently. In addition, it has been shown that it is possible to expect positive learning results already after one year of learning, which is relatively short when compared to the lifespan of a building (Yang et al. 2015).

Finally, the interaction between individual systems and between occupants and systems are the key to achieve true balance between occupant comfort/satisfaction and energy efficient operation (Cook 2012; Mozer 1998). Since human inputs are required for the algorithms to be successful, the user interface between the occupants and the building systems is key. This could be done either by using the existing infrastructure, in which the occupants keep using the systems as provided, but are limited to the installed hardware and data logging options in the building management system. The other option is to install and upgrade new hardware (voice recognition, motion control, smartphone apps). However, the installation of such novel approaches needs to keep in mindthat occupants tend to use easy-to-access and familiar interfaces (Luria et al. 2017; Sadeghi et al. 2016). In other words, in addition to the technical development of the control system, the occupant's perception of it is also important.

37.5 Conclusion

In this chapter, we have introduced reinforcement learning (RL) algorithms. Starting with basic Q-learning, we showed how mapping techniques, such as neural networks can deal with the curse of dimensionality, and how batch reinforcement learning and memory replay can improve the learning process. We have also provided typical algorithms in pseudo-code. We showed examples for opportunities for RL implementations in the built environment, from human–building interaction, to building energy optimization, to urban scale energy use coordination.

We discussed the major challenges of applying RL, and showed that the generally slow learning times might pose a barrier for success. Furthermore, the interesting and important application of multiple agents interacting with and learning from each other, will require significant progress in the theory of multi-agent systems.

The human, i.e., trial-and-error, nature of RL is interesting because the agent can learn from direct feedback or observation of a human. In addition, it becomes easier to communicate to the occupants of how the learning procedure in their smart building may happen. Such improved communication will lead to improved acceptance, and as a consequence to improved satisfaction with, and success of, the learning system. As reinforcement learning inherently supports interaction, it is vital that researchers of the built environment embrace these opportunities and include learning approaches in their work, modify them and give practical guidance. This chapter hopes to provide a humble contribution in bridging these disciplines.

References

ASHRAE. (2012). *ANSI/ASHRAE 55:2010 Thermal Environmental Conditions for Human Occupancy* (Vol. 2004).

Babuska, R., Schutter, B.D., and Buoniu, L. (2008). A comprehensive survey of multiagent. *Ieee Transactions on Systems, Man, and Cybernetics Part C: Applications and Reviews, 38*(2), 156–72.

Cheng, Z., Zhao, Q., Wang, F., Jiang, Y., Xia, L., and Ding, J. (2016). Satisfaction based Q-learning for integrated lighting and blind control. *Energy and Buildings, 127*, 43–55.

Cook, D.J. (2012). How smart is your home? *Science 335* (6076), 1579–81.

De Somer, O., Soares, A., Kuijpers, T., Vossen, K., Vanthournout, K., and Spiessens, F. (2017). Using reinforcement learning for demand response of domestic hot water buffers: a real-life demonstration. *CoRR*, 1–6. https://arxiv.org/pdf/1703.05486.pdf (last accessed August 20, 2018).

Dounis, A.I. and Caraiscos, C. (2009). Advanced control systems engineering for energy and comfort management in a building environment – a review. *Renewable and Sustainable Energy Reviews, 13*(6-7), 1246–61.

Ernst, D., Geurts, P., and Wehenkel, L. (2005). Tree-based batch mode reinforcement learning. *Journal of Machine Learning Research, 6*(1), 503–56.

Fanger, P.O. (1970). Thermal comfort – analysis and applications in environmental engineering. *McGraw-Hill Book Company.*

Gunay, H.B., O'Brien, W., and Beausoleil-Morrison, I. (2013). A critical review of observation studies, modeling, and simulation of adaptive occupant behaviors in offices. *Building and Environment, 70*(0), 31–47.

Haykin, S. (2009). *Neural Networks and Learning Machines* (3rd ed.). Upper Saddle River, New Jersey 07458: Pearson Education.

Jordan, M.I. and Mitchell, T.M. (2015). Machine learning: Trends, perspectives, and prospects. *Science, 349*(6245), 255–60.

Kaelbling, L.P., Littman, M.L., and Moore, A.W. (1996). Reinforcement learning: A survey. *Journal of Artificial Intelligence Research, 4*, 237–85.

Kalyanakrishnan, S. and Stone, P. (2007). Batch reinforcement learning in a complex domain. In *6th Int'l Conf. on Autonomous Agents and Multiagent Systems (AAMAS)* (pp. 650–7). Honolulu, Hawai.

Kazmi, H. and D'Oca, S. (2017). Demonstrating model-based reinforcement learning for energy efficiency and demand response using hot water vessels in net-zero energy buildings. *IEEE PES Innovative Smart Grid Technologies Conference Europe.*

Knox, W.B. and Stone, P. (2010). Training a tetris agent via interactive shaping: A demonstration of the TAMER framework. In *9th Int'l Conf. on Autonomous Agents and Multiagent Systems (AAMAS 2010)* (pp. 1767–8). Toronto.

Knox, W B. and Stone, P. (2015). Framing reinforcement learning from human reward: Reward positivity, temporal discounting, episodicity, and performance. *Artificial Intelligence 225*, 24–50.

Krarti, M. (2003). An overview of artificial intelligence-based methods for building energy systems. *Journal of Solar Energy Engineering, 125*(3), 331.

Lin, L.J. (1992). Self-improving reactive agents based on reinforcement learning, Planning and teaching. *Machine Learning, 8*(3), 293–321.

Lucon, O. and Ürge-Vorsatz, D. (2014). Fifth assessment report, mitigation of climate change. *Intergovernmental Panel on Climate Change, 674*–738.

Luria, M., Hoffman, G., and Zuckerman, O. (2017). Comparing social robot, screen and voice interfaces for smart-home control. In *Proceedings of the 2017 Chi Conference on Human Factors in Computing Systems – Chi'17* (pp. 580–628). New York, USA: ACM Press.

Miller, C., Nagy, Z., and Schlueter, A. (2015). Automated daily pattern filtering of measured building performance data. *Automation in Construction, 49*(A) 1–17.

Miller, C., Nagy, Z., and Schlueter, A. (2018). A review of unsupervised statistical learning and visual analytics techniques applied to performance analysis of non-residential buildings. *Renewable and Sustainable Energy Reviews, 81*, 1365–77.

Mitchell, T.M. (1997). *Machine Learning.* New York: McGraw-Hill Book Company.

Mnih, V., Kavukcuoglu, K., Silver, D., Graves, A., Antonoglou, I., Wierstra, D., and Riedmiller, M. (2013). Playing Atari with deep reinforcement learning. *arXiv preprint:1312.5602.* http://arxiv.org/abs/1312.5602 (last accessed August 20, 2018).

Mnih, V., Kavukcuoglu, K., Silver, D., Rusu, A.A., Veness, J., Bellemare, M.G., … Hassabis, D. (2015). Human-level control through deep reinforcement learning. *Nature 518*(7540), 529–33.

Mozer, M.C. (1998). The neural network house: An environment that adapts to its inhabitants. *American Association for Artificial Intelligence Spring Symposium on Intelligent Environments*, 110–14.

Park, J.Y. and Nagy, Z. (2018). Comprehensive analysis of the relationship between thermal comfort and building control research: A data-driven literature review. *Renewable and Sustainable Energy Reviews 82P3*, 2664–79.

Prívara, S., Cigler, J., Váa, Z., Oldewurtel, F., Sagerschnig, C., and Žáčeková, E. (2013). Building modeling as a crucial part for building predictive control. *Energy and Buildings, 56*, 8–22.

Reddy, T.A. (2011). *Applied Data Analysis and Modeling for Energy Engineers and Scientists.* Boston, MA: Springer US.

Russell, S. and Norvig, P. (2010). *Artificial Intelligence: A Modern Approach, 3rd edition*. London: Pearson.

Sadeghi, S.A., Karava, P., Konstantzos, I., and Tzempelikos, A. (2016). Occupant interactions with shading and lighting systems using different control interfaces: A pilot field study. *Building and Environment, 97*, 177–95.

Silver, D., Schrittwieser, J., Simonyan, K., Antonoglou, I., Huang, A., Guez, A., ... Sifre, L. (2017). Article mastering the game of Go without human knowledge. *Nature, 550*(7676), 354–59.

Sutton, R. and Barto, A. (1998). *Reinforcement Learning: An Introduction*.

Tuyls, K., and Weiss, G. (2012). Multiagent Learning: and Prospects. *AI Magazine, Fall 2012*, 41–52.

Vázquez-Canteli, J., Kämpf, J., and Nagy, Z. (2017, sep). Balancing comfort and energy consumption of a heat pump using batch reinforcement learning with fitted Q-iteration. *Energy Procedia, 122*, 415–420. Retrieved from http://linkinghub.elsevier.com/retrieve/pii/S1876610217332629

Wang, S. (2012). Machine learning algorithms in bipedal robot control. *Systems, Man, and ..., 42*(5), 728–43.

Watkins, C.J.C.H. (1992). Q-learning. *Machine Learning, 8*, 279–92.

Yang, L., Nagy, Z., Goffin, P., and Schlueter, A. (2015). Reinforcement learning for optimal control of low exergy buildings. *Applied Energy, 156*, 577–586.

Part X
Multi-objective optimization

Resilience-based restoration optimization, resource location, and importance measures

Kash Barker[1] and Yasser Almoghathawi[2]

[1] SCHOOL OF INDUSTRIAL AND SYSTEMS ENGINEERING, UNIVERSITY OF OKLAHOMA, USA

[2] DEPARTMENT OF SYSTEMS ENGINEERING, KING FAHD UNIVERSITY OF PETROLEUM AND MINERALS, DHAHRAN, SAUDI ARABIA

38.1 Introduction

Where previous work in planning for disruptions to critical infrastructure networks emphasized prevention and protection, such planning has recently shifted more broadly to capture the ability of infrastructure networks to withstand a disruption and recovery timely from it. The ability to withstand, adapt to, and recover from a disruption is generally referred to as *resilience* (Turnquist & Vugrin 2013), a definition with which many would largely agree (Haimes 2009; Aven 2011; Ayyub 2013). For critical infrastructures in particular, the Infrastructure Security Partnership (2011) described that planners for a resilient infrastructure network would "prepare for, prevent, protect against, respond or mitigate any anticipated or unexpected significant threat or event" as well as "rapidly recover and reconstitute critical assets, operations, and services with minimum damage and disruption."

These infrastructure networks rely on each other in different ways for them to be functional. As a result, they are increasingly becoming more interdependent (i.e., two infrastructure networks are said to be interdependent if there is a bidirectional relationship between them through which the state of each infrastructure is dependent on the other one) (Rinaldi et al. 2001). Therefore, US federal planning documents suggest (as do many across the globe) the importance of addressing critical infrastructure network resilience in such a way that reflects their "interconnectedness and interdependency" (White House 2013).

This chapter provides an overview of a resilience-based perspective on: (i) optimizing the restoration of interdependent infrastructure networks, (ii) measuring the importance of their components, and (iii) locating work crews and resources for efficient restoration.

38.2 Methodological background

There has been a significant amount of research in the area of critical infrastructure restoration (e.g., Nurre et al. (2012) for single infrastructure networks, González et al. (2016) for interdependent networks). Lee et al. (2007) propose a model to restore disrupted components in a set of interdependent infrastructure networks by minimizing the cost associated with unmet demand. The model, however, does not consider the cost associated with the restoration process, is not time dependent, and does not associate work crews with the restoration process. Gong et al. (2009) propose a multiobjective optimization model to schedule work crews for restoration of interdependent networks with the objectives of minimizing the cost, time to restoration, and delay in restoration time. The model also assigns available work crews to each restoration task. Cavdaroglu et al. (2013) combine the work of Lee et al. (2007) and Gong et al. (2009) by specifically accounting for the interdependencies that exist between critical infrastructure networks. This work specifically uses a network flow model to determine which disrupted components should be restored, create a schedule for restoration, and assign restoration to tasks to available work crews, with the objective of minimizing the total cost including flow cost, restoration cost, and cost of unmet demand.

The work discussed in this chapter restores interdependent networks with the objective of maximizing a measure of resilience. Several approaches have recently been offered in the literature to quantify the resilience (Hosseini et al. 2016). In this work, we consider the resilience paradigm based on network performance shown in Figure 38.1 (Henry & Ramirez-Marquez 2012). Two primary dimensions of resilience, vulnerability and recoverability, are illustrated in Figure 38.1. The vulnerability of a network can be defined as the magnitude of the damage to the network caused by a disruptive event (Jönsson et al. 2008), while the recoverability of a network refers to the speed at which the network recovers to a desired level of performance following a disruptive event (Rose 2007).

Figure 38.1 shows the performance of a network across different states over time, measured by function $\varphi(t)$, which describes the behavior of the network before, during and after the occurrence of a disruptive event, e^j. Accordingly, network resilience, $Я$, can be defined as the time dependent ratio of network recovery over its loss (i.e., $Я(t) = \text{Recovery}(t)\,/\,\text{Loss}(t)$ (Henry & Ramirez-Marquez 2012)) and can be mathematically represented by Equation (38.1), where

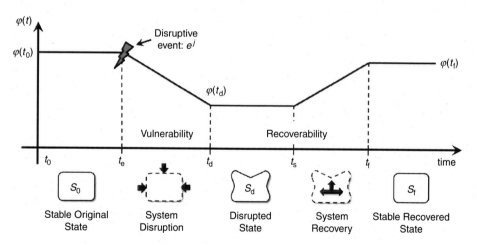

Figure 38.1 Network performance, $\varphi(t)$ across state transitions before, during, and after the occurrence of a disruptive event, e^j.

Source: Adapted from Henry and Ramirez-Marquez 2012.

t_d is the time at which the maximum disruption occurs and t_s and t_f are the starting and finishing time of the recovery process, respectively. The value of the network resilience, $Я_\varphi(t\,|\,e^j)$, at time t given the occurrence of a disruptive event, e^j, is between 0 and 1 where $Я_\varphi(t\,|\,e^j) = 1$ indicates that the network is fully resilient.

$$Я_\varphi(t\,|\,e^j) = \frac{\varphi(t\,|\,e^j) - \varphi(t_d\,|\,e^j)}{\varphi(t_o) - \varphi(t_d\,|\,e^j)}, t \in (t_s, t_f). \tag{38.1}$$

38.3 Restoration optimization

This work, adapted from Almoghathawi et al. (2017a), develops a multiobjective mixed integer programming formulation for the restoration of interdependent networks. This model contains a set of networks, $K = \{1, \dots, \kappa\}$, and a set of time periods, $T = \{1, \dots, \tau\}$. In each network $k \in K$ there is a set of nodes, N^k, and a set of links between nodes, L^k. Each network $k \in K$ has a set of source nodes, $N_s^k \subseteq N^k$, and a set of demand nodes, $N_d^k \subseteq N^k$. There is a set of disrupted nodes $N'^k \subseteq N^k$ and disrupted links $L'^k \subseteq L^k$ for each network $k \in K$ following a disruption.

Supply for each node $i \in N_s^k$ in network $k \in K$ is denoted by b_i^k and is considered to be independent of time. Unmet demand for network $k \in K$ during time $t \in T$ in node $i \in N_d^k$ is represented as slack, s_{it}^k. Each network $k \in K$ has a weight μ^k such that $\sum_{k \in K} \mu^k = 1$. The total slack at all demand nodes in network $k \in K$ prior to a disruption and immediately following a disruption are represented by S_0^k and S_d^k, respectively (according to the time periods t_0 and t_d in Figure 38.1). Accordingly, the slacks in the model represent the loss in the maximum flow, and reducing them to a desired level represents a means to measure the effectiveness of the restoration process. Hence, with Equation (38.1) in mind, the resilience of the system of interdependent infrastructure networks can be represented mathematically by Equation (38.2).

$$\sum_{k \in K} \mu^k \left[\frac{\sum_{t=1}^{\tau} \left[t \left(S_d^k - \sum_{i \in N_d^k} s_{it}^k \right) - (t-1) \left(S_d^k - \sum_{i \in N_d^k} s_{t(t-1)}^k \right) \right]}{\tau(S_d^k - S_0^k)} \right]. \tag{38.2}$$

Another important and conflicting objective for the restoration process is the total cost of the restoration itself. Let the fixed restoration cost for node $i \in N'^k$ and link $(i, j) \in L'^k$ in network $k \in K$ be denoted by fn_i^k and fl_{ij}^k, respectively. The flow unitary cost through link $(i, j) \in L^k$ in network $k \in K$ is represented by c_{ij}^k, and p_i^k denotes the unit cost of unmet demand in node $i \in N^k$ in network $k \in K$. Hence, the system cost, which includes restoration cost, flow cost, and disruption cost (i.e., unmet demand), can be represented mathematically by Equation (38.3), where z_i^k is a binary decision variable that equals 1 if node $i \in N'^k$ in network $k \in K$ is to be restored and 0 otherwise, y_{ij}^k is a binary decision variable that equals 1 if link $(i, j) \in L'^k$ in network $k \in K$ is to be restored and 0 otherwise, and x_{ijt}^k is a non-negative decision variable that represents the flow through link $(i, j) \in L^k$ in network $k \in K$ at time period $t \in T$.

$$\sum_{k \in K} \left(\sum_{i \in N'^k} fn_i^k z_i^k + \sum_{(i,j) \in L'^k} fl_{ij}^k y_{ij}^k + \sum_{t \in T} \left[\sum_{(i,j) \in L^k} c_{ij}^k x_{ijt}^k + \sum_{i \in N_d^k} p_i^k s_{it}^k \right] \right). \tag{38.3}$$

Let the restoration duration of node $i \in N^k$ and link $(i,j) \in L^k$ in network $k \in K$ be denoted by dn_i^k and dl_{ij}^k, respectively. Each link $(i,j) \in L^k$ in network $k \in K$ has a capacity of u_{ij}^k. The status of each component at time period $t \in T$ is represented by two binary decision variables: β_{it}^k equals 1 if node $i \in N^k$ in network $k \in K$ is operational at time period $t \in T$ and 0 otherwise, and similarly, α_{ijt}^k equals 1 if link $(i,j) \in L^k$ in network $k \in K$ is operational at time period $t \in T$ and 0 otherwise. For each network $k \in K$, there is a set of available work crews or resources, R^k, that are specific to network k (e.g., expertise or equipment necessary to restore network k). The binary decision variables denoted by γ_{it}^{kr} and δ_{ijt}^{kr} represent the scheduling variables of the model, where γ_{it}^{kr} equals 1 if node $i \in N^k$ in network $k \in K$ is restored by work crew $r \in R^k$ in time period $t \in T$ and 0 otherwise. Likewise, δ_{ijt}^{kr} equals 1 if link $(i,j) \in L^k$ in network $k \in K$ is restored by work crew $r \in R^k$ in time period $t \in T$ and 0 otherwise. Finally, the interdependence between the networks is captured by Ψ, where $\left((i,k),(\bar{i},\bar{k})\right) \in \Psi$ denote that node $\bar{i} \in N^{\bar{k}}$ in network $\bar{k} \in K$ depends physically on node $i \in N^k$ in network $k \in K$ in order to be operational.

In this multiobjective problem, resilience as measured in Equation (38.2) is maximized while cost in Equation (38.3) is minimized. The constraints for this problem are as follows. Constraints (38.4)–(38.10) represent the flow constraints for each infrastructure network. Constraints (38.4)–(38.6) are the flow conservation constraints at node $i \in N^k$ in network $k \in K$ at time $t \in T$. Constraints (38.7)–(38.10) are the capacity constraints on link $(i,j) \in L^k$ in network $k \in K$ at time $t \in T$ where constraints (38.7) consider undisrupted components, constraints (38.8) and (38.9) consider disrupted nodes, and constraints (38.10) consider disrupted links. Constraints (38.11) are the interdependent constraints which ensure that for a node $\bar{i} \in N^{\bar{k}}$ in network $\bar{k} \in K$ to be operational at time $t \in T$, node $i \in N^k$ in network $k \in K$ must be operational at time $t \in T$ as well. Constraints (38.12)–(38.20) are the assignment and scheduling constraints. Constraints (38.12) and (38.13) ensure that if a component (node or link) in network $k \in K$ is to be restored, it is scheduled to be restored by work crew $r \in R^k$ at time $t \in T$. Constraints (38.14) ensure that at most one component (node or link) in network $k \in K$ can be restored during time $t \in T$ by work crew $r \in R^k$. Constraints (38.15) and (38.16) ensure that a component (node or link) in network $k \in K$ is operational at time $t \in T$ and completed by work crew $r \in R^k$. Constraints (38.17)–(38.20) ensure that a component (node or link) in network $k \in K$ cannot be operational or completed by work crew $r \in R^k$ prior to its restoration time. Finally, constraints (38.21)–(38.28) represent the nature of the decision variables of the restoration model.

$$\sum_{(i,j) \in L^k} x_{ijt}^k \leq b_i^k, \quad \forall i \in N_s^k, k \in K, t \in T \tag{38.4}$$

$$\sum_{(i,j) \in L^k} x_{ijt}^k - \sum_{(j,i) \in L^k} x_{jit}^k = 0, \quad \forall i \in N^k \setminus \{N_s^k, N_d^k\}, k \in K, t \in T \tag{38.5}$$

$$\sum_{(j,i) \in L^k} x_{jit}^k + s_{it}^k = b_i^k, \quad \forall i \in N_d^k, k \in K, t \in T \tag{38.6}$$

$$x_{ijt}^k - u_{ij}^k \leq 0, \quad \forall (i,j) \in L^k, k \in K, t \in T \tag{38.7}$$

$$x_{ijt}^k - u_{ij}^k \beta_{it}^k \leq 0, \quad \forall (i,j) \in L^k, i \in N^k, k \in K, t \in T \tag{38.8}$$

$$x_{ijt}^k - u_{ij}^k \beta_{jt}^k \leq 0, \quad \forall (i,j) \in L^k, j \in N^k, k \in K, t \in T \tag{38.9}$$

$$x_{ijt}^k - u_{ij}^k \alpha_{ijt}^k \leq 0, \quad \forall (i,j) \in L^k, \, k \in K, \, t \in T \tag{38.10}$$

$$\beta_{\bar{7}t}^{\bar{\imath}} - \beta_{it}^k \leq 0, \quad \forall \left((i,k), (\bar{7}, \bar{k}) \right) \in \Psi, \, t \in T \tag{38.11}$$

$$y_{ij}^k = \sum_{r \in R^k} \sum_{t \in T} \delta_{ijt}^{kr}, \quad \forall (i,j) \in L^k, \, k \in K \tag{38.12}$$

$$z_i^k = \sum_{r \in R^k} \sum_{t \in T} \gamma_{it}^{kr}, \quad \forall i \in N^k, \, k \in K \tag{38.13}$$

$$\sum_{(i,j) \in L^k} \sum_{l=t}^{\min\{\tau, t+dl_{ij}^k -1\}} \delta_{ijl}^{kr} + \sum_{i \in N^k} \sum_{l=t}^{\min\{\tau, t+dn_i^k -1\}} \gamma_{il}^{kr} \leq 1, \quad \forall k \in K, \, r \in R^k, t \in T \tag{38.14}$$

$$\alpha_{ijt}^k \leq \sum_{r \in R^k} \sum_{l=1}^{t} \delta_{ijl}^{kr}, \quad \forall (i,j) \in L^k, \, k \in K, \, t \in T \tag{38.15}$$

$$\beta_{it}^k \leq \sum_{r \in R^k} \sum_{l=1}^{t} \gamma_{il}^{kr}, \quad \forall i \in N^k, \, k \in K, \, t \in T \tag{38.16}$$

$$\sum_{t=1}^{dl_{ij}^k -1} \alpha_{ijt}^k = 0, \quad \forall (i,j) \in L^k, \, k \in K \tag{38.17}$$

$$\sum_{t=1}^{dn_i^k -1} \beta_{it}^k = 0, \quad \forall i \in N^k, \, k \in K \tag{38.18}$$

$$\sum_{r \in R^k} \sum_{t=1}^{dl_{ij}^k -1} \delta_{ijt}^{kr} = 0, \quad \forall (i,j) \in L^k, \, k \in K \tag{38.19}$$

$$\sum_{r \in R^k} \sum_{t=1}^{dn_i^k -1} \gamma_{it}^{kr} = 0, \quad \forall i \in N^k, \, k \in K \tag{38.20}$$

$$s_{it}^k \geq 0, \quad \forall i \in N^k, \, k \in K, \, t \in T \tag{38.21}$$

$$x_{ijt}^k \geq 0, \quad \forall (i,j) \in L^k, \, k \in K, \, t \in T \tag{38.22}$$

$$y_{ij}^k \in \{0,1\}, \quad \forall (i,j) \in L^k, \, k \in K \tag{38.23}$$

$$z_i^k \in \{0,1\}, \quad \forall i \in N^k, \, k \in K \tag{38.24}$$

$$\alpha_{ijt}^k \in \{0,1\}, \quad \forall (i,j) \in L^k, \, k \in K, \, t \in T \tag{38.25}$$

$$\beta_{it}^k \in \{0,1\}, \quad \forall i \in N^k, \, k \in K, \, t \in T \tag{38.26}$$

$$\delta_{ijt}^{kr} \in \{0,1\}, \quad \forall (i,j) \in L^k, k \in K, t \in T, r \in R^k \tag{38.27}$$

$$\gamma_{it}^{kr} \in \{0,1\}, \quad \forall i \in N^k, k \in K, t \in T, r \in R^k. \tag{38.28}$$

38.3.1 Illustrative example

Due to the difficulty of obtaining real data for interdependent infrastructure networks, the proposed restoration model is illustrated with realistic fictional interdependent networks which are generated using the extended algorithm for the proximal topology generator proposed by Xin-Jian et al. (2007). The generation process of these fictional interdependent networks is performed in two steps: (i) we generate the individual networks, and then (ii) we build the interdependencies between them.

In this work, we illustrate our restoration model considering two infrastructure networks, namely simulated power and water networks. For the power network, the power generators represent the supply nodes, substations represent the demand nodes, and the lines between these nodes represent the links. For the water network, water pumps and storage tanks represent the supply and demand nodes, respectively and the pipelines between the nodes within this network represent the links. These two networks are interdependent since the water network depends on the power network for operation and the power network depends on the water network for cooling and emission control (Dueñas-Osorio et al. 2007; Zhang et al. 2016).

During the first step of the fictional interdependent networks generation process, each network will initially be seeded with independent and randomly distributed supply nodes. Hence, these supply nodes are located randomly with no links between them. Next, we add randomly distributed nodes to the network one at a time and connect them with a new undirected link to the nearest existing node based on Euclidean distance. Finally, we add a sparse random graph to the generated network upon adding the required number of nodes.

In the proposed restoration model, we consider the physical dependence between the infrastructure networks to describe their interdependence; that is, the functionality of a node in one network is dependent on the functionality of a node or multiple nodes from another network or multiple nodes from other multiple different networks. As such, for the second step of the fictional interdependent network generation process, we connect each water pump and storage tank in the water network to the nearest power generator or substation in the power network, based on Euclidean distance. Similarly, we connect each power generator in the power network to the nearest water pump in the water network, also based on Euclidean distance.

As a result, the two interdependent infrastructure networks generated by the two steps described earlier are illustrated in Figure 38.2. Furthermore, the general properties for the interdependent power and water networks are depicted in Table 38.1, that includes number of nodes, number of undirected links, number of supply nodes, number of demand nodes, and the average node degree for each network, respectively.

We consider the occurrence of a random disruption to the interdependent infrastructure networks where some of the components, either nodes or links, in each infrastructure network are randomly disrupted. Accordingly, a set of 12 components (i.e., four nodes and eight bi-directional links) from each infrastructure network are randomly selected to be disrupted as shown in Figure 38.3, where the yellow nodes and thick links are the disrupted networks components. Hence, the percentage of disrupted components in the interdependent power-water networks is 32 percent representing the total of 24 disrupted components in both infrastructure networks.

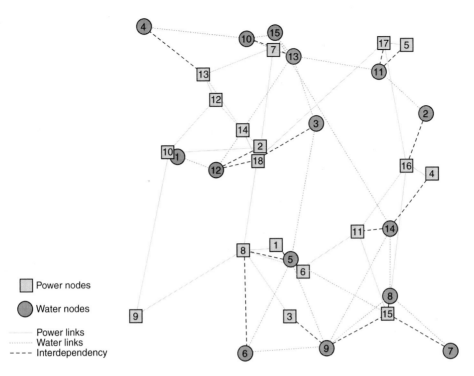

Figure 38.2 An interdependent network example.

Table 38.1 General properties of the interdependent networks

Network	N	L	N_s	N_d	deg
Power	18	24	5	7	2.67
Water	15	19	4	6	2.53

Without loss of generality, we consider the following parameters distributions and values for illustrative purposes of the proposed multi-objective restoration model: $\mu^k = 1/\kappa$ where $\kappa = 2$, $\tau = 40$, b_i^k, $u_{ij}^k \sim U(0,100)$, fn_i^k, $fl_{ij}^k \sim U(1,100)$, $c_{ij}^k \sim U(1,10)$, $p_i^k = 1000$, and dn_i^k, $dl_{ij}^k \sim U(1,5)$. The disruption cost for node $i \in \mathcal{N}^k$ in network $k \in K$ (i.e., unmet demand cost, p_i^k) is considered higher than its restoration cost, fn_i^k, since we are aiming to maximize the resilience of the system of interdependent infrastructure networks. Hence, both objectives will be focusing on minimizing the unmet demand at node $i \in \mathcal{N}^k$ in network $k \in K$. The multiobjective optimization model for the interdependent networks restoration is solved using LINGO 17.0.

Figure 38.4 depicts the trajectory of interdependent infrastructure network resilience considering the three different scenarios for availability of the work crews (WC): one, two, and three work crews. This could help decision makers when developing their recovery plans following a disruptive event (e.g., considering more work crews for one network than the other).

As can be observed from Figure 38.4, considering more work crews helps in achieving full resilience of the interdependent infrastructure networks earlier. However, though they are assigned same number of work crews, it could take longer time in an individual network than

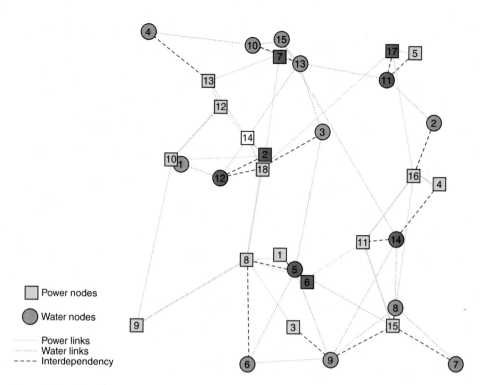

Figure 38.3 The interdependent networks example with the randomly disrupted components.

the others due to the interdependencies among both infrastructure networks, see Figure 38.4(a) and (b). Hence, assigning more work crews to restore the disrupted components in one network than the other could help in reaching the maximum level of resilience of the system of interdependent infrastructure networks faster considering the available time periods for the recovery process. In general, there are three factors that affect the progress of improvement for the resilience of the system of interdependent infrastructure networks: (i) the set of disrupted components in the interdependent networks, (ii) the nature of the interdependencies among the infrastructure networks, and (iii) the number of available work crews for each infrastructure network during the restoration process. Furthermore, the available time period and budget for the restoration process can influence the maximum level of resilience that the system of interdependent infrastructure networks can achieve. Accordingly, what are the disrupted components in each of the interdependent networks that have more influence on the resilience of the system of interdependent infrastructure networks than other disrupted components? These components will naturally be restored first.

The proposed resilience-driven multi-objective restoration model focuses on maximizing the resilience of the interdependent infrastructure networks to retain their performance level prior to the disruption. Hence, the disrupted components might not be all restored, especially if they do not have an effect on the resilience of the other networks. Accordingly, the full resilience of the interdependent infrastructure networks could be achieved prior to complete restoration of these networks (i.e., time to full resilience (TFR) $\leq$ time to complete restoration (TCR) (Barker et al. 2013; Baroud et al. 2014)), where if TFR = TCR, all the disrupted components have some influence on the resilience of the interdependent infrastructure networks.

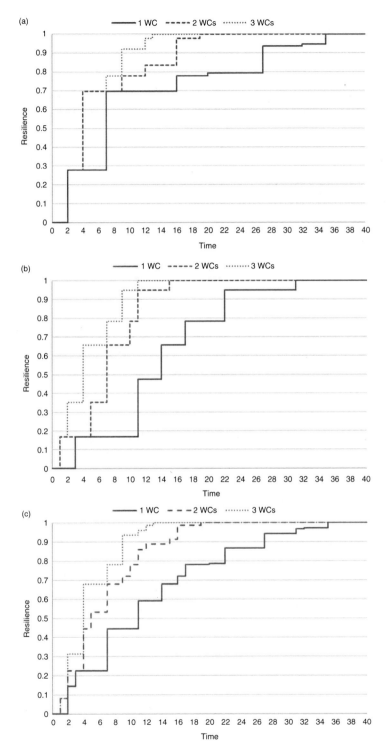

Figure 38.4 Network resilience measure over the recovery time horizon with different number of work crews for the (a) power network, (b) water network, and (c) collective set of inter-dependent networks.

Table 38.2 Comparison between time to full resilience (TFR) and time to complete restoration (TCR) for the collective set of interdependent networks with different number of work crews and different considerations of recovery time

Recovery time	One work crew		Two work crews		Three work crews	
	TFR	TCR	TFR	TCR	TFR	TCR
Fixed	10	12	5	6	3	4
Different	34	40	18	19	12	13

Table 38.2 shows a comparison between the time when the interdependent power-water networks are fully resilient and the time when all the disrupted components are restored with different considerations of recovery times for the disrupted components. Two scenarios are considered for the recovery time: (i) fixed recovery time, that is all the disrupted components have the same recovery time of one time unite; and (ii) different recovery time, as described earlier where $dn_i^k, dl_{ij}^k \sim U(1,5)$. As shown in Table 38.2, the time required to have a fully resilient system of interdependent networks is less than the time needed to recover all the disrupted components in the system. Consequently, there are some disrupted components that have no influence the resilience of the interdependent networks, hence they are not restored. The difference between TFR and TCR decreases as the number of work crews increase due to the availability of multiple work crews in each network.

38.4 Facility location

This work, adapted from Mooney et al. (2017), integrates the initial restoration optimization model discussed previously with a facility location model to determine where work crews in each network should dispatch from.

Many of the parameters and decision variables introduced in Section 38.3 are used here, though a few new terms are introduced to reflect the specific properties associated with facility location. Work crews are assigned to origin locations such that the fixed cost of establishment and the distance travelled is minimized. There is a set of candidate sites, M, where work crews must be assigned prior to a disruptive event (we distinguish between *sites* as candidates and *facilities* as the sites chosen among the candidates). Before a work crew can be assigned to a facility, the facility must be established in a candidate location. Binary decision variable v_m equals 1 if candidate site $m \in M$ is established and is 0 otherwise. There is a fixed cost associated with establishing a resource facility; this cost is represented by cs_m for site $m \in M$. Further, if work crew $r \in R^k$ in network $k \in K$ is stationed at site $m \in M$, the binary decision variable w_m^{kr} equals 1 and is 0 otherwise. Of course, each candidate site is positioned some distance from all disrupted components in network $k \in K$. For nodes, this distance is the Euclidean distance from candidate site $m \in M$ to node $i \in N'^k$ in network $k \in K$ and is represented by ns_{im}^k. For links, the Euclidean distance from candidate site $m \in M$ to the midpoint of link $(i, j) \in L^k$ in network $k \in K$ is represented by ls_{ijm}^k. There is also a unitary cost associated with the distance a work crew must travel from each candidate site to a disrupted element. This cost is captured by ds_m for site $m \in M$.

This formulation is also a multiobjective mixed-integer programming formulation. The first objective maximizes resilience, as in Equation (38.2). As costs associated with facility location and travel to facilities are included in this model, the total cost objective to be minimized is altered to Equation (38.29). Total cost of restoration is a function of fixed restoration costs, unitary flow cost, the cost of unmet demand, the cost of establishing a facility, and the cost associated with the travel distance from candidate sites. The travel distance is multiplied by 2 considering that a work crew dispatches from a candidate site to which they return after each restoration activity.

$$
\sum_{k \in K} \left(\sum_{i \in N^k} fn_i^k z_i^k + \sum_{(i,j) \in L^k} fl_{ij}^k y_{ij}^k + \sum_{t \in T} \left[\sum_{(i,j) \in L^k} c_{ij}^k x_{ijt}^k + \sum_{i \in N_j^k} p_i^k s_{it}^k \right] \right)
$$
$$
+ \sum_{m \in M} \left[cs_m v_m + \sum_{t \in T} \sum_{r \in R^k} 2 \left[\sum_{i \in N^k} ns_{im}^k ds_m w_m^{kr} \gamma_{it}^{kr} + \sum_{(i,j) \in L^k} ls_{ijm}^k ds_m w_m^{kr} \delta_{ijt}^{kr} \right] \right]. \tag{38.29}
$$

Constraints (38.4) through (38.28) remain the same. The facility location decisions are made by constraints (38.30) through (38.32). Constraints (38.30) state that candidate site $m \in M$ may be assigned to at most one work crew $r \in R^k$ in network $k \in K$. This also implies that there may not be work crews from different networks assigned the same site. It is also important to consider the fact that a work crew cannot be assigned to a site that is not established; thus, constraints (38.31) are in place so that work crew $r \in R^k$ for network $k \in K$ may not be assigned to site $m \in M$ unless it has been selected to be established. It should be noted that a work crew may not change locations. Therefore, each work crew $r \in R^k$ in network $k \in K$ may only be assigned to one selected site, as described by constraints (38.32). The nature of the newly introduced decisions variables v_m and w_{mr}^k is provided in constraints (38.33) and (38.34).

$$
\sum_{k \in K} \sum_{r \in R^k} w_{mr}^k \leq 1, \quad \forall m \in M \tag{38.30}
$$

$$
v_m \geq w_{mr}^k, \quad \forall m \in M, r \in R^k, k \in K \tag{38.31}
$$

$$
\sum_{m \in M} w_{mr}^k = 1, \quad \forall r \in R^k, k \in K \tag{38.32}
$$

$$
v_m \in \{0,1\}, \quad \forall m \in M \tag{38.33}
$$

$$
w_{mr}^k \in \{0,1\}, \quad \forall m \in M, r \in R^k, k \in K. \tag{38.34}
$$

The proposed multi-objective optimization model is a mixed integer nonlinear program due to products of binary variables in two terms in the cost objective, Equation (38.29) (i.e., $w_m^{kr} \gamma_{it}^{kr}$ and $w_m^{kr} \delta_{ijt}^{kr}$). However, we would like to linearize the objective function so we can simplify the model and continue using a linear solver. Hence, both nonlinearities can be linearized by introducing two binary variables, G_{imt}^{kr} and H_{ijmt}^{kr}, that satisfy constraints (38.35) through (38.39).

$$
G_{imt}^{kr} \leq \gamma_{it}^{kr}, \quad \forall i \in N^k, t \in T, m \in M, r \in R^k, k \in K \tag{38.35}
$$

$$
H_{ijmt}^{kr} \leq \delta_{ijt}^{kr}, \quad \forall i(i,j) \in L^k, t \in T, m \in M, r \in R^k, k \in K \tag{38.36}
$$

$$
G_{imt}^{kr}, H_{ijmt}^{kr} \leq w_m^{kr}, \quad \forall i \in N^k, (i,j) \in L^k, t \in T, m \in M, r \in R^k, k \in K \tag{38.37}
$$

$$
G_{imt}^{kr} \geq \gamma_{it}^{kr} + w_m^{kr} - 1, \quad \forall i \in N^k, t \in T, m \in M, r \in R^k, k \in K \tag{38.38}
$$

$$
H_{ijmt}^{kr} \geq \delta_{ijt}^{kr} + w_m^{kr} - 1, \quad \forall (i,j) \in L^k, t \in T, m \in M, r \in R^k, k \in K. \tag{38.39}
$$

759

38.4.1 Illustrative example

The proposed facility location model for interdependent infrastructure network recovery is illustrated with the generated interdependent infrastructure networks, power and water, in Section 38.3.1. In addition, candidate sites are placed on the graph in a 4×4 grid resulting in a total of 16 candidate sites. The candidate locations are equally spaced in vertical and horizontal directions, as shown in Figure 38.5. Note that candidate sites set in a grid makes for a more interesting illustration, though it is more likely that a (perhaps smaller) discrete set of candidate sites would realistically be available.

As for the parameters distributions and values for illustrative purposes of the proposed facility location model, they are the same as described in Section 38.3.1 with the addition of the two following parameters: $cs_m \sim U(1,100)$ and $ds_m \sim U(1,10)$. We consider the same set of disrupted components as in Section 38.3.1, that is a total of 24 disrupted components (four nodes and eight bi-directional links for each network). The proposed facility location model is solved using LINGO 17.0.

Figure 38.6 shows the resilience across the available time periods for restoring the disrupted components of interdependent infrastructure network considering three different scenarios for site selection: one, two, and three sites for work crews in each network. As shown in Figure 38.6, increasing the number of facilities and, in turn, increasing the number of work crews in each network, reduces the time to full resilience for the set of interdependent infrastructure networks. It should also be noted that because of the interdependencies between the two networks, one network may reach full resilience before the other. The model inherently prioritizes the recovery of interdependent nodes, but one network may take longer to reach full resilience.

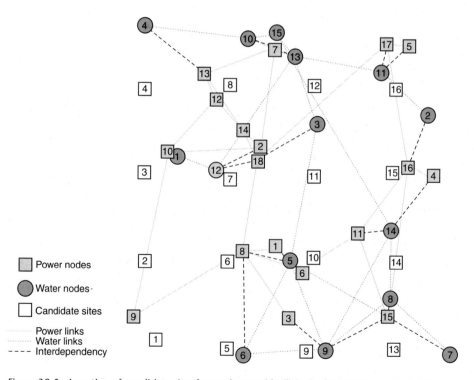

Figure 38.5 Location of candidate sites for work crews' facilities in the interdependent networks.

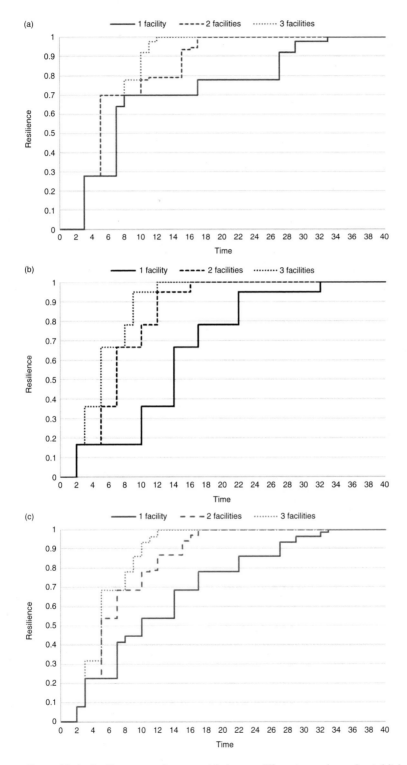

Figure 38.6 Resilience vs. time considering a different number of established facilities for (a) power network, (b) water network, and (c) collective set of interdependent networks.

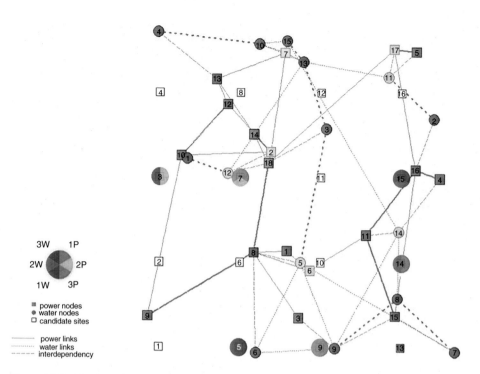

Figure 38.7 The interdependent networks with the disrupted components and the selected sites for work crew facilities.

There exists a tradeoff when increasing the number of facilities. As the number of established facilities increases, additional fixed facility costs increase too. However, there may exist some benefits to increasing the number of facilities. By establishing additional facilities, the distance each work crew must travel to repair a disrupted component and the number of time periods with unmet demand are decreased. As such, determining the number of facilities to establish is dependent upon the cost parameters associated with these decision variables. In the case of this experiment, increasing the number of established facilities decreases the total cost of restoration for the interdependent infrastructure network because the fixed cost of establishing a facility is small compared to the cost of unmet demand in each network.

The selected sites in which work crews' facilities to be established considering the three different scenarios for site selection: one, two, and three sites for work crews in each network are shown in Figure 38.7, where ("1P"), ("2P"), and ("3P") represent the three different scenarios for site selection for power network (i.e., one, two, and three sites, respectively). Similarly, ("1W"), ("2W"), and ("3W") represent the scenarios of one, two, and three sites for work crews in water network, respectively.

38.5 Importance measures

This work, adapted from Almoghathawi and Barker (2017), reformulates the interdependent network restoration optimization approach to develop two measures of importance or criticality of components of interdependent infrastructure networks.

An important part of analyzing critical infrastructure networks is understanding which components of the network adversely affect the performance of the entire network when disrupted. For example, in electric power networks, such an exercise would include identifying the key substations that, when disrupted, could result in large numbers of customers without power. In transportation networks, one may be concerned with the bridges that lead to heavy congestion or delays in travel time when inoperable. The field of reliability engineering has long sought to identify system components that can cause a degradation in system perform-ance, where performance is often measured with reliability or availability (Kuo & Zhu 2012).

Several component importance measures (CIMs) have been proposed in literature to iden-tify the critical and influential components that could be reinforced or protected prior to a disruptive event and prioritized or expedited during the recovery process after a disruptive event (Nicholson et al. 2016, Almoghathawi et al. 2017b). Most of the proposed CIMs are based on network vulnerability analysis, involving the identification of critical components that most affect network performance when disrupted. These CIMs include topological-based CIMs (e.g., average path length (Newman 2003), network efficiency (Nagurney & Qiang 2009), eccentricity and heterogeneity (Guidotti et al. 2017), reliability-based CIMs (e.g., reliability achievement worth (Ramirez-Marquez & Coit 2005), availability (Gravette & Barker 2014)), resilience-based CIMs (e.g., resilience worth (Barker et al. 2013)), flow-based CIMs (e.g., flow vulnerability (Ouyang et al. 2014), flow capacity rate (Nicholson et al. 2016)), and, especially for transportation networks, travel-related CIMs (e.g., travel time and distance (Erath et al. 2009), cost of travel time (Jenelius et al. 2006), and accessibility (Chen et al. 2007)), among others. Some other proposed CIMs are based on analyzing network recoverability following a disrup-tive event by assessing the effect of the disrupted networks components on the performance of their networks when they are restored, including optimal repair time and resilience reduction worth (Fang et al. 2016).

Inspired by the work of Fang et al. (2016) and Barker et al. (2013), we develop two resilience-based component importance measures that extend from the restoration optimization formu-lation in Section 28.3. Let f_{it}^k be the maximum flow from supply node $i \in N_s^k$ to all demand nodes in network $k \in K$ after recovery at time period $t \in T$ obtained by solving the traditional maximum flow problem (Ford & Fulkerson 1956). Hence, the total maximum flow supplied from all supply nodes and received by all demand nodes in network $k \in K$ after recovery at time period $t \in T$ equals $\sum_{i \in N_s^k} f_{it}^k$. The total maximum flow from all supply nodes to all demand nodes in network $k \in K$ prior to and after a disruptive event are represented by F_0^k and F_d^k, respectively (i.e., F_0^k refers to the original maximum flow at time t_0, and F_d^k refers to the maximum flow at time t_d following a disruptive event). Accordingly, the resilience of the system of interdependent networks can be represented mathematically by Equation (38.40), weighted with μ^k for network $k \in K$. Note that Equation (38.40), based on maximum flow, provides a different perspective on resilience relative to Equation (38.2), which was calculated as a function of unmet demand in the networks.

$$\sum_{k \in K} \mu^k \left[\frac{\sum_{t=1}^{\tau} \left[\sum_{i \in N_s^k} f_{it}^k - \sum_{i \in N_s^k} f_{i(t-1)}^k \right]}{F_0^k - F_d^k} \right]. \tag{38.40}$$

Equation (38.40) serves as the objective function to be maximized, subject to the following constraints in addition to constraints (38.7)–(38.11), (38.22), (38.25), and (38.26). All disrupted components (nodes or links) are assumed to have the same recovery time of one time unit.

$$\sum_{(i,j)\in L^k} x_{ijt}^k - \sum_{(j,i)\in L^k} x_{jit}^k = f_{it}^k, \quad \forall i \in \mathcal{N}_s^k, k \in K, t \in T \tag{38.41}$$

$$\sum_{(i,j)\in L^k} x_{ijt}^k - \sum_{(j,i)\in L^k} x_{jit}^k = 0, \quad \forall i \in \mathcal{N}^k \setminus \{\mathcal{N}_s^k, \mathcal{N}_d^k\}, k \in K, t \in T \tag{38.42}$$

$$\sum_{(i,j)\in L^k} x_{ijt}^k - \sum_{(j,i)\in L^k} x_{jit}^k = -f_{it}^k, \quad \forall i \in \mathcal{N}_d^k, k \in K, t \in T \tag{38.43}$$

$$\alpha_{ijt}^k - \alpha_{ij(t+1)}^k \leq 0, \quad \forall (i,j) \in L^k, k \in K, t \in T \tag{38.44}$$

$$\beta_{it}^k - \beta_{i(t+1)}^k \leq 0, \quad \forall i \in \mathcal{N}^k, k \in K, t \in T \tag{38.45}$$

$$\sum_{i\in \mathcal{N}^k} \left[\beta_{it}^k - \beta_{i(t-1)}^k \right] + \sum_{(i,j)\in L^k} \left[\alpha_{ijt}^k - \alpha_{ij(t-1)}^k \right] \leq 1, \quad \forall k \in K, t \in T \tag{38.46}$$

$$\alpha_{ij0}^k = 0, \quad \forall (i,j) \in L^k, k \in K, t \in T \tag{38.47}$$

$$\beta_{i0}^k = 0, \quad \forall i \in \mathcal{N}^k, k \in K, t \in T. \tag{38.48}$$

Constraints (38.41)–(38.43) are flow conservation constraints at node $i \in \mathcal{N}^k$ in network $k \in K$ at time $t \in T$. Constraints (38.44) and (38.45) ensure that once a link or node, respectively, in network $k \in K$ is recovered or operational at time $t \in T$, it will remain operational thereafter. Constraints (38.46) ensure that at most one component (node or link) in network $k \in K$ can be recovered during time $t \in T$. Constraints (38.47) and (38.48) reflect the initial status of the disrupted links and nodes, respectively, in network $k \in K$.

The *optimal recovery time* (ORT) CIM a disrupted network component $e \in E^k = \mathcal{N}^k \cup L^k$ in network $k \in K$, denoted as I_e^{ORT}, is defined in Equation (38.49), where ω_{et}^k represents the status of each component at time period $t \in T$ such that ω_{et}^k equals 1 if component $e \in E^k$ in network $k \in K$ is operational at time period $t \in T$ and 0 otherwise. The ORT represents the optimal time to recover a disrupted network component (node or link) such that the resilience of the interdependent infrastructure networks is maximized over the recovery time horizon. It quantifies the effect of the disrupted components on the resilience of the interdependent infrastructure networks once they are recovered and prioritizes them accordingly where the lower value of the ORT indicates the extent to which the component is more important to the resilience of the interdependent networks. This CIM extends the importance measure proposed by Fang et al. (2016) to interdependent infrastructure networks.

$$I_e^{ORT} = 1 + \sum_{t\in T}(1 - \omega_{et}^k), \tag{38.49}$$

where

$$\omega_{et}^k = \begin{cases} \beta_{it}^k, & \text{if } e \text{ is as node, } e = i \\ \alpha_{ijt}^k, & \text{if } e \text{ is a link, } e = (i,j). \end{cases}$$

The *resilience reduction worth* (ЯRW) CIM of a disrupted network component $e \in E^k = \mathcal{N}^k \cup L^k$ in network $k \in K$, denoted as $I_e^{\text{ЯRW}}$, is defined in Equation (38.50), where $Я(\tau)$ is the optimal resilience of the interdependent networks at time τ and $\Re(\tau | \sum_{t \in T} \omega_{et}^k = 0)$ is the optimal resilience of the interdependent networks at time τ when network component $e \in E^{\cdot k}$ is not recovered. The ЯRW represents the ratio of the optimal system resilience at recovery time τ to the optimal system resilience when a disrupted network component (node or link) is not recovered at recovery time τ. It measures the potential impact on the resilience of the interdependent infrastructure networks caused by a specific disrupted network element (i.e., when this specific disrupted network element is not recovered during the recovery time horizon). The higher value of ЯRW indicates the more critical the component is to the resilience of the interdependent networks. This CIM is inspired by the performance reduction worth importance measure (Levitin et al. 2003) and the reliability reduction worth importance measure (Espiritu et al. 2007), both of which are defined by the ratio of actual system performance to the system performance when a specific component is always considered to be failed or not working.

$$I_e^{\text{ЯRW}} = \frac{\Re(\tau)}{R(\tau | \sum_{t \in T} \omega_{et}^k = 0)}. \tag{38.50}$$

38.5.1 Illustrative example

We illustrate our two proposed resilience-based components importance measures, ORT and ЯRW, with the generated interdependent infrastructure networks, power, and water, in Section 38.3.1. As described earlier in Section 38.3.1, the two interdependent infrastructure networks were disrupted randomly, targeting the same number and type of disrupted components in both networks (i.e., 4 nodes and 8 bi-directional links are randomly disrupted for each network). The set of disrupted components in power and water networks are shown in Table 38.3, respectively. Table 38.3 shows the importance of each disrupted component in power and water, respectively according to the two proposed resilience-based CIMs. The two CIMs are solved using LINGO 17.0, considering the physical interdependency between the infrastructure networks.

The parameters used to illustrate the proposed CIMs are the same as described in Section 38.3.1 with the exception of recovery time for the disrupted components (nodes or links) as they are assumed to have the same recovery time of one time unit each. Two main assumptions are considered in the interdependent network resilience optimization model that is used for the two proposed CIMs: (i) the disrupted network components for both infrastructure networks are considered completely disrupted, and (ii) the recovery time is fixed for all the disrupted components in both infrastructure networks.

According to the proposed ORT and ЯRW importance measures, the disrupted components in both interdependent infrastructure networks have different ranks based on their importance and effect on the resilience of the interdependent networks, see Table 38.3. For example, link (4,16) in the power network is the most important component with the highest restoration priority according to ORT importance measure. However, node 7 in the same network is the most critical component to be restored according to ЯRW importance measure, as shown in Table 38.3. Similarly, node 14 in the water network is the most important component with the highest restoration priority according to ORT importance measure, while it is not the most important component according to ЯRW importance measure, as shown in Table 38.3.

Table 38.3 Restoration priorities for the disrupted components in the interdependent power networkaccording to multiple resilience-based CIMs

Power network				Water network			
Disrupted component		Restoration order		Disrupted component		Restoration order	
		ORT	ЯRW			ORT	ЯRW
node	2	2	2	node	5	8	6
node	6	8	5	node	11	6	2
node	7	4	1	node	12	2	1
node	17	6	3	node	14	1	3
link	(2,14)	9	9	link	(1,12)	3	8
link	(4,16)	1	4	link	(2,11)	7	4
link	(5,17)	7	6	link	(3,5)	10	10
link	(8,9)	5	8	link	(3,13)	5	5
link	(8,18)	10	10	link	(4,10)	4	7
link	(10,12)	3	7	link	(7,8)	11	11
link	(11,15)	11	11	link	(8,9)	12	12
link	(11,16)	12	12	link	(13,15)	9	9

The two proposed CIMs, ORT and ЯRW, provide decision makers with the restoration priorities of the only disrupted networks components that have influence on the resilience of the interdependent networks, which satisfy the objective of the interdependent network resilience optimization model. Accordingly, there could be some disrupted networks components that do not enhance the resilience of the interdependent networks when restored such as links (11,15) and (11,16) in the power network and links (7,8) and (8,9) in the water network, which are ranked arbitrary as shown in Table 38.3. Hence, their restoration priorities are left for decision makers preferences.

Figure 38.8 shows the improvement in the resilience of each of the two considered interdependent infrastructure networks, power and water, by restoring the disrupted components in both interdependent networks according to their importance (i.e. restoration priorities) based on the ORT importance measure. Three restoration scenarios for restoring the disrupted components in the power and water networks are considered in Figure 38.8 which are: (i) restoring all the disrupted components in both network ("Both"), (ii) restoring the disrupted components in the power network only ("P only"), and (iii) restoring the disrupted components in the water network only ("W only"). Though there is a slight improvement in the resilience of the interdependent networks individually when restoring the disrupted components in one network only, as in scenario (ii) or (iii), the resilience will only reach a certain level of improvement as it requires the restoration of the disrupted components from the other network due to their interdependency, as shown in Figure 38.8. However, if the components of one network do not depend on any of the disrupted components in the other one to be functional, their network can be fully resilient when restoring all its disrupted components. Moreover, the set of disrupted components have for each infrastructure network have resulted in zero unit of flow from all supply nodes to all demand nodes in each network. Accordingly, if the decision maker decides to restore the disrupted components in the water network only, the resilience of the power network will remain zero, as shown in Figure 39.8(a); and vice versa, as shown in Figure 39.8(b). Figure 39.8 serves to illustrate the importance of considering the interdependent nature of the two networks when making restoration decisions.

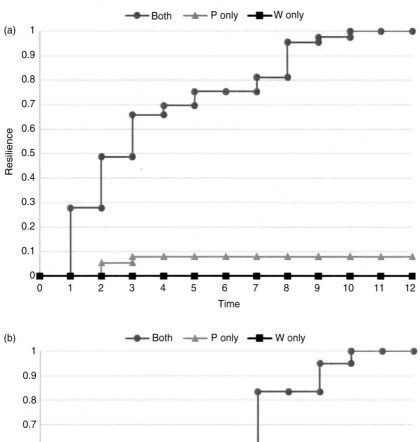

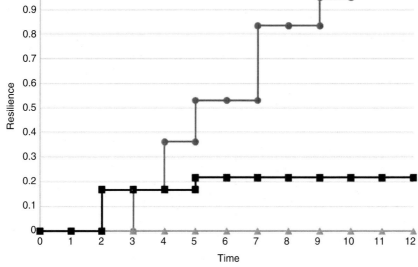

Figure 38.8 Network resilience considering different restoration scenarios based on the ORT for the (a) power network and (b) water network.

38.6 Conclusions

This chapter discusses some new developments in resilience planning for interdependent infrastructure networks, while setting up several areas for future work, which include:

- Valuing the tradeoff between pre-disruption mitigation investments to reduce vulnerability and post-disruption contingency investments to enhance recoverability,
- Improving the realism of modeling restoration activities with the integration of more operational models of work crew behavior (e.g., work crew routing),
- Considering other service network groups beside infrastructure restoration work crews (e.g., emergency response) that are engaged after a disruptive event, and
- Exploring community and economic impacts, and how resilience planning changes when such considerations are made, for an improved understanding of community resilience.

References

Almoghathawi, Y. and K. Barker. 2017. Component importance measures for interdependent infrastructure network resilience. Manuscript submitted for publication.

Almoghathawi, Y., K. Barker, and L.A. McLay. 2017a. Resilience-driven restoration model for interdependent infrastructure networks. Manuscript submitted for publication.

Almoghathawi, Y., K. Barker, C.M. Rocco, and C.D. Nicholson. 2017b. A multi-criteria decision analysis approach for importance identification and ranking of network components. *Reliability Engineering and System Safety*, **158**:142–51.

Aven, T. 2011. On some recent definitions and analysis frameworks for risk, vulnerability, and resilience. *Risk Analysis*, **31**(4): 515–22.

Ayyub, B. 2013. Systems resilience for multihazard environments: Definition, metrics, and valuation for decision making. *Risk Analysis*, **34**(2): 340–55.

Barker, K., J.E. Ramirez-Marquez, and C.M. Rocco. 2013. Resilience-based network component importance measures. *Reliability Engineering and System Safety*, **117**(1): 89–97.

Baroud, H., J.E. Ramirez-Marquez, K. Barker, and C.M. Rocco. 2014. Stochastic measures of network resilience: applications to waterway commodity flows. *Risk Analysis*, **34**(7): 1317–35.

Cavdaroglu, B., E. Hammel, J.E. Mitchell, T.C. Sharkey, and W.A. Wallace. 2013. Integrating restoration and scheduling decisions for disrupted interdependent infrastructure systems. *Annals of Operations Research*, **203**(1): 279–94.

Chen, A., C. Yang, S. Kongsomsaksakul, and M. Lee. 2007. Network-based accessibility measures for vulnerability analysis of degradable transportation networks. *Networks and Spatial Economics*, **7**(3): 241–56.

Dueñas-Osorio, L., J.I. Craig, and B.J. Goodno. 2007. Seismic response of critical interdependent networks. *Earthquake Engineering and Structural Dynamics*, **36**(2): 285–306.

Erath, A., J. Birdsall, K.W. Axhausen, and R. Hajdin. 2009. Vulnerability assessment methodology for Swiss road network. *Transportation Research Record*, **2137**(1): 118–26.

Espiritu, J.F., D.W. Coit, and U. Prakash. 2007. Component criticality importance measures for the power industry. *Electric Power Systems Research*, **77**(5): 407–20.

Fang, Y.P., N. Pedroni, and E. Zio. 2016. Resilience-based component importance measures for critical infrastructure network systems. *IEEE Transactions on Reliability*, **65**(2): 502–12.

Gong, J., E.E. Lee, J.E. Mitchell, and W.A. Wallace. 2009. Logic-based multiobjective optimization for restoration planning. In *Optimization and Logistics Challenges in the Enterprise* (pp. 305–24). Springer US.

González, A.D., L. Dueñas-Osorio, M. Sánchez-Silva, and A.L. Medaglia. 2016. The interdependent network design problem for optimal infrastructure system restoration. *Computer-Aided Civil and Infrastructure Engineering*, **31**(5): 334–50.

Gravette, M.A., and K. Barker. 2014. Achieved availability importance measures for enhancing reliability centered maintenance decisions. *Journal of Risk and Reliability*, **229**(1): 62–72.

Guidotti, R., P. Gardoni, and Y. Chen. 2017. Network reliability analysis with link and nodal weights and auxiliary nodes. *Structural Safety*, **65**, 12–26.

Haimes, Y.Y. 2009. On the definition of resilience in systems. *Risk Analysis*, **29**(4): 498–501.

Henry, D., and J.E. Ramirez-Marquez. 2012. Generic metrics and quantitative approaches for system resilience as a function of time. *Reliability Engineering and System Safety*, **99**(1): 114–22.

Hosseini, S., K. Barker, and J.E. Ramirez-Marquez. 2016. A review of definitions and measures of system resilience. *Reliability Engineering and System Safety*, **145**: 47–61.

Infrastructure Security Partnership. 2011. *Regional Disaster Resilience Guide for Developing an Action Plan*. Technical report, American Society of Civil Engineers.

Jenelius, E., T. Petersen, and L.G. Mattsson. 2006. Importance and exposure in road network vulnerability analysis. *Transportation Research Part A*, **40**(7): 537–60.

Jönsson, H., J. Johansson, and H. Johansson. 2008. Identifying critical components in technical infrastructure networks. *Journal of Risk and Reliability*, **222**(2): 235–43.

Kuo, W. and X. Zhu. 2012. *Importance Measures in Reliability, Risk, and Optimization: Principles and Applications*. New York: Wiley.

Lee, E.E., J.E. Mitchell, and W.A. Wallace. 2007. Restoration of services in interdependent infrastructure systems: A network flows approach. *Systems, Man, and Cybernetics, Part C: Applications and Reviews, IEEE Transactions on*, **37**(6): 1303–17.

Levitin, G., L. Podofillini, and E. Zio. 2003. Generalized importance measures for multi-state elements based on performance level restrictions. *Reliability Engineering and System Safety*, **82**(3): 287–98.

Mooney, E.L., Y. Almoghathawi, and K. Barker. 2017. Resource location for interdependent network recovery. Manuscript submitted for publication.

Nagurney, A. and Q. Qiang. 2009. *Fragile Networks: Identifying Vulnerabilities and Synergies in an Uncertain World*. New York: Wiley.

Newman, M.E. 2003. The structure and function of complex networks. *SIAM Review*, **45**(2): 167–256.

Nicholson, C.D., K. Barker, and J.E. Ramirez-Marquez. 2016. Flow-based vulnerability measures for network component importance: experimentation with preparedness planning. *Reliability Engineering and System Safety*, **145**: 62–73.

Nurre, S.G., B. Cavdaroglu, J.E. Mitchell, and T.C. Sharkey. 2012. Restoring infrastructure systems: an integrated network design and scheduling (INDS) problem. *European Journal of Operational Research*, **223**(3): 794–806.

Ouyang, M., L. Zhao, L. Hong, and Z. Pan. 2014. Comparisons of complex network based models and real train flow model to analyze Chinese railway vulnerability. *Reliability Engineering and System Safety*, **123**: 38–46.

Ramirez-Marquez, J.E. and D.W. Coit. 2005. Composite importance measures for multi-state systems with multi-state components. *IEEE Transactions on Reliability*, **54**(3): 517–29.

Rinaldi, S.M., J.P. Peerenboom, and T.K. Kelly. 2001. Identifying, understanding and analyzing critical infrastructure interdependencies. *IEEE Control Systems Magazine*, **21**(6): 11–25.

Rose, A. 2007. Economic resilience to natural and man-made disasters: Multidisciplinary origins and contextual dimensions. *Environmental Hazards*, **7**(4): 383–98.

Turnquist, M., and E. Vugrin, E. 2013. Design for Resilience in Infrastructure Distribution Networks. *Environment Systems and Decisions*, **33**(1): 104–20.

White House. 2013. *Presidential Policy Directive 21 -- Critical Infrastructure Security and Resilience*. Office of the Press Secretary: Washington, DC.

Xin-Jian, X., X. Zhang, and J.F.F. Mendes. 2007. Impacts of preference and geography on epidemic spreading, *Physical Review E*, **76**(5): 056109.

Zhang, Y., N. Yang, and U. Lall. 2016. Modeling and simulation of the vulnerability of interdependent power-water infrastructure networks to cascading failures. *Journal of Systems Science and Systems Engineering*, **25**(1): 102–18.

39

Lifecycle multi criteria decision analysis of buildings using generalized expected utility

Umberto Alibrandi[1] and Khalid M. Mosalam[2]

[1] BERKELEY EDUCATION ALLIANCE FOR RESEARCH IN SINGAPORE LIMITED (BEARS), CREATE TOWER, 1 CREATE WAY, #11-02, 138602 SINGAPORE; UMBERTOALIBRANDI@BEARS-BERKELEY.SG, UMBERTOALIBRANDI@GMAIL.COM

[2] DEPARTMENT OF CIVIL AND ENVIRONMENTAL ENGINEERING, UNIVERSITY OF CALIFORNIA, BERKELEY, 723 DAVIS HALL, BERKELEY, CA 94720-1710, USA; MOSALAM@BERKELEY.EDU

39.1 Introduction

It is estimated that by 2030, two-thirds of the world's population will live in megacities, characterized by dense urban communities, i.e. high population density and several high-rise buildings close to each other. Thus, there is immediate need for resilience against disruptive extreme events. This can be achieved only through a risk-informed analysis of the safety of structures. Moreover, a building should not only be safe, but also sustainable. Most countries worldwide are attempting to promote the adoption of "green" buildings, enabling sustainable development and quality of life. Such green buildings should be designed to be resilient, also because of environmental impact associated with post-hazard repairs. To this aim, the lifecycle analysis of the infrastructure systems, including buildings, should drive the design process.

In a decision-making process, an important step is represented by the selection of multiple design alternatives and/or actions through the building lifecycle. These alternatives are compared in terms of chosen suitable performance measures. The latter represent the criteria of the decision-making problem. An important challenge is represented by the different sources of uncertainty, giving rise to a problem of decision under uncertainty or under risk.

In this chapter, the probabilistic modeling of the performance measures is described through the Performance-based Engineering (PBE) approach (Cornell & Krawinkler 2000; Günay & Mosalam 2013; Alibrandi & Mosalam 2018), which is widely adopted in Civil and Mechanical Engineering. PBE approach links in a natural way the building design to the desired uncertain performances, denoted in the following as Performance Variables of the decision-making problem. Their distribution is obtained through the Kernel Density Maximum Entropy Method (KDMEM), recently proposed by the authors (Alibrandi & Mosalam 2017a). KDMEM is based on the Maximum Entropy (ME) approach, so that it provides the least biased and most honest distribution given the available information. Moreover, the adoption of fractional moments in KDMEM provides a good description of the tails of the distributions, from samples of small size.

The different design alternatives are typically compared and ranked through a suitable metric. The most popular approach is represented by the minimization of the Expected Cost (EC) (Benjamin & Cornell 1970). However, experience has shown that typically the decision makers are conservative with respect to a minimum lifecycle expected cost, because of their risk-aversion toward low-probability high-consequence events. Some researchers conjecture that the risk-aversion can be explained by the non-inclusion of follow-up consequences (Maes & Faber 2007). Therefore, the minimum EC should be adopted by considering complete cost models. This is the approach followed in (Gardoni et al. 2016), where a financial approach to the lifecycle cost analysis is pursued. However, it is underlined that in the real world, perfect information does not exist, especially with reference to the lifecycle analysis. Therefore, any decision under uncertainty is affected to some extent by the risk-attitude of the decision maker.

Differently from the EC approach, in the utility theory, it is recognized that subjective factors should be incorporated into the risk evaluation. This is accomplished through the utility function, which measures the desirability of the consequences. In such cases, the optimal alternative gives the maximum Expected Utility (EU) (Von Neumann and Morgenstern 1944). It has been recognized that also the EU is not able to provide an accurate description of the observed behavior of the decision makers (Allais & Hagen 1979; Kahneman & Tversky 1979). Therefore, the Cumulative Prospect Theory (CPT) (Tversky & Kahneman 1992) and the Rank-Dependent Utility Theory (Quiggin 1993) try to address these issues through the integration of the risk perception inside the formulation of the utility function, including the subjective evaluation of the probability of occurrence of the rare events. In this chapter, the alternatives are ranked through the broad Generalized Expected Utility (GEU) (Mosalam et al. 2018), where the risk perception is modeled through the application of suitable risk measures (e.g. quantiles, superquantiles) (Rockafellar 2007, Rockafellar & Royset 2015) of the utility of the decision maker, defined through its probability distribution. The joint adoption of PBE with GEU gives rise to the extended framework PBE-GEU. An attractive feature of PBE-GEU is its straightforward scalability to multiple criteria, obtained by applying the GEU to the multi-attribute utility function (Keeney & Raiffa 1993). This is useful, because the integrated design typically requires the joint consideration of multiple criteria, and even sometimes conflicting ones.

The decision-making process is dynamic in the sense that the optimal decision changes when new information is available. This is obtained through Bayesian analysis, which is implemented in PBE-GEU through the Bayesian Networks (BN) (Alibrandi & Mosalam 2017b). The formulation can be used for updating the distribution of the performance measures described through not only the Performance Variables $G_1, G_2, ..., G_n$, but also the subjective utilities expressing the degree of preference of the decision maker and of the different stakeholders (Konstantakopoulos et al. 2017).

After describing the main features of the framework, PBE-GEU is applied to a hypothetical office building located in California. The numerical application shows the capabilities of PBE-GEU for lifecycle integrated design under uncertainty of a building subjected to an extreme event represented by the seismic hazard.

39.2 Life cycle analyses: economic and environmental metrics

39.2.1 Life cycle cost

The Life cycle cost (LCC) represents the total cost incurred by the building during the lifecycle (Wen & Kang 2001a, 2001b; Gardoni et al. 2016), i.e.

$$LCC(t_n, \boldsymbol{x}) = C_0(\boldsymbol{x}) + \sum_{k=1}^{n} C_F(t_k, \boldsymbol{x}), \qquad (39.1)$$

where $\boldsymbol{x}$ collects the design parameters, t_n is the lifespan typically measured in years, i.e. t_k for $k = 1,\ldots,n$, C_0 is the initial cost, while $C_F(t_k, \boldsymbol{x})$ is the lifecycle failure cost. Typically, when the design is more conservative, the initial cost $C_0(\boldsymbol{x})$ increases, while the failure cost $C_F(t_k, \boldsymbol{x})$ decreases. The initial cost $C_0(\boldsymbol{x})$ is usually assumed deterministic, such that

$$C_0(\boldsymbol{x}) = C_0^m(\boldsymbol{x}) + C_0^t(\boldsymbol{x}) + C_0^s(\boldsymbol{x}), \qquad (39.2)$$

where $C_0^m(\boldsymbol{x})$, $C_0^t(\boldsymbol{x})$ and $C_0^s(\boldsymbol{x})$ denote the cost of the material in the respective material manufacturing, material transportation, and on-site construction phases. They are defined as follows:

$$\begin{cases} C_0^m(\boldsymbol{x}) = \sum_m Q_m(\boldsymbol{x}) \times UC_m \\ C_0^t(\boldsymbol{x}) = \sum_v H_v(\boldsymbol{x}) \times UC_{m,v}, \\ C_0^s(\boldsymbol{x}) = \sum_e H_e(\boldsymbol{x}) \times UC_e \end{cases} \qquad (39.3)$$

where Q_m (m^3 or ton) is the quantity of the material m, UC_m its unit cost ($\$ / m^3$ or $\$ / ton$), H_v is the usage hours (h) of vehicle v, $UC_{m,v}$ is the unit cost per unit hour ($\$ / h$) of vehicle v for the transportation of the material m, H_e is the on-site usage hours of the equipment e, and UC_e is the unit cost per unit hour ($\$ / h$) of equipment e.

The lifecycle failure cost represents a stochastic process because of the uncertainties related to the hazard(s) demands on the building, the capacities, and socio-economic changes, e.g. related to the use and occupation of the building. It is expressed as follows:

$$C_F(t_k, \boldsymbol{x}) = C_S(t_k, \boldsymbol{x}) + C_{NS}(t_k, \boldsymbol{x}) = \left[L_S(\boldsymbol{x}|ds) + L_{NS}(\boldsymbol{x}|ds) \right] \left(\frac{1 + \gamma_r}{1 + \gamma_d} \right)^{t_k}, \qquad (39.4)$$

where $C_S(t_k, \boldsymbol{x})$ and $C_{NS}(t_k, \boldsymbol{x})$ are the contributions of repair costs of structural and non-structural components, respectively, $L_S(\boldsymbol{x}|ds)$ and $L_{NS}(\boldsymbol{x}|ds)$ are the corresponding annual losses under the assumption that each year the existing damages are repaired, γ_r is the growth rate providing the revaluation of the asset, while γ_d represents the discounting rate, which may be considered if the decision maker considers less painful future costs which are discounted to the net present value. The repair costs of the structural elements are dependent upon the damage state ds (Wei et al. 2016) as follows:

$$L_S(\boldsymbol{x}|ds) = C_S^m(\boldsymbol{x}|ds) + C_S^t(\boldsymbol{x}|ds) + C_S^s(\boldsymbol{x}|ds) + C_S^d(\boldsymbol{x}|ds), \qquad (39.5)$$

where $C_S^m(\boldsymbol{x}|ds)$, $C_S^t(\boldsymbol{x}|ds)$, $C_S^s(\boldsymbol{x}|ds)$ and $C_S^d(\boldsymbol{x}|ds)$ denote the respective cost of the material in the material manufacturing, material transportation, and on-site construction phases and the debris disposal. Similar expression to that in Equation (39.5) can be used for the repair costs of the non-structural components.

A complete cost model needs to take into account possible revenues affecting the optimal decision in terms of Life Cycle Revenue (LCR). Here, the revenues are represented by the rent as follows:

$$LCR(t_n, x) = \sum_{k=1}^{n} R(x|ds) \left(\frac{1+\gamma_r}{1+\gamma_d} \right)^{t_k}, \tag{39.6}$$

where $R(x|ds)$ denotes the annual rent. It depends on the given damage state ds, since this may determine loss of functionality, and consequently a reduction of the rent.

The lifecycle economic benefit $B(t_n, x)$ is here given by the Net Present Value (NPV), defined as the difference between the revenues and the costs as follows:

$$B(t_n, x) \equiv NPV(t_n, x) = LCR(t_n, x) - LCC(t_n, x). \tag{39.7}$$

The economic benefit can also be described by different economic metrics, like the Life Profitability Method defined as an average of multiple financial indices, see (Gardoni et al. 2016).

39.2.2 Life cycle environmental analysis

In terms of environmental metric, the $CO_2(t_k)$ emission during the life cycle environment (LCE) is considered as follows:

$$LCE(t_n, x) = CO_2(t_0, x) + \sum_{k=1}^{n} CO_2(t_k, x), \tag{39.8}$$

where $CO_2(t_0, x)$ and $CO_2(t_k, x)$ for $k = 1,\ldots,n$ denote the CO_2 emissions during the construction stage and the lifecycle, respectively. The initial emission $CO_2(t_0, x)$ is assumed as follows:

$$CO_2(t_0, x) = CO_2^m(t_0, x) + CO_2^t(t_0, x) + CO_2^s(t_0, x), \tag{39.9}$$

where $CO_2^m(t_0, x)$, $CO_2^t(t_0, x)$ and $CO_2^s(t_0, x)$ denote the CO_2 emissions in the respective material manufacturing, material transportation, and on-site construction phases. They are defined as follows:

$$\begin{cases} CO_2^m(t_0, x) = \sum_m Q_m(x) \times EF_m \\ CO_2^t(t_0, x) = \sum_v H_v(x) \times DC_v \times EF_d \\ CO_2^s(t_0, x) = \sum_e H_e(x) \times DC_e \times EF_d, \end{cases} \tag{39.10}$$

where EF_m is the CO_2 emission factor of the material $(kg - CO_2/m^3$ or $kg - CO_2/ton)$, DC_v and DC_e are the diesel consumption per hour (l/h) of vehicle v and equipment e, respectively, while EF_d is the CO_2 emission factor of diesel $(kg - CO_2/l)$.

The lifecycle CO_2 emission represents a stochastic process because of the uncertainties related to the degrading properties of material, climate change, etc. Here, it is modeled as an ergodic stationary process as follows:

$$CO_2(t_k, \boldsymbol{x}) = \sum_{i=1}^{k} CO_2(\boldsymbol{x}|ds),$$

(39.11)

where $CO_2(t_k, \boldsymbol{x})$ is the CO_2 emission because of post-hazard repairs at year $t = t_k$, while $CO_2(\boldsymbol{x}|ds)$ is the annual emission under the assumption that each year the existing damages are repaired. In a lifecycle environmental analysis, it is assumed that no discount rate is applied, because inside a sustainability framework, the future generations have the same importance of the current ones. Similar to L_S in Equation (39.5), one has the following:

$$CO_2(\boldsymbol{x}|ds) = CO_2^m(\boldsymbol{x}|ds) + CO_2^t(\boldsymbol{x}|ds) + CO_2^s(\boldsymbol{x}|ds) + CO_2^d(\boldsymbol{x}|ds),$$

(39.12)

where $CO_2^m(\boldsymbol{x}|ds)$, $CO_2^t(\boldsymbol{x}|ds)$, $CO_2^s(\boldsymbol{x}|ds)$ and $CO_2^d(\boldsymbol{x}|ds)$ denote the respective cost of the material in the material manufacturing, material transportation, and on-site construction phases and the debris disposal.

39.3 PEER performance-based engineering

The main difficulty with the lifecycle analyses and the corresponding decision making is represented by the multiple sources of uncertainty. The Pacific Earthquake Engineering Research (PEER) Center developed a robust Performance-based Engineering (PBE) methodology (Cornell & Krawinkler 2000; Günay & Mosalam 2013; Alibrandi & Mosalam 2018) whose focus is the explicit determination of system performance measures meaningful to various stakeholders (e.g. losses, downtime, etc.). In PBE, the following four main steps can be delineated as follows: (i) characterization and assessment of the hazard, defined through its intensity measure, IM (ii) probabilistic assessment of the demand on the structure, described through the Engineering Demand Parameter, EDP (iii) probabilistic assessment of the resulting physical damage, described through the Damage Measure, DM, and (iv) assessment of the losses modeled through chosen performance variables, G. The latter step is one key feature of the PBE methodology, because it allows the explicit calculation of the performance measures, expressed in terms of the direct interest of various stakeholders. Therefore, the performance variables G_i may include not only structural losses, but also construction and maintenance costs, CO_2 emission during the construction and operation phases, etc.

The adoption of the PBE methodology (Cornell & Krawinkler 2000) has several advantages: (i) it is based on the total probability theorem, which requires elementary knowledge of probabilistic concepts and thus easily adopted and interpreted in practice, (ii) it is already applied for the evaluation of the safety of structures subjected to seismic hazard by practicing engineers, making the extension to different hazards and other G_i somewhat straightforward, and (iii) the different stages of the analysis can be performed by separate groups of a multi-disciplinary research team.

Following Alibrandi and Mosalam (2017b) and considering the Multi-Attribute Utility Theory (MAUT), it is natural to formulate the PBE-MAUT approach for sustainable and resilient building design inside the framework of the Bayesian Networks (BN), which are graphical probabilistic models that facilitate the efficient representation of the dependence among

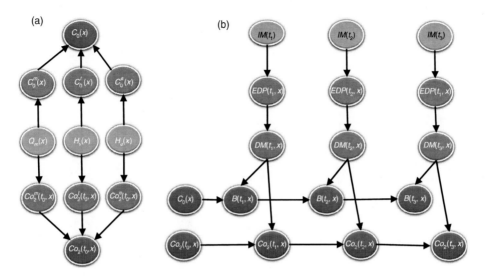

Figure 39.1 Schematic of lifecycle analyses through Bayesian networks. (a) construction stage, (b) lifecycle.

random variables (Nielsen & Jensen 2009). The BNs have a transparent modeling framework, and they can be adopted by users with limited background in probabilistic or reliability analyses. Figures 39.1(a) and 39.1(b) represent the PBE framework applied to the construction stage and to the lifecycle, respectively.

Note that some variables, including the performance variables G_S are expressed in terms of x, to denote their dependence on the design variables. In Figure 39.1(b), the links from $DM(t_k, x)$ (Damage Measure) to $B(t_k, x)$ indicate that the distribution of B is conditioned on DM (see Equations (39.4), (39.6), and (39.7)). In a similar manner, it is seen that the distribution of $CO_2(t_k, x)$ is conditioned on $DM(t_k, x)$ (see Equation (39.12)). The link between $CO_2(t_{k-1}, x)$ and $CO_2(t_k, x)$ indicates that the amount of emitted CO_2 at year $t = t_k$ is dependent upon the emitted CO_2 in the previous t_{k-1} years. There is no link between $DM(t_{k-1}, x)$ and $DM(t_k, x)$ since it is assumed that there is no degradation of the material and each damage is repaired across the year.

39.4 Kernel density maximum entropy method

Typically, in PEER PBE, the uncertain quantities are described from a probabilistic point of view by fitting a Lognormal (LN) distribution to the data. However, this choice has been sometimes questioned, because it might not represent the best statistical model given the available data. In this chapter, we adopt the Kernel Density Maximum Entropy Method (KDMEM) (Alibrandi & Mosalam 2017a), which is a kernel density approach based on the information theory.

The target Probability Density Function (PDF) of the uncertain quantity X, $f_X(x)$, is expressed as a linear superposition of Kernel Density Functions (KDFs) as follows:

$$f_X(x) \cong f_{kD}(x) = \sum_{i=1}^{N} p_i f_X^K(x; x_i, h),$$

(39.13)

where the coefficients p_i satisfy the constraints $0 \leq p_i \leq 1$, $\sum_i p_i = 1$, while $f_X^k(x; x_i, h)$ is the i-th basis KDF. The centers x_i, $i = 1,2,\ldots,N$, are uniformly spaced with a constant step $\Delta x = x_{i+1} - x_i$ in the range $[0, x_{max}]$. The bandwidth is $h = (2/3)\Delta x$, which is shown to be a suitable value under uniform spacing of the centers (Alibrandi & Ricciardi 2008; Alibrandi & Mosalam 2017a). It is noted that when $N \to \infty$, then $h \to 0$, and Equation (39.13) gives

$$f_{kD}(x) = \sum_{i=1}^{N} p_i \delta(x - x_i)$$

(39.14)

where δ is the Dirac Delta function. Therefore, the representation in Equations (39.13)–(39.14) can reconstruct any type of distribution. Multiplying both sides of Equation (39.14) by x^{α_k}, α_k being positive real number, $k = 1,2,\ldots,M$, arranged in the vector, $\boldsymbol{\alpha}$, and integrating over the domain, the following relationship holds:

$$\begin{cases} \mathbf{1}^T \boldsymbol{p} = 1 \\ \\ \boldsymbol{M}(\boldsymbol{\alpha})\boldsymbol{p} = \boldsymbol{\mu}(\boldsymbol{\alpha}) \end{cases}$$

(39.15)

where $\mathbf{1}$ is a vector of N unit entries, and $\boldsymbol{p}$ collects the N free parameters $p_1, p_2, \ldots, p_N$, while terms of the matrix $\boldsymbol{M}$ and vector $\boldsymbol{\mu}$ are given as follows:

$$M_{ki}(\boldsymbol{\alpha}) = \int x^{\alpha_k} \delta(x - x_i) dx = x_i^{\alpha_k}$$

$$\mu_k(\boldsymbol{\alpha}) = \int_{\Omega} x^{\alpha_k} f_X(x) dx = E[X^{\alpha_k}]$$

(39.16)

In Equations (39.15)–(39.16), $\boldsymbol{\mu}(\boldsymbol{\alpha})$ collects the fractional moments (Novi Inverardi & Tagliani 2003; Taufer et al. 2009; Zhang & Pandey 2013) of X. It is noted that the fractional moments can be defined for low values of α ($\alpha \leq 2$), such that the estimates of sample fractional moments derived from a small sample of n_s data can be robust enough. Moreover, it is seen that a reduced number of fractional moments, say $M = 4$, may provide a good description of the tails. To determine the free parameters $p_1, p_2, \ldots, p_N$, it is noted from Equations (39.15)–(39.16) that $\boldsymbol{p}$ can be considered as the Probability Mass Function (PMF) of a discrete valued random variable X_δ whose fractional moments $E[X_\delta^{\alpha_k}] = \sum_{i=1}^{N} x_i^{\alpha_k} p_i$ are the same of $f_X(x)$, i.e. $E[X_\delta^{\alpha_k}] = E[X^{\alpha_k}] = \mu_k(\boldsymbol{\alpha})$. According to Jaynes (1957, 1968), the ME probability distribution, $\boldsymbol{p}_{ME}$, is the least biased distribution, given the satisfaction of the available information. It is obtained through the maximization of the Shannon's entropy $H(\boldsymbol{p}) = -\sum_{i=1}^{N} p_i \ln(p_i)$ as follows:

$$\begin{cases} \max_{\boldsymbol{p}} H(\boldsymbol{p}) \\ \\ \mathbf{1}^T \boldsymbol{p} = 1 \\ \\ \boldsymbol{M}(\boldsymbol{\alpha})\boldsymbol{p} = \boldsymbol{\mu}(\boldsymbol{\alpha}) \end{cases}$$

(39.17)

The optimization problem in Equation (39.17) is convex, which implies the uniqueness of the ME distribution of X_δ, expressed as follows:

$$p_i^{ME}(\lambda_1, \lambda_2, \ldots, \lambda_M) = exp\left\{-\lambda_0(\lambda_1, \lambda_2, \ldots, \lambda_M) - \sum_{k=1}^{M} \lambda_k x_i^{\alpha_k}\right\} \quad i = 1, \ldots, N, \tag{39.18}$$

where

$$\lambda_0(\lambda_1, \lambda_2, \ldots, \lambda_M) = log\left\{\sum_{i=1}^{N} exp\left(-\sum_{k=1}^{M} \lambda_k x_i^{\alpha_k}\right)\right\}. \tag{39.19}$$

In Equations (39.18)–(39.19), the parameters $\lambda_1, \lambda_2, \ldots, \lambda_M$ can be determined as a solution of a linear system of M equations as follows:

$$\Theta(\alpha)\lambda = \rho(\alpha), \tag{39.20}$$

where

$$\Theta_{kj}(\alpha) = \alpha_k E\left[X^{\alpha_k + \alpha_j}\right], \quad \rho_j(\alpha) = (\alpha_j + 1)E\left[X^{\alpha_j}\right], \tag{39.21}$$

with $k = 1, 2, \ldots, M$ and $j = 0, 1, \ldots, M-1$. From Equations (39.20)–(39.21), the Lagrange multipliers $\lambda_1, \lambda_2, \ldots, \lambda_M$ are determined and substituted into Equations (39.18)–(39.19) to provide the ME distribution p_{ME} of X_δ. The substitution of p_{ME} into Equation (39.13) gives the KDME PDF $f_{KDME}(x)$. In the proposed procedure, a central role is played by the number M and values of the free parameters $\alpha_1, \alpha_2, \ldots, \alpha_M$. To this aim, it is useful to interpret the KDME PDF as a probabilistic model of parameters α as follows:

$$\tilde{f}_{KDME}(x;\alpha) = \sum_{i=1}^{N} p_{i,ME}(\alpha) f_X^K(x). \tag{39.22}$$

The model selection is pursued through the Akaike Information Criterion (AIC) (Akaike 1973) which suggests to maximize an unbiased estimation of the following logarithmic likelihood function:

$$L(\alpha_1, \alpha_2, \ldots, \alpha_M) = \frac{1}{n_s} \sum_{j=1}^{n_s} log\left[\tilde{f}_{KDME}\left(x^{(j)}; \alpha_1, \alpha_2, \ldots, \alpha_M\right)\right] - \frac{M}{n_s}, \tag{39.23}$$

where n_s is the number of data of the sample, $x^{(j)}$ is the j–th sample of X, $\alpha_1, \alpha_2, \ldots, \alpha_M$ are the M free parameters, while M / n_s penalizes the model complexity. It is of interest to note that for a given M, the maximization of $L(\alpha_1, \alpha_2, \ldots, \alpha_M)$ equals the minimization of the Kullback-Leibler divergence between the target PDF and the KDME approximation, i.e.

$$\max_{\alpha} L(\alpha_1, \alpha_2, \ldots, \alpha_M) = \min_{\alpha} D\left[f_X(x), \tilde{f}_{KDME}(x; \alpha_1, \alpha_2, \ldots, \alpha_M)\right] = D(M). \tag{39.24}$$

The optimal hyperparameters α^* minimize $D(M)$, i.e.

$$D_{min} = \min_{M} D(M) = min\{D(1), D(2),..., D(M),...\}.\tag{39.25}$$

The substitution of α^* in Equation (39.22) gives the required KDME PDF, i.e. $f_{KDME}(x) = f_{KDME}(x;\alpha^*)$.

39.5 Generalized expected utility theory

In the theory of decision under risk, the main focus is the choice of the optimal solution in terms of a given performance G, given a set of alternatives $G^{(i)}(t_n) = G[t_n, \mathbf{x}^{(i)}]$, $i = 1,2,...,m$. This is obtained through the definition of a functional $\mathcal{V}(\cdot)$ applied to the performance G, such that if $\mathcal{V}(G^{(1)}) \geq \mathcal{V}(G^{(2)})$, then the alternative $G^{(1)}$ is preferred over the alternative $G^{(2)}$. Here, the Generalized Expected Utility (*GEU*) (Mosalam et al. 2018) is adopted and expressed as follows:

$$GEU^{(i)} = \int u^{(i)} d\left[h\left(F_U^{(i)}\right)\right],\tag{39.26}$$

where $u^{(i)}$ is the utility of the i-th alternative, $F_U^{(i)}$ is its Cumulative Distribution Function (CDF), while $h(\cdot)$ is a suitable function describing the risk perception of the decision maker. The utility $u^{(i)}$ is defined through the *utility function* $u(g)$ which is a function expressing the degree of preference of the decision maker. The *GEU* embodies a distinction between the attitudes to the outcomes, measured by $u(g)$, and attitudes to the probabilities where "increased uncertainty hurts" (Yaari 1987) distorted through $h(F_U)$. The optimal decision maximizes the *GEU*.

If the probabilities are not distorted by the risk perception of the decision maker, i.e. $h(F_U) \equiv F_U$, then the *GEU* coincides with the largely adopted Expected Utility, *EU* (Von Neumann & Morgenstern 1944) which represents a class of functionals, which are state-independent and linear in the probabilities as follows:

$$GEU^{(i)} \equiv E[U^{(i)}] = \int u^{(i)} dF_U^{(i)}(u) = \int u(g) dF_G^{(i)}(g) \equiv EU^{(i)},\tag{39.27}$$

where $F_G^{(i)}$ is the CDF of the performance G. In the literature, it is recognized that a rational decision maker should be risk-neutral by considering complete consequence models. Thus, it is assumed that $u(g) = g$ and

$$GEU^{(i)} \equiv EU^{(i)} = \int g dF_G^{(i)}(g) = \int g f_G^{(i)}(g) dg \equiv E[G^{(i)}],\tag{39.28}$$

where $f_G^{(i)}(g)$ is the PDF of $G^{(i)}$. The optimal alternative provides the maximum *GEU*, i.e.

$$\max_{G^{(i)}} GEU \equiv \max_{G^{(i)}} EU \equiv \max_{G^{(i)}} E[G].\tag{39.29}$$

Thus, a rational decision maker will pursue the maximum expected performance(s) of the asset. In this chapter, the considered performances are the lifecycle economic benefit $B(t_n, \mathbf{x})$ and the lifecycle CO_2 emission, such that Equation (39.29) gives

$$\begin{cases} \max_{B^{(i)}} GEU \equiv \max_{B^{(i)}} E\left[B(t_n)\right] \\ \max_{co_2^{(i)}} GEU \equiv \min_{co_2^{(i)}} E\left[CO_2(t_n)\right]. \end{cases} \tag{39.30}$$

Research has shown that the choices of the decision makers are conservative with respect to the maximum expected values of the performances because of the risk perception which addresses overweighting of low probability events with extreme consequences (Kahneman & Tversky 1979; Tversky & Kahneman 1992). In this regard, here, we reduce the risk-aversion of the decision makers through (*i*) accurate modeling of the consequences, and (*ii*) probabilistic modeling of the uncertainties through the KDMEM. However, unavoidable uncertainties still arise and they may affect the risk perception. This can be modeled inside the *GEU* as suggested in (Mosalam et al. 2018) as follows:

$$h(F_U) = \begin{cases} \dfrac{1}{\alpha} F_U & 0 \le F_U \le \alpha \\ 0 & F_U > \alpha. \end{cases} \tag{39.31}$$

In this way, Equation (39.26) provides the following:

$$GEU(\alpha) = \frac{1}{\alpha} \int_0^\alpha u \, dF_U \equiv E\left[U|0 \le u \le u_\alpha\right], \tag{39.32}$$

where $u_\alpha = F_U^{-1}(\alpha)$ is the α-quantile of U while $GEU(\alpha)$ provides its α-superquantile (or conditional quantile) (Artzner et al. 1999; Rockafellar & Royset 2015). It is noted that Equation (39.32) provides the expected utility, conditioned on the $\alpha(\%)$ events providing the lowest utility values; for $\alpha = 1$, then $GEU \equiv EU$, while low values of α correspond to risk-averse decisions. For a chosen performance measure, the $GEU(\alpha)$ provides the directly expected value in the $\alpha(\%)$ worst scenarios of the performance itself, i.e.

$$GEU(\alpha) = \frac{1}{\alpha} \int_0^\alpha u(g) \, dF_U = \frac{1}{\alpha} \int_0^\alpha g \, dF_G \equiv E\left[G|0 \le g \le g_\alpha\right], \tag{39.33}$$

where $g_\alpha = F_G^{-1}(\alpha)$ is the α-quantile of G.

In the most general case, it is expected that the optimal design depends on multiple performances $G_1, G_2, \ldots, G_n$, which are typically conflicting one another. The utility function $u(\boldsymbol{G})$ is expressed as a combination of single attribute utility functions $u_j(G_j)$ of only one performance where the relative importance is defined by weights w_j, $0 \le w_j \le 1$, $\sum_{j=1}^n w_j = 1$. A simple rule of combination of the utilities is the linear model expressed as follows:

$$u(G_1, G_2, \ldots, G_n) = \sum_{j=1}^n w_j u_j(G_j). \tag{39.34}$$

This is generally valid if the consequences of the interaction between the performances G_j are negligible. Here, it is noted that the multi-attribute utility function of the ith alternative $U^{(i)} = u(\boldsymbol{G}^{(i)})$ is a random variable since $\boldsymbol{G}^{(i)}$ is a vector of random variables. It depends on the corresponding joint PDF $f_G^{(i)} = f_G^{(i)}(g)$ of the uncertain performances $\boldsymbol{G}^{(i)}$. Since $U^{(i)}$ is a random variable, it is completely defined by its CDF, $F_U^{(i)}$, whose knowledge allows to determine the *GEU* through Equation (39.26).

39.6 Application example

A hypothetical four-bay five-story Reinforced Concrete (RC) office building presented in (Mosalam et al. 2018) is considered herein, see Figure 39.2.

The floor-to-floor height is $3m$, the spacing of the columns is $5m$, the floor area is $A_f = 400\,m^2$, with a total area $A = 2,000\,m^2$. Two design alternatives are considered: (*i*) *D1*, where the columns are $300 \times 300\,mm$ with 8 reinforcing bars of $14\,mm$ diameter (1.37%), (*ii*) *D2*, where the columns are $300 \times 500\,mm$ with 8 reinforcing bars of $16\,mm$ diameter (1.07%). In both designs the beam sections are $300 \times 500\,mm$ with 8 reinforcing bars of $16\,mm$ diameter, providing 1.07% longitudinal reinforcement.

For the two designs, the construction cost is $C_0^{(1)} = 2.08\,\$M$ and $C_0^{(2)} = 2.60\,\$M$, corresponding to a unit cost of $1,040\$/m^2$ and $1,300\$/m^2$, respectively. These values are quite typical of constructions in California, Berkeley area, without considering the land cost, land development, local government fees, as well as local impact fees related to the cost of the service provided by the local agency. The corresponding emission of CO_2 is $CO_2^{(1)}(t_0) = 606.4\,ton$ and $CO_2^{(2)}(t_0) = 758.0\,ton$, whose respective unit emission is $303.2\,kg/m^2$ and $379.0\,kg/m^2$, derived from Wei et al. (2016).

39.6.1 Hazard analysis

It is assumed that the building is subjected to seismic hazard only. The building is located in Berkeley, CA whose latitude and longitude are respectively $37.877°$ and $-122.264°$. The chosen intensity measure *IM* is the Peak Ground Acceleration (*PGA*), whose hazard curve is

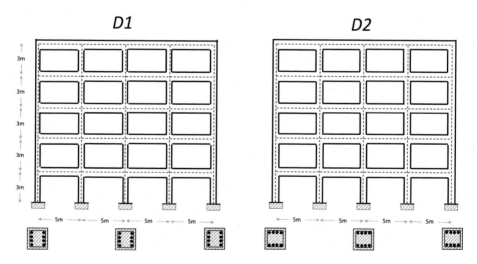

Figure 39.2 Representative 2D-model of the building for the two design alternatives: Design *D1*, more economic and sustainable during the construction stage, Design *D2*, more resilient, economic and sustainable during the lifecycle.

obtained by using the Hazard Curve Calculator application of OpenSHA (Field et al. 2003). Discrete values of *PGA* between 0.05*g* and 2*g* with 0.05*g* increments are chosen, for a total of 40 *IM* values. A set of 81 Ground Motions (*GMs*) compatible with the site class and the hazard curve are selected from the PEER Next Generation Attenuation (NGA) *GM* database (PEER 2011). The selection criteria for magnitude *M*, distance *R*, and shear wave velocity V_{s30}, are: $6 \leq M \leq 7.5, 0 \leq R \leq 20\,km, 360 \leq V_{s30} \leq 760\,m/sec$.

39.6.2 Structural analysis

Beams and columns are modeled using displacement-based beam-column elements with fiber discretized sections. The compressive strength of the concrete is 35 MPa and the concrete strain values at maximum strength and at crushing strength are 0.2% and 0.5%, respectively. The steel of the reinforcing bars is assumed to have yield strength 420 MPa with elastic modulus 200,000 MPa and strain hardening ratio $b = 0.05$. Sufficient shear reinforcement is assumed to be provided to eliminate any shear failure. The structural analyses are performed using the software OpenSees (McKenna 2010). The 81 GMs are scaled for each *IM*, giving a total number of nonlinear time history analyses of $81 \times 40 = 3,240$. For brevity, this study considers only the Maximum peak Interstory Drift Ratio (*MIDR*) as *EDP*. For each value of the intensity measures $IM_m, m = 1, \ldots, 40$, the conditional annual distribution for the two alternative designs $P^{(i)}\left[MIDR|\,IM_m\right], i = 1,2$ is determined through the KDMEM, which provides the most honest and least biased distribution given the available information (Jaynes 1968). The distribution of *MIDR* for the two design alternatives is given as follows:

$$P^{(i)}\left(MIDR\right) = \sum_{m=1}^{40} P^{(i)}\left(MIDR|\,IM_m\right) p\left(IM_m\right). \tag{39.35}$$

This distribution is represented in Figure 39.3.

39.6.3 Damage analysis

In the absence of available data to develop probabilistic capacity models, capacity values are based on HAZUS (FEMA 2013), which classifies buildings in terms of their use (occupancy

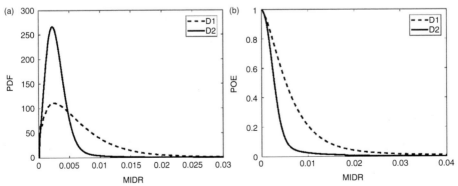

Figure 39.3 Distribution of the annual maximum peak interstory drift ratio, *MIDR*, for the two design alternatives (a) PDF, (b) Probability Of Exceedance (POE).

class) and in terms of their structural system (model building type). In HAZUS, four damage states are considered: slight $(DS_1 : ds_1 \leq MIDR \leq ds_2)$, moderate $(DS_2 : ds_2 \leq MIDR \leq ds_3)$, extensive $(DS_3 : ds_3 \leq MIDR \leq ds_4)$ and complete $(DS_4 : MIDR \geq ds_4)$, in addition to the "no damage state" $(DS_0 : MIDR \leq ds_1)$. The considered building belongs to the building structure C1M (Mid-Rise Concrete Moment Frame), where one has: $ds_1 = 0.33\%$, $ds_2 = 0.58\%$, $ds_3 = 1.56\%$ and $ds_4 = 4.00\%$ (mid-code values). These values are treated as median values of a lognormal distribution, while the dispersion value is assumed to be 0.3 (Wen et al. 2004). In Table 39.1, the annual probabilities of achieving the corresponding damage states are shown.

As expected, the first alternative requires less initial construction cost $(C_0^{(1)} < C_0^{(2)})$ and provides lower CO_2 emission during the construction stage $(CO_2^{(1)}(t_0) < C_0^{(2)}(t_0))$. However, it is more vulnerable to the seismic hazard during its lifecycle.

39.6.4 Loss analysis

The loss functions are derived from (Wei et al. 2016) assuming that the probability distributions $P^{(i)}\left[L_S | DM = DS_k\right]$ follow lognormal distributions, whose dispersion is assumed to be 0.3. The median values are presented in Table 39.2.

These values correspond to injecting epoxy resin for slight damage (DS_1), patching with shotcrete for moderate damage (DS_2), jacketing with RC for extensive damage (DS_3), demolition and reconstruction for complete damage (DS_4). It is seen that $L_S^{(1)} < L_S^{(2)}$, i.e. the first alternative is cheaper. However, damages during the lifecycle are more frequent. The distribution of the annual loss is given as follows:

$$P^{(i)}(L_S) = \sum_{k=1}^{4} P^{(i)}(L_S | DS_k) p^{(i)}(DS_k) \tag{39.36}$$

This is represented in Figure 39.4

39.6.5 Revenue analysis

The revenue functions are derived assuming that the probability distributions $P^{(i)}\left[R | DM = DS_k\right]$ follow lognormal distributions, whose dispersion is assumed to be 0.3. The median values are presented in Table 39.3.

Table 39.1 Probability of occurrence of the damage states for the two different design alternatives

Alternative	None (DS_0)	Slight (DS_1)	Moderate (DS_2)	Extensive (DS_3)	Complete (DS_4)
$p^{(1)}(DS_k)$	31.96%	23.10%	35.39%	8.47%	1.07%
$p^{(2)}(DS_k)$	62.47%	26.17%	9.95%	1.17%	0.23%

Table 39.2 Median values of the lifecycle annual losses corresponding to the post-hazard repair costs of the structural components

Alternative	None	Slight	Moderate	Extensive	Complete
$L_S^{(1)}(\$ / year)$	0	24,960	135,200	374,400	2,329,600
$L_S^{(2)}(\$ / year)$	0	31,200	169,000	468,000	2,912,000

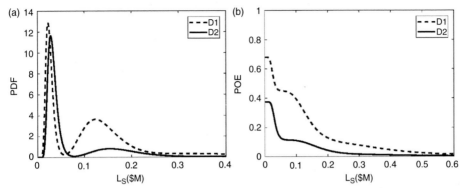

Figure 39.4 Distribution of the annual Structural Loss L_S for the two design alternatives (a) PDF, (b) POE.

Table 39.3 Median values of the lifecycle annual revenues corresponding to the rents, including loss of function because of seismic hazards

Alternative	None	Slight	Moderate	Extensive	Complete
$R^{(1)}\,(\$/\,year)$	273,750	272,250	267,000	219,750	165,750
$R^{(2)}\,(\$/\,year)$	365,000	363,000	356,000	293,000	221,000

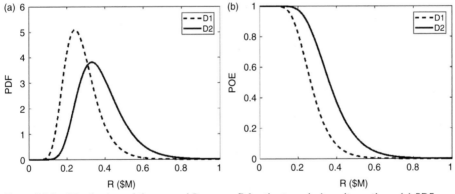

Figure 39.5 Distribution of the annual Revenue R for the two design alternatives. (a) PDF, (b) POE.

These values correspond to monthly rents $R^{(1)} = 22.5\$ / m^2$ and $R^{(2)} = 30\$ / m^2$, by assuming the first option as a lower rent building, also in terms of services and architectural design. A conservative scenario is chosen where on average only 50% of the available area will be rented. Following HAZUS, a loss of function of 2, 9, 72, and 144 days is assumed necessary to repair the four damage states, DS_1, DS_2, DS_3, and DS_4, respectively. These are median values for the probability of business or service interruption. Figure 39.5 represents the distribution of the annual rent, which is expressed as follows:

$$P^{(i)}(R) = \sum_{k=0}^{4} P^{(i)}(R|DS_k)\, p^{(i)}(DS_k). \tag{39.37}$$

39.6.6 Environmental analysis

The CO_2 emission functions are derived from (Wei et al. 2016) assuming that the probability distributions $P^{(i)}\left[CO_2\middle|DM = DS_k\right]$ follow lognormal distributions, whose dispersion is assumed to be 0.3. The median values are presented in Table 39.4.

It is seen that $CO_2^{(1)} < CO_2^{(2)}$, i.e. the first alternative provides for each repair minor CO_2 emission. However, damages are more frequent. The distribution of the annual CO_2 emission shown in Figure 39.6 is obtained from the following:

$$P^{(i)}\left(CO_2\right) = \sum_{k=1}^{4} P^{(i)}\left(CO_2\middle|DS_k\right) p^{(i)}\left(DS_k\right). \tag{39.38}$$

39.6.7 Lifecycle economic and environmental analyses

The lifecycle expected economic benefit $E\left[LCB(t)\right]$ and expected CO_2 emissions $E\left[LCA(t)\right]$ are shown in Figure 39.7, considering a lifetime of $t_n = 20$ years.

It is seen that for both performance metrics, the second option is better since it determines greater long-term economic benefit and less environmental impact. Of course, if longer lifespans are considered, the competitive advantages of the second option become more apparent. Since alternative D2 is less vulnerable to the hazard, it follows that: (i) a resilient building is sustainable, and (ii) a resilient building provides greater lifecycle economic benefit, although the initial cost of the construction can be greater. To rank the alternatives, a multi-attribute utility function is adopted, see Equation (39.34), expressed as follows:

$$u\left[b(t), co_2(t)\right] = w_B u_B\left[b(t)\right] + w_{CO_2} u_{CO_2}\left[co_2(t)\right], \tag{39.39}$$

Table 39.4 Median values of the lifecycle annual CO_2 emissions corresponding to the post-hazard repair of the structural components

Alternative	None	Slight	Moderate	Extensive	Complete
$CO_2^{(1)}$ (kg / year)	0	6,064	42,448	272,880	715,552
$CO_2^{(2)}$ (kg / year)	0	7,580	53,060	341,100	894,440

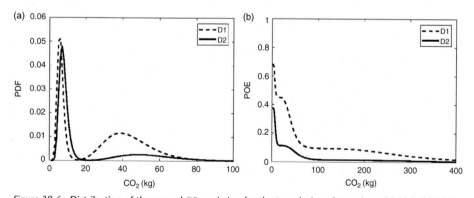

Figure 39.6 Distribution of the annual CO_2 emission for the two design alternatives. (a) PDF, (b) POE.

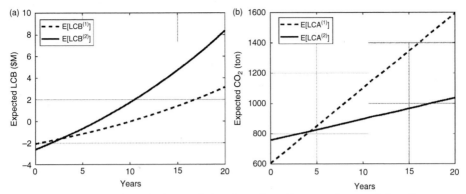

Figure 39.7 Lifecycle analyses for the two design alternatives. (a) expected economic benefit, (b) expected CO_2 emission.

where w_B and w_{CO_2} are the weights of the linear (i.e. risk-neutral) single-attribute utility functions, expressed as follows:

$$u_B\left[b(t)\right] = \begin{cases} 0 & b(t) < b_{min} \\ \dfrac{b(t)}{b_{max}} & b_{min} \le b(t) \le b_{max} \\ 1 & b(t) > b_{max} \end{cases} \tag{39.40}$$

$$u_{CO_2}\left[co_2(t)\right] = \begin{cases} 1 & co_2(t) < co_{2,min} \\ \dfrac{co_{2,max} - co_2(t)}{co_{2,max} - co_{2,min}} & co_{2,min} \le co_2(t) \le co_{2,max}, \\ 0 & co_2(t) > co_{2,max} \end{cases} \tag{39.41}$$

with $b_{min} = 0$, $b_{max} = 10 \ \$M$, and $co_{2,min} = 0$, $co_{2,max} = 2{,}000 \ ton$. Figure 39.8 shows the utility functions of the two design alternatives where $w_B = 0.5$ and $w_{CO_2} = 0.5$ are assumed.

Since the two criteria are not conflicting with each other (the more resilient option provides more economic benefit and less CO_2 emissions), the ranking of the alternatives is not modified by the choice of the weights or by the risk-aversion of the decision maker.

39.7 Conclusions

In this chapter, we have developed a framework of lifecycle analyses under uncertainty for sustainable and resilient building design. A numerical example has illustrated the main features of the method. Herein, the optimal decision is determined through the Generalized Expected Utility (GEU), which allows, if needed, to model the risk-aversion of the decision maker and his/her perception toward extreme events. It is a broadly general framework, which includes, as particular decision criteria, the maximization of the Expected Utility (EU) and the minimization of the Expected Cost (EC). In the presented example, two performance measures are considered: (*i*) lifecycle CO_2 emission and (*ii*) lifecycle economic benefit. Three decision criteria

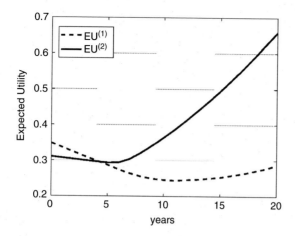

Figure 39.8 Lifecycle expected utility for the two design alternatives.

are considered: (*i*) maximization of the GEU applied to the two performances, (*ii*) maximization of the EU applied to the two performances, (iii) minimization of the expected lifecycle CO_2 emission and maximization of the expected lifecycle economic benefit. It is seen that in this case the three criteria coincide.

A major challenge in the decision making under risk is represented by the uncertainty quantification, given the small amount of available data. In this chapter, the random variables are characterized from a statistical point of view through the Kernel Density Maximum Entropy Method (KDMEM). This is a kernel density estimation method, based on the Maximum Entropy approach. As a consequence, it provides the least biased and most honest distribution given the available information.

In the numerical application, lifecycle analyses of economic and environmental metrics have been considered. The lifecycle economic analysis includes costs and revenues, and the performances are evaluated through the Net Present Value. Economic and environmental analyses include initial stage of construction as well as post-hazard repairs. The analyses show that design by resilience means design by sustainability since it provides less environmental impact along the lifecycle. Moreover, it is more advantageous from an economic point of view.

Future research will be devoted to the extension of the method considering the occurrence of multiple hazards, in addition to sustainability analysis. In this regard, several types of new design concepts and materials can be compared to determine the most sustainable site-dependent solution for each type of building.

Acknowledgements

This research was funded by the Republic of Singapore's National Research Foundation through a grant to the Berkeley Education Alliance for Research in Singapore (BEARS) for the Singapore Berkeley Building Efficiency and Sustainability in the Tropics (SinBerBEST) program. BEARS has been established by the University of California, Berkeley, as a center for intellectual excellence in research and education in Singapore. Khalid M. Mosalam is a principal investigator of the Tsinghua-Berkeley Shenzhen Institute (TBSI). The authors acknowledge the funding support from SinBerBEST and the partial support from TBSI.

References

Akaike H., 1973. Information theory and an extension of the maximum likelihood principle, *2nd Int. Symp. Inf. Theory*, 267–81.

Alibrandi U. and Mosalam K.M., 2017a. The Kernel Density Maximum Entropy with Generalized Moments for evaluating probability distributions, including tails, from small sample of data, *Int. J. Numer. Methods Eng.*, 113(13): 1904–28.

Alibrandi U. and Mosalam K.M. 2017b. A decision support tool for sustainable and resilient building design. In: Gardoni, P. (ed.), *Risk and Reliability Analysis: Theory and Applications – In Honor of Prof. Armen Der Kiureghian*, Springer Series in Reliability Engineering, pp. 509–36.

Alibrandi U. and Mosalam K.M. 2018. Code-conforming PEER performance based earthquake engineering using stochastic dynamic analysis and information theory, *KSCE Journal of Civil Engineering*, 22(3): 1002–15.

Alibrandi U. and Ricciardi G., 2008. Efficient evaluation of the pdf of a random variable through the kernel density maximum entropy approach, *Int. J. Numer. Methods Eng.*, 75: 1511–48.

Allais M. and Hagen O., 1979. *Expected Utility Hypotheses and the Allais Paradox*. Dordrecht. Reidel.

Artzner P., Delbaen, F, Eber, J-M, and Heath D., 1999. Coherent measures of risk, *Math. Financ.* 9: 203–28.

Benjamin J.R. and Cornell C.A., 1970. *Probability, Statistics and Decision for Civil Engineers*. New York: McGraw-Hill.

Cornell C.A. and Krawinkler H., 2000. Progress and challenges in seismic performance assessment. *PEER Cent. News* 3, 1–4.

FEMA, 2013. *Earthquake model HAZUS, MH Technical Manual*. Washington DC.

Field E.H., Jordan T.H., and Cornell C.A., 2003. OpenSHA: a developing community-modelling environment for seismic hazard analysis. *Seismol. Res. Lett.*, 74: 406–419.

Gardoni P., Guevara-Lopez F., and Contento A., 2016. The Life Profitability Method (LPM): A financial approach to engineering decisions, *Struct. Saf.*, 63: 11–20.

Günay S. and Mosalam K.M., 2013. PEER performance-based earthquake engineering methodology, revisited, *J. Earthq. Eng.*, 17: 829–58.

Jaynes E.T., 1957. Information theory and statistical mechanics, *Phys. Rev.*, 106: 620–30.

Jaynes E.T., 1968. Prior probabilities, *IEEE Trans. Syst. Sci. Cybern.*, 4: 227–41.

Kahneman D. and Tversky A., 1979. Prospect theory: an analysis of decision under risk, *Econometrica*, 47: 263–92.

Keeney R. and Raiffa H., 1993. *Decisions with Multiple Objectives: Preferences and Value Tradeoffs*. Cambridge: Cambridge University Press.

Konstantakopoulos I.C., Ratliff L.J., Jin M., Sastry S.S., and Spanos, C.J., 2017. A robust utility learning framework via inverse optimization, *IEEE Trans. Control Syst. Technol.*, 26(3): 954–70.

Maes M.A. and Faber M.H., 2007. Preferences utility and risk perception in engineering decision making, *Int. J. Risk Assess. Manag.*, 7: 807–27.

McKenna F., 2010. *Opensees User's Manual*. Pacific Earthquake Engineering Research Center, Univ. of California, Berkeley, Berkeley, CA.

Mosalam K.M., Alibrandi U., Lee H., and Armengou J. 2018. Performance based engineering and multi criteria decision analysis for sustainable and resilient building design, *Structural Safety*, 74: 1–13.

Nielsen T.D. and Jensen F.V. 2009. *Bayesian Network and Decision Graph*, Springer Science & Business Media.

Novi Inverardi P.L. and Tagliani A. 2003. Maximum entropy density estimation from fractional moments, *Commun. Stat. – Theory Methods*, 32: 327–45.

PEER, 2011. *PEER NGA Ground Motion Database*.

Quiggin J., 1993. *Generalized Expected Utility Theory. The Rank-Dependent Model*. Springer, Netherlands.

Rockafellar R.T. 2007. Coherent Approaches to Risk in Optimization Under Uncertainty. *INFORMS Tutorials Oper. Res.* 38–61.

Rockafellar R.T. and Royset J.O., 2015. Engineering decisions under risk averseness, *ASCE-ASME J. Risk Uncertain. Eng. Syst. Part A Civ. Eng.* 1(2).

Taufer E., Bose S., and Tagliani A. 2009. Optimal predictive densities and fractional moments. *Appl. Stoch. Model. Bus. Ind.*, 25: 57–71.

Tversky A. and Kahneman D., 1992. Advances in prospect theory: Cumulative representation of uncertainty. *J. Risk Uncertain.* 5: 297–323.

Von Neumann J. and Morgenstern O., 1944. *Theory of Games and Economic Behavior*. Princeton, NJ: Princeton University Press.

Wei H., Shohet I.M., Skibniewski M., Shapira S., and Yao X. 2016. Assessing the lifecycle sustainability costs and benefits of seismic mitigations designs for buildings, *J. Archit. Eng.* **22**(1): 04015011 (13 pp.).

Wen Y.K. and Kang Y.J. 2001a. Minimum building life-cycle cost design criteria. I: Methodology, *Journal of Structural Engineering*, 127(3): 330–7.

Wen Y.K. and Kang Y.J. 2001b. Minimum building life-cycle cost design criteria. II: Applications, *Journal of Structural Engineering*, 127(3): 338–46.

Wen Y.K., Ellingwood B.R., and Bracci J. 2004. Vulnerability function framework for consequence-based engineering, *Mid-America Earthq. Cent. Proj.* 1–101.

Yaari M.E. 1987. The dual theory of choice under risk, *Econometrica* **55**(1): 95–115.

Zhang X. and Pandey M.D., 2013. Structural reliability analysis based on the concepts of entropy, fractional moment and dimensional reduction method, *Structural Safety* **43**: 28–40.

Part XI

The role of urban planning and public policies

40

Addressing the infrastructure decay rate in US cities

The case for a paradigm shift in information and communication

Mark Reiner[1] and Jennifer E. Cross[2]

[1] WISRD, LLC, 6948 HOWELL STREET, ARVADA, COLORADO 80004, USA; TEL: 303-596-1401; MARK.REINER@WISRD.COM (CORRESPONDING AUTHOR)

[2] INSTITUTE FOR THE BUILT ENVIRONMENT AND COLORADO STATE UNIVERSITY, FT. COLLINS, COLORADO, USA; JENI.CROSS@COLOSTATE.EDU

40.1 Introduction

In early March 2017, the American Society of Civil Engineering (ASCE) issued their latest quadrennial report as to the status of infrastructure in the United States. The Infrastructure Report Card (Report Card)[1] gives an overall letter grade to infrastructure at the state and national levels, as well as individual sector grades. The current overall grade of a D+ for the United States did not change since the Report Card was last published in 2013. In fact, the ASCE has now issued six report cards since 1998, with the intention of influencing the planning, operation, and maintenance of major urban infrastructure, and the grade has never exceeded a D+. Consistent with these low ratings from the ASCE, throughout the country there are over 240,000 water main breaks every year and over 56,000 bridges that are over 50 years old and considered structurally deficient. The Report Card claims that $4.59 trillion is required to bring our systems to a B, or an adequate grade, by 2025. Despite the obvious need for investment in the nation's infrastructure, the onus of this expense rests at the municipalities which are struggling financially as needs increase and federal and state funds decrease.

The current paradigm used by municipal governments across the United States is to install new municipal infrastructure with an intended design-life of 80–100 years paired with a maintenance plan that replaces the infrastructure on a 200–400 year cycle (based on available funds). The ratio between an asset design-life and the replacement cycle of the asset represents an ***infrastructure 'decay rate'***. This decay rate paradigm, where planned replacement lags significantly behind the actual asset design life, means that cities must be reactive to infrastructure failures (e.g., replacing burst water mains) rather than planning and proactively replacing infrastructure. The current decay rate paradigm persists and is not only dangerous – posing great risk to human life and community well-being – but also costlier to maintain. So, if the current paradigm is costlier to maintain and operate and poses greater risk to human life and property, why then does it persist?

While the Report Card has sparked a conversation about the need to invest in municipal infrastructure, it has done little to provoke alarm at the public level or provide a clear path forward as to how to better communicate the problem. In this chapter, we examine the barriers to change that are preventing utilities and municipal governments from shifting from the decay rate paradigm, which uses a capital investment planning (CIP) process – where the replacement time horizon is three to five times longer than the design life of the infrastructure – to a resilient communications-based paradigm where planners, city decision makers, and the public are provided information to enable informed decisions regarding systems level assessments and prioritize investments that reduce risks and costs while maintaining a high quality infrastructure.

40.2 Barriers to change

The Report Card[2] clearly indicates a need for change, but how can utilities that serve municipalities (private) and municipal owned utilities (public) that often provide just single sector services, e.g. energy, take on a complex changing paradigm for planning, funding, and building comprehensive resilient infrastructure? After 20 years of a D or D+ letter grade, it is clear that information alone is not adequate to provoke a change in practices and planning paradigm. John Kotter (2012) has studied scores of change efforts across industries and found that organizational transformation efforts – a substantial revision of business practices and strategies – often fail. In order to be successful, organizations must traverse three major phases: (1) creating a climate for change, (2) engaging and enabling the whole organization, and (3) implementing and sustaining the change (Cohen 2005). In the first phase, creating a climate for change, the Report Card plays a crucial role in increasing urgency by building a clear understanding of the necessity of the change for the well-being and longevity of the organization. Creating a sense of urgency is a necessary first step in creating clarity and motivation for the change as well as reducing fear, anger, and complacency that have become part of general practice. However, the communication break-down begins with direct knowledge of the city's true conditions. The fear, anger, and complacency can be uncovered with a heartfelt talk with many utility directors in the country. One utility department head had this to say:

> Want to know what keeps me up at night? Installing infrastructure with a 100-year design life and replacing it on a 500-year cycle.[3]

How is this message of urgency passed from utility director to the elected officials of the city, and, subsequently, to the general public in a manner that elicits urgency rather than fear? While the Report Card has initiated a conversation about the urgency of managing the aging infrastructure, a paradigm shift in communication strategies is needed to engage the public in this urgency. This begins by evaluating the current baseline of communications in the CIP process: (1) how are needs communicated by each utility, (2) how are other city departments afforded an opportunity to provide input, and (3) how is all of this information communicated to the public – *without causing alarm*.

The second step in the change process is building guiding teams (Kotter 2012; Cohen 2005). In regards to infrastructure, there are many stakeholder groups including: planning, design, construction, and operations. Shifting the decay rate paradigm requires systems thinking and integration of knowledge across stakeholder groups (Stroh 2015; Meadows 2008). A paradigm shift requires not only the identification of "communication breakdowns" in the CIP process

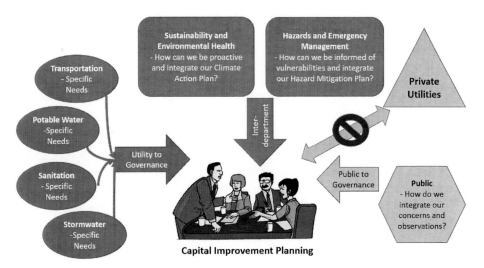

Figure 40.1   Communication breakdown groups in CIP process.

among key stakeholder groups, but also identification of *relevant information* for the stakeholders and tools to effectively integrate disparate priorities. This chapter identifies four such communication breakdowns in the typical municipal CIP process: (a) intra-departmental, (b) public to governance ("governance" refers to the CIP decision authority), (c) public utility to governance, and (d) private utility to governance. These breakdowns are represented on Figure 40.1.

Each of the groups in Figure 40.1 have different priorities because of their role in the system. Rather than immediately assume that each group's priorities compete with each other, this chapter proposes that a systems approach and the integrative use of data for decision-making regarding planning, funding, design, construction, and operations of infrastructure can resolve tensions across stakeholders and make a dramatic improvement in reducing risks and costs of decaying infrastructure. We propose a new process, the *Integrated Information CIP* (IICIP) process that would provide more transparent information to each group, facilitate systems thinking, and allow for longer-term life-cycle management and planning of infrastructure.

We argue that changing the current municipal CIP paradigm is urgent and requires three things: (1) an integrated data platform that communicates the true status of all the city's infrastructure vulnerabilities, (2) integrative decision-making process between the city governance and city utilities and departments, and (3) a robust public engagement process that better communicates the city's current infrastructure decay rate. Changing current practices from siloed and isolated decision-making into an integrative process will require organizational transformation.

40.3 Current paradigm: Evidence of the decay rate and the capital investment planning process

40.3.1 Urgency

The fact that our cities have dangerously aging infrastructure is not a secret. In addition to the ASCE Report Card, public works directors and other utility managers are continually trying to communicate the urgency for more funding to city governance. In turn, city governance hears these messages, but often perceive that Engineering, Procurement, and Construction

(EPC) contracts, or passing a bond is not possible within the current political realities with the public. Finally, the public, who make bond passing possible, are more likely to perceive that they are overtaxed than to understand the magnitude of resources needed to invest in public infrastructure maintenance and replacement and the extent of the risks they face from not investing in infrastructure. Information alone is not enough to compel action, human beings must be emotionally touched by the information and understand how the lack of investment is a risk to their personal well-being, their community, and others that they care about (Cohen 2005; Cialdini 2008).

The national message is currently that the US has over 56,000 bridges that are over 50 years old and considered structurally deficient[4] and there are still an estimated 240,000 water main breaks per year in the United States, wasting over two trillion gallons of treated drinking water.[5] But, this national-level message is too detached to create an emotional connection in the public. At the city-level, Los Angeles' system of water pipes has averaged about three water main breaks a day across the city.[6] And, at the household level, there are common articles such as:

> Anita Kramer had no idea that a 72-inch water main in her Maryland neighborhood was a ticking time bomb that was about to flood her home and ruin many of her most cherished possessions.[7]

While the city-level and personal stories present the risk of aging infrastructure, it is still an unseen risk and detached as a responsibility to the public (Morgan et al. 2002).

40.3.2 City's infrastructure stakeholders and approach to the CIP process

The CIP process is sanctioned by the legal mandate that a city is obligated to provide, or have franchise agreements to provide, basic services to all residents, businesses, and industry within the incorporated boundary. Standards as to the quantity, and often quality and reliability, of those basic services are typically developed and passed by city council. To support this mandate, and other aesthetic, economic, and livability initiatives – within defined budgets, the city planners and engineers contribute to the CIP process, as depicted on Figure 40.2.

In most cities, different city departments promote competing priorities that may be inconsistent with the stated long-term required provision of infrastructure, resulting in efforts that lag far behind their own planning documents. There are at least four substantial challenges in a city's CIP process (World Bank 2011):

1. Demands from multiple utilities and planners for capital investment are always higher than available funding; therefore, cities must make prioritized choices.
2. There is an intrinsic timing challenge. On the one hand, allocating funding for capital projects should be done annually within a city's budgeting cycle. On the other hand, complex infrastructure projects may require several years' preparation and "packaging" before external financing (grants or loans) can be sought.
3. Contemporary approaches to evaluate options for complex infrastructure projects usually exceed the local government's technical capacities, even in large cities. Therefore, consultants are brought in for a specific project, not the overall CIP process.
4. Capital investment planning is an evolving area of public management. Local governments across the world are continuously trying new approaches.

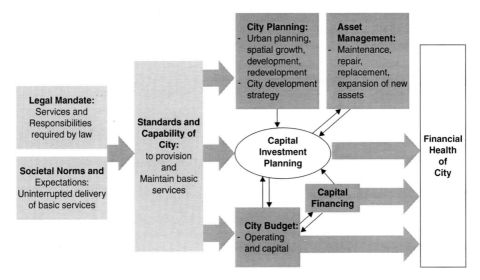

Figure 40.2   How CIP is related to other city functions.
Source: World Bank 2011.

Prioritizing projects within the CIP process, as championed from within city government, is challenging enough. The needs, and vulnerabilities, of private utilities that are franchised to provide basic services, are typically not integrated into the CIP process. However, these privately managed infrastructure assets represent another invisible risk because their assets are collocated with municipal assets and failure of one asset often leads to failure of other proximal assets.

The communication challenge begins with the lack of integrated data from each sector's asset management system, where the needs for keeping one system running are put forth as priority. Of course, this is logical from each utility's perspective, the motivation is to keep the systems working as efficiently and reliably as possible. However, from a city's perspective, the goal is a comprehensive view of all sectors to form a comprehensive plan. This gap in goals is due to a lack of integrated information as each infrastructure sector reports separately, and decision-makers do not receive a comprehensive baseline of all infrastructure systems within the city. Additional communication breakdowns occur within the CIP process as other city-departments also struggle to communicate their project priorities to city governance. Urban and transportation planners also need to understand the baseline of *existing* potential hazards and vulnerabilities of the city in order to develop a long-term city master plan as well as evaluate development proposals and permit requests. For emergency management planners that are focused on natural hazard mitigation and climate action planning, there is the difficulty of integrating resilience priorities into anything but new projects, as the existing systems are a mystery. These competing views of priorities and others lead to the communication breakdowns as outlined in the next section.

40.4 Communication as a problem, a tool, and a strategy for change

Current communication activities that are part of the existing CIP practices must be transformed in order to generate a paradigm shift for a city to claim resilient infrastructure. The stakeholders in the existing CIP process are not only driven by the immediate infrastructure priorities as seen from their perspective, but also the deeply entrenched assumptions of their respective professions. For hazard mitigation and climate action planning, the initial focus is to make incremental reactive improvements to the existing infrastructure – rather than be proactive in the CIP process. One of the key factors that has led to this reactive paradigm is directing the budget to emergency repairs rather than a proactive and integrated *vision of the city we want*. And in the case of the public, limited information impedes a deep engagement beyond the visual needs and costs of city infrastructure. Consider the following communication breakdowns.

40.4.1 Communication as a problem: Breakdowns in the existing paradigm

In this section, we argue that communication and lack of relevant information are the key problems with the existing CIP process and we enumerate the ways current practices prevent the adoption of an integrative paradigm. Then, we will discuss the ways in which communication and information must be leveraged as part of a change effort, and finally we will discuss specific tools, that can enhance change efforts.

Utility to governance – the role of the engineer
Curiously, despite the low letter grade in the Report Card, the ASCE seems to take full responsibility for the condition of our infrastructure by issuing definitions of what an engineer's role encompasses: "Civil engineers are responsible for the planning, design, construction, operation and maintenance of physical infrastructure." (ASCE 2015). But notice that the key task *not included* in this definition is to *secure the necessary funding* that allows an engineer to fulfill those stated roles in the first place. The securing of funding becomes a "not-my-job" communication breakdown. The ASCE recognizes funding as a key problem, but assigns the source of the problem to the Federal government – not the taxpayer, specifically:

> If the United States is serious about achieving an infrastructure system fit for the 21st century, some specific steps must be taken, beginning with increased, long-term, consistent investment. To continue to delay such investment only escalates the costs and risks of an aging infrastructure system – an option the country, the economy, and families can no longer afford. (Report Card)

While much of the current news on infrastructure funding is on the federal level, we must recognize that municipalities face the onus of the necessary $4.59 trillion, and the message of the infrastructure decay rate has to be tailored to the taxpayer directly. But, there are powerful forces that emanate from each public/private utility department and city governance that lead to this communication breakdown with the public. The public views basic infrastructure as the city's problem, and the city governance, in turn, defers to the priorities identified by the engineers that run the utilities for two reasons: (1) buy-in to ASCE's definition of an engineer's role as being "responsible for the planning, design, construction, operation and maintenance of physical infrastructure" without realizing funding is the key task, and (2) that all of the physical and operational data of our infrastructure systems reside in each utility's asset management system (if they have one) and are sector specific, not integrated. These data from asset management systems are deciphered by the engineers and department heads and communicated to city governance as a list of priorities by each isolated sector. Without a comprehensive view of all infrastructure vulnerabilities (i.e., an annually updated baseline of infrastructure conditions) the city governance is forced to consider these lists of priorities in a non-integrated manner.

Intra-departmental communication

Without being integrated into the CIP process, most departments can only react to the existing built environment by focusing on making the existing systems more resource efficient or attractive. Consider some aspects of municipal planning that have evolved to assume a reaction to existing infrastructure, rather than being a proactive participant in new systems planning.

- **Hazard mitigation planning:** The Federal Emergency Management Agency (FEMA) mandates that local governments produce a Hazard Mitigation Plan (HMP) in order to be eligible for post-disaster funding. However, aging and vulnerable infrastructure is *not* considered a hazard in the HMP. Per FEMA's guidance, communities only need to address natural hazards of concern, and are merely encouraged to address manmade and technological hazards. ("Manmade" refers to vulnerabilities of systems to terrorism[8] and "technological" refers to nuclear power plant incidents and US Army chemical stockpiles.[9]) The HMP does not require an overview of aging infrastructure in hazard analyses despite the potential of failing infrastructure to exacerbate disasters (Reiner & Rouse 2017).
- **Climate action planning:** The fundamental driver of the infrastructure *resilience* discussion is climate change. As cities are responsible for two-thirds of the worlds energy use and 70 percent of global carbon emissions, and more than 95 percent of US greenhouse gas (GHG) emissions can be attributed directly to our infrastructure systems (Ramaswami 2014). Yet, the standardized measurement and common reporting platform[10] that has been organized for global reporting[11] provides no actionable information for a city's Public Works Director as the data is typically at least a year or two old and the information is not tied to the condition of a city's infrastructure. But, with a baseline of infrastructure vulnerabilities and the ability to be proactive in the CIP process, new infrastructure can be planned proactively to reduce vulnerabilities *and* its contribution to the carbon footprint.
- **Sustainability planning:** Many frameworks for sustainable city planning focus on reacting to city infrastructure, rather than actively engaging in the management of existing systems. For example, the Sustainability Tools for Assessing and Rating (STAR™) Communities – that purports to be "the nation's leading comprehensive framework and certification program for evaluating local sustainability, encompassing economic, environmental, and social performance measures."[12] Yet, the condition of existing infrastructure is an extremely minor component of the STAR rating system and, in fact, can virtually be ignored and the city can still receive high marks (Reiner & Rouse 2017).

Public to governance

The public engagement in the CIP process falls far short of what is possible and what is required to fully engage the public in infrastructure decision-making – as evidenced by our aging infrastructure. The Public Participation Spectrum (IAP2)[13] identifies five levels of public participation from the lowest level of engagement: inform and consult to the more complex levels of engage, collaborate and empower. Current efforts through topical town meetings, task forces, and steering committees rarely do more than provide the public an opportunity to consult. Consulting is defined as obtaining public feedback on data and analyses in order that city official can made decisions. Public input is often desired and encouraged by city governance; but, coordinating comprehensive public priorities is often difficult due to the range of opinions and lack of a common source of integrated data and a process of deliberative decision-making

(Carcasson & Sprain 2016). Consider some of the communication channels of the current paradigm:

- **Community infrastructure task force:** In order to engage the public in the CIP process, a city may choose to form a community task force to provide input. Consider the example from Denver, Colorado in 2006, when, then Mayor Hickenlooper formed the "Infrastructure Priorities Task Force" to be proactively involved in the future of Denver's infrastructure.

  > Rather than approach Denver voters every few years with immediate needs, we really want to engage the community in proactively evaluating and prioritizing citywide infrastructure priorities – both short- and long-term – in hopes of preparing a forward-looking, comprehensive and prudent fiscal package, [said Hickenlooper][14]

  However, a task force, no matter how expert, is reliant on the data they receive from each separate utility's asset management system. They do not have their own information to counter or propose informed alternatives. As such, the task force relied on the data from each department's capital budget and list of capital, O&M, and deferred needs as reported by that department's staff. In the opinion of one of the Task Force members, the prioritization exercise did not involve a systems approach to infrastructure levels of service, efficiencies, critical paths, or collateral impacts to the city's economy and quality of life.[15] There was neither a methodology nor data to support credible prioritization of infrastructure needs, but merely a tally of budget needs of siloed departments that could justify an estimate for eight bond proposals on the November 2007 ballot.

- **Community input on infrastructure resilience:** Cities are also utilizing guidelines for engaging the community at-large as stakeholders in the infrastructure of their city. The National Institute for Standards and Technology (NIST) published the "Community Guide for Resilience" (NIST 2016) with the intent to engage a broad range of community stakeholders and representatives in a series of six steps that help to define how vital social functions – such as healthcare, education and public safety – are supported by buildings and infrastructure systems. The guide does provide important language on the importance of understanding existing infrastructure dependencies – "Understanding how a community's social institutions and needs depend on the built environment is key." But, the Guide also underplays this dependency by stating: "only a fraction of the built environment is essential and needs to be functional during and immediately after a disaster event to support social needs, such as emergency response and acute and emergency healthcare." This may be true during and after emergencies, but this is not a critical foundational block of resilient design for providing day-to-day reliable operations. Without understanding and prioritizing the value of all sectors of reliable infrastructure in the first place, how do we determine if we want our systems to "bounce back" to normal in planning for city resilience?

The existing strategies used by cities to communicate across organizations, across departments, and with the public are all limited by the current data paradigm where overwhelming amounts of data from each asset management system in a utility is continually pared down as it passes from one stakeholder to the next. And, regarding infrastructure budgets to maintain viability, these lists of needs for each sector do not communicate whether a system is continually applying *triage or pursuing a proactive approach* to reduce the city's infrastructure decay rate. By assuming the triage path to maintaining city services, costs for emergency infrastructure repairs come from operations and maintenance budgets and require all personnel to drop their daily responsibilities and respond immediately; while local businesses and residents have to go without services.

The third step in effecting organizational transformation efforts is crafting the right vision (Kotter 2012; Cohen 2005). A clear, inspiring, and achievable picture of the future is a necessity for motivating people to act and be willing to give up existing practices for something new. Regarding infrastructure, the current asset management system data paradigm is not capable of providing *information* (distinguished from data) to all stakeholders in ways that help to craft an inspiring and achievable view of the future. The key term here is *achievable*. A city cannot provide a vision were the financial needs are far outstripped by available resources. However, an achievable vision for a city is one that produces a comprehensive plan that shows the long-term fiscal responsibility of decreasing the city's infrastructure decay rate. Without a sense that a desired vision is achievable, no change effort can take root.

40.5 New paradigm – integrative data analysis and decision making

In this section, we shift our focus from communication as a problem in the CIP process towards the ways communications can be a specific tool for change and a strategy to enhance the change effort. The data and technology required to achieve these changes already currently exists. However, the paradigm shift is to transform the way existing data is organized, analyzed and shared as *information* with decision-makers and stakeholders. The new strategy is to ferret out relevant information in the mountains of data contained in asset management systems and other city databases. We propose that a new tool for compiling, analyzing, and visualizing data for stakeholders that can transform a currently frustrating and daunting process of prioritization into a much clearer picture of system-level priorities.

What we are proposing is a new communication tool for the Integrated Information CIP (IICIP) that is designed for these purposes:

- to integrate existing data from multiple existing sources,
- to comprehensively visualize data on all infrastructure systems within a city without being overwhelmed,
- to provide an understandable analysis that identifies key vulnerabilities on all infrastructure systems to find locations in the city of highest risk,
- to develop a baseline that enables systems thinking and proactive analysis,
- to streamline the process of analysis in order to facilitate the creation of a systems-level priority, and
- to make visible the risks and vulnerabilities in the infrastructure of a place.

The relevant information for this new paradigm already exists in asset management systems – but it is not currently available for analysis in ways that support systems thinking. For example, in many municipal water departments, despite knowing pressure zones, soil types, pipe material and age, and maintenance history; the replacement of assets is still governed by an estimated *remaining useful life* and can be governed by subjective, rather than objective rules. Therefore, the capacity of engineers and the wealth of data in asset management systems is not actualized effectively. Rather, the information that flows from asset management into of the current CIP process is a simplistic list of needs rather than a set of data that can be analyzed in relationship to data from the other utilities.

> *Communication is the key to the new IICIP paradigm and converting the existing data into relevant and integrated information for the stakeholder groups of the CIP process is not only achievable but also has the potential to radically transform the process and outcomes.*

Both planners and operators are in need of rich information on the status of the existing systems in order to plan everything from short-term maintenance, to mid-range replacements, to long-range planning. Meeting the information needs of various stakeholder groups requires a robust baseline database, which would include:

- the decay rate for each system,
- understanding the existing key vulnerability(ies) in each infrastructure system,
- identifying how vulnerabilities compound when collocated with other infrastructure systems,
- identifying all infrastructure assets by ownership to engage more stakeholders,
- how expected natural hazards may further expose infrastructure vulnerabilities,
- the degree and location of vulnerabilities provide valuable insight to the emergency management and other city departments that are responsible for maintenance and planning, and
- how a city's comprehensive plan addresses existing infrastructure vulnerabilities and how implementation of capital improvements is proactively addressing natural hazards and systems' vulnerabilities.

This begins by extracting the essential datasets from asset management systems, and adding new visualization capacity, which is required for systems analysis and integrative decision-making (Bammer 2011). This visualization would provide a bigger picture, spatially and in terms of integrated infrastructure sectors, of the condition and proximity of all of the city's infrastructure assets. However, the vision has to be achievable. The immediate mental image of this "bigger picture" may be an indecipherable array of data, but in order for this complex web of data to be useful and actionable, it must be simplified (Morgan et al. 2002). And, in order to simplify, a logic has to be applied that is known by all stakeholders; including any inherent limitations in the logic (Morgan et al. 2002; Carcasson & Sprain 2016).

An overall message of the city's decay rate and key vulnerabilities can easily be conveyed by paring down the data to pull just key vulnerability metrics of physical failure from each sector and subsector (e.g. natural gas mains are a subsector of the energy sector) and providing a common color code to convey that vulnerability. This concept is a Cross-Sector-Infrastructure Vulnerability Assessment Model (CSI-VAM) to analyze the *potential areas of physical failure* (additional analyses of the potential cascading *operational* failures that could result could also be added, but the complexity may be lost on the governance in the IICIP process) and the overall existing vulnerabilities of a city's infrastructure. The order of analyses would be: (1) analyze each subsector individually, (2) analyze the hazards associated with collocated infrastructure assets, and (3) incorporate future conditions of natural threats – as determined by the city's HMP.

There are existing infrastructure vulnerability models that start with the natural threats (i.e., the reverse of the proposed order) and predict damage estimates to the visible portions of the city (i.e., buildings and bridges). However, without starting with known and inherent infrastructure vulnerabilities, the predictions are based on generalized information, such as building codes and land use. Information alone does *not* have transformative power. What we do with the information sets the next critical steps of:

1. integrate what we know of current conditions of all infrastructure sectors into a common legend for understandability,
2. spatially identify areas of collocated critical condition assets that would not have been identified by approaching single sectors,

3. identify all owners of assets that are highly vulnerable to integrate the CIP process,
4. visualize the analysis in simple terms, as the ability to explain is the necessary communication tool (Bammer 2011), and
5. use the resulting baseline of infrastructure vulnerabilities as a baseline for discussions regarding the integration of green, restorative, and regenerative future infrastructure.

A new process must not only integrate complex information, but it must also analyze it according to the organizations goals (e.g. reducing vulnerability to natural hazards, or reducing carbon emissions), and produce visual results that help groups understand the whole system in order to set priorities.

40.5.1 Transcending the current paradigm – articulating the goals of the IICIP

The focus in the IICIP process shifts from the lists of needs from asset management systems to the informational needs of the key stakeholder group – the public. After all, the integrated information alone will not increase the city's budget, or re-prioritize an existing budget, without the consent of the governed. This, of course, is not news, but, consider the change in messaging available with the above integrated information. *How would the public react to a city-specific decay rate, or identification of local vulnerabilities rather than an ASCE national letter-grade?*

While this information exists and a common geospatial platform is currently possible to produce, the question for the IICIP process is "what is the effective level of information to the public?" How would the public react to knowing, quantitatively and spatially, where infrastructure vulnerabilities existed in their city? Would the knowledge that a 130-year-old pressurized gas main was right in front of Bob and Carol's house on Main and Elm Streets galvanize widespread city support for improvements? Human beings are more likely to take action against a specific and tangible threat than a vague and unknown risk (Morgan et al. 2002). So, if we can use existing data to create better lists and visualizations of risks, vulnerabilities, and associated costs, we would have an improved tool for engaging the public in conversations about the necessity of bonds and funding for infrastructure. Visualizations and carefully crafted messages can become part of the communication toolbox for helping to create a sense of urgency among city departments, across organizations, and with the public.

In addition, we argue for inclusion of the ownership of all infrastructure assets to be integrated into the visualizations and analyses. This would enable discussions as to how a private utility's CIP process directly interacts with public utilities and affects the City's CIP. For example, the City of Denver owns the streets, storm and wastewater systems – but not the potable water (Denver Water is a separate entity), energy (gas and electric), or communication systems. By viewing the totality of infrastructure vulnerabilities, the goal is to initiate a discussion of common goals among the stakeholders to form a partnership approach – and cross siloes. With new information, and a means to integrate priorities into the IICIP process, new goals should be considered and articulated and communicated to each stakeholder group.

Other key steps in the process of organizational change include enabling new action – this often includes changing existing processes, reorganizing teams, and aligning new processes (Kotter 2012; Cohen 2005). In the case of infrastructure planning and operations, we explore three key processes to change: (1) developing grades, as well as decay rates, for infrastructure, (2) identifying risks and vulnerabilities as part of cost analysis, and (3) creating new processes for cross-departmental priorities. We look further at how the decay rate is brought to the attention of the public, how grades could be assigned to the built environment, the potential for cost-savings, and how intra-departmental goals can better be prioritized.

1-Decay Rate – embracing the term for advancing improvement

For this chapter, the decay rate is simply determined as a ratio of the replacement cycle for a system's assets divided by the intended design life and represented as a scalar variable by which to compare against other systems and cities.[16] The term "decay rate," promoted in this chapter to describe the weakening of a city's foundational infrastructure may seem slightly organic when referring to the concrete, steel, and hard plastics of our infrastructure (aka, "gray" infrastructure). And, typically a decay rate is specifically referring to the time taken for a given amount of a radioactive substance to decay to half of its initial value. But, the term provides an immediate mental image of disrepair, old, and not able to support grandiose visions of the future of the city, i.e. *urban decay*. We have become accustomed to the term "aging infrastructure," but aging is natural and expected, thus, the term loses the capacity to communicate the risks, costs, and vulnerabilities of the actual decline in the condition of the system. Inspiring willingness to change requires messages that make the urgency for action both obvious and tangible (Cialidini 2008; Cohen 2005; Morgan et al. 2002).

Consider supplemental terms to the decay rate. When a city's infrastructure systems are being replaced at a rate matching the design-life of the system, the city has moved to *equilibrium* (i.e. a decay rate of 1). And, should the city be slightly ahead of equilibrium, say replacing when at 95 percent of design-life, we may even call the city *advanced and resilient* (i.e. a decay rate of 0.95). However, replacing infrastructure too quickly would represent the city as having *poor stewardship* (i.e. a decay rate < 0.9) of economic resources by not getting the most out of the life-cycle of our infrastructure. Engineers in the utility departments will be the first to decry simply using design-life and replacement rate as there are other factors to consider, and mountains of associated data. But, returning to the ASCE definition of an engineer's role, they are not responsible for the one thing that enables all of their roles – *funding. The data from asset management systems has to be converted to information that the public can use, and galvanize behind in order to affect funding.*

Grading infrastructure – the case for the simplistic approach at the city-level

The national/state message from ASCE regarding aging infrastructure is not reaching taxpayers and the elected officials that direct the funding at the city-level. The primary failure of this message is that the rating is at the wrong scale. People ignore information that is not apparently about them (Morgan et al. 2002). In order for the public to be motivated to action, this message must be shifted to address the specific local condition; it must grade both the local place, city or town, as well as identify specific risks within the place – perhaps even the neighborhood level to identify social inequalities.

The ASCE uses eight criteria[17] for assigning letter grades and has a consistent and vetted methodology for grading infrastructure and should continue to do so every four years. But cities must identify criteria for a more local scale and message in order to make specific targets actionable. When presented with too much information or too many choices, it is difficult to make decisions (Carcasson & Sprain 2016; Morgan 2002). Because the local considerations, challenges and risks are unique in each community, cities ought to simplify this grading paradigm to fit their own needs. This simplification begins by considering the definition of the term "system."

40.5.2 "System" [sis-tuh m]. noun. an assemblage of parts forming a complex or unitary whole

The point of highlighting this definition is that a system is only as reliable and resilient as its *weakest-link*. In the IICIP, all assessments of the city's "resilience" and of adding new assets would be done with the knowledge of existing vulnerabilities within the existing system (e.g., adding a new substation to an antiquated electrical distribution grid). Using a car as a meta-phor, would you feel safe driving down the interstate if you knew that 10 percent of the parts in the car were in extremely poor condition – and you did not know which 10 percent they were? If an infrastructure sector, like this car metaphor, has 10 percent parts that are of extreme concern, do you assign an "A" letter grade for the 90 percent of the system that is in good condition, or an "F" for the 10 percent that is failing? Similarly, for purposes of reliable and resilient infrastructure, it does not make sense to average a poor grade with good grades in ASCE's eight grading criteria, e.g. does an "F" in the "Condition" criteria and an "A" in the "Capacity" criteria equal a "C"? The IICIP would be centered around new analyses that assigns grades based on the existing vulnerability of the integrated system, not simply averaging grades across systems.

Reducing cost – the case for proactive vs reactive

Cities already face financial constraints. One of the greatest challenges of any new system is to enable a new decision-making paradigm that has the potential to make greater strides in resiliency and planning within the current financial paradigm. This is only possible through new analyses that allow for the assessment of data across systems, and prioritization of action which examines both short and long-term cost savings.

According to an American Water Works Association (AWWA) report, water utilities in the United States install water mains with a material and service lifespan (design life) of 75–100 years (AWWA 2010). Yet, these utilities are averaging a pipe replacement rate of 0.5 percent per year (i.e., an estimated 200-year replacement cycle – more than double the useful life of the pipes). However, there are utilities with even longer replacement cycles, even a well-managed and progressive utility, such as Denver Water. Their sophisticated asset management system promotes a "remaining useful life" over the suggested AWWA design life. In fact, the decay rate can easily be calculated from the information published on their website:

> The water distribution system contains more than 3,000 miles of water mains, and Denver Water crews install or replace an average of 60,000 feet of pipe a year.[18]

This equates to a 0.38 percent replacement rate (i.e., a 263-year replacement cycle) and, when divided by the intended design-life of approximately 85 years, a *decay rate of 3.1* is obtained. While there are other factors to consider, in addition to aging pipes, the fact is that the average age of the entire stock of pipes in the system continues to increase annually and this aging is increasing the costs to cities because they are spending more and more money in reaction to breaks rather than investing in strategically prioritized replacements. This non-sequitur of logic is known by our key engineering societies, but the message is not reaching the public:

> And, it is known that aging water mains are subject to more frequent breaks and other failures that can threaten public health and safety (such as compromising tap water quality and fire-fighting flows). Buried infrastructure failures also may impose significant damages (for example, through flooding and sinkholes), are costly to repair, disrupt businesses and residential communities, and waste precious water resources. These maladies weaken our economy and undermine our quality of life. As large as the cost of reinvestment may be, not undertaking it will be worse in the long run by almost any standard (AWWA, 2010).

Not replacing the pipes at the end of design life is always a costly decision. Again, using an example from Denver Water, on January 28, 2017, a 130-year-old, 24 in. diameter, water main broke near the corner of 29th Street and Zuni Street. In addition to emergency repairs, Denver Water compensated local residents for about $147k (although indemnified, Denver Water reserves $1000 for car damage and up to $8000 for business damage[19]). Perhaps not so interesting to these same residents, was that there had been a similar break on this line the previous year. To add to the frustration of this one neighborhood, the same location suffered yet a third break on July 5, 2017. So, while age is not the only factor, it is an increasingly significant vulnerability metric, and, despite the sophistication of Denver Water's asset management system, their current analysis and decision-making paradigm does not enable integrative action with all stakeholders in the city's infrastructure needs and this increases the costs of repairing and maintaining the system. New data integration and integrative analyses are required for the city to take new action. The other lesson from this series of failures on 29th and Zuni is that the *residents do not have their own source of information.*

The communication failure here is that the true cost of infrastructure is invisible to residents. Without tangible knowledge of the full costs of reliable and resilient infrastructure, the public cannot calculate their willingness to support new rates or bonds required for system performance. One of the key messages to the public, in addition to the decay rate, should be that – *replacing our infrastructure prior to failure is extremely cost effective in the life-cycle.* This message could be potentially powerful in garnering support for new bonds, especially if the inconvenience of every resident is factored into the cost (Moore et al. 2006). Using another example from Colorado, the City of Westminster significantly increased its investment in replacing aging water lines beginning in 2006. They went from an average of 150 breaks per year to around 50–60. The city estimated that by reducing the number of service interruptions and emergency staff time, they were saving the taxpayers of Westminster approximately $400,000 annually due to this strategy.[20] Tangible examples like this should include not only the total taxpayer savings, but also estimates of the hours and dollars saved by individuals NOT impacted by breaks.

40.6 Conclusions

In her book *Thinking in Systems* Donella Meadows (2008) outlines several leverage points for changing systems. In order to change the existing paradigm, and new integrative data platform provides on the foundation for change. In order to deliver on its potential, it must be integrated into new processes that:

- Change the structure of information flows,
- Increase a city's capacity to self-organize,
- Enhance the ability to make decisions based on community goals, and
- Enable a paradigm shift.

Enabling a paradigm shift is not only urgently needed, but also possible. An integrative data platform such as the IICIP can only change the structure of information flows when organizational leaders in cities and utilities establish regular processes whereby various departments come together to examine the information, discuss current goals for resiliency, mitigating risks, planning for climate change adaptation and mitigation, and setting priorities based on the system's level analysis. Using the platform in intra and inter-departmental meetings will not only change the structure of information flows, but will increase the capacity of the city to self-organize.

The potential of a new process cannot be realized unless city and utility leaders approach its adoption with a mindset for organizational transformation (Kotter 2012, Senge 2006). Our experience with individual city and utility employees and their increasing concern over the condition, risks and costs of the country's infrastructure leaves us feeling hopeful that conditions are ripe for change. The key strategies for invoking a paradigm shift in infrastructure operations and planning require that cities, not national organizations like ASCE, begin with clearly articulating the urgent need for a change in business strategy and investment infrastructure. Clearly articulating the urgency is an ongoing part of the change, it is not a one-time activity, and thus must be continually communicated until the new integrative practices are entrenched.

While it might seem daunting to launch a change of this magnitude, people who feel the urgent need for change, as many utility and city planners do, will eagerly engage in change efforts when the path forward is visible and apparently achievable. The integrative data platform we have described above has the potential to transform currently available data from an overwhelming mess of information into a clear picture with an obvious set of priorities. Tangible visualizations of system-level vulnerability and weaknesses not only *can* but *must* be presented in ways that simplify complex data into an actionable set of items for discussion, consideration, and prioritization. The same data set can be modified for public consideration in ways that communicate the urgent need for investment, the costs associated with inaction, and savings associated with bonds rather than reactive triage that is the status quo in cities. Because citizens experience the costs and inconvenience of responding to breaks, it is not only possible but also potentially empowering to communicate with the public about the urgent need for change.

The current paradigm for managing existing infrastructure is on a downward spiral. In order to address the $4.59 trillion needed for an adequate ASCE grade in 2025, a paradigm shift is required. Cities must begin by articulating the urgent need for investment to their citizens, stakeholders, and across the organization. Then, they must craft a vision that is aligned with local values and establish numerous communication channels for engaging the public, utilities partners, and departments within the city. The paradigm shift cannot happen without an integrative data platform that enable new analyses, the simplification of masses of data, and visualization of data to help all parties set priorities and communicate the urgent need for investment. Such a platform can be created from existing data, but the key to its success will the integration of that platform into existing city processes for planning, capital investment processes, budgeting, and public engagement. This is all possible, but requires the will and vision of city leaders and supporting teams within the city that are committed to planning and operating more robust systems.

Acknowledgements

We would like to thank the following people who provided insights and comments on this chapter:

David Rouse, David Rouse, FAICP, ASLA
American Planning Association. Managing Director of Research and Advisory Services

Ann Livingston, J.D.
Principal Planner in Sustainability, Sustainability Division, Public Works Department, City of Fort Lauderdale

Stephen Fisher, PhD, PE, QEP, ENV SP
Member, ASCE National Committee on Sustainability

Alan Mickelson, PhD.
Associate Professor, Electrical, Computer & Energy Engineering – Colorado University, Boulder

Notes

1 www.infrastructurereportcard.org/ (retrieved in March 2017).
2 www.infrastructurereportcard.org/ (retrieved in March 2017).
3 Personal communication between author and anonymous public works director
4 www.infrastructurereportcard.org/cat-item/bridges/ (retrieved in April 2017).
5 www.infrastructurereportcard.org/ (retrieved in March 2017).
6 www.infrastructurereportcard.org/this-week-in-infrastructure-state-solutions-innovations-for-infrastructure-improvement/ (retrieved in April 2017).
7 www.cnn.com/2011/US/01/20/water.main.infrastructure/index.html (retrieved in April 2017).
8 www.fema.gov/media-library/assets/documents/4528 (retrieved in April 2017).
9 www.fema.gov/technological-hazards (retrieved in April 2017).
10 www.ghgprotocol.org/greenhouse-gas-protocol-accounting-reporting-standard-cities (retrieved in March 2017).
11 www.compactofmayors.org/history/ (retrieved in March 2017).
12 www.starcommunities.org/ (retrieved in May 2017).
13 www.iap2.org/?219 (retrieved in June 2017).
14 www.denvergov.org/content/denvergov/en/mayors-office/newsroom/2006/mayor-hickenlooper-convenes-infrastructure-priorities-task-force.html (retrieved in May 2017).
15 Personal communication with Steve Fisher, April 17, 2017.
16 The theme of this chapter is to primarily focus on the communication needs of the public and elected officials. Advanced asset management systems will use a failure (hazard) function that is dependent on the age and design life of the asset, and with the distribution of all ages/design lives of the assets within a system, a replacement rate can be determined to keep the failure rates from increasing too rapidly, or even going exponential. However, there are three reasons for presenting the decay rate as a simple ratio: (1) most utilities, despite the analytic capabilities, fall back to subjective rules that are not data rigorous, (2) the key of this chapter is to present information in a way that the public can absorb, and (3) if the public and elected officials understand the reason for the decay rate, they are more likely to pass bond issues. For more on latter two points, please read the embedded article in the following link. http://mentalfloss.com/article/76144/why-no-one-wanted-aws-third-pound-burger.
17 www.infrastructurereportcard.org/making-the-grade/what-makes-a-grade/ (retrieved in April 2017).
18 www.denverwater.org/project-updates/pipe-replacement (retrieved in July 2017).
19 www.9news.com/news/local/who-pays-for-damage-after-water-main-breaks/407066100 (retrieved in July 2017).
20 www.ci.westminster.co.us/CityGovernment/PublicWorksUtilities/WaterandSewerRates (retrieved in July 2017).

References

ASCE, 2015. *Adapting Infrastructure and Civil Engineering Practice to a Changing Climate Committee on Adaptation to a Changing Climate*. Edited by J. Rolf Olsen, Ph.D.

ASCE, 2016. Failure to Act Report, 2016.

AWWA, 2010. Buried No Longer: Confronting America's Water Infrastructure Challenge.

Bammer, G., 2011. *Disciplining Interdisciplinarity: Integration and Implementation Sciences for Researching Complex Real-World Problems*. Canberra, Australia: ANU E Press.

Carcasson, M. and Sprain, L., 2016. Beyond problem solving: Reconceptualizing the work of public deliberation as deliberative inquiry. *Communication Theory*, 26(1), 41–63.

Cialdini, R.B., 2008. *Influence: Science and Practice*.5th Ed. Boston, MA: Allyn and Bacon.

Cohen, D.S., 2005. *The Heart of Change Field Guide: Tools and Tactics for Leading Change in Your Organization*. Boston, MA: Harvard Business Review Press.

Kotter, J.P., 2012. *Leading Change*. Boston, MA: Harvard Business Review Press.

Meadows, D., 2008. *Thinking in Systems: A Primer*. White River Junction, VT: Chelsea Green Publishing.

Moore, J.E., Little, R.G., Cho, S., and Lee, S., 2006. Using regional economic models to estimate the costs of infrastructure failures: the cost of a limited interruption in electric power in the Los Angeles region. *Public Works Management & Policy*, 10(3), 256–74.

Morgan, M.G., Fischoff, B., Bostrom, A., and Atman, C.J., 2002. *Risk Communication: A Mental Models Approach*. New York, NY: Cambridge University Press.

NIST, 2016. *Community Resilience Planning Guide for Buildings and Infrastructure Systems – Volume 1*. May, Special Publication 1190–1.

Ramaswami et al. Fall 2014 International, interdisciplinary education on sustainable infrastructure and sustainable cities: key concepts and skills. *NAE Bridge Magazine*,

Reiner, M., and Rouse, D. 2017. Dependency model: Reliable infrastructure and the resilient, sustainable, and livable city. Journal of Sustainable and Resilient Infrastructure. Accepted and forthcoming.

Senge, P., 2006. *The Fifth Discipline: The Art and Practice of the Learning Organization*. New York, NY: Doubleday/Currency.

Stroh, D.P., 2015. *Systems Thinking for Social Change: A Practical Guide to Solving Complex Problems, Avoiding Unintended Consequences, and Achieving Lasting Results*. White River Junction, VT: Chelsea Green Publishing.

World Bank. 2011. *Summary of: Guidebook on Capital Investment Planning for Local Governments*. October.

Balanced urban design process to create resilient and sustainable urban environments

¹Nuwan Dias, ²Dilanthi Amaratunga, ³Kaushal Keraminiyage, and ⁴Richard Haigh

¹²³⁴GLOBAL DISASTER RESILIENCE CENTRE, UNIVERSITY OF HUDDERSFIELD, UK
¹ N.DIAS@HUD.AC.UK,
² D.AMARATUNGA@HUD.AC.UK,
³ K.KERAMINIYAGE@HUD.AC.UK,
⁴ R.HAIGH@HUD.AC.UK

41.1 Introduction

The international conference that took place in 1956 at Harvard's Graduate School of Design on the future of cities, pioneered the creation of the discipline Urban Design (UD) in the 1960s. Carmona et al. (2010) state the profession was typified by the concept of city beautification by concentrating on the visual qualities and aesthetic experience of urban spaces, rather than the myriad cultural, social, economic, political and spatial factors and processes contributing to successful urban places.

Larice and Macdonald (2013) specify the specific reason for the emergence of the profession of urban design in the 1960s as being the beautification of cities. Cities in the 1960s were heavily polluted due to 100 years of industrialization and urban sprawl was seen everywhere in cities. In western countries industrialization had almost come to an end by this time and patterns of livelihood were changing to a more service-based economic sector. Therefore, there was an extensive need to regenerate cities from the increasingly deprived situations caused by declining industries and to bring life back into them. However, at that time, the architect's role was concentrated on designing buildings; urban planning was more policy-oriented and did not focus on specific town and street design. Therefore, there was no profession which could undertake the care of the aesthetic aspect of cities and concentrate on how to create beautiful cities. Consequently, an outcome of the international conference that took place at Harvard in 1956 was a discipline to bridge the gap between urban planning and architecture.

The discussion set out in this chapter reveals when and where the profession originated, its original scope and the key reason for the introduction of the profession. Section 41.2 will discuss the role of urban design in today's context and how it can contribute to the sustainable urban development.

Table 41.1 Distinction between urban design and urban planning

Urban Design	Urban Planning
Plans and designs streets, parks, transit stops on different scales such as at regional level, local level but does not plan overall scheme	Plans for larger regions, towns and villages as a whole
Orients designs for aesthetics as well as for functionality	Usually plans a utility
The treatment of space in urban design is three-dimensional, where vertical elements are as important as horizontal elements	Urban planning is customarily a two-dimensional activity where the majority of plans are visually represented from a two- dimensional view: not model, sectional, or elevation
More design and action oriented	More policy oriented
Urban design thinks about functionality – designs try to create houses as homes by mixing communities, using active frontages, etc.	Focus on land use rather than functionality (ex-planning identifies location for housing)
Urban design use visualization	Deals with known context
Make action-oriented strategies	Makes space-oriented strategies

41.2 Current scope of urban design and its role in urban development

In today's world, the scope of urban design is wider, endeavouring to enhance the socio, economic, and environmental life of a city. Urban design is the art of making places in an urban context which involves designing groups of buildings and the spaces and landscapes between them and also creating frameworks for successful development (Urban Design Group 2011).

There is a debate existing over the definition and scope of urban design and urban planning. In fact, the two disciplines are interrelated but there are certain features which distinguish urban design from urban planning. The urban planner perceives land-use, job creation, and equity in a two-dimensional sense whereas the urban designer thinks about how to make the area work as a place which is memorable and pleasant in a three-dimensional sense. As Madanipour (2006) states, "Urban planning and urban design are getting closer together" as urban design makes planning "more forward looking" and "by developing visions for the future of their area." However, it is important to distinguish between urban design and urban planning as this study is focused on urban design and not on urban planning. Accordingly, Table 41.1 distinguishes between urban design and urban planning:

As mentioned earlier, at the time urban design was introduced as a separate profession, city beautification was the fundamental purpose of urban design. Over time, the scope and objectives of urban design have changed so that now, urban design plays a vital role in city development. Today, urban design has become a collaborative discipline that combines with others to create three-dimensional forms and spaces that function effectively for people.

Today, the concept of sustainability has become integrated with urban design. As Ritchie and Thomas (2013) describe, sustainable urban design should share the values of social, economic, and environmental sustainability.

41.3 The urban design process (key stages in an UD process)

There are key stages in any urban design process. Roberts and Greed (2001) state that the urban design process occurs in four sequential stages which are called the framework for urban design and cover the following:

- Defining the problem.
- Developing a rationale.
- Summary of development opportunities and constraints.
- Conceptualising and evaluating urban design options. (Adapted from: Roberts & Greed 2001)

As Roberts and Greed (2001) discovered in the first stage, "defining the problem," the study area is defined, surveys of the study area are conducted and the urban form and activities are analyzed. Thereafter, the second stage, "developing a rationale," planning/socio-economic context, built form/townscape, land use/activity movement or access, physical and natural environment, socio-space and cultural space and public realms are assessed by means of SWOT analysis or scenario development. Thirdly, the development opportunities and constraints are developed and then, the developed urban design options are evaluated before finalizing the scheme.

Similarly, Moughtin (2003) describes the urban design process in line with the RIBA practice and management hand book of the time. He also explains that there are four main phases in the design process which are as follows:

- Phase 1 Assimilation: the accumulation of general information and information specifically related to the problem.
- Phase 2 General Study: the investigation of the nature of the problem: the investigation of possible solutions.
- Phase 3 Development: the development of one or more solutions.
- Phase 4 Communication: the communication of the chosen solution to the client. (Adapted from Moughtin 2003)

As Moughtin (2003) explains in phase 1, "Assimilation," the background of the urban design process is prepared including information specifically related to the urban design problem in question. Thereafter, in phase 2, "General Study," the urban analysis is conducted while investigating some possible solutions. In phase 3, "Development," possible solutions identified at the previous stage are further developed before communicating them to the client. With the exception of phase 4, "Communication," the previous three phases are all similar to those discovered by Roberts and Greed (2001).

Carmona et al. (2010) introduce the urban design process in stages and have stated that each stage represents a complex set of activities, which, while generally portrayed as a linear process, is iterative and cyclical. Each sequential stage is presented below:

- Setting goals – in conjunction with other actors (particularly clients and stakeholders), having regard to economic and political realities, proposed timescale and client and stakeholder requirements.
- Analysis – gathering and analysing information and ideas that might inform the design solutions.
- Visioning – generating and developing possible solutions through an iterative process of imaging and presentation, usually informed by personal experience and design philosophies.
- Synthesis and prediction – testing the generated solutions as a means of identifying workable alternatives.
- Decision making – identifying which alternatives can be discarded and which are worthy of further refinement or promotion as preferred design solutions.

- Evaluation – (appraisal) reviewing the finished product against the identified goals. (Adapted from Carmona et al. 2010)

When critically evaluating the stages introduced by different researchers for the urban design process, it can be noted that all of them generate common stages but use different names. Accordingly, based on different viewpoints, the authors have established five key stages in the urban design process. In other words, the literature informed the urban design process framework described in the latter part of the chapter which has been developed and explained using these five key stages for the urban design process. The five key stages are as follows:

1. The preparation stage – A platform for creating a project team, deciding deadlines etc. This stage must take place before assessing urban issues.
2. Problem identification stage – This is the point at which initial urban issues and problems are identified.
3. Urban analysis stage – A detailed analysis of the urban environment takes place at this stage which can lead to a SWOT analysis etc.
4. Vision and strategy generation – This is the stage where initial solutions are developed, assessed and refined.
5. Design development stage – The stage where the solutions that have been developed are individually assessed to form solutions that are realistic and feasible.

41.4 Urban design process in practice

The current process employed in urban design is often seen as too top-down in method and there are serious concerns and criticisms over this issue. The main criticism is that a top-down process does not help to achieve sustainability indicators usually explored in today's urban context (Roy & Ganguly 2009). The classic approach to urban development (top-down) generally provides early and high level planning. Greed and Roberts (2014) ask the question, "Who are the real designers?" which prompts two sub–questions: "professionals?" or "community groups?" The urban professional already has a contextual base, i.e., the "place" that requires development; understanding of "place" is strengthened with the help and participation of concerned stakeholders. In fact, "place making" is now recognized as a vitally important dimension of urban design facilitated by community engagement.

As stated above, the current urban design process is mainly top-down and dominated by urban planners and designers and offers few opportunities for the community to partake. However, there is no rigid urban design process in practice as most of the urban design processes are tailor made to the particular urban context. However, it is generally considered that the UD process is top-down where there are limited opportunities for the community. Roberts and Greed (2001) describe how the urban design process occurs in four sequential stages based on the behavior of project team members in these four stages. As they discovered, during the first stage, "defining the problem," the planning or design team appraises the study area by conducting surveys associated with the urban form by undertaking an activity analysis. Thereafter, based on the analysis, the team develops a rationale with a summary of development opportunities and constraints. In the latter stage, area strategies and urban design options are evaluated by team members who then finalize an urban design strategy for the area. This indicates that, in practice, the current urban design process is stiff and directly indicates that it is a totally top-down process.

There are several other urban design processes which are explained by different researchers and practitioners; some examples are the UD process explained by Moughtin (2003) in line with the RIBA practice and management handbook of the time. Boyko et al. (2006) identified a more recent development in the urban design process which has a better role for the stakeholder engagement. The Department of Infrastructure & Regional Development Australia (2013) has developed its own urban design process as a part of an urban design protocol for Australian cities.

Lawson (2006) describes the current process of urban design, which follows a sequence of activities, as unconvincing. He argues that many designers learn about the design problems largely by trying to solve them. As he explained, the current process does not allow a clear platform for in-depth analysis of urban problems and the process is led by designers.

41.5 Urban design process in practice and its implications on sustainable urban design

As mentioned in Section 41.4, the predominant urban design process has a high level, top-down approach. However, it is not justifiable to totally reject the current predominant top-down approach without assessing its positive and negative features. Accordingly, this section seeks to identify and analyse the positive and negative aspects of the current process in order to identify the implications for effective community engagement and, therefore, for sustainable development.

Fraser et al. (2006) state that design processes typically led by experts, simply comply with the funding agencies and this top-down process may alienate the community and fail to capture locally significant factors. The authors further state that projects designed using this top-down model do not necessarily engage community members nor ensure that indicators are relevant at the local level. However, as explained by the same authors, this type of top-down processes reduces the risk of being time and resource intensive. Larice and Macdonald (2013) specified that a top-down urban design process is less time consuming as the whole process is pre-defined and controlled by professional actors. Supporting the argument of Fraser et al. (2006) regarding the alienation of locally significant factors in a top-down process, Roy and Ganguly (2009) stated that a classic top-down process provides early, high level planning which may not deal with the real issues at ground level. As the same authors explained, a top-down process has no significant understanding of the specific issues, or their cause, at ground level. The Commission for Architecture & Built Environment (2000) argues that a blanket policy of using a top-down process across all locations at all times is not suitable for urban design because each design solution should be distinctive and specific to each context in which it is to be implemented.

The distinctiveness of the place has been widely discussed by the seminal author Norberg-Schulz (1980) who particularly explained that each location has its own distinct features which is, in effect, the "genius loci" of that particular place. Accordingly, the findings of the Commission for Architecture & Built Environment (2000) has been firmly entrenched with the findings of Norberg-Schulz (1980). Where Schulz identifies the distinctiveness of each place, the Commission for Architecture & Built Environment has gone one step beyond and explored the negative implications of a top-down process on the identification of distinctive features in a local context.

Carmona et al. (2003) maintain that the danger of the top-down process is the prior formation of the agenda which may lead to the manipulation of local opinion rather than addressing genuine community needs that emerge through effective participation. Supporting the argument of Carmona et al. (2003), and adding to that argument, the Commission for Architecture & Built Environment (2000) has stated that local stakeholders often have particular insight into specific urban design issues affecting a given context and, therefore, urban design solutions developed through a top-down process may not be accepted by the majority of stakeholders. While many authors have discovered the negative implications of the current top-down process, Larice and Macdonald (2007) exposed several of its positive implications. Accordingly, the authors have asserted that in a top-down process, development options or proposals are already prepared, therefore, it is easier to focus on the community consultation process. Furthermore, they discovered that a top-down process is less time consuming due to the whole process being predefined and controlled by professional actors. In addition, Larice and Macdonald (2007) argue that a top-down process is more effective in terms of resource mobilization because professional experts mobilise, co-ordinate and interpret community options.

Even though Larice and Macdonald (2007) are positive about the current process of urban design, Cooksey and Kikula (2005) argue there are more negative implications in the current process than positive implications. As they discovered, the key positive implications are: a top-down approach gives government planners and designers a sense of control and efficiency while donor agencies are keener to invest in projects which have a top-down process because they feel that budgets can be maintained along with pre-established targets and timetables. However, as has also been argued, there are numerous negative implications to the top-down process and these are presented below:

- Decisions are made centrally by organizations that are remote from the project area. Participation of stakeholders is limited to the provision of data or to approving and adhering to what has already been planned.
- Planners and bureaucrats proceed from a starting point of a clean slate and assume they are in possession of all the requisite knowledge for improving people's lives. In reality, they are making interventions in a well-established, community social system which has survived over generations of struggle and interaction with the local environment.
- Plans are generally based on quantitative data or numerical estimations collected through rapid diagnostic feasibility studies or project formulation missions.
- Planning (as well as implementation) follows a pre-conceived project design (a master plan) with a fixed time schedule often extending over several years and leading to rigid interventions that do not respect or consider environmental changes, local initiatives, and development choices.
- The process follows a predetermined project design usually based on assumptions of uniformity and cost-effectiveness regardless of specific conditions pertinent to the area where the project is to be implemented.
- Top-down process is usually based on poor assumptions of social and environmental behavior which are often proven to be incorrect because locality and social formations differ. (Cooksey & Kikula 2005)

Karsten (2009) describes the current top-down urban design process from the perspective of urban planning and city development. She states that three urban discourses exist: the attractive city, the creative city, and the emancipatory city. She has argued that all of these dominant discourses are top-down and tend to overlook the day-to-day life of residents and particularly, of family residents. She further stated that top-down processes focus only on city centres and not the needs and aspirations of local districts and residents.

Bell (2005) argued that to achieve good urban design, it is necessary to identify local features such as, social and cultural features, heritage, movement and access, environmental management, and so on. She also stated that the current process of urban design often fails to identify such features in the local context, and therefore, this makes creating a good urban design challenging. Accordingly, she suggests the need for a new progressive process for urban design which has the scope to include the local context. Directly supporting the argument of Bell (2005), Boyko et al. (2005) stated that the urban design process must be transformed to create sustainable urban environments.

Similarly, the Technical Manual for BREEAM Communities (BREEAM 2012) has also specified that to ensure the needs, ideas, and knowledge of the community are considered, it is vital to change the rigid top-down process model, and to ultimately, achieve sustainability in urban design. Based on the findings from the literature synthesis in this section, the positive and negative features of the top-down process model can be summarized as follows:

As described in Section 41.2, the current scope of urban design is to create sustainable urban designs. Sustainable urban design is about creating high quality neighbourhoods for people in terms of the "triple bottom line." Therefore, as determined in this section, to create sustainable environments, the urban design professional needs to diagnose the urban environment properly and create design solutions which match the needs and aspirations of the community.

Based on the findings from literature, the question can now be posed: How can this be achieved without the full engagement of the community, in every aspect of the design process, particularly urban analysis and vision creation? Without an in depth understanding of place, the "genius loci," designers tend to begin with a "clean sheet" and risk bringing development strategies that do not link the past, present and the future effectively through

Table 41.2 Positive and negative features of a top-down urban design process

Positive and Negative features of a top-down urban design process	
Positive Features	Negative Features
A top-down process gives planners and designers good control over the design project	Alienates local community members and fails to capture locally significant factors
Community consultation is easy in top-down process as the plans are already prepared	Provides early and high-level planning which may not deal with the real requirements at ground level
Less time consuming	Does not identify specifically the uniqueness of the local entity
Effective use of resources	Could lead to manipulation of local opinion rather than addressing genuine community needs that emerge through effective participation
Donor agencies are keener to invest in projects which use a top-down approach	Planners and bureaucrats proceed on the assumption that they possess all the knowledge required for improving people's lives. In reality, they often fail to understand the social system
	May not be accepted by the majority of the community
	Participation of stakeholders is limited to the provision of data or to approving and adhering to what has already been planned
	Generally based on quantitative and numeric analysis rather than identifying particular facts in the local context
	Often fails to identify the specific conditions of the area in which the project is to be implemented
	Usually based on poor assumptions of social and environmental behavior
	Overlooks the day-to-day life of residents and particularly of family residents
	Fails to capture local knowledge

the design solution. Therefore, as discovered in this review, using a top-down process may result in the roots of local problems and local significant factors being overlooked. When local significant factors and problems are not clearly identified in the urban design solutions developed by professionals, primarily working alone, there is every chance they will not fulfil the needs and aspirations of local communities. It can also be argued that a development solution, which does not fulfil community needs and aspirations, may not be acceptable to local communities.

In consequence, current problems and issues in the area remain unsolved and additional issues are created; loss of community commitment to the area could ensue, thus devaluing buildings and land which in the long term, could result in an unsustainable area. Accordingly, it can be noted that the current top-down process has many negative implications for sustainable development. However, as this section has established, a top-down process does have some positive implications, but on the whole, many authors and researchers reject a top-down urban design process and suggest that a bottom-up process is necessary to achieve sustainability in urban design. However, a fully bottom-up process has also been criticized by many authors and researchers citing loss of control and ineffectiveness. The nature of the bottom-up process proposed by many authors is discussed and criticisms relating to the bottom-up process are presented below.

41.6 Bottom-up urban design process against the top-down urban design process

To overcome the constraints identified in the top-down urban design process, many authors and researchers have discussed implementing a bottom-up approach in order to deliver sustainable urban designs. Roy and Ganguly (2009) support the development of a bottom-up urban design process and argued that its approach to designing makes more sense because a community intuitively understands their needs and aspirations better than professional actors. Therefore, the involvement of a community from the beginning to the end of a project will help to deliver more sustainable solutions.

Fraser et al. (2006) state that a proper bottom-up approach, where the community can engage actively in the development process, will capture locally significant factors and will help to achieve better results in relation to sustainability indicators. These authors (Fraser et al. 2006) provided many logical reasons as to why we should move to a proper bottom-up approach. Some of the key points that they make are as follows:

- A bottom-up approach provides a comprehensive assessment of local social, environmental and economic issues which help to diagnose the local context in a detailed manner rather than relying only on quantitative facts and figures.
- A bottom-up approach fills the gap between the problems identified by the planners and the actual problems that exist in an area. It also promotes increased sensitivity to local issues.
- Solutions generated through a bottom-up approach are grounded in the locality, and therefore, address local issues and provide sustainable solutions.
- A bottom-up approach increases a community's capacity to manage their environment, and therefore, the community is empowered.

Moughtin (2003) cites the Millgate Project implemented in Nottinghamshire by the Nottingham Community and Housing Association. This project adopted the fundamental theories of sustainable development and permaculture. The community was allowed to design their own homes. The impetus for this project came from Mark Vidal Hall, the vicar of Chellaston, Derbyshire, who argued that the methods used by the architects and planners to create communities were quite wrong. His criticism was that the professionals involved in the building industry put more effort into the physical structure rather than being concerned with the requirements of the community. In this project, the community took on many responsibilities in order to successfully complete it from beginning to end. They felt that the project belonged to them and that the development was not forcibly implemented from the "top."

Reed (2006) describes a whole system approach is needed to achieve real sustainability beyond the so-called "green design." He states that the whole process needs a change in thinking and in this model, he emphasizes the importance of having a proper bottom-up approach to understanding a place. This approach has been referred to as "regenerative design" because it seeks to restore the physical, social, and environmental systems to "good health."

Batty (2009) states that cities have been treated as systems, and in the last two decades, the focus of city treatment has changed more towards systems whose structure emerges from the bottom up. Consequently, the author stated, in a bottom-up process, cities are treated as an emergent phenomenon, generated through a combination of hierarchical levels of decision, driven in a decentralized fashion.

Greed and Roberts (2014) state that there has been considerable discussion on implementing a bottom-up urban design process. As they discuss in recent times, community members, residents and minority groups have had a particular interest in urban design issues where they believe "the feel" of the area is understood by the people who actually live in the area. Therefore, as described by the authors, non-professionals urgently want to have their say and look to bottom-up urban design processes.

Boyko et al. (2006) state that sustainability issues should be addressed early in the urban design process and therefore, people who live, work, and socialize in urban environments have a fundamental role to play in urban design. Accordingly, Boyko et al. (2006) suggest the constantly changing social, functional, aesthetic, and emotional needs should be addressed in the urban design process by providing community engagement opportunities throughout the process.

All the above literature suggests that the key characteristic of a bottom-up urban design process is community consultation and involvement from the beginning to the end of the project. This indicates the importance of consulting with the community at the urban analysis stage, as the early involvement of the community helps to properly diagnose the area. Likewise, as indicated in the above literature synthesis, consultation with the community should continue through all the stages from the urban analysis stage through to strategy generation and up to design finalization; the professional actor's role needs to focus on helping the community recognize the problems and the potential of their area.

This indicates that there is still a need for a proper bottom-up urban design process which actually identifies community needs and aspirations and delivers sustainable solutions.

While there are convincing facts for the implementation of a bottom-up process in urban design, there are strong arguments about the negative features of a bottom-up process which refute the adaptation of a bottom-up process for urban design. The next section discusses the drawbacks of the bottom-up process.

41.7 Bottom-up process: Is it a solid solution?

As evidenced in Section 41.6, the key characteristics of a bottom-up process is community engagement throughout the urban design process. Furthermore, the section indicated that a bottom-up process is more decentralized and operates in a more liberated manner. However, as will be shown, there are criticisms concerning a bottom-up urban approach to a design process.

Cliff (2014) states that the powerful role played by the non-designers in the urban design process is welcome and appreciated. The author further states that in order to understand the local context, the role of non-designers is crucial. However, the author argues against a design process which is fully grounded without the iterative mix of urban design philosophies and language. Similarly, Cooksey and Kikula (2005) state that a bottom-up process is ideal in order to understand the local context but it may reduce planners' and designers' control which will result in reducing the efficiency of the UD process.

On the other hand, the same authors speculate that donor agencies may not be particularly interested in projects which employ a bottom-up process as they are cautious that budgets and targets may not be pre-established. Larice and Macdonald (2007) also stated bottom-up processes may be time consuming and ineffective if they are not controlled by professionals but operate in a more decentralized manner. Pissourios (2014) argues bottom-up communicative planning lacks the crucial components of a typical planning theory. Consequently, he argues that bottom-up planning is more decentralised and community based rather than integrating essential theoretical support for the process. He argues that basic features, such as maintaining planning standards and classification of urban users, are totally absent in a bottom-up planning process.

The argument of Oakley and Tsao (2007) is quite different from other arguments that have already been discussed. They believe that it is extremely difficult to attract community contribution due to the enormous commitment required of them throughout the process. This indicates that in a bottom-up process, there are many instances when a project team needs to hold community participatory workshops or discussions which are sometimes ineffective at certain stages of the process. Larice and Macdonald (2013) share a similar theory to that put forward by Oakley and Tsao (2007) on the effectiveness of community engagement but are more focused on the management of the community. The authors have argued that in a bottom-up process, it is quite difficult to manage the community if the development options and proposals are not already prepared. Annibal et al. (2013) assert that local people have a unique perspective on their needs, joining up settlements, managing change through community-led planning and delivery of innovative services but the authors have stated that the community needs to be organised, and therefore, a statutory service needs to be engaged which can identify local priorities, secure resources, and undertake responsibilities.

Based on the above discussions it can be noted that even though the bottom-up process has been proposed as a potential process for urban design, it has its own weaknesses which can adversely affect the quality of the urban design project or its processes. Therefore, a pure bottom-up process itself may not be a complete solution as a new urban design process framework. Based on this argument, the following section explores the need for a new urban design process framework for sustainable urban designs.

41.8 The need for a new urban design process framework

As has been explored in Sections 41.4 and 41.5, the current urban design process is mainly top-down and it has a number of negative implications for the sustainable urban design. Therefore, as explored in Section 41.6, researchers and authors have discussed using a bottom-up process in urban design. Nevertheless, as outlined in Section 41.7, bottom-up processes have their own negative features which may adversely affect the creation of sustainable urban designs. Section 41.5 has explored the positive features of the current top-down urban design process which may positively affect the creation of sustainable urban designs. In order to avoid the drawbacks of both processes, researchers and authors have argued the need for a *"balanced"* urban design process integrating the positive features from both the bottom-up and top-down processes.

Pissourios (2014) suggested a combined bottom-up/top-down process for a broader context of urban planning. As the author argued, top-down process planning was approached mainly as a technocratic procedure of urban intervention and planning theory was explained in the political discourse. As a result of this, planning has become a subject that takes decisions based on technical aspects rather than considering the needs of people and their environment. On the other hand, Pissourios (2014) argues the emerging communicative urban planning process lacks the crucial components of a typical planning theory. He argues that bottom-up planning processes are more decentralized and community based rather than integrating essential theoretical support for the process. He suggests the need for an integrated process specifically in the context of urban planning. Similarly, Cliff (2014) has explored the need for an integrated process, but in particular, for the context of urban design. She argued that the involvement of the community in urban design is vital; it should be an iterative, community-based process combined with core design principles. For this reason, she emphasizes the need for a community embedded urban design process which has input from urban design professionals.

As Carmona et al. (2010) explain, the producer/consumer gap is a key issue in urban design. In this context, the "producer" is the urban designer and the people are the "consumers." The lack of direct consumer input is a key reason for the producer/consumer gap. Since the consumer does not have any input into the process, the producer produces "poor quality" developments serving narrower financial purposes. Accordingly, a combined methodology to bridge the producer/consumer gap is needed. Annibal et al. (2013) also emphasize the need for a community-based development but argued that it should be within a framework managed by urban designers. It was stated that a community needs to be organised to achieve successful engagement and therefore, a statutory service needs to be engaged which can identify local priorities, secure resources, and undertake responsibility.

Sections 41.5 to 41.7 have explored the literature conveying many different viewpoints about the urban design process. All of the points of view expressed within these sections have emphasized the need for a new urban design process framework which provides guidance on the tasks to be undertaken and how each task should be carried out at key stages in the urban design process. Accordingly, there is a strong need to develop a new urban design process framework which emphasizes community engagement but encompasses the essential positive features of a top-down urban design process.

Based on this, the next section explores the key factors of a good urban design process which leads to the creation of sustainable urban designs.

41.9 Literature-informed potential urban design process framework

As decisively discovered in previous sections (41.5–41.8), a new urban design process framework is required. However, there is still a question which needs to be answered about what factors are required for an urban design process which leads to the creation of sustainable urban designs. In fact, these factors have already been mentioned or discussed throughout the literature synthesis, as part of various topics. Here, the author's intention is to further clarify these factors and present them concisely in this section.

Carmona (2014) declares a dedicated role played by non-designers to be one of the key factors for a good urban design process which leads to the creation of sustainable urban designs.

The author emphasizes the need for the community to have a strong say in the urban design process, thus supporting the argument of Carmona (2014) and Boyko et al. (2006) who feel that ownership of the process should be given to the community.

According to this argument, a community should have an influential role, particularly in diagnosing the urban environment. BREEAM (2012) has stated that a sustainable urban design process should identify the needs, ideas, and knowledge of the local community. Adding to the findings of BREEAM (2012), Bell (2005) also avers that the professional actors should be responsive to community views and he suggests providing equal opportunities for the community, including wider stakeholders, to participate in the process and also specifies that professionals should acknowledge their participation.

Similarly, Walton et al. (2007) suggested in a sustainable urban design, stakeholders should have the opportunity to participate in the decision-making process. Adding to Walton et al. (2007), Lang (2005) argues that stakeholders should have opportunities for augmentation in the UD process. According to Cooksey and Kikula (2005), stakeholders should have real decision-making opportunities rather than being consulted just to get data. Boyko et al. (2010), maintain that in a sustainable process of urban design, the professional actors should understand the views of outsiders. The same authors (Boyko et al. 2006) have further emphasized the need for involvement of a broader spectrum of stakeholders in the urban design process. Adding to this, Bell (2005) stated there should be a cross-disciplinary partnership in the urban design process.

Based on these discussions, it is clear that two factors are required for the urban design process to create sustainable urban designs: they are the influential role provided by the community and participatory opportunities provided to a wide range of stakeholders.

As Lang (2005) described, in an urban design process there should be a leader who can control and manage the UD process. Supporting this argument, Carmona (2014) stated there should be a project champion to lead and control the UD process. Similarly, Cooksey and Kikula (2005) stated that control and efficiency should be maintained in the urban design process. According to Bell (2005), there should be a comprehensive scoping procedure in the UD process and there should be a leader to comprehensively scope the UD process. Based on the above stated viewpoints, it can clearly be seen that leadership is another factor essential to the urban design process.

Fraser et al. (2006) stated that to ensure sustainability in the UD process, it is necessary to assess the local context in a detailed manner using the qualitative facts rather than relying purely on quantitative data. Boyko et al. (2006) have declared a similar argument and stated that urban analysis should be focused on the local context rather than relying on quantitative methods. Cliff (2014) has also specified that a successful urban design process should be community based but should also be combined with design principles.

This section indicated another factor which is that a comprehensive urban analysis should be made based on both subjective and objective elements.

As Walton et al. (2007) discuss, a sustainable urban design process should provide a pathway to an in-depth understanding of the physical setting and should also appreciate local dynamics such as community values, customs, local history and so forth. According to Roy and Ganguly (2009), the urban design process should deal with requirements at ground level and in addition, Fraser et al. (2006) discovered that capturing locally significant factors is one of the key success factors for a sustainable UD process. Similarly, Bell (2005) stated that working with local cultures is also a success factor in the UD process. Accordingly, the two other factors that have emerged from this section are: "the need for conducting an in-depth urban analysis based on ground level facts" and "the need for addressing local needs in the design solutions."

Cooksey and Kikula (2005) argued that professional actors should not propose an UD based on pre-determined assumptions of uniformities. He particularly emphasized the need to understand specific local conditions in the UD process. In a similar way, Lang (2005) says that professionals should begin the UD process with an open mind, avoiding the use of generalized solutions. The Commission for Architecture & Built Enviornment (2000) has also specified the need for a fresh approach and has stressed the importance of designers avoiding the use of a blanket policy in the urban design process.

The final factor that has emerged from this section indicates that designers should avoid early decisions in the UD process and should always work according to the nature of the urban entity rather than using blanket policies.

Based on the factors that have been discussed in Section 41.8, a literature-informed potential urban design process framework can be presented, followed by a short description of what is expected to be done at each stage of the UD process.

The first key factor derived from the literature explains that a leader should be appointed to take overall control of the UD process at the preparation stage. This is supported by the next key factor from the literature review which explains that there should be a feeling of control and efficiency throughout the process. This indicates that the project leader should create an atmosphere of being in full control throughout the UD process. In addition to this, the third key factor reveals that comprehensive scoping should be undertaken in the UD process and the literature findings have revealed that to scope the project process and to make the process efficient, whilst also providing leadership, a project champion should be assigned at the preparation stage.

When it comes to the problem identification stage, there is a literature-informed key factor which advocates, "starting the problem identification with an open mind." This key factor has been further supported by another sub-factor saying that problem identification should begin as a fresh process. Additionally, another key factor revealed by the literature at the problem identification stage, describes how locally significant factors should be captured at the problem identification stage by identifying the needs, ideas, and knowledge of the community through community views and the views of professional actors.

The next key factor discovered is linked to the urban analysis stage where it was found that the project team should avoid early decisions in the UD process. The sub-factor for this key factor further describes this proposal and it explains that the project team should not make decisions about the urban environment based only on the findings from the problem identification stage. Generally, this may happen if the problem identification has provided a large amount of information about the urban environment. The next key factor discovered in the literature review under urban analysis is about conducting an in-depth urban analysis based on ground level facts. The sub-factors aligned with this key factor indicate that it is necessary to consider locally specific conditions about culture, values, identity, existing physical settings and so forth in the urban analysis by using data sources such as community members, professionals, local businessmen and secondary data.

The next key factor from the literature review indicates that the urban environment should be analyzed based on both subjective and objective elements rather than only relying on the quantified data analysed from secondary data sources.

The next two key factors in literature are concerned with the vision, mission and strategy generation stage. The first key factor has described how local requirements should be addressed in design solutions by providing decision-making opportunities to the wider community. There is another literature-informed key factor which mentions that it is necessary to "avoid clean slate design." The idea of this key factor, as identified in the sub-factor of the key factor, is that it is necessary to complement the existing economic activities in bringing new development

Litrature Informed Potential UD process Framework

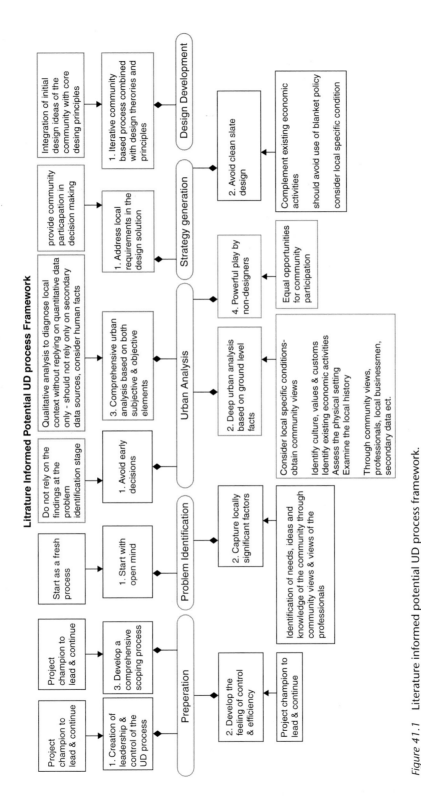

Figure 41.1   Literature informed potential UD process framework.

solutions and furthermore, the use of a blanket policy in the area avoiding local specific conditions should be avoided.

Finally, for the design development stage, one key factor was discovered and it states that the design development stage should be an iterative community-based process combined with design theories and principles. Furthermore, the sub-factor of the key factor explains that community design ideas should be integrated with the core design principles. In fact, this is a common idea that many authors promote for community engagement in urban development. According to them, they promote community engagement throughout the UD process without limiting it in certain stages.

41.10 Conclusions

The sustainable urban design/place making tradition is the newest and current tradition (scope) of urban design. Accordingly, in today's context the aim of an urban design project is to deliver a sustainable place which is socially, economically, and environmentally sustainable. In order to deliver sustainable urban design solutions, the urban design process plays a vital role. the current urban design process is mainly top-down, which is a professionally led process. This type of urban design process offered the community few opportunities, except in the latter stages of the urban design process. These top-down design processes are often critised and they have particularly emphasized the need for a pure-bottom up urban design process. However, this study revealed that the bottom-up process has also been criticized by many practitioners in urban design as well as some authors citing loss of control and ineffectiveness. Accordingly, this study revealed that there is a definite need to introduce a new urban design process framework to enable urban design to achieve its current scope. But, as revealed from the literature, neither a pure bottom-up process or a pure top-down process is not the sole solution to this issue. Therefore, based on literature, this study introduced a new community embedded, but balanced urban design process framework for urban design. This new process is benefitted from positive features of both top-down and bottom-up processes. However, a further study has been carried out on this and accordingly, a new community embedded sustainable urban design process framework has been developed after triangulating this literature informed urban design process with empirically developed two urban design processes.

References

Annibal, I., Liddle, J., and McElwee, G. 2013. Animating "bottom-up" sustainable strategies in village settings. *International Journal of Sociology and Social Policy*, 33, 742–61.
Batty, M. 2009. Cities as complex systems: Scaling, interaction, networks, dynamics and urban morphologies. *UCL Working Papers Series*.
Bell, W. 2005. Progressing process in urban design. *Urban Policy and Research*, 23, 371–6.
Boyko, C.T., Cooper, R., and Davey, C. (2005). Sustainability and the urban design process. *Proceedings of the ICE-Engineering Sustainability*, 158(3), 119–25.
Boyko, C.T., Cooper, R., Davey, C.L., and Wootton, A.B. 2006. Addressing sustainability early in the urban design process. *Management of Environmental Quality: An International Journal*, 17, 689–706.
Boyko, C.T., Cooper, R., Davey, C.L., and Wootton, A.B. 2010. Informing an urban design process by way of a practical example. *Proceedings of the ICE-Urban Design and Planning*, 163, 17–30.
BREEAM 2012. Technical Manual for BREEAM Communities.
Carmona, M. 2014. The place-shaping continuum: A theory of urban design process. *Journal of Urban Design*, 19, 2–36.
Carmona, M., Heath, T., Oc, T., and Tiesdell, S. 2003. *Public Places Urban Spaces*, Oxford, Architectural Press.
Carmona, M., Heath, T., Oc, T., and Tiesdell, S. 2010. *Public Places Urban Spaces*, USA, Routledge.

Cliff, E. 2014. Process and principles in urban design. *Journal of Urban Design*, 19(1), 47–8.

Commission for Architecture and Built Enviornment (CFAB)2000. By design: Urban design in the planning system: Towards better practice In: *Environment*, ed. CFAB. www.gov.uk/government/uploads/system/uploads/attachment_data/file/7665/158490.pdf (last accessed August 20, 2018).

Cooksey, B. and Kikula, I. 2005. *When Bottom-up Meets Top-down: The Limits of Local Participation in Local Government Planning in Tanzania.* Mkuki na Nyota Publishers.

Department of Infrastructure & Regional Development Australia 2013. *Urban Design Model Process: An Urban Design Protocol for Australian Cities.*

Fraser, E.D., Dougill, A.J., Mabee, W.E., Reed, M., and McAlpine, P. 2006. Bottom up and top down: Analysis of participatory processes for sustainability indicator identification as a pathway to community empowerment and sustainable environmental management. *Journal of Environmental Management,* 78, 114–27.

Greed, C. & Roberts, M. 2014. *Introducing Urban Design: Interventions and Responses.* New York: Routledge.

Lang, J.T. 2005. *Urban Design: A Typology of Procedures and Products.* New York: Routledge.

Larice, M. and MacDonald, E. 2007. *The Urban Design Reader.* New York: Routledge.

Larice, M. and MacDonald, E. 2013. *The Urban Design Reader.* New York: Routledge.

Lawson, B. 2006. *How Designers Think: The Design Process Demystified.* New York: Routledge.

Moughtin, J.C. 2003. *Urban Design: Method and Techniques.* New York: Routledge.

Oakley, D. and Tsao, H.-S. 2007. The bottom-up mandate: Fostering community partnerships and combating economic distress in Chicago's empowerment zone. *Urban Studies,* 44, 819–43.

Pissourios, I. 2014. Top-down and bottom-up urban and regional planning: Towards a framework for the use of planning standards. *European Spatial Research and Policy,* 83–99.

Reed, B. 2006. Shifting our mental model – "sustainability" to regeneration. *Rethinking Sustainable Construction 2006: Next Generation Green Buildings* Florida, USA.

Ritchie, A. and Thomas, R. 2013. *Sustainable Urban Design: An Environmental Approach.* New York: Taylor & Francis.

Roberts, M. and Greed, C. 2001. *Approaching Urban Design: The Design Process* Essex: Pearson Education Ltd.

Roy, U. and Ganguly, M. 2009. *Integration of Top down & Bottom Up Approach in Urban and Regional Planning: West Bengal Experience of Draft Development Plans (DDP) and Beyond.* National Town & Country Planners Congress. Goa: India.

Urban Design Group 2011. What is urban design? www.udg.org.uk/about/what-is-urban-design (last accessed August 20, 2018).

Walton, D., Lally, M., Septiana, H., Taylor, D., Thorne, R., and Cameron, A. 2007. Urban design compendium. *Reino Unido: English Partnerships,* 2.

Part XII

Economic considerations and the role of insurance and re-insurance

42

Defining economic recovery

An application of the synthetic control method

Ryan Levitt[1] and Sammy Zahran[1,2]

[1] DEPARTMENT OF ECONOMICS, COLORADO STATE UNIVERSITY,
FORT COLLINS, COLORADO 80523–1771, USA

[2] DEPARTMENT OF EPIDEMIOLOGY, COLORADO SCHOOL OF PUBLIC HEALTH,
FORT COLLINS, COLORADO, USA

42.1 Introduction

A considerable amount of scientific research has gone into quantifying the immediate impacts of natural disasters. The long-term impacts, and the recovery process in particular, have received less attention. Community recovery is often cited as the least understood "phase" of a natural disaster (Mileti et al. 1975; Chang 2010; Cheng et al. 2015). This lack of understanding originates from the difficulty in defining community recovery.

Defining community recovery requires a non-arbitrary *threshold* that must be overcome for a community to be considered *recovered*. Traditionally, this threshold has been defined as the return to pre-disaster conditions. Researchers have questioned the *return back* criterion for defining community recovery (Chang & Rose 2012; Cheng et al. 2015). Defining recovery as returning to pre-disaster conditions inadequately accounts for pre-disaster community dynamics. For example, if an area's economy is growing or contracting prior to the disaster, these dynamics will influence post-disaster outcomes. Additionally, post-disaster shocks unrelated to the disaster itself might similarly confound understanding of post-disaster outcomes. For example, a large macroeconomic event, such as the 2008 recession, will influence many of the community outcome variables we care about, such as employment, housing, and income.

Forwarding a definition of recovery that addresses both pre-disasters dynamics and post-disaster confounding events necessitates counterfactual reasoning. Although we observe post-disaster community outcomes we do not observe what these outcomes would have been had the disaster not taken place, or the counterfactual trajectory of a community. Naïve extrapolation from pre-disaster trends on community variables of interest can substantially miss the counterfactual trajectory of a community if a non-disaster related event like the Great Recession intervenes. Thus, a major aspect of defining disaster recovery involves constructing a counterfactual history for damaged areas.

The purpose of this chapter is to provide a list of definitions of disaster recovery. Our list of definitions are illustrated with analyses of *total employment* in four Louisiana parishes impacted by Hurricanes Katrina and Rita in 2005. The purpose of reasoning through different definitions of recovery is not to formulate an argument for the superiority of one definition over another. Certain definitions may be more or less appropriate depending on the community variable being considered. To address the problem of the counterfactual trajectory of a community, this chapter introduces and then deploys a statistical methodology referred to as *synthetic control* (Abadie & Gardeazabal 2003; Abadie et al. 2010) to estimate what total employment would have been in these damaged areas had Hurricanes Katrina and Rita not occurred.

42.2 Study area

Hurricane Katrina made landfall on the Louisiana/Mississippi border on August 29, 2005. The storm was one of the most destructive disasters in United States history. Katrina laid waste to 90,000 square miles of land along the Gulf Coast, devastating communities in Florida, Alabama, Mississippi, and Louisiana, and caused a catastrophic failure of the levee system surrounding the city of New Orleans. The storm caused approximately $100 billion in losses, damaging more than 300,000 homes and 150,000 businesses, displaced 1.5 million people, and claimed over 1,800 lives (Zahran et al. 2011). With residents of the Gulf Coast still staggering from the devastation caused by Katrina, Hurricane Rita made landfall on September 23. Rita caused over $10 billion in damages and resulted in the forced evacuation of over 2 million people. Rita's storm surge topped the half-repaired Katrina-damaged levees of New Orleans. This chapter focuses on the four parishes of Metropolitan New Orleans that were substantially affected by Hurricanes Katrina and Rita. These parishes include: (1) Jefferson, (2) Orleans, (3) St. Bernard, and (4) St. John the Baptist (Figure 42.1).

The Department of Homeland Security, in cooperation with Federal Emergency Management Agency (FEMA) and the Department of Housing and Urban Development (HUD) provided an assessment of the level of housing damage in counties impacted by Hurricanes Katrina and Rita, defined as the count of damaged homes over the total number of occupied homes. Reported damages in Jefferson, Orleans, St. Bernard, and St. John the Baptist were 53.3%, 71.5%, 80.6% and 46.3% respectively. Table 42.1 presents a more detailed description of these damages.

The table delineates damage in terms of minor, major, and severe categories. These categories are based on direct housing inspections performed by FEMA after Katrina. Each category corresponds with one of the three available reimbursement levels, less than $5,200, $5,200, and $10,500. Reimbursements constitute a fraction of the total damage sustained. In Orleans Parish, for instance, the median verified loss for homes classified as suffering severe damage was $107,815. Since assessments were done to determine eligibility for FEMA housing assistance, any individual who did not register with FEMA is not included in these damage counts. Additionally, vacant houses and second homes were not included.

Although a significant fraction of the housing stock was damaged in all four areas, the severity of that damage differed. For example, a much larger percent of housing damage in Orleans and St. Bernard was characterized as either major or severe. In contrast, a majority of housing damage in St. John the Baptist was categorized as minor. Importantly, each parish had a unique experience in the disaster, which is partially reflected in these different damage levels.

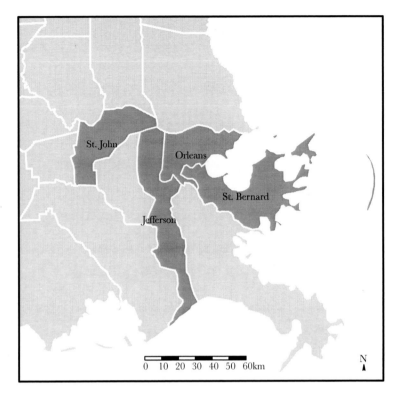

Figure 42.1 Map of Jefferson Parish, Orleans Parish, St. Bernard Parish, and St. John the Baptist Parish.

Source: Shapefile provided by TIGER/Line US Census Bureau.

Table 42.1 Reported housing damages from Hurricane Katrina and Rita

Louisiana Parish	Minor	Major	Severe	Total
Jefferson	33.80%	16.80%	2.70%	53.3%
Orleans	15.50%	14.00%	41.90%	71.5%
St. Bernard	2.20%	23.60%	54.70%	80.6%
St. John the Baptist	44.30%	1.70%	0.30%	46.3%

Note: Damages are defined as the count of homes that sustained either minor, major, or severe damages relative to the total number of occupied homes in the area. These estimates are provided by the Department of Homeland Security.

These divergent experiences are relevant both for defining recovery and ultimately comparing recovery across areas.

43.3 Standard definitions of recovery

There are two standard definitions for recovery: (1) *the return to pre-disaster conditions*, and (2) *the recuperation of after-shock losses*. To illustrate these definitions, we analyze the behavior of total employment across our four Louisiana parishes. Data on total employment are provided by

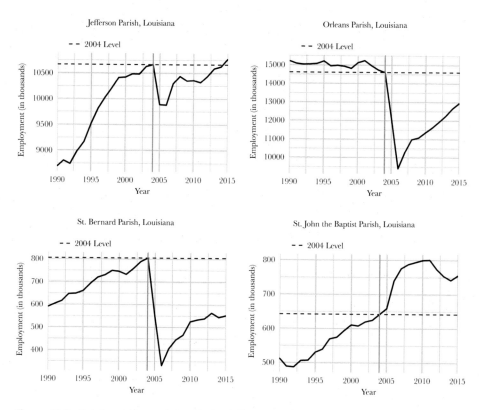

Figure 42.2 Total employment trends for Jefferson, Orleans, St. Bernard and St. John the Baptist. The dashed line corresponds to 2004 employment levels.

Source: Data are provided by the Bureau of Economic Analysis.

the Bureau of Economic Analysis (BEA). These data reflect the count of jobs in an area and are based on the location of the job, rather than the residence of the worker. Data are provided for 1990 until 2015. This sample period results in 15 pre-treatment years and 10 post-treatment years.

Figure 42.2 plots total employment over time for each parish. The solid black line in each plot corresponds to the observed employment level, measured in thousands of jobs. The dashed line represents employment in 2004. The grey line separates the pre- and post-Katrina/Rita periods.

As noted above, community recovery is typically defined *as a return to pre-disaster conditions.* In this example, an area is recovered if it eclipses the 2004 employment level. Applying this definition to Figure 42.2, both Orleans and St. Bernard remain unrecovered, and Jefferson surpasses its pre-disaster level in 2015. While 46.3 percent of the housing stock in St. John the Baptist suffered measurable damage, total employment remained above the 2004 level throughout the post-disaster period. With *a return to pre-disaster condition* definition of recovery, one might be tempted to conclude that Hurricanes Katrina and Rita either did not affect employment, or might have caused an increase employment, in St. John the Baptist Parish. Because St. John the Baptist was experiencing positive employment growth prior to Hurricanes Katrina and Rita, the observed increase in employment following the disaster might simply reflect a continuation of this trend. Moreover, given the close proximity of St. John the Baptist to other highly damaged areas, the

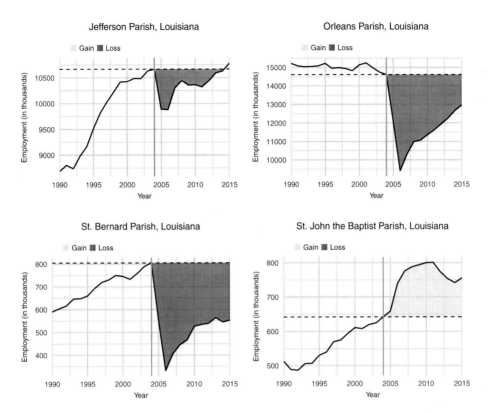

Figure 42.3 Total employment loss or gain in tirne. Plots illustrate our second definition, in which recovery can be defined as the time it takes to recuperate losses attributable to the disaster. The light gray shading corresponds to employment gains relative to pre-disaster levels. The dark gray shading corresponds to lost employment relative to pre-disaster levels.

observed increase in employment might reflect a spillover effect, with displaced workers finding jobs in less damaged neighboring areas (Xiao & Nilawar 2013). Whatever the precise reason, the post-disaster behavior of total employment in St. John the Baptist frustrates a straightforward definition of recovery like *returning back to pre-disaster conditions*.

A second threshold definition of recovery can be defined as the moment in which losses from a disaster event are recuperated. For example, if gross domestic product (GDP) is 5 percent lower in an area due to a disaster, this definition requires GDP to be 5 percent higher in that area for an equivalent amount of time. Figure 42.3 provides an illustration of this concept across our four parishes. For these parishes to be fully recovered, employment losses, defined by the area of dark gray shading, need to be recuperated. This requires future employment gains to offset these identified losses. Jefferson parish is the only area in our example in which we see both losses and gains based on a 2004 reference level (though these gains are minimal and fractionally small). While Jefferson parish satisfies the first definition of recovery by eclipsing the 2004 employment level in 2015, it is short of satisfying the second definition of recovery given employment-years un-recuperated. Applying this second definition to St. John the Baptist, it appears that the parish immediately recovered after the disaster, given that employment gains in the following year surpassed any associated losses.

While the definitions of recovery illustrated by the examples in Figures 42.2 and 42.3 have the merit of being simple and measurable, they inadequately address the confounding effects of pre-disasters trends and post-disaster events that shape community recovery. In the next section we detail a statistical methodology designed to resolve these inadequacies, allowing one to advance a series of counterfactual-based definitions of recovery.

42.4 Counterfactual definitions of recovery

It is not clear that a return to pre-disaster conditions is the correct benchmark for defining recovery. Xiao (2011) and Cheng et al. (2015) instead construct control cases for identifying the effects of a natural disaster. Building on this work, we follow Abadie and Gardeazabal (2003) and Abadie et al. (2010), and estimate a "synthetic" control for each of the four parishes to trace counter-factual trajectories of recovery. Economists have applied this methodology to the identification of long-term impacts of natural disasters (e.g. Coffman & Noy 2012; Cavallo et al., 2013; Barone & Mocetti 2014; duPont & Noy 2016).

Abadie and Gardeazabal (2003) and Abadie et al. (2010) describe a data-driven procedure for constructing a control case to identify the effects of an event or policy intervention. The synthetic control method was originally applied in context of identifying growth impacts of terrorism (Abadie & Gardeazabal 2003), and the influence of Proposition 99 on smoking consumption in California (Abadie et al. 2010). Synthetic controls are constructed by taking a weighted average of *control* areas that were unaffected by an event or policy intervention of interest. Weights are chosen to minimize a cost function that depends on pre-period lags of the outcome variable and several predictor variables. If this weighted average roughly matches outcome variable in the treated area prior to the event, the intuition is that it will provide an approximation of the evolution of this outcome had the event or intervention not occurred.

In our case, the effects of Hurricane Katrina and Rita are represented as the difference between the observed behavior of total employment in our *treated parishes* versus the counterfactual behavior of total employment in our *synthetic control* parishes. Additionally, a placebo analysis is undertaken to investigate the statistical significance of these estimated effects. A more detailed description of the synthetic control method is provided below.

42.4.1 Synthetic control method

Assume there are $J+1$ geographic areas, where the first area is *treated* by Hurricane Katrina. The remaining J areas represent potential controls counties – which hence forward will be referred to as the *donor pool*. Let Y_{it} be observed employment for area i at time t, and T_0 be the number of periods prior to the disaster. In the treated area, Y_{1t}, employment is being affected by the hurricane for $t > T_0$. Additionally, let Y_{it}^0 be what employment would have been absent the disaster. The method assumes that for $t \leq T_0$, $Y_{it}^1 = Y_{it}^0$. Intuitively, this implies that the disaster has no impact on employment prior to occurring, and thus is an exogenous event. For $t > T_0$, the effect of the disaster will be the deviation of Y_{it} from Y_{it}^0. Given that Y_{1t} is observed, to identify the effect of a disaster, Y_{1t}^0 must be estimated. Abadie et al. (2010) suggests estimating Y_{1t}^0 by taking a weighted average across a donor pool of unaffected areas. Thus, for our treated area, the effect of Hurricane Katrina, α, can be expressed as:

$$\alpha_{1t} = Y_{1t} - \sum_{j=2}^{J+1} w_j * Y_{jt},$$

(42.1)

where w_j is a non-negative weight applied to county j. These weights are estimated by minimizing the cost function described in Equation (42.2). W is a $(1 \times \mathcal{J})$ vector encompassing these $\mathcal{J}$ weights. X_1 is a $(1 \times K)$ vector of predictors for the treated region, and X_0 is the corresponding $(\mathcal{J} \times K)$ matrix of these same predictors for each potential control county. Additionally, let V be a $(K \times K)$ symmetric and positive semidefinite matrix, with the diagonal elements representing the "importance" of each predictor (Smith 2015). County weights are thus chosen by minimizing the following cost function:

$$\|X_1 - X_0 W\|_v = \sqrt{(X_1 - X_0 W)' V (X_1 - X_0 W)}$$
$$s.t. w_j \geq 0$$
$$\sum_{j=2}^{\mathcal{J}+1} w_j = 1 \tag{42.2}$$

Abadie et al. (2010) state that the above inferential procedure is valid for any choice of V, however suggest choosing V such that the mean squared prediction error of the outcome variable is minimized for the pre-period. In context of this example, this implies minimizing the mean squared prediction error between the synthetic employment and observed employment during the years prior to Hurricane Katrina. Employment data have been normalized to 2004 values, so that level differences do not significantly impact matches arrived at by the synthetic control analysis. Predictor variables of county employment are provided by the 2000 Decennial Census and the Bureau of Economic Analysis. These predictors and their respective sources are listed in Table 42.2.

42.4.2 Defining the donor pool

The synthetic control method is typically applied in the context of one treated area and a small pool of donors. For example, in Abadie Gardeazabal (2003), the authors estimate the economic impact of terrorist activities in Basque Country Spain by utilizing a donor pool of the

Table 42.2 List of predictor variables and their respective sources

Predictor Variables	Source
Population density (population per square mile)	2000 Decennial Census
Median housing value	2000 Decennial Census
Median age	2000 Decennial Census
Median income	2000 Decennial Census
Poverty rate	2000 Decennial Census
Labor force participation rate	2000 Decennial Census
Service occupations (% of employed population)	2000 Decennial Census
Farming, fishing, and forestry occupations (% of employed population)	2000 Decennial Census
Production, transportation, and material moving occupations (% of employed population)	2000 Decennial Census
Percent bachelor degree or higher (% of population 25 and older)	2000 Decennial Census
Average population growth: 1990–2004	Bureau of Economic Analysis
Average employment growth: 1990–2004	Bureau of Economic Analysis
Lagged employment level: 1990, 1994, 1998, 2002	Bureau of Economic Analysis

16 remaining autonomous communities in Spain. Abadie et al. (2010) examine the effects of proposition 99, a large-scale tobacco control initiative, on California's tobacco consumption. They construct a synthetic control for California using the remaining 38 states that had not adopted large-scale tobacco programs during their sample period.

In applying the synthetic control method to Louisiana parishes, there are over 3,000 counties (or county equivalents) which could constitute our donor pool. This results in a substantially larger donor pool relative to these previous applications. A donor pool of this size introduces the potential for interpolation bias, particularly if weighted counties are substantially different from the treated unit. Following a suggestion made in Abadie et al. (2010), and to guard against this bias, we restrict the donor pool to a smaller size.

First, we eliminate any county that experienced housing damages from Hurricane Katrina, Rita, or Wilma. Next, we construct a "distance" metric based on the covariates described in Table 42.2. All predictor variables are normalized by dividing by associated standard deviations to control for difference in units. Using the "distance" between treated and donor (j) county predictors (X) (see Equation 42.3), we identify a unique set of 20 control areas with the smallest "distance" for each of our four treated parishes.

$$Distance_j = \sqrt{\left(X_1 - X_j\right)'\left(X_1 - X_j\right)}. \tag{42.3}$$

Lists of these included areas and corresponding weights are provided in Table 42.3 (for Jefferson and Orleans parishes) and in Table 42.4 (for St. Bernard and St. John the Baptist parishes). Each synthetic control arrived at involves some combination of five to 10 donor counties, depending on the parish.

Table 42.3 List of counties included in the donor pool for Jefferson Parish and Orleans Parish and their corresponding weight

Jefferson Parish Control Counties	Weight	Orleans Parish Control Counties	Weight
Kenton County, Kentucky	35.5%	Jackson County, Illinois	35.6%
Bibb County, Georgia	24.9%	Richmond city, Virginia	19.5%
Montgomery County, Alabama	20.5%	St. Louis city, Missouri	15.8%
Scott County, Iowa	11.2%	Roanoke city, Virginia	15.8%
Escambia County, Florida	7.7%	Norfolk city, Virginia	12.8%
Pulaski County, Arkansas	0.2%	Milwaukee County, Wisconsin	0.4%
Jefferson County, Alabama	0%	Roosevelt County, Montana	0%
Cascade County, Montana	0%	Caddo Parish, Louisiana	0%
St. Clair County, Illinois	0%	Orangeburg County, South Carolina	0%
Jefferson County, Kentucky	0%	Wayne County, Michigan	0%
Pennington County, South Dakota	0%	Bibb County, Georgia	0%
Summit County, Ohio	0%	Richmond County, Georgia	0%
Spokane County, Washington	0%	Macon County, Alabama	0%
Dauphin County, Pennsylvania	0%	Adair County, Missouri	0%
Franklin County, Kentucky	0%	Dougherty County, Georgia	0%
Hamilton County, Tennessee	0%	Delaware County, Indiana	0%
Marion County, Indiana	0%	Custer County, Oklahoma	0%
Shelby County, Tennessee	0%	Coahoma County, Mississippi	0%
Oklahoma County, Oklahoma	0%	Sumter County, Georgia	0%
Chatham County, Georgia	0%	McDonough County, Illinois	0%

Table 42.4 List of counties included in the donor pool for St. Bernard Parish and St. John the Baptist Parish and their corresponding weight

St. Bernard Control Counties	Weight	St. John Control Counties	Weight
Bay County, Florida	41.3%	Berkeley County, SC	33.7%
Campbell County, Kentucky	24.1%	Peach County, Georgia	26.5%
Raleigh County, West Virginia	18.7%	Bowie County, Texas	25.5%
Bossier Parish, Louisiana	13.3%	Houston County, Alabama	10.9%
Williamson County, Illinois	2.1%	Nueces County, Texas	3.4%
Polk County, Florida	0.1%	El Paso County, Texas	0%
Cheyenne County, Nebraska	0.1%	Bossier Parish, Louisiana	0%
Natrona County, Wyoming	0.1%	Lowndes County, Georgia	0%
Lawrence County, Ohio	0.1%	Gregg County, Texas	0%
Caroline County, Virginia	0.1%	San Patricio County, Texas	0%
Bowie County, Texas	0%	Madison County, Kentucky	0%
Austin County, Texas	0%	McLennan County, Texas	0%
Wagoner County, Oklahoma	0%	Smith County, Texas	0%
Houston County, Alabama	0%	Spalding County, Georgia	0%
Pottawattamie County, Iowa	0%	Craighead County, Arkansas	0%
Escambia County, Florida	0%	Meade County, Kentucky	0%
Jefferson County, Missouri	0%	Madison County, Tennessee	0%
Androscoggin County, Maine	0%	Cumberland County, NC	0%
Washington County, Maryland	0%	Caldwell County, Texas	0%
Perry County, Pennsylvania	0%	Victoria County, Texas	0%

42.4.3 The synthetic control method and definitions of recovery

Figure 42.4 plots the results of the synthetic control analysis for each parish. The black line on the graph corresponds to observed employment levels and the dashed line corresponds to the synthetic control. Each synthetic control consists of a weighted average across the donor counties listed in Tables 42.3 and 42.4. Note the precision of the statistical match of synthetic controls to the behavior of observed total employment in the pre-disaster period.

Because our synthetic controls represent the counter-factual behavior of total employment in damaged parishes had Hurricanes Katrina and Rita not occurred, we can advance a third definition of community recovery. *A community is recovered when the observed behavior of a variable of interest converges on the counter-factual behavior of that variable.*

With respect to this third definition, results for Orleans and St. Bernard parishes are not especially revealing. Synthetic controls for Orleans and St. Bernard parishes roughly obey pre-period trajectories. Jefferson parish's synthetic control, on the other hand, is informative. In Figure 42.2, employment in Jefferson surpassed pre-disaster levels by the end of the sample period. If we instead utilize Jefferson's synthetic control, we see a missing gap between observed employment and what employment would have been had the disaster not occurred. Thus, under our third definition, Jefferson remains unrecovered. Applying the logic of this third definition to St. John the Baptist, we see that employment increased above its associated synthetic control, suggesting that Hurricanes Katrina and Rita had a positive impact on the area's employment. This supports previous findings, in which the disaster appears to have pushed economic activity into less damaged areas (Xiao & Nilawar 2013). By the end of the sample period, however, St. John the Baptist returns to its synthetic control level, suggesting that this positive spillover was transitory.

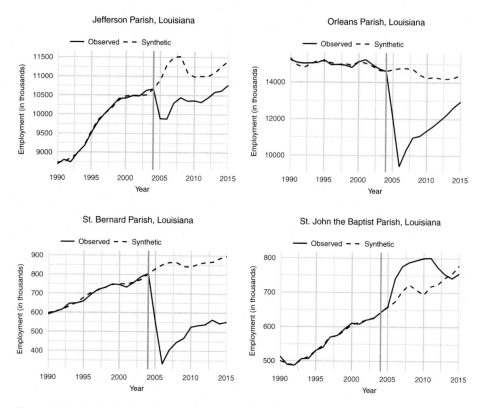

Figure 42.4 Synthetic control results for Jefferson, Orleans, St. Bernard, and St. John the Baptist Parish. Dashed lines in the post-disaster period reflect the expected behavior of total employment absent the disaster shock. This counterfactual is constructed by taking a weighted average of control areas.

To compare these different experiences, Figure 42.5 plots the estimated effects of Hurricanes Katrina and Rita across each parish. These effects reflect the statistical difference between observed and synthetic employment defined by Equation (42.1).

42.4.4 Placebo analysis

Previous applications of the synthetic control method employ a "placebo" analysis to measure the statistical significance of estimated effects. This entails repeating the synthetic control procedure for a series of non-treated areas, typically the areas that constitute the donor pool. The process of repeating the synthetic control procedure for each control county results in a distribution of results. It is then possible to compare the estimated effect in each treated area, relative to this distribution of placebo cases. Following the synthetic control method literature (e.g. Abadie et al. 2010; Cavallo et al. 2013), we repeat the same procedure for each of the control counties listed in Table 42.3 and 42.4. This is done with the same predictor variables and donor pool restrictions. Figure 42.6 plots four placebo examples to highlight the intuition of the method. Given that these areas were not impacted by Hurricanes Katrina and Rita, the difference between the synthetic control and the observed trends should be approximately zero. In

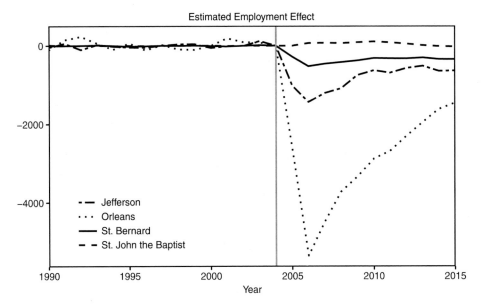

Figure 42.5 Estimated employment effects of Hurricane Katrina over time for each of the four parishes. Employment effects reflect the difference between observed outcomes relative to estimated synthetic controls.

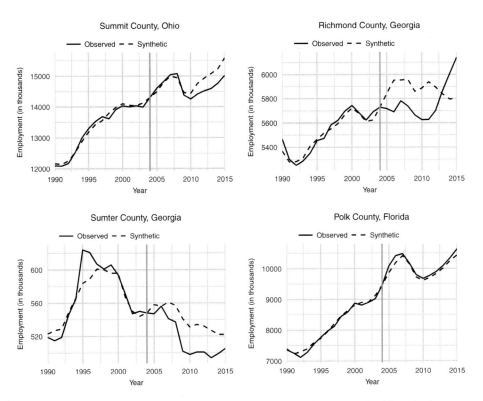

Figure 42.6 Synthetic control method applied to non-treated areas. Dashed lines in the post-disaster period reflect the expected behavior of total employment. Given that these areas were unaffected by Hurricane Katrina and Rita, the difference between observed and synthetic outcomes should approximately match.

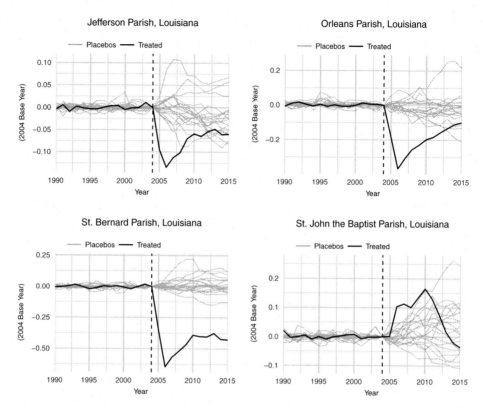

Figure 42.7 Placebo analysis for Jefferson, Orleans, St. Bernard, and St. John the Baptist. Each line corresponds to the difference between observed outcomes relative to estimated synthetic controls. The black lines coincide with the four treated areas, and the light gray lines their associated placebos.

the context of Summit County Ohio and Polk County Florida, the synthetic control nearly perfectly matches observed trends during the post-treatment period. However, due to idiosyncratic shocks not all placebos result in strong post-treatment period matches. For example, Sumter County Georgia and Richmond County Georgia, illustrate scenarios in which the synthetic control deviates from observed trends during the post-treatment period.

Figure 42.7 plots the results for all 20 placebo cases associated with each treated area. The black line represents the difference between observed employment totals in treated parishes relative to their synthetic controls. The light gray lines correspond to this same difference for each of the 20 placebo counties. Total employment in each year has been normalized by a 2004 base employment level so that county comparisons can more readily be made. Results from the placebo analysis show that the estimated effects across Jefferson, Orleans, St. Bernard, and St. John the Baptist are all initially outside their associated bands of placebo cases. With the exception of St. Bernard, the effects of Hurricane Katrina appear to dissipate in the later years. Trends in Orleans, Jefferson, and St. John the Baptist all approach or enter their corresponding placebo bands by the end of the period. St. Bernard, in contrast, appears permanently impacted by the event, and its estimated effect is significantly larger than any of the placebo cases across the entire post-period.

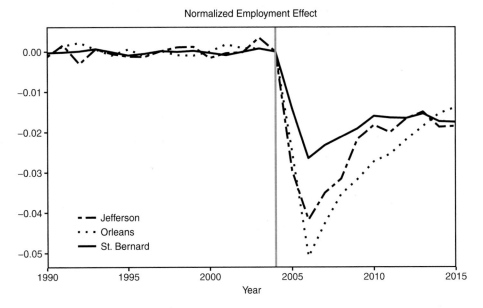

Normalized Employment Effect

Figure 42.8 Damage normalized employment effects for Jefferson, Orleans, and St. Bernard. Employment effects are divided by the count of major and severe damages accruing from Hurricane Katrina and Rita.

42.5 Evaluating recovery by controlling for severity

While our third definition and accompanying methodology address the confounding effects of pre-disasters trends and post-disaster events that shape community recovery, the economic trajectory of an area visited by a natural disaster might overwhelmingly reflect the severity of the initial shock. Controlling for the severity of a disaster strike can allow one to evaluate the economic recovery of an area relative to the initial damages incurred. To illustrate the value in controlling for disaster severity, we normalize the estimated disaster effects, derived through our synthetic control method, by the count of occupied housing that experienced major and severe damages. Since St. John the Baptist experienced a positive and temporary impact from the disaster, we drop it from this portion of the analysis.

Figure 42.8 plots these normalized effects for Jefferson, Orleans, and St. Bernard. This figure shows that once you control for differences in damages, Jefferson and Orleans had remarkably similar recovery experiences. The negative impacts of Katrina and Rita on employment in St. Bernard was initially smaller than in Jefferson and Orleans, perhaps reflecting varying underlying resilience to the negative employment effects of Katrina and Rita. By the end of the series all three parishes appear to roughly match one another in terms of long-terms effects.

42.6 Conclusions

Disaster recovery tends to be defined as the time it takes to return to pre-disaster conditions or the *return back criterion*. This basic definition fails to account pre-disaster trends or other post-disaster shocks that shape observed outcomes. We illustrated definitions of recovery: (1) with analyses of total employment in four Louisiana parishes that were impacted by Hurricanes

Katrina and Rita. We highlighted differences between using the pre-disaster return criterion versus counterfactually defined criteria in the determination of whether a community has *recovered*.

To estimate counter-factual trajectories of community recovery, we deployed the synthetic control method, which constructs a weighted average out a pool of potential disaster-unaffected control counties. Using the estimated effects derived from our synthetic control analysis, we then plotted differences in recovery experiences across our four parishes. Results suggest unique experiences. For example, St. John the Baptist experienced a temporary boom in employment following the disaster, whereas employment in St. Bernard appeared to be permanently suppressed. To control for incurred damage, we then normalized employments effects by the count of occupied housing that incurred either major or severe damage. Examining these normalized trends suggests remarkably similar recovery experiences for Jefferson and Orleans. St. Bernard, in contrast, initially appeared more insulated relative to Jefferson and Orleans, however lagged during the recovery process. By the end of the series all three parishes had roughly similar long-term employment losses.

Future analysis could extend this framework to other aspects of the community recovery process. In particular, these concepts can be applied to a wider range of relevant variables capturing the multidimensionality of communities. Additionally, differences in damaged-normalized recovery experiences can be exploited to identify the factors that determine the underlying resiliency of an area to the negative consequences of disaster events, including policy interventions meant to enhance community resilience.

References

Abadie, A. and Gardeazabal, J. (2003). The economic costs of conflict: A case study of the Basque Country. *The American Economic Review, 93*(1), 113–32.

Abadie, A., Diamond, A., and Hainmueller, J. (2010). Synthetic control methods for comparative case studies: Estimating the effect of California's tobacco control program. *Journal of the American statistical Association, 105*(490), 493–505.

Barone, G. and Mocetti, S. (2014). Natural disasters, growth and institutions: A tale of two earthquakes. *Journal of Urban Economics, 84*, 52–66.

Cavallo, E., Galiani, S., Noy, I., and Pantano, J., (2013). Catastrophic natural disasters and economic growth. *Review of Economics and Statistics, 95*(5), pp.1549–61.

Chang, S.E. (2010). Urban disaster recovery: A measurement framework and its application to the 1995 Kobe earthquake. *Disasters, 34*(2), 303–27.

Chang, S.E. and Rose, A.Z. (2012). Towards a theory of economic recovery from disasters. *International Journal of Mass Emergencies and Disasters.*

Cheng, S., Ganapati, E., and Ganapati, S. (2015). Measuring disaster recovery: bouncing back or reaching the counterfactual state?. *Disasters, 39*(3), 427–46.

Coffman, M. and Noy, I. (2012). Hurricane Iniki: measuring the long-term economic impact of a natural disaster using synthetic control. *Environment and Development Economics, 17*(2), 187–205.

duPont IV, W. and Noy, I. (2015). What happened to Kobe? A reassessment of the impact of the 1995 earthquake in Japan. *Economic Development and Cultural Change, 63*(4), 777–812.

Mileti, D.S., Drabek, T.E., and Haas, J.E. (1975). *Human Systems in Extreme Environments: A Sociological Perspective* (Vol. 21). Institute of Behavioral Science, University of Colorado.

Smith, B. (2015). The resource curse exorcised: Evidence from a panel of countries. *Journal of Development Economics, 116*, 57–73.

Xiao, Y. (2011). Local economic impacts of natural disasters. *Journal of Regional Science, 51*(4), 804–20.

Xiao, Y. and Nilawar, U. (2013). Winners and losers: analysing post-disaster spatial economic demand shift. *Disasters, 37*(4), 646–68.

Zahran, S., Peek, L., Snodgrass, J.G., Weiler, S., and Hempel, L. (2011). Economics of disaster risk, social vulnerability, and mental health resilience. *Risk Analysis*, 31 (7), 1107–19.

43

Modeling business interruption as a function of the reliability and resilience of physical infrastructure and social systems

Fabrizio Nocera[1] and Paolo Gardoni[2]

[1] DEPARTMENT OF CIVIL AND ENVIRONMENTAL ENGINEERING, MAE CENTER: CREATING A MULTI- HAZARD APPROACH TO ENGINEERING, UNIVERSITY OF ILLINOIS AT URBANA- CHAMPAIGN, URBANA, IL, USA; FNOCERA@ILLINOIS.EDU

[2] DEPARTMENT OF CIVIL AND ENVIRONMENTAL ENGINEERING, MAE CENTER: CREATING A MULTI- HAZARD APPROACH TO ENGINEERING, UNIVERSITY OF ILLINOIS AT URBANA- CHAMPAIGN, URBANA, IL, USA; GARDONI@ILLINOIS.EDU

43.1 Introduction

Critical infrastructure such as transportation, electric power, water, and wastewater underpin the national well-being and economic prosperity by providing a continuous flow of goods and services (PCCIP 1997; Corotis 2009; Ellingwood et al. 2016; Gardoni et al. 2016; Gardoni & Murphy 2018). Past disasters continue to show the vulnerability of critical infrastructure to multiple hazards (i.e., natural and anthropogenic) and emphasize the need of risk mitigation and management (Murphy & Gardoni 2006; Gardoni & Murphy 2014; Gardoni et al. 2016). Buildings, bridges, and other structures and infrastructure may experience natural hazards (e.g., floods, earthquakes, hurricanes) and anthropogenic hazards (e.g., accidents and terrorist attacks), which may lead to reduction or loss of functionality of physical infrastructure (Gardoni & LaFave 2016; Guidotti et al. 2016). Businesses may experience disruptions by either direct damage to properties, or (reduction or) loss of functionality of the supporting critical infrastructure (e.g., electric power, water and wastewater). In addition, disruptions of the transportation network may result in business interruption because of impaired access of employees and customers, as well as of delivery of supplies. Business disruptions might lead to reduction or loss of production and sales, reduced income for shareholders and employees, as well as temporary or permanent closure (May 2001; Chang 2016). The impact on the business interruption of the loss of functionality of critical infrastructure depends on the type of business and the direction of the loss of functionality. For example, the impact of the loss of electric power, potable water, and wastewater ranges from minor inconveniences up to immediate shutdown of the business activities.

The impacts of natural hazards on critical infrastructure networks has been the subject of much research. Significant progress has been made in predicting the damage of physical components of critical infrastructure networks such as bridges and pipes, as well as in predicting the consequences in terms of provision of goods and services (e.g., Guidotti et al. 2017a,b; Guikema & Gardoni 2009; Kang et al. 2008; Lee et al. 2007; Gardoni & LaFave 2016; Gardoni 2017). In addition, interdisciplinary research has improved the understanding of the effects of critical infrastructure disruptions on the population well-being and the economy (e.g., Murphy & Gardoni 2006, 2007, 2008 2010; Chang et al. 2009; Gardoni & Murphy 2009, 2010, 2018; Rosenheim et al. 2018; Guidotti et al. 2018). Estimating the losses due to business interruption is needed to quantify the severity and extent of a hazard impact, understand businesses' vulnerabilities, support mitigation and recovery decisions, and inform insurers of their liability (e.g., Sheets 1994; Insurance Research Council 1995; Rhinesmith 1997). Nevertheless, past studies (e.g., Shinozuka et al. 1998; May 2001) focused primarily on qualitative approaches to estimate business interruption losses, without modeling the functionality of the business facilities and the supporting infrastructure. In terms of modeling the duration of the business interruption, Rose (2004) discussed about economic resilience to disasters, identifying inherent resilience as the result of the reliance of businesses on critical infrastructure, as well as adaptive resilience as the ability of businesses to modify regular activities after the occurrence of a hazard event. Kajitani and Tatano (2009) investigated the impacts on business interruption with and without backup plans, such as backup power generators and water storage, yet only on a survey basis.

This chapter proposes a probabilistic procedure that addresses the limitation in the current approaches. In particular, the proposed procedure models and quantifies business interruption incorporating the dependency on physical infrastructure and social systems. The proposed procedure includes a reliability analysis to model the direct physical damage to the business properties and the impact to the network functionality, as well as a resilience analysis to model the recovery of structures and infrastructure and estimate the duration of business interruptions.

Following this introduction, Section 43.2 discusses the fundamental aspects of business interruption. Section 43.3 presents the proposed probabilistic procedure to integrate physical infrastructure and social systems in the modeling of business interruption. Section 43.4 introduces mathematical models that can be adopted in the proposed probabilistic procedure. Finally, Section 43.5 illustrates the proposed procedure considering the business interruption of a hypothetical food retail store following a seismic event.

43.2 Business interruption

Business interruption is an anticipated or unanticipated disruption of the normal operations of a firm (Spedding & Rose 2008). Business interruption can be classified into ordinary and contingent (Rose & Huyck 2016). Ordinary business interruption refers to the drop of profit due to a reduction in the flows of services of a given business (e.g., due to property damage). Contingent business interruption arises from disruptions to off-site sources, such as disruption in the supply chain or supporting critical infrastructure on which the business depends. Modeling and predicting business interruption requires considering both ordinary and contingent business interruption to properly estimate the likelihood of survival of a business after the occurrence of a damaging event (Jain & Guin 2009) and the duration of the interruption.

The estimation of the likelihood and duration of business interruption requires including the following contributing factors (Rose & Lim 2002; Rose & Huyck 2016):

i) **Physical damage to plants/facilities and/or equipment.** There is a need to specify the role of buildings and equipment because the effect on business interruption is different if, for example, a damaged building is an office building, a warehouse, or a factory. Activities carried in office headquarters can be reallocated more easily, whereas it may not be possible to reallocate activities carried in factories (e.g., production.)

ii) **Supply-chain disruptions.** Businesses can experience interruptions when there is a loss (or reduction) of inputs in the supply chain. Business interruption losses are related to the interdependencies between suppliers, customers, and the business itself. If suppliers are disrupted, a business may not be able to restock and will eventually have to close. Similarly, if customers are disrupted, a business might not be able to sell its products or services. Therefore, even businesses that are physically undamaged may be forced to close if suppliers or customers experience damage due to the occurrence of a hazard. The consequences of a damaging event can be felt even across different countries. For example, after the 2011 Great East Japan Earthquake, damage to part producers in Japan caused interruption to the supply chain of automobile manufacturers located in the United States and in Europe (Norio et al. 2011; Todo et al. 2014).

iii) **Redundancy in the business network.** Redundancy and a large footprint of the business network can help mitigate business interruption by shifting the business activities to different sites that have suffered less damage, or for which inputs are less affected.

In addition to these more intuitive and direct contributing factors, the likelihood and duration of business interruption are also affected by the following two factors (Rose et al. 2009, Shinozuka et al. 1998), which are more indirect:

iv) **Damage to supporting infrastructure.** Businesses are typically dependent on critical infrastructure (e.g., water network, electrical power network, transportation network) to be functional. For example, a factory may be forced to close due to outage of electricity due to an earthquake induced damage to substations, transmission lines, or distribution lines, while the business facilities themselves might not experience structural damage.

v) **Social systems and employees' profile.** In the immediate aftermath of a disaster, workers tend to make their own safety (and the one of their family) a priority rather than their job. Similarly, meeting physiological needs (like having a shelter) might lead to population dislocation reducing the available workforce at the site. Guidotti et al. (2018) showed the relevance of integrating physical infrastructure and social systems in communities' reliability and resilience analysis to estimate population dislocation. If there are no or fewer employees attending work, a business may not be able to stay open or function as usual.

In the remaining of this section, we provide more details about these two indirect factors that have been less studied in the literature. Section 43.3 proposes a probabilistic procedure to model business interruption incorporating the dependency on physical infrastructure and social systems.

43.2.1 The role of critical infrastructure on business interruption

Critical infrastructure provide the conveyance of goods, services, and resources to communities, such as electric power, water and wastewater, transportation, and telecommunications that are vital for economic activities (Corotis 2009; Ellingwood et al. 2016; Gardoni et al. 2016). Critical infrastructure networks are independent or (inter)dependent systems that jointly operate supporting the production and distribution of goods and services (PCCIP 1997). They can experience direct damage as well as reduction or loss of functionality if the supporting infrastructure are not functional (e.g., Rinaldi et al. 2001; Dueñas-Osorio et al. 2007; Kim et al. 2007; Vespignani 2010; Chang, 2014; Franchin 2014; Franchin & Cavalieri 2015; Guidotti et al. 2017a,b). For example, an industrial building might be directly damaged by an earthquake (Bai et al. 2014; Xu & Gardoni 2016) but could also experience a loss of functionality due to damage to the supporting water and power networks.

As a result, business interruption may be experienced also as a consequence of disruption in the supporting critical infrastructure. Businesses need to have access to infrastructure services (e.g., electric power, water, and wastewater) to run their activities. Electric power and water networks are designed to deliver critical resources from a source to the location where people and businesses use them. Previous studies (e.g., Shinozuka et al. 1998; Chang 2014) noted that businesses typically consider electric power crucial for their ability to do business, such that they would shut down immediately due to lack of electric power. Additionally, businesses might be able to tolerate the loss of water and wastewater services only for a relatively short time of period – approximately two days (Shinozuka et al. 1998).

Similarly, employees and customers need to have physical access to businesses to conduct regular business activities, and supplies and products need to be able to go in and out of the business facilities. The transportation infrastructure allows for the connection across space safely and efficiently (Fricker & Whitford 2005). The different modes of transport are air, water, and land transport, which includes rail, road, and off-road transport. Air transportation infrastructure are composed of airports and their related structures such as terminal buildings and control towers. Water transportation infrastructure comprise different type of port facilities, including wharves, cranes, and piers. Rail transportation infrastructure are composed of tracks, bridges, tunnels, and stations. Road infrastructure systems include surface roads (e.g., local roads, highways, and interstate), as well as tunnels and bridges. In general, different modes of transportation are functionally interconnected. For example, moving a manufactured product from the factory to the retail store may involve different modes of transportation such as sea, rail, and road. Disruptions in the transportation infrastructure may result in business interruption due to obstructions in the employees' ability to go to work, delivery and transport of products or supplies, and customers' access.

43.2.2 The role of social systems on business interruption

Modeling business interruption also needs to account for the impact of a hazard on social systems to properly estimate the available workforce (Rose & Huyck 2016). The workforce might be impacted because employees may be unable to go to work because of lack of access to businesses (as discussed earlier), as well as because of possible casualties and population dislocation. The number and the severity of casualties are generally correlated with building damage, including nonstructural and structural damage (FEMA 2015, Noh et al. 2017) as well as other socio-economic factors that define the individuals' vulnerability (Wang et al. 2018). For instance, nonstructural damage usually controls the casualty estimates in smaller earthquakes, whereas a larger number of casualties is expected in severe earthquakes due to a larger number of structural collapses and/or partial collapses. It is crucial, in business interruption loss estimations, to predict the number and severity of casualties to obtain an estimate of the available workforce. The severity of casualties are classified into four different levels (FEMA 2015; Durkin et al.

1991; Coburn et al. 1992). Severity 1 is defined as injuries that require basic medical aid such as bandages or observations; Severity 2 is defined as injuries that involve medical technology such as x-rays or surgery, yet do not expect to evolve into a life-threatening status; Severity 3 is defined as injuries that immediately constitute a life-threatening status; Severity 4 is defined as instantaneous mortality. Each severity of casualties has different implications in terms of the ability of a person to go to work.

In addition, the human response after the occurrence of a damaging event depends on the goods and services provided by the complex system of physical infrastructure. The inability of physical infrastructure to provide goods and services (e.g., potable water, power, and housing) might lead to population dislocation, thereby affecting the available workforce. Namely, possible responses might include the decision to leave the community (e.g., external dislocation) or to relocate within the community (e.g., internal dislocation). In the first case, population dislocation results in a reduction of the size of a community. In the case of internal dislocation, there is an increase of the population size at assembly points (e.g., shelters, local schools) keeping the overall population of a community constant. Population dislocation generally impacts the available workforce. As a result, it is important to include the effects of population dislocation on the predictions of business interruption.

43.3 Integration of physical infrastructure and social systems in the modeling of business interruption

This chapter proposes a probabilistic procedure for modeling business interruption incorporating the dependencies on physical infrastructure and social systems. The proposed procedure includes a reliability analysis to model the direct physical damage to the business properties and the impact to the network functionality and social systems, as well as a resilience analysis to model the recovery of structures, infrastructure, and communities needed to estimate the duration of business interruption. The proposed probabilistic procedure is general and applicable to different category of businesses, physical infrastructure, and hazards. The proposed procedure has the following five steps:

Step 1: Definition of the critical infrastructure network models

The first step requires representing the critical infrastructure networks, and defining their spatial extensions (or footprints) and their modeling granularity as further discussed in Section 43.4.1. The spatial extension is defined in order to include the nodes of the supply-chain that can be affected by the occurrence of a damaging event (e.g., distribution centers and warehouses). The granularity is defined depending on the purpose of network modeling and affects the ability to capture the spatial variability in the network functionality. In this step, we need to define the constituting elements (or network components) as well as the network topology.

Step 2: Generation of the hazard intensity measure(s) over the area of interest

Intensity measures of the hazards are obtained over the hazard footprint capturing the spatial variations in the intensity measures. The vulnerability of critical infrastructure networks and their components depends on the type of hazard. For example, extreme winds mainly cause damage to components above ground like transmission lines in electric power networks, while earthquakes tend to have a larger impact on bridges in transportation networks. Therefore, in this step of the procedure, we need to use hazard-specific models to generate spatial maps of the relevant intensity measures.

Step 3: Assessment of the physical damage to the components of the critical infrastructure network

In this step, fragility functions and repair rate curves are used to obtain probabilistic estimates of the direct damage to the components of the critical infrastructure networks. Fragility functions are used for point (or nodal) elements, such as buildings, bridges, distribution nodes, and are defined as the conditional probability of attaining or exceeding a specified performance level given a (set of) hazard intensity measure(s) (Gardoni et al. 2002; Gardoni 2017). Repair rate curves are used for linear elements, such as roads, pipelines, electric power distribution lines. They provide the number of expected repairs per unit length of a linear element of interest, for a given hazard intensity measure (e.g. ALA 2001; O'Rourke & Ayala 1993; O'Rourke & Deyoe 2004).

Step 4: Estimation of the physical damage to the building inventory and estimation of the resulting available workforce

This step consists in estimating the structural and non-structural damage to the building inventory. This is estimated probabilistically using fragility functions (e.g., Ramamoorthy 2006, 2008; Bai et al. 2011, 2014; Xu & Gardoni 2016). Once we obtain the estimate of the physical damage to buildings, the corresponding casualties are estimated (e.g., Steelman et al. 2007; FEMA 2015; Noh et al. 2017; Wang et al. 2018). Workers estimated to be casualties with Severity 1 or higher, for example, can be removed from the set of available workers. In addition, the workforce could be reduced also because of population dislocation, which could be due to physical damage to residential buildings or lack of services (e.g., water and power) to the residential buildings (Guidotti et al. 2018; Rosenheim et al. 2018). Therefore, also workers estimated to dislocate could be removed from the set of available workers (e.g., in the case of external dislocation).

Step 5: Assessment of the post-event functionality over time

This step consists in assessing the functionality of the damaged networks in terms of the ability to provide services in the aftermath, as well as the post-event functionality over time of buildings, infrastructure, and social systems. The resilience of the critical infrastructure networks plays a critical role in the duration of business interruption. Resilience has been defined as the ability to prepare for and adapt to changing conditions and withstand and recover rapidly from disruptions (Bruneau et al. 2003; McAllister 2013; Caverzan & Solomos 2014; Ellingwood et al. 2016; Guidotti et al. 2016, 2017; Sharma et al. 2018a; Doorn et al. 2018). The recovery of structures and infrastructure can be estimated using empirical recovery functions (e.g., FEMA 2015). Alternatively, physics-based recovery functions can be used (Sharma et al. 2018a,b). Physics-based recovery functions are developed based on the actual work plan of activities involved in the recovery process, taking into account the amount of available resources (Sharma et al. 2018a), as well as their optimal allocation at the regional scale (Sharma et al. 2018b). In this step, we need to estimate the post-event functionality in terms of connectivity between the different origin-destination nodes by a topology-based method or in terms of the actual flow of goods, services, and resources (including workforce) using a flow-based method (Guidotti & Gardoni 2018). The severity of casualties can also be used to predict the duration of workers unavailability by considering a corresponding recovery time from the specific casualty. Repopulation models can be used to predict the returning population after an external dislocation.

43.4 Modeling business interruption as a function of transportation network

In this section, we introduce the models needed in the proposed formulation to model business interruption as a function of the reliability and resilience of the transportation network subject to seismic hazards.

43.4.1 Models for physical infrastructure: Graph theory-based models

The modeling of transportation networks for business interruption requires a clear description of the taxonomy and the granularity of the network. As previously discussed, critical infrastructure networks enable the movement of goods and services. Thus, we need to identify: (1) origin nodes that originate the goods and services (e.g., distribution centers and warehouses, and employees); and (2) destination nodes that receive and use the goods (e.g., retail stores and factories). The granularity of the network depends on the purpose of network modeling. As an example, if we are interested in modeling the movement of goods (e.g., from distribution centers to retail stores) on a road transportation network, we might confine the model only to major roads, such as highways and main routes with no need to model minor and local roads. On the other hand, modeling the accessibility of workers might require a finer resolution, including in the model all different types of roads. A spatially hybrid modeling granularity is also possible when we model business interruption over a large region. For example, the granularity within the area of interest can be more refined, while beyond the geographical boundaries of the area of interest we can only consider major roads to model the flow in and out of the region of interest of goods and services.

Critical infrastructure networks are often represented mathematically based on concepts of graph theory (e.g., Ruohonen 2013, Guidotti & Gardoni 2018). Defining a network mathematically as $G = (V, E)$ means expressing the graph $G = (V, E)$ in terms of the set V of $\mathcal{N}$ vertices, as well as the set E of M edges. Two generic nodes v_i and v_j are connected if there is a finite sequence of nodes and edges that lead from v_i to v_j. The finite sequence of nodes and edges is named a walk in the graph $G = (V, E)$. To fully characterize mathematically a network, we can use adjacency tables (Guidotti et al. 2016, 2017a,b) that provide information on the connectivity of the network.

For a transportation network, edges represent the line segment (e.g., roads and rail lines) between different nodes. Nodes represent the points of interest that form the set of origins and destinations (e.g., distribution centers, employees, and business plants/facilities); furthermore, nodes can also include bridges (i.e., bridges over waterways, highways), as commonly done in bridge engineering (e.g., Liu & Frangopol 2005).

The availability of goods and services depends on the connectivity along the supply chain of the business of interest. Let the subset $V_{SC} = (v_{SC,1}, v_{SC,2}, ..., v_{SC,N_{SC}})$ define the nodes in the supply chain including the business facilities and bridges in the transportation network. Also, let the subset $V_W = (v_{W,1}, v_{W,2}, ..., v_{W,N_W})$ define the set of nodes involved in the analysis to estimate the available workforce including workers' residencies and bridges.

In a topology-based method, a connectivity analysis consists in finding the existence of a path from the origins to the destinations. This can be done using algorithms for the lightest path (e.g., shortest path) such as Dijkstra's algorithm or Floyd's Algorithm (Ruohonen 2013), a matrix-based system reliability method (Kang et al. 2008), as well as improved simulation methods to obtain estimates of the probability of connectivity in a computationally efficient manner (Guikema & Gardoni 2009). In a flow-based method it is possible to associate to each node and edge of the defined network G a mapping or values (i.e., weights) (Guidotti et al. 2016, 2018). As an example, the mapping for a node may correspond to physical characteristics (e.g., traffic capacity for a bridge); similarly, for edges the mapping may capture the flow of goods from one node to the other. The flow through a link can be expressed as a function of time, specifying the input and output node.

Under normal conditions, critical infrastructure ensure the connectivity between the different origin-destination nodes (for a topology-based method), as well as the sufficient supply of goods or services (for a flow-based method.) However, after the occurrence of a damaging event, nodes may fail and need to be removed from the network. The removal of a node from a network may imply changes in the connectivity, as well as the ability of meeting the imposed demand at time t_{0^+} (the time immediately after the occurrence of the damaging event). After the occurrence of a damaging event, recovery activities start to reestablish the functionality of the network (Sharma et al. 2018a). As a result, nodes (e.g., bridges) are gradually restored to their functional state, and can be re-included in the set V of the nodes of G.

43.4.2 Models for the reliability of nodes: Fragility functions

Fragility functions are commonly used to estimate the vulnerability of structures and infrastructure components subject to hazards. A fragility function is defined as the conditional probability of attaining or exceeding a specified performance level given a (set of) hazard intensity measure(s) (Gardoni et al. 2002, 2003; Gardoni 2017).

Methods to develop fragility functions can be classified into empirical, analytical, and physics-based. Empirical fragility functions are developed based on observations of actual damage and post-seismic surveys (e.g., Basöz & Kiremidjian 1998; FEMA 2003). Analytical fragility functions are developed from the results of static or dynamic analyses of structural models of specific bridges (e.g., Choi et al. 2004). These two types of fragility functions share four common limitations: (1) the fragility functions are structure-specific; thus they cannot be used for different structures; (2) the fragility functions are developed considering the models for the entire structural system (i.e., full bridge); thus, they cannot include information from experimental test data, typically obtained at the structural component level; (3) the fragility functions are constructed assuming an arbitrary shape (e.g., a lognormal cumulative distribution function) with parameters that have no physical meaning; and (4) the fragility functions typically do not account for all of the prevailing sources of uncertainty.

To overcome these limitations, Gardoni et al. (2002, 2003) proposed a physics-based method to develop fragility functions (named physics-based fragility functions). In a physics-based method, probabilistic capacity, and demand models for the modes of failure of interest are first developed based on rule of physics and mechanics, as well as information from computer simulations, laboratory tests, and field data. The capacity may be defined as, for example, the maximum load/deformation that the infrastructure component can experience before entering a certain damage state (in the extreme case failure). The demand is the corresponding force or deformation imposed on the infrastructure component given a (set of) hazard intensity measure(s). After developing probabilistic capacity and demand models, fragility functions can be obtained by conducting a rigorous reliability analysis, which does not require to make any assumptions on the shape of the fragility function.

Following Gardoni et al. (2002, 2003), a multivariate probabilistic predictive model for both capacity and demand quantities can be written as

$$T_k\left[Y_k\left(\mathbf{r},\boldsymbol{\Theta}_{T,k}\right)\right]=T_k\left[\hat{y}_k\left(\mathbf{r}\right)\right]+\gamma_k\left(\mathbf{r},\theta_{T,k}\right)+\sigma_{T,k}\varepsilon_{T,k}, \quad k=1,\ldots,q, \tag{43.1}$$

where $T_k(\cdot)$ is a variance stabilizing transformation function; $Y_k(\mathbf{r},\boldsymbol{\Theta}_{T,k})$ is the kth predicted quantity of interest; $\hat{y}_k(\mathbf{r})$ is an existing deterministic model to predict Y_k (typically based on first principles, i.e. rules of physics and mechanics); $\gamma_k(\mathbf{r},\theta_{T,k})$ is a correction term for the bias in $\hat{y}_k(\mathbf{r})$ (also constructed in part based on the rules of physics and mechanics); $\mathbf{r}$ is a vector of basic variables that might influence Y_k; $\boldsymbol{\Theta}_{T,k}=(\boldsymbol{\theta}_{T,k},\sigma_{T,k})$ is a vector of unknown model parameters that needs to be estimated; and $\sigma_{T,k}\varepsilon_{T,k}$ is the (additive) model error of Y_k (additivity assumption), in which $\sigma_{T,k}$ is the standard deviation of the model error, assumed not to depend on $\mathbf{r}$ (homoskedasticity assumption), and $\varepsilon_{T,k}$ is a standard normal random variable (normality assumption). In general, $(\varepsilon_{T,1},\ldots,\varepsilon_{T,q})$ form a vector of dependent random variables. Let Σ denote the covariance matrix of $(\sigma_{T,1}\varepsilon_{T,1},\ldots,\sigma_{T,q}\varepsilon_{T,q})$. The collection of all of the unknown model parameters is then $\boldsymbol{\Theta}=(\boldsymbol{\theta},\Sigma)$, where $\boldsymbol{\theta}=(\boldsymbol{\theta}_{T,1},\ldots,\boldsymbol{\theta}_{T,q})$. The transformation $T_k(\cdot)$ is used to (approximately) satisfy the additivity, homoskedasticity, and normality assumptions.

To estimate $\boldsymbol{\Theta}$, Gardoni et al. (2002) developed a Bayesian approach that combines the prior information about $\boldsymbol{\Theta}$ with the objective information from the observed data. The Bayesian approach allows to capture the statistical uncertainty in the estimates of $\boldsymbol{\Theta}$ through its posterior probability density function (PDF). Also, the Bayesian approach allows us to update the probabilistic models as new data become available (Gardoni et al. 2003; Choe et al. 2007). Specifically, the calibration of the probabilistic capacity and demand models can involve both the real data (i.e., laboratory tests and/or from field data as in Gardoni et al. 2002, 2003; Zhong et al. 2009) and virtual data (i.e., computer simulations as in Gardoni et al 2003; Zhong et al. 2008; Huang et al. 2010).

Once we obtain the probabilistic capacity and demand models as described in Equation (43.1), we can write the limit-state function, $g_k(\mathbf{r},\boldsymbol{\Theta}_k)$, for the kth failure mode as (Gardoni 2017)

$$g_k\left(\mathbf{r},\boldsymbol{\Theta}_k\right)=C_k\left(\mathbf{r},\boldsymbol{\Theta}_{C,k}\right)-D_k\left(\mathbf{r},\boldsymbol{\Theta}_{D,k}\right) \quad k=1,\ldots,q, \tag{43.2}$$

where $C_k(\mathbf{r},\boldsymbol{\Theta}_{C,k})$ is the capacity model for the kth failure mode; $D_k(\mathbf{r},\boldsymbol{\Theta}_{D,k})$ is the corresponding demand model; and $\boldsymbol{\Theta}_k=(\boldsymbol{\Theta}_{C,k},\boldsymbol{\Theta}_{D,k})$. Both $C_k(\mathbf{r},\boldsymbol{\Theta}_{C,k})$ and $D_k(\mathbf{r},\boldsymbol{\Theta}_{D,k})$ are special cases of $T_k[Y_k(\mathbf{r},\boldsymbol{\Theta}_{T,k})]$. By writing $\mathbf{r}$ as $\mathbf{r}=(\mathbf{x},\mathbf{s})$, where $\mathbf{x}$ is a vector of state variables that define the infrastructure component (e.g., material properties) and $\mathbf{s}$ is a vector of demand variables (e.g., hazard intensity measure(s)), we can write the fragility function as

$$F\left(\mathbf{s},\boldsymbol{\Theta}\right)=\mathbf{P}\left\{\bigcup_k\left[g_k\left(\mathbf{x},\mathbf{s},\boldsymbol{\Theta}_k\right)\leq 0\right]\Big|\mathbf{s},\boldsymbol{\Theta}\right\}. \tag{43.3}$$

Depending on the treatment of the uncertainties in $\boldsymbol{\Theta}$, two possible estimates of the fragility functions can be obtained (Gardoni et al. 2002). The first option is to obtain a point-estimate of the fragility $\hat{F}(\mathbf{s})=F(\mathbf{s},\hat{\boldsymbol{\Theta}})$, obtained by replacing $\boldsymbol{\Theta}$ in Equation (43.3) with a fixed value $\hat{\boldsymbol{\Theta}}$ (e.g., the posterior mode of $\boldsymbol{\Theta}$.) Alternatively, to incorporate the uncertainty $\boldsymbol{\Theta}$ one can write a predictive estimate as

$$\tilde{F}\left(\mathbf{s}\right)=\int F\left(\mathbf{s},\boldsymbol{\Theta}\right)f\left(\boldsymbol{\Theta}\right)d\boldsymbol{\Theta}. \tag{43.4}$$

Considering the reliability index $\beta(\mathbf{s},\Theta)$ (Ditlevsen & Madsen 1996; Gardoni 2017) corresponding to the conditional fragility function in Equation (43.3), confidence intervals on the predictive estimate in Equation (43.4) can be developed (Gardoni et al. 2002). Using a first-order Taylor expansion around the mean point, the variance of $\beta(\mathbf{s},\Theta)$ is (approximately)

$$\sigma_\beta^2(\mathbf{s}) \approx \nabla_\Theta \beta(\mathbf{s}) \Sigma_{\Theta\Theta} \nabla_\Theta \beta(\mathbf{s})^T,$$

(43.5)

where $\nabla_\Theta \beta(\mathbf{s})$ is the gradient row vector of $\beta(\mathbf{s},\Theta)$ evaluated at the mean point and computed by first-order reliability analysis, and $\Sigma_{\Theta\Theta}$ is the estimated covariance matrix of Θ. Therefore, one can obtain, for example, one standard deviation bounds, which represent approximatively 15 percent and 85 percent probability levels as

$$\left\{ \Phi\left[-\tilde{\beta}(\mathbf{s}) - \sigma_\beta(\mathbf{s})\right], \Phi\left[-\tilde{\beta}(\mathbf{s}) + \sigma_\beta(\mathbf{s})\right] \right\},$$

(43.6)

where $\tilde{\beta}(\mathbf{s}) = \Phi^{-1}[1 - \tilde{F}(\mathbf{s})]$. A more detailed review of the physics-based method to develop fragility functions and of a number of applications can be found in Chapter 13 of this volume.

43.5 Example: A food retailer in Seaside, Oregon

In this section we used the presented probabilistic procedure to study the business interruption of a hypothetical food retail store located in Seaside, Oregon after the occurrence of an earthquake originated from the Cascadia Subduction Zone. Specifically, we consider the dependency of the retail store on the transportation network. Seaside is a coastal city located in Clatsop County with 6,440 off-season inhabitants, according to the 2010 census data (Rosenheim et al. 2018).

Step 1: Definition of the critical infrastructure network models

The model of the transportation road network is available from the Census Bureau (www.census.gov/geo/maps-data/data/tiger.html). The data include the different type of roads (i.e., local roads, routes, highways, and interstates), which are used to define the edges of the network. We model all of the roads within the city of Seaside, and the major roads, such as highways and main routes as links between the retail store located in Seaside and the distribution centers, assumed to be located in Portland, Oregon. Based on this information, we developed the model with hybrid granularity for the road network shown in Figure 43.1.

The nodes of the network considered for modeling the business interruption are the bridges along the road network, the selected food retail store, the corresponding distribution centers, and the workers' residences. The bridge inventory is available from the US Department of Transportation in the Federal Highway Administration section (www.fhwa.dot.gov/bridge/nbi/ascii.cfm). Data include bridge locations, as well as geometry characteristics, year built, and maintenance responsibility (information used in the modeling of the bridge recovery in Step 5). In this example, the food retail store receives its supply from two distribution centers located in Portland, Oregon. Finally, as for the workforce of the retails store, 200 workers are randomly placed within Seaside so that their expected incomes have a spatial distribution consistent with the information from the census data. Figure 43.1 shows the location of the considered nodes and the shortest path between the distribution centers and the food retail store, assumed to be

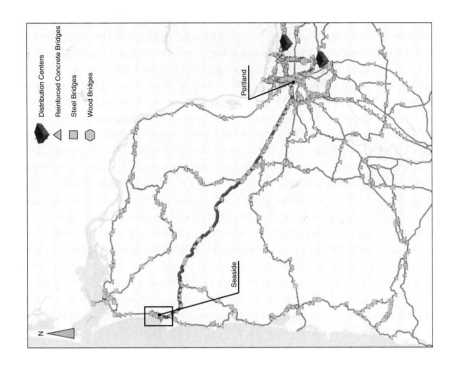

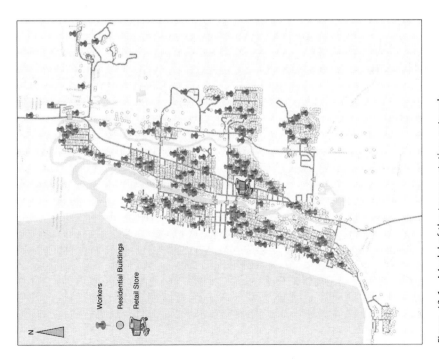

Figure 43.1 Model of the transportation network.

the route used during normal operations. Figure 43.1 also shows the bridge nodes by their construction material (i.e., reinforced concrete, steel, and wood).

Step 2: Generation of the hazard intensity measure(s) over the area of interest

The second step of the proposed procedure involves generating the hazard intensity measure(s) over the area of interest. In this example, the city of Seaside is subject to a seismic hazard generated from the Cascadia Subduction Zone. We consider a seismic event of magnitude $M_W = 7.0$, located 25 km southwest of the city. Ground Motion Prediction Equations (Boore & Atkinson 2008) are used to obtain maps of two seismic intensity measures: the Peak Ground Acceleration (PGA) and the Spectral Acceleration (S_a) at the natural period of the components of the critical infrastructure network (i.e., the bridges).

Step 3: Assessment of the physical damage to the components of the critical infrastructure network

In this example, the bridges are considered as the vulnerable nodes. As discussed earlier, the conditional probability for a selected bridge of being in a specified damage state is obtained using fragility functions. We consider five different damage states: none, slight, moderate, heavy, and complete. Since the fragility functions are the conditional probability of attaining or exceeding a specified performance level given a (set of) hazard intensity measure(s), the conditional probability $\mathbf{P}(DS_{p,i} \mid \mathbf{s})$ of being in the pth damage state for the ith bridge, $DS_{p,i}$, given the set of demand variables, $\mathbf{s}$, is calculated as the difference between the fragility curves following Bai et al. (2009).

For the reinforced concrete bridges, we used the probabilistic capacity and demand models in Gardoni et al. (2002, 2003) and obtained the estimates of the fragility functions performing a reliability analysis. The fragility functions corresponding to the probability of attaining or exceeding the complete damage state is obtained directly based on Gardoni et al. (2002, 2003). The fragility functions for the slight, moderate, and heavy damage states are obtained considering capacity drift values of 1, 2, and 4 percent based on Simon et al. (2010). To compute the capacity and demand models, we use the values of the state variables in $\mathbf{x}$ (e.g., span length, deck width, concrete strength) obtained from the blueprints, provided by the Oregon Department of Transportation. Also, we consider typical values of a few missing state variables in $\mathbf{x}$ (e.g., reinforcement ratio) provided by the Oregon Department of Transportation in the bridge design guidelines (www.oregon.gov/ODOT/Bridge/Pages/Bridge-Design-Manual.aspx) considering whether a bridge is seismically designed or not (based on the year built.) For the steel and wood bridges, we adopt fragility curves from HAZUS-MH (FEMA 2015).

Step 4: Estimation of the physical damage to the building inventory and estimation of the resulting available workforce

A building damage analysis is performed using different fragility functions (e.g., HAZUS-MH (FEMA 2015), and Steelman et al. 2007) considering five possible damage states (DS_p where $p = 1,\ldots,5$). Figure 43.2 shows the mean damage to the buildings, where the mean is computed following Bai et al. (2009).

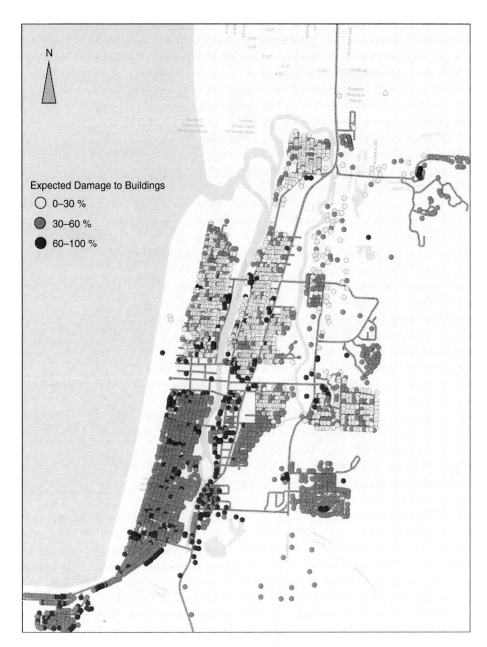

Figure 43.2 Expected physical damage to the Seaside buildings.

We then estimate the probability of a worker to be unavailable considering the conditional probability of the severity of the casualties for a given $\mathbf{s}$, coupled with the probability of household dislocation due to structural damage of residential buildings. We estimate the conditional probability mass function (PMF) of the casualty severity (CS_l where $l = 1,\ldots,4$ indicates the level of severity), for a given $\mathbf{s}$, $\mathbf{P}(CS_l \mid \mathbf{s})$, using the total probability rule

$$\mathbf{P}(CS_l|\mathbf{s}) = \sum_{p=1}^{5} \mathbf{P}(CS_l|DS_p) \times \mathbf{P}(DS_p|\mathbf{s}), \tag{43.7}$$

where $\mathbf{P}(CS_l \mid DS_p)$ is the conditional probability of the lth (indoor) casualty severity given the pth damage state of the building, obtained from HAZUS-MH (FEMA 2015); $\mathbf{P}(DS_p \mid \mathbf{s})$ is the probability of being in each damage state given the set of demand variables (e.g. hazard intensity measure(s)), obtained from the fragility functions.

The probability of household dislocation due to structural damage of residential buildings is obtained using a logistic regression model (Rosenheim et al. 2018). In this example, we only consider external dislocation. Thus, the probability that the zth worker is temporary unavailable $\mathbf{P}(U_{w_z} \mid \mathbf{s})$ is estimated as

$$\mathbf{P}(U_{w_z}|\mathbf{s}) = \sum_{l=1}^{3} \mathbf{P}(CS_{l,w_z}|\mathbf{s}) + \mathbf{P}(ED_{w_z}|\mathbf{s}) - \sum_{l=1}^{3} \mathbf{P}(CS_{l,w_z}|\mathbf{s}) \times \mathbf{P}(ED_{w_z}|\mathbf{s}), \tag{43.8}$$

where $\sum_{l=1}^{3} \mathbf{P}(CS_{l,w_z} \mid \mathbf{s})$ is the probability of the zth worker of being in either casualty severity 1, 2, or 3, as defined in Section 43.2.2 (namely, that a worker is injured, yet not instantaneously killed or fatally injured); $\mathbf{P}(ED_{w_z} \mid \mathbf{s})$ is the probability of external dislocation of the zth worker. In addition, if the zth worker happens to be instantaneously killed or mortally injured (i.e., Severity Casualty 4), the worker is permanently removed from the set of available workers.

Step 5: Assessment of the post-event functionality over time

The final step of the proposed procedure is the assessment of the post-event functionality of the network over time. To assess the post-event functionality, we consider the network connectivity to check whether there is a possible path between the different origin and destination nodes. Under the considered seismic scenario, the ith bridge v_i is estimated to be closed for an expected time $\mathbf{E}[t_{CL,i} \mid \mathbf{s}]$

$$\mathbf{E}[t_{CL,i}|\mathbf{s}] = \sum_{p=1}^{5} \mathbf{E}(t_{CL,i} \mid DS_{p,i}) \times \mathbf{P}(DS_{p,i}|\mathbf{s}), \tag{43.9}$$

where $\mathbf{E}(t_{CL,i} \mid DS_{p,i})$ is the expected recovery time given the bridge is in the pth damage state, obtained from HAZUS-MH (FEMA 2015). Consequently, if the ith bridge v_i belongs to the kth edge e_k, the expected closure time of the kth edge e_k is

$$\max_{i \in e_k} \mathbf{E}[t_{CL,i}|\mathbf{s}]. \tag{43.10}$$

Figure 43.3 shows the bridges that are expected to be closed at time t_{0^+}.

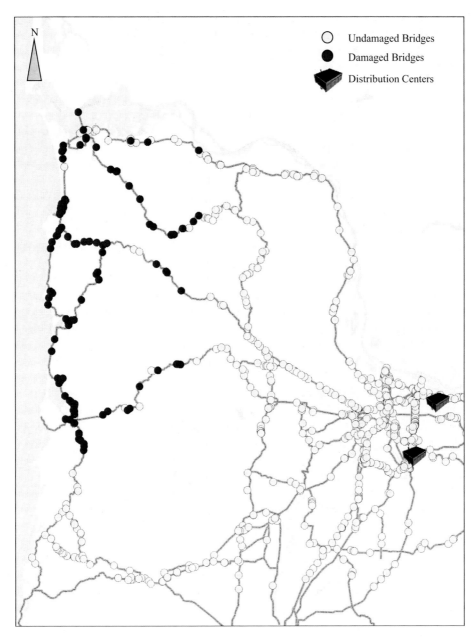

Figure 43.3 Expected closed bridges and corresponding route from the distribution centers to the food retail store at time l_{0^+}.

In this example, immediately after the occurrence of the earthquake, there are no available routes from the distribution centers to the retail store (as shown in Figure 43.3). Similarly, the available workforce is reduced to about 16%, as shown in Figure 43.4. The available workforce is estimated considering workers that are not injured, dead, or dislocated and that have physical access to the store.

After the occurrence of the seismic event, recovery activities start to restore the functionality of the network. Bridges are restored during the recovery process, implying changes in the connectivity over time. The estimate in Equation (43.9) defines the expected time to fully repair each bridge after the occurrence of the damaging event. Nevertheless, the mobilization and the allocation of resources in the recovery process are factors difficult to predict and to model. In this example, we consider the allocation of resources based on the maintenance responsibility of the bridges in a hierarchical fashion (i.e., the federal government may recover simultaneously more bridges than the state, as well as the state may recover simultaneously more bridges than the county and the city/town). Based on the hierarchical allocation of resources, along with the possibility of having recovery activities in parallel (e.g., while the state is repairing six bridges under their responsibility, the county can repair four under their responsibility), we estimate the time to reopen a generic edge in the network. We also consider emergency/priority repairs such as shoring or building temporary bridges to allow at least one available link between origins and destinations. Specifically, we select bridges for emergency repairs to provide at least a path between the different origin and destination nodes. The selection is based on the minimization of the time needed for reestablishing a path. Based on the expected closure time of the kth edge e_k, bridges are first shored in the north side of the region to re-open a possible path between origin and destination nodes (i.e., distribution centers and retail store) in the shortest possible time. Figure 43.5 shows the connectivity between the distribution centers and the food retail store after 90 days from the occurrence of the earthquake when a possible path is available even though through a longer route than the one adopted in the normal conditions (shown in Figure 43.1). Because of the lack of connectivity that impairs bringing the needed resources into Seaside, we assumed that bridges within Seaside cannot start being repaired before day 90 after the earthquake.

Figure 43.6 shows the available workforce at time $t = 90$ days. For this example, since the focus is on the role of the transportation network, we estimate the available workforce as the number of original workers that can now access the retail store (after removing the deceased workers). This is equivalent to assuming that after the 90 days all of the injured workers recovered and that those who had dislocated returned to their original residence. The connectivity analysis shows that there is an increase in the available workforce from 16 percent to 40 percent, yet it is not fully restored. For a more detailed analysis, we could use the severity of casualties to predict the duration of workers unavailability (by considering a corresponding recovery time from the specific casualty) and we could use repopulation models to predict the rate of returning workers after an external dislocation. In addition, the retail store may generally decide to hire temporary workers, as well as redeploy the workforce among different stores located in the area, yet this factor is not considered in this example.

As the recovery activities continue to restore bridges to their functional state, more workers regain access to the retail store. In the considered example, the workforce is restored to full capacity at time $t = 120$ days, as shown in Figure 43.7.

Finally, the end of the recovery activities – from the business perspective – is at time $t = 370$ days, when the route between the distribution centers and the retail store is again the shortest possible one as in the pre-hazard condition, and all of the workers (and customers) have full

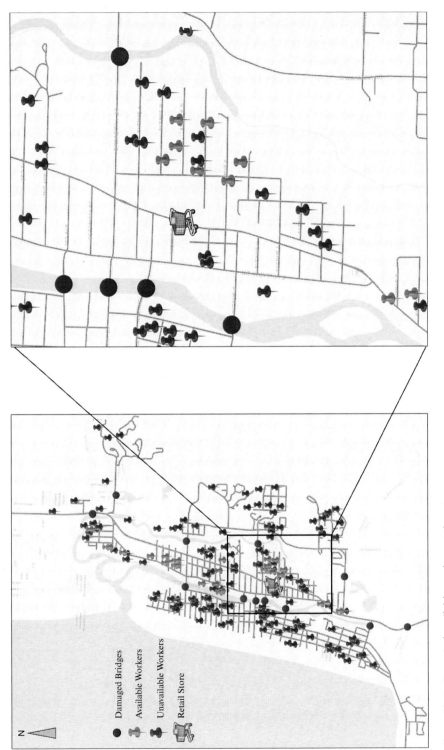

Figure 43.4 Expected available workers at time t_0.

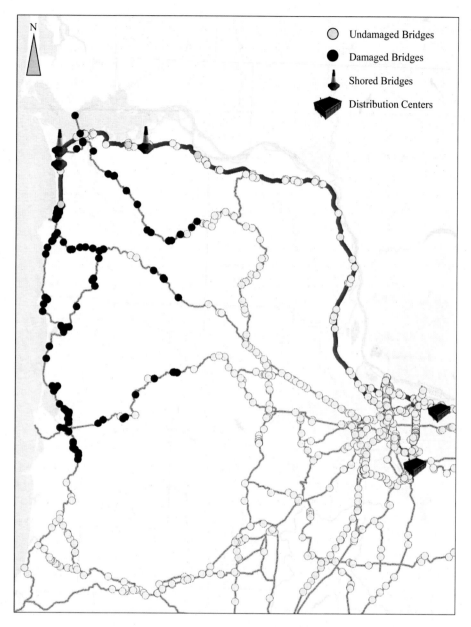

Figure 43.5 Connectivity between the distribution centers and the food retail store at time $t = 90$ days.

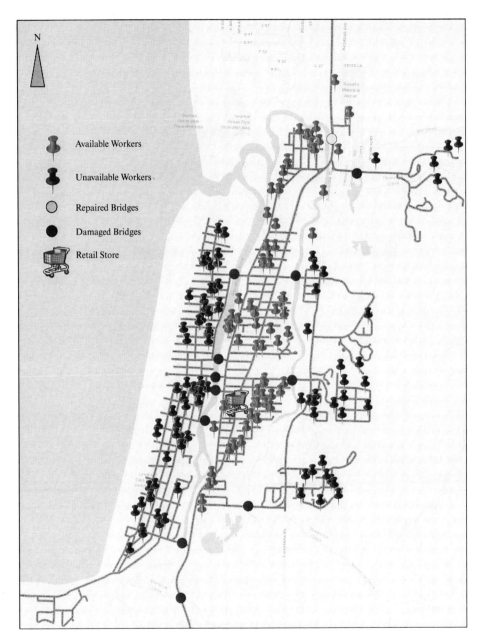

Figure 43.6 Expected available workers at time $t = 90$ days.

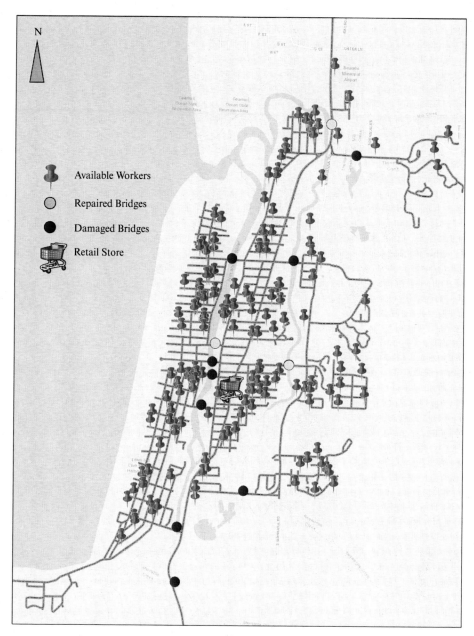

Figure 43.7 Expected available workers at time $t = 120$ days.

access to the retail store, allowing the business to go back to the regular pre-hazard condition activities.

43.6 Conclusions

This chapter proposed a probabilistic procedure for modeling business interruption incorporating the dependency of business operations on physical infrastructure and social systems. The proposed procedure included a reliability analysis to model the direct physical damage to the business properties and the impact to the network functionality and social systems, as well as a resilience analysis to model the recovery of structures, infrastructure, and communities needed to estimate the duration of business interruption. The proposed probabilistic procedure is general and applicable to different category of businesses, physical infrastructure, and hazards.

The chapter illustrated the proposed procedure investigating the duration of business interruption of a hypothetical food retail store located in Seaside, Oregon as a function of the reliability and resilience of the transportation network. The example included several contributing factors that can affect the duration of business interruption such as the supply-chain connectivity and the remaining available workforce. The example considered an earthquake scenario and used fragility functions to estimate the probability of bridge closure. The example also incorporated social systems to estimate the remaining available workforce due to casualties and population dislocation after the occurrence of the earthquake. In this example, the considered functionality metric for the transportation network is the accessibility (connectivity) of the retail store by its suppliers such as distribution centers, as well as by the workers. Finally, a recovery analysis estimated the time needed for the business operation to return to full functionality.

Acknowledgments

This work was supported in part by the National Science Foundation (NSF) under Award No. 1638346 and by the National Institute of Standards and Technology (NIST) through the Center for Risk-Based Community Resilience Planning under Award No. 70NANB15H044. Opinions and findings presented are those of the authors and do not necessarily reflect the views of the sponsor.

References

ALA (2001) *Seismic fragility formulations for water Systems: Part 1 – guideline, American lifelines alliance, April, ASCE.* Retrieved from www.americanlifelinesalliance.org/

Bai J.-W., Hueste M.B.D., and Gardoni P. (2009) "Probabilistic assessment of structural damage due to earthquakes for buildings in mid-America." *Journal of Structural Engineering* 135, 1155–63.

Bai J.-W., Gardoni P., and Hueste M.B.D. (2011) "Story-specific demand models and seismic fragility estimates for multi-story buildings." *Structural Safety* 33 96–107.

Bai J.-W., Hueste M.B.D., and Gardoni, P. (2014) "Seismic vulnerability assessment of tilt-up concrete structures." *Structure and Infrastructure Engineering*, 11: 1131–46.

Basöz N.I. and Kiremidjian A.S. (1998) "Evaluation of bridge damage data from the Loma Prieta and Northridge, California earthquakes." *Technical Report MCEER. No. 98-0004. US Multidisciplinary Center for Earthquake Engineering Research* (MCEER), Buffalo, NY.

Boore D.M. and Atkinson G.M. (2008) "Ground-motion prediction equations for the average horizontal component of PGA, PGV, and 5%-damped PSA at spectral periods between 0.01 s and 10.0 s." *Earthquake Spectra* 24, 99–138.

Bruneau M., Chang S.E., Eguchi R.T., Lee G.C., O'Rourke T.D., Reinhorn A.M., Shinozuka M., Tierney K., Wallace W.A., and von Winterfeldt D. (2003). "A Framework to quantitatively assess and enhance the seismic resilience of communities." *Earthquake Spectra* 19733–752.

Caverzan A. and Solomos G. (2014) "Review on resilience in literature and standards codes for critical built-infrastructures." *JRC Science and Policy Report*

Chang S.E. (2014) "Infrastructure resilience to disasters." *The Bridge* 44, 36–41.

Chang S.E. (2016) "Socioeconomic impacts of infrastructure disruptions." *Oxford Research Encyclopedia of Natural Hazard Science.* http://naturalhazardscience.oxfordre.com/view/10.1093/acrefore/9780199389407.001.0001/acrefore-9780199389407-e-66 (last accessed September 13, 2018).

Chang S.E., Pasion C., Yavari S., and Elwood K. (2009) "Social impacts of lifeline losses: Modeling displaced populations and health care functionality." *ASCE Technical Council on Lifeline Earthquake Engineering*, Oakland, CA

Choe D., Gardoni P., and Rosowsky D. (2007) "Closed-form fragility estimates, parameter sensitivity and Bayesian updating for RC columns." *Journal of Engineering Mechanics* 133, 833–43.

Choi E., DesRoches R., and Nielson B. (2004) "Seismic fragility of typical bridges in moderate seismic zones." *Engineering Structures* 26, 187–99.

Coburn A.W., Spence R.J.S., and Pomonis A. (1992) "Factors determining human casualty levels in earthquakes: Mortality prediction in building collapse." *10th World Conference on Earthquake Engineering*, Madrid (Spain).

Corotis R. (2009) "Societal issues in adopting life-cycle concepts within the political system." *Structure and Infrastructure Engineering* 5, 59–65.

Ditlevsen O. and Madsen H.O. (1996). *Structural Reliability Methods*, New York: Wiley.

Doorn N., Gardoni P., and Murphy C. (2018) "A multidisciplinary definition and evaluation of resilience: the role of social justice in defining resilience." *Sustainable and Resilient Infrastructure*. DOI: 10.1080/23789689.2018.1428162

Dueñas-Osorio L., Craig J.I., and Goodno B.J. (2007) "Seismic response of critical interdependent networks." *Earthquake Engineering & Structural Dynamics* 36, 285–306.

Durkin M.E., Thiel C.C., Schneider J.E., and De Vriend T. (1991) "Injuries and emergency medical response in the Loma Prieta earthquake." *Bulletin of the Seismological Society of America* 81, 2143–66.

Ellingwood B.R., Cutler H., Gardoni P., Peacock W.G., van de Lindt J.W., and Wang N. (2016) "The Centerville Virtual Community: A fully integrated decision model of interacting physical and social infrastructure systems." *Sustainable and Resilient Infrastructure* 1, 95–107.

FEMA (2015) *Hazus 2.1 technical and user's manuals*, available at www.fema.gov/media-library/assets/documents/24609 (last accessed February 21, 2018).

Franchin P. (2014) "A computational framework for systemic seismic risk analysis of civil infrastructural systems," in K. Pitilakis, P. Franchin, B. Khazai, and H. Wenzel (eds.), *SYNER-G: Systemic Seismic Vulnerability and Risk Assessment of Complex Urban, Utility, Lifeline Systems and Critical Facilities* (pp. 23–56), New York: Springer.

Franchin P. and Cavalieri F. (2015) "Probabilistic assessment of civil infrastructure resilience to earthquakes." *Computer-Aided Civil and Infrastructure Engineering* 30, 583–600.

Fricker J.D. and Whitford R.K. eds. (2005). *Fundamentals of Transportation Engineering. A Multimodal Systems Approach.* Pearson Prentice Hall.

Gardoni P. ed. (2017) *Risk and Reliability Analysis: Theory and Applications.* New York: Springer.

Gardoni P. and LaFave J.M. eds. (2016) *Multi-hazard Approaches to Civil Infrastructure Engineering.* New York: Springer.

Gardoni P. and Murphy C. (2009). "Capabilities-based approach to measuring the societal impacts of natural and man-made hazards in risk analysis." *ASCE Natural Hazards Review* 10, 29–37.

Gardoni P. and Murphy C. (2010) "Gauging the societal impacts of natural disasters using a Capabilities-based Approach." *Disasters* 34, 619–36.

Gardoni P. and Murphy C. (2014) "A scale of risk." *Risk Analysis*, 34, 1208–27.

Gardoni P. and Murphy C. (2018) "Society-based design: promoting societal well-being by designing sustainable and resilient infrastructure." *Sustainable and Resilient Infrastructure*. DOI: 10.1080/23789689.2018.1448667.

Gardoni P., Der Kiureghian A., and Mosalam K.M. (2002) "Probabilistic capacity models and fragility estimates for reinforced concrete columns based on experimental observations." *Journal of Engineering Mechanics* 128, 1024–38.

Gardoni P., Mosalam K.M., and Der Kiureghian A. (2003) "Probabilistic seismic demand models and fragility estimates for RC bridges." *Journal of Earthquake Engineering* 7, 79–106.

Gardoni P., Reinschmidt K.F., and Kumar R. (2007) "A probabilistic framework for Bayesian adaptive forecasting of project progress." *Computer-Aided Civil and Infrastructure Engineering* 22, 182–96.

Gardoni P., Murphy C., and Rowell A. eds. (2016) *Societal Risk Management of Natural Hazards,* New York: Springer.

Guidotti R., Chmielewski H., Unnikrishnan V., Gardoni P., McAllister T., and van de Lindt J.W. (2016). "Modeling the resilience of critical infrastructure: the role of network dependencies." *Sustainable and Resilient Infrastructure* 1, 153–68.

Guidotti R., Gardoni P., and Chen Y. (2017a) "Network reliability analysis with link and nodal weights and auxiliary nodes." *Structural Safety* 65, 12–26.

Guidotti R., Gardoni P., and Chen Y. (2017b) "Multi-layer heterogeneous network model for interdependent infrastructure systems," *12th International Conference on Structural Safety & Reliability (ICOSSAR 2017),* TU Wien, Vienna (Austria).

Guidotti R. and Gardoni P. (2018) "Modeling of interdependent critical infrastructure for regional risk and resilience analysis." in Gardoni P. ed., *Handbook of Sustainable and Resilient Infrastructure.* New York: Routledge.

Guidotti R., Gardoni P., and Rosenheim N. (2018) "Integration of physical infrastructure and social systems in communities' reliability and resilience analysis." *Reliability Engineering and System Safety* (submitted).

Guikema S. and Gardoni P. (2009) "Reliability estimation for networks of reinforced concrete bridges." *ASCE Journal of Infrastructure Systems* 15, 61–9.

Huang Q., Gardoni P., and Hurlebaus S. (2010) "Probabilistic seismic demand models and fragility estimates for reinforced concrete highway bridges with one single-column bent." *Journal of Engineering Mechanics* 136, 1340–53.

Insurance Research Council and Insurance Institute of Property Loss Reduction (1995) *Coastal Exposure and Community Protection: Hurricane Andrew's Legacy,* Wheaton, IL.

Jain V.K. and Guin J. (2009) "Modeling business interruption losses for insurance portfolios." *11th America's Conference on Wind Engineering,* San Juan (Puerto Rico).

Kajitani Y. and Tatano H. (2009) "Estimation of lifeline resilience factors based on surveys of Japanese industries." *Earthquake Spectra* 25, 755–76.

Kang W.-H., Song, J., and Gardoni P. (2008) "Matrix-based system reliability method and applications to bridge networks." *Reliability Engineering and System Safety* 93, 1584–93.

Kim Y.S., Spencer B.F. Jr, Song J., Elnashai A.S., and Stokes T. (2007) "Seismic performance assessment of interdependent lifeline systems." *MAE Center CD Release 0716.* http://mae.cee.illinois.edu/publications/reports/Report07-16.pdf (last accessed September 13, 2018).

Lee E.E., Mitchell J.E., and Wallace W.A. (2007) "Restoration of services in interdependent infrastructure systems: A network flows approach." *IEEE Transactions on Systems, Man and Cybernetics Part C: Applications and Reviews* 37, 1303–17.

Liu M. and Frangopol D. M. (2005) "Balancing connectivity of deteriorating bridge networks and long-term maintenance cost through optimization." *Journal of Bridge Engineering* 10, 468–81.

May P. (2001) *Organizational and Societal Consequences for Performance-Based Earthquake Engineering.* PEER 2001/04. Berkeley, CA: Pacific Earthquake Engineering Research Center, College of Engineering, University of California, Berkeley.

McAllister T. (2013) *Developing Guidelines and Standards for Disaster Resilience of the Built Environment: A Research Needs Assessment.* Gaithersburg, MD.

Murphy C. and Gardoni P. (2006) "The role of society in engineering risk analysis: a capabilities-based approach." *Risk Analysis* 26, 1073–83.

Murphy C. and Gardoni P. (2007) "Determining public policy and resource allocation priorities for mitigating natural hazards: a capabilities-based approach." *Science and Engineering Ethics* 13, 489–504.

Murphy C. and Gardoni P. (2008) "The acceptability and the tolerability of societal risks: A capabilities-based approach." *Science and Engineering Ethics* 14, 77–92.

Murphy C. and Gardoni P. (2010) "Assessing capability instead of achieved functionings in risk analysis." *Journal of Risk Research* 13, 137–47.

Noh H.-Y., Kiremidjian A., Ceferino L., and So E. (2017) "Bayesian updating of earthquake vulnerability functions with application to mortality rates." *Earthquake Spectra* 33, 1173–89.

Norio O., Ye T., Kajitani Y., Shi P., and Tatano H. (2011) "The 2011 Eastern Japan Great Earthquake Disaster: Overview and Comments." *International Journal of Disaster Risk Science* 2, 34–42.

O'Rourke M.J. and Ayala G. (1993) "Pipeline damage due to wave propagation." *Journal of Geotechnical Engineering* 119, 1490–8.

O'Rourke M.J. and Deyoe E. (1993) "Seismic damage to segmented buried pipe." *Earthquake Spectra* 20, 1167–83.

PCCIP (1997, October) *Critical Foundations: Protecting America's Infrastructures: The Report of the President's Commission on Critical Infrastructure Protection.* Retrieved from www.fas.org/sgp/library/pccip.pdf (last accessed August 20, 2018).

PPD-21 (2013, February 12) *Presidential Policy Directive/ PPD-21 – Critical Infrastructure Security and Resilience.* Washington, DC: The White House.

Ramamoorthy K.S., Gardoni P., and Bracci M.J. (2006) "Probabilistic demand models and fragility curves for reinforced concrete frames." *ASCE Journal of Structural Engineering* 132, 1563–72.

Ramamoorthy K.S., Gardoni P., and Bracci M.J. (2008) "Seismic fragility and confidence bounds for gravity load designed reinforced concrete frames of varying height." *ASCE Journal of Structural Engineering* 134, 639–50.

Rhinesmith A. (1997) *The Federal Budget and Federal Disaster Assistance. Presentation before the Committee on Assessing the Costs of Natural Disasters of the National Research Council*, Washington, DC.

Rinaldi S.M., Peerenboom J.P., and Kelly T.K. (2001) "Identifying, understanding, and analyzing critical infrastructure interdependencies." *IEEE Control Systems Magazine* 21, 11–25.

Rose A. (2004) "Defining and measuring economic resilience to disasters." *Disaster Prevention and Management* 13, 307–14.

Rose A. and Huyck C. K. (2016) "Improving catastrophe modeling for business interruption insurance needs." *Risk Analysis* 36, 1896–1915.

Rose A. and Lim D. (2002) "Business interruption losses from natural hazards: conceptual and methodological issues in the case of the Northridge Earthquake." *Environmental Hazards* 4, 1–14.

Rose A., Oladosu G., Lee B., and Beeler-Asay G. (2009) "The economic impacts of the 2001 terrorist attacks on the World Trade Center: A computable general equilibrium analysis." *Peace Economics, Pease Science, and Publicy Policy* 15, 1–31.

Rosenheim N., Guidotti R., and Gardoni P. (2018) "Integration of detailed household characteristic data with critical infrastructure and its implementation to post-hazard resilience modeling." *2nd International Workshop on Modelling of Physical, Economic and Social Systems for Resilience Assessment*, Ispra (Italy).

Ruohonen K. (2013) *Graph Theory.* Tampereen teknillinen yliopisto. Originally titled Graafiteoria, lecture notes translated by Tamminen, J., Lee, K.C., and Piché, R. http://math.tut.fi/~ruohonen/GT_English.pdf (last accessed August 20, 2018).

Sharma N., Tabandeh A., and Gardoni P. (2018a) "Resilience analysis: A mathematical formulation to model resilience of engineering systems." *Sustainable and Resilient Infrastructure* 3, 49–67.

Sharma N., Tabandeh A., and Gardoni P. (2018b) "Regional resilience analysis: A multi-scale approach to model and optimize the recovery of interdependent infrastructure" in Gardoni P. ed., *Handbook of Sustainable and Resilient Infrastructure.* New York: Routledge.

Sheets R. (1994) "Statement before hearing of the House Committee on Public Works and Transportation on H.R. 2873, The Natural Disaster Prevention act of 1993." Subcommittee on Water Resources and Environment.

Shinozuka M., Rose A., and Eguchi R. T. (1998) "Engineering and socioeconomic impacts of earthaquakes: An analysis of electricity lifeline disruptions in the New Madrid area." Multidisciplinary Center for Earthquake Engineering Research, Buffalo, NY.

Simon J., Bracci J.M., and Gardoni P. (2010) "Seismic response and fragility of deteriorated reinforced concrete bridges." *ASCE Journal of Structural Engineering* 136, 1273–81.

Spedding L. and Rose A. eds. (2008) *Business Risk Management Handbook.* New York: Elsevier.

Steelman J., Song J., and Hajjar J.F. (2007) "Integrated data flow and risk aggregation for consequence-based risk management of seismic regional losses." MAE Center. http://mae.cee.illinois.edu/publications/reports/Report_Jan_07.pdf (last accessed August 20, 2018).

Todo Y., Nakajima K., and Matous P. (2014) "How do supply chain networks affect the resilience of firms to natural disasters? Evidence from the Great East Japan Earthquake." *Journal of Regional Science* 55, 209–29.

Vespignani A. (2010) "Complex networks: The fragility of interdependency." *Nature* 464, 984–5.

Wang Y., Gardoni P., Murphy C., and Guerrier S. (2018) "Predicting fatality rates due to earthquakes accounting for community vulnerability." *Earthquake Spectra* (under review).

Xu H. and Gardoni P. (2016) "Probabilistic capacity and seismic demand models and fragility estimates for reinforced concrete buildings based on three-dimensional analyses." *Engineering Structures* 112, 200–14.

Zhong J., Gardoni P., Rosowsky D., and Haukaas T. (2008) "Probabilistic seismic demand models and fragility estimates for reinforced concrete bridges with two-column bents." *Journal of Engineering Mechanics* 134, 495–504.

Zhong, J. Gardoni P., and Rosowsky D. (2009) "Bayesian updating of seismic demand models and fragility estimates for reinforced concrete bridges with two-column bents." *Journal of Earthquake Engineering* 13, 716–35.

44

CAT bond pricing and coverage design against natural perils

Lorenzo Hofer,[1] *Paolo Gardoni,*[2] *and Mariano Angelo Zanini*[3]

[1] DEPARTMENT OF CIVIL, ENVIRONMENTAL AND ARCHITECTURAL ENGINEERING,
UNIVERSITY OF PADOVA, ITALY; LORENZO.HOFER@DICEA.UNIPD.IT

[2] DEPARTMENT OF CIVIL AND ENVIRONMENTAL ENGINEERING,
UNIVERSITY OF ILLINOIS AT URBANA-CHAMPAIGN, USA; GARDONI@ILLINOIS.EDU

[3] DEPARTMENT OF CIVIL, ENVIRONMENTAL AND ARCHITECTURAL ENGINEERING,
UNIVERSITY OF PADOVA, ITALY; MARIANOANGELO.ZANINI@DICEA.UNIPD.IT

44.1 Introduction

The development of preparedness programs against natural disasters is a relevant issue for individuals, corporations and governments. Natural disasters can have devastating effects on the communities, in terms of costs for repairing damaged structures, interruption of business operations and human losses. Every year, rainfalls windstorm, tornadoes, floods, and earthquakes cause billion dollars losses (Gardoni et al. 2016; Gardoni & LaFave 2016). Munich Re estimated more than 380 billion dollars of insurance claims induced by natural catastrophes in 2011 (Munich Re 2011). From the analysis of past events, losses amplitude seems to increase over time; furthermore, this worldwide increasing trend is expected to continue since higher concentrations of population and built environment develop in areas susceptible to natural hazard (Grossi & Kunreuther 2005; Murphy et al. 2018).

The trend of catastrophe losses over the last two decades stresses the need to manage such risks both on national, as well as on a global scale. Exposure can be partially reduced by private insurance/reinsurance companies, especially when dealing with events able to disrupt the entire economy of a region. In some countries (e.g., Greece, Italy, and Mexico), national governments and public authorities entirely manage such risks and sometimes have to face significant losses. In this context, householders are not encouraged to subscribe private insurance coverage and have a low perception of risk (Zanini et al. 2015).

Capital capacity needs therefore to be secured to provide coverage to significant losses by using sophisticated Alternative Risk Transfer products (ART). One ART solution is represented by the insurance-linked securitization, an alternative way to transfer catastrophe risk into securities (i.e., Catastrophe (CAT) bonds) and selling them to financial entities able to absorb such high levels of losses (i.e., financial markets). In this way, CAT bonds are able to provide an important supply for governments and public authorities, surpassing the capacity of traditional providers and are therefore well suited to offer coverage for substantial losses (Kunreuther 2001).

CAT bonds are usually structured as coupon-paying bonds with a default linked to the occurrence of a trigger event or events during the period of coverage. In case of default, the principal, which has been held in trust, is used to pay the losses of the issuing company; on the contrary if there is no default, the principal is returned to the investor at maturity and coupons are also paid as counterweight to the assumed risk. The description of a typical securitization structure can be found for example in Grossi and Kunreuther (2005). One key point in CAT bond design is the definition of the trigger event. The literature categorizes five types of triggering variables, i.e. indemnity, industry index, modeled loss indices, parametric indices, and hybrid triggers (Hagedorn et al. 2009, Burnecki et al. 2011). Some studies on trigger types and their effectiveness can be found in Franco (2010) and Goda (2013). Among the different options, a commonly used trigger event is the overcoming of a loss threshold, called indemnity trigger (Kunreuther & Pauly 2010). In the United States, data provided by the PCS® (Property Claim Services) are widely accepted as reference industry index triggers for CAT bonds and other catastrophe-linked instruments (Lin & Wang 2009; Ma & Ma 2013). When the information used to calibrate a CAT bond are obtained from models (e.g., by performing a regional analysis), triggers can be based on modeled losses, rather than on actual realized losses (Grossi & Kunreuther 2005). In case of parametric CAT bonds, triggers are typically based on parameters directly related to the specific risk for which a coverage is designed, such as magnitude values for earthquakes (Härdle & Cabrera 2010), wind speeds for hurricanes, rainfall total for flooding. Among the hybrid triggers, Takahashi (2017) developed new financial derivatives for encouraging earthquake protection, in which the building owner has to pay for the earthquake protection only when the specified earthquake occurs.

Despite their growing importance, limited research on CAT bond pricing can be found in literature (Shao 2015; Braun 2016), and mainly focused on specific aspects, like pricing (Burnecki et al. 2011; Shao et al. 2015), trigger consistency (Franco 2010; Goda 2013), accuracy of models (Jaeger et al. 2010; Galeotti et al. 2013). Further work is needed to improve the pricing of CAT bonds and reduce errors associated with the definition of the trigger mechanism. In particular, there is a need to propagate the uncertainties in the model parameters on the CAT bond default probability and pricing. Assessing the role of such uncertainties underlying the CAT bonds issuance is a crucial step for a rational pricing and economic sustainability of these financial products. For this reason, Hofer et al. (2018a) proposed a risk-based CAT bond pricing procedure that allows to compute a CAT bond pricing surface characterized by a desired level of assumed risk. The next section gives an overview of the risk-based CAT bond pricing procedure. In the following of this chapter, we present a practical implementation of a CAT bond coverage policy for an area subject to catastrophe risks. The method is general and can be used by different stakeholders (e.g., issuing companies, insurance/reinsurance companies, and national governments) for covering different types of losses arising from different natural perils. Finally, an application to a case-study is presented considering the entire Italian territory.

44.2 Risk-based CAT bond pricing

CAT bonds are usually structured as coupon-paying bonds with a default linked to the occurrence of a trigger event. In particular, this work focuses on CAT bonds whose trigger event is the overcoming of a loss threshold. In this case, bonds are priced for a set of possible combinations of a threshold D of monetary losses (trigger event) and maturity time T; this information is thus summarized into a pricing surface, function of D and T. The mathematical formulation summarized in this chapter uses a compound doubly stochastic Poisson process as the underlying stochastic process for the CAT bond pricing (Burnecki & Kukla 2003; Baryshnikov et al. 2001; Burnecki et al. 2011) and it is able to consider uncertainties in model parameters (Hofer et al. 2018a). In particular, accounting for the uncertainties in the model parameters allows for the definition of CAT bond pricing based on a fixed level of risk. Additional details of the mathematical method described in this section, can be found in Hofer et al. (2018a).

The main assumption is that perils follow a doubly stochastic Poisson process $M(s)$ ($s \in [0, T]$), either with constant (homogeneous Poisson process – HPP) or more generally with a varying intensity over time (non-homogeneous Poisson process – NHPP). In the most general case, the intensity function $m(s)$ that defines the Poisson process varies over time and the probability of n events in the interval $[0, t]$, with $t \in [0, T]$, is given by

$$P[M(t) = n] = \frac{\left[\int_0^t m(s)\,ds\right]^n \cdot e^{-\int_0^t m(s)\,ds}}{n!} \qquad n = 0, 1, \ldots \tag{44.1}$$

Economic losses X_i associated to each catastrophic event at time t_i ($i = 1, 2, \ldots n$) are traditionally assumed to be independent, identically distributed random variables with a common distribution (Baryshnikov et al. 2001). This distribution (also known as the loss distribution) has to correctly fit the observed or simulated claims or losses. The distribution parameters describing the Poisson process and the loss distribution are referred respectively as Θ_P and Θ_L.

The accumulated losses at time instant t are represented by a predictable, left-continuous and increasing aggregate loss process $L(t)$ (Burnecki et al. 2011), defined as

$$L(t) = \sum_{i=1}^{M(t)} X_i. \tag{44.2}$$

As a consequence, "failure" of the system, which corresponds to CAT bond's default, occurs when the accumulated losses exceed the threshold level D. The associated probability of failure P_f, i.e. the probability that the accumulated losses exceed the threshold D before the bond expiration time T, has to be assessed for each D-T combination, given the parameters $\Theta = [\Theta_P, \Theta_L]$, as

$$P_f(T, D; \Theta) = P[L(T; \Theta) \geq D]. \tag{44.3}$$

Using Equation (44.2) for the accumulated losses by time T, and conditioning on the number of events, Equation (44.3) becomes

$$P_f(T, D; \Theta) = \sum_{n=1}^{\infty} P\left[\left(\sum_{i=1}^{n} X_i(\Theta_L)\right) \geq D \,\middle|\, M(T; \Theta_P) = n\right] \cdot P[M(T; \Theta_P) = n], \tag{44.4}$$

which can be simplified by considering the independence between the Poisson point process and the incurred losses in the following way

$$P_f(T, D; \Theta) = \sum_{n=1}^{\infty} \left[1 - F_X^n(D; \Theta_L)\right] \cdot P[M(T; \Theta_P) = n]. \tag{44.5}$$

In Equation (44.5), $F_X^n(D;\Theta_L) = \int_0^\infty F_X^{n-1}(D-x;\Theta_L)\, dF_X(x;\Theta_L)$ is the n-fold convolution of the loss distribution evaluated at D, which represents the cumulative density function (CDF) of $(X_1 + X_2 + \ldots + X_n)$ (Nakagawa 2011; Sánchez-Silva & Klutke 2016). In the most general case, $P[M(T;\Theta_P) = n]$ is given by Equation (44.1). Similar approaches have been used to model the failure probability of deteriorating engineering systems (Kumar et al. 2015). This formulation is general and can be applied for computing P_f with every loss distribution type.

Risk-based CAT bond pricing calculates the CAT bond pricing surface, characterized by a desired risk value for each D-T combination. The issuer defines a quantile q on the P_f distribution and finds the corresponding CAT bond price on the price distribution V_t. Figure 44.1 shows an example of P_f curve for a fixed threshold D and the corresponding CAT bond price. Following Gardoni et al. (2002), the solid line is a point estimate $\hat{P}_f(T,D)$ of P_f obtained by computing $P_f(T,D;\Theta)$ at a point estimate of Θ (i.e., $\Theta = \hat{\Theta}$, where $\hat{\Theta}$ could be the mean or median of Θ, $\hat{P}_f(T,D) = P_f(T,D;\hat{\Theta}))$, or the predictive estimate $\tilde{P}_f(T,D)$ of P_f computed as the expected value of $P_f(T,D;\Theta)$ over Θ. Similarly, $\tilde{V}_t(T,D)$ (or $\hat{V}_t(T,D)$) is a predictive (or point) estimate of the CAT bond price obtained from $\tilde{P}_f(T,D)$ (or $\hat{P}_f(T,D)$). At each value of T, q is the probability that the default probability P_f is smaller than the probability $P_{f,d}$ assumed for the pricing design as the fixed risk, where d in the subscript stands for *design value*. $P_{f,d}$ is then needed for the calculation of the related CAT bond design price $V_{t,d}$ on the price distribution V_t.

Assuming a quantile on P_f implies considering the same probability that the CAT bond is under-priced. Formally, this statement is given by the following expression (Hofer et al. 2018a)

$$P\left[P_f < P_{f,d}\right] = P\left[V_t > V_{t,d}\right] = q. \tag{44.6}$$

The distribution of P_f is then needed to compute $P_{f,d}$ for a given quantile q. The exact evaluation of the distribution of P_f due to the uncertainties in Θ requires nested reliability calculations (Der Kiureghian 1989; Gardoni et al. 2002). As a computationally more efficient approach, uncertainty inherent in the calculations due to the uncertainties in the parameters can be assessed through approximate quantiles obtained by first-order analysis (Gardoni et al. 2002). The design default probability $P_{f,d}$ can thus be calculated as (Hofer et al. 2018a)

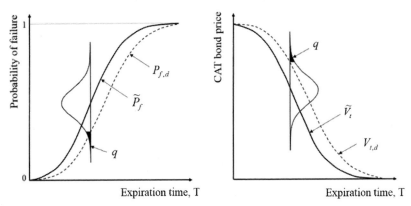

Figure 44.1 Relationship between failure probabilities $\tilde{P}_f$, $P_{f,d}$ and CAT bond prices $\tilde{V}_t$, $V_{t,d}$, given a quantile q.

$$P_{f,d}(T,D) = \Phi\left[-\tilde{\beta}(T,D) - k \cdot \sigma_\beta(T,D)\right], \tag{44.7}$$

where $\Phi(\cdot)$ is the standard normal cumulative density function, $\tilde{\beta}(T,D)$ is the reliability index calculated as $\tilde{\beta}(T,D) = \Phi^{-1}\left[1 - \tilde{P}_f(T,D)\right]$ and $k\,\sigma_\beta$ represents the quantile of the β distribution reflecting the acceptable level of risk. Note that k is a constant and it is calculated starting from the assumed quantile q as follows (Hofer et al. 2018a)

$$k = \Phi^{-1}\left[1 - q\right]. \tag{44.8}$$

Following Gardoni et al. (2002), the variance of the reliability index $\beta(T,D;\Theta)$ can be approximated using a first-order Taylor series expansion around M_Θ, as

$$\sigma_\beta^2(T,D) \approx \nabla_\Theta \beta(T,D)^{\mathrm{T}} \Sigma_{\Theta\Theta} \nabla_\Theta \beta(T,D), \tag{44.9}$$

where M_Θ is the mean vector of the model parameters Θ. The vector M_Θ can be estimated either with the maximum likelihood estimation method or, more precisely, with the Bayesian updating technique, as the posterior mean vector (Gardoni et al. 2002). In Equation (44.9), $\Sigma_{\Theta\Theta}$ is the covariance matrix of the model parameters that contains the variances of the model parameters and their possible correlation. The term $\Sigma_{\Theta\Theta}$ can be computed in first approximation as the negative of the inverse of the Hessian of the log-likelihood function (Richards 1961) or, again, more accurately with a Bayesian updating technique (Gardoni et al. 2002). The gradient of β is computed by applying the chain rule to the definition of β, and the gradient of P_f can be computed using the definition of derivative as

$$\nabla_\Theta \beta(T,D) = -\frac{1}{\varphi\left[\tilde{\beta}(T,D)\right]} \nabla_\Theta P_f(T,D) \tag{44.10}$$

$$\nabla_\Theta P_f(T,D) = \left[\frac{P_f(T,D;\Theta + \delta\Theta) - P_f(T,D;\Theta)}{\delta\Theta}\right]_{M_\Theta}. \tag{44.11}$$

Once $P_{f,d}$ is calculated, the corresponding CAT bond price can be computed. In the following, the pricing formula for the *zero-coupon* and *coupon* CAT bond are provided. The *zero-coupon* CAT bond is a debt security that does not pay interest but renders profit only at maturity, while the *coupon* CAT bond pays the principal value at maturity, and also coupons over the bond's life.

Following Burnecki and Kukla (2003), the proposed formulations derive CAT bond price as discounted expected value of the future payoff under the risk-neutral measure (or equivalent martingale measure), considering an arbitrage-free opportunities financial market. In particular the following equations are written by assuming that the instantaneous interest rate process follows the square-root process of Cox et al. 1985, and that the aggregate loss process $L(t)$, retains its original distributional characteristics after changing from the historical estimated actual probability measure, to the risk-neutral probability measure (Cox & Pedersen 2000).

Given the threshold D, the price of the *zero-coupon* CAT bond ($V_{t,d}^{zc}$) paying the principal Z at maturity time T and correspondent to the assumed quantile q is (Hofer et al. 2018a)

$$V_{t,d}^{zc}(T,D) = B_{CIR}(t,T) Z \left[1 - P_{f,d}(T,D) \right].$$

(44.12)

Finally, the price of the *coupon CAT* bond $(V_{t,d}^{c})$ paying the principal value PV at maturity, and coupon payments $C(s)$, which cease if the bond is triggered, can be obtained as (Hofer et al. 2018a)

$$V_{t,d}^{c}(T,D) = B_{CIR}(t,T) \cdot PV \left[1 - P_{f,d}(T,D) \right] + \int_{t}^{T} B_{CIR}(t,s) C(s) \left[1 - P_{f,d}(s,D) \right] ds .$$

(44.13)

In Equations (44.12)–(44.13), $B_{CIR}(t,T)$ represents the expected value of the stochastic discount factor, under the risk neutral measure, and assuming the Cox-Ingersoll-Ross model (CIR model) it is equal to

$$B_{CIR}(t,T) = E \left[\exp \left(-\int_{t}^{T} r(\xi) d\xi \right) \middle| F_{t} \right] = A(t,T) \exp \left[-B(t,T) r \right].$$

(44.14)

Further details and the definition of $A(t,T)$ and $B(t,T)$ can be found in Cox et al. 1985. In Equation 44.14 $\exp \left[-\int_{t}^{T} r(\xi) d\xi \right]$ represents a continuous progressive process of the discount interest rate r, describing the value at time t of 1 US\$ paid at time T (with $T > t$). For both *zero-coupon* and *coupon* CAT bond, the bond principal is assumed to be completely lost, in case the bond is triggered.

With this procedure, we can use the information related to the parameter uncertainties and find pricing surfaces $V_{t,d}^{zc}$ and $V_{t,d}^{c}$ where all points are characterized by a desired level of risk. Note that, when $q = 0.5$ the point or predictive estimate of P_f, and consequently of V_t^{zc} (or V_t^{c}), is computed without any further information related to parameter uncertainties ($k=0$). In addition, $k = +/-1$ represent the approximate 15 percent and 85 percent percentile bounds of P_f and V_t^{zc} (or V_t^{c}), containing 70 percent of the probability (Gardoni et al. 2002).

44.3 CAT bond coverage design method

CAT bond pricing is a specific step in the more general method in which CAT bonds are used as a risk-transfer tool. This section describes a method for the implementation of a CAT bond coverage policy. The method is general since issuing companies may be of different nature and may be interested in facing different types of losses. For example, private insurance/reinsurance companies may want to protect their insured portfolio from the insolvency risk, whereas national governments may be interest in covering significant losses on the entire national building stock (Grossi & Kunreuther 2005). The method is divided into four main steps. The first step requires the identification of the region of interest based on the spatial distribution of the portfolio to be covered. In the second step, the distribution parameters needed for the CAT bond pricing have to be calculated. The third step consists in the definition of the financial characteristics of the CAT bond. Lastly, the fourth step consists in the application of the risk-based CAT bond pricing procedure described above. A description of the main details of each step is given in the following.

Step 1: Definition of the region of interest

The first step of the CAT bond coverage design method consists in the definition of the region of interest based on the spatial distribution of the portfolio that the issuing company wants to cover. The definition of the region of interest has a direct implication in the pricing process since only perils or damage occurring inside this area can potentially trigger the bond, and in addition, only past events located within this area are considered for the calibration of the hazard models. Private insurance/reinsurance companies, may be interested in transferring risk associated to a portfolio, or a part of it, of point-like structures highly scattered over a territory. On the contrary, when the issuing company coincides with a national authority, the entire portfolio of structures over the national territory may be of interest. In both cases, different risk levels can be observed within the same region of interest. For this reason, a common practice is to tailor CAT bonds associated to different risk levels for the same combinations of D-T, in order to meet the needs of different types of investors, via the subdivision of the region of interest in smaller zones.

This subdivision process is typically case-specific, however, some general aspects should be considered in all cases. In particular, since the pricing described above is substantially influenced by magnitude and frequency of the losses, the subdivision should be able to capture both aspects (i.e., magnitude and frequency), identifying zones characterized by levels of risk that are similar within a zone and different among zones. A zone with frequent and highly impacting losses leads to calibrate high-risk CAT bonds with related high gains for risk-seeking investors, whereas a zone with rare and low-impact events leads to low-risk CAT bonds, more attractive for risk-averse investors. In the case of a portfolio located in a wide region with a homogeneous spatial distribution of vulnerability and exposure, the subdivision in zones can be based directly on the hazard of interest. For example, when dealing with natural disasters like floods, tsunamis, and hurricanes, areas close to river banks or sea coastlines are usually higher-risk zones; in case of earthquakes, size and location of past events can help in the zoning process.

Step 2: Definition of the distribution parameters

Once the zoning is defined, the second step of the CAT bond coverage design method consists in the estimation of the Poisson process and loss distribution parameters, respectively Θ_P and Θ_L, for each zone, which have to be used in the pricing calculation. The crucial aspect in this step is the correct calibration of model parameters, since a more accurate knowledge of the problem implies fewer uncertainties in the final pricing outcomes. For the calibration of the Poisson process, the frequency of the past events occurred in each zone has to be considered. Recent studies have shown how climate change is affecting the likelihood of occurrence, magnitude and consequences of specific natural hazards like heat waves and droughts, severe precipitations, and hurricanes (Gardoni et al. 2016; Murphy et al. 2018), leading to the adoption of non-Poissonian processes. More complex models for accounting for the effects of climate change could be used. Regarding the loss distribution, it has to be able to represent the amount of losses associated to each event occurred inside each zone of interest. The calibration of the loss distribution can rely on historical data or simulated/modelled estimates. Usually historical data on extreme events are few, difficult to find and sometimes not accurate (especially for older events). In addition, building vulnerability can be reduced over time with respect to the vulnerability at the time of the occurrence of a historical event associate with a certain loss, since the reconstruction process that follows is typically carried out with higher safety standards to mitigate the likelihood of new damage in the future. Computer simulations can be carried out to predict potential losses that can arise for the portfolio of interest. Catastrophe models are thus needed to simulate losses considering a specific metric, e.g. direct structural damage (i.e., the costs to be sustained to repair structural damage) for residential buildings, or losses due to business interruption for industrial plants (Hofer et al. 2018b).

Step 3: Definition of the financial characteristics of the CAT bond

In the third step of the method, CAT bond financial characteristics have to be decided. First, the type of bond have to be set. *Zero-coupon* or *coupon* CAT bonds are the most common financial products adopted when dealing with natural perils. The *zero-coupon* CAT bond pays Z at maturity if it is not triggered, on the contrary, if the trigger occurs, the investor loses his/her capital. When *coupon* CAT bond are structured, the benefit for the investor is the payment of PV at maturity if it is not triggered plus a series of coupon payments $C(s)$ periodically cashed (e.g., quarterly, semi-annually, or annually). Usually, it is assumed that if the bond is triggered the investor completely loses the principal. A continuously compounded discount rate $r(\xi)$ has also to be set, and it can be assumed constant and equal to the London Inter-Bank Offered Rate (LIBOR) (Härdle & Cabrera 2010; Burnecki et al. 2011). Another financial characteristic of the bond is the definition of D and T. These values are crucial for the success of the bond mechanism and have to be specified in the contract. The definition of D is case-specific and clearly has to be set in relation to the frequency and magnitude of losses potentially impacting each zone, whereas T typically ranges between 2–4 years.

Step 4: Application of the risk-based CAT bond pricing procedure

Lastly, the fourth step of the method consists in the application of the risk-based CAT bond pricing detailed in the previous sections for each zone in which the region of interest is subdivided.

44.4 Case-study application

This section uses the risk-based CAT bond pricing and the CAT bond coverage design method to design a CAT bond-based coverage against earthquake-induced losses to the residential building asset of Italy. In this application, the issuing entity is taken to be the Italian government, needing a full risk-transfer in case of losses arising from earthquakes with moment magnitude $M_W \geq 4.5$.

Step 1: Definition of the region of interest

The region of interest is the entire Italian territory. The Italian territory is subdivided into three zones (i.e., Zone 1 – high-risk, Zone 2 – medium-risk, and Zone 3 – low-risk) in order to develop three different default-risk CAT bond products and show how CAT bond price reflects the risk of each zone. Figure 44.2 shows the three zones, with overlapped the historical earthquakes with $M_W \geq 4.5$ occurred in Italy since 1005 (Rovida et al. 2015).

Step 2: Definition of the distribution parameters

Once the default-risk zoning is defined, parameters of the Poisson process and the loss distribution have to be determined for each zone. The considered losses are the direct structural losses (i.e., the sum of all costs to be sustained for repairing seismic damage on residential structures).

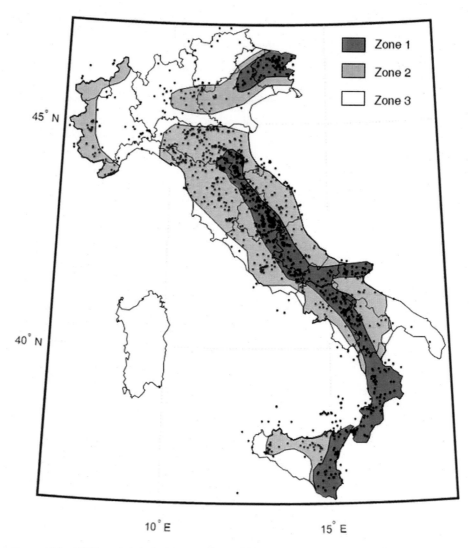

Figure 44.2   CAT bond default-risk zonation vs. historical seismicity ($M_w \geq 4.5$).

Such losses are a significant component of the total losses induced by earthquakes, and currently has to be covered by the Italian government with public funding.

The parameters of the Poisson process that describe the occurrence of events in each zone can be derived using the historical catalogue of Italian earthquakes (available since year 1005). In particular, since the majority of (recorded) earthquakes are concentrated in the last century, thus evidencing the well-known problem of catalogue-completeness (i.e., lack of data related to low-to-medium events during the Middle Ages), we use the time window 1890–2015 for the calibration of the Poisson processes. Such time window of 125 years is characterized by the occurrence of 383, 295 and 61 events respectively in Zones 1, 2, and 3. Figure 44.3 shows the aggregate number of earthquakes occurred over the years in each zone. It can be

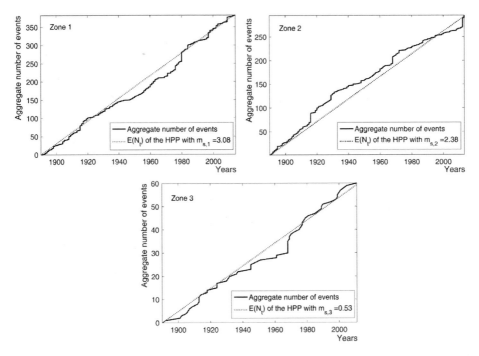

Figure 44.3 Comparison between the aggregate number of earthquakes and the expected number of events of the HPP (E[N$_t$]) for each zone.

seen that the sequence of events can be represented with a homogeneous Poisson process (HPP) characterized by a constant intensity (i.e. slope of the curve) within the considered time window.

For each ith zone (i=1, 2, 3), Table 44.1 lists the posterior mean $\mathbf{M}_{\Theta_{P,i}}$ and covariance matrix $\mathbf{\Sigma}_{\Theta_{P,i}\Theta_{P,i}}$, containing in this case the intensity m_i of the Poisson process, and its variance $\sigma^2_{m_i}$ (calculated via Bayesian updating, Gardoni et al. 2002) for each zone. Table 44.1 shows that the m_3 is significantly smaller than m_1 and m_2 values.

Due to the limited record of real losses and claim data, losses are estimated considering scenario earthquakes and estimating the corresponding direct structural loss. For performing scenario analysis, a detailed description of vulnerability and exposure of the region of interest is required. Earthquake scenarios corresponding to each historical event with $M_W \geq 4.5$ occurred within each zone are generated considering the peak ground acceleration (PGA) as reference intensity measure. The ground motion prediction equation (GMPE) proposed by Bindi et al. (2011) that are specific for the Italian territory is used to estimate the PGA on rock at the centroid of each Italian municipality. Uncertainty in scenario predictions is taken into account by simulating ten spatially-correlated ground motion fields, in accordance to Goda and Hong (2008), and Goda and Atkinson (2009, 2010). A total of 11 shake fields (1 mean and 10 spatially-correlated) are considered for each event, for a total of 4,213, 3,245 and 671 shake fields respectively in Zones 1, 2, and 3. For each shake field, the values of PGA at the centroid of each Italian municipality are amplified with a topographic-stratigraphic coefficient (Italian Building Code for Constructions 2008) based on a v_{S30} (i.e., the time-averaged shear-wave velocity to 30 m depth) site classification (Wald & Allen 2007) to take into account soil amplification phenomena.

Table 44.1 Mean and variance of the intensity of the Poisson process for the three zones

	$\mathbf{M}_{\Theta_{P,j}} = [m_i]$	$\mathbf{\Sigma}_{\Theta_{P,j}, \Theta_{P,j}} = [\sigma_{m_i}^2]$
Zone 1	3.08	0.025
Zone 2	2.38	0.019
Zone 3	0.53	0.005

Table 44.2 Number of residential buildings per construction period vs. construction material in Italy

Construction period	Construction material			Total
	Masonry	RC	Other	
Pre 1919	1,725,486	–	107,018	1,832,504
1919–1945	1,149,082	77,122	100,803	1,327,007
1946–1960	1,212,279	303,903	184,654	1,700,836
1961–1970	1,087,428	676,242	28,163	1,791,833
1971–1980	863,668	907,046	34,937	1,805,651
1981–1990	467,821	737,632	25,314	1,230,767
1991–2000	251,721	455,906	16,390	724,017
2001–2005	125,719	247,516	9,869	383,104
post 2005	92,773	189,328	77,878	359,979
Total	6,975,977	3,594,695	585,026	11,155,698

Source: Istituto Nazionale di Statistica 2011.

The spatial distribution of the residential building stock is modeled at the municipality scale, in accordance to the 15th census database provided by the Italian National Institute of Statistics (Istituto Nazionale di Statistica 2011). This database stores the number of residential buildings for each municipality, their different construction materials (i.e., masonry, reinforced concrete (RC), and "other") and the age of construction (i.e., pre 1919, 1919–45, 1946–60, 1961–70, 1971–80, 1981–90, 1991–2000, 2001–05, post 2005). Table 44.2 lists the number of buildings per construction period and construction material for the entire Italian stock. Most of the buildings are masonry structures built before 1919. For each construction period, masonry buildings are more numerous than RC structures up to 1971–80, after that period, construction of RC buildings becomes more common than the construction of masonry buildings. As in Asprone et al. (2013), "other" category is considered populated by combined RC-masonry structures, since in Italy such structural type constitutes a significant portion of structures other than masonry and RC ones.

Figure 44.4 shows the residential-use built area for each municipality, evidencing a higher distribution in the Po plain and around the metropolitan areas of the main cities outside of the Po plan (from North to South: Florence, Rome, Naples, Bari, and Palermo).

The exposed value, i.e. the economic quantification of the replacement cost of the entire residential asset, is calculated for each municipality as the product between the residential-use built area and the average unit replacement cost RC_{ave}, taken to be 1,500 €/m² based on information from the Centre for Sociological, Economics and Market Research (CRESME) (2011), and considered constant over the Italian territory.

Fragility models available in literature and classified per structural category are used to represent the structural vulnerability of the Italian residential building stock. An extensive

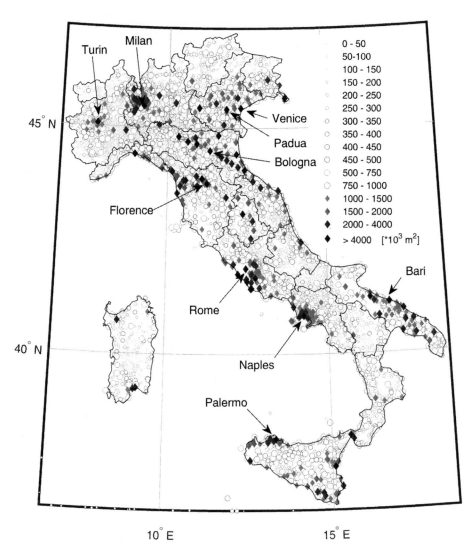

Figure 44.4   Residential-use built-area for each Italian municipality.

literature survey is performed for identifying the most suitable fragility functions to be used in the loss-calculation model. A total of eight categories of structural type are defined in accordance with the available census data. In particular, two categories of masonry buildings (built before or after 1919) are considered according to Kostov et al. (2004). For RC and combined RC-masonry buildings, a distinction is made between gravity-load and seismic-load designed structures by considering the age of construction with respect to the temporal evolution of Italian seismic codes (Legge 64, 1974; DM 1984), to know whether or not each municipality was classified as a seismic risk-prone area or not. For each municipality currently classified as a seismic risk-prone area, structures built before the year in which the municipality was classified as a seismic risk-prone area, are considered as gravity-load designed, whereas

877

structures built after that year are considered as seismic-load designed. A further subdivision is also performed both for RC-gravity and RC-seismic buildings, considering the number of storeys and thus defining two additional classes (low-raise buildings: 1–2 story, and medium- or high-raise buildings: 3 or more stories). Summarizing, the following taxonomy is adopted in the loss-calculation model:

1. Masonry structures built before 1919;
2. Masonry structures built after 1919;
3. RC structures, gravity-design, 1–2 storey;
4. RC structures, gravity-design, 3+ storeys;
5. RC structures, seismic-design, 1–2 storey;
6. RC structures, seismic-design, 3+ storeys;
7. Other structures, gravity-design;
8. Other structures, seismic-design.

Table 44.3 lists the values of the mean and standard deviation (characterizing the analytical lognormal fragility functions) of the curves corresponding to a set of increasing damage states (from slight damage to collapse) for each structural type. The values are obtained from Kostov et al. (2004) and Ahmad et al. (2011).

The built area values for each structural type in each municipality is estimated by a disaggregation of the value of the municipal built area based on the ratio of buildings belonging to a structural type with respect to the total number of buildings at municipality level (Istituto Nazionale di Statistica 2011).

Loss-calculations are then performed for each shake field according to Bai et al. (2009) considering municipalities within a radius of 200 km. We do not consider losses beyond 200 km both because of limitations in the applicability of the GMPE and the negligible effects in terms of seismic damage beyond such source-to-site distance. A set of repair cost ratios (i.e., ratio between unit cost to repair a building in a specific damage state and the unit replacement cost RC_{ave}) is derived from Dolce and Manfredi (2015), assuming the same deterministic values for all the considered structural types, with values equal to 0.15, 0.4, 0.65, 1, respectively for

Table 44.3 Mean and standard deviation of the adopted fragility curves for each structural type

Structural type	Damage State								Authors
	Slight DS_1		Moderate DS_2		Extensive DS_3		Complete DS_4		
	Mean [g]	St. Dev. [g]	Mean [g]	St. Dev. [g]	Mean [g]	St. Dev. [g]	Mean [g]	St. Dev. [g]	
#1	0.14	0.13	0.20	0.19	0.23	0.22	0.33	0.31	Kostov et al. 2004
#2	0.16	0.15	0.23	0.22	0.26	0.24	0.45	0.42	Kostov et al. 2004
#3	0.090	0.031	0.130	0.060	0.263	0.101	0.350	0.130	Ahmad et al. 2011
#4	0.085	0.028	0.122	0.055	0.187	0.078	0.235	0.093	Ahmad et al. 2011
#5	0.090	0.031	0.130	0.060	0.262	0.100	0.517	0.192	Ahmad et al. 2011
#6	0.085	0.028	0.121	0.052	0.185	0.075	0.328	0.123	Ahmad et al. 2011
#7	0.15	0.14	0.22	0.20	0.36	0.330	0.48	0.45	Kostov et al. 2004
#8	0.16	0.15	0.26	0.24	0.41	0.380	0.56	0.52	Kostov et al. 2004

Table 44.4 Parameters of the fitted Lognormal distribution for the three zones

	$\Theta_{L,1}$ – *Zone 1*		$\Theta_{L,2}$ – *Zone 2*		$\Theta_{L,3}$ – *Zone 3*	
	λ	ζ	λ	ζ	λ	ζ
Mean	20.303	1.548	20.279	1.640	20.133	1.469
St. Dev.	0.0248	0.0175	0.0303	0.0214	0.0616	0.0436
	Correlation coefficients					
ζ	0		0		0	

the Slight Damage (DS_1), Moderate Damage (DS_2), Extensive Damage (DS_3), and Complete Damage $(DS_4.)$ Once a wide number of losses are simulated (i.e., 4,213, 3,245 and 671 loss values in Zones 1, 2, and 3, respectively), Lognormal CDFs (Cumulative Density Function) are fitted on the cumulative losses to obtain the loss distribution parameters Θ_L for each zone. Table 44.4 gives the values of Θ_L (i.e., the two parameters λ and ζ of the Lognormal distribution) and correlation coefficient for the two model parameters for each fitted Lognormal distribution. The values of the mean loss distribution decrease from Zone 1 to 3, meaning that the biggest losses are expected to happen in Zone 1 (as expected.) Figure 44.5 shows the comparison between the empirical CDFs obtained from the modeled losses and the fitted Lognormal CDFs. In the remaining of this example, we assume that Θ_P and Θ_L are uncorrelated.

Step 3: Definition of the financial characteristics of the CAT bond

CAT bond price is evaluated a time $t = 0$, assuming a principal equal to 1 € (Burnecki et al. 2011). Two different products are considered for the pricing, a *zero-coupon* and a *coupon* CAT bond, both with a full loss of the principal in case of bond triggering. In the first case, the *zero-coupon* CAT bond is assumed to be priced at 3.5 percent over LIBOR (Burnecki et al. 2011) so that if no trigger event occurs, the total yield is 6 percent, and consequently $Z = 1.06$ €. For the *coupon* CAT bond, the yearly coupon payments $C(s) = 0.06$ € and $Z = 1.00$ € are considered. A continuous discount rate r equivalent to LIBOR = 2.5 percent is assumed constant and equal to $ln(1.025)$. Threshold level D and expiration time T are considered respectively ranging between [3, 30] *bn* € and [0.25, 4] years. The integration domain in the D-T space is considered sufficiently broad to show variation of CAT bond pricing for a wide range of possible combinations. The bond for a zone is triggered when the accumulated losses caused by earthquakes occurred within the zone are greater than the set threshold before the set expiration time.

Step 4: Application of the risk-based CAT bond pricing procedure

For using the information related to the parameter uncertainties to obtain a risk-based CAT bond price, we consider the quantile $q = 0.2$. In this way, all points of the D-T domain are characterized by a constant level of risk and the probability of the bond to be under-priced is fixed and equal to $q = 0.2$, corresponding to $k = 0.84$ in Equation (44.8). For comparison, also the bound corresponding to $q = 0.5$ and $q = 1 - 0.2 = 0.8$ are plotted in the following figures. Consequently, there is a 0.6 probability that P_f and V_t^{zc} (or V_t^c) are within the lower and upper limits. The specific choices of the desired level of acceptable risk and the optimal

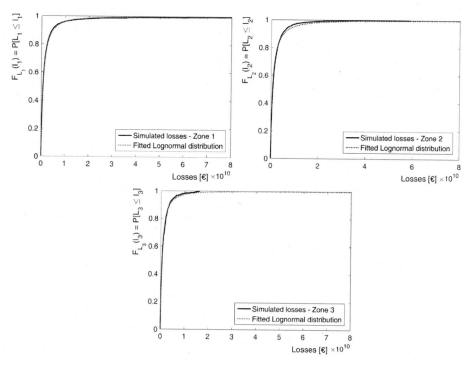

Figure 44.5 Modeled loss data fitting with Lognormal distribution for each zone.

D-T combination have to be made by a financial market analyst and are beyond the scope of this work.

Figure 44.6 shows the P_f surfaces for Zones 1, 2, and 3, calculated according to Equations (44.5)–(44.7). Two cuts of the surface are also shown, corresponding to planes with $T = 1$, and $D = 10$ *bn* €. As a general behavior common for all of the three zones, for a given threshold level D, P_f increases from 0 to 1 over time, whereas for a given expiration time T, P_f decreases as the threshold level D increases. The distance between $\tilde{P}_f$ and P_{fd} $(q = 0.2)$ increases for higher D and T values due to the higher uncertainties associated to the underlying stochastic process. As expected, for a fixed D-T combination, the P_f values of Zone 1 are always bigger than the ones associated with Zones 2 and 3. In fact, Zone 1 is the most risky one, since the probability of CAT bond triggering is the highest. In relative terms, a remarkable difference can be observed between the outcomes of Zone 3 and those of the other two zones. For example, considering a threshold level $D = 10$ *bn* €, after 4 years $\tilde{P}_f$ for Zones 1 and 2 is respectively equal to 0.85 and 0.65, whereas for Zone 3 it is only about 0.10.

Figure 44.7 shows the *Zero-coupon* CAT bond pricing surfaces associated with the threshold D paying $Z = 1.06$ € at maturity, for each Zone. The CAT bond price is proportional to the survival probability. Consequently, for a given D, the CAT bond price decreases over time, whereas for a set T, the CAT bond value increases as D increases. Figure 44.7 shows also the *iso-value* lines corresponding to the *predictive value* $\tilde{V}_t^{zc}$ and $V_{t,d}^{zc}$ with $q = 0.2$ and 0.8, that are useful for the CAT-bond price design.

Finally, Figure 44.8 shows the *coupon* CAT bond pricing surfaces. The overall trend is similar to the *zero-coupon* one, due to the high ratio intercurrent between the principal and the entity of

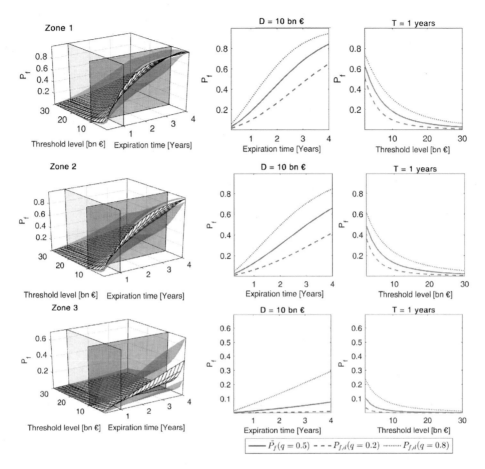

Figure 44.6 Failure probability P_f surface for the three zones.

coupons. For a set T, the price of *coupon* CAT bond increases as D increases, while increasing T leads generally to a lower *coupon* CAT bond price since the chance of receiving more coupons is greater. At the same time the possibility of losing the principal of the bond increases. As for the *zero-coupon* CAT bond surfaces, also the *coupon* CAT bond price reflects the different seismic risk-levels of the three zones. For a given D-T combination, the price for a bond in Zone 1 is the lowest while the price in Zone 3 is the highest.

44.4.1 Influence of covariance matrix and quantile choice

The uncertainty in model parameters is captured by the covariance matrix $\mathbf{\Sigma}_{\Theta\Theta}$. High values along the diagonal reflect high uncertainties in the corresponding distribution parameters. For this reason, it is crucial to use all of the available knowledge to obtain accurate estimates of $\mathbf{\Theta}$. To show the influence of the covariance matrix on the final results, a fictitious covariance matrix $\mathbf{\Sigma}'_{\Theta\Theta}$ is considered, in which the variances in the diagonal are $1/10$ of the original ones. Table 44.5 shows values of $\mathbf{\Sigma}'_{\Theta\Theta}$ for Zone 1.

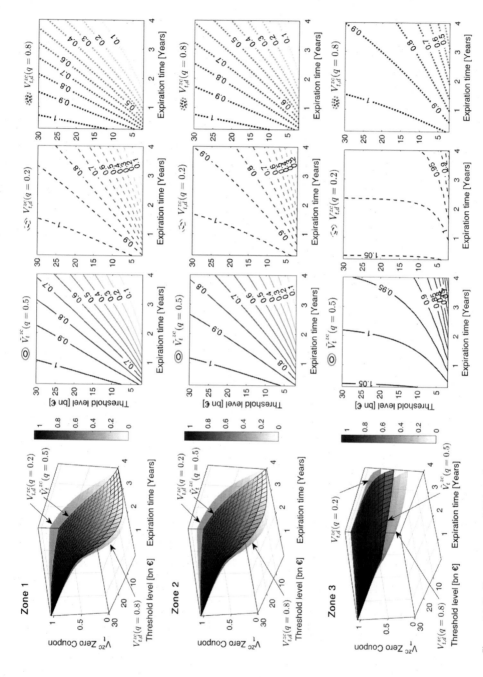

Figure 44.7 Zero-coupon CAT bond price for the three zones.

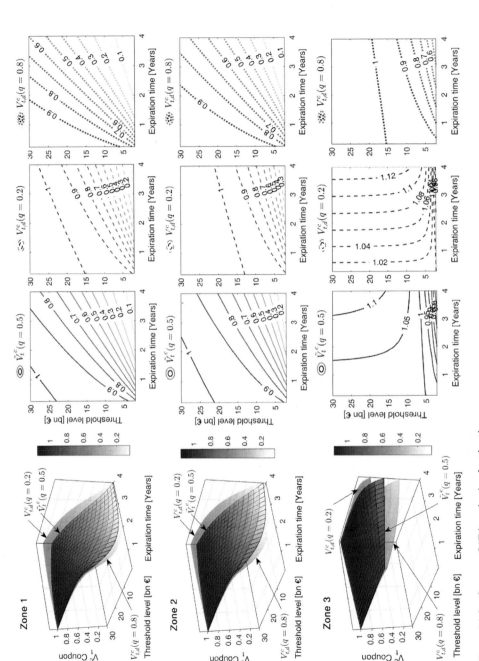

Figure 44.8 Coupon CAT bond price for the three zones.

Table 44.5 Model parameters and values of the reduced covariance matrix $\Sigma'_{\theta\theta}$ for Zone 1

Zone 1	$\Theta_{P,1}$	$\Theta_{L,1}$	
	m	λ	ζ
Mean	3.08	20.303	1.548
St. Dev.	0.05	0.0079	0.0056
	Correlation coefficients		
λ	0		
ζ	0	0	

The new covariance matrix $\Sigma'_{\theta\theta}$ represents a hypothetical case in which a more accurate knowledge of the distribution parameters is available with respect to the case analyzed earlier. For sake of brevity, this comparison is performed only for the *coupon* CAT bond price V_t^c of Zone 1. Furthermore, to show the influence of the choice of quantile (previously assumed equal to 0.2), the calculation is now performed both for $q = 0.2$ and $q = 0.1$, i.e. $k = 1.28$ (the other bound is obtained for $q = 0.9$, i.e. $k = -1.28$). Figure 44.9 shows the influence on the results of the different level of uncertainty and of the choice of quantile q.

For all values of q, the $P_{f,d}$ curves calculated with the smaller values in the covariance matrix (bottom row in Figure 44.9) are closer to the expected P_f then when computed using the larger values in the covariance matrix (top row in Figure 44.9). This means that, as expected, a better knowledge on the model parameters, i.e. smaller values of their variances, implies less spread in the price distribution for all D-T combinations. Also, for $q = 0.2$ and $q = 0.1$, we see that better knowledge allows the issuing company to set lower CAT bond prices with the same risk level, i.e. with the same probability that the bond is under-priced. The ratio $V_{t,d}^c / \tilde{V}_t^c$ is not constant within the D-T domain, meaning that the price distribution dispersion is not the same for every D-T combination. Results show that CAT bond pricing surfaces obtained with the formulations proposed by Burnecki and Kukla (2003) that corresponds to $q = 0.5$ (i.e., no information about uncertainties in model parameters) may be acceptable for some D-T combinations. However, several D-T combinations are less attractive since thay are too risky (e.g., for low values of D and high values of T) or too safe (e.g., fr for high values of D and low values of T). More generally, the parameter uncertainties have to be taken into account with the use of the proposed risk-based CAT bond pricing procedure since uncertainties play a key role in a rational risk assumption.

44.5 Conclusions

This chapter presented a general method for designing a CAT bond coverage for a portfolio subject to possible losses due to the occurrence of natural perils. The presented method is general and can be used by different issuing entities, against losses caused by different types of natural hazards. In particular, two main contributions are presented. First, the chapter presented a risk-based formulation that defines the CAT bond price based on a desired level of assumed risk. The level of assumed risk is defined based on the uncertainties in the model parameters that define the frequency of occurrence of catastrophic events and the loss distribution. With a risk-based formulation, the related CAT bond pricing surface is characterized by a constant risk value for each combination of loss threshold level D and expiration time T. Then, the chapter presented a CAT bond coverage design method for an area subject to catastrophe

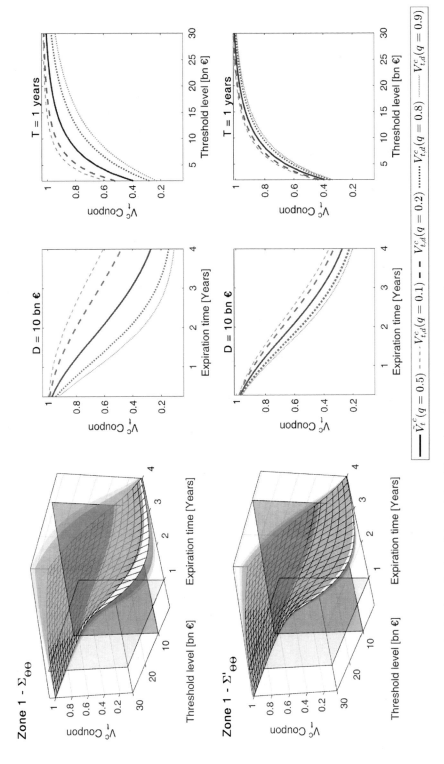

Figure 44.9 Coupon CAT bond price of Zone 1 for different *q* values and covariance matrixes.

risks, describing in detail the main steps to properly transfer potential future losses to capital markets. The second part of the chapter presented a case-study in which a possible CAT bond-based coverage configuration is designed for the residential building portfolio of Italy against earthquake-induced losses. The results can be considered as a possible solution adoptable by the Italian authorities for transferring seismic risk to capital markets and thus reducing what can be a significant burden on public finances. The Italian territory was subdivided into three zones based on their seismic risk, and three different CAT bonds were priced. The example clearly showed the importance of considering uncertainty in the model parameters in defining a CAT bond pricing.

References

Ahmad N., Crowley H., and Pinho R. (2011) "Analytical fragility functions for reinforced concrete and masonry buildings aggregates of Euro-Mediterranean regions – UPAV methodology," *Internal report, Syner-G Project*, 2009/2012.

Asprone D., Jalayer F., Simonelli S., Acconcia A., Prota A., and Manfredi G. (2013) "Seismic insurance model for the Italian residential building stock," *Structural Safety*, 44: 70–9.

Bai J.W., Hueste M.B.D., and Gardoni P. (2009) "Probabilistic Assessment of Structural Damage due to Earthquakes for Buildings in Mid-America," *Journal of Structural Engineering*, 135(10): 1155–63.

Baryshnikov Y., Mayo A., and Taylor D. (2001) "*Pricing of CAT Bonds*", Preprint.

Bindi D., Pacor F., Luzi L., Puglia R., Massa M., Ameri G., and Paolucci R. (2011) "Ground motion prediction equations derived from the Italian strong motion database." *Bulletin of Earthquake Engineering*, 2011, 9(6): 1899–1920.

Braun A. (2016) "Pricing in the primary market for CAT bonds: New empirical evidence", *The Journal of Risk and Insurance*, 83(4): 811–47.

Burnecki K. and Kukla G. (2003) "Pricing of zero-coupon and coupon CAT bonds", *Applied Mathematics*, 30: 315–24.

Burnecki K., Kukla G., and Taylor D. (2011) "Pricing of catastrophe bond," in Čížek P., Härdle W.K, and Weron, F. eds., *Statistical Tools for Finance and Insurance*, Second edition, New York: Springer.

Cox J.C., Ingersoll Jr. J.E., and Ross S.A. (1985) "A theory of the term structure of interest rates," *Econometrica*, 53(2): 385–407.

Cox S.H. and Pedersen H.W. (2000) "Catastrophe risk bonds," *North American Actuarial Journal*, 4(4): 56–82.

CRESME – Italian Centre for Sociological, Economics and Market Researc, Fondazione Housing Sociale (2011), *Il mercato delle costruzioni 2012. XIX Rapporto Congiunturale e previsionale CRESME*. Lo scenario di breve periodo, 2015.

Der Kiureghian A. (1989), "Measures of structural safety under imperfect states of knowledge", *Journal of Structural Engineering*, 115(5), 1119–40.

Dolce M. and Manfredi G. (2015) "White book on private 480 reconstruction outside the historical centers in the municipalities hit by the 6th April 2009 Abruzzo earthquake," Ed. Doppiavoce. www.reluis.it/doc/pdf/Libro-bianco.pdf (last accessed September 29, 2017).

Franco G. (2010) "Minimization of trigger error in Cat-in-a-Box parametric earthquake catastrophe bonds with an application to Costa Rica," *Earthquake Spectra*, 26(4): 983–98.

Galeotti M., Gürtler M., and Winkelvos C. (2013) "Accuracy of premium calculation models for cat bonds – an empirical analysis," *Journal of Risk and Insurance*, 80(2): 401–21.

Gardoni P. and LaFave J. eds. (2016) *Multi-hazard Approaches to Civil Infrastructure Engineering*. New York: Springer.

Gardoni P., Der Kiureghian A., and Mosalam K.M. (2002) "Probabilistic capacity models and fragility estimates for reinforced concrete columns based on experimental observations," *Journal of Engineering Mechanics*, 128(10): 1024–38.

Gardoni P., Murphy C., and Rowell A., eds. (2016) *Societal Risk Management of Natural Hazards*. New York: Springer.

Goda K. (2013) "Basis risk of earthquake catastrophe bond trigger using scenario-based versus station intensity-based approaches: a case study for southwestern British Columbia," *Earthquake Spectra*, 29(3): 757–75.

Goda K. and Atkinson G.M. (2009) "Interperiod dependence of ground-motion prediction equations: a copula prospective," *Bulletin of the Seismological Society of America*, 99(2A): 922–7.

Goda K. and Atkinson G.M. (2010) "Intraevent spatial correlation of ground-motion parameters using SK-net data," *Bulletin of the Seismological Society of America*, 100(6): 3055–67.

Goda K. and Hong H.P. (2008) "Spatial correlation of peak ground motions and response spectra," *Bulletin of the Seismological Society of America*, 98(1): 354–65.

Grossi P. and Kunreuther H. eds. (2005) *Catastrophe Modeling: A New Approach to Managing Risk*. New York: Springer.

Hagedorn D., Heigl C., Mueller A., and Seidler G. (2009) "Choice of triggers," *The Handbook of Insurance-Linked Securities*, The Wiley Finance Series, pp. 37–48.

Härdle W.K. and Cabrera B.L. (2010) "Calibrating CAT Bonds for Mexican Earthquakes", *The Journal of Risk and Insurance*, 77(3): 625–50.

Hofer L., Gardoni P., and Zanini M.A. (2018a) "Risk-based CAT bond pricing considering parameter uncertainties." (Submitted – Quantitative Finance.)

Hofer L., Zanini M.A., Faleschini F., and Pellegrino C. (2018b) "Profitability analysis for assessing the optimal seismic retrofit strategy of industrial productive processes with business-interruption consequences," *Journal of Structural Engineering*, 144(2): 04017205.

ISTAT – Istituto Nazionale di Statistica, *15° Censimento generale della popolazione e delle abitazioni* (2011). http://dawinci.istat.it/MD/dawinciMD.jsp. (last accessed September 27, 2017.

Italian Building Code for Constructions (2008) Norme tecniche per le costruzioni 2008, CS.LL.PP. DM 14 Gennaio, *Gazzetta Ufficiale della Repubblica Italiana 29*, 2008. (in Italian).

Jaeger L., Mueller S., and Scherling S. (2010) "Insurance-linked securities: What drives their returns?" *Journal of Alternative Investments*, 13(2): 9–34.

Kostov M., Vaseva E., Kaneva A., Koleva N., Verbanov G., Stefanov D., Darvarova E., Salakov D., Simeonova S., and Cristoskov L. (2004) "Application to Sofia," RISK-UE WP13.

Kumar R., Cline D.B.H., and Gardoni P. (2015) "A stochastic framework to model deterioration in engineering systems," *Structural Safety*, 53: 36–43.

Kunreuter H. (2001) "Mitigation and financial risk management for natural hazard," *The Geneva Papers on Risk and Insurance*, 26(2): 277–96.

Kunreuther H. and Pauly M. (2001) "Insuring against catastrophes," in Diebold F.X., Doherty N.A., and Herring J.R. eds., *The Known, the Unknown, and the Unknowable in Financial Risk Management: Measurement and Theory Advancing Practice*. Princeton, NJ: Princeton University Press, pp. 210–38.

Legge 2 (1974) *Provvedimenti per le costruzioni con particolari prescrizioni per le zone sismiche*.

Lin X.S. and Wang T. (2009) "Pricing perpetual American catastrophe put options: a penalty function approach," *Insurance: Mathematics and Economics*, 44(2): 287–95.

Ma Z.-G. and Ma C.-Q. (2013) "Pricing catastrophe risk bonds: A mixed approximation method," *Insurance: Mathematics and Economics*, 52(2): 243–54.

Ministro dei LL.PP di concerto con il Ministro dell'Interno (1984) *Decreto Ministeriale 19 giugno 1984. Norme tecniche relative alle costruzioni in zone sismiche*.

Munich Re, NatCatSERVICE (2011) *NATHAN World Map of Natural Hazards, version 2011*. Munchener Ruckversicherungs-Gesellschaft, Geo Risks Research, NatCatSERVICE.

Murphy C., Gardoni P., and McKim R. (2018) *Climate Change and Its Impact: Risks and Inequalities*. New York: Springer.

Nakagawa T. (ed.) (2011) *Stochastic Processes: With Applications to Reliability Theory*. New York: Springer.

Richards F.S.G. (1961) "A method of maximum likelihood estimation," *Journal of the Royal Statistical Society*, 23: 469–75.

Rovida A., Locati M., Camassi R., Lolli B., and Gasperini P. (2015) "*CPTI15, the 2015 version of the Parametric Catalogue of Italian Earthquakes.*" Istituto Nazionale di Geofisica e Vulcanologia, 2016. http://doi.org/10.6092/INGV.IT-CPTI15.

Sánchez-Silva M. and Klutke G.A. (eds.) (2016) *Reliability and Life-Cycle Analysis of Deteriorating Systems*. New York: Springer.

Shao J. (2015) "*Modelling Catastrophe Risk Bond*," PhD Thesis in Mathematical Science – University of Liverpool.

Takahasci Y. (2017) "Innovative derivatives to drive investment in earthquake protection technologies," in Gardoni P. ed, *Risk and Reliability Analysis: Theory and Applications.* New York: Springer.

Wald D.J. and Allen T.I. (2007) "Topographic slope as a proxy for seismic site conditions and amplification," *Bulletin of the Seismological Society of America,* 97(5): 1379–95.

Zanini M.A., Hofer L., and Pellegrino C. (2015) "Le polizze assicurative come strumento finanziario per il trasferimento del rischio sismico: stato dell'arte," *Proceedings of the 15th Italian Conference on Earthquake Engineering – ANIDIS,* L'Aquila, September 13–17, 2015 (in Italian).

Index